discontinued

United States Foreign Trade Highlights

Trends in the Global Market

United States Foreign Trade Highlights

Trends in the Global Market

Editors
Diane Werneke
Mark Siegal
Katherine DeBrandt
Mary Meghan Ryan

BERNAN PRESS
Lanham, MD

ISBN: 1-886222-26-6

Printed by Automated Graphic Systems, Inc., White Plains, MD, on acid-free paper that meets the American National Standards Institute Z39-48 standard.

2006 2005   4 3 2 1

BERNAN PRESS
4611-F Assembly Drive
Lanham, MD 20706
800-274-4447
email: info@bernan.com
www.bernanpress.com

CONTENTS

SECTION C. U.S. COMMODITY TRADE BY GEOGRAPHIC AREA

SECTION D. U.S. COMMODITY TRADE HIGHLIGHTS

SECTION E. EXPORTS OF GOODS BY STATE

PREFACE

This publication brings together a wide variety of government data to assist the user in assessing trends in U.S. international trade. Building on the Commerce Department's *Foreign Trade Highlights*, last published in 2002 with data now available only on its Internet Web site, and updating many of the features of Bernan Press' discontinued publication *Foreign Trade of the United States, Second Edition, 2001*, this publication includes the following:

- U.S. international transactions data, the most comprehensive measure of international trade, including the external position of the United States with respect to its financial balances with the rest of the world;

- U.S. aggregate foreign trade data, which include trade balances in goods and services classified in several ways, trade in services by major category, and information on the U.S. trade performance with regard to its top trading partners;

- U.S. commodity trade by geographical area and trade with our largest trading partners;

- U.S. commodity trade by detailed product categories;

- State exports of goods, including figures that show the distribution of exported goods among manufactured, agricultural, and other goods; and

- An explanatory discussion of the foreign trade data sources and uses to assist the user in ferreting out the multiple statistics that appear in the media as well as in academic discussions of trade issues.

The uses of these trade data are numerous: they show historic trends in trade in goods and services; they reveal how well the United States is doing in trade with its chief foreign competitors; and they provide a source of information on how trade affects not only the country as a whole but also each state, as available data include state exports of goods and their largest markets abroad.

Public policy analysts use such data to evaluate and plan programs such as export expansion, agricultural assistance under the Foreign Assistance and Merchant Marine Acts; to measure the impact of tariff and trade concessions under the General Agreement on Tariffs and Trade (GATT) and the General System of Preferences; and to analyze operations under various trade agreements such as the North American Free Trade Agreement, the Multi-Fiber Agreement, and others. These trade data are also useful for analysis of market share and product penetration, and in general for

determining marketing policies and product development.

This publication has five sections, each of which highlights a particular facet of U.S. foreign trade. Sections A through D provide information on the U.S. economy as a whole while Section E affords a view of export activity at the state level.

Section A provides information on U.S. international transactions, the "balance of payments" data, as well as the capital flows that are required to finance these balances. The data are provided by the Department of Commerce's Bureau of Economic Analysis (BEA) and the Census Bureau, and are available on a quarterly and annual basis from two different data systems. The International Transactions Accounts provide information on financial flows as well as the exchange of goods and services. A widely used statistic from the accounts is the current account balance—the most comprehensive measure of trade in goods and services—and its cumulation, which determines the net international investment position (whether the United States is a net creditor or debtor nation). The alternate data system, the National Income and Product Accounts (NIPA), provide data that differ somewhat in concept, scope, and definitions from the international transactions accounts. These are the numbers that are published each quarter with the release of the gross domestic product—the broadest measure of U.S. domestic economic activity in the United States. These data are published as annual data in this volume.

Section B provides aggregate data on foreign trade in goods and services on a balance of payments basis and is available monthly, quarterly, and annually from the BEA; it is compatible with the international transactions accounts. These data are the most prominent source of information relating to trade in services, including passenger fares paid by the residents of one country to another; other transportation, such as freight charges, royalties, and licensing fees; and other private services, which include education, financial, insurance, telecommunications, business, professional, and technical services. However, the main focus of Section B is the export and import of goods or merchandise provided by the Census Bureau. These are shown in several detailed product groupings and in terms of bilateral trade with other countries. The data in this volume appear on an annual basis.

U.S. commodity trade with the major regions of the world and with its top trading partners is presented in **Section C** and includes data on trade in the top 20 commodities (based on the 2003 dollar value) that the United States exports and imports. The tables also provide regional aggregation.

The data are collected by the Census Bureau and complied by the Office of Trade and Economic Analysis (OTEA) in the Commerce Department's International Trade Administration (ITA). These data appear in this publication as annual data.

Section D provides highlights of these commodity trade data cross-classified by the top countries to which the United States exports these commodities and those from which the United States imports these goods, and also shows U.S. trade balances with other nations.

The final part, **Section E**, focuses on trade activity at the state level. It includes exports of goods by each state's top exports and the top countries purchasing these exports.

As noted above, the data in this volume are annual time series. The data cover different time spans depending on data availability. In general, the data in this volume are presented through 2003 with some series updated through 2004. These data are the latest available as of February 2005.

The tables presented in this publication follow the layout of tables in *U.S. Foreign Trade Highlights*, previously published in document form by the OTEA and now available on their Web site at <www.ita.doc.gov/td/industry/otea/usfth/>. This volume expands that coverage to include aggregate international transactions and state-level data.

All statistical data are subject to errors due to sample variability, incomplete coverage, reporting and classification errors, and other causes. The responsibility of the editor and publisher of this volume is limited to reasonable care in the reproduction and presentation of the data obtained from established government sources.

In this publication, Bernan Press is pleased to assemble foreign trade data in one convenient volume and welcomes user comment on improvements and refinements for future editions.

This edition has been edited by Diane Werneke, in association with Mark Siegal, Katherine A. DeBrandt, and Mary Meghan Ryan.

Diane Werneke was formerly an economist and senior congressional liaison at the Federal Reserve Board and has also served on the House Budget Committee, the President's Commission on Employment and Unemployment Statistics, and in the International Labor Office in Geneva, Switzerland, specializing in macroeconomic and labor market policy and analysis. She holds a B.A. from the University of California at Berkeley and an M.A. from The George Washington University, both in economics.

Mark Siegal is a research editor with Bernan Press. He previously worked as a staff assistant with the USDA Human Nutrition Research Center on Aging at Tufts University, and has a background in researching government data; statistics and data management; technical writing; and editing. Also an assistant editor on *Business Statistics* and *Vital Statistics of the United States*, he has a B.S. in communication (with distinction in research) from Cornell University and a certificate in epidemiology from Tufts University.

Katherine A. DeBrandt is a senior data analyst team leader with Bernan Press. She received her B.A. in political science from Colgate University. She is also a co-editor of *The Who, What, and Where of America: Understanding the Census Results*; *State Profiles: The Population and Economy of Each U.S. State*; and *Social Change in America: The Historical Handbook*, all published by Bernan Press.

Mary Meghan Ryan is a data analyst with Bernan Press. She received her bachelor's degree in economics from the University of Maryland and is a former economist with the American Economic Group. Additionally, she has worked as a research assistant for FRANDATA. She is also an associate editor of the eighth edition of *Business Statistics of the United States* and the first edition of *Vital Statistics of the United States*, both published by Bernan Press.

Bernan Press' editorial and production departments, under the direction of Tamera Wells-Lee, did the copy editing, layout, and graphics preparation. Kara Prezocki, the production team leader, capably managed the production aspects of this volume as well as prepared the graphics and cover design. Production assistant Rebecca Zayas assisted Kara in coordinating this project. With support from Automated Graphics Systems and Publications Professionals, Kara and Rebecca assisted the editor tremendously with finalizing this publication.

As always, special thanks are due to the many federal agency personnel who assisted us in obtaining the data, provided excellent resources on their Web sites, and patiently answered our questions.

INTRODUCTION

In today's global economy, the world trade patterns that had captured little public attention in the United States for much of the post–Second World War period have now moved to a more prominent position in discussions not only among economists but also among public policy makers and the general public. A greater attention to international economic issues is partly due to ongoing increases in the interdependence of the world's economies. But this focus has been accentuated by two trends that have intensified in recent years.

One trend is the emergence of several developing countries, most notably China and India, as economic forces, and the consequent reorganization of production processes that has changed the nature and location of jobs. The second is the substantial widening of the U.S. trade deficit to a record level, which is raising concerns about its sustainability.

Job reorganization has resulted from the integration of other countries into the global economy—not only China and other developing countries, but also those of the former Soviet Union and its Eastern Bloc allies. It has also resulted from a heightened pace of technological change especially manifest in the declining cost of generating information. Cheaper access to information has boosted the integration and coordination of diverse production processes and the ability to transfer production to locations where costs (both labor and materials) are less expensive.

This type of shifting has long been evident in manufacturing industries in response to economic development and technological change, but what has emerged in recent years is the increasing array of services that can be carried out anywhere in the world, and with it, the restructuring of production processes and jobs around the world.

The deterioration of the U.S. trade situation is not a new phenomenon, as the U.S. balance of trade has generally trended downward since the mid-1980s. However, since the beginning of the 1990s, trade deficits have risen sharply both in dollar terms and relative to the U.S. economy, so that in 2004 the deficit on the current account—the broadest measure of international trade—was 5.7 percent of gross domestic product. As the U.S. trade deficits have mounted, the U.S. indebtedness to foreigners has consequently risen sharply from inconsequential amounts in the mid-1980s to nearly 25 percent of the U.S. gross domestic product in 2004. As of the end of 2003, foreign-owned assets in the United States totaled $9.6 trillion while U.S. holdings of foreign assets were $7.2 trillion, meaning the United States was in debt to the rest of the world by some $2.4 trillion.

U.S. exports contribute to the economy of most state and local areas while imports allow the U.S. consumer to choose from a wide variety of goods and services. Price competition from abroad restrains inflation, but noticeably impacts domestic jobs and profits of companies that are subject to the competition.

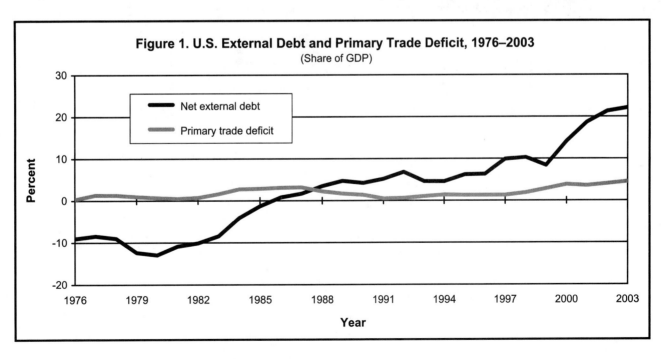

Figure 1. U.S. External Debt and Primary Trade Deficit, 1976–2003
(Share of GDP)

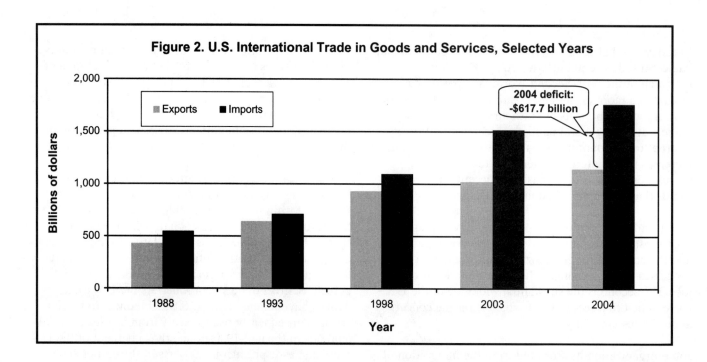

Figure 2. U.S. International Trade in Goods and Services, Selected Years

Recent years have shown a marked decline in various measures of the trade balance, as export expansion has been overwhelmed by the growth of imported goods and services, as depicted in Figure 2.

There are several reasons for the deterioration of the U.S. external sector. Until recently, the high and appreciating value of the dollar lessened the competitiveness of U.S. products. The reasons for the rise in the value of the dollar are many, including the attractiveness of investments in the United States (including the stock market during the 1990s), which increased the demand for the dollar; the role of the dollar as a reserve currency; and the dollar's use as a store of value for many lesser-developed countries. Even with the dollar's steady decline since 2002, the adjustment of the quantities demanded to the price changes transmitted by currency changes takes some time to work its way through economic systems. Moreover, with some trading partners, notably, but not solely, China, keeping the value of their currency tied or closely aligned to the dollar, the market signals of changing prices are blocked.

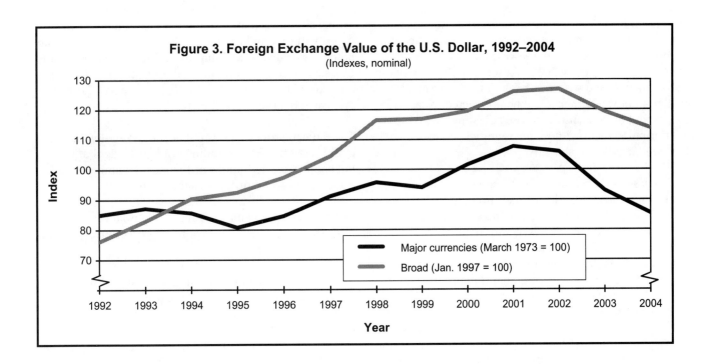

Figure 3. Foreign Exchange Value of the U.S. Dollar, 1992–2004
(Indexes, nominal)

Another reason for this decline is that the U.S. economy has tended to be stronger over significant periods than that of its chief trading partners, again supporting U.S. demand for imports relative to the weaker foreign demand for U.S. exports. Indeed, even without a growth differential between the economies of the United States and U.S. foreign trading partners, historically, the responsiveness of U.S. imports to income has been greater than the responsiveness of U.S. exports to income in the rest of the world. This means that even at similar growth rates, the United States tends to import more relative to those abroad.

Oil imports have also exacerbated the U.S. trade balance, as the recent sharp rise in the price of oil has pushed up the value of these imports. Although the United States does not consume as much energy per unit of output as it did three decade ago when the first energy crisis occurred, the country remains the world's largest importer of petroleum products.

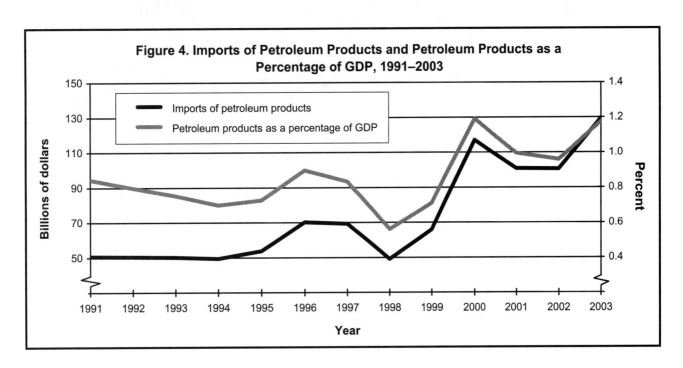

Figure 4. Imports of Petroleum Products and Petroleum Products as a Percentage of GDP, 1991–2003

The reason for concern about foreign trade deficits is that many worry that these current trends cannot continue without abatement. Federal Reserve Board Chairman Alan Greenspan said in 2000, "At some point something has got to give, and we don't know what it's going to be. We don't know whether it will be protracted over a very long period of time, in which case adjustments will occur in a normal manner without any significance, or whether they will occur more abruptly."

Four years later, Chairman Greenspan continued to express his worries, and his former director of the International Finance Division of the Federal Reserve Board, Edwin Truman, now with the Institute for International Economics, said, "When I left the Federal Reserve in 1998, when the current account deficit was 2.3 percent of the U.S. GDP [gross domestic product], the staff had concluded that deficits on that scale were not sustainable indefinitely. Six years later, the deficit is twice that size and not likely to narrow over the next two years....This history should give us pause, but it does not undermine the basic conclusion that sooner or later the U.S. current account deficit will narrow substantially....The adjustment is uncertain not only with respect to timing but also with respect to size."

These adjustments could occur through one or more mechanisms including: a further depreciation of the dollar against the currencies of our trading partners, rendering U.S. exports relatively cheaper and our imports more expensive; faster growth in markets abroad, stimulating demand for our exports, and conversely, slower growth in U.S. consumer spending, which has a relatively high propensity toward imported goods; continuing productivity growth that makes U.S. goods and services more competitive worldwide; and improved domestic trends in the U.S. saving rate, both public and private, which includes the federal budget deficit as well as a variety of other cyclical and structural adjustments.

The data contained in this publication are fully discussed in the section "Understanding Foreign Trade Statistics," but some brief definitions of the most commonly used trade terms are in order. To summarize:

- The **current account balance** is the broadest measure of trade, as it includes exports, imports, current income flows, and transfers.

- The **international transactions accounts**, of which the current account is a subset, are also known as the balance of payments, and they provide a comprehensive view of both economic transactions (the current account) and the financial transactions that accompany them.

- **Trade in goods and services**, also called the foreign trade statistics, are monthly data that are presented on a "balance of payments" basis and are the basis for the exports and imports of goods and services in the current account.

- **Trade in goods, merchandise, and commodities** all refer to exports and imports of products, as opposed to services.

UNDERSTANDING FOREIGN TRADE STATISTICS

This article is intended to serve as a guide to the various sources of foreign trade statistics. It also describes other types and sources of international data that are beyond the scope of this volume.

INTERNATIONAL TRANSACTIONS ACCOUNTS

The U.S. International Transactions Accounts, or balance of payment accounts, provide a comprehensive and detailed view of economic and financial transactions between the United States and foreign nations and of the accumulated value of U.S.-owned assets abroad and foreign-owned assets in the United States, known as the "net international investment position of the United States"—whether the nation is a net creditor or debtor to the rest of the world. Major transactions include merchandise trade, travel, transportation, other services, and governmental and private capital flows.

The Bureau of Economic Analysis (BEA) in the U.S. Department of Commerce prepares these statistics on a quarterly basis, and for the net international investment status, on an annual basis. The quarterly data are released in March, June, September, and December of each calendar year (most recently for this publication in December 2004 for data through the third quarter of 2004). With each quarterly release, data for the previous quarter are revised to incorporate additional information that has become available. Annual revisions to the data are made in June of each year to incorporate definitional, statistical, methodological, and presentational revisions. Most recently, the BEA has focused on improving the data collected for the service sector and on addressing gaps in the data that have arisen because of the dynamic nature of international financial markets. Also, in June of each year, the data showing the net international investment position of the United States as of the end of the previous year are published along with revisions to the prior year's data. All of this information is available on the BEA's Web site at <www.bea.gov> and in the *Survey of Current Business* by subscription to this publication at the U.S. Government Printing Office, Washington, DC 20402.

The U.S. international transactions accounts may be visualized as a balance sheet (hence the term "balance of payments") with credits, or additions to the accounts, and debits, or subtractions from the accounts. *Credits* to the accounts include the export of U.S. goods and services, receipts of income, unilateral current transfers to the United States (which includes government grants and pensions), and net capital and financial inflows to the United States, that is, increases in foreign-owned assets in the United States or decreases in U.S.-owned assets

abroad. *Debits* to the accounts include imports of foreign goods and services, income payments, current unilateral transfers to foreigners, and net capital and financial outflows from the United States to foreign countries, that is, decreases in foreign-owned assets in the United States or increases in U.S.-owned assets abroad.

These international transactions are divided into three sets of accounts, each comprising credit and debit items: the current account, the capital account, and the financial account; credits minus debits equal the balance on these three accounts.

The **current account balance** is the most widely used statistic to gauge the impact of trade on U.S. economic activity. Often referred to erroneously as the "trade" balance, which is defined more precisely below, the current account balance refers to the export of goods and services, income receipts, and unilateral transfers less imports of goods and services, income payments, and unilateral transfers abroad.

The **capital account balance**, the smallest of the international transactions accounts, includes the net effect (inflows less outflows) of debt forgiveness, the value of assets accompanying immigrants, such as bank accounts transferred by foreigners immigrating to the United States and vice versa, and the buying and selling of "non-produced," or existing nonfinancial assets, such as the rights to natural resources, patents, copyrights, trademarks, and leases.

The **financial account** measures the flow of capital between the United States and foreign nations, that is, the flows of private and governmental capital, including direct investment and purchases and sales of securities (equities and bonds), which are among the largest items that finance the current account balance.

The central relationship between these accounts is that the net inflow or outflow of capital into the United States, as measured by the capital and financial accounts, must balance the net flow of goods and services, income receipts, and unilateral transfers, that is, the current account. When the current account balance is negative, as it currently is, purchases of foreign goods and services, that is, imports (and other outflows), exceed sales of goods and services to foreigners, that is, exports (and other inflows). A negative account balance requires a net positive inflow of capital from foreigners to finance the current account deficit that is reflected in additional claims on the United States held by foreigners, whether these claims are held in the form of U.S. currency, securities, loans, or other forms of ownership of U.S. assets.

This conceptual identify in practice must be modified because of different and incomplete international data sources. The modification is known as the "statistical discrepancy," which is a separate item in the international accounts. It represents the amount by which the value of capital flows must be augmented to exactly offset the current account balance. Thus, in reality, the identity is

modified as follows: the absolute value of the current account equals the absolute value of capital and financial inflows plus the statistical discrepancy.

To visualize these balance sheets and ascertain the contribution of the major items in the international transactions account, the simplified table below may be useful.

U.S. INTERNATIONAL TRANSACTIONS, 2003

Item	Billions of dollars
1. Current account balance (2 + 5 + 8 + 9)	-530.7
2. Trade balance in goods	-547.6
3. Exports	713.1
4. Imports	-1,260.7
5. Trade balance in services	51.0
6. Exports	307.4
7. Imports	-256.4
8. Unilateral transfers (net)[1]	-67.4
9. Income receipts (net)[2]	33.3
10. Financial account balance[3] (11 + 12 + 13)	545.8
11. Direct investment (net)	-133.9
12. Portfolio investment (net)[4]	292.1
13. Other[5]	387.6
14. Capital account balance (net)	-3.1
15. Statistical discrepancy	-12.0

This table shows the accounting identity that the current account (-$530.7 billion) exactly balances the capital flows with the adjustment for the statistical discrepancy ($545.8 billion less $3.1 billion less $12.0 billion). Detailed items of the international transactions accounts are shown in Section A, Table A-1, together with footnotes that give precise definitions.

Unlike the international transactions accounts discussed above that depict the flows of goods and services and

capital, the **U.S. international investment position** is a stock concept; that is, it measures the total holdings of money, stocks, bonds, and other assets that the United States owns abroad and vice versa, the total holdings by foreigners of U.S. assets. The net international investment position thus depicts the extent to which U.S. claims on foreign assets exceed or fall short of foreign claims on U.S. assets, that is, whether the United States is a creditor or debtor nation. These data, derived from the compilation of flows in the international transactions accounts,

[1] Exports less imports (refers to unilateral transfers).

[2] Receipts less payments.

[3] U.S.-owned assets in foreign countries (outflow [-]) less foreign-owned assets in the United States (inflow [+]).

[4] Foreign-owned U.S. securities (equities and bonds) less U.S.-owned foreign securities (equities and bonds).

[5] Official and governmental assets (U.S. assets [-] less foreign official and government assets [+] and U.S. liabilities to foreigners less U.S. claims on foreigners).

are published by the BEA on an annual basis and are calculated using one of two methods, based on different methods of valuing direct investment. One is the current cost method, which values the investments of U.S. and foreign parent companies' affiliates in plants and equipment at replacement cost in today's prices, in land using general price indices, and in inventories using estimates of their replacement costs. The other method is the market value method, which values the owners' equity component of their direct investment using indices of stock market prices. Although broad secular trends are similar, market-valued direct investment is more volatile than the current cost method, reflecting volatility in the stock market. Again, a simplified table shows the components:

INTERNATIONAL INVESTMENT POSITION OF THE UNITED STATES AT YEAR-END, 2002 AND 2003 (BILLIONS OF DOLLARS, CURRENT COST VALUATION.)

Investment item	Position 2002	Change 2002–2003 (+/-) due to:			Position 2003
		Financial flows	Price changes	Exchange rate and other changes	
1. Net investment position (2 - 9)	-2,233.0	-545.8	37.1	311.0	-2,430.6
2. U.S.-owned assets abroad (3 + 4 + 5)	6,413.5	283.4	355.7	150.1	7,202.7
3. U.S. official assets	158.6	-1.5	18.1	8.4	183.6
4. U.S. governmental assets	85.3	-0.5			84.8
5. U.S. private assets (6 + 7 + 8)	6,189.6	285.5	337.6	141.7	6,934.3
6. Direct investment abroad	1,840.0	173.8	9.5	45.7	2,069.0
7. Foreign securities (stocks and bonds)	1,846.9	72.3	328.1	227.0	2,474.4
8. U.S. claims on foreigners[1]	2,482.7	39.3		-131.2	2,391.0
9. Foreign-owned assets in the United States (10 + 11)	8,646.6	829.2	318.6	-160.9	9,633.4
10. Foreign official assets	1,212.7	248.6	3.9	8.9	1,474.2
11. Other foreign assets[2]	7,433.8	580.6	314.6	-169.8	8,159.2

In general, changes in the net investment position can arise from inflows of capital that increase U.S. indebtedness to foreigners, while a net outflow increases foreigners' indebtedness to the United States. As described above, a deficit in the U.S. current account requires an equivalent inflow of foreign capital while a current account surplus would require an equal outflow of U.S. capital. Referring back to the previous table on U.S. international transactions, it is evident that much of the deterioration in our financial status in relation to the rest of the world was due to large inflows of capital ($545.8 billion) necessary to finance the current account deficit, as shown on the transactions table, that increased foreign investment in the United States and thus enlarged the tally of what the United States owed to foreigners (the change in the net position as a result of financial flows, shown in the table above). As depicted in this table, changes in the net investment position can also be a result of valuation adjustments such as changes in prices and exchange rates.

FOREIGN TRANSACTIONS IN THE NATIONAL INCOME AND PRODUCT ACCOUNTS

In addition to the international transaction accounts and the net investment status of the United States, the BEA also produces quarterly and annual data on foreign transactions that are compatible with the domestic-based

---

[1] U.S. claims on unaffiliated foreigners reported by nonbank concerns and by banks (such as commercial paper and loans).

[2] Includes official and governmental assets, direct private investment, investments in securities, and foreign claims.

National Income and Product Accounts (NIPA). These data show trends in price and quantity, which the international transactions accounts do not. Because of differences in scope, concept, and definitions, the aggregate value of the foreign transactions in the NIPA accounts are not exactly the same as estimates from the international transactions accounts. The chief differences are the NIPA inclusion of only the 50 states and the District of Columbia. The international transactions also include Puerto Rico and the U.S. territories, in addition to a differing treatment of gold and of some services. More data and information can be found in *Business Statistics of the United States: Patterns of Economic Change, 10th Edition, 2005,* Bernan Press. A reconciliation of the two sets of international transactions is published by the BEA's *Survey of Current Business*, most recently in June 2004.

U.S. INTERNATIONAL TRADE IN GOODS AND SERVICES

The key building blocks for the aggregate foreign trade statistics described above are the data on exports and imports of goods and services produced by the Census Bureau and the Bureau of Economic Analysis (BEA), both agencies of the Commerce Department. These data are commonly referred to as "foreign trade" or "balance of payments" statistics. These trade data are published monthly by the BEA and the Census Bureau in their release, *U.S. International Trade in Goods and Services,* often referred to as the FT900 release, and they provide an earlier view of U.S. trade patterns than the quarterly trade aggregates. They are also available in considerably more detail. For example, the greater detail shows specific industry products, such as petroleum or advanced technology, and these products can be cross-classified to show U.S. trade with individual countries and regions. Exports of goods are also available by states.

TRADE IN GOODS

Monthly data on exports and imports of goods are compiled by the Census Bureau and, as such, these goods are said to be measured on a "Census basis." Unlike the Census Bureau economic survey data that are based on solicited responses such as the population and labor force data, the trade data are compiled from the U.S. Customs Service reports on virtually all goods shipments leaving or entering the United States (exports and imports, respectively). Since 1990, exports to Canada are compiled using Canadian import data. (This requires several alignments, which are described in the monthly FT900 release and at <www.bea.gov>.)

The data reflect the exports and imports of the 50 states, the District of Columbia, Puerto Rico, the U.S. Virgin Islands, and U.S. Foreign Trade Zones (these are enclosed areas under the control of U.S. Customs with facilities for handling, storing, assembly, manufacturing, and processing goods without being subject to formal Customs entry procedures and payment of duties and tariffs until the foreign merchandise enters Customs territories for domestic consumption).

In general, the statistics record the physical movement of merchandise between the United States and foreign countries. The data include both government and nongovernmental shipments, but exclude those transactions between U.S. territories and possessions (treated as domestic trade), transactions with the U.S. military, diplomatic, and consular operations abroad, U.S. goods returned to the United States by the Armed Forces, the personal and household belongings of travelers, and in-transit shipments. Imports are arrivals of merchandise from foreign countries that enter consumption channels (for example, stores), warehouses, or Foreign Trade Zones.

Valuation. The value of merchandise exports and imports is measured in accordance with Census Bureau definitions. Exports are valued at "f.a.s.," or free alongside of ship at the port of exportation, based on the transaction price including inland freight, insurance, and other charges incurred in placing the goods alongside of a carrier at the U.S. port of exportation. The value, as defined, excludes the cost of loading the goods aboard the ship and other costs beyond the port of exportation.

For imports of goods, the value is measured on the appraised value reported to the U.S. Customs Service, "Customs," which is generally, the price paid for the merchandise for export to the United States. U.S. import duties, freight, insurance, and other charges incurred in bringing the merchandise to the United States are excluded.

Statistical Month. The month of exportation is based on the date when the merchandise leaves the United States. The month of importation is the month in which the U.S. Customs Service releases the merchandise to the importer.

Classifications of goods exports and imports. The export statistics are initially collected and compiled in terms of about 8,000 commodity classifications called Schedule B, as determined by the Census Bureau, and are based on the **Harmonized Commodity Description and Coding System** (the "Harmonized System" or "HS"), which describes and measures the characteristics of the goods. The Harmonized System is an international system established by the United Nations to classify products for tariff and statistical purposes and enhance comparability of data among nations. The import statistics are initially collected and compiled by about 14,000 commodity classifications, as determined by the U.S. International Trade Commission, also based on the HS system.

Under the international HS system, individual product categories are represented by 6-digit codes (the number of digits represents the level of detail a product is shown in) and are aggregated to higher levels of classification. The United States defines products using 10-digit codes, which are allowed under HS so long as the country definitions are within the HS 6-digit framework. In this volume, HS statistics are shown nationally at the 2-digit level, and by 6-digit code for the state tables in Section E.

These basic classifications are summarized and rearranged into other classification systems.

The HS and Schedule B classifications are summarized in six **end-use** categories which allow the examination of goods by their principal uses: foods, feeds, and beverages; industrial supplies and materials; capital goods, except automobile products; vehicles, parts, and engines; consumer goods except foods and autos; and other merchandise. The end-use demand concept was developed by the BEA for the purpose of estimating balance of payments data and is supplied by the Census Bureau for use in the international transactions or balance of payments accounts, as well as the National Income and Product Accounts.

Another universally used grouping is the **Standard International Trade Classification (SITC)**, a statistical classification of commodities designed by the U.N. and compatible with the HS. It is designed to provide commodity aggregations that are needed for the purposes of economic analysis and to facilitate the international comparison of trade by commodity. There are 10 broad groupings under the SITC system: (1) foods and live animals; (2) beverages and tobacco; (3) crude materials inedible, except fuels; (4) minerals, fuels, lubricants, and related materials; (5) animal and vegetable oils, fats and waxes; (6) chemicals and related products; (7) manufactured goods classified chiefly by material; (8) machinery and transport equipment; (9) miscellanous manufactured articles; and (10) commodities and transactions not classified elsewhere. These 10 groups of commodities represent the aggregation of approximately 3,000 5-digit SITC codes that reflect detailed products in each of the broad categories. In this volume, commodities are presented at the 1-, 2-, and 3-digit level of aggregation. The full list of SITC codes is given at <www.census.gov/foreign-trade/reference/codes/index.html>.

Goods are also classified according to the **North American Industry Classification System (NAICS)**, which was jointly created by the United States, Canada, and Mexico following the ratification of the North American Free Trade Agreement. This system is designed to promote comparability for data within North American and is not strictly comparable to the SITC system because product descriptions under NAICS may not fit neatly into the SITC classification scheme. NAICS replaced the Standard Industrial Classification (SIC) system beginning in 1997.

Because of the growing importance of technology goods in the U.S. economy and in world trade, the Census Bureau also provides a separate classification of **advanced technology products**, shown in Figure B-8 in the Section B highlights. Approximately 500 of the Schedule B and HS commodity classification codes used in reporting U.S. exports and imports are identified as "high technology," meeting the criteria that the products are from a high technology field (such as biotechnology), and they represent leading edge technology in that field.

To highlight **trade with other areas of the world**, merchandise trade data are also presented both bilaterally (individual countries' trade with the United States) and organized into geographical and economic groupings, both of which are presented in this volume. Section C contains the major groupings, their definitions, as well as the United States' top 80 trading partners. Section B also includes detailed data for countries and regions. With the release of the January 2005 trade statistics by the Census Buraeu and the BEA in March (not available for this publication), more detailed data will become available on countries that have accounted for increased trade activity in recent years.

For the purposes of bilateral trade, the country of destination of exports is defined as the country where the goods are to be consumed, further processed, or manufactured, as known to the shipper at the time of exportation. If the shipper does not know the country of ultimate destination, the shipment is credited to the last country where the shipper knows that the merchandise will be shipped in the same form as when exported. The country of origin of imports is the country where the goods are grown, manufactured, or mined. In instances where the country of origin cannot be identified, transactions are credited to the country of shipment.

Merchandise export data are also available by **state** and are shown in this volume in Section E. They denote the state from which the export actually starts its journey, or origin of movement, to the port of exportation. This may not necessarily be where the product is actually grown or produced or the actual location of the exporter. A further description is given in Section E.

Adjusting Goods Trade to a Balance of Payments Basis. Merchandise trade on a Census basis is adjusted to a balance of payments basis as it appears in the FT900 monthly release in order to bring the data into line with the concepts and definitions used to prepare the international transactions accounts as well as the National Income and Product Accounts. Generally, these adjustments include changes in ownership that occur without the goods passing into or out of the customs territory of the United States. These adjustments are necessary to supplement the coverage of the basic Census data, to eliminate the duplication of transactions recorded elsewhere in the international accounts, and to value transactions according to a standard definition.

The adjustments to exports include:

- The deduction of military sales contracts is made because the Census data include these contracts as goods while the BEA includes such sales as services;

- An addition is made for private gift parcels mailed to foreigners by individuals mailed through the U.S. Postal System because only commercial shipments are covered in Census goods exports; and

- Gold (nonmonetary) exports purchased by foreign official agencies from private dealers in the United States and held at the Federal Reserve Bank of New York are added to Census figures because Census data only include gold that leaves the customs territory.

Adjustments to imports include:

- An addition is made to imports for inland freight in Canada. Imports of goods from all countries are valued at the port of export, including inland freight charges (Customs value), but in the case of Canada this should be the cost of the goods at the U.S. border. However, the Customs value for certain Canadian goods is the point of origin in Canada. Therefore, the BEA makes an addition for the inland freight charges of transporting these goods to the U.S. border to make the value comparable to the Customs value reported by all other countries.

- An addition is made for gold sold by foreign official agencies to private purchasers out of their stock of gold held at the Federal Reserve Bank of New York. Census data only include gold that enters the customs territory.

- Imports by U.S. military agencies is deducted because these military sales contracts have been in the Census goods data while the BEA includes them in services.

Revision Policy. Each month the aggregate goods data published in the FT900 release contains the current month preliminary estimates together with revisions of the prior month's estimates, reflecting additional data that has become available since the previous month's release. Trade classified by "end-use" category is similarly revised. SITC and country detail are not revised monthly. In this volume, these data appear on an annual basis. Annual revisions for the monthly data are made in June of each year.

Further detailed discussion of foreign trade in goods can be found at <www.census.gov/foreign-trade/guide/> and in the *Survey of Current Business* (March, June, September, and December issues) as well as at <www.census.gov/foreign-trade/aip/index.html#infopapers>, where information is available on reporting and nonsampling errors, undocumented shipments, timeliness errors, undocumented shipments, and low-valued transactions. This information is also available from the Foreign Trade Division, Census Bureau, Room 2179, Federal Office Building #3, Washington, DC 20233.

TRADE IN SERVICES

Monthly service trade data are prepared by the BEA and generally refer to services provided by the U.S. government, businesses, or individuals to residents of other countries and for similar services provided by foreigners to U.S. residents. The data for services trade are far less detailed than for goods trade although research has focused on expanding the data. Estimates of the export and import of services sum with little adjustment to the aggregates displayed in the quarterly and annual international transactions accounts. The statistics reflect transactions between foreign countries and the 50 states, the District of Columbia, Puerto Rico, and the other U.S. territories and possessions. Transactions with U.S. military, diplomatic, and consular facilities abroad are excluded because they are considered part of the U.S. economy.

As detailed in BEA's *Survey of Current Business* as well as the FT900 release, the data are divided into seven broad categories. The types of services are the same for exports and imports in six of the categories while in the seventh, exports are defined as "transfers under U.S. military sales contracts" and imports are "direct defense expenditures." The following is a brief description of each of these categories:

- **Travel** includes purchases of services and some goods by U.S. travelers abroad and by foreign visitors to the United States. A traveler is defined as a person who stays less than one year and who is not a resident of the foreign country. The category includes food, lodging, recreation, gifts, and other items incidental to a foreign visit.

- **Passenger fares** are fares paid by residents of one country to those of another. Receipts (exports) consist of fares received by U.S. carriers for travel between the United States and foreign countries and payments (imports) are fares paid by U.S. residents to foreign carriers for such travel.

- **Other transportation** consists of charges for the transportation of goods by air, ocean, waterway, pipeline, and rail to and from the United States. It includes freight charges, operating expenses that transportation companies incur in foreign ports, and payments for vessel charter and aircraft rental with a crew.

- **Royalties and license fees** are transactions with foreign residents involving intangible assets and proprietary rights, such as the use of patents, techniques, processes, formulas, designs, trademarks, copyrights, franchises, and manufacturing rights. The term "royalties" generally refers to the utilization of copyrights or trademarks while license fees pertain to payments for the use of patents or industrial processes.

- **Other private services** include transactions with affiliated foreigners for which there is no identification available by type and transactions with unaffiliated foreigners. The term "affiliated" refers to a direct investment relationship, which is said to exist when a U.S. person has ownership or control, directly or indirectly, of 10 percent or more of a foreign business enterprise's voting securities or the equivalent, or when a foreign person has a similar interest in a U.S. enterprise. Transactions with unaffiliated foreigners consist of educational service, financial services (including commissions and other transaction fees associated with the purchase and sale of securities and the noninterest income of banks but excluding investment income), insurance and telecommunications services, and business, professional, and technical services. The latter includes advertising, computer, data processing, database and other information services, research, development, and testing services, management, consulting, public relations services, legal services, construction, engineering, architectural, and mining services, industrial engineering services, installation, maintenance, and repair of equipment, and other services such as medical services and film and tape rentals.

- **Transfers under U.S. military sales contracts** are exports of services as well as goods in which the U.S. military agencies participate, including exports of equipment and services such as repair and training

services that cannot be separately identified. **Direct Defense Department expenditures** (imports) include expenditures by U.S. personnel, payments of wages to foreign residents' construction expenditures, payment for foreign contractual services, and procurement of foreign goods.

- **U.S. government miscellaneous services** are transactions with foreign residents generally involving the provision of services by foreigners.

Service estimates are based on quarterly, annual, and benchmark surveys, as well as partial information generated from monthly reports. They are valued at market prices.

Revision Policy. Each month, a preliminary estimate for the current month and a revised estimate of the preceding month are released. After a revision is released, no further changes are made to that month's estimate until more complete data become available in March, June, September, and December. When these data become available, the estimates are then revised for the six preceding months. For example, in December 2004 (the latest data available in this volume) service trade data were revised for the July–December period. As it is the established procedure, the March 2005 release will also contain revisions for all months in 2004, and the June 2005 release will contain annual revisions which reflect updated data source and changes in estimating methodologies.

Further information on trade in services may be found on the BEA Web site at <www.bea.gov> or by contacting the BEA at the Balance of Payments Division, Bureau of Economic Analysis, Department of Commerce, Washington, DC 20230, or by telephone at (202) 606-9545.

WORLD TRADE STATISTICS

In addition to U.S. foreign trade data, there are many sources of information on the foreign trade of other countries. The World Trade Organization (WTO) publishes *International Trade Statistics,* an annual report on global trade (most recently in October 2004 for the 2003 data), which contains detailed analysis and tables for most countries, leading trading nations, trade by sector and product, and regional trade. These data are supplemented by monthly press releases. The information is available on the WTO's Web site at <www.wto.org>.

The Organisation for Economic Co-operation and Development (OECD) provides detailed trade data on both goods and services on their member countries, which include Australia, Austria, Belgium, Canada, the Czech Republic, Denmark, Finland, France, Germany, Greece, Hungary, Iceland, Ireland, Italy, Japan, South Korea, Luxembourg, Mexico, the Netherlands, New Zealand, Norway, Poland, Portugal, the Slovak Republic, Spain, Sweden, Switzerland, Turkey, the United Kingdom, and the United States. The OECD Web site at <www.oecd.org> also provides links to the trade databases of other key international organizations, such as the United Nations, the World Bank, the International Monetary Fund, as well as regional development banks and organizations. The Web site also has links to nongovernmental sources such as research institutions that produce trade data and analysis.

The International Monetary Fund is a source of international statistics on all aspects of international finance. It reports, for most countries of the world, data on international transactions, government accounts, exchange rates, and other relevant data needed in analyses of balance of payments issues. The data are published monthly, and are available from their Web site at <www.imf.org> for a fee.

In addition, the Office of Trade and Economic Analysis (OTEA), part of the Commerce Department's International Trade Administration provides, links to regional trade data for Asian/Pacific nations, Europe, and developing countries; to data on trade in services; and to data from many other sources in the Foreign Trade Highlight's Frequently Asked Questions section at <www.ita.doc.gov/td/industry/otea/usfth/fth_faq.html>.

INTERNATIONAL COMPARISONS

U.S. trade patterns are influenced by a variety of factors including, importantly, economic developments abroad such as growth rates, productivity, and prices. This subject is beyond the scope of this volume, but is covered in *Business Statistics*, published by Bernan Press. Sources of these data are also detailed.

FOREIGN EXCHANGE RATES

The value of one currency versus another or against a group of currencies is a necessary tool in analyzing foreign trade patterns. This volume shows both trade-weighted indexes, compiled by the Federal Reserve Board, and bilateral exchange rates, from the International Monetary Fund. The Federal Reserve indexes measure the value of the dollar against groups of foreign countries. The **broad** index, shown in Figure 3 of the Introduction, measures the change in the value of the dollar relative to the currencies of a broad group of trading partners. The **major** index, also shown in Figure 3, is a subset of the broad index and features the currencies of countries that circulate widely outside the home country of issue, and are of particular relevance to international capital flows. These indexes are weighted on the basis of trade flows. The broad index includes 26 countries' economies whose bilateral shares of U.S. imports or exports exceeded 0.5 percent. Seven of the 26 currencies in the broad index—the euro, the Canadian dollar, the Japanese yen, the British pound, the Swiss franc, the Australian dollar, and the Swedish krona—along with the U.S. dollar are referred to as major currencies.

Bilateral foreign exchange rates, which are mainly composed of market and official rates, are published for most world economies by the International Monetary Fund and appear in this volume in Table B-34. Exchange rates and indexes can also be found at <www.federalreserve.gov/releases/>.

SECTION A. U.S. INTERNATIONAL TRANSACTIONS AND INVESTMENT POSITION

ABOUT THE DATA

Section A provides an overview of U.S. international transactions and the net international investment position of the United States. This is important background for the foreign trade data that composes the rest of this volume.

Table A-1 shows **U.S. international transactions**: the current account balance and the capital flows that finance it.

Table A-2 shows the **net international investment position of the United States**: the accumulated values of U.S.-owned assets abroad and foreign-owned assets in the United States, which show whether the United States is a net creditor or debtor nation in the global economy.

These data are shown on an annual basis through 2003, the latest available annual data as of February 2005. Annual revisions are made to the data in June of each

year and are published by the Bureau of Economic Analysis (BEA) in the July *Survey of Current Business*. The data is also available on the BEA's Web site at <www.bea.gov>.

The latest revision for the international transactions data covers the 1989–2003 period. Estimates for the international investment position were revised for 1994–2002 (consequently, 2003 data for this series remain as preliminary estimates). These revisions appeared in the July 2004 *Survey of Current Business*.

See "Understanding Foreign Trade Statistics" for more detailed information and definitions.

Tables A-1 and A-2 contain the many footnotes published by the BEA that specifically define the components of the U.S. international transactions accounts. These tables also provide the detailed data underpinning the following figures.

1

HIGHLIGHTS

Since 1994, the current account deficit has exceeded $100 billion every year. This deficit is primarily because of a deficit on goods, meaning that U.S. imports of goods outstripped U.S. exports of goods. By 2003, these persistent annual deficits resulted in a $2.4 trillion debt to the rest of the world.

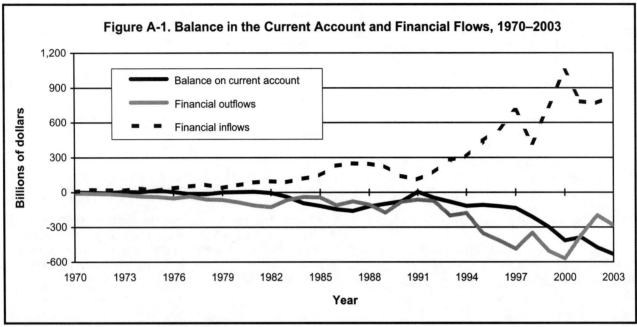

Figure A-1. Balance in the Current Account and Financial Flows, 1970–2003

Source: Bureau of Economic Analysis.

Figure A-1 shows that the current account was roughly in balance until the early 1980s. Since 1982, there has been a deficit every year except for 1991. After 1991, a more substantial gap began to grow. By the end of 2003, the current account deficit had reached $531 billion, and the preliminary data for 2004 shows a deficit of $666 billion.

The current account deficit was financed by inflows of foreign capital that, until recently, largely consisted of private investments by foreigners in U.S. stocks, bonds, interests in companies, or other assets as foreigners sought higher returns on investments than they thought were attainable elsewhere. However, since the early 2000s, private capital flows from abroad have ceased their rapid expansion, and foreign governments, especially Japan and China, have taken up the slack by buying U.S. Treasury securities.

Financial outflows—that is, U.S. investments abroad—largely consist of U.S. private direct investments and, to a lesser extent, purchases of foreign securities. Overall, financial outflows have slowed since the early 2000s.

As seen in Figure A-2, the current account balance has declined significantly over the past decade, primarily because imports of foreign goods greatly exceed exports of U.S. goods. While exports of U.S. goods are growing, imports are increasing more than twice as fast, causing the deficit to continue to climb. In 1996, the deficit in goods was about 2.4 percent of gross domestic product. This grew to 5.7 percent in 2004, when the current account balance reached a deficit of $666 billion.

Trade in services has maintained a small but positive balance since the early 1970s. However, this surplus in services trade has been declining since 1997, as services imports are rising much more rapidly than exports.

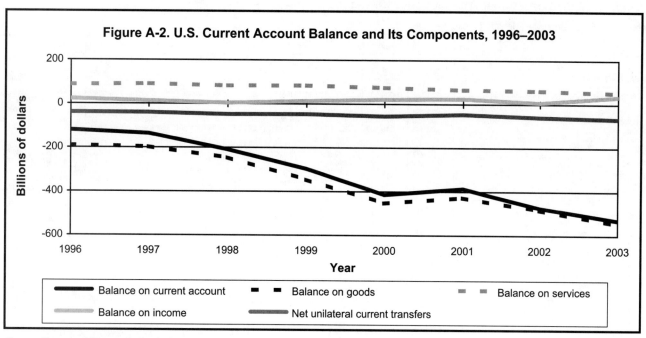

Figure A-2. U.S. Current Account Balance and Its Components, 1996–2003

Source: Bureau of Economic Analysis.

The result of ongoing current account deficits can be seen in Figure A-3, which shows the rapid decline of the United States' net international investment position. Using the current, or replacement, cost valuation of direct investment in plants, equipment, inventories, land, etc., the United States became a substantial debtor nation by the mid-1990s. This trend sharpened in 1999 and by year-end 2003 (the latest available data), the United States had amassed a debt to the rest of the world of $2.4 trillion.

From 2002 to 2003, the net international investment position deteriorated by $198 billion due primarily to large net foreign purchases of U.S. securities (mostly corporate bonds and U.S. Treasury securities). In 2003, foreign acquisitions of U.S. assets reached $829 billion, which was the second highest value ever. Foreign official purchases more than doubled from 2002 to 2003. Private investment in U.S. Treasury securities increased, but purchases of other securities have declined since 2000.

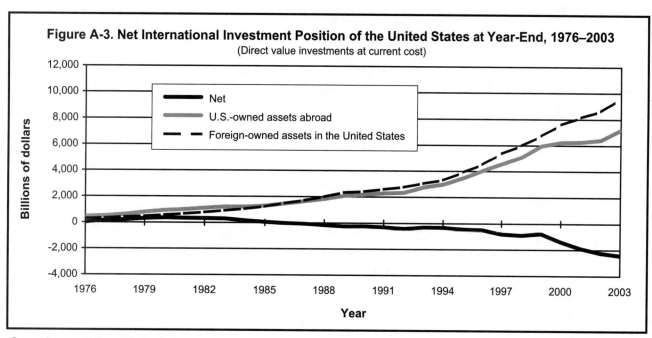

Figure A-3. Net International Investment Position of the United States at Year-End, 1976–2003
(Direct value investments at current cost)

Source: Bureau of Economic Analysis.

Table A-1. U.S. International Transactions, 1994–2003

(Millions of dollars; credits [+], debits [-] [1], except as noted.)

Item	1994	1995	1996	1997	1998	1999	2000	2001	2002	2003
CURRENT ACCOUNT										
Exports of goods and services and income receipts	869 775	1 004 631	1 077 731	1 191 441	1 194 803	1 259 665	1 421 429	1 293 345	1 242 739	1 314 888
Exports of goods and services	703 254	794 387	851 602	934 637	933 495	966 443	1 070 980	1 006 653	975 940	1 020 503
Goods, balance of payments basis [2]	502 859	575 204	612 113	678 366	670 416	683 965	771 994	718 712	681 833	713 122
Services [3]	200 395	219 183	239 489	256 271	263 079	282 478	298 986	287 941	294 107	307 381
Transfers under U.S. military agency sales contracts [4]	12 787	14 643	16 446	16 675	17 405	15 928	13 790	12 539	11 943	12 491
Travel	58 417	63 395	69 809	73 426	71 325	74 801	82 400	71 893	66 728	64 509
Passenger fares	16 997	18 909	20 422	20 868	20 098	19 785	20 687	17 926	17 046	15 693
Other transportation	23 754	26 081	26 074	27 006	25 604	26 916	29 803	28 442	29 195	31 833
Royalties and license fees [5]	26 712	30 289	32 470	33 228	35 626	39 670	43 233	40 696	44 219	48 227
Other private services [5]	60 841	65 048	73 340	84 113	92 095	104 493	108 287	115 614	124 181	133 818
U.S. government miscellaneous services	887	818	928	955	926	885	786	831	795	810
Income receipts	166 521	210 244	226 129	256 804	261 308	293 222	350 449	286 692	266 799	294 385
Income receipts on U.S.-owned assets abroad	164 578	208 065	223 948	254 534	258 871	290 474	347 614	283 761	263 861	291 354
Direct investment receipts	77 344	95 260	102 505	115 323	103 963	131 626	151 839	128 665	147 291	187 522
Other private receipts	83 106	108 092	116 852	135 652	151 307	155 651	191 929	151 535	113 267	99 135
U.S. government receipts	4 128	4 713	4 591	3 559	3 601	3 197	3 846	3 561	3 303	4 697
Compensation of employees	1 943	2 179	2 181	2 270	2 437	2 748	2 835	2 931	2 938	3 031
Imports of goods and services and income payments	-951 008	-1 080 005	-1 159 355	-1 287 010	-1 355 917	-1 509 732	-1 779 188	-1 632 465	-1 657 301	-1 778 117
Imports of goods and services	-801 633	-890 652	-955 544	-1 042 815	-1 098 363	-1 229 695	-1 449 324	-1 369 345	-1 397 675	-1 517 011
Goods, balance of payments basis [2]	-668 690	-749 374	-803 113	-876 470	-917 103	-1 029 980	-1 224 408	-1 145 900	-1 164 728	-1 260 674
Services [3]	-132 943	-141 278	-152 431	-166 345	-181 260	-199 715	-224 916	-223 445	-232 947	-256 337
Direct defense expenditures	-10 217	-10 043	-11 061	-11 707	-12 185	-13 335	-13 473	-14 835	-19 101	-25 117
Travel	-43 782	-44 916	-48 078	-52 051	-56 483	-58 963	-64 705	-60 200	-58 044	-56 613
Passenger fares	-13 062	-14 663	-15 809	-18 138	-19 971	-21 315	-24 274	-22 633	-19 969	-20 957
Other transportation	-26 019	-27 034	-27 403	-28 959	-30 363	-34 139	-41 425	-38 682	-38 407	-44 768
Royalties and license fees [5]	-5 852	-6 919	-7 837	-9 161	-11 235	-13 107	-16 468	-16 538	-19 235	-20 049
Other private services [5]	-31 451	-35 080	-39 556	-43 567	-48 174	-56 035	-61 688	-67 675	-75 271	-85 829
U.S. government miscellaneous services	-2 560	-2 623	-2 687	-2 762	-2 849	-2 821	-2 883	-2 882	-2 920	-3 004
Income payments	-149 375	-189 353	-203 811	-244 195	-257 554	-280 037	-329 864	-263 120	-259 626	-261 106
Income payments on foreign-owned assets in the United States	-143 423	-183 090	-197 511	-237 529	-250 560	-272 082	-322 345	-255 034	-251 246	-252 573
Direct investment payments	-22 150	-30 318	-33 093	-42 950	-38 418	-53 437	-56 910	-12 783	-46 460	-68 657
Other private payments	-77 081	-97 149	-97 800	-112 878	-127 988	-138 120	-180 918	-159 825	-128 672	-111 874
U.S. government payments	-44 192	-55 623	-66 618	-81 701	-84 154	-80 525	-84 517	-82 426	-76 114	-72 042
Compensation of employees	-5 952	-6 263	-6 300	-6 666	-6 994	-7 955	-7 519	-8 086	-8 380	-8 533
Unilateral current transfers, net	-36 799	-34 104	-38 583	-40 410	-48 443	-46 755	-55 684	-46 581	-59 382	-67 439
U.S. government grants [4]	-14 978	-11 190	-15 401	-12 472	-13 270	-13 774	-16 714	-11 517	-17 097	-21 865
U.S. government pensions and other transfers	-4 556	-3 451	-4 466	-4 191	-4 305	-4 406	-4 705	-5 798	-5 125	-5 341
Private remittances and other transfers [6]	-17 265	-19 463	-18 716	-23 747	-30 868	-28 575	-34 265	-29 266	-37 160	-40 233
CAPITAL AND FINANCIAL ACCOUNT										
Capital Account										
Capital account transactions, net	-1 723	-927	-654	-1 044	-740	-4 843	-809	-1 083	-1 260	-3 079
Financial Account										
U.S.-owned assets abroad, net (increase/financial outflow (-))	-178 937	-352 264	-413 409	-485 475	-347 829	-503 640	-569 798	-366 768	-198 014	-283 414
U.S. official reserve assets, net	5 346	-9 742	6 668	-1 010	-6 783	8 747	-290	-4 911	-3 681	1 523
Gold [7]	0	0	0	0	0	0	0	0	0	0
Special drawing rights	-441	-808	370	-350	-147	10	-722	-630	-475	601
Reserve position in the International Monetary Fund	494	-2 466	-1 280	-3 575	-5 119	5 484	2 308	-3 600	-2 632	1 494
Foreign currencies	5 293	-6 468	7 578	2 915	-1 517	3 253	-1 876	-681	-574	-572
U.S. government assets, other than official reserve assets, net	-390	-984	-989	68	-422	2 750	-941	-486	345	537
U.S. credits and other long-term assets	-5 383	-4 859	-5 025	-5 417	-4 678	-6 175	-5 182	-4 431	-5 251	-7 279
Repayments on U.S. credits and other long-term assets [8]	5 088	4 125	3 930	5 438	4 111	9 559	4 265	3 873	5 701	7 981
U.S. foreign currency holdings and U.S. short-term assets, net	-95	-250	106	47	145	-634	-24	72	-105	-165
U.S. private assets, net	-183 893	-341 538	-419 088	-484 533	-340 624	-515 137	-568 567	-361 371	-194 678	-285 474
Direct investment	-80 167	-98 750	-91 885	-104 803	-142 644	-224 934	-159 212	-142 349	-134 835	-173 799
Foreign securities	-63 190	-122 394	-149 315	-116 852	-124 204	-116 236	-121 908	-84 644	15 889	-72 337
U.S. claims on unaffiliated foreigners reported by U.S. nonbanking concerns	-36 336	-45 286	-86 333	-121 760	-38 204	-97 704	-138 790	-8 520	-45 425	-28 932
U.S. claims reported by U.S. banks, not included elsewhere	-4 200	-75 108	-91 555	-141 118	-35 572	-76 263	-148 657	-125 858	-30 307	-10 406

[1]Credits, +: Exports of goods and services and income receipts; unilateral current transfers to the United States; capital account transactions receipts; financial inflows—increase in foreign-owned assets (U.S. liabilities) or decrease in U.S.-owned assets (U.S. claims). Debits, -: Imports of goods and services and income payments; unilateral current transfers to foreigners; capital account transactions payments; financial outflows—decrease in foreign-owned assets (U.S. liabilities) or increase in U.S.-owned assets (U.S. claims).
[2]Excludes exports of goods under U.S. military agency sales contracts identified in Census export documents, excludes imports of goods under direct defense expenditures identified in Census import documents, and reflects various other adjustments (for valuation, coverage, and timing) of Census statistics to balance of payments basis.
[3]Includes some goods: Mainly military equipment; major equipment, other materials, supplies, and petroleum products purchased abroad by U.S. military agencies; and fuels purchased by airline and steamship operators.
[4]Includes transfers of goods and services under U.S. military grant programs.
[5]Beginning in 1982, these lines are presented on a gross basis. The definition of exports is revised to exclude U.S. parents' payments to foreign affiliates and to include U.S. affiliates' receipts from foreign parents. The definition of imports is revised to include U.S. parents' payments to foreign affiliates and to exclude U.S. affiliates' receipts from foreign parents.
[6]Beginning in 1982, the "other transfers" component includes taxes paid by U.S. private residents to foreign governments and taxes paid by private nonresidents to the U.S. government.
[7]At the present time, all U.S.-Treasury-owned gold is held in the United States.
[8]Includes sales of foreign obligations to foreigners.

Table A-1. U.S. International Transactions, 1994–2003—*Continued*

(Millions of dollars; credits [+], debits [-] [1], except as noted.)

Item	1994	1995	1996	1997	1998	1999	2000	2001	2002	2003
Foreign-owned assets in the United States, net (increase/financial inflow (+))	305 989	438 562	551 096	706 809	423 569	740 210	1 046 896	782 859	768 246	829 173
Foreign official assets in the United States, net	39 583	109 880	126 724	19 036	-19 903	43 543	42 758	28 059	113 990	248 573
U.S. government securities	36 827	72 712	120 679	-2 161	-3 589	32 527	35 710	54 620	89 016	194 568
U.S. Treasury securities [9]	30 750	68 977	115 671	-6 690	-9 921	12 177	-5 199	33 700	60 466	169 685
Other [10]	6 077	3 735	5 008	4 529	6 332	20 350	40 909	20 920	28 550	24 883
Other U.S. government liabilities [11]	1 564	-105	-982	-881	-3 326	-2 863	-1 825	-2 309	137	-564
U.S. liabilities reported by U.S. banks, not included elsewhere	3 665	34 008	5 704	22 286	-9 501	12 964	5 746	-29 978	21 221	49 420
Other foreign official assets [12]	-2 473	3 265	1 323	-208	-3 487	915	3 127	5 726	3 616	5 149
Other foreign assets in the United States, net	266 406	328 682	424 372	687 773	443 472	696 667	1 004 138	754 800	654 256	580 600
Direct investment	46 121	57 776	86 502	105 603	179 045	289 444	321 274	167 021	72 411	39 890
U.S. Treasury securities	34 274	91 544	130 435	130 435	28 581	-44 497	-69 983	-14 378	100 432	113 432
U.S. securities other than U.S. Treasury securities	56 971	77 249	103 272	161 409	156 315	298 834	459 889	393 885	285 500	250 981
U.S. currency	23 400	12 300	17 362	24 782	16 622	22 407	5 315	23 783	21 513	16 640
U.S. liabilities to unaffiliated foreigners reported by U.S. nonbanking concerns	1 302	59 637	53 736	116 518	23 140	76 247	170 672	66 110	77 990	84 014
U.S. liabilities reported by U.S. banks, not included elsewhere	104 338	30 176	16 478	149 026	39 769	54 232	116 971	118 379	96 410	75 643
Statistical discrepancy (sum of above items with sign reversed)	-7 297	24 107	-16 826	-84 311	134 557	65 095	-62 846	-29 307	-95 028	-12 012
Of which: Seasonal adjustment discrepancy	0	0	0	0	0	0	0	0	0	0
MEMORANDA:										
Balance on goods	-165 831	-174 170	-191 000	-198 104	-246 687	-346 015	-452 414	-427 188	-482 895	-547 552
Balance on services	67 452	77 905	87 058	89 926	81 819	82 763	74 070	64 496	61 160	51 044
Balance on goods and services	-98 379	-96 265	-103 942	-108 178	-164 868	-263 252	-378 344	-362 692	-421 735	-496 508
Balance on income	17 146	20 891	22 318	12 609	3 754	13 185	20 585	23 572	7 173	33 279
Unilateral current transfers, net	-36 799	-34 104	-38 583	-40 410	-48 443	-46 755	-55 684	-46 581	-59 382	-67 439
Balance on current account [13]	-118 032	-109 478	-120 207	-135 979	-209 557	-296 822	-413 443	-385 701	-473 944	-530 668

[1]Credits, +: Exports of goods and services and income receipts; unilateral current transfers to the United States; capital account transactions receipts; financial inflows—increase in foreign-owned assets (U.S. liabilities) or decrease in U.S.-owned assets (U.S. claims). Debits, -: Imports of goods and services and income payments; unilateral current transfers to foreigners; capital account transactions payments; financial outflows—decrease in foreign-owned assets (U.S. liabilities) or increase in U.S.-owned assets (U.S. claims).
[9]Consists of bills, certificates, marketable bonds and notes, and nonmarketable convertible and nonconvertible bonds and notes.
[10]Consists of U.S. Treasury and Export-Import Bank obligations, not included elsewhere, and of debt securities of U.S. government corporations and agencies.
[11]Includes, primarily, U.S. government liabilities associated with military agency sales contracts and other transactions arranged with or through foreign official agencies.
[12]Consists of investments in U.S. corporate stocks and in debt securities of private corporations and state and local governments.
[13]Conceptually, the sum of "balance on current account" and "capital account transactions, net" is equal to "net lending or net borrowing" in the national income and product accounts (NIPAs). However, the foreign transactions account in the NIPAs (a) includes adjustments to the international transactions accounts for the treatment of gold, (b) includes adjustments for the different geographical treatment of transactions with U.S. territories and Puerto Rico, and (c) includes services furnished without payment by financial pension plans except life insurance carriers and private noninsured pension plans. A reconciliation of the balance on goods and services from the international accounts and the NIPA net exports appears in reconciliation table 2 in appendix A in the *Survey of Current Business*. A reconciliation of the other foreign transactions in the two sets of accounts appears in table 4.3B of the full set of NIPA tables.

Table A-2. International Investment Position of the United States at Year-End, 1994–2003

(Millions of dollars.)

Type of investment	1994	1995	1996	1997	1998	1999	2000	2001	2002	2003 p
Net international investment position of the United States										
With direct investment positions at current cost	-323 397	-458 462	-495 055	-820 682	-899 966	-775 488	-1 388 745	-1 889 680	-2 233 018	-2 430 682
With direct investment positions at market value	-135 251	-305 836	-360 024	-822 732	-1 075 377	-1 046 688	-1 588 556	-2 308 161	-2 553 407	-2 650 990
U.S.-owned assets abroad										
With direct investment at current cost	2 987 118	3 486 272	4 032 307	4 567 906	5 090 938	5 965 143	6 231 236	6 270 408	6 413 535	7 202 692
With direct investment at market value	3 315 135	3 964 558	4 650 837	5 379 128	6 174 518	7 390 427	7 393 643	6 898 707	6 613 320	7 863 968
U.S. official reserve assets	163 394	176 061	160 739	134 836	146 006	136 418	128 400	129 961	158 602	183 577
Gold [1]	100 110	101 279	96 698	75 929	75 291	75 950	71 799	72 328	90 806	108 866
Special drawing rights	10 039	11 037	10 312	10 027	10 603	10 336	10 539	10 783	12 166	12 638
Reserve position in the International Monetary Fund	12 030	14 649	15 435	18 071	24 111	17 950	14 824	17 869	21 979	22 535
Foreign currencies	41 215	49 096	38 294	30 809	36 001	32 182	31 238	28 981	33 651	39 538
U.S. government assets, other than official reserve assets	83 908	85 064	86 123	86 198	86 768	84 227	85 168	85 654	85 309	84 772
U.S. credits and other long-term assets [2]	81 884	82 802	83 999	84 130	84 850	81 657	82 574	83 132	82 682	81 980
Repayable in dollars	81 389	82 358	83 606	83 780	84 528	81 367	82 293	82 854	82 406	81 706
Other [3]	495	444	393	350	322	290	281	278	276	274
U.S. foreign currency holdings and U.S. short-term assets	2 024	2 262	2 124	2 068	1 918	2 570	2 594	2 522	2 627	2 792
U.S. private assets										
With direct investment at current cost	2 739 816	3 225 147	3 785 445	4 346 872	4 858 164	5 744 498	6 017 668	6 054 793	6 169 624	6 934 343
With direct investment at market value	3 067 833	3 703 433	4 403 975	5 158 094	5 941 744	7 169 782	7 180 075	6 683 092	6 369 409	7 595 619
Direct investment abroad										
At current cost [4]	786 565	885 506	989 810	1 068 063	1 196 021	1 414 355	1 531 607	1 686 635	1 839 995	2 069 013
At market value [4]	1 114 582	1 363 792	1 608 340	1 879 285	2 279 601	2 839 639	2 694 014	2 314 934	2 039 780	2 730 289
Foreign securities [5]	937 153	1 203 925	1 487 546	1 751 183	2 052 995	2 525 341	2 385 353	2 114 734	1 846 879	2 474 374
Bonds [5]	310 391	413 310	481 411	543 396	578 012	521 625	532 511	502 061	501 762	502 130
Corporate stocks [5]	626 762	790 615	1 006 135	1 207 787	1 474 983	2 003 716	1 852 842	1 612 673	1 345 117	1 972 244
U.S. claims on unaffiliated foreigners reported by U.S. nonbanking concerns [6]	322 980	367 567	450 578	545 524	588 322	704 517	836 559	839 303	908 024	614 672
U.S. claims reported by U.S. banks, not included elsewhere [7]	693 118	768 149	857 511	982 102	1 020 826	1 100 285	1 264 149	1 414 121	1 574 726	1 776 284
Foreign-owned assets in the United States										
With direct investment at current cost	3 310 515	3 944 734	4 527 362	5 388 588	5 990 904	6 740 631	7 619 981	8 160 088	8 646 553	9 633 374
With direct investment at market value	3 450 386	4 270 394	5 010 861	6 201 860	7 249 895	8 437 115	8 982 199	9 206 868	9 166 727	10 514 958
Foreign official assets in the United States	535 227	682 873	820 823	873 716	896 174	951 088	1 030 708	1 082 296	1 212 723	1 474 161
U.S. government securities	407 152	507 460	631 088	648 188	669 768	693 781	756 155	831 459	954 896	1 145 029
U.S. Treasury securities [8]	396 887	489 952	606 427	615 076	622 921	617 680	639 796	704 603	796 449	956 663
Other [8]	10 265	17 508	24 661	33 112	46 847	76 101	116 359	126 856	158 447	188 366
Other U.S. government liabilities [9]	23 678	23 573	22 592	21 712	18 386	21 141	19 316	17 007	17 144	16 580
U.S. liabilities reported by U.S. banks, not included elsewhere	73 386	107 394	113 098	135 384	125 883	138 847	153 403	123 425	144 646	190 601
Other foreign official assets [8]	31 011	44 446	54 045	68 432	82 137	97 319	101 834	110 405	96 037	121 951
Other foreign assets										
With direct investment at current cost	2 775 288	3 261 861	3 706 539	4 514 872	5 094 730	5 789 543	6 589 273	7 077 792	7 433 830	8 159 213
With direct investment at market value	2 915 159	3 587 521	4 190 038	5 328 144	6 353 721	7 486 027	7 951 491	8 124 572	7 954 004	9 040 797
Direct investment in the United States										
At current cost [10]	617 982	680 066	745 619	824 136	920 044	1 101 709	1 421 017	1 513 514	1 505 171	1 553 955
At market value [10]	757 853	1 005 726	1 229 118	1 637 408	2 179 035	2 798 193	2 783 235	2 560 294	2 025 345	2 435 539
U.S. Treasury securities [8]	235 684	326 995	433 903	538 137	543 323	440 685	381 630	358 483	457 670	542 542
U.S. securities other than U.S. Treasury securities [8]	739 695	969 849	1 165 113	1 512 725	1 903 443	2 351 291	2 623 014	2 821 372	2 786 647	3 391 050
Corporate and other bonds [8]	368 077	459 080	539 308	618 837	724 619	825 175	1 068 566	1 343 071	1 600 414	1 852 971
Corporate stocks [8]	371 618	510 769	625 805	893 888	1 178 824	1 526 116	1 554 448	1 478 301	1 186 233	1 538 079
U.S. currency	157 185	169 484	186 846	211 628	228 250	250 657	255 972	279 755	301 268	317 908
U.S. liabilities to unaffiliated foreigners reported by U.S. nonbanking concerns [11]	239 817	300 424	346 810	459 407	485 675	578 046	738 904	798 314	864 632	466 543
U.S. liabilities reported by U.S. banks, not included elsewhere [12]	784 925	815 043	828 248	968 839	1 013 995	1 067 155	1 168 736	1 306 354	1 518 442	1 887 215

pPreliminary.
[1]U.S. official gold stock is valued at market price.
[2]Also includes paid-in capital subscriptions to international financial institutions and resources provided to foreigners under foreign assistance programs requiring repayment over several years. Excludes World War I debts that are not being serviced.
[3]Includes indebtedness that the borrower may contractually, or at its option, repay with its currency, with a third country's currency, or by delivery of materials or transfer of services.
[4]A break in series in 1994 reflects the reclassification of intercompany debt positions between parent companies and affiliates that are not depository institutions and that are primarily engaged in financial intermediation from the direct investment accounts to the nonbank investment accounts. Estimates for 1976 forward are linked to the 1977, 1982, 1989, 1994, and 1999 benchmark surveys of U.S. direct investment abroad.
[5]Estimates include results of the 1994, 1997, and 2001 Benchmark Surveys of U.S. Ownership of Foreign Long-term Securities conducted by the U.S. Department of the Treasury.
[6]A break in series in 1983 reflects the introduction of counterparty data from the United Kingdom and from the Bank for International Settlements (BIS) for several European countries, Caribbean banking centers, and Asian banking centers. Additional coverage from BIS data was introduced in 1986, 1989, 1993, and 1994. In 1994, intercompany debt positions between parent companies and affiliates that are not depository institutions and that are primarily engaged in financial intermediation are reclassified from the direct investment accounts to the nonbank investment accounts. A break in series in 2003 reflects the reclassification of assets reported by U.S. securities brokers from nonbank-reported assets to bank-reported assets, and a reduction in counterparty balances to eliminate double counting.
[7]A break in series in 1988 reflects the introduction of data on holdings of foreign commercial paper. A break in series in 2003 reflects the reclassification of assets reported by U.S. securities brokers from nonbank-reported assets to bank-reported assets.
[8]Estimates include results of 1978, 1984, 1989, 1994, and 2000 Benchmark Surveys of Foreign Portfolio Investment in the United States, and the results of the 2002 and 2003 Annual Surveys of Foreign Holdings of U.S. Securities, conducted by the U.S. Department of the Treasury.
[9]Primarily U.S. government liabilities associated with military sales contracts and other transactions arranged with or through foreign official agencies.
[10]Estimates for 1976 forward are linked to the 1980, 1987, 1992, and 1997 benchmark surveys of foreign direct investment in the United States.
[11]A break in series in 1983 reflects the introduction of counterparty data from the United Kingdom. A break in series in 1994 reflects the reclassification of intercompany debt positions between parent companies and affiliates that are not depository institutions and that are primarily engaged in financial intermediation from the direct investment accounts to the nonbank investment accounts. A break in series in 1996 reflects the introduction of counterparty data from the Bank of International Settlements (BIS) for several European countries. A break in series in 2003 reflects the reclassification of liabilities reported by U.S. securities brokers from nonbank-reported liabilities to bank-reported liabilities, and a reduction in counterparty balances to eliminate double counting.
[12]A break in series in 2003 reflects the reclassification of liabilities reported by U.S. securities brokers from nonbank-reported liabilities to bank-reported liabilities.

SECTION B. U.S. FOREIGN TRADE IN GOODS AND SERVICES

ABOUT THE DATA

This section provides a detailed picture of the overall U.S. foreign trade situation. Aggregate statistics appear first in this section, starting with trade in goods and services arranged by major category (Tables B-1 through B-4). Table B-5 is based on the National Income and Product Accounts and differs from the totals shown on the balance of payments basis, as explained in "Understanding Foreign Trade Statistics."

The next several tables give a variety of information on the goods sector of the U.S. economy including bilateral exports and imports, trade with the top purchasers of U.S. goods exports and sellers of goods imports to the United States (Tables B-6 through B-22), and exports of goods by detailed product groupings (Tables B-23 through B-32). In addition, Table B-33 contains data on U.S. petroleum product suppliers, and foreign exchange rates appear in Table B-34. Data for the North American Industry Classification System (NAICS) of product groupings are contained in Tables B-35 through B-43. NAICS replaced the old Standard Industrial Classification (SIC) system commencing in 1997. Tables B-44 through B-60 examine shares of foreign trade and other detailed data by country.

Annual data is provided in these tables, and time spans vary according to availability. The latest year for most tables is 2003. Some tables include data for 2004 and revised data for prior years, as available by February 2005. These tables are: B-1 to B-4, B-35 to B-37, and B-46 to B-49. As a result, the 2003 data in these tables may not match the 2003 data in other tables.

These data are taken from the Office of Trade and Economic Analysis (OTEA) in the Commerce Department's International Trade Administration (ITA). In turn, the OTEA presents data that were collected by the Bureau of Economic Analysis (BEA) and the Census Bureau, also within the Commerce Department. The data are generally revised annually.

The arrangement of tables in this section generally matches *U.S. Foreign Trade Highlights*, formerly published by the OTEA. These tables are now available online on the OTEA's Web site at <www.ita.doc.gov/td/industry/otea/usfth/>.

Some of these data are published monthly in the FT900 release by the BEA and the Census Bureau, including the goods and services data, trade by principal end-use category, petroleum exports and imports, and goods trade by NAICS and Standard International Trade Classification (SITC) product codes (see "Understanding Foreign Trade Statistics" for definitions). These monthly data are subsequently published in the BEA's *Survey of Current Business*. Other data on trade in goods are available from the Foreign Trade Division of the Census Bureau and at <www.census.gov/foreign-trade/www>. Additional data on trade in services are attainable from the Balance of Payments Division at the BEA and at <www.bea.gov>.

All geographic areas are defined in Section C.

Data may not add to total or may appear as zero because of rounding.

HIGHLIGHTS

A number of interesting trends in foreign trade are emerging, as detailed in the figures in this section. The overall major trend has been a growing U.S. trade deficit, mainly because of rising imports. Exports have also risen, but at a significantly lower rate. The trade deficit with China in particular has grown considerably in the last 15 years and is now roughly a quarter of the total U.S. trade deficit.

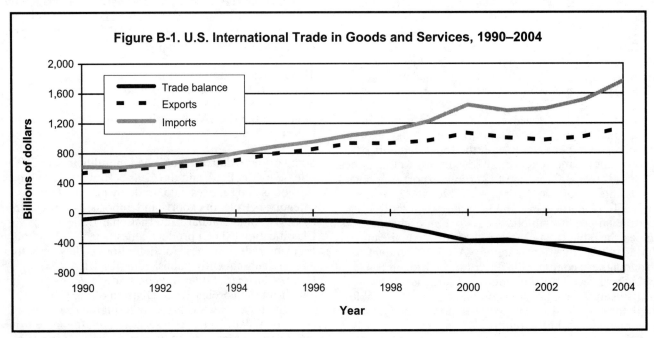

Source: Bureau of Economic Analysis.

Figure B-1 traces recent trends in trade in goods and services. While exports rose steadily over the period, the influx of imports was much more rapid. By the end of 2004, the trade deficit was nearly $618 billion, an increase of $121 billion from the 2003 deficit. Exports increased 12.3 percent in 2004 following a period of weakness earlier in the decade; imports rose more than 16 percent, also following a sluggish period as a result of the fall-off in U.S. demand during the 2001 recession. (See Table B-1.) The rapid rise in imports was widespread, but it was particularly evident in the capital and consumer goods groups and in petroleum and consumer goods. (See Table B-4.)

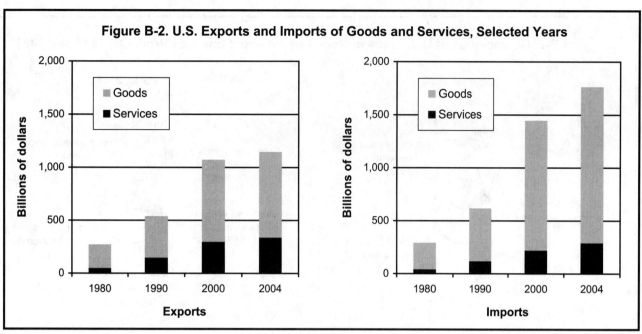

Figure B-2. U.S. Exports and Imports of Goods and Services, Selected Years

Source: Bureau of Economic Analysis.

The contribution of the goods and services sectors to U.S. foreign trade is shown in Figure B-2. Exports of services in 2004 accounted for about 30 percent, or $339 million, of total exports; their share of imports was much smaller—about 16 percent, or $290 million—so that the positive trade balance in the service sector only slightly offset the deficit in the goods sector. In the goods sector, the trade balances in manufacturing and mineral fuel products deteriorated. (See Table B-3.) In the service sector, other private services, which include business services and professional services, maintained a positive trade balance of $48 billion, which slowed the decline of the sector's trade balance. (See Table B-2.)

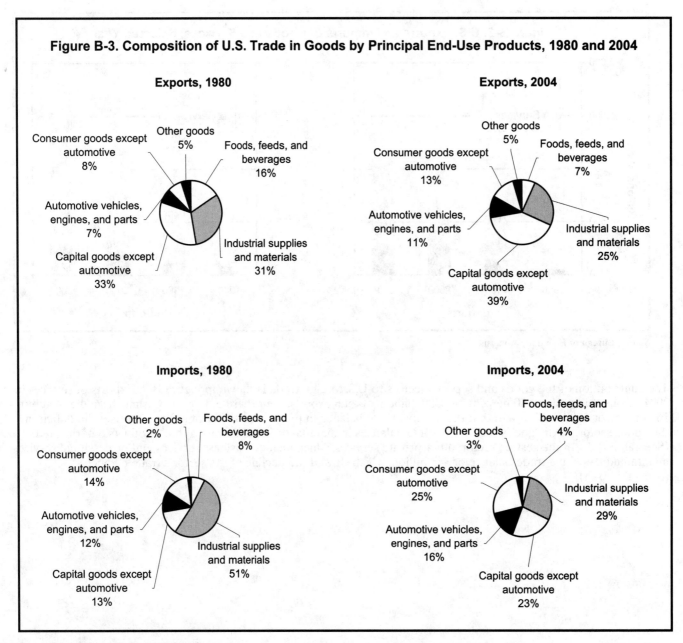

Figure B-3. Composition of U.S. Trade in Goods by Principal End-Use Products, 1980 and 2004

Source: International Trade Administration.

Figure B-3 shows the changing composition of U.S. trade in goods between 1980 and 2004. U.S. exports of capital goods (less automotive goods); autos; and consumer goods (less autos) all expanded their share of total U.S. goods exports, while the share of foods, feeds, and beverages, as well as industrial supplies and materials, declined significantly. On the import side, U.S. purchases of foreign capital goods, consumer goods, and autos as a share of all goods imports were up over the period while imports of industrial supplies and food items became less important. (See Table B-4.)

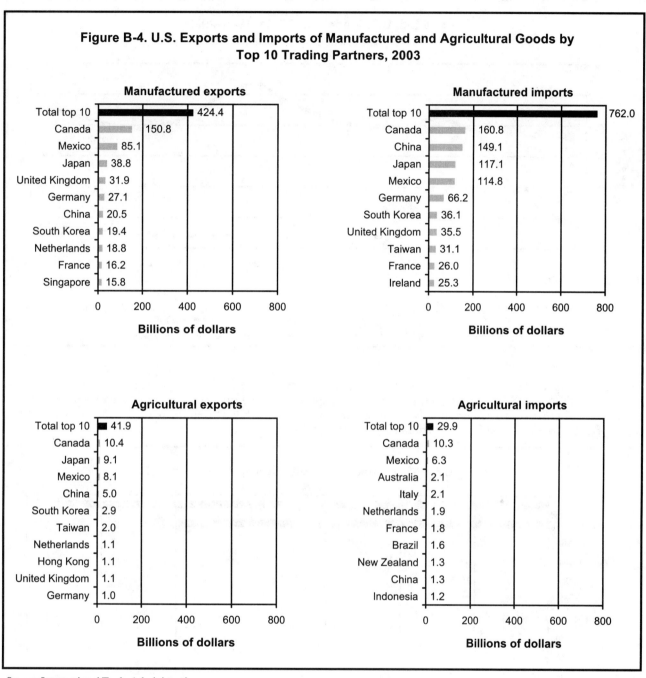

Figure B-4. U.S. Exports and Imports of Manufactured and Agricultural Goods by Top 10 Trading Partners, 2003

Manufactured exports

	Billions of dollars
Total top 10	424.4
Canada	150.8
Mexico	85.1
Japan	38.8
United Kingdom	31.9
Germany	27.1
China	20.5
South Korea	19.4
Netherlands	18.8
France	16.2
Singapore	15.8

Manufactured imports

	Billions of dollars
Total top 10	762.0
Canada	160.8
China	149.1
Japan	117.1
Mexico	114.8
Germany	66.2
South Korea	36.1
United Kingdom	35.5
Taiwan	31.1
France	26.0
Ireland	25.3

Agricultural exports

	Billions of dollars
Total top 10	41.9
Canada	10.4
Japan	9.1
Mexico	8.1
China	5.0
South Korea	2.9
Taiwan	2.0
Netherlands	1.1
Hong Kong	1.1
United Kingdom	1.1
Germany	1.0

Agricultural imports

	Billions of dollars
Total top 10	29.9
Canada	10.3
Mexico	6.3
Australia	2.1
Italy	2.1
Netherlands	1.9
France	1.8
Brazil	1.6
New Zealand	1.3
China	1.3
Indonesia	1.2

Source: International Trade Administration.

Exports of manufactured and agricultural goods to the top 10 foreign purchasers and imports from the top 10 suppliers are shown in Figure B-4. Canada and Mexico are the principal trading partners of the United States, with relations governed by the North American Free Trade Agreement (NAFTA). Exports to these two countries were nearly 45 percent greater than exports to the European Union (EU-15). While U.S. imports from Canada and Mexico roughly equaled the sum of imports from Japan, China, and the newly industrialized countries (NICs) of Asia (Hong Kong, Singapore, South Korea, and Taiwan), exports to Canada and Mexico were about 43 percent higher than exports to these Asian countries. (See Tables B-6, B-7, and B-8.)

Based

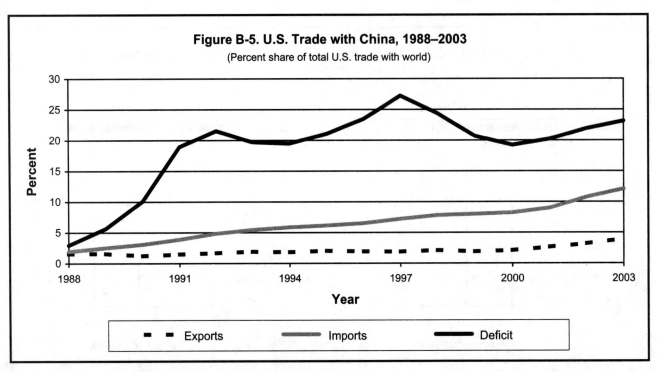

Source: International Trade Administration.

Figure B-5 shows the rapid growth of trade with China. From 1988 to 2003, imports from China rose from 2 percent to 12 percent of total U.S. imports from the world, while exports to China only rose from just under 2 percent to 4 percent of total U.S. exports. Consequently, the trade deficit with China has soared from 3 percent ($3.5 billion) to 23 percent ($124 billion) of total U.S. trade deficit. (See Table B-26.)

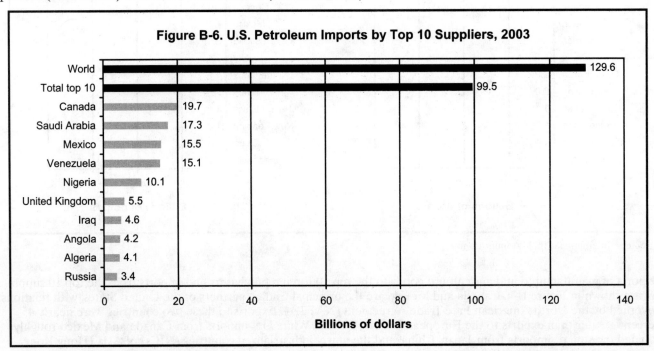

Source: International Trade Administration.

As noted at the outset of this volume, the United States is heavily dependent on foreigners for its supply of petroleum products. Figure B-6 details the major suppliers—Canada ranks first with almost $20 billion and Mexico third with over $15 billion. Among the top 20 suppliers are six of the 11 Organization of Petroleum Exporting Countries (OPEC) members. Led by Saudi Arabia, with $17 billion, these six countries together supply the United States with 41 percent of its petroleum imports. (See Table B-33.)

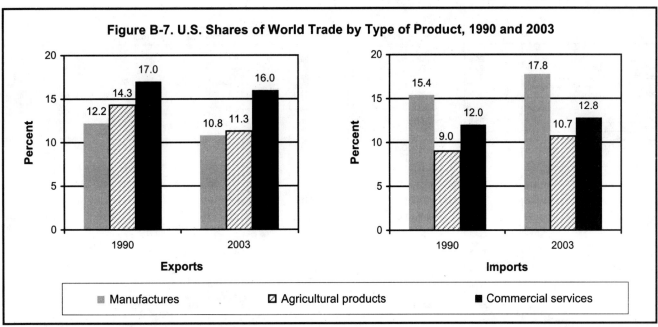

Source: Bureau of Economic Analysis and International Trade Administration.

Figure B-7 shows the U.S. share of global trade for selected product types in 1990 and 2003. During this period, U.S. shares of world exports declined, with agricultural exports falling the most. In general, this trend indicates a decline in the competitiveness of these products. U.S. shares of world imports rose over the period, reflecting the deteriorating trade balance; our share of manufactured imports rose the most. (See Table B-54.)

Figure B-8. Advanced Technology Products in U.S. Goods Trade, 1995–2003

Year	Value of advanced technology products trade (billions of dollars)			Percent of total goods	
	Exports	Imports	Balance	Exports	Imports
1995	138.5	124.8	13.7	23.7	16.8
1996	154.9	130.4	24.5	24.8	16.4
1997	179.5	147.3	32.2	26.0	16.9
1998	186.4	156.8	29.6	27.3	17.2
1999	200.3	181.2	19.1	28.8	17.7
2000	227.4	222.1	5.3	29.1	18.2
2001	199.6	195.2	4.4	27.4	17.1
2002	178.6	195.2	-16.6	25.8	16.8
2003	180.2	207.0	-26.8	24.9	16.5

Source: Census Bureau.

Advanced technology is a new product grouping of U.S. trade in goods; the series was initiated in 2000 with data available from 1995 to 2003. As noted in the volume's section "Understanding Foreign Trade Statistics," the Census Bureau has classified about 500 commodity groupings as "high technology," meeting the criteria that the products are from a high technology field such as biotechnology, and that they represent leading edge technology. In 2003, exports of these goods amounted to $180 billion or about 25 percent of our exports of goods, while representing less than 17 percent of total goods imports. However, exports have trended down since highs in 2000, both in value and as a share of all goods exports, while imports have held relatively steady and a trade deficit in advanced technology products was posted in 2002 and 2003.

Table B-1. U.S. International Trade in Goods and Services, 1960–2004

(Billions of dollars; balance of payments basis; domestic and foreign exports, f.a.s.; general imports, Customs.)

Year	Exports			Imports			Trade balance		
	Total	Goods	Services	Total	Goods	Services	Total	Goods	Services
1960	25.9	19.7	6.3	22.4	14.8	7.7	3.5	4.9	-1.4
1961	26.4	20.1	6.3	22.2	14.5	7.7	4.2	5.6	-1.4
1962	27.7	20.8	6.9	24.4	16.3	8.1	3.4	4.5	-1.2
1963	29.6	22.3	7.3	25.4	17.0	8.4	4.2	5.2	-1.0
1964	33.3	25.5	7.8	27.3	18.7	8.6	6.0	6.8	-0.8
1965	35.3	26.5	8.8	30.6	21.5	9.1	4.7	5.0	-0.3
1966	38.9	29.3	9.6	36.0	25.5	10.5	2.9	3.8	-0.9
1967	41.3	30.7	10.7	38.7	26.9	11.9	2.6	3.8	-1.2
1968	45.5	33.6	11.9	45.3	33.0	12.3	0.2	0.6	-0.4
1969	49.2	36.4	12.8	49.1	35.8	13.3	0.1	0.6	-0.5
1970	56.6	42.5	14.2	54.4	39.9	14.5	2.3	2.6	-0.3
1971	59.7	43.3	16.4	61.0	45.6	15.4	-1.3	-2.3	1.0
1972	67.2	49.4	17.8	72.7	55.8	16.9	-5.4	-6.4	1.0
1973	91.2	71.4	19.8	89.3	70.5	18.8	1.9	0.9	1.0
1974	120.9	98.3	22.6	125.2	103.8	21.4	-4.3	-5.5	1.2
1975	132.6	107.1	25.5	120.2	98.2	22.0	12.4	8.9	3.5
1976	142.7	114.7	28.0	148.8	124.2	24.6	-6.1	-9.5	3.4
1977	152.3	120.8	31.5	179.5	151.9	27.6	-27.2	-31.1	3.8
1978	178.4	142.1	36.4	208.2	176.0	32.2	-29.8	-33.9	4.2
1979	224.1	184.4	39.7	248.7	212.0	36.7	-24.6	-27.6	3.0
1980	271.8	224.3	47.6	291.2	249.8	41.5	-19.4	-25.5	6.1
1981	294.4	237.0	57.4	310.6	265.1	45.5	-16.2	-28.0	11.9
1982	275.2	211.2	64.1	299.4	247.6	51.7	-24.2	-36.5	12.3
1983	266.0	201.8	64.2	323.8	268.9	54.9	-57.8	-67.1	9.3
1984	290.9	219.9	71.0	400.1	332.4	67.7	-109.2	-112.5	3.3
1985	288.8	215.9	72.9	410.9	338.1	72.8	-122.1	-122.2	0.1
1986	309.7	223.3	86.4	450.3	368.4	81.8	-140.6	-145.1	4.5
1987	348.8	250.2	98.6	502.1	409.8	92.3	-153.3	-159.6	6.2
1988	431.3	320.2	111.1	547.2	447.2	100.0	-115.9	-127.0	11.1
1989	489.4	362.1	127.2	581.6	477.4	104.2	-92.2	-115.2	23.0
1990	537.2	389.3	147.9	618.4	498.3	120.0	-81.1	-109.0	27.9
1991	581.3	416.9	164.3	611.9	490.7	121.2	-30.7	-73.8	43.1
1992	616.5	439.6	176.8	654.6	536.5	118.1	-38.2	-96.9	58.7
1993	642.4	456.9	185.4	711.5	589.4	122.1	-69.2	-132.5	63.3
1994	702.6	502.9	199.8	799.8	668.7	131.1	-97.2	-165.8	68.6
1995	793.7	575.2	218.5	888.8	749.4	139.4	-95.1	-174.2	79.1
1996	850.9	612.1	238.8	953.7	803.1	150.6	-102.9	-191.0	88.1
1997	933.9	678.4	255.5	1 040.9	876.5	164.4	-107.0	-198.1	91.1
1998	932.6	670.4	262.1	1 095.7	917.1	178.6	-163.2	-246.7	83.5
1999	965.5	684.0	281.5	1 226.7	1 030.0	196.7	-261.2	-346.0	84.8
2000	1 070.1	772.0	298.1	1 445.4	1 224.4	221.0	-375.4	-452.4	77.0
2001	1 006.7	718.7	287.9	1 369.3	1 145.9	223.4	-362.7	-427.2	64.5
2002	975.9	681.8	294.1	1 397.7	1 164.7	232.9	-421.7	-482.9	61.2
2003	1 020.5	713.1	307.4	1 517.0	1 260.7	256.3	-496.5	-547.6	51.0
2004	1 146.1	807.6	338.6	1 763.9	1 473.8	290.1	-617.7	-666.2	48.5

Note: Balance of payments basis for goods reflects adjustments for timing, coverage, and valuation to the data compiled by the Census Bureau. The major adjustments concern military trade of U.S. defense agencies, additional nonmonetary gold transactions, and inland freight in Canada and Mexico.

Table B-2. U.S. Trade in Services by Major Category, 1978–2004

(Billions of dollars; balance of payments basis; domestic and foreign exports, f.a.s.; general imports, Customs.)

Year	Total services			Travel			Passenger fares			Other transportation		
	Exports	Imports	Balance	Exports	Imports	Balance	Exports	Imports	Balance	Exports	Imports	Balance
1978	36.4	32.2	4.2	7.2	8.5	-1.3	1.6	2.9	-1.3	8.1	9.1	-1.0
1979	39.7	36.7	3.0	8.4	9.4	-1.0	2.2	3.2	-1.0	10.0	10.9	-0.9
1980	47.6	41.5	6.1	10.6	10.4	0.2	2.6	3.6	-1.0	11.6	11.8	-0.2
1981	57.4	45.5	11.9	12.9	11.5	1.4	3.1	4.5	-1.4	12.6	12.5	0.1
1982	64.1	51.7	12.3	12.4	12.4	0.0	3.2	4.8	-1.6	12.3	11.7	0.6
1983	64.2	54.9	9.3	10.9	13.1	-2.2	3.6	6.0	-2.4	12.6	12.2	0.4
1984	71.0	67.7	3.3	17.2	22.9	-5.7	4.1	5.7	-1.7	13.8	14.8	-1.0
1985	72.9	72.8	0.1	17.8	24.6	-6.8	4.4	6.4	-2.0	14.7	15.6	-1.0
1986	86.4	81.8	4.5	20.4	25.9	-5.5	5.6	6.5	-0.9	15.4	17.8	-2.3
1987	98.6	92.3	6.2	23.6	29.3	-5.7	7.0	7.3	-0.3	17.0	19.0	-2.0
1988	111.1	100.0	11.1	29.4	32.1	-2.7	9.0	7.7	1.2	19.3	20.9	-1.6
1989	127.2	104.2	23.0	36.3	33.4	2.8	10.6	8.2	2.4	20.5	22.2	-1.6
1990	147.9	120.0	27.9	43.0	37.3	5.7	15.3	10.5	4.8	22.0	25.0	-2.9
1991	164.3	121.2	43.1	48.4	35.3	13.1	15.9	10.0	5.8	22.6	25.0	-2.3
1992	176.9	116.5	60.4	54.7	38.6	16.2	16.6	10.6	6.0	21.5	23.8	-2.2
1993	185.9	122.3	63.7	57.9	40.7	17.2	16.5	11.4	5.1	22.0	24.5	-2.6
1994	201.0	131.9	69.2	58.4	43.8	14.6	17.0	13.1	3.9	23.8	26.0	-2.3
1995	219.2	141.4	77.8	63.4	44.9	18.5	18.9	14.7	4.2	26.1	27.0	-1.0
1996	240.0	150.9	89.2	69.8	48.1	21.7	20.4	15.8	4.6	26.1	27.4	-1.3
1997	256.6	166.3	90.4	73.4	52.1	21.4	20.9	18.1	2.7	27.0	29.0	-2.0
1998	262.3	182.5	79.8	71.3	56.5	14.8	20.1	20.0	0.1	25.6	30.4	-4.8
1999	273.2	189.4	83.8	74.7	58.9	15.9	19.8	21.3	-1.5	26.9	34.1	-7.2
2000	292.2	218.5	73.7	82.3	64.8	17.5	20.8	24.3	-3.5	30.1	41.6	-11.5
2001	288.9	219.5	69.4	71.9	60.2	11.7	17.9	22.6	-4.7	28.4	38.7	-10.2
2002	294.1	232.9	61.2	66.7	58.0	8.7	17.0	20.0	-2.9	29.2	38.4	-9.2
2003	307.4	256.3	51.0	64.5	56.6	7.9	15.7	21.0	-5.3	31.8	44.8	-12.9
2004	338.6	290.1	48.5	74.7	64.6	10.0	18.8	23.2	-4.4	37.3	53.7	-16.4

Year	Royalties and license fees			Other private services			Military-defense transfers/expenditures			U.S. government miscellaneous services		
	Exports	Imports	Balance	Exports	Imports	Balance	Exports	Imports	Balance	Exports	Imports	Balance
1978	5.9	0.7	5.2	4.7	2.6	2.1	8.2	7.4	0.9	0.6	1.1	-0.5
1979	6.2	0.8	5.4	5.4	2.8	2.6	7.0	8.3	-1.3	0.5	1.2	-0.7
1980	7.1	0.7	6.4	6.3	2.9	3.4	9.0	10.9	-1.8	0.4	1.2	-0.8
1981	7.3	0.7	6.6	10.3	3.6	6.7	10.7	11.6	-0.8	0.5	1.3	-0.8
1982	5.6	0.8	4.8	17.4	8.2	9.3	12.6	12.5	0.1	0.6	1.5	-0.9
1983	5.7	0.9	4.8	18.1	7.9	10.2	12.5	13.1	-0.6	0.7	1.6	-0.9
1984	6.1	1.2	4.9	19.1	9.0	10.2	10.0	12.5	-2.5	0.7	1.5	-0.8
1985	6.6	1.2	5.4	19.9	10.2	9.7	8.7	13.1	-4.4	0.9	1.7	-0.9
1986	7.9	1.4	6.5	27.7	14.8	12.9	8.5	13.7	-5.2	0.6	1.7	-1.1
1987	9.9	1.8	8.1	29.2	18.0	11.1	11.1	15.0	-3.8	0.5	1.9	-1.4
1988	11.8	2.6	9.2	31.3	19.1	12.1	9.3	15.6	-6.3	0.7	1.9	-1.3
1989	13.8	2.5	11.3	36.9	20.6	16.2	8.6	15.3	-6.7	0.6	1.9	-1.3
1990	17.1	3.2	13.9	40.3	24.6	15.8	9.7	17.5	-7.8	0.7	1.9	-1.3
1991	18.5	4.2	14.3	47.8	28.3	19.5	10.5	16.4	-5.9	0.7	2.1	-1.4
1992	20.8	5.2	15.7	50.0	22.3	27.7	12.4	13.8	-1.4	0.8	2.3	-1.4
1993	21.7	5.0	16.7	53.5	26.3	27.3	13.5	12.1	1.4	0.9	2.3	-1.4
1994	26.7	5.9	20.9	61.5	30.4	31.1	12.8	10.2	2.6	0.9	2.6	-1.7
1995	30.3	6.9	23.4	65.1	35.2	29.8	14.6	10.0	4.6	0.8	2.6	-1.8
1996	32.5	7.8	24.6	73.9	38.0	35.9	16.4	11.1	5.4	0.9	2.7	-1.8
1997	33.2	9.2	24.1	84.5	43.5	41.0	16.7	11.7	5.0	1.0	2.8	-1.8
1998	35.6	11.2	24.4	91.3	49.4	41.9	17.4	12.2	5.2	0.9	2.8	-1.9
1999	36.9	12.6	24.3	98.2	46.3	51.8	15.8	13.3	2.5	0.9	2.8	-1.9
2000	39.6	16.1	23.5	104.7	55.3	49.5	14.0	13.6	0.4	0.8	2.9	-2.1
2001	41.1	16.7	24.4	116.1	63.4	52.8	12.5	15.0	-2.4	0.8	2.9	-2.1
2002	44.2	19.2	25.0	124.2	75.3	48.9	11.9	19.1	-7.2	0.8	2.9	-2.1
2003	48.2	20.0	28.2	133.8	85.8	48.0	12.5	25.1	-12.6	0.8	3.0	-2.2
2004	51.1	22.6	28.5	142.3	94.3	48.0	13.6	28.3	-14.7	0.7	3.2	-2.5

Note: Military-defense transfers/expenditures are defined as transfers under U.S. military sales contracts for exports and direct defense expenditures for imports. Balance numbers do not always agree due to rounding.

Table B-3. U.S. Trade in Goods, 1979–2004

(Billions of dollars; Census basis; domestic and foreign exports, f.a.s.; general imports, Customs.)

Year	Total goods [1]			Manufactured goods [2,3]			Agricultural products [3,4]			Mineral fuels [3]			Other goods [3]		
	Exports	Imports	Balance	Exports	Imports	Balance	Exports	Imports	Balance	Exports	Imports	Balance	Exports	Imports	Balance
1979	186.5	209.5	-22.9	132.7	117.1	15.6	35.2	16.9	18.3	5.7	59.9	-54.2	12.9	15.5	-2.7
1980	225.7	245.3	-19.5	160.7	133.0	27.7	41.8	17.4	24.3	8.2	78.9	-70.7	15.1	15.9	-0.8
1981	238.7	261.0	-22.3	171.7	149.8	22.0	43.8	17.2	26.6	10.3	81.2	-70.9	12.8	12.8	0.0
1982	216.4	244.0	-27.5	155.3	151.7	3.6	37.0	15.7	21.3	12.8	65.3	-52.5	11.3	11.3	0.1
1983 [5]	205.6	258.0	-52.4	148.5	171.2	-22.7	36.5	16.5	19.9	9.8	57.8	-48.0	10.9	12.5	-1.6
1983	205.6	258.0	-52.4	148.7	170.9	-22.2	36.1	16.0	20.2	9.8	57.8	-48.0	11.0	13.4	-2.4
1984	224.0	330.7	-106.7	164.1	230.9	-66.8	37.9	19.3	18.6	9.7	60.8	-51.1	12.3	19.6	-7.3
1985	218.8	336.5	-117.7	168.0	257.5	-89.5	29.3	19.5	9.8	10.3	53.7	-43.4	11.2	5.9	5.3
1986	227.2	365.4	-138.3	179.8	296.7	-116.8	26.3	20.9	5.4	8.4	37.2	-28.8	12.6	10.7	1.9
1987	254.1	406.2	-152.1	199.9	324.4	-124.6	28.7	20.3	8.4	8.0	44.1	-36.1	17.5	17.4	0.1
1988	322.4	441.0	-118.5	255.6	361.4	-105.7	37.1	20.7	16.4	8.5	41.0	-32.5	21.2	17.8	3.3
1989	363.8	473.2	-109.4	287.0	379.4	-92.4	41.6	21.1	20.5	9.9	52.6	-42.7	25.3	20.0	5.2
1990	393.6	495.3	-101.7	315.4	388.8	-73.5	39.6	22.3	17.2	12.4	64.7	-52.3	26.3	19.5	6.8
1991	421.7	488.5	-66.7	345.1	392.4	-47.3	39.4	22.1	17.2	12.3	54.1	-41.8	24.9	19.8	5.1
1992	448.2	532.7	-84.5	368.5	434.3	-65.9	43.1	23.4	19.8	11.3	55.3	-43.9	25.2	19.7	5.5
1993	465.1	580.7	-115.6	388.7	479.9	-91.2	42.8	23.6	19.2	9.9	55.9	-46.0	23.7	21.2	2.5
1994	512.6	663.3	-150.6	431.1	557.3	-126.3	45.9	26.0	20.0	9.0	56.4	-47.4	26.7	23.6	3.1
1995	584.7	743.4	-158.7	486.7	629.7	-143.0	56.0	29.3	26.8	10.5	59.1	-48.6	31.6	25.4	6.2
1996	625.1	795.3	-170.2	524.7	658.8	-134.1	60.6	32.6	28.1	12.4	78.1	-65.7	27.4	25.8	1.5
1997	689.2	870.7	-181.5	592.5	728.9	-136.4	57.1	35.2	21.9	13.0	78.3	-65.3	26.7	28.3	-1.7
1998	682.1	911.9	-229.8	596.6	790.8	-194.2	52.0	35.7	16.3	10.4	57.3	-47.0	23.2	28.1	-4.9
1999	695.8	1 024.6	-328.8	611.6	882.7	-271.1	48.2	36.7	11.5	9.9	75.2	-65.3	26.1	30.0	-3.9
2000	781.9	1 218.0	-436.1	691.5	1 012.9	-321.3	53.0	39.2	13.8	13.4	135.4	-122.0	26.9	30.6	-3.7
2001	729.1	1 141.0	-411.9	640.2	950.7	-310.4	55.2	39.5	15.7	12.7	121.9	-109.2	20.9	28.9	-7.9
2002	693.1	1 164.7	-471.6	606.3	974.6	-368.3	54.8	42.0	12.8	11.7	115.7	-104.0	20.3	32.4	-12.1
2003	724.8	1 257.1	-532.4	627.1	1 027.4	-400.3	61.4	47.5	13.9	14.1	153.3	-139.2	22.2	29.0	-6.8
2004	819.0	1 470.5	-651.5	709.7	1 175.5	-465.8	63.4	54.3	9.1	18.9	205.9	-187.0	27.0	34.9	-7.9

Note: Data for 1983–1988 are estimated, based on the HS. Pre-1983 data are on a Schedule A/E basis and adjusted to match the latest trade definitions as closely as possible.

[1]Includes nonmonetary gold, military grant aid, special category shipments, trade between the U.S. Virgin Islands and foreign countries, and undocumented exports to Canada. Adjustments were also made for carryover.

[2]Manufactured goods include commodity sections 5–9 under Schedules A and E for 1970–1982 and SITC Rev. 3 for 1983 forward. Manufactures include undocumented exports to Canada, nonmonetary gold (excluding gold ore, scrap, and base bullion) and special category shipments.

[3]1991 imports include revisions for passenger cars, trucks, petroleum and petroleum products not included elsewhere.

[4]Agricultural products for 1983 forward use the latest Census definition that excludes goods previously classified as manufactured agricultural products.

[5]Data for 1983 are on the old (non-HS) basis of commodity classification.

Table B-4. U.S. Trade in Goods by Principal End-Use Category, 1980–2004

(Billions of dollars; Census basis; domestic and foreign exports, f.a.s.; general imports, Customs.)

Year	Foods, feeds, and beverages			Industrial supplies			Capital goods except automotive		
	Exports	Imports	Balance	Exports	Imports	Balance	Exports	Imports	Balance
1980	36.0	18.5	17.5	70.6	124.7	-54.1	74.8	31.1	43.7
1981	38.6	18.5	20.1	67.7	130.7	-63.0	82.5	37.0	45.5
1982	32.0	17.5	14.5	62.1	107.7	-45.6	75.1	38.4	36.7
1983	30.7	18.5	12.2	57.4	105.3	-47.8	70.6	39.4	31.2
1984	31.3	21.5	9.8	62.6	121.6	-59.1	76.4	58.0	18.5
1985	24.1	22.3	1.8	59.2	114.1	-54.9	78.9	62.4	16.4
1986	22.5	24.5	-2.0	62.0	102.9	-40.9	81.8	72.6	9.2
1987	24.3	26.8	-2.6	66.7	117.3	-50.6	86.2	87.0	-0.8
1988	32.3	24.8	7.5	85.1	118.3	-33.2	109.2	101.4	7.8
1989	37.2	25.1	12.1	99.3	132.3	-33.0	138.8	113.3	25.5
1990	35.1	26.6	8.4	104.4	143.2	-38.8	152.7	116.4	36.3
1991	35.7	26.5	9.2	109.7	131.6	-21.9	166.7	120.7	45.9
1992	40.3	27.6	12.7	109.1	138.6	-29.5	175.9	134.3	41.7
1993	40.6	27.9	12.8	111.8	145.6	-33.8	181.7	152.4	29.3
1994	42.0	31.0	11.0	121.4	162.1	-40.7	205.0	184.4	20.7
1995	50.5	33.2	17.3	146.2	181.8	-35.6	233.0	221.4	11.6
1996	55.5	35.7	19.8	147.7	204.5	-56.8	252.9	229.1	23.8
1997	51.5	39.7	11.8	158.2	213.8	-55.5	294.5	253.3	41.3
1998	46.4	41.2	5.2	148.3	200.1	-51.9	299.6	269.6	30.1
1999	46.0	43.6	2.4	147.5	221.4	-73.9	311.0	295.7	15.3
2000	47.9	46.0	1.9	172.6	300.0	-127.4	356.9	347.0	9.9
2001	49.4	46.6	2.8	160.1	273.9	-113.8	321.7	298.0	23.7
2002	49.6	49.7	-0.1	156.8	267.7	-110.8	290.5	283.3	7.2
2003	55.0	55.8	-0.8	173.0	313.8	-140.8	293.6	295.8	-2.2
2004	56.3	62.2	-5.8	203.6	412.4	-208.9	331.1	343.8	-12.7

Year	Automotive vehicles, engines, and parts			Consumer goods except automotives			Other goods		
	Exports	Imports	Balance	Exports	Imports	Balance	Exports	Imports	Balance
1980	16.0	28.2	-12.1	17.2	34.3	-17.2	11.1	4.6	6.5
1981	18.3	30.7	-12.5	17.1	38.4	-21.2	14.4	5.7	8.8
1982	16.0	34.3	-18.3	15.7	39.6	-24.0	15.6	6.5	9.1
1983	15.4	42.1	-26.7	16.2	46.3	-30.1	15.3	6.5	8.8
1984	18.6	55.1	-36.5	16.4	61.4	-45.0	17.9	8.1	9.8
1985	20.6	66.6	-46.0	15.8	69.9	-54.1	20.7	10.0	10.7
1986	19.9	78.5	-58.6	17.8	80.3	-62.5	23.6	11.2	12.3
1987	24.6	87.5	-62.8	17.7	93.6	-76.0	34.6	12.2	22.4
1988	29.3	87.7	-58.4	23.1	95.9	-72.8	43.4	12.8	30.6
1989	34.8	86.1	-51.3	36.4	102.9	-66.4	17.2	13.6	3.6
1990	37.4	87.3	-49.9	43.3	105.7	-62.4	20.7	16.1	4.6
1991	40.0	85.7	-45.6	45.9	108.0	-62.1	23.7	15.9	7.7
1992	47.0	91.8	-44.8	51.4	122.7	-71.2	24.4	17.7	6.7
1993	52.4	102.4	-50.0	54.7	134.0	-79.4	23.9	18.4	5.5
1994	57.8	118.3	-60.5	60.0	146.3	-86.3	26.5	21.3	5.2
1995	61.8	123.8	-62.0	64.4	159.9	-95.5	28.7	23.4	5.3
1996	65.0	128.9	-63.9	70.1	171.0	-100.9	33.8	26.1	7.7
1997	74.0	139.8	-65.8	77.4	193.8	-116.4	33.5	29.3	4.2
1998	73.2	149.1	-75.9	79.3	216.5	-137.3	35.4	35.4	0.1
1999	75.3	179.0	-103.7	80.9	241.9	-161.0	35.3	43.0	-7.7
2000	80.4	195.9	-115.5	89.4	281.8	-192.5	34.8	48.3	-13.6
2001	75.4	189.8	-114.3	88.3	284.3	-196.0	34.1	48.4	-14.3
2002	78.9	203.7	-124.8	84.4	307.9	-223.5	32.9	49.1	-16.2
2003	80.7	210.2	-129.5	89.9	333.9	-244.0	32.5	47.6	-15.1
2004	88.2	228.4	-140.2	102.8	373.2	-270.4	37.0	50.5	-13.5

Note: Because of rounding and revisions, categories may not sum to totals as shown in Table B-3 and balances may not agree with exports and imports.

Table B-5. International Trade in Goods and Services, 1974–2003

(Billions of dollars; National Income and Product Accounts basis; domestic and foreign exports, f.a.s.; general imports, Customs.)

Year	GDP	Net exports	Exports			Imports		
			Total	Goods	Services	Total	Goods	Services
1974	1 500.0	-0.8	126.7	101.0	25.7	127.5	104.5	22.9
1975	1 638.3	16.0	138.7	109.6	29.1	122.7	99.0	23.7
1976	1 825.3	-1.6	149.5	117.8	31.7	151.1	124.6	26.5
1977	2 030.9	-23.0	159.4	123.7	35.7	182.4	152.6	29.8
1978	2 294.7	-25.4	186.9	145.4	41.5	212.3	177.4	34.8
1979	2 563.3	-22.6	230.1	184.0	46.1	252.7	212.8	39.9
1980	2 789.5	-13.0	280.8	225.8	55.0	293.8	248.6	45.3
1981	3 128.4	-12.6	305.2	239.1	66.1	317.8	267.8	49.9
1982	3 255.0	-20.0	283.2	215.0	68.2	303.2	250.5	52.6
1983	3 536.7	-51.6	277.0	207.3	69.7	328.6	272.7	56.0
1984	3 933.2	-102.7	302.4	225.6	76.7	405.1	336.3	68.8
1985	4 220.3	-115.2	302.0	222.2	79.8	417.2	343.3	73.9
1986	4 462.8	-132.8	320.5	226.0	94.5	453.3	370.0	83.3
1987	4 739.5	-145.2	363.9	257.5	106.4	509.1	414.8	94.3
1988	5 103.8	-110.4	444.1	325.8	118.3	554.5	452.1	102.4
1989	5 484.4	-88.2	503.3	369.4	134.0	591.5	484.8	106.7
1990	5 803.1	-77.9	552.4	396.6	155.7	630.3	508.1	122.3
1991	5 995.9	-27.5	596.8	423.5	173.3	624.3	500.7	123.6
1992	6 337.7	-33.3	635.3	448.0	187.4	668.6	544.9	123.6
1993	6 657.4	-65.1	655.8	459.9	195.9	720.9	592.8	128.1
1994	7 072.2	-93.6	720.9	510.1	210.8	814.5	676.8	137.7
1995	7 397.7	-91.4	812.2	583.3	228.9	903.6	757.4	146.1
1996	7 816.9	-96.2	868.6	618.3	250.2	964.8	807.4	157.4
1997	8 304.3	-101.6	955.3	687.7	267.6	1 056.9	885.3	171.5
1998	8 747.0	-160.0	955.9	680.9	275.1	1 115.9	929.0	186.9
1999	9 268.4	-260.5	991.2	697.2	294.0	1 251.7	1 045.5	206.3
2000	9 817.0	-379.5	1 096.3	784.3	311.9	1 475.8	1 243.5	232.3
2001	10 100.8	-366.6	1 035.1	731.5	303.6	1 401.7	1 168.0	233.6
2002	10 480.8	-426.3	1 006.8	697.8	309.1	1 433.1	1 190.3	242.7
2003	10 987.9	-494.9	1 048.9	725.5	323.4	1 543.8	1 283.3	260.5

Note: National Income and Product Accounts basis for goods and services reflects adjustments for statistical differences and coverage to the Balance of Payments basis. The major adjustments concern the treatment of U.S. territories and nonmonetary gold transactions. Totals will not always equal the sum of the components because of rounding and use of the chained price methodology.

Table B-6. U.S. Total Exports of Goods to Individual Countries, 1997–2003

(Millions of dollars, except as noted; Census basis; domestic and foreign exports, f.a.s.)

Region and country	1997	1998	1999	2000	2001	2002	2003	1997–2003 change	
								Value	Percent
WORLD	689 182	682 138	695 797	781 918	729 100	693 103	724 006	34 824	5.1
EUROPE	163 273	170 008	171 834	187 448	181 529	163 625	172 013	8 740	5.4
Western Europe	155 384	162 571	165 952	181 509	174 696	157 029	164 899	9 515	6.1
European Union (EU-15)	140 774	149 034	151 814	165 064	158 768	143 691	150 549	9 776	6.9
Austria	2 075	2 143	2 588	2 592	2 605	2 427	1 793	-282	-13.6
Belgium	13 420	13 918	12 381	13 926	13 502	13 326	15 218	1 798	13.4
Denmark	1 757	1 874	1 726	1 507	1 609	1 496	1 548	-209	-11.9
Finland	1 741	1 915	1 669	1 571	1 554	1 535	1 714	-27	-1.6
France	15 965	17 729	18 877	20 362	19 864	19 016	17 068	1 103	6.9
Germany	24 458	26 657	26 800	29 448	29 995	26 630	28 848	4 390	17.9
Greece	949	1 355	996	1 222	1 294	1 152	1 191	242	25.5
Ireland	4 642	5 647	6 384	7 714	7 144	6 745	7 699	3 056	65.8
Italy	8 995	8 991	10 091	11 060	9 916	10 057	10 570	1 575	17.5
Luxembourg	712	606	983	397	549	480	279	-433	-60.8
Netherlands	19 827	18 978	19 437	21 836	19 485	18 311	20 703	876	4.4
Portugal	954	888	1 092	984	1 240	861	863	-91	-9.6
Spain	5 539	5 454	6 133	6 322	5 756	5 298	5 935	397	7.2
Sweden	3 314	3 822	4 251	4 554	3 541	3 153	3 226	-89	-2.7
United Kingdom	36 425	39 058	38 407	41 570	40 714	33 204	33 895	-2 530	-6.9
Non-EU Western Europe	14 611	13 536	14 138	16 445	15 929	13 339	14 350	-261	-1.8
Bosnia-Herzegovina	103	40	44	44	43	32	21	-81	-79.3
Croatia	139	97	108	90	110	78	197	58	41.9
Cyprus	245	162	192	190	268	193	327	82	33.7
Gibraltar	9	9	4	15	10	26	14	5	59.1
Iceland	179	237	298	256	225	219	242	63	35.2
Liechtenstein	13	7	9	14	7	15	16	3	27.2
Macedonia	34	15	56	69	33	19	26	-8	-22.2
Malta and Gozo	121	267	190	335	259	210	202	81	66.7
Norway	1 721	1 709	1 439	1 547	1 835	1 407	1 468	-254	-14.7
Other Non-EU Western Europe	40	43	37	43	51	36	84	44	109.8
Serbia and Montenegro	49	74	59	30	66	78	50	1	1.8
Slovenia	113	123	114	139	119	131	140	26	23.3
Switzerland	8 307	7 247	8 371	9 954	9 807	7 783	8 660	353	4.3
Turkey	3 540	3 506	3 217	3 720	3 095	3 113	2 904	-635	-17.9
Eastern Europe	7 889	7 438	5 882	5 939	6 832	6 596	7 114	-775	-9.8
Albania	3	15	25	21	16	15	10	7	212.9
Baltic States	353	336	447	281	268	275	407	55	15.5
Estonia	47	87	163	88	58	82	121	73	154.4
Latvia	218	187	218	134	111	91	124	-94	-43.1
Lithuania	87	62	66	59	100	103	163	75	86.0
Bulgaria	110	112	103	114	108	101	156	46	42.2
Czech Republic	590	569	610	736	706	654	672	83	14.0
Hungary	486	483	504	569	686	688	934	448	92.3
Poland	1 170	882	826	757	788	686	759	-411	-35.1
Romania	258	337	176	233	374	248	367	109	42.2
Slovakia	82	111	127	110	70	93	115	33	40.5
Newly Independent States (NIS)	4 838	4 593	3 064	3 118	3 817	3 836	3 694	-1 144	-23.6
Armenia	62	51	51	56	50	112	103	41	65.5
Azerbaijan	62	123	55	210	64	70	121	59	94.5
Belarus	41	30	26	31	35	19	84	44	107.1
Georgia	141	137	84	110	106	99	132	-9	-6.5
Kazakhstan	346	103	180	124	160	605	168	-178	-51.4
Kyrgyzstan	28	21	23	23	28	31	39	11	37.7
Moldova	20	21	11	27	36	31	25	6	27.9
Russia	3 365	3 553	2 060	2 092	2 716	2 397	2 450	-915	-27.2
Tajikistan	19	12	14	12	29	33	50	31	168.8
Turkmenistan	118	28	18	84	248	47	34	-84	-70.9
Ukraine	403	368	205	191	200	255	231	-172	-42.7
Uzbekistan	234	147	339	158	145	139	257	23	9.7
WESTERN HEMISPHERE	286 183	298 781	308 668	349 576	322 992	309 976	319 266	33 083	11.6
NAFTA	223 155	235 376	253 509	290 290	264 721	258 393	267 227	44 072	19.7
Canada	151 767	156 603	166 600	178 941	163 424	160 923	169 770	18 003	11.9
Mexico	71 388	78 773	86 909	111 349	101 296	97 470	97 457	26 069	36.5
Caribbean	9 522	10 165	9 832	10 872	10 644	10 474	10 813	1 291	13.6
Aruba	238	351	307	291	277	465	355	117	48.9
Bahamas	810	816	842	1 069	1 026	975	1 084	275	33.9
Barbados	281	281	305	307	287	268	302	21	7.4
Cayman Islands	270	422	369	355	262	232	310	39	14.5
Dominican Republic	3 924	3 944	4 100	4 473	4 398	4 262	4 214	290	7.4
Haiti	499	549	614	577	550	573	640	141	28.2
Jamaica	1 417	1 304	1 293	1 376	1 406	1 420	1 470	53	3.7
Leeward and Windward Islands	444	701	525	563	459	465	557	113	25.5
Netherlands Antilles	475	751	597	674	816	741	747	272	57.2
Trinidad and Tobago	1 106	983	785	1 100	1 087	1 020	1 064	-42	-3.8
Turks and Caicos Islands	59	64	95	89	77	54	72	13	22.7
Central America	9 114	10 275	10 333	10 926	10 604	11 393	12 907	3 793	41.6
Belize	115	120	136	208	173	138	199	85	73.7
Costa Rica	2 024	2 297	2 381	2 460	2 502	3 132	3 414	1 390	68.7
El Salvador	1 400	1 514	1 519	1 780	1 870	1 664	1 824	424	30.3
Guatemala	1 730	1 938	1 812	1 901	1 870	2 044	2 274	544	31.5
Honduras	2 019	2 318	2 370	2 584	2 416	2 571	2 845	826	40.9
Nicaragua	290	337	374	380	443	437	503	213	73.5
Panama	1 536	1 753	1 742	1 612	1 330	1 407	1 848	312	20.3

Note: Because of rounding, aggregations may differ slightly from values in other published sources.

Table B-6. U.S. Total Exports of Goods to Individual Countries, 1997–2003—*Continued*

(Millions of dollars, except as noted; Census basis; domestic and foreign exports, f.a.s.)

Region and country	1997	1998	1999	2000	2001	2002	2003	1997–2003 change	
								Value	Percent
South America	43 453	42 211	34 347	36 925	36 427	28 837	27 430	-16 023	-36.9
Argentina	5 810	5 886	4 950	4 696	3 920	1 585	2 435	-3 375	-58.1
Bolivia	295	417	298	253	216	192	182	-113	-38.4
Brazil	15 915	15 142	13 203	15 321	15 879	12 376	11 218	-4 696	-29.5
Chile	4 368	3 979	3 078	3 460	3 118	2 609	2 719	-1 649	-37.8
Colombia	5 197	4 816	3 560	3 671	3 583	3 583	3 755	-1 442	-27.8
Ecuador	1 526	1 683	910	1 038	1 412	1 606	1 448	-78	-5.1
Guyana	143	146	145	159	141	128	117	-25	-17.8
Paraguay	913	786	515	446	389	433	489	-425	-46.5
Peru	1 953	2 063	1 697	1 660	1 564	1 563	1 707	-247	-12.6
Suriname	183	187	144	134	155	125	193	10	5.4
Uruguay	548	591	495	537	406	209	327	-221	-40.3
Venezuela	6 602	6 516	5 354	5 550	5 642	4 430	2 840	-3 762	-57.0
Other Western Hemisphere	940	753	647	563	596	879	889	-51	-5.4
Bermuda	338	400	344	429	371	415	401	63	18.7
Cuba	10	4	5	7	7	146	261	251	2 645.3
Falkland Islands	0	3	0	0	0	0	1	1	X
French Guiana	494	247	194	17	130	250	156	-338	-68.5
Greenland	5	6	3	1	5	4	3	-2	-38.8
Guadeloupe	58	64	63	86	59	40	45	-12	-21.2
Martinique	34	26	35	22	23	24	22	-12	-36.0
St. Pierre and Miquelon	2	3	3	2	1	1	0	-2	X
ASIA	213 547	187 566	190 881	218 796	198 929	193 494	206 631	-6 915	-3.2
Japan	65 549	57 831	57 466	64 924	57 452	51 449	52 064	-13 485	-20.6
Korea, South	25 046	16 486	22 958	27 830	22 181	22 576	24 099	-948	-3.8
Taiwan	20 366	18 165	19 131	24 406	18 122	18 382	17 488	-2 878	-14.1
China	12 862	14 241	13 111	16 185	19 182	22 128	28 419	15 556	120.9
Hong Kong	15 117	12 925	12 652	14 582	14 028	12 594	13 542	-1 575	-10.4
Macao	65	41	42	71	70	79	55	-10	-16.0
ASEAN	48 271	39 368	39 941	47 139	43 788	41 924	45 280	-2 991	-6.2
Brunei	178	123	67	156	104	46	36	-142	-79.9
Burma	20	32	9	17	11	10	7	-13	-65.3
Cambodia	19	11	20	32	29	29	58	39	211.3
Indonesia	4 522	2 299	2 038	2 402	2 521	2 556	2 520	-2 002	-44.3
Laos	3	4	2	4	4	4	5	2	74.1
Malaysia	10 780	8 957	9 060	10 938	9 358	10 344	10 921	141	1.3
Philippines	7 417	6 737	7 222	8 799	7 660	7 276	7 992	575	7.8
Singapore	17 696	15 694	16 247	17 806	17 652	16 218	16 576	-1 121	-6.3
Thailand	7 349	5 239	4 985	6 618	5 989	4 860	5 842	-1 508	-20.5
Vietnam	287	274	292	368	460	580	1 324	1 038	362.1
Middle East	20 928	23 661	20 885	19 015	19 278	18 930	19 365	-1 563	-7.5
Bahrain	406	295	348	449	433	419	509	103	25.3
Gaza Strip and West Bank	1	4	8	9	2	0	1	-1	-61.5
Iran	1	0	48	17	8	32	99	98	8 881.8
Iraq	82	106	10	10	46	32	316	234	285.0
Israel	5 995	6 983	7 691	7 746	7 475	7 027	6 878	884	14.7
Jordan	403	353	276	317	339	404	492	90	22.2
Kuwait	1 390	1 524	864	787	902	1 015	1 509	119	8.6
Lebanon	552	514	357	355	418	317	314	-238	-43.1
Oman	341	303	188	200	306	356	323	-18	-5.2
Qatar	379	354	146	191	336	314	409	30	7.8
Saudi Arabia	8 438	10 520	7 912	6 234	5 958	4 781	4 596	-3 842	-45.5
Syria	180	161	173	226	231	274	214	34	18.6
United Arab Emirates	2 607	2 366	2 708	2 285	2 638	3 593	3 510	903	34.6
Yemen Arab Republic	153	178	157	189	185	366	195	42	27.3
Other Asia	5 342	4 848	4 696	4 644	4 829	5 432	6 321	979	18.3
Afghanistan	12	7	18	8	6	80	61	49	427.8
Bangladesh	259	318	274	239	307	269	227	-33	-12.5
India	3 608	3 564	3 688	3 667	3 757	4 101	4 986	1 379	38.2
Korea, North	2	5	11	3	1	25	8	6	233.3
Mongolia	34	20	10	18	12	66	21	-14	-39.7
Nepal	27	16	21	35	14	20	16	-10	-39.0
Pakistan	1 240	720	497	462	541	693	840	-401	-32.3
South Asia NEC	6	8	9	7	8	5	8	2	32.8
Sri Lanka	155	190	167	205	183	172	155	0	0.1
AUSTRALIA AND OCEANIA	14 450	14 216	14 163	14 825	13 379	15 184	15 251	801	5.5
Australia	12 063	11 918	11 818	12 482	10 931	13 085	13 104	1 041	8.6
Australian Island Dependencies	5	3	5	4	5	3	2	-2	-48.9
Fiji	33	74	126	23	19	17	20	-13	-40.2
French Pacific Islands	140	119	119	113	108	116	135	-4	-3.1
New Zealand	1 962	1 887	1 923	1 970	2 111	1 813	1 849	-113	-5.8
New Zealand Island Dependencies	39	12	7	12	11	19	17	-21	-54.9
Other Pacific Islands NEC	8	13	8	12	9	14	8	-1	-9.5
Papua New Guinea	117	65	37	23	22	23	30	-86	-74.0
Southern Pacific Islands	6	46	16	14	20	12	8	2	31.6
Trust Territory (former)	68	70	75	108	74	74	68	0	-0.3
Western Samoa	11	10	12	64	70	8	11	0	0.0

Note: Because of rounding, aggregations may differ slightly from values in other published sources.

X = Not applicable.

Table B-6. U.S. Total Exports of Goods to Individual Countries, 1997–2003—*Continued*

(Millions of dollars, except as noted; Census basis; domestic and foreign exports, f.a.s.)

Region and country	1997	1998	1999	2000	2001	2002	2003	1997–2003 change Value	1997–2003 change Percent
AFRICA	11 390	11 167	9 880	10 966	12 119	10 663	10 685	-705	-6.2
Algeria	692	651	459	862	1 038	984	487	-204	-29.5
Angola	281	355	252	225	276	374	492	211	75.3
Benin	52	44	31	26	32	35	30	-21	-41.5
Botswana	43	36	33	31	43	32	26	-17	-39.9
Br. Indian Ocean Territory	1	1	1	1	0	0	4	3	600.0
Burkina Faso	18	16	11	16	4	19	11	-7	-39.9
Burundi	1	5	3	2	5	2	3	3	500.0
Cameroon	121	75	37	59	184	156	91	-31	-25.2
Cape Verde	10	10	8	7	8	10	9	-1	-9.0
Central African Republic	4	5	4	2	4	6	7	4	105.6
Chad	3	4	3	11	137	127	64	61	1 977.4
Comoros	0	1	0	1	1	0	1	0	X
Congo	75	92	47	82	90	52	79	4	5.5
Dem. Rep. of the Congo (Zaire)	38	34	21	10	19	28	31	-7	-19.0
Djibouti	7	20	26	17	19	59	34	27	369.9
Egypt	3 835	3 059	3 001	3 334	3 564	2 868	2 660	-1 175	-30.6
Equatorial Guinea	47	87	221	96	80	109	336	289	612.5
Eritrea	16	25	4	17	22	29	87	71	434.4
Ethiopia	121	89	164	165	61	61	409	288	237.5
Fr. Indian Ocean Areas	3	4	4	5	3	3	2	-1	-17.2
Gabon	85	62	45	64	73	66	63	-22	-25.4
Gambia	10	9	10	9	8	10	27	17	175.3
Ghana	315	225	233	191	200	193	209	-106	-33.5
Guinea	83	65	55	68	73	63	36	-47	-56.8
Guinea-Bissau	3	1	1	0	1	3	1	-1	-52.0
Ivory Coast	151	151	104	95	97	76	103	-48	-31.9
Kenya	225	199	189	238	578	271	197	-29	-12.7
Lesotho	2	1	1	1	1	2	5	3	112.5
Liberia	43	50	45	43	37	28	33	-10	-22.1
Libya	0	0	0	18	9	18	0	0	X
Madagascar	12	15	106	15	21	15	46	35	303.5
Malawi	18	15	7	14	13	30	17	-1	-5.7
Mali	26	25	30	32	33	11	32	5	20.2
Mauritania	21	20	25	16	25	23	35	14	67.0
Mauritius	31	23	39	24	29	28	32	1	1.9
Mayotte	0	0	0	0	0	0	0	0	X
Morocco	435	561	566	523	282	565	465	30	7.0
Mozambique	46	46	35	57	28	95	63	17	37.1
Namibia	25	51	196	80	256	58	28	3	12.0
Niger	25	18	19	37	63	41	34	9	35.5
Nigeria	813	817	628	722	955	1 058	1 029	216	26.6
Rwanda	35	22	48	19	17	10	8	-27	-77.4
Sao Tome and Principe	13	9	1	1	11	2	1	-12	-89.2
Senegal	52	59	63	82	80	75	102	50	96.9
Seychelles	6	10	8	7	176	8	7	1	18.0
Sierra Leone	16	24	13	19	28	26	28	13	80.3
Somalia	3	3	3	5	7	6	7	4	150.0
South Africa	2 997	3 628	2 586	3 090	2 960	2 526	2 821	-176	-5.9
St. Helena	3	0	2	0	4	2	2	0	-14.8
Sudan	36	7	9	17	17	11	26	-10	-28.3
Swaziland	5	8	9	67	12	12	8	3	57.7
Tanzania	65	67	68	45	64	63	66	1	1.7
Togo	26	25	26	11	16	14	15	-10	-40.6
Tunisia	252	196	280	289	276	195	171	-82	-32.4
Uganda	35	30	25	28	32	24	43	8	21.3
Western Sahara	0	0	0	0	0	0	0	0	X
Zambia	29	22	20	19	16	36	20	-10	-33.4
Zimbabwe (Rhodesia)	82	93	61	52	31	49	42	-40	-49.1
OTHER	341	400	371	307	262	187	186	-155	-45.5
International Organizations	0	0	0	0	0	0	0	0	X
Unidentified Countries	341	400	371	307	262	187	186	-155	-45.5
MISCELLANEOUS [1]	0	0	0	1	-110	-26	-26	-26	X
ADDENDUM									
Developed Countries	389 722	394 437	406 345	442 917	411 573	386 825	404 507	14 785	3.8
Developing Countries	299 120	287 301	289 081	338 694	317 265	306 092	319 314	20 194	6.8
APEC (20 countries)	434 153	417 809	439 351	506 992	459 890	448 892	469 908	35 755	8.2
EU-10 (joined 5/1/2004)	3 158	2 933	3 011	3 117	3 164	2 930	3 555	397	12.6
EU-25 (EU-15 + EU-10)	143 932	151 967	154 825	168 181	161 931	146 621	154 105	10 173	7.1

Note: Because of rounding, aggregations may differ slightly from values in other published sources.

[1]Includes transshipments, carryover, and timing adjustments, revisions not accounted for elsewhere, and roundoff.
X = Not applicable.

Table B-7. U.S. Total Imports of Goods from Individual Countries, 1997–2003

(Millions of dollars, except as noted; Census basis; general imports, Customs.)

Region and country	1997	1998	1999	2000	2001	2002	2003	1997–2003 change Value	1997–2003 change Percent
WORLD	870 671	911 896	1 024 618	1 218 022	1 140 999	1 161 366	1 259 705	389 035	44.7
EUROPE	181 441	202 874	224 790	256 765	253 767	260 813	284 549	103 107	56.8
Western Europe	172 958	191 971	212 968	240 660	239 424	245 915	266 224	93 265	53.9
European Union (EU-15)	157 528	176 380	195 227	220 019	220 058	225 719	244 811	87 283	55.4
Austria	2 368	2 561	2 909	3 227	3 969	3 815	4 489	2 121	89.5
Belgium	7 912	8 440	9 196	9 929	10 158	9 807	10 141	2 229	28.2
Denmark	2 138	2 395	2 819	2 965	3 407	3 237	3 718	1 581	73.9
Finland	2 392	2 596	2 908	3 251	3 394	3 444	3 598	1 207	50.4
France	20 636	24 016	25 709	29 800	30 408	28 240	29 221	8 585	41.6
Germany	43 122	49 842	55 228	58 513	59 077	62 506	68 047	24 926	57.8
Greece	453	467	563	591	505	546	616	163	35.9
Ireland	5 867	8 401	10 994	16 464	18 499	22 388	25 841	19 974	340.5
Italy	19 408	20 959	22 357	25 043	23 790	24 220	25 437	6 029	31.1
Luxembourg	239	373	314	332	306	300	265	26	10.8
Netherlands	7 293	7 599	8 475	9 671	9 515	9 849	10 972	3 679	50.4
Portugal	1 138	1 265	1 356	1 579	1 555	1 673	1 967	829	72.9
Spain	4 606	4 780	5 059	5 713	5 197	5 733	6 708	2 102	45.6
Sweden	7 299	7 848	8 103	9 597	8 909	9 216	11 125	3 826	52.4
United Kingdom	32 659	34 838	39 237	43 345	41 369	40 745	42 667	10 008	30.6
Non-EU Western Europe	15 430	15 591	17 742	20 642	19 366	20 197	21 412	5 982	38.8
Bosnia-Herzegovina	8	7	15	18	12	16	12	3	41.0
Croatia	83	73	110	141	129	146	181	98	118.2
Cyprus	16	32	31	23	35	26	25	8	51.2
Gibraltar	3	6	10	1	3	1	3	0	3.6
Iceland	231	268	304	260	233	297	283	52	22.5
Liechtenstein	117	243	277	278	224	238	262	145	123.8
Macedonia	147	175	137	152	112	73	61	-86	-58.7
Malta and Gozo	224	340	325	482	369	310	373	149	66.7
Norway	3 752	2 872	4 043	5 706	5 203	5 843	5 212	1 460	38.9
Other Non-EU Western Europe	36	42	43	63	31	34	49	13	36.7
Serbia and Montenegro	10	13	5	2	6	10	15	4	40.4
Slovenia	277	287	276	313	286	307	482	205	74.1
Switzerland	8 405	8 690	9 539	10 160	9 670	9 382	10 668	2 263	26.9
Turkey	2 121	2 543	2 629	3 042	3 055	3 516	3 788	1 667	78.6
Eastern Europe	8 483	10 903	11 821	16 105	14 343	14 897	18 325	9 842	116.0
Albania	12	12	9	8	7	6	4	-7	-62.4
Baltic States	302	321	563	996	550	660	906	605	200.4
Estonia	77	125	237	573	241	164	182	105	136.5
Latvia	145	115	229	288	145	197	377	232	160.1
Lithuania	80	81	97	135	164	300	347	268	335.2
Bulgaria	171	219	199	236	337	340	441	270	157.5
Czech Republic	610	673	754	1 070	1 116	1 233	1 394	785	128.6
Hungary	1 079	1 567	1 893	2 715	2 965	2 637	2 699	1 620	150.2
Poland	696	784	816	1 041	953	1 109	1 326	630	90.6
Romania	400	393	442	473	520	695	730	330	82.6
Slovakia	166	166	169	241	238	260	1 013	847	511.7
Newly Independent States (NIS)	5 048	6 768	6 977	9 325	7 658	7 957	9 810	4 762	94.3
Armenia	6	17	15	23	33	31	38	32	526.7
Azerbaijan	6	5	26	21	21	34	10	4	66.7
Belarus	66	105	94	104	108	126	215	149	226.4
Georgia	7	14	18	32	31	18	54	47	671.4
Kazakhstan	129	169	229	429	352	335	392	263	204.3
Kyrgyzstan	2	0	1	2	3	5	11	9	358.3
Moldova	54	109	87	105	68	39	43	-11	-20.1
Russia	4 319	5 747	5 921	7 659	6 264	6 870	8 598	4 279	99.1
Tajikistan	9	33	23	9	5	1	7	-1	-14.1
Turkmenistan	2	3	9	28	46	60	76	74	3 538.1
Ukraine	410	531	529	872	674	362	282	-128	-31.2
Uzbekistan	39	34	26	41	54	77	84	45	114.1
WESTERN HEMISPHERE	306 878	318 163	366 915	440 136	415 008	413 233	441 113	134 235	43.7
NAFTA	253 172	267 885	308 432	366 765	347 606	343 703	362 239	109 068	43.1
Canada	167 234	173 256	198 711	230 838	216 268	209 088	224 166	56 932	34.0
Mexico	85 938	94 629	109 721	135 926	131 338	134 616	138 073	52 136	60.7
Caribbean	7 907	7 512	8 016	10 275	9 314	9 035	11 854	3 947	49.9
Aruba	610	470	675	1 536	1 034	774	964	354	58.0
Bahamas	155	142	195	275	314	450	479	325	209.5
Barbados	42	35	59	39	40	34	44	1	3.3
Cayman Islands	20	18	9	7	7	9	12	-8	-39.8
Dominican Republic	4 327	4 441	4 287	4 383	4 183	4 169	4 455	128	3.0
Haiti	188	272	301	297	263	255	332	144	76.6
Jamaica	738	755	678	648	461	396	495	-243	-33.0
Leeward and Windward Islands	108	89	135	137	140	141	125	17	16.1
Netherlands Antilles	580	308	384	719	485	362	620	40	7.0
Trinidad and Tobago	1 134	977	1 287	2 229	2 380	2 440	4 322	3 187	281.0
Turks and Caicos Islands	5	5	6	6	8	5	6	1	15.1
Central America	8 866	9 630	11 492	12 158	11 473	12 242	12 810	3 944	44.5
Belize	77	66	81	94	97	78	101	24	31.2
Costa Rica	2 323	2 745	3 968	3 539	2 886	3 142	3 362	1 038	44.7
El Salvador	1 346	1 438	1 605	1 933	1 880	1 982	2 019	673	50.0
Guatemala	1 990	2 072	2 265	2 607	2 589	2 796	2 945	955	48.0
Honduras	2 322	2 544	2 713	3 090	3 127	3 261	3 312	989	42.6
Nicaragua	439	453	495	589	604	680	769	330	75.1
Panama	367	312	365	307	291	303	301	-66	-18.0

Note: Because of rounding, aggregations may differ slightly from values in other published sources.

Table B-7. U.S. Total Imports of Goods from Individual Countries, 1997–2003—*Continued*

(Millions of dollars, except as noted; Census basis; general imports, Customs.)

Region and country	1997	1998	1999	2000	2001	2002	2003	1997–2003 change Value	1997–2003 change Percent
South America	36 886	33 106	38 922	50 859	46 499	48 179	54 166	17 281	46.8
Argentina	2 228	2 231	2 598	3 100	3 013	3 187	3 169	941	42.2
Bolivia	223	224	224	185	166	160	185	-39	-17.2
Brazil	9 626	10 102	11 314	13 853	14 466	15 781	17 884	8 259	85.8
Chile	2 293	2 453	2 953	3 269	3 495	3 785	3 703	1 410	61.5
Colombia	4 737	4 656	6 259	6 968	5 710	5 604	6 386	1 648	34.8
Ecuador	2 055	1 752	1 821	2 238	2 010	2 143	2 721	666	32.4
Guyana	113	137	121	140	140	116	118	6	4.9
Paraguay	41	34	48	41	33	44	53	13	31.0
Peru	1 772	1 976	1 928	1 995	1 844	1 939	2 407	635	35.8
Suriname	92	106	123	135	143	133	140	49	53.1
Uruguay	229	256	199	313	228	193	256	27	11.8
Venezuela	13 477	9 181	11 335	18 623	15 251	15 094	17 144	3 667	27.2
Other Western Hemisphere	49	30	53	79	116	74	44	-5	-9.9
Bermuda	30	12	25	39	66	23	15	-15	-49.0
Cuba	0	0	1	0	0	0	0	0	X
Falkland Islands	1	0	1	3	7	6	5	5	920.0
French Guiana	2	3	4	2	0	8	3	1	41.7
Greenland	8	7	13	16	29	23	14	6	75.9
Guadeloupe	4	2	3	10	11	11	3	-1	-30.0
Martinique	2	1	1	2	1	1	1	-1	-70.0
St. Pierre and Miquelon	2	5	5	6	3	4	3	1	23.8
ASIA	354 997	367 661	408 542	484 650	437 749	456 094	492 503	137 506	38.7
Japan	121 663	121 845	130 864	146 479	126 473	121 429	118 029	-3 634	-3.0
Korea, South	23 173	23 942	31 179	40 308	35 181	35 572	36 963	13 790	59.5
Taiwan	32 629	33 125	35 204	40 503	33 375	32 199	31 600	-1 029	-3.2
China	62 558	71 169	81 788	100 018	102 278	125 193	152 379	89 822	143.6
Hong Kong	10 288	10 538	10 528	11 449	9 646	9 328	8 850	-1 437	-14.0
Macao	1 021	1 109	1 124	1 266	1 225	1 233	1 356	335	32.8
ASEAN	71 013	73 395	77 658	87 945	76 385	78 339	81 878	10 865	15.3
Brunei	56	211	389	384	399	287	423	367	657.2
Burma	115	164	232	471	470	356	276	161	139.9
Cambodia	103	365	593	826	963	1 071	1 263	1 160	1 126.0
Indonesia	9 188	9 341	9 525	10 367	10 104	9 643	9 520	332	3.6
Laos	14	21	13	10	4	3	4	-10	-70.6
Malaysia	18 027	19 000	21 424	25 568	22 340	24 009	25 438	7 411	41.1
Philippines	10 445	11 947	12 353	13 935	11 325	10 980	10 061	-384	-3.7
Singapore	20 075	18 356	18 191	19 178	15 000	14 802	15 158	-4 916	-24.5
Thailand	12 602	13 436	14 330	16 385	14 727	14 793	15 181	2 579	20.5
Vietnam	389	554	608	821	1 053	2 395	4 555	4 166	1 072.4
Middle East	20 403	18 766	25 422	38 967	36 412	34 302	41 477	21 074	103.3
Bahrain	116	156	225	338	424	395	378	262	225.0
Gaza Strip and West Bank	0	0	4	5	6	7	2	2	X
Iran	0	0	2	169	143	156	161	161	X
Iraq	312	1 183	4 226	6 066	5 820	3 548	4 574	4 262	1 366.4
Israel	7 326	8 640	9 864	12 964	11 959	12 416	12 770	5 444	74.3
Jordan	25	16	31	73	229	412	674	648	2 562.1
Kuwait	1 816	1 266	1 439	2 781	1 991	1 940	2 277	460	25.3
Lebanon	78	83	51	77	90	62	92	15	18.6
Oman	242	217	220	258	420	401	695	452	186.6
Qatar	157	220	272	486	502	485	331	174	110.5
Saudi Arabia	9 365	6 241	8 254	14 365	13 272	13 150	18 069	8 704	92.9
Syria	28	46	95	159	159	161	259	231	828.0
United Arab Emirates	920	660	714	972	1 194	923	1 129	209	22.7
Yemen Arab Republic	16	38	24	256	202	246	66	50	313.1
Other Asia	12 250	13 773	14 775	17 715	16 774	18 500	19 971	7 721	63.0
Afghanistan	10	17	9	1	1	3	56	46	461.0
Bangladesh	1 679	1 846	1 918	2 418	2 359	2 134	2 074	394	23.5
India	7 322	8 237	9 071	10 687	9 737	11 818	13 053	5 730	78.3
Korea, North	0	0	0	0	0	0	0	0	X
Mongolia	42	42	61	117	144	162	183	141	332.5
Nepal	114	139	178	229	200	152	171	58	50.9
Pakistan	1 442	1 692	1 741	2 167	2 249	2 305	2 532	1 089	75.5
South Asia NEC	20	34	55	95	99	114	95	75	365.7
Sri Lanka	1 620	1 767	1 742	2 002	1 984	1 810	1 807	187	11.6
AUSTRALIA AND OCEANIA	6 465	7 373	7 381	8 831	9 034	9 126	9 196	2 731	42.2
Australia	4 602	5 387	5 280	6 438	6 478	6 479	6 414	1 812	39.4
Australian Island Dependencies	1	1	1	2	1	1	2	1	155.6
Fiji	85	101	100	147	182	156	175	90	106.4
French Pacific Islands	87	54	51	75	63	54	61	-27	-30.7
New Zealand	1 579	1 645	1 748	2 080	2 199	2 282	2 403	824	52.2
New Zealand Island Dependencies	4	4	6	8	11	4	9	6	154.1
Other Pacific Islands NEC	3	6	5	6	8	10	13	10	346.7
Papua New Guinea	65	130	145	35	39	90	66	2	2.5
Southern Pacific Islands	4	9	4	3	5	5	4	0	-9.1
Trust Territory (former)	32	30	36	32	42	40	43	11	33.5
Western Samoa	3	7	5	6	7	6	4	2	76.0

Note: Because of rounding, aggregations may differ slightly from values in other published sources.

X = Not applicable.

Table B-7. U.S. Total Imports of Goods from Individual Countries, 1997–2003—*Continued*

(Millions of dollars, except as noted; Census basis; general imports, Customs.)

Region and country	1997	1998	1999	2000	2001	2002	2003	1997–2003 change Value	1997–2003 change Percent
AFRICA	19 925	15 824	16 991	27 642	25 436	22 100	32 036	12 111	60.8
Algeria	2 440	1 638	1 824	2 724	2 702	2 360	4 753	2 313	94.8
Angola	2 779	2 241	2 418	3 555	3 096	3 123	4 264	1 485	53.4
Benin	8	4	18	2	1	1	1	-7	-92.2
Botswana	25	20	17	41	21	29	14	-11	-44.3
Br. Indian Ocean Territory	11	1	0	3	0	0	1	-10	-88.3
Burkina Faso	1	1	3	3	5	3	1	0	-10.0
Burundi	14	8	6	8	3	1	6	-8	-57.2
Cameroon	57	53	77	155	102	172	214	157	274.1
Cape Verde	1	0	0	4	2	2	6	5	460.0
Central African Republic	1	3	2	3	2	2	2	1	53.8
Chad	3	8	7	5	6	6	22	20	672.4
Comoros	3	1	2	4	11	5	4	1	53.8
Congo	472	315	415	532	474	204	433	-39	-8.2
Dem. Rep. of the Congo (Zaire)	282	172	229	215	154	182	175	-107	-38.1
Djibouti	0	1	0	0	1	2	1	1	X
Egypt	658	660	618	888	882	1 356	1 144	486	74.0
Equatorial Guinea	30	67	43	155	464	502	904	873	2 891.7
Eritrea	1	1	1	0	0	0	0	-1	X
Ethiopia	70	52	30	29	29	26	31	-40	-56.4
Fr. Indian Ocean Areas	1	1	0	1	1	3	2	2	266.7
Gabon	2 202	1 259	1 543	2 197	1 660	1 588	1 970	-233	-10.6
Gambia	3	2	0	0	1	0	0	-3	X
Ghana	155	143	209	205	187	116	82	-73	-47.3
Guinea	128	115	117	88	88	72	69	-59	-45.8
Guinea-Bissau	0	0	0	1	0	0	2	2	X
Ivory Coast	289	426	350	384	333	376	490	201	69.4
Kenya	114	99	106	110	128	189	249	135	118.6
Lesotho	87	100	111	140	215	322	393	307	354.7
Liberia	5	25	30	45	45	46	60	55	1 139.6
Libya	0	0	0	0	0	0	0	0	X
Madagascar	63	71	80	158	272	216	384	321	512.9
Malawi	83	60	73	55	78	71	77	-6	-7.1
Mali	4	3	9	10	6	3	2	-1	-36.8
Mauritania	0	0	1	0	0	1	1	1	X
Mauritius	238	272	259	286	278	281	298	60	25.0
Mayotte	0	0	0	0	0	0	0	0	X
Morocco	296	343	386	441	435	392	385	89	30.2
Mozambique	31	26	10	24	7	9	8	-22	-72.5
Namibia	63	52	30	45	37	57	123	60	95.6
Niger	30	2	12	7	5	1	4	-26	-86.6
Nigeria	6 349	4 194	4 385	10 538	8 775	5 945	10 394	4 044	63.7
Rwanda	4	4	4	5	7	3	3	-1	-33.3
Sao Tome and Principe	0	1	3	1	0	0	0	0	X
Senegal	7	5	9	4	104	4	5	-2	-33.8
Seychelles	2	2	5	8	24	26	13	11	441.7
Sierra Leone	18	12	10	4	5	4	7	-12	-64.7
Somalia	0	1	0	1	3	0	0	0	X
South Africa	2 510	3 049	3 194	4 210	4 433	4 034	4 638	2 128	84.8
St. Helena	1	0	0	3	3	4	6	5	460.0
Sudan	12	3	0	2	3	1	3	-9	-76.9
Swaziland	44	25	38	53	65	115	162	118	267.6
Tanzania	27	32	35	32	28	25	24	-2	-9.0
Togo	9	2	3	6	13	3	6	-4	-40.4
Tunisia	63	62	75	94	122	93	100	37	58.6
Uganda	38	15	20	29	18	15	35	-3	-7.7
Western Sahara	0	0	0	0	0	0	0	0	X
Zambia	56	47	38	18	16	8	13	-43	-77.6
Zimbabwe (Rhodesia)	140	127	133	112	91	103	57	-83	-59.4
OTHER	0	0	0	0	0	0	0	0	X
International Organizations	0	0	0	0	0	0	0	0	X
Unidentified Countries	0	0	0	0	0	0	0	0	X
MISCELLANEOUS 1	965	1	0	-1	5	0	309	-655	-67.9
ADDENDUM									
Developed Countries	470 547	497 152	552 766	630 706	595 275	589 226	621 874	151 326	32.2
Developing Countries	400 123	414 744	471 852	587 316	545 725	572 140	637 832	237 708	59.4
APEC (20 countries)	588 893	618 685	692 791	813 636	749 828	765 778	813 988	225 095	38.2
EU-10 (joined 5/1/2004)	3 368	4 169	4 827	6 882	6 511	6 542	8 218	4 850	144.0
EU-25 (EU-15 + EU-10)	160 897	180 550	200 053	226 901	226 568	232 261	253 030	92 133	57.3

Note: Because of rounding, aggregations may differ slightly from values in other published sources.

1Includes transshipments, carryover, and timing adjustments, revisions not accounted for elsewhere, and roundoff.
X = Not applicable.

Table B-8. U.S. Total Balances of Goods with Individual Countries, 1997–2003

(Millions of dollars, except as noted; Census basis; foreign and domestic exports, f.a.s.; general imports, Customs.)

Region and country	1997	1998	1999	2000	2001	2002	2003	1997–2003 change Value	1997–2003 change Percent
WORLD	-181 488	-229 758	-328 821	-436 104	-411 899	-468 263	-532 350	-350 862	193.3
EUROPE	-18 169	-32 864	-52 957	-69 319	-72 268	-97 239	-111 555	-93 386	514.0
Western Europe	-17 575	-29 399	-47 018	-59 153	-64 738	-88 938	-100 321	-82 746	470.8
European Union (EU-15)	-16 755	-27 345	-43 412	-54 954	-61 290	-82 080	-93 095	-76 340	455.6
Austria	-294	-418	-321	-635	-1 364	-1 388	-2 724	-2 430	827.4
Belgium	5 508	5 478	3 185	3 996	3 344	3 519	5 095	-413	-7.5
Denmark	-381	-521	-1 093	-1 458	-1 798	-1 741	-2 161	-1 780	467.4
Finland	-650	-681	-1 239	-1 680	-1 840	-1 912	-1 889	-1 239	190.4
France	-4 672	-6 287	-6 831	-9 439	-10 544	-9 224	-12 166	-7 495	160.4
Germany	-18 663	-23 185	-28 428	-29 064	-29 081	-35 876	-39 281	-20 618	110.5
Greece	496	889	432	630	788	606	1 893	1 396	281.4
Ireland	-1 224	-2 754	-4 611	-8 750	-11 355	-15 693	-18 051	-16 827	1 374.3
Italy	-10 413	-11 968	-12 266	-13 982	-13 874	-14 164	-14 854	-4 441	42.6
Luxembourg	473	233	670	66	243	180	14	-459	-97.0
Netherlands	12 534	11 378	10 962	12 166	9 969	8 462	9 742	-2 792	-22.3
Portugal	-184	-377	-264	-594	-316	-811	-1 105	-921	501.0
Spain	933	673	1 074	609	559	-435	-747	-1 680	-180.0
Sweden	-3 985	-4 026	-3 852	-5 044	-5 368	-6 063	-7 896	-3 911	98.1
United Kingdom	3 766	4 220	-830	-1 775	-655	-7 540	-8 967	-12 733	-338.1
Non-EU Western Europe	-820	-2 054	-3 605	-4 199	-3 447	-6 858	-7 225	-6 405	781.4
Bosnia-Herzegovina	94	33	29	26	31	16	9	-85	-90.0
Croatia	56	24	-3	-51	-29	-68	16	-40	-71.4
Cyprus	228	130	160	167	233	168	187	-41	-17.9
Gibraltar	6	3	-6	14	8	25	11	5	86.7
Iceland	-52	-31	-6	-4	-7	-78	-40	12	-23.1
Liechtenstein	-104	-235	-268	-264	-217	-223	-246	-142	136.4
Macedonia	-113	-161	-80	-83	-79	-55	-35	79	-69.4
Malta and Gozo	-103	-73	-135	-148	-110	-100	-171	-68	66.1
Norway	-2 031	-1 162	-2 603	-4 159	-3 368	-4 436	-3 766	-1 735	85.5
Other Non-EU Western Europe	3	1	-7	-22	20	2	35	32	1 053.3
Serbia and Montenegro	39	62	54	28	60	69	35	-4	-9.3
Slovenia	-164	-164	-162	-175	-167	-176	-345	-181	110.8
Switzerland	-98	-1 443	-1 167	-206	138	-1 599	-2 029	-1 931	1 966.1
Turkey	1 419	963	588	679	40	-403	-888	-2 307	-162.6
Eastern Europe	-594	-3 465	-5 939	-10 166	-7 531	-8 301	-11 234	-10 640	1 791.0
Albania	-9	3	16	13	8	9	5	14	-161.6
Baltic States	51	15	-115	-715	-302	-385	-499	-550	-1 079.0
Estonia	-29	-38	-74	-485	-183	-82	-61	-32	108.2
Latvia	73	72	-11	-154	-34	-106	-254	-326	-449.0
Lithuania	8	-19	-31	-76	-84	-197	-185	-192	-2 528.9
Bulgaria	-62	-107	-96	-122	-229	-238	-286	-224	362.3
Czech Republic	-20	-104	-144	-334	-410	-580	-722	-702	3 509.0
Hungary	-594	-1 084	-1 389	-2 146	-2 279	-1 950	-1 767	-1 174	197.8
Poland	474	98	10	-284	-165	-422	-566	-1 040	-219.2
Romania	-142	-57	-266	-240	-145	-447	-363	-222	156.2
Slovakia	-84	-55	-42	-131	-168	-168	-894	-811	969.5
Newly Independent States (NIS)	-210	-2 174	-3 913	-6 207	-3 842	-4 121	-6 142	-5 932	2 822.1
Armenia	56	35	36	33	17	81	65	9	16.2
Azerbaijan	57	118	29	189	44	35	110	54	94.9
Belarus	-25	-75	-68	-73	-73	-106	-131	-106	416.9
Georgia	134	122	65	78	75	81	77	-57	-42.3
Kazakhstan	217	-66	-50	-305	-192	270	-244	-462	-212.3
Kyrgyzstan	26	20	22	21	24	26	28	2	8.5
Moldova	-34	-89	-77	-78	-33	-9	-18	16	-47.6
Russia	-954	-2 195	-3 861	-5 566	-3 548	-4 473	-6 171	-5 217	546.8
Tajikistan	10	-21	-9	3	23	32	43	33	326.0
Turkmenistan	116	25	10	57	203	-13	-42	-158	-136.5
Ukraine	-7	-164	-324	-681	-474	-108	-32	-25	349.3
Uzbekistan	195	113	313	117	91	61	173	-23	-11.6
WESTERN HEMISPHERE	-20 696	-19 383	-58 247	-90 559	-93 296	-103 284	-119 216	-98 519	476.0
NAFTA	-30 016	-32 509	-54 923	-76 475	-82 885	-85 310	-92 319	-62 303	207.6
Canada	-15 467	-16 653	-32 111	-51 897	-52 844	-48 165	-51 671	-36 204	234.1
Mexico	-14 549	-15 857	-22 812	-24 577	-30 041	-37 146	-40 648	-26 099	179.4
Caribbean	1 614	2 653	1 816	597	1 331	1 427	-1 005	-2 620	-162.3
Aruba	-372	-118	-368	-1 244	-758	-309	-600	-228	61.2
Bahamas	655	673	647	794	713	526	595	-59	-9.0
Barbados	239	247	246	268	247	233	257	18	7.5
Cayman Islands	251	404	359	348	255	223	297	47	18.6
Dominican Republic	-403	-497	-186	89	214	81	-250	153	-38.0
Haiti	311	277	313	280	287	318	307	-4	-1.2
Jamaica	678	549	615	728	945	1 024	1 047	368	54.3
Leeward and Windward Islands	336	612	390	426	319	323	430	94	28.1
Netherlands Antilles	-105	442	213	-45	332	380	115	220	-209.9
Trinidad and Tobago	-28	6	-501	-1 129	-1 293	-1 420	-3 271	-3 242	11 456.5
Turks and Caicos Islands	53	59	89	83	69	49	66	13	23.5
Central America	248	645	-1 159	-1 232	-979	-864	57	-191	-76.9
Belize	38	54	55	115	76	60	97	60	159.7
Costa Rica	-299	-449	-1 587	-1 078	-384	-25	49	348	-116.5
El Salvador	54	76	-86	-153	-121	-318	-199	-253	-469.7
Guatemala	-261	-134	-453	-707	-719	-752	-683	-423	162.2
Honduras	-303	-227	-344	-506	-711	-690	-486	-183	60.3
Nicaragua	-150	-116	-122	-208	-161	-243	-268	-119	79.3
Panama	1 169	1 441	1 378	1 305	1 040	1 104	1 547	378	32.4

Note: Because of rounding, aggregations may differ slightly from values in other published sources.

Table B-8. U.S. Total Balances of Goods with Individual Countries, 1997–2003—*Continued*

(Millions of dollars, except as noted; Census basis; foreign and domestic exports, f.a.s.; general imports, Customs.)

Region and country	1997	1998	1999	2000	2001	2002	2003	1997–2003 change Value	Percent
South America	6 567	9 105	-4 576	-13 934	-11 242	-19 342	-26 792	-33 359	-508.0
Argentina	3 582	3 655	2 352	1 596	907	-1 602	-733	-4 314	-120.5
Bolivia	72	193	75	68	50	32	-2	-74	-102.8
Brazil	6 289	5 040	1 889	1 468	1 413	-3 405	-6 699	-12 989	-206.5
Chile	2 075	1 527	125	191	-377	-1 176	-990	-3 066	-147.7
Colombia	460	160	-2 699	-3 297	-3 297	-2 022	-2 629	-3 089	-672.0
Ecuador	-529	-69	-911	-1 200	-598	-538	-1 275	-746	141.1
Guyana	30	9	25	19	1	13	-2	-31	-105.1
Paraguay	873	752	467	405	356	389	430	-442	-50.7
Peru	181	87	-232	-335	-280	-377	-710	-891	-492.4
Suriname	92	81	21	-1	12	-8	53	-39	-42.5
Uruguay	319	336	296	224	179	15	71	-248	-77.8
Venezuela	-6 876	-2 666	-5 981	-13 073	-9 608	-10 664	-14 305	-7 430	108.1
Other Western Hemisphere	891	723	594	485	480	805	844	-47	-5.3
Bermuda	308	389	319	390	305	392	386	78	25.2
Cuba	10	4	4	7	7	145	259	249	2 624.2
Falkland Islands	0	3	-1	-3	-7	-6	-4	-4	X
French Guiana	491	243	190	15	130	242	152	-339	-69.0
Greenland	-3	-1	-10	-15	-24	-19	-11	-8	260.0
Guadeloupe	54	62	60	76	48	29	43	-11	-20.6
Martinique	31	25	34	20	23	23	21	-10	-31.9
St. Pierre and Miquelon	0	-2	-2	-5	-3	-3	-3	-2	X
ASIA	-141 450	-180 095	-217 661	-265 854	-238 732	-262 548	-286 416	-144 966	102.5
Japan	-56 115	-64 014	-73 398	-81 555	-69 022	-69 979	-66 032	-9 918	17.7
Korea, South	1 873	-7 456	-8 220	-12 478	-13 001	-12 996	-13 157	-15 030	-802.4
Taiwan	-12 263	-14 960	-16 073	-16 097	-15 253	-13 766	-14 152	-1 889	15.4
China	-49 695	-56 927	-68 677	-83 833	-83 096	-103 065	-124 068	-74 373	149.7
Hong Kong	4 829	2 387	2 124	3 133	4 381	3 266	4 669	-160	-3.3
Macao	-956	-1 068	-1 083	-1 196	-1 155	-1 153	-1 301	-345	36.1
ASEAN	-22 742	-34 027	-37 717	-40 805	-32 506	-36 415	-36 606	-13 864	61.0
Brunei	122	-88	-322	-228	-295	-241	-385	-507	-414.8
Burma	-95	-132	-224	-454	-458	-346	-269	-174	182.9
Cambodia	-84	-354	-573	-794	-933	-1 042	-1 204	-1 120	1 326.8
Indonesia	-4 666	-7 042	-7 487	-7 965	-7 583	-7 088	-6 999	-2 333	50.0
Laos	-12	-17	-11	-6	0	2	1	12	-105.2
Malaysia	-7 247	-10 043	-12 364	-14 631	-12 893	-13 665	-14 526	-7 279	100.5
Philippines	-3 028	-5 211	-5 131	-5 136	-3 665	-3 704	-2 072	956	-31.6
Singapore	-2 378	-2 662	-1 944	-1 372	2 652	1 416	1 422	3 801	-159.8
Thailand	-5 252	-8 198	-9 345	-9 768	-8 738	-9 933	-9 343	-4 091	77.9
Vietnam	-102	-280	-317	-454	-593	-1 815	-3 231	-3 129	3 070.9
Middle East	526	4 895	-4 537	-19 952	-17 135	-15 372	-22 109	-22 635	-4 302.4
Bahrain	290	139	122	111	9	24	130	-160	-55.1
Gaza Strip and West Bank	1	4	5	4	-4	-7	-1	-2	-175.0
Iran	1	0	46	-152	-135	-125	-62	-63	-6 330.0
Iraq	-230	-1 077	-4 217	-6 055	-5 774	-3 517	-4 275	-4 045	1 759.3
Israel	-1 331	-1 657	-2 174	-5 219	-4 484	-5 389	-5 877	-4 546	341.5
Jordan	377	337	245	243	110	-8	-181	-558	-148.0
Kuwait	-426	258	-575	-1 994	-1 088	-926	-770	-343	80.5
Lebanon	474	431	305	278	329	256	222	-252	-53.2
Oman	98	86	-31	-58	-114	-45	-372	-471	-478.4
Qatar	222	134	-127	-295	-168	-171	76	-146	-65.7
Saudi Arabia	-927	4 279	-342	-8 131	-7 315	-8 369	-13 473	-12 546	1 353.4
Syria	153	116	78	67	73	113	-32	-185	-121.0
United Arab Emirates	1 687	1 706	1 994	1 313	1 444	2 670	2 380	693	41.1
Yemen Arab Republic	137	140	133	-66	-17	120	125	-12	-8.9
Other Asia	-6 908	-8 925	-10 079	-13 071	-11 945	-13 068	-13 660	-6 752	97.7
Afghanistan	2	-10	9	7	5	77	5	3	206.7
Bangladesh	-1 420	-1 528	-1 644	-2 178	-2 052	-1 865	-1 848	-428	30.1
India	-3 715	-4 673	-5 383	-7 020	-5 980	-7 717	-8 076	-4 361	117.4
Korea, North	2	5	11	3	1	25	8	6	233.3
Mongolia	-8	-22	-51	-99	-132	-95	-163	-155	1 907.4
Nepal	-87	-124	-156	-194	-186	-132	-155	-68	78.9
Pakistan	-202	-971	-1 244	-1 705	-1 708	-1 612	-1 688	-1 486	734.8
South Asia NEC	-14	-26	-46	-88	-91	-109	-90	-76	531.5
Sri Lanka	-1 465	-1 576	-1 575	-1 797	-1 801	-1 639	-1 653	-188	12.8
AUSTRALIA AND OCEANIA	7 986	6 844	6 783	5 995	4 345	6 058	6 038	-1 948	-24.4
Australia	7 461	6 531	6 538	6 044	4 453	6 606	6 674	-787	-10.5
Australian Island Dependencies	4	3	4	3	4	2	0	-4	X
Fiji	-52	-27	27	-124	-163	-139	-156	-104	199.6
French Pacific Islands	52	65	84	38	46	62	75	22	42.6
New Zealand	383	242	175	-110	-89	-469	-555	-938	-245.1
New Zealand Island Dependencies	35	8	0	4	0	15	8	-27	-77.7
Other Pacific Islands NEC	6	7	3	6	1	4	-6	-12	-196.7
Papua New Guinea	52	-64	-107	-12	-17	-67	-36	-88	-168.7
Southern Pacific Islands	1	37	12	12	15	8	4	2	200.0
Trust Territory (former)	36	40	40	75	32	34	25	-11	-31.1
Western Samoa	9	4	7	59	63	1	6	-3	-29.1

Note: Because of rounding, aggregations may differ slightly from values in other published sources.

X = Not applicable.

Table B-8. U.S. Total Balances of Goods with Individual Countries, 1997–2003—*Continued*

(Millions of dollars, except as noted; Census basis; foreign and domestic exports, f.a.s.; general imports, Customs.)

Region and country	1997	1998	1999	2000	2001	2002	2003	1997–2003 change	
								Value	Percent
AFRICA	-8 534	-4 658	-7 111	-16 674	-13 312	-11 085	-22 490	-13 956	163.5
Algeria	-1 748	-987	-1 366	-1 863	-1 664	-1 376	-4 261	-2 513	143.8
Angola	-2 499	-1 886	-2 166	-3 330	-2 820	-2 749	-3 776	-1 278	51.1
Benin	44	40	14	24	31	35	30	-14	-32.8
Botswana	19	16	17	-10	22	2	12	-6	-34.1
Br. Indian Ocean Territory	-11	0	1	-2	0	0	2	13	-120.8
Burkina Faso	17	16	8	13	-1	16	10	-7	-41.6
Burundi	-13	-3	-4	-6	3	1	-3	10	-78.2
Cameroon	64	22	-40	-96	82	-16	-1 204	-1 269	-1 972.8
Cape Verde	10	9	7	3	6	8	4	-7	-65.0
Central African Republic	2	2	1	-1	1	4	6	3	139.1
Chad	0	-4	-4	6	131	122	42	42	X
Comoros	-2	0	-2	-3	-9	-5	-3	-1	54.5
Congo	-397	-223	-368	-450	-384	-130	-354	43	-10.7
Dem. Rep. of the Congo (Zaire)	-244	-138	-208	-205	-135	176	-144	100	-41.1
Djibouti	7	20	26	16	18	57	31	24	326.0
Egypt	3 178	2 398	2 383	2 446	2 682	1 513	1 464	-1 714	-53.9
Equatorial Guinea	17	20	178	-59	-384	-393	-568	-585	-3 459.8
Eritrea	15	24	3	17	22	28	87	72	479.3
Ethiopia	52	37	133	137	32	35	379	327	628.1
Fr. Indian Ocean Areas	2	3	3	4	3	1	0	-2	X
Gabon	-2 118	-1 197	-1 498	-2 133	-1 587	-1 522	-1 907	211	-10.0
Gambia	7	7	9	9	8	9	27	20	289.7
Ghana	160	82	24	-13	13	76	127	-33	-20.3
Guinea	-45	-50	-62	-20	-15	-9	-33	12	-25.6
Guinea-Bissau	2	1	1	0	1	3	-1	-3	-135.0
Ivory Coast	-138	-275	-246	-289	-236	-300	-387	-249	180.2
Kenya	111	100	83	128	449	83	-53	-164	-147.4
Lesotho	-84	-99	-110	-140	-215	-320	-388	-304	360.8
Liberia	38	25	14	-2	-6	-18	-26	-64	-168.8
Libya	0	0	0	18	9	18	0	0	X
Madagascar	-51	-57	26	-142	-251	-200	-337	-286	561.6
Malawi	-65	-46	-65	-42	-65	-41	-60	5	-8.3
Mali	22	22	21	22	27	9	29	7	30.5
Mauritania	21	19	24	16	25	22	34	13	65.0
Mauritius	-207	-248	-220	-262	-249	-253	-266	-59	28.5
Mayotte	0	0	0	0	0	0	0	0	X
Morocco	139	218	180	82	-152	173	83	-56	-40.0
Mozambique	15	20	25	33	21	86	54	39	255.6
Namibia	-38	-1	166	35	218	0	-95	-57	150.1
Niger	-5	16	6	30	59	40	30	35	-692.0
Nigeria	-5 536	-3 377	-3 757	-9 816	-7 820	-4 888	-9 377	-3 840	69.4
Rwanda	31	18	44	14	10	7	5	-26	-83.0
Sao Tome and Principe	13	9	-2	1	11	2	1	-12	-90.0
Senegal	45	54	54	78	-24	71	97	52	116.7
Seychelles	4	8	2	-1	153	-18	-6	-10	-252.6
Sierra Leone	-3	11	3	15	23	22	22	24	-903.7
Somalia	2	2	3	4	6	6	7	4	183.3
South Africa	487	579	-609	-1 121	-1 473	-1 509	-1 805	-2 292	-470.5
St. Helena	2	0	1	-3	1	-2	-3	-5	-294.1
Sudan	24	4	9	16	14	10	23	-1	-3.7
Swaziland	-39	-17	-28	15	-53	-103	-154	-115	295.9
Tanzania	38	35	33	13	36	38	41	2	5.7
Togo	16	23	23	5	4	11	9	-7	-42.0
Tunisia	189	134	206	195	154	102	68	-121	-64.0
Uganda	-3	15	5	-1	14	9	7	9	-376.0
Western Sahara	0	0	0	0	0	0	0	0	X
Zambia	-27	-26	-18	1	0	28	7	34	-126.3
Zimbabwe (Rhodesia)	-58	-34	-72	-60	-60	-53	-15	43	-74.1
OTHER	341	0	371	307	262	187	186	-155	-45.5
International Organizations	0	0	0	0	0	0	0	0	X
Unidentified Countries	341	0	371	307	262	187	186	-155	-45.5
MISCELLANEOUS [1]	-966	397	1	-1	1 102	-352	1 102	2 068	-214.0
ADDENDUM									
Developed Countries	-80 826	-102 714	-146 423	-187 792	-183 712	-202 454	-213 711	-132 885	164.4
Developing Countries	-100 662	-127 044	-182 399	-248 312	-228 187	-265 809	-318 640	-217 978	216.5
APEC (20 countries)	-154 739	-200 876	-253 439	-306 644	-289 848	-316 834	-341 981	-187 242	121.0

Note: Because of rounding, aggregations may differ slightly from values in other published sources.

[1]Includes transshipments, carryover, and timing adjustments, revisions not accounted for elsewhere, and roundoff.
X = Not applicable.

Table B-9. Top 50 Partners in Total U.S. Trade, 1997–2003

(Millions of dollars, except as noted; top 50 based on 2003 value; Census basis; foreign and domestic exports, f.a.s.; general imports, Customs.)

Country	1997	1998	1999	2000	2001	2002	2003	Percent change, 1997–2003
TOTAL OF TOP 50	1 491 933	1 526 817	1 653 278	1 921 550	1 792 779	1 778 430	1 897 903	27.2
Canada	319 001	329 860	365 311	409 779	379 692	370 010	393 936	23.5
Mexico	157 326	173 402	196 630	247 275	232 634	232 086	235 531	49.7
China	75 420	85 410	94 899	116 204	121 461	147 320	180 798	139.7
Japan	187 212	179 676	188 330	211 404	183 925	172 878	170 093	-9.1
Germany	67 580	76 499	82 029	87 961	89 072	89 135	96 895	43.4
United Kingdom	69 085	73 896	77 644	84 916	82 083	73 949	76 562	10.8
South Korea	48 219	40 427	54 137	68 138	57 362	58 148	61 062	26.6
Taiwan	52 994	51 289	54 336	64 909	51 496	50 581	49 088	-7.4
France	36 601	41 745	44 586	50 162	50 273	47 256	46 289	26.5
Malaysia	28 807	27 957	30 484	36 506	31 698	34 353	36 358	26.2
Italy	28 402	29 950	32 447	36 103	33 706	34 277	36 007	26.8
Ireland	10 509	14 048	17 378	24 177	25 643	29 133	33 539	219.2
Singapore	37 771	34 049	34 439	36 985	32 652	31 020	31 734	-16.0
Netherlands	27 120	26 577	27 912	31 507	29 000	28 159	31 675	16.8
Brazil	25 540	25 244	24 516	29 173	30 346	28 157	29 102	13.9
Belgium	21 332	22 358	21 577	23 855	23 661	23 133	25 359	18.9
Saudi Arabia	17 803	16 761	16 165	20 599	19 230	17 931	22 665	27.3
Hong Kong	25 405	23 464	23 180	26 031	23 674	21 923	22 393	-11.9
Thailand	19 951	18 675	19 315	23 003	20 717	19 653	21 022	5.4
Venezuela	20 079	15 697	16 688	24 173	20 893	19 523	19 984	-0.5
Israel	13 321	15 624	17 555	20 710	19 434	19 442	19 649	47.5
Australia	16 665	17 304	17 099	18 920	17 408	19 564	19 518	17.1
Switzerland	16 712	15 938	17 910	20 114	19 477	17 165	19 328	15.7
Philippines	17 862	18 684	19 575	22 734	18 985	18 256	18 053	1.1
India	10 930	11 802	12 759	14 354	13 494	15 919	18 039	65.0
Sweden	10 613	11 670	12 353	14 151	12 450	12 369	14 350	35.2
Spain	10 144	10 234	11 193	12 036	10 953	11 031	12 643	24.6
Indonesia	13 711	11 640	11 564	12 769	12 624	12 199	12 040	-12.2
Nigeria	7 163	5 011	5 013	11 259	9 730	7 003	11 423	59.5
Russia	7 684	9 300	7 981	9 751	8 980	9 267	11 048	43.8
Colombia	9 934	9 472	9 819	10 639	9 293	9 187	10 140	2.1
Dominican Republic	8 251	8 385	8 387	8 856	8 581	8 431	8 669	5.1
South Africa	5 507	6 677	5 780	7 300	7 392	6 560	7 459	35.4
Costa Rica	4 348	5 041	6 348	5 999	5 388	6 273	6 776	55.9
Turkey	5 661	6 048	5 847	6 762	6 149	6 629	6 692	18.2
Norway	5 473	4 581	5 482	7 253	7 038	7 249	6 680	22.0
Chile	6 662	6 432	6 031	6 729	6 614	6 394	6 422	-3.6
Austria	4 443	4 704	5 498	5 818	6 573	6 242	6 282	41.4
Honduras	4 341	4 862	5 083	5 674	5 542	5 832	6 156	41.8
Vietnam	675	828	900	1 189	1 513	2 975	5 879	770.9
Argentina	8 038	8 117	7 548	7 795	6 934	4 773	5 605	-30.3
Trinidad and Tobago	2 240	1 960	2 072	3 328	3 467	3 461	5 386	140.4
Finland	4 133	4 510	4 577	4 822	4 948	4 979	5 312	28.5
Denmark	3 895	4 269	4 544	4 472	5 016	4 733	5 267	35.2
Algeria	3 131	2 289	2 283	3 586	3 740	3 345	5 240	67.4
Guatemala	3 720	4 009	4 077	4 508	4 458	4 841	5 219	40.3
Iraq	394	1 290	4 236	6 076	5 867	3 580	4 890	1 141.3
Angola	3 060	2 596	2 670	3 781	3 372	3 497	4 756	55.4
United Arab Emirates	3 527	3 026	3 422	3 257	3 832	4 516	4 639	31.5
New Zealand	3 541	3 531	3 672	4 051	4 310	4 095	4 252	20.1

Note: Total U.S. trade equals total U.S. exports to purchasers plus total U.S. imports from suppliers (detail may not add due to rounding).

Table B-10. Top 50 Purchasers of U.S. Exports, 1997–2003

(Millions of dollars; top 50 based on 2003 value; Census basis; foreign and domestic exports, f.a.s.)

Country	1997	1998	1999	2000	2001	2002	2003	Percent change, 1997–2003
TOTAL OF TOP 50	661 740	655 064	671 459	756 693	701 796	666 125	694 863	5.0
Canada	151 767	156 603	166 600	178 941	163 424	160 923	169 770	11.9
Mexico	71 388	78 773	86 909	111 349	101 296	97 470	97 457	36.5
Japan	65 549	57 831	57 466	64 924	57 452	51 449	52 064	-20.6
United Kingdom	36 425	39 058	38 407	41 570	40 714	33 204	33 895	-6.9
Germany	24 458	26 657	26 800	29 448	29 995	26 630	28 848	17.9
China	12 862	14 241	13 111	16 185	19 182	22 128	28 419	120.9
South Korea	25 046	16 486	22 958	27 830	22 181	22 576	24 099	-3.8
Netherlands	19 827	18 978	19 437	21 836	19 485	18 311	20 703	4.4
Taiwan	20 366	18 165	19 131	24 406	18 122	18 382	17 488	-14.1
France	15 965	17 729	18 877	20 362	19 864	19 016	17 068	6.9
Singapore	17 696	15 694	16 247	17 806	17 652	16 218	16 576	-6.3
Belgium	13 420	13 918	12 381	13 926	13 502	13 326	15 218	13.4
Hong Kong	15 117	12 925	12 652	14 582	14 028	12 594	13 542	-10.4
Australia	12 063	11 918	11 818	12 482	10 931	13 085	13 104	8.6
Brazil	15 915	15 142	13 203	15 321	15 879	12 376	11 218	-29.5
Malaysia	10 780	8 957	9 060	10 938	9 358	10 344	10 921	1.3
Italy	8 995	8 991	10 091	11 060	9 916	10 057	10 570	17.5
Switzerland	8 307	7 247	8 371	9 954	9 807	7 783	8 660	4.3
Philippines	7 417	6 737	7 222	8 799	7 660	7 276	7 992	7.8
Ireland	4 642	5 647	6 384	7 714	7 144	6 745	7 699	65.8
Israel	5 995	6 983	7 691	7 746	7 475	7 027	6 878	14.7
Spain	5 539	5 454	6 133	6 322	5 756	5 298	5 935	7.2
Thailand	7 349	5 239	4 985	6 618	5 989	4 860	5 842	-20.5
India	3 608	3 564	3 688	3 667	3 757	4 101	4 986	38.2
Saudi Arabia	8 438	10 520	7 912	6 234	5 958	4 781	4 596	-45.5
Dominican Republic	3 924	3 944	4 100	4 473	4 398	4 262	4 214	7.4
Colombia	5 197	4 816	3 560	3 671	3 583	3 583	3 755	-27.8
United Arab Emirates	2 607	2 366	2 708	2 285	2 638	3 593	3 510	34.6
Costa Rica	2 024	2 297	2 381	2 460	2 502	3 132	3 414	68.7
Sweden	3 314	3 822	4 251	4 554	3 541	3 153	3 226	-2.7
Turkey	3 540	3 506	3 217	3 720	3 095	3 113	2 904	-17.9
Honduras	2 019	2 318	2 370	2 584	2 416	2 571	2 845	40.9
Venezuela	6 602	6 516	5 354	5 550	5 642	4 430	2 840	-57.0
South Africa	2 997	3 628	2 586	3 090	2 960	2 526	2 821	-5.9
Chile	4 368	3 979	3 078	3 460	3 118	2 609	2 719	-37.8
Egypt	3 835	3 059	3 001	3 334	3 564	2 868	2 660	-30.6
Indonesia	4 522	2 299	2 038	2 402	2 521	2 556	2 520	-44.3
Russia	3 365	3 553	2 060	2 092	2 716	2 397	2 450	-27.2
Argentina	5 810	5 886	4 950	4 696	3 920	1 585	2 435	-58.1
Guatemala	1 730	1 938	1 812	1 901	1 870	2 044	2 274	31.5
New Zealand	1 962	1 887	1 923	1 970	2 111	1 813	1 849	-5.8
Panama	1 536	1 753	1 742	1 612	1 330	1 407	1 848	20.3
El Salvador	1 400	1 514	1 519	1 780	1 870	1 664	1 824	30.3
Austria	2 075	2 143	2 588	2 592	2 605	2 427	1 793	-13.6
Finland	1 741	1 915	1 669	1 571	1 554	1 535	1 714	-1.6
Peru	1 953	2 063	1 697	1 660	1 564	1 563	1 707	-12.6
Denmark	1 757	1 874	1 726	1 507	1 609	1 496	1 548	-11.9
Kuwait	1 390	1 524	864	787	902	1 015	1 509	8.6
Jamaica	1 417	1 304	1 293	1 376	1 406	1 420	1 470	3.7
Norway	1 721	1 709	1 439	1 547	1 835	1 407	1 468	-14.7

Table B-11. Top 50 Suppliers of U.S. Imports, 1997–2003

(Millions of dollars; top 50 based on 2003 value; Census basis; general imports, Customs.)

Country	1997	1998	1999	2000	2001	2002	2003	Percent change, 1997–2003
TOTAL OF TOP 50	839 099	880 796	990 761	1 174 021	1 099 339	1 119 770	1 211 233	44.3
Canada	167 234	173 256	198 711	230 838	216 268	209 088	224 166	34.0
China	62 558	71 169	81 788	100 018	102 278	125 193	152 379	143.6
Mexico	85 938	94 629	109 721	135 926	131 338	134 616	138 073	60.7
Japan	121 663	121 845	130 864	146 479	126 473	121 429	118 029	-3.0
Germany	43 122	49 842	55 228	58 513	59 077	62 506	68 047	57.8
United Kingdom	32 659	34 838	39 237	43 345	41 369	40 745	42 667	30.6
South Korea	23 173	23 942	31 179	40 308	35 181	35 572	36 963	59.5
Taiwan	32 629	33 125	35 204	40 503	33 375	32 199	31 600	-3.2
France	20 636	24 016	25 709	29 800	30 408	28 240	29 221	41.6
Ireland	5 867	8 401	10 994	16 464	18 499	22 388	25 841	340.5
Malaysia	18 027	19 000	21 424	25 568	22 340	24 009	25 438	41.1
Italy	19 408	20 959	22 357	25 043	23 790	24 220	25 437	31.1
Saudi Arabia	9 365	6 241	8 254	14 365	13 272	13 150	18 069	92.9
Brazil	9 626	10 102	11 314	13 853	14 466	15 781	17 884	85.8
Venezuela	13 477	9 181	11 335	18 623	15 251	15 094	17 144	27.2
Thailand	12 602	13 436	14 330	16 385	14 727	14 793	15 181	20.5
Singapore	20 075	18 356	18 191	19 178	15 000	14 802	15 158	-24.5
India	7 322	8 237	9 071	10 687	9 737	11 818	13 053	78.3
Israel	7 326	8 640	9 864	12 964	11 959	12 416	12 770	74.3
Sweden	7 299	7 848	8 103	9 597	8 909	9 216	11 125	52.4
Netherlands	7 293	7 599	8 475	9 671	9 515	9 849	10 972	50.4
Switzerland	8 405	8 690	9 539	10 160	9 670	9 382	10 668	26.9
Nigeria	6 349	4 194	4 385	10 538	8 775	5 945	10 394	63.7
Belgium	7 912	8 440	9 196	9 929	10 158	9 807	10 141	28.2
Philippines	10 445	11 947	12 353	13 935	11 325	10 980	10 061	-3.7
Indonesia	9 188	9 341	9 525	10 367	10 104	9 643	9 520	3.6
Hong Kong	10 288	10 538	10 528	11 449	9 646	9 328	8 850	-14.0
Russia	4 319	5 747	5 921	7 659	6 264	6 870	8 598	99.1
Spain	4 606	4 780	5 059	5 713	5 197	5 733	6 708	45.6
Australia	4 602	5 387	5 280	6 438	6 478	6 479	6 414	39.4
Colombia	4 737	4 656	6 259	6 968	5 710	5 604	6 386	34.8
Norway	3 752	2 872	4 043	5 706	5 203	5 843	5 212	38.9
Algeria	2 440	1 638	1 824	2 724	2 702	2 360	4 753	94.8
South Africa	2 510	3 049	3 194	4 210	4 433	4 034	4 638	84.8
Iraq	312	1 183	4 226	6 066	5 820	3 548	4 574	1 366.4
Vietnam	389	554	608	821	1 053	2 395	4 555	1 072.4
Austria	2 368	2 561	2 909	3 227	3 969	3 815	4 489	89.5
Dominican Republic	4 327	4 441	4 287	4 383	4 183	4 169	4 455	3.0
Trinidad and Tobago	1 134	977	1 287	2 229	2 380	2 440	4 322	281.0
Angola	2 779	2 241	2 418	3 555	3 096	3 123	4 264	53.4
Turkey	2 121	2 543	2 629	3 042	3 055	3 516	3 788	78.6
Denmark	2 138	2 395	2 819	2 965	3 407	3 237	3 718	73.9
Chile	2 293	2 453	2 953	3 269	3 495	3 785	3 703	61.5
Finland	2 392	2 596	2 908	3 251	3 394	3 444	3 598	50.4
Costa Rica	2 323	2 745	3 968	3 539	2 886	3 142	3 362	44.7
Honduras	2 322	2 544	2 713	3 090	3 127	3 261	3 312	42.6
Argentina	2 228	2 231	2 598	3 100	3 013	3 187	3 169	42.2
Guatemala	1 990	2 072	2 265	2 607	2 589	2 796	2 945	48.0
Ecuador	2 055	1 752	1 821	2 238	2 010	2 143	2 721	32.4
Hungary	1 079	1 567	1 893	2 715	2 965	2 637	2 699	150.2

Table B-12. Top 50 Surplus Countries in U.S. Trade, 1997–2003

(Millions of dollars; top 50 based on 2003 value; Census basis; foreign and domestic exports, f.a.s.; general imports, Customs.)

Country	1997	1998	1999	2000	2001	2002	2003	Percent change, 1997–2003
TOTAL OF TOP 50	41 701	36 790	31 990	34 259	35 930	35 307	40 919	-1.9
Netherlands	12 534	11 378	10 962	12 165	9 969	8 462	9 731	-22.4
Australia	7 461	6 531	6 538	6 044	4 453	6 606	6 690	-10.3
Belgium	5 508	5 478	3 185	3 997	3 344	3 519	5 077	-7.8
Hong Kong	4 829	2 387	2 124	3 133	4 381	3 266	4 692	-2.8
United Arab Emirates	1 687	1 706	1 994	1 313	1 444	2 670	2 381	41.2
Panama	1 169	1 441	1 378	1 305	1 040	1 104	1 547	32.3
Egypt	3 178	2 398	2 383	2 446	2 682	1 512	1 516	-52.3
Singapore	-2 378	-2 662	-1 944	-1 372	2 652	1 416	1 418	-159.6
Jamaica	679	549	615	728	945	1 024	975	43.7
Bahamas	655	673	647	794	712	526	605	-7.6
Greece	496	889	432	630	788	606	575	15.9
Paraguay	873	752	467	405	356	389	436	-50.1
Leeward and Windward Islands	336	612	390	425	319	323	432	28.5
Bermuda	308	389	319	390	305	392	386	25.2
Ethiopia	51	37	134	136	32	35	379	639.5
Haiti	311	277	313	280	287	318	308	-1.1
Cyprus	228	130	160	167	233	168	302	32.4
Cayman Islands	251	404	359	348	255	223	298	18.8
Cuba	10	4	4	7	7	145	261	2 642.1
Barbados	239	247	246	268	247	233	258	8.2
Lebanon	474	431	305	278	329	256	222	-53.2
Unidentified Countries	341	400	371	307	262	187	186	-45.5
Uzbekistan	195	113	313	117	91	61	173	-11.3
French Guiana	491	243	190	15	130	242	152	-69.0
Bahrain	290	139	122	111	9	24	131	-55.0
Yemen Arab Republic	137	140	133	-66	-17	120	129	-6.0
Ghana	160	82	24	-13	13	76	128	-20.2
Netherlands Antilles	-105	443	213	-45	332	380	127	-220.9
Azerbaijan	57	118	29	189	44	35	112	97.3
Belize	38	54	55	115	76	60	98	161.3
Senegal	45	54	54	78	-24	71	98	116.7
Eritrea	15	24	3	17	22	28	87	467.3
Morocco	139	218	179	82	-152	173	80	-42.4
Georgia	134	122	65	78	75	81	78	-42.0
Qatar	222	134	-127	-295	-166	-171	77	-65.2
French Pacific Islands	52	65	84	38	46	62	75	43.0
Uruguay	319	336	296	224	179	15	71	-77.7
Tunisia	189	134	206	195	154	102	70	-62.8
Turks and Caicos Islands	53	59	89	83	69	49	66	23.5
Armenia	56	35	36	33	17	81	65	16.2
Mozambique	15	20	25	33	21	86	54	258.3
Suriname	92	81	21	-1	12	-8	53	-42.3
Costa Rica	-299	-448	-1 587	-1 078	-384	-10	53	-117.6
Tajikistan	10	-20	-9	3	23	32	43	322.8
Guadeloupe	54	62	60	76	48	29	43	-20.5
Chad	0	-4	-4	6	131	122	42	X
Tanzania	38	35	33	13	36	38	42	9.1
Serbia and Montenegro	39	62	54	28	60	69	35	-8.5
Mauritania	21	19	24	16	25	22	34	64.3
Djibouti	7	20	26	16	18	57	34	361.6

X = Not applicable.

Table B-13. Top 50 Deficit Countries in U.S. Trade, 1997–2003

(Millions of dollars; top 50 based on 2003 value; Census basis; foreign and domestic exports, f.a.s.; general imports, Customs.)

Country	1997	1998	1999	2000	2001	2002	2003	Percent change, 1997–2003
TOTAL OF TOP 50	-221 816	-264 522	-357 003	-461 526	-440 975	-495 292	-564 306	154.4
China	-49 695	-56 927	-68 677	-83 833	-83 096	-103 065	-123 961	149.4
Japan	-56 115	-64 014	-73 398	-81 555	-69 022	-69 979	-65 965	17.6
Canada	-15 467	-16 653	-32 111	-51 897	-52 844	-48 165	-54 396	251.7
Mexico	-14 549	-15 857	-22 812	-24 577	-30 041	-37 146	-40 616	179.2
Germany	-18 663	-23 185	-28 428	-29 064	-29 081	-35 876	-39 199	110.0
Ireland	-1 224	-2 754	-4 611	-8 750	-11 355	-15 643	-18 142	1 381.7
Italy	-10 413	-11 968	-12 266	-13 982	-13 874	-14 164	-14 867	42.8
Malaysia	-7 247	-10 043	-12 364	-14 631	-12 983	-13 665	-14 517	100.3
Venezuela	-6 876	-2 666	-5 981	-13 073	-9 608	-10 664	-14 305	108.1
Taiwan	-12 263	-14 960	-16 073	-16 097	-15 253	-13 818	-14 112	15.1
Saudi Arabia	-927	4 279	-342	-8 131	-7 315	-8 369	-13 473	1 353.4
South Korea	1 873	-7 456	-8 220	-12 478	-13 001	-12 996	-12 865	-786.8
France	-4 672	-6 287	-6 831	-9 439	-10 544	-9 224	-12 153	160.2
Nigeria	-5 536	-3 377	-3 757	-9 816	-7 820	-4 888	-9 365	69.1
Thailand	-5 252	-8 198	-9 345	-9 768	-8 738	-9 933	-9 339	77.8
United Kingdom	3 766	4 220	-830	-1 775	-655	-7 541	-8 772	-332.9
India	-3 715	-4 673	-5 383	-7 019	-5 980	-7 717	-8 067	117.1
Sweden	-3 985	-4 026	-3 852	-5 043	-5 367	-6 063	-7 899	98.2
Indonesia	-4 666	-7 042	-7 487	-7 965	-7 583	-7 088	-7 000	50.0
Brazil	6 289	5 040	1 889	1 468	1 413	-3 405	-6 666	-206.0
Russia	-954	-2 195	-3 861	-5 566	-3 548	-4 473	-6 148	544.4
Israel	-1 331	-1 657	-2 174	-5 219	-4 484	-5 389	-5 892	342.6
Algeria	-1 748	-987	-1 366	-1 863	-1 664	-1 376	-4 266	144.0
Iraq	-230	-1 077	-4 217	-6 056	-5 774	-3 517	-4 258	1 752.2
Angola	-2 499	-1 886	-2 166	-3 330	-2 820	-2 749	-3 772	51.0
Norway	-2 031	-1 162	-2 603	-4 159	-3 368	-4 436	-3 745	84.4
Trinidad and Tobago	-28	6	-501	-1 129	-1 293	-1 420	-3 258	11 370.8
Vietnam	-102	-280	-317	-454	-593	-1 815	-3 231	3 070.3
Austria	-294	-418	-321	-635	-1 364	-1 388	-2 697	818.2
Colombia	460	160	-2 700	-3 297	-2 127	-2 022	-2 631	-672.3
Denmark	-381	-521	-1 093	-1 458	-1 798	-1 741	-2 170	469.9
Philippines	-3 028	-5 211	-5 131	-5 136	-3 665	-3 704	-2 069	-31.7
Switzerland	-98	-1 443	-1 167	-206	138	-1 600	-2 008	1 944.6
Gabon	-2 118	-1 197	-1 498	-2 133	-1 587	-1 522	-1 907	-10.0
Finland	-650	-681	-1 239	-1 680	-1 840	-1 909	-1 884	189.7
Bangladesh	-1 420	-1 528	-1 644	-2 179	-2 052	-1 865	-1 847	30.0
South Africa	487	579	-609	-1 121	-1 473	-1 509	-1 816	-472.9
Hungary	-593	-1 084	-1 389	-2 146	-2 279	-1 950	-1 766	197.5
Pakistan	-202	-971	-1 244	-1 705	-1 708	-1 612	-1 692	737.2
Sri Lanka	-1 465	-1 576	-1 575	-1 797	-1 801	-1 639	-1 653	12.8
Macao	-956	-1 068	-1 083	-1 196	-1 155	-1 154	-1 301	36.1
Ecuador	-529	-69	-911	-1 200	-598	-538	-1 273	140.6
Cambodia	-84	-354	-573	-794	-933	-1 042	-1 205	1 327.6
Portugal	-184	-377	-264	-594	-316	-811	-1 105	500.9
Chile	2 075	1 527	125	191	-377	-1 176	-984	-147.4
Slovakia	-84	-55	-42	-131	-168	-168	-898	973.9
Turkey	1 418	963	588	679	40	-403	-884	-162.3
Spain	933	673	1 074	609	559	-435	-773	-182.8
Kuwait	-426	258	-575	-1 994	-1 088	-926	-768	80.0
Argentina	3 582	3 655	2 352	1 596	907	-1 602	-734	-120.5

Table B-14. U.S. Manufactures Exports to Individual Countries, 1996–2002

(Millions of dollars; Census basis; foreign and domestic exports, f.a.s.)

Region and country	1996	1997	1998	1999	2000	2001	2002	1996–2002 change Value	1996–2002 change Percent
WORLD	522 660	591 233	595 218	611 781	689 524	641 885	606 558	83 899	16.1
EUROPE	126 467	141 712	151 682	156 146	171 264	166 027	148 946	22 478	17.8
Western Europe	122 086	136 386	146 191	151 747	166 543	160 725	143 468	21 382	17.5
European Union (EU-15)	110 025	123 656	134 254	138 917	151 676	146 210	131 614	21 589	19.6
Austria	1 945	2 012	2 450	2 535	2 499	2 572	2 374	428	22.0
Belgium	9 546	10 711	11 451	10 655	12 318	12 002	11 970	2 423	25.4
Denmark	1 468	1 484	1 633	1 532	1 330	1 438	1 331	-137	-9.3
Finland	2 128	1 484	1 730	1 490	1 395	1 362	1 376	-752	-35.4
France	13 199	14 769	16 648	17 965	19 349	18 998	18 157	4 959	37.6
Germany	21 177	22 201	24 544	25 081	27 364	28 288	24 845	3 668	17.3
Greece	618	750	1 193	861	1 088	1 144	1 001	383	62.1
Ireland	3 377	4 334	5 268	6 089	7 354	6 837	6 446	3 069	90.9
Italy	6 820	7 108	7 375	8 690	9 398	8 336	8 613	1 792	26.3
Luxembourg	238	710	602	979	392	548	464	226	94.9
Netherlands	13 415	16 763	16 562	17 097	19 563	17 210	16 442	3 027	22.6
Portugal	561	606	648	843	741	1 012	580	19	3.4
Spain	3 737	3 700	3 775	4 868	5 029	4 544	3 884	147	3.9
Sweden	3 137	3 025	3 539	3 995	4 313	3 283	2 910	-226	-7.2
United Kingdom	28 658	33 997	36 836	36 237	39 544	38 637	31 221	2 563	8.9
Non-EU Western Europe	12 061	12 730	11 937	12 830	14 867	14 515	11 854	-207	-1.7
Bosnia-Herzegovina	28	70	17	31	32	23	21	-7	-24.4
Croatia	84	107	76	102	86	103	69	-15	-17.8
Cyprus	73	75	74	86	76	173	158	85	116.1
Gibraltar	2	3	3	3	9	4	13	10	491.4
Iceland	218	149	204	246	229	194	197	-22	-9.9
Liechtenstein	9	12	7	9	14	7	14	5	57.9
Macedonia	11	25	11	45	45	25	11	0	0.0
Malta and Gozo	103	109	254	172	303	245	194	90	87.4
Norway	1 362	1 576	1 572	1 294	1 417	1 692	1 261	-101	-7.4
Other Non-EU Western Europe	23	33	29	30	41	45	29	6	25.8
Serbia and Montenegro	32	47	59	46	15	30	61	29	89.1
Slovenia	110	82	100	98	114	106	113	3	2.7
Switzerland	8 155	8 062	6 999	8 153	9 716	9 597	7 535	-620	-7.6
Turkey	1 850	2 381	2 532	2 514	2 771	2 270	2 179	329	17.8
Eastern Europe	4 381	5 326	5 491	4 399	4 721	5 302	5 478	1 096	25.0
Albania	4	1	5	18	12	7	6	1	36.0
Baltic States	174	183	166	164	144	186	209	35	20.1
Estonia	54	21	34	34	40	48	73	18	33.5
Latvia	71	98	73	68	51	59	53	-19	-26.2
Lithuania	48	64	59	61	54	78	83	35	73.2
Bulgaria	46	45	60	67	60	73	70	24	53.8
Czech Republic	376	543	504	557	677	656	620	244	64.8
Hungary	320	458	458	479	546	659	658	338	105.8
Poland	711	1 002	711	704	675	652	576	-135	-19.0
Romania	131	124	249	146	192	346	203	73	55.4
Slovakia	61	80	109	125	108	68	92	30	49.6
Newly Independent States (NIS)	2 559	2 890	3 230	2 138	2 306	2 655	3 044	485	19.0
Armenia	16	39	24	38	48	42	106	90	575.0
Azerbaijan	48	48	48	30	192	63	57	9	19.7
Belarus	37	34	26	24	30	34	18	-19	-51.4
Georgia	35	110	74	38	56	62	62	28	80.2
Kazakhstan	128	253	88	176	122	151	596	468	366.5
Kyrgyzstan	30	16	11	15	13	23	27	-3	-11.5
Moldova	9	16	14	7	25	16	16	7	77.5
Russia	1 550	1 744	2 501	1 291	1 435	1 711	1 762	212	13.7
Tajikistan	5	3	2	3	3	9	23	18	322.3
Turkmenistan	188	117	28	15	69	247	45	-143	-76.2
Ukraine	244	278	269	169	165	180	235	-9	-3.7
Uzbekistan	269	232	145	331	150	117	97	-172	-64.0
WESTERN HEMISPHERE	213 030	253 139	265 138	275 968	312 076	287 841	274 331	61 302	28.8
NAFTA	168 730	198 709	209 615	227 402	259 891	236 368	229 991	61 261	36.3
Canada	119 952	135 823	139 834	149 585	160 662	146 906	144 628	24 676	20.6
Mexico	48 778	62 885	69 781	77 817	99 229	89 463	85 363	36 585	75.0
Caribbean	6 091	7 349	8 172	7 746	8 583	8 425	8 158	2 067	33.9
Aruba	134	167	282	241	218	211	375	241	180.1
Bahamas	481	610	620	651	826	760	642	161	33.4
Barbados	155	205	223	237	248	222	210	55	35.3
Cayman Islands	179	219	368	319	289	209	191	13	7.1
Dominican Republic	2 637	3 221	3 338	3 386	3 715	3 700	3 505	869	32.9
Haiti	248	275	312	370	372	351	386	139	56.1
Jamaica	1 105	1 032	983	939	983	1 039	1 031	-74	-6.7
Leeward and Windward Islands	273	312	587	419	445	342	351	78	28.7
Netherlands Antilles	357	308	574	440	441	579	541	184	51.5
Trinidad and Tobago	486	950	830	661	966	946	878	392	80.7
Turks and Caicos Islands	37	51	56	83	78	68	47	9	25.3

Note: Data are based on the Harmonized System of commodity classification and converted to other classification systems using recent Census data concordances to produce consistent time series. Therefore, the data in this table differs from values in other published sources. Manufactured goods are defined as SITC (Rev. 3) 5–9. Table B-3 provides revised data for this table's world values.

Table B-14. U.S. Manufactures Exports to Individual Countries, 1996–2002—*Continued*

(Millions of dollars; Census basis; foreign and domestic exports, f.a.s.)

Region and country	1996	1997	1998	1999	2000	2001	2002	1996–2002 change Value	1996–2002 change Percent
Central America	6 229	7 365	8 478	8 785	9 165	8 788	9 493	3 264	52.4
Belize	86	89	100	116	163	141	110	23	27.0
Costa Rica	1 540	1 778	2 015	2 130	2 192	2 213	2 814	1 274	82.7
El Salvador	821	1 088	1 223	1 281	1 513	1 485	1 370	549	66.9
Guatemala	1 172	1 330	1 514	1 446	1 469	1 448	1 549	378	32.2
Honduras	1 398	1 717	2 052	2 098	2 291	2 190	2 289	891	63.7
Nicaragua	186	210	249	280	298	332	348	162	87.1
Panama	1 026	1 152	1 325	1 434	1 240	980	1 014	-13	-1.2
South America	31 392	38 894	38 256	31 503	33 975	33 762	26 040	-5 352	-17.0
Argentina	4 213	5 305	5 570	4 719	4 445	3 732	1 484	-2 729	-64.8
Bolivia	223	259	378	289	235	199	171	-52	-23.2
Brazil	11 279	14 594	14 049	12 550	14 528	15 170	11 590	312	2.8
Chile	3 766	4 006	3 740	2 829	3 212	2 929	2 409	-1 357	-36.0
Colombia	3 907	4 471	4 138	3 014	3 172	3 082	2 984	-923	-23.6
Ecuador	1 046	1 224	1 369	746	860	1 219	1 361	315	30.1
Guyana	105	111	117	118	130	114	102	-3	-2.8
Paraguay	821	833	721	479	410	382	429	-392	-47.8
Peru	1 409	1 725	1 646	1 356	1 444	1 294	1 272	-137	-9.7
Suriname	191	153	159	124	113	137	105	-86	-45.2
Uruguay	440	509	563	464	509	385	186	-255	-57.8
Venezuela	3 991	5 705	5 806	4 814	4 919	5 119	3 947	-44	-1.1
Other Western Hemisphere	587	822	617	532	462	497	650	63	10.7
Bermuda	192	241	289	246	341	299	341	148	77.0
Cuba	5	9	3	5	7	3	6	1	10.3
Falkland Islands	0	0	3	0	0	0	0	0	X
French Guiana	300	492	245	191	18	128	249	-51	-17.0
Greenland	4	5	2	3	1	2	2	-2	-49.2
Guadeloupe	55	46	50	55	76	44	30	-25	-45.4
Martinique	28	28	21	30	18	20	21	-7	-25.8
St. Pierre and Miquelon	2	1	2	2	1	0	0	-1	X
ASIA	162 859	174 465	156 544	159 130	184 068	165 602	160 940	-1 919	-1.2
Japan	46 969	47 621	42 824	42 205	48 972	43 622	38 649	-8 319	-17.7
Korea, South	20 413	19 959	13 202	18 825	23 444	18 096	18 411	-2 002	-9.8
Taiwan	14 404	16 830	15 650	16 511	21 668	15 602	15 906	1 502	10.4
China	9 131	10 357	12 234	11 406	13 128	15 465	18 034	8 903	97.5
Hong Kong	11 781	12 817	10 981	11 093	12 966	12 512	11 158	-623	-5.3
Macao	29	65	39	39	67	67	76	47	162.0
ASEAN	38 933	44 266	36 483	36 578	43 525	39 655	37 654	-1 279	-3.3
Brunei	371	175	122	65	153	102	42	-329	-88.6
Burma	30	19	31	8	16	9	8	-22	-73.3
Cambodia	18	15	8	13	15	17	21	4	21.1
Indonesia	2 856	3 461	1 672	1 199	1 612	1 415	1 571	-1 285	-45.0
Laos	3	3	4	2	4	3	3	-1	-17.2
Malaysia	7 747	10 210	8 586	8 681	10 581	8 836	9 825	2 078	26.8
Philippines	5 001	6 447	5 943	6 343	7 791	6 794	6 424	1 423	28.5
Singapore	15 955	17 089	15 197	15 606	17 133	16 890	15 260	-694	-4.4
Thailand	6 379	6 619	4 674	4 412	5 922	5 234	4 039	-2 340	-36.7
Vietnam	573	228	247	250	299	355	460	-113	-19.7
Middle East	17 132	18 221	21 128	18 500	16 365	16 769	16 587	-545	-3.2
Bahrain	188	364	248	309	415	376	379	191	101.1
Gaza Strip and West Bank	0	0	4	6	9	2	0	0	X
Iran	0	1	0	0	2	3	3	3	X
Iraq	0	0	10	0	2	39	32	32	X
Israel	5 167	5 266	6 374	7 011	7 004	6 807	6 342	1 175	22.7
Jordan	172	240	236	163	179	186	286	114	66.1
Kuwait	1 888	1 298	1 377	795	691	806	935	-953	-50.5
Lebanon	286	258	236	179	170	239	157	-128	-45.0
Oman	193	317	262	156	174	278	329	137	71.0
Qatar	194	344	336	129	175	318	292	98	50.6
Saudi Arabia	6 468	7 555	9 753	7 161	5 395	5 243	4 211	-2 257	-34.9
Syria	153	104	101	99	110	118	139	-15	-9.6
United Arab Emirates	2 288	2 384	2 090	2 430	1 957	2 266	3 222	934	40.8
Yemen Arab Republic	133	87	99	62	82	88	260	126	94.7
Other Asia	4 067	4 332	4 003	3 971	3 933	3 815	4 466	399	9.8
Afghanistan	8	7	5	13	2	1	80	72	911.3
Bangladesh	110	133	149	140	141	154	124	14	12.4
India	2 928	3 243	3 171	3 353	3 204	3 130	3 571	643	22.0
Korea, North	1	1	0	5	0	1	1	1	109.4
Mongolia	4	32	15	8	12	12	66	62	1 692.7
Nepal	8	26	15	20	34	12	17	9	114.8
Pakistan	890	771	515	314	388	389	468	-421	-47.3
South Asia NEC	3	6	7	9	6	7	5	2	77.4
Sri Lanka	117	113	125	110	145	108	135	18	15.1
AUSTRALIA AND OCEANIA	13 170	13 474	13 343	13 310	13 948	12 587	14 288	1 118	8.5
Australia	11 347	11 380	11 325	11 203	11 841	10 371	12 446	1 098	9.7
Australian Island Dependencies	2	4	3	4	4	5	2	1	48.4
Fiji	22	27	67	123	20	15	15	-7	-33.5
French Pacific Islands	65	80	65	82	64	65	68	3	4.1
New Zealand	1 573	1 782	1 718	1 781	1 827	1 970	1 654	81	5.2
New Zealand Island Dependencies	32	38	6	6	10	8	14	-18	-55.8
Other Pacific Islands NEC	65	110	61	34	19	21	21	-45	-68.3
Papua New Guinea	12	5	45	16	13	17	9	-3	-26.6
Southern Pacific Islands	42	37	37	48	80	44	45	2	5.1
Trust Territory (former)	6	6	6	8	59	65	3	-3	-48.6
Western Samoa	3	5	10	5	10	7	12	9	292.3

Note: Data are based on the Harmonized System of commodity classification and converted to other classification systems using recent Census data concordances to produce consistent time series. Therefore, the data in this table differs from values in other published sources. Manufactured goods are defined as SITC (Rev. 3) 5–9. Table B-3 provides revised data for this table's world values.

X = Not applicable.

Table B-14. U.S. Manufactures Exports to Individual Countries, 1996–2002—*Continued*

(Millions of dollars; Census basis; foreign and domestic exports, f.a.s.)

Region and country	1996	1997	1998	1999	2000	2001	2002	1996–2002 change Value	1996–2002 change Percent
AFRICA	7 133	8 443	8 435	7 228	8 167	9 826	7 976	844	11.8
Algeria	321	361	372	220	592	797	694	374	116.6
Angola	231	242	320	226	167	243	319	88	38.1
Benin	13	29	22	16	12	21	24	11	85.7
Botswana	27	40	35	32	30	42	32	4	15.7
Br. Indian Ocean Territory	0	0	1	1	1	0	0	0	X
Burkina Faso	5	10	5	3	9	3	11	6	116.5
Burundi	1	1	1	2	2	3	2	0	16.4
Cameroon	59	105	58	21	47	177	144	85	142.2
Cape Verde	62	4	3	4	5	7	7	-55	-88.7
Central African Republic	3	3	4	3	2	3	4	1	36.7
Chad	1	1	3	1	8	133	124	123	8 916.0
Comoros	0	0	0	0	1	1	0	0	X
Congo	55	65	77	34	61	74	46	-9	-16.2
Dem. Rep. of the Congo (Zaire)	39	18	22	17	6	11	20	-19	-49.5
Djibouti	2	2	10	12	11	15	14	12	577.8
Egypt	1 723	2 710	1 987	1 859	2 184	2 642	1 935	213	12.3
Equatorial Guinea	17	47	86	220	94	78	107	91	545.5
Eritrea	6	12	10	4	5	7	6	-1	-8.4
Ethiopia	110	102	58	135	50	35	50	-60	-54.6
Fr. Indian Ocean Areas	3	3	3	3	5	3	3	-1	-24.1
Gabon	54	81	57	39	56	67	59	5	8.4
Gambia	5	6	4	5	5	5	6	1	18.9
Ghana	206	233	161	156	136	139	139	-67	-32.5
Guinea	59	61	52	32	46	67	41	-18	-30.8
Guinea-Bissau	3	1	1	0	0	1	2	-1	-37.5
Ivory Coast	110	124	137	75	76	74	60	-50	-45.7
Kenya	89	188	133	153	205	550	221	132	148.2
Lesotho	1	1	0	1	0	1	1	1	167.1
Liberia	13	20	33	24	27	25	17	4	29.8
Libya	0	0	0	0	0	0	0	0	X
Madagascar	10	7	9	104	10	16	8	-2	-22.4
Malawi	10	15	14	7	11	13	16	6	64.7
Mali	16	18	18	27	26	31	9	-7	-41.4
Mauritania	10	9	5	12	14	23	21	11	112.4
Mauritius	25	31	22	38	23	29	27	2	8.4
Mayotte	0	0	0	0	0	0	0	0	X
Morocco	136	211	372	374	297	159	420	284	209.7
Mozambique	10	13	14	13	19	9	14	4	45.4
Namibia	17	25	51	195	78	245	52	35	204.3
Niger	7	8	7	10	28	52	27	20	309.4
Nigeria	617	653	636	424	524	692	718	101	16.4
Rwanda	3	7	12	30	9	9	3	-1	-25.6
Sao Tome and Principe	0	13	9	1	1	11	2	2	X
Senegal	33	31	31	46	56	59	60	28	85.0
Seychelles	102	5	10	7	7	176	8	-94	-92.2
Sierra Leone	9	4	6	7	12	12	11	2	17.3
Somalia	1	1	1	1	3	3	4	4	648.4
South Africa	2 597	2 598	3 255	2 276	2 819	2 759	2 260	-336	-12.9
St. Helena	0	0	0	0	0	4	2	2	X
Sudan	34	26	0	0	0	1	2	-32	-94.5
Swaziland	2	4	7	8	67	11	11	9	380.1
Tanzania	34	42	51	44	31	45	40	6	18.4
Togo	13	10	23	21	8	13	9	-4	-33.8
Tunisia	84	119	104	201	195	167	96	12	13.9
Uganda	12	17	16	16	19	21	17	5	38.5
Western Sahara	0	0	0	0	0	0	0	0	X
Zambia	43	26	19	19	18	14	21	-22	-52.0
Zimbabwe (Rhodesia)	89	79	88	50	49	31	32	-57	-63.5
OTHER	2	0	76	0	1	0	77	75	4 545.7
International Organizations	2	0	76	0	1	0	77	75	4 545.7
Unidentified Countries	0	0	0	0	0	0	0	0	X
MISCELLANEOUS [1]	0	0	0	0	0	0	0	0	X
ADDENDUM									
Developed Countries	304 524	335 590	345 147	358 797	392 664	366 352	343 105	38 581	12.7
Developing Countries	218 136	255 643	250 071	252 983	296 860	275 533	263 453	45 317	20.8
APEC (20 countries)	333 631	377 296	366 661	388 280	450 554	405 391	396 708	63 076	18.9

Note: Data are based on the Harmonized System of commodity classification and converted to other classification systems using recent Census data concordances to produce consistent time series. Therefore, the data in this table differs from values in other published sources. Manufactured goods are defined as SITC (Rev. 3) 5–9. Table B-3 provides revised data for this table's world values.

[1]Includes transshipments, carryover, and timing adjustments, revisions not accounted for elsewhere, and roundoff.
X = Not applicable.

Table B-15. U.S. Manufactures Imports from Individual Countries, 1996–2002

(Millions of dollars; Census basis; general imports, Customs.)

Region and country	1996	1997	1998	1999	2000	2001	2002	1996–2002 change Value	1996–2002 change Percent
WORLD	659 867	728 574	792 422	882 729	1 013 480	950 680	975 381	315 514	47.8
EUROPE	147 152	164 164	186 631	204 835	230 354	228 576	231 617	84 465	57.4
Western Europe	141 175	156 672	176 762	194 857	216 494	216 407	220 367	79 192	56.1
European Union (EU-15)	129 993	144 498	163 534	180 479	200 905	201 596	205 441	75 449	58.0
Austria	2 138	2 277	2 464	2 794	3 092	3 803	3 608	1 469	68.7
Belgium	6 375	7 415	7 920	8 630	9 006	9 080	8 773	2 398	37.6
Denmark	1 733	1 752	1 969	2 403	2 406	2 912	2 748	1 016	58.6
Finland	2 100	2 190	2 421	2 664	2 861	3 071	2 994	894	42.6
France	16 861	18 683	21 875	23 404	26 990	27 673	25 684	8 824	52.3
Germany	37 901	41 995	48 688	53 895	57 214	57 696	60 859	22 958	60.6
Greece	276	296	319	331	377	315	323	47	17.1
Ireland	4 463	5 505	7 955	10 572	15 883	18 090	21 918	17 455	391.1
Italy	16 680	17 730	19 374	20 731	22 758	21 533	21 826	5 145	30.8
Luxembourg	198	234	373	313	332	305	298	100	50.3
Netherlands	5 238	5 665	5 927	6 731	7 527	7 192	7 303	2 066	39.4
Portugal	835	907	1 056	1 138	1 357	1 334	1 455	619	74.1
Spain	3 451	3 753	3 887	4 078	4 538	3 982	4 567	1 115	32.3
Sweden	6 880	6 890	7 450	7 653	8 862	8 077	8 491	1 611	23.4
United Kingdom	24 862	29 207	31 857	35 141	37 703	36 533	34 594	9 732	39.1
Non-EU Western Europe	11 182	12 174	13 229	14 378	15 589	14 811	14 926	3 744	33.5
Bosnia-Herzegovina	10	8	7	14	17	11	13	3	32.8
Croatia	57	71	64	101	131	111	134	77	134.1
Cyprus	15	13	28	27	18	31	21	6	42.6
Gibraltar	6	3	6	10	1	3	1	-5	-82.5
Iceland	45	37	66	55	61	70	109	64	142.1
Liechtenstein	89	116	242	276	293	224	236	147	164.5
Macedonia	99	124	157	104	127	96	52	-48	-48.1
Malta and Gozo	208	222	334	323	460	362	303	95	45.9
Norway	1 436	1 451	1 430	1 578	1 547	1 606	1 562	125	8.7
Other Non-EU Western Europe	13	21	31	20	25	17	19	6	49.1
Serbia and Montenegro	6	9	12	4	2	5	6	0	0.4
Slovenia	276	268	280	270	306	278	300	24	8.8
Switzerland	7 636	8 195	8 509	9 406	9 942	9 392	9 177	1 541	20.2
Turkey	1 286	1 635	2 060	2 191	2 657	2 605	2 993	1 707	132.8
Eastern Europe	5 977	7 492	9 868	9 978	13 860	12 169	11 250	5 272	88.2
Albania	7	4	4	6	3	2	2	-5	-78.0
Baltic States	90	135	187	186	212	198	196	105	116.7
Estonia	49	56	62	48	64	60	83	33	67.9
Latvia	18	46	74	91	86	59	55	37	202.5
Lithuania	23	33	51	48	63	80	58	35	154.0
Bulgaria	107	154	182	154	205	247	282	175	163.4
Czech Republic	471	598	658	741	1 050	1 078	1 190	719	152.7
Hungary	608	1 021	1 516	1 858	2 675	2 927	2 596	1 988	327.0
Poland	559	614	683	697	916	778	897	337	60.3
Romania	206	329	374	389	461	484	522	316	153.2
Slovakia	120	164	163	166	238	233	249	129	107.1
Newly Independent States (NIS) ...	3 808	4 473	6 100	5 780	8 098	6 221	5 316	1 508	39.6
Armenia	1	5	16	14	21	31	28	27	2 024.0
Azerbaijan	3	4	4	6	12	6	7	4	107.3
Belarus	51	65	102	86	96	99	94	43	85.0
Georgia	7	6	12	15	11	7	11	4	53.6
Kazakhstan	112	114	163	222	414	333	307	195	174.6
Kyrgyzstan	5	2	0	0	2	3	5	0	-8.2
Moldova	26	48	108	87	102	67	38	12	44.9
Russia	3 057	3 814	5 139	4 825	6 558	5 015	4 387	1 330	43.5
Tajikistan	29	8	32	23	9	5	1	-28	-96.2
Turkmenistan	0	0	2	8	27	35	51	51	X
Ukraine	492	369	490	472	813	567	330	-162	-33.0
Uzbekistan	24	37	32	21	32	52	57	33	139.9
WESTERN HEMISPHERE	202 503	225 293	249 579	285 636	325 511	307 965	308 945	106 442	52.6
NAFTA	181 409	201 318	223 365	255 639	291 722	274 770	274 296	92 887	51.2
Canada	120 444	129 523	140 048	159 441	175 241	160 262	158 679	38 235	31.7
Mexico	60 965	71 795	83 317	96 198	116 482	114 508	115 617	54 652	89.6
Caribbean	4 667	5 225	5 395	5 544	5 920	5 538	5 319	652	14.0
Aruba	9	11	22	37	74	20	25	16	172.0
Bahamas	87	83	76	87	125	113	135	48	54.4
Barbados	36	36	30	53	33	32	24	-13	-34.7
Cayman Islands	8	12	15	6	6	4	7	0	-5.5
Dominican Republic	3 087	3 633	3 829	3 847	3 931	3 717	3 696	609	19.7
Haiti	135	173	256	287	283	254	241	106	78.6
Jamaica	589	541	496	476	479	268	185	-404	-68.6
Leeward and Windward Islands	78	81	79	118	124	101	104	26	33.0
Netherlands Antilles	119	138	125	116	125	128	108	-12	-9.8
Trinidad and Tobago	518	515	466	514	738	897	795	277	53.5
Turks and Caicos Islands	2	1	1	3	2	4	1	-1	-58.1

Note: Data are based on the Harmonized System of commodity classification and converted to other classification systems using recent Census data concordances to produce consistent time series. Therefore, the data in this table differs from values in other published sources. Manufactured goods are defined as SITC (Rev. 3) 5–9. Table B-3 provides revised data for this table's world values.

X = Not applicable.

Table B-15. U.S. Manufactures Imports from Individual Countries, 1996–2002—*Continued*

(Millions of dollars; Census basis; general imports, Customs.)

Region and country	1996	1997	1998	1999	2000	2001	2002	1996–2002 change Value	1996–2002 change Percent
Central America	4 765	5 949	6 966	8 895	9 242	8 852	9 489	4 724	99.1
Belize	22	21	24	24	24	19	20	-3	-11.9
Costa Rica	1 229	1 494	1 908	3 059	2 647	1 997	2 241	1 012	82.4
El Salvador	931	1 158	1 271	1 474	1 736	1 773	1 896	965	103.6
Guatemala	914	1 091	1 302	1 446	1 718	1 845	1 910	995	108.9
Honduras	1 366	1 842	2 077	2 410	2 650	2 707	2 828	1 462	107.0
Nicaragua	192	230	276	325	358	407	470	278	144.7
Panama	110	114	109	157	110	104	125	15	13.4
South America	11 644	12 763	13 834	15 525	18 575	18 733	19 802	8 158	70.1
Argentina	652	848	985	1 054	1 294	1 205	1 204	551	84.5
Bolivia	200	149	156	163	137	125	128	-72	-35.9
Brazil	6 522	7 178	7 697	8 572	10 681	11 224	12 269	5 748	88.1
Chile	885	875	845	1 205	1 271	1 516	1 541	656	74.1
Colombia	1 064	1 077	1 212	1 527	1 675	1 446	1 420	357	33.5
Ecuador	112	121	128	157	165	185	159	47	41.9
Guyana	39	36	34	29	32	32	29	-10	-26.4
Paraguay	32	28	18	28	20	12	17	-15	-45.9
Peru	702	1 019	1 376	1 384	1 505	1 326	1 341	639	91.0
Suriname	14	7	7	16	9	7	6	-8	-57.0
Uruguay	177	145	176	110	215	137	133	-45	-25.2
Venezuela	1 244	1 280	1 200	1 280	1 570	1 517	1 555	310	24.9
Other Western Hemisphere	18	37	18	33	51	72	39	21	119.4
Bermuda	10	29	10	24	38	61	21	10	101.1
Cuba	0	0	0	1	0	0	0	0	X
Falkland Islands	0	0	0	0	1	0	0	0	X
French Guiana	5	2	3	4	2	0	7	3	55.1
Greenland	1	1	2	1	0	0	0	0	X
Guadeloupe	1	3	2	3	9	10	9	8	738.1
Martinique	1	2	1	1	0	0	1	0	-30.1
St. Pierre and Miquelon	0	0	0	0	0	0	0	0	X
ASIA	304 103	332 063	347 915	383 727	447 418	403 188	424 021	119 918	39.4
Japan	114 503	120 461	121 102	130 409	145 482	125 630	120 590	6 087	5.3
Korea, South	22 275	22 710	23 423	30 650	39 272	34 075	34 716	12 441	55.9
Taiwan	29 517	32 192	32 660	34 696	40 038	32 826	31 749	2 232	7.6
China	49 928	60 708	69 484	80 139	97 658	100 109	122 558	72 630	145.5
Hong Kong	9 742	10 172	10 433	10 426	11 334	9 556	9 217	-525	-5.4
Macao	855	1 019	1 106	1 122	1 264	1 222	1 230	375	43.8
ASEAN	60 171	64 484	66 747	70 948	80 281	69 378	71 675	11 504	19.1
Brunei	49	56	124	128	186	216	198	150	309.1
Burma	89	98	149	213	429	433	322	233	262.7
Cambodia	3	102	364	590	824	961	1 069	1 066	34 203.9
Indonesia	5 831	6 813	7 144	7 501	8 363	8 249	7 782	1 951	33.5
Laos	16	14	21	12	9	4	2	-13	-84.3
Malaysia	17 265	17 302	18 332	20 713	24 532	21 594	23 382	6 117	35.4
Philippines	7 436	9 638	11 160	11 719	13 304	10 722	10 362	2 925	39.3
Singapore	20 093	19 780	18 032	17 841	18 686	14 671	14 508	-5 585	-27.8
Thailand	9 318	10 545	11 259	12 021	13 718	12 296	12 649	3 331	35.7
Vietnam	72	136	163	210	229	233	1 400	1 328	1 845.2
Middle East	7 781	9 146	10 342	11 821	15 807	14 977	15 227	7 446	95.7
Bahrain	105	117	144	219	326	404	395	290	275.7
Gaza Strip and West Bank	0	0	0	3	5	6	7	7	X
Iran	0	0	0	2	137	136	149	149	X
Iraq	0	0	0	0	0	0	0	0	X
Israel	6 320	7 205	8 488	9 733	12 795	11 807	12 226	5 905	93.4
Jordan	23	24	15	30	72	225	409	386	1 699.7
Kuwait	28	17	29	36	68	113	62	33	116.1
Lebanon	15	52	57	38	49	54	45	30	198.8
Oman	129	161	189	209	211	199	256	126	97.7
Qatar	157	130	197	179	379	388	310	153	97.5
Saudi Arabia	538	534	572	651	831	728	533	-5	-0.9
Syria	10	11	35	48	89	76	48	38	382.0
United Arab Emirates	454	894	610	671	836	838	786	332	73.0
Yemen Arab Republic	0	0	6	1	8	4	2	1	X
Other Asia	9 331	11 171	12 618	13 516	16 280	15 415	17 060	7 729	82.8
Afghanistan	1	3	5	4	1	1	4	3	490.0
Bangladesh	1 231	1 544	1 751	1 801	2 269	2 257	2 044	813	66.1
India	5 395	6 475	7 280	8 021	9 499	8 568	10 554	5 158	95.6
Korea, North	0	0	0	0	0	0	0	0	X
Mongolia	26	35	40	60	116	141	159	133	512.9
Nepal	109	110	138	177	229	200	152	43	39.6
Pakistan	1 203	1 401	1 653	1 695	2 117	2 202	2 263	1 060	88.1
South Asia NEC	12	20	33	55	95	98	114	102	879.5
Sri Lanka	1 355	1 584	1 720	1 703	1 956	1 948	1 771	416	30.7
AUSTRALIA AND OCEANIA	2 771	3 257	4 006	3 884	4 434	4 701	4 469	1 698	61.3
Australia	2 035	2 437	3 181	3 063	3 379	3 623	3 424	1 389	68.2
Australian Island Dependencies	1	1	1	1	1	1	1	0	-34.6
Fiji	56	59	69	73	113	105	82	27	47.9
French Pacific Islands	45	48	43	46	69	50	40	-5	-10.4
New Zealand	604	658	636	652	825	865	869	265	43.9
New Zealand Island Dependencies ...	4	3	4	6	7	6	3	0	-7.6
Other Pacific Islands NEC	1	8	37	3	2	2	5	4	608.3
Papua New Guinea	2	1	2	1	1	2	1	0	-7.6
Southern Pacific Islands	22	38	30	33	32	40	35	13	59.6
Trust Territory (former)	0	2	2	2	2	3	3	3	X
Western Samoa	2	1	3	2	3	3	4	2	117.7

Note: Data are based on the Harmonized System of commodity classification and converted to other classification systems using recent Census data concordances to produce consistent time series. Therefore, the data in this table differs from values in other published sources. Manufactured goods are defined as SITC (Rev. 3) 5–9. Table B-3 provides revised data for this table's world values.

X = Not applicable.

Table B-15. U.S. Manufactures Imports from Individual Countries, 1996–2002—*Continued*

(Millions of dollars; Census basis; general imports, Customs.)

Region and country	1996	1997	1998	1999	2000	2001	2002	1996–2002 change Value	1996–2002 change Percent
AFRICA	3 338	3 797	4 292	4 647	5 764	6 251	6 328	2 990	89.6
Algeria	30	30	7	62	8	39	11	-19	-63.5
Angola	9	6	4	11	13	7	8	-2	-17.2
Benin	5	1	1	0	0	0	0	-5	X
Botswana	27	25	20	17	41	18	29	2	7.5
Br. Indian Ocean Territory	3	1	0	0	2	0	0	-3	X
Burkina Faso	0	1	1	0	1	5	3	3	X
Burundi	0	0	0	0	0	0	0	0	X
Cameroon	7	9	12	10	7	6	8	1	13.8
Cape Verde	0	0	0	0	1	1	2	2	X
Central African Republic	0	0	0	0	1	2	1	1	X
Chad	2	0	0	0	0	0	0	-2	X
Comoros	0	0	0	0	0	0	0	0	X
Congo	24	18	12	22	30	17	18	-6	-26.0
Dem. Rep. of the Congo (Zaire)	116	125	95	121	36	36	34	-82	-70.7
Djibouti	0	0	0	0	0	1	2	2	X
Egypt	411	545	585	533	731	691	1 103	692	168.6
Equatorial Guinea	1	2	2	1	2	28	57	57	8 250.8
Eritrea	1	0	0	0	0	0	0	-1	X
Ethiopia	8	3	3	1	1	2	3	-4	-54.2
Fr. Indian Ocean Areas	1	1	0	0	0	1	0	0	X
Gabon	4	6	19	62	9	10	13	9	247.6
Gambia	2	3	2	0	0	0	0	-2	X
Ghana	114	118	88	133	69	58	50	-65	-56.6
Guinea	6	12	14	18	11	16	21	15	271.4
Guinea-Bissau	0	0	0	0	1	0	0	0	X
Ivory Coast	32	16	14	9	14	12	15	-17	-52.1
Kenya	46	57	49	70	74	88	149	103	222.0
Lesotho	65	86	100	111	140	215	322	256	392.0
Liberia	27	3	0	1	2	1	2	-24	-91.3
Libya	0	0	0	0	0	0	0	0	X
Madagascar	15	19	26	50	115	186	93	77	508.7
Malawi	2	0	0	2	7	11	12	10	552.1
Mali	4	4	3	6	9	6	2	-2	-45.9
Mauritania	0	0	0	1	0	0	1	1	X
Mauritius	193	208	252	251	262	261	270	77	40.2
Morocco	129	166	213	235	284	248	227	97	75.3
Mozambique	1	2	1	1	0	0	1	0	45.9
Namibia	14	32	18	2	9	24	50	36	255.7
Niger	1	41	1	5	7	4	1	0	35.5
Nigeria	13	8	13	14	11	9	18	5	41.4
Rwanda	0	0	0	0	0	0	0	0	X
Sao Tome and Principe	0	0	1	1	0	0	0	0	X
Senegal	5	6	4	8	3	96	3	-1	-28.5
Seychelles	2	2	2	5	7	8	6	3	139.1
Sierra Leone	20	18	12	9	4	4	3	-17	-84.0
Somalia	0	0	0	0	0	0	0	0	X
South Africa	1 789	1 985	2 476	2 636	3 618	3 922	3 539	1 750	97.8
St. Helena	0	0	0	0	0	0	0	0	X
Sudan	2	2	0	0	0	0	0	-2	X
Swaziland	19	20	20	28	37	56	104	85	456.0
Tanzania	12	17	20	17	20	15	12	0	0.4
Togo	2	1	1	1	2	8	1	-1	-39.0
Tunisia	34	47	47	60	53	56	61	27	80.5
Uganda	0	1	2	0	8	2	1	1	X
Western Sahara	0	0	0	0	0	0	0	0	X
Zambia	64	55	46	35	16	14	6	-57	-89.8
Zimbabwe (Rhodesia)	77	94	103	98	95	64	65	-12	-15.1
OTHER	0	0	0	0	0	0	0	0	X
International Organizations	0	0	0	0	0	0	0	0	X
Unidentified Countries	0	0	0	0	0	0	0	0	X
MISCELLANEOUS [1]	0	0	0	0	0	0	1	1	X
ADDENDUM									
Developed Countries	380 550	411 735	444 206	491 059	545 038	510 709	507 468	126 919	33.4
Developing Countries	279 318	316 839	348 216	391 670	468 442	439 972	467 913	188 595	67.5
APEC (20 countries)	474 721	520 643	557 894	623 224	718 065	657 292	674 973	200 252	42.2

Note: Data are based on the Harmonized System of commodity classification and converted to other classification systems using recent Census data concordances to produce consistent time series. Therefore, the data in this table differs from values in other published sources. Manufactured goods are defined as SITC (Rev. 3) 5–9. Table B-3 provides revised data for this table's world values.

[1]Includes transshipments, carryover, and timing adjustments, revisions not accounted for elsewhere, and roundoff.
X = Not applicable.

Table B-16. U.S. Manufactures Trade Balances with Individual Countries, 1996–2002

(Millions of dollars; Census basis; foreign and domestic exports, f.a.s.; general imports, Customs.)

Region and country	1996	1997	1998	1999	2000	2001	2002	1996–2002 change Value	1996–2002 change Percent
WORLD	-137 207	-137 341	-197 204	-270 948	-323 956	-308 796	-368 823	-231 615	168.8
EUROPE	-20 684	-22 453	-34 949	-48 690	-59 090	-62 548	-82 672	-61 988	299.7
Western Europe	-19 089	-20 286	-30 572	-43 110	-49 951	-55 682	-76 900	-57 811	302.9
European Union (EU-15)	-19 968	-20 843	-29 280	-41 562	-49 229	-55 386	-73 827	-53 859	269.7
Austria	-193	-265	-14	-259	-593	-1 231	-1 234	-1 041	539.4
Belgium	3 172	3 296	3 531	2 025	3 312	2 922	3 197	25	0.8
Denmark	-265	-268	-336	-871	-1 076	-1 474	-1 418	-1 153	435.2
Finland	28	-706	-691	-1 174	-1 467	-1 709	-1 618	-1 646	-5 782.9
France	-3 662	-3 913	-5 226	-5 439	-7 641	-8 675	-7 527	-3 865	105.5
Germany	-16 724	-19 794	-24 144	-28 814	-29 849	-29 409	-36 014	-19 290	115.3
Greece	342	455	874	530	711	829	678	336	98.3
Ireland	-1 086	-1 171	-2 687	-4 483	-8 529	-11 253	-15 472	-14 386	1 324.3
Italy	-9 860	-10 622	-11 999	-12 040	-13 359	-13 198	-13 213	-3 353	34.0
Luxembourg	40	476	229	666	60	243	166	126	317.6
Netherlands	8 178	11 098	10 635	10 366	12 036	10 018	9 139	961	11.8
Portugal	-275	-301	-408	-295	-617	-322	-875	-600	218.5
Spain	286	-53	-111	789	491	562	-683	-969	-338.7
Sweden	-3 744	-3 865	-3 911	-3 658	-4 549	-4 794	-5 581	-1 837	49.1
United Kingdom	3 796	4 790	4 979	1 096	1 841	2 105	-3 373	-7 169	-188.9
Non-EU Western Europe	879	557	-1 292	-1 549	-722	-296	-3 073	-3 952	-449.6
Bosnia-Herzegovina	18	62	10	17	14	12	8	-10	-56.0
Croatia	27	35	12	1	-45	-8	-65	-92	-342.2
Cyprus	58	62	45	59	58	142	137	78	134.9
Gibraltar	-4	0	-3	-7	8	1	11	16	-365.7
Iceland	173	111	138	191	168	124	87	-86	-49.6
Liechtenstein	-80	-103	-235	-267	-279	-217	-222	-142	176.2
Macedonia	-88	-100	-146	-58	-82	-71	-40	48	-54.3
Malta and Gozo	-104	-113	-81	-151	-157	-117	-109	-5	4.8
Norway	-74	126	141	-284	-131	86	-300	-226	304.7
Other Non-EU Western Europe	11	12	-2	10	16	28	10	0	-1.9
Serbia and Montenegro	26	37	47	42	13	24	54	28	107.0
Slovenia	-166	-185	-180	-172	-192	-172	-187	-21	12.9
Switzerland	519	-134	-1 510	-1 252	-226	205	-1 642	-2 161	-416.4
Turkey	565	745	471	322	113	-334	-814	-1 378	-244.1
Eastern Europe	-1 595	-2 167	-4 377	-5 579	-9 139	-6 866	-5 772	-4 177	261.9
Albania	-3	-3	0	12	9	5	4	7	-256.0
Baltic States	85	48	-21	-22	-69	-13	13	-71	-84.3
Estonia	5	-36	-28	-13	-24	-12	-10	-15	-292.3
Latvia	54	52	-1	-22	-35	1	-2	-56	-104.1
Lithuania	25	31	8	13	-9	-1	25	0	0.4
Bulgaria	-62	-108	-122	-87	-145	-174	-212	-151	244.3
Czech Republic	-95	-55	-154	-184	-374	-422	-570	-476	502.5
Hungary	-288	-562	-1 059	-1 379	-2 129	-2 268	-1 938	-1 650	572.2
Poland	152	388	28	7	-241	-126	-321	-472	-311.6
Romania	-75	-205	-125	-244	-270	-138	-319	-244	322.7
Slovakia	-59	-84	-55	-41	-130	-165	-157	-98	166.6
Newly Independent States (NIS)	-1 249	-1 584	-2 870	-3 641	-5 792	-3 566	-2 271	-1 022	81.8
Armenia	14	34	8	24	26	11	78	63	440.2
Azerbaijan	45	44	44	24	179	57	51	6	13.3
Belarus	-14	-31	-76	-61	-66	-65	-76	-62	432.6
Georgia	27	103	61	23	45	55	51	24	87.4
Kazakhstan	16	139	-75	-46	-292	-182	289	273	1 706.6
Kyrgyzstan	25	14	11	14	11	20	22	-3	-12.1
Moldova	-17	-33	-93	-80	-77	-51	-22	-5	27.4
Russia	-1 506	-2 070	-2 638	-3 533	-5 123	-3 303	-2 624	-1 118	74.2
Tajikistan	-24	-5	-30	-19	-6	4	22	46	-192.0
Turkmenistan	188	117	25	8	42	212	-6	-194	-103.3
Ukraine	-248	-91	-221	-303	-649	-387	-95	153	-61.7
Uzbekistan	245	196	114	310	118	65	40	-205	-83.7
WESTERN HEMISPHERE	10 526	27 846	15 559	-9 668	-13 435	-20 125	-34 614	-45 140	-428.8
NAFTA	-12 679	-2 609	-13 750	-28 237	-31 831	-38 401	-44 305	-31 626	249.4
Canada	-492	6 301	-215	-9 856	-14 579	-13 357	-14 051	-13 559	2 756.4
Mexico	-12 187	-8 910	-13 536	-18 381	-17 252	-25 045	-30 254	-18 067	148.2
Caribbean	1 424	2 124	2 777	2 202	2 663	2 886	2 838	1 415	99.4
Aruba	125	156	260	204	144	190	350	225	180.7
Bahamas	393	527	545	564	701	647	507	113	28.8
Barbados	119	168	193	185	216	190	186	67	56.7
Cayman Islands	171	207	354	312	283	206	184	13	7.6
Dominican Republic	-450	-412	-492	-461	-216	-17	-191	259	-57.6
Haiti	113	102	56	83	89	97	145	33	29.1
Jamaica	516	490	487	463	504	771	846	330	64.0
Leeward and Windward Islands	195	231	508	301	321	239	248	53	27.0
Netherlands Antilles	238	170	449	324	316	451	433	196	82.3
Trinidad and Tobago	-32	434	364	148	228	48	83	115	-363.8
Turks and Caicos Islands	36	50	55	80	77	64	46	10	29.3

Note: Data are based on the Harmonized System of commodity classification and converted to other classification systems using recent Census data concordances to produce consistent time series. Therefore, the data in this table differs from values in other published sources. Manufactured goods are defined as SITC (Rev. 3) 5–9. Table B-3 provides revised data for this table's world values.

Table B-16. U.S. Manufactures Trade Balances with Individual Countries, 1996–2002—*Continued*

(Millions of dollars; Census basis; foreign and domestic exports, f.a.s.; general imports, Customs.)

Region and country	1996	1997	1998	1999	2000	2001	2002	1996–2002 change Value	Percent
Central America	1 464	1 415	1 512	-110	-78	-64	5	-1 460	-99.7
Belize	64	69	76	92	139	122	90	26	40.6
Costa Rica	311	284	107	-929	-456	216	573	262	84.1
El Salvador	-110	-70	-47	-193	-223	-289	-526	-416	376.7
Guatemala	257	240	213	1	-249	-397	-360	-618	-240.0
Honduras	32	-126	-26	-312	-359	-516	-539	-571	-1 776.0
Nicaragua	-6	-20	-27	-45	-60	-75	-122	-116	1 863.1
Panama	917	1 038	1 216	1 277	1 130	875	889	-27	-3.0
South America	19 749	26 131	24 421	15 978	15 400	15 029	6 238	-13 511	-68.4
Argentina	3 560	4 457	4 584	3 665	3 151	2 527	280	-3 280	-92.1
Bolivia	23	110	222	127	97	74	43	20	85.8
Brazil	4 757	7 416	6 352	3 978	3 846	3 946	-679	-5 436	-114.3
Chile	2 881	3 131	2 895	1 624	1 940	1 413	868	-2 013	-69.9
Colombia	2 843	3 394	2 925	1 487	1 496	1 636	1 564	-1 280	-45.0
Ecuador	934	1 103	1 242	588	695	1 034	1 202	268	28.7
Guyana	66	75	84	89	98	82	74	7	11.2
Paraguay	789	805	703	451	390	370	412	-378	-47.9
Peru	708	706	270	-28	-61	-32	-68	-776	-109.6
Suriname	177	146	152	109	104	130	98	-78	-44.2
Uruguay	263	363	387	354	294	248	53	-210	-79.8
Venezuela	2 747	4 426	4 606	3 534	3 349	3 602	2 392	-355	-12.9
Other Western Hemisphere	569	785	599	499	411	425	611	42	7.3
Bermuda	182	213	279	222	303	239	320	138	75.7
Cuba	5	9	3	4	6	3	6	0	4.6
Falkland Islands	0	0	3	0	0	0	0	0	X
French Guiana	295	490	242	187	16	128	242	-53	-18.1
Greenland	3	4	0	1	1	2	2	-2	-48.1
Guadeloupe	54	43	48	53	67	35	21	-33	-61.8
Martinique	28	26	20	29	17	19	20	-7	-25.7
St. Pierre and Miquelon	1	1	2	2	1	0	0	-1	X
ASIA	-141 244	-157 598	-191 371	-224 598	-263 350	-237 585	-263 081	-121 837	86.3
Japan	-67 534	-72 840	-78 278	-88 204	-96 510	-82 008	-81 941	-14 407	21.3
Korea, South	-1 862	-2 751	-10 221	-11 825	-15 828	-15 979	-16 305	-14 443	775.9
Taiwan	-15 112	-15 363	-17 010	-18 184	-18 370	-17 225	-15 843	-730	4.8
China	-40 797	-50 351	-57 250	-68 733	-84 530	-84 644	-104 525	-63 727	156.2
Hong Kong	2 039	2 644	549	668	1 631	2 956	1 941	-98	-4.8
Macao	-826	-954	-1 067	-1 083	-1 197	-1 155	-1 154	-328	39.7
ASEAN	-21 238	-20 219	-30 264	-34 370	-36 755	-29 724	-34 021	-12 782	60.2
Brunei	323	119	-2	-63	-33	-114	-156	-479	-148.3
Burma	-58	-79	-117	-206	-413	-424	-314	-255	437.3
Cambodia	15	-87	-356	-577	-809	-944	-1 048	-1 062	-7 298.7
Indonesia	-2 974	-3 352	-5 472	-6 303	-6 752	-6 834	-6 211	-3 237	108.8
Laos	-12	-11	-17	-11	-6	-1	0	13	X
Malaysia	-9 518	-7 092	-9 746	-12 032	-13 951	-12 758	-13 557	-4 039	42.4
Philippines	-2 436	-3 190	-5 217	-5 376	-5 512	-3 928	-3 938	-1 502	61.7
Singapore	-4 138	-2 692	-2 835	-2 235	-1 553	2 220	753	4 891	-118.2
Thailand	-2 939	-3 926	-6 585	-7 609	-7 796	-7 063	-8 610	-5 670	192.9
Vietnam	501	92	84	41	70	122	-940	-1 441	-287.8
Middle East	9 351	9 075	10 785	6 680	557	1 792	1 361	-7 990	-85.5
Bahrain	83	247	103	90	89	-28	-16	-99	-119.1
Gaza Strip and West Bank	0	0	4	2	4	-5	-7	-7	X
Iran	0	1	0	-2	-135	-132	-146	-146	X
Iraq	0	0	10	0	1	39	32	32	X
Israel	-1 153	-1 939	-2 113	-2 721	-5 791	-5 000	-5 883	-4 730	410.3
Jordan	150	217	222	133	107	-39	-123	-272	-182.0
Kuwait	1 860	1 281	1 348	759	623	693	873	-986	-53.0
Lebanon	271	206	179	141	121	185	112	-159	-58.6
Oman	63	156	73	-53	-37	79	73	10	16.3
Qatar	37	214	139	-50	-203	-70	-18	-55	-149.0
Saudi Arabia	5 930	7 022	9 181	6 510	4 563	4 516	3 678	-2 252	-38.0
Syria	143	93	66	51	21	43	91	-53	-36.7
United Arab Emirates	1 833	1 490	1 480	1 759	1 121	1 428	2 436	602	32.9
Yemen Arab Republic	133	87	93	61	74	84	258	125	94.1
Other Asia	-5 264	-6 839	-8 615	-9 545	-12 348	-11 599	-12 594	-7 330	139.3
Afghanistan	7	4	0	9	2	1	76	69	947.6
Bangladesh	-1 121	-1 410	-1 602	-1 661	-2 128	-2 102	-1 920	-799	71.3
India	-2 468	-3 233	-4 108	-4 668	-6 295	-5 438	-6 983	-4 515	183.0
Korea, North	1	1	0	5	0	1	1	1	107.5
Mongolia	-22	-3	-25	-51	-104	-129	-93	-71	318.3
Nepal	-101	-84	-123	-157	-195	-188	-136	-34	33.9
Pakistan	-313	-630	-1 137	-1 382	-1 729	-1 813	-1 794	-1 481	472.5
South Asia NEC	-9	-14	-25	-47	-89	-91	-109	-100	1 126.8
Sri Lanka	-1 238	-1 471	-1 595	-1 593	-1 811	-1 840	-1 636	-398	32.2
AUSTRALIA AND OCEANIA	10 399	10 217	9 337	9 426	9 514	7 886	9 819	-580	-5.6
Australia	9 312	8 943	8 144	8 139	8 462	6 748	9 022	-291	-3.1
Australian Island Dependencies	0	3	3	4	3	4	1	1	X
Fiji	-34	-32	-2	49	-93	-90	-68	-34	100.3
French Pacific Islands	21	32	23	36	-5	15	28	7	35.3
New Zealand	969	1 124	1 082	1 129	1 002	1 105	785	-184	-19.0
New Zealand Island Dependencies	28	35	3	1	3	2	11	-17	-61.9
Other Pacific Islands NEC	65	102	24	31	17	19	16	-49	-75.6
Papua New Guinea	10	4	43	14	12	15	7	-3	-29.5
Southern Pacific Islands	20	-2	7	15	48	3	9	-11	-54.6
Trust Territory (former)	6	4	4	6	57	62	0	-6	X
Western Samoa	1	4	7	2	7	4	8	7	576.3

Note: Data are based on the Harmonized System of commodity classification and converted to other classification systems using recent Census data concordances to produce consistent time series. Therefore, the data in this table differs from values in other published sources. Manufactured goods are defined as SITC (Rev. 3) 5–9. Table B-3 provides revised data for this table's world values.

X = Not applicable.

Table B-16. U.S. Manufactures Trade Balances with Individual Countries, 1996–2002—*Continued*

(Millions of dollars; Census basis; foreign and domestic exports, f.a.s.; general imports, Customs.)

Region and country	1996	1997	1998	1999	2000	2001	2002	1996–2002 change Value	1996–2002 change Percent
AFRICA	3 794	4 646	4 143	2 581	2 403	3 575	1 648	-2 147	-56.6
Algeria	291	332	364	158	584	757	683	393	135.0
Angola	222	236	316	215	154	236	311	89	40.4
Benin	8	29	21	15	12	20	24	16	204.3
Botswana	1	15	15	15	-11	25	3	2	339.4
Br. Indian Ocean Territory	-3	0	0	0	-1	0	0	3	X
Burkina Faso	5	9	5	3	9	-2	8	3	65.6
Burundi	1	1	1	2	1	2	2	1	50.3
Cameroon	53	95	47	11	40	170	136	84	158.9
Cape Verde	62	4	3	4	4	5	5	-57	-91.5
Central African Republic	3	2	3	3	1	1	3	0	-6.1
Chad	-1	1	3	1	8	133	124	124	-17 892.9
Comoros	0	0	0	0	0	1	0	0	X
Congo	31	46	65	12	31	57	28	-3	-8.5
Dem. Rep. of the Congo (Zaire)	-77	-108	-74	-104	-30	-25	-14	63	-81.4
Djibouti	2	2	10	12	10	14	12	10	488.9
Egypt	1 312	2 165	1 402	1 326	1 453	1 951	833	-480	-36.5
Equatorial Guinea	16	45	83	219	92	50	50	34	213.3
Eritrea	5	12	10	4	4	7	5	0	9.7
Ethiopia	102	99	55	133	50	33	46	-56	-54.6
Fr. Indian Ocean Areas	3	2	3	3	4	2	2	-1	-20.6
Gabon	51	75	39	-23	47	57	46	-5	-9.7
Gambia	3	3	3	5	5	5	6	3	80.4
Ghana	91	115	73	22	67	81	89	-2	-2.4
Guinea	53	49	37	13	35	51	20	-33	-62.1
Guinea-Bissau	3	1	1	0	0	1	2	-1	-37.6
Ivory Coast	78	108	123	65	62	62	45	-34	-43.0
Kenya	43	131	84	83	130	462	72	29	68.4
Lesotho	-65	-85	-100	-110	-140	-214	-320	-255	393.8
Liberia	-14	17	32	24	26	24	14	28	-203.4
Libya	0	0	0	0	0	0	0	0	X
Madagascar	-5	-12	-17	55	-105	-170	-85	-80	1 476.0
Malawi	8	14	13	5	4	2	5	-3	-40.6
Mali	11	15	16	21	17	25	7	-5	-39.7
Mauritania	10	9	5	11	14	23	21	11	108.6
Mauritius	-168	-177	-230	-212	-239	-233	-243	-75	44.8
Mayotte	0	0	0	0	0	0	0	0	X
Morocco	6	45	160	139	13	-89	193	187	2 985.3
Mozambique	9	12	14	12	19	8	14	4	45.3
Namibia	3	-7	33	194	69	221	2	-1	-36.1
Niger	6	-34	6	5	22	48	26	20	340.2
Nigeria	604	645	623	410	513	683	700	96	15.9
Rwanda	3	7	11	29	8	8	2	-1	-28.2
Sao Tome and Principe	0	13	9	-1	0	10	2	2	X
Senegal	28	25	27	38	52	-37	57	29	103.3
Seychelles	100	4	8	2	0	168	2	-98	-97.9
Sierra Leone	-11	-14	-6	-1	9	8	7	19	-166.3
Somalia	1	1	1	1	3	3	4	4	721.9
South Africa	808	613	779	-359	-799	-1 164	-1 279	-2 087	-258.4
St. Helena	0	0	0	0	0	4	2	2	X
Sudan	32	24	0	0	0	1	2	-31	-94.4
Swaziland	-16	-15	-13	-19	30	-44	-93	-76	466.7
Tanzania	22	25	30	27	10	30	28	6	28.0
Togo	11	10	22	20	7	5	7	-4	-32.9
Tunisia	51	72	57	140	142	111	35	-15	-30.5
Uganda	12	16	14	15	11	20	15	4	30.9
Western Sahara	0	0	0	0	0	0	0	0	X
Zambia	-21	-29	-27	-16	2	0	14	35	-167.7
Zimbabwe (Rhodesia)	13	-15	-15	-48	-46	-33	-32	-45	-359.4
OTHER	2	0	76	0	1	0	77	75	4 545.7
International Organizations	2	0	76	0	1	0	77	75	4 545.7
Unidentified Countries	0	0	0	0	0	0	0	0	X
MISCELLANEOUS [1]	-1	0	0	0	0	1	0	1	X
ADDENDUM									
Developed Countries	-76 026	-76 146	-99 059	-132 261	-152 374	-144 357	-164 364	-88 338	116.2
Developing Countries	-61 181	-61 195	-98 145	-138 687	-171 582	-164 439	-204 459	-143 277	234.2
APEC (20 countries)	-144 700	-149 377	-195 956	-240 731	-274 728	-257 707	-285 639	-140 940	97.4

Note: Data are based on the Harmonized System of commodity classification and converted to other classification systems using recent Census data concordances to produce consistent time series. Therefore, the data in this table differs from values in other published sources. Manufactured goods are defined as SITC (Rev. 3) 5–9. Table B-3 provides revised data for this table's world values.

[1]Includes transshipments, carryover, and timing adjustments, revisions not accounted for elsewhere, and roundoff.
X = Not applicable.

Table B-17. Top 30 Purchasers and Suppliers of U.S. Manufactures Products, 1997–2003

(Millions of dollars; top 30 based on 2003 value; Census basis; foreign and domestic exports, f.a.s.; general imports, Customs.)

Country	1997	1998	1999	2000	2001	2002	2003	Percent change, 1997–2003
TOTAL OF TOP 30 PURCHASERS (EXPORTS)	525 217	528 156	553 554	628 452	579 132	550 404	569 632	8.5
Canada	135 823	139 834	149 585	160 662	146 906	144 628	150 828	11.0
Mexico	62 885	69 781	77 817	99 229	89 463	85 363	85 082	35.3
Japan	47 621	42 824	42 205	48 972	43 622	38 649	38 845	-18.4
United Kingdom	33 997	36 836	36 237	39 544	38 637	31 221	31 908	-6.1
Germany	22 201	24 544	25 081	27 364	28 288	24 845	27 067	21.9
China	10 357	12 234	11 406	13 128	15 465	18 034	20 499	97.9
South Korea	19 959	13 202	18 825	23 444	18 096	18 411	19 361	-3.0
Netherlands	16 763	16 562	17 097	19 563	17 210	16 442	18 823	12.3
France	14 769	16 648	17 965	19 349	18 998	18 157	16 198	9.7
Singapore	17 089	15 197	15 606	17 133	16 890	15 260	15 766	-7.7
Taiwan	16 830	15 650	16 511	21 668	15 602	15 906	14 862	-11.7
Belgium	10 711	11 451	10 655	12 318	12 002	11 970	13 782	28.7
Australia	11 380	11 325	11 203	11 841	10 371	12 446	12 242	7.6
Hong Kong	12 817	10 981	11 093	12 966	12 512	11 158	12 056	-5.9
Malaysia	10 210	8 586	8 681	10 581	8 836	9 825	10 371	1.6
Brazil	14 594	14 049	12 550	14 528	15 170	11 590	10 358	-29.0
Italy	7 108	7 375	8 690	9 398	8 336	8 613	9 073	27.6
Switzerland	8 062	6 999	8 153	9 716	9 597	7 535	8 299	2.9
Ireland	4 334	5 268	6 089	7 354	6 837	6 446	7 428	71.4
Philippines	6 447	5 943	6 343	7 791	6 794	6 424	7 296	13.2
Israel	5 266	6 374	7 011	7 004	6 807	6 342	6 202	17.8
Thailand	6 619	4 674	4 412	5 922	5 234	4 039	4 874	-26.4
Spain	3 700	3 775	4 868	5 029	4 544	3 884	4 492	21.4
India	3 243	3 171	3 353	3 204	3 130	3 571	4 297	32.5
Saudi Arabia	7 555	9 753	7 161	5 395	5 243	4 211	4 036	-46.6
Dominican Republic	3 221	3 338	3 386	3 715	3 700	3 505	3 257	1.1
United Arab Emirates	2 384	2 090	2 430	1 957	2 266	3 222	3 173	33.1
Colombia	4 471	4 138	3 014	3 172	3 082	2 984	3 133	-29.9
Costa Rica	1 778	2 015	2 130	2 192	2 213	2 814	3 042	71.1
Sweden	3 025	3 539	3 995	4 313	3 283	2 910	2 979	-1.5
TOTAL OF TOP 30 SUPPLIERS (IMPORTS)	691 681	750 388	835 485	958 084	895 425	918 702	963 032	39.2
Canada	129 523	140 048	159 441	175 241	160 262	158 679	160 819	24.2
China	60 708	69 484	80 139	97 658	100 109	122 558	149 110	145.6
Japan	120 461	121 102	130 409	145 482	125 630	120 590	117 115	-2.8
Mexico	71 795	83 317	96 198	116 482	114 508	115 617	114 775	59.9
Germany	41 995	48 688	53 895	57 214	57 696	60 859	66 195	57.6
South Korea	22 710	23 423	30 650	39 272	34 075	34 716	36 093	58.9
United Kingdom	29 207	31 857	35 141	37 703	36 533	34 594	35 473	21.5
Taiwan	32 192	32 660	34 696	40 038	32 826	31 749	31 124	-3.3
France	18 683	21 875	23 404	26 990	27 673	25 684	26 010	39.2
Ireland	5 505	7 955	10 572	15 883	18 090	21 918	25 265	359.0
Malaysia	17 302	18 332	20 713	24 532	21 594	23 382	24 589	42.1
Italy	17 730	19 374	20 731	22 758	21 533	21 826	22 592	27.4
Singapore	19 802	18 032	17 841	18 686	14 671	14 508	14 929	-24.5
Brazil	7 178	7 697	8 572	10 681	11 224	12 269	13 135	83.0
Thailand	10 545	11 259	12 021	13 718	12 296	12 649	12 757	21.0
Israel	7 205	8 488	9 733	12 795	11 807	12 226	12 575	74.5
India	6 475	7 280	8 021	9 499	8 568	10 554	11 698	80.6
Switzerland	8 195	8 509	9 406	9 942	9 392	9 177	10 417	27.1
Sweden	6 890	7 450	7 653	8 862	8 077	8 491	10 235	48.6
Philippines	9 638	11 160	11 719	13 304	10 722	10 362	9 358	-2.9
Belgium	7 415	7 920	8 630	9 006	9 080	8 773	8 831	19.1
Hong Kong	10 172	10 433	10 426	11 334	9 556	9 217	8 761	-13.9
Netherlands	5 665	5 927	6 731	7 527	7 192	7 303	7 856	38.7
Indonesia	6 813	7 144	7 501	8 363	8 249	7 782	7 340	7.7
Spain	3 753	3 887	4 078	4 538	3 982	4 567	5 385	43.5
Russia	3 814	5 139	4 825	6 558	5 015	4 387	4 847	27.1
Austria	2 277	2 464	2 794	3 092	3 803	3 608	4 169	83.1
Republic of South Africa	1 985	2 476	2 636	3 618	3 922	3 539	4 123	107.7
Dominican Republic	3 633	3 829	3 847	3 931	3 717	3 696	3 950	8.7
Australia	2 437	3 181	3 063	3 379	3 623	3 424	3 507	43.9

Table B-18. U.S. Total Agricultural Exports to Individual Countries, 1996–2002

(Millions of dollars; Census basis; foreign and domestic exports, f.a.s.)

Region and country	1996	1997	1998	1999	2000	2001	2002	1996–2002 change Value	1996–2002 change Percent
WORLD	61 707	58 673	53 255	49 634	53 507	55 291	54 732	-6 975	-11.3
EUROPE	12 328	12 208	10 373	8 611	8 666	9 113	8 331	-3 997	-32.4
Western Europe	10 216	10 506	9 015	7 576	7 521	7 807	7 580	-2 636	-25.8
European Union (EU-15)	9 072	9 002	7 951	6 478	6 329	6 510	6 254	-2 818	-31.1
Austria	29	27	22	14	18	16	13	-15	-53.0
Belgium	729	672	644	551	558	628	558	-172	-23.5
Denmark	247	308	224	172	161	168	157	-90	-36.5
Finland	131	132	75	81	62	60	46	-84	-64.5
France	517	575	498	367	333	395	403	-113	-22.0
Germany	1 479	1 334	1 233	928	915	944	993	-486	-32.9
Greece	140	149	119	89	76	101	101	-39	-27.6
Ireland	221	236	276	204	288	243	215	-5	-2.4
Italy	795	762	688	502	563	571	546	-248	-31.2
Luxembourg	1	1	3	4	5	2	14	13	2 073.7
Netherlands	2 064	1 953	1 565	1 548	1 451	1 372	1 183	-881	-42.7
Portugal	290	249	157	139	126	151	212	-77	-26.7
Spain	1 069	1 146	1 054	683	614	648	678	-391	-36.6
Sweden	136	131	130	101	99	115	92	-44	-32.2
United Kingdom	1 225	1 328	1 263	1 095	1 061	1 097	1 041	-184	-15.0
Non-EU Western Europe	1 144	1 504	1 064	1 097	1 192	1 297	1 326	182	15.9
Bosnia-Herzegovina	30	31	23	7	12	19	11	-20	-64.7
Croatia	19	28	19	3	1	5	7	-13	-65.6
Cyprus	37	37	11	21	18	21	22	-15	-40.3
Gibraltar	0	0	0	1	0	0	0	0	X
Iceland	18	16	20	30	19	20	14	-4	-22.1
Liechtenstein	0	0	0	0	0	0	1	1	X
Macedonia	3	8	3	10	23	8	7	5	174.4
Malta and Gozo	20	8	7	11	10	9	13	-8	-37.8
Norway	129	81	74	65	61	66	58	-71	-55.0
Other Non-EU Western Europe	12	4	5	4	0	4	4	-8	-69.2
Serbia and Montenegro	13	1	10	13	15	14	9	-4	-32.5
Slovenia	17	28	19	10	6	3	6	-11	-62.4
Switzerland	228	518	206	433	356	547	499	270	118.4
Turkey	616	743	666	489	669	579	676	60	9.7
Eastern Europe	2 112	1 703	1 358	1 036	1 144	1 305	750	-1 361	-64.5
Albania	8	2	10	7	8	8	9	1	18.5
Baltic States	133	160	170	281	126	69	44	-89	-66.8
Estonia	27	26	58	133	46	15	9	-19	-68.4
Latvia	92	119	111	146	77	42	31	-61	-66.3
Lithuania	15	15	2	2	2	13	5	-10	-66.4
Bulgaria	30	6	10	9	7	15	13	-17	-55.4
Czech Republic	13	16	10	7	8	10	13	0	-1.4
Hungary	10	25	18	20	18	24	27	17	167.7
Poland	227	121	121	67	53	90	68	-159	-70.0
Romania	48	16	27	15	19	25	43	-5	-11.3
Slovakia	1	2	2	2	1	1	1	0	-14.4
Newly Independent States (NIS)	1 641	1 355	991	627	905	1 063	697	-944	-57.5
Armenia	42	22	23	11	8	7	8	-34	-81.8
Azerbaijan	6	6	9	13	3	2	9	4	66.0
Belarus	11	1	0	0	0	0	0	-10	X
Georgia	48	30	62	32	47	38	31	-17	-34.7
Kazakhstan	1	0	12	2	1	7	8	6	497.5
Kyrgyzstan	17	11	9	7	12	4	5	-12	-72.5
Moldova	12	4	6	3	2	20	15	2	17.6
Russia	1 355	1 235	843	517	812	919	553	-801	-59.2
Tajikistan	12	16	10	9	10	20	10	-2	-13.0
Turkmenistan	12	0	0	3	3	2	2	-10	-83.6
Ukraine	44	30	16	23	7	19	14	-31	-69.6
Uzbekistan	81	0	0	6	1	27	43	-39	-47.8
WESTERN HEMISPHERE	17 595	18 287	19 545	18 246	19 561	20 986	21 734	4 139	23.5
NAFTA	12 506	12 986	14 215	13 709	15 270	16 575	17 080	4 574	36.6
Canada	7 037	7 759	8 006	8 024	8 520	9 010	9 588	2 551	36.3
Mexico	5 469	5 227	6 209	5 686	6 749	7 565	7 492	2 023	37.0
Caribbean	1 358	1 461	1 416	1 450	1 365	1 379	1 378	20	1.4
Aruba	29	29	29	29	29	30	29	0	-0.1
Bahamas	136	115	110	117	130	133	130	-6	-4.5
Barbados	52	49	42	46	42	50	41	-11	-21.1
Cayman Islands	20	35	43	36	38	34	29	9	47.8
Dominican Republic	417	540	507	563	515	520	543	125	30.1
Haiti	191	201	214	218	181	177	172	-19	-9.8
Jamaica	207	205	194	188	177	185	191	-16	-7.7
Leeward and Windward Islands	81	79	75	65	68	68	61	-21	-25.3
Netherlands Antilles	86	85	85	77	72	61	57	-29	-33.5
Trinidad and Tobago	134	118	111	103	108	116	120	-14	-10.4
Turks and Caicos Islands	4	5	6	8	7	5	4	0	-7.3

Note: Developing countries sum equals world minus developed countries sum.

X = Not applicable.

Table B-18. U.S. Total Agricultural Exports to Individual Countries, 1996–2002—*Continued*

(Millions of dollars; Census basis; foreign and domestic exports, f.a.s.)

Region and country	1996	1997	1998	1999	2000	2001	2002	1996–2002 change Value	1996–2002 change Percent
Central America	1 055	1 102	1 279	1 150	1 127	1 242	1 263	208	19.7
Belize	16	16	17	17	21	21	20	4	23.7
Costa Rica	221	192	206	183	187	201	228	7	3.1
El Salvador	192	231	245	201	215	240	213	21	10.7
Guatemala	275	264	314	278	260	298	343	67	24.4
Honduras	134	165	189	195	197	201	188	55	40.7
Nicaragua	65	68	76	85	75	103	85	20	30.4
Panama	151	166	231	192	172	178	187	36	23.6
South America	2 596	2 661	2 560	1 866	1 731	1 727	1 816	-780	-30.1
Argentina	165	355	206	150	156	119	53	-112	-67.8
Bolivia	40	31	29	20	14	15	19	-21	-52.1
Brazil	587	542	488	219	272	229	338	-249	-42.5
Chile	131	128	138	153	117	101	113	-18	-13.4
Colombia	623	542	579	438	422	454	524	-99	-15.9
Ecuador	159	191	181	107	102	110	145	-13	-8.4
Guyana	29	29	22	23	23	23	23	-7	-22.9
Paraguay	33	32	10	10	10	5	3	-30	-90.9
Peru	309	196	358	297	172	213	215	-94	-30.5
Suriname	26	24	23	17	17	19	18	-8	-32.6
Uruguay	17	15	13	13	17	25	19	1	8.3
Venezuela	477	577	514	421	411	414	347	-130	-27.3
Other Western Hemisphere	79	77	76	71	68	63	197	118	148.7
Bermuda	70	67	67	61	60	52	52	-18	-25.4
Cuba	0	0	0	0	0	4	139	139	X
Falkland Islands	0	0	0	0	0	0	0	0	X
French Guiana	1	1	1	1	1	0	1	0	-38.4
Greenland	0	0	0	0	0	0	2	2	X
Guadeloupe	5	5	4	6	4	4	2	-3	-57.5
Martinique	4	3	3	3	2	2	1	-2	-62.1
St. Pierre and Miquelon	0	1	0	0	0	0	0	0	X
ASIA	27 935	25 004	20 359	19 803	22 157	22 336	21 555	-6 380	-22.8
Japan	11 766	10 617	9 192	9 008	9 595	9 111	8 537	-3 230	-27.4
Korea, South	3 856	2 866	2 229	2 457	2 652	2 621	2 702	-1 154	-29.9
Taiwan	2 969	2 622	1 804	1 962	2 043	2 028	2 028	-941	-31.7
China	2 081	1 604	1 340	856	1 744	1 964	1 989	-92	-4.4
Hong Kong	1 501	1 726	1 515	1 222	1 300	1 239	1 109	-393	-26.2
Macao	0	1	2	2	1	1	1	1	X
ASEAN	3 277	3 005	2 109	2 308	2 710	3 003	2 927	-350	-10.7
Brunei	1	2	1	1	1	2	4	2	216.2
Burma	2	1	0	1	1	2	2	0	1.1
Cambodia	2	2	1	2	12	9	4	3	172.0
Indonesia	855	776	456	541	685	917	815	-39	-4.6
Laos	0	0	0	0	0	0	2	2	X
Malaysia	616	483	283	315	301	388	373	-243	-39.4
Philippines	899	877	717	788	911	796	778	-121	-13.4
Singapore	287	280	212	217	240	233	258	-29	-10.1
Thailand	583	543	418	412	506	576	614	31	5.3
Vietnam	33	41	21	32	53	80	78	44	132.4
Middle East	1 828	1 799	1 540	1 551	1 682	1 658	1 598	-231	-12.6
Bahrain	19	9	22	27	13	30	29	10	53.7
Gaza Strip and West Bank	0	0	0	0	0	0	0	0	X
Iran	0	0	0	48	15	5	11	11	X
Iraq	3	82	96	9	8	8	0	-3	X
Israel	618	538	367	425	484	429	467	-151	-24.5
Jordan	151	143	88	90	92	126	94	-57	-37.9
Kuwait	42	46	50	57	49	59	55	13	31.0
Lebanon	134	99	69	77	82	81	65	-69	-51.2
Oman	14	12	18	18	13	17	17	2	16.8
Qatar	6	8	10	10	9	10	15	9	138.4
Saudi Arabia	554	621	505	449	481	431	343	-210	-38.0
Syria	50	63	49	57	88	80	113	63	126.8
United Arab Emirates	123	112	189	189	242	286	283	160	130.3
Yemen Arab Republic	114	65	76	95	107	97	105	-9	-8.2
Other Asia	655	764	628	439	429	711	665	10	1.5
Afghanistan	8	2	0	5	5	4	0	-8	X
Bangladesh	88	120	160	123	86	140	132	44	49.9
India	113	155	202	157	216	356	278	165	145.9
Korea, North	0	2	4	7	2	0	24	24	X
Mongolia	0	2	5	2	5	0	0	0	X
Nepal	1	0	1	1	1	2	3	2	246.0
Pakistan	352	442	194	89	57	135	197	-156	-44.2
South Asia NEC	0	0	0	0	0	0	0	0	X
Sri Lanka	92	41	62	56	56	74	31	-61	-66.5
AUSTRALIA AND OCEANIA	495	559	556	497	503	483	522	27	5.5
Australia	327	358	339	327	326	296	344	17	5.3
Australian Island Dependencies	0	1	0	0	0	0	0	0	X
Fiji	5	5	6	3	3	3	2	-3	-65.6
French Pacific Islands	36	38	37	32	35	33	32	-4	-11.6
New Zealand	93	116	125	104	101	114	109	16	17.4
New Zealand Island Dependencies	0	0	5	0	1	1	1	0	X
Other Pacific Islands NEC	2	2	2	2	3	2	2	-1	-26.9
Papua New Guinea	4	6	4	3	1	1	2	-1	-33.8
Southern Pacific Islands	0	0	0	0	1	2	3	3	X
Trust Territory (former)	24	28	31	21	28	26	25	2	7.6
Western Samoa	5	4	4	4	5	4	3	-2	-30.6

Note: Developing countries sum equals world minus developed countries sum.

X = Not applicable.

Table B-18. U.S. Total Agricultural Exports to Individual Countries, 1996–2002—*Continued*

(Millions of dollars; Census basis; foreign and domestic exports, f.a.s.)

Region and country	1996	1997	1998	1999	2000	2001	2002	1996–2002 change Value	Percent
AFRICA	2 693	2 248	2 087	2 087	2 305	2 103	2 292	-402	-14.9
Algeria	294	316	257	221	258	230	270	-24	-8.1
Angola	28	29	28	23	55	28	46	18	63.9
Benin	2	5	6	2	4	4	5	3	174.9
Botswana	1	3	1	1	1	1	0	-1	X
Br. Indian Ocean Territory	0	0	0	0	0	0	0	0	X
Burkina Faso	3	7	9	6	5	1	7	4	126.1
Burundi	0	0	3	1	0	3	0	0	X
Cameroon	3	12	7	6	5	2	4	1	24.3
Cape Verde	5	6	6	3	2	1	2	-3	-61.8
Central African Republic	0	1	0	0	0	0	2	2	X
Chad	2	2	0	1	3	3	2	0	-11.3
Comoros	0	0	0	0	0	0	0	0	X
Congo	7	5	8	9	16	14	4	-3	-37.9
Dem. Rep. of the Congo (Zaire)	24	14	10	3	2	6	7	-18	-72.9
Djibouti	2	2	5	13	2	2	41	38	1 708.6
Egypt	1 257	966	904	980	1 049	1 025	861	-396	-31.5
Equatorial Guinea	0	0	0	1	0	1	1	1	X
Eritrea	8	4	14	0	12	14	23	15	202.0
Ethiopia	36	18	29	30	114	26	11	-25	-70.2
French Indian Ocean Area	0	0	1	0	0	0	0	0	X
Gabon	0	1	1	2	3	4	4	4	X
Gambia	2	2	2	2	3	3	3	2	99.2
Ghana	64	52	46	51	38	41	48	-17	-25.7
Guinea	12	10	5	8	7	8	9	-3	-24.6
Guinea-Bissau	0	1	0	1	0	0	1	1	X
Heard Island and McDonald Islands	0	0	0	0	0	0	0	0	X
Ivory Coast	20	19	6	21	12	12	13	-8	-37.8
Kenya	10	32	61	29	28	19	43	33	312.3
Kiribati (Gilbert Islands)	0	0	1	0	0	0	0	0	X
Lesotho	2	1	1	0	0	0	1	-1	-68.4
Liberia	37	18	13	16	13	9	9	-28	-74.7
Libya	0	0	0	0	18	9	18	18	X
Madagascar	2	5	6	2	5	5	7	6	340.4
Malawi	0	0	0	0	2	1	13	13	X
Mali	0	3	2	1	0	2	2	1	X
Mauritania	1	3	2	1	2	2	1	1	108.5
Mauritius	0	0	1	0	1	0	1	0	X
Morocco	233	163	122	155	166	91	124	-109	-47.0
Mozambique	10	26	29	18	30	15	66	56	566.5
Namibia	5	1	0	0	2	5	6	1	13.4
Nauru	0	0	0	0	0	0	0	0	X
Niger	1	2	2	0	2	5	9	8	1 223.8
Nigeria	177	116	151	172	178	243	301	124	70.1
Republic of South Africa	298	223	200	181	136	101	149	-148	-49.8
Sao Tome and Principe	0	0	0	0	0	0	0	0	X
Senegal	7	7	16	4	6	7	7	0	-1.9
Seychelles	1	1	0	0	0	0	0	0	X
Sierra Leone	15	9	16	5	6	14	13	-2	-12.7
Somalia	3	1	2	2	2	3	2	-1	-43.9
St. Helena	0	0	0	0	0	0	0	0	X
Sudan	16	11	7	8	17	17	10	-6	-39.5
Swaziland	0	1	2	1	1	1	1	1	X
Tanzania	5	13	8	17	4	10	11	7	141.0
Togo	5	3	0	3	0	1	3	-2	-36.1
Tunisia	90	118	81	71	85	104	96	6	6.6
Uganda	4	17	11	7	6	9	4	0	8.0
Western Sahara	0	0	0	0	0	0	0	0	X
Zambia	0	0	1	1	0	1	14	14	X
Zimbabwe (Rhodesia)	1	1	4	9	4	0	17	16	1 814.8
OTHER	0	0	0	0	0	0	0	0	X
International Organizations	0	0	0	0	0	0	0	0	X
Unidentified Countries	0	0	0	0	0	0	0	0	X
MISCELLANEOUS [1]	663	369	338	392	319	273	299	-365	-54.9
ADDENDUM									
Developed Countries	29 736	29 579	26 877	25 218	26 199	26 438	26 486	-3 251	-10.9
Developing Countries	31 971	29 094	26 378	24 416	27 309	28 853	28 247	-3 724	-11.6
APEC (20 countries)	40 172	37 462	34 210	32 918	36 830	38 173	37 702	-2 470	-6.1

Note: Developing countries sum equals world minus developed countries sum.

[1]Includes transshipments, carryover, and timing adjustments, revisions not accounted for elsewhere, and roundoff.
X = Not applicable.

Table B-19. U.S. Total Agricultural Imports from Individual Countries, 1996–2002

(Millions of dollars; Census basis; general imports, Customs.)

Region and country	1996	1997	1998	1999	2000	2001	2002	1996–2002 change Value	1996–2002 change Percent
WORLD	33 805	36 381	37 105	37 997	39 187	39 541	42 041	8 236	24.4
EUROPE	7 666	7 936	8 305	8 901	8 918	8 853	9 582	1 915	25.0
Western Europe	7 284	7 704	8 050	8 648	8 631	8 542	9 232	1 948	26.7
European Union (EU-15)	6 630	7 042	7 437	8 056	8 140	7 985	8 703	2 073	31.3
Austria	40	45	40	44	70	116	113	73	182.2
Belgium	150	172	189	170	168	186	190	40	26.6
Denmark	420	420	417	428	483	502	504	85	20.2
Finland	59	68	71	65	57	85	91	32	53.2
France	1 101	1 267	1 368	1 656	1 513	1 357	1 518	418	37.9
Germany	776	786	835	804	812	762	780	4	0.5
Greece	159	135	125	204	130	130	164	4	2.7
Ireland	319	293	340	309	327	293	293	-26	-8.1
Italy	1 320	1 388	1 389	1 459	1 553	1 566	1 794	474	35.9
Luxembourg	1	2	0	0	0	0	0	-1	X
Netherlands	1 186	1 260	1 352	1 412	1 565	1 608	1 756	571	48.1
Portugal	65	72	68	75	67	65	83	18	28.2
Spain	522	565	628	737	705	670	758	236	45.3
Sweden	80	111	109	89	77	86	95	15	18.6
United Kingdom	431	458	506	603	613	559	562	131	30.3
Non-EU Western Europe	654	662	613	591	490	556	529	-125	-19.2
Bosnia-Herzegovina	0	0	0	0	0	1	2	1	X
Croatia	13	10	7	8	9	10	9	-4	-29.3
Cyprus	2	1	2	2	2	2	2	1	42.0
Gibraltar	0	0	0	0	0	0	0	0	X
Iceland	2	1	2	1	2	2	1	0	-24.0
Liechtenstein	2	1	1	1	0	1	1	-1	-60.8
Macedonia	26	23	18	32	10	16	21	-5	-17.6
Malta and Gozo	0	0	0	0	1	0	0	0	X
Norway	29	31	35	40	48	43	45	16	55.4
Other Non-EU Western Europe	0	0	0	1	3	0	0	0	X
Serbia and Montenegro	2	1	1	1	0	0	2	0	8.1
Slovenia	14	9	6	5	7	6	5	-9	-62.7
Switzerland	145	160	141	140	151	147	166	21	14.7
Turkey	420	425	399	359	257	329	274	-146	-34.8
Eastern Europe	383	232	256	254	288	311	350	-33	-8.6
Albania	4	8	8	3	5	5	4	1	22.1
Baltic States	12	12	20	26	40	44	38	25	208.7
Estonia	0	0	0	1	3	4	2	1	X
Latvia	0	0	2	1	1	4	2	2	X
Lithuania	11	11	18	23	36	36	33	22	191.1
Bulgaria	21	20	34	46	28	31	35	15	72.7
Czech Republic	11	12	15	15	18	26	30	19	172.5
Hungary	69	61	52	35	43	39	43	-26	-37.4
Poland	75	70	81	86	100	124	152	77	102.2
Romania	1	2	1	2	3	2	4	2	181.5
Slovakia	3	2	3	3	2	3	3	0	0.3
Newly Independent States (NIS)	186	47	42	38	49	37	40	-146	-78.6
Armenia	0	1	0	0	1	1	1	1	X
Azerbaijan	1	1	1	2	3	3	2	1	225.4
Belarus	1	0	0	0	0	1	1	0	-1.9
Georgia	0	0	2	3	2	3	3	2	X
Kazakhstan	1	0	0	0	0	0	0	-1	X
Kyrgyzstan	0	0	0	0	0	0	0	0	X
Moldova	4	3	4	2	3	1	1	-2	-67.1
Russia	36	30	27	18	26	15	17	-19	-53.0
Tajikistan	3	0	0	0	0	0	0	-3	X
Turkmenistan	0	2	0	1	1	2	2	2	X
Ukraine	7	5	5	7	11	11	11	3	44.3
Uzbekistan	134	2	2	4	2	2	2	-131	-98.4
WESTERN HEMISPHERE	17 978	19 820	20 035	20 498	21 113	21 838	22 954	4 976	27.7
NAFTA	10 634	11 601	12 537	12 945	13 789	15 162	15 879	5 246	49.3
Canada	6 821	7 470	7 826	8 023	8 695	9 890	10 358	3 538	51.9
Mexico	3 813	4 131	4 711	4 922	5 094	5 272	5 521	1 708	44.8
Caribbean	460	546	460	323	328	336	355	-104	-22.7
Aruba	0	0	0	0	0	0	0	0	X
Bahamas	3	3	3	3	3	4	4	1	49.6
Barbados	1	1	1	1	1	1	1	0	9.1
Cayman Islands	0	0	0	0	0	1	1	1	X
Dominican Republic	370	452	372	241	244	254	260	-110	-29.8
Haiti	8	11	10	10	10	6	11	3	39.9
Jamaica	50	49	51	50	49	53	58	8	15.7
Leeward and Windward Islands	2	8	5	4	4	3	6	3	148.9
Netherlands Antilles	2	2	2	1	2	1	0	-2	X
Trinidad and Tobago	23	21	15	13	16	14	14	-9	-39.0
Turks and Caicos Islands	0	0	0	0	0	0	0	0	X

Note: Developing countries sum equals world minus developed countries sum.

X = Not applicable.

Table B-19. U.S. Total Agricultural Imports from Individual Countries, 1996–2002—*Continued*

(Millions of dollars; Census basis; general imports, Customs.)

Region and country	1996	1997	1998	1999	2000	2001	2002	1996–2002 change Value	1996–2002 change Percent
Central America	1 948	2 221	2 065	1 943	2 132	1 906	1 965	18	0.9
Belize	32	36	20	23	35	38	31	0	-1.5
Costa Rica	683	748	773	830	813	804	803	120	17.5
El Salvador	101	154	131	101	168	87	74	-26	-25.9
Guatemala	661	779	687	696	705	610	691	30	4.5
Honduras	277	296	302	134	249	231	233	-44	-15.9
Nicaragua	79	95	93	74	112	95	98	18	23.0
Panama	115	115	60	85	50	41	35	-80	-69.3
South America	4 937	5 451	4 973	5 287	4 863	4 432	4 753	-184	-3.7
Argentina	753	715	648	700	699	608	589	-164	-21.8
Bolivia	14	20	17	15	16	16	21	7	51.0
Brazil	1 402	1 559	1 330	1 491	1 200	1 048	1 215	-187	-13.4
Chile	754	747	781	911	1 027	1 027	1 154	400	53.1
Colombia	1 126	1 432	1 300	1 189	1 124	926	927	-199	-17.7
Ecuador	539	549	520	569	451	485	505	-34	-6.2
Guyana	10	10	8	6	15	6	6	-3	-35.1
Paraguay	11	13	14	16	15	15	16	5	47.5
Peru	158	276	228	222	196	206	246	88	55.8
Suriname	0	1	0	0	0	0	0	0	X
Uruguay	62	60	54	62	64	60	34	-28	-45.5
Venezuela	108	69	73	106	55	34	40	-69	-63.3
Other Western Hemisphere	0	0	1	1	0	1	1	1	X
Bermuda	0	0	1	1	0	0	1	0	X
Cuba	. . .	. . .	. . .	. . .	. . .	. . .	. . .	. . .	. . .
Falkland Islands	0	0	0	0	0	0	0	0	X
French Guiana	0	0	0	0	0	0	0	0	X
Greenland	0	0	0	0	0	0	0	0	X
Guadeloupe	0	0	0	0	0	1	0	0	X
Martinique	0	0	0	0	0	0	0	0	X
St. Pierre and Miquelon	0	0	0	0	0	0	0	0	X
ASIA	5 597	5 859	5 667	5 419	5 499	4 915	5 399	-198	-3.5
Japan	285	302	300	350	370	359	374	89	31.2
Korea, South	93	89	90	102	114	128	151	58	63.0
Taiwan	160	173	172	179	189	178	175	14	8.9
China	596	682	742	770	812	819	1 007	411	69.0
Hong Kong	98	89	77	78	86	77	93	-5	-4.8
Macao	0	0	1	1	1	0	1	0	X
ASEAN	3 595	3 670	3 326	2 849	2 871	2 413	2 665	-930	-25.9
Brunei	0	0	0	0	0	0	0	0	X
Burma	9	7	6	6	8	6	1	-8	-91.5
Cambodia	1	1	0	1	1	1	1	0	-20.7
Indonesia	1 539	1 553	1 340	1 047	997	833	932	-607	-39.4
Laos	0	0	0	0	0	0	0	0	X
Malaysia	379	405	367	370	353	262	309	-69	-18.3
Philippines	595	629	604	479	468	417	439	-156	-26.2
Singapore	48	60	78	102	61	45	56	8	16.1
Thailand	892	856	743	688	784	697	737	-155	-17.4
Vietnam	132	158	187	157	200	153	190	58	44.1
Middle East	130	130	154	169	169	193	195	65	49.7
Bahrain	0	0	0	0	0	0	0	0	X
Gaza Strip and West Bank	0	0	0	0	0	0	0	0	X
Iran	0	0	0	0	1	3	3	3	X
Iraq	. . .	. . .	. . .	. . .	. . .	. . .	. . .	. . .	. . .
Israel	96	101	119	125	122	133	141	46	47.5
Jordan	1	1	1	0	1	1	1	0	-5.5
Kuwait	0	0	0	0	0	0	0	0	X
Lebanon	24	19	25	13	27	35	15	-9	-36.9
Oman	0	0	0	0	1	1	1	1	X
Qatar	0	0	0	0	0	0	0	0	X
Saudi Arabia	1	1	0	1	2	1	1	0	52.4
Syria	5	4	4	23	11	12	9	4	67.8
United Arab Emirates	1	1	2	3	2	3	20	19	2 461.0
Yemen Arab Republic	3	3	2	3	3	4	3	0	18.4
Other Asia	639	724	805	922	887	747	738	99	15.5
Afghanistan	5	7	3	6	0	0	0	-5	X
Bangladesh	1	2	3	2	1	1	1	0	-4.3
India	550	651	730	852	823	685	672	122	22.1
Korea, North	. . .	. . .	. . .	. . .	. . .	. . .	. . .	. . .	. . .
Mongolia	2	2	0	0	0	0	1	-1	-41.2
Nepal	8	3	2	1	0	0	0	-7	X
Pakistan	43	26	29	31	32	34	31	-12	-28.0
South Asia NEC	0	0	0	0	0	0	0	0	X
Sri Lanka	30	33	39	30	30	27	33	2	7.0
AUSTRALIA AND OCEANIA	1 657	1 865	2 161	2 315	2 789	3 093	3 155	1 498	90.4
Australia	845	960	1 131	1 288	1 596	1 787	1 890	1 044	123.6
Australian Island Dependencies	0	0	0	0	0	0	0	0	X
Fiji	12	11	12	13	8	10	7	-4	-37.2
French Pacific Islands	1	5	3	4	3	7	8	8	1 291.5
New Zealand	771	859	964	954	1 157	1 255	1 206	436	56.5
New Zealand Island Dependencies	0	0	0	1	0	4	0	0	X
Other Pacific Islands NEC	1	0	2	1	1	1	2	1	194.1
Papua New Guinea	25	26	41	52	23	29	41	16	64.9
Southern Pacific Islands	1	0	4	2	1	1	0	-1	X
Trust Territory (former)	2	3	1	1	0	0	0	-2	X
Western Samoa	0	0	2	0	0	0	0	0	X

Note: Developing countries sum equals world minus developed countries sum.

. . . = Not available.
X = Not applicable.

Table B-19. U.S. Total Agricultural Imports from Individual Countries, 1996–2002—*Continued*

(Millions of dollars; Census basis; general imports, Customs.)

Region and country	1996	1997	1998	1999	2000	2001	2002	1996–2002 change Value	1996–2002 change Percent
AFRICA	899	899	935	862	865	837	948	50	5.5
Algeria	0	1	2	1	0	0	0	0	X
Angola	...	...	...	...	...	...	...	...	...
Benin	0	0	2	15	0	0	0	0	X
Botswana	0	0	0	0	0	0	0	0	X
Br. Indian Ocean Territory	0	0	0	0	0	0	0	0	X
Burkina Faso	4	0	0	2	2	0	0	-4	X
Burundi	1	14	6	6	8	2	1	0	30.0
Cameroon	21	20	10	10	11	6	19	-2	-11.7
Cape Verde	0	0	0	0	0	0	0	0	X
Central African Republic	0	1	2	3	2	1	0	0	X
Chad	0	0	1	0	0	0	0	0	X
Comoros	2	2	1	2	3	10	5	3	111.8
Congo	3	7	1	4	3	1	4	1	41.7
Dem. Rep. of the Congo (Zaire)	3	2	2	2	2	1	1	-1	-48.9
Djibouti	0	0	0	0	0	0	0	0	X
Egypt	26	15	23	27	41	26	44	18	69.1
Equatorial Guinea	...	...	...	...	...	0	0	0	...
Eritrea	0	0	0	0	0	0	0	0	X
Ethiopia	24	66	44	28	26	26	22	-2	-8.1
French Indian Ocean Areas	0	0	0	0	0	0	0	0	X
Gabon	1	0	0	1	0	1	1	-1	-64.1
Gambia	0	0	0	0	0	0	0	0	X
Ghana	32	12	26	43	71	58	28	-3	-10.1
Guinea	2	6	4	1	0	3	1	-1	-33.1
Guinea-Bissau	0	0	0	0	0	0	0	0	X
Heard Island and McDonald Islands	0	0	0	0	0	0	0	0	X
Ivory Coast	310	238	387	297	261	227	281	-29	-9.5
Kenya	55	55	48	35	34	39	37	-18	-33.2
Kiribati (Gilbert Islands)	...	...	...	...	...	...	...	...	...
Lesotho	...	...	...	...	...	...	...	...	...
Liberia	0	2	25	29	43	41	43	43	X
Libya	...	...	...	...	...	...	...	...	...
Madagascar	26	40	41	28	38	85	122	96	364.7
Malawi	71	82	60	71	48	67	59	-12	-16.8
Mali	1	0	0	3	0	0	0	-1	X
Mauritania	0	0	0	0	0	0	0	0	X
Mauritius	12	14	10	3	5	14	6	-6	-50.5
Morocco	50	52	42	53	40	37	54	4	7.6
Mozambique	25	28	23	8	24	7	7	-19	-74.1
Namibia	0	0	1	0	0	0	0	0	X
Niger	0	0	0	0	0	0	0	0	X
Nigeria	34	24	13	8	4	8	13	-21	-62.5
Republic of South Africa	109	103	111	106	133	108	137	28	25.6
Sao Tome and Principe	0	0	0	0	0	0	0	0	X
Senegal	0	0	0	0	0	7	0	0	X
Seychelles	0	0	0	0	0	0	0	0	X
Sierra Leone	0	0	0	0	0	0	0	0	X
Somalia	0	0	0	0	0	0	0	0	X
St. Helena	0	0	0	0	0	0	0	0	X
Sudan	7	4	0	0	0	0	0	-7	X
Swaziland	8	23	3	8	13	7	7	-1	-9.9
Tanzania	4	5	6	9	8	7	6	2	40.4
Togo	1	0	1	2	1	1	1	0	-6.4
Tunisia	0	3	4	5	11	10	4	3	X
Uganda	16	37	12	17	16	12	11	-5	-29.8
Western Sahara	0	0	0	0	0	0	0	0	X
Zambia	0	0	1	2	1	1	1	0	X
Zimbabwe (Rhodesia)	49	40	21	32	14	23	34	-15	-31.1
OTHER	0	0	0	0	0	0	0	0	X
International Organizations	0	0	0	0	0	0	0	0	X
Unidentified Countries	0	0	0	0	0	0	0	0	X
MISCELLANEOUS [1]	7	3	2	2	2	4	2	-5	-72.8
ADDENDUM									
Developed Countries	16 115	17 397	18 382	19 368	20 582	21 941	23 197	7 083	44.0
Developing Countries	17 690	18 984	18 723	18 630	18 605	17 600	18 843	1 153	6.5
APEC (20 countries)	18 039	19 497	20 409	20 710	22 248	23 450	24 897	6 858	38.0

Note: Developing countries sum equals world minus developed countries sum.

[1]Includes transshipments, carryover, and timing adjustments, revisions not accounted for elsewhere, and roundoff.
. . . = Not available.
X = Not applicable.

Table B-20. U.S. Total Agricultural Trade Balances with Individual Countries, 1996–2002

(Millions of dollars; Census basis; foreign and domestic exports, f.a.s.; general imports, Customs.)

Region and country	1996	1997	1998	1999	2000	2001	2002	1996–2002 change Value	1996–2002 change Percent
WORLD	27 902	22 292	16 150	11 637	14 321	15 751	12 691	-15 211	-54.5
EUROPE	4 661	4 272	2 068	-290	-253	260	-1 086	-5 747	-123.3
Western Europe	2 932	2 802	965	-1 072	-1 109	-734	-1 652	-4 584	-156.3
European Union (EU-15)	2 443	1 960	514	-1 578	-1 811	-1 475	-2 449	-4 891	-200.2
Austria	-11	-18	-18	-30	-52	-101	-100	-88	768.8
Belgium	579	500	454	381	390	442	368	-211	-36.5
Denmark	-173	-112	-193	-256	-322	-334	-348	-175	101.0
Finland	72	64	3	16	5	-24	-45	-116	-162.4
France	-584	-692	-870	-1 289	-1 180	-962	-1 115	-531	91.0
Germany	704	549	398	124	103	181	213	-490	-69.7
Greece	-19	13	-6	-114	-54	-28	-62	-43	220.6
Ireland	-98	-57	-64	-105	-39	-50	-78	20	-20.7
Italy	-526	-627	-701	-958	-990	-995	-1 248	-722	137.3
Luxembourg	0	-2	3	4	5	1	13	14	X
Netherlands	878	692	213	135	-114	-236	-573	-1 452	-165.3
Portugal	225	177	89	64	58	86	129	-96	-42.6
Spain	547	581	426	-54	-91	-22	-81	-627	-114.8
Sweden	56	20	21	12	22	28	-3	-59	-105.1
United Kingdom	794	870	757	492	448	538	479	-315	-39.6
Non-EU Western Europe	490	842	451	506	702	741	797	307	62.8
Bosnia-Herzegovina	30	31	23	7	12	19	9	-21	-69.4
Croatia	6	17	12	-6	-9	-5	-3	-9	-141.1
Cyprus	36	36	9	19	16	20	20	-16	-43.9
Gibraltar	0	0	0	1	0	0	0	0	X
Iceland	16	15	18	29	17	18	13	-4	-21.9
Liechtenstein	-2	0	-1	-1	0	-1	0	2	X
Macedonia	-23	-15	-15	-21	13	-8	-14	9	-39.7
Malta and Gozo	20	8	7	11	10	9	12	-7	-37.6
Norway	99	50	39	25	14	23	13	-87	-87.4
Other Non-EU Western Europe	12	4	4	3	-2	4	4	-8	-69.3
Serbia and Montenegro	12	0	10	12	15	14	7	-4	-38.2
Slovenia	3	19	13	5	0	-3	1	-2	-60.7
Switzerland	83	358	65	292	205	400	332	249	299.1
Turkey	196	318	268	130	412	250	402	206	104.7
Eastern Europe	1 729	1 470	1 103	782	857	994	566	-1 163	-67.3
Albania	4	-6	2	5	3	3	5	1	15.5
Baltic States	121	148	150	256	85	26	7	-114	-94.3
Estonia	27	26	57	132	43	11	7	-20	-74.7
Latvia	91	119	109	145	76	38	28	-63	-68.9
Lithuania	3	4	-17	-21	-34	-23	-28	-32	-990.9
Bulgaria	10	-14	-23	-36	-21	-16	-22	-32	-328.1
Czech Republic	2	4	-5	-8	-10	-16	-17	-19	-834.6
Hungary	-59	-35	-34	-15	-25	-16	-16	43	-72.3
Poland	151	50	40	-20	-47	-34	-84	-236	-155.7
Romania	47	15	25	14	16	22	39	-8	-16.8
Slovakia	-2	0	-1	-1	-1	-2	-2	0	7.9
Newly Independent States (NIS)	1 454	1 308	949	589	857	1 026	657	-798	-54.8
Armenia	42	21	23	10	8	7	7	-35	-84.0
Azerbaijan	5	4	8	10	0	-1	7	2	47.0
Belarus	10	1	0	0	0	0	-1	-10	-105.9
Georgia	47	29	60	29	45	35	28	-19	-40.0
Kazakhstan	1	0	11	2	0	7	8	7	1 318.5
Kyrgyzstan	17	11	9	6	11	4	4	-12	-73.7
Moldova	9	0	2	1	-1	19	14	5	50.9
Russia	1 319	1 205	816	499	786	904	536	-783	-59.3
Tajikistan	8	15	10	9	10	20	10	2	21.4
Turkmenistan	12	-2	0	2	2	0	0	-12	X
Ukraine	37	24	11	16	-4	8	3	-34	-92.2
Uzbekistan	-52	-2	-2	2	-1	25	40	93	-177.4
WESTERN HEMISPHERE	-384	-1 533	-490	-2 252	-1 552	-852	-1 221	-837	218.2
NAFTA	1 873	1 385	1 678	764	1 480	1 413	1 201	-672	-35.9
Canada	217	289	180	1	-175	-880	-770	-987	-455.7
Mexico	1 656	1 096	1 498	764	1 655	2 293	1 971	315	19.0
Caribbean	898	915	956	1 127	1 037	1 043	1 022	124	13.8
Aruba	29	29	29	29	29	30	29	0	-0.2
Bahamas	134	113	108	114	127	129	126	-8	-5.7
Barbados	51	49	42	45	41	50	40	-11	-21.6
Cayman Islands	20	35	43	36	38	33	28	8	42.6
Dominican Republic	47	88	134	322	271	266	283	236	496.8
Haiti	183	190	203	207	171	171	161	-22	-11.9
Jamaica	157	156	143	138	128	133	133	-24	-15.3
Leeward and Windward Islands	79	70	70	62	64	65	55	-24	-30.4
Netherlands Antilles	84	83	83	76	70	60	57	-27	-31.7
Trinidad and Tobago	111	97	95	90	92	102	106	-5	-4.4
Turks and Caicos Islands	4	5	6	7	7	5	4	0	-9.2

Note: Developing countries sum equals world minus developed countries sum.

X = Not applicable.

Table B-20. U.S. Total Agricultural Trade Balances with Individual Countries, 1996–2002—*Continued*

(Millions of dollars; Census basis; foreign and domestic exports, f.a.s.; general imports, Customs.)

Region and country	1996	1997	1998	1999	2000	2001	2002	1996–2002 change Value	1996–2002 change Percent
Central America	-893	-1 119	-786	-793	-1 005	-664	-702	191	-21.3
Belize	-16	-19	-3	-7	-14	-17	-12	4	-26.9
Costa Rica	-462	-556	-567	-646	-626	-602	-575	-113	24.5
El Salvador	92	77	114	100	48	153	138	47	50.8
Guatemala	-385	-515	-373	-418	-446	-312	-348	37	-9.6
Honduras	-143	-130	-112	61	-52	-31	-45	99	-68.9
Nicaragua	-14	-27	-17	10	-37	8	-13	2	-10.4
Panama	36	51	172	107	122	137	151	116	323.5
South America	-2 341	-2 790	-2 413	-3 420	-3 132	-2 706	-2 938	-597	25.5
Argentina	-589	-361	-442	-550	-543	-490	-536	53	-9.0
Bolivia	26	11	12	5	-3	-1	-2	-28	-105.9
Brazil	-816	-1 017	-842	-1 272	-928	-819	-877	-62	7.6
Chile	-623	-619	-643	-758	-911	-926	-1 041	-418	67.0
Colombia	-503	-891	-721	-751	-703	-472	-403	100	-19.9
Ecuador	-380	-358	-339	-462	-349	-375	-360	20	-5.3
Guyana	19	18	14	17	8	17	16	-3	-16.8
Paraguay	23	18	-4	-6	-5	-11	-13	-35	-155.8
Peru	152	-81	130	75	-25	6	-31	-183	-120.3
Suriname	26	24	23	17	16	19	17	-9	-33.3
Uruguay	-45	-45	-41	-49	-47	-34	-15	30	-66.3
Venezuela	369	508	441	315	355	380	307	-62	-16.8
Other Western Hemisphere	79	77	75	70	67	62	196	117	148.4
Bermuda	69	67	67	61	60	52	51	-18	-26.0
Cuba	0	0	0	0	0	4	139	139	X
Falkland Islands	0	0	0	0	0	0	0	0	X
French Guiana	1	1	1	1	1	0	1	0	-38.9
Greenland	0	0	0	0	0	0	2	2	X
Guadeloupe	5	5	4	6	4	3	2	-3	-62.6
Martinique	4	3	3	3	2	2	1	-2	-62.1
St. Pierre and Miquelon	0	1	0	0	0	0	0	0	X
ASIA	22 338	19 145	14 692	14 384	16 658	17 420	16 094	-6 244	-28.0
Japan	11 481	10 315	8 892	8 658	9 225	8 752	8 163	-3 319	-28.9
Korea, South	3 764	2 777	2 139	2 355	2 538	2 492	2 551	-1 213	-32.2
Taiwan	2 809	2 450	1 631	1 783	1 855	1 849	1 793	-1 016	-36.2
China	1 485	922	598	86	933	1 145	982	-503	-33.9
Hong Kong	1 403	1 636	1 438	1 144	1 213	1 162	1 015	-388	-27.6
Macao	0	1	1	1	1	1	. . .	0	X
ASEAN	-318	-665	-1 216	-541	-161	589	262	580	-182.4
Brunei	1	2	1	1	2	2	4	2	216.7
Burma	-7	-6	-6	-5	-7	-4	1	8	-113.2
Cambodia	0	1	0	1	11	8	3	3	X
Indonesia	-684	-777	-884	-506	-312	84	-117	568	-83.0
Laos	0	0	0	0	0	0	1	1	X
Malaysia	237	78	-84	-55	-52	126	64	-173	-73.1
Philippines	304	247	113	309	443	379	339	35	11.4
Singapore	239	219	133	115	179	188	202	-37	-15.4
Thailand	-310	-313	-324	-276	-278	-121	-123	187	-60.2
Vietnam	-99	-117	-166	-125	-147	-73	-112	-14	14.1
Middle East	1 698	1 669	1 386	1 382	1 513	1 465	1 403	-295	-17.4
Bahrain	19	9	22	27	13	30	29	10	53.7
Gaza Strip and West Bank	0	0	0	0	0	0	0	0	X
Iran	0	0	0	48	14	2	8	8	X
Iraq	3	82	96	9	8	8	0	-3	X
Israel	522	437	248	300	363	296	325	-197	-37.7
Jordan	150	142	87	89	92	125	93	-57	-38.2
Kuwait	42	46	50	57	49	59	55	13	30.7
Lebanon	111	80	45	64	55	46	51	-60	-54.3
Oman	14	12	18	18	12	16	15	1	7.7
Qatar	6	8	10	10	9	10	15	9	138.5
Saudi Arabia	553	620	504	448	480	430	342	-211	-38.1
Syria	45	59	44	34	77	68	105	60	133.7
United Arab Emirates	122	112	186	187	240	283	264	141	115.7
Yemen Arab Republic	112	62	74	92	103	93	102	-10	-8.8
Other Asia	16	40	-177	-483	-459	-36	-74	-90	-561.6
Afghanistan	4	-5	-2	-1	5	4	0	-4	X
Bangladesh	87	119	157	121	85	139	131	44	50.7
India	-437	-496	-529	-695	-607	-330	-394	43	-9.9
Korea, North	0	2	4	7	2	0	24	24	X
Mongolia	-1	0	5	2	5	0	-1	1	-36.5
Nepal	-7	-3	-1	0	1	2	3	9	-140.7
Pakistan	309	415	165	58	25	102	166	-144	-46.5
South Asia NEC	0	0	0	0	0	0	0	0	X
Sri Lanka	61	7	23	26	26	47	-2	-63	-103.0
AUSTRALIA AND OCEANIA	-1 162	-1 306	-1 605	-1 818	-2 286	-2 610	-2 636	-1 474	126.9
Australia	-519	-602	-791	-960	-1 270	-1 491	-1 546	-1 027	198.0
Australian Island Dependencies	0	1	0	0	0	0	0	0	X
Fiji	-7	-6	-6	-9	-5	-6	-6	1	-16.7
French Pacific Islands	35	33	34	28	31	26	24	-12	-33.3
New Zealand	-678	-742	-839	-850	-1 057	-1 141	-1 098	-420	61.8
New Zealand Island Dependencies	0	0	5	0	1	-3	0	0	X
Other Pacific Islands NEC	2	2	5	0	1	2	1	0	0	-2	X
Papua New Guinea	-21	-20	-36	-49	-22	-28	-38	-17	81.9
Southern Pacific Islands	-1	0	-4	-2	0	1	2	3	-367.7
Trust Territory (former)	22	26	30	20	28	26	25	4	16.4
Western Samoa	5	4	2	4	4	4	. . .	-5	X

Note: Developing countries sum equals world minus developed countries sum.

. . . = Not available.
X = Not applicable.

Table B-20. U.S. Total Agricultural Trade Balances with Individual Countries, 1996–2002—*Continued*

(Millions of dollars; Census basis; foreign and domestic exports, f.a.s.; general imports, Customs.)

Region and country	1996	1997	1998	1999	2000	2001	2002	1996–2002 change Value	1996–2002 change Percent
AFRICA	1 795	1 349	1 152	1 226	1 440	1 265	1 343	-452	-25.2
Algeria	294	315	255	221	258	230	270	-24	-8.1
Angola	28	29	28	23	55	28	46	18	63.9
Benin	2	5	5	-12	4	4	5	3	175.0
Botswana	1	3	1	1	1	1	0	-1	X
Br. Indian Ocean Territory	0	0	0	0	0	0	0	0	X
Burkina Faso	0	7	9	3	3	1	7	8	X
Burundi	-1	-14	-3	-5	-8	0	-1	0	26.0
Cameroon	-18	-7	-3	-4	-6	-4	-15	3	-18.1
Cape Verde	5	6	6	3	2	1	2	-3	-61.7
Central African Republic	0	-1	-2	-2	-2	-1	1	2	X
Chad	2	2	-1	1	3	2	2	0	-10.5
Comoros	-2	-2	-1	-2	-3	-10	-5	-3	111.8
Congo	4	-2	6	5	13	13	1	-4	-84.9
Dem. Rep. of the Congo (Zaire)	22	12	8	1	0	5	5	-16	-75.9
Djibouti	2	2	5	13	2	2	41	38	1 706.7
Egypt	1 231	951	882	952	1 008	1 000	817	-414	-33.6
Equatorial Guinea	0	0	0	1	0	1	1	1	X
Eritrea	8	4	14	0	12	14	23	15	201.4
Ethiopia	12	-48	-15	2	88	1	-12	-23	-199.8
French Indian Ocean Areas	0	0	1	0	0	0	0	0	X
Gabon	-1	0	1	1	3	3	4	5	-474.0
Gambia	2	2	2	2	3	3	3	2	98.8
Ghana	33	39	21	9	-33	-17	19	-13	-40.7
Guinea	10	4	1	7	6	4	8	-2	-23.3
Guinea-Bissau	0	1	0	1	0	0	1	1	X
Heard Island and McDonald Islands	0	0	0	0	0	0	0	0	X
Ivory Coast	-290	-219	-380	-277	-249	-215	-268	22	-7.5
Kenya	-45	-24	13	-7	-6	-20	6	51	-114.1
Kiribati (Gilbert Islands)	0	0	1	0	0	0	0	0	X
Lesotho	2	1	1	0	0	0	1	-1	-68.6
Liberia	37	16	-12	-13	-31	-32	-34	-71	-192.9
Libya	0	0	0	0	18	9	18	18	X
Madagascar	-25	-36	-36	-27	-33	-80	-114	-90	366.6
Malawi	-70	-82	-60	-71	-46	-66	-45	25	-35.4
Mali	-1	3	1	-2	0	1	1	2	-261.5
Mauritania	1	3	2	1	2	2	1	1	108.8
Mauritius	-12	-13	-10	-3	-4	-14	-6	6	-52.7
Morocco	183	111	80	101	126	54	70	-113	-61.8
Mozambique	-15	-2	5	10	7	9	60	75	-488.5
Namibia	5	1	-1	0	2	5	5	1	16.3
Niger	1	2	2	0	2	5	9	8	1 244.6
Nigeria	143	92	138	164	174	235	288	145	101.6
Republic of South Africa	189	120	89	75	3	-8	13	-176	-93.3
Sao Tome and Principe	0	0	0	0	0	0	0	0	X
Senegal	7	7	16	4	6	0	7	0	-2.8
Seychelles	1	0	0	0	0	0	0	0	X
Sierra Leone	15	9	15	5	5	14	13	-2	-13.5
Somalia	3	1	1	2	2	3	2	-1	-44.8
St. Helena	0	0	0	0	0	0	0	0	X
Sudan	9	7	6	8	17	16	10	1	9.4
Swaziland	-8	-22	-2	-8	-12	-6	-6	2	-20.5
Tanzania	0	8	2	8	-4	3	5	5	X
Togo	4	3	0	1	0	0	2	-2	-42.0
Tunisia	90	114	78	66	74	94	92	3	2.8
Uganda	-12	-20	-1	-10	-10	-3	-7	5	-41.7
Western Sahara	0	0	0	0	0	0	0	0	X
Zambia	0	0	0	-1	0	0	13	13	X
Zimbabwe (Rhodesia)	-48	-39	-17	-23	-10	-23	-17	31	-64.3
OTHER	0	0	0	0	0	0	0	0	X
International Organizations	0	0	0	0	0	0	0	0	X
Unidentified Countries	0	0	0	0	0	0	0	0	X
MISCELLANEOUS [1]	653	364	333	387	314	267	197	-457	-69.9
ADDENDUM									
Developed Countries	13 622	12 182	8 496	5 850	5 617	4 497	3 110	-10 512	-77.2
Developing Countries	14 281	10 110	7 655	5 786	8 704	11 253	9 581	-4 699	-32.9
APEC (20 countries)	22 817	18 743	14 686	12 714	14 893	14 639	. . .	X	X

Note: Developing countries sum equals world minus developed countries sum.

[1] Includes transshipments, carryover, and timing adjustments, revisions not accounted for elsewhere, and roundoff.
. . . = Not available.
X = Not applicable.

Table B-21. Top 30 Purchasers and Suppliers of U.S. Agricultural Products, 1997–2003

(Millions of dollars; top 30 based on 2003 value; Census basis; foreign and domestic exports, f.a.s.; general imports, Customs.)

Country	1997	1998	1999	2000	2001	2002	2003	Percent change, 1997–2003
TOTAL OF TOP 30 PURCHASERS (EXPORTS)	49 950	45 341	42 205	46 418	47 819	46 982	53 362	6.8
Canada	7 759	8 006	8 024	8 520	9 010	9 588	10 421	34.3
Japan	10 617	9 192	9 008	9 595	9 111	8 537	9 113	-14.2
Mexico	5 227	6 209	5 686	6 749	7 565	7 492	8 067	54.3
China	1 604	1 340	856	1 744	1 964	1 989	4 986	210.8
South Korea	2 866	2 229	2 457	2 652	2 621	2 702	2 914	1.7
Taiwan	2 622	1 804	1 962	2 043	2 028	1 967	2 048	-21.9
Netherlands	1 953	1 565	1 548	1 451	1 372	1 183	1 144	-41.4
Hong Kong	1 726	1 515	1 222	1 300	1 239	1 109	1 131	-34.5
United Kingdom	1 328	1 263	1 095	1 061	1 097	1 041	1 073	-19.2
Germany	1 334	1 233	928	915	944	993	1 048	-21.5
Egypt	966	904	980	1 049	1 025	861	1 002	3.7
Indonesia	776	456	541	685	917	815	1 000	28.9
Turkey	743	666	489	669	579	676	926	24.6
Spain	1 146	1 054	683	614	648	678	855	-25.4
Thailand	543	418	412	506	576	614	689	26.8
Belgium	672	644	551	558	628	558	639	-4.9
Philippines	877	717	788	911	796	778	631	-28.0
Australia	358	339	327	326	296	344	618	72.7
Russia	1 235	843	517	812	919	553	580	-53.1
Colombia	542	579	438	422	454	524	513	-5.2
Italy	762	688	502	563	571	546	495	-35.0
Dominican Republic	540	507	563	515	520	543	451	-16.5
France	575	498	367	333	395	403	437	-24.1
Israel	538	367	425	484	429	467	427	-20.6
Brazil	542	488	219	272	229	338	393	-27.4
Malaysia	483	283	315	301	388	373	382	-21.0
Venezuela	577	514	421	411	414	347	375	-35.0
Guatemala	264	314	278	260	298	343	351	32.7
Saudi Arabia	621	505	449	481	431	343	333	-46.4
India	155	202	157	216	356	278	322	107.7
TOTAL OF TOP 30 SUPPLIERS (IMPORTS)	32 855	33 717	34 657	35 698	36 117	38 357	43 198	31.5
Canada	7 470	7 826	8 023	8 695	9 890	10 358	10 317	38.1
Mexico	4 131	4 711	4 922	5 094	5 272	5 521	6 316	52.9
Australia	960	1 131	1 288	1 596	1 787	1 890	2 106	119.5
Italy	1 388	1 389	1 459	1 553	1 566	1 794	2 092	50.7
Netherlands	1 260	1 352	1 412	1 565	1 608	1 756	1 884	49.5
France	1 267	1 368	1 656	1 513	1 357	1 518	1 797	41.8
Brazil	1 559	1 330	1 491	1 200	1 048	1 215	1 557	-0.1
New Zealand	859	964	954	1 157	1 255	1 206	1 337	55.7
China	682	742	770	812	819	1 007	1 284	88.4
Indonesia	1 553	1 340	1 047	997	833	932	1 232	-20.7
Ireland	293	340	309	327	293	293	1 226	319.0
Chile	747	781	911	1 027	1 027	1 154	1 215	62.6
Colombia	1 432	1 300	1 189	1 124	926	927	1 031	-28.0
Thailand	856	743	688	784	697	737	917	7.1
Spain	565	628	737	705	670	758	872	54.4
Germany	786	835	804	812	762	780	870	10.8
Costa Rica	748	773	830	813	804	803	865	15.7
Guatemala	779	687	696	705	610	691	757	-2.8
India	651	730	852	823	685	672	687	5.7
Argentina	715	648	700	699	608	589	560	-21.7
Ecuador	549	520	569	451	485	505	558	1.6
United Kingdom	458	506	603	613	559	562	555	21.1
Denmark	420	417	428	483	502	504	553	31.8
Philippines	629	604	479	468	417	439	486	-22.8
Malaysia	405	367	370	353	262	309	445	9.7
Ivory Coast	238	387	297	261	227	281	412	73.0
Japan	302	300	350	370	359	374	373	23.6
Turkey	425	399	359	257	329	274	337	-20.8
Dominican Republic	452	372	241	244	254	260	280	-38.0
Peru	276	228	222	196	206	246	277	0.2

Table B-22. U.S. Manufactures Trade, 1998–2003

(Millions of dollars; top 10 based on 2003 value; Census basis; foreign and domestic exports, f.a.s.; general imports, Customs.)

SITC product	1998	1999	2000	2001	2002	2003	1998–2003 change	
							Value	Percent
TOTAL OF TOP 10 EXPORTS	409 636	422 690	473 256	436 477	407 507	412 733	3 097	0.8
77 – Electrical machinery, apparatus, and appliances	76 872	88 655	110 095	88 557	82 657	85 910	9 038	11.8
78 – Motor vehicles	56 469	56 640	59 992	56 703	60 329	63 130	6 661	11.8
79 – Transport equipment	55 724	52 742	43 399	48 025	46 148	42 510	-13 214	-23.7
75 – Office machines and a.d.p. equipment	47 759	48 604	57 595	49 404	39 744	41 054	-6 706	-14.0
89 – Miscellaneous manufactured articles	31 798	32 206	35 538	35 431	33 226	34 621	2 822	8.9
71 – Power generating machinery	29 963	32 380	34 345	36 181	34 381	33 642	3 680	12.3
74 – General industrial machinery	30 999	30 729	34 455	33 748	31 839	32 183	1 184	3.8
87 – Professional scientific instruments	25 386	26 905	32 326	31 274	29 210	30 977	5 591	22.0
72 – Machinery specialized	28 688	26 120	32 529	27 491	25 091	25 000	-3 688	-12.9
76 – Telecommunications equipment	25 978	27 709	32 980	29 664	24 882	23 706	-2 272	-8.7
TOTAL OF TOP 10 IMPORTS	545 802	628 649	768 423	701 881	719 152	773 076	227 275	41.6
78 – Motor vehicles	121 310	146 202	161 682	157 409	168 173	172 578	51 268	42.3
33 – Petroleum, petroleum products	49 370	65 887	117 174	100 668	101 152	129 600	80 230	162.5
77 – Electrical machinery, apparatus, and appliances	79 366	88 592	108 813	84 710	81 288	82 545	3 178	4.0
75 – Office machines and a.d.p. equipment	76 846	84 443	92 165	75 861	76 970	80 826	3 981	5.2
76 – Telecommunications equipment	42 462	50 959	70 487	62 821	66 268	71 137	28 674	67.5
84 – Articles of apparel and clothing	53 743	56 413	64 296	63 862	63 810	68 162	14 419	26.8
89 – Miscellaneous manufactured articles	47 470	51 313	56 718	57 538	62 044	64 401	16 931	35.7
74 – General industrial machinery	28 802	31 447	34 709	33 258	35 201	38 467	9 665	33.6
51 – Organic chemicals	18 300	21 860	28 563	29 626	30 213	32 876	14 575	79.6
71 – Power generating machinery	28 132	31 533	33 815	36 127	34 032	32 485	4 353	15.5
TOTAL OF TOP 10 SURPLUSES	72 096	66 164	64 166	65 633	61 871	58 181	-13 915	-19.3
79 – Transport equipment	39 606	34 465	22 346	24 481	25 890	22 995	-16 610	-41.9
57 – Plastics in primary form	6 476	6 330	7 439	7 189	7 472	7 761	1 285	19.9
87 – Professional scientific instruments	9 881	9 264	10 312	9 874	8 301	7 316	-2 565	-26.0
59 – Chemical materials	6 192	6 261	6 943	6 857	6 556	6 558	366	5.9
72 – Machinery specialized	5 718	4 488	9 796	7 938	6 721	4 271	-1 447	-25.3
77 – Electrical machinery, apparatus, and appliances	-2 495	63	1 282	3 847	1 368	3 365	5 860	-234.9
53 – Dyeing, tanning, and coloring materials	1 058	1 055	1 529	1 400	1 619	1 802	744	70.3
58 – Plastics in nonprimary form	1 834	1 529	1 982	1 715	1 656	1 709	-125	-6.8
55 – Essential oils	1 995	1 862	2 005	2 278	1 940	1 245	-749	-37.6
71 – Power generating machinery	1 831	847	531	53	349	1 157	-674	-36.8
TOTAL OF TOP 10 DEFICITS	-208 621	-262 715	-304 730	-296 576	-341 853	-364 535	-155 914	74.7
78 – Motor vehicles	-64 842	-89 561	-101 690	-100 705	-107 844	-109 448	-44 606	68.8
84 – Articles of apparel and clothing	-44 950	-48 145	-55 668	-56 849	-57 778	-62 625	-17 675	39.3
76 – Telecommunications equipment	-16 484	-23 250	-37 507	-33 157	-41 386	-47 430	-30 946	187.7
75 – Office machines and a.d.p. equipment	-29 086	-35 839	-34 570	-26 458	-37 226	-39 773	-10 686	36.7
89 – Miscellaneous manufactured articles	-15 672	-19 107	-21 180	-22 107	-28 818	-29 780	-14 108	90.0
82 – Furniture and bedding	-8 664	-11 478	-13 725	-13 892	-17 217	-20 090	-11 426	131.9
66 – Nonmetallic mineral	-11 551	-13 706	-15 199	-13 096	-14 956	-15 748	-4 197	36.3
85 – Footwear	-13 029	-13 229	-13 987	-14 429	-14 683	-14 909	-1 880	14.4
51 – Organic chemicals	-3 119	-6 106	-9 632	-12 679	-13 373	-12 425	-9 305	298.3
54 – Medicinal and pharmaceutical products	-1 224	-2 295	-1 572	-3 203	-8 570	-12 307	-11 083	905.1

Table B-23. U.S. Total Exports by 2-Digit SITC Product Groups, 1998–2003

(Millions of dollars; Census basis; foreign and domestic exports, f.a.s.; general imports, Customs.)

SITC product	1998	1999	2000	2001	2002	2003	1998–2003 change Value	1998–2003 change Percent
TOTAL	680 474	692 821	780 419	731 026	693 257	723 743	43 269	6.4
00–49 Non-manufacturing	85 256	81 040	90 895	89 141	86 699	97 667	12 412	14.6
50–99 Manufacturing	595 219	611 781	689 524	641 885	606 558	626 076	30 857	5.2
00 – Live animals	683	658	864	898	642	792	109	15.9
01 – Meat and meat preparations	6 431	6 372	7 549	7 379	6 477	7 379	949	14.8
02 – Dairy products and birds' eggs ...	808	747	822	871	764	822	14	1.7
03 – Fish (except marine mammals)	2 272	2 858	2 956	3 207	3 135	3 283	1 011	44.5
04 – Cereals and cereal preparation ...	11 491	11 652	11 060	11 094	11 856	12 376	886	7.7
05 – Vegetables and fruit	7 942	7 779	8 165	8 111	8 365	9 001	1 060	13.3
06 – Sugars, sugar preparations	668	638	694	733	648	716	48	7.1
07 – Coffee, tea, cocoa	1 047	1 012	1 071	1 218	1 141	1 276	229	21.8
08 – Feeding stuff for animals	4 305	3 635	4 088	4 478	4 114	4 159	-146	-3.4
09 – Miscellaneous edible	2 671	2 886	2 992	3 186	3 154	3 471	800	29.9
11 – Beverages	1 524	1 566	1 551	1 605	1 638	1 864	340	22.3
12 – Tobacco and tobacco manufactures	6 309	5 198	5 269	4 040	3 033	2 924	-3 386	-53.7
21 – Hides, skins, and furskins	1 279	1 156	1 667	1 998	1 758	1 811	532	41.6
22 – Oil seeds and oleaginous fruits ...	5 441	5 037	5 818	5 930	6 197	8 427	2 986	54.9
23 – Crude rubber	1 173	1 186	1 454	1 436	1 423	1 616	443	37.8
24 – Cork and wood	4 133	4 299	4 415	3 628	3 440	3 480	-653	-15.8
25 – Pulp and waste paper	3 485	3 616	4 714	3 769	3 940	4 216	732	21.0
26 – Textile fibers	3 942	2 232	3 248	3 368	3 335	4 729	788	20.0
27 – Crude fertilizers	1 676	1 614	1 790	1 718	1 571	1 634	-42	-2.5
28 – Metalliferous ores	3 627	3 558	4 357	4 541	4 682	5 749	2 122	58.5
29 – Crude animal and vegetable materials	1 504	1 479	1 568	1 692	1 782	1 882	378	25.1
32 – Coal, coke, and briquettes	3 192	2 261	2 174	1 947	1 676	1 629	-1 563	-49.0
33 – Petroleum, petroleum products ...	6 138	6 760	9 466	8 544	8 018	9 634	3 496	57.0
34 – Gas, natural and manufactured ...	555	699	1 302	1 116	1 692	2 068	1 513	272.5
35 – Electric current	185	206	398	1 258	304	716	531	287.7
41 – Animal oils and fats	686	516	385	365	524	548	-138	-20.1
42 – Fixed vegetable fats and oils	1 830	1 184	826	801	1 077	1 168	-662	-36.2
43 – Animal or vegetable fats and oils, processed	259	234	229	213	314	296	37	14.3
51 – Organic chemicals	15 181	15 754	18 931	16 946	16 839	20 451	5 270	34.7
52 – Inorganic chemicals	4 842	4 701	5 514	5 730	5 612	5 756	914	18.9
53 – Dyeing, tanning, and coloring materials	3 528	3 687	4 205	3 879	3 976	4 282	755	21.4
54 – Medicinal and pharmaceutical products	9 661	11 247	13 122	15 421	16 150	19 209	9 548	98.8
55 – Essential oils	4 888	5 013	5 546	6 031	6 135	6 857	1 969	40.3
56 – Fertilizers	3 282	3 117	2 485	2 247	2 262	2 552	-730	-22.3
57 – Plastics in primary form	11 560	11 771	13 873	13 511	13 896	15 128	3 568	30.9
58 – Plastics in nonprimary form	5 315	5 364	6 191	5 772	5 993	6 504	1 189	22.4
59 – Chemical materials	11 014	11 333	12 675	12 784	12 730	13 416	2 401	21.8
61 – Leather, leather manufactures	1 026	1 042	1 121	1 011	969	1 017	-9	-0.8
62 – Rubber manufactures	4 902	4 901	5 383	5 085	4 941	4 913	10	0.2
63 – Cork and wood manufactures	1 801	1 857	1 997	1 692	1 702	1 751	-49	-2.7
64 – Paper, paperboard	10 082	10 100	11 118	10 430	9 895	10 205	123	1.2
65 – Textile yarn, fabrics	9 205	9 504	10 952	10 473	10 665	10 893	1 689	18.3
66 – Nonmetallic mineral	7 968	8 744	10 515	10 350	10 353	11 199	3 231	40.5
67 – Iron and steel	6 026	5 450	6 319	5 970	5 713	6 775	748	12.4
68 – Nonferrous metals	7 575	6 910	8 272	7 410	6 746	6 772	-802	-10.6
69 – Manufactures of metals	13 221	13 650	16 312	14 237	14 074	14 172	951	7.2
71 – Power generating machinery	29 963	32 380	34 345	36 181	34 381	33 642	3 680	12.3
72 – Machinery specialized	28 688	26 120	32 529	27 491	25 091	25 000	-3 688	-12.9
73 – Metalworking machinery	5 717	5 718	6 808	5 296	4 664	4 622	-1 095	-19.1
74 – General industrial machinery	30 999	30 729	34 455	33 748	31 839	32 183	1 184	3.8
75 – Office machines and a.d.p. equipment	47 759	48 604	57 595	49 404	39 744	41 054	-6 706	-14.0
76 – Telecommunications equipment ...	25 978	27 709	32 980	29 664	24 882	23 706	-2 272	-8.7
77 – Electrical machinery, apparatus, and appliances	76 872	88 655	110 095	88 557	82 657	85 910	9 038	11.8
78 – Motor vehicles	56 469	56 640	59 992	56 703	60 329	63 130	6 661	11.8
79 – Transport equipment	55 724	52 742	43 399	48 025	46 148	42 510	-13 214	-23.7
81 – Prefab buildings; sanitary, plumbing, etc.	1 462	1 377	1 476	1 417	1 451	1 489	27	1.9
82 – Furniture and bedding	4 675	4 701	5 202	4 720	4 355	4 265	-409	-8.8
83 – Travel goods, handbags	343	384	422	414	382	430	87	25.3
84 – Articles of apparel and clothing ...	8 793	8 269	8 629	7 012	6 032	5 537	-3 256	-37.0
85 – Footwear	851	839	867	806	703	694	-157	-18.5
87 – Professional scientific instruments	25 386	26 905	32 326	31 274	29 210	30 977	5 591	22.0
88 – Photography apparatus, equipment, and optical goods	6 381	6 950	8 724	7 451	6 779	6 851	470	7.4
89 – Miscellaneous manufactured articles	31 798	32 206	35 538	35 431	33 226	34 621	2 822	8.9
93 – Special transactions	5 287	5 500	5 666	6 483	6 554	6 215	928	17.6
95 – Coin including gold	40	37	87	20	35	34	-5	-13.0
96 – Coin (other than gold)	6	5	4	4	4	5	-1	-22.0
97 – Gold, nonmonetary	5 407	5 225	6 015	4 881	3 359	4 832	-575	-10.6
99 – Low value shipments	15 547	15 940	17 836	17 925	16 081	16 519	972	6.2

Note: Unrevised data. Revised total and manufactures are shown in Table B-3.

Table B-24. U.S. Total Imports by 2-Digit SITC Product Groups, 1998–2003

(Millions of dollars; Census basis; foreign and domestic exports, f.a.s.; general imports, Customs.)

SITC product	1998	1999	2000	2001	2002	2003	1998–2003 change Value	1998–2003 change Percent
TOTAL	913 885	1 024 766	1 216 888	1 141 959	1 163 549	1 259 396	345 511	37.8
00–49 Non-manufacturing	121 463	142 037	203 407	191 279	188 168	232 037	110 574	91.0
50–99 Manufacturing	792 422	882 729	1 013 480	950 680	975 381	1 027 358	234 936	29.6
00 – Live animals	1 718	1 642	1 929	2 239	2 120	1 619	-99	-5.8
01 – Meat and meat preparations	2 847	3 258	3 840	4 254	4 269	4 403	1 555	54.6
02 – Dairy products and birds' eggs	904	1 018	984	1 058	1 085	1 195	292	32.3
03 – Fish (except marine mammals)	8 105	8 902	9 906	9 750	10 005	10 930	2 825	34.9
04 – Cereals and cereal preparation	2 350	2 480	2 559	2 779	3 022	3 269	919	39.1
05 – Vegetables and fruit	8 372	9 261	9 283	9 522	10 196	11 454	3 082	36.8
06 – Sugars, sugar preparations	1 687	1 626	1 582	1 622	1 884	2 161	474	28.1
07 – Coffee, tea, cocoa	5 782	5 136	4 849	3 940	4 215	5 305	-477	-8.2
08 – Feeding stuff for animals	658	599	636	621	664	697	38	5.8
09 – Miscellaneous edible	991	1 171	1 223	1 443	1 728	1 868	877	88.4
11 – Beverages	6 493	7 405	8 132	8 498	9 452	10 678	4 186	64.5
12 – Tobacco and tobacco manufactures	1 263	1 210	1 127	1 237	1 318	1 300	37	2.9
21 – Hides, skins, and furskins	172	149	167	162	142	133	-39	-22.8
22 – Oil seeds and oleaginous fruits	376	326	346	285	251	262	-115	-30.5
23 – Crude rubber	1 675	1 451	1 689	1 427	1 548	1 833	157	9.4
24 – Cork and wood	7 625	8 925	8 235	7 969	7 874	7 276	-349	-4.6
25 – Pulp and waste paper	2 443	2 597	3 381	2 631	2 363	2 597	154	6.3
26 – Textile fibers	737	744	636	601	644	650	-87	-11.8
27 – Crude fertilizers	1 298	1 270	1 401	1 321	1 279	1 340	42	3.2
28 – Metalliferous ores	4 101	3 657	3 829	3 237	3 091	3 142	-959	-23.4
29 – Crude animal and vegetable materials	2 675	2 601	2 684	2 620	2 579	2 783	107	4.0
32 – Coal, coke, and briquettes	726	665	805	1 022	993	1 176	449	61.9
33 – Petroleum, petroleum products	49 370	65 887	117 174	100 668	101 152	129 600	80 230	162.5
34 – Gas, natural and manufactured	6 511	7 316	12 899	18 503	13 789	23 404	16 893	259.5
35 – Electric current	1 039	1 334	2 711	2 681	1 160	1 382	343	33.0
41 – Animal oils and fats	47	47	51	54	59	62	15	32.8
42 – Fixed vegetable fats and oils	1 324	1 219	1 188	995	1 131	1 340	16	1.2
43 – Animal or vegetable fats and oils, processed	174	142	160	141	153	182	8	4.6
51 – Organic chemicals	18 300	21 860	28 563	29 626	30 213	32 876	14 575	79.6
52 – Inorganic chemicals	5 118	5 173	6 096	6 193	6 018	7 419	2 301	45.0
53 – Dyeing, tanning, and coloring materials	2 470	2 632	2 676	2 480	2 358	2 480	11	0.4
54 – Medicinal and pharmaceutical products	10 885	13 542	14 694	18 624	24 719	31 516	20 631	189.5
55 – Essential oils	2 893	3 151	3 541	3 753	4 195	5 611	2 718	94.0
56 – Fertilizers	1 568	1 500	1 689	1 890	1 619	2 130	562	35.8
57 – Plastics in primary form	5 084	5 442	6 434	6 322	6 425	7 366	2 282	44.9
58 – Plastics in nonprimary form	3 480	3 835	4 208	4 057	4 336	4 794	1 314	37.8
59 – Chemical materials	4 822	5 072	5 731	5 927	6 174	6 857	2 035	42.2
61 – Leather, leather manufactures	1 236	1 185	1 330	1 221	1 170	1 122	-114	-9.2
62 – Rubber manufactures	6 463	7 156	7 584	7 001	7 724	8 531	2 068	32.0
63 – Cork and wood manufactures	5 799	7 254	7 394	7 185	8 042	9 491	3 692	63.7
64 – Paper, paperboard	12 796	13 407	15 184	14 819	14 434	14 849	2 053	16.0
65 – Textile yarn, fabrics	12 890	13 575	15 175	14 613	16 099	17 257	4 366	33.9
66 – Nonmetallic mineral	19 519	22 450	25 714	23 446	25 310	26 947	7 427	38.1
67 – Iron and steel	19 190	15 132	17 818	13 858	14 477	12 944	-6 246	-32.5
68 – Nonferrous metals	16 145	17 208	21 783	19 606	16 658	16 807	662	4.1
69 – Manufactures of metals	18 029	19 627	21 987	21 311	23 023	24 978	6 949	38.5
71 – Power generating machinery	28 132	31 533	33 815	36 127	34 032	32 485	4 353	15.5
72 – Machinery specialized	22 970	21 632	22 733	19 552	18 370	20 729	-2 241	-9.8
73 – Metalworking machinery	7 928	6 787	7 731	6 589	5 082	5 335	-2 593	-32.7
74 – General industrial machinery	28 802	31 447	34 709	33 258	35 201	38 467	9 665	33.6
75 – Office machines and a.d.p. equipment	76 846	84 443	92 165	75 861	76 970	80 826	3 981	5.2
76 – Telecommunications equipment	42 462	50 959	70 487	62 821	66 268	71 137	28 674	67.5
77 – Electrical machinery, apparatus, and appliances	79 366	88 592	108 813	84 710	81 288	82 545	3 178	4.0
78 – Motor vehicles	121 310	146 202	161 682	157 409	168 173	172 578	51 268	42.3
79 – Transport equipment	16 118	18 277	21 053	23 544	20 259	19 515	3 396	21.1
81 – Prefab buildings; sanitary, plumbing, etc.	3 391	4 327	5 106	4 895	5 566	6 003	2 612	77.0
82 – Furniture and bedding	13 338	16 178	18 927	18 612	21 572	24 356	11 017	82.6
83 – Travel goods, handbags	3 944	4 148	4 432	4 301	4 392	4 842	898	22.8
84 – Articles of apparel and clothing	53 743	56 413	64 296	63 862	63 810	68 162	14 419	26.8
85 – Footwear	13 879	14 068	14 854	15 235	15 386	15 603	1 723	12.4
87 – Professional scientific instruments	15 505	17 641	22 014	21 399	20 909	23 661	8 156	52.6
88 – Photography apparatus, equipment, and optical goods	11 700	12 585	14 554	12 245	11 554	11 911	211	1.8
89 – Miscellaneous manufactured articles	47 470	51 313	56 718	57 538	62 044	64 401	16 931	35.7
93 – Special transactions	26 419	31 783	34 572	35 367	35 893	33 622	7 203	27.3
95 – Coin including gold	291	367	89	99	130	199	-92	-31.7
96 – Coin (other than gold)	20	11	652	7	12	8	-12	-59.6
97 – Gold, nonmonetary	3 571	3 034	2 659	2 078	2 429	2 932	-639	-17.9
98 – Estimate of low valued import transactions	8 526	11 788	13 818	13 237	13 045	14 067	5 541	65.0

Note: Unrevised data. Revised total and manufactures are shown in Table B-3.

Table B-25. U.S. Total Trade Balances by 2-Digit SITC Product Groups, 1998–2003

(Millions of dollars; Census basis; foreign and domestic exports, f.a.s.; general imports, Customs.)

SITC product	1998	1999	2000	2001	2002	2003	1998–2003 change Value	1998–2003 change Percent
TOTAL	-233 411	-331 945	-436 469	-410 933	-470 291	-535 652	-302 242	129.5
00–49 Non-manufacturing	-36 208	-60 997	-112 513	-102 137	-101 469	-134 370	-98 163	271.1
50–99 Manufacturing	-197 203	-270 948	-323 956	-308 796	-368 823	-401 282	-204 079	103.5
00 – Live animals	-1 035	-984	-1 065	-1 341	-1 478	-827	208	-20.1
01 – Meat and meat preparations	3 583	3 114	3 709	3 125	2 208	2 977	-607	-16.9
02 – Dairy products and birds' eggs	-96	-272	-162	-186	-321	-374	-278	290.6
03 – Fish (except marine mammals)	-5 833	-6 044	-6 950	-6 543	-6 871	-7 647	-1 814	31.1
04 – Cereals and cereal preparation	9 141	9 172	8 501	8 315	8 834	9 108	-33	-0.4
05 – Vegetables and fruit	-430	-1 481	-1 118	-1 411	-1 831	-2 453	-2 023	470.2
06 – Sugars, sugar preparations	-1 019	-988	-888	-889	-1 237	-1 445	-426	41.8
07 – Coffee, tea, cocoa	-4 735	-4 124	-3 778	-2 722	-3 074	-4 029	706	-14.9
08 – Feeding stuff for animals	3 646	3 037	3 452	3 857	3 450	3 462	-185	-5.1
09 – Miscellaneous edible	1 680	1 714	1 769	1 743	1 426	1 603	-77	-4.6
11 – Beverages	-4 969	-5 839	-6 581	-6 894	-7 814	-8 815	-3 846	77.4
12 – Tobacco and tobacco manufactures	5 046	3 988	4 142	2 803	1 715	1 624	-3 422	-67.8
21 – Hides, skins, and furskins	1 108	1 007	1 501	1 836	1 616	1 679	571	51.6
22 – Oil seeds and oleaginous fruits	5 064	4 712	5 472	5 645	5 946	8 165	3 101	61.2
23 – Crude rubber	-502	-265	-235	9	-125	-217	286	-56.8
24 – Cork and wood	-3 492	-4 626	-3 820	-4 341	-4 434	-3 796	-303	8.7
25 – Pulp and waste paper	1 042	1 019	1 333	1 138	1 577	1 620	578	55.5
26 – Textile fibers	3 204	1 488	2 613	2 766	2 691	4 079	874	27.3
27 – Crude fertilizers	378	344	389	397	292	294	-84	-22.2
28 – Metalliferous ores	-474	-99	528	1 304	1 591	2 607	3 081	-650.0
29 – Crude animal and vegetable materials	-1 171	-1 122	-1 116	-928	-797	-900	271	-23.1
32 – Coal, coke, and briquettes	2 466	1 595	1 369	925	683	454	-2 012	-81.6
33 – Petroleum, petroleum products	-43 232	-59 127	-107 709	-92 124	-93 134	-119 966	-76 734	177.5
34 – Gas, natural and manufactured	-5 956	-6 617	-11 597	-17 387	-12 098	-21 336	-15 380	258.3
35 – Electric current	-854	-1 127	-2 313	-1 423	-857	-666	189	-22.1
41 – Animal oils and fats	639	469	333	310	465	486	-153	-24.0
42 – Fixed vegetable fats and oils	506	-35	-363	-194	-55	-172	-678	-134.0
43 – Animal or vegetable fats and oils, processed	85	93	68	72	161	114	29	34.4
51 – Organic chemicals	-3 119	-6 106	-9 632	-12 679	-13 373	-12 425	-9 305	298.3
52 – Inorganic chemicals	-276	-472	-583	-462	-406	-1 663	-1 387	502.7
53 – Dyeing, tanning, and coloring materials	1 058	1 055	1 529	1 400	1 619	1 802	744	70.3
54 – Medicinal and pharmaceutical products	-1 224	-2 295	-1 572	-3 203	-8 570	-12 307	-11 083	905.1
55 – Essential oils	1 995	1 862	2 005	2 278	1 940	1 245	-749	-37.6
56 – Fertilizers	1 714	1 617	797	356	643	422	-1 292	-75.4
57 – Plastics in primary form	6 476	6 330	7 439	7 189	7 472	7 761	1 285	19.9
58 – Plastics in nonprimary form	1 834	1 529	1 982	1 715	1 656	1 709	-125	-6.8
59 – Chemical materials	6 192	6 261	6 943	6 857	6 556	6 558	366	5.9
61 – Leather, leather manufactures	-210	-143	-209	-209	-201	-104	105	-50.3
62 – Rubber manufactures	-1 560	-2 255	-2 200	-1 917	-2 783	-3 618	-2 058	131.9
63 – Cork and wood manufactures	-3 998	-5 397	-5 397	-5 493	-6 340	-7 740	-3 742	93.6
64 – Paper, paperboard	-2 714	-3 307	-4 065	-4 389	-4 539	-4 644	-1 930	71.1
65 – Textile yarn, fabrics	-3 686	-4 071	-4 222	-4 141	-5 433	-6 363	-2 678	72.6
66 – Nonmetallic mineral	-11 551	-13 706	-15 199	-13 096	-14 956	-15 748	-4 197	36.3
67 – Iron and steel	-13 164	-9 683	-11 498	-7 888	-8 763	-6 170	6 994	-53.1
68 – Nonferrous metals	-8 571	-10 298	-13 512	-12 196	-9 912	-10 035	-1 464	17.1
69 – Manufactures of metals	-4 809	-5 977	-5 675	-7 074	-8 949	-10 806	-5 997	124.7
71 – Power generating machinery	1 831	847	531	53	349	1 157	-674	-36.8
72 – Machinery specialized	5 718	4 488	9 796	7 938	6 721	4 271	-1 447	-25.3
73 – Metalworking machinery	-2 211	-1 068	-922	-1 293	-417	-713	1 499	-67.8
74 – General industrial machinery	2 197	-718	-253	489	-3 362	-6 285	-8 482	-386.0
75 – Office machines and a.d.p. equipment	-29 086	-35 839	-34 570	-26 458	-37 226	-39 773	-10 686	36.7
76 – Telecommunications equipment	-16 484	-23 250	-37 507	-33 157	-41 386	-47 430	-30 946	187.7
77 – Electrical machinery, apparatus, and appliances	-2 495	63	1 282	3 847	1 368	3 365	5 860	-234.9
78 – Motor vehicles	-64 842	-89 561	-101 690	-100 705	-107 844	-109 448	-44 606	68.8
79 – Transport equipment	39 606	34 465	22 346	24 481	25 890	22 995	-16 610	-41.9
81 – Prefab buildings; sanitary, plumbing, etc.	-1 929	-2 950	-3 630	-3 479	-4 114	-4 514	-2 585	134.0
82 – Furniture and bedding	-8 664	-11 478	-13 725	-13 892	-17 217	-20 090	-11 426	131.9
83 – Travel goods, handbags	-3 600	-3 764	-4 011	-3 887	-4 010	-4 411	-811	22.5
84 – Articles of apparel and clothing	-44 950	-48 145	-55 668	-56 849	-57 778	-62 625	-17 675	39.3
85 – Footwear	-13 029	-13 229	-13 987	-14 429	-14 683	-14 909	-1 880	14.4
87 – Professional scientific instruments	9 881	9 264	10 312	9 874	8 301	7 316	-2 565	-26.0
88 – Photography apparatus, equipment, and optical goods	-5 320	-5 635	-5 830	-4 794	-4 775	-5 060	259	-4.9
89 – Miscellaneous manufactured articles	-15 672	-19 107	-21 180	-22 107	-28 818	-29 780	-14 108	90.0
93 – Special transactions	-21 132	-26 283	-28 905	-28 885	-29 340	-27 407	-6 275	29.7
95 – Coin including gold	-252	-330	-3	-79	-96	-165	87	-34.6
96 – Coin (other than gold)	-14	-6	-647	-3	-8	-3	10	-76.5
97 – Gold, nonmonetary	1 836	2 191	3 357	2 803	930	1 901	64	3.5
98 – Estimate of low valued import transactions	-8 526	-11 788	-13 818	-13 237	-13 045	-14 067	-5 541	65.0
99 – Low value shipments	15 547	15 940	17 836	17 925	16 081	16 519	972	6.0

Note: Unrevised data. Revised total and manufactures are shown in Table B-3.

Table B-26. U.S. Total Goods Exports, Imports, and Balances by Area and Year, 1984–2003

(Millions of dollars; Census basis; foreign and domestic exports, f.a.s.; general imports, Customs.)

Year and trade type	World	NAFTA	Japan	China	EU-15	Other Americas	ASEAN-10	Rest of world
EXPORTS								
1984	223 141	63 522	23 173	3 004	46 725	17 545	9 478	59 695
1985	219 182	66 479	22 191	3 852	46 255	17 042	7 891	55 473
1986	227 483	67 402	26 619	3 105	49 713	18 501	8 457	53 686
1987	252 866	73 900	27 808	3 488	56 504	20 257	9 872	61 036
1988	322 718	91 713	37 431	5 033	78 825	23 120	12 507	74 090
1989	363 766	103 235	44 584	5 807	91 574	24 089	16 061	78 415
1990	392 976	111 342	48 585	4 807	103 426	25 702	18 975	80 139
1991	421 854	118 422	48 147	6 287	108 501	30 197	20 819	89 481
1992	447 471	130 754	47 764	7 470	107 733	35 145	24 011	94 595
1993	464 858	141 826	47 950	8 767	101 483	36 844	28 326	99 663
1994	512 416	165 095	53 481	9 287	107 750	41 759	32 119	102 926
1995	583 031	172 336	64 298	11 748	123 599	50 011	39 676	121 362
1996	622 827	189 345	67 536	11 978	127 511	52 522	43 556	130 380
1997	687 598	221 503	65 673	12 805	140 803	63 041	48 368	135 405
1998	680 474	233 162	57 888	14 258	149 470	63 444	39 330	122 922
1999	692 821	250 957	57 484	13 118	151 645	55 205	39 862	124 550
2000	780 419	288 151	65 254	16 253	164 825	59 260	47 369	139 307
2001	731 026	265 234	57 639	19 235	159 175	58 404	43 840	127 500
2002	693 257	258 330	51 639	22 053	143 747	51 647	41 950	123 891
2003	723 743	266 938	52 064	28 418	150 549	52 039	45 280	128 455
IMPORTS								
1984	325 726	84 498	57 135	3 065	61 828	29 869	15 943	73 388
1985	345 276	88 138	68 783	3 862	70 288	27 772	14 718	71 715
1986	369 961	85 554	81 911	4 771	77 921	24 641	14 253	80 910
1987	405 901	91 356	84 575	6 293	83 704	26 591	17 028	96 354
1988	441 282	104 198	89 802	8 512	92 227	27 992	20 838	97 712
1989	473 397	115 396	93 586	11 989	92 521	30 204	24 772	104 929
1990	496 038	121 544	90 433	15 224	99 381	33 762	27 250	108 443
1991	488 873	122 335	92 333	18 976	93 346	31 407	28 969	101 507
1992	532 017	133 681	97 181	25 676	101 258	33 534	35 851	104 836
1993	580 469	150 851	107 268	31 535	105 559	34 478	42 327	108 451
1994	663 830	178 440	119 149	38 781	119 457	38 504	52 062	117 437
1995	743 505	206 824	123 577	45 555	131 910	42 250	62 176	131 213
1996	791 315	229 469	115 218	51 495	142 718	48 847	66 373	137 194
1997	870 213	253 923	121 359	62 552	157 544	53 676	70 982	150 178
1998	913 885	269 552	121 982	71 156	176 367	50 418	73 394	151 017
1999	1 024 766	308 030	131 404	81 786	195 368	58 400	77 669	172 109
2000	1 216 888	365 120	146 577	100 063	220 366	73 322	87 977	223 462
2001	1 141 959	348 402	126 602	102 280	220 031	67 488	76 367	200 788
2002	1 163 549	345 322	121 494	125 168	226 115	69 570	78 342	197 537
2003	1 259 396	363 239	118 029	152 379	244 811	78 874	81 877	220 187
BALANCES								
1984	-102 585	-20 976	-33 962	-61	-15 103	-12 325	-6 465	-13 693
1985	-126 093	-21 659	-46 592	-10	-24 033	-10 731	-6 827	-16 242
1986	-142 478	-18 153	-55 292	-1 666	-28 208	-6 140	-5 796	-27 224
1987	-153 035	-17 456	-56 767	-2 805	-27 200	-6 333	-7 156	-35 318
1988	-118 564	-12 486	-52 371	-3 479	-13 402	-4 873	-8 331	-23 622
1989	-109 631	-12 161	-49 002	-6 181	-947	-6 115	-8 711	-26 514
1990	-103 062	-10 202	-41 849	-10 417	4 045	-8 060	-8 275	-28 304
1991	-67 020	-3 913	-44 187	-12 689	15 155	-1 210	-8 150	-12 026
1992	-84 546	-2 928	-49 418	-18 206	6 475	1 611	-11 840	-10 241
1993	-115 610	-9 025	-59 318	-22 768	-4 076	2 366	-14 001	-8 788
1994	-151 415	-13 345	-65 669	-29 494	-11 707	3 255	-19 943	-14 511
1995	-160 475	-34 488	-59 280	-33 807	-8 311	7 761	-22 500	-9 850
1996	-168 488	-40 124	-47 683	-39 517	-15 208	3 675	-22 817	-6 814
1997	-182 615	-32 420	-55 686	-49 747	-16 741	9 365	-22 614	-14 773
1998	-233 411	-36 390	-64 094	-56 898	-26 897	13 026	-34 064	-28 095
1999	-331 945	-57 073	-73 920	-68 668	-43 723	-3 195	-37 807	-47 559
2000	-436 469	-76 969	-81 322	-83 810	-55 541	-14 063	-40 609	-84 155
2001	-410 933	-83 168	-68 963	-83 046	-60 856	-9 085	-32 527	-73 288
2002	-470 291	-86 992	-69 855	-103 115	-82 368	-17 923	-36 392	-73 646
2003	-535 652	-95 301	-65 965	-123 961	-94 262	-26 835	-36 597	-92 731

Note: NAFTA includes Canada and Mexico. EU-15 (European Union) consists of Austria, Belgium, Denmark, Finland, France, Germany, Greece, Ireland, Italy, Luxembourg, Netherlands, Portugal, Spain, Sweden, and the United Kingdom. ASEAN-10 (Association of Southeast Asian Nations) consists of Brunei, Burma (Myanmar), Cambodia, Indonesia, Laos, Malaysia, Philippines, Singapore, Thailand, and Vietnam. Other Americas includes North, Central, and South America less Mexico and Canada. Rest of world equals all other countries not listed above. Unrevised data.

Table B-27. U.S. Total Exports by Area and 3-Digit SITC Product Groups, 2003

(Millions of dollars; Census basis; foreign and domestic exports, f.a.s.)

SITC product	World	NAFTA	Japan	EU-15	Other Americas	ASEAN-10	Rest of world
000 – TOTAL	**723 743**	**266 938**	**52 064**	**150 549**	**52 039**	**45 280**	**156 873**
001 – Live animals other than animals of division 03	792	168	75	147	34	19	350
011 – Meat of bovine animals	3 069	877	1 157	10	40	21	963
012 – Other meat and edible offal	3 571	862	973	78	206	35	1 417
016 – Meat and edible meat offal, salted, in brine, dried or smoked; edible flours and meals of meat or meat offal	135	98	15	1	9	2	11
017 – Meat and edible meat offal, prepared or preserved, n.e.s. ...	605	337	103	6	39	15	104
022 – Milk, cream, milk products except butter or cheese	480	219	32	16	29	59	124
023 – Butter and other fats and oils derived from milk	20	13	0	0	2	0	4
024 – Cheese and curd	158	70	23	5	25	7	27
025 – Birds' eggs and egg yolks, fresh, dried or otherwise preserved, sweetened or not; egg albumin	164	69	18	20	33	2	22
034 – Fish, fresh, chilled or frozen	2 138	350	832	326	16	33	582
035 – Fish, dried, salted, or in brine; smoked fish	61	5	17	8	1	1	30
036 – Crustaceans	728	306	125	157	17	14	109
037 – Fish, crustaceans, molluscs and other aquatic invertebrates, prepared or preserved, n.e.s.	356	155	22	84	17	21	58
041 – Wheat and meslin, unmilled	3 958	406	482	231	794	336	1 710
042 – Rice	1 031	216	114	70	332	55	244
043 – Barley, unmilled	103	23	52	4	12	0	13
044 – Maize (not including sweet corn) unmilled	4 972	1 084	1 602	72	683	43	1 487
045 – Cereals, unmilled (other than wheat, rice, barley, and maize) ..	615	361	135	70	11	4	33
046 – Meal and flour of wheat and flour of meslin	88	23	1	3	17	1	44
047 – Cereal meals and flours, n.e.s.	106	60	1	4	13	1	27
048 – Cereal preparations and preparations of flour or starch of fruits or vegetables	1 503	1 151	94	34	87	22	116
054 – Vegetables, roots, tubers and other edible vegetable products ..	1 954	1 355	186	129	81	19	185
056 – Vegetables, roots and tubers, prepared or preserved, n.e.s. ...	1 101	381	276	77	72	71	223
057 – Fruit and nuts (not including oil nuts), fresh or dried	4 668	1 756	581	1 064	92	222	953
058 – Fruit preserved, and fruit preparations (excluding fruit juices) ..	547	201	66	133	22	19	106
059 – Fruit juices and vegetable juices, unfermented and not containing added spirits	733	361	95	130	53	11	82
061 – Sugars, molasses, and honey	413	178	59	41	28	35	71
062 – Sugar confectionery	303	189	6	47	21	6	34
071 – Coffee and coffee substitutes	403	272	28	35	8	15	44
072 – Cocoa	212	201	1	3	2	1	4
073 – Chocolate and other food preparations containing cocoa, n.e.s. ..	512	311	26	12	43	30	89
074 – Tea and mate	74	46	3	10	4	4	7
075 – Spices	75	31	4	15	12	2	11
081 – Feeding stuff for animals	4 159	1 101	733	643	523	411	748
091 – Margarine and shortening	96	59	2	2	22	2	9
098 – Edible products and preparations, n.e.s.	3 375	1 433	282	227	332	216	885
111 – Nonalcoholic beverages, n.e.s.	401	232	83	9	40	4	34
112 – Alcoholic beverages	1 463	341	139	670	94	19	200
121 – Tobacco, unmanufactured; tobacco refuse	1 041	3	128	503	74	66	266
122 – Tobacco, manufactured	1 883	49	1 013	170	43	27	581
211 – Hides and skins (except furskins), raw	1 669	128	105	119	20	71	1 226
212 – Furskins, raw (including furskin heads, tails and other pieces or cuttings, suitable for furriers' use)	142	48	1	17	0	1	77
222 – Oil seeds and oleaginous fruits	8 303	1 354	973	1 222	147	599	4 008
223 – Oil seeds and oleaginous fruits, whole or broken, of a kind used for extracting other fixed vegetalbe oils	124	35	21	16	12	13	28
231 – Natural rubber in primary forms	94	42	2	5	6	5	33
232 – Synthetic rubber; reclaimed rubber; waste, pairings and scrap of unhardened rubber	1 522	467	42	529	153	63	268
244 – Cork, natural, raw and waste (including natural cork in blocks or sheets)	1	0	0	1	0	0	1
245 – Fuel wood (excluding wood waste) and wood charcoal	10	6	0	0	1	0	2
246 – Wood in chips or particles and wood waste	174	69	79	10	2	0	15
247 – Wood in the rough or roughly squared	1 275	404	452	133	20	34	231
248 – Wood, simply worked	2 020	914	127	454	90	81	353
251 – Pulp and waste paper	4 216	881	371	1 155	220	207	1 382
261 – Silk textile fibers	3	0	0	0	0	0	2
263 – Cotton textile fibers	3 454	558	116	91	280	467	1 942
264 – Jute and other textile bast fibers, n.e.s., raw or processed but not spun; tow and waste of these fibres (including yarn) ...	1	0	0	0	0	0	0
265 – Vegetable textile fibers (other than cotton and jute), raw or processed but not spun; waste of these fibers	4	1	0	1	1	0	0
266 – Synthetic fibers suitable for spinning	473	216	21	70	103	4	59
267 – Manmade fibers, n.e.s. suitable for spinning and waste of manmade fibers	449	30	8	136	17	54	205
268 – Wool and other animal hair (including wool tops)	59	11	0	20	7	0	20
269 – Worn clothing and other worn textile articles; rags	288	60	26	13	67	12	109
272 – Fertilizer, crude, except those of division 56 (imports only) ..	0	0	0	0	0	0	0
273 – Stone, sand and gravel	324	134	22	63	20	9	76
274 – Sulfur and unroasted iron pyrites	46	8	0	0	7	0	31
277 – Natural abrasives, n.e.s. (including industrial diamonds)	108	15	20	31	9	5	29
278 – Crude minerals, n.e.s.	1 156	341	174	315	70	54	203

Note: NAFTA includes Canada and Mexico. EU-15 (European Union) consists of Austria, Belgium, Denmark, Finland, France, Germany, Greece, Ireland, Italy, Luxembourg, Netherlands, Portugal, Spain, Sweden, and the United Kingdom. ASEAN-10 (Association of Southeast Asian Nations) consists of Brunei, Burma (Myanmar), Cambodia, Indonesia, Laos, Malaysia, Philippines, Singapore, Thailand, and Vietnam. Other Americas includes North, Central, and South America less Mexico and Canada. Rest of world equals all other countries not listed above.

Table B-27. U.S. Total Exports by Area and 3-Digit SITC Product Groups, 2003—*Continued*

(Millions of dollars; Census basis; foreign and domestic exports, f.a.s.)

SITC product	World	NAFTA	Japan	EU-15	Other Americas	ASEAN-10	Rest of world
281 – Iron ore and concentrates	248	241	0	0	0	0	7
282 – Ferrous waste and scrap; remelting ingots of iron or steel	1 945	326	31	156	18	162	1 251
283 – Copper ores and concentrates; copper mattes; cement copper	88	57	1	24	1	0	6
284 – Nickel ores and concentrates; nickel mattes, nickel oxide sinters and other intermediate products of nickel metallurgy	10	7	1	1	1	0	1
285 – Aluminum ores and concentrates	344	211	15	59	7	5	47
286 – Ores and concentrates of uranium or thorium	0	0	0	0	0	0	0
287 – Ores and concentrates of base metals	762	208	79	330	13	1	130
288 – Nonferrous base metal waste and scrap	1 525	324	65	50	54	16	1 017
289 – Ores and concentrates of precious metals; waste, scrap and sweepings of precious metals (other than gold)	826	172	64	451	6	0	133
291 – Crude animal materials, n.e.s.	634	308	86	55	24	17	144
292 – Crude vegetable materials, n.e.s.	1 248	496	69	288	107	31	257
321 – Coal, pulverized or not	1 549	631	1	580	173	0	164
322 – Briquettes, lignite and peat	10	5	0	1	1	1	2
325 – Coke and semicoke (including char) of coal, of lignite or of peat, agglomerated or not; retort carbon	70	64	0	2	1	0	3
333 – Crude oil	155	154	0	0	0	0	1
334 – Oil (not crude)	7 350	3 215	266	180	2 743	463	482
335 – Residual petroleum products	2 129	479	142	385	207	84	832
342 – Liquefied propane and butane	473	304	32	11	76	0	50
343 – Natural gas, whether or not liquefied	1 300	1 152	148	0	0	0	0
344 – Petroleum gases and other gaseous hydrocarbons, n.e.s.	294	234	3	11	6	28	12
345 – Coal gas, water gas, producer gas and similar gases, other than petroleum gases and other gaseous hydrocarbons	1	0	0	0	0	0	1
351 – Electric current	716	716	0	0	0	0	0
411 – Animal oils and fats	548	213	10	6	162	1	156
421 – Fixed vegetable fats and oils, soft, crude, refined or fractioned	1 002	279	36	50	155	3	479
422 – Fixed vegetable fats and oils (other than soft), crude, refined or fractioned	165	24	6	38	8	4	87
431 – Animal or vegetable fats and oils processed; waxes and inedible mixtures or preparations of animal or vegetable fats	296	137	18	48	25	6	63
511 – Hydrocarbons and specified derivatives	4 394	1 497	250	613	511	141	1 383
512 – Alcohols, phenols, and halogenated derivatives ..	2 398	634	137	410	238	154	824
513 – Carboxylic acids, halides, and derivities	2 855	757	124	1 010	345	88	530
514 – Nitrogen-function compounds	3 682	622	265	1 029	318	190	1 257
515 – Organo-inorganic and heterocyclic compounds ...	4 819	462	179	2 873	415	182	707
516 – Organic chemicals	2 304	648	229	658	199	130	441
522 – Inorganic chemical elements	2 170	549	372	406	271	95	477
523 – Metallic salts and peroxysalts of inorganic acids .	1 550	448	120	316	257	141	268
524 – Inorganic chemicals, n.e.s.; organic and inorganic compounds of precious metals	429	161	50	89	12	17	101
525 – Radioactive and associated materials	1 606	80	817	351	12	6	340
531 – Synthetic organic coloring matter and color lakes and preparations based thereon	565	175	29	188	52	33	87
532 – Dyeing and tanning extracts, and synthetic tanning materials	61	9	3	22	6	4	17
533 – Pigments, paints, varnishes and related materials	3 656	1 647	126	695	374	164	651
541 – Medicinal products, except medicaments	8 181	960	701	4 999	281	147	1 092
542 – Medicaments (including veterinary medicaments) ..	11 028	2 351	506	5 874	523	87	1 686
551 – Essential oils, perfume and flavor materials	1 253	428	108	291	107	103	216
553 – Perfumery, cosmetics, or toilet preparations, excluding soaps	3 688	1 258	324	883	334	141	747
554 – Soap, cleansing and polishing preparations	1 916	973	112	263	141	97	330
562 – Fertilizers (except crude)	2 552	565	162	25	641	112	1 047
571 – Polymers of ethylene	2 845	1 450	68	405	427	106	389
572 – Polymers of styrene, in primary forms	859	602	22	100	39	20	75
573 – Polymers of vinyl chloride or other halogenated olefins, in primary forms	1 170	528	47	160	86	36	314
574 – Polyacetals, other polyethers and epoxide resins, in primary forms; polycarbonates, alkyd resins and other polyesters	3 100	1 221	156	383	336	197	807
575 – Plastics	6 859	2 706	387	1 430	556	337	1 443
579 – Waste, parings and scrap, of plastics	294	83	1	18	7	3	183
581 – Tubes, pipes and hoses of plastics	1 088	664	32	124	114	41	113
582 – Plates, sheets, film, foil and strip of plastics	5 134	2 538	218	975	274	276	853
583 – Monofilament with a cross-sectional dimension exceeding 1 mm, rods, sticks, and profile shapes of plastics	282	72	5	27	156	4	18
591 – Insecticides, fungicides, herbicides, plant growth regulators, etc., disinfectants and similar products	1 457	621	40	293	321	39	144
592 – Starches, inulin and wheat gluten; albuminoidal substances	1 304	561	113	202	94	54	279
593 – Explosives and pyrotechnic products	394	207	27	60	13	18	70
597 – Prepared additives for mineral oils, etc.; liquids for hydraulic transmissions; antifreezes and deicing fluids; lubricating preparations	1 880	496	138	304	222	293	428
598 – Miscellaneous chemical products	8 381	1 830	935	2 880	436	346	1 954
611 – Leather	878	288	12	137	57	20	362
612 – Manufactures of leather or composition leather, n.e.s.; saddlery and harness	122	78	12	12	3	1	14
613 – Furskins, tanned or dressed (including pieces or cuttings), assembled or unassembled without the addition of other materials	18	4	0	7	2	0	5
621 – Materials of rubber, including pastes, plates, sheets, rods, thread, tubes, etc.	1 053	715	59	139	39	17	84
625 – Rubber tires, interchangeable tire treads, tire flaps and inner tubes for wheels of all kinds	2 320	1 666	105	202	159	22	167
629 – Articles of rubber, n.e.s.	1 540	1 038	31	227	61	43	141

Note: NAFTA includes Canada and Mexico. EU-15 (European Union) consists of Austria, Belgium, Denmark, Finland, France, Germany, Greece, Ireland, Italy, Luxembourg, Netherlands, Portugal, Spain, Sweden, and the United Kingdom. ASEAN-10 (Association of Southeast Asian Nations) consists of Brunei, Burma (Myanmar), Cambodia, Indonesia, Laos, Malaysia, Philippines, Singapore, Thailand, and Vietnam. Other Americas includes North, Central, and South America less Mexico and Canada. Rest of world equals all other countries not listed above.

Table B-27. U.S. Total Exports by Area and 3-Digit SITC Product Groups, 2003—*Continued*

(Millions of dollars; Census basis; foreign and domestic exports, f.a.s.)

SITC product	World	NAFTA	Japan	EU-15	Other Americas	ASEAN-10	Rest of world
633 – Cork manufactures	49	10	1	7	6	1	23
634 – Veneers, plywood, particle board, and other wood, worked, n.e.s.	1 028	578	11	247	43	20	129
635 – Wood manufactures, n.e.s.	674	358	74	99	59	9	76
641 – Paper and paperboard	6 265	2 950	528	686	728	201	1 172
642 – Paper and paperboard, cut to size or shape, and articles of paper or paperboard	3 939	2 904	79	325	271	77	283
651 – Textile yarn	1 852	710	51	253	538	33	266
652 – Cotton fabrics, woven	1 350	722	5	50	505	12	56
653 – Woven fabrics of manmade textile materials	1 321	851	6	53	280	12	118
654 – Woven fabrics of textile materials, other than cotton or manmade fibers and narrow or special fabrics	214	97	5	30	47	3	33
655 – Knitted or crocheted fabrics	1 419	512	6	27	811	11	53
656 – Tulles, lace, embroidery, ribbons, trimmings and other small wares	620	268	9	30	230	10	74
657 – Special yarns, special textile fabrics and related products	2 693	1 525	94	389	175	80	431
658 – Made-up articles of textile materials	706	378	34	122	61	15	96
659 – Floor coverings, etc.	718	523	23	53	36	11	72
661 – Lime, cement, and fabricated construction materials	301	200	6	12	33	4	47
662 – Clay construction materials and refractory construction materials	322	158	21	33	37	12	61
663 – Mineral manufactures, n.e.s.	1 641	643	91	397	135	48	328
664 – Glass	2 565	1 437	180	411	62	66	408
665 – Glassware	731	317	50	150	52	31	130
666 – Pottery	120	65	4	21	15	2	14
667 – Pearls, precious and semiprecious stones	5 518	169	95	1 603	93	139	3 421
671 – Pig iron and iron and steel powders	159	93	4	31	11	1	19
672 – Iron or steel ingots and other primary forms, and semifinished products of iron or steel	190	65	14	32	17	13	49
673 – Iron or nonalloy steel flat-rolled products, not clad, plated or coated	1 509	973	8	173	21	16	318
674 – Iron and nonalloy steel flat-rolled products, clad, plated or coated	640	521	3	25	9	8	73
675 – Alloy steel flat-rolled products	1 080	655	4	148	13	19	242
676 – Iron and steel bars, rods, angles, shapes and sections, including sheet piling	923	714	5	69	66	14	56
677 – Iron and steel rails and railway track construction material	69	49	0	8	5	0	7
678 – Iron and steel wire	241	163	3	33	12	3	27
679 – Iron and steel tubes, pipes and fittings	1 963	1 155	51	194	130	62	371
681 – Silver, platinum, and other platinum group metals	1 230	181	157	586	11	9	287
682 – Copper	1 349	729	42	155	24	53	345
683 – Nickel	436	82	24	242	9	9	70
684 – Aluminum	3 045	2 205	123	258	111	66	282
685 – Lead	80	28	1	40	2	2	8
686 – Zinc	57	38	0	6	3	1	8
687 – Tin	45	24	2	3	1	8	8
689 – Miscellaneous nonferrous base metals employed in metallurgy and cermets	530	56	70	235	10	3	154
691 – Metal structures and parts, n.e.s., of iron, steel or aluminum	712	313	26	88	111	38	136
692 – Metal containers for storage or transport	661	368	28	109	57	12	88
693 – Wire products (excluding insulated electrical wiring) and fencing grills	430	261	11	53	29	12	64
694 – Nails, screws, nuts, bolts, rivets and similar articles, of iron, steel, copper or aluminum	1 700	1 192	26	243	47	56	138
695 – Tools for use in the hand or in machines	2 416	1 131	95	537	153	91	408
696 – Cutlery	447	215	8	92	37	14	80
697 – Household equipment of base metal, n.e.s.	574	316	45	90	29	10	84
699 – Manufactures of base metal	7 232	4 870	243	880	249	370	619
711 – Steam or other vapor generating boilers, super-heated water boilers and auxiliary plant for use therewith; and parts thereof	337	99	3	26	34	12	162
712 – Steam turbines and other vapor turbines, and parts thereof, n.e.s.	279	41	8	86	24	26	94
713 – Internal combustion piston engines	12 619	8 469	637	1 813	406	185	1 109
714 – Nonelectric engines and motors	15 609	2 162	1 063	7 761	1 092	1 105	2 426
716 – Rotating electric plant and parts	3 920	1 883	117	566	290	171	892
718 – Power generating machinery and parts thereof, n.e.s.	879	267	42	187	62	28	294
721 – Agricultural machinery (excluding tractors) and parts	2 545	1 091	89	642	206	36	480
722 – Tractors (other than mechanical handling equipment)	1 371	587	23	308	73	18	362
723 – Civil engineering and contractors' plant and equipment	8 860	2 156	85	1 330	1 534	645	3 110
724 – Textile and leather machinery, and parts thereof, n.e.s.	1 164	357	27	145	212	40	383
725 – Paper mill and pulp mill machinery, paper cutting machines and machinery for the manufacture of paper articles; parts thereof	602	222	16	149	60	39	116
726 – Printing and bookbinding machinery, and parts thereof	1 090	309	72	305	99	42	263
727 – Food-processing machines (excluding domestic)	572	172	23	154	78	29	116
728 – Machinery and equipment specialized for particular industries	8 795	2 137	902	1 530	420	606	3 202
731 – Machine tools working by removing metal or other material	1 692	409	204	365	45	139	530
733 – Machine tools for working metal, sintered metal carbides or cermets, without removing material	493	195	17	87	24	15	155
735 – Parts and accessories suitable for use solely or principally with metal working machine tools, whether or not removing materials	1 378	341	116	337	105	108	370
737 – Metalworking machinery (other than machine tools) and parts thereof, n.e.s.	1 060	332	58	196	74	68	332
741 – Heating and cooling equipment	6 059	2 746	272	891	420	241	1 489
742 – Pumps for liquids, whether or not fitted with a measuring device; liquid elevators; parts for such pumps and liquid elevators	3 318	1 422	103	676	265	159	694
743 – Pumps, air or gas compressors and fans	7 411	3 052	379	1 248	541	456	1 734
744 – Mechanical handling equipment	3 669	1 358	71	651	592	158	838
745 – Nonelectrical machinery, tools and mechanical apparatus, and parts thereof, n.e.s.	3 481	1 228	129	1 056	216	139	712
746 – Ball or roller bearings	1 198	620	34	250	86	46	162

Note: NAFTA includes Canada and Mexico. EU-15 (European Union) consists of Austria, Belgium, Denmark, Finland, France, Germany, Greece, Ireland, Italy, Luxembourg, Netherlands, Portugal, Spain, Sweden, and the United Kingdom. ASEAN-10 (Association of Southeast Asian Nations) consists of Brunei, Burma (Myanmar), Cambodia, Indonesia, Laos, Malaysia, Philippines, Singapore, Thailand, and Vietnam. Other Americas includes North, Central, and South America less Mexico and Canada. Rest of world equals all other countries not listed above.

Table B-27. U.S. Total Exports by Area and 3-Digit SITC Product Groups, 2003—Continued

(Millions of dollars; Census basis; foreign and domestic exports, f.a.s.)

SITC product	World	NAFTA	Japan	EU-15	Other Americas	ASEAN-10	Rest of world
747 – Taps, cocks, valves and similar appliances for pipes, boiler shells, tanks, etc.	3 665	2 048	127	605	163	130	592
748 – Transmission shafts and cranks; bearing housings and plain shaft bearings; gears and gearing; ball screws; gear boxes	1 913	1 200	37	323	93	41	218
749 – Nonelectric parts and accessories of machinery, n.e.s.	1 471	761	63	224	99	53	270
751 – Office machines	717	260	24	152	97	39	145
752 – Automatic data processing machines	21 595	7 820	1 650	5 379	1 596	1 190	3 961
759 – Parts for office machines and a.d.p. machines	18 742	5 908	1 012	5 580	1 573	1 951	2 719
761 – Television receivers	1 264	849	37	173	92	30	84
762 – Radio-broadcast receivers	820	657	30	21	40	10	63
763 – Sound and television recorders	1 258	525	87	161	167	15	303
764 – Telecommunications equipment	20 364	6 716	1 569	4 515	1 981	782	4 800
771 – Electric power machinery (other than rotating electric plant of power generating machinery) and parts thereof	2 815	1 351	109	508	163	191	493
772 – Electrical apparatus for switching or protecting elec. circuits	11 841	6 654	376	1 922	504	754	1 632
773 – Equipment for distributing electricity	4 691	3 272	105	515	159	201	439
774 – Electro-diagnostic apparatus	5 428	517	774	2 483	266	132	1 255
775 – Household type electrical and nonelectrical equipment	2 478	1 502	57	351	174	35	358
776 – Thermionic, cold cathode, and photocathode valves	47 770	8 486	2 499	4 610	1 816	15 208	15 152
778 – Electrical machinery and apparatus	10 888	4 981	526	1 867	618	566	2 330
781 – All motor vehicles	22 777	13 589	474	5 615	413	61	2 625
782 – Special purpose motor vehicles	7 870	6 490	26	209	315	60	769
783 – Road motor vehicles, n.e.s.	1 696	1 388	0	45	51	10	200
784 – Parts and accessories of motor vehicles	28 327	22 159	1 071	2 582	736	146	1 634
785 – Motorcycles (including mopeds) and cycles, motorized and not motorized; invalid carriages	1 298	374	169	506	33	13	203
786 – Trailers and semi-trailers; other vehicles, not mechanically propelled; specially designed and equipped transport containers	1 162	990	22	49	36	4	60
791 – Railway vehicles (including hovertrains) and associated equipment	1 537	949	22	182	88	26	269
792 – Aircraft and associated equipment	39 638	2 464	4 844	12 474	1 626	4 575	13 656
793 – Ships, boats, and floating structures	1 335	401	35	390	235	10	265
811 – Prefabricated buildings	314	126	44	30	26	6	83
812 – Sanitary, plumbing and heating fixtures and fittings, n.e.s.	332	271	2	19	9	2	30
813 – Lighting fixtures and fittings, n.e.s.	843	474	42	125	48	16	138
821 – Furniture and bedding accessories	4 265	2 982	339	343	191	51	360
831 – Trunks, suitcases, vanity cases, binocular and camera cases, handbags, wallets, etc. of leather, etc.	430	113	144	55	15	14	90
841 – Men's or boys' coats, jackets, etc. not knit	707	261	28	34	361	3	20
842 – Women's or girls' coats, jackets, etc. not knit	437	280	20	31	77	4	24
843 – Men's or boys' coats, jackets, etc. knit	396	109	21	14	236	2	13
844 – Women's or girls' coats, jackets, etc. knit	434	178	17	24	187	2	26
845 – Articles of apparel of textile fabrics	2 203	1 014	109	92	911	13	63
846 – Clothing accessories	937	421	15	41	423	6	31
848 – Apparel and accessories except textile; headgear	423	140	73	74	60	12	65
851 – Footwear	694	278	33	82	101	45	154
871 – Optical instruments and apparatus, n.e.s.	1 893	622	300	500	58	52	362
872 – Medical instruments and appliances	8 930	1 862	1 201	3 842	426	177	1 422
873 – Meters and counters, n.e.s.	748	542	13	62	28	17	86
874 – Measuring/checking/analysing instruments	19 406	4 577	2 068	5 405	734	1 708	4 913
881 – Photographic apparatus and equipment, n.e.s.	973	218	141	292	96	30	196
882 – Photographic and cinematographic supplies	2 897	1 094	183	801	205	100	514
883 – Cinematographic film, exposed and developed, whether or not incorporating sound track or consisting only of sound track	33	7	1	7	3	2	14
884 – Optical goods, n.e.s.	2 479	564	470	547	93	121	683
885 – Watches and clocks	468	125	25	61	73	13	172
891 – Arms and ammunition	2 425	199	295	611	52	31	1 237
892 – Printed matter	4 875	2 739	198	888	234	145	671
893 – Articles of plastics	7 213	4 869	285	841	419	168	631
894 – Baby carriages, toys, games and sporting goods	3 989	1 692	363	876	266	97	695
895 – Office and stationery supplies, n.e.s.	666	329	22	128	70	26	91
896 – Works of art, collectors' pieces, and antiques	2 735	95	122	1 566	22	11	920
897 – Jewelry, goldsmiths' and silversmiths' wares	2 768	514	346	380	581	102	845
898 – Musical instruments and accessories	4 991	1 926	396	967	340	417	946
899 – Miscellaneous manufactured articles	4 958	772	534	2 572	225	58	798
931 – Special transactions not classified by kind	6 215	1 552	785	1 390	573	337	1 578
950 – Coin, including gold coin; proof and presentation sets and current coin	34	4	1	4	12	0	15
961 – Coin (other than gold coin), not being legal tender	5	1	0	2	1	0	1
971 – Gold, nonmonetary	4 832	582	4	1 348	93	26	2 779
984 – Estimate of low value import transactions	0	0	0	0	0	0	0
992 – Export shipments valued not over $10,000, not identified by kind	692	394	38	60	77	12	112
994 – Estimated low value shipments	15 826	6 657	550	3 435	1 769	745	2 670

Note: NAFTA includes Canada and Mexico. EU-15 (European Union) consists of Austria, Belgium, Denmark, Finland, France, Germany, Greece, Ireland, Italy, Luxembourg, Netherlands, Portugal, Spain, Sweden, and the United Kingdom. ASEAN-10 (Association of Southeast Asian Nations) consists of Brunei, Burma (Myanmar), Cambodia, Indonesia, Laos, Malaysia, Philippines, Singapore, Thailand, and Vietnam. Other Americas includes North, Central, and South America less Mexico and Canada. Rest of world equals all other countries not listed above.

Table B-28. U.S. Total Imports by Area and 3-Digit SITC Product Groups, 2003

(Millions of dollars; Census basis; general imports, Customs.)

SITC product	World	NAFTA	Japan	EU-15	Other Americas	ASEAN-10	Rest of world
000 – TOTAL	1 259 396	362 239	118 029	244 811	78 874	81 877	373 565
001 – Live animals other than animals of division 03	1 619	1 354	4	199	12	8	41
011 – Meat of bovine animals	2 351	869	0	0	119	0	1 363
012 – Other meat and edible offal	1 327	735	0	177	2	2	411
016 – Meat and edible meat offal, salted, in brine, dried or smoked; edible flours and meals of meat or meat offal	201	135	0	46	3	0	16
017 – Meat and edible meat offal, prepared or preserved, n.e.s.	524	193	1	67	219	0	43
022 – Milk, cream, milk products except butter or cheese	219	55	0	34	6	1	123
023 – Butter and other fats and oils derived from milk	63	17	0	12	1	0	33
024 – Cheese and curd	891	32	0	578	45	0	236
025 – Birds' eggs and egg yolks, fresh, dried or otherwise preserved, sweetened or not; egg albumin	22	15	0	2	0	1	5
034 – Fish, fresh, chilled or frozen	3 401	794	55	108	1 069	359	1 016
035 – Fish, dried, salted, or in brine; smoked fish	160	56	5	5	19	11	63
036 – Crustaceans	5 101	1 374	61	16	967	1 315	1 368
037 – Fish, crustaceans, molluscs and other aquatic invertebrates, prepared or preserved, n.e.s.	2 268	312	35	42	239	1 200	441
041 – Wheat and meslin, unmilled	141	135	0	6	0	0	0
042 – Rice	208	0	0	6	0	132	69
043 – Barley, unmilled	49	34	0	12	3	0	0
044 – Maize (not including sweet corn) unmilled	151	42	0	1	107	0	0
045 – Cereals, unmilled (other than wheat, rice, barley, and maize)	224	153	0	68	1	0	1
046 – Meal and flour of wheat and flour of meslin	72	68	1	0	0	0	3
047 – Cereal meals and flours, n.e.s.	52	43	0	0	4	3	1
048 – Cereal preparations and preparations of flour or starch of fruits or vegetables	2 372	1 524	43	509	67	71	158
054 – Vegetables, roots, tubers and other edible vegetable products	3 529	2 858	2	185	301	4	178
056 – Vegetables, roots and tubers, prepared or preserved, n.e.s.	1 588	768	17	414	74	53	262
057 – Fruit and nuts (not including oil nuts), fresh or dried	4 363	949	2	139	2 533	165	576
058 – Fruit preserved, and fruit preparations (excluding fruit juices) ...	1 138	315	20	71	140	318	273
059 – Fruit juices and vegetable juices, unfermented and not containing added spirits	836	84	1	41	448	96	165
061 – Sugars, molasses, and honey	1 039	242	2	18	517	94	167
062 – Sugar confectionery	1 122	625	8	222	107	38	121
071 – Coffee and coffee substitutes	1 961	260	0	168	1 240	176	116
072 – Cocoa	1 357	31	0	224	219	392	490
073 – Chocolate and other food preparations containing cocoa, n.e.s. ...	1 077	750	1	229	45	1	51
074 – Tea and mate	265	68	5	39	33	11	109
075 – Spices	645	36	1	41	65	151	351
081 – Feeding stuff for animals	697	450	14	77	36	34	85
091 – Margarine and shortening	30	20	0	5	3	0	2
098 – Edible products and preparations, n.e.s.	1 839	830	84	341	79	135	369
111 – Nonalcoholic beverages, n.e.s.	967	457	8	367	22	34	80
112 – Alcoholic beverages	9 711	2 125	26	6 385	264	5	906
121 – Tobacco, unmanufactured; tobacco refuse	690	42	0	73	304	44	228
122 – Tobacco, manufactured	610	55	26	45	382	12	89
211 – Hides and skins (except furskins), raw	74	65	0	2	1	1	5
212 – Furskins, raw (including furskin heads, tails and other pieces or cuttings, suitable for furriers' use)	59	29	0	25	0	0	4
222 – Oil seeds and oleaginous fruits	180	127	0	2	28	0	24
223 – Oil seeds and oleaginous fruits, whole or broken, of a kind used for extracting other fixed vegetalbe oils	81	40	0	2	2	6	32
231 – Natural rubber in primary forms	1 047	5	0	4	1	968	70
232 – Synthetic rubber; reclaimed rubber; waste, pairings and scrap of unhardened rubber	785	292	95	245	45	7	101
244 – Cork, natural, raw and waste (including natural cork in blocks or sheets)	2	0	0	1	0	0	0
245 – Fuel wood (excluding wood waste) and wood charcoal	20	11	0	1	4	0	4
246 – Wood in chips or particles and wood waste	114	108	0	1	4	0	1
247 – Wood in the rough or roughly squared	227	215	0	3	5	1	4
248 – Wood, simply worked	6 913	5 080	0	400	897	99	438
251 – Pulp and waste paper	2 597	1 989	0	122	446	3	37
261 – Silk textile fibers	1	0	0	0	0	0	0
263 – Cotton textile fibers	34	3	0	2	0	0	28
264 – Jute and other textile bast fibers, n.e.s., raw or processed but not spun; tow and waste of these fibres (including yarn)	0	0	0	0	0	0	0
265 – Vegetable textile fibers (other than cotton and jute), raw or processed but not spun; waste of these fibers	19	11	0	5	0	0	4
266 – Synthetic fibers suitable for spinning	437	66	44	71	0	30	225
267 – Manmade fibers, n.e.s. suitable for spinning and waste of manmade fibers	51	11	0	37	0	1	2
268 – Wool and other animal hair (including wool tops)	61	2	0	13	2	0	44
269 – Worn clothing and other worn textile articles; rags	46	27	0	3	6	0	10
272 – Fertilizer, crude, except those of division 56 (imports only) ...	80	6	0	3	23	0	48
273 – Stone, sand and gravel	276	181	4	26	35	1	29
274 – Sulfur and unroasted iron pyrites	72	59	0	1	12	0	0
277 – Natural abrasives, n.e.s. (including industrial diamonds)	114	1	5	55	1	0	51
278 – Crude minerals, n.e.s.	799	280	18	75	119	1	306

Note: NAFTA includes Canada and Mexico. EU-15 (European Union) consists of Austria, Belgium, Denmark, Finland, France, Germany, Greece, Ireland, Italy, Luxembourg, Netherlands, Portugal, Spain, Sweden, and the United Kingdom. ASEAN-10 (Association of Southeast Asian Nations) consists of Brunei, Burma (Myanmar), Cambodia, Indonesia, Laos, Malaysia, Philippines, Singapore, Thailand, and Vietnam. Other Americas includes North, Central, and South America less Mexico and Canada. Rest of world equals all other countries not listed above.

Table B-28. U.S. Total Imports by Area and 3-Digit SITC Product Groups, 2003—*Continued*

(Millions of dollars; Census basis; general imports, Customs.)

SITC product	World	NAFTA	Japan	EU-15	Other Americas	ASEAN-10	Rest of world
281 – Iron ore and concentrates	328	196	0	5	126	0	1
282 – Ferrous waste and scrap; remelting ingots of iron or steel	511	348	1	127	15	0	19
283 – Copper ores and concentrates; copper mattes; cement copper	18	8	0	0	10	0	0
284 – Nickel ores and concentrates; nickel mattes, nickel oxide sinters and other intermediate products of nickel metallurgy	1	1	0	0	0	0	0
285 – Aluminum ores and concentrates	749	31	12	56	405	0	244
286 – Ores and concentrates of uranium or thorium	27	0	0	0	0	0	27
287 – Ores and concentrates of base metals	465	82	0	19	34	8	321
288 – Nonferrous base metal waste and scrap	823	535	6	70	56	3	153
289 – Ores and concentrates of precious metals; waste, scrap and sweepings of precious metals (other than gold)	219	74	10	51	28	16	38
291 – Crude animal materials, n.e.s.	534	75	0	43	95	22	299
292 – Crude vegetable materials, n.e.s.	2 249	502	35	509	623	51	529
321 – Coal, pulverized or not	779	94	0	0	598	60	27
322 – Briquettes, lignite and peat	158	154	0	1	0	0	2
325 – Coke and semicoke (including char) of coal, of lignite or of peat, agglomerated or not; retort carbon	239	13	110	0	7	0	109
333 – Crude oil	101 722	28 624	0	4 501	18 748	1 001	48 848
334 – Oil (not crude)	26 735	6 185	86	5 856	7 058	322	7 229
335 – Residual petroleum products	1 143	392	37	291	219	26	179
342 – Liquefied propane and butane	2 422	1 515	0	92	143	2	669
343 – Natural gas, whether or not liquefied	20 621	18 250	0	0	1 783	11	577
344 – Petroleum gases and other gaseous hydrocarbons, n.e.s.	361	266	0	42	12	0	40
345 – Coal gas, water gas, producer gas and similar gases, other than petroleum gases and other gaseous hydrocarbons	0	0	0	0	0	0	0
351 – Electric current	1 382	1 382	0	0	0	0	0
411 – Animal oils and fats	62	15	6	15	1	3	23
421 – Fixed vegetable fats and oils, soft, crude, refined or fractioned	896	306	14	496	25	1	53
422 – Fixed vegetable fats and oils (other than soft), crude, refined or fractioned	444	13	0	45	10	339	37
431 – Animal or vegetable fats and oils processed; waxes and inedible mixtures or preparations of animal or vegetable fats	182	71	3	26	10	54	17
511 – Hydrocarbons and specified derivatives	2 021	1 080	73	439	134	4	290
512 – Alcohols, phenols, and halogenated derivatives	2 032	249	87	332	771	140	453
513 – Carboxylic acids, halides, and derivities	2 736	307	693	684	43	37	973
514 – Nitrogen-function compounds	2 916	128	335	1 777	23	24	629
515 – Organo-inorganic and heterocyclic compounds	20 973	75	877	16 485	35	2 219	1 283
516 – Organic chemicals	2 197	115	330	664	250	68	770
522 – Inorganic chemical elements	3 142	775	150	474	945	10	788
523 – Metallic salts and peroxysalts of inorganic acids	980	420	46	244	54	7	208
524 – Inorganic chemicals, n.e.s.; organic and inorganic compounds of precious metals	318	71	43	62	25	1	116
525 – Radioactive and associated materials	2 979	227	132	1 303	0	0	1 318
531 – Synthetic organic coloring matter and color lakes and preparations based thereon	725	50	39	317	9	12	298
532 – Dyeing and tanning extracts, and synthetic tanning materials	70	6	8	17	13	0	26
533 – Pigments, paints, varnishes and related materials	1 686	646	198	605	9	21	206
541 – Medicinal products, except medicaments	7 839	301	354	5 669	25	70	1 420
542 – Medicaments (including veterinary medicaments)	23 677	1 822	2 040	17 425	8	12	2 371
551 – Essential oils, perfume and flavor materials	1 391	55	10	1 068	103	21	134
553 – Perfumery, cosmetics, or toilet preparations, excluding soaps	3 250	713	77	1 934	34	25	468
554 – Soap, cleansing and polishing preparations	970	475	50	291	22	13	120
562 – Fertilizers (except crude)	2 130	1 142	14	99	128	26	721
571 – Polymers of ethylene	2 163	1 960	39	102	22	31	9
572 – Polymers of styrene, in primary forms	633	266	46	80	89	23	130
573 – Polymers of vinyl chloride or other halogenated olefins, in primary forms	534	224	115	162	23	2	9
574 – Polyacetals, other polyethers and epoxide resins, in primary forms; polycarbonates, alkyd resins and other polyesters	1 327	524	122	228	18	231	204
575 – Plastics	2 561	702	391	1 138	37	8	284
579 – Waste, parings and scrap, of plastics	150	61	3	59	3	1	23
581 – Tubes, pipes and hoses of plastics	735	306	58	180	10	11	170
582 – Plates, sheets, film, foil and strip of plastics	3 670	1 382	458	814	133	94	789
583 – Monofilament with a cross-sectional dimension exceeding 1 mm, rods, sticks, and profile shapes of plastics	389	347	4	20	0	0	18
591 – Insecticides, fungicides, herbicides, plant growth regulators, etc., disinfectants and similar products	622	99	28	369	20	4	102
592 – Starches, inulin and wheat gluten; albuminoidal substances	1 204	166	43	527	39	11	419
593 – Explosives and pyrotechnic products	341	86	2	51	8	1	192
597 – Prepared additives for mineral oils, etc.; liquids for hydraulic transmissions; antifreezes and deicing fluids; lubricating preparations	304	114	23	147	1	12	6
598 – Miscellaneous chemical products	4 386	754	1 127	1 829	28	99	548
611 – Leather	744	65	0	289	271	15	103
612 – Manufactures of leather or composition leather, n.e.s.; saddlery and harness	349	45	1	70	18	14	201
613 – Furskins, tanned or dressed (including pieces or cuttings), assembled or unassembled without the addition of other materials	29	4	0	12	5	0	8
621 – Materials of rubber, including pastes, plates, sheets, rods, thread, tubes, etc.	915	423	115	208	25	42	101
625 – Rubber tires, interchangeable tire treads, tire flaps and inner tubes for wheels of all kinds	5 258	1 427	1 210	702	288	97	1 534
629 – Articles of rubber, n.e.s.	2 358	895	360	453	62	108	480

Note: NAFTA includes Canada and Mexico. EU-15 (European Union) consists of Austria, Belgium, Denmark, Finland, France, Germany, Greece, Ireland, Italy, Luxembourg, Netherlands, Portugal, Spain, Sweden, and the United Kingdom. ASEAN-10 (Association of Southeast Asian Nations) consists of Brunei, Burma (Myanmar), Cambodia, Indonesia, Laos, Malaysia, Philippines, Singapore, Thailand, and Vietnam. Other Americas includes North, Central, and South America less Mexico and Canada. Rest of world equals all other countries not listed above.

Table B-28. U.S. Total Imports by Area and 3-Digit SITC Product Groups, 2003—*Continued*

(Millions of dollars; Census basis; general imports, Customs.)

SITC product	World	NAFTA	Japan	EU-15	Other Americas	ASEAN-10	Rest of world
633 – Cork manufactures	202	2	0	191	0	0	9
634 – Veneers, plywood, particle board, and other wood, worked, n.e.s.	4 952	3 181	3	507	520	338	403
635 – Wood manufactures, n.e.s.	4 336	2 055	6	320	404	366	1 186
641 – Paper and paperboard	11 073	7 496	443	2 211	127	79	716
642 – Paper and paperboard, cut to size or shape, and articles of paper or paperboard	3 775	1 981	70	391	145	127	1 062
651 – Textile yarn	2 045	837	122	385	55	122	524
652 – Cotton fabrics, woven	1 500	144	76	248	11	111	911
653 – Woven fabrics of manmade textile materials	1 180	280	69	219	9	104	498
654 – Woven fabrics of textile materials, other than cotton or manmade fibers and narrow or special fabrics	640	99	8	245	9	6	274
655 – Knitted or crocheted fabrics	1 031	327	8	115	14	13	555
656 – Tulles, lace, embroidery, ribbons, trimmings and other small wares	579	127	15	103	34	18	282
657 – Special yarns, special textile fabrics and related products	1 961	624	177	554	70	45	491
658 – Made-up articles of textile materials	6 636	852	32	434	342	259	4 717
659 – Floor coverings, etc.	1 685	194	1	327	7	17	1 139
661 – Lime, cement, and fabricated construction materials	2 881	676	9	870	397	120	809
662 – Clay construction materials and refractory construction materials	1 682	237	25	1 043	191	62	125
663 – Mineral manufactures, n.e.s.	2 526	764	270	635	76	29	753
664 – Glass	2 336	1 068	225	403	38	153	448
665 – Glassware	1 904	369	47	760	53	24	652
666 – Pottery	1 764	52	49	387	18	192	1 066
667 – Pearls, precious and semiprecious stones	13 854	85	95	2 864	139	216	10 455
671 – Pig iron and iron and steel powders	1 832	122	22	84	852	0	752
672 – Iron or steel ingots and other primary forms, and semifinished products of iron or steel ..	1 318	516	9	275	386	0	133
673 – Iron or nonalloy steel flat-rolled products, not clad, plated or coated	1 369	484	32	278	55	26	493
674 – Iron and nonalloy steel flat-rolled products, clad, plated or coated	1 132	601	30	157	82	12	250
675 – Alloy steel flat-rolled products	1 220	408	121	535	35	10	111
676 – Iron and steel bars, rods, angles, shapes and sections, including sheet piling	2 354	840	151	574	236	14	538
677 – Iron and steel rails and railway track construction material	163	34	56	17	1	0	55
678 – Iron and steel wire	564	187	75	137	20	2	142
679 – Iron and steel tubes, pipes and fittings	2 992	1 030	310	561	138	96	857
681 – Silver, platinum, and other platinum group metals	3 425	609	41	725	140	0	1 910
682 – Copper	3 160	1 273	117	409	946	37	378
683 – Nickel	1 170	345	23	264	11	13	513
684 – Aluminum	7 238	4 190	84	684	628	20	1 633
685 – Lead	104	94	0	3	0	0	6
686 – Zinc	828	622	1	29	61	0	115
687 – Tin	189	4	2	5	140	12	26
689 – Miscellaneous nonferrous base metals employed in metallurgy and cermets	694	103	71	142	32	5	341
691 – Metal structures and parts, n.e.s., of iron, steel or aluminum	1 705	1 055	34	353	20	13	229
692 – Metal containers for storage or transport	664	373	41	110	23	16	101
693 – Wire products (excluding insulated electrical wiring) and fencing grills	756	249	44	139	19	20	285
694 – Nails, screws, nuts, bolts, rivets and similar articles, of iron, steel, copper or aluminum ..	2 930	379	492	318	28	62	1 651
695 – Tools for use in the hand or in machines	3 873	424	739	900	42	29	1 740
696 – Cutlery	1 236	116	48	200	28	28	815
697 – Household equipment of base metal, n.e.s.	4 337	702	31	383	67	270	2 886
699 – Manufactures of base metal	9 477	3 648	696	1 455	152	165	3 361
711 – Steam or other vapor generating boilers, super-heated water boilers and auxiliary plant for use therewith; and parts thereof	266	177	0	27	1	24	36
712 – Steam turbines and other vapor turbines, and parts thereof, n.e.s.	397	65	92	181	0	2	57
713 – Internal combustion piston engines	15 933	6 431	4 771	3 560	615	72	485
714 – Nonelectric engines and motors	8 714	1 788	593	5 458	7	64	803
716 – Rotating electric plant and parts	6 170	2 449	774	1 412	190	139	1 206
718 – Power generating machinery and parts thereof, n.e.s.	1 004	217	134	544	12	11	87
721 – Agricultural machinery (excluding tractors) and parts	1 530	637	30	588	18	4	253
722 – Tractors (other than mechanical handling equipment)	2 170	160	865	824	44	3	275
723 – Civil engineering and contractors' plant and equipment	4 983	905	1 464	1 950	179	39	446
724 – Textile and leather machinery, and parts thereof, n.e.s.	1 800	36	235	1 013	37	22	458
725 – Paper mill and pulp mill machinery, paper cutting machines and machinery for the manufacture of paper articles; parts thereof	809	108	20	540	17	0	123
726 – Printing and bookbinding machinery, and parts thereof	1 607	107	237	1 036	12	4	210
727 – Food-processing machines (excluding domestic)	652	54	40	470	7	3	79
728 – Machinery and equipment specialized for particular industries	7 179	1 131	1 503	3 138	35	80	1 293
731 – Machine tools working by removing metal or other material	2 134	45	1 080	615	6	25	363
733 – Machine tools for working metal, sintered metal carbides or cermets, without removing material	710	77	212	314	10	3	94
735 – Parts and accessories suitable for use solely or principally with metal working machine tools, whether or not removing materials	1 051	159	319	403	4	6	160
737 – Metalworking machinery (other than machine tools) and parts thereof, n.e.s.	1 440	259	593	402	19	9	158
741 – Heating and cooling equipment	5 391	2 163	360	1 049	77	156	1 588
742 – Pumps for liquids, whether or not fitted with a measuring device; liquid elevators; parts for such pumps and liquid elevators	3 240	913	411	1 269	65	17	566
743 – Pumps, air or gas compressors and fans	8 105	2 181	1 229	1 990	317	259	2 128
744 – Mechanical handling equipment	5 139	1 737	689	1 950	15	26	722
745 – Nonelectrical machinery, tools and mechanical apparatus, and parts thereof, n.e.s.	4 318	643	541	1 962	26	16	1 130
746 – Ball or roller bearings	1 414	213	424	312	51	65	350

Note: NAFTA includes Canada and Mexico. EU-15 (European Union) consists of Austria, Belgium, Denmark, Finland, France, Germany, Greece, Ireland, Italy, Luxembourg, Netherlands, Portugal, Spain, Sweden, and the United Kingdom. ASEAN-10 (Association of Southeast Asian Nations) consists of Brunei, Burma (Myanmar), Cambodia, Indonesia, Laos, Malaysia, Philippines, Singapore, Thailand, and Vietnam. Other Americas includes North, Central, and South America less Mexico and Canada. Rest of world equals all other countries not listed above.

Table B-28. U.S. Total Imports by Area and 3-Digit SITC Product Groups, 2003—*Continued*

(Millions of dollars; Census basis; general imports, Customs.)

SITC product	World	NAFTA	Japan	EU-15	Other Americas	ASEAN-10	Rest of world
747 – Taps, cocks, valves and similar appliances for pipes, boiler shells, tanks, etc.	5 532	1 568	807	1 567	56	70	1 462
748 – Transmission shafts and cranks; bearing housings and plain shaft bearings; gears and gearing; ball screws; gear boxes	3 540	792	860	1 304	142	11	431
749 – Nonelectric parts and accessories of machinery, n.e.s.	1 788	822	354	387	11	13	200
751 – Office machines	3 852	333	941	249	5	228	2 096
752 – Automatic data processing machines	52 012	6 926	3 403	2 251	37	16 410	22 986
759 – Parts for office machines and a.d.p. machines	24 962	1 909	4 663	2 322	130	5 117	10 822
761 – Television receivers	11 874	5 255	1 924	116	14	1 776	2 790
762 – Radio-broadcast receivers	5 937	1 620	318	102	115	1 258	2 523
763 – Sound and television recorders	12 794	195	4 051	113	5	1 863	6 567
764 – Telecommunications equipment	40 531	10 257	2 538	3 833	1 066	5 410	17 427
771 – Electric power machinery (other than rotating electric plant of power generating machinery) and parts thereof	6 427	2 006	372	815	116	640	2 479
772 – Electrical apparatus for switching or protecting elec. circuits	12 476	4 809	1 530	2 232	394	655	2 854
773 – Equipment for distributing electricity	8 763	6 013	227	404	201	637	1 282
774 – Electro-diagnostic apparatus	4 868	573	921	2 629	2	70	674
775 – Household type electrical and nonelectrical equipment	8 604	2 328	128	963	71	254	4 859
776 – Thermionic, cold cathode, and photocathode valves	25 417	2 320	2 804	2 642	652	8 536	8 462
778 – Electrical machinery and apparatus	15 989	4 435	2 943	2 242	211	586	5 574
781 – All motor vehicles	114 721	42 625	32 227	29 835	546	4	9 483
782 – Special purpose motor vehicles	17 293	16 302	473	445	26	0	47
783 – Road motor vehicles, n.e.s.	1 838	1 619	0	149	0	0	70
784 – Parts and accessories of motor vehicles	32 888	16 563	7 286	4 844	708	231	3 256
785 – Motorcycles (including mopeds) and cycles, motorized and not motorized; invalid carriages	4 745	123	2 149	590	64	53	1 765
786 – Trailers and semi-trailers; other vehicles, not mechanically propelled; specially designed and equipped transport containers	1 093	603	4	78	6	8	395
791 – Railway vehicles (including hovertrains) and associated equipment	933	505	89	235	22	0	81
792 – Aircraft and associated equipment	16 990	6 409	854	6 764	1 846	91	1 025
793 – Ships, boats, and floating structures	1 592	501	17	522	17	105	430
811 – Prefabricated buildings	347	267	0	20	0	1	59
812 – Sanitary, plumbing and heating fixtures and fittings, n.e.s.	783	386	10	61	129	39	158
813 – Lighting fixtures and fittings, n.e.s.	4 873	1 001	32	276	9	75	3 479
821 – Furniture and bedding accessories	24 356	8 827	135	2 491	609	1 888	10 406
831 – Trunks, suitcases, vanity cases, binocular and camera cases, handbags, wallets, etc. of leather, etc.	4 842	107	9	637	46	376	3 666
841 – Men's or boys' coats, jackets, etc. not knit	12 637	2 560	4	560	2 263	2 021	5 228
842 – Women's or girls' coats, jackets, etc. not knit	15 903	1 723	25	680	1 232	3 120	9 124
843 – Men's or boys' coats, jackets, etc. knit	3 900	335	1	43	1 154	884	1 483
844 – Women's or girls' coats, jackets, etc. knit	5 947	663	7	96	1 208	1 124	2 850
845 – Articles of apparel of textile fabrics	22 225	3 039	178	626	4 673	3 457	10 251
846 – Clothing accessories	2 296	341	10	249	359	117	1 220
848 – Apparel and accessories except textile; headgear	5 254	279	30	327	90	1 063	3 466
851 – Footwear	15 603	340	2	1 768	1 206	1 195	11 092
871 – Optical instruments and apparatus, n.e.s.	1 579	88	411	441	8	80	552
872 – Medical instruments and appliances	7 699	2 055	406	2 725	899	369	1 246
873 – Meters and counters, n.e.s.	1 388	963	166	109	14	29	107
874 – Measuring/checking/analysing instruments	12 994	3 392	2 206	4 545	51	664	2 136
881 – Photographic apparatus and equipment, n.e.s.	3 103	340	946	849	17	80	870
882 – Photographic and cinematographic supplies	1 943	214	960	629	16	9	115
883 – Cinematographic film, exposed and developed, whether or not incorporating sound track or consisting only of sound track	273	241	0	15	0	0	16
884 – Optical goods, n.e.s.	2 992	124	626	990	3	269	980
885 – Watches and clocks	3 600	105	794	152	2	260	2 288
891 – Arms and ammunition	1 338	278	62	628	48	7	315
892 – Printed matter	4 148	1 592	84	963	50	181	1 279
893 – Articles of plastics	10 216	3 473	328	1 063	184	284	4 882
894 – Baby carriages, toys, games and sporting goods	21 566	1 156	886	860	70	713	17 881
895 – Office and stationery supplies, n.e.s.	1 532	187	378	216	37	51	663
896 – Works of art, collectors' pieces, and antiques	4 398	66	46	3 536	44	10	697
897 – Jewelry, goldsmiths' and silversmiths' wares	7 499	369	22	1 658	449	921	4 080
898 – Musical instruments and accessories	5 852	773	1 517	642	12	229	2 679
899 – Miscellaneous manufactured articles	7 854	608	91	2 667	128	414	3 946
931 – Special transactions not classified by kind	33 622	14 258	2 208	8 192	1 965	1 663	5 337
950 – Coin, including gold coin; proof and presentation sets and current coin	199	51	0	68	1	0	79
961 – Coin (other than gold coin), not being legal tender	8	4	0	1	0	0	3
971 – Gold, nonmonetary	2 932	1 593	1	41	1 254	9	35
984 – Estimate of low value import transactions	14 067	5 368	1 317	3 746	554	537	2 546
992 – Export shipments valued not over $10,000, not identified by kind	0	0	0	0	0	0	0
994 – Estimated low value shipments	0	0	0	0	0	0	0

Note: NAFTA includes Canada and Mexico. EU-15 (European Union) consists of Austria, Belgium, Denmark, Finland, France, Germany, Greece, Ireland, Italy, Luxembourg, Netherlands, Portugal, Spain, Sweden, and the United Kingdom. ASEAN-10 (Association of Southeast Asian Nations) consists of Brunei, Burma (Myanmar), Cambodia, Indonesia, Laos, Malaysia, Philippines, Singapore, Thailand, and Vietnam. Other Americas includes North, Central, and South America less Mexico and Canada. Rest of world equals all other countries not listed above.

Table B-29. U.S. Total Trade Balances by Area and 3-Digit SITC Product Groups, 2003

(Millions of dollars; Census basis; foreign and domestic exports, f.a.s.; general imports, Customs.)

SITC product	World	NAFTA	Japan	EU-15	Other Americas	ASEAN-10	Rest of world
000 – TOTAL	-535 652	-95 301	-65 965	-94 262	-26 835	-36 597	-216 692
001 – Live animals other than animals of division 03	-827	-1 186	71	-52	21	11	308
011 – Meat of bovine animals	718	9	1 157	10	-79	21	-400
012 – Other meat and edible offal	2 243	127	973	-99	204	33	1 006
016 – Meat and edible meat offal, salted, in brine, dried or smoked; edible flours and meals of meat or meat offal	-65	-38	15	-45	6	2	-5
017 – Meat and edible meat offal, prepared or preserved, n.e.s.	81	144	103	-61	-180	15	61
022 – Milk, cream, milk products except butter or cheese	261	165	32	-18	23	58	2
023 – Butter and other fats and oils derived from milk	-43	-4	0	-11	1	0	-30
024 – Cheese and curd	-734	38	23	-573	-20	6	-209
025 – Birds' eggs and egg yolks, fresh, dried or otherwise preserved, sweetened or not; egg albumin	142	54	18	18	33	1	17
034 – Fish, fresh, chilled or frozen	-1 262	-444	777	218	-1 054	-326	-433
035 – Fish, dried, salted, or in brine; smoked fish	-99	-50	11	2	-17	-11	-33
036 – Crustaceans	-4 373	-1 069	65	141	-951	-1 301	-1 259
037 – Fish, crustaceans, molluscs and other aquatic invertebrates, prepared or preserved, n.e.s.	-1 912	-157	-12	42	-222	-1 180	-383
041 – Wheat and meslin, unmilled	3 818	271	482	225	794	336	1 710
042 – Rice	823	215	114	65	332	-77	176
043 – Barley, unmilled	54	-11	52	-8	9	0	13
044 – Maize (not including sweet corn) unmilled	4 821	1 042	1 602	71	576	43	1 487
045 – Cereals, unmilled (other than wheat, rice, barley, and maize)	391	208	135	2	11	3	32
046 – Meal and flour of wheat and flour of meslin	15	-45	0	2	17	1	40
047 – Cereal meals and flours, n.e.s.	54	16	0	4	9	-2	26
048 – Cereal preparations and preparations of flour or starch of fruits or vegetables	-869	-374	51	-476	21	-49	-42
054 – Vegetables, roots, tubers and other edible vegetable products	-1 574	-1 503	183	-57	-220	14	8
056 – Vegetables, roots and tubers, prepared or preserved, n.e.s.	-488	-387	259	-337	-3	19	-39
057 – Fruit and nuts (not including oil nuts), fresh or dried	304	807	579	925	-2 441	57	377
058 – Fruit preserved, and fruit preparations (excluding fruit juices)	-592	-114	46	61	-118	-298	-168
059 – Fruit juices and vegetable juices, unfermented and not containing added spirits	-103	277	93	89	-395	-85	-84
061 – Sugars, molasses, and honey	-627	-64	57	23	-489	-58	-97
062 – Sugar confectionery	-819	-437	-2	-175	-86	-32	-87
071 – Coffee and coffee substitutes	-1 558	12	28	-133	-1 232	-160	-72
072 – Cocoa	-1 145	169	1	-221	-217	-391	-486
073 – Chocolate and other food preparations containing cocoa, n.e.s.	-565	-439	25	-217	-3	29	38
074 – Tea and mate	-191	-22	-2	-29	-30	-7	-102
075 – Spices	-570	-5	3	-25	-53	-150	-340
081 – Feeding stuff for animals	3 462	651	719	566	487	376	663
091 – Margarine and shortening	66	39	2	-3	19	2	8
098 – Edible products and preparations, n.e.s.	1 537	603	198	-114	253	80	516
111 – Nonalcoholic beverages, n.e.s.	-566	-225	75	-358	18	-29	-46
112 – Alcoholic beverages	-8 248	-1 784	113	-5 715	-170	14	-706
121 – Tobacco, unmanufactured; tobacco refuse	350	-39	128	430	-229	22	39
122 – Tobacco, manufactured	1 274	-6	987	125	-339	14	492
211 – Hides and skins (except furskins), raw	1 595	64	105	117	18	70	1 221
212 – Furskins, raw (including furskin heads, tails and other pieces or cuttings, suitable for furriers' use)	84	18	1	-9	0	1	73
222 – Oil seeds and oleaginous fruits	8 122	1 227	973	1 220	120	599	3 983
223 – Oil seeds and oleaginous fruits, whole or broken, of a kind used for extracting other fixed vegetalbe oils	43	-5	21	13	11	7	-4
231 – Natural rubber in primary forms	-954	37	2	2	5	-963	-37
232 – Synthetic rubber; reclaimed rubber; waste, pairings and scrap of unhardened rubber	737	176	-53	283	108	56	167
244 – Cork, natural, raw and waste (including natural cork in blocks or sheets)	0	0	0	-1	0	0	0
245 – Fuel wood (excluding wood waste) and wood charcoal	-10	-5	0	-1	-2	0	-2
246 – Wood in chips or particles and wood waste	61	-40	79	9	-2	0	15
247 – Wood in the rough or roughly squared	1 048	189	452	131	15	34	228
248 – Wood, simply worked	-4 894	-4 165	127	55	-807	-18	-85
251 – Pulp and waste paper	1 620	-1 108	371	1 033	-226	204	1 345
261 – Silk textile fibers	2	0	0	0	0	0	2
263 – Cotton textile fibers	3 420	555	116	88	280	467	1 914
264 – Jute and other textile bast fibers, n.e.s., raw or processed but not spun; tow and waste of these fibres (including yarn)	0	0	0	0	0	0	0
265 – Vegetable textile fibers (other than cotton and jute), raw or processed but not spun; waste of these fibers	-16	-9	0	-3	1	0	-3
266 – Synthetic fibers suitable for spinning	35	150	-24	-1	102	-27	-166
267 – Manmade fibers, n.e.s. suitable for spinning and waste of manmade fibers	398	19	7	99	17	53	204
268 – Wool and other animal hair (including wool tops)	-2	9	0	7	4	0	-23
269 – Worn clothing and other worn textile articles; rags	242	34	26	10	61	12	99
272 – Fertilizer, crude, except those of division 56 (imports only)	-80	-6	0	-3	-23	0	-48
273 – Stone, sand and gravel	48	-47	18	37	-15	9	47
274 – Sulfur and unroasted iron pyrites	-26	-52	0	-1	-4	0	31
277 – Natural abrasives, n.e.s. (including industrial diamonds)	-6	13	14	-24	8	5	-22
278 – Crude minerals, n.e.s.	357	61	156	240	-49	53	-103

Note: NAFTA includes Canada and Mexico. EU-15 (European Union) consists of Austria, Belgium, Denmark, Finland, France, Germany, Greece, Ireland, Italy, Luxembourg, Netherlands, Portugal, Spain, Sweden, and the United Kingdom. ASEAN-10 (Association of Southeast Asian Nations) consists of Brunei, Burma (Myanmar), Cambodia, Indonesia, Laos, Malaysia, Philippines, Singapore, Thailand, and Vietnam. Other Americas includes North, Central, and South America less Mexico and Canada. Rest of world equals all other countries not listed above.

Table B-29. U.S. Total Trade Balances by Area and 3-Digit SITC Product Groups, 2003—*Continued*

(Millions of dollars; Census basis; foreign and domestic exports, f.a.s.; general imports, Customs.)

SITC product	World	NAFTA	Japan	EU-15	Other Americas	ASEAN-10	Rest of world
281 – Iron ore and concentrates	-80	45	0	-5	-126	0	5
282 – Ferrous waste and scrap; remelting ingots of iron or steel	1 434	-22	31	29	3	162	1 232
283 – Copper ores and concentrates; copper mattes; cement copper	70	49	1	24	-9	0	6
284 – Nickel ores and concentrates; nickel mattes, nickel oxide sinters and other intermediate products of nickel metallurgy	9	6	1	0	1	0	1
285 – Aluminum ores and concentrates	-405	179	4	3	-398	5	-198
286 – Ores and concentrates of uranium or thorium	-27	0	0	0	0	0	-27
287 – Ores and concentrates of base metals	297	126	79	311	-21	-7	-191
288 – Nonferrous base metal waste and scrap	702	-211	59	-20	-2	12	864
289 – Ores and concentrates of precious metals; waste, scrap and sweepings of precious metals (other than gold)	607	97	54	400	-23	-16	94
291 – Crude animal materials, n.e.s.	100	233	86	12	-71	-5	-155
292 – Crude vegetable materials, n.e.s.	-1 001	-6	34	-221	-516	-20	-272
321 – Coal, pulverized or not	769	536	1	580	-425	-60	137
322 – Briquettes, lignite and peat	-147	-150	0	0	1	1	0
325 – Coke and semicoke (including char) of coal, of lignite or of peat, agglomerated or not; retort carbon	-168	51	-110	2	-5	0	-106
333 – Crude oil	-101 567	-28 469	0	-4 501	-18 748	-1 001	-48 848
334 – Oil (not crude)	-19 385	-2 970	179	-5 676	-4 314	142	-6 746
335 – Residual petroleum products	986	87	105	94	-12	59	653
342 – Liquefied propane and butane	-1 949	-1 212	32	-81	-67	-2	-619
343 – Natural gas, whether or not liquefied	-19 321	-17 098	148	0	-1 783	-11	-577
344 – Petroleum gases and other gaseous hydrocarbons, n.e.s.	-67	-32	3	-32	-6	28	-28
345 – Coal gas, water gas, producer gas and similar gases, other than petroleum gases and other gaseous hydrocarbons	1	0	0	0	0	0	1
351 – Electric current	-666	-666	0	0	0	0	0
411 – Animal oils and fats	486	199	4	-9	160	-2	133
421 – Fixed vegetable fats and oils, soft, crude, refined or fractionated	107	-27	22	-446	130	2	426
422 – Fixed vegetable fats and oils (other than soft), crude, refined or fractionated	-279	11	5	-8	-2	-335	50
431 – Animal or vegetable fats and oils processed; waxes and inedible mixtures or preparations of animal or vegetable fats	114	66	15	21	15	-48	45
511 – Hydrocarbons and specified derivatives	2 373	417	177	173	376	137	1 092
512 – Alcohols, phenols, and halogenated derivatives	365	385	51	78	-533	14	371
513 – Carboxylic acids, halides, and derivities	119	450	-569	326	303	52	-443
514 – Nitrogen-function compounds	765	494	-69	-748	294	167	628
515 – Organo-inorganic and heterocyclic compounds	-16 154	387	-698	-13 611	380	-2 036	-575
516 – Organic chemicals	107	533	-101	-7	-51	62	-329
522 – Inorganic chemical elements	-971	-226	222	-68	-674	85	-310
523 – Metallic salts and peroxysalts of inorganic acids	571	28	75	72	203	134	59
524 – Inorganic chemicals, n.e.s.; organic and inorganic compounds of precious metals	111	89	7	27	-13	16	-15
525 – Radioactive and associated materials	-1 373	-147	685	-951	12	6	-978
531 – Synthetic organic coloring matter and color lakes and preparations based thereon	-160	124	-10	-129	44	22	-210
532 – Dyeing and tanning extracts, and synthetic tanning materials	-9	3	-5	5	-6	3	-9
533 – Pigments, paints, varnishes and related materials	1 971	1 001	-72	90	364	143	445
541 – Medicinal products, except medicaments	342	659	347	-670	256	77	-327
542 – Medicaments (including veterinary medicaments)	-12 649	530	-1 533	-11 552	515	76	-685
551 – Essential oils, perfume and flavor materials	-138	373	98	-777	5	82	82
553 – Perfumery, cosmetics, or toilet preparations, excluding soaps	438	545	247	-1 052	300	117	279
554 – Soap, cleansing and polishing preparations	946	499	63	-28	120	83	209
562 – Fertilizers (except crude)	422	-577	148	-74	512	86	326
571 – Polymers of ethylene	682	-510	29	302	406	75	379
572 – Polymers of styrene, in primary forms	227	336	-24	21	-49	-3	-54
573 – Polymers of vinyl chloride or other halogenated olefins, in primary forms	636	304	-68	-2	63	34	305
574 – Polyacetals, other polyethers and epoxide resins, in primary forms; polycarbonates, alkyd resins and other polyesters	1 774	696	33	155	319	-33	603
575 – Plastics	4 299	2 003	-4	292	519	329	1 160
579 – Waste, parings and scrap, of plastics	144	22	-2	-41	4	2	159
581 – Tubes, pipes and hoses of plastics	353	358	-26	-56	104	30	-57
582 – Plates, sheets, film, foil and strip of plastics	1 463	1 156	-240	160	141	182	64
583 – Monofilament with a cross-sectional dimension exceeding 1 mm, rods, sticks, and profile shapes of plastics	-107	-275	1	8	155	4	0
591 – Insecticides, fungicides, herbicides, plant growth regulators, etc., disinfectants and similar products	835	522	12	-76	300	35	42
592 – Starches, inulin and wheat gluten; albuminoidal substances	99	395	69	-325	55	44	-140
593 – Explosives and pyrotechnic products	54	121	24	8	5	17	-122
597 – Prepared additives for mineral oils, etc.; liquids for hydraulic transmissions; antifreezes and deicing fluids; lubricating preparations	1 576	382	115	157	220	281	421
598 – Miscellaneous chemical products	3 994	1 076	-191	1 050	408	247	1 406
611 – Leather	134	224	12	-152	-214	5	259
612 – Manufactures of leather or composition leather, n.e.s.; saddlery and harness	-227	34	11	-57	-15	-13	-187
613 – Furskins, tanned or dressed (including pieces or cuttings), assembled or unassembled without the addition of other materials	-11	0	0	-5	-3	0	-4
621 – Materials of rubber, including pastes, plates, sheets, rods, thread, tubes, etc.	137	292	-57	-69	14	-26	-17
625 – Rubber tires, interchangeable tire treads, tire flaps and inner tubes for wheels of all kinds	-2 938	239	-1 105	-500	-129	-75	-1 367
629 – Articles of rubber, n.e.s.	-818	142	-329	-226	0	-65	-339

Note: NAFTA includes Canada and Mexico. EU-15 (European Union) consists of Austria, Belgium, Denmark, Finland, France, Germany, Greece, Ireland, Italy, Luxembourg, Netherlands, Portugal, Spain, Sweden, and the United Kingdom. ASEAN-10 (Association of Southeast Asian Nations) consists of Brunei, Burma (Myanmar), Cambodia, Indonesia, Laos, Malaysia, Philippines, Singapore, Thailand, and Vietnam. Other Americas includes North, Central, and South America less Mexico and Canada. Rest of world equals all other countries not listed above.

Table B-29. U.S. Total Trade Balances by Area and 3-Digit SITC Product Groups, 2003—*Continued*

(Millions of dollars; Census basis; foreign and domestic exports, f.a.s.; general imports, Customs.)

SITC product	World	NAFTA	Japan	EU-15	Other Americas	ASEAN-10	Rest of world
633 – Cork manufactures	-154	9	1	-184	6	1	14
634 – Veneers, plywood, particle board, and other wood, worked, n.e.s.	-3 924	-2 603	8	-260	-477	-318	-274
635 – Wood manufactures, n.e.s.	-3 662	-1 697	68	-220	-345	-357	-1 110
641 – Paper and paperboard	-4 808	-4 546	85	-1 526	601	122	455
642 – Paper and paperboard, cut to size or shape, and articles of paper or paperboard	164	923	8	-65	127	-50	-778
651 – Textile yarn	-192	-127	-71	-131	483	-88	-258
652 – Cotton fabrics, woven	-150	578	-71	-198	495	-99	-855
653 – Woven fabrics of manmade textile materials	141	571	-62	-166	271	-92	-380
654 – Woven fabrics of textile materials, other than cotton or manmade fibers and narrow or special fabrics	-426	-2	-3	-215	38	-3	-241
655 – Knitted or crocheted fabrics	388	185	-2	-88	797	-3	-501
656 – Tulles, lace, embroidery, ribbons, trimmings and other small wares	42	141	-6	-73	196	-8	-207
657 – Special yarns, special textile fabrics and related products	733	901	-84	-165	105	35	-60
658 – Made-up articles of textile materials	-5 930	-474	2	-312	-281	-244	-4 621
659 – Floor coverings, etc.	-967	329	22	-275	30	-6	-1 066
661 – Lime, cement, and fabricated construction materials	-2 580	-476	-3	-858	-364	-116	-763
662 – Clay construction materials and refractory construction materials	-1 361	-80	-4	-1 009	-154	-50	-64
663 – Mineral manufactures, n.e.s.	-884	-121	-178	-238	60	19	-425
664 – Glass	229	369	-45	8	24	-86	-41
665 – Glassware	-1 173	-51	3	-610	0	7	-522
666 – Pottery	-1 644	13	-45	-367	-4	-190	-1 052
667 – Pearls, precious and semiprecious stones	-8 336	84	-1	-1 261	-46	-78	-7 034
671 – Pig iron and iron and steel powders	-1 673	-29	-18	-53	-841	1	-733
672 – Iron or steel ingots and other primary forms, and semifinished products of iron or steel	-1 129	-451	5	-243	-368	13	-84
673 – Iron or nonalloy steel flat-rolled products, not clad, plated or coated	141	490	-24	-105	-34	-11	-175
674 – Iron and nonalloy steel flat-rolled products, clad, plated or coated	-493	-81	-27	-132	-73	-4	-177
675 – Alloy steel flat-rolled products	-140	247	-117	-387	-22	9	130
676 – Iron and steel bars, rods, angles, shapes and sections, including sheet piling	-1 430	-127	-146	-505	-171	0	-482
677 – Iron and steel rails and railway track construction material	-95	14	-56	-9	4	0	-49
678 – Iron and steel wire	-323	-24	-72	-104	-9	2	-115
679 – Iron and steel tubes, pipes and fittings	-1 029	126	-259	-367	-8	-35	-486
681 – Silver, platinum, and other platinum group metals	-2 195	-428	116	-139	-129	8	-1 623
682 – Copper	-1 811	-543	-75	-254	-921	16	-33
683 – Nickel	-734	-263	1	-22	-2	-4	-443
684 – Aluminum	-4 193	-1 985	39	-426	-516	46	-1 351
685 – Lead	-24	-67	1	37	2	2	2
686 – Zinc	-771	-584	-1	-22	-57	1	-107
687 – Tin	-144	20	0	-2	-139	-4	-18
689 – Miscellaneous nonferrous base metals employed in metallurgy and cermets	-164	-47	-1	93	-21	-2	-186
691 – Metal structures and parts, n.e.s., of iron, steel or aluminum	-993	-742	-8	-265	91	24	-93
692 – Metal containers for storage or transport	-3	-6	-13	-1	34	-4	-13
693 – Wire products (excluding insulated electrical wiring) and fencing grills	-326	12	-33	-86	11	-8	-221
694 – Nails, screws, nuts, bolts, rivets and similar articles, of iron, steel, copper or aluminum	-1 229	813	-466	-75	19	-7	-1 513
695 – Tools for use in the hand or in machines	-1 457	707	-644	-362	111	62	-1 332
696 – Cutlery	-789	99	-40	-109	9	-13	-735
697 – Household equipment of base metal, n.e.s.	-3 764	-386	14	-293	-37	-260	-2 802
699 – Manufactures of base metal	-2 245	1 222	-453	-575	98	205	-2 742
711 – Steam or other vapor generating boilers, super-heated water boilers and auxiliary plant for use therewith; and parts thereof	71	-78	3	-2	33	-12	126
712 – Steam turbines and other vapor turbines, and parts thereof, n.e.s.	-118	-24	-84	-95	24	24	36
713 – Internal combustion piston engines	-3 314	2 038	-4 134	-1 747	-209	113	625
714 – Nonelectric engines and motors	6 895	374	470	2 302	1 084	1 041	1 623
716 – Rotating electric plant and parts	-2 250	-566	-657	-846	100	33	-314
718 – Power generating machinery and parts thereof, n.e.s.	-125	50	-93	-357	51	17	207
721 – Agricultural machinery (excluding tractors) and parts	1 015	454	60	54	188	32	227
722 – Tractors (other than mechanical handling equipment)	-799	427	-841	-516	29	15	87
723 – Civil engineering and contractors' plant and equipment	3 877	1 251	-1 379	-620	1 355	607	2 664
724 – Textile and leather machinery, and parts thereof, n.e.s.	-636	321	-208	-868	176	18	-75
725 – Paper mill and pulp mill machinery, paper cutting machines and machinery for the manufacture of paper articles; parts thereof	-207	114	-4	-391	43	39	-7
726 – Printing and bookbinding machinery, and parts thereof	-517	202	-165	-731	87	38	53
727 – Food-processing machines (excluding domestic)	-79	119	-17	-316	72	26	37
728 – Machinery and equipment specialized for particular industries	1 616	1 007	-601	-1 609	385	525	1 909
731 – Machine tools working by removing metal or other material	-442	364	-877	-250	40	114	167
733 – Machine tools for working metal, sintered metal carbides or cermets, without removing material	-217	118	-195	-226	14	13	60
735 – Parts and accessories suitable for use solely or principally with metal working machine tools, whether or not removing materials	326	183	-204	-66	101	102	210
737 – Metalworking machinery (other than machine tools) and parts thereof, n.e.s.	-380	73	-534	-206	54	59	174
741 – Heating and cooling equipment	668	583	-87	-158	343	85	-98
742 – Pumps for liquids, whether or not fitted with a measuring device; liquid elevators; parts for such pumps and liquid elevators	78	509	-308	-593	199	143	128
743 – Pumps, air or gas compressors and fans	-694	872	-850	-742	224	197	-394
744 – Mechanical handling equipment	-1 470	-378	-618	-1 299	577	132	116
745 – Nonelectrical machinery, tools and mechanical apparatus, and parts thereof, n.e.s.	-837	586	-412	-906	190	123	-419
746 – Ball or roller bearings	-217	407	-390	-62	35	-19	-188

Note: NAFTA includes Canada and Mexico. EU-15 (European Union) consists of Austria, Belgium, Denmark, Finland, France, Germany, Greece, Ireland, Italy, Luxembourg, Netherlands, Portugal, Spain, Sweden, and the United Kingdom. ASEAN-10 (Association of Southeast Asian Nations) consists of Brunei, Burma (Myanmar), Cambodia, Indonesia, Laos, Malaysia, Philippines, Singapore, Thailand, and Vietnam. Other Americas includes North, Central, and South America less Mexico and Canada. Rest of world equals all other countries not listed above.

Table B-29. U.S. Total Trade Balances by Area and 3-Digit SITC Product Groups, 2003—*Continued*

(Millions of dollars; Census basis; foreign and domestic exports, f.a.s.; general imports, Customs.)

SITC product	World	NAFTA	Japan	EU-15	Other Americas	ASEAN-10	Rest of world
747 – Taps, cocks, valves and similar appliances for pipes, boiler shells, tanks, etc.	-1 867	480	-680	-963	108	59	-870
748 – Transmission shafts and cranks; bearing housings and plain shaft bearings; gears and gearing; ball screws; gear boxes	-1 628	408	-822	-981	-49	30	-213
749 – Nonelectric parts and accessories of machinery, n.e.s.	-317	-61	-291	-163	88	40	70
751 – Office machines	-3 135	-72	-917	-97	93	-189	-1 951
752 – Automatic data processing machines	-30 417	894	-1 753	3 129	1 559	-15 220	-19 026
759 – Parts for office machines and a.d.p. machines	-6 220	3 999	-3 651	3 258	1 443	-3 167	-8 103
761 – Television receivers	-10 610	-4 406	-1 887	57	78	-1 746	-2 707
762 – Radio-broadcast receivers	-5 117	-963	-288	-81	-75	-1 249	-2 460
763 – Sound and television recorders	-11 536	330	-3 964	48	162	-1 848	-6 264
764 – Telecommunications equipment	-20 168	-3 541	-969	682	915	-4 627	-12 628
771 – Electric power machinery (other than rotating electric plant of power generating machinery) and parts thereof ...	-3 612	-655	-264	-307	48	-448	-1 985
772 – Electrical apparatus for switching or protecting elec. circuits	-635	1 844	-1 154	-310	110	98	-1 223
773 – Equipment for distributing electricity	-4 073	-2 741	-122	111	-43	-436	-843
774 – Electro-diagnostic apparatus	560	-56	-146	-146	264	62	581
775 – Household type electrical and nonelectrical equipment	-6 126	-827	-71	-612	104	-219	-4 501
776 – Thermionic, cold cathode, and photocathode valves	22 353	6 166	-305	1 968	1 163	6 672	6 689
778 – Electrical machinery and apparatus	-5 101	546	-2 416	-375	408	-20	-3 244
781 – All motor vehicles	-91 944	-29 036	-31 754	-24 220	-133	57	-6 858
782 – Special purpose motor vehicles	-9 423	-9 811	-447	-236	289	60	722
783 – Road motor vehicles, n.e.s.	-143	-231	0	-104	51	10	130
784 – Parts and accessories of motor vehicles	-4 561	5 596	-6 215	-2 262	27	-85	-1 622
785 – Motorcycles (including mopeds) and cycles, motorized and not motorized; invalid carriages	-3 446	252	-1 980	-84	-31	-40	-1 562
786 – Trailers and semi-trailers; other vehicles, not mechanically propelled; specially designed and equipped transport containers	68	387	19	-28	30	-4	-335
791 – Railway vehicles (including hovertrains) and associated equipment	604	444	-67	-53	66	26	188
792 – Aircraft and associated equipment	22 648	-3 945	3 989	5 710	-220	4 484	12 631
793 – Ships, boats, and floating structures	-257	-100	18	-132	218	-95	-165
811 – Prefabricated buildings	-34	-142	43	10	26	5	24
812 – Sanitary, plumbing and heating fixtures and fittings, n.e.s.	-452	-115	-8	-43	-120	-37	-129
813 – Lighting fixtures and fittings, n.e.s.	-4 029	-527	10	-151	39	-60	-3 341
821 – Furniture and bedding accessories	-20 090	-5 844	204	-2 148	-418	-1 837	-10 047
831 – Trunks, suitcases, vanity cases, binocular and camera cases, handbags, wallets, etc. of leather, etc.	-4 411	6	135	-582	-31	-363	-3 577
841 – Men's or boys' coats, jackets, etc. not knit	-11 929	-2 299	24	-527	-1 902	-2 018	-5 208
842 – Women's or girls' coats, jackets, etc. not knit	-15 466	-1 442	-5	-649	-1 155	-3 115	-9 100
843 – Men's or boys' coats, jackets, etc. knit	-3 504	-226	20	-30	-918	-881	-1 469
844 – Women's or girls' coats, jackets, etc. knit	-5 513	-485	11	-71	-1 021	-1 122	-2 824
845 – Articles of apparel of textile fabrics	-20 022	-2 025	-70	-533	-3 762	-3 444	-10 188
846 – Clothing accessories	-1 359	80	5	-208	64	-111	-1 190
848 – Apparel and accessories except textile; headgear	-4 831	-139	42	-253	-30	-1 050	-3 401
851 – Footwear	-14 909	-61	31	-1 686	-1 105	-1 150	-10 938
871 – Optical instruments and apparatus, n.e.s.	314	534	-111	59	49	-28	-190
872 – Medical instruments and appliances	1 230	-193	795	1 117	-472	-192	176
873 – Meters and counters, n.e.s.	-640	-421	-153	-47	14	-12	-21
874 – Measuring/checking/analysing instruments	6 412	1 186	-138	860	683	1 044	2 777
881 – Photographic apparatus and equipment, n.e.s.	-2 130	-121	-805	-557	78	-50	-674
882 – Photographic and cinematographic supplies	954	880	-776	172	189	91	399
883 – Cinematographic film, exposed and developed, whether or not incorporating sound track or consisting only of sound track	-239	-235	1	-7	2	2	-2
884 – Optical goods, n.e.s.	-514	440	-156	-443	90	-148	-298
885 – Watches and clocks	-3 132	20	-769	-90	71	-247	-2 116
891 – Arms and ammunition	1 087	-79	233	-17	4	24	922
892 – Printed matter	727	1 147	114	-75	184	-35	-608
893 – Articles of plastics	-3 003	1 395	-44	-223	235	-116	-4 251
894 – Baby carriages, toys, games and sporting goods	-17 577	536	-524	17	196	-615	-17 186
895 – Office and stationery supplies, n.e.s.	-866	142	-356	-88	33	-24	-572
896 – Works of art, collectors' pieces and antiques	-1 662	29	76	-1 970	-22	2	223
897 – Jewelry, goldsmiths' and silversmiths' wares	-4 731	145	324	-1 278	132	-820	-3 235
898 – Musical instruments and accessories	-861	1 153	-1 121	324	328	188	-1 733
899 – Miscellaneous manufactured articles	-2 896	164	443	-95	97	-356	-3 149
931 – Special transactions not classified by kind	-27 407	-12 706	-1 423	-6 802	-1 392	-1 326	-3 759
950 – Coin, including gold coin; proof and presentation sets and current coin	-165	-48	1	-64	10	0	-64
961 – Coin (other than gold coin), not being legal tender	-3	-3	0	1	1	0	-2
971 – Gold, nonmonetary	1 901	-1 011	3	1 308	-1 161	17	2 744
984 – Estimate of low value import transactions	-14 067	-5 368	-1 317	-3 746	-554	-537	-2 546
992 – Export shipments valued not over $10,000, not identified by kind	692	394	38	60	77	12	112
994 – Estimated low value shipments	15 826	6 657	550	3 435	1 769	745	2 670

Note: NAFTA includes Canada and Mexico. EU-15 (European Union) consists of Austria, Belgium, Denmark, Finland, France, Germany, Greece, Ireland, Italy, Luxembourg, Netherlands, Portugal, Spain, Sweden, and the United Kingdom. ASEAN-10 (Association of Southeast Asian Nations) consists of Brunei, Burma (Myanmar), Cambodia, Indonesia, Laos, Malaysia, Philippines, Singapore, Thailand, and Vietnam. Other Americas includes North, Central, and South America less Mexico and Canada. Rest of world equals all other countries not listed above.

Table B-30. U.S. Total Exports by 2-Digit HS Product Groups, 1999–2003

(Millions of dollars; Census basis; foreign and domestic exports, f.a.s.)

HS product	1999	2000	2001	2002	2003	1999–2003 change Value	1999–2003 change Percent
TOTAL	692 821	780 419	731 026	693 257	723 743	30 923	4.5
01 – Live animals	658	864	898	642	792	134	20.4
02 – Meat and edible meat offal	5 933	7 063	6 807	5 911	6 781	848	14.3
03 – Fish, crustaceans and aquatic invertebrates ...	2 536	2 663	2 855	2 774	2 928	392	15.5
04 – Dairy products; birds eggs; honey; edible animal products, n.e.s.o.i.	669	809	829	687	763	93	13.9
05 – Products of animal origin, n.e.s.o.i.	365	438	585	591	635	271	74.2
06 – Live trees, plants, bulbs, etc.; cut flowers, etc.	302	291	279	269	289	-13	-4.3
07 – Edible vegetables and certain roots and tubers	1 786	1 890	1 869	1 933	2 052	266	14.9
08 – Edible fruit and nuts; citrus fruit or melon peels ...	3 660	3 980	4 055	4 241	4 761	1 101	30.1
09 – Coffee, tea, mate, and spices	417	390	360	351	399	-19	-4.5
10 – Cereals	10 338	9 733	9 653	10 245	10 680	341	3.3
11 – Milling products; malt; starch; inulin; wheat gluten ...	520	462	505	648	661	140	27.0
12 – Oil seeds, etc.; miscellaneous grains, seeds, fruits, plants, etc. ...	5 996	6 830	6 868	7 330	9 631	3 635	60.6
13 – Lac; gums, resins and other vegetable sap and extract ...	222	255	293	286	308	86	38.8
14 – Vegetable plaiting materials and products, n.e.s.o.i. ...	28	37	22	28	26	-2	-7.9
15 – Animal or vegetable fats, oils, etc. and waxes ...	1 964	1 473	1 420	1 950	2 035	70	3.6
16 – Edible preparations of meat, fish, crustaceans, etc.	773	791	938	933	964	191	24.7
17 – Sugars and sugar confectionary	622	683	724	635	703	81	12.9
18 – Cocoa and cocoa preparations	495	584	732	655	724	229	46.3
19 – Prepared cereal, flour, starch or milk; bakers wares ...	1 341	1 424	1 494	1 470	1 587	246	18.4
20 – Prepared vegetables, fruit, nuts or other plant parts ...	2 236	2 217	2 103	2 131	2 109	-126	-5.6
21 – Miscellaneous edible preparations	2 556	2 564	2 798	2 865	3 147	592	23.2
22 – Beverages, spirits, and vinegar	1 674	1 707	1 788	1 765	2 015	341	20.4
23 – Food industry residues and waste; prepared animal feed ...	3 294	3 688	4 114	3 642	3 636	342	10.4
24 – Tobacco and manufactured tobacco substitutes ...	5 198	5 269	4 040	3 033	2 924	-2 275	-43.8
25 – Salt; sulfur; earth and stone; lime and cement plaster ...	1 489	1 652	1 606	1 485	1 544	55	3.7
26 – Ores, slag, and ash	1 075	1 155	1 146	1 109	1 269	194	18.0
27 – Mineral fuel, oil, etc.; bitumin substances; mineral wax ...	9 966	13 384	12 898	11 719	14 079	4 113	41.3
28 – Inorganic chemicals; precious and rare-earth metals and radioactive compounds ...	5 074	5 934	6 123	5 938	6 088	1 013	20.0
29 – Organic chemicals	17 664	21 023	19 312	19 434	23 206	5 541	31.4
30 – Pharmaceutical products	8 921	10 532	12 508	13 073	15 939	7 018	78.7
31 – Fertilizers	3 117	2 485	2 247	2 262	2 552	-566	-18.1
32 – Tanning and dye extracts, etc.; dye, paint, putty, etc.; inks ...	3 799	4 306	3 978	4 069	4 374	575	15.1
33 – Essential oils, etc.; perfumery, cosmetic, etc. preparations ...	3 532	3 971	4 359	4 443	4 941	1 409	39.9
34 – Soap, etc.; waxes, polish, etc.; candles; dental preparations ...	2 146	2 329	2 379	2 469	2 757	611	28.4
35 – Albuminoidal substances; modified starch; glue; enzymes ...	1 428	1 567	1 817	1 696	1 488	60	4.2
36 – Explosives; pyrotechnics; matches; pyrotechnic alloys, etc. ...	281	338	284	306	421	140	49.8
37 – Photographic or cinematographic goods	2 705	3 451	2 584	2 869	2 931	225	8.3
38 – Miscellaneous chemical products	9 549	10 657	10 592	10 565	11 327	1 778	18.6
39 – Plastics and articles thereof	23 778	28 148	26 868	27 204	28 932	5 155	21.7
40 – Rubber and articles thereof	6 181	6 943	6 654	6 447	6 614	432	7.0
41 – Raw hides and skins (no furskins) and leather ...	1 920	2 442	2 718	2 444	2 546	627	32.6
42 – Leather articles; saddlery, etc.; handbags, etc.; gut articles ...	636	730	657	615	679	43	6.8
43 – Furskins and artificial fur; manufactures thereof ...	203	213	218	205	183	-19	-9.5
44 – Wood and articles of wood; wood charcoal ...	6 082	6 343	5 278	5 097	5 181	-900	-14.8
45 – Cork and articles of cork	74	69	42	46	50	-23	-31.7
46 – Manufactures of straw, esparto, etc.; basketware and wickerwork ...	21	24	17	26	26	5	25.2
47 – Wood pulp, etc.; recovered (waste and scrap) paper and paperboard ...	3 616	4 714	3 769	3 940	4 216	600	16.6
48 – Paper and paperboard and articles (including paper pulp articles) ...	10 491	11 607	10 899	10 337	10 672	181	1.7
49 – Printed books, newspapers, etc.; manuscripts, etc. ...	4 322	4 508	4 593	4 246	4 410	88	2.0
50 – Silk, including yarns and woven fabric thereof ...	21	25	26	28	31	10	47.7
51 – Wool and animal hair, including yarn and woven fabric ...	122	134	126	120	122	0	-0.1
52 – Cotton, including yarn and woven fabric thereof ...	2 473	3 785	4 032	3 983	5 229	2 756	111.4
53 – Vegetable textile fibers, n.e.s.o.i.; vegetable fibers and paper yarns and woven fabrics ...	26	37	30	45	31	5	19.5
54 – Manmade filaments, including yarns and woven fabrics ...	2 048	2 512	2 002	1 921	1 779	-269	-13.1
55 – Manmade staple fibers, including yarns and woven fabrics ...	1 412	1 558	1 475	1 545	1 570	158	11.2
56 – Wadding, felt, etc.; spun yarn; twine, ropes, etc. ...	944	1 073	1 055	1 100	1 278	334	35.4
57 – Carpets and other textile floor coverings	808	812	730	710	710	-98	-12.1
58 – Special woven fabrics; tufted fabrics; lace; tapestries, etc. ...	752	807	839	924	715	-37	-4.9
59 – Impregnated, etc. textile fabrics; textile articles for industry ...	1 186	1 213	1 286	1 293	1 456	270	22.8
60 – Knitted or crocheted fabrics	629	807	949	1 101	1 419	790	125.5
61 – Apparel articles and accessories, knit or crochet ...	4 120	4 580	3 896	3 225	3 030	-1 091	-26.5
62 – Apparel articles and accessories, not knit, etc. ...	3 683	3 548	2 590	2 376	2 085	-1 598	-43.4
63 – Textile articles, n.e.s.o.i.; needlecraft sets; worn textile articles ...	1 017	1 102	987	956	988	-29	-2.9
64 – Footwear, gaiters, etc. and parts thereof	839	867	806	703	694	-145	-17.3
65 – Headgear and parts thereof	101	120	133	112	111	10	9.6
66 – Umbrellas, walking-sticks, riding-crops, etc., parts ...	15	14	14	11	10	-5	-34.0
67 – Prepared feathers, down, etc.; artifical flowers; human hair articles ...	52	50	52	50	51	0	-0.9
68 – Articles of stone, plaster, cement, asbestos, mica, etc. ...	1 201	1 316	1 254	1 250	1 379	178	14.9
69 – Ceramic products	934	1 044	1 023	926	908	-26	-2.8
70 – Glass and glassware	3 181	3 815	3 781	3 441	3 565	384	12.1

Note: Unrevised data.

Table B-30. U.S. Total Exports by 2-Digit HS Product Groups, 1999–2003—*Continued*

(Millions of dollars; Census basis; foreign and domestic exports, f.a.s.)

HS product	1999	2000	2001	2002	2003	1999–2003 change	
						Value	Percent
71 – Pearls, precious, etc. stones, precious metals, etc.; coin	12 663	15 352	14 655	13 540	15 266	2 604	20.6
72 – Iron and steel	4 240	5 227	5 008	4 979	6 639	2 399	56.6
73 – Articles of iron or steel	8 120	9 149	8 321	8 003	8 166	47	0.6
74 – Copper and articles thereof	1 881	3 415	2 119	2 088	2 497	617	32.8
75 – Nickel and articles thereof	460	586	696	607	581	121	26.4
76 – Aluminum and articles thereof	5 346	5 591	4 977	4 923	4 996	-350	-6.5
78 – Lead and articles thereof	157	172	80	75	122	-35	-22.2
79 – Zinc and articles thereof	117	118	100	96	108	-10	-8.2
80 – Tin and articles thereof	105	107	67	61	62	-43	-40.7
81 – Base metals, n.e.s.o.i.; cermets; articles thereof	866	1 039	1 119	1 014	1 142	275	31.8
82 – Tools, cutlery, etc. of base metal and parts thereof	2 751	3 009	2 870	2 800	2 874	124	4.5
83 – Miscellaneous articles of base metal	2 673	3 205	3 011	3 023	3 043	370	13.8
84 – Nuclear reactors, boilers, machinery, etc.; parts	137 321	158 919	145 087	130 207	130 804	-6 518	-4.7
85 – Electric machinery, etc.; sound equipment; TV equipment; parts	121 601	148 287	122 559	110 451	112 598	-9 003	-7.4
86 – Railway or tramway stock, etc.; traffic signal equipment	1 605	1 412	1 506	1 093	1 609	3	0.2
87 – Vehicles, except railway or tramway, and parts, etc.	58 563	61 928	58 750	62 511	65 182	6 619	11.3
88 – Aircraft, spacecraft, and parts thereof	49 629	40 976	44 705	43 901	39 670	-9 959	-20.1
89 – Ships, boats, and floating structures	1 672	1 114	1 899	1 239	1 335	-337	-20.1
90 – Optical, photographic, etc., medical or surgical instruments, etc.	38 012	45 019	44 224	41 178	44 034	6 022	15.8
91 – Clocks and watches and parts thereof	520	517	449	415	468	-52	-9.9
92 – Musical instruments; parts and accessories thereof	397	416	447	429	454	56	14.1
93 – Arms and ammunition; parts and accessories thereof	2 179	2 172	2 168	2 095	1 786	-394	-18.1
94 – Furniture; bedding, etc.; lamps, n.e.s.o.i., etc.; prefabricated buildings	5 910	6 542	6 107	5 731	5 650	-260	-4.4
95 – Toys, games and sport equipment; parts and accessories	3 903	4 139	3 858	3 639	3 967	64	1.6
96 – Miscellaneous manufactured articles	1 175	1 232	1 105	1 087	1 088	-87	-7.4
97 – Works of art, collectors' pieces and antiques	2 298	3 425	4 070	2 558	2 735	438	19.0
98 – Special classification provisions, n.e.s.o.i.	21 440	23 502	24 407	22 635	22 734	1 293	6.0

Note: Unrevised data.

Table B-31. U.S. Total Imports by 2-Digit HS Product Groups, 1999–2003

(Millions of dollars; Census basis; general imports, Customs.)

HS product	1999	2000	2001	2002	2003	1999–2003 change Value	1999–2003 change Percent
TOTAL	1 024 766	1 216 888	1 141 959	1 163 549	1 259 396	234 630	22.9
01 – Live animals	1 642	1 929	2 239	2 120	1 619	-23	-1.4
02 – Meat and edible meat offal	2 798	3 393	3 801	3 790	3 880	1 081	38.6
03 – Fish, crustaceans and aquatic invertebrates	7 279	8 153	7 868	7 923	8 663	1 383	19.0
04 – Dairy products; birds eggs; honey; edible animal products, n.e.s.o.i.	1 075	1 064	1 123	1 242	1 390	315	29.3
05 – Products of animal origin, n.e.s.o.i.	462	540	516	552	538	76	16.3
06 – Live trees, plants, bulbs, etc.; cut flowers, etc.	1 099	1 160	1 150	1 132	1 249	150	13.6
07 – Edible vegetables and certain roots and tubers	2 528	2 649	2 961	3 138	3 608	1 080	42.7
08 – Edible fruit and nuts; citrus fruit or melon peels	4 009	3 919	3 892	4 229	4 578	569	14.2
09 – Coffee, tea, mate, and spices	3 368	3 200	2 160	2 198	2 594	-774	-23.0
10 – Cereals	858	806	884	854	772	-86	-10.0
11 – Milling products; malt; starch; inulin; wheat gluten	268	313	303	383	451	183	68.5
12 – Oil seeds, etc.; miscellaneous grains, seeds, fruits, plants, etc.	832	853	756	687	742	-90	-10.8
13 – Lac; gums, resins and other vegetable sap and extract	547	493	496	460	526	-20	-3.7
14 – Vegetable plaiting materials and products, n.e.s.o.i.	50	53	67	51	49	-1	-2.0
15 – Animal or vegetable fats, oils, etc. and waxes	1 404	1 398	1 181	1 328	1 537	133	9.5
16 – Edible preparations of meat, fish, crustaceans, etc.	2 083	2 202	2 336	2 563	2 792	709	34.0
17 – Sugars and sugar confectionary	1 528	1 480	1 536	1 702	1 933	404	26.5
18 – Cocoa and cocoa preparations	1 527	1 408	1 539	1 762	2 434	907	59.4
19 – Prepared cereal, flour, starch or milk; bakers wares	1 667	1 778	1 923	2 222	2 536	869	52.1
20 – Prepared vegetables, fruit, nuts or other plant parts	2 688	2 678	2 639	2 802	3 225	538	20.0
21 – Miscellaneous edible preparations	1 223	1 247	1 424	1 629	1 790	567	46.4
22 – Beverages, spirits, and vinegar	7 578	8 339	8 729	9 704	10 940	3 362	44.4
23 – Food industry residues and waste; prepared animal feed	583	615	594	644	677	95	16.3
24 – Tobacco and manufactured tobacco substitutes	1 210	1 127	1 237	1 318	1 300	90	7.4
25 – Salt; sulfur; earth and stone; lime and cement plaster	2 096	2 097	2 006	1 920	2 081	-15	-0.7
26 – Ores, slag, and ash	1 671	1 641	1 512	1 488	1 459	-211	-12.7
27 – Mineral fuel, oil, etc.; bitumin substances; mineral wax	75 311	133 730	122 983	117 228	155 600	80 289	106.6
28 – Inorganic chemicals; precious and rare-earth metals and radioactive compounds	5 916	6 909	6 800	6 551	7 884	1 969	33.3
29 – Organic chemicals	23 673	30 495	31 739	32 835	36 130	12 456	52.6
30 – Pharmaceutical products	11 247	12 177	15 943	21 514	27 630	16 384	145.7
31 – Fertilizers	1 527	1 714	1 914	1 640	2 168	641	42.0
32 – Tanning and dye extracts, etc.; dye, paint, putty, etc.; inks	2 670	2 716	2 501	2 380	2 500	-170	-6.4
33 – Essential oils, etc.; perfumery, cosmetic, etc. preparations	2 450	2 750	2 948	3 268	4 641	2 191	89.4
34 – Soap, etc.; waxes, polish, etc.; candles; dental preparations	1 356	1 493	1 431	1 571	1 672	317	23.4
35 – Albuminoidal substances; modified starch; glue; enzymes	1 091	1 248	1 220	1 159	1 319	227	20.8
36 – Explosives; pyrotechnics; matches; pyrotechnic alloys, etc.	270	267	288	307	357	88	32.5
37 – Photographic or cinematographic goods	2 554	2 734	2 335	2 276	2 216	-339	-13.3
38 – Miscellaneous chemical products	3 832	4 367	4 577	4 834	5 276	1 444	37.7
39 – Plastics and articles thereof	16 670	19 088	19 116	20 345	22 852	6 182	37.1
40 – Rubber and articles thereof	9 503	10 187	9 334	10 195	11 404	1 900	20.0
41 – Raw hides and skins (no furskins) and leather	1 052	1 168	1 033	935	818	-234	-22.2
42 – Leather articles; saddlery, etc.; handbags, etc.; gut articles	6 038	7 157	7 121	7 094	7 500	1 462	24.2
43 – Furskins and artificial fur; manufactures thereof	225	331	364	334	375	150	66.7
44 – Wood and articles of wood; wood charcoal	16 015	15 453	14 967	15 725	16 563	548	3.4
45 – Cork and articles of cork	163	175	187	191	204	41	25.0
46 – Manufactures of straw, esparto, etc.; basketware and wickerwork	277	302	324	375	408	131	47.3
47 – Wood pulp, etc.; recovered (waste and scrap) paper and paperboard	2 597	3 381	2 631	2 363	2 597	0	0.0
48 – Paper and paperboard and articles (including paper pulp articles)	13 580	15 390	15 006	14 650	15 095	1 515	11.2
49 – Printed books, newspapers, etc.; manuscripts, etc.	3 163	3 491	3 536	3 744	3 902	739	23.4
50 – Silk, including yarns and woven fabric thereof	269	294	235	235	247	-23	-8.4
51 – Wool and animal hair, including yarn and woven fabric	371	414	362	289	305	-65	-17.6
52 – Cotton, including yarn and woven fabric thereof	2 064	2 113	1 807	1 975	1 823	-241	-11.7
53 – Vegetable textile fibers, n.e.s.o.i.; vegetable fibers and paper yarns and woven fabrics	202	185	140	143	149	-53	-26.2
54 – Manmade filaments, including yarns and woven fabrics	1 945	2 103	1 824	1 872	1 856	-89	-4.6
55 – Manmade staple fibers, including yarns and woven fabrics	1 142	1 171	1 077	1 157	1 143	1	0.0
56 – Wadding, felt, etc.; spun yarn; twine, ropes, etc.	726	851	902	962	1 060	334	46.0
57 – Carpets and other textile floor coverings	1 253	1 469	1 415	1 535	1 667	414	33.0
58 – Special woven fabrics; tufted fabrics; lace; tapestries, etc.	521	592	543	589	624	103	19.7
59 – Impregnated, etc. textile fabrics; textile articles for industry	700	792	778	934	1 043	344	49.2
60 – Knitted or crocheted fabrics	929	1 005	1 015	1 080	1 031	102	11.0
61 – Apparel articles and accessories, knit or crochet	23 712	26 405	26 858	27 823	29 719	6 007	25.3
62 – Apparel articles and accessories, not knit, etc.	28 692	32 801	31 691	30 896	33 189	4 497	15.7
63 – Textile articles, n.e.s.o.i.; needlecraft sets; worn textile articles	3 984	4 583	4 880	5 690	6 681	2 696	67.7
64 – Footwear, gaiters, etc. and parts thereof	14 068	14 854	15 235	15 386	15 603	1 535	10.9
65 – Headgear and parts thereof	1 064	1 246	1 289	1 280	1 359	296	27.8
66 – Umbrellas, walking-sticks, riding-crops, etc., parts	249	284	293	275	310	62	24.7
67 – Prepared feathers, down, etc.; artifical flowers; human hair articles	1 030	1 092	1 122	1 197	1 234	203	19.7
68 – Articles of stone, plaster, cement, asbestos, mica, etc.	3 030	3 433	3 509	3 753	4 096	1 065	35.2
69 – Ceramic products	3 645	4 074	3 758	3 940	4 295	650	17.8
70 – Glass and glassware	4 053	4 393	4 155	4 265	4 500	447	11.0

Note: Unrevised data.

Table B-31. U.S. Total Imports by 2-Digit HS Product Groups, 1999–2003—*Continued*

(Millions of dollars; Census basis; general imports, Customs.)

HS product	1999	2000	2001	2002	2003	1999–2003 change	
						Value	Percent
71 – Pearls, precious, etc. stones, precious metals, etc.; coin	24 545	29 923	26 153	26 543	28 209	3 663	14.9
72 – Iron and steel	12 904	14 665	10 484	11 522	10 241	-2 663	-20.6
73 – Articles of iron or steel	11 949	14 150	13 891	14 358	15 168	3 220	26.9
74 – Copper and articles thereof	4 064	5 113	4 749	4 141	3 823	-241	-5.9
75 – Nickel and articles thereof	942	1 541	1 175	1 001	1 283	341	36.2
76 – Aluminum and articles thereof	8 394	9 187	8 478	8 996	9 626	1 231	14.7
78 – Lead and articles thereof	202	213	162	145	117	-85	-42.1
79 – Zinc and articles thereof	1 298	1 342	1 099	1 086	949	-349	-26.9
80 – Tin and articles thereof	318	339	277	231	246	-72	-22.6
81 – Base metals, n.e.s.o.i.; cermets; articles thereof	1 070	1 107	1 173	856	885	-185	-17.3
82 – Tools, cutlery, etc. of base metal and parts thereof	4 177	4 554	4 309	4 668	5 178	1 000	23.9
83 – Miscellaneous articles of base metal	4 176	4 686	4 608	5 083	5 418	1 242	29.7
84 – Nuclear reactors, boilers, machinery, etc.; parts	165 575	180 908	161 305	161 872	170 680	5 105	3.1
85 – Electric machinery, etc.; sound equipment; TV equipment; parts	145 901	186 099	154 593	152 087	157 675	11 774	8.1
86 – Railway or tramway stock, etc.; traffic signal equipment	2 308	1 828	1 357	1 040	1 105	-1 203	-52.1
87 – Vehicles, except railway or tramway, and parts, etc.	148 129	163 854	159 341	170 516	175 165	27 036	18.3
88 – Aircraft, spacecraft, and parts thereof	14 988	18 167	21 098	17 996	17 001	2 013	13.4
89 – Ships, boats, and floating structures	1 127	1 178	1 206	1 329	1 592	464	41.2
90 – Optical, photographic, etc., medical or surgical instruments, etc.	30 710	36 620	34 874	34 805	38 776	8 066	26.3
91 – Clocks and watches and parts thereof	3 257	3 485	3 048	3 204	3 600	343	10.5
92 – Musical instruments; parts and accessories thereof	1 262	1 423	1 306	1 309	1 365	103	8.2
93 – Arms and ammunition; parts and accessories thereof	702	839	852	974	1 092	391	55.7
94 – Furniture; bedding, etc.; lamps, n.e.s.o.i., etc.; prefabricated buildings	20 378	23 833	23 230	26 717	29 722	9 344	45.9
95 – Toys, games and sport equipment; parts and accessories	18 227	19 254	20 265	21 443	21 044	2 817	15.5
96 – Miscellaneous manufactured articles	2 738	2 865	2 765	2 833	2 914	176	6.4
97 – Works of art, collectors' pieces and antiques	4 903	5 858	5 450	5 186	4 381	-522	-10.6
98 – Special classification provisions, n.e.s.o.i.	31 829	34 623	35 417	35 934	33 668	1 839	5.8
99 – Special import provisions, n.e.s.o.i.	11 788	13 818	13 237	13 045	14 067	2 279	19.3

Note: Unrevised data.

Table B-32. U.S. Total Trade Balances by 2-Digit HS Product Groups, 1999–2003

(Millions of dollars; Census basis; foreign and domestic exports, f.a.s.; general imports, Customs.)

HS product	1999	2000	2001	2002	2003	1999–2003 change	
						Value	Percent
TOTAL	-331 945	-436 469	-410 933	-470 291	-535 652	-203 707	61.4
01 – Live animals	-984	-1 065	-1 341	-1 478	-827	157	-16.0
02 – Meat and edible meat offal	3 135	3 670	3 005	2 121	2 901	-233	-7.4
03 – Fish, crustaceans and aquatic invertebrates	-4 743	-5 490	-5 013	-5 149	-5 735	-992	20.9
04 – Dairy products; birds eggs; honey; edible animal products, n.e.s.o.i.	-406	-255	-294	-555	-627	-221	54.6
05 – Products of animal origin, n.e.s.o.i.	-98	-102	70	39	97	195	-199.7
06 – Live trees, plants, bulbs, etc.; cut flowers, etc.	-797	-869	-871	-863	-960	-163	20.4
07 – Edible vegetables and certain roots and tubers	-741	-759	-1 092	-1 206	-1 555	-814	109.8
08 – Edible fruit and nuts; citrus fruit or melon peels	-349	61	163	11	184	532	-152.7
09 – Coffee, tea, mate, and spices	-2 951	-2 809	-1 800	-1 847	-2 196	756	-25.6
10 – Cereals	9 480	8 928	8 769	9 391	9 908	427	4.5
11 – Milling products; malt; starch; inulin; wheat gluten	252	150	202	265	209	-43	-17.1
12 – Oil seeds, etc.; miscellaneous grains, seeds, fruits, plants, etc.	5 164	5 977	6 112	6 643	8 889	3 725	72.1
13 – Lac; gums, resins and other vegetable sap and extract	-325	-238	-202	-174	-218	107	-32.8
14 – Vegetable plaiting materials and products, n.e.s.o.i.	-22	-16	-44	-23	-23	-1	5.7
15 – Animal or vegetable fats, oils, etc. and waxes	560	75	239	621	497	-63	-11.2
16 – Edible preparations of meat, fish, crustaceans, etc.	-1 310	-1 411	-1 397	-1 629	-1 828	-518	39.5
17 – Sugars and sugar confectionery	-906	-797	-812	-1 066	-1 230	-324	35.7
18 – Cocoa and cocoa preparations	-1 033	-825	-808	-1 107	-1 710	-677	65.6
19 – Prepared cereal, flour, starch or milk; bakers wares	-326	-354	-428	-752	-949	-622	190.8
20 – Prepared vegetables, fruit, nuts or other plant parts	-452	-461	-536	-671	-1 116	-664	147.0
21 – Miscellaneous edible preparations	1 333	1 317	1 374	1 236	1 358	25	1.8
22 – Beverages, spirits, and vinegar	-5 904	-6 633	-6 941	-7 939	-8 926	-3 021	51.2
23 – Food industry residues and waste; prepared animal feed	2 712	3 073	3 520	2 998	2 959	247	9.1
24 – Tobacco and manufactured tobacco substitutes	3 988	4 142	2 803	1 715	1 624	-2 365	-59.3
25 – Salt; sulfur; earth and stone; lime and cement plaster	-606	-445	-401	-435	-537	70	-11.5
26 – Ores, slag, and ash	-596	-486	-366	-379	-191	405	-68.0
27 – Mineral fuel, oil, etc.; bitumin substances; mineral wax	-65 345	-120 346	-110 084	-105 509	-141 520	-76 176	116.6
28 – Inorganic chemicals; precious and rare-earth metals and radioactive compounds	-841	-975	-676	-614	-1 797	-955	113.5
29 – Organic chemicals	-6 009	-9 472	-12 427	-13 400	-12 924	-6 915	115.1
30 – Pharmaceutical products	-2 326	-1 645	-3 435	-8 440	-11 691	-9 365	402.7
31 – Fertilizers	1 590	772	333	622	384	-1 206	-75.8
32 – Tanning and dye extracts, etc.; dye, paint, putty, etc.; inks	1 129	1 590	1 476	1 689	1 874	745	66.0
33 – Essential oils, etc.; perfumery, cosmetic, etc. preparations	1 081	1 221	1 412	1 175	300	-782	-72.3
34 – Soap, etc.; waxes, polish, etc.; candles; dental preparations	791	836	948	898	1 084	294	37.1
35 – Albuminoidal substances; modified starch; glue; enzymes	336	319	597	537	169	-167	-49.6
36 – Explosives; pyrotechnics; matches; pyrotechnic alloys, etc.	12	71	-4	-1	64	52	448.5
37 – Photographic or cinematographic goods	151	717	249	594	715	564	374.1
38 – Miscellaneous chemical products	5 716	6 290	6 015	5 731	6 051	334	5.8
39 – Plastics and articles thereof	7 108	9 060	7 752	6 859	6 081	-1 027	-14.4
40 – Rubber and articles thereof	-3 322	-3 243	-2 680	-3 748	-4 790	-1 468	44.2
41 – Raw hides and skins (no furskins) and leather	868	1 274	1 686	1 510	1 728	860	99.1
42 – Leather articles; saddlery, etc.; handbags, etc.; gut articles	-5 402	-6 428	-6 465	-6 478	-6 821	-1 419	26.3
43 – Furskins and artificial fur; manufactures thereof	-22	-118	-146	-128	-192	-169	753.4
44 – Wood and articles of wood; wood charcoal	-9 934	-9 110	-9 689	-10 628	-11 382	-1 448	14.6
45 – Cork and articles of cork	-89	-107	-145	-146	-154	-64	71.7
46 – Manufactures of straw, esparto, etc.; basketware and wickerwork	-256	-278	-307	-349	-382	-126	49.1
47 – Wood pulp, etc.; recovered (waste and scrap) paper and paperboard	1 019	1 333	1 138	1 577	1 620	601	58.9
48 – Paper and paperboard and articles (including paper pulp articles)	-3 089	-3 782	-4 108	-4 312	-4 423	-1 333	43.2
49 – Printed books, newspapers, etc.; manuscripts, etc.	1 159	1 017	1 058	502	509	-650	-56.1
50 – Silk, including yarns and woven fabric thereof	-248	-269	-209	-207	-216	33	-13.1
51 – Wool and animal hair, including yarn and woven fabric	-249	-280	-236	-169	-184	65	-26.1
52 – Cotton, including yarn and woven fabric thereof	409	1 671	2 225	2 008	3 406	2 997	732.8
53 – Vegetable textile fibers, n.e.s.o.i.; vegetable fibers and paper yarns and woven fabrics	-176	-148	-110	-98	-118	58	-32.9
54 – Manmade filaments, including yarns and woven fabrics	103	409	178	50	-76	-179	-174.3
55 – Manmade staple fibers, including yarns and woven fabrics	270	387	399	389	427	158	58.4
56 – Wadding, felt, etc.; spun yarn; twine, ropes, etc.	218	222	153	138	218	0	-0.1
57 – Carpets and other textile floor coverings	-445	-658	-684	-825	-957	-512	114.9
58 – Special woven fabrics; tufted fabrics; lace; tapestries, etc.	230	216	296	335	91	-140	-60.7
59 – Impregnated, etc. textile fabrics; textile articles for industry	486	421	508	359	413	-73	-15.1
60 – Knitted or crocheted fabrics	-300	-199	-66	20	388	687	-229.3
61 – Apparel articles and accessories, knit or crochet	-19 592	-21 825	-22 962	-24 598	-26 690	-7 097	36.2
62 – Apparel articles and accessories, not knit, etc.	-25 009	-29 253	-29 102	-28 520	-31 104	-6 095	24.4
63 – Textile articles, n.e.s.o.i.; needlecraft sets; worn textile articles	-2 968	-3 482	-3 894	-4 735	-5 693	-2 726	91.8
64 – Footwear, gaiters, etc. and parts thereof	-13 229	-13 987	-14 429	-14 683	-14 909	-1 680	12.7
65 – Headgear and parts thereof	-963	-1 126	-1 156	-1 168	-1 249	-286	29.7
66 – Umbrellas, walking-sticks, riding-crops, etc., parts	-233	-270	-279	-264	-300	-67	28.6
67 – Prepared feathers, down, etc.; artifical flowers; human hair articles	-978	-1 042	-1 069	-1 147	-1 182	-204	20.8
68 – Articles of stone, plaster, cement, asbestos, mica, etc.	-1 830	-2 117	-2 254	-2 503	-2 717	-887	48.5
69 – Ceramic products	-2 711	-3 030	-2 734	-3 014	-3 387	-677	25.0
70 – Glass and glassware	-871	-578	-374	-825	-935	-63	7.2

Note: Unrevised data.

Table B-32. U.S. Total Trade Balances by 2-Digit HS Product Groups, 1999–2003—*Continued*

(Millions of dollars; Census basis; foreign and domestic exports, f.a.s.; general imports, Customs.)

HS product	1999	2000	2001	2002	2003	1999–2003 change	
						Value	Percent
71 – Pearls, precious, etc. stones, precious metals, etc.; coin	-11 883	-14 570	-11 497	-13 003	-12 943	-1 060	8.9
72 – Iron and steel	-8 664	-9 438	-5 477	-6 544	-3 602	5 062	-58.4
73 – Articles of iron or steel	-3 829	-5 001	-5 570	-6 355	-7 002	-3 173	82.9
74 – Copper and articles thereof	-2 183	-1 698	-2 630	-2 052	-1 326	857	-39.3
75 – Nickel and articles thereof	-483	-956	-479	-394	-703	-220	45.5
76 – Aluminum and articles thereof	-3 048	-3 596	-3 501	-4 074	-4 629	-1 581	51.9
78 – Lead and articles thereof	-45	-41	-83	-69	5	50	-111.0
79 – Zinc and articles thereof	-1 181	-1 224	-999	-990	-841	339	-28.7
80 – Tin and articles thereof	-213	-232	-210	-169	-184	29	-13.7
81 – Base metals, n.e.s.o.i.; cermets; articles thereof	-204	-67	-53	158	257	461	-226.1
82 – Tools, cutlery, etc. of base metal and parts thereof	-1 427	-1 546	-1 439	-1 868	-2 304	-877	61.5
83 – Miscellaneous articles of base metal	-1 503	-1 481	-1 596	-2 060	-2 375	-872	58.0
84 – Nuclear reactors, boilers, machinery, etc.; parts	-28 254	-21 989	-16 218	-31 665	-39 876	-11 622	41.1
85 – Electric machinery, etc.; sound equipment; TV equipment; parts	-24 300	-37 812	-32 035	-41 636	-45 077	-20 777	85.5
86 – Railway or tramway stock, etc.; traffic signal equipment	-702	-416	149	53	503	1 206	-171.7
87 – Vehicles, except railway or tramway, and parts, etc.	-89 566	-101 927	-100 592	-108 005	-109 982	-20 416	22.8
88 – Aircraft, spacecraft, and parts thereof	34 641	22 809	23 607	25 905	22 669	-11 972	-34.6
89 – Ships, boats, and floating structures	545	-65	693	-90	-257	-801	-147.1
90 – Optical, photographic, etc., medical or surgical instruments, etc.	7 302	8 399	9 350	6 373	5 257	-2 045	-28.0
91 – Clocks and watches and parts thereof	-2 738	-2 968	-2 599	-2 789	-3 132	-394	14.4
92 – Musical instruments; parts and accessories thereof	-865	-1 007	-860	-880	-912	-47	5.5
93 – Arms and ammunition; parts and accessories thereof	1 477	1 333	1 315	1 121	693	-784	-53.1
94 – Furniture; bedding, etc.; lamps, n.e.s.o.i., etc.; prefabricated buildings	-14 468	-17 290	-17 123	-20 985	-24 072	-9 604	66.4
95 – Toys, games and sport equipment; parts and accessories	-14 324	-15 116	-16 408	-17 804	-17 077	-2 753	19.2
96 – Miscellaneous manufactured articles	-1 563	-1 634	-1 661	-1 747	-1 827	-263	16.8
97 – Works of art, collectors' pieces and antiques	-2 605	-2 433	-1 380	-2 628	-1 646	960	-36.8
98 – Special classification provisions, n.e.s.o.i.	-10 389	-11 121	-11 010	-13 299	-10 934	-545	5.2
99 – Special import provisions, n.e.s.o.i.	-11 788	-13 818	-13 237	-13 045	-14 067	-2 279	19.3

Note: Unrevised data.

Table B-33. Top 20 Suppliers of Petroleum Products to the United States, 1997–2003

(Millions of dollars, except as noted; top 20 based on 2003 value; Census basis; foreign and domestic exports, f.a.s.; general imports, Customs.)

Source	1997	1998	1999	2000	2001	2002	2003	Percent of world in 2003	Percent change, 1997–2003
WORLD	69 249	49 370	65 887	117 174	100 668	101 152	129 600	100.0	87.2
Total of Top 20 Suppliers	63 448	44 656	59 772	104 816	89 527	91 300	117 453	90.6	85.1
Canada	10 070	7 514	8 935	16 679	14 478	15 518	19 724	15.2	95.9
Saudi Arabia	9 000	5 736	7 569	13 356	12 485	12 597	17 308	13.4	92.3
Mexico	8 439	5 293	7 204	12 747	10 201	12 189	15 477	11.9	83.4
Venezuela	11 648	7 638	9 488	16 578	13 275	13 134	15 147	11.7	30.0
Nigeria	6 303	4 129	4 302	10 432	8 525	5 908	10 058	7.8	59.6
United Kingdom	2 143	1 514	2 380	4 104	3 308	4 694	5 469	4.2	155.1
Iraq	286	1 199	4 193	6 109	5 801	3 593	4 573	3.5	1 500.1
Angola	2 778	2 247	2 414	3 543	3 093	3 107	4 238	3.3	52.6
Algeria	2 076	1 311	1 563	2 442	2 237	2 125	4 092	3.2	97.1
Russia	119	224	523	829	876	2 009	3 361	2.6	2 725.7
Norway	2 068	1 228	2 223	3 929	3 339	4 024	3 123	2.4	51.0
Colombia	2 060	1 986	3 356	3 893	2 919	2 889	2 762	2.1	34.1
Kuwait	1 796	1 240	1 410	2 693	1 856	1 879	2 107	1.6	17.3
Gabon	2 169	1 232	1 431	2 172	1 622	1 558	1 937	1.5	-10.7
Brazil	141	262	289	787	1 102	1 201	1 919	1.5	1 265.2
Ecuador	660	400	530	1 221	971	1 041	1 467	1.1	122.2
Argentina	568	533	747	1 037	1 106	1 299	1 334	1.0	134.9
Trinidad and Tobago	534	444	603	1 108	928	1 019	1 237	1.0	131.6
Netherlands	327	272	259	488	590	691	1 076	0.8	229.1
Belgium	264	254	351	668	815	826	1 046	0.8	296.2
OPEC (million dollars)	31 611	21 686	29 104	52 330	45 120	39 873	53 940	41.6	70.6
OPEC (percent of world)	45.6	43.9	44.2	44.7	44.8	39.4	41.6	41.6	-8.8
SITC 333 (crude oil)									
Billion barrels	3.08	3.26	3.22	3.40	3.48	3.43	3.67	X	19.4
Billion dollars	54.43	37.53	50.66	89.79	74.43	77.37	99.10	X	82.1
Dollars per barrel	17.69	11.52	15.71	26.41	21.41	22.59	26.97	X	52.5

Note: OPEC (Organization of Petroleum Exporting Countries) consists of 11 countries: Algeria, Indonesia, Iran, Iraq, Kuwait, Libya, Nigeria, Qatar, Saudi Arabia, the United Arab Emirates, and Venezuela. Petroleum products are defined as SITC (Rev. 3) 33 and include crude, refined and residual petroleum products. Unrevised data.

X = Not applicable.

Table B-34. Foreign Exchange Rates, 1996–2003

(Annual average, foreign currency units per U.S. dollar.)

Country (currency)	1996	1997	1998	1999	2000	2001	2002	2003
Afghanistan (Afghanis) [3]	. . .	. . .	. . .	. . .	. . .	. . .	50.00	50.00
Albania (Leks)	104.50	148.93	150.63	137.69	143.71	143.49	140.15	121.86
Algeria (Algerian Dinars)	54.75	57.71	58.74	66.57	75.26	77.22	79.68	77.40
Angola (Kwanzas)	0.13	0.23	0.39	2.79	10.04	22.06	43.53	74.61
Antigua Barbuda (E. Caribbean Dollars)	2.70	2.70	2.70	2.70	2.70	2.70	2.70	2.70
Argentina (Argentine Pesos)	1.00	1.00	1.00	1.00	1.00	1.00	3.06	2.90
Armenia (Drams)	414.04	490.85	504.92	535.06	539.53	555.08	573.35	578.76
Aruba (Aruban Florins)	1.79	1.79	1.79	1.79	1.79	1.79	1.79	1.79
Australia (Australian Dollars)	1.28	1.35	1.59	1.55	1.72	1.93	1.84	1.53
Austria (Natl Currency) [4]	10.59	12.20	12.38	. . .	. . .	. . .	. . .	. . .
Azerbaijan (Manat)	4 301.26	3 985.37	3 869.00	4 120.17	4 474.15	4 656.58	4 860.82	4 910.73
Bahamas (Bahamian Dollars)	1.00	1.00	1.00	1.00	1.00	1.00	1.00	1.00
Bahrain (Bahrain Dinars)	0.38	0.38	0.38	0.38	0.38	0.38	0.38	0.38
Bangladesh (Taka)	41.79	43.89	46.91	49.09	52.14	55.81	57.89	58.15
Barbados (Barbados Dollars)	2.00	2.00	2.00	2.00	2.00	2.00	2.00	2.00
Belarus (Belarusian Rubel)	13.23	26.02	46.13	248.80	876.75	1 390.00	1 790.92	2 053.58
Belgium (Natl Currency) [4]	30.96	35.77	36.30	. . .	. . .	. . .	. . .	. . .
Belize (Belize Dollars)	2.00	2.00	2.00	2.00	2.00	2.00	2.00	2.00
Benin (Cfa Francs)	511.55	583.67	589.95	615.70	711.98	733.04	696.99	581.20
Bhutan (Ngultrum)	35.43	36.31	41.26	43.06	44.94	47.19	48.61	46.58
Bolivia (Bolivianos)	5.07	5.25	5.51	5.81	6.18	6.61	7.17	7.66
Bosnia-Herzegovina (Convertible Mark)	. . .	1.73	1.76	1.84	2.12	2.19	1.73	1.73
Botswana (Pula)	3.32	3.65	4.23	4.62	5.10	5.84	6.33	4.95
Brazil (Reais)	1.01	1.08	1.16	1.81	1.83	2.36	2.92	3.08
Brunei (Brunei Dollars) [3]	1.41	1.48	1.67	1.69	1.72	1.79	1.79	1.74
Bulgaria (Leva)	0.18	1.68	1.76	1.84	2.12	2.18	2.08	1.73
Burkina (Upper Volta) (Cfa Francs)	511.55	583.67	589.95	615.70	711.98	733.04	696.99	581.20
Burundi (Burundi Francs)	302.75	352.35	447.77	563.56	720.67	830.35	930.75	1 082.62
Cambodia (Kampuchea) (Riel)	2 624.08	2 946.25	3 744.42	3 807.83	3 840.75	3 916.33	3 912.10	3 973.33
Cameroon (Cfa Francs)	511.55	583.67	589.95	615.70	711.98	733.04	696.99	581.20
Canada (Canadian Dollars)	1.36	1.38	1.48	1.49	1.49	1.55	1.57	1.40
Cape Verde (Escudos)	82.59	93.18	98.16	102.70	115.88	123.21	117.26	97.70
Central African Rep. (Cfa Francs)	511.55	583.67	589.95	615.70	711.98	733.04	696.99	581.20
Chad (Cfa Francs)	511.55	583.67	589.95	615.70	711.98	733.04	696.99	581.20
Chile (Chilean Pesos)	412.27	419.30	460.29	508.78	535.47	634.94	688.94	691.43
China (Yuan)	8.31	8.29	8.28	8.28	8.28	8.28	8.28	8.28
Colombia (Colombian Pesos)	1 036.69	1 140.96	1 426.04	1 756.23	2 087.90	2 299.63	2 504.24	2 877.65
Comoros (Comorian Francs)	383.66	437.75	442.46	461.78	533.98	549.78	522.74	435.90
Congo, Republic (Cfa Francs)	511.55	583.67	589.95	615.70	711.98	733.04	696.99	581.20
Costa Rica (Colones)	207.69	232.60	257.23	285.69	308.19	328.87	359.82	398.66
Croatia (Kunas)	5.43	6.10	6.36	7.11	8.28	8.34	7.87	6.70
Cuba (Peso) [3]	1.00	1.00	1.00	1.00	1.00	1.00	1.00	1.00
Cyprus (Cyprus Pounds)	0.47	0.51	0.52	0.54	0.62	0.64	0.61	0.52
Czech Republic (Koruny)	27.14	31.70	32.28	34.57	38.60	38.04	32.74	28.21
Denmark (Kroner)	5.80	6.60	6.70	6.98	8.08	8.32	7.89	6.59
Dem. Rep. of the Congo (Zaire) (Congo Francs)	0.50	1.31	1.61	4.02	21.82	206.62	346.49	405.34
Djibouti (Djibouti Francs)	177.72	177.72	177.72	177.72	177.72	177.72	177.72	177.72
Dominica (E. Caribbean Dollars)	2.70	2.70	2.70	2.70	2.70	2.70	2.70	2.70
Dominican Republic (Dominican Pesos)	13.77	14.27	15.27	16.03	16.42	16.95	18.61	30.83
Ecuador (U.S. Dollars)	3 189.47	3 998.27	5 446.57	11 786.80	24 988.40	25 000.00	25 000.00	25 000.00
Egypt (Egyptian Pounds)	3.39	3.39	3.39	3.40	3.47	3.97	4.50	5.85
El Salvador (Colones)	8.76	8.76	8.76	8.76	8.76	8.75	8.75	8.75
Equatorial Guinea (Cfa Francs)	511.55	583.67	589.95	615.70	711.98	733.04	696.99	581.20
Eritrea (Nafka)	. . .	. . .	. . .	7.60	9.50	11.31	13.96	. . .
Estonia (Krooni)	12.03	13.88	14.07	14.68	16.97	17.56	16.61	13.86
Ethiopia (Birr)	6.35	6.71	7.12	7.94	8.22	8.46	8.57	8.60
EURO Area, 11 Cty. (Euros) [4]	. . .	. . .	. . .	0.94	1.09	1.12	1.06	0.89
Fed States Micronesia (U.S. Dollars)	1.00	1.00	1.00	1.00	1.00	1.00	1.00	1.00
Fiji (Fiji Dollars)	1.40	1.44	1.99	1.97	2.13	2.28	2.19	1.90
Finland (Natl Currency)	4.59	5.19	5.34	. . .	. . .	. . .	. . .	. . .
France (Natl Currency)	5.12	5.84	5.90	. . .	. . .	. . .	. . .	. . .
Gabon (Cfa Francs)	511.55	583.67	589.95	615.70	711.98	733.04	696.99	581.20
Georgia (Lari)	1.26	1.30	1.39	2.02	1.98	2.07	2.20	2.15
Germany (Natl Currency) [4]	1.50	1.73	1.76	. . .	. . .	. . .	. . .	. . .
Ghana (Cedis)	1 637.23	2 050.17	2 314.15	2 669.30	5 455.06	7 170.76	7 932.70	2.70
Greece (Natl Currency) [4]	240.71	273.06	295.53	305.65	365.40	. . .	2.70	2.70
Grenada (E. Caribbean Dollars)	2.70	2.70	2.70	2.70	2.70	2.70	2.70	7.94
Guatemala (Quetzales)	6.05	6.07	6.39	7.39	7.76	7.86	7.82	. . .
Guinea (Guinean Francs)	1 004.02	1 095.33	1 236.83	1 387.40	1 746.87	1 950.56	1 975.80	581.20
Guinea-Bissau (Cfa Francs)	405.75	583.67	589.95	615.70	711.98	733.04	696.99	

[1] FXRs included market, official, principal and secondary rates, as published by the IMF. RF and RH are the main rates used.

[2] One should review IMF publications for methods and definitions prior to using these rates in calculations. Market rates can be as much as 100 times higher than official rates (for example, North Korea in 2001).

[3] Some values were estimated using partial year data. End-of-year values used if annual average unavailable.

[4] The Euro became the official currency of 11 Euro Area nations on January 1, 1999, and of Greece in 2001.

. . . = Not available.

Table B-34. Foreign Exchange Rates, 1996–2003—*Continued*

(Annual average, foreign currency units per U.S. dollar.)

Country (currency)	1996	1997	1998	1999	2000	2001	2002	2003
Guyana (Guyana Dollars)	140.38	142.40	150.52	178.00	182.43	187.32	190.70	193.90
Haiti (Gourdes)	15.70	16.65	16.77	16.94	21.17	24.43	29.25	40.50
Honduras (Lempiras)	11.71	13.00	13.39	14.21	14.84	15.47	16.43	17.35
Hong Kong (Hong Kong Dollars)	7.73	7.74	7.75	7.76	7.79	7.80	7.80	7.79
Hungary (Forint)	152.65	186.79	214.40	237.15	282.18	286.49	257.89	224.31
Iceland (Kronur)	66.50	70.90	70.96	72.34	78.62	97.42	91.66	76.71
India (Indian Rupees)	35.43	36.31	41.26	43.06	44.94	47.19	48.61	46.58
Indonesia (Rupiah)	2 342.30	2 909.38	10 013.60	7 855.15	8 421.77	10 260.90	9 311.20	8 577.13
Iran (Rials)	1 750.76	1 752.92	1 751.86	1 752.93	1 764.43	1 753.56	6 906.96	8 193.89
Iraq (Dinars)	...	...	...	...	...	...	...	1 890.00
Ireland (Natl Currency) [4]	0.63	0.66	0.70	...	...	...	...	...
Israel (New Sheqalim)	3.19	3.45	3.80	4.14	4.08	4.21	4.74	4.55
Italy (Natl Currency) [4]	1 542.95	1 703.10	1 736.21	...	...	...	...	...
Ivory Coast (Cfa Francs)	511.55	583.67	589.95	615.70	711.98	733.04	696.99	581.20
Jamaica (Jamaica Dollars)	37.12	35.40	36.55	39.04	42.70	46.00	48.42	57.74
Japan (Yen)	108.78	120.99	130.91	113.91	107.77	121.53	125.39	115.93
Jordan (Jordanian Dinars)	0.71	0.71	0.71	0.71	0.71	0.71	0.71	0.71
Kazakhstan (Tenge)	67.30	75.44	78.30	119.52	142.13	146.74	153.28	149.58
Kenya (Kenya Shillings)	57.11	58.73	60.37	70.33	76.18	78.56	78.75	75.94
Kiribati (Gilbert I) (Australian Dollars) [3]	1.28	1.35	1.59	1.55	1.72	1.93	1.94	1.54
Korea, North (NK Won)	2.15	2.15	2.15	2.15	2.15	2.15	2.15	150.00
Korea, South (Won)	804.45	951.29	1 401.44	1 188.82	1 130.96	1 290.99	1 251.09	1 191.61
Kuwait (Kuwaiti Dinars)	0.30	0.30	0.30	0.30	0.31	0.31	0.30	0.30
Kyrgyz (Som)	12.81	17.36	20.84	39.01	47.70	48.38	46.94	43.65
Laos (Kip)	921.02	1 259.98	3 298.33	7 102.02	7 887.64	8 954.58	10 056.33	10 443.00
Latvia (Lats)	0.55	0.58	0.59	0.59	0.61	0.63	0.62	0.57
Lebanon (Lebanese Pounds)	1 571.44	1 539.45	1 516.13	1 507.84	1 507.50	1 507.50	1 507.50	1 507.50
Lesotho (Maloti)	4.30	4.61	5.53	6.11	6.94	8.61	10.54	7.56
Liberia (Liberian Dollars)	1.00	1.00	41.51	41.90	40.95	48.58	61.75	...
Libya (Libyan Dinars)	0.36	0.38	0.39	0.50	0.51	0.60	1.21	1.29
Lithuania (Litai)	4.00	4.00	4.00	4.00	4.00	4.00	3.68	3.06
Luxembourg (Natl Currency) [4]	30.96	35.77	36.30	...	...	...	...	...
Macao (Patacas)	7.97	7.98	7.98	7.99	8.03	8.03	8.03	8.02
Macedonia (Denars)	39.98	50.00	54.46	56.90	65.90	68.04	64.35	54.32
Madagascar (Malagasy Francs)	4 061.25	5 090.89	5 441.40	6 283.77	6 767.48	6 588.49	6 832.00	6 191.64
Malawi (Kwacha)	15.31	16.44	31.07	44.09	59.54	72.20	76.69	97.43
Malaysia (Ringgit)	2.52	2.81	3.92	3.80	3.80	3.80	3.80	3.80
Maldive Islands (Rufiyaa)	11.77	11.77	11.77	11.77	11.77	12.24	12.80	12.80
Mali (Cfa Francs)	511.55	583.67	589.95	615.70	711.98	733.04	696.99	581.20
Malta and Gozo (Maltese Liri)	0.36	0.39	0.39	0.40	0.44	0.45	0.43	0.38
Mauritania (Ouguiyas)	137.22	151.85	188.48	209.51	238.92	255.63	271.74	263.03
Mauritius (Mauritian Rupees)	17.95	21.06	23.99	25.19	26.25	29.13	29.96	27.90
Mexico (Mexican Pesos)	7.60	7.92	9.14	9.56	9.46	9.34	9.66	10.79
Moldova (Lei)	4.60	4.62	5.37	10.52	12.43	12.87	13.57	13.94
Mongolia (Togrogs)	548.40	789.99	840.83	1 021.87	1 076.67	1 097.70	1 110.31	1 171.00
Morocco (Dirhams)	8.72	9.53	9.60	9.80	10.63	11.30	11.02	9.57
Myanmar (Kyat)	5.92	6.24	6.34	6.29	6.52	6.68	6.57	6.08
Mozambique (Meticais)	11 517.80	11 772.60	12 110.20	13 028.60	15 447.10	20 703.60	23 678.00	23 782.30
Namibia (Namibia Dollars)	4.30	4.61	5.53	6.11	6.94	8.61	10.54	7.56
Nepal (Nepalese Rupees)	56.69	58.01	65.98	68.24	71.09	74.95	77.88	76.14
Netherlands (Natl Currency) [4]	1.69	1.95	1.98	...	...	...	...	...
New Zealand (New Zealand Dollars)	1.45	1.51	1.87	1.89	2.20	2.38	2.16	1.72
Nicaragua (Cordobas)	8.44	9.45	10.58	11.81	12.68	13.37	14.25	14.25
Niger (Cfa Francs)	511.55	583.67	589.95	615.70	711.98	733.04	696.99	581.20
Nigeria (Naira)	21.88	21.89	21.89	92.34	101.70	111.23	120.58	129.22
Norway (Norwegian Kroner)	6.45	7.07	7.55	7.80	8.80	8.99	7.98	7.08
Oman (Rials Omani)	0.38	0.38	0.38	0.38	0.38	0.38	0.38	0.38
Pakistan (Pakistan Rupees)	35.91	40.92	44.94	49.12	53.65	61.93	59.72	57.75
Panama (Balboas)	1.00	1.00	1.00	1.00	1.00	1.00	1.00	1.00
Papua New Guinea (Kina)	1.32	1.44	2.07	2.57	2.78	3.39	3.89	3.56
Paraguay (Guaranies)	2 056.81	2 177.86	2 726.49	3 119.07	3 486.35	4 105.92	5 716.30	6 424.34
Peru (Nuevos Soles)	2.45	2.66	2.93	3.38	3.49	3.51	3.52	3.48
Philippines (Philippine Pesos)	26.22	29.47	40.89	39.09	44.19	50.99	51.60	54.20
Poland (Zlotys)	2.70	3.28	3.48	3.97	4.35	4.09	4.08	3.89
Portugal (Natl Currency) [4]	154.24	175.31	180.10	...	...	...	...	...
Qatar (Qatar Riyals)	3.64	3.64	3.64	3.64	3.64	3.64	3.64	3.64
Rep. South Africa (Rand)	4.30	4.61	5.53	6.11	6.94	8.61	10.54	7.56
Romania (Lei)	3 084.22	7 167.94	8 875.58	15 332.80	21 708.70	29 060.80	33 055.40	33 200.10
Russia (Russian Rubles)	5.12	5.78	9.71	24.62	28.13	29.17	31.35	30.69
Rwanda (Rwanda Francs)	306.82	301.53	312.31	333.94	389.70	442.99	475.37	537.66

[1]FXRs included market, official, principal and secondary rates, as published by the IMF. RF and RH are the main rates used.
[2]One should review IMF publications for methods and definitions prior to using these rates in calculations. Market rates can be as much as 100 times higher than official rates (for example, North Korea in 2001).
[3]Some values were estimated using partial year data. End-of-year values used if annual average unavailable.
[4]The Euro became the official currency of 11 Euro Area nations on January 1, 1999, and of Greece in 2001.
. . . = Not available.

Table B-34. Foreign Exchange Rates, 1996–2003—*Continued*

(Annual average, foreign currency units per U.S. dollar.)

Country (currency)	1996	1997	1998	1999	2000	2001	2002	2003
San Marino (Euros)	1 542.95	1 703.10	1 736.21	. . .	. . .	. . .	. . .	. . .
Sao Tome and Principe (Dobras)	2 203.16	4 552.51	6 883.24	7 118.96	7 978.17	8 842.11	9 088.30	9 347.58
Saudi Arabia (Saudi A. Rial)	3.75	3.75	3.75	3.75	3.75	3.75	3.75	3.75
Senegal (Cfa Francs)	511.55	583.67	589.95	615.70	711.98	733.04	696.99	581.20
Seychelles (Seychelles Rupee)	4.97	5.03	5.26	5.34	5.71	5.86	5.48	5.40
Sierra Leone (Leones)	920.73	981.48	1 563.62	1 804.19	2 092.12	1 986.15	2 099.03	2 347.94
Singapore (Singapore Dollars)	1.41	1.48	1.67	1.69	1.72	1.79	1.79	1.74
Slovakia (Koruny)	30.65	33.62	35.23	41.36	46.04	48.35	45.33	36.77
Slovenia (Tolars)	135.36	159.69	166.13	181.77	222.66	242.75	240.25	207.11
Solomon Islands (Solomon Isl Dollars) 3	3.57	3.72	4.82	4.84	5.09	5.27	5.37	7.51
Spain (Natl Currency) 4	126.66	146.41	149.40	. . .	. . .	. . .	. . .	. . .
Sri Lanka (Ceylon) (Sri Lanka Rupees)	55.27	58.99	64.45	70.64	77.01	89.38	95.66	96.52
St. Christopher-Nevis (E. Caribbean Dollars)	2.70	2.70	2.70	2.70	2.70	2.70	2.70	2.70
St. Lucia (E. Caribbean Dollars)	2.70	2.70	2.70	2.70	2.70	2.70	2.70	2.70
St. Vincent/Grenadines (E. Caribbean Dollars)	2.70	2.70	2.70	2.70	2.70	2.70	2.70	2.70
Sudan (Sudanese Dinars)	125.08	157.57	200.80	252.55	257.12	258.70	263.31	260.98
Suriname (Suriname Guilder)	401.26	401.00	401.00	859.44	1 322.47	2 178.50	2 346.75	2 601.30
Swaziland (Emalangeni)	4.30	4.61	5.53	6.11	6.94	8.61	10.48	7.56
Sweden (Swedish Kronor)	6.71	7.63	7.95	8.26	9.16	10.33	9.74	8.09
Switzerland (Swiss Francs)	1.24	1.45	1.45	1.50	1.69	1.69	1.56	1.35
Syria (Syrian Pounds)	11.23	11.23	11.23	11.23	11.23	11.23	11.23	11.23
Tajikistan (Tajik Somoni)	0.30	0.56	0.78	1.24	2.08	2.37	2.76	3.06
Tanzania (Tanzania Shillin)	579.98	612.12	664.67	744.76	800.41	876.41	966.58	1 038.42
Thailand (Baht)	25.34	31.36	41.36	37.81	40.11	44.43	42.96	41.48
Togo (Cfa Francs)	511.55	583.67	589.95	615.70	711.98	733.04	696.99	581.20
Tonga (Pa'Anga)	1.23	1.26	1.49	1.60	1.76	2.12	2.20	2.14
Trinidad and Tobago (TT Dollars)	6.01	6.25	6.30	6.30	6.30	6.23	6.25	6.30
Tunisia (Tunisian Dinars)	0.97	1.11	1.14	1.19	1.37	1.44	1.42	1.29
Turkey (Liras)	81 404.90	151 865.00	260 724.00	418 783.00	625 219.00	1 225 588.00	1 507 226.00	1 500 885.00
Turkmenistan (Manat) 3	3 257.67	4 143.42	4 890.17	5 200.00	5 200.00	5 200.00	5 200.00	5 200.00
Uganda (Uganda Shillings)	1 046.08	1 083.01	1 240.31	1 454.83	1 644.48	1 755.66	1 797.60	1 963.72
Ukraine (Hryvnias)	1.83	1.86	2.45	4.13	5.44	5.37	5.33	5.33
United Arab Emirates (Dirhams)	3.67	3.67	3.67	3.67	3.67	3.67	3.67	3.67
United Kingdom (Pounds Sterling)	0.64	0.61	0.60	0.62	0.66	0.69	0.67	0.61
United States (U.S. Dollars)	1.00	1.00	1.00	1.00	1.00	1.00	1.00	1.00
Uruguay (Uruguayan Pesos)	7.97	9.44	10.47	11.34	12.10	13.32	21.26	28.21
Uzbekistan (Sum) 3	40.07	62.92	94.49	124.63	236.61	. . .	125.30	115.90
Vanuatu (New Hebrides) (Vatu)	111.72	115.87	127.52	129.08	137.64	145.31	139.20	122.19
Venezuela (Bolivares)	417.33	488.64	547.56	605.72	679.96	723.67	1 160.95	1 606.96
Vietnam (Dong)	11 032.60	11 683.30	13 268.00	13 943.20	14 167.70	14 725.20	15 280.00	15 279.50
Western Samoa (Tala)	2.46	2.56	2.95	3.01	3.29	3.48	. . .	2.97
Yemen (Rial)	94.76	129.28	135.88	155.72	161.72	168.67	175.63	183.45
Zambia (Zambian Kwacha)	1 207.90	1 314.50	1 862.07	2 388.02	3 110.84	3 610.94	4 398.60	4 733.27
Zimbabwe (Rhodesia) (Zimbabwe Dollars)	10.00	12.11	23.68	38.30	44.42	55.05	55.05	250.00

1FXRs included market, official, principal and secondary rates, as published by the IMF. RF and RH are the main rates used.
2One should review IMF publications for methods and definitions prior to using these rates in calculations. Market rates can be as much as 100 times higher than official rates (for example, North Korea in 2001).
3Some values were estimated using partial year data. End-of-year values used if annual average unavailable.
4The Euro became the official currency of 11 Euro Area nations on January 1, 1999, and of Greece in 2001.
. . . = Not available.

Table B-35. U.S. Total Exports by 3-Digit NAICS Product Groups, 1998–2004

(Millions of dollars; Census basis; foreign and domestic exports, f.a.s.)

NAICS product	1998	1999	2000	2001	2002	2003	2004	Percent change, 1998–2004
TOTAL	680 474	692 821	780 419	731 026	693 257	723 743	817 936	20.2
111 – Agricultural products	25 034	22 733	24 449	24 861	25 797	30 359	33 210	32.7
112 – Livestock and livestock products	1 121	1 039	1 266	1 325	1 032	1 194	982	-12.4
113 – Forestry and logging	1 550	1 568	1 673	1 472	1 450	1 515	1 700	9.7
114 – Fishing, hunting, and trapping	2 127	2 601	2 810	2 969	2 941	3 056	3 461	62.7
211 – Oil and gas extraction	1 257	1 460	1 747	1 339	1 727	2 177	3 112	147.6
212 – Mining	5 411	4 451	4 537	4 240	3 911	4 020	5 733	5.9
311 – Processed foods	25 168	24 118	25 750	27 089	25 856	27 496	26 646	5.9
312 – Beverages and tobacco products	6 523	5 531	5 675	4 435	3 659	3 797	3 758	-42.4
313 – Fabric mill products	5 672	6 055	7 284	7 365	7 642	7 805	8 638	52.3
314 – Non-apparel textile products	2 218	2 211	2 333	2 083	1 982	2 004	2 235	0.8
315 – Apparel manufactures	8 708	8 194	8 558	6 956	5 994	5 470	4 962	-43.0
316 – Leather and related products	2 693	2 570	2 688	2 709	2 593	2 717	2 931	8.8
321 – Wood products	4 651	4 859	5 022	4 099	3 948	4 036	4 492	-3.4
322 – Paper products	13 820	14 131	15 979	14 496	14 107	14 504	15 732	13.8
323 – Printing and related products	4 955	4 866	5 097	5 125	4 774	4 984	5 233	5.6
324 – Petroleum and coal products	5 388	6 007	9 029	8 416	8 049	9 659	12 829	138.1
325 – Chemical manufactures	67 531	69 870	80 259	79 034	80 504	91 017	108 484	60.6
326 – Plastics and rubber products	14 522	15 197	17 715	16 508	16 169	16 510	18 332	26.2
327 – Non-metallic mineral products	6 211	6 527	8 173	7 745	6 326	6 405	6 925	11.5
331 – Primary metal manufactures	20 130	18 667	21 498	19 312	16 689	19 125	22 790	13.2
332 – Fabricated metal products	19 985	20 136	22 913	20 699	20 187	20 365	22 614	13.2
333 – Machinery manufactures	79 392	76 335	89 768	81 380	74 945	74 925	92 674	16.7
334 – Computer and electronic products	147 475	161 543	196 234	165 345	145 848	149 993	164 200	11.3
335 – Electrical equipment, appliances, and parts ...	22 383	23 716	27 478	24 923	22 848	23 292	26 828	19.9
336 – Transportation equipment	131 943	132 095	128 255	130 365	130 897	128 854	140 439	6.4
337 – Furniture and related products	2 613	2 563	3 024	2 588	2 323	2 546	2 868	9.8
339 – Miscellaneous manufactures	20 478	21 970	24 452	25 779	26 661	29 401	34 247	67.2
511 – Publishing industries (except Internet) ...	0	0	0	0	324	336	511	X
910 – Waste and scrap	3 570	3 623	5 129	4 824	5 165	6 564	8 755	145.3
920 – Public administration	3 330	2 848	4 021	4 644	3 179	3 441	4 367	31.1
980 – Goods returned to Canada (exports only); U.S. goods returned and reimported items (imports only) ...	1 933	1 703	1 905	1 880	1 339	1 173	837	-56.7
990 – Special classification provisions	22 682	23 635	25 695	27 019	24 392	25 002	27 411	20.9

Note: Unrevised data.

X = Not applicable.

Table B-36. U.S. Total Imports by 3-Digit NAICS Product Groups, 1998–2004

(Millions of dollars; Census basis; general imports, Customs.)

NAICS product	1998	1999	2000	2001	2002	2003	2004	Percent change, 1998–2004
TOTAL	913 885	1 024 766	1 216 888	1 141 959	1 163 549	1 259 396	1 469 671	60.8
111 – Agricultural products	12 364	12 237	11 742	11 313	11 737	12 966	14 344	16.0
112 – Livestock and livestock products	2 522	2 504	2 859	3 202	3 187	2 784	2 498	-0.9
113 – Forestry and logging	1 512	1 242	1 409	1 158	1 288	1 612	2 019	33.6
114 – Fishing, hunting, and trapping	6 761	7 303	8 339	7 953	8 076	8 768	8 947	32.3
211 – Oil and gas extraction	45 362	59 475	104 614	94 724	92 913	124 831	162 183	257.5
212 – Mining	2 891	2 566	2 711	2 877	2 797	3 052	3 687	27.5
311 – Processed foods	17 371	18 432	19 078	19 770	21 196	23 882	27 876	60.5
312 – Beverages and tobacco products	6 987	7 870	8 699	9 035	10 089	11 298	12 060	72.6
313 – Fabric mill products	6 533	6 481	7 071	6 357	6 804	6 830	7 423	13.6
314 – Non-apparel textile products	5 615	6 362	7 364	7 612	8 651	9 877	11 752	109.3
315 – Apparel manufactures	52 376	55 141	63 042	62 501	62 407	66 600	70 652	34.9
316 – Leather and related products	19 554	20 025	21 495	21 824	22 172	22 905	24 746	26.5
321 – Wood products	13 288	16 003	15 393	14 970	15 725	16 585	22 870	72.1
322 – Paper products	15 610	16 435	19 092	18 179	17 543	18 428	20 662	32.4
323 – Printing and related products	3 475	3 789	4 196	4 140	4 433	4 701	5 155	48.4
324 – Petroleum and coal products	10 490	13 713	25 479	24 402	21 817	27 922	39 861	280.0
325 – Chemical manufactures	53 722	60 963	71 898	76 890	83 770	97 984	108 843	102.6
326 – Plastics and rubber products	14 226	15 984	17 515	17 032	18 690	20 648	24 304	70.8
327 – Non-metallic mineral products	11 512	13 224	14 802	13 557	13 549	14 415	16 497	43.3
331 – Primary metal manufactures	40 622	36 930	43 855	36 818	34 794	33 866	56 156	38.2
332 – Fabricated metal products	22 797	24 487	28 256	26 664	28 773	30 378	36 119	58.4
333 – Machinery manufactures	70 879	72 093	79 939	72 471	69 119	77 930	94 943	34.0
334 – Computer and electronic products	181 202	205 604	251 639	205 545	206 295	213 487	249 122	37.5
335 – Electrical equipment, appliances, and parts	30 256	34 811	39 910	39 325	40 211	42 575	49 426	63.4
336 – Transportation equipment	164 528	193 686	213 384	211 689	219 243	222 566	240 417	46.1
337 – Furniture and related products	10 797	13 173	15 612	15 274	17 496	19 644	22 569	109.0
339 – Miscellaneous manufactures	47 144	50 961	56 702	56 509	61 861	65 482	72 558	53.9
511 – Publishing industries (except Internet)	214	163	162	175	133	122	98	-54.2
910 – Waste and scrap	1 756	1 710	1 871	1 588	1 614	1 808	3 051	73.7
920 – Public administration	4 593	5 424	6 342	5 902	5 669	4 757	5 714	24.4
980 – Goods returned to Canada (exports only); U.S. goods returned and reimported items (imports only)	25 363	30 888	33 706	34 675	34 753	32 953	33 178	30.8
990 – Special classification provisions	11 563	15 089	18 711	17 831	16 745	17 743	19 939	72.4

Note: Unrevised data.

Table B-37. U.S. Total Trade Balances by 3-Digit NAICS Product Groups, 1998–2004

(Millions of dollars; Census basis; foreign and domestic exports, f.a.s.; general imports, Customs.)

NAICS product	1998	1999	2000	2001	2002	2003	2004	Percent change, 1998–2004
TOTAL	-233 411	-331 945	-436 469	-410 933	-470 291	-535 652	-651 735	179.2
111 – Agricultural products	12 670	10 496	12 707	13 548	14 060	17 393	18 866	48.9
112 – Livestock and livestock products	-1 401	-1 465	-1 593	-1 877	-2 155	-1 591	-1 516	8.2
113 – Forestry and logging	39	326	264	314	162	-97	-319	-925.8
114 – Fishing, hunting, and trapping	-4 634	-4 701	-5 529	-4 983	-5 135	-5 712	-5 486	18.4
211 – Oil and gas extraction	-44 105	-58 016	-102 867	-93 385	-91 186	-122 654	-159 070	260.7
212 – Mining	2 520	1 885	1 826	1 363	1 114	968	2 046	-18.8
311 – Processed foods	7 797	5 686	6 671	7 319	4 660	3 614	-1 231	-115.8
312 – Beverages and tobacco products	-464	-2 339	-3 024	-4 600	-6 430	-7 501	-8 303	1 688.8
313 – Fabric mill products	-860	-426	213	1 008	838	975	1 215	-241.2
314 – Non-apparel textile products	-3 397	-4 151	-5 031	-5 529	-6 670	-7 872	-9 517	180.2
315 – Apparel manufactures	-43 668	-46 947	-54 484	-55 545	-56 413	-61 130	-65 690	50.4
316 – Leather and related products	-16 861	-17 455	-18 807	-19 115	-19 579	-20 188	-21 815	29.4
321 – Wood products	-8 637	-11 144	-10 371	-10 871	-11 776	-12 548	-18 378	112.8
322 – Paper products	-1 790	-2 304	-3 113	-3 683	-3 436	-3 923	-4 930	175.4
323 – Printing and related products	1 480	1 077	901	984	341	283	78	-94.7
324 – Petroleum and coal products	-5 102	-7 706	-16 450	-15 986	-13 768	-18 263	-27 032	429.8
325 – Chemical manufactures	13 809	8 908	8 361	2 144	-3 266	-6 967	-358	-102.6
326 – Plastics and rubber products	296	-787	200	-523	-2 521	-4 138	-5 972	-2 114.7
327 – Non-metallic mineral products	-5 301	-6 698	-6 628	-5 812	-7 223	-8 010	-9 573	80.6
331 – Primary metal manufactures	-20 492	-18 262	-22 357	-17 506	-18 105	-14 741	-33 365	62.8
332 – Fabricated metal products	-2 812	-4 351	-5 343	-5 964	-8 586	-10 013	-13 505	380.3
333 – Machinery manufactures	8 513	4 242	9 829	8 910	5 826	-3 004	-2 269	-126.7
334 – Computer and electronic products	-33 728	-44 061	-55 405	-40 199	-60 448	-63 493	-84 923	151.8
335 – Electrical equipment, appliances, and parts	-7 873	-11 095	-12 433	-14 402	-17 363	-19 283	-22 598	187.0
336 – Transportation equipment	-32 584	-61 591	-85 129	-81 324	-88 345	-93 712	-99 978	206.8
337 – Furniture and related products	-8 184	-10 610	-12 588	-12 686	-15 172	-17 098	-19 701	140.7
339 – Miscellaneous manufactures	-26 666	-28 991	-32 250	-30 730	-35 200	-36 081	-38 311	43.7
511 – Publishing industries (except Internet)	-214	-163	-162	-175	191	214	413	-293.0
910 – Waste and scrap	1 813	1 913	3 258	3 236	3 551	4 756	5 705	214.6
920 – Public administration	-1 262	-2 576	-2 321	-1 257	-2 489	-1 316	-1 347	6.7
980 – Goods returned to Canada (exports only); U.S. goods returned and reimported items (imports only)	-23 430	-29 185	-31 801	-32 795	-33 414	-31 780	-32 342	38.0
990 – Special classification provisions	11 118	8 546	6 984	9 188	7 647	7 259	7 471	-32.8

Note: Unrevised data.

Table B-38. U.S. Total Exports by 4-Digit NAICS Product Groups, 1998–2003

(Millions of dollars; Census basis; foreign and domestic exports, f.a.s.)

NAICS product	1998	1999	2000	2001	2002	2003	Percent change, 1998–2003
TOTAL	680 474	692 821	780 419	731 026	693 257	723 743	6.4
1111 – Oilseeds and grains	14 938	14 614	14 842	15 013	15 789	18 395	23.1
1112 – Vegetables and melons	1 542	1 531	1 668	1 675	1 772	1 906	23.6
1113 – Fruits and tree nuts	3 431	3 187	3 547	3 595	3 796	4 294	25.1
1114 – Mushrooms, nursery and related products	320	334	335	334	332	366	14.3
1119 – Other agricultural products	4 802	3 067	4 057	4 244	4 107	5 397	12.4
1121 – Cattle	240	242	337	341	183	117	-51.0
1122 – Swine	23	19	12	12	38	34	43.6
1123 – Poultry and eggs	259	218	207	218	216	223	-13.9
1124 – Sheep, goats and fine animal hair	42	43	37	27	31	31	-26.2
1125 – Farmed fish and related products	47	49	58	64	41	51	9.2
1129 – Other animals	510	469	617	663	523	738	44.7
1132 – Forestry products	191	201	214	196	205	263	37.2
1133 – Timber and logs	1 359	1 366	1 460	1 276	1 245	1 252	-7.9
1141 – Fish, fresh, chilled, and frozen, and other marine products	2 127	2 601	2 810	2 969	2 941	3 056	43.7
2111 – Oil and gas	1 257	1 460	1 747	1 339	1 727	2 177	73.2
2121 – Coal and petroleum gases	3 036	2 136	2 042	1 833	1 607	1 554	-48.8
2122 – Metal ores	998	991	1 039	1 043	1 030	1 140	14.2
2123 – Nonmetallic minerals	1 377	1 325	1 456	1 364	1 274	1 326	-3.7
3111 – Animal foods	1 327	1 251	1 450	1 641	1 356	1 358	2.3
3112 – Grain and oilseed milling products	6 641	5 582	5 161	5 618	5 819	5 829	-12.2
3113 – Sugar and confectionery products	899	921	1 096	1 280	1 129	1 216	35.2
3114 – Fruits and vegetable preserves and specialty foods	2 803	2 933	2 838	2 736	2 751	2 785	-0.6
3115 – Dairy products	1 033	1 030	1 154	1 222	1 081	1 181	14.4
3116 – Meat products and meat packaging products	8 505	8 201	9 843	10 104	9 210	10 253	20.6
3117 – Seafood products, prepared, canned, and packaged	299	427	334	382	337	346	15.4
3118 – Bakery and tortilla products	617	626	642	651	664	777	25.8
3119 – Foods, n.e.s.o.i.	3 044	3 147	3 232	3 457	3 509	3 751	23.2
3121 – Beverages	1 681	1 634	1 641	1 685	1 699	1 914	13.8
3122 – Tobacco products	4 842	3 897	4 035	2 750	1 960	1 883	-61.1
3131 – Fibers, yarns, and threads	557	627	762	620	604	736	32.1
3132 – Fabrics	4 470	4 778	5 864	5 951	6 230	6 104	36.5
3133 – Finished and coated textile fabrics	645	650	658	794	808	966	49.7
3141 – Textile furnishings	1 349	1 253	1 292	1 194	1 134	1 120	-17.0
3149 – Other textile products	870	958	1 041	889	847	885	1.7
3151 – Knit apparel	420	449	437	367	348	344	-18.1
3152 – Apparel	6 367	6 239	6 612	5 288	4 505	4 092	-35.7
3159 – Apparel accessories	1 920	1 506	1 509	1 301	1 141	1 033	-46.2
3161 – Leather and hide tanning	1 404	1 235	1 238	1 395	1 409	1 476	5.1
3162 – Footwear	551	533	559	529	515	510	-7.3
3169 – Other leather products	738	801	892	785	670	731	-1.0
3211 – Sawmill and wood products	2 596	2 729	2 751	2 191	2 060	2 048	-21.1
3212 – Veneer, plywood, and engineered wood products	1 168	1 182	1 266	1 085	1 101	1 098	-6.0
3219 – Other wood products	888	948	1 004	824	787	890	0.3
3221 – Pulp, paper, and paperboard mill products	8 947	8 850	10 276	8 849	7 809	7 922	-11.5
3222 – Converted paper products	4 873	5 281	5 702	5 647	6 299	6 582	35.1
3231 – Printing, publishing, and similar products	4 955	4 866	5 097	5 125	4 774	4 984	0.6
3241 – Petroleum and coal products	5 388	6 007	9 029	8 416	8 049	9 659	79.3
3251 – Basic chemicals	23 555	24 447	28 854	26 823	26 659	30 908	31.2
3252 – Resin, synthetic rubber, artificial and synthetic fibers and filaments	13 926	13 963	16 514	15 710	16 160	17 462	25.4
3253 – Pesticides, fertilizers, and other agricultural chemicals	5 269	4 885	4 219	4 071	4 019	4 229	-19.7
3254 – Pharmaceuticals and medicines	12 221	13 814	16 034	18 547	19 258	23 043	88.6
3255 – Paints, coatings, and adhesives	1 925	2 088	2 351	2 263	2 293	2 359	22.5
3256 – Soaps, cleaning compounds, and toilet preparations	4 886	5 067	5 577	5 948	6 034	6 687	36.9
3259 – Other chemical products and preparations	5 749	5 606	6 710	5 671	6 081	6 330	10.1
3261 – Plastics products	9 592	10 387	12 442	11 552	11 498	11 805	23.1
3262 – Rubber products	4 931	4 810	5 273	4 957	4 671	4 704	-4.6
3271 – Clay and refractory products	1 179	1 190	1 367	1 292	1 183	1 147	-2.7
3272 – Glass and glass products	3 374	3 755	5 021	4 678	3 451	3 499	3.7
3273 – Cement and concrete products	171	167	180	167	175	185	8.1
3274 – Lime and gypsum products	74	78	89	88	93	100	35.9
3279 – Other nonmetallic mineral products	1 413	1 337	1 517	1 519	1 423	1 474	4.3
3311 – Iron and steel and ferroalloy	5 044	4 570	5 351	5 061	4 831	5 845	15.9
3312 – Steel products from purchased steel	325	341	340	342	320	313	-3.7
3313 – Alumina and aluminum and processing	4 176	4 017	4 254	3 662	3 274	3 256	-22.0
3314 – Nonferrous (excluding aluminum) and processing	10 079	9 219	11 111	9 855	7 901	9 309	-7.6
3315 – Foundries	505	520	443	392	363	402	-20.4
3321 – Crowns, closures, seals, and other packing accessories	276	268	267	279	258	269	-2.3
3322 – Cutlery and handtools	1 543	1 730	1 750	1 700	1 682	1 728	12.0

Note: Unrevised data.

Table B-38. U.S. Total Exports by 4-Digit NAICS Product Groups, 1998–2003—*Continued*

(Millions of dollars; Census basis; foreign and domestic exports, f.a.s.)

NAICS product	1998	1999	2000	2001	2002	2003	Percent change, 1998–2003
3323 – Architectural and structural metals	961	912	907	850	804	891	-7.3
3324 – Boilers, tanks, and shipping containers	2 048	1 762	1 652	1 556	1 407	1 483	-27.6
3325 – Hardware	1 682	1 898	2 339	2 189	2 194	2 078	23.5
3326 – Springs and wire products	818	803	943	776	746	808	-1.2
3327 – Bolts, nuts, screws, rivets, washers, and other turned products ...	1 522	1 593	1 790	1 581	1 597	1 632	7.2
3329 – Other fabricated metal products	11 135	11 171	13 264	11 766	11 499	11 476	3.1
3331 – Agricultural, construction, and mining machinery	20 243	16 053	17 599	17 787	17 424	17 904	-11.6
3332 – Industrial machinery	8 718	9 861	14 228	9 488	8 062	7 824	-10.3
3333 – Commercial and service industry machinery	7 280	7 013	9 269	8 499	7 061	7 108	-2.4
3334 – HVAC and commercial refrigeration equipment	5 646	5 519	5 693	5 492	5 234	5 075	-10.1
3335 – Metalworking machinery	5 801	5 331	6 242	5 432	4 947	4 924	-15.1
3336 – Engines, turbines, and power transmission equipment ...	11 528	11 687	12 373	12 496	12 591	12 332	7.0
3339 – Other general purpose machinery	20 175	20 871	24 364	22 187	19 627	19 759	-2.1
3341 – Computer equipment	44 825	45 994	54 801	46 876	38 109	39 575	-11.7
3342 – Communications equipment	17 125	18 799	21 631	18 767	15 450	13 981	-18.4
3343 – Audio and video equipment	5 699	5 110	5 915	5 548	5 445	5 214	-8.5
3344 – Semiconductors and other electronic components	53 703	64 391	83 319	64 259	58 301	61 360	14.3
3345 – Navigational, measuring, medical, and control instruments	23 571	25 053	28 674	28 336	27 074	28 231	19.8
3346 – Magnetic and optical media	2 552	2 195	1 893	1 560	1 469	1 632	-36.0
3351 – Electric lighting equipment	1 567	1 572	1 711	1 602	1 596	1 545	-1.4
3352 – Household appliances and miscellaneous machines, n.e.s.o.i.	3 469	3 445	3 698	3 407	3 158	3 272	-5.7
3353 – Electrical equipment	7 548	8 088	8 841	8 487	7 885	8 411	11.4
3359 – Electrical equipment and components, n.e.s.o.i.	9 799	10 611	13 228	11 427	10 209	10 063	2.7
3361 – Motor vehicles	24 531	23 813	24 708	24 177	27 689	30 870	25.8
3362 – Motor vehicle bodies and trailers	1 524	1 531	1 559	1 318	1 322	1 593	4.5
3363 – Motor vehicle parts	38 621	41 211	44 767	41 600	41 592	39 590	2.5
3364 – Aerospace products and parts	62 368	61 070	53 470	58 474	56 372	52 281	-16.2
3365 – Railroad rolling stock	1 432	1 240	1 191	1 306	965	1 418	-1.0
3366 – Ships and boats	1 702	1 619	992	1 839	1 182	1 273	-25.2
3369 – Transportation equipment, n.e.s.o.i.	1 765	1 611	1 568	1 652	1 775	1 828	3.6
3371 – Household and institutional furniture and kitchen cabinets	1 449	1 404	1 585	1 402	1 301	1 338	-7.6
3372 – Office furniture (including fixtures)	1 082	1 078	1 360	1 102	932	1 105	2.1
3379 – Furniture related products, n.e.s.o.i.	82	80	79	84	90	103	25.9
3391 – Medical equipment and supplies	8 663	9 137	10 043	11 178	11 704	13 437	55.1
3399 – Miscellaneous manufactured commodities	11 814	12 833	14 410	14 601	14 957	15 964	35.1
5112 – Software publishers	0	0	0	0	324	336	X
9100 – Waste and scrap	3 570	3 623	5 129	4 824	5 165	6 564	83.9
9200 – Used or second-hand merchandise	3 330	2 848	4 021	4 644	3 179	3 441	3.3
9800 – Goods returned to Canada (exports only); U.S. goods returned and reimported items (imports only)	1 933	1 703	1 905	1 880	1 339	1 173	-39.3
9900 – Special classification provisions, n.e.s.o.i.	22 682	23 635	25 695	27 019	24 392	25 002	10.2

Note: Unrevised data.

X = Not applicable.

Table B-39. U.S. Total Imports by 4-Digit NAICS Product Groups, 1998–2003

(Millions of dollars; Census basis; general imports, Customs.)

NAICS product	1998	1999	2000	2001	2002	2003	Percent change, 1998–2003
TOTAL	913 885	1 024 766	1 216 888	1 141 959	1 163 549	1 259 396	37.8
1111 – Oilseeds and grains	1 097	996	959	1 038	1 041	945	-13.8
1112 – Vegetables and melons	2 445	2 358	2 445	2 728	2 798	3 226	32.0
1113 – Fruits and tree nuts	6 401	6 348	6 009	5 137	5 542	6 334	-1.0
1114 – Mushrooms, nursery and related products	1 123	1 156	1 223	1 217	1 212	1 335	18.8
1119 – Other agricultural products	1 298	1 379	1 105	1 194	1 144	1 125	-13.3
1121 – Cattle	1 158	1 020	1 171	1 477	1 463	883	-23.8
1122 – Swine	273	216	290	349	301	391	43.3
1123 – Poultry and eggs	26	31	31	37	41	38	47.6
1124 – Sheep, goats and fine animal hair	105	59	54	47	36	31	-70.4
1125 – Farmed fish and related products	543	638	703	764	792	848	56.2
1129 – Other animals	417	539	609	529	555	593	42.2
1132 – Forestry products	1 388	1 074	1 175	948	1 059	1 403	1.0
1133 – Timber and logs	124	167	234	210	229	209	69.2
1141 – Fish, fresh, chilled, and frozen, and other marine products	6 761	7 303	8 339	7 953	8 076	8 768	29.7
2111 – Oil and gas	45 362	59 475	104 614	94 724	92 913	124 831	175.2
2121 – Coal and petroleum gases	281	280	377	673	599	788	180.5
2122 – Metal ores	1 610	1 272	1 228	1 100	1 131	1 145	-28.9
2123 – Nonmetallic minerals	1 000	1 015	1 107	1 103	1 067	1 119	11.9
3111 – Animal foods	377	368	390	390	407	393	4.0
3112 – Grain and oilseed milling products	2 357	2 225	2 231	2 046	2 299	2 707	14.8
3113 – Sugar and confectionery products	2 524	2 404	2 402	2 550	2 877	3 584	42.0
3114 – Fruits and vegetable preserves and specialty foods	2 882	3 329	3 242	3 208	3 521	4 043	40.3
3115 – Dairy products	1 301	1 370	1 439	1 508	1 491	1 679	29.1
3116 – Meat products and meat packaging products	3 300	3 710	4 307	4 740	4 766	4 891	48.2
3117 – Seafood products, prepared, canned, and packaged	954	1 107	1 018	1 198	1 310	1 493	56.6
3118 – Bakery and tortilla products	1 155	1 257	1 356	1 424	1 571	1 834	58.8
3119 – Foods, n.e.s.o.i.	2 522	2 661	2 692	2 705	2 955	3 258	29.2
3121 – Beverages	6 504	7 414	8 141	8 508	9 472	10 688	64.3
3122 – Tobacco products	484	456	559	527	617	610	26.1
3131 – Fibers, yarns, and threads	652	716	806	701	670	700	7.3
3132 – Fabrics	5 424	5 319	5 742	5 169	5 555	5 440	0.3
3133 – Finished and coated textile fabrics	457	446	523	487	579	690	51.2
3141 – Textile furnishings	3 666	4 217	5 026	5 113	6 092	7 063	92.7
3149 – Other textile products	1 949	2 145	2 338	2 498	2 559	2 813	44.4
3151 – Knit apparel	681	844	947	920	1 029	1 085	59.3
3152 – Apparel	48 799	51 301	58 517	57 990	57 770	61 700	26.4
3159 – Apparel accessories	2 896	2 997	3 578	3 591	3 609	3 815	31.7
3161 – Leather and hide tanning	1 607	1 668	2 032	2 100	2 171	2 187	36.1
3162 – Footwear	13 344	13 622	14 495	14 876	15 079	15 287	14.6
3169 – Other leather products	4 604	4 735	4 968	4 848	4 923	5 430	18.0
3211 – Sawmill and wood products	7 165	8 305	7 574	7 334	7 113	6 437	-10.2
3212 – Veneer, plywood, and engineered wood products	3 375	4 441	4 213	4 018	4 608	5 948	76.2
3219 – Other wood products	2 747	3 257	3 605	3 619	4 004	4 200	52.9
3221 – Pulp, paper, and paperboard mill products	12 222	12 643	14 501	13 389	12 337	12 718	4.1
3222 – Converted paper products	3 388	3 792	4 591	4 790	5 206	5 710	68.5
3231 – Printing, publishing, and similar products	3 475	3 789	4 196	4 140	4 433	4 701	35.3
3241 – Petroleum and coal products	10 490	13 713	25 479	24 402	21 817	27 922	166.2
3251 – Basic chemicals	18 964	19 788	22 916	23 187	22 908	25 721	35.6
3252 – Resin, synthetic rubber, artificial and synthetic fibers and filaments	6 989	7 343	8 522	8 274	8 401	9 351	33.8
3253 – Pesticides, fertilizers, and other agricultural chemicals	2 578	2 498	2 878	3 327	2 822	4 112	59.5
3254 – Pharmaceuticals and medicines	17 769	23 467	28 960	33 755	41 002	49 548	178.8
3255 – Paints, coatings, and adhesives	687	931	1 012	988	885	966	40.6
3256 – Soaps, cleaning compounds, and toilet preparations	2 671	2 958	3 415	3 621	4 057	4 597	72.1
3259 – Other chemical products and preparations	4 065	3 977	4 195	3 739	3 695	3 690	-9.2
3261 – Plastics products	8 169	9 262	10 384	10 475	11 479	12 671	55.1
3262 – Rubber products	6 057	6 722	7 131	6 557	7 211	7 977	31.7
3271 – Clay and refractory products	3 614	3 916	4 404	4 037	4 196	4 546	25.8
3272 – Glass and glass products	3 859	4 585	5 295	4 615	4 299	4 436	15.0
3273 – Cement and concrete products	1 419	1 745	1 877	1 820	1 853	1 861	31.2
3274 – Lime and gypsum products	175	340	150	123	96	90	-48.5
3279 – Other nonmetallic mineral products	2 445	2 638	3 077	2 961	3 105	3 482	42.4
3311 – Iron and steel and ferroalloy	18 329	14 216	16 790	12 808	13 479	11 977	-34.7
3312 – Steel products from purchased steel	1 016	1 070	1 110	1 013	1 109	1 184	16.6
3313 – Alumina and aluminum and processing	6 605	6 829	7 528	6 785	7 062	7 448	12.8
3314 – Nonferrous (excluding aluminum) and processing	14 183	14 348	17 935	15 782	12 715	12 807	-9.7
3315 – Foundries	489	467	493	429	429	450	-8.0
3321 – Crowns, closures, seals, and other packing accessories	115	134	150	177	192	237	106.0
3322 – Cutlery and handtools	2 870	3 109	3 318	3 228	3 494	3 831	33.5

Note: Unrevised data.

Table B-39. U.S. Total Imports by 4-Digit NAICS Product Groups, 1998–2003—*Continued*

(Millions of dollars; Census basis; general imports, Customs.)

NAICS product	1998	1999	2000	2001	2002	2003	Percent change, 1998–2003
3323 – Architectural and structural metals	970	1 209	1 524	1 736	1 837	1 792	84.7
3324 – Boilers, tanks, and shipping containers	1 015	1 169	1 478	1 647	1 984	1 772	74.5
3325 – Hardware	2 695	2 916	3 290	3 143	3 446	3 668	36.1
3326 – Springs and wire products	1 556	1 698	1 745	1 581	1 610	1 690	8.6
3327 – Bolts, nuts, screws, rivets, washers, and other turned products	2 054	2 049	2 355	2 018	2 109	2 371	15.4
3329 – Other fabricated metal products	11 520	12 203	14 395	13 134	14 102	15 016	30.3
3331 – Agricultural, construction, and mining machinery	12 195	11 585	11 790	11 083	11 384	13 309	9.1
3332 – Industrial machinery	10 676	10 480	11 517	9 859	8 720	9 005	-15.7
3333 – Commercial and service industry machinery	11 204	11 135	12 743	9 560	8 151	11 284	0.7
3334 – HVAC and commercial refrigeration equipment	2 898	3 428	4 062	4 041	4 553	5 299	82.8
3335 – Metalworking machinery	9 334	8 264	8 922	7 572	6 424	6 912	-25.9
3336 – Engines, turbines, and power transmission equipment	8 114	9 740	11 077	12 163	11 803	11 870	46.3
3339 – Other general purpose machinery	16 458	17 461	19 828	18 191	18 085	20 250	23.0
3341 – Computer equipment	55 017	61 278	68 538	59 049	62 323	64 021	16.4
3342 – Communications equipment	15 616	20 326	31 162	27 275	28 024	30 448	95.0
3343 – Audio and video equipment	22 840	24 512	29 036	27 483	31 112	32 098	40.5
3344 – Semiconductors and other electronic components	68 400	78 528	98 418	66 993	58 574	57 585	-15.8
3345 – Navigational, measuring, medical, and control instruments	17 002	18 423	21 785	22 118	23 326	26 031	53.1
3346 – Magnetic and optical media	2 327	2 537	2 701	2 627	2 937	3 304	42.0
3351 – Electric lighting equipment	4 371	5 201	5 970	5 823	6 170	6 380	46.0
3352 – Household appliances and miscellaneous machines, n.e.s.o.i.	6 834	7 725	8 644	9 465	10 755	11 983	75.3
3353 – Electrical equipment	9 319	11 185	12 613	12 424	12 563	13 052	40.1
3359 – Electrical equipment and components, n.e.s.o.i.	9 732	10 701	12 683	11 612	10 723	11 159	14.7
3361 – Motor vehicles	94 270	114 966	126 284	124 237	131 842	132 141	40.2
3362 – Motor vehicle bodies and trailers	1 043	1 211	1 889	1 375	1 262	1 472	41.2
3363 – Motor vehicle parts	41 665	47 745	51 812	48 428	53 653	58 022	39.3
3364 – Aerospace products and parts	22 033	23 581	26 694	31 380	26 131	24 237	10.0
3365 – Railroad rolling stock	1 896	2 055	1 615	1 163	871	852	-55.0
3366 – Ships and boats	1 071	1 062	1 103	1 127	1 174	1 283	19.8
3369 – Transportation equipment, n.e.s.o.i.	2 550	3 065	3 987	3 979	4 309	4 558	78.8
3371 – Household and institutional furniture and kitchen cabinets	7 911	9 784	11 585	11 547	13 448	15 001	89.6
3372 – Office furniture (including fixtures)	2 417	2 884	3 489	3 156	3 387	3 852	59.4
3379 – Furniture related products, n.e.s.o.i.	469	505	538	572	661	791	68.5
3391 – Medical equipment and supplies	6 736	7 243	8 076	9 031	10 355	12 882	91.2
3399 – Miscellaneous manufactured commodities	40 408	43 718	48 627	47 478	51 506	52 601	30.2
5112 – Software publishers	214	163	162	175	133	122	-42.8
9100 – Waste and scrap	1 756	1 710	1 871	1 588	1 614	1 808	2.9
9200 – Used or second-hand merchandise	4 593	5 424	6 342	5 902	5 669	4 757	3.6
9800 – Goods returned to Canada (exports only); U.S. goods returned and reimported items (imports only)	25 363	30 888	33 706	34 675	34 753	32 953	29.9
9900 – Special classification provisions, n.e.s.o.i.	11 563	15 089	18 711	17 831	16 745	17 743	53.4

Note: Unrevised data.

Table B-40. U.S. Total Trade Balances by 4-Digit NAICS Product Groups, 1998–2003

(Millions of dollars; Census basis; foreign and domestic exports, f.a.s.; general imports, Customs.)

NAICS product	1998	1999	2000	2001	2002	2003	Percent change, 1998–2003
TOTAL	-233 411	-331 945	-436 469	-410 933	-470 291	-535 652	129.5
1111 – Oilseeds and grains	13 842	13 618	13 883	13 976	14 749	17 450	26.1
1112 – Vegetables and melons	-903	-827	-778	-1 053	-1 026	-1 320	46.2
1113 – Fruits and tree nuts	-2 969	-3 160	-2 462	-1 542	-1 746	-2 040	-31.3
1114 – Mushrooms, nursery and related products	-803	-822	-888	-882	-880	-969	20.6
1119 – Other agricultural products	3 504	1 688	2 952	3 050	2 963	4 272	21.9
1121 – Cattle	-918	-778	-835	-1 136	-1 280	-765	-16.7
1122 – Swine	-250	-198	-279	-337	-263	-358	43.3
1123 – Poultry and eggs	233	187	175	181	175	185	-20.7
1124 – Sheep, goats and fine animal hair	-63	-16	-17	-20	-4	0	-99.7
1125 – Farmed fish and related products	-496	-589	-646	-700	-751	-797	60.6
1129 – Other animals	93	-71	8	135	-32	145	56.1
1132 – Forestry products	-1 197	-873	-961	-751	-854	-1 140	-4.7
1133 – Timber and logs	1 235	1 199	1 226	1 066	1 016	1 043	-15.6
1141 – Fish, fresh, chilled, and frozen, and other marine products	-4 634	-4 701	-5 529	-4 983	-5 135	-5 712	23.3
2111 – Oil and gas	-44 105	-58 016	-102 867	-93 385	-91 186	-122 654	178.1
2121 – Coal and petroleum gases	2 756	1 856	1 666	1 160	1 007	767	-72.2
2122 – Metal ores	-612	-281	-189	-57	-100	-5	-99.1
2123 – Nonmetallic minerals	376	310	349	261	207	207	-45.0
3111 – Animal foods	950	883	1 060	1 252	949	965	1.7
3112 – Grain and oilseed milling products	4 284	3 357	2 930	3 572	3 520	3 122	-27.1
3113 – Sugar and confectionery products	-1 625	-1 483	-1 306	-1 271	-1 749	-2 368	45.7
3114 – Fruits and vegetable preserves and specialty foods	-79	-397	-404	-472	-769	-1 258	1 490.7
3115 – Dairy products	-268	-340	-285	-286	-409	-498	85.7
3116 – Meat products and meat packaging products	5 205	4 491	5 536	5 363	4 445	5 362	3.0
3117 – Seafood products, prepared, canned, and packaged	-654	-680	-684	-816	-973	-1 148	75.4
3118 – Bakery and tortilla products	-537	-632	-715	-773	-907	-1 058	96.8
3119 – Foods, n.e.s.o.i.	522	487	540	751	554	493	-5.6
3121 – Beverages	-4 823	-5 780	-6 500	-6 824	-7 772	-8 775	81.9
3122 – Tobacco products	4 358	3 441	3 476	2 223	1 343	1 274	-70.8
3131 – Fibers, yarns, and threads	-95	-88	-44	-81	-66	36	-137.9
3132 – Fabrics	-954	-541	122	782	675	664	-169.6
3133 – Finished and coated textile fabrics	189	204	135	307	229	275	46.1
3141 – Textile furnishings	-2 318	-2 964	-3 734	-3 919	-4 958	-5 943	156.5
3149 – Other textile products	-1 079	-1 187	-1 297	-1 610	-1 712	-1 929	78.7
3151 – Knit apparel	-261	-395	-510	-553	-680	-741	184.1
3152 – Apparel	-42 431	-45 061	-51 905	-52 702	-53 264	-57 608	35.8
3159 – Apparel accessories	-976	-1 491	-2 069	-2 290	-2 468	-2 781	185.0
3161 – Leather and hide tanning	-203	-433	-795	-705	-763	-711	251.2
3162 – Footwear	-12 793	-13 089	-13 936	-14 347	-14 564	-14 777	15.5
3169 – Other leather products	-3 865	-3 933	-4 076	-4 063	-4 253	-4 700	21.6
3211 – Sawmill and wood products	-4 570	-5 577	-4 823	-5 143	-5 053	-4 389	-4.0
3212 – Veneer, plywood, and engineered wood products	-2 207	-3 258	-2 947	-2 933	-3 506	-4 850	119.7
3219 – Other wood products	-1 859	-2 309	-2 601	-2 795	-3 217	-3 309	78.0
3221 – Pulp, paper, and paperboard mill products	-3 275	-3 793	-4 225	-4 540	-4 528	-4 796	46.4
3222 – Converted paper products	1 485	1 489	1 112	857	1 093	873	-41.2
3231 – Printing, publishing, and similar products	1 480	1 077	901	984	341	283	-80.9
3241 – Petroleum and coal products	-5 102	-7 706	-16 450	-15 986	-13 768	-18 263	258.0
3251 – Basic chemicals	4 591	4 659	5 938	3 636	3 751	5 187	13.0
3252 – Resin, synthetic rubber, artificial and synthetic fibers and filaments	6 937	6 620	7 992	7 436	7 759	8 111	16.9
3253 – Pesticides, fertilizers, and other agricultural chemicals	2 690	2 387	1 341	745	1 196	117	-95.7
3254 – Pharmaceuticals and medicines	-5 548	-9 653	-12 927	-15 208	-21 744	-26 505	377.7
3255 – Paints, coatings, and adhesives	1 238	1 156	1 339	1 276	1 408	1 393	12.5
3256 – Soaps, cleaning compounds, and toilet preparations	2 215	2 108	2 162	2 327	1 977	2 090	-5.6
3259 – Other chemical products and preparations	1 685	1 629	2 516	1 933	2 386	2 640	56.7
3261 – Plastics products	1 423	1 125	2 058	1 077	18	-866	-160.8
3262 – Rubber products	-1 126	-1 912	-1 858	-1 601	-2 539	-3 273	190.5
3271 – Clay and refractory products	-2 435	-2 726	-3 037	-2 745	-3 013	-3 399	39.6
3272 – Glass and glass products	-484	-830	-274	63	-848	-937	93.4
3273 – Cement and concrete products	-1 248	-1 578	-1 697	-1 654	-1 677	-1 676	34.3
3274 – Lime and gypsum products	-101	-262	-61	-34	-3	10	-110.0
3279 – Other nonmetallic mineral products	-1 033	-1 301	-1 560	-1 442	-1 682	-2 008	94.5
3311 – Iron and steel and ferroalloy	-13 285	-9 645	-11 438	-7 746	-8 647	-6 133	-53.8
3312 – Steel products from purchased steel	-690	-729	-770	-672	-789	-871	26.1
3313 – Alumina and aluminum and processing	-2 429	-2 812	-3 274	-3 123	-3 788	-4 192	72.6
3314 – Nonferrous (excluding aluminum) and processing	-4 104	-5 129	-6 823	-5 927	-4 815	-3 498	-14.8
3315 – Foundries	16	53	-51	-38	-66	-48	-393.8
3321 – Crowns, closures, seals, and other packing accessories	161	134	117	103	66	32	-80.0
3322 – Cutlery and handtools	-1 328	-1 379	-1 568	-1 528	-1 812	-2 103	58.4

Note: Unrevised data.

Table B-40. U.S. Total Trade Balances by 4-Digit NAICS Product Groups, 1998–2003—*Continued*

(Millions of dollars; Census basis; foreign and domestic exports, f.a.s.; general imports, Customs.)

NAICS product	1998	1999	2000	2001	2002	2003	Percent change, 1998–2003
3323 – Architectural and structural metals	-9	-297	-617	-886	-1 034	-901	9 778.9
3324 – Boilers, tanks, and shipping containers	1 033	593	174	-90	-577	-290	-128.0
3325 – Hardware	-1 013	-1 018	-951	-954	-1 252	-1 590	57.0
3326 – Springs and wire products	-738	-895	-802	-804	-864	-882	19.5
3327 – Bolts, nuts, screws, rivets, washers, and other turned products ...	-532	-455	-565	-437	-511	-738	38.8
3329 – Other fabricated metal products	-385	-1 032	-1 130	-1 368	-2 602	-3 540	818.7
3331 – Agricultural, construction, and mining machinery	8 048	4 468	5 808	6 703	6 040	4 595	-42.9
3332 – Industrial machinery	-1 959	-619	2 711	-371	-657	-1 181	-39.7
3333 – Commercial and service industry machinery	-3 924	-4 122	-3 474	-1 062	-1 090	-4 177	6.4
3334 – HVAC and commercial refrigeration equipment	2 748	2 091	1 631	1 451	681	-224	-108.1
3335 – Metalworking machinery	-3 533	-2 934	-2 681	-2 140	-1 478	-1 989	-43.7
3336 – Engines, turbines, and power transmission equipment ...	3 414	1 948	1 297	333	788	462	-86.5
3339 – Other general purpose machinery	3 717	3 410	4 536	3 996	1 542	-491	-113.2
3341 – Computer equipment	-10 191	-15 283	-13 737	-12 173	-24 214	-24 446	139.9
3342 – Communications equipment	1 509	-1 527	-9 530	-8 508	-12 574	-16 467	-1 191.4
3343 – Audio and video equipment	-17 141	-19 402	-23 120	-21 935	-25 667	-26 883	56.8
3344 – Semiconductors and other electronic components	-14 698	-14 137	-15 098	-2 734	-273	3 775	-125.7
3345 – Navigational, measuring, medical, and control instruments	6 568	6 630	6 889	6 218	3 747	2 200	-66.5
3346 – Magnetic and optical media	225	-342	-807	-1 067	-1 468	-1 672	-842.5
3351 – Electric lighting equipment	-2 804	-3 629	-4 260	-4 221	-4 574	-4 835	72.4
3352 – Household appliances and miscellaneous machines, n.e.s.o.i.	-3 365	-4 280	-4 946	-6 059	-7 596	-8 710	158.9
3353 – Electrical equipment	-1 771	-3 096	-3 772	-3 937	-4 678	-4 641	162.0
3359 – Electrical equipment and components, n.e.s.o.i.	67	-90	545	-185	-515	-1 097	-1 726.9
3361 – Motor vehicles	-69 739	-91 154	-101 576	-100 060	-104 154	-101 271	45.2
3362 – Motor vehicle bodies and trailers	481	319	-330	-57	61	121	-74.9
3363 – Motor vehicle parts	-3 044	-6 534	-7 046	-6 828	-12 061	-18 432	505.5
3364 – Aerospace products and parts	40 335	37 489	26 776	27 094	30 240	28 044	-30.5
3365 – Railroad rolling stock	-463	-815	-424	143	95	566	-222.2
3366 – Ships and boats	630	557	-111	711	7	-10	-101.6
3369 – Transportation equipment, n.e.s.o.i.	-785	-1 453	-2 419	-2 327	-2 534	-2 730	247.8
3371 – Household and institutional furniture and kitchen cabinets	-6 462	-8 379	-10 001	-10 145	-12 147	-13 663	111.4
3372 – Office furniture (including fixtures)	-1 335	-1 806	-2 129	-2 054	-2 455	-2 747	105.8
3379 – Furniture related products, n.e.s.o.i.	-387	-425	-459	-487	-571	-688	77.5
3391 – Medical equipment and supplies	1 927	1 894	1 967	2 147	1 349	555	-71.2
3399 – Miscellaneous manufactured commodities	-28 594	-30 885	-34 217	-32 877	-36 549	-36 636	28.1
5112 – Software publishers	-214	-163	-162	-175	191	214	-199.8
9100 – Waste and scrap	1 813	1 913	3 258	3 236	3 551	4 756	162.3
9200 – Used or second-hand merchandise	-1 262	-2 576	-2 321	-1 257	-2 489	-1 316	4.3
9800 – Goods returned to Canada (exports only); U.S. goods returned and reimported items (imports only)	-23 430	-29 185	-31 801	-32 795	-33 414	-31 780	35.6
9900 – Special classification provisions, n.e.s.o.i.	11 118	8 546	6 984	9 188	7 647	7 259	-34.7

Note: Unrevised data.

Table B-41. U.S. Total Exports by 6-Digit NAICS Product Groups, 1998–2003

(Millions of dollars; Census basis; foreign and domestic exports, f.a.s.)

NAICS product	1998	1999	2000	2001	2002	2003	Percent change, 1998–2003
TOTAL	680 474	692 821	780 419	731 026	693 257	723 743	6.4
111110 – Soybeans	4 885	4 557	5 313	5 451	5 624	7 936	62.5
111120 – Oilseeds (except soybean)	247	180	165	191	210	198	-19.9
111130 – Dry peas and beans	386	327	286	274	287	291	-24.8
111140 – Wheat	3 714	3 581	3 388	3 382	3 632	3 958	6.6
111150 – Corn	4 619	5 127	4 714	4 765	5 128	4 972	7.6
111160 – Rice	416	157	181	161	199	322	-22.6
111199 – Other grains	672	685	796	789	710	718	6.9
111211 – Potatoes	93	92	93	90	123	89	-4.1
111219 – Other vegetables (excluding potatoes) and melons	1 449	1 438	1 574	1 585	1 649	1 817	25.4
111310 – Oranges	357	172	304	314	325	358	0.5
111320 – Citrus fruits (except oranges)	309	340	331	316	320	322	4.2
111331 – Apples	350	372	388	412	380	364	4.0
111332 – Grapes	335	382	455	476	494	515	54.0
111333 – Strawberries	93	108	119	115	136	196	110.3
111334 – Berries (except strawberries)	30	38	47	50	59	72	137.8
111335 – Tree nuts	1 101	946	1 042	1 047	1 224	1 520	38.1
111339 – Other noncitrus fruits	857	828	861	865	859	947	10.6
111411 – Mushrooms	23	29	30	27	21	27	15.9
111421 – Nursery products and trees	212	217	219	222	219	250	17.8
111422 – Fresh flowers, seeds and foliage	85	88	86	86	91	89	5.1
111910 – Tobacco	1 469	1 302	1 237	1 292	1 075	1 043	-29.0
111920 – Cotton	2 589	1 011	1 967	2 234	2 113	3 452	33.3
111930 – Sugarcane	0	0	1	2	0	1	X
111940 – Hay, alfalfa hay, and clover	244	269	332	320	427	462	89.4
111991 – Sugar beets	3	3	3	3	3	3	0.4
111992 – Peanuts	160	159	197	121	173	116	-27.2
111998 – Other miscellaneous agricultural products	337	323	320	273	316	321	-4.8
11211X – Cattle	240	242	337	341	183	117	-51.0
112210 – Swine	23	19	12	12	38	34	43.6
1123XX – Poultry and eggs	259	218	207	218	216	223	-13.9
112410 – Sheep and wool	30	22	21	21	24	20	-32.3
112420 – Goats and other fine animal hair	12	21	16	6	8	11	-11.1
112511 – Fish, farmed	46	49	57	64	40	51	9.2
112512 – Shellfish, farmed	0	0	0	0	0	0	X
112910 – Bees and honey	9	9	8	6	7	9	1.5
112920 – Horses and other equine	318	295	424	451	315	536	68.5
112930 – Rabbits, foxes, furskins, and cuttings	149	127	145	164	158	143	-3.9
112990 – All other live animals	34	38	39	42	43	49	46.6
113210 – Forestry products	191	201	214	196	205	263	37.2
113310 – Timber and logs	1 359	1 366	1 460	1 276	1 245	1 252	-7.9
114111 – Finfish fresh, chilled, frozen; finfish products	1 462	1 766	1 872	2 182	2 167	2 243	53.4
114112 – Shellfish fresh, chilled, frozen; shellfish products	527	683	732	641	671	720	36.7
114119 – Other marine products	138	152	207	146	104	94	-32.0
211111 – Crude petroleum and natural gas	919	1 004	893	787	1 082	1 424	55.0
211112 – Liquid natural gas	338	456	854	553	645	753	122.5
212112 – Coal (excluding anthracite) and petroleum gases	2 991	2 101	2 008	1 803	1 581	1 543	-48.4
212113 – Anthracite coal, not agglomerated	45	34	35	30	25	11	-75.2
212210 – Iron ores	245	243	246	229	249	248	1.5
212221 – Gold ores	8	5	14	15	18	20	163.2
212222 – Silver ores	5	41	26	72	57	16	243.4
212231 – Lead ores and zinc ores	363	388	362	396	445	484	33.5
212234 – Copper ores and nickel ores	68	97	181	91	86	81	19.4
212291 – Uranium-radium-vanadium ores	1	0	0	2	1	2	120.3
212299 – All other metal ores	310	218	209	237	174	288	-7.0
212311 – Dimension stone	60	52	66	93	66	72	18.8
212319 – Other crushed and broken stone	56	46	41	44	47	41	-27.0
212322 – Industrial sand	180	156	198	166	165	174	-3.7
212324 – Kaolin and other kaolinic clays	582	574	622	575	547	574	-1.4
212325 – Other clay, ceramic and refractory minerals	224	204	218	216	222	229	2.3
212391 – Borate minerals and potassium salts	25	16	16	14	15	14	-44.5
212393 – Other chemical and fertilizer minerals	72	77	94	77	63	77	7.0
212399 – All other nonmetallic minerals	178	200	200	179	149	147	-17.3
311111 – Dog and cat foods	748	725	825	925	699	707	-5.4
311119 – Other animal foods	579	526	625	716	657	651	12.4
311211 – Flour and other grain mill products	310	348	319	301	359	263	-15.1
311212 – Milled rice and by-products	805	800	668	567	588	726	-9.8
311213 – Malts	44	39	35	45	36	30	-31.9
311221 – Wet corn milling products	1 488	1 276	1 253	1 249	1 241	1 348	-9.4
311222 – Soybean oil and by-products	2 752	2 101	1 983	2 467	2 381	2 099	-23.7
311223 – Other oilseed products	633	552	440	450	500	483	-23.6
311225 – Margarine and edible fats and oils	406	269	268	242	310	363	-10.7
311230 – Breakfast cereals	203	195	194	297	403	516	154.9

Note: Unrevised data.

X = Not applicable.

Table B-41. U.S. Total Exports by 6-Digit NAICS Product Groups, 1998–2003—*Continued*

(Millions of dollars; Census basis; foreign and domestic exports, f.a.s.)

NAICS product	1998	1999	2000	2001	2002	2003	Percent change, 1998–2003
31131X – Sugars	171	163	174	214	198	176	2.8
311320 – Chocolate and confectionery products	424	461	556	714	624	689	62.5
311340 – Nonchocolate confectionery products	304	296	366	352	307	350	15.4
311411 – Frozen fruits, juices and vegetables	964	987	994	928	918	826	-14.4
311421 – Fruits and vegetables preserved	1 208	1 275	1 252	1 205	1 247	1 329	10.0
311422 – Specialty canned foods	72	87	82	97	99	105	46.1
311423 – Dried and dehydrated foods	559	584	509	505	488	525	-6.0
311511 – Fluid milk, cream and related products	44	33	37	45	56	54	24.9
311512 – Creamery butter	14	5	9	6	7	20	37.6
311513 – Cheese	135	152	149	171	169	159	18.1
311514 – Dry, condensed and evaporated dairy products	752	752	868	914	769	888	18.0
311520 – Ice cream and frozen desserts	88	89	91	86	79	60	-31.1
311611 – Meat products (excluding poultry)	5 586	5 807	7 326	7 244	6 775	7 587	35.8
311613 – Animal fats, oils and by-products	717	580	494	453	601	624	-13.0
311615 – Poultry, prepared or preserved	2 202	1 814	2 023	2 407	1 834	2 042	-7.2
311711 – Seafood products, prepared, canned and packaged	299	427	334	382	337	346	15.4
31181X – Bread and bakery products	425	421	418	429	444	487	14.7
311822 – Prepared flour mixes and dough	138	143	154	154	159	218	57.9
311823 – Pasta	55	62	69	68	61	71	30.8
311911 – Roasted nuts and peanut butter	193	162	181	197	218	240	24.4
311919 – Other snack foods	304	322	300	256	247	211	-30.7
311920 – Coffee and tea	356	387	350	391	398	450	26.3
311930 – Flavoring extracts and syrups	519	519	504	588	515	501	-3.4
311941 – Mayonnaise, dressings and other prepared sauces	211	216	243	258	263	275	30.7
311942 – Spices and extracts	113	129	127	142	144	159	40.5
311999 – Other foods, n.e.s.o.i.	1 348	1 413	1 526	1 626	1 724	1 915	42.0
312111 – Soft drinks	254	252	239	215	231	289	14.0
312112 – Bottled waters	9	13	15	19	12	19	117.7
312113 – Ice	8	12	12	16	23	16	102.5
312120 – Malt and beer	336	278	251	277	253	260	-22.6
312130 – Wines	552	564	584	572	566	658	19.3
312140 – Distilled liquors	523	514	540	586	614	670	28.2
312221 – Cigarettes	4 175	3 245	3 328	2 127	1 472	1 424	-65.9
312229 – Other tobacco products	667	652	706	623	488	459	-31.2
313111 – Yarns	355	384	438	417	431	574	61.8
313113 – Threads	202	244	324	203	174	162	-20.0
313210 – Broadwoven fabrics	2 490	2 748	3 478	3 393	3 427	2 946	18.3
313221 – Narrow fabrics	563	672	757	778	801	669	18.9
313230 – Nonwoven fabrics	741	686	778	775	842	1 018	37.3
313249 – Knit fabrics and lace	676	672	852	1 005	1 160	1 471	117.4
313312 – Textile, fabric finishing mill products	59	53	43	46	56	72	21.6
313320 – Coated fabrics	586	597	615	748	751	894	52.5
314110 – Carpets and rugs	860	808	812	730	710	710	-17.4
314121 – Curtains and draperies	39	39	42	37	41	34	-14.2
314129 – Other household textile products	450	406	438	427	383	376	-16.4
314911 – Textile sacks and bags	40	40	40	43	48	46	16.6
314912 – Canvas and related products	48	53	48	42	44	49	2.1
314991 – Ropes, cordage and twine	81	74	85	89	93	102	26.0
314992 – Tire cords and tire fabrics	154	162	158	135	126	116	-25.1
314999 – All other miscellaneous textile products	547	628	711	581	535	572	4.6
31511X – Hosiery and socks	420	449	437	367	348	344	-18.1
315221 – Men's, boys' underwear, nightwear	708	776	910	805	664	672	-5.1
315222 – Men's, boys' suits, coats, overcoats	111	86	87	76	52	49	-56.0
315223 – Men's, boys' shirts (excluding work)	1 145	1 404	1 521	1 035	774	714	-37.6
315224 – Men's, boys' trousers, slacks, jeans	1 066	901	861	685	592	549	-48.5
315228 – Men's, boys' other outerwear	388	366	430	319	284	281	-27.6
315231 – Women's, girls' lingerie	808	816	733	592	571	449	-44.4
315232 – Women's, girls' blouses and shirts	439	420	465	444	437	377	-14.2
315233 – Women's, girls' dresses	128	107	114	94	76	70	-45.3
315234 – Women's, girls' suits, coats, skirts	312	236	241	213	162	146	-53.1
315239 – Women's, girls' other outerwear	920	841	969	833	757	651	-29.2
315291 – Infants' apparel	208	156	148	69	37	33	-84.0
315292 – Fur and leather apparel	134	132	134	124	101	100	-25.6
315991 – Hats and caps	53	51	56	59	49	51	-3.6
315992 – Gloves and mittens	67	57	66	57	51	54	-19.9
315993 – Men's and boys' neckwear	19	14	14	10	12	12	-37.3
315999 – Other apparel accessories	1 781	1 383	1 373	1 175	1 028	916	-48.5
316110 – Leather and hide tanning	1 404	1 235	1 238	1 395	1 409	1 476	5.1
316211 – Rubber and plastic footwear	81	69	93	61	50	42	-48.7
316212 – House slippers	15	22	14	9	8	13	-12.4
316213 – Men's footwear (excluding athletic)	179	177	165	185	171	188	4.5
316214 – Women's footwear (excluding athletic)	107	107	111	114	115	120	12.1
316219 – Other footwear	168	158	176	161	170	148	-11.8
316991 – Luggage	256	278	284	270	237	254	-0.7
316992 – Women's handbags and purses	49	56	80	95	94	123	150.4

Note: Unrevised data.

Table B-41. U.S. Total Exports by 6-Digit NAICS Product Groups, 1998–2003—*Continued*

(Millions of dollars; Census basis; foreign and domestic exports, f.a.s.)

NAICS product	1998	1999	2000	2001	2002	2003	Percent change, 1998–2003
316993 – Personal leather goods (excluding purses)	45	54	59	51	57	61	35.9
316999 – All other articles of leather	389	413	468	368	282	293	-24.7
321113 – Sawmill products	2 463	2 614	2 638	2 113	1 984	1 953	-20.7
321114 – Treated wood products, n.e.s.o.i.	133	115	114	78	76	94	-28.8
321211 – Hardwood veneer and plywood	416	448	493	446	498	512	23.3
321212 – Softwood veneer and plywood	227	203	206	150	150	156	-31.4
321213 – Engineered wood (excluding truss)	215	193	201	157	124	125	-42.2
321219 – Reconstituted wood products	310	338	367	331	329	306	-1.4
321911 – Wood windows and doors	137	140	150	131	129	148	7.5
321918 – Other millwork (including flooring)	210	222	229	209	221	258	22.9
321920 – Wood containers and pallets	133	171	196	150	132	142	6.6
321991 – Mobile homes and trailers	27	17	22	17	12	14	-49.0
321992 – Prefabricated wood buildings	53	56	48	43	38	42	-20.5
321999 – Miscellaneous wood products	327	343	358	273	255	287	-12.4
322110 – Pulp mill products	2 806	2 874	3 614	2 913	2 886	2 861	2.0
322121 – Paper (except newsprint) mill products	5 474	5 367	5 909	5 305	4 400	4 578	-16.4
322122 – Newsprint mill products	606	561	684	583	473	443	-26.8
322130 – Paperboard mill products	63	49	70	48	50	40	-36.3
322211 – Corrugated and solid fiber boxes	891	936	1 023	921	932	964	8.2
322212 – Folding paperboard boxes	266	262	286	363	301	283	6.6
322213 – Setup paperboard boxes	47	58	69	71	63	56	18.2
322214 – Fiber can, tube, drum and similar products	42	44	40	33	33	43	3.0
322215 – Nonfolding sanitary food containers	182	185	216	209	194	199	9.6
322222 – Coated and laminated paper	1 580	1 736	1 867	1 759	2 065	2 204	39.6
322223 – Foil and coated paper and plastic bags	414	455	491	511	526	566	36.8
322224 – Uncoated paper and multiwall bags	44	39	43	44	45	45	2.8
322232 – Envelopes	54	58	51	50	53	56	2.7
322233 – Stationery, tablets and related products	232	234	279	246	682	754	224.5
322291 – Sanitary paper products	734	878	930	1 061	968	937	27.8
322299 – All other converted paper products	387	397	406	377	436	473	22.3
323116 – Manifold business forms	18	16	15	12	10	12	-32.4
323117 – Books printing	2 070	2 062	2 097	1 996	1 955	1 995	-3.7
323118 – Blankbook, binders and stationery articles, n.e.s.o.i.	220	193	199	193	166	178	-19.2
323119 – Printed matter, n.e.s.o.i.	2 619	2 562	2 738	2 882	2 605	2 766	5.6
323122 – Printing type, plates, cylinders, etc., n.e.s.o.i.	28	32	48	41	37	33	18.7
324110 – Petroleum refinery products	5 292	5 877	8 894	8 276	7 885	9 471	79.0
324121 – Asphalt paving mixtures	21	20	21	26	24	32	50.4
324122 – Asphalt shingle and coating materials	75	109	114	114	139	156	108.6
325110 – Petrochemicals	436	504	633	478	549	648	48.7
325120 – Industrial gases	196	187	236	226	188	207	5.6
325131 – Inorganic dyes and pigments	925	947	1 172	1 050	1 174	1 345	45.3
325132 – Synthetic organic dyes and pigments	699	683	727	632	586	565	-19.2
325181 – Alkalies and chlorine	841	789	869	1 062	855	903	7.4
325182 – Carbon black	140	144	184	171	164	197	41.4
325188 – All other basic inorganic chemicals	4 195	4 122	4 930	5 014	5 145	5 247	25.1
325191 – Gum and wood chemicals	161	155	163	158	121	139	-13.7
325192 – Cyclic crude and intermediates	1 915	2 260	2 983	2 063	2 398	3 242	69.3
325193 – Ethyl alcohols	58	58	92	127	72	104	79.6
325199 – All other basic organic chemicals	13 989	14 598	16 867	15 842	15 406	18 310	30.9
325211 – Plastics materials and resins	10 415	10 570	12 595	12 155	12 483	13 502	29.6
325212 – Synthetic rubbers	1 503	1 571	1 923	1 899	1 944	2 173	44.5
325221 – Cellulose organic fibers	549	480	496	507	481	481	-12.4
325222 – Noncellulosic organic fibers	1 459	1 343	1 500	1 148	1 252	1 306	-10.5
325311 – Nitrogenous fertilizers	3 294	3 128	2 501	2 267	2 282	2 570	-22.0
325312 – Phosphatic fertilizers	62	63	72	74	66	76	22.8
325320 – Pesticides and other agricultural chemicals	1 913	1 693	1 646	1 730	1 671	1 583	-17.3
325411 – Medicinal and botanical drugs and vitamins	3 965	3 984	4 393	4 580	4 886	5 844	47.4
325412 – Pharmaceutical preparations	6 256	7 829	9 425	11 631	11 624	13 633	117.9
325414 – Biological products (excluding diagnostic)	2 000	2 001	2 215	2 336	2 749	3 566	78.4
325510 – Paints and coatings	1 293	1 398	1 547	1 498	1 491	1 542	19.2
325520 – Adhesives	632	690	804	765	802	817	29.3
325611 – Soaps and other detergents	1 083	1 112	1 201	1 305	1 309	1 446	33.5
325612 – Polishes and other sanitation goods	228	237	257	270	325	346	51.9
325613 – Surface active agents	976	1 120	1 212	1 128	1 180	1 336	36.9
325620 – Perfumes, makeups and other toiletries	2 599	2 598	2 906	3 245	3 220	3 559	36.9
325910 – Printing inks	400	444	525	452	431	512	28.2
325920 – Explosives and accessories	273	230	274	225	258	375	37.1
325992 – Photo films, papers, plates and chemicals	2 544	2 577	3 322	2 438	2 721	2 790	9.7
325998 – All other miscellaneous chemical products and preparations (including natural)	2 532	2 356	2 589	2 557	2 670	2 653	4.8
326113 – Not reinforced plastics plates, sheets, etc. (excluding packaging)	2 647	2 580	2 944	2 753	2 722	2 872	8.5
326121 – Plastics rods, sticks and profile shapes	184	187	276	268	324	402	118.6
326122 – Plastics tubes, hoses, pipes and pipe fittings	318	318	489	453	448	492	54.8
326160 – Plastics bottles	244	251	311	329	363	387	58.5
326191 – Plastics plumbing fixtures	41	44	44	52	41	42	1.7
326192 – Plastic floor coverings	145	148	161	122	115	114	-20.8

Note: Unrevised data.

Table B-41. U.S. Total Exports by 6-Digit NAICS Product Groups, 1998–2003—*Continued*

(Millions of dollars; Census basis; foreign and domestic exports, f.a.s.)

NAICS product	1998	1999	2000	2001	2002	2003	Percent change, 1998–2003
326199 – All other plastics products	6 013	6 860	8 217	7 575	7 484	7 495	24.6
326211 – Tires and tire parts (excluding retreadings)	2 591	2 476	2 521	2 387	2 339	2 300	-11.2
326212 – Tire retreadings	25	23	13	13	9	11	-54.6
326220 – Rubber and plastics hoses and belting	1 210	1 151	1 363	1 254	1 086	1 131	-6.5
326299 – Other rubber products	1 105	1 160	1 377	1 303	1 238	1 262	14.2
327111 – China plumb fixtures and china and earthen bath access	79	68	75	76	85	98	24.8
327112 – China, fine earthenware and other pottery products	468	468	550	556	506	475	1.5
327113 – Porcelain electrical supplies	147	169	226	187	162	136	-7.5
327121 – Brick and structural ceramics	16	12	16	12	14	16	-1.6
327122 – Ceramic wall and floor tiles	31	30	32	34	33	32	3.7
327123 – Other structural ceramic products	11	8	8	11	9	11	4.6
327124 – Clay and alumina articles	128	118	154	120	113	114	-10.8
327125 – Nonclay refractory articles	300	318	307	296	261	265	-11.7
327211 – Drawn, blown, float and flat glass	753	722	816	776	783	843	12.0
327212 – Other pressed and blown glass and glassware	1 097	1 147	1 427	1 370	1 196	1 208	10.1
327213 – Glass containers	179	180	182	218	172	174	-2.9
327215 – Glass products, n.e.s.o.i.	1 345	1 705	2 596	2 314	1 300	1 274	-5.3
327310 – Cements	59	59	68	61	62	69	15.4
327320 – Wet, nonrefractory mortars and concretes	0	1	0	0	1	1	X
327331 – Concrete bricks and blocks	12	12	20	20	21	16	37.2
327390 – Other concrete products	100	96	91	86	91	99	-0.8
327410 – Lime and calcined dolomite	7	7	9	11	12	12	67.0
327420 – Gypsum products	67	71	80	78	81	88	32.4
327910 – Abrasive products	520	496	523	536	494	512	-1.5
327991 – Cut stone and stone products	40	38	44	44	34	35	-11.5
327992 – Ground or treated mineral and earth	147	155	176	194	190	193	31.1
327993 – Mineral wool and glass fibers	412	395	451	427	394	429	4.1
327999 – All other miscellaneous nonmetallic mineral products	294	253	322	319	312	304	3.6
331111 – Iron and steel	4 911	4 461	5 227	4 962	4 757	5 771	17.5
331112 – Electrometallurgical ferroalloy product	133	109	125	100	74	73	-44.8
331222 – Steel wire drawing	325	341	340	342	320	313	-3.7
331311 – Alumina refining	452	373	420	393	325	332	-26.6
331312 – Primary aluminum	571	626	662	475	445	397	-30.5
331314 – Secondary smelting and alloying of aluminum	37	36	49	43	42	51	37.0
331315 – Aluminum sheets, plates and foils	2 368	2 276	2 331	2 075	1 863	1 886	-20.3
331316 – Aluminum extruded products	381	341	438	412	386	386	1.2
331319 – Other aluminum rolling and drawing	366	365	355	264	213	204	-44.2
331411 – Primary smelting and refining of copper	279	207	357	211	208	398	42.5
331419 – Other nonferrous metals primary smelting, refining	7 099	6 412	7 492	6 333	4 619	5 825	-17.9
331421 – Copper rolling, drawing and extruding	580	517	611	479	422	494	-14.8
331422 – Copper wire (except mechanical) drawing	731	666	871	781	768	719	-1.6
331491 – Other nonferrous metals roll, draw, extruding	1 260	1 269	1 578	1 739	1 542	1 563	24.1
331492 – Other nonferrous secondary smelt, refine, alloying	131	147	202	313	342	309	136.5
331511 – Iron foundries	505	520	443	392	363	402	-20.4
332115 – Crowns, closures, seals and other packing accessories	276	268	267	279	258	269	-2.3
332211 – Cutlery and flatware (excluding precious)	377	467	386	417	426	429	13.6
332212 – Hand and edge tools	1 009	1 095	1 171	1 073	1 065	1 105	9.5
332213 – Saw blades and handsaws	139	148	173	193	171	176	26.3
332214 – Kitchen utensils, pots and pans	17	20	20	18	20	18	10.4
332311 – Prefab metal buildings and components	203	161	174	161	148	165	-18.5
332312 – Fabricated structural metals	479	480	469	421	400	471	-1.7
332321 – Metal windows and doors	190	185	176	174	163	170	-10.1
332322 – Sheet metal works	66	62	65	63	60	58	-12.0
332323 – Ornamental and architectural metal works	23	24	23	32	33	25	12.3
332410 – Power boilers and heat exchangers	1 012	868	737	745	612	711	-29.7
332420 – Metal tanks (heavy gauge)	571	501	512	398	371	383	-32.9
332431 – Metal cans	111	67	77	95	123	107	-4.0
332439 – Other metal containers	354	326	326	318	301	282	-20.5
332510 – Hardware	1 682	1 898	2 339	2 189	2 194	2 078	23.5
332611 – Springs (heavy gauge)	327	302	338	269	259	298	-9.0
332618 – Other fabricated wire products	491	501	606	508	488	510	4.0
332722 – Bolts, nuts, screws, rivets, washers, and other turned products	1 522	1 593	1 790	1 581	1 597	1 632	7.2
332911 – Industrial valves	2 560	2 647	2 930	2 999	2 843	3 058	19.5
332912 – Fluid power valves and hose fittings	368	410	503	505	463	486	31.9
332913 – Plumbing fixtures fittings and trim	75	87	90	101	155	149	97.2
332919 – Other metal valves and pipe fittings	883	760	913	840	775	839	-5.0
332991 – Ball and roller bearings	1 032	1 038	1 149	1 128	1 186	1 265	22.5
332992 – Small arms ammunition	1 619	1 597	1 482	1 522	1 537	1 304	-19.5
332994 – Small arms	250	218	193	182	268	269	7.3
332995 – Other ordnances and accessories	620	328	488	453	285	203	-67.3
332997 – Industrial patterns	70	67	83	38	29	41	-41.8
332998 – Enameled iron and metal sanitary wares	73	69	75	63	65	67	-7.4
332999 – Other miscellaneous fabricated metal products	3 584	3 951	5 358	3 935	3 893	3 796	5.9
333111 – Farm machinery and equipment	5 152	4 165	4 375	4 177	4 424	4 800	-6.8
333120 – Construction machinery	7 259	6 743	7 779	7 310	6 370	6 844	-5.7

Note: Unrevised data.

X = Not applicable.

Table B-41. U.S. Total Exports by 6-Digit NAICS Product Groups, 1998–2003—*Continued*

(Millions of dollars; Census basis; foreign and domestic exports, f.a.s.)

NAICS product	1998	1999	2000	2001	2002	2003	Percent change, 1998–2003
333131 – Mining machinery and equipment	1 245	974	1 115	1 039	903	1 039	-16.5
333132 – Oil and gas field machinery and equipment	6 587	4 171	4 329	5 261	5 726	5 220	-20.8
333210 – Sawmill and woodworking machinery	205	208	223	211	201	193	-5.9
333220 – Plastics and rubber industry machinery	1 161	1 090	1 305	1 149	1 015	998	-14.1
333291 – Paper industry machinery	829	762	811	705	589	671	-19.0
333292 – Textile machinery	775	720	800	772	758	741	-4.4
333293 – Printing machinery and equipment	1 524	1 442	1 695	1 336	1 100	1 105	-27.5
333294 – Food product machinery	830	761	818	744	778	724	-12.8
333295 – Semiconductor machinery	3 153	4 635	8 315	4 344	3 413	3 156	0.1
333298 – Other miscellaneous industrial machinery	240	243	260	228	208	236	-1.8
333311 – Automatic vending machines	305	252	221	230	175	175	-42.6
333313 – Office machinery	1 547	1 452	1 605	1 613	1 251	1 252	-19.0
333314 – Optical instruments and lenses	2 554	2 696	4 874	4 256	3 736	4 028	57.7
333315 – Photographic and photocopying equipment	2 528	2 288	2 226	2 036	1 546	1 343	-46.9
333319 – Other commercial, service industry machinery	347	324	343	363	352	309	-10.7
333411 – Air purification equipment	244	212	202	205	200	207	-15.2
333412 – Industrial and commercial fans and blowers	298	327	368	343	295	320	7.2
333414 – Heating equipment (excluding warm air furnaces)	347	281	272	302	305	274	-21.1
333415 – AC, warm air heating and commercial refrigeration equipment	4 757	4 700	4 852	4 642	4 433	4 275	-10.1
333511 – Industrial molds	835	839	945	842	746	713	-14.7
333512 – Machine tools (metal cutting types)	2 178	1 948	2 636	2 149	1 795	1 767	-18.8
333513 – Machine tools (metal forming types)	1 363	1 280	1 248	1 074	998	1 047	-23.2
333514 – Special dies, tools, die sets, jigs and fixtures	370	290	371	344	470	439	18.8
333515 – Cutting tools and machine tool accessories	878	876	937	856	804	832	-5.2
333516 – Rolling mill machinery and equipment	178	98	105	166	134	125	-29.5
333611 – Turbines and turbine generator sets	3 792	3 668	3 607	4 969	4 350	3 715	-2.0
333612 – Speed changers, industrial high-speed drives, gears	655	541	594	623	611	700	6.9
333613 – Mechanical power transmission equipment	660	648	786	676	670	712	7.8
333618 – Other engine equipment	6 420	6 830	7 386	6 228	6 959	7 205	12.2
333911 – Pumps and pumping equipment	1 551	1 543	1 724	1 775	1 694	1 676	8.0
333912 – Air and gas compressors	1 733	1 725	1 929	1 894	1 785	1 862	7.4
333913 – Measuring and dispensing pumps	273	239	241	252	232	243	-11.0
333921 – Elevators and moving stairways	143	146	151	136	156	168	17.2
333922 – Conveyors and conveying equipment	869	906	891	803	548	513	-41.0
333923 – Overhead cranes, hoists and monorail systems	220	202	257	187	178	189	-14.0
333924 – Industrial trucks, tractors, trailers, stacker machinery	1 322	1 396	1 457	1 501	1 214	1 174	-11.3
333991 – Power-driven handtools	857	870	876	806	754	782	-8.7
333992 – Welding and soldering equipment	1 094	1 230	1 292	965	914	1 003	-8.3
333993 – Packaging machinery	851	808	870	777	709	718	-15.6
333994 – Industrial furnaces and ovens	805	844	1 208	957	788	784	-2.6
333995 – Fluid power cylinders and actuators	203	167	164	159	170	193	-4.9
333996 – Fluid power pumps and motors	708	730	784	851	782	824	16.3
333997 – Scales and balances (except laboratory)	158	156	178	190	181	174	10.0
333999 – Other miscellaneous general purpose machinery	9 387	9 909	12 342	10 933	9 521	9 457	0.7
334111 – Electronic computers	9 101	9 179	10 730	9 871	8 571	7 968	-12.4
334112 – Computer storage devices	5 528	5 419	5 006	4 450	3 618	3 492	-36.8
334119 – Other computer equipment	30 196	31 397	39 065	32 554	25 921	28 114	-6.9
334210 – Telephone apparatus	7 736	9 169	11 954	10 390	8 229	7 260	-6.1
334220 – Radio, TV broadcast and wireless communication equipment	8 862	9 044	9 071	7 773	6 671	6 170	-30.4
334290 – Other communications equipment	527	586	607	604	550	551	4.6
334310 – Audio and video equipment	5 699	5 110	5 915	5 548	5 445	5 214	-8.5
334411 – Picture, microwave, amp, electron, cathode and sim tubes	2 539	2 481	2 815	2 522	2 270	1 613	-36.5
334412 – Printed circuits	2 347	2 561	3 074	2 355	2 194	2 009	-14.4
334413 – Semiconductors and related devices	37 235	46 464	59 223	44 202	41 752	45 909	23.3
334414 – Electronic capacitors and parts	1 622	1 922	3 316	1 791	1 631	1 619	-0.2
334415 – Electronic resistors and parts	600	710	978	756	630	613	2.2
334416 – Electronic coils, transformers, other inductors	512	618	924	627	461	461	-9.9
334417 – Electronic connectors	2 330	2 515	3 506	2 968	2 554	2 484	6.6
334418 – Printed circuit assemblies (electronic assemblies)	1 539	1 681	2 441	2 252	1 479	1 146	-25.5
334419 – Other electronic components	4 980	5 439	7 042	6 786	5 329	5 506	10.6
334510 – Electromedical apparatus	3 887	4 240	4 526	5 067	4 708	4 778	22.9
334511 – Search, detection and navigation instruments	2 598	2 633	2 775	3 204	3 708	3 768	45.0
334512 – Automatic environmental controls	308	341	340	278	275	264	-14.4
334513 – Industrial process controls	3 911	4 160	4 814	4 690	4 593	4 853	24.1
334514 – Total fluid meters and counting devices	255	264	282	295	360	358	40.1
334515 – Electricity measuring, testing instruments	5 428	6 060	8 179	6 479	5 464	5 411	-0.3
334516 – Analytical laboratory instruments	2 951	3 206	3 510	3 667	3 454	3 844	30.2
334517 – Irradiation apparatus	1 528	1 596	1 704	1 959	2 053	2 308	51.1
334518 – Watches, clocks and parts	402	465	469	408	368	429	6.7
334519 – Other measuring and controlling devices	2 302	2 087	2 075	2 289	2 091	2 218	-3.7
334612 – Prerecorded CDs, tapes, records	324	336	330	328	290	308	-4.8
334613 – Unrecorded magnetic and optical media	2 228	1 859	1 563	1 231	1 179	1 324	-40.6
335110 – Electric lamp bulbs and parts	837	836	868	776	747	718	-14.2
335121 – Residential electric lighting fixtures	80	75	88	93	96	83	4.2
335129 – Lighting equipment, n.e.s.o.i.	650	660	754	734	753	744	14.4

Note: Unrevised data.

Table B-41. U.S. Total Exports by 6-Digit NAICS Product Groups, 1998–2003—*Continued*

(Millions of dollars; Census basis; foreign and domestic exports, f.a.s.)

NAICS product	1998	1999	2000	2001	2002	2003	Percent change, 1998–2003
335211 – Electric housewares and household fans	835	796	784	685	617	710	-15.0
335212 – Household vacuum cleaner and floor polishers	441	436	401	390	411	363	-17.8
335221 – Household cooking appliances	335	324	342	349	320	341	1.6
335222 – Household refrigerators and freezers	800	739	757	764	697	703	-12.1
335224 – Household laundry equipment	617	596	641	659	648	683	10.7
335228 – Major appliances and miscellaneous machines, n.e.s.o.i.	441	553	771	559	465	473	7.4
335311 – Power, distribution, specialty transformers	615	566	545	543	499	500	-18.7
335312 – Motors and generators	3 018	3 042	3 226	3 621	3 120	3 213	6.5
335313 – Switchgear and switchboard apparatus	1 519	1 559	1 814	1 584	1 496	1 591	4.7
335314 – Relays and industrial controls	2 396	2 922	3 256	2 738	2 769	3 108	29.7
335911 – Storage batteries	845	859	932	894	780	722	-14.5
335912 – Primary batteries	577	717	656	631	546	616	6.7
335921 – Fiber optic cable	229	267	452	599	209	194	-15.2
335929 – Communication and energy wire, n.e.s.o.i.	2 161	2 345	3 221	2 667	2 331	2 276	5.3
335931 – Current-carrying wiring devices	1 637	2 056	2 440	2 032	1 966	1 976	20.7
335932 – Noncurrent-carrying wiring devices	119	179	194	146	157	140	17.3
335991 – Carbon and graphite products	601	530	565	519	482	479	-20.3
335999 – Miscellaneous electrical equipment and components, n.e.s.o.i.	3 629	3 657	4 760	3 938	3 736	3 659	0.8
336111 – Autos and light duty motor vehicles, including chassis	16 265	16 606	16 816	17 973	20 724	22 299	37.1
336120 – Heavy duty trucks and chassis	8 267	7 207	7 892	6 203	6 965	8 571	3.7
336211 – Motor vehicle bodies	180	213	160	141	113	125	-30.1
336212 – Truck trailers	539	517	562	372	352	381	-29.4
336213 – Motor homes	203	197	193	159	184	231	13.8
336214 – Transportation equipment, n.e.s.o.i., including trailers and campers	602	603	644	646	673	856	42.1
33631X – Motor vehicle gasoline engines and engine parts	4 945	6 141	7 103	7 013	6 688	6 311	27.6
336321 – Vehicular lighting equipment	544	605	666	618	636	589	8.3
336322 – Motor vehicle electrical and electronic equipment, n.e.s.o.i.	3 178	3 085	3 083	2 699	2 938	2 835	-10.8
336330 – Motor vehicle steering and suspension parts	1 096	1 194	1 297	1 181	1 258	1 257	14.7
336340 – Motor vehicle brake systems	1 745	1 864	1 936	1 818	1 914	2 015	15.5
336350 – Motor vehicle transmission and power train parts	4 333	4 379	5 330	4 913	4 894	4 486	3.5
336360 – Motor vehicle seating and interior trim	1 855	2 150	2 232	2 032	1 854	1 507	-18.8
336370 – Motor vehicle metal stampings	1 454	1 579	1 705	1 524	1 585	1 592	9.5
336391 – Motor vehicle air-conditioning	458	471	562	529	516	510	11.4
336399 – Motor vehicle parts, n.e.s.o.i.	19 013	19 745	20 853	19 273	19 308	18 489	-2.8
336411 – Aircraft	35 674	33 260	25 179	28 035	28 356	24 231	-32.1
336412 – Aircraft engines and engine parts	11 418	12 443	13 087	14 245	13 336	13 191	15.5
336413 – Aircraft parts and auxiliary equipment, n.e.s.o.i.	14 919	15 091	14 962	15 925	14 092	14 336	-3.9
336414 – Guided missiles and space vehicles	46	4	3	7	6	3	-94.3
336415 – Missile, space vehicle propulsion units and parts	21	27	21	10	32	32	53.6
336419 – Missile, space vehicle parts and auxiliary equipment, n.e.s.o.i.	289	246	216	253	550	489	69.1
336510 – Railroad rolling stock	1 432	1 240	1 191	1 306	965	1 418	-1.0
336611 – Ships	1 018	919	326	1 276	571	445	-56.3
336612 – Boats	684	701	666	563	611	829	21.2
336991 – Motorcycles, bicycles and parts	969	918	998	1 021	1 054	1 182	21.9
336992 – Military armored vehicles, tanks and tank components	795	693	571	631	722	647	-18.7
337110 – Wood kitchen cabinets and countertops	20	25	35	33	39	63	207.1
337121 – Upholstered household furniture	220	206	220	210	199	216	-1.9
337124 – Metal household furniture	68	65	70	59	53	55	-19.9
337127 – Institutional furniture	1 136	1 104	1 255	1 095	1 005	1 002	-11.8
337129 – Wood sewing machine cabinets	5	4	5	5	4	3	-27.8
337211 – Wood office furniture	89	80	103	100	84	71	-20.4
337214 – Office furniture (except wood)	262	249	278	226	167	148	-43.7
337215 – Showcases, partitions, shelvings and lockers	731	750	979	776	681	887	21.3
337910 – Mattresses	45	44	49	58	61	70	57.1
337920 – Blinds and shades	37	36	31	26	29	33	-11.5
339112 – Surgical and medical instruments	4 538	4 812	5 057	5 794	5 777	6 832	50.6
339113 – Surgical appliances and supplies	2 572	2 686	3 279	3 540	4 031	4 765	85.3
339114 – Dental equipment and supplies	656	662	664	708	760	768	17.1
339115 – Ophthalmic goods	898	976	1 042	1 135	1 136	1 072	19.4
339911 – Jewelry (except costume)	1 205	1 667	1 858	2 273	2 424	2 462	104.3
339912 – Silverware, platedware and holloware	98	100	116	107	110	99	0.8
339913 – Jewelers' material and lapidary work	3 009	3 628	4 557	4 501	4 914	5 548	84.4
339914 – Costume jewelry and novelties	161	174	169	168	155	160	-0.6
339920 – Sporting and athletic goods	2 066	1 932	2 021	2 012	1 880	1 936	-6.3
339931 – Dolls and stuffed toys	147	168	190	160	126	117	-20.6
339932 – Games, toys and children's vehicles	1 210	1 183	1 206	1 190	1 161	1 326	9.6
339941 – Pens and mechanical pencils	336	316	276	255	262	243	-27.8
339942 – Lead pencils and art goods	95	86	95	80	74	77	-19.6
339943 – Marking devices	12	15	17	16	17	17	33.5
339944 – Carbon paper and inked ribbon	401	370	375	362	361	357	-11.0
339950 – Signs	58	59	67	58	58	59	2.3
339991 – Gaskets, packing and sealing devices	864	953	1 142	1 135	1 157	1 203	39.2
339992 – Musical instruments	414	381	406	435	418	447	8.1
339993 – Fasteners, buttons, needles and pins	254	266	351	275	289	275	8.4
339994 – Brooms, brushes and mops	172	202	240	215	225	243	41.3
339999 – Miscellaneous manufactured commodities, n.e.s.o.i.	1 312	1 335	1 324	1 358	1 324	1 396	6.4
511210 – Software publishing	0	0	0	0	324	336	X
910000 – Waste and scrap	3 570	3 623	5 129	4 824	5 165	6 564	83.9
920000 – Used or second-hand merchandise	3 330	2 848	4 021	4 644	3 179	3 441	3.3
980000 – Goods returned to Canada (exports only); U.S. goods returned and reimported (imports only)	1 933	1 703	1 905	1 880	1 339	1 173	-39.3
990000 – Special classification provisions, n.e.s.o.i.	22 682	23 635	25 695	27 019	24 392	25 002	10.2

Note: Unrevised data.

X = Not applicable.

Table B-42. U.S. Total Imports by 6-Digit NAICS Product Groups, 1998–2003

(Millions of dollars; Census basis; general imports, Customs.)

NAICS product	1998	1999	2000	2001	2002	2003	Percent change, 1998–2003
TOTAL	913 885	1 024 766	1 216 888	1 141 959	1 163 549	1 259 396	37.8
111110 – Soybeans	54	29	34	31	28	47	-11.8
111120 – Oilseeds (except soybean)	263	207	192	167	165	195	-26.1
111130 – Dry peas and beans	72	89	107	124	156	139	92.6
111140 – Wheat	284	273	229	282	266	141	-50.4
111150 – Corn	142	156	160	135	137	151	6.1
111160 – Rice	0	0	0	0	0	0	X
111199 – Other grains	282	242	236	299	289	273	-3.1
111211 – Potatoes	97	89	77	67	104	90	-7.4
111219 – Other vegetables (excluding potatoes) and melons	2 348	2 269	2 368	2 661	2 694	3 136	33.6
111310 – Oranges	35	82	41	40	46	50	42.2
111320 – Citrus fruits (except oranges)	101	168	183	178	176	248	145.0
111331 – Apples	77	112	92	95	108	133	74.1
111332 – Grapes	438	539	552	572	680	677	54.5
111333 – Strawberries	67	63	53	46	59	57	-15.5
111334 – Berries (except strawberries)	67	67	80	93	108	139	107.5
111335 – Tree nuts	1 175	1 204	1 055	947	1 056	1 339	13.9
111339 – Other noncitrus fruits	4 440	4 112	3 953	3 166	3 308	3 690	-16.9
111411 – Mushrooms	26	34	42	48	59	71	171.1
111421 – Nursery products and trees	417	456	490	529	535	578	38.8
111422 – Fresh flowers, seeds and foliage	681	666	691	640	618	686	0.7
111910 – Tobacco	780	754	569	711	701	690	-11.5
111920 – Cotton	31	182	62	43	51	32	5.1
111930 – Sugarcane	0	0	0	0	0	0	X
111940 – Hay, alfalfa hay, and clover	8	7	9	9	8	7	-9.0
111991 – Sugar beets	0	3	2	4	0	1	X
111992 – Peanuts	38	41	71	40	18	3	-93.1
111998 – Other miscellaneous agricultural products	440	392	393	387	366	391	-11.1
11211X – Cattle	1 158	1 020	1 171	1 477	1 463	883	-23.8
112210 – Swine	273	216	290	349	301	391	43.3
1123XX – Poultry and eggs	26	31	31	37	41	38	47.6
112410 – Sheep and wool	90	49	45	39	29	26	-70.9
112420 – Goats and other fine animal hair	14	10	9	9	6	5	-66.9
112511 – Fish, farmed	529	622	682	743	771	823	55.6
112512 – Shellfish, farmed	14	16	22	21	21	25	79.2
112910 – Bees and honey	88	98	97	77	168	212	140.9
112920 – Horses and other equine	206	326	386	319	252	246	19.6
112930 – Rabbits, foxes, furskins, and cuttings	62	49	59	63	59	60	-3.7
112990 – All other live animals	61	67	67	70	76	75	22.5
113210 – Forestry products	1 388	1 074	1 175	948	1 059	1 403	1.0
113310 – Timber and logs	124	167	234	210	229	209	69.2
114111 – Finfish fresh, chilled, frozen; finfish products	2 227	2 442	2 542	2 343	2 537	2 688	20.7
114112 – Shellfish fresh, chilled, frozen; shellfish products	4 427	4 737	5 670	5 487	5 427	5 965	34.7
114119 – Other marine products	107	123	127	123	112	115	7.2
211111 – Crude petroleum and natural gas	42 872	56 966	100 751	90 729	89 592	119 715	179.2
211112 – Liquid natural gas	2 491	2 510	3 862	3 995	3 321	5 115	105.4
212112 – Coal (excluding anthracite) and petroleum gases	280	278	375	669	564	737	163.2
212113 – Anthracite coal, not agglomerated	1	1	1	4	35	51	6 841.1
212210 – Iron ores	527	399	420	293	313	328	-37.8
212221 – Gold ores	13	2	9	11	26	22	70.0
212222 – Silver ores	43	2	0	3	3	1	-96.8
212231 – Lead ores and zinc ores	84	98	79	35	45	60	-28.2
212234 – Copper ores and nickel ores	231	82	2	58	105	18	-92.0
212291 – Uranium-radium-vanadium ores	0	62	55	65	45	28	X
212299 – All other metal ores	712	628	662	636	594	688	-3.4
212311 – Dimension stone	29	33	40	43	55	50	75.6
212319 – Other crushed and broken stone	104	113	134	102	113	125	19.7
212322 – Industrial sand	13	23	35	40	48	48	255.7
212324 – Kaolin and other kaolinic clays	11	11	18	18	21	33	191.4
212325 – Other clay, ceramic and refractory minerals	36	35	38	35	38	43	19.6
212391 – Borate minerals and potassium salts	10	13	13	9	4	8	-18.4
212392 – Phosphate rock	38	39	31	36	50	42	11.8
212393 – Other chemical and fertilizer minerals	322	268	282	338	254	376	17.0
212399 – All other nonmetallic minerals	438	479	515	483	483	395	-9.8
311111 – Dog and cat foods	149	138	126	132	154	142	-5.1
311119 – Other animal foods	228	230	264	257	253	251	10.1
311211 – Flour and other grain mill products	97	120	126	140	184	185	90.8
311212 – Milled rice and by-products	187	194	188	176	171	216	15.6
311213 – Malts	17	24	40	46	56	64	275.8
311221 – Wet corn milling products	303	284	289	254	283	350	15.4
311222 – Soybean oil and by-products	19	30	32	31	53	52	172.1
311223 – Other oilseed products	1 470	1 323	1 317	1 116	1 219	1 469	-0.1
311225 – Margarine and edible fats and oils	129	111	97	93	103	118	-8.8
311230 – Breakfast cereals	136	140	141	190	229	254	87.5

Note: Unrevised data.

X = Not applicable.

Table B-42. U.S. Total Imports by 6-Digit NAICS Product Groups, 1998–2003—*Continued*

(Millions of dollars; Census basis; general imports, Customs.)

NAICS product	1998	1999	2000	2001	2002	2003	Percent change, 1998–2003
31131X – Sugars	873	706	600	643	672	680	-22.1
311320 – Chocolate and confectionery products	1 012	958	1 001	1 103	1 253	1 737	71.6
311340 – Nonchocolate confectionery products	639	740	801	805	953	1 166	82.6
311411 – Frozen fruits, juices and vegetables	948	1 063	1 085	1 038	1 170	1 365	44.0
311421 – Fruits and vegetables preserved	1 698	2 001	1 920	1 936	2 068	2 349	38.3
311422 – Specialty canned foods	73	79	78	80	80	70	-4.6
311423 – Dried and dehydrated foods	163	186	160	154	203	259	59.4
311511 – Fluid milk, cream and related products	16	19	14	22	19	21	31.0
311512 – Creamery butter	81	53	35	98	61	63	-21.7
311513 – Cheese	643	720	697	750	796	891	38.7
311514 – Dry,condensed and evaporated dairy products	554	541	675	622	595	677	22.1
311520 – Ice cream and frozen desserts	7	37	18	17	20	27	299.2
311611 – Meat products (excluding poultry)	3 141	3 539	4 074	4 499	4 512	4 652	48.1
311613 – Animal fats, oils and by-products	109	111	160	148	141	118	8.9
311615 – Poultry, prepared or preserved	50	60	74	94	113	121	143.1
311711 – Seafood products, prepared, canned and packaged	954	1 107	1 018	1 198	1 310	1 493	56.6
31181X – Bread and bakery products	795	913	1 016	1 111	1 252	1 460	83.7
311822 – Prepared flour mixes and dough	112	121	123	112	108	152	35.8
311823 – Pasta	248	224	217	201	211	222	-10.5
311911 – Roasted nuts and peanut butter	58	64	68	73	75	85	47.6
311919 – Other snack foods	42	57	75	93	99	137	226.5
311920 – Coffee and tea	954	858	821	777	786	858	-10.1
311930 – Flavoring extracts and syrups	27	32	32	32	41	79	198.2
311941 – Mayonnaise, dressings and other prepared sauces	179	232	259	285	294	307	71.4
311942 – Spices and extracts	435	489	507	402	419	423	-2.7
311999 – Other foods, n.e.s.o.i.	828	928	929	1 044	1 240	1 369	65.3
312111 – Soft drinks	238	307	377	436	468	602	153.4
312112 – Bottled waters	268	237	201	186	196	331	23.5
312113 – Ice	50	70	89	107	140	15	-69.8
312120 – Malt and beer	1 736	1 917	2 210	2 377	2 608	2 708	56.0
312130 – Wines	2 330	2 705	2 815	2 841	3 318	3 950	69.6
312140 – Distilled liquors	1 883	2 177	2 449	2 562	2 743	3 082	63.7
312221 – Cigarettes	103	151	259	239	317	300	191.4
312229 – Other tobacco products	381	305	300	288	300	310	-18.6
313111 – Yarns	600	669	760	658	620	656	9.4
313113 – Threads	52	47	45	42	50	43	-16.5
313210 – Broadwoven fabrics	3 956	3 692	3 922	3 354	3 578	3 391	-14.3
313221 – Narrow fabrics	375	394	439	408	444	506	35.0
313230 – Nonwoven fabrics	277	286	355	373	425	486	75.8
313249 – Knit fabrics and lace	817	947	1 026	1 035	1 108	1 057	29.4
313312 – Textile, fabric finishing mill products	55	31	49	42	39	38	-31.8
313320 – Coated fabrics	401	415	475	445	540	653	62.6
314110 – Carpets and rugs	1 114	1 253	1 469	1 415	1 535	1 667	49.6
314121 – Curtains and draperies	194	268	362	397	576	725	273.6
314129 – Other household textile products	2 358	2 695	3 195	3 301	3 982	4 671	98.1
314911 – Textile sacks and bags	141	161	206	211	241	221	57.5
314912 – Canvas and related products	248	251	236	253	265	324	30.7
314991 – Ropes, cordage and twine	231	221	251	260	271	288	24.8
314992 – Tire cords and tire fabrics	210	208	214	210	247	268	27.3
314999 – All other miscellaneous textile products	1 120	1 304	1 432	1 565	1 535	1 713	53.0
31511X – Hosiery and socks	681	844	947	920	1 029	1 085	59.3
315221 – Men's, boys' underwear, nightwear	1 949	2 232	2 266	2 181	2 293	2 338	20.0
315222 – Men's, boys' suits, coats, overcoats	1 422	1 470	1 567	1 288	1 197	1 399	-1.6
315223 – Men's, boys' shirts (excluding work)	7 803	8 109	8 935	8 516	8 342	8 998	15.3
315224 – Men's, boys' trousers, slacks, jeans	4 548	5 010	5 822	5 553	5 676	5 975	31.4
315228 – Men's, boys' other outerwear	4 581	4 351	4 973	4 989	4 664	4 959	8.3
315231 – Women's, girls' lingerie	3 492	3 997	4 279	4 264	4 535	4 481	28.3
315232 – Women's, girls' blouses and shirts	6 710	7 808	8 802	8 923	9 399	10 227	52.4
315233 – Women's, girls' dresses	1 962	2 074	2 107	1 824	1 565	1 632	-16.9
315234 – Women's, girls' suits, coats, skirts	3 266	3 051	3 497	3 482	3 350	3 748	14.8
315239 – Women's, girls' other outerwear	10 551	10 633	12 538	13 052	13 216	14 323	35.8
315291 – Infants' apparel	1 422	1 404	1 757	1 868	1 808	1 942	36.6
315292 – Fur and leather apparel	1 093	1 161	1 974	2 050	1 724	1 677	53.4
315991 – Hats and caps	750	804	924	944	924	987	31.6
315992 – Gloves and mittens	611	560	608	602	584	645	5.6
315993 – Men's and boys' neckwear	194	202	203	163	178	181	-6.4
315999 – Other apparel accessories	1 342	1 431	1 842	1 881	1 923	2 002	49.2
316110 – Leather and hide tanning	1 607	1 668	2 032	2 100	2 171	2 187	36.1
316211 – Rubber and plastic footwear	448	527	580	590	493	413	-7.8
316212 – House slippers	134	147	148	162	142	161	19.6
316213 – Men's footwear (excluding athletic)	3 227	3 304	3 593	3 747	3 548	3 568	10.6
316214 – Women's footwear (excluding athletic)	5 640	5 620	6 014	6 252	6 320	6 500	15.3
316219 – Other footwear	3 894	4 025	4 160	4 126	4 575	4 645	19.3
316991 – Luggage	2 431	2 585	2 679	2 599	2 543	2 668	9.8
316992 – Women's handbags and purses	1 015	1 038	1 218	1 208	1 352	1 621	59.7

Note: Unrevised data.

Table B-42. U.S. Total Imports by 6-Digit NAICS Product Groups, 1998–2003—*Continued*

(Millions of dollars; Census basis; general imports, Customs.)

NAICS product	1998	1999	2000	2001	2002	2003	Percent change, 1998–2003
316993 – Personal leather goods (excluding purses)	545	566	589	551	572	633	16.1
316999 – All other articles of leather	613	546	482	490	456	508	-17.1
321113 – Sawmill products	7 113	8 249	7 526	7 285	7 049	6 385	-10.2
321114 – Treated wood products, n.e.s.o.i.	53	56	49	48	64	52	-1.0
321211 – Hardwood veneer and plywood	985	1 127	1 146	1 058	1 266	1 262	28.2
321212 – Softwood veneer and plywood	150	283	271	341	423	571	281.8
321213 – Engineered wood (excluding truss)	554	790	664	666	799	914	64.8
321214 – Truss (imports only)	39	71	76	71	76	96	142.7
321219 – Reconstituted wood products	1 647	2 169	2 056	1 882	2 045	3 105	88.5
321911 – Wood windows and doors	328	423	517	571	626	653	99.2
321918 – Other millwork (including flooring)	598	807	811	773	879	931	55.7
321920 – Wood containers and pallets	309	339	402	395	429	414	33.9
321991 – Mobile homes and trailers	6	9	5	9	18	14	143.9
321992 – Prefabricated wood buildings	56	89	104	133	156	156	178.5
321999 – Miscellaneous wood products	1 450	1 589	1 766	1 737	1 895	2 031	40.1
322110 – Pulp mill products	2 392	2 545	3 302	2 614	2 333	2 573	7.6
322121 – Paper (except newsprint) mill products	4 289	4 643	5 313	4 945	4 848	5 088	18.6
322122 – Newsprint mill products	5 458	5 336	5 761	5 721	5 062	4 975	-8.8
322130 – Paperboard mill products	84	119	125	108	93	82	-2.5
322211 – Corrugated and solid fiber boxes	151	174	219	211	218	241	59.8
322212 – Folding paperboard boxes	351	347	385	430	482	528	50.6
322213 – Setup paperboard boxes	20	24	32	40	49	62	211.8
322214 – Fiber can, tube, drum and similar products	7	9	14	14	16	18	161.6
322215 – Nonfolding sanitary food containers	19	21	27	28	25	27	46.2
322222 – Coated and laminated paper	854	937	1 001	899	932	984	15.2
322223 – Foil and coated paper and plastic bags	748	843	1 041	1 150	1 260	1 515	102.5
322224 – Uncoated paper and multiwall bags	38	46	49	61	72	66	72.8
322232 – Envelopes	21	24	27	30	35	42	104.5
322233 – Stationery, tablets and related products	350	427	625	607	430	575	64.2
322291 – Sanitary paper products	504	578	737	894	1 014	1 062	110.9
322299 – All other converted paper products	326	360	433	426	674	590	80.8
323116 – Manifold business forms	6	8	8	7	11	13	108.4
323117 – Books printing	1 446	1 538	1 682	1 719	1 732	1 835	26.9
323118 – Blankbook, binders and stationery articles, n.e.s.o.i.	581	628	703	633	719	784	34.9
323119 – Printed matter, n.e.s.o.i.	1 422	1 599	1 791	1 772	1 954	2 054	44.4
323122 – Printing type, plates, cylinders, etc., n.e.s.o.i.	19	16	11	10	17	15	-19.2
324110 – Petroleum refinery products	10 413	13 634	25 393	24 309	21 706	27 800	167.0
324121 – Asphalt paving mixtures	31	29	38	31	42	46	46.6
324122 – Asphalt shingle and coating materials	46	50	48	62	70	77	66.9
325110 – Petrochemicals	470	478	701	639	670	893	90.3
325120 – Industrial gases	116	124	116	107	125	128	10.1
325131 – Inorganic dyes and pigments	691	752	832	746	807	850	22.9
325132 – Synthetic organic dyes and pigments	970	940	844	683	716	730	-24.7
325181 – Alkalies and chlorine	194	128	164	221	168	207	6.8
325182 – Carbon black	94	93	104	138	176	171	81.0
325188 – All other basic inorganic chemicals	4 055	4 270	4 956	5 084	4 981	5 712	40.9
325191 – Gum and wood chemicals	121	110	119	105	101	110	-9.5
325192 – Cyclic crude and intermediates	1 065	1 111	1 588	1 446	1 481	1 642	54.3
325193 – Ethyl alcohols	124	130	162	178	170	193	55.0
325199 – All other basic organic chemicals	11 064	11 652	13 330	13 840	13 513	15 084	36.3
325211 – Plastics materials and resins	4 542	4 852	5 784	5 625	5 664	6 580	44.9
325212 – Synthetic rubbers	869	937	1 073	1 101	1 109	1 128	29.8
325221 – Cellulose organic fibers	150	126	99	76	91	83	-44.9
325222 – Noncellulosic organic fibers	1 427	1 427	1 565	1 471	1 537	1 560	9.4
325311 – Nitrogenous fertilizers	1 180	1 150	1 514	1 911	1 400	2 517	113.3
325312 – Phosphatic fertilizers	916	868	905	892	922	981	7.0
325320 – Pesticides and other agricultural chemicals	482	481	459	524	500	615	27.6
325411 – Medicinal and botanical drugs and vitamins	9 117	12 592	17 361	18 523	19 826	22 169	143.1
325412 – Pharmaceutical preparations	7 798	9 591	10 136	13 491	·19 179	24 604	215.5
325414 – Biological products (excluding diagnostic)	853	1 285	1 463	1 741	1 997	2 775	225.2
325510 – Paints and coatings	480	674	742	732	597	629	31.1
325520 – Adhesives	208	257	270	255	288	338	62.7
325611 – Soaps and other detergents	505	578	684	741	833	889	76.1
325612 – Polishes and other sanitation goods	105	107	124	103	107	120	14.5
325613 – Surface active agents	312	311	362	346	401	476	52.7
325620 – Perfumes, makeups and other toiletries	1 749	1 962	2 244	2 431	2 715	3 112	77.9
325910 – Printing inks	309	220	208	261	235	253	-18.0
325920 – Explosives and accessories	143	142	155	160	167	199	39.3
325992 – Photo films, papers, plates and chemicals	2 320	2 359	2 513	2 044	1 938	1 801	-22.3
325998 – All other miscellaneous chemical products and preparations (including natural)	1 293	1 256	1 318	1 274	1 356	1 436	11.1
326112 – Reinforced plastics packaging films and sheets	23	36	38	23	29	61	169.9
326113 – Not reinforced plastics plates, sheets, etc. (excluding packaging)	1 762	1 837	2 026	1 918	2 035	2 309	31.0
326121 – Plastics rods, sticks and profile shapes	212	258	302	304	325	350	65.4
326122 – Plastics tubes, hoses, pipes and pipe fittings	231	288	309	301	285	311	34.4
326160 – Plastics bottles	217	231	276	310	342	385	77.6
326191 – Plastics plumbing fixtures	89	121	120	112	114	122	36.9
326192 – Plastic floor coverings	239	287	341	342	383	427	79.0
326199 – All other plastics products	5 397	6 203	6 971	7 164	7 966	8 706	61.3
326211 – Tires and tire parts (excluding retreadings)	4 043	4 587	4 739	4 181	4 733	5 223	29.2
326212 – Tire retreadings	15	14	13	9	9	15	-2.8

Note: Unrevised data.

Table B-42. U.S. Total Imports by 6-Digit NAICS Product Groups, 1998–2003—*Continued*

(Millions of dollars; Census basis; general imports, Customs.)

NAICS product	1998	1999	2000	2001	2002	2003	Percent change, 1998–2003
326220 – Rubber and plastics hoses and belting	934	990	1 098	1 062	1 078	1 198	28.3
326299 – Other rubber products	1 065	1 131	1 281	1 305	1 391	1 542	44.7
327111 – China plumb fixtures and china and earthen bath access	237	284	314	357	438	525	121.5
327112 – China, fine earthenware and other pottery products	1 955	1 957	2 160	1 988	1 912	1 981	1.3
327113 – Porcelain electrical supplies	221	243	299	260	226	226	2.3
327121 – Brick and structural ceramics	6	9	16	11	11	12	93.8
327122 – Ceramic wall and floor tiles	862	1 020	1 117	1 112	1 290	1 430	66.0
327123 – Other structural ceramic products	13	16	19	19	24	26	93.9
327124 – Clay and alumina articles	85	156	258	98	93	111	30.3
327125 – Nonclay refractory articles	234	231	221	191	202	234	0.0
327211 – Drawn, blown, float and flat glass	515	559	576	599	583	629	22.1
327212 – Other pressed and blown glass and glassware	1 877	2 097	2 138	1 941	1 976	2 014	7.3
327213 – Glass containers	452	526	586	538	608	607	34.3
327215 – Glass products, n.e.s.o.i.	1 015	1 403	1 994	1 537	1 132	1 186	16.9
327310 – Cements	963	1 145	1 074	987	940	941	-2.3
327320 – Wet, nonrefractory mortars and concretes	1	1	1	0	0	0	X
327331 – Concrete bricks and blocks	24	39	47	43	50	64	167.7
327390 – Other concrete products	431	561	755	790	864	856	98.5
327410 – Lime and calcined dolomite	20	14	12	14	18	20	-1.3
327420 – Gypsum products	155	326	137	109	78	70	-54.7
327910 – Abrasive products	867	821	948	787	781	837	-3.5
327991 – Cut stone and stone products	872	1 019	1 280	1 393	1 537	1 807	107.3
327992 – Ground or treated mineral and earth	171	176	193	162	173	179	5.0
327993 – Mineral wool and glass fibers	240	314	331	330	332	360	49.8
327999 – All other miscellaneous nonmetallic mineral products	296	309	325	288	282	299	1.1
331111 – Iron and steel	17 158	13 127	15 524	11 989	12 559	10 832	-36.9
331112 – Electrometallurgical ferroalloy product	1 171	1 089	1 266	819	920	1 145	-2.2
331222 – Steel wire drawing	1 016	1 070	1 110	1 013	1 109	1 184	16.6
331311 – Alumina refining	842	743	812	607	533	465	-44.7
331312 – Primary aluminum	3 776	3 992	4 266	4 085	4 213	4 435	17.5
331314 – Secondary smelting and alloying of aluminum	7	10	14	16	14	18	153.1
331315 – Aluminum sheets, plates and foils	1 392	1 449	1 630	1 450	1 580	1 672	20.1
331316 – Aluminum extruded products	393	422	529	416	485	530	35.0
331319 – Other aluminum rolling and drawing	195	214	276	210	237	327	68.0
331411 – Primary smelting and refining of copper	1 784	1 938	2 366	2 469	2 040	1 639	-8.1
331419 – Other nonferrous metals primary smelting, refining	9 682	9 487	12 008	10 295	8 190	8 679	-10.4
331421 – Copper rolling, drawing and extruding	708	699	994	815	688	685	-3.3
331422 – Copper wire (except mechanical) drawing	332	535	775	670	661	705	112.3
331491 – Other nonferrous metals roll, draw, extruding	1 327	1 394	1 370	1 218	897	871	-34.3
331492 – Other nonferrous secondary smelt, refine, alloying	350	295	421	315	239	229	-34.7
331511 – Iron foundries	489	467	493	429	429	450	-8.0
332115 – Crowns, closures, seals and other packing accessories	115	134	150	177	192	237	106.0
332211 – Cutlery and flatware (excluding precious)	650	720	761	773	819	960	47.7
332212 – Hand and edge tools	1 611	1 713	1 837	1 767	1 911	2 031	26.1
332213 – Saw blades and handsaws	270	288	306	290	331	368	36.2
332214 – Kitchen utensils, pots and pans	339	388	413	397	433	471	39.0
332311 – Prefab metal buildings and components	58	73	65	73	65	74	26.9
332312 – Fabricated structural metals	562	716	936	1 095	1 204	1 099	95.7
332321 – Metal windows and doors	261	315	391	401	432	470	80.0
332322 – Sheet metal works	22	27	42	39	40	42	89.1
332323 – Ornamental and architectural metal works	67	77	91	129	97	107	59.3
332410 – Power boilers and heat exchangers	357	436	761	920	1 144	660	84.9
332420 – Metal tanks (heavy gauge)	315	360	327	327	433	654	107.7
332431 – Metal cans	60	80	71	70	82	113	87.0
332439 – Other metal containers	283	293	318	330	324	345	21.9
332510 – Hardware	2 695	2 916	3 290	3 143	3 446	3 668	36.1
332611 – Springs (heavy gauge)	708	832	859	709	762	786	11.1
332618 – Other fabricated wire products	849	867	886	872	848	904	6.6
332722 – Bolts, nuts, screws, rivets, washers, and other turned products	2 054	2 049	2 355	2 018	2 109	2 371	15.4
332911 – Industrial valves	3 307	3 411	3 918	3 750	3 966	4 206	27.2
332912 – Fluid power valves and hose fittings	359	427	560	495	553	629	75.2
332913 – Plumbing fixtures fittings and trim	402	580	660	685	774	801	99.0
332919 – Other metal valves and pipe fittings	660	672	829	812	792	765	15.9
332991 – Ball and roller bearings	1 638	1 479	1 626	1 429	1 410	1 497	-8.6
332992 – Small arms ammunition	197	196	262	239	281	328	66.0
332994 – Small arms	393	466	525	548	630	696	76.9
332995 – Other ordnances and accessories	21	23	33	40	37	43	109.7
332997 – Industrial patterns	15	17	19	20	19	19	22.2
332998 – Enameled iron and metal sanitary wares	155	175	200	214	279	311	100.7
332999 – Other miscellaneous fabricated metal products	4 373	4 756	5 764	4 904	5 359	5 722	30.9
333111 – Farm machinery and equipment	3 612	3 075	3 419	3 374	3 598	4 198	16.2
333120 – Construction machinery	7 778	7 707	7 458	6 796	6 856	8 043	3.4
333131 – Mining machinery and equipment	487	534	604	540	501	586	20.4
333132 – Oil and gas field machinery and equipment	318	269	308	374	429	482	51.5
333210 – Sawmill and woodworking machinery	839	923	970	814	817	930	10.9

Note: Unrevised data.

X = Not applicable.

Table B-42. U.S. Total Imports by 6-Digit NAICS Product Groups, 1998–2003—*Continued*

(Millions of dollars; Census basis; general imports, Customs.)

NAICS product	1998	1999	2000	2001	2002	2003	Percent change, 1998–2003
333220 – Plastics and rubber industry machinery	2 080	2 156	1 992	1 449	1 556	1 806	-13.2
333291 – Paper industry machinery	1 025	995	1 112	1 078	711	859	-16.3
333292 – Textile machinery	1 859	1 398	1 235	855	713	721	-61.2
333293 – Printing machinery and equipment	2 198	2 277	2 107	1 908	1 586	1 639	-25.4
333294 – Food product machinery	657	669	605	588	629	766	16.5
333295 – Semiconductor machinery	1 804	1 831	3 257	2 970	2 451	1 957	8.5
333298 – Other miscellaneous industrial machinery	213	231	237	198	258	328	53.6
333311 – Automatic vending machines	105	120	123	115	130	163	54.6
333313 – Office machinery	2 598	2 421	2 645	2 308	2 576	5 644	117.2
333314 – Optical instruments and lenses	2 093	2 716	4 510	3 391	2 213	2 443	16.7
333315 – Photographic and photocopying equipment	6 193	5 644	5 216	3 507	2 983	2 738	-55.8
333319 – Other commercial, service industry machinery	215	234	248	239	249	297	37.8
333411 – Air purification equipment	152	168	210	243	264	330	117.1
333412 – Industrial and commercial fans and blowers	491	581	729	628	616	621	26.3
333414 – Heating equipment (excluding warm air furnaces)	300	393	460	465	486	561	86.7
333415 – AC, warm air heating and commercial refrigeration equipment	1 955	2 286	2 662	2 705	3 186	3 787	93.8
333511 – Industrial molds	1 235	1 333	1 348	1 161	1 324	1 369	10.9
333512 – Machine tools (metal cutting types)	4 381	3 535	3 914	3 105	2 299	2 346	-46.5
333513 – Machine tools (metal forming types)	1 704	1 599	1 801	1 651	1 065	1 174	-31.1
333514 – Special dies, tools, die sets, jigs and fixtures	630	578	564	546	729	891	41.4
333515 – Cutting tools and machine tool accessories	1 022	994	1 144	1 013	931	1 006	-1.6
333516 – Rolling mill machinery and equipment	360	225	151	95	77	126	-65.0
333611 – Turbines and turbine generator sets	1 064	1 584	2 670	4 846	3 830	2 417	127.2
333612 – Speed changers, industrial high-speed drives, gears	1 290	1 644	1 436	1 433	1 467	1 584	22.7
333613 – Mechanical power transmission equipment	845	903	996	870	925	1 034	22.4
333618 – Other engine equipment	4 914	5 609	5 975	5 014	5 581	6 835	39.1
333911 – Pumps and pumping equipment	1 025	1 059	1 169	1 159	1 236	1 422	38.7
333912 – Air and gas compressors	1 299	1 321	1 440	1 253	1 239	1 357	4.5
333913 – Measuring and dispensing pumps	49	67	93	104	73	73	49.3
333921 – Elevators and moving stairways	211	243	264	288	317	322	52.3
333922 – Conveyors and conveying equipment	748	734	900	810	732	806	7.8
333923 – Overhead cranes, hoists and monorail systems	428	445	400	355	449	425	-0.8
333924 – Industrial trucks, tractors, trailers, stacker machinery	1 550	1 644	1 817	1 531	1 354	1 506	-2.8
333991 – Power-driven handtools	1 438	1 652	1 833	1 797	2 123	2 514	74.9
333992 – Welding and soldering equipment	862	706	842	846	868	1 045	21.3
333993 – Packaging machinery	1 072	1 117	1 246	1 302	1 332	1 505	40.3
333994 – Industrial furnaces and ovens	410	379	539	478	436	368	-10.2
333995 – Fluid power cylinders and actuators	262	320	366	343	317	396	51.2
333996 – Fluid power pumps and motors	692	701	790	783	770	915	32.2
333997 – Scales and balances (except laboratory)	224	266	295	280	294	377	68.5
333999 – Other miscellaneous general purpose machinery	6 189	6 806	7 834	6 864	6 546	7 219	16.6
334111 – Electronic computers	7 266	10 118	13 494	12 134	15 576	19 714	171.3
334112 – Computer storage devices	18 152	16 866	16 286	13 353	12 167	11 522	-36.5
334119 – Other computer equipment	29 598	34 294	38 758	33 561	34 580	32 784	10.8
334210 – Telephone apparatus	7 340	8 948	13 109	8 100	8 163	8 681	18.3
334220 – Radio, TV broadcast and wireless communication equipment	7 521	10 606	17 255	18 392	19 066	20 999	179.2
334290 – Other communications equipment	755	772	798	783	795	769	1.8
334310 – Audio and video equipment	22 840	24 512	29 036	27 483	31 112	32 098	40.5
334411 – Picture, microwave, amp, electron, cathode and sim tubes	1 006	942	869	950	913	813	-19.2
334412 – Printed circuits	2 193	2 266	3 007	2 173	1 921	1 815	-17.2
334413 – Semiconductors and related devices	33 448	37 684	48 226	30 811	26 520	25 216	-24.6
334414 – Electronic capacitors and parts	1 337	1 694	2 816	1 499	1 309	1 205	-9.9
334415 – Electronic resistors and parts	650	687	1 003	715	685	634	-2.5
334416 – Electronic coils, transformers, other inductors	1 106	1 210	1 676	1 016	779	748	-32.4
334417 – Electronic connectors	2 236	2 501	3 274	2 303	2 041	2 109	-5.7
334418 – Printed circuit assemblies (electronic assemblies)	19 141	23 522	27 948	20 219	17 453	17 950	-6.2
334419 – Other electronic components	7 283	8 020	9 599	7 307	6 952	7 096	-2.6
334510 – Electromedical apparatus	2 241	2 635	3 147	3 693	4 551	5 306	136.8
334511 – Search, detection and navigation instruments	1 188	1 301	1 565	1 675	1 671	2 058	73.1
334512 – Automatic environmental controls	509	571	623	649	718	733	44.0
334513 – Industrial process controls	3 461	3 709	4 360	4 195	4 460	4 801	38.7
334514 – Total fluid meters and counting devices	204	219	243	274	279	313	53.6
334515 – Electricity measuring, testing instruments	2 482	2 700	3 684	3 393	2 871	3 194	28.7
334516 – Analytical laboratory instruments	1 685	1 942	2 499	2 645	2 528	2 745	62.9
334517 – Irradiation apparatus	1 298	1 323	1 490	1 744	2 092	2 298	77.1
334518 – Watches, clocks and parts	3 029	3 074	3 313	2 898	3 029	3 411	12.6
334519 – Other measuring and controlling devices	906	949	863	952	1 126	1 173	29.5
334612 – Prerecorded CDs, tapes, records	286	365	351	319	294	272	-4.9
334613 – Unrecorded magnetic and optical media	2 040	2 172	2 350	2 308	2 642	3 032	48.6
335110 – Electric lamp bulbs and parts	1 153	1 267	1 391	1 614	1 476	1 515	31.4
335121 – Residential electric lighting fixtures	1 157	1 343	1 573	1 443	1 712	1 780	53.9
335129 – Lighting equipment, n.e.s.o.i.	2 061	2 591	3 006	2 766	2 982	3 085	49.7
335211 – Electric housewares and household fans	3 272	3 658	4 154	4 491	4 909	5 193	58.7
335212 – Household vacuum cleaner and floor polishers	517	524	580	701	944	1 291	149.8
335221 – Household cooking appliances	1 628	1 855	2 181	2 273	2 490	2 651	62.9

Note: Unrevised data.

Table B-42. U.S. Total Imports by 6-Digit NAICS Product Groups, 1998–2003—*Continued*

(Millions of dollars; Census basis; general imports, Customs.)

NAICS product	1998	1999	2000	2001	2002	2003	Percent change, 1998–2003
335222 – Household refrigerators and freezers	551	630	670	950	1 160	1 242	125.5
335224 – Household laundry equipment	335	398	405	371	512	731	117.8
335228 – Major appliances and miscellaneous machines, n.e.s.o.i.	531	660	654	680	740	874	64.5
335311 – Power, distribution, specialty transformers	1 034	1 284	1 556	1 691	1 669	1 488	44.0
335312 – Motors and generators	4 052	5 110	5 336	5 467	5 415	5 580	37.7
335313 – Switchgear and switchboard apparatus	1 231	1 451	1 803	1 707	1 649	1 732	40.6
335314 – Relays and industrial controls	3 002	3 339	3 919	3 560	3 831	4 252	41.6
335911 – Storage batteries	1 591	1 818	2 122	1 828	1 623	1 517	-4.7
335912 – Primary batteries	357	453	466	418	433	499	39.6
335921 – Fiber optic cable	72	128	402	659	153	151	110.4
335929 – Communication and energy wire, n.e.s.o.i.	2 670	2 935	3 362	2 989	2 873	2 991	12.0
335931 – Current-carrying wiring devices	1 711	1 844	2 072	1 769	1 785	1 887	10.3
335932 – Noncurrent-carrying wiring devices	123	136	158	133	91	95	-22.6
335991 – Carbon and graphite products	454	363	393	387	404	480	5.8
335999 – Miscellaneous electrical equipment and components, n.e.s.o.i.	2 754	3 023	3 707	3 428	3 361	3 540	28.5
336111 – Autos and light duty motor vehicles, including chassis	80 869	96 544	109 267	106 622	114 063	114 371	41.4
336120 – Heavy duty trucks and chassis	13 401	18 423	17 017	17 615	17 779	17 771	32.6
336211 – Motor vehicle bodies	353	319	411	437	395	490	38.9
336212 – Truck trailers	246	430	387	397	346	451	83.4
336213 – Motor homes	116	114	100	105	113	118	2.3
336214 – Transportation equipment, n.e.s.o.i., including trailers and campers	328	348	991	435	408	412	25.8
33631X – Motor vehicle gasoline engines and engine parts	9 415	10 719	11 409	10 290	10 801	11 047	17.3
336321 – Vehicular lighting equipment	623	714	817	789	1 030	1 155	85.2
336322 – Motor vehicle electrical and electronic equipment, n.e.s.o.i.	6 231	7 035	7 419	6 938	7 685	7 936	27.4
336330 – Motor vehicle steering and suspension parts	1 826	2 213	2 300	2 228	2 732	3 079	68.6
336340 – Motor vehicle brake systems	2 276	2 520	2 562	2 456	2 824	3 124	37.2
336350 – Motor vehicle transmission and power train parts	6 721	7 815	8 568	7 936	8 281	8 737	30.0
336360 – Motor vehicle seating and interior trim	2 788	3 068	2 959	2 663	3 078	3 522	26.3
336370 – Motor vehicle metal stampings	537	576	608	500	506	468	-12.9
336391 – Motor vehicle air-conditioning	892	1 039	1 237	1 167	1 384	1 517	70.0
336399 – Motor vehicle parts, n.e.s.o.i.	10 355	12 045	13 934	13 462	15 331	17 439	68.4
336411 – Aircraft	6 939	8 780	12 399	14 711	12 680	12 334	77.7
336412 – Aircraft engines and engine parts	9 494	9 239	8 902	10 669	8 714	7 431	-21.7
336413 – Aircraft parts and auxiliary equipment, n.e.s.o.i.	5 405	5 317	5 018	5 658	4 610	4 199	-22.3
336414 – Guided missiles and space vehicles	0	38	102	71	0	112	X
336415 – Missile, space vehicle propulsion units and parts	10	24	47	44	30	40	300.4
336419 – Missile, space vehicle parts and auxiliary equipment, n.e.s.o.i.	185	183	226	226	98	121	-34.8
336510 – Railroad rolling stock	1 896	2 055	1 615	1 163	871	852	-55.0
336611 – Ships	232	104	76	59	54	124	-46.5
336612 – Boats	839	958	1 027	1 069	1 120	1 159	38.2
336991 – Motorcycles, bicycles and parts	2 445	2 993	3 899	3 895	4 057	4 312	76.3
336992 – Military armored vehicles, tanks and tank components	104	71	88	83	252	246	135.8
337110 – Wood kitchen cabinets and countertops	322	395	474	526	579	644	100.0
337121 – Upholstered household furniture	784	972	1 251	1 269	1 539	1 878	139.6
337124 – Metal household furniture	1 100	1 354	1 542	1 480	1 666	2 032	84.7
337127 – Institutional furniture	5 696	7 055	8 310	8 262	9 656	10 439	83.3
337129 – Wood sewing machine cabinets	8	8	8	9	7	8	-3.4
337211 – Wood office furniture	491	550	677	555	606	694	41.4
337214 – Office furniture (except wood)	458	501	636	516	402	407	-11.0
337215 – Showcases, partitions, shelvings and lockers	1 468	1 833	2 175	2 084	2 379	2 751	87.3
337910 – Mattresses	48	56	64	62	54	86	81.7
337920 – Blinds and shades	422	448	474	510	607	704	67.1
339112 – Surgical and medical instruments	2 251	2 724	3 022	3 528	4 147	5 493	144.0
339113 – Surgical appliances and supplies	2 424	2 385	2 678	3 084	3 619	4 526	86.7
339114 – Dental equipment and supplies	349	403	437	500	578	725	107.7
339115 – Ophthalmic goods	1 711	1 730	1 939	1 919	2 012	2 138	24.9
339911 – Jewelry (except costume)	4 566	5 079	5 754	5 538	6 294	6 602	44.6
339912 – Silverware, plateware and hollowware	575	632	721	667	721	737	28.2
339913 – Jewelers' material and lapidary work	9 451	11 011	13 228	11 567	13 078	13 850	46.6
339914 – Costume jewelry and novelties	597	678	792	831	919	988	65.6
339920 – Sporting and athletic goods	3 506	3 500	4 128	4 203	4 466	4 790	36.6
339931 – Dolls and stuffed toys	4 359	4 202	4 030	3 641	3 551	3 526	-19.1
339932 – Games, toys and children's vehicles	8 616	8 901	9 366	10 567	11 519	10 651	23.6
339941 – Pens and mechanical pencils	671	811	957	840	850	870	29.7
339942 – Lead pencils and art goods	251	233	281	293	321	372	48.1
339943 – Marking devices	57	57	60	57	55	62	8.1
339944 – Carbon paper and inked ribbon	291	294	314	300	314	246	-15.6
339950 – Signs	67	83	84	99	113	143	111.8
339991 – Gaskets, packing and sealing devices	1 125	1 195	1 326	1 303	1 478	1 558	38.5
339992 – Musical instruments	1 067	1 121	1 283	1 168	1 207	1 291	20.9
339993 – Fasteners, buttons, needles and pins	335	348	315	283	266	270	-19.2
339994 – Brooms, brushes and mops	490	624	635	708	827	860	75.5
339999 – Miscellaneous manufactured commodities, n.e.s.o.i.	4 383	4 948	5 353	5 412	5 526	5 784	32.0
511210 – Software publishing	214	163	162	175	133	122	-42.8
910000 – Waste and scrap	1 756	1 710	1 871	1 588	1 614	1 808	2.9
920000 – Used or second-hand merchandise	4 593	5 424	6 342	5 902	5 669	4 757	3.6
980000 – Goods returned to Canada (exports only); U.S. goods returned and reimported (imports only)	25 363	30 888	33 706	34 675	34 753	32 953	29.9
990000 – Special classification provisions, n.e.s.o.i.	11 563	15 089	18 711	17 831	16 745	17 743	53.4

Note: Unrevised data.

X = Not applicable.

Table B-43. U.S. Total Trade Balances by 6-Digit NAICS Product Groups, 1998–2003

(Millions of dollars; Census basis; foreign and domestic exports, f.a.s.; general imports, Customs.)

NAICS product	1998	1999	2000	2001	2002	2003	Percent change, 1998–2003
TOTAL	-233 411	-331 945	-436 469	-410 933	-470 291	-535 652	129.5
111110 – Soybeans	4 831	4 528	5 279	5 420	5 596	7 889	63.3
111120 – Oilseeds (except soybean)	-16	-27	-27	24	45	3	-120.8
111130 – Dry peas and beans	314	238	178	150	131	152	-51.7
111140 – Wheat	3 430	3 308	3 159	3 100	3 366	3 818	11.3
111150 – Corn	4 477	4 971	4 554	4 630	4 990	4 821	7.7
111160 – Rice	416	157	181	161	199	322	-22.6
111199 – Other grains	390	443	560	490	421	445	14.2
111211 – Potatoes	-4	3	16	23	19	-1	-79.9
111219 – Other vegetables (excluding potatoes) and melons	-899	-830	-794	-1 076	-1 045	-1 319	46.8
111310 – Oranges	321	90	263	274	279	308	-4.1
111320 – Citrus fruits (except oranges)	208	172	148	138	144	74	-64.4
111331 – Apples	274	261	296	317	271	231	-15.6
111332 – Grapes	-104	-157	-97	-96	-187	-162	56.3
111333 – Strawberries	26	44	65	69	77	139	442.0
111334 – Berries (except strawberries)	-37	-29	-32	-43	-49	-68	82.8
111335 – Tree nuts	-75	-258	-13	100	168	180	-341.8
111339 – Other noncitrus fruits	-3 583	-3 284	-3 092	-2 300	-2 449	-2 743	-23.4
111411 – Mushrooms	-3	-5	-12	-22	-37	-44	1 248.9
111421 – Nursery products and trees	-205	-238	-271	-307	-316	-328	60.4
111422 – Fresh flowers, seeds and foliage	-595	-578	-605	-554	-527	-596	0.1
111910 – Tobacco	689	548	668	581	374	353	-48.8
111920 – Cotton	2 559	829	1 906	2 191	2 062	3 420	33.7
111930 – Sugarcane	0	0	1	2	0	0	X
111940 – Hay, alfalfa hay, and clover	236	261	324	311	419	454	92.8
111991 – Sugar beets	2	0	1	-1	3	2	-26.5
111992 – Peanuts	122	118	126	81	155	114	-6.4
111998 – Other miscellaneous agricultural products	-103	-69	-72	-114	-50	-71	-31.5
11211X – Cattle	-918	-778	-835	-1 136	-1 280	-765	-16.7
112210 – Swine	-250	-198	-279	-337	-263	-358	43.3
1123XX – Poultry and eggs	233	187	175	181	175	185	-20.7
112410 – Sheep and wool	-61	-28	-24	-17	-6	-6	-89.9
112420 – Goats and other fine animal hair	-2	11	7	-3	1	6	-353.2
112511 – Fish, farmed	-483	-574	-625	-680	-731	-773	60.1
112512 – Shellfish, farmed	-14	-16	-21	-20	-20	-25	80.1
112910 – Bees and honey	-79	-89	-89	-70	-161	-203	157.4
112920 – Horses and other equine	112	-31	38	132	63	290	158.5
112930 – Rabbits, foxes, furskins, and cuttings	87	78	86	101	99	84	-4.0
112990 – All other live animals	-28	-29	-28	-28	-34	-26	-6.8
113210 – Forestry products	-1 197	-873	-961	-751	-854	-1 140	-4.7
113310 – Timber and logs	1 235	1 199	1 226	1 066	1 016	1 043	-15.6
114111 – Finfish fresh, chilled, frozen; finfish products	-764	-676	-670	-160	-370	-445	-41.7
114112 – Shellfish fresh, chilled, frozen; shellfish products ...	-3 901	-4 054	-4 939	-4 846	-4 756	-5 245	34.5
114119 – Other marine products	31	29	80	23	-9	-21	-168.9
211111 – Crude petroleum and natural gas	-41 953	-55 962	-99 858	-89 943	-88 509	-118 291	182.0
211112 – Liquid natural gas	-2 152	-2 053	-3 009	-3 442	-2 677	-4 363	102.7
212112 – Coal (excluding anthracite) and petroleum gases ...	2 711	1 823	1 632	1 134	1 017	806	-70.3
212113 – Anthracite coal, not agglomerated	44	33	33	26	-9	-40	-189.4
212210 – Iron ores	-283	-156	-174	-63	-64	-80	-71.7
212221 – Gold ores	-5	3	5	4	-8	-2	-63.3
212222 – Silver ores	-38	38	26	69	55	15	-139.4
212231 – Lead ores and zinc ores	279	290	284	361	400	424	51.9
212234 – Copper ores and nickel ores	-163	15	179	33	-19	63	-138.5
212291 – Uranium-radium-vanadium ores	1	-62	-55	-63	-44	-26	-3 597.3
212299 – All other metal ores	-403	-410	-453	-399	-421	-400	-0.7
212311 – Dimension stone	32	18	26	51	11	22	-32.1
212319 – Other crushed and broken stone	-48	-68	-92	-58	-67	-84	73.5
212322 – Industrial sand	167	133	164	126	116	126	-24.5
212324 – Kaolin and other kaolinic clays	571	564	604	558	526	541	-5.2
212325 – Other clay, ceramic and refractory minerals ...	188	169	180	181	184	186	-1.0
212391 – Borate minerals and potassium salts	15	4	3	5	11	6	-60.8
212392 – Phosphate rock	-38	-39	-31	-36	-50	-42	11.8
212393 – Other chemical and fertilizer minerals	-250	-191	-188	-261	-192	-300	19.8
212399 – All other nonmetallic minerals	-260	-279	-315	-304	-333	-248	-4.7
311111 – Dog and cat foods	599	588	699	793	545	565	-5.5
311119 – Other animal foods	351	295	361	459	404	400	13.9
311211 – Flour and other grain mill products	213	228	193	161	176	78	-63.4
311212 – Milled rice and by-products	618	606	480	390	417	510	-17.5
311213 – Malts	28	15	-6	-1	-20	-33	-221.0
311221 – Wet corn milling products	1 185	993	965	995	958	998	-15.7
311222 – Soybean oil and by-products	2 733	2 071	1 951	2 436	2 328	2 047	-25.1
311223 – Other oilseed products	-837	-771	-877	-666	-719	-985	17.7
311225 – Margarine and edible fats and oils	277	158	171	149	207	245	-11.5
311230 – Breakfast cereals	67	55	53	107	174	262	291.2

Note: Unrevised data.

X = Not applicable.

Table B-43. U.S. Total Trade Balances by 6-Digit NAICS Product Groups, 1998–2003—*Continued*

(Millions of dollars; Census basis; foreign and domestic exports, f.a.s.; general imports, Customs.)

NAICS product	1998	1999	2000	2001	2002	2003	Percent change, 1998–2003
31131X – Sugars	-702	-543	-426	-429	-474	-504	-28.2
311320 – Chocolate and confectionery products	-588	-496	-444	-389	-629	-1 048	78.2
311340 – Nonchocolate confectionery products	-335	-443	-436	-452	-646	-816	143.5
311411 – Frozen fruits, juices and vegetables	16	-76	-90	-109	-252	-539	-3 432.8
311421 – Fruits and vegetables preserved	-490	-726	-668	-731	-821	-1 019	108.1
311422 – Specialty canned foods	-1	7	5	17	19	35	-2 767.4
311423 – Dried and dehydrated foods	396	398	349	351	285	266	-32.9
311511 – Fluid milk, cream and related products	27	14	22	23	38	33	21.3
311512 – Creamery butter	-66	-47	-26	-92	-54	-43	-34.6
311513 – Cheese	-508	-569	-547	-579	-627	-732	44.1
311514 – Dry, condensed and evaporated dairy products	198	211	193	292	175	211	6.4
311520 – Ice cream and frozen desserts	81	52	74	70	60	34	-58.2
311611 – Meat products (excluding poultry)	2 445	2 268	3 252	2 745	2 263	2 935	20.0
311613 – Animal fats, oils and by-products	609	468	334	305	461	506	-16.9
311615 – Poultry, prepared or preserved	2 152	1 754	1 950	2 313	1 721	1 922	-10.7
311711 – Seafood products, prepared, canned and packaged	-654	-680	-684	-816	-973	-1 148	75.4
31181X – Bread and bakery products	-370	-491	-598	-682	-809	-973	163.1
311822 – Prepared flour mixes and dough	26	22	32	42	52	66	152.7
311823 – Pasta	-194	-162	-148	-133	-151	-151	-22.1
311911 – Roasted nuts and peanut butter	135	98	113	124	143	155	14.5
311919 – Other snack foods	262	265	226	162	148	74	-71.9
311920 – Coffee and tea	-597	-471	-471	-386	-388	-407	-31.8
311930 – Flavoring extracts and syrups	492	486	472	556	474	422	-14.3
311941 – Mayonnaise, dressings and other prepared sauces	32	-16	-16	-27	-30	-32	-199.6
311942 – Spices and extracts	-322	-360	-380	-260	-276	-264	-17.9
311999 – Other foods, n.e.s.o.i.	520	485	596	582	484	546	5.0
312111 – Soft drinks	16	-56	-138	-221	-237	-312	-2 021.2
312112 – Bottled waters	-259	-224	-186	-167	-183	-311	20.2
312113 – Ice	-42	-58	-78	-91	-117	1	-102.7
312120 – Malt and beer	-1 400	-1 639	-1 959	-2 100	-2 355	-2 448	74.8
312130 – Wines	-1 778	-2 141	-2 231	-2 269	-2 751	-3 292	85.2
312140 – Distilled liquors	-1 360	-1 663	-1 908	-1 976	-2 129	-2 412	77.4
312221 – Cigarettes	4 072	3 094	3 070	1 888	1 155	1 124	-72.4
312229 – Other tobacco products	287	347	406	335	188	149	-48.0
313111 – Yarns	-245	-285	-322	-241	-190	-82	-66.4
313113 – Threads	150	197	278	160	124	119	-21.2
313210 – Broadwoven fabrics	-1 467	-943	-443	39	-152	-444	-69.7
313221 – Narrow fabrics	189	278	317	370	358	164	-13.2
313230 – Nonwoven fabrics	465	400	423	403	417	531	14.4
313249 – Knit fabrics and lace	-140	-275	-175	-30	52	413	-394.7
313312 – Textile, fabric finishing mill products	4	22	-5	4	18	34	730.6
313320 – Coated fabrics	184	182	140	303	211	241	30.7
314110 – Carpets and rugs	-255	-445	-658	-684	-825	-957	275.6
314121 – Curtains and draperies	-155	-229	-320	-361	-534	-691	346.5
314129 – Other household textile products	-1 908	-2 290	-2 756	-2 874	-3 599	-4 295	125.1
314911 – Textile sacks and bags	-101	-122	-167	-168	-192	-175	73.6
314912 – Canvas and related products	-200	-197	-188	-211	-221	-275	37.5
314991 – Ropes, cordage and twine	-150	-147	-166	-172	-178	-186	24.1
314992 – Tire cords and tire fabrics	-56	-46	-56	-75	-121	-152	172.0
314999 – All other miscellaneous textile products	-573	-676	-721	-984	-1 000	-1 141	99.2
31511X – Hosiery and socks	-261	-395	-510	-553	-680	-741	184.1
315221 – Men's, boys' underwear, nightwear	-1 241	-1 457	-1 356	-1 376	-1 629	-1 666	34.3
315222 – Men's, boys' suits, coats, overcoats	-1 311	-1 384	-1 480	-1 211	-1 145	-1 351	3.0
315223 – Men's, boys' shirts (excluding work)	-6 659	-6 705	-7 414	-7 481	-7 568	-8 284	24.4
315224 – Men's, boys' trousers, slacks, jeans	-3 482	-4 109	-4 961	-4 868	-5 084	-5 427	55.9
315228 – Men's, boys' other outerwear	-4 193	-3 985	-4 543	-4 670	-4 380	-4 678	11.6
315231 – Women's, girls' lingerie	-2 684	-3 181	-3 546	-3 673	-3 964	-4 031	50.2
315232 – Women's, girls' blouses and shirts	-6 271	-7 388	-8 338	-8 479	-8 963	-9 850	57.1
315233 – Women's, girls' dresses	-1 834	-1 968	-1 993	-1 730	-1 489	-1 561	-14.9
315234 – Women's, girls' suits, coats, skirts	-2 954	-2 815	-3 257	-3 269	-3 188	-3 601	21.9
315239 – Women's, girls' other outerwear	-9 631	-9 792	-11 570	-12 220	-12 459	-13 672	42.0
315291 – Infants' apparel	-1 214	-1 248	-1 609	-1 800	-1 771	-1 909	57.3
315292 – Fur and leather apparel	-959	-1 030	-1 839	-1 926	-1 622	-1 577	64.5
315991 – Hats and caps	-697	-753	-868	-885	-875	-935	34.3
315992 – Gloves and mittens	-544	-503	-542	-545	-533	-591	8.7
315993 – Men's and boys' neckwear	-175	-188	-189	-153	-166	-170	-3.1
315999 – Other apparel accessories	439	-47	-469	-706	-894	-1 086	-347.1
316110 – Leather and hide tanning	-203	-433	-795	-705	-763	-711	251.2
316211 – Rubber and plastic footwear	-367	-458	-487	-529	-443	-372	1.2
316212 – House slippers	-120	-124	-133	-153	-134	-148	23.6
316213 – Men's footwear (excluding athletic)	-3 048	-3 127	-3 428	-3 562	-3 377	-3 380	10.9
316214 – Women's footwear (excluding athletic)	-5 533	-5 512	-5 902	-6 138	-6 205	-6 380	15.3
316219 – Other footwear	-3 726	-3 868	-3 985	-3 965	-4 405	-4 496	20.7
316991 – Luggage	-2 175	-2 307	-2 395	-2 329	-2 306	-2 414	11.0
316992 – Women's handbags and purses	-966	-982	-1 137	-1 113	-1 257	-1 498	55.1

Note: Unrevised data.

Table B-43. U.S. Total Trade Balances by 6-Digit NAICS Product Groups, 1998–2003—*Continued*

(Millions of dollars; Census basis; foreign and domestic exports, f.a.s.; general imports, Customs.)

NAICS product	1998	1999	2000	2001	2002	2003	Percent change, 1998–2003
316993 – Personal leather goods (excluding purses)	-501	-512	-530	-500	-515	-572	14.3
316999 – All other articles of leather	-224	-133	-14	-122	-174	-215	-3.9
321113 – Sawmill products	-4 650	-5 635	-4 888	-5 173	-5 065	-4 431	-4.7
321114 – Treated wood products, n.e.s.o.i.	80	59	65	30	12	42	-47.2
321211 – Hardwood veneer and plywood	-569	-679	-653	-612	-767	-750	31.8
321212 – Softwood veneer and plywood	77	-80	-65	-191	-273	-416	-639.2
321213 – Engineered wood (excluding truss)	-339	-597	-464	-508	-674	-789	132.8
321214 – Truss (imports only)	-39	-71	-76	-71	-76	-96	142.7
321219 – Reconstituted wood products	-1 337	-1 831	-1 689	-1 551	-1 716	-2 800	109.4
321911 – Wood windows and doors	-190	-283	-367	-440	-497	-505	165.4
321918 – Other millwork (including flooring)	-389	-585	-582	-563	-658	-674	73.3
321920 – Wood containers and pallets	-176	-168	-205	-245	-297	-272	54.7
321991 – Mobile homes and trailers	21	7	17	8	-6	-1	-103.1
321992 – Prefabricated wood buildings	-3	-34	-56	-91	-118	-113	4 231.3
321999 – Miscellaneous wood products	-1 123	-1 247	-1 408	-1 464	-1 641	-1 745	55.4
322110 – Pulp mill products	414	329	312	298	553	287	-30.6
322121 – Paper (except newsprint) mill products	1 184	724	596	360	-448	-510	-143.0
322122 – Newsprint mill products	-4 852	-4 775	-5 077	-5 139	-4 589	-4 532	-6.6
322130 – Paperboard mill products	-21	-70	-55	-60	-44	-42	96.8
322211 – Corrugated and solid fiber boxes	740	761	804	710	715	723	-2.3
322212 – Folding paperboard boxes	-85	-85	-99	-66	-181	-244	189.1
322213 – Setup paperboard boxes	28	34	37	31	15	-6	-121.5
322214 – Fiber can, tube, drum and similar products	35	34	26	19	17	25	-27.5
322215 – Nonfolding sanitary food containers	163	164	189	181	170	172	5.4
322222 – Coated and laminated paper	725	799	866	860	1 132	1 220	68.3
322223 – Foil and coated paper and plastic bags	-334	-389	-550	-640	-734	-948	183.9
322224 – Uncoated paper and multiwall bags	6	-7	-6	-16	-27	-21	-476.0
322232 – Envelopes	34	33	24	20	18	14	-59.7
322233 – Stationery, tablets and related products	-118	-193	-346	-361	252	180	-252.8
322291 – Sanitary paper products	230	301	193	167	-46	-125	-154.3
322299 – All other converted paper products	61	37	-27	-49	-239	-117	-293.3
323116 – Manifold business forms	11	8	6	5	-1	-1	-110.1
323117 – Books printing	624	524	416	278	223	160	-74.4
323118 – Blankbook, binders and stationery articles, n.e.s.o.i.	-361	-435	-505	-440	-553	-606	67.8
323119 – Printed matter, n.e.s.o.i.	1 197	964	947	1 110	651	713	-40.4
323122 – Printing type, plates, cylinders, etc., n.e.s.o.i.	9	16	37	32	20	18	98.6
324110 – Petroleum refinery products	-5 121	-7 757	-16 499	-16 033	-13 821	-18 328	257.9
324121 – Asphalt paving mixtures	-10	-8	-16	-5	-17	-14	38.3
324122 – Asphalt shingle and coating materials	29	59	65	52	69	79	174.8
325110 – Petrochemicals	-34	26	-69	-161	-121	-245	626.1
325120 – Industrial gases	80	64	120	118	64	79	-1.1
325131 – Inorganic dyes and pigments	234	195	340	304	367	495	111.6
325132 – Synthetic organic dyes and pigments	-271	-257	-117	-50	-130	-165	-39.0
325181 – Alkalies and chlorine	647	662	705	841	687	696	7.5
325182 – Carbon black	45	51	80	33	-12	27	-40.8
325188 – All other basic inorganic chemicals	140	-148	-27	-70	164	-466	-432.3
325191 – Gum and wood chemicals	40	45	44	53	20	29	-26.4
325192 – Cyclic crude and intermediates	851	1 149	1 395	617	917	1 600	88.1
325193 – Ethyl alcohols	-66	-72	-69	-51	-98	-88	33.4
325199 – All other basic organic chemicals	2 925	2 946	3 537	2 002	1 893	3 226	10.3
325211 – Plastics materials and resins	5 872	5 717	6 811	6 530	6 819	6 923	17.9
325212 – Synthetic rubbers	634	633	850	798	835	1 045	64.8
325221 – Cellulose organic fibers	399	354	397	431	390	398	-0.2
325222 – Noncellulosic organic fibers	32	-84	-65	-323	-285	-254	-901.2
325311 – Nitrogenous fertilizers	2 114	1 979	987	356	882	54	-97.5
325312 – Phosphatic fertilizers	-855	-804	-833	-818	-856	-905	5.9
325320 – Pesticides and other agricultural chemicals	1 431	1 213	1 187	1 206	1 171	968	-32.4
325411 – Medicinal and botanical drugs and vitamins	-5 152	-8 608	-12 968	-13 943	-14 941	-16 325	216.9
325412 – Pharmaceutical preparations	-1 542	-1 762	-711	-1 860	-7 555	-10 971	611.4
325414 – Biological products (excluding diagnostic)	1 146	716	752	595	752	791	-31.0
325510 – Paints and coatings	814	723	806	766	894	913	12.2
325520 – Adhesives	424	433	533	509	514	480	13.0
325611 – Soaps and other detergents	578	534	518	564	476	557	-3.6
325612 – Polishes and other sanitation goods	123	130	133	167	218	226	83.5
325613 – Surface active agents	664	809	850	783	779	860	29.5
325620 – Perfumes, makeups and other toiletries	849	636	662	813	505	447	-47.4
325910 – Printing inks	91	224	316	191	197	259	185.2
325920 – Explosives and accessories	130	87	118	65	91	176	34.7
325992 – Photo films, papers, plates and chemicals	224	218	810	394	783	989	341.1
325998 – All other miscellaneous chemical products and preparations (including natural)	1 240	1 100	1 271	1 283	1 315	1 217	-1.8
326112 – Reinforced plastics packaging films and sheets	-23	-36	-38	-23	-29	-61	169.9
326113 – Not reinforced plastics plates, sheets, etc. (excluding packaging)	884	743	918	835	688	564	-36.3
326121 – Plastics rods, sticks and profile shapes	-28	-72	-26	-36	-1	52	-289.6
326122 – Plastics tubes, hoses, pipes and pipe fittings	87	29	180	151	162	181	109.4
326160 – Plastics bottles	27	19	34	19	21	2	-92.0
326191 – Plastics plumbing fixtures	-48	-77	-76	-61	-72	-80	67.1
326192 – Plastic floor coverings	-94	-139	-180	-220	-268	-313	232.5
326199 – All other plastics products	616	657	1 246	411	-482	-1 211	-296.5
326211 – Tires and tire parts (excluding retreadings)	-1 452	-2 112	-2 218	-1 795	-2 394	-2 923	101.3
326212 – Tire retreadings	10	10	0	4	0	-3	-130.6

Note: Unrevised data.

Table B-43. U.S. Total Trade Balances by 6-Digit NAICS Product Groups, 1998–2003—*Continued*

(Millions of dollars; Census basis; foreign and domestic exports, f.a.s.; general imports, Customs.)

NAICS product	1998	1999	2000	2001	2002	2003	Percent change, 1998–2003
326220 – Rubber and plastics hoses and belting	276	161	265	192	8	-67	-124.2
326299 – Other rubber products	39	29	95	-2	-153	-280	-810.5
327111 – China plumb fixtures and china and earthen bath access	-158	-216	-239	-282	-353	-427	169.7
327112 – China, fine earthenware and other pottery products	-1 488	-1 489	-1 610	-1 432	-1 406	-1 507	1.3
327113 – Porcelain electrical supplies	-74	-74	-73	-73	-64	-90	21.8
327121 – Brick and structural ceramics	10	3	0	1	3	3	-64.3
327122 – Ceramic wall and floor tiles	-830	-990	-1 085	-1 078	-1 257	-1 397	68.3
327123 – Other structural ceramic products	-3	-8	-11	-9	-15	-15	438.3
327124 – Clay and alumina articles	43	-38	-104	22	20	3	-92.6
327125 – Nonclay refractory articles	66	86	86	105	58	31	-53.2
327211 – Drawn, blown, float and flat glass	238	164	240	177	200	214	-9.8
327212 – Other pressed and blown glass and glassware	-779	-951	-712	-572	-780	-806	3.4
327213 – Glass containers	-273	-346	-403	-320	-436	-433	58.6
327215 – Glass products, n.e.s.o.i.	330	302	601	777	168	88	-73.4
327310 – Cements	-904	-1 086	-1 006	-926	-877	-872	-3.5
327320 – Wet, nonrefractory mortars and concretes	-1	0	1	0	1	1	-248.6
327331 – Concrete bricks and blocks	-12	-27	-27	-24	-28	-48	295.2
327390 – Other concrete products	-331	-465	-664	-704	-773	-757	128.5
327410 – Lime and calcined dolomite	-13	-8	-4	-3	-6	-8	-39.9
327420 – Gypsum products	-88	-254	-57	-31	3	18	-120.4
327910 – Abrasive products	-347	-325	-425	-252	-288	-324	-6.5
327991 – Cut stone and stone products	-832	-980	-1 236	-1 349	-1 502	-1 772	113.0
327992 – Ground or treated mineral and earth	-23	-21	-17	31	16	14	-161.2
327993 – Mineral wool and glass fibers	172	81	120	97	62	69	-59.8
327999 – All other miscellaneous nonmetallic mineral products	-2	-56	-2	31	30	5	-308.5
331111 – Iron and steel	-12 247	-8 665	-10 297	-7 027	-7 801	-5 061	-58.7
331112 – Electrometallurgical ferroalloy product	-1 038	-980	-1 142	-719	-846	-1 072	3.2
331222 – Steel wire drawing	-690	-729	-770	-672	-789	-871	26.1
331311 – Alumina refining	-390	-370	-392	-214	-208	-134	-65.7
331312 – Primary aluminum	-3 205	-3 366	-3 604	-3 609	-3 768	-4 039	26.0
331314 – Secondary smelting and alloying of aluminum	30	26	35	26	28	33	8.9
331315 – Aluminum sheets, plates and foils	976	827	700	625	283	214	-78.0
331316 – Aluminum extruded products	-12	-80	-91	-4	-98	-144	1 150.1
331319 – Other aluminum rolling and drawing	171	151	79	53	-24	-123	-171.5
331411 – Primary smelting and refining of copper	-1 505	-1 731	-2 009	-2 258	-1 832	-1 241	-17.5
331419 – Other nonferrous metals primary smelting, refining	-2 583	-3 075	-4 516	-3 963	-3 571	-2 854	10.5
331421 – Copper rolling, drawing and extruding	-127	-181	-382	-336	-266	-190	49.5
331422 – Copper wire (except mechanical) drawing	399	131	96	110	107	15	-96.3
331491 – Other nonferrous metals roll, draw, extruding	-68	-125	208	521	645	692	-1 120.3
331492 – Other nonferrous secondary smelt, refine, alloying	-220	-148	-219	-2	102	81	-136.7
331511 – Iron foundries	16	53	-51	-38	-66	-48	-393.9
332115 – Crowns, closures, seals and other packing accessories	161	134	117	103	66	32	-80.0
332211 – Cutlery and flatware (excluding precious)	-273	-253	-376	-357	-393	-532	95.0
332212 – Hand and edge tools	-602	-617	-666	-694	-846	-926	54.0
332213 – Saw blades and handsaws	-131	-140	-133	-98	-160	-192	46.6
332214 – Kitchen utensils, pots and pans	-322	-368	-393	-380	-413	-453	40.5
332311 – Prefab metal buildings and components	145	88	109	88	82	92	-36.7
332312 – Fabricated structural metals	-82	-236	-467	-674	-804	-628	662.8
332321 – Metal windows and doors	-72	-130	-215	-227	-268	-300	317.7
332322 – Sheet metal works	44	35	23	24	20	17	-62.3
332323 – Ornamental and architectural metal works	-44	-54	-67	-97	-64	-81	83.2
332410 – Power boilers and heat exchangers	655	432	-24	-175	-531	52	-92.1
332420 – Metal tanks (heavy gauge)	256	141	185	71	-63	-271	-206.1
332431 – Metal cans	51	-13	6	25	41	-6	-112.1
332439 – Other metal containers	71	33	8	-11	-24	-64	-189.7
332510 – Hardware	-1 013	-1 018	-951	-954	-1 252	-1 590	57.0
332611 – Springs (heavy gauge)	-380	-529	-522	-440	-504	-488	28.4
332618 – Other fabricated wire products	-358	-366	-280	-364	-361	-394	10.1
332722 – Bolts, nuts, screws, rivets, washers, and other turned products	-532	-455	-565	-437	-511	-738	38.8
332911 – Industrial valves	-747	-764	-988	-751	-1 123	-1 147	53.6
332912 – Fluid power valves and hose fittings	9	-17	-56	10	-90	-143	-1 659.4
332913 – Plumbing fixtures fittings and trim	-327	-493	-570	-584	-619	-652	99.4
332919 – Other metal valves and pipe fittings	223	87	83	29	-17	74	-66.9
332991 – Ball and roller bearings	-605	-441	-477	-301	-224	-233	-61.6
332992 – Small arms ammunition	1 422	1 400	1 220	1 284	1 256	976	-31.3
332994 – Small arms	-143	-248	-332	-366	-362	-427	198.7
332995 – Other ordnances and accessories	600	305	456	413	247	160	-73.4
332997 – Industrial patterns	54	50	64	19	10	22	-60.0
332998 – Enameled iron and metal sanitary wares	-82	-107	-124	-151	-214	-244	196.1
332999 – Other miscellaneous fabricated metal products	-789	-805	-406	-969	-1 466	-1 926	144.1
333111 – Farm machinery and equipment	1 540	1 090	956	802	826	602	-60.9
333120 – Construction machinery	-520	-965	321	514	-486	-1 199	130.7
333131 – Mining machinery and equipment	759	440	511	499	402	454	-40.2
333132 – Oil and gas field machinery and equipment	6 269	3 902	4 021	4 887	5 297	4 738	-24.4
333210 – Sawmill and woodworking machinery	-633	-716	-747	-603	-616	-737	16.3

Note: Unrevised data.

Table B-43. U.S. Total Trade Balances by 6-Digit NAICS Product Groups, 1998–2003—*Continued*

(Millions of dollars; Census basis; foreign and domestic exports, f.a.s.; general imports, Customs.)

NAICS product	1998	1999	2000	2001	2002	2003	Percent change, 1998–2003
333220 – Plastics and rubber industry machinery	-919	-1 066	-687	-301	-540	-808	-12.1
333291 – Paper industry machinery	-197	-233	-301	-373	-122	-188	-4.6
333292 – Textile machinery	-1 084	-678	-436	-82	46	20	-101.9
333293 – Printing machinery and equipment	-674	-835	-412	-572	-486	-534	-20.7
333294 – Food product machinery	173	92	213	156	149	-42	-124.2
333295 – Semiconductor machinery	1 348	2 804	5 058	1 374	962	1 199	-11.1
333298 – Other miscellaneous industrial machinery	27	12	23	30	-50	-92	-440.6
333311 – Automatic vending machines	200	132	97	115	46	13	-93.7
333313 – Office machinery	-1 051	-969	-1 040	-695	-1 325	-4 392	317.7
333314 – Optical instruments and lenses	461	-19	364	865	1 523	1 585	243.4
333315 – Photographic and photocopying equipment	-3 665	-3 356	-2 991	-1 471	-1 437	-1 395	-61.9
333319 – Other commercial, service industry machinery	131	90	95	124	103	13	-90.2
333411 – Air purification equipment	92	44	-9	-38	-64	-123	-234.0
333412 – Industrial and commercial fans and blowers	-193	-254	-361	-286	-321	-301	55.9
333414 – Heating equipment (excluding warm air furnaces)	47	-112	-188	-163	-181	-287	-716.2
333415 – AC, warm air heating and commercial refrigeration equipment	2 802	2 414	2 189	1 938	1 247	488	-82.6
333511 – Industrial molds	-400	-494	-403	-320	-577	-657	64.2
333512 – Machine tools (metal cutting types)	-2 204	-1 587	-1 278	-956	-504	-579	-73.7
333513 – Machine tools (metal forming types)	-342	-319	-554	-577	-67	-126	-63.0
333514 – Special dies, tools, die sets, jigs and fixtures	-260	-288	-193	-202	-259	-452	73.7
333515 – Cutting tools and machine tool accessories	-145	-118	-208	-157	-127	-173	20.0
333516 – Rolling mill machinery and equipment	-183	-127	-46	71	57	-1	-99.5
333611 – Turbines and turbine generator sets	2 729	2 084	937	123	520	1 298	-52.4
333612 – Speed changers, industrial high-speed drives, gears	-635	-1 102	-842	-810	-856	-883	39.0
333613 – Mechanical power transmission equipment	-185	-255	-210	-194	-255	-323	74.5
333618 – Other engine equipment	1 506	1 222	1 412	1 214	1 378	370	-75.4
333911 – Pumps and pumping equipment	526	485	555	616	459	254	-51.8
333912 – Air and gas compressors	434	404	489	641	546	504	16.3
333913 – Measuring and dispensing pumps	224	172	148	148	159	169	-24.2
333921 – Elevators and moving stairways	-68	-96	-113	-152	-161	-154	126.7
333922 – Conveyors and conveying equipment	121	172	-10	-8	-183	-293	-342.9
333923 – Overhead cranes, hoists and monorail systems	-208	-243	-143	-168	-271	-235	13.0
333924 – Industrial trucks, tractors, trailers, stacker machinery	-227	-248	-360	-29	-140	-332	46.3
333991 – Power-driven handtools	-581	-782	-957	-991	-1 368	-1 732	198.1
333992 – Welding and soldering equipment	232	524	450	120	46	-42	-118.1
333993 – Packaging machinery	-222	-309	-376	-525	-623	-787	255.2
333994 – Industrial furnaces and ovens	395	465	669	480	352	416	5.2
333995 – Fluid power cylinders and actuators	-58	-154	-203	-184	-147	-202	246.4
333996 – Fluid power pumps and motors	17	29	-5	68	12	-91	-645.5
333997 – Scales and balances (except laboratory)	-66	-111	-116	-90	-113	-203	209.6
333999 – Other miscellaneous general purpose machinery	3 199	3 103	4 508	4 069	2 975	2 238	-30.0
334111 – Electronic computers	1 834	-939	-2 764	-2 263	-7 005	-11 746	-740.4
334112 – Computer storage devices	-12 624	-11 448	-11 280	-8 903	-8 549	-8 030	-36.4
334119 – Other computer equipment	598	-2 897	307	-1 007	-8 659	-4 670	-880.8
334210 – Telephone apparatus	396	221	-1 156	2 290	66	-1 420	-458.9
334220 – Radio, TV broadcast and wireless communication equipment	1 341	-1 562	-8 184	-10 619	-12 395	-14 829	-1 205.9
334290 – Other communications equipment	-228	-186	-191	-179	-245	-217	-4.6
334310 – Audio and video equipment	-17 141	-19 402	-23 120	-21 953	-25 667	-26 883	56.8
334411 – Picture, microwave, amp, electron, cathode and sim tubes	1 533	1 539	1 946	1 572	1 357	800	-47.8
334412 – Printed circuits	154	295	67	183	273	194	25.7
334413 – Semiconductors and related devices	3 788	8 780	10 997	13 391	15 232	20 692	446.3
334414 – Electronic capacitors and parts	285	228	499	292	322	414	45.5
334415 – Electronic resistors and parts	-50	23	-24	41	-54	-21	-58.9
334416 – Electronic coils, transformers, other inductors	-594	-592	-752	-389	-318	-287	-51.8
334417 – Electronic connectors	93	14	232	665	513	375	302.8
334418 – Printed circuit assemblies (electronic assemblies)	-17 603	-21 841	-25 507	-17 967	-15 974	-16 804	-4.5
334419 – Other electronic components	-2 303	-2 581	-2 557	-521	-1 623	-1 590	-31.0
334510 – Electromedical apparatus	1 646	1 605	1 380	1 373	157	-529	-132.1
334511 – Search, detection and navigation instruments	1 410	1 331	1 211	1 529	2 037	1 710	21.3
334512 – Automatic environmental controls	-201	-230	-282	-371	-443	-470	133.7
334513 – Industrial process controls	449	451	454	495	132	53	-88.2
334514 – Total fluid meters and counting devices	51	44	39	22	80	45	-13.1
334515 – Electricity measuring, testing instruments	2 946	3 360	4 495	3 085	2 593	2 216	-24.8
334516 – Analytical laboratory instruments	1 267	1 264	1 011	1 022	926	1 100	-13.2
334517 – Irradiation apparatus	230	273	214	215	-39	11	-95.3
334518 – Watches, clocks and parts	-2 627	-2 609	-2 844	-2 490	-2 661	-2 982	13.5
334519 – Other measuring and controlling devices	1 397	1 138	1 212	1 338	965	1 045	-25.2
334612 – Prerecorded CDs, tapes, records	37	-29	-20	9	-4	36	-3.7
334613 – Unrecorded magnetic and optical media	188	-314	-787	-1 077	-1 463	-1 708	-1 008.3
335110 – Electric lamp bulbs and parts	-316	-431	-522	-838	-729	-797	151.9
335121 – Residential electric lighting fixtures	-1 077	-1 268	-1 486	-1 351	-1 616	-1 697	57.6
335129 – Lighting equipment, n.e.s.o.i.	-1 411	-1 930	-2 252	-2 032	-2 229	-2 341	65.9
335211 – Electric housewares and household fans	-2 437	-2 861	-3 369	-3 806	-4 292	-4 484	84.0
335212 – Household vacuum cleaner and floor polishers	-76	-88	-178	-310	-533	-929	1 128.8
335221 – Household cooking appliances	-1 292	-1 531	-1 839	-1 924	-2 170	-2 311	78.8

Note: Unrevised data.

Table B-43. U.S. Total Trade Balances by 6-Digit NAICS Product Groups, 1998–2003—*Continued*

(Millions of dollars; Census basis; foreign and domestic exports, f.a.s.; general imports, Customs.)

NAICS product	1998	1999	2000	2001	2002	2003	Percent change, 1998–2003
335222 – Household refrigerators and freezers	249	109	88	-186	-462	-539	-316.5
335224 – Household laundry equipment	281	198	237	288	136	-48	-117.1
335228 – Major appliances and miscellaneous machines, n.e.s.o.i.	-90	-107	117	-121	-275	-401	343.1
335311 – Power, distribution, specialty transformers	-419	-718	-1 011	-1 148	-1 169	-989	135.9
335312 – Motors and generators	-1 033	-2 069	-2 110	-1 846	-2 295	-2 366	129.0
335313 – Switchgear and switchboard apparatus	288	108	11	-123	-153	-141	-149.1
335314 – Relays and industrial controls	-607	-417	-663	-821	-1 062	-1 145	88.7
335911 – Storage batteries	-746	-958	-1 190	-935	-843	-795	6.5
335912 – Primary batteries	220	264	190	213	114	117	-46.8
335921 – Fiber optic cable	157	139	50	-60	56	43	-72.5
335929 – Communication and energy wire, n.e.s.o.i.	-509	-590	-141	-321	-541	-714	40.4
335931 – Current-carrying wiring devices	-74	213	368	263	181	89	-221.4
335932 – Noncurrent-carrying wiring devices	-3	44	36	13	66	45	-1 536.2
335991 – Carbon and graphite products	147	167	171	132	78	-1	-100.5
335999 – Miscellaneous electrical equipment and components, n.e.s.o.i.	875	633	1 062	510	375	118	-86.5
336111 – Autos and light duty motor vehicles, including chassis	-64 605	-79 938	-92 451	-88 648	-93 339	-92 071	42.5
336120 – Heavy duty trucks and chassis	-5 134	-11 216	-9 125	-11 412	-10 815	-9 200	79.2
336211 – Motor vehicle bodies	-174	-106	-251	-296	-282	-365	110.3
336212 – Truck trailers	293	88	175	-25	7	-70	-124.0
336213 – Motor homes	87	83	93	54	71	112	29.0
336214 – Transportation equipment, n.e.s.o.i., including trailers and campers	274	255	-347	211	265	444	61.7
33631X – Motor vehicle gasoline engines and engine parts	-4 470	-4 578	-4 306	-3 276	-4 112	-4 736	5.9
336321 – Vehicular lighting equipment	-80	-109	-151	-171	-394	-566	611.6
336322 – Motor vehicle electrical and electronic equipment, n.e.s.o.i.	-3 053	-3 950	-4 336	-4 239	-4 746	-5 101	67.1
336330 – Motor vehicle steering and suspension parts	-730	-1 018	-1 003	-1 048	-1 473	-1 822	149.6
336340 – Motor vehicle brake systems	-531	-657	-625	-638	-910	-1 109	108.8
336350 – Motor vehicle transmission and power train parts	-2 389	-3 436	-3 238	-3 023	-3 387	-4 251	78.0
336360 – Motor vehicle seating and interior trim	-932	-919	-727	-630	-1 224	-2 015	116.1
336370 – Motor vehicle metal stampings	918	1 002	1 098	1 024	1 078	1 124	22.6
336391 – Motor vehicle air-conditioning	-435	-567	-675	-638	-868	-1 007	131.8
336399 – Motor vehicle parts, n.e.s.o.i.	8 658	7 699	6 919	5 810	3 976	1 049	-87.9
336411 – Aircraft	28 735	24 480	12 780	13 324	15 676	11 897	-58.6
336412 – Aircraft engines and engine parts	1 925	3 204	4 185	3 576	4 622	5 759	199.2
336413 – Aircraft parts and auxiliary equipment, n.e.s.o.i.	9 514	9 774	9 944	10 266	9 482	10 137	6.5
336414 – Guided missiles and space vehicles	46	-34	-98	-64	6	-110	-338.5
336415 – Missile, space vehicle propulsion units and parts	11	2	-26	-34	2	-7	-167.5
336419 – Missile, space vehicle parts and auxiliary equipment, n.e.s.o.i.	104	63	-9	26	452	368	255.0
336510 – Railroad rolling stock	-463	-815	-424	143	95	566	-222.2
336611 – Ships	786	814	250	1 217	517	320	-59.2
336612 – Boats	-155	-257	-361	-506	-509	-331	112.8
336991 – Motorcycles, bicycles and parts	-1 476	-2 075	-2 901	-2 875	-3 004	-3 131	112.1
336992 – Military armored vehicles, tanks and tank components	691	621	482	548	470	401	-41.9
337110 – Wood kitchen cabinets and countertops	-302	-369	-439	-493	-540	-581	92.7
337121 – Upholstered household furniture	-564	-765	-1 031	-1 059	-1 340	-1 662	194.9
337124 – Metal household furniture	-1 032	-1 289	-1 472	-1 421	-1 613	-1 977	91.6
337127 – Institutional furniture	-4 561	-5 951	-7 056	-7 167	-8 651	-9 437	106.9
337129 – Wood sewing machine cabinets	-4	-4	-3	-4	-3	-5	28.0
337211 – Wood office furniture	-402	-470	-575	-456	-523	-623	55.1
337214 – Office furniture (except wood)	-195	-253	-358	-290	-235	-260	32.9
337215 – Showcases, partitions, shelvings and lockers	-737	-1 084	-1 196	-1 308	-1 697	-1 864	152.8
337910 – Mattresses	-3	-12	-15	-4	7	-16	447.8
337920 – Blinds and shades	-384	-412	-443	-483	-578	-671	74.7
339112 – Surgical and medical instruments	2 286	2 087	2 035	2 266	1 630	1 339	-41.4
339113 – Surgical appliances and supplies	148	301	602	456	413	239	61.9
339114 – Dental equipment and supplies	307	259	228	209	181	43	-86.0
339115 – Ophthalmic goods	-814	-754	-898	-783	-875	-1 066	31.0
339911 – Jewelry (except costume)	-3 361	-3 412	-3 896	-3 265	-3 870	-4 140	23.2
339912 – Silverware, platedware and hollowware	-476	-532	-605	-561	-611	-638	33.9
339913 – Jewelers' material and lapidary work	-6 441	-7 383	-8 671	-7 066	-8 164	-8 302	28.9
339914 – Costume jewelry and novelties	-436	-504	-623	-663	-764	-828	90.0
339920 – Sporting and athletic goods	-1 441	-1 568	-2 106	-2 191	-2 585	-2 854	98.1
339931 – Dolls and stuffed toys	-4 212	-4 034	-3 840	-3 481	-3 426	-3 410	-19.0
339932 – Games, toys and children's vehicles	-7 406	-7 718	-8 161	-9 377	-10 357	-9 325	25.9
339941 – Pens and mechanical pencils	-335	-495	-682	-585	-587	-627	87.3
339942 – Lead pencils and art goods	-156	-146	-186	-213	-247	-295	89.4
339943 – Marking devices	-45	-42	-43	-41	-38	-46	1.2
339944 – Carbon paper and inked ribbon	110	76	61	62	47	111	1.2
339950 – Signs	-10	-25	-16	-41	-55	-84	757.6
339991 – Gaskets, packing and sealing devices	-261	-242	-184	-167	-320	-355	36.3
339992 – Musical instruments	-654	-740	-877	-733	-789	-843	29.0
339993 – Fasteners, buttons, needles and pins	-81	-83	35	-9	22	5	-105.8
339994 – Brooms, brushes and mops	-318	-422	-395	-493	-602	-617	94.0
339999 – Miscellaneous manufactured commodities, n.e.s.o.i.	-3 071	-3 613	-4 028	-4 053	-4 202	-4 388	42.9
511210 – Software publishing	-214	-163	-162	-175	191	214	-199.8
910000 – Waste and scrap	1 813	1 913	3 258	3 236	3 551	4 756	162.3
920000 – Used or second-hand merchandise	-1 262	-2 576	-2 321	-1 257	-2 489	-1 316	4.3
980000 – Goods returned to Canada (exports only); U.S. goods returned and reimported (imports only)	-23 430	-29 185	-31 801	-32 795	-33 414	-31 780	35.6
990000 – Special classification provisions, n.e.s.o.i.	11 118	8 546	6 984	9 188	7 647	7 259	-34.7

Note: Unrevised data.

Table B-44. U.S. Shares of Other Nations' Imports, 1993–2003

(Percent of total.)

Importer	1993	1994	1995	1996	1997	1998	1999	2000	2001	2002	2003	Year of maximum
WORLD	12.9	12.8	12.4	12.8	13.5	13.6	13.2	12.8	12.2	11.2	10.0	1998
Afghanistan	2.2	1.5	1.1	2.8	2.1	1.6	4.0	1.9	1.1	8.7	4.8	2002
Albania	0.4	0.3	0.3	1.2	0.1	0.3	0.5	1.5	1.1	1.7	0.6	2002
Algeria	15.0	14.3	13.2	10.2	10.6	10.5	8.4	11.6	10.5	9.8	3.6	1993
Angola	12.8	15.4	15.1	14.2	12.2	17.5	12.4	11.0	8.6	13.2	12.1	1998
Antigua Barbuda	47.7	17.8	35.8	28.3	31.6	25.3	12.8	16.4	18.1	13.0	23.2	1993
Argentina	23.0	22.0	19.1	19.6	20.0	19.1	19.6	19.1	18.6	20.1	21.5	1993
Armenia	10.4	24.3	16.4	12.0	13.0	10.7	10.2	11.6	9.6	14.0	9.9	1994
Aruba	. . .	. . .	58.6	59.2	57.5	66.4	66.1	51.4	55.0	54.7	55.2	1998
Australia	21.5	22.0	21.9	23.3	22.1	22.4	21.1	20.1	18.4	18.3	16.0	1996
Austria	4.5	4.4	4.2	4.5	5.4	5.3	4.1	4.1	3.8	3.5	2.3	1997
Azerbaijan	1.9	1.3	2.0	1.7	2.8	3.7	8.0	10.0	16.1	5.9	5.2	2001
Bahamas	23.7	28.5	33.2	20.9	90.8	32.1	29.0	29.4	32.9	18.4	18.2	1997
Bahrain	16.6	10.8	8.1	6.7	10.5	8.4	11.5	12.7	13.0	11.4	11.2	1993
Bangladesh	4.3	4.7	6.1	3.6	4.2	3.3	5.3	2.4	2.9	3.0	2.6	1995
Barbados	38.2	40.8	40.9	43.5	45.4	41.8	41.0	41.5	42.1	41.1	37.7	1997
Belarus	3.5	1.7	1.8	2.2	1.6	1.5	1.9	1.6	1.6	0.2	0.8	1993
Belgium	. . .	. . .	. . .	. . .	7.7	7.7	7.5	7.6	7.0	6.4	5.9	1998
Belgium and Luxembourg	5.3	5.2	5.4	5.9	. . .	. . .	. . .	. . .	. . .	. . .	. . .	1996
Belize	56.6	53.2	54.1	55.1	51.8	49.4	52.6	50.3	39.4	12.0	39.1	1993
Benin	5.3	4.5	5.6	3.6	7.6	6.6	5.1	4.1	4.8	2.9	1.9	1997
Bermuda	70.2	36.2	71.6	72.7	28.4	32.3	11.7	11.0	8.2	8.3	7.6	1996
Bolivia	22.2	19.3	21.7	27.7	23.0	25.5	32.2	22.5	18.4	15.6	11.4	1999
Bosnia-Herzegovina	3.9	5.5	3.3	3.3	4.7	1.7	1.8	1.8	1.7	1.0	0.6	1994
Brazil	23.5	20.6	21.2	22.1	23.2	23.6	23.8	23.1	23.4	22.1	21.4	1999
Brunei	25.1	11.3	8.8	17.5	10.0	5.8	13.1	10.8	8.7	3.1	2.1	1993
Bulgaria	2.8	2.6	2.2	2.3	3.3	4.1	3.3	3.0	2.7	2.2	2.6	1998
Burkina (Upper Volta)	4.5	6.0	4.7	4.1	4.2	2.3	2.2	3.4	0.9	3.1	1.4	1994
Burundi	2.1	3.6	4.9	4.6	1.9	1.5	2.2	2.6	3.1	1.3	2.0	1995
Cambodia (Kampuchea)	2.0	0.7	1.9	1.4	2.4	3.5	3.1	2.3	1.1	1.3	2.2	1998
Cameroon	7.1	8.0	1.9	8.3	8.3	8.1	5.0	4.8	7.9	8.6	5.7	2002
Canada	65.0	65.8	66.7	67.4	67.5	68.0	67.0	64.4	63.7	62.6	60.6	1998
Cape Verde	10.8	2.2	3.0	21.9	9.9	5.7	5.2	4.5	3.2	3.2	2.8	1996
Central African Republic	1.3	1.8	2.5	2.2	3.0	3.2	2.5	2.0	2.9	4.9	5.4	2003
Chad	7.5	7.4	7.1	2.1	2.7	2.3	2.1	6.7	39.7	29.2	18.6	2001
Chile	22.6	22.7	24.5	21.0	20.5	20.3	18.8	17.8	16.1	14.9	13.0	1995
China	10.3	12.1	12.2	11.6	11.5	12.1	11.8	9.6	10.8	9.2	8.2	1995
Colombia	35.6	32.1	39.1	36.2	35.3	32.2	37.3	35.4	34.7	31.8	29.6	1995
Comoros	0.2	0.1	0.4	0.0	0.0	0.2	0.2	1.4	1.9	0.1	0.6	2001
Congo	5.4	9.9	9.7	4.3	8.9	9.1	7.2	9.4	8.9	4.9	6.8	1994
Costa Rica	47.2	44.4	45.3	46.4	31.2	28.8	25.8	23.6	22.9	35.3	33.4	1993
Croatia	2.6	3.3	2.7	2.7	2.9	3.3	3.1	2.9	3.2	2.7	2.4	1998
Cuba	0.2	0.3	0.2	0.2	0.4	0.1	0.2	0.1	0.2	5.3	8.3	2003
Cyprus	9.3	10.4	13.0	16.8	19.0	12.4	10.8	10.4	11.5	2.7	3.4	1997
Czech Republic	3.0	3.4	3.7	3.4	3.8	3.7	3.9	4.3	4.1	3.3	3.1	2000
Dem. Rep. of the Congo (Zaire)	5.0	4.5	6.3	6.0	4.2	4.3	3.6	1.4	2.7	3.3	3.0	1995
Denmark	4.8	5.1	4.9	5.1	5.0	5.0	4.5	4.3	4.4	3.9	2.9	1996
Djibouti	3.1	1.9	2.4	2.2	2.0	3.9	3.2	3.0	3.2	9.3	5.0	2002
Dominica	35.9	34.6	32.0	39.4	41.5	42.4	40.4	37.5	36.3	23.4	18.1	1998
Dominican Republic	38.7	21.1	16.5	10.5	62.0	65.3	65.2	60.5	58.6	51.0	49.5	1998
Ecuador	31.7	26.2	30.8	31.5	30.5	30.1	32.2	28.4	27.4	26.6	23.1	1999
Egypt	15.0	17.1	18.8	20.0	13.1	12.6	14.4	17.0	14.4	16.1	13.4	1996
El Salvador	43.8	48.6	44.2	40.0	41.4	38.5	37.3	35.1	34.3	38.4	36.4	1994
Equatorial Guinea	5.6	3.2	4.3	11.8	25.7	34.7	58.2	33.3	27.9	27.3	31.0	1999
Estonia	2.7	2.5	2.5	2.3	3.7	4.6	4.4	2.3	2.3	2.8	2.9	1998
Ethiopia	9.5	12.3	12.8	5.3	4.6	5.5	4.7	9.0	4.2	3.7	16.6	2003
Falkland Islands	0.0	0.0	0.7	0.2	0.2	3.7	0.0	0.2	0.7	0.8	1.4	1998
Faroe Islands	2.9	1.4	0.1	0.6	0.2	1.0	0.0	0.8	4.3	1.1	2.5	2001
Fiji	7.6	14.4	9.7	9.3	5.2	4.7	14.0	3.4	2.8	2.2	2.2	1994
Finland	7.2	7.6	6.5	7.3	7.4	8.3	5.6	4.8	4.2	3.7	3.7	1998
France	8.7	8.3	7.5	7.8	8.5	8.7	8.0	7.4	7.4	6.8	5.4	1998
French Guiana	2.6	2.9	3.3	11.6	. . .	. . .	. . .	. . .	. . .	. . .	. . .	1996
French Polynesia	15.4	12.7	10.0	11.7	14.5	12.6	12.0	11.2	9.3	6.5	5.8	1993
Gabon	5.8	11.8	6.4	10.4	7.5	6.3	3.4	5.1	5.6	6.3	5.3	1994
Georgia	1.1	1.5	3.8	4.8	13.2	12.2	8.5	10.1	11.9	10.7	10.9	1997
Germany	7.3	7.4	7.1	7.3	7.7	8.3	8.3	8.6	8.3	7.7	7.3	2000
Ghana	11.4	6.6	6.7	10.0	10.3	7.2	8.1	6.5	7.2	6.5	5.6	1993
Gibraltar	1.3	2.8	2.6	1.1	0.5	0.8	0.3	0.7	0.7	1.6	0.9	1994
Greece	4.1	3.5	3.2	3.3	3.4	4.0	5.4	3.2	3.5	4.7	5.2	1999
Greenland	4.0	3.3	2.4	3.6	3.1	2.1	0.7	0.4	1.2	1.0	0.7	1993
Grenada	34.8	35.0	41.5	42.4	41.1	40.0	41.9	44.8	32.2	29.9	29.3	2000

Note: U.S. share equals a nation's merchandise imports from the United States divided by its imports from the world. China's values (from the IMF) differ significantly from values derived from U.S. data. The United States and China differ considerably on treatment of trade moving through Hong Kong.

. . . = Not available.

Table B-44. U.S. Shares of Other Nations' Imports, 1993–2003—*Continued*

(Percent of total.)

Importer	1993	1994	1995	1996	1997	1998	1999	2000	2001	2002	2003	Year of maximum
Guadeloupe	3.3	2.2	2.4	2.1	. . .	. . .	. . .	. . .	. . .	. . .	. . .	1993
Guatemala	46.1	44.1	44.9	44.8	41.1	38.4	35.4	35.1	34.2	34.3	33.3	1993
Guinea	8.7	8.1	7.0	7.6	8.2	8.6	6.1	5.6	7.1	8.3	4.5	1993
Guinea-Bissau	1.3	0.7	0.6	6.9	3.4	1.2	1.1	0.6	0.9	2.4	0.9	1996
Guyana	26.6	30.6	30.0	24.2	24.2	25.2	25.4	27.0	22.5	25.1	19.7	1994
Haiti	55.7	60.8	62.2	58.0	55.8	57.7	57.8	50.0	51.2	52.4	52.4	1995
Honduras	45.6	37.4	42.9	46.6	48.1	46.2	57.7	55.4	53.7	53.2	52.1	1999
Hong Kong	7.4	7.1	7.7	7.9	7.8	7.5	7.1	6.8	6.7	5.7	5.5	1996
Hungary	4.0	3.1	3.1	3.5	3.8	3.9	3.5	3.8	4.2	3.7	2.0	2001
Iceland	9.3	8.9	8.3	9.4	9.6	10.5	10.9	11.0	11.4	10.9	7.5	2001
India	10.2	9.5	9.7	8.8	9.1	8.7	7.5	6.3	7.2	6.9	6.7	1993
Indonesia	11.5	11.2	11.7	11.8	13.1	12.9	11.8	10.1	10.4	8.5	8.3	1997
Iran	4.1	2.9	3.9	0.5	0.2	0.0	0.0	0.1	0.5	0.3	0.4	1993
Iraq	0.8	0.2	0.0	0.5	7.9	6.3	1.0	0.3	0.9	0.6	7.4	1997
Ireland	17.4	18.5	17.9	15.8	15.0	16.2	15.6	16.2	15.0	15.3	15.8	1994
Israel	17.4	18.0	18.7	20.0	18.8	19.6	20.3	18.1	20.1	18.5	19.7	1999
Italy	5.3	4.6	4.8	4.9	5.0	5.0	4.9	5.3	4.9	4.9	4.0	1993
Ivory Coast	5.1	6.6	5.4	5.7	6.1	4.5	4.9	3.2	4.8	3.4	3.2	1994
Jamaica	55.5	53.7	54.1	56.0	50.8	51.3	49.2	47.2	45.4	44.0	39.3	1996
Japan	23.2	23.0	22.6	22.9	22.4	24.0	21.7	19.1	18.3	17.4	15.6	1998
Jordan	12.4	9.7	9.2	9.6	9.6	9.6	10.0	9.9	8.1	7.9	7.7	1993
Kazakhstan	4.4	3.3	1.7	1.6	4.7	6.2	9.5	5.5	5.4	7.0	2.0	1999
Kenya	5.8	7.3	3.9	5.3	7.4	7.9	6.7	9.4	16.7	8.1	5.2	2001
Kiribati (Gilbert Islands)	39.2	28.4	3.2	4.3	3.4	4.2	14.7	9.3	13.3	4.9	2.9	1993
Korea, South	20.7	21.1	22.5	22.2	20.7	21.9	20.8	18.2	15.9	15.2	14.2	1995
Kuwait	15.8	14.5	16.1	16.7	13.7	15.4	12.3	12.1	12.9	12.8	15.0	1996
Laos	1.0	0.2	0.3	0.2	0.1	0.6	0.1	0.7	0.6	0.6	0.6	1993
Latvia	1.2	2.0	1.9	2.3	2.4	2.0	2.0	2.0	1.8	1.6	2.0	1997
Lebanon	9.0	8.8	9.6	10.9	9.2	9.3	8.1	7.3	7.2	5.6	4.4	1996
Liberia	0.4	0.8	0.8	1.4	1.2	0.9	1.5	0.9	0.9	0.6	0.8	1999
Libya	0.0	0.0	0.0	0.0	0.0	1.4	0.0	0.5	0.2	0.4	0.0	1998
Lithuania	4.5	2.0	1.9	2.1	2.9	2.9	3.8	2.4	3.1	2.8	3.0	1993
Luxembourg	. . .	. . .	. . .	. . .	5.7	4.4	8.8	3.4	4.9	3.9	2.2	1999
Macao	5.8	6.8	7.3	5.9	5.8	4.7	5.0	4.5	4.2	4.1	2.5	1995
Macedonia	2.2	3.3	3.4	4.2	4.7	5.3	4.0	4.0	3.1	1.0	1.3	1998
Madagascar	6.4	4.5	3.9	4.2	4.5	3.9	3.9	17.1	15.5	18.8	5.4	2002
Malawi	3.4	3.5	2.6	2.6	3.2	2.8	1.5	2.5	3.2	5.4	2.7	2002
Malaysia	16.9	16.6	16.3	15.5	16.8	19.6	17.4	16.6	16.1	16.5	12.1	1998
Maldive Islands	0.9	0.4	0.4	1.2	1.5	0.9	2.0	2.2	2.1	1.3	1.3	2000
Mali	4.9	2.9	2.6	1.8	2.5	2.3	2.6	3.0	2.6	0.9	2.3	1993
Malta and Gozo	8.7	5.1	6.0	6.9	7.9	7.9	8.4	10.6	6.0	4.6	3.7	2000
Martinique	2.9	2.7	2.9	2.1	. . .	. . .	. . .	. . .	. . .	. . .	. . .	1993
Mauritania	3.7	2.7	7.2	2.8	3.2	3.6	4.7	2.7	4.0	2.9	3.7	1995
Mauritius	2.3	2.3	2.6	3.1	2.9	3.3	3.3	2.9	3.1	3.2	1.2	1999
Mexico	71.2	71.8	74.5	75.6	74.8	74.5	74.1	73.1	67.6	63.2	61.8	1996
Moldova	2.3	2.9	1.3	3.1	3.5	3.0	3.8	6.2	3.1	4.6	2.5	2000
Mongolia	4.5	4.4	3.5	2.5	7.8	7.2	6.1	4.6	2.3	3.4	2.6	1997
Morocco	10.1	7.7	5.9	6.6	5.7	7.3	4.8	4.6	3.7	4.6	3.1	1993
Mozambique	2.9	5.0	6.7	4.1	3.6	4.9	3.7	3.5	3.0	5.2	3.9	1995
Myanmar	. . .	. . .	. . .	1.3	0.8	1.5	0.5	0.6	0.5	0.4	0.2	1998
Nauru	70.8	0.4	1.6	0.0	4.2	4.4	4.1	20.6	18.1	10.2	7.1	1993
Nepal	1.1	1.3	1.4	1.0	0.9	1.5	2.0	2.8	1.7	2.5	1.8	2000
Netherlands	8.7	8.3	8.9	9.1	9.8	9.9	9.4	10.2	9.9	9.1	8.0	2000
New Caledonia	5.4	4.6	4.2	4.6	5.3	4.0	6.1	3.5	3.9	4.4	3.6	1999
New Zealand	18.0	19.2	18.7	16.7	17.8	19.0	16.7	17.4	16.1	13.6	11.8	1994
Nicaragua	26.2	24.4	29.9	31.9	36.4	31.4	34.2	25.0	27.5	23.6	22.6	1997
Niger	4.4	3.3	5.6	5.4	5.6	6.4	3.3	1.8	5.7	5.1	5.5	1998
Nigeria	12.9	10.3	11.4	13.3	12.8	11.8	9.2	8.8	9.0	9.0	7.7	1996
Norway	8.3	7.4	6.7	6.6	6.7	7.6	7.4	6.9	6.9	6.2	3.9	1993
Oman	8.1	6.7	6.5	7.5	8.0	7.0	6.4	4.1	5.8	6.9	5.6	1993
Pakistan	9.3	9.8	9.3	10.6	11.8	9.8	6.4	6.1	5.6	6.4	5.8	1997
Panama	36.8	39.3	40.6	44.1	37.3	40.1	35.4	32.9	29.5	34.3	12.8	1996
Papua New Guinea	3.8	4.6	3.9	4.0	6.6	5.4	3.6	2.1	2.2	2.1	2.4	1997
Paraguay	13.9	11.8	12.3	10.9	16.8	20.4	20.3	16.4	16.4	21.9	20.9	2002
Peru	30.1	28.2	26.7	30.7	31.8	32.5	31.6	29.2	29.7	27.0	28.6	1998
Philippines	20.0	18.5	18.5	19.7	19.5	22.2	20.7	18.6	19.4	20.6	17.9	1998
Poland	5.2	3.9	3.9	4.4	4.5	3.8	3.6	4.4	3.4	3.3	1.2	1993
Portugal	3.1	3.6	3.3	3.2	3.2	2.8	2.8	3.1	3.8	2.2	1.9	2001
Qatar	11.6	11.3	10.6	11.4	11.1	14.0	11.4	10.3	13.7	8.4	8.4	1998
Republic of South Africa	13.2	16.2	11.9	12.9	12.4	13.1	13.7	11.9	11.5	9.5	8.3	1994

Note: U.S. share equals a nation's merchandise imports from the United States divided by its imports from the world. China's values (from the IMF) differ significantly from values derived from U.S. data. The United States and China differ considerably on treatment of trade moving through Hong Kong.

. . . = Not available.

Table B-44. U.S. Shares of Other Nations' Imports, 1993–2003—*Continued*

(Percent of total.)

Importer	1993	1994	1995	1996	1997	1998	1999	2000	2001	2002	2003	Year of maximum
Reunion	0.2	1.9	0.6	0.1	. . .	. . .	. . .	. . .	. . .	. . .	. . .	1994
Romania	5.7	6.5	4.0	3.8	4.0	4.2	3.5	3.0	3.2	3.0	2.0	1994
Russia	8.6	5.4	5.7	6.5	7.8	9.4	7.9	8.0	8.7	6.4	4.6	1998
Rwanda	2.8	16.1	14.9	12.7	11.8	8.6	18.3	7.9	6.9	3.7	2.5	1999
SACCA, excluding South Africa	. . .	. . .	. . .	. . .	. . .	5.5	9.9	16.0	16.4	16.1	16.0	2001
Sao Tome and Principe	6.7	26.2	4.5	0.6	34.6	21.1	0.6	2.5	21.9	3.5	2.7	1997
Saudi Arabia	20.6	21.3	21.4	21.9	22.4	21.3	18.9	19.2	15.4	11.0	9.5	1997
Senegal	5.6	4.9	5.6	5.3	4.8	5.6	4.1	3.9	4.2	5.4	3.6	1998
Seychelles	7.7	3.8	3.8	26.4	2.1	3.3	1.7	1.8	26.3	1.4	0.9	1996
Sierra Leone	9.2	10.4	8.0	10.6	7.3	13.2	7.9	6.2	7.1	5.6	5.4	1998
Singapore	16.3	15.2	15.1	16.4	16.9	18.5	17.1	15.1	16.5	14.3	14.1	1998
Slovakia	1.8	2.8	2.5	2.7	3.1	2.9	2.6	2.1	1.9	2.1	0.5	1997
Slovenia	2.7	2.5	3.0	3.5	3.0	2.9	3.0	3.0	2.9	2.9	1.0	1996
Solomon Islands	2.2	0.9	1.9	4.7	1.3	2.1	1.1	5.2	7.2	2.0	1.7	2001
Somalia	11.5	11.1	3.6	1.6	1.1	1.1	1.1	1.6	2.1	1.9	2.0	1993
Spain	6.9	7.3	6.4	6.3	6.3	5.6	4.8	4.6	4.2	3.7	3.1	1994
Sri Lanka (Ceylon)	3.3	6.7	3.9	4.2	3.5	3.7	3.5	3.8	4.6	3.6	2.2	1994
St. Christopher-Nevis	47.8	46.3	36.4	43.1	36.7	38.2	58.6	56.9	43.6	39.3	35.7	1999
St. Helena	23.8	17.7	1.3	32.3	6.6	0.4	0.6	1.3	11.7	5.3	5.7	1996
St. Lucia	40.6	39.4	38.1	37.0	39.3	40.4	42.8	40.9	18.0	18.5	19.3	1999
St. Pierre and Miquelon	0.8	0.5	1.2	3.7	3.1	6.8	2.2	1.7	0.6	0.7	0.0	1998
St. Vincent and Grenadines	36.9	35.8	37.2	38.8	41.2	40.0	38.4	38.2	12.5	11.2	10.4	1997
Sudan	5.0	5.2	3.8	4.3	2.7	0.5	0.5	1.2	1.0	0.6	1.0	1994
Suriname	40.7	45.9	42.3	37.2	31.7	36.9	32.8	30.1	26.9	22.7	30.5	1994
Sweden	9.6	9.2	5.4	5.8	6.0	5.8	6.3	6.7	5.4	4.8	3.9	1993
Switzerland	6.5	6.6	6.4	7.1	8.4	7.3	7.1	7.8	6.7	6.6	8.1	1997
Syria	6.4	6.0	6.8	7.3	6.5	4.8	4.6	4.3	3.9	4.3	2.8	1996
Taiwan	. . .	. . .	. . .	19.5	20.3	18.8	17.8	17.9	17.0	16.1	13.2	1997
Tajikistan	1.6	5.8	3.1	2.4	0.4	4.6	0.3	0.0	0.0	0.0	0.6	1994
Tanzania	2.5	3.5	3.9	3.1	4.7	5.1	6.0	3.9	3.7	5.2	3.4	1999
Thailand	11.7	11.9	11.5	12.6	13.8	14.0	12.8	11.8	11.6	9.6	9.5	1998
Togo	2.2	1.9	5.8	6.7	4.9	2.5	2.2	1.6	2.9	4.7	1.2	1996
Tonga	9.0	8.3	10.4	11.3	12.3	18.6	12.9	10.3	7.2	14.3	6.3	1998
Trinidad and Tobago	39.4	46.6	44.6	38.1	52.2	45.0	40.3	34.3	34.0	37.5	31.8	1997
Tunisia	5.8	6.6	4.9	4.5	3.3	3.3	3.8	4.6	4.1	3.2	2.0	1994
Turkey	11.4	10.4	10.4	7.5	8.9	8.8	7.6	7.2	7.9	6.0	4.4	1993
Turkmenistan	8.5	16.7	3.9	30.1	7.2	7.2	4.5	3.5	9.4	6.5	1.9	1996
Tuvalu	18.8	0.9	3.7	0.0	0.0	0.0	0.0	0.0	0.0	0.0	0.0	1993
Uganda	5.0	4.9	2.8	2.2	4.8	3.8	3.5	3.3	3.9	2.5	3.7	1993
Ukraine	8.2	1.7	1.2	3.2	3.8	4.0	3.4	2.6	2.9	2.8	1.1	1993
United Arab Emirates	9.2	8.7	8.4	11.0	11.3	10.1	8.2	7.9	7.6	7.7	7.6	1997
United Kingdom	12.0	12.0	12.2	12.7	13.6	13.8	12.9	13.4	14.0	11.9	10.2	2001
United States	0.0	0.0	0.0	0.0	0.0	0.0	0.0	0.0	0.0	0.0	0.0	1993
Uruguay	9.6	9.3	9.9	12.2	11.7	12.1	10.6	9.8	9.0	8.8	11.1	1996
Uzbekistan	8.8	4.0	2.3	8.0	5.7	5.5	15.6	8.8	7.1	7.3	11.5	1999
Vanuatu (New Hebrides)	0.6	0.7	0.8	0.4	0.3	31.4	4.5	1.2	0.5	0.5	1.0	1998
Venezuela	47.7	45.8	42.6	39.3	41.5	39.1	40.7	31.3	30.2	31.8	27.4	1993
Vietnam	0.1	0.8	1.6	2.2	2.1	2.9	2.8	2.3	2.5	2.3	5.7	2003
Western Samoa	10.5	11.4	5.7	8.0	8.4	7.3	7.9	26.1	28.4	4.3	5.1	2001
Yugoslavia (Serbia/Montenegro)	0.0	0.0	0.0	2.1	1.9	2.6	2.7	1.1	1.5	1.8	1.0	1999
Zambia	2.8	2.5	3.6	4.9	4.2	2.6	3.0	5.0	1.6	3.3	1.5	2000
Zimbabwe (Rhodesia)	8.9	5.3	4.5	3.4	5.1	5.6	4.8	6.0	2.8	3.1	2.2	1993

Note: U.S. share equals a nation's merchandise imports from the United States divided by its imports from the world. China's values (from the IMF) differ significantly from values derived from U.S. data. The United States and China differ considerably on treatment of trade moving through Hong Kong.

. . . = Not available.

Table B-45. U.S. Shares of Other Nations' Exports, 1993–2003

(Percent of total.)

Exporter	1993	1994	1995	1996	1997	1998	1999	2000	2001	2002	2003	Year of maximum
WORLD	15.6	15.6	14.6	14.8	15.4	16.5	17.7	18.5	17.9	17.6	16.4	2000
Afghanistan	0.4	5.5	3.2	12.5	7.0	10.6	6.8	1.8	0.7	4.3	26.2	2003
Albania	3.7	11.0	3.4	1.2	1.5	1.7	0.5	0.9	0.7	1.6	1.0	1994
Algeria	15.9	16.5	16.7	15.3	16.0	15.4	14.0	16.7	14.3	14.2	18.7	2003
Angola	70.5	68.5	63.7	57.1	62.6	64.1	53.2	45.6	47.7	41.0	48.1	1993
Antigua Barbuda	56.7	14.8	6.3	11.7	5.6	5.7	6.7	1.6	1.1	0.5	3.4	1993
Argentina	9.7	10.6	7.4	8.2	7.8	7.8	11.4	12.0	10.9	11.5	9.7	2000
Armenia	0.1	0.2	0.2	1.5	3.1	5.2	6.9	12.6	15.3	8.3	6.4	2001
Aruba	...	...	21.3	24.7	35.4	35.4	45.8	5.8	5.4	12.2	8.8	1999
Australia	8.0	7.0	6.3	6.4	7.4	9.5	9.6	9.9	9.7	9.6	8.7	2000
Austria	3.5	3.5	3.0	3.2	3.7	4.1	4.6	5.0	5.1	4.9	4.9	2001
Azerbaijan	0.4	0.1	0.2	0.8	0.3	2.3	3.2	0.5	0.6	2.4	0.6	1999
Bahamas	39.2	34.4	26.0	27.9	77.1	25.8	23.6	29.3	34.7	38.1	39.3	1997
Bahrain	4.2	4.4	3.1	2.3	1.8	2.4	3.3	4.1	5.1	4.5	3.5	2001
Bangladesh	33.6	33.4	31.9	30.9	35.5	35.8	31.2	31.8	29.6	27.6	23.8	1998
Barbados	23.2	21.9	14.6	14.1	14.7	16.5	16.7	3.8	15.0	14.7	18.7	1993
Belarus	2.0	2.2	1.2	1.5	1.3	1.5	1.4	1.4	1.0	2.0	2.8	2003
Belgium	...	...	...	...	4.9	5.1	5.4	5.9	5.6	7.9	6.7	2002
Belgium and Luxembourg	4.4	4.4	3.6	4.0	...	...	...	...	...	...	...	1993
Belize	43.8	44.4	36.6	42.1	46.7	36.0	44.3	52.3	35.7	12.6	39.0	2000
Benin	0.8	1.7	0.8	0.1	0.1	1.1	4.2	0.6	0.3	0.1	0.2	1999
Bermuda	4.2	80.3	49.7	3.5	8.8	6.0	3.0	4.5	4.5	2.3	1.2	1994
Bolivia	26.5	26.9	27.2	26.1	20.7	22.9	32.6	24.0	13.9	14.1	10.9	1999
Bosnia-Herzegovina	8.5	11.5	6.3	4.8	2.1	1.4	2.4	2.6	1.6	1.9	1.0	1994
Brazil	20.7	20.6	18.9	19.5	17.5	19.4	22.5	22.4	24.6	26.1	22.4	2002
Brunei	0.6	1.4	2.0	2.1	2.5	10.3	15.3	12.0	11.6	8.1	10.0	1999
Bulgaria	6.7	6.4	3.1	2.4	2.8	2.7	3.8	4.0	5.6	4.8	5.8	1993
Burkina (Upper Volta)	0.3	0.1	0.3	0.3	1.8	0.1	1.5	1.7	2.6	1.5	0.3	2001
Burundi	0.5	0.2	0.2	0.1	0.9	1.7	3.6	0.7	0.1	2.6	14.1	2003
Cambodia (Kampuchea)	0.2	0.4	1.4	1.4	13.7	31.4	22.7	65.9	64.2	58.7	57.6	2000
Cameroon	4.9	1.7	1.8	2.3	0.7	1.1	2.5	1.5	2.1	6.8	7.5	2003
Canada	81.3	82.5	80.4	82.3	83.2	86.5	87.6	87.4	87.6	87.7	86.6	2002
Cape Verde	43.4	1.3	1.3	1.6	4.8	0.5	0.8	12.3	17.7	8.1	18.2	1993
Central African Republic	0.0	0.0	0.0	0.0	0.1	1.1	0.7	1.0	1.3	1.1	1.5	2003
Chad	0.4	2.3	2.6	5.7	2.9	5.9	7.3	6.0	7.4	8.3	24.3	2003
Chile	17.4	17.2	14.5	13.9	13.4	14.4	18.1	16.8	18.5	19.1	16.2	2002
China	18.5	17.7	16.6	17.7	17.9	20.7	21.5	22.7	20.4	21.5	21.1	2000
Colombia	40.5	36.3	34.1	40.5	37.9	38.3	50.0	50.4	43.4	44.2	47.1	2000
Comoros	39.7	31.2	17.7	40.6	17.0	2.0	15.0	18.1	24.7	16.7	11.2	1996
Congo	47.7	41.2	22.6	16.5	20.2	19.5	22.8	15.8	20.1	9.9	15.2	1993
Costa Rica	55.4	43.4	40.1	36.9	24.8	20.0	15.0	15.5	16.3	29.1	25.0	1993
Croatia	2.1	2.2	1.9	2.0	2.2	2.0	2.0	1.8	1.8	1.6	2.3	2003
Cuba	...	...	...	...	...	...	0.0	0.0	...	0.0	0.0	1999
Cyprus	1.9	1.6	1.2	0.7	1.1	1.9	4.0	2.3	1.7	1.9	1.5	1999
Czech Republic	1.9	2.2	1.8	2.1	2.4	2.2	2.4	2.8	3.0	2.9	2.5	2001
Dem. Rep. of the Congo (Zaire)	22.5	14.1	16.2	16.1	21.6	15.9	19.7	19.2	13.5	13.4	15.5	1993
Denmark	5.3	5.5	4.2	4.3	4.6	4.7	5.5	5.9	6.9	6.4	6.2	2001
Djibouti	...	...	...	...	...	0.6	0.1	0.3	0.4	1.2	0.3	2002
Dominica	4.8	7.7	7.8	7.0	5.1	5.2	6.5	7.4	6.0	7.7	8.4	2003
Dominican Republic	50.5	10.0	10.6	10.6	83.3	87.1	88.6	87.3	86.5	85.2	84.5	1999
Ecuador	46.3	42.4	42.8	37.9	38.2	39.0	36.6	39.7	38.2	40.2	41.5	1993
Egypt	13.9	10.6	15.2	13.0	11.4	12.2	12.3	12.9	8.3	18.4	13.6	2002
El Salvador	30.2	48.9	17.5	19.3	19.2	21.5	21.1	23.6	18.8	62.9	57.5	2002
Equatorial Guinea	6.4	0.5	25.3	41.3	8.5	16.3	6.6	13.8	27.8	29.0	33.3	1996
Estonia	1.9	1.8	2.4	2.2	1.8	1.9	2.5	1.8	2.2	2.2	2.3	1999
Ethiopia	9.1	6.3	6.3	6.1	11.3	8.7	7.9	5.1	6.5	4.5	5.1	1997
Falkland Islands	0.0	1.5	1.7	0.8	0.8	0.1	2.0	1.9	8.8	6.9	3.5	2001
Faroe Islands	2.5	2.9	2.3	2.1	3.6	2.8	0.0	5.7	3.1	3.7	3.4	2000
Fiji	10.5	17.9	11.5	8.3	10.7	16.3	14.8	21.4	28.9	25.4	23.4	2001
Finland	7.9	7.2	6.7	8.0	7.0	7.4	8.0	7.4	9.8	9.0	8.2	2001
France	6.8	6.8	5.8	6.0	6.3	7.3	7.9	8.7	8.6	7.8	6.8	2000
French Guiana	1.9	5.0	1.0	4.4	...	...	...	...	...	...	...	1994
French Polynesia	8.7	10.7	12.4	10.6	18.0	18.8	17.2	20.8	20.5	17.7	9.1	2000
Gabon	41.8	49.9	53.0	64.1	61.4	50.3	43.3	52.8	45.6	50.7	51.4	1996
Georgia	0.3	2.4	0.4	0.7	1.8	4.2	4.5	1.9	5.6	2.9	6.4	2003
Germany	7.8	8.0	7.5	7.8	8.6	9.4	10.2	10.3	10.6	10.3	9.3	2001
Ghana	17.3	12.3	12.4	10.5	9.4	7.9	10.4	13.2	12.0	6.8	4.2	1993
Gibraltar	6.4	5.8	5.2	5.6	3.1	8.9	3.8	1.9	1.8	0.6	0.9	1998
Greece	4.2	5.2	3.2	3.8	4.4	4.5	5.7	5.4	5.6	5.3	6.5	2003
Greenland	1.9	1.0	0.6	0.1	2.1	1.7	3.1	4.8	7.6	5.5	2.9	2001
Grenada	33.6	31.9	29.9	20.5	22.8	37.3	44.6	49.2	29.7	14.5	15.6	2000

Note: U.S. share equals a nation's exports to the United States divided by its exports from the world. China's values (from the IMF) differ significantly from values derived from U.S. data. The United States and China differ considerably on treatment of trade moving through Hong Kong.

... = Not available.

Table B-45. U.S. Shares of Other Nations' Exports, 1993–2003—*Continued*

(Percent of total.)

Exporter	1993	1994	1995	1996	1997	1998	1999	2000	2001	2002	2003	Year of maximum
Guadeloupe	3.6	1.5	1.2	1.3	. . .	. . .	. . .	. . .	. . .	. . .	. . .	1993
Guatemala	38.0	32.1	31.3	36.8	45.5	52.2	55.9	57.1	57.0	59.0	55.5	2002
Guinea	24.8	15.3	22.0	30.9	23.2	19.7	20.2	11.5	17.7	9.5	9.2	1996
Guinea-Bissau	0.6	0.0	0.0	0.0	0.2	0.1	0.2	0.4	0.0	0.0	1.6	2003
Guyana	22.4	21.3	22.3	16.8	18.2	22.3	21.7	24.4	25.4	22.3	21.2	2001
Haiti	84.1	68.9	60.8	77.1	86.4	86.4	87.8	86.5	84.2	84.4	83.9	1999
Honduras	49.8	46.7	48.4	44.6	42.4	38.5	68.8	69.4	69.6	69.0	65.2	2001
Hong Kong	23.1	23.2	21.8	21.3	21.8	23.4	23.9	23.3	22.3	21.4	18.7	1999
Hungary	4.3	4.1	3.2	3.5	3.2	4.5	5.2	5.3	5.0	3.5	6.4	2003
Iceland	15.8	14.4	12.3	12.5	14.3	12.7	15.1	12.4	10.5	10.9	9.9	1993
India	18.5	19.3	17.4	19.1	19.5	21.1	22.5	21.3	20.7	22.3	20.3	1999
Indonesia	14.2	14.6	13.9	13.6	13.4	14.4	14.2	13.7	13.8	13.2	12.1	1994
Iran	7.8	13.9	4.1	0.0	0.0	0.0	0.0	0.6	0.6	0.7	0.5	1994
Iraq	0.0	0.0	0.0	0.0	9.9	24.3	40.0	40.0	51.8	37.4	45.4	2001
Ireland	9.0	8.4	8.4	9.5	11.5	13.5	15.2	17.0	16.8	16.7	20.5	2003
Israel	31.3	31.6	29.9	30.8	32.1	35.6	35.5	36.8	38.2	40.2	37.3	2002
Italy	7.7	7.8	7.3	7.4	7.9	8.6	9.3	10.4	9.7	9.8	8.5	2000
Ivory Coast	5.7	4.0	4.4	7.0	7.5	8.4	8.7	7.8	7.0	7.5	7.1	1999
Jamaica	46.8	44.3	44.9	41.9	38.4	39.8	37.2	37.9	31.2	28.1	29.3	1993
Japan	29.5	30.0	27.5	27.5	28.1	30.9	31.1	30.1	30.4	28.8	24.8	1999
Jordan	1.0	1.1	1.5	1.3	0.5	0.6	1.1	4.9	10.2	14.6	19.0	2003
Kazakhstan	3.4	2.3	0.8	1.0	2.1	1.4	1.4	2.1	1.8	1.2	2.5	1993
Kenya	3.7	3.9	2.7	2.8	3.0	3.6	4.9	5.2	5.7	8.1	8.8	2003
Kiribati (Gilbert Islands)	27.0	11.6	10.4	11.1	16.5	11.1	16.9	6.0	3.0	3.4	5.4	1993
Korea, South	21.2	20.4	18.5	16.0	15.2	17.4	20.6	22.0	20.9	20.4	17.9	2000
Kuwait	20.3	15.2	0.2	11.8	12.3	13.1	11.1	14.3	12.3	11.7	12.0	1993
Laos	4.4	1.7	1.7	0.8	3.6	5.4	2.7	2.3	1.0	0.7	0.9	1998
Latvia	0.6	1.2	1.3	0.7	1.4	2.9	5.7	3.8	2.8	4.3	10.0	2003
Lebanon	4.0	3.7	3.0	2.8	6.2	6.6	6.2	6.8	8.6	6.2	7.6	2001
Liberia	0.8	0.5	1.0	2.4	0.6	2.7	5.2	7.1	4.2	4.0	5.5	2000
Libya	0.0	0.0	0.0	0.0	0.0	0.0	0.0	0.0	0.0	0.0	0.0	1993
Lithuania	1.4	0.6	0.7	0.8	1.6	2.8	4.4	4.9	3.8	3.6	2.8	2000
Luxembourg	. . .	. . .	. . .	. . .	3.6	5.4	3.7	4.1	2.8	2.7	1.9	1998
Macao	33.4	37.2	41.8	40.1	45.0	47.7	47.0	48.3	48.2	48.6	49.4	2003
Macedonia	5.8	3.6	3.0	6.2	9.5	13.3	11.4	16.8	11.2	9.6	6.1	2000
Madagascar	6.7	8.7	6.8	3.9	4.7	6.0	5.4	19.2	16.9	19.8	35.0	2003
Malawi	14.6	12.1	13.5	15.4	14.9	12.3	14.3	12.8	16.1	14.8	13.1	2001
Malaysia	20.3	21.2	20.8	18.2	18.4	21.6	21.9	20.5	20.2	20.2	19.5	1999
Maldive Islands	11.3	18.0	19.2	10.3	18.2	20.7	35.4	44.7	38.5	38.4	32.5	2000
Mali	0.7	2.3	2.2	1.8	1.3	1.2	3.3	3.8	3.8	1.5	1.2	2000
Malta and Gozo	7.5	7.5	9.6	13.5	15.0	17.1	21.3	27.4	15.1	11.5	12.0	2000
Martinique	0.6	1.1	2.6	0.5	. . .	. . .	. . .	. . .	. . .	. . .	. . .	1995
Mauritania	1.5	0.9	1.2	1.1	0.1	0.1	0.1	0.1	0.1	0.2	0.1	1993
Mauritius	17.9	18.1	14.8	13.4	14.3	16.7	18.0	20.2	19.8	19.7	14.4	2000
Mexico	83.3	85.3	83.6	84.0	85.6	87.9	88.3	88.7	88.5	89.0	87.6	2002
Moldova	0.2	0.3	1.1	1.4	6.7	2.8	3.1	3.3	4.9	5.8	4.3	1997
Mongolia	1.1	3.5	5.5	4.2	5.6	8.5	12.9	24.3	27.7	31.6	32.0	2003
Morocco	3.4	3.3	3.2	3.2	3.2	3.6	4.6	5.2	4.0	4.7	4.0	2000
Mozambique	5.3	8.7	5.5	11.4	11.8	5.5	4.6	4.7	0.9	1.6	0.8	1997
Myanmar	. . .	. . .	. . .	8.9	9.9	14.0	15.9	22.3	17.4	13.1	9.7	2000
Nauru	0.2	0.0	0.0	0.7	0.3	0.4	0.4	4.2	0.0	3.1	0.9	2000
Nepal	27.3	33.4	30.5	28.5	26.2	25.9	30.4	32.6	32.3	27.7	26.0	1994
Netherlands	4.3	4.2	3.6	3.6	4.2	4.3	4.0	4.4	4.2	4.6	4.5	2002
New Caledonia	7.5	4.9	8.5	9.4	10.3	4.1	5.7	5.2	2.5	1.9	1.4	1997
New Zealand	11.7	11.0	10.0	9.3	10.6	13.0	13.8	14.8	15.1	15.5	14.6	2002
Nicaragua	44.3	39.7	38.2	39.3	42.0	38.0	38.6	39.8	30.2	59.4	58.3	2002
Niger	0.2	0.2	0.2	0.1	0.3	1.1	0.1	2.5	0.0	0.0	0.2	2000
Nigeria	44.0	37.8	37.5	34.8	37.0	36.4	31.9	44.4	41.5	33.6	41.4	2000
Norway	6.7	6.5	6.2	7.5	6.3	6.3	8.3	8.0	8.0	8.6	7.4	2002
Oman	3.9	5.4	3.3	4.6	1.5	1.6	1.2	2.8	4.5	4.4	6.7	2003
Pakistan	14.5	15.8	15.1	16.7	18.8	21.6	22.9	25.2	24.3	24.5	22.6	2000
Panama	37.2	40.7	14.7	11.7	48.0	42.2	44.6	45.4	48.6	47.8	19.7	2001
Papua New Guinea	4.2	3.6	1.6	2.7	2.3	5.3	4.6	1.3	1.5	3.3	1.8	1998
Paraguay	6.9	7.0	4.8	3.7	4.1	2.6	4.6	3.6	2.6	3.4	3.2	1994
Peru	21.2	16.6	17.3	19.9	23.4	32.9	29.3	28.1	25.5	26.2	27.1	1998
Philippines	38.6	38.5	35.8	33.9	35.1	34.4	29.6	29.9	28.0	24.7	20.4	1993
Poland	2.9	3.4	2.7	2.3	2.6	2.7	2.8	3.2	2.4	2.7	2.7	1994
Portugal	4.4	5.1	4.5	4.6	4.8	4.9	4.9	6.0	5.8	5.8	5.8	2000
Qatar	2.0	2.5	2.4	3.4	2.8	4.4	4.2	4.2	3.1	4.2	2.3	1998
Republic of South Africa	6.9	4.9	4.8	5.4	5.5	7.0	7.8	11.1	12.9	12.7	12.4	2001

Note: U.S. share equals a nation's exports to the United States divided by its exports from the world. China's values (from the IMF) differ significantly from values derived from U.S. data. The United States and China differ considerably on treatment of trade moving through Hong Kong.

. . . = Not available.

Table B-45. U.S. Shares of Other Nations' Exports, 1993–2003—*Continued*

(Percent of total.)

Exporter	1993	1994	1995	1996	1997	1998	1999	2000	2001	2002	2003	Year of maximum
Reunion	0.1	0.2	0.6	0.0	. . .	. . .	. . .	. . .	. . .	. . .	. . .	1995
Romania	1.4	3.1	2.5	2.4	3.7	3.8	3.7	3.7	3.1	4.4	4.1	2002
Russia	4.5	5.9	6.6	7.6	5.8	8.4	8.9	7.7	7.2	6.1	4.6	1999
Rwanda	3.6	2.4	2.6	4.9	3.1	3.6	4.2	5.3	5.7	2.1	1.7	2001
SACCA, excluding South Africa	. . .	. . .	. . .	. . .	. . .	2.2	2.8	3.0	3.0	3.0	3.0	2000
Sao Tome and Principe	7.1	1.0	1.4	6.0	1.9	4.0	8.0	2.6	2.4	3.3	0.0	1999
Saudi Arabia	17.5	18.5	17.0	17.6	15.3	16.4	16.2	17.6	19.2	18.9	20.9	2003
Senegal	1.6	1.0	0.5	0.2	0.2	0.4	0.2	0.5	0.3	0.3	0.7	1993
Seychelles	0.1	0.0	0.2	31.3	0.4	0.0	0.0	0.1	0.0	0.0	0.8	1996
Sierra Leone	34.7	8.8	5.0	3.3	1.5	4.0	26.7	2.9	8.2	3.6	4.6	1993
Singapore	20.4	18.7	18.3	18.4	18.4	19.9	19.2	17.3	15.4	15.3	14.3	1993
Slovakia	1.1	1.6	1.3	1.3	1.6	1.2	1.4	1.4	1.3	1.4	4.6	2003
Slovenia	3.5	3.5	3.1	3.0	2.9	2.8	3.0	3.1	2.7	2.8	3.6	2003
Solomon Islands	2.1	0.5	2.4	0.9	0.5	1.7	0.7	0.8	3.3	0.8	1.1	2001
Somalia	0.1	0.0	0.0	0.0	0.1	0.4	0.2	0.7	0.4	0.3	0.0	2000
Spain	4.7	4.9	4.2	4.2	4.4	4.3	4.6	5.0	4.6	4.6	4.2	2000
Sri Lanka (Ceylon)	35.2	34.9	35.6	34.1	36.0	39.2	38.8	40.2	40.8	37.7	33.4	2001
St. Christopher-Nevis	36.4	54.9	54.3	58.4	56.0	63.2	68.5	65.9	62.6	65.1	58.7	1999
St. Helena	14.8	0.0	0.0	34.1	15.4	3.1	1.1	25.8	29.6	22.1	26.9	1996
St. Lucia	27.3	28.2	26.3	14.9	19.9	14.4	13.6	17.8	33.4	27.7	25.1	2001
St. Pierre and Miquelon	0.0	2.1	53.5	4.8	17.7	39.9	39.4	32.0	18.8	33.1	24.4	1995
St. Vincent and Grenadines	7.4	9.4	12.5	7.6	7.1	5.4	3.3	2.6	11.3	7.1	1.9	1995
Sudan	3.2	7.0	4.0	3.6	2.3	0.6	0.0	0.1	0.2	0.1	0.3	1994
Suriname	20.0	17.1	21.0	19.4	17.6	19.4	20.4	24.7	26.0	25.8	22.7	2001
Sweden	9.0	8.6	7.9	8.3	8.3	8.6	9.2	10.2	11.1	11.4	11.5	2003
Switzerland	9.0	9.2	8.7	9.4	10.5	11.0	12.4	13.1	11.6	12.0	10.1	2000
Syria	1.9	1.3	0.9	0.2	0.2	0.6	1.3	3.0	2.5	2.2	3.9	2003
Taiwan	. . .	. . .	. . .	. . .	24.2	26.6	25.4	23.5	22.5	20.5	18.0	1998
Tajikistan	4.3	5.5	2.0	1.4	0.6	0.3	0.1	0.1	0.2	0.1	0.1	1994
Tanzania	2.5	2.7	3.2	2.4	1.9	2.3	3.2	2.1	2.0	1.4	2.6	1995
Thailand	21.5	20.9	17.6	18.0	19.4	22.3	21.7	21.3	20.3	19.6	17.0	1998
Togo	1.7	1.5	0.1	1.1	0.2	0.1	0.8	0.3	2.4	0.4	1.3	2001
Tonga	20.8	26.6	25.8	24.5	10.3	16.6	23.5	30.4	34.5	38.2	49.0	2003
Trinidad and Tobago	46.8	37.6	33.2	48.8	43.9	39.9	41.4	46.8	57.1	54.6	63.4	2003
Tunisia	0.7	1.0	1.2	1.4	0.6	0.5	0.6	0.7	1.0	0.8	0.8	1996
Turkey	6.4	8.4	7.0	7.1	7.7	8.2	9.2	11.3	10.0	9.2	8.0	2000
Turkmenistan	0.3	0.1	1.7	2.6	0.2	0.2	0.8	0.5	1.2	1.7	1.6	1996
Tuvalu	62.0	0.0	0.0	0.0	0.0	0.0	0.0	0.0	0.0	0.0	0.0	1993
Uganda	7.4	8.8	2.3	2.7	6.0	3.5	5.3	8.9	6.1	4.7	9.0	2003
Ukraine	4.5	3.5	2.8	2.6	2.1	4.0	3.8	5.0	3.5	2.9	1.3	2000
United Arab Emirates	3.3	2.0	1.8	1.8	2.8	2.5	2.4	2.2	3.0	2.3	2.3	1993
United Kingdom	12.9	13.0	12.2	12.2	12.5	13.4	14.8	15.8	15.9	15.5	15.7	2001
United States	. . .	. . .	. . .	. . .	. . .	. . .	. . .	. . .	. . .	. . .	. . .	. . .
Uruguay	8.9	6.3	6.0	7.1	6.0	5.8	6.9	8.4	8.6	8.4	9.0	2003
Uzbekistan	0.9	0.1	0.5	5.7	1.3	1.3	1.3	1.6	2.5	4.8	4.2	1996
Vanuatu (New Hebrides)	7.7	12.4	0.0	1.6	3.4	5.9	23.6	9.8	1.0	3.2	1.0	1999
Venezuela	58.0	51.0	50.5	46.3	47.3	42.1	49.6	51.9	47.7	45.1	48.1	1993
Vietnam	0.0	2.3	3.0	2.7	3.0	5.0	4.4	5.1	7.1	14.7	20.9	2003
Western Samoa	12.6	3.1	0.9	1.7	6.4	26.5	10.8	10.8	12.6	9.2	4.9	1998
Yugoslavia (Serbia/Montenegro)	0.0	0.0	0.0	1.2	0.8	0.9	0.7	0.3	0.5	0.7	0.8	1996
Zambia	0.3	0.7	9.4	2.8	7.1	2.2	0.8	1.6	1.9	0.9	1.2	1995
Zimbabwe (Rhodesia)	7.1	6.3	4.7	6.2	5.7	6.7	5.8	3.2	2.7	4.1	2.0	1993

Note: U.S. share equals a nation's exports to the United States divided by its exports from the world. China's values (from the IMF) differ significantly from values derived from U.S. data. The United States and China differ considerably on treatment of trade moving through Hong Kong.

. . . = Not available.

Table B-46. Top 50 Country-Product Export Changes, 2003–2004

(Millions of dollars; top 50 based on 2003–2004 change; Census basis; foreign and domestic exports, f.a.s.)

SITC product	Buyer	2003	2004	Change
TOTAL OF TOP 50		95 511	127 793	32 282
784 – Parts and accessories of motor vehicles	Canada	16 222	17 869	1 647
792 – Aircraft and associated equipment	France	1 541	3 103	1 562
752 – Automatic data process machines	Mexico	2 688	4 000	1 312
776 – Thermionic, cold cathode and photocathode valves	Hong Kong	2 838	3 995	1 157
994 – Estimated low value shipments	Canada	3 654	4 634	979
667 – Pearls, precious and semiprecious stones	Israel	2 046	3 001	955
542 – Medicaments (including veterinary medicaments)	Netherlands	821	1 766	945
728 – Machinery specialized for particular industries	Taiwan	760	1 657	897
343 – Natural gas, whether or not liquefied	Canada	1 078	1 947	869
541 – Medicinal products, except medicaments	Germany	821	1 662	841
776 – Thermionic, cold cathode and photocathode valves	Canada	2 423	3 179	757
792 – Aircraft and associated equipment	Pakistan	83	833	750
714 – Nonelectric engines and motors	France	2 371	3 116	745
782 – Special purpose motor vehicles	Canada	5 684	6 384	699
776 – Thermionic, cold cathode and photocathode valves	Singapore	2 375	3 062	687
263 – Cotton textile fibers	China	769	1 434	665
772 – Electrical apparatus for switching or protecting	Mexico	4 253	4 917	664
541 – Medicinal products, except medicaments	Netherlands	1 130	1 786	655
874 – Measuring/checking/analyzing instuments	Taiwan	922	1 563	641
792 – Aircraft and associated equipment	Ireland	911	1 533	622
792 – Aircraft and associated equipment	Greece	213	812	599
781 – All motor vehicles	Mexico	2 511	3 107	596
511 – Hydrocarbons and specified derivatives	Taiwan	336	920	584
713 – Internal combustion piston engines	Mexico	2 000	2 575	575
764 – Telecommunications equipment	Netherlands	1 074	1 635	561
792 – Aircraft and associated equipment	Brazil	736	1 275	539
673 – Iron and nonalloy steel flat-roll products	Canada	695	1 218	523
723 – Civil engineering and contractors' plant and equipment	Canada	1 635	2 145	511
044 – Maize (not including sweet corn) unmilled	South Korea	48	548	500
728 – Machinery specialized for particular industries	Singapore	303	799	497
792 – Aircraft and associated equipment	Israel	726	1 222	496
821 – Furniture and bedding accessories	Canada	2 174	2 661	488
783 – Road motor vehicles	Canada	1 305	1 784	479
764 – Telecommunications equipment	Canada	3 609	4 082	473
776 – Thermionic, cold cathode and photocathode valves	China	2 475	2 936	462
041 – Wheat and meslin, unmilled	China	35	495	460
334 – Oil (not crude)	Mexico	2 164	2 621	457
874 – Measuring/checking/analyzing instuments	Mexico	1 276	1 732	456
776 – Thermionic, cold cathode and photocathode valves	Thailand	905	1 360	455
511 – Hydrocarbons and specified derivatives	South Korea	580	1 033	453
511 – Hydrocarbons and specified derivatives	Mexico	1 028	1 469	441
728 – Machinery specialized for particular industries	China	646	1 084	438
731 – Machine tools working by removing metal or other	Taiwan	155	587	432
971 – Gold, nonmonetary	Canada	445	872	427
684 – Aluminum	Canada	1 545	1 960	415
776 – Thermionic, cold cathode and photocathode valves	Mexico	6 063	6 450	387
321 – Coal, pulverized or not	Japan	1	387	386
784 – Parts and accessories of motor vehicles	Mexico	5 937	6 320	382
781 – All motor vehicles	Saudi Arabia	648	1 030	381
541 – Medicinal products, except medicaments	France	853	1 233	380

Note: Unrevised data.

Table B-47. Top 50 Country-Product Export Changes, 1999–2004

(Millions of dollars; top 50 based on 1999–2004 change; Census basis; foreign and domestic exports, f.a.s.)

SITC product	Buyer	1999	2004	Change
TOTAL OF TOP 50		60 933	117 629	56 696
994 – Estimated low value shipments	Canada	1 750	4 634	2 883
781 – All motor vehicles	Germany	1 178	4 012	2 834
759 – Parts for office machines and a.d.p. machines	Mexico	1 805	4 162	2 357
782 – Special purpose motor vehicles	Canada	4 033	6 384	2 351
752 – Automatic data process machines	Mexico	1 840	4 000	2 160
776 – Thermionic, cold cathode and photocathode valves	China	812	2 936	2 124
222 – Oil seeds and oleaginous fruit	China	354	2 333	1 979
343 – Natural gas, whether or not liquefied	Canada	58	1 947	1 889
667 – Pearls, precious and semiprecious stones	Israel	1 127	3 001	1 873
776 – Thermionic, cold cathode and photocathode valves	Hong Kong	2 392	3 995	1 603
542 – Medicaments (including veterinary medicaments)	Netherlands	339	1 766	1 427
541 – Medicinal products, except medicaments	Netherlands	371	1 786	1 415
263 – Cotton textile fibers	China	24	1 434	1 410
781 – All motor vehicles	Canada	9 509	10 811	1 303
541 – Medicinal products, except medicaments	Germany	466	1 662	1 195
713 – Internal combustion piston engines	Mexico	1 425	2 575	1 150
542 – Medicaments (including veterinary medicaments)	United Kingdom	718	1 841	1 123
899 – Miscellaneous manufactured articles	Ireland	89	1 181	1 092
792 – Aircraft and associated equipment	Ireland	515	1 533	1 018
542 – Medicaments (including veterinary medicaments)	Belgium	138	1 098	960
781 – All motor vehicles	Mexico	2 175	3 107	932
511 – Hydrocarbons and specified derivatives	Mexico	551	1 469	918
511 – Hydrocarbons and specified derivatives	South Korea	142	1 033	891
334 – Oil (not crude)	Mexico	1 743	2 621	878
776 – Thermionic, cold cathode and photocathode valves	Malaysia	4 693	5 567	874
874 – Measuring/checking/analyzing instuments	China	467	1 340	873
784 – Parts and accessories of motor vehicles	Mexico	5 460	6 320	859
728 – Machinery specialized for particular industries	China	231	1 084	853
282 – Ferrous waste and scrap	China	97	933	837
288 – Nonferrous base metal waste and scrap	China	144	976	832
792 – Aircraft and associated equipment	Singapore	1 546	2 350	804
723 – Civil engineering and contractors' plant and equipment	Canada	1 347	2 145	798
792 – Aircraft and associated equipment	Pakistan	39	833	795
764 – Telecommunications equipment	Netherlands	847	1 635	788
542 – Medicaments (including veterinary medicaments)	Canada	1 317	2 085	768
667 – Pearls, precious and semiprecious stones	Belgium	775	1 506	731
515 – Organo-inorganic and heterocyclic compounds	Belgium	417	1 141	725
782 – Special purpose motor vehicles	Mexico	296	1 019	723
673 – Iron and nonalloy steel flat-roll products	Canada	513	1 218	705
541 – Medicinal products, except medicaments	France	562	1 233	671
776 – Thermionic, cold cathode and photocathode valves	Costa Rica	182	844	662
334 – Oil (not crude)	Canada	703	1 359	657
781 – All motor vehicles	Saudi Arabia	376	1 030	653
792 – Aircraft and associated equipment	Greece	165	812	647
872 – Medical instruments and appliances	Netherlands	635	1 260	625
351 – Electric current	Canada	206	829	623
511 – Hydrocarbons and specified derivatives	Taiwan	307	920	613
874 – Measuring/checking/analyzing instuments	Taiwan	956	1 563	607
575 – Plastics	Mexico	783	1 389	606
772 – Electrical apparatus for switching or protecting	Mexico	4 315	4 917	602

Note: Unrevised data.

Table B-48. Top 50 Country-Product Import Changes, 2003–2004

(Millions of dollars; top 50 based on 2003–2004 change; Census basis; general imports, Customs.)

SITC product	Seller	2003	2004	Change
TOTAL OF TOP 50		304 621	399 795	95 170
752 – Automatic data process machines	China	15 268	24 461	9 192
333 – Crude oil	Nigeria	9 629	15 402	5 773
333 – Crude oil	Venezuela	12 691	18 398	5 706
781 – All motor vehicles	Canada	30 799	36 248	5 449
333 – Crude oil	Canada	14 196	18 966	4 770
764 – Telecommunications equipment	China	7 922	12 097	4 175
333 – Crude oil	Iraq	4 562	8 352	3 791
333 – Crude oil	Mexico	14 428	17 999	3 571
764 – Telecommunications equipment	South Korea	6 289	9 218	2 929
759 – Parts for office machines and a.d.p. machines	China	6 560	9 266	2 706
333 – Crude oil	Saudi Arabia	16 887	19 398	2 511
763 – Sound recorders and TV recorders	China	5 327	7 605	2 278
761 – Television receivers	Mexico	5 249	7 416	2 167
248 – Wood, simply worked	Canada	5 018	7 181	2 163
821 – Furniture and bedding accessories	China	8 750	10 910	2 160
333 – Crude oil	Algeria	2 858	5 007	2 148
781 – All motor vehicles	South Korea	7 938	10 040	2 103
784 – Parts and accessories of motor vehicles	Japan	7 286	8 931	1 644
333 – Crude oil	Ecuador	1 393	2 835	1 442
334 – Oil (not crude)	Venezuela	2 329	3 640	1 311
343 – Natural gas, whether or not liquefied	Canada	18 249	19 481	1 232
334 – Oil (not crude)	Canada	5 149	6 363	1 213
872 – Medical instruments and appliances	Ireland	1 064	2 276	1 212
334 – Oil (not crude)	United Kingdom	1 071	2 247	1 177
764 – Telecommunications equipment	Mexico	7 258	8 405	1 147
634 – Veneers, plywood and particle board	Canada	3 157	4 291	1 134
894 – Toys and sporting goods	China	16 448	17 569	1 120
667 – Pearls, precious and semiprecious stones	Israel	6 113	7 181	1 068
713 – Internal combustion piston engines	Mexico	2 867	3 878	1 011
784 – Parts and accessories of motor vehicles	Mexico	5 661	6 671	1 010
723 – Civil engineering and contractors' plant and equipment	Japan	1 464	2 401	937
333 – Crude oil	Kuwait	1 977	2 904	927
343 – Natural gas, whether or not liquefied	Trinidad and Tobago	1 767	2 630	864
761 – Television receivers	China	1 446	2 288	842
333 – Crude oil	Norway	2 690	3 517	827
542 – Medicaments (including veterinary medicaments)	France	2 171	2 994	822
699 – Manufactures of base metal	China	1 976	2 787	811
334 – Oil (not crude)	Aruba	930	1 729	798
684 – Aluminum	Canada	4 136	4 932	797
851 – Footwear	China	10 565	11 351	785
778 – Electrical machinery and apparatus	China	3 135	3 908	773
775 – Household type electric and nonelectric equipment	China	3 774	4 546	772
764 – Telecommunications equipment	Thailand	832	1 595	763
334 – Oil (not crude)	Netherlands	1 004	1 751	747
334 – Oil (not crude)	Russia	1 846	2 588	742
971 – Gold, nonmonetary	Peru	342	1 081	739
781 – All motor vehicles	Austria	521	1 257	736
551 – Essential oils, perfume and flavor materials	Ireland	908	1 636	728
831 – Trunks, suitcases, vanity cases, and briefcases	China	3 320	4 044	724
641 – Paper and paperboard	Canada	7 401	8 124	723

Note: Unrevised data.

Table B-49. Top 50 Country-Product Import Changes, 1999–2004

(Millions of dollars; top 50 based on 1999–2004 change; Census basis; general imports, Customs.)

SITC product	Seller	1999	2004	Change
TOTAL OF TOP 50		208 330	422 433	214 102
343 – Natural gas, whether or not liquefied	Canada	5 184	18 249	13 064
752 – Automatic data process machines	China	2 809	15 268	12 459
333 – Crude oil	Saudi Arabia	5 538	16 887	11 349
333 – Crude oil	Mexico	5 007	14 428	9 421
781 – All motor vehicles	Germany	11 096	19 726	8 629
333 – Crude oil	Canada	5 580	14 196	8 616
515 – Organo-inorganic and heterocyclic compounds	Ireland	3 556	11 649	8 094
781 – All motor vehicles	Japan	24 686	32 227	7 541
333 – Crude oil	Venezuela	5 211	12 691	7 480
821 – Furniture and bedding accessories	China	2 183	8 750	6 567
781 – All motor vehicles	South Korea	1 696	7 938	6 242
333 – Crude oil	Nigeria	3 828	9 629	5 801
894 – Toys and sporting goods	China	11 167	16 449	5 282
764 – Telecommunications equipment	South Korea	1 161	6 289	5 128
764 – Telecommunications equipment	China	2 823	7 922	5 100
542 – Medicaments (including veterinary medicaments)	Ireland	226	5 126	4 900
752 – Automatic data process machines	Malaysia	3 008	7 782	4 774
759 – Parts for office machines and a.d.p. machines	China	2 468	6 560	4 093
763 – Sound recorders and TV recorders	China	1 321	5 327	4 005
782 – Special purpose motor vehicles	Mexico	3 513	7 226	3 713
333 – Crude oil	United Kingdom	915	4 368	3 452
334 – Oil (not crude)	Canada	1 743	5 149	3 407
333 – Crude oil	Iraq	1 199	4 562	3 362
781 – All motor vehicles	United Kingdom	1 811	5 006	3 195
784 – Parts and accessories of motor vehicles	Canada	7 826	10 902	3 076
782 – Special purpose motor vehicles	Canada	6 013	9 075	3 062
764 – Telecommunications equipment	Mexico	4 221	7 258	3 037
792 – Aircraft and associated equipment	Canada	3 472	6 343	2 871
764 – Telecommunications equipment	Malaysia	969	3 837	2 868
333 – Crude oil	Algeria	88	2 858	2 770
542 – Medicaments (including veterinary medicaments)	United Kingdom	1 303	4 031	2 727
781 – All motor vehicles	Mexico	9 147	11 827	2 680
851 – Footwear	China	8 008	10 565	2 557
667 – Pearls, precious and semiprecious stones	Israel	3 572	6 113	2 541
752 – Automatic data process machines	Mexico	3 622	6 138	2 516
775 – Household type electric and nonelectric equipment	China	1 466	3 774	2 308
784 – Parts and accessories of motor vehicles	Mexico	3 500	5 661	2 161
821 – Furniture and bedding accessories	Mexico	2 317	4 275	1 958
515 – Organo-inorganic and heterocyclic compounds	Singapore	275	2 214	1 940
333 – Crude oil	Angola	2 180	4 105	1 925
542 – Medicaments (including veterinary medicaments)	France	293	2 171	1 879
778 – Electrical machinery and apparatus	China	1 288	3 120	1 832
893 – Articles of plastics	China	1 784	3 611	1 826
781 – All motor vehicles	Canada	29 024	30 799	1 775
343 – Natural gas, whether or not liquefied	Trinidad and Tobago	0	1 767	1 767
931 – Special transactions not classified by kind	Canada	8 306	10 008	1 702
761 – Television receivers	Japan	255	1 924	1 669
899 – Miscellaneous manufactured articles	Ireland	59	1 726	1 667
334 – Oil (not crude)	Russia	179	1 846	1 667
813 – Lighting fixtures and fittings	China	1 434	3 081	1 647

Note: Unrevised data.

Table B-50. U.S. Total Exports by 3-Digit End-Use Product Groups, 1999–2003

(Millions of dollars; Census basis; foreign and domestic exports, f.a.s.)

End-use product	1999	2000	2001	2002	2003	1999–2003 change Value	1999–2003 change Percent
TOTAL	692 821	780 419	731 026	693 257	723 743	30 923	4.5
000 – Wheat, rice, and other food grains	4 743	4 402	4 254	4 594	5 103	359	7.6
001 – Soybeans and other oil seeds and food oils	5 962	6 386	6 543	6 993	9 433	3 470	58.2
002 – Feedstuff	9 169	9 254	9 714	9 758	9 763	594	6.5
003 – Other agricultural foods	21 961	24 087	24 441	23 551	25 790	3 829	17.4
010 – Nonagricultural (fish, beverages)	3 944	4 136	4 529	4 600	5 004	1 060	26.9
100 – Cotton, including linters, raw	985	1 936	2 179	2 065	3 399	2 414	245.1
101 – Other agricultural materials for industry and farm	6 372	6 937	7 572	7 169	7 200	828	13.0
110 – Coals and related fuels	2 738	2 605	2 262	1 919	1 815	-924	-33.7
111 – Petroleum and products, excluding natural gas	8 638	11 992	10 682	10 336	12 717	4 079	47.2
112 – Gas-natural	218	411	538	994	1 300	1 082	496.4
113 – Nuclear fuel materials and fuels	953	1 176	1 245	1 520	1 571	618	64.8
114 – Electric energy	206	398	1 258	304	716	510	247.1
120 – Steelmaking and ferroalloying materials	1 407	1 700	1 765	1 854	2 609	1 202	85.4
121 – Iron and steel products	5 725	6 829	6 202	5 986	7 078	1 354	23.6
122 – Nonferrous and other metals-crude and	13 495	16 068	14 233	12 126	13 969	474	3.5
123 – Finished metal shapes and advanced metal manufactures	8 428	10 487	8 804	8 725	8 951	523	6.2
124 – Paper and paper base stocks	12 197	14 161	12 415	12 209	12 849	652	5.3
125 – Chemicals, excluding medicinals and food additives	45 974	52 471	49 780	52 311	57 954	11 980	26.1
126 – Industrial textile fibers, yarn, fabric	9 812	11 374	10 875	11 148	11 349	1 537	15.7
127 – Other nonagricultural industrial materials	22 212	25 684	23 218	20 543	21 668	-544	-2.4
131 – Lumber and other wood supplies	5 105	5 353	4 488	4 443	4 588	-516	-10.1
132 – Building materials, except metals	3 032	3 423	3 302	3 168	3 238	206	6.8
200 – Electric and electric generating equipment	29 202	35 810	30 954	27 568	27 393	-1 809	-6.2
210 – Oil drilling, mining and construction machinery	11 849	12 658	14 112	12 928	12 809	960	8.1
211 – Industrial and service machinery, n.e.c.	71 483	84 651	74 731	69 272	69 699	-1 784	-2.5
212 – Agricultural machinery and equipment	3 201	3 428	3 320	3 526	3 791	590	18.4
213 – Computers, peripherals and semiconductors	93 416	115 625	92 748	80 815	86 083	-7 333	-7.8
214 – Telecommunications equipment	25 315	31 241	27 920	22 210	20 747	-4 567	-18.0
215 – Business machinery and equipment, except computers	2 996	3 196	2 892	2 040	1 925	-1 071	-35.7
216 – Scientific, hospital and medical machinery	16 788	19 191	20 091	19 336	20 872	4 084	24.3
220 – Civilian aircraft, engines, parts	52 952	48 031	52 846	50 436	46 845	-6 107	-11.5
221 – Railway transportation equipment	1 621	1 465	1 603	1 244	1 738	117	7.2
222 – Vessels (except military and pleasure craft)	1 081	1 001	1 016	1 142	1 024	-58	-5.3
223 – Spacecraft, engines and parts, except military	30	24	16	37	34	4	13.2
300 – Passenger cars, new and used	16 576	16 739	17 863	20 535	22 111	5 536	33.4
301 – Trucks, buses and special purpose vehicles	8 824	9 529	7 550	8 349	10 236	1 412	16.0
302 – Parts, engines, bodies, and chassis	48 947	53 203	49 362	49 554	47 779	-1 168	-2.4
400 – Apparel, footwear, and household goods	10 427	10 888	9 120	8 061	7 709	-2 718	-26.1
401 – Other consumer nondurables	28 189	31 418	32 608	32 119	35 871	7 682	27.3
410 – Household goods	16 179	17 749	17 742	16 872	18 359	2 179	13.5
411 – Recreational equipment and materials	7 955	8 109	7 742	7 577	7 913	-42	-0.5
412 – Home entertainment equipment	9 176	10 040	9 158	8 713	8 130	-1 046	-11.4
413 – Coins, gems, jewelry, and collectibles	4 982	6 343	7 448	5 924	6 148	1 166	23.4
420 – Nondurables, unmanufactured	302	291	279	269	289	-13	-4.3
421 – Durables, unmanufactured	3 544	4 459	4 423	4 842	5 479	1 935	54.6
500 – Military-type goods	13 989	11 301	11 611	11 770	10 942	-3 047	-21.8
600 – Domestic exports, n.e.c.	20 521	22 760	23 573	21 806	21 753	1 232	6.0

Note: Unrevised data.

Table B-51. U.S. Total Imports by 3-Digit End-Use Product Groups, 1999–2003

(Millions of dollars; Census basis; general imports, Customs.)

End-use product	1999	2000	2001	2002	2003	1999–2003 change Value	1999–2003 change Percent
TOTAL	1 024 766	1 216 888	1 141 959	1 163 549	1 259 396	234 630	22.9
000 – Green coffee, cocoa beans, and cane sugar	3 716	3 257	2 306	2 437	2 882	-835	-22.5
001 – Other agricultural foods	26 521	28 039	29 582	31 996	36 247	9 726	36.7
002 – Feedstuff and foodgrains	1 487	1 475	1 541	1 612	1 605	119	8.0
010 – Nonagricultural products	11 891	13 202	13 211	13 655	15 066	3 175	26.7
100 – Petroleum and products, excluding gas	67 530	120 139	103 709	103 566	133 180	65 650	97.2
101 – Fuels, n.e.s., coal and gas	7 008	11 818	17 350	13 247	21 855	14 847	211.9
103 – Nuclear fuel materials and fuels	1 698	2 045	2 101	2 189	2 919	1 221	71.9
104 – Electric energy	1 334	2 711	2 681	1 160	1 382	48	3.6
110 – Paper base stocks	2 598	3 384	2 632	2 365	2 601	2	0.1
111 – Newsprint and other paper products	9 019	10 340	9 705	9 106	9 253	234	2.6
120 – Agricultural products	5 564	5 613	5 315	5 257	5 825	260	4.7
121 – Textile supplies and related materials	10 304	11 260	10 313	10 867	10 806	501	4.9
123 – Other materials, except chemicals	1 730	1 841	1 584	1 527	1 480	-249	-14.4
125 – Chemicals, excluding medicinals and food additives	29 481	33 657	33 999	33 108	36 668	7 188	24.4
130 – Lumber and other unfinished building materials	12 439	12 177	11 935	12 263	12 043	-396	-3.2
131 – Building materials, finished	9 380	9 622	9 352	10 233	12 135	2 755	29.4
140 – Steelmaking and ferroalloying materials, unmanufactured	2 793	3 104	2 239	2 459	2 839	45	1.6
141 – Iron and steel mill products, semifinished	10 091	11 590	8 202	9 066	7 404	-2 688	-26.6
142 – Major nonferrous metals, crude and semifinished	19 983	23 542	21 078	18 423	18 811	-1 173	-5.9
150 – Iron and steel products, except advanced manufactured	3 960	4 637	4 336	4 231	4 100	140	3.5
151 – Iron and steel manufactures, advanced	4 075	4 675	4 202	4 403	4 839	763	18.7
152 – Finished metal shapes and advanced manufactures	5 916	7 176	6 783	6 917	7 624	1 708	28.9
160 – Unfinished	1 683	1 885	1 827	1 770	1 890	208	12.3
161 – Finished	14 164	16 114	15 769	16 918	18 660	4 496	31.7
200 – Electric and electric generating equipment	32 825	39 756	34 790	32 911	33 289	464	1.4
210 – Oil drilling, mining and construction machinery	6 985	7 176	6 888	6 575	7 523	538	7.7
211 – Industrial and service machinery, n.e.c.	66 497	75 270	69 810	67 782	72 177	5 681	8.5
212 – Agricultural machinery and equipment	3 694	4 039	3 877	4 155	4 814	1 120	30.3
213 – Computers, peripherals and semiconductors	119 050	138 140	104 454	101 297	101 132	-17 918	-15.1
214 – Telecommunications equipment	21 268	32 401	24 448	23 176	24 763	3 495	16.4
215 – Business machinery and equipment, except computers	6 438	6 143	4 866	4 463	7 135	697	10.8
216 – Scientific, hospital and medical machinery	11 424	14 210	15 256	16 030	18 435	7 011	61.4
220 – Civilian aircraft, engines and parts	23 307	26 347	31 170	25 843	24 183	876	3.8
221 – Railway transportation equipment	2 211	1 763	1 292	999	1 006	-1 204	-54.5
222 – Vessels, except military and pleasure craft, miscellaneous	522	689	616	702	1 021	499	95.5
223 – Spacecraft, engines and parts, except military	66	151	116	37	165	98	148.2
300 – Passenger cars, new and used	96 543	109 264	106 621	114 062	114 365	17 822	18.5
301 – Trucks, buses, and special-purpose vehicles	20 088	18 642	19 240	19 400	19 828	-260	-1.3
302 – Parts, engines, bodies, and chassis	62 547	68 219	63 936	70 417	75 958	13 411	21.4
400 – Apparel, footwear, and household goods	77 662	87 438	86 904	88 307	94 319	16 658	21.4
401 – Other consumer nondurables	37 568	44 611	49 587	57 727	67 217	29 649	78.9
410 – Household goods	47 205	56 187	58 862	66 241	73 749	26 543	56.2
411 – Recreational equipment and materials	27 151	30 513	30 276	31 591	31 919	4 769	17.6
412 – Home entertainment equipment	26 060	32 058	29 858	32 641	34 395	8 335	32.0
413 – Coins, gems, jewelry, and collectibles	14 960	17 303	15 509	16 280	16 188	1 228	8.2
420 – Nondurables, unmanufactured	1 099	1 160	1 150	1 132	1 249	150	13.6
421 – Durables, unmanufactured	11 339	13 668	12 111	13 720	14 637	3 297	29.1
500 – Imports, n.e.s.	43 893	48 437	48 572	49 286	47 816	3 924	8.9

Note: Unrevised data.

Table B-52. Countries' Shares of World Merchandise Imports, 1992–2002

(Percent.)

Country	1992	1993	1994	1995	1996	1997	1998	1999	2000	2001	2002	1992–2002 change
Afghanistan	0.01	0.01	0.01	0.01	0.01	0.01	0.01	0.01	0.01	0.01	0.01	0.00
Albania	0.01	0.01	0.00	0.01	0.02	0.01	0.01	0.01	0.01	0.02	0.02	0.01
Algeria	0.21	0.22	0.21	0.20	0.16	0.14	0.16	0.15	0.14	0.17	0.17	-0.04
Angola	0.06	0.04	0.03	0.03	0.04	0.04	0.04	0.04	0.03	0.05	0.05	-0.01
Antigua Barbuda	0.00	0.00	0.01	0.01	0.01	0.00	0.01	0.01	0.01	0.01	0.01	0.01
Argentina	0.36	0.41	0.48	0.35	0.42	0.50	0.54	0.41	0.36	0.29	0.22	-0.14
Armenia	0.00	0.01	0.01	0.01	0.01	0.01	0.02	0.01	0.01	0.01	0.01	0.01
Aruba	...	...	...	0.01	0.01	0.01	0.01	0.01	0.01	0.01	0.01	...
Australia	2.08	2.21	2.28	2.21	2.25	2.16	2.14	2.19	1.99	1.84	2.05	-0.03
Austria	1.32	1.19	1.20	1.21	1.17	1.07	1.12	1.13	1.01	1.08	1.07	-0.25
Azerbaijan	0.02	0.02	0.02	0.01	0.02	0.01	0.02	0.02	0.02	0.02	0.02	0.00
Bahamas	0.06	0.08	0.06	0.04	0.07	0.03	0.05	0.05	0.05	0.05	0.06	0.00
Bahrain	0.11	0.11	0.08	0.07	0.07	0.07	0.06	0.05	0.05	0.05	0.05	-0.06
Bangladesh	0.09	0.10	0.10	0.12	0.12	0.11	0.12	0.13	0.13	0.13	0.11	0.02
Barbados	0.01	0.01	0.01	0.01	0.01	0.02	0.02	0.02	0.02	0.02	0.01	0.00
Belarus	0.08	0.06	0.06	0.10	0.12	0.14	0.14	0.11	0.12	0.12	0.13	0.05
Belgium	...	...	...	...	...	2.61	2.73	2.51	2.46	2.58	2.71	...
Belgium and Luxembourg	3.03	2.81	2.87	2.90	2.79	...	...	...	...	...	...	...
Belize	0.01	0.01	0.01	0.00	0.00	0.00	0.01	0.01	0.01	0.01	0.01	0.00
Benin	0.01	0.01	0.01	0.01	0.01	0.01	0.01	0.01	0.02	0.02	0.02	0.01
Bermuda	0.03	0.03	0.04	0.02	0.02	0.04	0.04	0.10	0.12	0.14	0.10	0.07
Bolivia	0.03	0.03	0.03	0.03	0.03	0.03	0.04	0.03	0.03	0.02	0.02	-0.01
Bosnia-Herzegovina	...	0.01	0.02	0.02	0.03	0.04	0.04	0.04	0.04	0.04	0.05	...
Brazil	1.05	1.46	1.51	1.90	1.95	2.16	2.02	1.66	1.66	1.69	1.59	0.54
Brunei	0.06	0.08	0.06	0.05	0.06	0.05	0.04	0.02	0.02	0.02	0.02	-0.04
Bulgaria	0.11	0.11	0.10	0.10	0.08	0.06	0.08	0.08	0.09	0.10	0.10	-0.01
Burkina (Upper Volta)	0.01	0.01	0.01	0.01	0.01	0.01	0.01	0.01	0.01	0.01	0.01	0.00
Burundi	0.01	0.00	0.01	0.00	0.00	0.00	0.00	0.00	0.00	0.00	0.00	-0.01
Cambodia (Kampuchea)	0.02	0.02	0.02	0.03	0.03	0.02	0.02	0.02	0.02	0.02	0.03	0.01
Cameroon	0.03	0.02	0.02	0.02	0.02	0.02	0.03	0.02	0.02	0.03	0.03	0.00
Canada	6.38	7.01	6.90	6.27	6.20	6.82	7.00	7.16	7.04	6.72	6.61	0.23
Cape Verde	0.00	0.00	0.00	0.00	0.01	0.00	0.00	0.00	0.00	0.00	0.00	0.00
Central African Republic	0.00	0.00	0.00	0.00	0.00	0.00	0.00	0.00	0.00	0.00	0.00	0.00
Chad	0.00	0.00	0.00	0.00	0.00	0.00	0.00	0.00	0.00	0.01	0.01	0.01
Chile	0.24	0.27	0.25	0.28	0.34	0.35	0.33	0.26	0.26	0.26	0.24	0.00
China	1.99	2.56	2.51	2.42	2.41	2.36	2.35	2.64	3.16	3.52	3.86	1.87
Colombia	0.16	0.24	0.26	0.25	0.25	0.26	0.25	0.17	0.16	0.19	0.17	0.01
Comoros	0.00	0.00	0.00	0.00	0.00	0.00	0.00	0.00	0.00	0.00	0.00	0.00
Congo	0.02	0.01	0.01	0.01	0.03	0.02	0.02	0.01	0.01	0.02	0.01	-0.01
Costa Rica	0.07	0.08	0.07	0.06	0.06	0.08	0.10	0.10	0.09	0.09	0.11	0.04
Croatia	...	0.12	0.11	0.14	0.14	0.15	0.14	0.12	0.11	0.13	0.15	...
Cuba	0.04	0.04	0.04	0.05	0.05	0.04	0.05	0.05	0.04	0.04	0.04	0.00
Cyprus	0.08	0.06	0.07	0.07	0.07	0.06	0.06	0.06	0.05	0.06	0.07	-0.01
Czech Republic	...	0.65	0.68	0.80	1.02	0.94	1.02	0.95	0.94	1.05	1.09	...
Czechoslovakia	0.65	...	...	...	...	...	...	...	...	...	...	...
Dem. Rep. of the Congo (Zaire)	0.02	0.02	0.02	0.02	0.02	0.02	0.01	0.01	0.01	0.01	0.01	-0.01
Denmark	0.86	0.73	0.74	0.77	0.71	0.74	0.77	0.71	0.64	0.64	0.68	-0.18
Djibouti	0.01	0.01	0.01	0.01	0.01	0.01	0.01	0.01	0.01	0.01	0.01	0.00
Dominica	0.00	0.00	0.00	0.00	0.00	0.00	0.00	0.00	0.00	0.00	0.00	0.00
Dominican Republic	0.13	0.14	0.21	0.19	0.21	0.24	0.27	0.27	0.28	0.27	0.26	0.13
Ecuador	0.06	0.06	0.08	0.08	0.06	0.07	0.09	0.05	0.05	0.08	0.08	0.02
Egypt	0.20	0.20	0.20	0.21	0.23	0.22	0.28	0.25	0.31	0.18	0.25	0.05
El Salvador	0.04	0.05	0.06	0.05	0.05	0.05	0.05	0.05	0.05	0.06	0.06	0.02
Equatorial Guinea	0.00	0.00	0.00	0.00	0.00	0.00	0.00	0.01	0.00	0.00	0.01	0.01
Estonia	0.01	0.02	0.04	0.05	0.06	0.07	0.08	0.07	0.07	0.08	0.09	0.08
Ethiopia	0.02	0.02	0.02	0.02	0.02	0.02	0.02	0.03	0.02	0.02	0.02	0.00
Falkland Islands	0.00	0.00	0.00	0.00	0.00	0.00	0.00	0.00	0.00	0.00	0.00	0.00
Faroe Islands	0.01	0.01	0.01	0.00	0.01	0.01	0.01	0.01	0.01	0.01	0.01	0.00
Fiji	0.02	0.02	0.02	0.02	0.02	0.02	0.01	0.02	0.01	0.01	0.01	-0.01
Finland	0.51	0.45	0.50	0.51	0.51	0.49	0.52	0.52	0.48	0.47	0.47	-0.04
France	5.88	5.01	5.08	5.09	4.79	4.55	4.86	4.99	4.66	4.75	4.53	-1.35
French Guiana	0.02	0.01	0.01	0.01	0.05	...	...	...	...	...	...	...
French Polynesia	0.02	0.02	0.01	0.02	0.01	0.01	0.01	0.01	0.01	0.01	0.02	0.00
Gabon	0.02	0.02	0.02	0.02	0.02	0.02	0.02	0.02	0.02	0.02	0.02	0.00
Georgia	0.00	0.01	0.01	0.01	0.01	0.02	0.02	0.01	0.01	0.01	0.02	0.02
Germany	9.83	8.16	8.05	8.12	7.72	7.25	7.76	7.39	7.03	7.11	6.84	-2.99
Ghana	0.05	0.05	0.04	0.05	0.06	0.06	0.06	0.05	0.04	0.04	0.05	0.00
Gibraltar	0.02	0.02	0.02	0.01	0.02	0.03	0.02	0.03	0.03	0.02	0.02	0.00
Greece	0.56	0.50	0.45	0.47	0.50	0.45	0.48	0.45	0.39	0.41	0.44	-0.12
Greenland	0.01	0.01	0.01	0.01	0.01	0.01	0.01	0.01	0.01	0.01	0.00	-0.01
Grenada	0.00	0.00	0.00	0.00	0.00	0.00	0.00	0.00	0.00	0.00	0.00	0.00
Guadeloupe	0.04	0.04	0.06	0.05	0.06	...	...	...	...	...	...	...
Guatemala	0.06	0.06	0.06	0.06	0.05	0.07	0.09	0.09	0.08	0.09	0.09	0.03
Guinea	0.02	0.02	0.01	0.01	0.01	0.01	0.01	0.01	0.01	0.01	0.01	-0.01
Guinea-Bissau	0.00	0.00	0.00	0.00	0.00	0.00	0.00	0.00	0.00	0.00	0.00	0.00

... = Not available.

Table B-52. Countries' Shares of World Merchandise Imports, 1992–2002—*Continued*

(Percent.)

Country	1992	1993	1994	1995	1996	1997	1998	1999	2000	2001	2002	1992–2002 change
Guyana	0.01	0.01	0.01	0.01	0.01	0.01	0.01	0.01	0.01	0.01	0.01	0.00
Haiti	0.01	0.01	0.01	0.02	0.02	0.02	0.02	0.02	0.02	0.02	0.02	0.01
Honduras	0.03	0.03	0.04	0.03	0.03	0.04	0.04	0.07	0.07	0.07	0.07	0.04
Hong Kong	3.01	3.43	3.51	3.53	3.45	3.47	3.09	2.86	3.00	2.91	2.95	-0.06
Hungary	0.27	0.31	0.31	0.28	0.28	0.35	0.43	0.44	0.45	0.48	0.51	0.24
Iceland	0.04	0.03	0.03	0.03	0.04	0.03	0.04	0.04	0.04	0.03	0.03	-0.01
India	0.56	0.53	0.55	0.63	0.63	0.68	0.71	0.76	0.71	0.81	0.85	0.29
Indonesia	0.66	0.70	0.69	0.74	0.75	0.69	0.46	0.38	0.47	0.56	0.52	-0.14
Iran	0.73	0.50	0.26	0.23	0.26	0.26	0.24	0.20	0.23	0.26	0.25	-0.48
Iraq	0.01	0.01	0.01	0.01	0.01	0.02	0.03	0.03	0.05	0.08	0.07	0.06
Ireland	0.55	0.53	0.55	0.59	0.61	0.65	0.74	0.76	0.71	0.73	0.73	0.18
Israel	0.46	0.50	0.51	0.52	0.52	0.48	0.46	0.49	0.52	0.48	0.50	0.04
Italy	4.55	3.65	3.64	3.76	3.60	3.46	3.61	3.50	3.30	3.36	3.35	-1.20
Ivory Coast	0.06	0.05	0.04	0.06	0.05	0.05	0.05	0.05	0.04	0.04	0.04	-0.02
Jamaica	0.05	0.05	0.05	0.05	0.05	0.05	0.05	0.05	0.04	0.05	0.05	0.00
Japan	5.67	5.98	5.94	6.15	6.07	5.63	4.70	4.94	5.33	5.04	4.69	-0.98
Jordan	0.08	0.09	0.07	0.07	0.07	0.07	0.06	0.06	0.06	0.07	0.07	-0.01
Kazakhstan	0.01	0.04	0.07	0.07	0.07	0.07	0.07	0.06	0.07	0.09	0.10	0.09
Kenya	0.04	0.04	0.05	0.06	0.05	0.05	0.06	0.05	0.05	0.05	0.05	0.01
Kiribati (Gilbert Islands)	0.00	0.00	0.00	0.00	0.00	0.00	0.00	0.00	0.00	0.00	0.00	0.00
Korea, South	2.02	2.14	2.22	2.47	2.61	2.40	1.56	1.91	2.25	2.04	2.19	0.17
Kuwait	0.18	0.17	0.15	0.14	0.15	0.14	0.14	0.12	0.10	0.11	0.11	-0.07
Laos	0.01	0.01	0.01	0.01	0.01	0.01	0.01	0.01	0.01	0.01	0.01	0.00
Latvia	0.04	0.05	0.06	0.06	0.08	0.09	0.10	0.09	0.09	0.10	0.13	0.09
Lebanon	0.10	0.11	0.12	0.12	0.13	0.12	0.12	0.10	0.09	0.09	0.09	-0.01
Liberia	0.14	0.13	0.13	0.10	0.07	0.06	0.10	0.06	0.08	0.06	0.06	-0.08
Libya	0.13	0.14	0.09	0.09	0.10	0.09	0.09	0.07	0.06	0.06	0.07	-0.06
Lithuania	0.01	0.03	0.05	0.07	0.08	0.09	0.10	0.08	0.08	0.09	0.10	0.09
Luxembourg	0.00	0.00	0.00	0.00	0.00	0.16	0.17	0.18	0.16	0.18	0.18	0.18
Macao	0.05	0.05	0.05	0.04	0.03	0.04	0.03	0.03	0.03	0.03	0.04	-0.01
Macedonia	0.00	0.03	0.03	0.03	0.03	0.03	0.03	0.03	0.03	0.03	0.03	0.03
Madagascar	0.01	0.01	0.01	0.01	0.01	0.01	0.01	0.01	0.01	0.02	0.01	0.00
Malawi	0.02	0.01	0.01	0.01	0.01	0.01	0.01	0.01	0.01	0.01	0.01	-0.01
Malaysia	0.97	1.13	1.29	1.42	1.36	1.31	0.98	1.04	1.15	1.07	1.19	0.22
Maldive Islands	0.00	0.00	0.00	0.01	0.01	0.01	0.01	0.01	0.01	0.01	0.01	0.01
Mali	0.02	0.02	0.02	0.02	0.02	0.02	0.02	0.02	0.02	0.02	0.02	0.00
Malta and Gozo	0.06	0.05	0.05	0.05	0.05	0.04	0.06	0.05	0.05	0.07	0.07	0.01
Martinique	0.04	0.04	0.04	0.04	0.03	...	...	...	...	...	...	...
Mauritania	0.01	0.01	0.01	0.01	0.01	0.01	0.01	0.01	0.01	0.01	0.01	0.00
Mauritius	0.04	0.04	0.04	0.04	0.04	0.04	0.04	0.04	0.03	0.03	0.03	-0.01
Mexico	3.18	3.39	3.61	2.78	3.26	3.83	4.40	4.74	5.14	5.11	4.15	0.97
Moldova	0.02	0.02	0.01	0.02	0.02	0.02	0.02	0.01	0.01	0.01	0.02	0.00
Mongolia	0.01	0.01	0.01	0.01	0.01	0.01	0.01	0.01	0.01	0.01	0.01	0.00
Morocco	0.20	0.17	0.17	0.17	0.16	0.15	0.14	0.19	0.17	0.16	0.19	-0.01
Mozambique	0.02	0.03	0.03	0.01	0.01	0.02	0.01	0.02	0.01	0.01	0.02	0.00
Nauru	0.00	0.00	0.00	0.00	0.00	0.00	0.00	0.00	0.00	0.00	0.00	0.00
Nepal	0.01	0.01	0.01	0.01	0.02	0.03	0.02	0.02	0.01	0.01	0.01	0.00
Netherlands	3.16	2.80	2.84	2.88	2.80	2.63	2.66	3.31	3.03	3.01	3.04	-0.12
New Caledonia	0.02	0.02	0.02	0.02	0.02	0.02	0.02	0.02	0.01	0.01	0.01	-0.01
New Zealand	0.22	0.24	0.26	0.25	0.26	0.24	0.21	0.23	0.20	0.19	0.21	-0.01
Nicaragua	0.02	0.02	0.02	0.02	0.02	0.02	0.02	0.03	0.03	0.03	0.03	0.01
Niger	0.01	0.01	0.00	0.01	0.01	0.00	0.01	0.01	0.00	0.00	0.01	0.00
Nigeria	0.23	0.19	0.12	0.11	0.12	0.12	0.13	0.12	0.13	0.17	0.16	-0.07
Norway	0.63	0.56	0.59	0.60	0.59	0.59	0.60	0.53	0.45	0.46	0.46	-0.17
Oman	0.09	0.10	0.08	0.08	0.08	0.08	0.10	0.07	0.07	0.08	0.08	-0.01
Pakistan	0.23	0.23	0.19	0.21	0.21	0.19	0.16	0.16	0.16	0.15	0.16	-0.07
Panama	0.05	0.05	0.05	0.05	0.04	0.05	0.06	0.06	0.05	0.04	0.16	0.11
Papua New Guinea	0.07	0.07	0.06	0.05	0.06	0.06	0.04	0.04	0.03	0.03	0.03	-0.04
Paraguay	0.07	0.08	0.10	0.11	0.10	0.13	0.14	0.09	0.08	0.07	0.07	0.00
Peru	0.19	0.21	0.25	0.29	0.28	0.29	0.28	0.22	0.21	0.21	0.19	0.00
Philippines	0.35	0.44	0.49	0.52	0.55	0.65	0.49	0.49	0.44	0.43	0.56	0.21
Poland	0.37	0.47	0.47	0.53	0.65	0.70	0.79	0.73	0.69	0.73	0.77	0.40
Portugal	0.75	0.60	0.59	0.61	0.59	0.58	0.62	0.64	0.54	0.55	0.54	-0.21
Qatar	0.05	0.05	0.04	0.04	0.06	0.05	0.06	0.04	0.05	0.06	0.05	0.00
Republic of South Africa	0.94	0.94	0.99	1.03	0.98	0.98	0.94	0.80	0.77	0.75	0.76	-0.18
Reunion	0.06	0.09	0.05	0.05	0.04	...	...	...	...	...	...	...
Romania	0.29	0.31	0.29	0.36	0.33	0.35	0.38	0.32	0.35	0.43	0.48	0.19
Russia	0.85	0.66	0.84	0.85	0.77	0.87	0.72	0.48	0.48	0.53	0.64	-0.21
Rwanda	0.01	0.01	0.01	0.01	0.01	0.01	0.00	0.00	0.00	0.00	0.00	-0.01
SACCA, excluding South Africa	...	...	...	...	...	...	0.02	0.02	0.02	0.02	0.02	...
Sao Tome and Principe	0.00	0.00	0.00	0.00	0.00	0.00	0.00	0.00	0.00	0.00	0.00	0.00
Saudi Arabia	0.81	0.70	0.51	0.50	0.48	0.47	0.50	0.45	0.43	0.61	0.63	-0.18
Senegal	0.03	0.03	0.02	0.02	0.02	0.02	0.03	0.03	0.02	0.03	0.03	0.01
Seychelles	0.00	0.01	0.00	0.00	0.01	0.01	0.01	0.01	0.01	0.01	0.01	0.01
Sierra Leone	0.01	0.01	0.01	0.00	0.01	0.00	0.00	0.00	0.00	0.01	0.01	0.00

. . . = Not available.

Table B-52. Countries' Shares of World Merchandise Imports, 1992–2002—*Continued*

(Percent.)

Country	1992	1993	1994	1995	1996	1997	1998	1999	2000	2001	2002	1992–2002 change
Singapore	1.76	2.11	2.22	2.28	2.28	2.20	1.70	1.77	1.89	1.68	1.64	-0.12
Slovakia	...	0.33	0.30	0.34	0.40	0.41	0.46	0.38	0.38	0.45	0.45	...
Slovenia	...	0.17	0.17	0.18	0.16	0.16	0.17	0.16	0.14	0.15	0.16	...
Solomon Islands	0.01	0.01	0.01	0.01	0.01	0.01	0.00	0.01	0.00	0.00	0.00	-0.01
Somalia	0.01	0.01	0.01	0.00	0.00	0.00	0.00	0.00	0.00	0.00	0.01	0.00
Spain	2.43	2.02	2.00	2.11	2.12	2.04	2.18	2.15	2.03	2.06	2.13	-0.30
Sri Lanka (Ceylon)	0.08	0.10	0.09	0.08	0.08	0.09	0.10	0.10	0.09	0.08	0.08	0.00
St. Christopher-Nevis	0.01	0.00	0.00	0.00	0.00	0.00	0.00	0.00	0.00	0.00	0.00	-0.01
St. Helena	0.00	0.00	0.00	0.00	0.00	0.00	0.00	0.00	0.00	0.00	0.00	0.00
St. Lucia	0.01	0.01	0.01	0.01	0.01	0.01	0.01	0.01	0.00	0.01	0.01	0.00
St. Pierre and Miquelon	0.00	0.00	0.00	0.00	0.00	0.00	0.00	0.00	0.00	0.00	0.00	0.00
St. Vincent and Grenadines	0.00	0.00	0.00	0.00	0.00	0.00	0.00	0.00	0.00	0.00	0.01	0.01
Sudan	0.03	0.03	0.02	0.02	0.02	0.03	0.03	0.03	0.02	0.03	0.03	0.00
Suriname	0.01	0.03	0.01	0.01	0.01	0.01	0.01	0.01	0.01	0.01	0.01	0.00
Sweden	1.11	0.97	1.04	1.18	1.16	1.09	1.14	1.00	0.97	0.87	0.97	-0.14
Switzerland	1.60	1.50	1.47	1.46	1.36	1.26	1.34	1.27	1.16	1.21	1.36	-0.24
Syria	0.08	0.10	0.11	0.09	0.09	0.07	0.07	0.06	0.08	0.09	0.10	0.02
Tajikistan	0.00	0.01	0.01	0.01	0.01	0.01	0.01	0.01	0.01	0.01	0.01	0.01
Tanzania	0.04	0.04	0.03	0.03	0.03	0.02	0.03	0.03	0.02	0.02	0.02	-0.02
Thailand	0.99	1.14	1.18	1.35	1.27	1.04	0.72	0.80	0.87	0.90	0.91	-0.08
Togo	0.02	0.02	0.02	0.01	0.01	0.01	0.01	0.01	0.00	0.01	0.01	-0.01
Tonga	0.00	0.00	0.00	0.00	0.00	0.00	0.00	0.00	0.00	0.00	0.00	0.00
Trinidad and Tobago	0.03	0.03	0.03	0.04	0.04	0.05	0.05	0.04	0.03	0.04	0.04	0.01
Tunisia	0.16	0.15	0.14	0.15	0.13	0.15	0.14	0.16	0.12	0.14	0.13	-0.03
Turkey	0.59	0.73	0.50	0.65	0.74	0.81	0.77	0.66	0.77	0.60	0.66	0.07
Turkmenistan	0.00	0.01	0.02	0.02	0.02	0.02	0.02	0.02	0.03	0.02	0.02	0.02
Tuvalu	0.00	0.00	0.00	0.00	0.00	0.00	0.00	0.00	0.00	0.00	0.00	0.00
Uganda	0.01	0.01	0.01	0.02	0.01	0.01	0.01	0.01	0.01	0.01	0.01	0.00
Ukraine	0.05	0.10	0.24	0.37	0.31	0.28	0.25	0.19	0.20	0.24	0.26	0.21
United Arab Emirates	0.42	0.48	0.46	0.38	0.39	0.38	0.41	0.57	0.57	0.64	0.64	0.22
United Kingdom	5.39	5.08	4.90	4.80	4.93	5.03	5.19	5.11	4.70	4.66	4.71	-0.68
United States	13.45	14.91	14.94	14.10	14.21	14.93	15.82	16.68	17.39	17.04	16.90	3.45
Uruguay	0.05	0.06	0.06	0.05	0.06	0.06	0.06	0.06	0.05	0.06	0.05	0.00
Uzbekistan	0.01	0.02	0.05	0.06	0.08	0.08	0.05	0.04	0.03	0.03	0.03	0.02
Vanuatu (New Hebrides)	0.00	0.00	0.00	0.00	0.00	0.00	0.00	0.00	0.00	0.00	0.00	0.00
Venezuela	0.63	0.59	0.33	0.38	0.35	0.47	0.52	0.40	0.47	0.48	0.44	-0.19
Vietnam	0.07	0.10	0.13	0.15	0.20	0.20	0.19	0.19	0.22	0.24	0.25	0.18
Western Samoa	0.00	0.00	0.00	0.00	0.00	0.00	0.00	0.00	0.00	0.00	0.00	0.00
Yugoslavia (former)	0.30	...	...	...	...	...	...	...	...	...	...	...
Yugoslavia (Serbia/Montenegro)	...	0.00	0.00	0.01	0.04	0.05	0.05	0.04	0.05	0.06	0.06	...
Zambia	0.02	0.02	0.01	0.01	0.01	0.01	0.02	0.01	0.02	0.01	0.02	0.00
Zimbabwe (Rhodesia)	0.10	0.09	0.09	0.10	0.14	0.10	0.08	0.06	0.05	0.05	0.05	-0.05

. . . = Not available.

Table B-53. Countries' Shares of World Merchandise Exports, 1992–2002

(Percent.)

Country	1992	1993	1994	1995	1996	1997	1998	1999	2000	2001	2002	1992–2002 change
Afghanistan	0.00	0.02	0.00	0.00	0.00	0.00	0.00	0.00	0.00	0.00	0.00	0.00
Albania	0.00	0.00	0.00	0.00	0.00	0.00	0.00	0.00	0.00	0.00	0.01	0.01
Algeria	0.31	0.28	0.21	0.19	0.21	0.25	0.19	0.23	0.33	0.30	0.30	-0.01
Angola	0.10	0.08	0.07	0.07	0.09	0.08	0.07	0.08	0.12	0.10	0.12	0.02
Antigua Barbuda	0.00	0.00	0.00	0.00	0.00	0.00	0.00	0.00	0.00	0.00	0.01	0.01
Argentina	0.34	0.36	0.39	0.41	0.47	0.47	0.50	0.41	0.42	0.43	0.41	0.07
Armenia	0.00	0.00	0.01	0.01	0.01	0.00	0.00	0.00	0.00	0.01	0.01	0.01
Aruba	...	...	...	0.00	0.00	0.00	0.00	0.00	0.00	0.00	0.00	...
Australia	1.16	1.17	1.14	1.07	1.16	1.17	1.06	1.01	1.02	1.02	1.05	-0.11
Austria	1.22	1.09	1.08	1.16	1.12	1.09	1.16	1.19	1.09	1.14	1.26	0.04
Azerbaijan	0.04	0.03	0.02	0.01	0.01	0.01	0.01	0.02	0.03	0.04	0.03	-0.01
Bahamas	0.03	0.02	0.01	0.01	0.01	0.00	0.01	0.01	0.01	0.01	0.02	-0.01
Bahrain	0.05	0.07	0.08	0.08	0.09	0.12	0.12	0.12	0.12	0.13	0.14	0.09
Bangladesh	0.06	0.06	0.06	0.06	0.06	0.07	0.07	0.08	0.09	0.09	0.09	0.03
Barbados	0.00	0.00	0.00	0.00	0.01	0.01	0.00	0.00	0.00	0.00	0.00	0.00
Belarus	0.09	0.05	0.06	0.09	0.11	0.13	0.13	0.11	0.12	0.12	0.10	0.01
Belgium	...	...	...	...	...	3.19	3.38	3.15	3.01	3.03	3.44	...
Belgium and Luxembourg	3.38	3.35	3.51	3.56	3.38	...	...	...	...	...	...	...
Belize	0.00	0.00	0.00	0.00	0.00	0.00	0.00	0.00	0.00	0.00	0.01	0.01
Benin	0.00	0.00	0.00	0.00	0.01	0.00	0.00	0.00	0.00	0.00	0.00	0.00
Bermuda	0.00	0.01	0.00	0.00	0.01	0.01	0.00	0.01	0.01	0.02	0.01	0.01
Bolivia	0.02	0.02	0.03	0.02	0.02	0.02	0.03	0.03	0.02	0.02	0.02	0.00
Bosnia-Herzegovina	...	0.00	0.00	0.00	0.00	0.01	0.01	0.01	0.01	0.01	0.01	...
Brazil	1.02	1.07	1.05	0.94	0.92	1.00	0.97	0.87	0.90	0.95	0.97	-0.05
Brunei	0.11	0.10	0.08	0.07	0.07	0.07	0.04	0.05	0.05	0.05	0.06	-0.05
Bulgaria	0.07	0.06	0.08	0.11	0.09	0.08	0.08	0.07	0.08	0.08	0.09	0.02
Burkina (Upper Volta)	0.00	0.00	0.00	0.00	0.00	0.00	0.00	0.00	0.00	0.00	0.00	0.00
Burundi	0.00	0.00	0.00	0.00	0.00	0.00	0.00	0.00	0.00	0.00	0.00	0.00
Cambodia (Kampuchea)	0.00	0.01	0.01	0.01	0.01	0.01	0.02	0.02	0.02	0.02	0.03	0.03
Cameroon	0.05	0.04	0.03	0.03	0.03	0.03	0.03	0.03	0.03	0.03	0.03	-0.02
Canada	3.66	3.88	3.88	3.83	3.87	3.95	4.00	4.28	4.43	4.21	4.07	0.41
Cape Verde	0.00	0.00	0.00	0.00	0.00	0.00	0.00	0.00	0.00	0.00	0.00	0.00
Central African Republic	0.00	0.00	0.00	0.00	0.00	0.00	0.00	0.00	0.00	0.00	0.00	0.00
Chad	0.00	0.00	0.00	0.00	0.00	0.00	0.00	0.00	0.00	0.00	0.00	0.00
Chile	0.28	0.26	0.28	0.33	0.33	0.34	0.31	0.31	0.31	0.30	0.29	0.01
China	2.35	2.53	2.91	3.00	2.92	3.39	3.48	3.52	4.01	4.30	5.25	2.90
Colombia	0.19	0.21	0.22	0.20	0.20	0.21	0.21	0.21	0.21	0.20	0.19	0.00
Comoros	0.00	0.00	0.00	0.00	0.00	0.00	0.00	0.00	0.00	0.00	0.00	0.00
Congo	0.03	0.03	0.02	0.02	0.04	0.04	0.03	0.03	0.05	0.04	0.03	0.00
Costa Rica	0.05	0.08	0.05	0.05	0.05	0.08	0.10	0.13	0.09	0.08	0.17	0.12
Croatia	...	0.11	0.10	0.09	0.09	0.08	0.09	0.08	0.07	0.07	0.08	...
Cuba	0.03	0.03	0.03	0.03	0.04	0.03	0.03	0.03	0.02	0.03	0.02	-0.01
Cyprus	0.03	0.02	0.02	0.02	0.03	0.02	0.02	0.02	0.02	0.02	0.02	-0.01
Czech Republic	...	0.32	0.34	0.35	0.43	0.42	0.50	0.47	0.47	0.54	0.61	...
Czechoslovakia	0.34	...	...	...	...	...	...	...	...	...	...	...
Dem. Rep. of the Congo (Zaire)	0.04	0.03	0.03	0.03	0.03	0.02	0.02	0.02	0.02	0.02	0.02	-0.02
Denmark	1.13	0.99	0.96	0.96	0.91	0.90	0.91	0.89	0.82	0.82	0.90	-0.23
Djibouti	0.00	0.00	0.00	0.00	0.00	0.00	0.00	0.00	0.00	0.00	0.00	0.00
Dominica	0.00	0.00	0.00	0.00	0.00	0.00	0.00	0.00	0.00	0.00	0.00	0.00
Dominican Republic	0.02	0.02	0.08	0.07	0.08	0.09	0.09	0.09	0.09	0.09	0.07	0.05
Ecuador	0.08	0.08	0.09	0.09	0.09	0.10	0.08	0.09	0.09	0.09	0.08	0.00
Egypt	0.08	0.09	0.08	0.07	0.07	0.07	0.06	0.06	0.10	0.07	0.11	0.03
El Salvador	0.02	0.02	0.03	0.02	0.02	0.03	0.02	0.02	0.02	0.02	0.05	0.03
Equatorial Guinea	0.00	0.00	0.00	0.00	0.00	0.01	0.01	0.01	0.02	0.03	0.03	0.03
Estonia	0.01	0.02	0.03	0.04	0.04	0.05	0.06	0.05	0.06	0.06	0.07	0.06
Ethiopia	0.01	0.01	0.01	0.01	0.01	0.01	0.01	0.01	0.01	0.01	0.01	0.00
Falkland Islands	0.00	0.00	0.00	0.00	0.00	0.00	0.00	0.00	0.00	0.00	0.00	0.00
Faroe Islands	0.01	0.01	0.01	0.01	0.01	0.01	0.01	0.01	0.01	0.01	0.01	0.00
Fiji	0.01	0.01	0.01	0.01	0.01	0.01	0.01	0.01	0.01	0.01	0.01	0.00
Finland	0.65	0.64	0.71	0.80	0.74	0.73	0.80	0.76	0.74	0.70	0.72	0.07
France	6.49	5.98	5.79	5.83	5.55	5.42	5.75	5.85	5.21	5.20	5.33	-1.16
French Guiana	0.00	0.00	0.00	0.00	0.00	...	...	...	...	...	...	...
French Polynesia	0.00	0.00	0.00	0.00	0.00	0.00	0.00	0.00	0.00	0.00	0.00	0.00
Gabon	0.06	0.06	0.06	0.05	0.06	0.06	0.05	0.06	0.06	0.06	0.05	-0.01
Georgia	0.00	0.01	0.00	0.00	0.00	0.00	0.01	0.01	0.01	0.01	0.01	0.01
Germany	11.66	10.04	10.14	10.27	9.90	9.48	10.24	9.67	8.84	9.19	9.73	-1.93
Ghana	0.03	0.03	0.04	0.03	0.03	0.03	0.03	0.03	0.03	0.03	0.03	0.00
Gibraltar	0.00	0.00	0.00	0.00	0.00	0.00	0.00	0.00	0.00	0.00	0.00	0.00
Greece	0.26	0.25	0.21	0.22	0.23	0.21	0.20	0.19	0.17	0.16	0.17	-0.09
Greenland	0.01	0.01	0.01	0.01	0.01	0.01	0.00	0.01	0.01	0.01	0.01	0.00
Grenada	0.00	0.00	0.00	0.00	0.00	0.00	0.00	0.00	0.00	0.00	0.00	0.00
Guadeloupe	0.00	0.00	0.00	0.00	0.00	...	...	...	...	...	...	...
Guatemala	0.04	0.04	0.04	0.04	0.04	0.06	0.07	0.07	0.07	0.07	0.07	0.03
Guinea	0.02	0.01	0.02	0.01	0.01	0.01	0.01	0.01	0.01	0.01	0.01	-0.01
Guinea-Bissau	0.00	0.00	0.00	0.00	0.00	0.00	0.00	0.00	0.00	0.00	0.00	0.00

... = Not available.

Table B-53. Countries' Shares of World Merchandise Exports, 1992–2002—*Continued*

(Percent.)

Country	1992	1993	1994	1995	1996	1997	1998	1999	2000	2001	2002	1992–2002 change
Guyana	0.01	0.01	0.01	0.01	0.01	0.01	0.01	0.01	0.01	0.01	0.01	0.00
Haiti	0.00	0.00	0.00	0.00	0.00	0.00	0.01	0.01	0.01	0.00	0.00	0.00
Honduras	0.02	0.02	0.02	0.02	0.03	0.03	0.03	0.07	0.07	0.07	0.07	0.05
Hong Kong	3.28	3.72	3.64	3.50	3.49	3.48	3.29	3.14	3.25	3.06	3.22	-0.06
Hungary	0.29	0.24	0.25	0.26	0.25	0.35	0.44	0.45	0.45	0.49	0.55	0.26
Iceland	0.04	0.04	0.04	0.04	0.04	0.03	0.04	0.04	0.03	0.03	0.04	0.00
India	0.53	0.58	0.58	0.62	0.62	0.64	0.64	0.65	0.69	0.71	0.80	0.27
Indonesia	0.93	1.02	0.96	0.92	0.96	0.99	0.92	0.88	1.00	0.91	0.92	-0.01
Iran	0.54	0.50	0.47	0.37	0.43	0.34	0.25	0.38	0.41	0.39	0.36	-0.18
Iraq	0.02	0.01	0.01	0.01	0.01	0.05	0.10	0.17	0.23	0.18	0.15	0.13
Ireland	0.77	0.80	0.82	0.88	0.91	0.97	1.22	1.29	1.23	1.34	1.41	0.64
Israel	0.36	0.40	0.40	0.38	0.39	0.42	0.44	0.47	0.51	0.47	0.47	0.11
Italy	4.87	4.64	4.57	4.70	4.84	4.41	4.59	4.24	3.81	3.88	4.05	-0.82
Ivory Coast	0.08	0.07	0.07	0.08	0.10	0.08	0.09	0.08	0.06	0.06	0.08	0.00
Jamaica	0.04	0.04	0.04	0.04	0.04	0.03	0.02	0.02	0.02	0.02	0.02	-0.02
Japan	9.32	10.00	9.51	8.93	7.94	7.80	7.35	7.57	7.70	6.50	6.71	-2.61
Jordan	0.03	0.03	0.03	0.03	0.03	0.02	0.02	0.02	0.02	0.04	0.02	-0.01
Kazakhstan	0.01	0.03	0.08	0.11	0.11	0.12	0.10	0.10	0.16	0.15	0.16	0.15
Kenya	0.04	0.04	0.04	0.04	0.04	0.04	0.04	0.04	0.03	0.04	0.04	0.00
Kiribati (Gilbert Islands)	0.00	0.00	0.00	0.00	0.00	0.00	0.00	0.00	0.00	0.00	0.00	0.00
Korea, South	2.12	2.37	2.44	2.65	2.65	2.67	2.51	2.59	2.77	2.41	2.60	0.48
Kuwait	0.12	0.25	0.23	0.26	0.26	0.27	0.19	0.23	0.30	0.26	0.25	0.13
Laos	0.00	0.01	0.01	0.01	0.01	0.00	0.01	0.01	0.01	0.01	0.01	0.01
Latvia	0.03	0.03	0.02	0.03	0.03	0.03	0.03	0.03	0.03	0.03	0.04	0.01
Lebanon	0.02	0.02	0.02	0.01	0.02	0.01	0.01	0.01	0.01	0.02	0.02	0.00
Liberia	0.02	0.01	0.01	0.02	0.02	0.01	0.02	0.01	0.01	0.02	0.02	0.00
Libya	0.27	0.21	0.19	0.17	0.20	0.18	0.11	0.14	0.20	0.18	0.16	-0.11
Lithuania	0.02	0.03	0.05	0.05	0.06	0.07	0.07	0.05	0.06	0.07	0.09	0.07
Luxembourg	. . .	. . .	. . .	. . .	. . .	0.12	0.15	0.15	0.13	0.17	0.16	. . .
Macao	0.05	0.05	0.04	0.04	0.04	0.04	0.04	0.04	0.04	0.04	0.04	-0.01
Macedonia	. . .	0.03	0.03	0.02	0.02	0.02	0.02	0.02	0.02	0.02	0.02	. . .
Madagascar	0.01	0.01	0.01	0.01	0.01	0.00	0.00	0.00	0.01	0.01	0.01	0.00
Malawi	0.01	0.01	0.01	0.01	0.01	0.01	0.01	0.01	0.01	0.01	0.01	0.00
Malaysia	1.12	1.30	1.41	1.49	1.51	1.46	1.39	1.53	1.58	1.42	1.50	0.38
Maldive Islands	0.00	0.00	0.00	0.00	0.00	0.00	0.00	0.00	0.01	0.00	0.00	0.00
Mali	0.01	0.01	0.00	0.00	0.01	0.01	0.01	0.00	0.00	0.00	0.00	-0.01
Malta and Gozo	0.04	0.04	0.04	0.04	0.03	0.03	0.03	0.04	0.04	0.04	0.04	0.00
Martinique	0.01	0.00	0.01	0.00	0.00	0.00	0.00	0.00	0.00	0.00	0.00	-0.01
Mauritania	0.01	0.01	0.01	0.01	0.01	0.01	0.01	0.01	0.01	0.01	0.01	0.00
Mauritius	0.04	0.04	0.03	0.03	0.03	0.03	0.03	0.03	0.02	0.02	0.03	-0.01
Mexico	1.27	1.43	1.46	1.60	1.85	2.05	2.23	2.46	2.68	2.55	2.59	1.32
Moldova	0.01	0.01	0.01	0.02	0.02	0.02	0.01	0.01	0.01	0.01	0.01	0.00
Mongolia	0.00	0.01	0.01	0.01	0.01	0.01	0.01	0.01	0.01	0.01	0.01	0.01
Morocco	0.12	0.10	0.10	0.10	0.10	0.09	0.09	0.15	0.13	0.11	0.13	0.01
Mozambique	0.00	0.00	0.00	0.00	0.00	0.00	0.00	0.00	0.01	0.01	0.01	0.01
Nauru	0.00	0.00	0.00	0.00	0.00	0.00	0.00	0.00	0.00	0.00	0.00	0.00
Nepal	0.01	0.01	0.01	0.01	0.01	0.01	0.01	0.01	0.01	0.01	0.01	0.00
Netherlands	3.80	3.54	3.52	3.58	3.43	3.20	3.20	3.97	3.70	3.72	3.92	0.12
New Caledonia	0.01	0.01	0.01	0.01	0.01	0.01	0.01	0.01	0.01	0.01	0.01	0.00
New Zealand	0.26	0.29	0.29	0.28	0.28	0.26	0.22	0.22	0.20	0.22	0.23	-0.03
Nicaragua	0.01	0.01	0.01	0.01	0.01	0.01	0.01	0.01	0.01	0.01	0.02	0.01
Niger	0.01	0.01	0.00	0.00	0.00	0.00	0.00	0.00	0.00	0.00	0.00	-0.01
Nigeria	0.34	0.32	0.27	0.25	0.31	0.31	0.21	0.24	0.34	0.32	0.27	-0.07
Norway	0.96	0.85	0.83	0.83	0.94	0.88	0.75	0.81	0.93	0.93	0.97	0.01
Oman	0.15	0.15	0.13	0.12	0.14	0.14	0.10	0.13	0.15	0.15	0.13	-0.02
Pakistan	0.20	0.18	0.18	0.16	0.18	0.16	0.16	0.15	0.15	0.15	0.16	-0.04
Panama	0.01	0.01	0.01	0.04	0.06	0.01	0.01	0.01	0.01	0.01	0.01	0.00
Papua New Guinea	0.05	0.07	0.07	0.06	0.06	0.05	0.04	0.05	0.05	0.04	0.04	-0.01
Paraguay	0.02	0.02	0.02	0.02	0.02	0.03	0.02	0.02	0.02	0.02	0.02	0.00
Peru	0.10	0.10	0.11	0.11	0.11	0.12	0.11	0.11	0.11	0.11	0.12	0.02
Philippines	0.27	0.31	0.32	0.35	0.40	0.47	0.56	0.64	0.61	0.52	0.57	0.30
Poland	0.36	0.39	0.41	0.46	0.47	0.48	0.53	0.49	0.51	0.58	0.66	0.30
Portugal	0.52	0.42	0.43	0.47	0.46	0.44	0.46	0.44	0.38	0.38	0.41	-0.11
Qatar	0.10	0.09	0.08	0.07	0.08	0.10	0.09	0.11	0.19	0.20	0.19	0.09
Republic of South Africa	0.65	0.67	0.61	0.57	0.57	0.58	0.51	0.44	0.43	0.35	0.34	-0.31
Reunion	0.01	0.00	0.00	0.00	0.00	. . .	. . .	. . .	. . .	. . .	. . .	. . .
Romania	0.12	0.13	0.15	0.16	0.15	0.16	0.16	0.15	0.17	0.18	0.22	0.10
Russia	1.09	1.21	1.52	1.56	1.62	1.58	1.35	1.31	1.66	1.33	1.73	0.64
Rwanda	0.01	0.00	0.00	0.00	0.00	0.00	0.00	0.00	0.00	0.00	0.00	-0.01
SACCA, excluding South Africa	. . .	. . .	. . .	. . .	. . .	. . .	0.04	0.04	0.04	0.04	0.04	. . .
Sao Tome and Principe	0.00	0.00	0.00	0.00	0.00	0.00	0.00	0.00	0.00	0.00	0.00	0.00
Saudi Arabia	1.38	1.17	1.02	1.01	1.17	1.12	0.73	0.88	1.19	1.10	0.99	-0.39
Senegal	0.02	0.02	0.01	0.01	0.01	0.01	0.02	0.01	0.01	0.01	0.02	0.00
Seychelles	0.00	0.00	0.00	0.00	0.00	0.00	0.00	0.00	0.00	0.00	0.01	0.01
Sierra Leone	0.00	0.00	0.00	0.00	0.00	0.00	0.00	0.00	0.00	0.00	0.00	0.00

. . . = Not available.

Table B-53. Countries' Shares of World Merchandise Exports, 1992–2002—*Continued*

(Percent.)

Country	1992	1993	1994	1995	1996	1997	1998	1999	2000	2001	2002	1992–2002 change
Singapore	1.74	2.04	2.33	2.38	2.42	2.32	2.08	2.07	2.22	1.96	2.01	0.27
Slovakia	. . .	0.15	0.16	0.17	0.17	0.18	0.20	0.18	0.19	0.20	0.23	. . .
Slovenia	. . .	0.17	0.17	0.17	0.16	0.16	0.17	0.15	0.14	0.15	0.17	. . .
Solomon Islands	0.00	0.00	0.00	0.00	0.00	0.00	0.00	0.00	0.00	0.00	0.00	0.00
Somalia	0.00	0.00	0.00	0.00	0.00	0.00	0.00	0.00	0.00	0.00	0.00	0.00
Spain	1.76	1.73	1.76	1.85	1.97	1.93	2.03	1.87	1.74	1.75	1.90	0.14
Sri Lanka (Ceylon)	0.08	0.08	0.08	0.08	0.08	0.09	0.09	0.08	0.09	0.08	0.07	-0.01
St. Christopher-Nevis	0.00	0.00	0.00	0.00	0.00	0.00	0.00	0.00	0.00	0.00	0.00	0.00
St. Helena	0.00	0.00	0.00	0.00	0.00	0.00	0.00	0.00	0.00	0.00	0.00	0.00
St. Lucia	0.00	0.00	0.00	0.00	0.00	0.00	0.00	0.00	0.00	0.00	0.00	0.00
St. Pierre and Miquelon	0.00	0.00	0.00	0.00	0.00	0.00	0.00	0.00	0.00	0.00	0.00	0.00
St. Vincent and Grenadines	0.00	0.00	0.00	0.00	0.00	0.00	0.00	0.00	0.00	0.00	0.00	0.00
Sudan	0.01	0.01	0.01	0.01	0.01	0.01	0.01	0.01	0.03	0.03	0.03	0.02
Suriname	0.01	0.03	0.01	0.01	0.01	0.01	0.01	0.01	0.01	0.01	0.01	0.00
Sweden	1.43	1.28	1.37	1.60	1.63	1.53	1.60	1.53	1.37	1.19	1.28	-0.15
Switzerland	1.80	1.73	1.70	1.64	1.53	1.41	1.49	1.45	1.30	1.32	1.41	-0.39
Syria	0.08	0.09	0.08	0.08	0.15	0.13	0.05	0.06	0.08	0.10	0.10	0.02
Tajikistan	0.00	0.01	0.01	0.02	0.01	0.01	0.01	0.01	0.01	0.01	0.01	0.01
Tanzania	0.01	0.01	0.01	0.01	0.01	0.01	0.01	0.01	0.01	0.01	0.02	0.01
Thailand	0.89	1.02	1.10	1.15	1.08	1.07	1.03	1.06	1.11	1.05	1.11	0.22
Togo	0.01	0.01	0.01	0.00	0.00	0.00	0.00	0.00	0.00	0.00	0.00	-0.01
Tonga	0.00	0.00	0.00	0.00	0.00	0.00	0.00	0.00	0.00	0.00	0.00	0.00
Trinidad and Tobago	0.05	0.04	0.06	0.06	0.05	0.05	0.04	0.05	0.05	0.07	0.07	0.02
Tunisia	0.11	0.10	0.11	0.12	0.11	0.11	0.11	0.13	0.10	0.11	0.11	0.00
Turkey	0.40	0.42	0.44	0.44	0.45	0.49	0.51	0.50	0.45	0.50	0.56	0.16
Turkmenistan	0.00	0.02	0.03	0.04	0.03	0.01	0.01	0.02	0.04	0.04	0.04	0.04
Tuvalu	0.00	0.00	0.00	0.00	0.00	0.00	0.00	0.00	0.00	0.00	0.00	0.00
Uganda	0.00	0.00	0.01	0.01	0.01	0.01	0.01	0.01	0.01	0.00	0.01	0.01
Ukraine	0.04	0.11	0.23	0.30	0.28	0.26	0.24	0.21	0.23	0.26	0.29	0.25
United Arab Emirates	0.62	0.59	0.52	0.49	0.53	0.58	0.49	0.51	0.62	0.61	0.59	-0.03
United Kingdom	5.21	4.97	4.91	4.83	4.99	5.18	5.08	4.87	4.56	4.33	4.45	-0.76
United States	12.27	12.84	12.33	11.76	12.03	12.74	12.89	12.47	12.44	11.77	11.16	-1.11
Uruguay	0.04	0.05	0.05	0.04	0.05	0.05	0.05	0.04	0.04	0.03	0.03	-0.01
Uzbekistan	0.00	0.02	0.05	0.05	0.05	0.05	0.04	0.04	0.03	0.03	0.03	0.03
Vanuatu (New Hebrides)	0.00	0.00	0.00	0.00	0.00	0.00	0.00	0.00	0.00	0.00	0.00	0.00
Venezuela	0.39	0.41	0.41	0.38	0.51	0.49	0.38	0.38	0.54	0.43	0.43	0.04
Vietnam	0.08	0.08	0.10	0.11	0.14	0.18	0.18	0.21	0.23	0.24	0.25	0.17
Western Samoa	0.00	0.00	0.00	0.00	0.00	0.00	0.00	0.00	0.00	0.00	0.00	0.00
Yugoslavia (former)	0.30	. . .	. . .	. . .	. . .	. . .	. . .	. . .	. . .	. . .	. . .	. . .
Yugoslavia (Serbia/Montenegro)	. . .	0.00	0.00	0.00	0.01	0.02	0.03	0.01	0.02	0.02	0.02	. . .
Zambia	0.02	0.02	0.02	0.02	0.02	0.02	0.02	0.01	0.01	0.01	0.01	-0.01
Zimbabwe (Rhodesia)	0.03	0.04	0.05	0.04	0.04	0.04	0.03	0.03	0.05	0.04	0.04	0.01

. . . = Not available.

Table B-54. U.S. Shares of World Trade by Type, 1980–2003

(Percent.)

Type	1980	1990	2000	2003
EXPORTS				
Merchandise	. . .	11.4	12.1	9.7
Manufactures	13.0	12.2	14.0	10.8
Chemicals	14.8	13.3	14.1	11.5
Clothing	3.1	2.4	4.3	2.5
Iron and steel products	4.2	3.3	4.5	3.7
Machinery and transport equipment	16.4	15.1	16.1	. . .
Automotive products	11.9	10.2	11.9	9.6
Office machines and telecom equipment	19.5	17.3	16.3	12.1
Textiles	6.8	4.8	7.0	6.4
Agricultural products	17.0	14.3	13.0	11.3
Commercial services	. . .	17.0	18.8	16.0
Transportation services	. . .	16.7	15.5	11.7
Travel services	. . .	19.0	21.6	16.0
Other commercial services	. . .	15.3	19.2	18.1
IMPORTS				
Merchandise	. . .	14.6	18.8	16.8
Manufactures	11.2	15.4	20.0	17.8
Chemicals	6.2	7.7	12.5	12.7
Clothing	16.4	23.8	31.6	29.1
Iron and steel products	10.1	9.5	12.5	7.2
Machinery and transport equipment	12.1	17.5	21.6	. . .
Automotive products	20.3	24.7	29.4	25.0
Office machines and telecom equipment	15.9	21.1	22.5	17.9
Textiles	4.5	6.2	9.4	10.3
Agricultural products	8.7	9.0	11.7	10.7
Commercial services	. . .	12.0	14.2	12.8
Transportation services	. . .	13.6	15.8	13.6
Travel services	. . .	14.6	15.5	12.0
Other commercial services	. . .	8.2	11.3	12.9
BALANCES				
Merchandise	. . .	-3.2	-6.7	-7.1
Manufactures	1.8	-3.3	-6.0	-7.0
Chemicals	8.6	5.6	1.6	-1.2
Clothing	-13.3	-21.4	-27.3	-26.7
Iron and steel products	-5.9	-6.2	-8.0	-3.5
Machinery and transport equipment	4.3	-2.4	-5.5	. . .
Automotive products	-8.4	-14.5	-17.5	-15.4
Office machines and telecom equipment	3.6	-3.8	-6.2	-5.8
Textiles	2.3	-1.4	-2.4	-3.9
Agricultural products	8.3	5.3	1.3	0.6
Commercial services	. . .	5.0	4.6	3.2
Transportation services	. . .	3.1	-0.3	-1.9
Travel services	. . .	4.4	6.1	4.0
Other commercial services	. . .	7.1	7.9	5.2

Note: Balance percent = (exports percent) – (imports percent).

. . . = Not available.

Table B-55. U.S. Exports of Goods by Country, 1985–2003

(Millions of dollars; Census basis; foreign and domestic exports, f.a.s.)

Country	1985	1986	1987	1988	1989	1990	1991	1992	1993	1994
WORLD	219 182	227 483	252 866	322 718	363 765	392 976	421 854	447 471	464 858	512 416
Afghanistan	3	8	8	6	5	4	3	4	9	5
Albania	12	5	3	7	5	10	18	36	34	16
Algeria	406	451	426	731	758	948	727	677	898	1 191
Andorra	0	0	0	44	52	40	17	16	15	5
Angola	137	86	95	101	98	150	188	158	169	197
Anguilla	0	0	0	14	17	15	11	11	14	13
Antigua Barbuda	0	0	0	68	73	69	75	68	73	65
Argentina	717	943	1 089	1 055	1 037	1 179	2 049	3 222	3 772	4 466
Armenia	0	0	0	0	0	0	0	25	78	74
Aruba	0	0	0	98	127	202	235	288	266	274
Australia	5 123	5 252	5 467	6 913	8 347	8 535	8 416	8 913	8 272	9 781
Austria	436	461	530	722	873	873	1 055	1 257	1 326	1 373
Azerbaijan	0	0	0	0	0	0	0	0	37	27
Bahamas	786	761	782	739	773	801	721	713	704	685
Bahrain	104	89	106	269	489	718	501	489	653	443
Bangladesh	219	164	193	258	282	181	179	188	245	233
Barbados	173	147	132	159	179	162	167	128	145	161
Belarus	0	0	0	0	0	0	0	25	92	46
Belgium	0	0	0	7 260	8 514	10 314	10 574	9 779	8 876	10 944
Belgium and Luxembourg	4 792	5 361	6 152	0	0	0	0	0	0	0
Belize	56	59	72	103	101	106	114	117	136	115
Benin	67	17	18	21	18	24	26	27	22	26
Bermuda	258	236	261	286	354	255	233	242	265	300
Bhutan	0	0	0	0	0	1	0	1	0	0
Bolivia	118	111	139	147	144	139	190	222	216	186
Bosnia-Herzegovina	0	0	0	0	0	0	0	5	15	39
Botswana	16	19	28	41	30	19	31	47	25	23
British Indian Ocean Territory	0	0	0	0	0	0	0	0	0	1
Brazil	3 128	3 856	3 994	4 247	4 799	5 062	6 154	5 740	6 045	8 118
British Virgin Islands	0	0	0	39	49	60	45	44	46	47
Brunei	50	202	92	77	63	143	162	453	478	376
Bulgaria	104	97	89	127	181	84	142	85	115	110
Burkina (Upper Volta)	27	10	10	16	11	15	24	13	18	7
Burma (Myanmar)	10	14	8	11	5	20	24	4	12	11
Burundi	6	2	2	1	1	1	2	10	2	18
Cambodia (Kampuchea)	0	0	0	0	0	0	0	16	16	7
Cameroon	68	33	45	31	36	46	46	57	48	54
Canada	52 852	55 022	59 331	71 079	78 266	82 967	85 146	90 156	100 190	114 255
Cape Verde	0	0	0	4	3	6	5	4	5	5
Cayman Islands	75	82	127	104	202	185	116	267	179	202
Central African Republic	1	1	2	3	6	1	1	1	5	3
Chad	23	4	4	5	35	8	14	5	8	7
Chile	682	823	796	1 065	1 411	1 672	1 840	2 455	2 605	2 776
China	3 852	3 105	3 488	5 033	5 807	4 807	6 287	7 470	8 767	9 287
Christmas Island	0	0	0	0	0	1	0	0	2	1
Cocos (Keeling) Islands	0	0	0	1	0	3	0	0	0	7
Colombia	1 451	1 308	1 410	1 757	1 916	2 038	1 947	3 282	3 229	4 070
Comoros	2	0	2	1	0	0	0	1	0	0
Congo	19	10	9	21	12	90	43	60	27	38
Cook Islands	0	0	0	1	1	1	4	3	2	1
Costa Rica	421	482	581	695	880	992	1 034	1 351	1 547	1 867
Croatia	0	0	0	0	0	0	0	90	103	147
Cuba	1	2	1	3	3	1	1	1	3	4
Cyprus	45	54	65	117	109	129	119	166	138	209
Czech Republic	0	0	0	0	0	0	0	0	266	297
Czechoslovakia	63	72	47	55	54	89	124	413	0	0
Dem. Rep. of the Congo (Zaire)	103	104	103	122	122	138	62	33	35	40
Denmark	701	749	861	911	1 052	1 311	1 572	1 477	1 092	1 215
Djibouti	4	4	4	4	3	7	10	11	13	7
Dominica	0	0	0	3	31	31	42	34	27	26
Dominican Republic	741	918	1 140	1 359	1 646	1 658	1 743	2 098	2 350	2 799
East Timor	0	0	0	0	0	0	0	0	0	0
Ecuador	590	595	615	680	641	680	948	999	1 098	1 196
Egypt	1 969	1 655	1 513	2 095	2 610	2 249	2 721	3 087	2 763	2 844
El Salvador	400	433	371	461	521	556	534	741	869	932
Equatorial Guinea	0	0	0	0	0	0	13	11	3	2
Eritrea	0	0	0	0	0	0	0	0	1	8
Estonia	0	0	0	0	0	0	0	59	54	33
Ethiopia	203	103	136	181	69	157	210	250	137	143
Falkland Islands	0	5	6	0	0	1	0	0	0	0
Faroe Islands	0	0	0	4	1	1	2	3	0	0
Federated States of Micronesia	0	0	22	27	27	25	46	32	25	25
Fiji	0	0	0	15	22	25	18	59	27	118
Finland	435	375	512	755	969	1 126	951	787	847	1 069
France	6 054	7 166	7 854	10 035	11 585	13 652	15 365	14 575	13 267	13 622
French Guiana	112	25	123	279	270	271	150	82	323	196
French Indian Ocean Areas	1	1	3	0	0	0	0	0	0	0
French Pacific Islands	113	90	82	0	0	0	0	0	0	0
French Polynesia	0	0	0	69	70	70	80	82	102	72
French S. Antarctic Territory	0	0	0	0	0	1	0	0	0	0

Note: Unrevised data. Countries are shown as they were for the year of the data and not with current country definitions.

Table B-55. U.S. Exports of Goods by Country, 1985–2003—*Continued*

(Millions of dollars; Census basis; foreign and domestic exports, f.a.s.)

Country	1995	1996	1997	1998	1999	2000	2001	2002	2003
WORLD	583 031	622 827	687 598	680 474	692 821	780 419	731 026	693 257	723 743
Afghanistan	4	17	11	7	18	8	6	80	61
Albania	14	12	3	15	25	21	15	15	10
Algeria	775	632	695	650	456	867	1 047	984	487
Andorra	16	24	21	23	8	10	8	11	8
Angola	260	268	281	354	252	226	276	372	492
Anguilla	15	13	18	17	22	30	20	20	21
Antigua Barbuda	97	82	85	96	96	139	96	81	127
Argentina	4 190	4 516	5 808	5 885	4 939	4 700	3 928	1 591	2 435
Armenia	70	57	62	51	50	57	50	112	103
Aruba	247	225	239	351	307	289	279	465	355
Australia	10 789	11 992	12 041	11 929	11 811	12 460	10 945	13 084	13 104
Austria	2 017	2 009	2 073	2 506	2 588	2 554	2 626	2 424	1 793
Azerbaijan	36	54	62	123	55	210	65	70	121
Bahamas	661	725	810	815	844	1 065	1 022	975	1 084
Bahrain	253	244	406	295	348	449	433	419	509
Bangladesh	325	210	259	318	275	239	308	269	227
Barbados	186	222	281	281	302	306	286	269	302
Belarus	48	53	41	30	26	31	35	19	84
Belgium	12 459	12 520	13 431	13 918	12 385	13 960	13 524	13 343	15 218
Belgium and Luxembourg	0	0	0	0	0	0	0	0	0
Belize	100	107	115	120	136	209	173	137	199
Benin	34	27	52	44	31	26	32	35	30
Bermuda	299	282	338	400	344	428	371	415	401
Bhutan	0	0	1	3	1	1	1	1	1
Bolivia	213	269	295	403	312	251	217	192	182
Bosnia-Herzegovina	28	59	102	40	44	44	43	32	21
Botswana	36	29	43	36	33	31	43	32	26
British Indian Ocean Territory	2	0	0	1	1	1	0	0	3
Brazil	11 444	12 699	15 912	15 157	13 249	15 360	15 929	12 409	11 218
British Virgin Islands	49	54	65	63	59	65	75	67	71
Brunei	189	375	178	123	67	156	104	46	36
Bulgaria	132	137	104	115	103	113	110	101	156
Burkina (Upper Volta)	15	10	18	16	11	16	4	19	11
Burma (Myanmar)	16	32	20	32	9	17	11	10	7
Burundi	3	2	1	5	3	2	5	2	3
Cambodia (Kampuchea)	27	21	18	11	20	32	30	29	58
Cameroon	46	71	122	75	37	59	184	156	91
Canada	126 024	132 584	150 124	154 152	163 913	176 430	163 724	160 799	169 481
Cape Verde	8	68	10	10	8	7	8	10	9
Cayman Islands	180	208	270	422	368	354	260	234	310
Central African Republic	6	4	4	4	4	2	4	6	7
Chad	11	3	3	3	3	11	137	127	64
Chile	3 613	4 132	4 375	3 985	3 079	3 455	3 131	2 612	2 719
China	11 748	11 978	12 805	14 258	13 118	16 253	19 235	22 053	28 418
Christmas Island	4	0	0	0	2	1	2	1	1
Cocos (Keeling) Islands	1	0	0	0	0	1	3	1	1
Colombia	4 628	4 709	5 199	4 817	3 532	3 689	3 606	3 589	3 755
Comoros	1	0	0	1	0	1	1	0	1
Congo	55	62	75	92	47	82	90	52	79
Cook Islands	1	1	1	1	1	1	1	1	2
Costa Rica	1 739	1 814	2 023	2 299	2 380	2 445	2 496	3 132	3 414
Croatia	140	106	139	97	108	90	110	78	197
Cuba	6	5	9	3	5	7	7	144	261
Cyprus	258	257	244	163	190	192	268	193	327
Czech Republic	363	410	592	568	610	733	707	654	672
Czechoslovakia	0	0	0	0	0	0	0	0	0
Dem. Rep. of the Congo (Zaire)	77	73	38	34	21	10	19	28	31
Denmark	1 517	1 730	1 758	1 874	1 719	1 513	1 611	1 496	1 548
Djibouti	8	8	7	20	27	17	19	56	34
Dominica	26	34	37	52	39	37	31	45	34
Dominican Republic	3 017	3 183	3 928	3 977	4 086	4 443	4 436	4 262	4 214
East Timor	0	0	0	0	0	0	1	0	0
Ecuador	1 538	1 257	1 523	1 687	920	1 037	1 420	1 607	1 448
Egypt	2 985	3 146	3 840	3 060	3 025	3 329	3 778	2 866	2 660
El Salvador	1 111	1 072	1 398	1 515	1 520	1 775	1 771	1 665	1 824
Equatorial Guinea	5	17	47	87	221	95	80	109	336
Eritrea	17	14	16	25	4	17	22	29	87
Estonia	139	83	48	87	162	90	58	82	121
Ethiopia	148	148	121	88	165	165	61	61	409
Falkland Islands	0	0	0	3	0	0	0	0	1
Faroe Islands	1	2	1	3	5	2	20	5	13
Federated States of Micronesia	23	25	29	31	25	29	30	27	24
Fiji	32	28	33	74	126	23	19	17	20
Finland	1 248	2 438	1 741	1 915	1 668	1 571	1 554	1 537	1 714
France	14 241	14 428	15 982	17 728	18 838	20 253	19 896	19 019	17 068
French Guiana	442	301	494	246	192	19	130	250	156
French Indian Ocean Areas	0	0	0	0	0	0	0	0	0
French Pacific Islands	0	0	0	0	0	0	0	0	0
French Polynesia	82	88	106	100	93	94	83	79	92
French S. Antarctic Territory	0	0	1	1	1	1	2	1	0

Note: Unrevised data. Countries are shown as they were for the year of the data and not with current country defintions.

Table B-55. U.S. Exports of Goods by Country, 1985–2003—*Continued*

(Millions of dollars; Census basis; foreign and domestic exports, f.a.s.)

Country	1985	1986	1987	1988	1989	1990	1991	1992	1993	1994
French West Indies	28	34	44	0	0	0	0	0	0	0
Gabon	91	25	52	54	46	49	85	55	48	40
Gambia	11	14	12	17	10	9	11	10	10	4
Gaza Strip	0	1	0	0	0	0	0	0	0	1
Georgia	0	0	0	0	0	0	0	16	47	79
Germany	8 925	10 374	11 559	14 015	16 883	18 690	21 316	21 236	18 957	19 237
Germany, East	73	68	54	109	94	62	1	0	0	0
Ghana	53	84	115	117	123	138	142	124	214	125
Gibraltar	13	32	4	6	2	32	10	11	9	23
Greece	395	324	348	553	706	765	1 036	896	884	830
Greenland	6	2	3	4	4	6	4	3	3	3
Grenada	0	0	0	26	28	35	32	24	24	23
Guadeloupe	0	0	0	29	33	54	83	60	49	51
Guatemala	404	399	478	582	662	759	951	1 204	1 310	1 355
Guinea	51	24	35	35	40	43	88	61	59	50
Guinea-Bissau	0	0	0	2	2	1	1	1	2	1
Guyana	43	47	60	68	78	76	86	118	123	110
Haiti	396	387	459	479	471	478	392	217	221	210
Heard Island and McDonald Islands	0	0	0	0	0	0	0	0	0	0
Honduras	295	329	393	454	515	563	627	808	898	1 012
Hong Kong	2 785	3 030	3 983	5 690	6 304	6 840	8 140	9 069	9 873	11 445
Hungary	94	98	95	78	122	157	256	295	434	309
Iceland	38	60	84	97	179	232	156	119	147	112
India	1 640	1 529	1 460	2 484	2 463	2 486	2 003	1 914	2 761	2 296
Indonesia	782	919	764	1 056	1 256	1 897	1 892	2 778	2 770	2 811
International Organizations	126	0	0	0	0	300	255	0	66	2
Iran	74	34	54	73	60	166	527	748	616	329
Iraq	427	527	683	1 156	1 174	732	0	0	4	1
Ireland	1 341	1 434	1 810	2 181	2 494	2 539	2 683	2 853	2 731	3 415
Israel	1 868	1 856	2 190	2 571	2 831	3 200	3 856	4 074	4 420	5 006
Italy	4 556	4 800	5 468	6 693	7 232	7 987	8 579	8 698	6 458	7 193
Ivory Coast	70	60	82	75	79	78	82	87	88	111
Jamaica	404	454	601	757	1 009	944	963	938	1 113	1 066
Japan	22 191	26 619	27 808	37 431	44 584	48 585	48 147	47 764	47 949	53 481
Jordan	267	263	291	326	381	309	220	250	363	288
Kazakhstan	0	0	0	0	0	0	0	15	68	131
Kenya	91	68	89	91	133	116	92	124	116	170
Kiribati (Gilbert Islands)	0	0	0	3	16	19	27	35	31	23
Korea, South	5 720	5 909	7 665	10 631	13 478	14 399	15 518	14 630	14 776	18 028
Korea, North	0	0	0	0	0	0	0	0	2	0
Kuwait	493	636	484	675	855	401	1 228	1 327	1 009	1 175
Kyrgyzstan	0	0	0	0	0	0	0	2	18	6
Laos	0	0	0	1	0	1	1	1	5	6
Latvia	0	0	0	0	0	0	0	54	90	101
Lebanon	117	101	92	113	94	98	165	311	376	443
Leeward and Windward Islands	198	224	238	0	0	0	0	0	0	0
Lesotho	7	8	7	4	4	3	3	3	4	3
Liberia	72	65	69	67	98	44	47	31	20	46
Libya	311	46	0	0	0	0	0	0	0	0
Liechtenstein	0	0	0	14	10	11	10	12	11	14
Lithuania	0	0	0	0	0	0	0	44	57	41
Luxembourg	0	0	0	108	142	134	217	272	561	228
Macao	1	3	5	7	11	8	10	19	28	21
Macedonia	0	0	0	0	0	0	0	4	11	14
Madagascar	33	25	18	12	7	11	14	6	11	48
Malawi	4	3	5	12	14	14	55	14	16	19
Malaysia	1 463	1 727	1 895	2 139	2 875	3 425	3 902	4 396	6 064	6 965
Maldive Islands	0	0	0	0	3	1	1	2	1	1
Mali	30	17	10	20	11	9	18	11	33	19
Malta and Gozo	26	24	97	102	48	45	57	58	172	88
Marshall Islands	0	0	22	38	33	27	38	34	36	33
Martinique	0	0	0	28	25	34	37	33	32	31
Mauritania	26	15	8	17	13	14	22	59	19	14
Mauritius	11	10	26	150	12	13	15	22	18	24
Mayotte	0	0	0	0	0	0	0	0	0	0
Mexico	13 628	12 379	14 570	20 633	24 969	28 375	33 276	40 597	41 635	50 840
Moldova	0	0	0	0	0	0	0	9	31	23
Monaco	0	0	0	3	4	10	7	6	6	6
Mongolia	0	0	1	0	0	0	12	2	17	6
Montserrat	0	0	0	6	11	11	8	13	6	7
Morocco	226	456	341	358	398	497	403	493	602	405
Mozambique	56	23	50	57	41	50	101	150	39	39
Namibia	19	20	1	2	13	44	33	34	20	16
Nauru	0	0	0	0	0	0	0	0	87	0
Nepal	7	8	56	64	9	10	6	5	5	7
Netherlands	7 218	7 741	8 101	9 901	11 393	13 016	13 528	13 740	12 839	13 591
Netherlands Antilles	427	398	507	432	412	542	629	476	523	520
Neutral Zone	0	0	0	0	5	0	0	0	0	0
New Caledonia	0	0	0	27	65	34	44	36	22	27
New Zealand	722	873	815	935	1 117	1 133	1 009	1 307	1 247	1 508
Nicaragua	42	3	3	6	2	68	147	188	150	185
Niger	13	2	2	8	9	12	10	13	16	12
Nigeria	652	403	295	356	492	551	833	1 001	891	509
Niue	0	0	0	0	0	0	0	0	0	0
Norfolk Island	0	0	0	1	1	3	1	2	1	1

Note: Unrevised data. Countries are shown as they were for the year of the data and not with current country defintions.

Table B-55.　U.S. Exports of Goods by Country, 1985–2003—*Continued*

(Millions of dollars; Census basis; foreign and domestic exports, f.a.s.)

Country	1995	1996	1997	1998	1999	2000	2001	2002	2003
French West Indies	0	0	0	0	0	0	0	0	0
Gabon	54	56	84	62	45	63	74	66	63
Gambia	6	8	10	9	10	9	8	10	27
Gaza Strip	0	0	0	2	1	0	0	0	0
Georgia	95	82	141	137	83	109	107	99	131
Germany	22 376	23 474	24 467	26 642	26 789	29 244	30 114	26 628	28 848
Germany, East	0	0	0	0	0	0	0	0	0
Ghana	167	295	314	223	235	191	200	193	209
Gibraltar	18	12	9	9	4	15	10	26	14
Greece	1 519	820	954	1 355	994	1 218	1 296	1 153	1 191
Greenland	2	4	5	6	3	1	5	4	3
Grenada	27	36	41	56	66	79	60	57	68
Guadeloupe	69	66	58	61	66	86	58	41	45
Guatemala	1 646	1 564	1 728	1 941	1 812	1 895	1 877	2 042	2 274
Guinea	67	87	83	65	55	67	78	63	36
Guinea-Bissau	1	7	2	1	1	0	1	3	1
Guyana	141	137	143	145	145	159	141	128	117
Haiti	551	474	500	548	615	576	550	583	640
Heard Island and McDonald Islands	0	0	0	0	0	1	0	0	0
Honduras	1 281	1 641	2 014	2 323	2 369	2 575	2 437	2 565	2 845
Hong Kong	14 220	13 956	15 115	12 923	12 647	14 625	14 072	12 612	13 542
Hungary	295	331	486	482	503	569	687	688	934
Iceland	171	257	179	237	298	256	226	219	242
India	3 296	3 318	3 616	3 545	3 707	3 663	3 764	4 098	4 986
Indonesia	3 356	3 965	4 532	2 291	1 939	2 547	2 499	2 581	2 520
International Organizations	0	2	0	76	0	1	0	77	0
Iran	277	0	1	0	48	17	8	27	99
Iraq	0	3	82	106	10	10	46	32	316
Ireland	4 095	3 660	4 641	5 653	6 375	7 727	7 150	6 749	7 699
Israel	5 593	6 009	5 992	6 977	7 694	7 750	7 482	7 039	6 878
Italy	8 862	8 785	8 973	9 027	10 094	11 000	9 916	10 089	10 570
Ivory Coast	173	141	151	152	104	95	97	76	103
Jamaica	1 421	1 491	1 417	1 304	1 295	1 378	1 407	1 420	1 470
Japan	64 298	67 536	65 673	57 888	57 484	65 254	57 639	51 440	52 064
Jordan	335	345	402	353	276	313	343	404	492
Kazakhstan	81	138	258	103	179	124	163	605	168
Kenya	114	104	226	199	189	238	577	271	197
Kiribati (Gilbert Islands)	2	4	3	3	7	4	6	4	1
Korea, South	25 413	26 583	25 067	16 538	22 954	27 902	22 197	22 596	24 099
Korea, North	5	1	2	4	11	3	1	25	8
Kuwait	1 416	1 979	1 394	1 479	909	791	906	1 015	1 509
Kyrgyzstan	25	47	28	21	21	24	28	31	39
Laos	2	3	3	4	2	4	4	4	5
Latvia	89	165	219	187	218	134	111	91	124
Lebanon	589	627	551	514	356	354	418	318	314
Leeward and Windward Islands	0	0	0	0	0	0	0	0	0
Lesotho	2	3	2	1	1	1	1	2	5
Liberia	42	50	43	50	45	43	37	28	33
Libya	0	0	0	0	0	18	9	18	0
Liechtenstein	15	9	12	7	9	14	7	15	16
Lithuania	52	63	87	62	66	59	100	103	163
Luxembourg	374	242	712	606	984	398	550	480	279
Macao	30	30	67	41	42	70	71	79	55
Macedonia	21	14	34	15	56	68	33	19	26
Madagascar	10	12	12	15	106	15	21	15	46
Malawi	18	13	18	14	7	14	15	30	17
Malaysia	8 818	8 521	10 828	8 953	9 079	10 996	9 380	10 348	10 921
Maldive Islands	1	2	6	5	8	6	6	4	7
Mali	23	18	26	25	30	32	33	11	31
Malta and Gozo	107	125	120	268	190	335	259	210	202
Marshall Islands	32	29	24	25	36	65	27	29	28
Martinique	38	35	34	26	35	22	23	24	22
Mauritania	43	15	21	20	25	16	25	23	35
Mauritius	24	25	31	23	39	24	29	27	32
Mayotte	0	0	0	0	0	0	0	0	0
Mexico	46 311	56 761	71 378	79 010	87 044	111 721	101 509	97 531	97 457
Moldova	10	22	20	21	11	27	36	31	25
Monaco	10	3	12	6	13	28	15	11	50
Mongolia	14	4	34	20	10	18	12	66	21
Montserrat	4	8	17	5	4	11	6	5	8
Morocco	521	476	435	552	574	525	286	566	465
Mozambique	49	23	46	46	34	58	28	98	63
Namibia	27	22	26	51	196	80	256	58	28
Nauru	1	0	1	1	1	6	4	3	2
Nepal	10	9	27	16	21	35	14	20	16
Netherlands	16 559	16 615	19 822	19 004	19 412	21 974	19 525	18 334	20 703
Netherlands Antilles	504	528	477	742	603	674	818	742	747
Neutral Zone	0	0	0	0	0	0	0	0	0
New Caledonia	22	29	34	19	42	19	25	37	43
New Zealand	1 693	1 727	1 957	1 885	1 934	1 974	2 134	1 814	1 849
Nicaragua	250	262	289	337	374	379	443	438	503
Niger	40	27	25	18	19	36	64	41	34
Nigeria	602	816	814	820	628	718	957	1 057	1 029
Niue	31	31	37	6	0	0	0	0	0
Norfolk Island	1	1	4	2	3	1	0	0	0

Note: Unrevised data. Countries are shown as they were for the year of the data and not with current country defintions.

Table B-55. U.S. Exports of Goods by Country, 1985–2003—*Continued*

(Millions of dollars; Census basis; foreign and domestic exports, f.a.s.)

Country	1985	1986	1987	1988	1989	1990	1991	1992	1993	1994
Norway	659	916	802	902	1 036	1 281	1 489	1 280	1 212	1 268
Oman	157	158	169	129	170	163	203	257	252	219
Other Pacific Islands, n.e.s.	9	15	16	0	0	0	0	0	0	0
Pacific Trust Territory (85-86)	33	58	0	0	0	0	0	0	0	0
Pacific Trust Territory (pre-85)	29	1	0	0	0	0	0	0	0	0
Pakistan	827	736	646	969	1 136	1 143	951	877	810	719
Palau	0	0	5	9	10	9	14	10	9	9
Panama	673	708	742	633	729	867	981	1 100	1 191	1 276
Papua New Guinea	40	51	51	113	121	54	96	72	50	65
Paraguay	99	171	183	194	167	307	375	415	521	794
Peru	492	692	810	793	690	778	840	1 002	1 069	1 408
Philippines	1 375	1 345	1 583	1 838	2 206	2 472	2 269	2 753	3 529	3 888
Pitcairn Island	0	0	0	0	0	0	0	0	0	0
Poland	238	151	239	304	414	406	458	637	916	625
Portugal	659	578	577	733	926	922	792	1 024	735	1 055
Qatar	61	62	75	98	101	115	147	189	166	162
Republic of South Africa	1 205	1 158	1 281	1 690	1 659	1 732	2 113	2 425	2 197	2 173
Reunion	0	0	0	1	1	5	2	3	2	4
Romania	208	251	193	202	156	369	209	248	324	337
Russia	0	0	0	0	0	0	0	2 098	2 967	2 579
Rwanda	6	4	4	2	2	1	2	3	7	35
San Marino	0	0	0	3	1	1	1	0	2	3
Sao Tome and Principe	0	0	0	11	4	13	4	3	3	13
Saudi Arabia	4 001	3 293	3 057	3 664	3 576	4 035	6 572	7 163	6 666	6 011
Senegal	60	50	49	69	69	53	76	80	69	42
Seychelles	1	1	1	2	82	2	2	2	65	6
Sierra Leone	13	23	26	17	25	27	25	28	21	24
Singapore	3 452	3 366	4 023	5 687	7 353	8 019	8 808	9 624	11 676	13 022
Slovakia	0	0	0	0	0	0	0	0	34	43
Slovenia	0	0	0	0	0	0	0	38	92	96
Solomon Islands	0	0	0	5	6	6	4	54	3	1
Somalia	51	57	36	27	21	12	7	21	31	30
South Asia, n.e.s.	2	1	4	0	0	0	0	0	0	0
Southern Pacific Islands	5	7	11	0	0	0	0	0	0	0
Soviet Union	2 423	1 248	1 480	2 768	4 271	3 088	3 577	1 036	0	0
Spain	2 496	2 576	3 093	4 015	4 798	5 208	5 482	5 487	4 181	4 625
Special Category Exports	5 446	4 364	5 422	5 339	0	0	0	0	0	0
Sri Lanka (Ceylon)	72	66	77	123	143	137	121	178	203	198
St. Christopher-Nevis	0	0	0	36	43	52	35	32	42	45
St. Helena	0	0	0	0	0	0	0	0	7	6
St. Lucia	0	0	0	71	76	83	89	82	99	81
St. Pierre and Miquelon	0	0	0	0	0	0	0	1	0	0
St. Vincent and Grenadines	0	0	0	36	41	35	43	35	38	38
Sudan	238	89	146	103	81	42	92	52	53	54
Suriname	86	84	72	93	138	157	135	139	118	122
Svalbard, Jan Mayen Island	0	0	0	0	0	0	2	1	0	2
Swaziland	1	1	6	5	3	8	5	4	2	5
Sweden	1 911	1 861	1 882	2 670	3 140	3 404	3 288	2 844	2 353	2 520
Switzerland	2 244	2 969	3 132	4 162	4 915	4 944	5 557	4 536	6 804	5 614
Syria	106	59	93	89	92	150	207	168	186	199
Taiwan	4 466	5 183	7 186	11 943	11 323	11 482	13 191	15 205	16 250	17 078
Tajikistan	0	0	0	0	0	0	0	9	12	15
Tanzania	46	38	34	28	29	48	35	34	33	49
Thailand	738	854	1 483	1 684	2 292	2 991	3 758	3 982	3 768	4 861
Togo	17	17	20	21	28	31	24	20	13	12
Tokelau Islands	0	0	0	0	0	1	0	1	1	1
Tonga	0	0	0	4	6	6	5	6	5	6
Transshipments	238	94	77	208	394	222	168	301	277	251
Trinidad and Tobago	504	532	361	328	562	430	469	447	529	541
Tunisia	111	155	103	175	160	179	171	233	232	327
Turkey	1 150	1 056	1 304	1 554	2 004	2 253	2 423	2 730	3 434	2 754
Turkmenistan	0	0	0	0	0	0	0	35	46	137
Turks and Caicos Islands	12	15	15	33	46	39	40	38	22	29
Tuvalu	0	0	0	0	0	0	0	0	0	0
Uganda	5	4	19	16	23	26	13	15	21	28
Ukraine	0	0	0	0	0	0	0	305	311	181
United Arab Emirates	576	492	545	703	1 240	998	1 456	1 552	1 811	1 593
United Kingdom	11 127	11 275	13 908	18 274	20 866	23 484	22 064	22 808	26 376	26 833
Uruguay	64	99	92	99	133	145	216	231	253	311
Uzbekistan	0	0	0	0	0	0	0	51	73	90
Vanuatu (New Hebrides)	0	0	0	2	1	6	1	2	1	1
Vatican City	0	0	0	0	0	0	0	0	0	0
Venezuela	3 159	3 137	3 560	4 573	3 036	3 107	4 668	5 438	4 599	4 042
Vietnam	20	30	23	16	11	7	4	4	7	172
Wallis and Futuna	0	0	0	0	0	0	0	0	0	0
West Bank	0	0	0	0	0	0	0	0	0	0
Western Africa, n.e.s.	24	24	24	0	0	0	0	0	0	0
Western Sahara	0	0	0	0	0	0	0	0	0	2
Western Samoa	2	2	3	4	4	4	7	73	10	7
Yemen (Aden) (S. Yemen)	9	17	14	7	8	4	3	0	0	0
Yemen (Sana)	41	83	115	78	71	107	189	321	318	178
Yugoslavia (former)	594	527	460	532	501	566	370	169	0	0
Yugoslavia (Serbia/Montenegro)	0	0	0	0	0	0	0	6	1	1
Zambia	59	35	47	26	50	80	23	68	42	33
Zimbabwe (Rhodesia)	46	54	75	34	121	135	53	143	84	93

Note: Unrevised data. Countries are shown as they were for the year of the data and not with current country defintions.

Table B-55. U.S. Exports of Goods by Country, 1985–2003—*Continued*

(Millions of dollars; Census basis; foreign and domestic exports, f.a.s.)

Country	1995	1996	1997	1998	1999	2000	2001	2002	2003
Norway	1 293	1 558	1 720	1 709	1 440	1 544	1 838	1 407	1 468
Oman	220	215	342	303	188	200	306	357	323
Other Pacific Islands, n.e.s.	0	0	0	0	0	0	0	0	0
Pacific Trust Territory (85-86)	0	0	0	0	0	0	0	0	0
Pacific Trust Territory (pre-85)	0	0	0	0	0	0	0	0	0
Pakistan	934	1 277	1 234	726	426	462	542	694	840
Palau	8	17	15	14	15	18	18	19	16
Panama	1 391	1 378	1 538	1 753	1 741	1 609	1 333	1 408	1 848
Papua New Guinea	51	69	117	65	37	21	22	23	30
Paraguay	993	897	913	786	515	444	397	433	489
Peru	1 775	1 767	1 960	2 056	1 701	1 662	1 567	1 556	1 707
Philippines	5 294	6 125	7 427	6 736	7 226	8 790	7 665	7 270	7 992
Pitcairn Island	2	0	0	0	0	3	6	6	3
Poland	776	968	1 171	882	825	757	788	687	759
Portugal	899	960	955	888	1 091	957	1 258	863	863
Qatar	223	207	360	354	146	192	336	314	408
Republic of South Africa	2 751	3 106	3 000	3 626	2 582	3 085	2 962	2 525	2 821
Reunion	4	3	2	3	2	3	3	2	2
Romania	256	266	254	340	177	233	375	248	367
Russia	2 826	3 340	3 289	3 585	1 845	2 318	2 724	2 399	2 450
Rwanda	38	37	35	22	47	19	17	10	8
San Marino	6	6	8	9	8	1	4	6	6
Sao Tome and Principe	2	0	13	9	1	1	11	2	1
Saudi Arabia	6 085	7 295	8 451	10 525	7 902	6 230	5 971	4 778	4 596
Senegal	68	56	52	59	63	82	85	75	102
Seychelles	7	103	6	10	8	7	176	8	7
Sierra Leone	18	28	16	23	13	19	28	25	28
Singapore	15 318	16 685	17 727	15 673	16 246	17 816	17 692	16 221	16 576
Slovakia	61	63	82	111	127	110	70	93	115
Slovenia	110	131	113	123	113	140	120	131	139
Solomon Islands	3	7	2	3	2	6	7	2	2
Somalia	8	4	3	3	3	5	7	6	7
South Asia, n.e.s.	0	0	0	0	0	0	0	0	0
Southern Pacific Islands	0	0	0	0	0	0	0	0	0
Soviet Union	0	0	0	0	0	0	0	0	0
Spain	5 529	5 486	5 544	5 465	6 132	6 323	5 811	5 226	5 935
Special Category Exports	0	0	0	0	0	0	0	0	0
Sri Lanka (Ceylon)	279	211	155	190	167	204	183	172	155
St. Christopher-Nevis	44	39	38	45	48	58	46	50	59
St. Helena	0	12	3	0	0	0	4	2	2
St. Lucia	81	84	89	92	98	105	89	98	121
St. Pierre and Miquelon	1	2	2	3	3	1	1	1	0
St. Vincent and Grenadines	42	45	54	274	92	37	39	41	46
Sudan	43	50	37	7	9	17	17	11	26
Suriname	190	222	183	187	144	131	158	125	193
Svalbard, Jan Mayen Island	1	2	1	1	1	0	1	1	3
Swaziland	3	2	5	8	9	67	12	11	8
Sweden	3 077	3 429	3 316	3 819	4 239	4 557	3 548	3 154	3 225
Switzerland	6 241	8 370	8 306	7 251	8 365	9 942	9 835	7 782	8 660
Syria	223	226	180	161	173	226	226	274	214
Taiwan	19 295	18 413	20 388	18 157	19 121	24 380	18 152	18 394	17 488
Tajikistan	18	17	19	12	13	13	29	33	50
Tanzania	66	50	65	67	68	45	64	62	66
Thailand	6 402	7 211	7 357	5 233	4 984	6 643	5 995	4 859	5 842
Togo	18	20	26	25	26	11	16	14	15
Tokelau Islands	0	0	0	5	6	10	10	18	15
Tonga	8	6	7	12	7	8	5	11	6
Transshipments	565	627	340	324	371	306	262	187	186
Trinidad and Tobago	689	665	1 106	983	785	1 097	1 090	1 018	1 064
Tunisia	215	189	251	197	280	289	278	195	171
Turkey	2 727	2 886	3 539	3 513	3 197	3 731	3 107	3 107	2 904
Turkmenistan	34	201	118	28	18	73	248	47	34
Turks and Caicos Islands	34	43	59	64	95	89	76	54	72
Tuvalu	0	0	0	0	0	0	0	0	0
Uganda	22	17	35	30	25	27	32	23	43
Ukraine	223	394	404	368	204	186	205	255	231
United Arab Emirates	1 994	2 527	2 606	2 370	2 713	2 291	2 640	3 598	3 510
United Kingdom	28 827	30 916	36 435	39 070	38 338	41 579	40 798	33 253	33 895
Uruguay	396	484	548	591	492	538	414	209	327
Uzbekistan	63	352	234	147	339	151	148	138	257
Vanuatu (New Hebrides)	1	1	1	40	7	1	1	1	1
Vatican City	0	0	1	1	2	2	3	3	3
Venezuela	4 641	4 741	6 607	6 520	5 373	5 552	5 684	4 447	2 840
Vietnam	253	616	278	274	291	368	461	580	1 324
Wallis and Futuna	0	0	0	0	0	0	0	0	1
West Bank	0	0	1	2	7	9	2	0	0
Western Africa, n.e.s.	0	0	0	0	0	0	0	0	0
Western Sahara	0	0	0	0	0	0	0	0	0
Western Samoa	8	12	11	10	12	64	70	7	11
Yemen (Aden) (S. Yemen)	1	0	0	0	0	0	0	0	0
Yemen (Sana)	185	256	154	177	157	189	185	366	195
Yugoslavia (former)	0	0	0	0	0	0	0	0	0
Yugoslavia (Serbia/Montenegro)	2	46	49	74	59	30	55	78	50
Zambia	49	46	30	22	20	19	16	36	19
Zimbabwe (Rhodesia)	122	91	82	93	60	53	31	49	42

Note: Unrevised data. Countries are shown as they were for the year of the data and not with current country defintions.

Table B-56. U.S. Imports of Goods by Country, 1985–2003

(Millions of dollars; Census basis; general imports, Customs.)

Country	1985	1986	1987	1988	1989	1990	1991	1992	1993	1994
WORLD	345 276	369 961	405 901	441 282	473 397	496 038	488 873	532 017	580 469	663 830
Afghanistan	7	5	6	5	5	5	4	2	3	6
Albania	3	3	2	2	3	2	3	5	8	6
Algeria	2 333	1 831	1 999	1 813	1 836	2 645	2 100	1 589	1 583	1 525
Andorra	0	0	0	1	0	0	0	0	0	0
Angola	1 053	677	1 294	1 216	1 863	1 958	1 786	2 303	2 090	2 061
Anguilla	0	0	0	0	0	0	1	0	0	0
Antigua Barbuda	25	12	9	7	12	4	4	5	15	5
Argentina	1 069	856	1 080	1 438	1 398	1 509	1 291	1 254	1 206	1 725
Armenia	0	0	0	0	0	0	0	1	1	1
Aruba	0	2	0	1	1	1	100	212	457	462
Australia	2 836	2 628	3 006	3 531	3 898	4 433	4 010	3 678	3 294	3 200
Austria	834	864	929	1 085	1 135	1 316	1 274	1 306	1 411	1 749
Azerbaijan	0	0	0	0	0	0	0	0	0	0
Bahamas	626	442	416	411	462	509	470	585	348	203
Bahrain	84	77	63	99	80	81	87	61	97	155
Bangladesh	196	230	370	368	429	538	524	832	886	1 080
Barbados	202	108	59	51	46	32	31	31	34	34
Belarus	0	0	0	0	0	0	0	25	34	53
Belgium	0	0	0	4 352	4 351	4 369	3 950	4 479	5 177	6 342
Belgium and Luxembourg	3 387	4 006	4 171	0	0	0	0	0	0	0
Belize	47	51	42	51	43	47	46	59	54	51
Benin	0	0	15	16	7	22	23	10	16	10
Bermuda	7	6	6	6	10	12	8	24	15	9
Bhutan	0	0	0	0	1	0	0	0	0	0
Bolivia	99	124	111	117	120	203	209	161	191	260
Bosnia-Herzegovina	0	0	0	0	0	0	0	10	7	4
Botswana	29	2	7	9	17	14	13	12	9	14
British Indian Ocean Territory	2	3	2	1	8	0	1	0	0	1
Brazil	7 526	6 813	7 865	9 324	8 379	7 976	6 727	7 611	7 466	8 708
British Virgin Islands	11	6	11	1	1	2	2	3	14	15
Brunei	2	60	15	28	75	96	26	30	30	46
Bulgaria	36	57	42	27	59	47	56	79	159	212
Burkina (Upper Volta)	1	1	0	2	0	1	1	0	0	0
Burma (Myanmar)	14	14	12	12	17	23	27	38	46	67
Burundi	1	10	5	1	5	8	8	8	3	8
Cambodia (Kampuchea)	0	1	0	0	0	0	0	0	1	1
Cameroon	324	305	414	219	415	158	127	84	101	55
Canada	69 006	68 253	71 085	80 921	88 210	91 372	91 141	98 497	110 921	128 947
Cape Verde	0	1	0	0	0	2	0	0	0	0
Cayman Islands	11	15	28	18	48	21	18	11	35	53
Central African Republic	1	4	5	3	3	2	1	1	1	0
Chad	0	0	0	0	0	0	1	0	0	2
Chile	745	820	981	1 162	1 308	1 321	1 304	1 387	1 462	1 822
China	3 862	4 771	6 293	8 512	11 989	15 224	18 976	25 676	31 535	38 781
Christmas Island	0	2	0	0	0	1	1	0	0	1
Cocos (Keeling) Islands	0	0	1	0	0	0	6	0	0	0
Colombia	1 331	1 874	2 232	2 167	2 548	3 175	2 734	2 849	3 033	3 172
Comoros	6	3	6	13	8	5	10	10	10	6
Congo	609	364	430	376	506	414	410	510	500	403
Cook Islands	1	1	2	13	0	0	0	0	1	2
Costa Rica	501	641	670	775	962	1 008	1 154	1 411	1 542	1 646
Croatia	0	0	0	0	0	0	0	43	106	115
Cuba	0	0	0	0	0	0	0	0	0	0
Cyprus	14	10	14	34	15	18	13	11	16	18
Czech Republic	0	0	0	0	0	0	0	0	277	316
Czechoslovakia	76	85	78	88	87	87	144	242	0	0
Dem. Rep. of the Congo (Zaire)	401	221	308	365	332	316	302	250	238	188
Denmark	1 665	1 757	1 779	1 666	1 537	1 678	1 666	1 668	1 664	2 122
Djibouti	0	0	0	0	0	0	0	0	0	0
Dominica	14	15	10	9	8	8	8	6	5	7
Dominican Republic	982	1 085	1 163	1 417	1 645	1 747	2 017	2 372	2 671	3 094
East Timor	0	0	0	0	0	0	0	0	0	0
Ecuador	1 837	1 464	1 266	1 231	1 484	1 377	1 328	1 332	1 399	1 727
Egypt	79	112	465	221	227	396	206	435	613	548
El Salvador	396	385	284	284	245	238	303	384	488	609
Equatorial Guinea	0	0	0	0	0	0	0	0	4	0
Eritrea	0	0	0	0	0	0	0	0	0	0
Estonia	0	0	0	0	0	0	0	12	20	29
Ethiopia	43	73	73	54	70	40	15	8	22	34
Falkland Islands	0	4	0	0	0	1	0	0	0	0
Faroe Islands	0	0	0	37	29	17	30	23	9	10
Federated States of Micronesia	0	0	5	0	1	6	5	13	14	13
Fiji	13	12	18	12	16	34	38	73	69	97
Finland	895	908	999	1 206	1 366	1 267	1 089	1 186	1 609	1 803
France	9 482	10 129	10 730	12 217	13 029	13 124	13 372	14 810	15 244	16 775
French Guiana	13	19	9	11	5	3	1	3	3	3
French Indian Ocean Areas	2	4	2	0	0	0	0	0	0	0
French Polynesia	4	6	10	11	9	11	12	11	8	14
French S. Antarctic Territory	0	0	0	1	0	0	0	0	0	0
French West Indies	3	3	2	0	0	0	0	0	0	0

Note: Unrevised data. Countries are shown as they were for the year of the data and not with current country defintions.

Table B-56. U.S. Imports of Goods by Country, 1985–2003—*Continued*

(Millions of dollars; Census basis; general imports, Customs.)

Country	1995	1996	1997	1998	1999	2000	2001	2002	2003
WORLD	743 505	791 315	870 213	913 885	1 024 766	1 216 888	1 141 959	1 163 549	1 259 396
Afghanistan	5	16	10	17	9	1	1	4	56
Albania	9	10	12	12	9	8	7	6	4
Algeria	1 668	2 103	2 439	1 631	1 831	2 724	2 694	2 365	4 753
Andorra	0	2	0	0	0	0	0	1	0
Angola	2 236	2 687	2 784	2 252	2 425	3 557	3 100	3 115	4 264
Anguilla	0	1	1	2	2	2	2	1	1
Antigua Barbuda	3	9	5	2	2	2	4	4	13
Argentina	1 760	2 278	2 212	2 252	2 599	3 102	3 016	3 185	3 169
Armenia	16	1	6	17	15	23	33	31	38
Aruba	420	558	610	471	675	1 511	1 052	771	964
Australia	3 319	3 854	4 601	5 382	5 290	6 439	6 479	6 478	6 414
Austria	1 964	2 199	2 365	2 558	2 910	3 233	3 990	3 817	4 489
Azerbaijan	1	5	6	5	26	21	21	34	9
Bahamas	156	165	166	143	195	275	313	458	479
Bahrain	134	115	118	155	225	338	424	395	378
Bangladesh	1 257	1 343	1 679	1 846	1 918	2 418	2 359	2 134	2 074
Barbados	38	41	42	35	59	39	40	34	43
Belarus	45	52	66	105	93	104	108	126	215
Belgium	6 050	6 779	7 910	8 422	9 208	9 931	10 129	9 835	10 141
Belgium and Luxembourg	0	0	0	0	0	0	0	0	0
Belize	52	68	77	66	80	94	97	78	101
Benin	10	18	8	4	18	2	1	1	1
Bermuda	10	11	30	12	25	39	66	23	15
Bhutan	0	0	1	1	0	1	1	1	1
Bolivia	263	275	223	224	218	191	166	160	185
Bosnia-Herzegovina	3	10	8	7	15	18	12	16	12
Botswana	21	27	25	20	17	41	21	30	14
British Indian Ocean Territory	2	3	11	0	0	3	0	0	1
Brazil	8 815	8 762	9 630	10 122	11 314	13 855	14 462	15 812	17 884
British Virgin Islands	11	7	17	8	23	31	12	40	35
Brunei	38	49	56	211	389	383	399	287	422
Bulgaria	183	126	172	219	200	235	336	340	441
Burkina (Upper Volta)	0	4	1	1	3	2	5	3	1
Burma (Myanmar)	81	108	115	164	232	471	470	356	276
Burundi	21	2	14	8	6	8	3	1	6
Cambodia (Kampuchea)	5	4	103	365	592	826	963	1 071	1 263
Cameroon	48	64	57	53	77	155	102	172	214
Canada	145 119	156 506	168 051	174 844	198 324	229 209	216 969	210 590	224 166
Cape Verde	0	0	0	0	0	4	1	2	6
Cayman Islands	18	17	20	18	9	7	7	9	12
Central African Republic	0	0	1	3	3	3	2	2	2
Chad	3	7	3	7	7	5	6	6	22
Chile	1 931	2 256	2 299	2 453	2 936	3 228	3 555	3 781	3 703
China	45 555	51 495	62 552	71 156	81 786	100 063	102 280	125 168	152 379
Christmas Island	0	0	1	0	0	0	0	1	0
Cocos (Keeling) Islands	0	0	0	0	0	0	1	0	0
Colombia	3 755	4 273	4 724	4 652	6 276	6 969	5 696	5 606	6 385
Comoros	2	6	3	1	2	4	11	5	4
Congo	207	315	472	315	415	510	491	201	433
Cook Islands	1	1	1	1	1	2	1	1	3
Costa Rica	1 845	1 974	2 323	2 745	3 958	3 547	2 887	3 142	3 362
Croatia	93	71	83	73	110	141	139	145	181
Cuba	0	0	0	0	1	0	0	0	0
Cyprus	13	17	16	32	31	23	35	26	25
Czech Republic	364	482	610	672	754	1 071	1 120	1 232	1 394
Czechoslovakia	0	0	0	0	0	0	0	0	0
Dem. Rep. of the Congo (Zaire)	262	250	291	172	229	212	154	202	174
Denmark	1 946	2 137	2 140	2 382	2 825	2 974	3 400	3 236	3 718
Djibouti	0	0	0	1	0	0	1	2	1
Dominica	7	8	9	6	23	7	5	5	5
Dominican Republic	3 397	3 575	4 329	4 443	4 282	4 384	4 183	4 169	4 455
East Timor	0	0	0	0	0	0	0	0	0
Ecuador	1 930	1 916	2 055	1 755	1 814	2 210	2 042	2 146	2 721
Egypt	606	665	658	660	617	888	879	1 352	1 144
El Salvador	813	1 074	1 347	1 438	1 605	1 933	1 882	1 982	2 019
Equatorial Guinea	31	76	30	67	43	155	445	520	904
Eritrea	0	2	1	1	0	0	0	0	0
Estonia	62	60	77	125	237	573	241	164	182
Ethiopia	33	35	70	52	30	29	29	26	30
Falkland Islands	0	0	1	0	1	3	7	6	5
Faroe Islands	8	8	14	11	22	31	13	15	17
Federated States of Micronesia	13	11	12	13	10	14	21	15	14
Fiji	78	75	85	101	100	146	183	156	175
Finland	2 269	2 345	2 397	2 595	2 910	3 250	3 394	3 444	3 598
France	17 177	18 630	20 725	24 077	25 910	29 782	30 296	28 408	29 221
French Guiana	5	5	2	3	4	2	0	7	3
French Indian Ocean Areas	0	0	0	0	0	0	0	0	0
French Polynesia	14	17	35	34	43	44	48	44	48
French S. Antarctic Territory	0	1	0	1	0	0	0	0	0
French West Indies	0	0	0	0	0	0	0	0	0

Note: Unrevised data. Countries are shown as they were for the year of the data and not with current country definitions.

Table B-56. U.S. Imports of Goods by Country, 1985–2003—*Continued*

(Millions of dollars; Census basis; general imports, Customs.)

Country	1985	1986	1987	1988	1989	1990	1991	1992	1993	1994
Gabon	502	207	358	175	418	720	712	928	941	1 155
Gambia	0	1	0	0	2	2	2	1	9	2
Gaza Strip	0	0	0	0	0	0	0	0	0	0
Georgia	0	0	0	0	0	0	0	7	21	1
Germany	20 239	25 124	27 069	26 503	24 834	28 109	26 229	28 829	28 605	31 749
Germany, East	91	86	85	110	139	85	0	0	0	0
Ghana	90	191	249	202	127	169	152	96	209	198
Gibraltar	1	4	2	2	1	1	1	7	4	4
Greece	395	394	480	529	476	507	433	370	348	455
Greenland	3	1	1	1	2	1	4	12	13	10
Grenada	1	3	4	7	8	8	8	7	8	7
Guadeloupe	0	0	0	1	2	1	2	1	5	2
Guatemala	409	601	495	433	609	795	900	1 075	1 194	1 283
Guinea	115	90	95	108	133	141	138	102	118	92
Guinea-Bissau	1	1	2	0	0	0	0	0	0	0
Guyana	47	64	59	50	56	52	84	101	91	98
Haiti	390	375	395	384	375	343	285	107	154	59
Heard Island and McDonald Islands	0	1	1	0	0	0	1	0	0	0
Honduras	375	433	489	442	459	492	557	783	915	1 097
Hong Kong	8 396	8 891	9 854	10 243	9 739	9 488	9 286	9 799	9 558	9 698
Hungary	218	225	279	294	329	349	367	349	401	470
Iceland	248	238	286	190	208	163	208	166	233	249
India	2 295	2 283	2 529	2 952	3 314	3 191	3 197	3 781	4 551	5 302
Indonesia	4 569	3 312	3 394	3 188	3 542	3 343	3 238	4 332	5 439	6 523
Iran	725	569	1 667	9	9	7	231	1	0	1
Iraq	474	440	495	1 488	2 408	3 015	6	0	0	0
Ireland	901	1 003	1 112	1 373	1 571	1 745	1 956	2 264	2 519	2 890
Israel	2 123	2 418	2 639	2 978	3 239	3 313	3 497	3 812	4 426	5 223
Italy	9 674	10 607	11 040	11 611	11 946	12 723	11 788	12 300	13 223	14 711
Ivory Coast	525	425	373	290	234	200	221	187	178	185
Jamaica	273	299	395	444	532	569	576	599	720	747
Japan	68 783	81 911	84 575	89 802	93 586	90 433	92 333	97 181	107 268	119 149
Jordan	14	10	11	12	8	11	6	18	19	29
Kazakhstan	0	0	0	0	0	0	0	21	39	60
Kenya	92	141	79	64	68	58	69	73	92	109
Kiribati (Gilbert Islands)	5	12	3	2	1	1	1	0	2	1
Korea, South	10 013	12 729	16 987	20 189	19 742	18 493	17 025	16 691	17 123	19 658
Korea, North	0	0	0	0	1	0	0	0	0	0
Kuwait	184	267	521	464	975	570	36	281	1 819	1 445
Kyrgyzstan	0	0	0	0	0	0	0	1	2	8
Laos	0	0	1	3	1	0	2	6	9	9
Latvia	0	0	0	0	0	0	0	10	23	50
Lebanon	19	29	33	40	31	24	27	27	27	25
Lesotho	1	3	5	13	19	25	27	53	56	63
Liberia	83	82	88	108	107	49	9	12	3	3
Libya	44	2	0	0	0	0	0	0	0	0
Liechtenstein	0	0	0	19	9	15	21	36	100	96
Lithuania	0	0	0	0	0	0	0	5	16	16
Luxembourg	0	0	0	166	218	210	188	227	253	288
Macao	342	411	510	551	653	736	583	721	669	791
Macedonia	0	0	0	0	0	0	0	46	111	82
Madagascar	52	63	71	49	38	42	47	54	43	57
Malawi	27	21	25	38	35	53	72	58	60	57
Malaysia	2 300	2 421	2 921	3 711	4 745	5 272	6 103	8 242	10 568	13 977
Maldive Islands	6	9	13	13	12	17	23	28	24	12
Mali	6	7	5	4	7	3	2	1	1	4
Malta and Gozo	34	34	48	74	60	40	65	91	104	96
Marshall Islands	0	0	0	1	3	3	3	8	11	8
Martinique	0	0	0	1	10	1	1	1	1	4
Mauritania	0	2	18	15	10	24	11	9	6	4
Mauritius	71	118	140	153	159	158	131	137	197	217
Mayotte	0	0	0	0	0	0	0	0	0	0
Mexico	19 132	17 302	20 271	23 277	27 186	30 172	31 194	35 184	39 930	49 493
Moldova	0	0	0	0	0	0	0	0	0	3
Monaco	0	0	0	10	14	13	14	13	16	18
Mongolia	4	1	1	1	2	2	1	7	34	27
Montserrat	4	3	2	2	2	1	2	2	1	1
Morocco	39	43	49	92	98	109	151	178	185	192
Mozambique	16	19	28	21	20	29	23	19	9	15
Namibia	12	21	8	5	15	33	35	23	22	28
Nauru	2	1	0	0	8	1	1	0	0	0
Nepal	44	32	32	53	47	50	55	73	91	117
Netherlands	4 081	4 066	3 964	4 587	4 796	4 972	4 827	5 287	5 451	6 015
Netherlands Antilles	808	470	520	411	384	421	656	646	397	424
Neutral Zone	0	0	0	1	0	0	0	0	0	0
New Caledonia	19	18	11	33	54	27	20	15	23	23
New Zealand	857	975	1 046	1 166	1 207	1 199	1 212	1 219	1 208	1 421
Nicaragua	41	1	1	1	0	15	60	69	126	167
Niger	9	12	7	5	2	46	5	3	6	2
Nigeria	3 002	2 530	3 573	3 298	5 227	5 977	5 360	5 074	5 301	4 430
Niue	0	1	1	0	0	0	0	0	0	0
Norfolk Island	0	1	0	0	0	0	0	0	0	0
Norway	1 164	1 079	1 404	1 452	1 989	1 848	1 626	1 976	1 938	2 373
Oman	46	38	216	76	117	292	115	182	277	459
Pacific Trust Territory (85-86)	6	2	0	0	0	0	0	0	0	0

Note: Unrevised data. Countries are shown as they were for the year of the data and not with current country defintions.

Table B-56. U.S. Imports of Goods by Country, 1985–2003—*Continued*

(Millions of dollars; Census basis; general imports, Customs.)

Country	1995	1996	1997	1998	1999	2000	2001	2002	2003
Gabon	1 449	1 949	2 201	1 268	1 520	2 209	1 655	1 592	1 970
Gambia	2	2	3	2	0	0	0	0	0
Gaza Strip	0	0	0	0	0	0	6	7	1
Georgia	11	8	7	14	18	32	31	17	54
Germany	36 847	38 943	43 069	49 824	55 094	58 737	59 151	62 480	68 047
Germany, East	0	0	0	0	0	0	0	0	0
Ghana	196	171	154	144	209	205	187	116	82
Gibraltar	5	6	3	6	10	1	3	1	3
Greece	398	496	453	467	571	592	506	546	616
Greenland	7	6	8	7	13	16	29	22	14
Grenada	5	4	6	12	20	27	24	7	8
Guadeloupe	1	1	4	2	3	10	11	10	3
Guatemala	1 527	1 673	1 990	2 072	2 266	2 605	2 589	2 800	2 945
Guinea	99	116	128	116	117	88	88	72	69
Guinea-Bissau	0	0	0	0	0	1	0	0	2
Guyana	108	109	112	135	122	141	140	116	118
Haiti	130	143	188	272	301	297	263	255	332
Heard Island and McDonald Islands	0	0	0	0	0	0	0	0	0
Honduras	1 442	1 796	2 322	2 545	2 713	3 090	3 126	3 264	3 312
Hong Kong	10 294	9 867	10 297	10 538	10 531	11 452	9 650	9 328	8 850
Hungary	547	677	1 078	1 567	1 892	2 716	2 965	2 639	2 699
Iceland	233	236	231	268	304	260	232	296	283
India	5 736	6 169	7 321	8 225	9 083	10 686	9 738	11 818	13 053
Indonesia	7 437	8 213	9 190	9 338	9 514	10 385	10 105	9 644	9 520
Iran	0	0	0	0	0	2	169	156	161
Iraq	0	0	286	1 199	4 193	6 111	5 801	3 593	4 574
Ireland	4 082	4 798	5 874	8 385	11 002	16 410	18 539	22 388	25 841
Israel	5 723	6 426	7 326	8 628	9 870	12 975	11 971	12 442	12 770
Italy	16 498	18 222	19 361	21 013	22 438	25 050	23 824	24 290	25 437
Ivory Coast	214	397	289	418	347	384	333	376	490
Jamaica	847	839	738	753	679	648	461	392	495
Japan	123 577	115 218	121 359	121 982	131 404	146 577	126 602	121 494	118 029
Jordan	29	25	25	16	31	73	229	412	673
Kazakhstan	125	114	116	169	228	425	351	335	392
Kenya	102	107	114	99	106	110	129	189	249
Kiribati (Gilbert Islands)	1	1	2	1	1	1	1	1	2
Korea, South	24 184	22 667	23 159	23 936	31 262	40 300	35 185	35 575	36 963
Korea, North	0	0	0	0	0	0	0	0	0
Kuwait	1 335	1 640	1 814	1 272	1 446	2 762	1 993	1 940	2 277
Kyrgyzstan	8	5	2	0	1	2	3	5	11
Laos	10	16	14	21	13	10	4	3	4
Latvia	86	99	149	115	229	287	144	197	377
Lebanon	35	41	78	82	51	77	90	62	92
Lesotho	62	65	86	100	111	140	215	322	393
Liberia	10	27	5	25	30	45	43	46	59
Libya	0	0	0	0	0	0	0	0	0
Liechtenstein	128	91	116	243	276	294	224	238	262
Lithuania	26	34	80	81	97	135	165	299	347
Luxembourg	233	203	239	374	314	332	306	299	265
Macao	895	858	1 021	1 109	1 124	1 266	1 224	1 232	1 356
Macedonia	89	125	147	175	136	137	112	74	61
Madagascar	57	46	62	71	80	158	272	216	384
Malawi	41	72	83	60	72	55	78	70	77
Malaysia	17 484	17 825	18 017	19 001	21 429	25 568	22 336	24 010	25 438
Maldive Islands	12	12	19	33	55	94	98	114	94
Mali	6	5	4	3	9	10	6	3	2
Malta and Gozo	132	208	224	341	323	484	369	310	373
Marshall Islands	13	5	17	6	10	5	6	9	27
Martinique	2	1	2	1	1	2	1	1	1
Mauritania	6	5	0	0	1	0	0	1	1
Mauritius	230	217	238	272	259	286	278	281	298
Mayotte	0	0	0	0	0	0	0	0	0
Mexico	61 705	72 963	85 872	94 709	109 706	135 911	131 433	134 732	138 073
Moldova	25	30	51	112	89	106	68	39	43
Monaco	12	16	20	26	14	23	15	15	22
Mongolia	23	31	42	42	61	117	144	161	183
Montserrat	2	5	5	0	0	0	0	0	1
Morocco	234	252	296	343	390	444	435	392	385
Mozambique	28	27	31	26	10	24	7	8	8
Namibia	12	27	63	52	30	42	37	57	123
Nauru	0	0	0	0	0	1	0	1	0
Nepal	96	117	113	139	177	229	200	152	171
Netherlands	6 378	6 617	7 278	7 591	8 473	9 704	9 500	9 864	10 972
Netherlands Antilles	288	663	582	308	383	718	488	362	620
Neutral Zone	0	0	0	0	0	0	0	0	0
New Caledonia	37	55	51	18	9	31	15	10	13
New Zealand	1 451	1 464	1 578	1 645	1 749	2 080	2 200	2 283	2 403
Nicaragua	238	350	439	453	493	590	605	679	769
Niger	2	1	42	2	12	7	5	1	4
Nigeria	4 775	5 849	6 349	4 195	4 361	10 549	8 786	5 964	10 394
Niue	0	0	0	0	0	0	0	0	2
Norfolk Island	79	1	0	0	0	1	0	0	0
Norway	3 091	3 869	3 735	2 874	4 051	5 710	5 207	5 830	5 212
Oman	295	411	242	217	219	257	420	401	695
Pacific Trust Territory (85–86)	0	0	0	0	0	0	0	0	0

Note: Unrevised data. Countries are shown as they were for the year of the data and not with current country definitions.

Table B-56. U.S. Imports of Goods by Country, 1985–2003—*Continued*

(Millions of dollars; Census basis; general imports, Customs.)

Country	1985	1986	1987	1988	1989	1990	1991	1992	1993	1994
Pacific Trust Territory (pre-85)	6	0	0	0	0	0	0	0	0	0
Pakistan	274	325	405	461	523	609	663	865	898	1 012
Palau	0	0	0	0	0	0	0	0	1	3
Panama	410	366	356	266	268	233	270	254	281	323
Papua New Guinea	34	45	22	34	29	22	34	64	98	108
Paraguay	24	30	22	37	45	51	43	35	50	80
Peru	1 087	803	769	656	815	803	778	739	754	840
Philippines	2 145	1 972	2 264	2 682	3 064	3 383	3 472	4 358	4 895	5 720
Pitcairn Island	2	1	1	1	0	0	0	0	0	0
Poland	220	233	296	378	387	409	357	374	454	651
Portugal	546	552	664	691	800	833	697	664	790	898
Qatar	16	64	3	1	50	53	30	70	65	81
Republic of South Africa	2 071	2 364	1 345	1 530	1 529	1 701	1 733	1 723	1 847	2 030
Reunion	0	0	0	3	4	1	1	0	0	1
Romania	882	754	715	681	354	231	69	87	69	195
Russia	0	0	0	0	0	0	0	480	1 744	3 235
Rwanda	6	11	11	12	7	31	7	5	4	2
San Marino	0	0	0	0	0	0	0	0	0	1
Sao Tome and Principe	1	0	1	2	0	0	0	0	1	0
Saudi Arabia	1 907	3 612	4 433	5 594	7 181	9 974	10 978	10 367	7 710	7 687
Senegal	5	7	7	8	41	4	12	10	7	11
Seychelles	9	8	14	5	6	1	1	1	4	3
Sierra Leone	16	11	20	41	53	46	48	61	47	51
Singapore	4 260	4 725	6 201	7 996	8 950	9 839	9 976	11 317	12 796	15 360
Slovakia	0	0	0	0	0	0	0	0	65	129
Slovenia	0	0	0	0	0	0	0	99	230	265
Solomon Islands	3	1	3	3	1	0	0	1	3	1
Somalia	2	0	4	1	0	0	3	2	0	0
Soviet Union	409	558	425	578	703	1 065	813	189	0	0
Spain	2 515	2 702	2 839	3 205	3 329	3 310	2 854	3 001	2 997	3 554
Sri Lanka (Ceylon)	282	337	417	424	449	538	605	789	1 002	1 093
St. Christopher-Nevis	16	24	24	21	21	16	15	23	24	22
St. Helena	0	1	2	4	1	0	0	0	1	0
St. Lucia	14	12	18	26	24	27	22	28	31	26
St. Pierre and Miquelon	5	6	8	2	6	4	6	2	0	0
St. Vincent and Grenadines	10	8	9	16	11	9	8	5	5	5
Sudan	9	22	22	23	20	16	16	11	12	35
Suriname	60	39	46	88	74	50	52	46	58	43
Svalbard, Jan Mayen Island	0	0	0	0	0	0	0	0	0	0
Swaziland	15	21	10	19	27	34	28	23	21	38
Sweden	4 124	4 419	4 758	4 995	4 890	4 931	4 502	4 716	4 532	5 044
Switzerland	3 476	5 253	4 249	4 638	4 699	5 452	5 585	5 643	5 979	6 376
Syria	3	8	59	37	98	52	25	42	130	64
Taiwan	16 396	19 791	24 622	24 804	24 326	22 667	23 036	24 601	25 105	26 711
Tajikistan	0	0	0	0	0	0	0	0	2	18	60
Tanzania	10	12	13	18	53	15	15	11	11	15
Thailand	1 428	1 748	2 220	3 218	4 378	5 294	6 125	7 528	8 542	10 307
Togo	11	24	23	5	3	4	3	6	3	4
Tokelau Islands	2	5	4	4	24	22	3	1	6	4
Tonga	1	1	1	1	3	3	5	4	4	6
Trinidad and Tobago	1 258	793	815	719	768	1 016	856	861	803	1 109
Tunisia	13	10	69	42	56	32	33	48	41	54
Turkey	602	633	821	983	1 377	1 180	1 009	1 109	1 196	1 575
Turkmenistan	0	0	0	0	0	0	0	1	2	2
Turks and Caicos Islands	4	5	5	4	3	4	4	6	4	4
Tuvalu	0	0	0	0	0	0	0	0	0	0
Uganda	113	133	81	58	40	16	18	12	10	35
Ukraine	0	0	0	0	0	0	0	89	172	327
United Arab Emirates	671	356	664	578	685	889	714	812	727	449
United Kingdom	14 937	15 396	17 341	18 042	18 242	20 288	18 520	20 151	21 736	25 063
Uruguay	557	472	344	275	218	208	238	266	266	167
Uzbekistan	0	0	0	0	0	0	0	1	7	3
Vanuatu (New Hebrides)	4	3	0	7	14	1	2	5	4	3
Vatican City	0	0	0	1	1	1	1	0	0	3
Venezuela	6 537	5 097	5 579	5 228	6 786	9 447	8 229	8 168	8 140	8 378
Vietnam	0	0	0	0	0	0	0	0	0	50
Wallis and Futuna	0	0	0	0	0	0	0	0	0	0
West Bank	0	0	0	0	0	0	0	0	0	0
Western Sahara	0	0	0	0	0	0	0	0	0	1
Western Samoa	23	1	2	2	3	1	1	1	1	0
Yemen (Aden) (S. Yemen)	1	0	1	16	1	21	0	0	0	0
Yemen (Sana)	1	1	4	120	260	378	116	41	98	183
Yugoslavia (former)	542	646	797	847	802	773	677	225	0	0
Yugoslavia (Serbia/Montenegro)	0	0	0	0	0	0	0	41	0	0
Zambia	58	65	50	20	24	29	42	70	41	63
Zimbabwe (Rhodesia)	52	70	70	120	127	119	89	107	111	102

Note: Unrevised data. Countries are shown as they were for the year of the data and not with current country defintions.

Table B-56. U.S. Imports of Goods by Country, 1985–2003—*Continued*

(Millions of dollars; Census basis; general imports, Customs.)

Country	1995	1996	1997	1998	1999	2000	2001	2002	2003
Pacific Trust Territory (pre-85)	0	0	0	0	0	0	0	0	0
Pakistan	1 197	1 266	1 442	1 691	1 740	2 167	2 249	2 305	2 531
Palau	6	9	13	14	16	14	15	15	2
Panama	307	346	367	313	365	307	293	302	301
Papua New Guinea	50	86	65	130	144	35	39	90	66
Paraguay	55	42	41	33	48	41	33	44	53
Peru	1 035	1 261	1 773	1 977	1 928	1 996	1 840	1 932	2 407
Philippines	7 006	8 162	10 436	11 949	12 380	13 937	11 331	10 985	10 061
Pitcairn Island	0	1	0	0	0	0	0	0	0
Poland	664	627	698	783	813	1 040	953	1 101	1 326
Portugal	1 055	1 016	1 138	1 266	1 357	1 579	1 556	1 673	1 967
Qatar	91	157	157	220	266	488	506	483	331
Republic of South Africa	2 209	2 323	2 500	1	0	0	1	3	2
Reunion	0	0	1	0	0	0	1		
Romania	222	249	400	393	434	470	520	695	730
Russia	4 035	3 561	4 290	5 734	5 805	7 796	6 261	6 825	8 598
Rwanda	2	9	4	4	4	5	7	3	3
San Marino	1	0	0	4	6	7	2	1	9
Sao Tome and Principe	0	0	0	1	3	1	0	0	0
Saudi Arabia	8 233	8 781	9 563	6 339	8 237	14 219	13 334	13 143	18 069
Senegal	6	5	7	5	9	4	104	4	4
Seychelles	2	3	2	2	5	8	24	26	13
Sierra Leone	28	22	18	12	10	4	5	4	7
Singapore	18 564	20 340	20 067	18 357	18 188	19 186	14 979	14 793	15 158
Slovakia	129	124	166	166	169	241	237	255	1 013
Slovenia	289	290	277	287	276	314	286	306	482
Solomon Islands	4	2	1	3	1	0	3	1	1
Somalia	0	0	0	1	0	0	0	0	0
Soviet Union	0	0	0	0	0	0	0	0	0
Spain	3 876	4 281	4 605	4 784	5 055	5 731	5 192	5 678	6 708
Sri Lanka (Ceylon)	1 260	1 393	1 620	1 766	1 742	2 002	1 984	1 810	1 807
St. Christopher-Nevis	22	23	30	32	33	37	41	49	45
St. Helena	0	2	1	0	0	3	3	4	6
St. Lucia	35	22	34	22	28	22	29	19	13
St. Pierre and Miquelon	3	0	2	5	5	6	3	4	3
St. Vincent and Grenadines	8	7	4	5	8	9	23	16	4
Sudan	23	19	12	3	0	2	3	1	3
Suriname	100	97	92	106	123	135	143	133	140
Svalbard, Jan Mayen Island	0	1	0	1	1	0	0	0	0
Swaziland	32	30	44	25	38	53	65	115	162
Sweden	6 246	7 158	7 302	7 837	8 111	9 603	8 851	9 287	11 125
Switzerland	7 596	7 793	8 392	8 676	9 596	10 174	9 574	9 382	10 668
Syria	56	15	28	46	95	158	159	148	259
Taiwan	28 975	29 911	32 624	33 123	35 198	40 514	33 391	32 199	31 600
Tajikistan	41	33	9	33	23	9	5	1	7
Tanzania	22	19	27	32	35	34	28	25	24
Thailand	11 351	11 336	12 595	13 434	14 324	16 389	14 729	14 799	15 181
Togo	29	4	9	2	3	6	13	3	6
Tokelau Islands	6	3	3	3	6	5	10	3	6
Tonga	6	4	3	6	5	5	8	9	13
Trinidad and Tobago	972	1 017	1 133	971	1 294	2 228	2 381	2 437	4 322
Tunisia	70	76	63	62	74	94	122	94	100
Turkey	1 800	1 777	2 119	2 546	2 627	3 042	3 054	3 515	3 788
Turkmenistan	1	0	2	3	8	28	45	60	76
Turks and Caicos Islands	5	5	5	5	6	6	8	5	6
Tuvalu	0	0	0	0	0	0	0	0	0
Uganda	13	16	38	15	20	29	18	15	35
Ukraine	409	507	414	531	518	873	670	406	282
United Arab Emirates	454	496	920	661	711	972	1 194	937	1 129
United Kingdom	26 891	28 892	32 689	34 792	39 191	43 459	41 397	40 870	42 667
Uruguay	167	260	228	256	199	313	228	193	256
Uzbekistan	19	157	39	34	26	35	54	77	84
Vanuatu (New Hebrides)	0	1	2	4	2	1	1	3	1
Vatican City	5	0	1	0	0	2	0	2	1
Venezuela	9 711	12 903	13 448	9 282	11 269	18 648	15 236	15 108	17 144
Vietnam	199	319	388	553	609	822	1 053	2 395	4 555
Wallis and Futuna	0	0	0	0	0	0	0	0	0
West Bank	0	0	0	0	3	5	0	0	0
Western Sahara	0	0	0	0	0	0	0	0	0
Western Samoa	0	1	3	7	5	5	7	6	4
Yemen (Aden) (S. Yemen)	0	0	0	0	0	0	0	0	0
Yemen (Sana)	42	27	16	38	19	248	210	246	66
Yugoslavia (former)	0	0	0	0	0	0	0	0	0
Yugoslavia (Serbia/Montenegro)	0	8	10	13	5	2	6	10	15
Zambia	33	64	56	47	38	18	16	8	12
Zimbabwe (Rhodesia)	98	133	139	127	133	112	91	103	57

Note: Unrevised data. Countries are shown as they were for the year of the data and not with current country definitions.

Table B-57. U.S. Trade Balances of Goods by Country, 1985–2003

(Millions of dollars; Census basis; foreign and domestic exports, f.a.s.; general imports, Customs.)

Country	1985	1986	1987	1988	1989	1990	1991	1992	1993	1994
WORLD	-126 093	-142 478	-153 035	-118 564	-109 631	-103 062	-67 020	-84 546	-115 611	-151 415
Afghanistan	-3	3	2	1	0	-1	-2	2	7	-1
Albania	9	1	1	5	2	8	15	31	27	10
Algeria	-1 927	-1 381	-1 573	-1 082	-1 078	-1 698	-1 372	-912	-685	-334
Andorra	0	0	0	43	51	40	16	16	14	5
Angola	-916	-591	-1 199	-1 115	-1 766	-1 808	-1 598	-2 145	-1 921	-1 864
Anguilla	0	0	0	14	17	15	10	10	14	13
Antigua Barbuda	-25	-12	-9	61	61	65	71	63	58	59
Argentina	-352	87	9	-383	-362	-330	758	1 967	2 566	2 741
Armenia	0	0	0	0	0	0	0	23	77	73
Aruba	0	-2	0	97	126	201	134	76	-191	-188
Australia	2 287	2 625	2 462	3 382	4 449	4 102	4 406	5 235	4 978	6 581
Austria	-397	-403	-399	-363	-262	-442	-219	-49	-85	-376
Azerbaijan	0	0	0	0	0	0	0	0	36	27
Bahamas	160	319	366	329	311	292	251	127	356	482
Bahrain	21	11	43	170	409	638	414	428	556	288
Bangladesh	23	-65	-177	-110	-147	-357	-345	-644	-641	-846
Barbados	-29	39	73	109	133	130	135	97	111	127
Belarus	0	0	0	0	0	0	0	0	58	-7
Belgium	0	0	0	2 908	4 163	5 946	6 623	5 300	3 699	4 602
Belgium and Luxembourg	1 405	1 354	1 981	0	0	0	0	0	0	0
Belize	9	8	29	52	58	59	69	58	82	64
Benin	67	17	3	5	10	2	4	17	6	16
Bermuda	251	230	255	279	344	242	224	219	250	291
Bhutan	0	0	0	0	0	0	0	1	0	0
Bolivia	20	-13	29	30	24	-65	-19	61	25	-74
Bosnia-Herzegovina	0	0	0	0	0	0	0	-4	8	34
Botswana	-13	17	22	32	13	5	18	34	16	9
British Indian Ocean Territory	-2	-3	-2	-1	-8	0	-1	0	0	0
Brazil	-4 398	-2 956	-3 871	-5 077	-3 580	-2 915	-573	-1 871	-1 420	-590
British Virgin Islands	-11	-6	-11	38	48	58	43	41	32	32
Brunei	48	141	77	49	-12	47	136	423	448	330
Bulgaria	68	40	47	100	122	37	86	6	-43	-102
Burkina (Upper Volta)	26	9	10	14	10	14	23	13	17	7
Burma (Myanmar)	-4	-1	-4	-1	-12	-3	-3	-34	-34	-56
Burundi	5	-8	-3	0	-4	-7	-6	1	0	10
Cambodia (Kampuchea)	0	0	0	0	0	0	0	16	15	6
Cameroon	-255	-272	-369	-188	-379	-112	-81	-27	-53	-2
Canada	-16 155	-13 230	-11 754	-9 842	-9 944	-8 405	-5 995	-8 341	-10 731	-14 693
Cape Verde	0	-1	0	4	1	6	5	4	5	5
Cayman Islands	64	68	99	86	154	164	99	256	145	150
Central African Republic	1	-2	-3	0	3	-1	0	0	4	2
Chad	23	4	4	5	35	7	14	5	7	6
Chile	-63	3	-185	-97	103	351	536	1 068	1 143	954
China	-10	-1 666	-2 805	-3 479	-6 181	-10 417	-12 689	-18 206	-22 768	-29 494
Christmas Island	0	-2	0	0	-1	0	0	0	1	0
Cocos (Keeling) Islands	0	0	-1	1	0	2	-6	0	0	6
Colombia	120	-566	-823	-410	-632	-1 136	-787	433	196	898
Comoros	-5	-3	-4	-13	-8	-5	-9	-10	-9	-6
Congo	-590	-354	-421	-355	-493	-324	-366	-450	-473	-365
Cook Islands	-1	-1	-2	-12	1	1	4	2	2	-1
Costa Rica	-80	-159	-89	-79	-81	-17	-120	-60	6	220
Croatia	0	0	0	0	0	0	0	48	-3	32
Cuba	1	2	1	3	3	1	1	1	3	4
Cyprus	31	43	51	83	94	111	106	155	122	191
Czech Republic	0	0	0	0	0	0	0	0	-11	-18
Czechoslovakia	-13	-13	-31	-32	-33	2	-20	171	0	0
Dem. Rep. of the Congo (Zaire)	-298	-117	-205	-243	-210	-178	-240	-217	-203	-148
Denmark	-963	-1 008	-918	-755	-485	-367	-94	-191	-572	-907
Djibouti	4	4	3	4	3	7	10	11	13	7
Dominica	-14	-15	-10	-5	26	22	37	29	22	19
Dominican Republic	-241	-167	-23	-58	1	-89	-274	-274	-322	-294
East Timor	0	0	0	0	0	0	0	0	0	0
Ecuador	-1 247	-870	-650	-551	-843	-697	-380	-333	-301	-531
Egypt	1 890	1 543	1 048	1 874	2 383	1 852	2 514	2 653	2 150	2 295
El Salvador	4	47	87	177	276	318	231	357	381	323
Equatorial Guinea	0	0	0	0	0	0	12	11	0	2
Eritrea	0	0	0	0	0	0	0	0	1	8
Estonia	0	0	0	0	0	0	0	46	34	4
Ethiopia	160	30	63	127	-2	117	196	241	115	109
Falkland Islands	0	2	6	0	1	-1	0	0	0	0
Faroe Islands	0	0	0	-33	-29	-16	-28	-20	-8	-9
Federated States of Micronesia	0	0	17	26	26	19	40	19	11	11
Fiji	-13	-12	-18	3	6	-9	-20	-14	-42	21
Finland	-460	-532	-487	-452	-397	-141	-138	-399	-762	-734
France	-3 428	-2 963	-2 876	-2 181	-1 444	528	1 993	-236	-1 977	-3 152
French Guiana	100	6	114	268	265	269	149	78	320	193
French Indian Ocean Areas	-1	-3	1	0	0	0	0	0	0	0
French Pacific Islands	113	90	82	0	0	0	0	0	0	0
French Polynesia	-4	-6	-10	58	62	60	67	71	94	58
French S. Antarctic Territory	0	0	0	0	-1	0	0	0	0	0

Note: Unrevised data. Countries are shown as they were for the year of the data and not with current country definitions.

Table B-57. U.S. Trade Balances of Goods by Country, 1985–2003—*Continued*

(Millions of dollars; Census basis; foreign and domestic exports, f.a.s.; general imports, Customs.)

Country	1995	1996	1997	1998	1999	2000	2001	2002	2003
WORLD	-160 475	-168 488	-182 615	-233 411	-331 945	-436 469	-410 933	-470 291	-535 652
Afghanistan	-1	0	1	-10	9	7	5	76	5
Albania	4	2	-9	2	16	13	8	9	5
Algeria	-893	-1 471	-1 744	-981	-1 374	-1 857	-1 647	-1 380	-4 266
Andorra	16	22	21	23	8	10	8	10	8
Angola	-1 977	-2 419	-2 504	-1 897	-2 173	-3 331	-2 824	-2 742	-3 772
Anguilla	15	12	17	15	20	28	18	19	20
Antigua Barbuda	94	73	80	94	94	136	92	78	115
Argentina	2 430	2 237	3 595	3 633	2 340	1 598	913	-1 595	-734
Armenia	54	56	56	35	34	34	17	81	65
Aruba	-172	-333	-371	-120	-368	-1 221	-774	-306	-609
Australia	7 470	8 137	7 439	6 547	6 520	6 021	4 466	6 606	6 690
Austria	53	-190	-292	-52	-323	-679	-1 365	-1 394	-2 697
Azerbaijan	35	49	57	118	29	189	44	35	112
Bahamas	504	560	644	673	648	790	709	517	605
Bahrain	119	129	288	139	123	111	9	24	131
Bangladesh	-932	-1 133	-1 420	-1 528	-1 642	-2 179	-2 051	-1 865	-1 847
Barbados	148	181	239	246	243	267	247	234	258
Belarus	3	1	-25	-75	-66	-73	-73	-107	-131
Belgium	6 409	5 741	5 521	5 496	3 177	4 029	3 395	3 508	5 077
Belgium and Luxembourg	0	0	0	0	0	0	0	0	0
Belize	48	38	38	54	56	115	76	60	98
Benin	24	9	44	40	13	24	31	34	30
Bermuda	288	270	308	389	319	389	306	392	386
Bhutan	0	0	0	2	0	0	0	0	1
Bolivia	-49	-6	72	179	94	61	51	32	-3
Bosnia-Herzegovina	25	49	94	33	29	26	31	16	9
Botswana	15	2	19	16	17	-9	23	2	12
British Indian Ocean Territory	0	-3	-11	0	1	-2	0	0	2
Brazil	2 628	3 938	6 283	5 035	1 935	1 505	1 466	-3 403	-6 666
British Virgin Islands	38	47	48	55	36	34	63	26	36
Brunei	151	327	122	-88	-322	-227	-295	-241	-387
Bulgaria	-51	11	-67	-104	-97	-123	-226	-239	-286
Burkina (Upper Volta)	14	6	17	15	8	13	-1	16	10
Burma (Myanmar)	-65	-76	-95	-132	-223	-454	-459	-346	-269
Burundi	-18	0	-13	-3	-3	-6	3	1	-3
Cambodia (Kampuchea)	22	17	-84	-354	-572	-794	-933	-1 042	-1 205
Cameroon	-2	6	65	22	-40	-96	82	-16	-123
Canada	-19 095	-23 922	-17 926	-20 692	-34 411	-52 779	-53 244	-49 790	-54 685
Cape Verde	7	67	9	9	7	3	6	8	3
Cayman Islands	162	191	251	404	359	347	253	225	298
Central African Republic	6	4	2	2	1	-1	1	4	5
Chad	8	-4	0	-4	-4	6	131	122	42
Chile	1 682	1 876	2 076	1 532	143	227	-424	-1 169	-984
China	-33 807	-39 517	-49 747	-56 898	-68 668	-83 810	-83 046	-103 115	-123 961
Christmas Island	4	0	0	0	1	1	1	1	1
Cocos (Keeling) Islands	1	0	0	0	0	1	2	1	0
Colombia	873	435	474	165	-2 744	-3 280	-2 091	-2 018	-2 631
Comoros	-2	-6	-2	0	-2	-3	-9	-5	-3
Congo	-152	-253	-396	-223	-368	-428	-401	-148	-354
Cook Islands	0	0	0	0	0	-1	0	0	-1
Costa Rica	-106	-160	-300	-446	-1 579	-1 102	-391	-10	53
Croatia	47	35	56	24	-2	-51	-30	-67	16
Cuba	6	5	9	3	4	6	7	144	261
Cyprus	245	239	227	131	158	168	233	168	302
Czech Republic	-1	-71	-18	-104	-145	-337	-413	-578	-722
Czechoslovakia	0	0	0	0	0	0	0	0	0
Dem. Rep. of the Congo (Zaire)	-185	-177	-253	-138	-208	-202	-135	-174	-144
Denmark	-428	-408	-381	-507	-1 106	-1 462	-1 790	-1 740	-2 170
Djibouti	8	8	7	20	27	16	18	54	34
Dominica	20	26	28	46	16	30	25	40	29
Dominican Republic	-381	-392	-401	-466	-196	59	253	93	-242
East Timor	0	0	0	0	0	0	1	0	0
Ecuador	-392	-659	-533	-69	-894	-1 173	-622	-539	-1 273
Egypt	2 379	2 481	3 183	2 399	2 408	2 441	2 899	1 514	1 516
El Salvador	298	-2	52	77	-85	-158	-110	-318	-196
Equatorial Guinea	-26	-59	17	20	178	-60	-365	-412	-567
Eritrea	16	12	15	24	3	16	22	28	87
Estonia	77	23	-29	-38	-75	-484	-183	-82	-61
Ethiopia	115	113	51	36	134	136	32	35	379
Falkland Islands	0	0	0	3	-1	-3	-6	-6	-4
Faroe Islands	-8	-7	-14	-8	-17	-30	7	-11	-4
Federated States of Micronesia	10	13	17	18	15	16	9	12	9
Fiji	-46	-47	-52	-27	27	-123	-164	-139	-156
Finland	-1 021	93	-657	-680	-1 242	-1 679	-1 841	-1 907	-1 884
France	-2 937	-4 202	-4 743	-6 349	-7 071	-9 530	-10 400	-9 389	-12 153
French Guiana	436	296	491	243	188	17	130	242	152
French Indian Ocean Areas	0	0	0	0	0	0	0	0	0
French Pacific Islands	0	0	0	0	0	0	0	0	0
French Polynesia	68	71	71	66	51	50	35	35	44
French S. Antarctic Territory	0	0	1	0	1	2	0	1	0

Note: Unrevised data. Countries are shown as they were for the year of the data and not with current country definitions.

Table B-57. U.S. Trade Balances of Goods by Country, 1985–2003—*Continued*

(Millions of dollars; Census basis; foreign and domestic exports, f.a.s.; general imports, Customs.)

Country	1985	1986	1987	1988	1989	1990	1991	1992	1993	1994
French West Indies	25	30	42	0	0	0	0	0	0	0
Gabon	-411	-182	-306	-121	-371	-671	-627	-873	-892	-1 114
Gambia	11	13	12	16	9	7	9	9	1	1
Gaza Strip	0	1	0	0	0	0	0	0	0	1
Georgia	0	0	0	0	0	0	0	9	26	77
Germany	-11 314	-14 750	-15 510	-12 488	-7 951	-9 419	-4 913	-7 593	-9 648	-12 512
Germany, East	-19	-19	-31	-1	-45	-23	1	0	0	0
Ghana	-36	-107	-134	-85	-5	-30	-10	27	6	-74
Gibraltar	12	28	2	5	1	31	10	4	5	19
Greece	0	-70	-133	24	230	258	603	527	536	375
Greenland	4	1	3	3	3	5	0	-8	-10	-6
Grenada	-1	-3	-4	18	20	27	23	16	16	16
Guadeloupe	0	0	0	28	31	53	82	59	44	49
Guatemala	-5	-202	-17	150	53	-36	51	128	116	72
Guinea	-64	-65	-59	-74	-93	-98	-50	-41	-59	-42
Guinea-Bissau	-1	-1	-2	2	2	1	1	1	1	1
Guyana	-4	-17	1	17	22	24	3	17	32	12
Haiti	6	12	64	95	96	135	107	110	67	152
Heard Island and McDonald Islands	0	-1	-1	0	0	0	0	0	0	0
Honduras	-81	-104	-96	12	55	71	70	26	-17	-86
Hong Kong	-5 611	-5 861	-5 871	-4 553	-3 435	-2 648	-1 146	-731	315	1 748
Hungary	-124	-127	-184	-216	-207	-192	-110	-54	33	-161
Iceland	-210	-177	-202	-92	-29	69	-52	-47	-86	-137
India	-655	-754	-1 069	-469	-851	-705	-1 195	-1 866	-1 790	-3 005
Indonesia	-3 787	-2 393	-2 630	-2 132	-2 286	-1 446	-1 347	-1 554	-2 669	-3 712
International Organizations	126	0	0	0	0	300	255	0	66	2
Iran	-651	-535	-1 613	64	51	159	296	747	616	328
Iraq	-47	87	189	-331	-1 235	-2 283	-6	0	4	1
Ireland	440	431	699	808	923	794	727	589	211	525
Israel	-255	-561	-449	-407	-408	-112	359	262	-6	-217
Italy	-5 118	-5 807	-5 572	-4 918	-4 714	-4 736	-3 209	-3 602	-6 764	-7 518
Ivory Coast	-455	-366	-291	-215	-155	-121	-139	-100	-90	-74
Jamaica	131	155	205	314	478	375	387	340	393	320
Japan	-46 592	-55 292	-56 767	-52 371	-49 002	-41 848	-44 187	-49 417	-59 318	-65 669
Jordan	253	253	281	314	372	298	213	232	344	259
Kazakhstan	0	0	0	0	0	0	0	-6	29	71
Kenya	-1	-73	9	27	65	58	23	51	24	61
Kiribati (Gilbert Islands)	-5	-12	-3	1	14	18	27	35	29	22
Korea, South	-4 293	-6 820	-9 322	-9 558	-6 264	-4 094	-1 506	-2 061	-2 347	-1 629
Korea, North	0	0	0	0	-1	0	0	0	2	0
Kuwait	309	369	-37	211	-120	-169	1 192	1 046	-810	-270
Kyrgyzstan	0	0	0	0	0	0	0	1	16	-2
Laos	0	0	-1	-2	-1	0	-1	-5	-3	-3
Latvia	0	0	0	0	0	0	0	45	67	51
Lebanon	98	72	60	73	63	74	138	283	350	418
Leeward and Windward Islands	198	224	238	0	0	0	0	0	0	0
Lesotho	6	5	2	-9	-15	-22	-24	-50	-52	-60
Liberia	-11	-17	-19	-40	-9	-5	38	18	17	43
Libya	267	45	0	0	0	0	0	0	0	0
Liechtenstein	0	0	0	-4	1	-3	-10	-23	-89	-82
Lithuania	0	0	0	0	0	0	0	39	41	26
Luxembourg	0	0	0	-58	-76	-76	29	45	308	-59
Macao	-341	-408	-504	-544	-642	-728	-573	-702	-640	-770
Macedonia	0	0	0	0	0	0	0	-42	-99	-68
Madagascar	-20	-37	-52	-37	-30	-30	-32	-47	-32	-9
Malawi	-22	-18	-20	-26	-21	-39	-18	-45	-44	-38
Malaysia	-837	-693	-1 026	-1 573	-1 870	-1 848	-2 201	-3 846	-4 504	-7 012
Maldive Islands	-6	-9	-13	-13	-9	-16	-21	-26	-23	-11
Mali	24	10	5	16	3	6	17	10	31	15
Malta and Gozo	-8	-10	49	27	-12	5	-9	-33	68	-8
Marshall Islands	0	0	21	36	30	25	35	26	24	25
Martinique	0	0	0	27	15	33	36	31	31	28
Mauritania	26	14	-10	1	2	-9	10	51	13	10
Mauritius	-60	-108	-114	-3	-147	-146	-116	-114	-179	-193
Mayotte	0	0	0	0	0	0	0	0	0	0
Mexico	-5 504	-4 922	-5 701	-2 644	-2 217	-1 797	2 081	5 413	1 706	1 347
Moldova	0	0	0	0	0	0	0	9	31	20
Monaco	0	0	0	-7	-10	-3	-7	-6	-10	-12
Mongolia	-4	-1	-1	-1	-2	-2	11	-4	-17	-20
Montserrat	-4	-3	-2	3	8	10	6	11	4	6
Morocco	187	413	292	266	300	388	251	315	417	213
Mozambique	40	5	22	35	21	21	78	130	31	24
Namibia	7	-1	-7	-3	-2	11	-3	11	-2	-11
Nauru	-2	-1	0	0	-8	-1	-1	0	86	0
Nepal	-36	-24	24	11	-38	-41	-49	-68	-86	-109
Netherlands	3 137	3 675	4 138	5 314	6 597	8 044	8 701	8 453	7 388	7 576
Netherlands Antilles	-381	-72	-13	21	29	121	-27	-170	126	95
Neutral Zone	0	0	0	0	4	1	0	0	0	0
New Caledonia	-19	-18	-11	-6	11	7	24	21	-1	5
New Zealand	-135	-102	-231	-231	-90	-66	-202	88	39	88
Nicaragua	1	2	2	5	2	53	87	119	24	19
Niger	4	-10	-5	2	7	-34	5	10	10	10
Nigeria	-2 350	-2 128	-3 279	-2 942	-4 735	-5 426	-4 527	-4 073	-4 410	-3 921
Niue	0	-1	-1	0	0	0	0	0	0	0
Norfolk Island	0	-1	0	0	1	3	1	2	1	1

Note: Unrevised data. Countries are shown as they were for the year of the data and not with current country definitions.

Table B-57. U.S. Trade Balances of Goods by Country, 1985–2003—*Continued*

(Millions of dollars; Census basis; foreign and domestic exports, f.a.s.; general imports, Customs.)

Country	1995	1996	1997	1998	1999	2000	2001	2002	2003
French West Indies	0	0	0	0	0	0	0	0	0
Gabon	-1 395	-1 893	-2 117	-1 206	-1 474	-2 145	-1 581	-1 527	-1 907
Gambia	4	7	7	7	9	9	8	9	27
Gaza Strip	0	0	0	2	1	0	-6	-7	-1
Georgia	85	75	134	122	65	77	76	81	77
Germany	-14 470	-15 469	-18 602	-23 182	-28 305	-29 493	-29 037	-35 852	-39 199
Germany, East	0	0	0	0	0	0	0	0	0
Ghana	-29	124	160	79	26	-14	13	76	128
Gibraltar	14	5	6	3	-5	14	8	25	11
Greece	1 121	324	501	888	423	626	790	607	575
Greenland	-5	-2	-3	-1	-10	-15	-24	-18	-11
Grenada	22	32	34	44	46	52	36	50	61
Guadeloupe	68	65	54	59	63	76	47	30	43
Guatemala	119	-109	-262	-131	-454	-710	-713	-758	-672
Guinea	-32	-29	-45	-50	-62	-21	-10	-9	-33
Guinea-Bissau	1	7	2	1	1	0	1	3	-1
Guyana	34	27	31	10	23	18	1	13	-1
Haiti	421	330	312	276	314	279	287	328	307
Heard Island and McDonald Islands	0	0	0	0	0	0	0	0	0
Honduras	-161	-155	-309	-222	-344	-515	-690	-699	-467
Hong Kong	3 926	4 088	4 818	2 385	2 116	3 173	4 423	3 283	4 692
Hungary	-252	-346	-592	-1 085	-1 389	-2 146	-2 278	-1 951	-1 765
Iceland	-62	21	-51	-31	-6	-4	-7	-77	-41
India	-2 440	-2 851	-3 705	-4 680	-5 376	-7 024	-5 973	-7 720	-8 067
Indonesia	-4 081	-4 248	-4 659	-7 047	-7 575	-7 839	-7 605	-7 063	-7 000
International Organizations	0	2	0	76	0	1	0	77	0
Iran	277	0	1	0	46	-152	-135	-129	-62
Iraq	0	3	-204	-1 093	-4 184	-6 101	-5 754	-3 561	-4 258
Ireland	13	-1 139	-1 232	-2 732	-4 628	-8 683	-11 390	-15 639	-18 142
Israel	-130	-417	-1 334	-1 650	-2 175	-5 224	-4 489	-5 403	-5 892
Italy	-7 635	-9 437	-10 387	-11 986	-12 344	-14 050	-13 908	-14 201	-14 867
Ivory Coast	-41	-256	-138	-266	-243	-289	-236	-300	-387
Jamaica	574	652	680	550	616	730	946	1 028	975
Japan	-59 280	-47 683	-55 687	-64 094	-73 920	-81 322	-68 963	-70 055	-65 965
Jordan	306	320	377	337	245	239	114	-8	-181
Kazakhstan	-44	24	142	-66	-49	-300	-188	270	-224
Kenya	12	-2	112	101	83	128	449	83	-52
Kiribati (Gilbert Islands)	1	3	1	2	5	3	5	3	0
Korea, South	1 230	3 916	1 908	-7 398	-8 308	-12 398	-12 988	-12 979	-12 865
Korea, North	5	1	2	4	11	3	1	25	8
Kuwait	82	340	-420	207	-537	-1 970	-1 087	-926	-768
Kyrgyzstan	16	42	26	20	21	23	24	26	28
Laos	-9	-13	-12	-17	-11	-6	0	2	1
Latvia	3	66	70	72	-11	-153	-34	-106	-253
Lebanon	554	586	474	432	305	277	328	256	222
Leeward and Windward Islands	0	0	0	0	0	0	0	0	0
Lesotho	-60	-63	-84	-99	-110	-139	-214	-320	-388
Liberia	32	23	38	25	14	-2	-6	-18	-26
Libya	0	0	0	0	0	18	9	18	0
Liechtenstein	-113	-82	-104	-236	-267	-280	-217	-223	-246
Lithuania	25	29	8	-19	-31	-76	-65	-197	-185
Luxembourg	141	38	473	232	670	65	245	181	14
Macao	-866	-828	-954	-1 068	-1 083	-1 197	-1 153	-1 153	-1 301
Macedonia	-68	-110	-113	-161	-79	-69	-79	-55	-34
Madagascar	-47	-34	-51	-57	26	-142	-251	-201	-337
Malawi	-23	-59	-65	-46	-65	-42	-63	-40	-60
Malaysia	-8 666	-9 303	-7 189	-10 049	-12 350	-14 573	-12 956	-13 662	-14 517
Maldive Islands	-11	-9	-14	-28	-46	-88	-91	-110	-88
Mali	18	13	22	22	21	22	26	9	29
Malta and Gozo	-26	-83	-104	-72	-133	-150	-110	-100	-171
Marshall Islands	18	24	7	19	26	60	21	19	1
Martinique	36	34	31	25	34	20	23	23	21
Mauritania	38	10	21	19	24	16	25	22	34
Mauritius	-205	-192	-207	-248	-220	-262	-249	-253	-266
Mayotte	0	0	0	0	0	0	0	0	0
Mexico	-15 394	-16 202	-14 494	-15 699	-22 662	-24 190	-29 924	-37 202	-40 616
Moldova	-15	-8	-32	-91	-78	-78	-33	-8	-18
Monaco	-3	-13	-7	-19	-2	5	0	-4	29
Mongolia	-9	-27	-7	-21	-51	-99	-132	-95	-163
Montserrat	2	3	12	5	4	10	6	5	7
Morocco	286	224	139	209	183	80	-148	173	80
Mozambique	22	-4	15	20	24	34	21	89	54
Namibia	15	-5	-37	-1	166	38	218	0	-95
Nauru	1	0	1	1	1	4	4	2	2
Nepal	-86	-108	-87	-124	-156	-194	-186	-132	-155
Netherlands	10 180	9 997	12 543	11 413	10 939	12 270	10 024	8 471	9 731
Netherlands Antilles	216	-135	-105	435	220	-44	330	380	127
Neutral Zone	0	0	0	0	0	0	0	0	0
New Caledonia	-15	-26	-17	2	33	-12	11	27	31
New Zealand	241	263	378	240	185	-107	-65	-468	-555
Nicaragua	12	-88	-150	-117	-119	-211	-162	-242	-266
Niger	38	26	-17	16	6	29	59	40	30
Nigeria	-4 172	-5 033	-5 535	-3 375	-3 733	-9 830	-7 829	-4 907	-9 365
Niue	31	31	37	5	0	0	0	0	0
Norfolk Island	-77	0	4	2	2	1	0	0	-1

Note: Unrevised data. Countries are shown as they were for the year of the data and not with current country defintions.

Table B-57. U.S. Trade Balances of Goods by Country, 1985–2003—*Continued*

(Millions of dollars; Census basis; foreign and domestic exports, f.a.s.; general imports, Customs.)

Country	1985	1986	1987	1988	1989	1990	1991	1992	1993	1994
Norway	-505	-163	-603	-550	-952	-567	-138	-695	-726	-1 105
Oman	111	120	-47	53	53	-129	88	75	-26	-239
Other Pacific Islands, n.e.s.	9	15	16	0	0	0	0	0	0	0
Pacific Trust Territory (85-86)	27	56	0	0	0	0	0	0	0	0
Pacific Trust Territory (pre-85)	23	1	0	0	0	0	0	0	0	0
Pakistan	553	411	241	508	612	534	288	12	-87	-293
Palau	0	0	5	9	10	9	13	9	8	6
Panama	263	343	386	367	461	634	711	847	910	954
Papua New Guinea	7	6	28	79	92	32	61	8	-47	-43
Paraguay	75	141	161	157	122	256	332	380	471	713
Peru	-594	-111	41	137	-126	-25	63	263	315	568
Philippines	-770	-627	-681	-845	-858	-911	-1 203	-1 604	-1 366	-1 832
Pitcairn Island	-2	-1	-1	-1	0	0	0	0	0	0
Poland	18	-81	-57	-74	27	-2	101	262	462	-26
Portugal	112	26	-88	42	126	90	95	360	-55	156
Qatar	46	-1	72	98	50	62	118	119	101	81
Republic of South Africa	-866	-1 206	-64	161	130	32	380	702	350	143
Reunion	0	0	0	-2	-3	4	1	3	2	3
Romania	-673	-503	-523	-478	-199	138	140	161	254	142
Russia	0	0	0	0	0	0	0	1 618	1 223	-656
Rwanda	-1	-6	-7	-10	-4	-30	-5	-2	3	33
San Marino	0	0	0	3	1	1	0	0	2	2
Sao Tome and Principe	-1	-1	-1	10	4	13	4	2	2	13
Saudi Arabia	2 094	-318	-1 376	-1 930	-3 605	-5 939	-4 406	-3 204	-1 044	-1 676
Senegal	56	43	42	62	27	48	65	70	62	31
Seychelles	-8	-7	-13	-3	77	2	1	1	60	3
Sierra Leone	-3	13	6	-24	-28	-19	-23	-33	-27	-27
Singapore	-808	-1 360	-2 178	-2 309	-1 597	-1 820	-1 169	-1 694	-1 121	-2 339
Slovakia	0	0	0	0	0	0	0	0	-31	-86
Slovenia	0	0	0	0	0	0	0	-61	-137	-169
Solomon Islands	-3	-1	-3	2	5	6	4	53	-1	0
Somalia	49	56	32	26	21	11	5	18	30	30
South Asia, n.e.s.	2	1	4	0	0	0	0	0	0	0
Southern Pacific Islands	5	7	11	0	0	0	0	0	0	0
Soviet Union	2 014	689	1 055	2 190	3 569	2 022	2 765	847	0	0
Spain	-19	-126	254	810	1 468	1 899	2 627	2 487	1 184	1 071
Special Category Exports	5 446	4 364	5 422	5 339	0	0	0	0	0	0
Sri Lanka (Ceylon)	-210	-271	-340	-301	-306	-401	-484	-612	-799	-895
St. Christopher-Nevis	-16	-24	-24	16	22	36	20	9	18	23
St. Helena	0	-1	-2	-4	-1	0	0	0	6	6
St. Lucia	-14	-12	-18	45	52	56	67	54	67	54
St. Pierre and Miquelon	-5	-6	-8	-2	-6	-4	-6	-1	0	0
St. Vincent and Grenadines	-10	-8	-9	20	30	26	36	30	33	33
Sudan	229	67	123	79	61	26	77	41	41	19
Suriname	25	46	26	6	65	107	83	93	60	78
Svalbard, Jan Mayen Island	0	0	0	0	0	0	2	1	0	1
Swaziland	-14	-20	-4	-15	-24	-26	-23	-20	-19	-32
Sweden	-2 213	-2 559	-2 876	-2 325	-1 750	-1 527	-1 214	-1 872	-2 178	-2 524
Switzerland	-1 232	-2 284	-1 117	-476	216	-507	-27	-1 107	825	-762
Syria	104	52	34	51	-7	98	182	126	55	134
Taiwan	-11 930	-14 608	-17 436	-12 861	-13 003	-11 184	-9 845	-9 397	-8 855	-9 633
Tajikistan	0	0	0	0	0	0	0	7	-6	-44
Tanzania	36	26	21	10	-24	33	20	23	21	34
Thailand	-690	-893	-737	-1 534	-2 086	-2 302	-2 368	-3 546	-4 773	-5 446
Togo	5	-7	-3	15	25	27	21	13	9	8
Tokelau Islands	-2	-5	-4	-4	-24	-21	-3	0	-5	-3
Tonga	-1	-1	-1	3	4	3	0	2	1	0
Transshipments	238	94	77	208	394	222	168	301	277	251
Trinidad and Tobago	-755	-261	-454	-391	-206	-586	-387	-414	-273	-569
Tunisia	99	145	34	132	104	146	138	184	192	273
Turkey	548	423	483	570	627	1 073	1 414	1 621	2 238	1 178
Turkmenistan	0	0	0	0	0	0	0	0	44	136
Turks and Caicos Islands	8	10	10	29	43	36	36	34	18	25
Tuvalu	0	0	0	0	0	0	0	32	0	0
Uganda	-108	-129	-62	-42	-17	10	-5	3	11	-7
Ukraine	0	0	0	0	0	0	0	216	139	-146
United Arab Emirates	-95	136	-119	126	555	110	742	740	1 085	1 144
United Kingdom	-3 810	-4 121	-3 433	232	2 624	3 196	3 544	2 657	4 640	1 770
Uruguay	-493	-373	-252	-175	-85	-63	-21	-35	-13	143
Uzbekistan	0	0	0	0	0	0	0	50	66	87
Vanuatu (New Hebrides)	-4	-3	0	-6	-13	5	-1	-3	-3	-2
Vatican City	0	0	0	-1	-1	0	0	0	0	-2
Venezuela	-3 378	-1 960	-2 019	-655	-3 750	-6 339	-3 560	-2 729	-3 541	-4 337
Vietnam	20	30	23	16	11	7	4	4	7	122
Wallis and Futuna	0	0	0	0	0	0	0	0	0	0
West Bank	0	0	0	0	0	0	0	0	0	0
Western Africa, n.e.s.	24	24	24	0	0	0	0	0	0	0
Western Sahara	0	0	0	0	0	0	0	0	0	0
Western Samoa	-21	1	1	2	0	4	6	72	9	7
Yemen (Aden) (S. Yemen)	8	17	13	-9	7	-17	3	0	0	0
Yemen (Sana)	40	82	111	-42	-189	-271	73	281	220	-5
Yugoslavia (former)	52	-118	-337	-316	-301	-207	-306	-56	0	0
Yugoslavia (Serbia/Montenegro)	0	0	0	0	0	0	0	-35	0	0
Zambia	2	-30	-3	6	26	52	-19	-2	1	1
Zimbabwe (Rhodesia)	-6	-16	6	-85	-6	16	-35	37	-27	-10

Note: Unrevised data. Countries are shown as they were for the year of the data and not with current country defintions.

Table B-57. U.S. Trade Balances of Goods by Country, 1985–2003—*Continued*

(Millions of dollars; Census basis; foreign and domestic exports, f.a.s.; general imports, Customs.)

Country	1995	1996	1997	1998	1999	2000	2001	2002	2003
Norway	-1 798	-2 312	-2 015	-1 164	-2 612	-4 167	-3 369	-4 423	-3 745
Oman	-75	-195	100	86	-32	-57	-114	-44	-372
Other Pacific Islands, n.e.s.	0	0	0	0	0	0	0	0	0
Pacific Trust Territory (85-86)	0	0	0	0	0	0	0	0	0
Pacific Trust Territory (pre-85)	0	0	0	0	0	0	0	0	0
Pakistan	-263	11	-208	-965	-1 314	-1 705	-1 707	-1 611	-1 692
Palau	2	8	2	0	-1	5	2	3	14
Panama	1 084	1 032	1 170	1 440	1 376	1 302	1 040	1 105	1 547
Papua New Guinea	1	-16	52	-64	-107	-13	-17	-67	-36
Paraguay	938	855	872	752	467	403	364	390	435
Peru	740	505	187	79	-227	-334	-273	-375	-700
Philippines	-1 712	-2 038	-3 008	-5 213	-5 153	-5 147	-3 666	-3 715	-2 069
Pitcairn Island	2	-1	0	0	0	2	5	6	3
Poland	113	341	473	99	12	-283	-165	-414	-567
Portugal	-157	-56	-183	-378	-266	-623	-297	-810	-1 104
Qatar	132	50	203	134	-120	-296	-170	-169	77
Republic of South Africa	541	784	500	571	-613	-1 119	-1 467	-1 502	-1 816
Reunion	3	3	2	3	2	3	2	0	0
Romania	34	16	-146	-54	-258	-237	-145	-447	-363
Russia	-1 208	-221	-1 001	-2 149	-3 960	-5 478	-3 537	-4 426	-6 148
Rwanda	37	29	31	18	44	14	10	7	5
San Marino	5	6	7	5	2	-6	1	5	-3
Sao Tome and Principe	2	0	13	9	-2	0	11	2	1
Saudi Arabia	-2 148	-1 486	-1 113	4 186	-336	-7 989	-7 363	-8 364	-13 473
Senegal	61	50	45	54	54	78	-19	71	97
Seychelles	5	100	4	8	2	-1	153	-18	-6
Sierra Leone	-11	6	-3	11	3	15	23	22	22
Singapore	-3 246	-3 655	-2 340	-2 684	-1 941	-1 370	2 712	1 429	1 418
Slovakia	-68	-62	-84	-55	-42	-131	-167	-162	-898
Slovenia	-179	-159	-163	-164	-163	-173	-166	-175	-342
Solomon Islands	-2	5	2	0	1	6	5	1	1
Somalia	8	4	2	2	3	4	6	6	7
South Asia, n.e.s.	0	0	0	0	0	0	0	0	0
Southern Pacific Islands	0	0	0	0	0	0	0	0	0
Soviet Union	0	0	0	0	0	0	0	0	0
Spain	1 653	1 205	938	680	1 076	592	619	-452	-773
Special Category Exports	0	0	0	0	0	0	0	0	0
Sri Lanka (Ceylon)	-981	-1 181	-1 465	-1 576	-1 575	-1 798	-1 801	-1 639	-1 653
St. Christopher-Nevis	21	16	8	13	16	21	5	1	14
St. Helena	0	10	2	0	0	-3	1	-2	-3
St. Lucia	46	62	55	70	70	83	60	79	108
St. Pierre and Miquelon	-3	1	0	-2	-2	-5	-3	-3	-3
St. Vincent and Grenadines	34	38	50	269	84	28	17	24	42
Sudan	21	32	25	4	9	15	14	10	23
Suriname	90	126	92	81	21	-4	15	-8	53
Svalbard, Jan Mayen Island	1	1	1	0	0	0	1	1	3
Swaziland	-29	-28	-39	-17	-28	15	-53	-103	-154
Sweden	-3 169	-3 730	-3 986	-4 017	-3 872	-5 046	-5 303	-6 133	-7 899
Switzerland	-1 355	578	-85	-1 425	-1 232	-231	261	-1 600	-2 008
Syria	168	211	153	116	78	68	68	126	-45
Taiwan	-9 680	-11 498	-12 236	-14 966	-16 077	-16 134	-15 240	-13 805	-14 112
Tajikistan	-23	-16	10	-20	-10	4	24	32	43
Tanzania	44	31	38	35	33	11	36	38	42
Thailand	-4 949	-4 125	-5 238	-8 201	-9 340	-9 747	-8 733	-9 940	-9 339
Togo	-11	16	16	23	23	5	4	11	10
Tokelau Islands	-6	-3	-2	2	0	5	0	15	9
Tonga	1	3	5	6	2	3	-3	2	-7
Transshipments	565	627	340	324	371	306	262	187	186
Trinidad and Tobago	-283	-352	-27	12	-508	-1 132	-1 291	-1 419	-3 258
Tunisia	145	113	188	135	206	195	156	102	70
Turkey	927	1 109	1 421	967	570	689	52	-408	-884
Turkmenistan	33	200	116	25	10	45	203	-12	-42
Turks and Caicos Islands	29	38	53	59	88	83	68	49	66
Tuvalu	0	0	0	0	0	-2	0	0	0
Uganda	9	1	-2	15	5	-2	15	8	8
Ukraine	-186	-113	-10	-163	-314	-687	-465	-151	-51
United Arab Emirates	1 540	2 031	1 686	1 709	2 002	1 319	1 446	2 661	2 381
United Kingdom	1 936	2 024	3 746	4 278	-853	-1 880	-599	-7 617	-8 772
Uruguay	229	224	319	336	294	225	186	16	71
Uzbekistan	45	194	195	113	313	117	94	61	173
Vanuatu (New Hebrides)	1	0	-1	36	5	1	0	-2	1
Vatican City	-4	0	1	0	2	0	3	0	2
Venezuela	-5 070	-8 162	-6 841	-2 763	-5 896	-13 096	-9 552	-10 662	-14 305
Vietnam	54	297	-110	-279	-318	-454	-592	-1 815	-3 230
Wallis and Futuna	0	0	0	0	0	0	0	0	1
West Bank	0	0	1	2	4	4	2	0	0
Western Africa, n.e.s.	0	0	0	0	0	0	0	0	0
Western Sahara	0	0	0	0	0	0	0	0	0
Western Samoa	7	11	8	4	7	59	63	1	7
Yemen (Aden) (S. Yemen)	1	0	0	0	0	0	0	0	0
Yemen (Sana)	144	228	138	140	138	-59	-24	120	129
Yugoslavia (former)	0	0	0	0	0	0	0	0	0
Yugoslavia (Serbia/Montenegro)	2	38	39	61	54	28	49	69	35
Zambia	16	-19	-26	-26	-18	1	0	28	7
Zimbabwe (Rhodesia)	24	-42	-57	-34	-73	-59	-59	-53	-15

Note: Unrevised data. Countries are shown as they were for the year of the data and not with current country definitions.

Table B-58. Ranks of U.S. Trading Partners, 1984, 1994, 2002

Country	Exports			Imports			Total trade		
	1984	1994	2002	1984	1994	2002	1984	1994	2002
Afghanistan	144	188	115	122	155	174	140	180	150
Albania	139	161	178	148	154	167	150	170	184
Algeria	58	47	55	17	44	49	28	45	53
Andorra	171	190	185	227	208	201	238	196	194
Angola	85	84	74	41	35	44	52	48	51
Anguilla	172	167	169	221	201	197	237	178	183
Antigua Barbuda	173	116	114	129	159	178	156	135	149
Arbitarily Small Items	174	247	249	158	230	239	177	247	249
Argentina	36	23	44	43	41	42	43	30	42
Armenia	175	113	104	201	187	137	231	133	129
Aruba	176	74	68	197	62	66	201	68	69
Australia	13	13	13	23	29	28	17	19	19
Austria	62	41	38	50	39	35	53	41	38
Azerbaijan	177	144	123	210	200	135	236	163	142
Bahamas	52	57	56	38	77	72	44	64	67
Bahrain	79	62	71	95	86	76	94	71	78
Bangladesh	67	76	81	80	52	53	76	58	59
Barbados	70	93	82	71	123	136	75	106	105
Belarus	178	124	170	222	112	113	212	123	127
Belgium	179	12	12	192	20	22	199	15	16
Belgium and Luxembourg	9	231	233	19	219	229	15	231	233
Belize	109	101	99	99	115	121	109	113	120
Benin	136	146	145	171	144	203	148	156	170
Bermuda	71	71	72	130	147	143	87	90	91
Bhutan	180	220	214	187	215	200	197	223	218
Bolivia	84	86	93	78	73	106	83	78	98
Bosnia-Herzegovina	181	133	147	214	160	148	221	150	162
Botswana	129	155	148	94	140	138	119	155	156
British Indian Ocean Territory	166	213	220	174	192	210	187	211	221
Brazil	20	15	15	11	15	13	12	16	14
British Virgin Islands	182	123	124	151	138	133	172	141	139
Brunei	119	65	138	125	118	91	128	80	100
Bulgaria	114	104	107	106	76	82	120	88	90
Burkina (Upper Volta)	126	176	171	176	195	180	139	189	182
Burma (Myanmar)	132	170	187	121	101	81	132	130	97
Burundi	140	159	210	152	151	202	151	166	214
Cambodia (Kampuchea)	156	175	153	175	185	64	173	186	72
Cameroon	103	118	96	49	110	103	65	120	101
Canada	1	1	1	1	1	1	1	1	1
Cape Verde	183	191	189	157	206	189	175	198	195
Cayman Islands	97	81	86	134	113	159	114	96	114
Central African Republic	157	198	193	142	204	187	164	205	197
Chad	133	173	102	177	179	168	145	184	131
Chile	38	31	34	48	37	36	46	34	36
China	19	14	7	21	4	3	19	6	4
Christmas Island	184	210	212	183	194	205	191	212	219
Cocos (Keeling) Islands	185	180	213	234	197	216	234	191	220
Colombia	30	24	29	39	30	32	34	28	30
Comoros	162	224	227	149	156	169	167	194	206
Congo	137	135	134	42	67	99	55	79	110
Cook Islands	186	209	217	161	180	196	180	206	217
Costa Rica	56	37	31	58	42	43	58	38	37
Croatia	187	94	118	207	89	111	207	95	118
Cuba	158	192	97	191	234	214	176	201	128
Cyprus	98	80	91	107	133	140	108	101	119
Czech Republic	188	72	62	194	70	62	203	70	61
Czechoslovakia	108	240	242	87	224	233	97	237	239
Dem. Rep. of the Congo (Zaire)	94	131	156	55	81	98	71	100	116
Denmark	50	45	47	33	34	41	40	40	43
Djibouti	143	179	132	181	213	188	154	192	158
Dominica	189	147	139	178	153	172	189	160	161
Dominican Republic	47	30	26	40	31	33	45	31	31
East Timor	190	248	226	238	240	220	246	248	228
Ecuador	45	46	43	32	40	52	37	43	47
Egypt	24	28	33	76	60	60	35	39	45
El Salvador	60	53	42	63	59	54	66	57	48
Equatorial Guinea	167	200	105	165	198	70	181	207	83
Eritrea	191	172	155	218	214	211	241	187	175
Estonia	192	137	113	206	125	104	214	140	112
Ethiopia	75	95	129	88	124	141	86	110	148
Falkland Islands	169	228	221	182	202	166	192	220	202
Faroe Islands	193	217	198	229	145	150	218	183	187
Federated States of Micronesia	194	148	159	219	141	151	217	153	165
Fiji	195	100	176	113	94	108	137	103	124
Finland	64	49	46	47	38	39	51	44	40
France	7	8	8	9	9	9	8	9	9
French Guiana	100	85	84	115	170	162	113	105	109
French Indian Ocean Areas	159	246	248	135	229	238	158	244	246
French Pacific Islands	96	238	240	244	244	244	117	240	242
French Polynesia	196	114	117	141	139	131	165	128	133
French S. Antarctic Territory	197	226	218	235	238	224	247	227	222
French West Indies	117	241	243	119	227	236	125	241	243
Gabon	118	130	126	52	48	59	68	62	66
Gambia	134	193	190	163	177	213	144	193	196
Gaza Strip	170	203	230	170	232	163	186	213	199

Table B-58. Ranks of U.S. Trading Partners, 1984, 1994, 2002—*Continued*

Country	Exports			Imports			Total trade		
	1984	1994	2002	1984	1994	2002	1984	1994	2002
Georgia	198	112	108	203	184	146	230	129	136
Germany	5	5	5	4	5	5	5	5	5
Germany, East	80	236	238	79	222	232	82	235	237
Ghana	113	98	92	98	78	114	112	87	103
Gibraltar	146	154	161	145	165	194	159	164	176
Greece	59	54	51	66	64	69	67	60	65
Greenland	153	196	201	123	146	144	146	179	178
Grenada	199	151	131	159	152	164	179	161	155
Guadeloupe	200	119	140	212	178	154	227	145	160
Guatemala	61	42	40	60	47	45	62	46	41
Guinea	120	120	127	83	97	124	98	116	130
Guinea-Bissau	201	207	205	231	237	219	245	215	213
Guyana	112	105	101	89	93	115	103	104	113
Haiti	57	79	64	64	107	93	63	93	76
Heard Island and McDonald Islands	202	222	228	239	210	227	240	222	229
Honduras	66	52	36	62	50	40	69	50	39
Hong Kong	18	11	14	8	14	25	11	12	17
Hungary	91	70	60	73	61	46	81	67	54
Iceland	111	102	87	75	74	90	85	84	86
India	28	35	27	24	23	19	27	26	25
Indonesia	32	29	35	13	18	23	18	24	27
International Organizations	203	199	120	209	236	241	249	209	152
Iran	77	67	160	51	190	107	60	86	123
Iraq	44	211	149	82	223	37	64	216	49
Ireland	31	27	21	45	32	12	38	29	13
Israel	25	20	20	31	24	18	30	22	21
Italy	14	16	17	10	11	10	9	11	10
Ivory Coast	104	103	121	59	82	79	73	91	89
Jamaica	54	50	48	65	57	78	59	53	62
Japan	2	2	3	2	2	4	2	2	3
Jordan	68	73	73	139	126	73	84	89	77
Kazakhstan	204	97	63	195	105	83	210	108	75
Kenya	99	91	80	92	90	102	100	92	88
Kiribati (Gilbert Islands)	205	152	202	169	189	195	185	167	207
Korea, South	8	6	6	7	8	7	7	8	7
Korea, North	206	221	163	189	233	222	198	225	179
Kuwait	49	48	54	70	45	55	61	47	57
Kyrgyzstan	207	183	150	215	150	171	220	175	169
Laos	163	186	199	150	148	184	170	173	200
Latvia	208	106	112	205	116	100	213	115	107
Lebanon	76	63	77	131	130	126	95	77	96
Leeward and Windward Islands	72	235	237	243	243	243	91	236	238
Lesotho	138	195	208	162	104	84	149	137	102
Liberia	87	125	157	85	168	130	93	147	153
Libya	73	230	174	126	228	237	90	230	188
Liechtenstein	209	165	179	225	95	96	208	119	111
Lithuania	210	129	106	202	135	88	216	142	95
Luxembourg	211	77	67	196	71	89	204	74	80
Macao	154	156	116	68	56	61	80	66	68
Macedonia	212	163	172	223	98	123	209	124	145
Madagascar	116	122	177	90	108	97	104	122	115
Malawi	151	158	152	104	109	125	130	132	143
Malaysia	26	17	16	22	12	11	25	13	11
Maldive Islands	213	205	200	127	142	117	155	176	134
Mali	131	157	183	154	162	185	143	168	190
Malta and Gozo	123	110	88	116	96	85	129	109	85
Marshall Islands	214	138	154	217	149	157	219	152	167
Martinique	215	140	164	220	166	204	222	157	180
Mauritania	122	164	167	155	167	198	133	171	181
Mauritius	142	150	158	96	75	92	122	99	104
Mayotte	216	249	231	241	241	226	248	249	232
Mexico	4	3	2	3	3	2	3	3	2
Moldova	217	153	151	216	171	134	223	165	154
Monaco	218	187	182	226	134	153	215	169	177
Mongolia	164	181	125	147	128	105	169	159	117
Montserrat	219	178	197	156	186	208	174	188	205
Morocco	53	64	66	103	80	77	74	72	73
Mozambique	124	132	110	109	136	160	127	143	141
Namibia	148	160	130	144	127	128	160	148	137
Nauru	220	219	204	185	211	207	193	221	212
Nepal	147	174	168	133	88	109	152	118	125
Netherlands	6	9	10	14	21	21	10	14	15
Netherlands Antilles	46	60	58	29	66	80	33	63	71
Neutral Zone	221	250	250	248	248	248	250	250	250
New Caledonia	222	145	143	120	131	156	147	146	163
New Zealand	41	39	41	46	46	51	48	42	46
Nicaragua	82	87	69	93	85	68	96	85	70
Niger	155	169	141	166	176	199	171	174	166
Nigeria	51	61	52	25	26	29	31	33	33
Niue	223	215	222	184	217	223	194	219	225
Norfolk Island	224	208	225	168	212	218	184	214	226
Norway	37	44	50	30	33	30	32	37	32
Oman	78	78	76	77	63	75	79	69	81
Other Pacific Islands, n.e.s.	128	243	245	251	251	251	142	243	245
Pacific Trust Territory (85-86)	225	251	251	249	249	249	251	251	251

Table B-58. Ranks of U.S. Trading Partners, 1984, 1994, 2002—*Continued*

Country	Exports			Imports			Total trade		
	1984	1994	2002	1984	1994	2002	1984	1994	2002
Pacific Trust Territory (pre-85)	92	237	239	112	225	234	105	238	240
Pakistan	43	56	59	72	53	50	56	54	55
Palau	226	171	173	224	172	149	224	182	173
Panama	39	43	49	67	69	87	54	56	64
Papua New Guinea	110	115	165	108	91	120	115	111	138
Paraguay	105	55	70	100	100	132	107	65	87
Peru	40	40	45	35	55	56	39	49	50
Philippines	27	26	19	27	22	20	26	23	22
Pitcairn Island	227	225	195	188	205	217	196	224	203
Poland	65	58	61	74	58	63	72	61	63
Portugal	35	51	57	57	54	58	49	52	58
Qatar	93	92	78	97	99	71	102	98	79
Republic of South Africa	22	36	37	26	36	34	24	36	35
Reunion	228	194	206	232	188	186	232	199	208
Romania	69	66	85	44	79	67	50	73	74
Russia	229	33	39	193	28	27	200	32	29
Rwanda	141	136	188	117	182	179	134	154	192
San Marino	230	197	196	228	193	192	233	202	198
Sao Tome and Principe	231	166	209	233	209	209	239	177	215
Saudi Arabia	10	18	24	16	17	17	14	18	23
Senegal	88	128	122	146	143	176	110	144	151
Seychelles	161	182	191	172	173	139	178	185	171
Sierra Leone	127	149	162	101	114	175	123	131	174
Singapore	15	10	11	15	10	16	16	10	12
Slovakia	232	127	111	204	87	94	206	112	99
Slovenia	233	107	100	200	72	86	205	82	92
Solomon Islands	234	206	211	179	191	206	190	210	216
Somalia	101	141	194	160	207	212	121	162	201
South Asia, n.e.s.	152	245	247	247	247	247	168	246	248
Southern Pacific Islands	145	244	246	246	246	246	161	245	247
Soviet Union	17	233	235	54	220	230	29	233	235
Spain	21	22	22	28	27	31	22	25	28
Special Category Exports	11	232	234	242	242	242	21	232	234
Sri Lanka (Ceylon)	89	83	95	69	51	57	78	59	60
St. Christopher-Nevis	235	126	135	110	132	129	136	136	144
St. Helena	165	184	207	138	216	173	163	195	204
St. Lucia	236	111	109	132	129	145	157	121	135
St. Pierre and Miquelon	168	218	216	137	196	177	162	217	210
St. Vincent and Grenadines	237	134	142	143	158	147	166	149	159
Sudan	81	117	186	114	121	191	99	127	193
Suriname	86	99	103	84	119	112	92	114	108
Svalbard, Jan Mayen Island	238	202	219	236	199	225	235	208	223
Swaziland	160	189	181	111	120	116	135	151	132
Sweden	29	34	30	18	25	26	23	27	26
Switzerland	23	19	18	20	19	24	20	21	24
Syria	83	82	79	153	102	110	106	94	93
Taiwan	12	7	9	5	6	8	6	7	8
Tajikistan	239	162	146	213	106	193	211	134	172
Tanzania	115	121	128	124	137	142	124	138	147
Thailand	34	21	23	36	13	15	36	17	18
Togo	135	168	180	102	163	183	126	172	189
Tokelau Islands	240	212	175	173	164	182	188	197	185
Tonga	241	185	184	164	157	158	182	181	186
Transshipments	63	75	94	250	250	250	77	97	122
Trinidad and Tobago	48	59	53	34	49	47	41	55	52
Tunisia	74	68	90	105	111	119	88	81	106
Turkey	33	32	32	61	43	38	47	35	34
Turkmenistan	242	96	137	211	181	127	228	117	140
Turks and Caicos Islands	130	142	133	140	161	170	141	158	157
Tuvalu	243	223	229	240	218	228	242	226	230
Uganda	150	143	166	86	122	152	111	139	168
Ukraine	244	88	83	198	68	74	202	75	82
United Arab Emirates	42	38	28	37	65	65	42	51	44
United Kingdom	3	4	4	6	7	6	4	4	6
Uruguay	95	69	89	53	84	101	70	76	94
Uzbekistan	245	109	98	199	174	122	225	126	121
Vanuatu (New Hebrides)	246	204	215	186	169	181	195	200	211
Vatican City	247	216	203	230	175	190	226	204	209
Venezuela	16	25	25	12	16	14	13	20	20
Vietnam	125	90	65	180	117	48	138	102	56
Wallis and Futuna	248	229	224	167	231	240	183	229	227
West Bank	249	227	223	237	239	215	244	228	224
Western Africa, n.e.s.	121	242	244	245	245	245	131	242	244
Western Sahara	250	201	232	190	183	221	229	203	231
Western Samoa	149	177	192	136	203	165	153	190	191
Yemen (Sana)	102	89	75	128	83	95	118	83	84
Yemen (Aden) (S. Yemen)	107	239	241	118	226	235	116	239	241
Yugoslavia (former)	55	234	236	56	221	231	57	234	236
Yugoslavia (Serbia/Montenegro)	251	214	119	208	235	155	243	218	146
Zambia	90	139	144	81	103	161	89	125	164
Zimbabwe (Rhodesia)	106	108	136	91	92	118	101	107	126

Table B-59. United States' and China's Shares of Imports by Top 50 Importers, 1994–2003

(Percent, except as noted; top 50 based on 2003 imports value; Census basis; foreign and domestic exports, f.a.s.; general imports, Customs.)

Country	Imports 2003 (millions of dollars)	United States shares			China shares		
		1994	2003	1994–2003 change	1994	2003	1994–2003 change
WORLD	7 723 523	12.8	9.8	-3.0	4.5	7.7	3.2
Total of top 50	7 223 982	X	X	X	X	X	X
United States	1 305 250	X	X	X	6.0	12.5	6.5
Germany	596 449	7.4	7.3	-0.1	2.6	4.7	2.1
China	412 836	12.1	8.2	-3.9	X	X	X
France	390 008	8.3	5.4	-2.9	1.7	2.8	1.1
United Kingdom	383 671	12.0	10.2	-1.8	1.1	3.7	2.6
Japan	383 000	23.0	15.6	-7.4	10.1	19.7	9.6
Italy	291 103	4.6	4.0	-0.6	1.9	3.7	1.8
Canada	263 333	65.8	55.5	-10.3	1.9	5.1	3.2
Netherlands	261 256	8.3	8.0	-0.3	1.4	6.2	4.8
Hong Kong	232 545	7.1	5.5	-1.6	37.6	43.5	5.9
Belgium	224 950	. . .	5.9	. . .	. . .	2.6	. . .
Spain	201 262	7.3	3.1	-4.2	1.9	3.2	1.3
Mexico	187 600	71.8	61.8	-10.0	0.5	5.5	5.0
South Korea	186 782	21.1	14.2	-6.9	5.3	11.8	6.5
Singapore	127 996	15.2	14.1	-1.1	2.8	8.7	5.9
Switzerland	117 762	6.6	4.5	-2.1	1.2	1.5	0.3
Malaysia	98 909	16.6	12.1	-4.5	2.3	6.8	4.5
Austria	97 964	4.4	2.3	-2.1	1.5	1.8	0.3
Australia	93 203	22.0	15.0	-7.0	4.9	10.3	5.4
Sweden	83 259	9.2	3.9	-5.3	2.3	2.3	0.0
India	81 705	9.5	6.7	-2.8	2.4	4.5	2.1
Thailand	75 809	11.9	9.5	-2.4	2.6	8.0	5.4
Poland	70 077	3.9	1.2	-2.7	1.4	2.5	1.1
Turkey	68 724	10.4	5.1	-5.3	1.1	3.8	2.7
Russia	63 031	5.4	4.7	-0.7	2.5	5.2	2.7
Denmark	57 796	5.1	2.9	-2.2	1.9	2.8	0.9
Brazil	57 744	20.6	21.4	0.8	1.4	4.1	2.7
Czech Republic	56 128	3.4	2.8	-0.6	0.7	4.8	4.1
Ireland	53 317	18.5	15.8	-2.7	1.2	2.3	1.1
Saudi Arabia	53 208	21.3	9.5	-11.8	2.2	4.4	2.2
United Arab Emirates	50 947	8.7	7.6	-1.1	6.7	10.9	4.2
Hungary	50 920	3.1	2.0	-1.1	0.7	4.9	4.2
Philippines	47 041	18.5	17.9	-0.6	1.4	6.7	5.3
Portugal	45 033	3.6	1.9	-1.7	0.6	0.9	0.3
Greece	43 686	3.5	5.2	1.7	1.3	3.2	1.9
Finland	41 987	7.6	3.7	-3.9	1.5	3.1	1.6
Norway	41 755	7.4	3.9	-3.5	1.9	2.4	0.5
Israel	38 328	18.0	19.7	1.7	0.3	3.3	3.0
Republic of South Africa	37 173	16.2	8.3	-7.9	1.7	6.0	4.3
Indonesia	32 544	11.2	8.3	-2.9	4.3	9.1	4.8
Iran	28 921	2.9	0.4	-2.5	1.2	8.8	7.6
Vietnam	25 705	0.8	5.7	4.9	2.5	13.6	11.1
Romania	24 116	6.5	2.0	-4.5	0.9	2.3	1.4
Ukraine	23 476	1.7	1.1	-0.6	0.3	4.4	4.1
Slovakia	23 163	2.8	0.5	-2.3	0.6	0.7	0.1
Egypt	21 793	17.1	13.4	-3.7	2.1	4.7	2.6
Chile	19 413	22.7	13.0	-9.7	2.4	6.6	4.2
New Zealand	18 466	19.2	11.8	-7.4	3.3	9.0	5.7
Morocco	16 532	7.7	3.1	-4.6	1.5	4.6	3.1
Luxembourg	16 306	. . .	2.2	. . .	. . .	10.9	. . .

Note: Top 50 importing countries accounted for 93.5 percent of world's imports.

. . . = Not available.
X = Not applicable.

Table B-60. Business Environment Indicators by Country

(Low numbers are better.)

Country	Economic freedom 2004	Economic freedom 1997–2004 change	Trade freedom 2004	Trade freedom 1997–2004 change	Competitive-ness rank	Technology rank	Days to start a business	Corruption index	Personal freedom index
Albania	3.10	-0.49	4	1	...	...	47	7.5	3.0
Algeria	3.31	-0.32	5	0	74	96	26	7.4	5.5
Angola	...	...	...	...	100	98	146	8.2	5.5
Argentina	3.48	0.73	4	0	78	45	32	7.5	2.0
Armenia	2.63	-0.87	2	0	...	...	25	7.0	4.0
Australia	1.88	-0.31	2	0	10	19	2	1.2	1.0
Austria	2.08	0.06	2	-1	17	27	29	2.0	1.0
Azerbaijan	3.39	-1.19	3	-2	...	...	123	8.2	5.5
Bahamas	2.25	0.20	5	0	...	...	...	...	1.0
Bahrain	2.08	0.28	3	1	...	...	...	3.9	5.0
Bangladesh	3.70	-0.06	5	0	98	95	35	8.7	4.0
Barbados	2.41	-0.52	4	0	...	...	...	...	1.0
Belarus	4.09	0.14	4	-1	...	...	79	5.8	6.0
Belgium	2.19	0.17	2	0	27	29	34	2.4	1.0
Belize	2.69	-0.02	4	-1	...	...	...	5.5	1.5
Benin	3.44	0.00	4	0	...	...	32	...	2.0
Bolivia	2.59	0.03	3	1	85	88	59	7.7	3.0
Bosnia and Herzegovina	3.30	...	3	...	...	...	54	6.7	4.0
Botswana	2.55	-0.20	3	-2	36	59	108	4.3	2.0
Brazil	3.10	-0.18	4	0	54	35	155	6.1	2.5
Bulgaria	3.08	-0.45	4	1	64	63	32	6.1	1.5
Burkina Faso	3.28	-0.53	4	-1	...	...	135	...	4.0
Burundi	...	...	...	...	...	...	43	...	5.0
Cambodia	2.90	-0.78	4	-1	...	...	94	...	5.5
Cameroon	3.63	-0.32	5	0	91	93	37	8.2	6.0
Canada	1.98	-0.10	2	0	16	11	3	1.3	1.0
Cape Verde	2.86	-0.94	5	0	...	...	...	...	...
Central African Republic	3.38	...	5	...	...	...	14	...	6.0
Chad	3.54	-0.70	5	0	101	102	75	...	5.5
Chile	1.91	-0.35	2	0	28	31	28	2.6	1.0
China	3.64	-0.09	5	0	44	65	41	6.6	6.5
Colombia	3.13	-0.10	4	0	63	60	43	6.3	4.0
Congo, Rep.	3.90	-0.43	5	1	...	...	67	7.8	4.5
Costa Rica	2.71	-0.32	3	-1	51	46	77	5.7	1.5
Croatia	3.11	-0.45	4	1	53	41	49	6.3	2.0
Cuba	4.08	-0.82	3	-2	...	...	...	5.4	7.0
Cyprus	1.95	-0.68	2	-1	...	...	...	3.9	1.0
Czech Republic	2.39	0.10	3	2	39	21	40	6.1	1.5
Denmark	1.80	-0.18	2	0	4	8	4	0.5	1.0
Dem. Rep. of the Congo (Zaire)	...	...	...	...	...	...	188	...	6.0
Djibouti	3.23	0.06	5	1	...	...	...	...	...
Dominican Republic	3.51	0.27	5	0	62	52	78	6.7	2.5
Ecuador	3.60	0.39	4	1	86	76	92	7.8	3.0
Egypt	3.28	-0.21	4	-1	58	68	43	6.7	6.0
El Salvador	2.24	-0.36	2	-1	48	67	115	6.3	2.5
Equatorial Guinea	3.69	...	5	...	...	...	...	...	...
Estonia	1.76	-0.70	1	-1	22	10	72	4.5	1.5
Ethiopia	3.33	-0.47	4	0	92	100	32	7.5	5.0
Fiji	3.06	-0.17	4	-1	...	...	...	...	3.5
Finland	1.95	-0.23	2	0	1	2	14	0.3	1.0
France	2.63	0.31	2	0	26	28	8	3.1	1.0
Gabon	3.43	0.12	5	0	...	...	...	7.5	4.5
Gambia	3.54	-0.01	4	0	55	80	...	7.5	4.0
Georgia	3.19	-0.69	4	1	...	...	25	8.2	4.0
Germany	2.03	-0.22	2	0	13	14	45	2.3	1.0
Ghana	3.40	-0.13	4	-1	71	86	85	6.7	2.0
Greece	2.80	-0.01	2	0	25	30	38	5.7	1.5
Guatemala	3.16	0.27	3	0	89	79	39	7.6	4.0
Guinea	3.24	-0.15	5	0	...	...	49	...	5.0
Guinea Bissau	3.90	...	5	...	...	...	...	...	...
Guyana	3.13	-0.22	4	0	...	...	...	...	...
Haiti	3.78	-0.57	4	0	102	101	203	8.5	6.0
Honduras	3.53	-0.05	3	-1	94	87	62	7.7	3.0
Hong Kong	1.34	-0.20	1	0	24	37	11	2.0	4.0
Hungary	2.60	-0.44	3	-1	33	32	52	5.2	1.5
Iceland	2.00	-0.30	2	0	8	15	...	0.4	1.0
India	3.53	-0.35	5	0	56	64	89	7.2	2.5
Indonesia	3.76	0.71	3	1	72	78	151	8.1	3.5
Iran	4.26	-0.54	2	-3	...	...	48	7.0	6.0
Iraq	...	...	...	...	...	...	...	7.8	6.0
Ireland	1.74	-0.40	2	0	30	38	24	2.5	1.0
Israel	2.36	-0.28	2	0	20	9	34	3.0	2.0
Italy	2.26	-0.15	2	-1	41	44	13	4.7	1.0
Ivory Coast	3.18	-0.62	4	-1	...	...	58	7.9	5.5
Jamaica	2.81	-0.05	4	2	67	53	31	6.2	2.5
Japan	2.53	0.37	2	0	11	5	31	3.0	1.5
Jordan	2.73	-0.12	4	0	34	48	36	5.4	5.0
Kazakhstan	3.70	...	4	...	...	...	25	7.6	5.5
Kenya	3.26	0.00	5	1	83	75	47	8.1	3.0
Korea, North	5.00	0.05	5	0	...	...	...	...	...
Korea, South	2.69	0.38	4	1	18	6	22	5.7	2.0
Kuwait	2.70	0.31	2	0	...	...	35	4.7	4.5
Kyrgyzstan	3.36	...	4	...	...	...	21	7.9	5.5
Laos	4.45	-0.25	5	0	...	...	198	...	6.5
Latvia	2.36	-0.55	2	-2	37	26	18	6.2	1.5

... = Not available.

Table B-60. Business Environment Indicators by Country—*Continued*

(Low numbers are better.)

Country	Economic freedom		Trade freedom		Competitive-ness rank	Technology rank	Days to start a business	Corruption index	Personal freedom index
	2004	1997–2004 change	2004	1997–2004 change					
Lebanon	3.13	0.36	4	2	...	...	46	7.0	5.5
Lesotho	3.50	-0.20	4	0	...	...	92	...	2.5
Libya	4.55	-0.40	5	0	...	...	...	7.9	7.0
Liechtenstein	...	...	...	...	...	...	...	...	1.0
Lithuania	2.19	-0.86	2	0	40	36	26	5.3	1.5
Luxembourg	1.71	-0.25	2	0	21	42	...	1.3	1.0
Macedonia	3.04	...	4	...	81	70	48	7.7	3.0
Madagascar	3.14	-0.30	3	-1	96	97	44	7.4	3.0
Malawi	3.46	-0.40	3	-2	76	94	35	7.2	3.5
Malaysia	3.16	0.31	3	-2	29	20	30	4.8	4.5
Mali	3.34	-0.16	3	0	99	99	42	7.0	2.0
Malta and Gozo	2.51	-0.74	4	0	19	17	...	...	1.0
Mauritania	2.94	-1.09	3	-2	...	...	82	...	5.5
Mauritius	2.99	...	5	...	46	49	...	5.6	1.5
Mexico	2.90	-0.45	2	-1	47	43	58	6.4	2.0
Moldova	3.09	-0.56	2	-1	...	...	30	7.6	3.5
Mongolia	2.90	-0.33	2	-1	...	...	20	...	2.0
Morocco	2.93	-0.07	5	1	61	71	11	6.7	5.0
Mozambique	3.28	-0.87	4	1	93	92	153	7.3	3.5
Myanmar	4.45	0.08	5	0	...	...	...	8.4	7.0
Namibia	2.96	0.16	4	0	52	62	85	5.3	2.5
Nepal	3.53	-0.36	5	1	...	...	21	...	4.5
Netherlands	2.04	0.17	2	0	12	18	11	1.1	1.0
New Zealand	1.70	-0.05	2	0	14	23	12	0.5	1.0
Nicaragua	2.94	-0.86	2	-3	90	85	45	7.4	3.0
Niger	3.43	-0.76	4	-1	...	...	27	...	4.0
Nigeria	3.95	0.53	5	0	87	82	44	8.6	4.0
Norway	2.35	-0.04	2	-1	9	13	23	1.2	1.0
Oman	2.80	0.01	3	0	...	...	34	3.7	5.5
Pakistan	3.40	0.11	5	0	73	83	24	7.5	5.5
Panama	2.83	0.29	3	-1	59	50	19	6.6	1.5
Papua New Guinea	...	...	...	...	...	...	56	7.9	3.0
Paraguay	3.39	0.48	3	1	95	91	74	8.4	3.0
Peru	2.83	-0.20	4	1	57	61	98	6.3	2.5
Philippines	3.05	-0.01	2	-3	66	56	50	7.5	2.5
Poland	2.81	-0.28	3	-1	45	34	31	6.4	1.5
Portugal	2.38	-0.03	2	0	25	22	78	3.4	1.0
Qatar	2.86	...	3	...	...	...	...	4.4	6.0
Romania	3.66	0.36	4	2	75	55	28	7.2	2.0
Russia	3.46	-0.37	3	-2	70	69	36	7.3	5.0
Rwanda	3.36	-1.24	3	-2	...	...	21	...	5.5
Samoa	...	-2.79	...	-3	...	...	...	...	7.0
Saudi Arabia	3.05	0.10	4	0	...	...	64	5.5	7.0
Senegal	3.00	-0.64	3	-2	79	89	57	6.8	2.5
Serbia and Montenegro	...	...	...	...	77	66	51	7.7	2.5
Sierra Leone	3.73	-0.06	5	1	...	...	26	7.8	3.5
Singapore	1.61	-0.06	1	0	6	12	8	0.6	4.5
Slovak Republic	2.44	-0.74	3	1	43	33	52	6.3	1.5
Slovenia	2.75	-0.70	3	-1	31	24	61	4.1	1.0
Somalia	...	...	...	...	...	...	...	...	...
South Africa	2.79	-0.20	4	-1	42	40	38	5.6	1.5
Spain	2.31	-0.19	2	0	23	25	108	3.1	1.0
Sri Lanka	3.06	0.45	3	0	68	72	50	6.6	3.0
Sudan	...	...	...	...	...	...	...	7.7	7.0
Suriname	3.96	-0.04	5	0	...	...	...	...	...
Swaziland	3.18	-0.13	4	0	...	...	...	...	1.5
Sweden	1.90	-0.35	2	0	3	4	16	0.7	1.0
Switzerland	1.84	-0.07	2	0	7	7	20	1.2	1.0
Syria	3.88	-0.26	4	-1	...	...	47	6.6	7.0
Taiwan	2.43	0.22	2	0	5	3	48	4.3	2.0
Tajikistan	4.15	...	3	...	...	...	...	8.2	5.5
Tanzania	3.29	-0.17	5	2	69	81	35	7.5	3.5
Thailand	2.86	0.29	4	1	32	39	33	6.7	2.5
Togo	3.73	...	3	...	...	...	53	...	5.5
Trinidad and Tobago	2.45	-0.23	2	-3	49	47	...	5.4	3.0
Tunisia	2.94	0.05	5	0	38	57	14	5.1	5.5
Turkey	3.39	0.69	3	2	65	54	9	6.9	3.5
Turkmenistan	4.31	...	5	...	...	...	...	...	...
Uganda	2.70	-0.05	3	-1	80	77	36	7.8	4.5
Ukraine	3.49	-0.34	3	-1	84	84	34	7.7	4.0
United Arab Emirates	2.60	0.25	2	0	...	...	54	4.8	6.0
United Kingdom	1.79	-0.16	2	0	15	16	18	1.3	1.0
United States	1.85	-0.02	2	0	2	1	5	2.5	1.0
Uruguay	2.55	-0.05	2	0	50	51	45	4.5	1.0
Uzbekistan	4.29	...	5	...	...	...	35	7.6	6.5
Venezuela	4.18	0.61	4	0	82	58	116	7.6	3.5
Vietnam	3.93	-0.53	5	0	60	73	56	7.6	6.5
Yemen	3.70	-0.25	3	-2	...	...	63	7.4	5.0
Zambia	3.50	0.63	4	2	88	90	35	7.5	4.0
Zimbabwe (Rhodesia)	4.54	0.85	5	0	97	75	96	7.7	6.0

. . . = Not available.

SECTION C. U.S. COMMODITY TRADE
BY GEOGRAPHIC AREA

ABOUT THE DATA

The tables presented in Section C provide a detailed picture of U.S. commodity trade with the major regions of the world and bilateral trade with individual countries. The tables in this section provide export and import data using 1-digit Standard International Classification (SITC) codes (see "Understanding Foreign Trade Statistics" for definitions), and include the top 20 3-digit SITC exports and imports. Tables C-1 to C-20 show data for major trading and economic areas, which are defined below. A second group of tables (C-21 to C-100) shows the same data for the United States' top 80 trading partners, which are ranked on the following page.

These data are taken from the Office of Trade and Economic Analysis (OTEA) in the Commerce Department's International Trade Administration (ITA). In turn, the OTEA presents data that were collected by the Bureau of Economic Analysis (BEA) and the Census Bureau.

The arrangement of tables in this section generally matches *U.S. Foreign Trade Highlights*, formerly published by the OTEA. These tables are now available online on the OTEA's Web site at <www.ita.doc.gov/td/industry/otea/usfth/>. Data for all 252 areas and trading partners can be found there as well. Custom tables can be created using multiple variables, including exports, imports, and trade balances; various product classification codes; and trading areas and individual countries, on the ITA's TradeStats Express at <tse.export.gov>.

For a variety of reasons, U.S. trade with the world does not equal the sum of trade with the developed and developing countries.

Data may not add to total or may appear as zero because of rounding.

Regional Definitions

Europe consists of Western Europe and Eastern Europe. **Western Europe** includes the European Union (EU-15) and non-EU Western Europe. The **European Union (EU-15)** includes Austria, Belgium, Denmark, Finland, France, Germany, Greece, Ireland, Italy, Luxembourg, the Netherlands, Portugal (including the Azores and the Madeira Islands), Spain (including Spanish Africa and the Canary Islands), Sweden, and the United Kingdom. The **non-EU Western Europe** countries in include Bosnia-Herzegovina, Croatia, Cyprus, Gibraltar, Iceland, Liechtenstein, Macedonia, Malta, Norway, Serbia and Montenegro, Slovenia, Switzerland, and Turkey; and, after

1987, Other Non-EU Western Europe (Andorra, Faroe Islands, Monaco, San Marino, Svalbard and Jan Mayen Island, and Vatican City). **Eastern Europe** includes Albania, the Baltic States (Estonia, Latvia, Lithuania), Bulgaria, the Czech Republic, Hungary, Poland, Romania, Slovakia, and the Newly Independent States (Armenia, Azerbaijan, Belarus, Georgia, Kazakhstan, Kyrgyzstan, Moldova, Russia, Tajikistan, Turkmenistan, Ukraine, and Uzbekistan). EU-10 is the group of 10 countries that joined the EU on 5/1/2004. They are: Cyprus, Czech Republic, Estonia, Hungary, Latvia, Lithuania, Malta, Poland, Slovakia, and Slovenia. EU-25 equals existing EU-15 plus the EU-10.

The **Western Hemisphere** includes all countries of the Western Hemisphere except for the United States. **North American Free Trade Agreement (NAFTA)** members are Canada, Mexico, and the United States. The **Caribbean** countries include Aruba, the Bahamas, Barbados, Cayman Islands, Dominican Republic, Haiti, Jamaica, Leeward and Windward Islands (i.e., Antigua, British Virgin Islands, Dominica, Grenada, Montserrat, St. Christopher-Nevis and Anguilla, St. Lucia, and St. Vincent), the Netherlands Antilles, Trinidad and Tobago, and Turks and Caicos Islands. The **Central American** countries consist of Belize, Costa Rica, El Salvador, Guatemala, Honduras, Nicaragua, and Panama. The countries of **South America** are Argentina, Bolivia, Brazil, Chile, Colombia, Ecuador, Guyana, Paraguay, Peru, Suriname, Uruguay, and Venezuela. The other countries of the Western Hemisphere include Bermuda, Cuba, Falkland Islands, French Guiana, Greenland, Guadeloupe, Martinique, and St. Pierre and Miquelon.

Asia includes Japan, South Korea, Taiwan plus China, Hong Kong, Macau plus the ASEAN-10, the Middle East, and Other Asia. The **Association of Southeast Asian Nations (ASEAN-10)** members are Brunei, Burma, Cambodia, Indonesia, Laos, Malaysia, the Philippines, Singapore, Thailand, and Vietnam. Cambodia was not a member in previous years. The **Middle East** includes Bahrain, Iran, Iraq, Israel (including the Gaza Strip and the West Bank), Jordan, Kuwait, Lebanon, the Neutral Zone, Oman, Qatar, Saudi Arabia, Syria, the United Arab Emirates, and the Yemen Arab Republic. The **Other Asia** countries are Afghanistan, Bangladesh, India, North Korea, Mongolia, Nepal, Pakistan, Sri Lanka, and Southern Asia NEC (not elsewhere classified). Southern Asia NEC includes Bhutan, East Timor, and Maldives Islands.

The **Asia-Pacific Economic Cooperation (APEC)** countries are Australia, Brunei, Canada, Chile, China, Hong Kong, Indonesia, Japan, Malaysia, Mexico, New Zealand, Papua New Guinea, Peru, Philippines, Russia, Singapore,

151

South Korea, Taiwan, Thailand, United States, and Vietnam.

Australia and Oceania consists of Australia, Australian island dependencies (i.e., Christmas Island, Cocos Island, Heard and McDonald Islands, and Norfolk Island), Fiji, French Pacific Islands (i.e., French Polynesia, New Caledonia, and Wallis and Futuna), New Zealand, New Zealand island dependencies (i.e., Cook Islands, Niue, and Tokelau Islands), Papua New Guinea, Southern Pacific Islands (i.e., Kiribati, Pitcairn Island, Solomon Islands, Tuvalu, and Vanuatu), Former Trust Territory (i.e., Federated States of Micronesia, Marshall Islands,

and Palau), Western Samoa, and Other Pacific Islands NEC (Nauru and Tonga).

Africa consists of all the countries on the continent. French Indian Ocean areas include Reunion and French Southern and Antarctic Lands. In January 1993, the U.S. Bureau of the Census began reporting trade values for Eritrea.

The **developed countries** of the world include Canada, Japan, all of Western Europe, Australia, New Zealand, and the Republic of South Africa. **Developing countries** include all other countries.

TOP 80 TRADING PARTNERS, 2003

1. Canada
2. Mexico
3. China
4. Japan
5. Germany
6. United Kingdom
7. Korea, South
8. Taiwan
9. France
10. Malaysia
11. Italy
12. Ireland
13. Singapore
14. Netherlands
15. Brazil
16. Belgium
17. Saudi Arabia
18. Hong Kong
19. Thailand
20. Venezuela
21. Israel
22. Australia
23. Switzerland
24. Philippines
25. India
26. Sweden
27. Spain
28. Indonesia
29. Nigeria
30. Russia
31. Colombia
32. Dominican Republic
33. Republic of South Africa
34. Costa Rica
35. Turkey
36. Norway
37. Chile
38. Austria
39. Honduras
40. Vietnam

41. Argentina
42. Trinidad and Tobago
43. Finland
44. Denmark
45. Algeria
46. Guatemala
47. Iraq
48. Angola
49. United Arab Emirates
50. New Zealand
51. Ecuador
52. Peru
53. El Salvador
54. Egypt
55. Kuwait
56. Hungary
57. Pakistan
58. Portugal
59. Bangladesh
60. Panama
61. Poland
62. Czech Republic
63. Gabon
64. Jamaica
65. Sri Lanka
66. Greece
67. Bahamas
68. Macau
69. Netherlands Antilles
70. Cambodia
71. Aruba
72. Nicaragua
73. Equatorial Guinea
74. Jordan
75. Slovakia
76. Romania
77. Oman
78. Haiti
79. Bahrain
80. Morocco

HIGHLIGHTS

In 2003, the United States ran a trade surplus with nearly half of its trading partners. However, the deficits with the other half were for much greater amounts, leaving the United States with a total trade deficit of nearly $536 billion. This deficit is up more than 60 percent from 1999, when it was $332 billion.

In 2003, the United States had its largest trade surplus with the Netherlands, and its largest deficit was with China. Figure C-1 ranks the countries with top five surpluses and top five deficits. The total of the top five deficits ($324.5 billion) was more than 11 times greater than the sum of the top five surpluses ($28.6 billion).

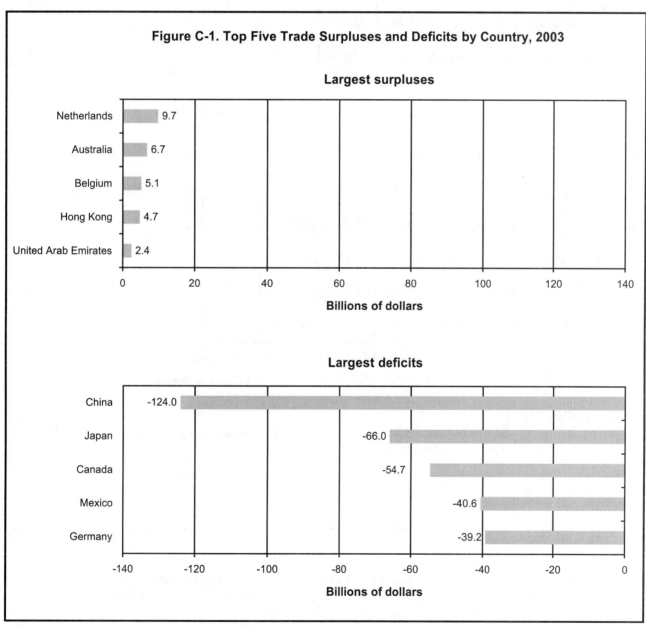

Figure C-1. Top Five Trade Surpluses and Deficits by Country, 2003

Largest surpluses

Country	Billions of dollars
Netherlands	9.7
Australia	6.7
Belgium	5.1
Hong Kong	4.7
United Arab Emirates	2.4

Largest deficits

Country	Billions of dollars
China	-124.0
Japan	-66.0
Canada	-54.7
Mexico	-40.6
Germany	-39.2

Source: International Trade Administration.

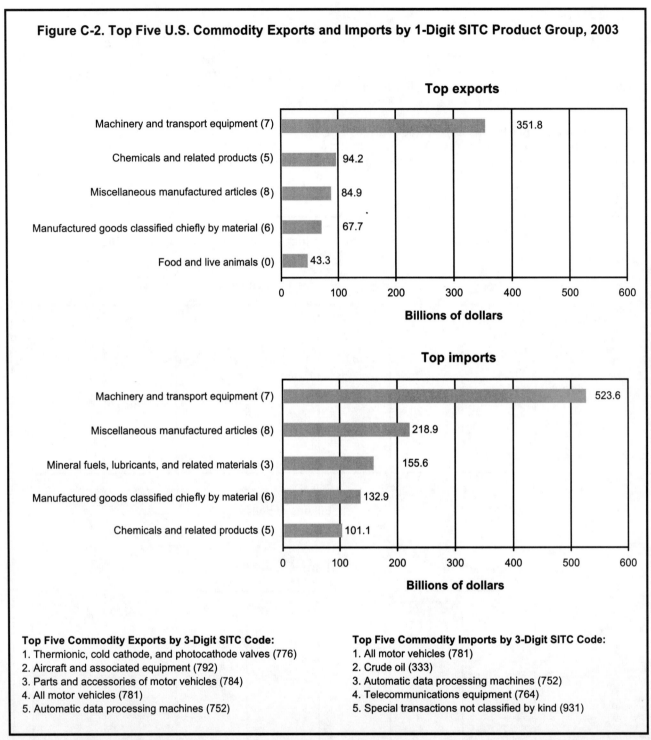

Figure C-2. Top Five U.S. Commodity Exports and Imports by 1-Digit SITC Product Group, 2003

Top exports

Machinery and transport equipment (7) — 351.8
Chemicals and related products (5) — 94.2
Miscellaneous manufactured articles (8) — 84.9
Manufactured goods classified chiefly by material (6) — 67.7
Food and live animals (0) — 43.3

Billions of dollars

Top imports

Machinery and transport equipment (7) — 523.6
Miscellaneous manufactured articles (8) — 218.9
Mineral fuels, lubricants, and related materials (3) — 155.6
Manufactured goods classified chiefly by material (6) — 132.9
Chemicals and related products (5) — 101.1

Billions of dollars

Top Five Commodity Exports by 3-Digit SITC Code:
1. Thermionic, cold cathode, and photocathode valves (776)
2. Aircraft and associated equipment (792)
3. Parts and accessories of motor vehicles (784)
4. All motor vehicles (781)
5. Automatic data processing machines (752)

Top Five Commodity Imports by 3-Digit SITC Code:
1. All motor vehicles (781)
2. Crude oil (333)
3. Automatic data processing machines (752)
4. Telecommunications equipment (764)
5. Special transactions not classified by kind (931)

Source: International Trade Administration.

Figure C-2 shows the value of the top five 1-digit SITC code exports and imports, both of which are led by machinery and transport equipment. Also included are the top five export and import commodities by 3-digit SITC codes. Among the major commodities supporting export growth is thermionic, cold cathode and photocathode valves, which are largely computer components, and are within the 1-digit SITC grouping of machinery and transport equipment. The chief imports are motor vehicles and crude oil, which when combined add up to 17 percent of U.S. imports. Crude oil imports have doubled from 1999 to 2003.

Table C-1. U.S. Trade by Commodity with World, 1999–2003

(Millions of dollars; total exports, f.a.s.; general imports, Customs; top 20 commodities based on 2003 dollar value.)

Commodity and SITC code	1999	2000	2001	2002	2003	Percent change, 1999–2003	Percent share of total, 2003
EXPORTS							
Total	692 821	780 419	731 026	693 257	723 743	4.5	100.0
Food and live animals (0)	38 237	40 263	41 173	40 295	43 275	13.2	6.0
Beverages and tobacco (1)	6 764	6 821	5 645	4 671	4 788	-29.2	0.7
Crude materials, inedible, except fuels (2)	24 178	29 032	28 080	28 128	33 545	38.7	4.6
Mineral fuels, lubricants and related materials (3)	9 926	13 340	12 865	11 689	14 047	41.5	1.9
Animal and vegetable oils, fats and waxes (4)	1 935	1 439	1 379	1 915	2 012	4.0	0.3
Chemicals and related products (5)	71 989	82 542	82 322	83 593	94 153	30.8	13.0
Manufactured goods classified chiefly by material (6)	62 157	71 990	66 658	65 059	67 696	8.9	9.4
Machinery and transport equipment (7)	369 298	412 200	375 068	349 736	351 757	-4.7	48.6
Miscellaneous manufactured articles (8)	81 630	93 184	88 524	82 137	84 864	4.0	11.7
Commodities and transactions not classified elsewhere (9)	26 707	29 609	29 312	26 033	27 605	3.4	3.8
Top 20 Commodities	348 559	392 960	362 815	341 021	347 880	-0.2	48.1
Thermionic, cold cathode, and photocathode valves (776)	49 351	62 824	47 622	44 518	47 770	-3.2	6.6
Aircraft and associated equipment (792)	49 611	40 954	44 689	43 876	39 638	-20.1	5.5
Parts and accessories of motor vehicles (784)	29 398	31 641	29 165	29 249	28 327	-3.6	3.9
All motor vehicles (781)	17 060	17 234	18 364	21 106	22 777	33.5	3.1
Automatic data processing machines (752)	26 715	30 929	27 386	21 812	21 595	-19.2	3.0
Telecommunications equipment (764)	24 381	29 163	26 133	21 587	20 364	-16.5	2.8
Measuring/checking/analyzing instruments (874)	18 156	22 152	20 388	18 640	19 406	6.9	2.7
Parts for office machines and a.d.p. machines (759)	20 811	25 467	20 869	17 175	18 742	-9.9	2.6
Estimated low value shipments (994)	13 757	15 707	16 842	15 280	15 826	15.0	2.2
Nonelectric engines and motors (714)	14 964	15 629	17 545	16 415	15 609	4.3	2.2
Internal combustion piston engines (713)	12 388	13 700	12 632	12 862	12 619	1.9	1.7
Electrical apparatus for switching or protecting elec. circuits (772)	12 413	15 129	12 498	11 648	11 841	-4.6	1.6
Medicaments (including veterinary medicaments) (542)	5 823	7 165	8 975	9 075	11 028	89.4	1.5
Electrical machinery and apparatus (778)	11 306	14 170	11 350	11 122	10 888	-3.7	1.5
Medical instruments and appliances (872)	6 722	7 115	8 088	7 941	8 930	32.8	1.2
Civil engineering and contractors' plant and equipment (723)	7 924	8 663	9 166	8 996	8 860	11.8	1.2
Machinery and equipment specialized for particular industries (728)	10 792	15 927	11 216	9 058	8 795	-18.5	1.2
Miscellaneous chemical products (598)	6 627	7 712	7 626	7 535	8 381	26.5	1.2
Oil seeds and oleaginous fruits (222)	4 936	5 722	5 815	6 051	8 303	68.2	1.1
Medicinal products, except medicaments (541)	5 424	5 957	6 446	7 075	8 181	50.8	1.1
IMPORTS							
Total	1 024 766	1 216 888	1 141 959	1 163 549	1 259 396	22.9	100.0
Food and live animals (0)	35 093	36 792	37 226	39 188	42 900	22.2	3.4
Beverages and tobacco (1)	8 615	9 259	9 736	10 770	11 978	39.0	1.0
Crude materials, inedible, except fuels (2)	21 719	22 366	20 254	19 772	20 014	-7.9	1.6
Mineral fuels, lubricants and related materials (3)	75 202	133 590	122 874	117 095	155 561	106.9	12.4
Animal and vegetable oils, fats and waxes (4)	1 409	1 400	1 190	1 344	1 584	12.4	0.1
Chemicals and related products (5)	62 206	73 633	78 871	86 057	101 050	62.4	8.0
Manufactured goods classified chiefly by material (6)	116 995	133 968	123 061	126 937	132 925	13.6	10.6
Machinery and transport equipment (7)	479 871	553 188	499 873	505 644	523 617	9.1	41.6
Miscellaneous manufactured articles (8)	176 673	200 902	198 087	205 233	218 938	23.9	17.4
Commodities and transactions not classified elsewhere (9)	46 983	51 790	50 789	51 510	50 828	8.2	4.0
Top 20 Commodities	520 959	650 165	600 964	613 497	668 136	28.3	53.1
All motor vehicles (781)	96 888	109 614	107 006	114 424	114 721	18.4	9.1
Crude oil (333)	50 662	89 786	75 263	79 368	101 722	100.8	8.1
Automatic data processing machines (752)	49 173	55 909	47 596	50 035	52 012	5.8	4.1
Telecommunications equipment (764)	29 082	44 349	37 937	37 690	40 531	39.4	3.2
Special transactions not classified by kind (931)	31 783	34 572	35 367	35 893	33 622	5.8	2.7
Parts and accessories of motor vehicles (784)	26 044	28 440	26 908	29 764	32 888	26.3	2.6
Oil (not crude) (334)	14 525	26 365	24 541	20 702	26 735	84.1	2.1
Thermionic, cold cathode, and photocathode valves (776)	38 564	49 210	31 405	26 955	25 417	-34.1	2.0
Parts for office machines and a.d.p. machines (759)	31 906	33 352	26 016	24 757	24 962	-21.8	2.0
Furniture and bedding accessories (821)	16 178	18 927	18 612	21 572	24 356	50.6	1.9
Medicaments (including veterinary medicaments) (542)	9 171	9 823	13 225	18 486	23 677	158.2	1.9
Articles of apparel of textile fabrics (845)	17 961	20 794	21 134	21 287	22 225	23.7	1.8
Toys and sporting goods (894)	18 991	20 017	20 909	22 059	21 566	13.6	1.7
Organo-inorganic and heterocyclic compounds (515)	12 242	16 868	17 840	19 378	20 973	71.3	1.7
Natural gas, whether or not liquefied (343)	6 304	10 966	16 303	12 220	20 621	227.1	1.6
Special purpose motor vehicles (782)	14 745	15 357	16 596	16 804	17 293	17.3	1.4
Aircraft and associated equipment (792)	14 982	18 160	21 091	17 984	16 990	13.4	1.3
Electrical machinery and apparatus (778)	14 254	17 149	14 719	14 917	15 989	12.2	1.3
Internal combustion piston engines (713)	14 785	15 771	13 850	14 695	15 933	7.8	1.3
Women's or girls' coats, jackets, etc. not knit (842)	12 719	14 736	14 646	14 507	15 903	25.0	1.3

Table C-2. U.S. Trade by Commodity with Europe, 1999–2003

(Millions of dollars; total exports, f.a.s.; general imports, Customs; top 20 commodities based on 2003 dollar value.)

Commodity and SITC code	1999	2000	2001	2002	2003	Percent change, 1999–2003	Percent share of total, 2003
EXPORTS							
Total	171 412	187 414	181 993	163 679	172 013	0.4	100.0
Food and live animals (0)	5 106	5 059	5 223	4 835	5 279	3.4	3.1
Beverages and tobacco (1)	2 317	2 116	2 000	1 616	1 701	-26.6	1.0
Crude materials, inedible, except fuels (2)	5 811	6 773	6 455	6 485	6 811	17.2	4.0
Mineral fuels, lubricants and related materials (3)	1 708	1 950	1 996	1 519	1 354	-20.7	0.8
Animal and vegetable oils, fats and waxes (4)	324	252	292	278	296	-8.6	0.2
Chemicals and related products (5)	21 276	24 833	25 855	26 570	31 155	46.4	18.1
Manufactured goods classified chiefly by material (6)	10 349	11 635	11 943	10 663	11 273	8.9	6.6
Machinery and transport equipment (7)	92 247	98 035	91 927	80 444	79 881	-13.4	46.4
Miscellaneous manufactured articles (8)	22 623	25 846	26 075	23 118	24 407	7.9	14.2
Commodities and transactions not classified elsewhere (9)	9 652	10 915	10 228	8 150	9 857	2.1	5.7
Top 20 Commodities	100 400	107 845	104 668	92 826	99 189	-1.2	57.7
Aircraft and associated equipment (792)	22 063	18 939	16 814	15 570	14 246	-35.4	8.3
Nonelectric engines and motors (714)	7 948	8 570	9 374	8 536	8 183	3.0	4.8
Medicaments (including veterinary medicaments) (542)	3 106	3 787	5 417	5 281	6 776	118.2	3.9
Measuring/checking/analyzing instruments (874)	5 888	6 696	6 461	5 631	6 025	2.3	3.5
All motor vehicles (781)	2 871	2 306	3 243	4 197	5 934	106.7	3.4
Parts for office machines and a.d.p. machines (759)	8 563	9 780	7 680	5 723	5 924	-30.8	3.4
Automatic data processing machines (752)	8 718	8 814	7 780	5 693	5 769	-33.8	3.4
Medicinal products, except medicaments (541)	3 024	3 591	3 812	4 467	5 409	78.9	3.1
Telecommunications equipment (764)	6 005	6 932	6 601	5 540	5 075	-15.5	3.0
Thermionic, cold cathode, and photocathode valves (776)	5 826	8 037	6 806	5 314	5 020	-13.8	2.9
Medical instruments and appliances (872)	3 152	3 249	3 795	3 681	4 124	30.8	2.4
Gold, nonmonetary (971)	4 042	4 913	4 099	2 573	4 076	0.8	2.4
Estimated low value shipments (994)	3 904	4 286	4 299	3 782	3 920	0.4	2.3
Miscellaneous chemical products (598)	2 462	2 764	2 710	2 701	3 053	24.0	1.8
Organo-inorganic and heterocyclic compounds (515)	1 911	2 488	2 110	1 995	2 956	54.7	1.7
Miscellaneous manufactured articles (899)	1 417	1 617	1 976	2 233	2 925	106.4	1.7
Parts and accessories of motor vehicles (784)	3 295	3 375	3 385	3 044	2 743	-16.8	1.6
Electro-diagnostic apparatus (774)	2 105	2 171	2 408	2 528	2 667	26.7	1.6
Works of art, collectors' pieces, and antiques (896)	1 947	2 847	3 480	2 197	2 309	18.6	1.3
Electrical apparatus for switching or protecting elec. circuits (772)	2 153	2 683	2 418	2 140	2 055	-4.6	1.2
IMPORTS							
Total	224 855	257 259	253 656	261 181	284 548	26.5	100.0
Food and live animals (0)	4 705	4 625	4 451	4 827	5 309	12.8	1.9
Beverages and tobacco (1)	5 418	5 657	5 798	6 411	7 229	33.4	2.5
Crude materials, inedible, except fuels (2)	2 075	2 115	2 016	2 234	2 280	9.9	0.8
Mineral fuels, lubricants and related materials (3)	7 429	14 032	12 377	15 567	18 678	151.4	6.6
Animal and vegetable oils, fats and waxes (4)	392	476	437	524	646	64.8	0.2
Chemicals and related products (5)	35 562	42 364	46 536	52 743	61 764	73.7	21.7
Manufactured goods classified chiefly by material (6)	29 906	35 512	30 751	29 061	30 236	1.1	10.6
Machinery and transport equipment (7)	94 297	102 807	101 766	100 175	106 428	12.9	37.4
Miscellaneous manufactured articles (8)	31 898	36 072	35 323	35 684	38 475	20.6	13.5
Commodities and transactions not classified elsewhere (9)	13 172	13 599	14 199	13 954	13 503	2.5	4.7
Top 20 Commodities	109 917	131 526	135 861	146 248	159 121	44.8	55.9
All motor vehicles (781)	20 216	22 156	23 101	26 408	30 745	52.1	10.8
Medicaments (including veterinary medicaments) (542)	7 354	7 594	10 156	14 892	18 587	152.7	6.5
Organo-inorganic and heterocyclic compounds (515)	10 302	14 769	15 477	16 292	17 132	66.3	6.0
Special transactions not classified by kind (931)	9 507	9 701	10 215	10 130	9 253	-2.7	3.3
Oil (not crude) (334)	3 448	7 205	6 834	6 899	9 142	165.1	3.2
Crude oil (333)	3 782	6 548	5 153	8 309	8 812	133.0	3.1
Aircraft and associated equipment (792)	7 875	9 969	10 639	8 825	7 091	-10.0	2.5
Alcoholic beverages (112)	4 826	5 045	5 161	5 810	6 556	35.8	2.3
Medicinal products, except medicaments (541)	3 205	3 730	4 280	5 072	6 479	102.2	2.3
Nonelectric engines and motors (714)	7 828	7 720	9 280	7 214	5 833	-25.5	2.0
Parts and accessories of motor vehicles (784)	4 043	4 082	4 023	4 444	5 375	32.9	1.9
Measuring/checking/analyzing instruments (874)	4 251	4 924	4 932	4 585	5 080	19.5	1.8
Telecommunications equipment (764)	2 473	3 823	3 912	4 534	4 105	66.0	1.4
Estimate of low value import transactions (984)	3 290	3 710	3 732	3 708	4 083	24.1	1.4
Works of art, collectors' pieces, and antiques (896)	4 341	5 149	4 919	4 703	3 895	-10.3	1.4
Internal combustion piston engines (713)	2 685	2 883	2 706	3 111	3 656	36.2	1.3
Miscellaneous manufactured articles (899)	842	1 131	1 808	2 545	3 626	330.6	1.3
Machinery and equipment specialized for particular industries (728)	3 942	4 078	3 475	2 970	3 417	-13.3	1.2
Pearls, precious and semiprecious stones (667)	2 832	3 448	2 793	2 834	3 193	12.7	1.1
Thermionic, cold cathode, and photocathode valves (776)	2 875	3 861	3 265	2 963	3 061	6.5	1.1

Table C-3. U.S. Trade by Commodity with Western Europe, 1999–2003

(Millions of dollars; total exports, f.a.s.; general imports, Customs; top 20 commodities based on 2003 dollar value.)

Commodity and SITC code	1999	2000	2001	2002	2003	Percent change, 1999–2003	Percent share of total, 2003
EXPORTS							
Total	165 753	181 270	175 137	157 080	164 899	-0.5	100.0
Food and live animals (0)	4 197	3 995	4 066	4 025	4 386	4.5	2.7
Beverages and tobacco (1)	2 159	1 958	1 828	1 494	1 604	-25.7	1.0
Crude materials, inedible, except fuels (2)	5 699	6 676	6 299	6 347	6 670	17.0	4.0
Mineral fuels, lubricants and related materials (3)	1 662	1 873	1 952	1 488	1 309	-21.2	0.8
Animal and vegetable oils, fats and waxes (4)	289	225	267	258	271	-6.2	0.2
Chemicals and related products (5)	20 988	24 331	25 189	25 906	30 431	45.0	18.5
Manufactured goods classified chiefly by material (6)	10 032	11 307	11 557	10 349	10 897	8.6	6.6
Machinery and transport equipment (7)	89 288	95 060	88 744	76 855	76 084	-14.8	46.1
Miscellaneous manufactured articles (8)	22 109	25 287	25 357	22 537	23 763	7.5	14.4
Commodities and transactions not classified elsewhere (9)	9 331	10 557	9 879	7 822	9 482	1.6	5.8
Top 20 Commodities	97 509	104 835	101 827	90 243	96 381	-1.2	58.4
Aircraft and associated equipment (792)	21 173	18 347	16 334	14 734	13 473	-36.4	8.2
Nonelectric engines and motors (714)	7 932	8 558	9 298	8 495	8 114	2.3	4.9
Medicaments (including veterinary medicaments) (542)	3 076	3 752	5 339	5 205	6 673	116.9	4.0
Measuring/checking/analyzing instruments (874)	5 715	6 516	6 264	5 419	5 811	1.7	3.5
All motor vehicles (781)	2 827	2 255	3 180	4 147	5 790	104.8	3.5
Parts for office machines and a.d.p. machines (759)	8 370	9 580	7 494	5 524	5 699	-31.9	3.5
Automatic data processing machines (752)	8 499	8 537	7 517	5 509	5 563	-34.5	3.4
Medicinal products, except medicaments (541)	2 986	3 552	3 758	4 421	5 360	79.5	3.3
Thermionic, cold cathode, and photocathode valves (776)	5 777	7 931	6 671	5 104	4 832	-16.4	2.9
Telecommunications equipment (764)	5 687	6 649	6 247	5 204	4 762	-16.3	2.9
Gold, nonmonetary (971)	4 041	4 909	4 093	2 567	4 068	0.7	2.5
Medical instruments and appliances (872)	3 093	3 198	3 682	3 619	4 044	30.7	2.5
Estimated low value shipments (994)	3 816	4 195	4 201	3 691	3 819	0.1	2.3
Miscellaneous chemical products (598)	2 433	2 715	2 657	2 658	3 005	23.5	1.8
Organo-inorganic and heterocyclic compounds (515)	1 907	2 479	2 096	1 987	2 953	54.9	1.8
Miscellaneous manufactured articles (899)	1 398	1 594	1 950	2 207	2 896	107.2	1.8
Parts and accessories of motor vehicles (784)	3 178	3 300	3 310	2 938	2 614	-17.7	1.6
Electro-diagnostic apparatus (774)	2 055	2 113	2 350	2 460	2 588	25.9	1.6
Works of art, collectors' pieces, and antiques (896)	1 943	2 798	3 327	2 187	2 298	18.3	1.4
Internal combustion piston engines (713)	1 603	1 857	2 059	2 167	2 019	26.0	1.2
IMPORTS							
Total	213 171	241 031	239 316	246 298	266 224	24.9	100.0
Food and live animals (0)	4 255	4 179	4 011	4 304	4 786	12.5	1.8
Beverages and tobacco (1)	5 257	5 508	5 598	6 199	7 031	33.7	2.6
Crude materials, inedible, except fuels (2)	1 914	1 929	1 848	2 035	2 077	8.5	0.8
Mineral fuels, lubricants and related materials (3)	6 497	12 446	11 015	12 868	14 361	121.0	5.4
Animal and vegetable oils, fats and waxes (4)	391	476	437	524	645	65.0	0.2
Chemicals and related products (5)	34 444	40 277	43 904	50 482	59 124	71.7	22.2
Manufactured goods classified chiefly by material (6)	24 902	28 759	26 212	24 918	26 324	5.7	9.9
Machinery and transport equipment (7)	91 893	99 593	98 839	97 416	102 368	11.4	38.5
Miscellaneous manufactured articles (8)	30 737	34 486	33 428	33 886	36 285	18.0	13.6
Commodities and transactions not classified elsewhere (9)	12 881	13 377	14 025	13 667	13 222	2.6	5.0
Top 20 Commodities	107 971	128 530	133 018	141 925	152 033	40.8	57.1
All motor vehicles (781)	20 167	21 954	22 766	26 170	29 836	47.9	11.2
Medicaments (including veterinary medicaments) (542)	7 353	7 594	10 153	14 889	18 585	152.8	7.0
Organo-inorganic and heterocyclic compounds (515)	10 268	14 723	15 415	16 181	17 009	65.7	6.4
Special transactions not classified by kind (931)	9 291	9 576	10 132	9 940	9 095	-2.1	3.4
Crude oil (333)	3 654	6 466	5 153	7 562	7 192	96.8	2.7
Aircraft and associated equipment (792)	7 812	9 843	10 525	8 770	6 919	-11.4	2.6
Oil (not crude) (334)	2 645	5 705	5 504	4 967	6 459	144.2	2.4
Medicinal products, except medicaments (541)	3 181	3 704	4 249	5 037	6 435	102.3	2.4
Alcoholic beverages (112)	4 700	4 921	4 995	5 649	6 391	36.0	2.4
Nonelectric engines and motors (714)	7 792	7 660	9 189	7 105	5 701	-26.8	2.1
Parts and accessories of motor vehicles (784)	3 929	3 947	3 898	4 227	5 026	27.9	1.9
Measuring/checking/analyzing instruments (874)	4 232	4 902	4 908	4 515	4 952	17.0	1.9
Telecommunications equipment (764)	2 440	3 773	3 843	4 464	3 988	63.4	1.5
Estimate of low value import transactions (984)	3 223	3 615	3 641	3 612	3 962	22.9	1.5
Works of art, collectors' pieces, and antiques (896)	4 276	4 983	4 853	4 641	3 833	-10.4	1.4
Miscellaneous manufactured articles (899)	833	1 121	1 797	2 527	3 605	332.8	1.4
Internal combustion piston engines (713)	2 663	2 840	2 667	3 070	3 585	34.6	1.3
Machinery and equipment specialized for particular industries (728)	3 916	4 046	3 454	2 944	3 382	-13.6	1.3
Pearls, precious and semiprecious stones (667)	2 775	3 378	2 661	2 746	3 074	10.8	1.2
Thermionic, cold cathode, and photocathode valves (776)	2 821	3 779	3 215	2 909	3 004	6.5	1.1

Table C-4. U.S. Trade by Commodity with European Union (EU-15), 1999–2003

(Millions of dollars; total exports, f.a.s.; general imports, Customs; top 20 commodities based on 2003 dollar value.)

Commodity and SITC code	1999	2000	2001	2002	2003	Percent change, 1999–2003	Percent share of total, 2003
EXPORTS							
Total	151 645	164 825	159 175	143 747	150 549	-0.7	100.0
Food and live animals (0)	3 741	3 539	3 672	3 622	3 916	4.7	2.6
Beverages and tobacco (1)	1 812	1 543	1 500	1 273	1 351	-25.4	0.9
Crude materials, inedible, except fuels (2)	5 461	6 208	5 826	5 764	5 817	6.5	3.9
Mineral fuels, lubricants and related materials (3)	1 543	1 721	1 821	1 338	1 171	-24.1	0.8
Animal and vegetable oils, fats and waxes (4)	170	139	147	137	142	-16.5	0.1
Chemicals and related products (5)	19 175	22 304	23 346	24 121	28 354	47.9	18.8
Manufactured goods classified chiefly by material (6)	9 166	10 376	10 648	9 260	10 049	9.6	6.7
Machinery and transport equipment (7)	84 474	89 487	83 279	72 290	72 199	-14.5	48.0
Miscellaneous manufactured articles (8)	19 812	22 826	22 629	20 287	21 311	7.6	14.2
Commodities and transactions not classified elsewhere (9)	6 290	6 683	6 307	5 655	6 239	-0.8	4.1
Top 20 Commodities	90 085	95 632	93 042	83 892	88 481	-1.8	58.8
Aircraft and associated equipment (792)	19 657	16 097	14 748	13 000	12 474	-36.5	8.3
Nonelectric engines and motors (714)	7 519	8 133	8 666	8 047	7 761	3.2	5.2
Medicaments (including veterinary medicaments) (542)	2 672	3 363	4 974	4 782	5 874	119.8	3.9
All motor vehicles (781)	2 707	2 128	3 032	4 039	5 615	107.4	3.7
Parts for office machines and a.d.p. machines (759)	8 051	9 254	7 234	5 387	5 580	-30.7	3.7
Measuring/checking/analyzing instruments (874)	5 365	6 174	5 912	5 056	5 405	0.7	3.6
Automatic data processing machines (752)	8 135	8 225	7 268	5 332	5 379	-33.9	3.6
Medicinal products, except medicaments (541)	2 773	3 178	3 504	4 181	4 999	80.3	3.3
Thermionic, cold cathode, and photocathode valves (776)	5 524	7 520	6 311	4 864	4 610	-16.5	3.1
Telecommunications equipment (764)	5 365	6 397	6 031	5 038	4 515	-15.8	3.0
Medical instruments and appliances (872)	2 943	3 033	3 509	3 442	3 842	30.5	2.6
Estimated low value shipments (994)	3 441	3 773	3 786	3 354	3 435	-0.2	2.3
Miscellaneous chemical products (598)	2 376	2 626	2 585	2 529	2 880	21.2	1.9
Organo-inorganic and heterocyclic compounds (515)	1 740	2 245	1 990	1 883	2 873	65.1	1.9
Parts and accessories of motor vehicles (784)	3 148	3 244	3 267	2 907	2 582	-18.0	1.7
Miscellaneous manufactured articles (899)	1 220	1 341	1 690	1 910	2 572	110.8	1.7
Electro-diagnostic apparatus (774)	1 953	2 014	2 240	2 356	2 483	27.1	1.6
Electrical apparatus for switching or protecting elec. circuits (772)	2 031	2 505	2 278	2 020	1 922	-5.4	1.3
Electrical machinery and apparatus (778)	1 902	2 563	2 127	1 851	1 867	-1.8	1.2
Internal combustion piston engines (713)	1 563	1 819	1 890	1 914	1 813	16.0	1.2
IMPORTS							
Total	195 368	220 366	220 031	226 115	244 811	25.3	100.0
Food and live animals (0)	3 547	3 522	3 441	3 661	4 105	15.7	1.7
Beverages and tobacco (1)	5 022	5 298	5 393	6 030	6 870	36.8	2.8
Crude materials, inedible, except fuels (2)	1 784	1 807	1 749	1 937	1 981	11.0	0.8
Mineral fuels, lubricants and related materials (3)	4 185	8 387	7 450	8 556	10 784	157.7	4.4
Animal and vegetable oils, fats and waxes (4)	351	448	402	490	583	66.1	0.2
Chemicals and related products (5)	31 737	37 576	40 976	47 396	55 595	75.2	22.7
Manufactured goods classified chiefly by material (6)	22 416	25 861	23 768	22 570	23 684	5.7	9.7
Machinery and transport equipment (7)	87 937	95 230	95 019	93 892	98 642	12.2	40.3
Miscellaneous manufactured articles (8)	26 856	29 915	29 119	29 051	30 521	13.6	12.5
Commodities and transactions not classified elsewhere (9)	11 533	12 323	12 714	12 533	12 047	4.5	4.9
Top 20 Commodities	99 479	117 288	122 988	131 357	142 028	42.8	58.0
All motor vehicles (781)	20 167	21 952	22 760	26 168	29 835	47.9	12.2
Medicaments (including veterinary medicaments) (542)	6 660	6 894	9 218	13 924	17 425	161.6	7.1
Organo-inorganic and heterocyclic compounds (515)	9 669	14 218	15 007	15 736	16 485	70.5	6.7
Special transactions not classified by kind (931)	8 226	8 772	9 169	9 036	8 192	-0.4	3.3
Aircraft and associated equipment (792)	7 666	9 652	10 334	8 606	6 764	-11.8	2.8
Alcoholic beverages (112)	4 688	4 915	4 990	5 643	6 385	36.2	2.6
Oil (not crude) (334)	2 344	5 036	4 895	4 483	5 856	149.8	2.4
Medicinal products, except medicaments (541)	2 775	3 245	3 732	4 460	5 669	104.3	2.3
Nonelectric engines and motors (714)	7 592	7 360	8 895	6 872	5 458	-28.1	2.2
Parts and accessories of motor vehicles (784)	3 768	3 789	3 743	4 062	4 844	28.6	2.0
Measuring/checking/analyzing instruments (874)	3 902	4 508	4 490	4 116	4 545	16.5	1.9
Crude oil (333)	1 692	3 113	2 308	3 829	4 501	166.0	1.8
Telecommunications equipment (764)	2 364	3 691	3 740	4 323	3 833	62.1	1.6
Estimate of low value import transactions (984)	3 031	3 403	3 437	3 418	3 746	23.6	1.5
Internal combustion piston engines (713)	2 650	2 822	2 654	3 055	3 560	34.3	1.5
Works of art, collectors' pieces, and antiques (896)	4 097	4 668	4 574	4 344	3 536	-13.7	1.4
Machinery and equipment specialized for particular industries (728)	3 644	3 748	3 186	2 698	3 138	-13.9	1.3
Pearls, precious and semiprecious stones (667)	2 414	2 993	2 487	2 598	2 864	18.6	1.2
Medical instruments and appliances (872)	1 399	1 544	1 791	1 952	2 725	94.8	1.1
Miscellaneous manufactured articles (899)	731	965	1 578	2 034	2 667	264.8	1.1

Table C-5. U.S. Trade by Commodity with Non-European Union Western Europe, 1999–2003

(Millions of dollars; total exports, f.a.s.; and general imports, Customs; top 20 commodities based on 2003 dollar value.)

Commodity and SITC code	1999	2000	2001	2002	2003	Percent change, 1999–2003	Percent share of total, 2003
EXPORTS							
Total	14 109	16 445	15 962	13 333	14 350	1.7	100.0
Food and live animals (0)	456	457	395	402	470	3.1	3.3
Beverages and tobacco (1)	347	414	328	221	253	-27.1	1.8
Crude materials, inedible, except fuels (2)	238	468	473	583	853	258.4	5.9
Mineral fuels, lubricants and related materials (3)	119	152	131	150	138	16.0	1.0
Animal and vegetable oils, fats and waxes (4)	119	87	120	122	130	9.2	0.9
Chemicals and related products (5)	1 813	2 027	1 843	1 784	2 077	14.6	14.5
Manufactured goods classified chiefly by material (6)	866	931	909	1 088	848	-2.1	5.9
Machinery and transport equipment (7)	4 814	5 573	5 465	4 565	3 885	-19.3	27.1
Miscellaneous manufactured articles (8)	2 297	2 461	2 728	2 250	2 452	6.7	17.1
Commodities and transactions not classified elsewhere (9)	3 040	3 874	3 572	2 167	3 244	6.7	22.6
Top 20 Commodities	8 823	11 132	10 424	8 363	9 623	9.1	67.1
Gold, nonmonetary (971)	2 564	3 356	3 057	1 707	2 720	6.1	19.0
Aircraft and associated equipment (792)	1 516	2 251	1 585	1 734	999	-34.1	7.0
Medicaments (including veterinary medicaments) (542)	404	389	364	424	799	97.8	5.6
Works of art, collectors' pieces, and antiques (896)	577	972	1 097	591	732	26.9	5.1
Cotton textile fibers (263)	55	216	177	251	422	667.3	2.9
Measuring/checking/analyzing instruments (874)	350	343	352	363	406	16.0	2.8
Estimated low value shipments (994)	375	422	415	337	384	2.4	2.7
Pearls, precious and semiprecious stones (667)	381	357	322	275	362	-5.0	2.5
Medicinal products, except medicaments (541)	213	374	254	240	361	69.5	2.5
Nonelectric engines and motors (714)	413	425	631	448	353	-14.5	2.5
Miscellaneous manufactured articles (899)	178	254	259	296	324	82.0	2.3
Telecommunications equipment (764)	322	252	216	167	247	-23.3	1.7
Jewelry, goldsmiths' and silversmiths' wares (897)	291	211	336	335	241	-17.2	1.7
Thermionic, cold cathode, and photocathode valves (776)	253	411	360	240	222	-12.3	1.5
Internal combustion piston engines (713)	40	38	169	253	207	417.5	1.4
Medical instruments and appliances (872)	150	165	173	178	202	34.7	1.4
Automatic data processing machines (752)	363	312	250	177	184	-49.3	1.3
All motor vehicles (781)	120	127	148	108	175	45.8	1.2
Civil engineering and contractors' plant and equipment (723)	150	135	153	151	148	-1.3	1.0
Tobacco, unmanufactured; tobacco refuse (121)	108	122	106	88	135	25.0	0.9
IMPORTS							
Total	17 804	20 665	19 285	20 183	21 412	20.3	100.0
Food and live animals (0)	709	657	570	642	682	-3.8	3.2
Beverages and tobacco (1)	235	209	205	169	162	-31.1	0.8
Crude materials, inedible, except fuels (2)	129	122	100	98	96	-25.6	0.4
Mineral fuels, lubricants and related materials (3)	2 312	4 060	3 565	4 312	3 577	54.7	16.7
Animal and vegetable oils, fats and waxes (4)	40	28	35	34	62	55.0	0.3
Chemicals and related products (5)	2 707	2 701	2 928	3 086	3 529	30.4	16.5
Manufactured goods classified chiefly by material (6)	2 486	2 898	2 443	2 348	2 640	6.2	12.3
Machinery and transport equipment (7)	3 956	4 363	3 820	3 525	3 725	-5.8	17.4
Miscellaneous manufactured articles (8)	3 882	4 572	4 309	4 834	5 763	48.5	26.9
Commodities and transactions not classified elsewhere (9)	1 347	1 054	1 311	1 134	1 176	-12.7	5.5
Top 20 Commodities	8 842	11 322	10 980	12 161	12 874	45.6	60.1
Crude oil (333)	1 962	3 353	2 844	3 733	2 690	37.1	12.6
Watches and clocks (885)	1 063	1 202	1 114	1 212	1 481	39.3	6.9
Medicaments (including veterinary medicaments) (542)	694	700	935	966	1 159	67.0	5.4
Miscellaneous manufactured articles (899)	102	156	219	492	938	819.6	4.4
Special transactions not classified by kind (931)	1 065	804	963	904	903	-15.2	4.2
Medicinal products, except medicaments (541)	405	459	517	577	766	89.1	3.6
Oil (not crude) (334)	301	669	610	484	602	100.0	2.8
Organo-inorganic and heterocyclic compounds (515)	598	505	408	446	525	-12.2	2.5
Women's or girls' coats, jackets, etc. not knit (842)	289	383	408	403	408	41.2	1.9
Measuring/checking/analyzing instruments (874)	330	394	418	398	407	23.3	1.9
Articles of apparel of textile fabrics (845)	273	331	317	383	389	42.5	1.8
Jewelry, goldsmiths' and silversmiths' wares (897)	255	338	314	298	370	45.1	1.7
Thermionic, cold cathode, and photocathode valves (776)	335	524	429	305	362	8.1	1.7
Works of art, collectors' pieces, and antiques (896)	179	315	280	297	297	65.9	1.4
Made-up articles of textile materials (658)	156	210	222	280	296	89.7	1.4
Women's or girls' coats, jackets, etc. knit (844)	204	232	219	250	285	39.7	1.3
Electrical apparatus for switching or protecting elec. circuits (772)	231	298	268	263	256	10.8	1.2
Lime, cement, and fabricated construction materials (661)	92	129	134	178	249	170.7	1.2
Liquefied propane and butane (342)	37	22	93	46	248	570.3	1.2
Machinery and equipment specialized for particular industries (728)	271	298	268	246	243	-10.3	1.1

Table C-6. U.S. Trade by Commodity with Eastern Europe, 1999–2003

(Millions of dollars; total exports, f.a.s.; general imports, Customs; top 20 commodities based on 2003 dollar value.)

Commodity and SITC code	1999	2000	2001	2002	2003	Percent change, 1999–2003	Percent share of total, 2003
EXPORTS							
Total	5 658	6 144	6 856	6 599	7 114	25.7	100.0
Food and live animals (0)	909	1 064	1 157	810	893	-1.8	12.6
Beverages and tobacco (1)	158	159	172	122	97	-38.6	1.4
Crude materials, inedible, except fuels (2)	112	97	156	139	141	25.9	2.0
Mineral fuels, lubricants and related materials (3)	46	77	44	31	45	-2.2	0.6
Animal and vegetable oils, fats and waxes (4)	35	27	25	20	24	-31.4	0.3
Chemicals and related products (5)	288	502	666	664	723	151.0	10.2
Manufactured goods classified chiefly by material (6)	317	328	387	314	375	18.3	5.3
Machinery and transport equipment (7)	2 959	2 975	3 183	3 589	3 797	28.3	53.4
Miscellaneous manufactured articles (8)	514	559	718	581	644	25.3	9.1
Commodities and transactions not classified elsewhere (9)	321	357	349	329	374	16.5	5.3
Top 20 Commodities	3 336	3 590	4 160	4 198	4 352	30.5	61.2
Aircraft and associated equipment (792)	890	591	480	836	773	-13.1	10.9
Other meat and edible offal (012)	441	656	908	560	608	37.9	8.5
Civil engineering and contractors' plant and equipment (723)	205	260	404	417	436	112.7	6.1
Telecommunications equipment (764)	318	284	354	336	313	-1.6	4.4
Special transactions not classified by kind (931)	210	240	236	225	258	22.9	3.6
Parts for office machines and a.d.p. machines (759)	192	200	186	199	226	17.7	3.2
Measuring/checking/analyzing instruments (874)	173	179	197	212	214	23.7	3.0
Automatic data processing machines (752)	219	277	263	183	206	-5.9	2.9
Thermionic, cold cathode, and photocathode valves (776)	49	106	135	210	188	283.7	2.6
All motor vehicles (781)	44	51	63	50	144	227.3	2.0
Parts and accessories of motor vehicles (784)	117	75	75	106	129	10.3	1.8
Radioactive and associated materials (525)	1	134	206	211	122	12 100.0	1.7
Medicaments (including veterinary medicaments) (542)	30	35	79	76	103	243.3	1.4
Estimated low value shipments (994)	88	91	98	91	101	14.8	1.4
Pumps for liquids and liquid elevators (742)	46	56	65	79	97	110.9	1.4
Machinery and equipment specialized for particular industries (728)	93	104	121	114	95	2.2	1.3
Electrical machinery and apparatus (778)	58	64	54	69	92	58.6	1.3
Agricultural machinery (excluding tractors) and parts (721)	54	77	63	95	89	64.8	1.3
Medical instruments and appliances (872)	59	52	114	61	80	35.6	1.1
Electro-diagnostic apparatus (774)	49	58	59	68	78	59.2	1.1
IMPORTS							
Total	11 684	16 227	14 339	14 883	18 325	56.8	100.0
Food and live animals (0)	450	446	440	523	523	16.2	2.9
Beverages and tobacco (1)	162	149	200	212	198	22.2	1.1
Crude materials, inedible, except fuels (2)	161	186	168	200	203	26.1	1.1
Mineral fuels, lubricants and related materials (3)	932	1 586	1 362	2 698	4 317	363.2	23.6
Animal and vegetable oils, fats and waxes (4)	0	0	0	0	0	X	0.0
Chemicals and related products (5)	1 118	2 087	2 632	2 261	2 641	136.2	14.4
Manufactured goods classified chiefly by material (6)	5 004	6 753	4 540	4 144	3 912	-21.8	21.3
Machinery and transport equipment (7)	2 404	3 214	2 927	2 759	4 061	68.9	22.2
Miscellaneous manufactured articles (8)	1 161	1 585	1 895	1 798	2 190	88.6	12.0
Commodities and transactions not classified elsewhere (9)	291	221	174	288	280	-3.8	1.5
Top 20 Commodities	7 135	10 526	8 749	9 071	12 187	70.8	66.5
Oil (not crude) (334)	803	1 499	1 329	1 932	2 683	234.1	14.6
Crude oil (333)	128	82	0	747	1 620	1 165.6	8.8
Aluminum (684)	1 229	1 317	720	1 108	1 083	-11.9	5.9
Radioactive and associated materials (525)	639	993	997	873	1 011	58.2	5.5
All motor vehicles (781)	48	202	336	238	909	1 793.8	5.0
Carboxylic acids, halides, and derivities (513)	14	392	683	660	558	3 885.7	3.0
Automatic data processing machines (752)	1 054	1 230	782	523	548	-48.0	3.0
Silver, platinum, and other platinum group metals (681)	1 442	2 261	1 500	513	465	-67.8	2.5
Women's or girls' coats, jackets, etc. not knit (842)	200	231	293	259	354	77.0	1.9
Parts and accessories of motor vehicles (784)	114	135	125	217	349	206.1	1.9
Pig iron and iron and steel powders (671)	297	371	164	238	331	11.4	1.8
Inorganic chemical elements (522)	123	197	298	187	330	168.3	1.8
Articles of apparel of textile fabrics (845)	124	196	228	258	296	138.7	1.6
Fertilizers (except crude) (562)	75	174	262	146	288	284.0	1.6
Men's or boys' coats, jackets, etc. not knit (841)	131	228	259	233	267	103.8	1.5
Furniture and bedding accessories (821)	87	146	142	188	244	180.5	1.3
Electrical machinery and apparatus (778)	241	364	235	198	236	-2.1	1.3
Nickel (683)	77	167	57	160	236	206.5	1.3
Crustaceans (036)	153	160	166	223	205	34.0	1.1
Glassware (665)	156	181	173	170	174	11.5	0.9

X = Not applicable.

Table C-7. U.S. Trade by Commodity with Western Hemisphere, 1999–2003

(Millions of dollars; total exports, f.a.s.; general imports, Customs; top 20 commodities based on 2003 dollar value.)

Commodity and SITC code	1999	2000	2001	2002	2003	Percent change, 1999–2003	Percent share of total, 2003
EXPORTS							
Total	306 162	347 410	323 637	309 977	318 977	4.2	100.0
Food and live animals (0)	14 740	15 600	16 921	17 205	18 459	25.2	5.8
Beverages and tobacco (1)	855	824	812	805	876	2.5	0.3
Crude materials, inedible, except fuels (2)	8 005	9 263	8 652	8 867	9 553	19.3	3.0
Mineral fuels, lubricants and related materials (3)	5 727	8 919	8 735	7 793	10 161	77.4	3.2
Animal and vegetable oils, fats and waxes (4)	867	727	677	976	1 003	15.7	0.3
Chemicals and related products (5)	29 321	33 529	33 176	32 808	35 921	22.5	11.3
Manufactured goods classified chiefly by material (6)	39 002	45 502	41 329	40 832	41 269	5.8	12.9
Machinery and transport equipment (7)	160 889	180 899	163 383	153 327	154 058	-4.2	48.3
Miscellaneous manufactured articles (8)	35 872	39 878	36 897	35 352	35 963	0.3	11.3
Commodities and transactions not classified elsewhere (9)	10 883	12 268	13 056	12 013	11 714	7.6	3.7
Top 20 Commodities	147 797	173 283	156 629	148 269	149 813	1.4	47.0
Parts and accessories of motor vehicles (784)	23 699	25 349	23 068	23 710	22 895	-3.4	7.2
All motor vehicles (781)	12 186	12 837	12 666	14 086	14 002	14.9	4.4
Thermionic, cold cathode, and photocathode valves (776)	13 192	17 668	12 958	10 746	10 301	-21.9	3.2
Automatic data processing machines (752)	9 706	11 411	10 350	9 170	9 415	-3.0	3.0
Internal combustion piston engines (713)	9 337	10 357	9 273	8 926	8 875	-4.9	2.8
Telecommunications equipment (764)	10 592	12 939	11 285	8 919	8 697	-17.9	2.7
Estimated low value shipments (994)	6 470	7 597	8 984	8 150	8 427	30.2	2.6
Parts for office machines and a.d.p. machines (759)	5 984	7 224	6 442	6 295	7 481	25.0	2.3
Electrical apparatus for switching or protecting elec. circuits (772)	7 816	9 516	7 642	7 029	7 158	-8.4	2.2
Special purpose motor vehicles (782)	4 737	5 676	4 928	5 656	6 805	43.7	2.1
Oil (not crude) (334)	3 316	5 599	4 731	4 505	5 959	79.7	1.9
Electrical machinery and apparatus (778)	6 516	7 705	6 062	5 843	5 599	-14.1	1.8
Measuring/checking/analyzing instruments (874)	5 267	5 945	5 894	5 357	5 311	0.8	1.7
Articles of plastics (893)	4 753	5 713	5 416	5 346	5 288	11.3	1.7
Manufactures of base metal (699)	5 034	7 011	5 519	5 393	5 119	1.7	1.6
Aircraft and associated equipment (792)	5 043	4 537	5 809	5 035	4 090	-18.9	1.3
Civil engineering and contractors' plant and equipment (723)	3 395	3 917	3 815	3 559	3 689	8.7	1.2
Paper and paperboard (641)	3 457	3 925	3 738	3 453	3 678	6.4	1.2
Pumps, air or gas compressors and fans (743)	3 412	3 766	3 921	3 485	3 593	5.3	1.1
Equipment for distributing electricity (773)	3 885	4 591	4 128	3 606	3 431	-11.7	1.1
IMPORTS							
Total	366 430	438 442	415 890	414 892	441 113	20.4	100.0
Food and live animals (0)	21 015	21 822	22 338	23 331	24 954	18.7	5.7
Beverages and tobacco (1)	2 666	2 971	3 167	3 438	3 650	36.9	0.8
Crude materials, inedible, except fuels (2)	15 608	15 712	14 316	13 641	13 484	-13.6	3.1
Mineral fuels, lubricants and related materials (3)	41 050	72 058	67 748	65 155	85 443	108.1	19.4
Animal and vegetable oils, fats and waxes (4)	455	369	357	382	451	-0.9	0.1
Chemicals and related products (5)	13 569	15 959	16 462	16 405	18 711	37.9	4.2
Manufactured goods classified chiefly by material (6)	45 075	49 843	47 429	48 836	50 184	11.3	11.4
Machinery and transport equipment (7)	160 387	183 562	171 115	168 322	168 289	4.9	38.2
Miscellaneous manufactured articles (8)	44 048	50 031	48 434	49 936	50 901	15.6	11.5
Commodities and transactions not classified elsewhere (9)	22 558	26 115	24 525	25 446	25 047	11.0	5.7
Top 20 Commodities	208 126	263 123	248 806	247 134	265 407	27.5	60.2
Crude oil (333)	24 456	42 906	34 312	39 007	47 372	93.7	10.7
All motor vehicles (781)	44 349	50 115	45 762	45 416	43 171	-2.7	9.8
Natural gas, whether or not liquefied (343)	6 120	10 697	15 841	12 006	20 033	227.3	4.5
Parts and accessories of motor vehicles (784)	14 132	15 074	14 173	15 913	17 271	22.2	3.9
Special purpose motor vehicles (782)	13 484	14 220	15 663	15 867	16 328	21.1	3.7
Special transactions not classified by kind (931)	14 717	16 979	16 870	17 480	16 223	10.2	3.7
Oil (not crude) (334)	7 520	13 081	12 126	10 418	13 243	76.1	3.0
Telecommunications equipment (764)	10 887	19 343	14 298	12 420	11 323	4.0	2.6
Furniture and bedding accessories (821)	7 558	8 520	8 176	8 854	9 435	24.8	2.1
Aircraft and associated equipment (792)	5 085	6 285	8 096	7 342	8 256	62.4	1.9
Articles of apparel of textile fabrics (845)	6 817	7 650	7 579	7 563	7 712	13.1	1.7
Paper and paperboard (641)	7 810	8 542	8 367	7 714	7 623	-2.4	1.7
Internal combustion piston engines (713)	6 705	7 007	5 790	6 330	7 046	5.1	1.6
Automatic data processing machines (752)	5 912	7 755	8 754	7 840	6 963	17.8	1.6
Equipment for distributing electricity (773)	5 892	6 482	5 919	6 268	6 214	5.5	1.4
Wood, simply worked (248)	8 157	7 300	6 946	6 592	5 976	-26.7	1.4
Estimate of low value import transactions (984)	5 057	5 999	5 774	5 568	5 922	17.1	1.3
Television receivers (761)	4 283	4 592	4 769	4 869	5 269	23.0	1.2
Electrical apparatus for switching or protecting elec. circuits (772)	4 400	5 382	4 825	4 950	5 204	18.3	1.2
Men's or boys' coats, jackets, etc. not knit (841)	4 785	5 194	4 766	4 717	4 823	0.8	1.1

Table C-8. U.S. Trade by Commodity with North American Free Trade Agreement (Canada and Mexico), 1999–2003

(Millions of dollars; total exports, f.a.s.; general imports, Customs; top 20 commodities based on 2003 dollar value.)

Commodity and SITC code	1999	2000	2001	2002	2003	Percent change, 1999–2003	Percent share of total, 2003
EXPORTS							
Total	250 957	288 151	265 234	258 330	266 938	6.4	100.0
Food and live animals (0)	11 156	12 304	13 412	13 632	14 726	32.0	5.5
Beverages and tobacco (1)	504	522	547	546	625	24.0	0.2
Crude materials, inedible, except fuels (2)	6 843	7 864	7 394	7 568	8 070	17.9	3.0
Mineral fuels, lubricants and related materials (3)	4 505	7 066	7 056	5 922	6 953	54.3	2.6
Animal and vegetable oils, fats and waxes (4)	547	504	456	671	653	19.4	0.2
Chemicals and related products (5)	22 012	25 095	24 384	25 112	27 802	26.3	10.4
Manufactured goods classified chiefly by material (6)	34 124	40 277	35 708	35 327	35 559	4.2	13.3
Machinery and transport equipment (7)	135 530	154 474	136 996	131 876	133 967	-1.2	50.2
Miscellaneous manufactured articles (8)	27 515	30 525	28 889	28 455	29 394	6.8	11.0
Commodities and transactions not classified elsewhere (9)	8 221	9 520	10 392	9 220	9 189	11.8	3.4
Top 20 Commodities	126 781	150 374	133 930	129 561	130 620	3.0	48.9
Parts and accessories of motor vehicles (784)	22 815	24 312	21 988	22 989	22 159	-2.9	8.3
All motor vehicles (781)	11 684	12 286	12 161	13 613	13 589	16.3	5.1
Thermionic, cold cathode, and photocathode valves (776)	12 125	16 069	11 662	9 102	8 486	-30.0	3.2
Internal combustion piston engines (713)	8 896	9 876	8 773	8 510	8 469	-4.8	3.2
Automatic data processing machines (752)	7 432	8 759	7 929	7 482	7 820	5.2	2.9
Telecommunications equipment (764)	6 921	9 243	8 247	6 816	6 716	-3.0	2.5
Estimated low value shipments (994)	4 651	5 659	7 107	6 479	6 657	43.1	2.5
Electrical apparatus for switching or protecting elec. circuits (772)	7 211	8 852	7 012	6 514	6 654	-7.7	2.5
Special purpose motor vehicles (782)	4 329	5 279	4 574	5 410	6 490	49.9	2.4
Parts for office machines and a.d.p. machines (759)	4 035	5 000	4 463	4 752	5 908	46.4	2.2
Electrical machinery and apparatus (778)	5 746	6 852	5 329	5 216	4 981	-13.3	1.9
Manufactures of base metal (699)	4 756	6 716	5 221	5 156	4 870	2.4	1.8
Articles of plastics (893)	4 335	5 208	4 899	4 890	4 869	12.3	1.8
Measuring/checking/analyzing instruments (874)	4 438	5 107	4 940	4 543	4 577	3.1	1.7
Equipment for distributing electricity (773)	3 615	4 218	3 767	3 447	3 272	-9.5	1.2
Oil (not crude) (334)	2 446	4 171	3 449	3 063	3 215	31.4	1.2
Pumps, air or gas compressors and fans (743)	2 917	3 228	3 315	2 952	3 052	4.6	1.1
Furniture and bedding accessories (821)	3 181	3 606	3 248	3 003	2 982	-6.3	1.1
Paper and paperboard (641)	2 576	3 029	2 932	2 749	2 950	14.5	1.1
Paper and paperboard, cut to size or shape, and articles (642)	2 672	2 904	2 914	2 875	2 904	8.7	1.1
IMPORTS							
Total	308 030	365 120	348 402	345 322	362 239	17.6	100.0
Food and live animals (0)	12 816	13 768	14 947	15 542	16 227	26.6	4.5
Beverages and tobacco (1)	1 930	2 223	2 361	2 514	2 679	38.8	0.7
Crude materials, inedible, except fuels (2)	12 798	12 831	11 538	10 836	10 459	-18.3	2.9
Mineral fuels, lubricants and related materials (3)	24 432	44 246	44 468	41 801	56 875	132.8	15.7
Animal and vegetable oils, fats and waxes (4)	416	329	319	333	404	-2.9	0.1
Chemicals and related products (5)	11 623	13 362	13 811	14 025	15 650	34.6	4.3
Manufactured goods classified chiefly by material (6)	39 006	42 705	40 866	41 533	42 717	9.5	11.8
Machinery and transport equipment (7)	154 140	176 936	164 075	160 604	160 064	3.8	44.2
Miscellaneous manufactured articles (8)	31 120	35 781	34 162	35 589	35 890	15.3	9.9
Commodities and transactions not classified elsewhere (9)	19 750	22 938	21 857	22 544	21 273	7.7	5.9
Top 20 Commodities	181 641	223 774	213 219	210 849	224 303	23.5	61.9
All motor vehicles (781)	44 347	49 948	45 137	44 794	42 625	-3.9	11.8
Crude oil (333)	13 352	24 669	19 656	22 725	28 624	114.4	7.9
Natural gas, whether or not liquefied (343)	6 015	10 370	15 355	11 440	18 250	203.4	5.0
Parts and accessories of motor vehicles (784)	13 436	14 397	13 619	15 260	16 563	23.3	4.6
Special purpose motor vehicles (782)	13 468	14 218	15 662	15 867	16 302	21.0	4.5
Special transactions not classified by kind (931)	13 259	15 130	15 226	15 719	14 258	7.5	3.9
Telecommunications equipment (764)	10 786	18 918	13 313	11 296	10 257	-4.9	2.8
Furniture and bedding accessories (821)	7 222	8 060	7 624	8 249	8 827	22.2	2.4
Paper and paperboard (641)	7 732	8 473	8 300	7 620	7 496	-3.1	2.1
Automatic data processing machines (752)	5 884	7 727	8 721	7 801	6 926	17.7	1.9
Internal combustion piston engines (713)	6 311	6 640	5 516	5 825	6 431	1.9	1.8
Aircraft and associated equipment (792)	3 880	4 808	6 144	5 490	6 409	65.2	1.8
Oil (not crude) (334)	2 557	4 430	4 716	4 629	6 185	141.9	1.7
Equipment for distributing electricity (773)	5 787	6 325	5 803	6 146	6 013	3.9	1.7
Estimate of low value import transactions (984)	4 569	5 434	5 281	5 088	5 368	17.5	1.5
Television receivers (761)	4 274	4 582	4 741	4 856	5 255	23.0	1.5
Wood, simply worked (248)	7 431	6 612	6 201	5 722	5 080	-31.6	1.4
Electrical apparatus for switching or protecting elec. circuits (772)	4 001	4 983	4 494	4 583	4 809	20.2	1.3
Electrical machinery and apparatus (778)	3 843	4 228	3 847	3 989	4 435	15.4	1.2
Aluminum (684)	3 487	3 822	3 863	3 750	4 190	20.2	1.2

Table C-9. U.S. Trade by Commodity with Caribbean, 1999–2003

(Millions of dollars; total exports, f.a.s.; general imports, Customs; top 20 commodities based on 2003 dollar value.)

Commodity and SITC code	1999	2000	2001	2002	2003	Percent change, 1999–2003	Percent share of total, 2003
EXPORTS							
Total	9 961	11 039	10 859	10 621	11 013	10.6	100.0
Food and live animals (0)	1 141	1 101	1 157	1 107	1 096	-3.9	10.0
Beverages and tobacco (1)	219	188	182	188	189	-13.7	1.7
Crude materials, inedible, except fuels (2)	270	270	260	268	275	1.9	2.5
Mineral fuels, lubricants and related materials (3)	374	664	631	716	1 249	234.0	11.3
Animal and vegetable oils, fats and waxes (4)	94	69	64	75	68	-27.7	0.6
Chemicals and related products (5)	649	771	824	859	811	25.0	7.4
Manufactured goods classified chiefly by material (6)	1 186	1 311	1 537	1 582	1 603	35.2	14.6
Machinery and transport equipment (7)	2 803	3 222	3 153	2 906	2 676	-4.5	24.3
Miscellaneous manufactured articles (8)	2 442	2 588	2 216	2 108	2 156	-11.7	19.6
Commodities and transactions not classified elsewhere (9)	782	855	837	812	888	13.6	8.1
Top 20 Commodities	3 954	4 654	4 759	5 006	5 502	39.2	50.0
Oil (not crude) (334)	356	636	614	690	1 200	237.1	10.9
Estimated low value shipments (994)	572	627	602	560	623	8.9	5.7
Jewelry, goldsmiths' and silversmiths' wares (897)	286	300	346	476	516	80.4	4.7
Telecommunications equipment (764)	308	374	459	406	401	30.2	3.6
Articles of apparel of textile fabrics (845)	412	481	365	354	391	-5.1	3.6
Cotton fabrics, woven (652)	42	61	216	297	239	469.0	2.2
Civil engineering and contractors' plant and equipment (723)	169	190	277	318	209	23.7	1.9
Special transactions not classified by kind (931)	86	76	152	181	200	132.6	1.8
Electrical apparatus for switching or protecting elec. circuits (772)	207	191	166	175	188	-9.2	1.7
Ships, boats, and floating structures (793)	59	73	72	104	159	169.5	1.4
All motor vehicles (781)	216	250	183	190	156	-27.8	1.4
Feeding stuff for animals (081)	121	134	148	145	152	25.6	1.4
Articles of plastics (893)	119	139	140	136	147	23.5	1.3
Automatic data processing machines (752)	144	174	212	185	141	-2.1	1.3
Maize (not including sweet corn) unmilled (044)	129	126	129	148	140	8.5	1.3
Knitted or crocheted fabrics (655)	41	42	64	80	137	234.1	1.2
Men's or boys' coats, jackets, etc. knit (843)	111	116	128	129	133	19.8	1.2
Men's or boys' coats, jackets, etc. not knit (841)	334	407	228	176	127	-62.0	1.2
Wheat and meslin, unmilled (041)	105	105	114	115	122	16.2	1.1
Edible products and preparations, n.e.s. (098)	137	152	144	141	121	-11.7	1.1
IMPORTS							
Total	8 103	10 343	9 433	9 110	11 955	47.5	100.0
Food and live animals (0)	443	459	448	465	519	17.2	4.3
Beverages and tobacco (1)	290	286	272	280	286	-1.4	2.4
Crude materials, inedible, except fuels (2)	182	167	221	196	311	70.9	2.6
Mineral fuels, lubricants and related materials (3)	1 619	3 486	2 934	2 830	4 617	185.2	38.6
Animal and vegetable oils, fats and waxes (4)	0	0	0	1	1	X	0.0
Chemicals and related products (5)	487	738	887	741	1 303	167.6	10.9
Manufactured goods classified chiefly by material (6)	315	451	292	364	369	17.1	3.1
Machinery and transport equipment (7)	441	473	390	411	475	7.7	4.0
Miscellaneous manufactured articles (8)	3 912	3 837	3 593	3 390	3 510	-10.3	29.4
Commodities and transactions not classified elsewhere (9)	412	446	396	432	564	36.9	4.7
Top 20 Commodities	6 674	8 689	7 988	7 662	10 296	54.3	86.1
Oil (not crude) (334)	1 181	2 533	1 934	1 642	2 042	72.9	17.1
Natural gas, whether or not liquefied (343)	105	327	486	566	1 767	1 582.9	14.8
Men's or boys' coats, jackets, etc. not knit (841)	905	967	924	902	883	-2.4	7.4
Articles of apparel of textile fabrics (845)	986	903	777	754	812	-17.6	6.8
Crude oil (333)	301	573	491	603	782	159.8	6.5
Inorganic chemical elements (522)	229	334	388	314	690	201.3	5.8
Medical instruments and appliances (872)	352	348	350	354	441	25.3	3.7
Special transactions not classified by kind (931)	329	363	317	338	421	28.0	3.5
Alcohols, phenols, and halogenated derivatives (512)	123	254	321	255	391	217.9	3.3
Men's or boys' coats, jackets, etc. knit (843)	241	229	235	292	329	36.5	2.8
Electrical apparatus for switching or protecting elec. circuits (772)	295	255	213	223	236	-20.0	2.0
Women's or girls' coats, jackets, etc. not knit (842)	377	428	385	287	234	-37.9	2.0
Jewelry, goldsmiths' and silversmiths' wares (897)	187	156	177	199	207	10.7	1.7
Aluminum ores and concentrates (285)	114	87	119	121	206	80.7	1.7
Tobacco, manufactured (122)	203	202	191	193	198	-2.5	1.7
Women's or girls' coats, jackets, etc. knit (844)	272	265	256	210	184	-32.4	1.5
Footwear (851)	237	182	193	140	139	-41.4	1.2
Crustaceans (036)	95	110	90	94	125	31.6	1.0
Pig iron and iron and steel powders (671)	50	77	48	80	109	118.0	0.9
Sugars, molasses, and honey (061)	92	96	93	95	100	8.7	0.8

X = Not applicable.

Table C-10. U.S. Trade by Commodity with Central America, 1999–2003

(Millions of dollars; total exports, f.a.s.; general imports, Customs; top 20 commodities based on 2003 dollar value.)

Commodity and SITC code	1999	2000	2001	2002	2003	Percent change, 1999–2003	Percent share of total, 2003
EXPORTS							
Total	10 196	10 678	10 357	11 248	12 707	24.6	100.0
Food and live animals (0)	907	884	988	970	1 043	15.0	8.2
Beverages and tobacco (1)	38	37	36	38	34	-10.5	0.3
Crude materials, inedible, except fuels (2)	173	211	215	241	300	73.4	2.4
Mineral fuels, lubricants and related materials (3)	294	469	391	513	1 129	284.0	8.9
Animal and vegetable oils, fats and waxes (4)	115	75	81	103	116	0.9	0.9
Chemicals and related products (5)	895	971	1 050	1 027	1 153	28.8	9.1
Manufactured goods classified chiefly by material (6)	1 234	1 378	1 816	2 218	2 390	93.7	18.8
Machinery and transport equipment (7)	3 033	2 684	2 414	3 136	3 600	18.7	28.3
Miscellaneous manufactured articles (8)	2 879	3 345	2 734	2 339	2 168	-24.7	17.1
Commodities and transactions not classified elsewhere (9)	628	623	633	663	775	23.4	6.1
Top 20 Commodities	4 904	5 479	5 202	6 144	7 368	50.2	58.0
Oil (not crude) (334)	277	439	356	457	1 054	280.5	8.3
Thermionic, cold cathode, and photocathode valves (776)	201	247	259	855	1 018	406.5	8.0
Knitted or crocheted fabrics (655)	50	63	207	446	663	1 226.0	5.2
Estimated low value shipments (994)	423	441	437	456	512	21.0	4.0
Articles of apparel of textile fabrics (845)	812	1 116	794	629	496	-38.9	3.9
Textile yarn (651)	71	127	188	265	399	462.0	3.1
Telecommunications equipment (764)	387	326	284	266	331	-14.5	2.6
Paper and paperboard (641)	313	329	318	297	325	3.8	2.6
Clothing accessories (846)	531	575	491	361	309	-41.8	2.4
Aircraft and associated equipment (792)	290	212	103	225	302	4.1	2.4
Parts for office machines and a.d.p. machines (759)	165	176	189	222	236	43.0	1.9
Maize (not including sweet corn) unmilled (044)	158	184	198	206	230	45.6	1.8
Men's or boys' coats, jackets, etc. not knit (841)	415	399	257	210	227	-45.3	1.8
Special transactions not classified by kind (931)	132	84	163	167	223	68.9	1.8
Cotton fabrics, woven (652)	69	106	245	334	217	214.5	1.7
Wheat and meslin, unmilled (041)	105	108	123	160	179	70.5	1.4
Automatic data processing machines (752)	204	218	193	163	171	-16.2	1.3
Feeding stuff for animals (081)	114	124	136	139	167	46.5	1.3
Polymers of ethylene (571)	136	141	154	162	160	17.6	1.3
Woven fabrics of manmade textile materials (653)	51	64	107	124	149	192.2	1.2
IMPORTS							
Total	11 400	12 072	11 383	12 169	12 708	11.5	100.0
Food and live animals (0)	2 197	2 420	2 181	2 230	2 379	8.3	18.7
Beverages and tobacco (1)	87	92	96	119	112	28.7	0.9
Crude materials, inedible, except fuels (2)	126	141	134	139	146	15.9	1.1
Mineral fuels, lubricants and related materials (3)	117	201	134	210	195	66.7	1.5
Animal and vegetable oils, fats and waxes (4)	2	0	5	3	3	50.0	0.0
Chemicals and related products (5)	100	102	74	80	77	-23.0	0.6
Manufactured goods classified chiefly by material (6)	228	228	211	260	250	9.6	2.0
Machinery and transport equipment (7)	1 853	1 398	727	877	1 124	-39.3	8.8
Miscellaneous manufactured articles (8)	6 324	7 185	7 451	7 711	7 939	25.5	62.5
Commodities and transactions not classified elsewhere (9)	366	305	370	542	482	31.7	3.8
Top 20 Commodities	10 055	10 672	10 080	10 707	11 261	12.0	88.6
Articles of apparel of textile fabrics (845)	2 262	2 832	2 982	3 244	3 354	48.3	26.4
Men's or boys' coats, jackets, etc. not knit (841)	1 264	1 276	1 213	1 141	1 137	-10.0	8.9
Fruit and nuts (not including oil nuts), fresh or dried (057)	798	855	963	981	1 013	26.9	8.0
Women's or girls' coats, jackets, etc. knit (844)	706	763	799	869	909	28.8	7.2
Women's or girls' coats, jackets, etc. not knit (842)	830	927	917	796	820	-1.2	6.5
Men's or boys' coats, jackets, etc. knit (843)	645	697	718	694	658	2.0	5.2
Thermionic, cold cathode, and photocathode valves (776)	72	204	327	450	628	772.2	4.9
Coffee and coffee substitutes (071)	595	732	395	387	459	-22.9	3.6
Medical instruments and appliances (872)	85	186	280	336	434	410.6	3.4
Special transactions not classified by kind (931)	240	205	230	367	304	26.7	2.4
Clothing accessories (846)	164	180	210	260	251	53.0	2.0
Crustaceans (036)	303	327	294	271	243	-19.8	1.9
Crude oil (333)	94	154	101	168	180	91.5	1.4
Sugars, molasses, and honey (061)	171	113	113	125	175	2.3	1.4
Fish, fresh, chilled or frozen (034)	77	109	120	146	151	96.1	1.2
Equipment for distributing electricity (773)	49	77	56	78	139	183.7	1.1
Vegetables, roots, tubers and other edible vegetable products (054)	102	99	101	106	115	12.7	0.9
Gold, nonmonetary (971)	51	26	78	106	103	102.0	0.8
Parts for office machines and a.d.p. machines (759)	1 470	832	105	109	102	-93.1	0.8
Miscellaneous manufactured articles (899)	77	78	78	73	86	11.7	0.7

Table C-11. U.S. Trade by Commodity with South America, 1999–2003

(Millions of dollars; total exports, f.a.s.; and general imports, Customs; top 20 commodities based on 2003 dollar value.)

Commodity and SITC code	1999	2000	2001	2002	2003	Percent change, 1999–2003	Percent share of total, 2003
EXPORTS							
Total	34 401	36 979	36 592	28 898	27 430	-20.3	100.0
Food and live animals (0)	1 462	1 241	1 297	1 341	1 376	-5.9	5.0
Beverages and tobacco (1)	84	67	39	26	22	-73.8	0.1
Crude materials, inedible, except fuels (2)	712	912	776	763	862	21.1	3.1
Mineral fuels, lubricants and related materials (3)	530	705	642	624	807	52.3	2.9
Animal and vegetable oils, fats and waxes (4)	110	79	76	104	114	3.6	0.4
Chemicals and related products (5)	5 736	6 656	6 884	5 765	6 115	6.6	22.3
Manufactured goods classified chiefly by material (6)	2 409	2 479	2 223	1 662	1 669	-30.7	6.1
Machinery and transport equipment (7)	19 231	20 372	20 546	14 984	13 501	-29.8	49.2
Miscellaneous manufactured articles (8)	2 950	3 290	2 984	2 374	2 165	-26.6	7.9
Commodities and transactions not classified elsewhere (9)	1 176	1 177	1 126	1 255	799	-32.1	2.9
Top 20 Commodities	17 606	19 364	19 116	14 637	13 789	-21.7	50.3
Automatic data processing machines (752)	1 908	2 242	1 997	1 322	1 265	-33.7	4.6
Civil engineering and contractors' plant and equipment (723)	1 375	1 593	1 642	1 325	1 258	-8.5	4.6
Parts for office machines and a.d.p. machines (759)	1 686	1 939	1 693	1 227	1 252	-25.7	4.6
Telecommunications equipment (764)	2 964	2 986	2 279	1 414	1 227	-58.6	4.5
Aircraft and associated equipment (792)	1 851	1 307	2 063	1 635	1 059	-42.8	3.9
Nonelectric engines and motors (714)	1 080	1 113	1 502	1 319	936	-13.3	3.4
Thermionic, cold cathode, and photocathode valves (776)	845	1 322	1 006	762	753	-10.9	2.7
Parts and accessories of motor vehicles (784)	715	924	961	602	612	-14.4	2.2
Estimated low value shipments (994)	760	792	780	600	577	-24.1	2.1
Fertilizers (except crude) (562)	285	345	380	344	555	94.7	2.0
Measuring/checking/analyzing instruments (874)	673	677	731	594	491	-27.0	1.8
Hydrocarbons and specified derivatives (511)	313	423	358	402	474	51.4	1.7
Oil (not crude) (334)	215	338	299	280	469	118.1	1.7
Wheat and meslin, unmilled (041)	303	216	257	420	455	50.2	1.7
Plastics (575)	398	442	431	421	447	12.3	1.6
Mechanical handling equipment (744)	467	697	622	498	440	-5.8	1.6
Pumps, air or gas compressors and fans (743)	386	439	501	435	419	8.5	1.5
Organo-inorganic and heterocyclic compounds (515)	513	574	644	308	386	-24.8	1.4
Electrical machinery and apparatus (778)	492	581	477	372	357	-27.4	1.3
Miscellaneous chemical products (598)	377	414	493	357	357	-5.3	1.3
IMPORTS							
Total	38 844	50 829	46 557	48 217	54 166	39.4	100.0
Food and live animals (0)	5 541	5 152	4 723	5 062	5 807	4.8	10.7
Beverages and tobacco (1)	358	369	438	523	572	59.8	1.1
Crude materials, inedible, except fuels (2)	2 501	2 572	2 421	2 470	2 567	2.6	4.7
Mineral fuels, lubricants and related materials (3)	14 882	24 123	20 208	20 314	23 755	59.6	43.9
Animal and vegetable oils, fats and waxes (4)	37	39	34	46	43	16.2	0.1
Chemicals and related products (5)	1 359	1 756	1 689	1 555	1 681	23.7	3.1
Manufactured goods classified chiefly by material (6)	5 525	6 459	6 060	6 679	6 847	23.9	12.6
Machinery and transport equipment (7)	3 952	4 747	5 915	6 421	6 625	67.6	12.2
Miscellaneous manufactured articles (8)	2 688	3 223	3 225	3 245	3 560	32.4	6.6
Commodities and transactions not classified elsewhere (9)	2 001	2 389	1 845	1 903	2 710	35.4	5.0
Top 20 Commodities	26 096	36 988	33 733	34 616	38 835	48.8	71.7
Crude oil (333)	10 709	17 509	14 063	15 510	17 787	66.1	32.8
Oil (not crude) (334)	3 759	6 069	5 443	4 107	5 000	33.0	9.2
Aircraft and associated equipment (792)	1 205	1 477	1 951	1 852	1 846	53.2	3.4
Fruit and nuts (not including oil nuts), fresh or dried (057)	1 282	1 349	1 304	1 472	1 474	15.0	2.7
Special transactions not classified by kind (931)	864	1 249	1 045	1 035	1 224	41.7	2.3
Gold, nonmonetary (971)	765	706	421	505	1 065	39.2	2.0
Footwear (851)	981	1 164	1 168	1 094	1 058	7.8	2.0
Telecommunications equipment (764)	63	391	950	1 085	996	1 481.0	1.8
Copper (682)	901	1 217	1 338	1 231	945	4.9	1.7
Wood, simply worked (248)	714	678	728	855	880	23.2	1.6
Fish, fresh, chilled or frozen (034)	524	685	668	689	867	65.5	1.6
Coffee and coffee substitutes (071)	1 212	851	575	639	767	-36.7	1.4
Pig iron and iron and steel powders (671)	479	643	598	680	742	54.9	1.4
Parts and accessories of motor vehicles (784)	691	663	545	640	694	0.4	1.3
Internal combustion piston engines (713)	393	365	272	504	613	56.0	1.1
Aluminum (684)	383	531	480	560	610	59.3	1.1
Coal, pulverized or not (321)	196	264	456	414	598	205.1	1.1
Crustaceans (036)	709	619	623	584	588	-17.1	1.1
All motor vehicles (781)	2	167	625	622	546	27 200.0	1.0
Furniture and bedding accessories (821)	264	391	480	538	535	102.7	1.0

Table C-12. U.S. Trade by Commodity with Asia, 1999–2003

(Millions of dollars; total exports, f.a.s.; general imports, Customs; top 20 commodities based on 2003 dollar value.)

Commodity and SITC code	1999	2000	2001	2002	2003	Percent change, 1999–2003	Percent share of total, 2003
EXPORTS							
Total	190 802	219 515	199 346	193 495	206 631	8.3	100.0
Food and live animals (0)	16 028	17 037	16 679	15 804	16 599	3.6	8.0
Beverages and tobacco (1)	3 270	3 679	2 698	2 120	2 071	-36.7	1.0
Crude materials, inedible, except fuels (2)	9 666	12 301	12 338	12 217	16 615	71.9	8.0
Mineral fuels, lubricants and related materials (3)	2 143	2 091	1 748	1 951	2 125	-0.8	1.0
Animal and vegetable oils, fats and waxes (4)	566	338	282	463	479	-15.4	0.2
Chemicals and related products (5)	18 728	21 256	20 133	21 443	24 102	28.7	11.7
Manufactured goods classified chiefly by material (6)	11 171	13 290	12 018	12 096	13 662	22.3	6.6
Machinery and transport equipment (7)	103 905	119 688	105 620	101 501	104 267	0.3	50.5
Miscellaneous manufactured articles (8)	20 490	24 672	22 949	21 146	21 864	6.7	10.6
Commodities and transactions not classified elsewhere (9)	4 836	5 162	4 884	4 753	4 848	0.2	2.3
Top 20 Commodities	108 079	125 656	110 845	106 697	114 543	6.0	55.4
Thermionic, cold cathode, and photocathode valves (776)	30 168	36 926	27 700	28 322	32 280	7.0	15.6
Aircraft and associated equipment (792)	19 478	13 918	17 731	17 891	17 632	-9.5	8.5
Measuring/checking/analyzing instruments (874)	6 536	9 078	7 528	7 214	7 564	15.7	3.7
Automatic data processing machines (752)	7 360	9 774	8 424	6 333	5 775	-21.5	2.8
Telecommunications equipment (764)	6 966	8 125	7 223	6 317	5 770	-17.2	2.8
Oil seeds and oleaginous fruits (222)	2 346	2 977	2 956	3 027	5 265	124.4	2.5
Parts for office machines and a.d.p. machines (759)	5 658	7 704	6 285	4 814	4 994	-11.7	2.4
Machinery and equipment specialized for particular industries (728)	5 009	8 826	5 392	4 398	4 249	-15.2	2.1
Nonelectric engines and motors (714)	3 249	3 174	3 494	3 637	3 668	12.9	1.8
Pearls, precious and semiprecious stones (667)	1 974	2 550	2 430	2 864	3 241	64.2	1.6
Electrical machinery and apparatus (778)	2 455	3 449	2 778	3 069	3 016	22.9	1.5
Miscellaneous chemical products (598)	1 899	2 362	2 413	2 421	2 831	49.1	1.4
Estimated low value shipments (994)	2 532	2 939	2 696	2 524	2 603	2.8	1.3
Electrical apparatus for switching or protecting elec. circuits (772)	2 292	2 759	2 264	2 277	2 461	7.4	1.2
Maize (not including sweet corn) unmilled (044)	2 872	2 465	2 398	2 426	2 411	-16.1	1.2
All motor vehicles (781)	1 674	1 762	2 003	2 284	2 265	35.3	1.1
Pumps, air or gas compressors and fans (743)	1 707	2 002	2 179	2 170	2 163	26.7	1.0
Medical instruments and appliances (872)	1 637	1 813	1 993	1 923	2 148	31.2	1.0
Meat of bovine animals (011)	1 806	2 188	1 729	1 599	2 114	17.1	1.0
Cotton textile fibers (263)	461	865	1 229	1 187	2 093	354.0	1.0
IMPORTS							
Total	409 132	484 718	437 951	456 205	492 503	20.4	100.0
Food and live animals (0)	6 717	7 295	7 216	7 607	8 868	32.0	1.8
Beverages and tobacco (1)	212	260	304	321	317	49.5	0.1
Crude materials, inedible, except fuels (2)	2 330	2 674	2 293	2 367	2 867	23.0	0.6
Mineral fuels, lubricants and related materials (3)	15 601	26 533	24 577	21 464	27 930	79.0	5.7
Animal and vegetable oils, fats and waxes (4)	544	539	373	425	469	-13.8	0.1
Chemicals and related products (5)	12 286	14 372	14 667	15 949	19 276	56.9	3.9
Manufactured goods classified chiefly by material (6)	38 814	44 571	40 909	45 397	48 636	25.3	9.9
Machinery and transport equipment (7)	223 578	264 897	224 827	234 973	246 642	10.3	50.1
Miscellaneous manufactured articles (8)	98 856	112 486	111 728	116 920	126 415	27.9	25.7
Commodities and transactions not classified elsewhere (9)	10 192	11 092	11 056	10 783	11 084	8.8	2.3
Top 20 Commodities	261 118	312 631	276 813	290 198	309 809	18.6	62.9
Automatic data processing machines (752)	38 823	43 896	35 798	39 475	42 159	8.6	8.6
All motor vehicles (781)	32 185	37 083	37 607	42 021	40 289	25.2	8.2
Crude oil (333)	13 915	23 519	21 169	19 212	25 193	81.0	5.1
Telecommunications equipment (764)	15 671	21 087	19 647	20 668	25 015	59.6	5.1
Parts for office machines and a.d.p. machines (759)	22 847	24 494	19 090	19 581	20 389	-10.8	4.1
Thermionic, cold cathode, and photocathode valves (776)	32 163	40 975	24 466	21 057	19 268	-40.1	3.9
Toys and sporting goods (894)	16 316	17 559	18 235	19 112	19 228	17.8	3.9
Sound and television recorders (763)	8 620	10 763	9 816	11 593	12 372	43.5	2.5
Articles of apparel of textile fabrics (845)	9 726	11 351	11 615	11 668	12 358	27.1	2.5
Footwear (851)	10 148	10 846	11 337	11 803	12 093	19.2	2.5
Furniture and bedding accessories (821)	6 150	7 587	7 784	9 997	11 971	94.7	2.4
Women's or girls' coats, jackets, etc. not knit (842)	8 145	9 354	9 334	9 542	10 949	34.4	2.2
Parts and accessories of motor vehicles (784)	7 614	8 978	8 471	9 121	9 899	30.0	2.0
Pearls, precious and semiprecious stones (667)	7 551	9 048	7 990	9 335	9 610	27.3	2.0
Electrical machinery and apparatus (778)	7 809	9 918	8 191	8 259	8 614	10.3	1.7
Special transactions not classified by kind (931)	6 792	7 050	7 415	7 100	7 125	4.9	1.4
Television receivers (761)	1 868	2 526	3 177	4 997	6 457	245.7	1.3
Men's or boys' coats, jackets, etc. not knit (841)	5 904	6 715	6 219	5 712	6 285	6.5	1.3
Articles of plastics (893)	3 502	4 029	4 136	4 736	5 354	52.9	1.1
Internal combustion piston engines (713)	5 369	5 853	5 316	5 209	5 181	-3.5	1.1

Table C-13. U.S. Trade by Commodity with Association of Southeast Asian Nations (ASEAN-10), 1999–2003

(Millions of dollars; total exports, f.a.s; general imports, Customs; top 20 commodities based on 2003 dollar value.)

Commodity and SITC code	1999	2000	2001	2002	2003	Percent change, 1999–2003	Percent share of total, 2003
EXPORTS							
Total	39 862	47 369	43 840	41 950	45 280	13.6	100.0
Food and live animals (0)	1 442	1 727	1 891	1 781	1 752	21.5	3.9
Beverages and tobacco (1)	190	225	202	177	116	-38.9	0.3
Crude materials, inedible, except fuels (2)	1 243	1 453	1 488	1 605	1 911	53.7	4.2
Mineral fuels, lubricants and related materials (3)	367	418	592	709	576	56.9	1.3
Animal and vegetable oils, fats and waxes (4)	41	20	13	25	13	-68.3	0.0
Chemicals and related products (5)	3 194	3 727	3 440	3 510	3 805	19.1	8.4
Manufactured goods classified chiefly by material (6)	1 690	1 954	1 745	1 714	1 788	5.8	3.9
Machinery and transport equipment (7)	26 794	32 085	29 931	28 151	30 748	14.8	67.9
Miscellaneous manufactured articles (8)	3 862	4 561	3 404	3 250	3 451	-10.6	7.6
Commodities and transactions not classified elsewhere (9)	1 039	1 199	1 136	1 030	1 120	7.8	2.5
Top 20 Commodities	29 047	34 421	31 649	30 310	33 364	14.9	73.7
Thermionic, cold cathode, and photocathode valves (776)	13 295	16 538	12 812	12 649	15 208	14.4	33.6
Aircraft and associated equipment (792)	2 675	1 810	4 926	4 277	4 575	71.0	10.1
Parts for office machines and a.d.p. machines (759)	1 618	2 133	1 788	1 654	1 951	20.6	4.3
Measuring/checking/analyzing instruments (874)	1 402	2 107	1 502	1 579	1 708	21.8	3.8
Automatic data processing machines (752)	1 809	1 884	1 602	1 273	1 190	-34.2	2.6
Nonelectric engines and motors (714)	838	766	934	1 052	1 105	31.9	2.4
Telecommunications equipment (764)	761	858	908	899	782	2.8	1.7
Electrical apparatus for switching or protecting elec. circuits (772)	787	1 014	729	758	754	-4.2	1.7
Estimated low value shipments (994)	719	867	754	708	745	3.6	1.6
Civil engineering and contractors' plant and equipment (723)	566	693	747	754	645	14.0	1.4
Machinery and equipment specialized for particular industries (728)	866	1 547	1 037	730	606	-30.0	1.3
Oil seeds and oleaginous fruits (222)	448	408	442	472	599	33.7	1.3
Electrical machinery and apparatus (778)	513	921	667	603	566	10.3	1.3
Cotton textile fibers (263)	137	271	360	379	467	240.9	1.0
Oil (not crude) (334)	291	313	494	622	463	59.1	1.0
Pumps, air or gas compressors and fans (743)	322	424	416	445	456	41.6	1.0
Musical instruments and accessories (898)	1 097	787	447	321	417	-62.0	0.9
Feeding stuff for animals (081)	300	452	542	499	411	37.0	0.9
Manufactures of base metal (699)	227	181	159	262	370	63.0	0.8
Miscellaneous chemical products (598)	376	447	383	374	346	-8.0	0.8
IMPORTS							
Total	77 669	87 977	76 367	78 342	81 877	5.4	100.0
Food and live animals (0)	3 818	4 190	4 145	4 099	4 772	25.0	5.8
Beverages and tobacco (1)	68	85	95	99	95	39.7	0.1
Crude materials, inedible, except fuels (2)	989	1 074	820	921	1 218	23.2	1.5
Mineral fuels, lubricants and related materials (3)	1 382	1 896	1 628	1 187	1 422	2.9	1.7
Animal and vegetable oils, fats and waxes (4)	464	452	302	361	396	-14.7	0.5
Chemicals and related products (5)	1 138	1 476	1 717	2 377	3 238	184.5	4.0
Manufactured goods classified chiefly by material (6)	3 677	4 037	3 486	3 520	3 526	-4.1	4.3
Machinery and transport equipment (7)	48 878	55 100	44 469	45 605	45 075	-7.8	55.1
Miscellaneous manufactured articles (8)	15 283	17 435	17 568	18 004	19 927	30.4	24.3
Commodities and transactions not classified elsewhere (9)	1 973	2 233	2 138	2 169	2 209	12.0	2.7
Top 20 Commodities	59 608	67 784	57 714	60 027	62 604	5.0	76.5
Automatic data processing machines (752)	16 323	16 336	14 709	16 355	16 410	0.5	20.0
Thermionic, cold cathode, and photocathode valves (776)	12 754	16 902	10 909	9 633	8 536	-33.1	10.4
Telecommunications equipment (764)	2 658	3 787	3 585	4 068	5 410	103.5	6.6
Parts for office machines and a.d.p. machines (759)	8 031	7 760	5 646	5 418	5 117	-36.3	6.2
Articles of apparel of textile fabrics (845)	2 341	3 050	3 212	3 204	3 457	47.7	4.2
Women's or girls' coats, jackets, etc. not knit (842)	1 731	2 136	2 260	2 382	3 120	80.2	3.8
Organo-inorganic and heterocyclic compounds (515)	519	565	795	1 512	2 219	327.6	2.7
Men's or boys' coats, jackets, etc. not knit (841)	1 637	1 792	1 681	1 661	2 021	23.5	2.5
Furniture and bedding accessories (821)	1 436	1 596	1 493	1 754	1 888	31.5	2.3
Sound and television recorders (763)	1 628	2 028	2 164	2 027	1 863	14.4	2.3
Television receivers (761)	1 190	1 388	1 320	2 044	1 776	49.2	2.2
Special transactions not classified by kind (931)	1 419	1 604	1 596	1 633	1 663	17.2	2.0
Crustaceans (036)	1 094	1 439	1 372	1 129	1 315	20.2	1.6
Radio-broadcast receivers (762)	1 548	1 666	1 551	1 450	1 258	-18.7	1.5
Fish, crustaceans and molluscs (37)	949	998	1 069	1 151	1 200	26.4	1.5
Footwear (851)	1 238	1 206	1 186	1 238	1 195	-3.5	1.5
Women's or girls' coats, jackets, etc. knit (844)	590	674	714	903	1 124	90.5	1.4
Apparel and accessories except textile; headgear (848)	947	986	989	1 002	1 063	12.2	1.3
Crude oil (333)	918	1 087	905	770	1 001	9.0	1.2
Natural rubber in primary forms (231)	657	784	558	693	968	47.3	1.2

Table C-14. U.S. Trade by Commodity with Middle East, 1999–2003

(Millions of dollars; total exports, f.a.s.; and general imports, Customs; top 20 commodities based on 2003 dollar value.)

Commodity and SITC code	1999	2000	2001	2002	2003	Percent change, 1999–2003	Percent share of total, 2003
EXPORTS							
Total	20 928	19 023	19 302	18 943	19 365	-7.5	100.0
Food and live animals (0)	1 234	1 431	1 408	1 266	1 285	4.1	6.6
Beverages and tobacco (1)	566	601	488	353	354	-37.5	1.8
Crude materials, inedible, except fuels (2)	331	378	381	420	427	29.0	2.2
Mineral fuels, lubricants and related materials (3)	158	161	168	211	195	23.4	1.0
Animal and vegetable oils, fats and waxes (4)	139	86	87	105	149	7.2	0.8
Chemicals and related products (5)	1 001	1 075	1 216	1 120	1 232	23.1	6.4
Manufactured goods classified chiefly by material (6)	2 121	2 411	2 417	2 805	3 033	43.0	15.7
Machinery and transport equipment (7)	12 422	10 174	10 350	9 948	9 865	-20.6	50.9
Miscellaneous manufactured articles (8)	2 048	1 785	1 957	1 854	1 966	-4.0	10.2
Commodities and transactions not classified elsewhere (9)	909	920	830	860	859	-5.5	4.4
Top 20 Commodities	14 156	11 897	11 986	11 931	12 157	-14.1	62.8
Aircraft and associated equipment (792)	5 480	3 037	2 914	2 536	2 320	-57.7	12.0
Pearls, precious and semiprecious stones (667)	1 147	1 480	1 530	1 909	2 108	83.8	10.9
All motor vehicles (781)	664	654	1 120	1 498	1 463	120.3	7.6
Civil engineering and contractors' plant and equipment (723)	425	370	503	853	614	44.5	3.2
Nonelectric engines and motors (714)	602	428	417	407	574	-4.7	3.0
Telecommunications equipment (764)	1 028	813	572	520	554	-46.1	2.9
Measuring/checking/analyzing instruments (874)	472	446	527	471	545	15.5	2.8
Special transactions not classified by kind (931)	438	458	325	431	460	5.0	2.4
Arms and ammunition (891)	631	300	401	376	412	-34.7	2.1
Automatic data processing machines (752)	437	481	441	332	361	-17.4	1.9
Estimated low value shipments (994)	354	353	380	377	357	0.8	1.8
Tobacco, manufactured (122)	551	586	470	330	326	-40.8	1.7
Pumps, air or gas compressors and fans (743)	346	300	383	328	318	-8.1	1.6
Heating and cooling equipment (741)	411	280	307	314	287	-30.2	1.5
Thermionic, cold cathode, and photocathode valves (776)	258	596	400	295	278	7.8	1.4
Rotating electric plant and parts (716)	105	98	116	116	268	155.2	1.4
Electrical machinery and apparatus (778)	208	250	259	285	238	14.4	1.2
Edible products and preparations, n.e.s. (098)	154	190	229	201	225	46.1	1.2
Special purpose motor vehicles (782)	283	583	425	169	225	-20.5	1.2
Miscellaneous chemical products (598)	162	194	267	183	224	38.3	1.2
IMPORTS							
Total	25 371	38 852	36 477	34 366	41 477	63.5	100.0
Food and live animals (0)	127	132	157	177	205	61.4	0.5
Beverages and tobacco (1)	12	27	37	16	34	183.3	0.1
Crude materials, inedible, except fuels (2)	75	67	72	57	70	-6.7	0.2
Mineral fuels, lubricants and related materials (3)	13 334	22 816	21 232	18 887	25 030	87.7	60.3
Animal and vegetable oils, fats and waxes (4)	2	2	2	3	4	100.0	0.0
Chemicals and related products (5)	1 188	1 724	1 946	1 747	2 176	83.2	5.2
Manufactured goods classified chiefly by material (6)	5 008	6 392	6 103	6 813	7 124	42.3	17.2
Machinery and transport equipment (7)	2 268	3 849	2 994	2 753	2 892	27.5	7.0
Miscellaneous manufactured articles (8)	2 394	2 867	2 896	2 854	2 919	21.9	7.0
Commodities and transactions not classified elsewhere (9)	964	976	1 037	1 059	1 024	6.2	2.5
Top 20 Commodities	22 401	34 967	32 661	30 757	37 664	68.1	90.8
Crude oil (333)	12 922	22 030	20 143	18 260	24 039	86.0	58.0
Pearls, precious and semiprecious stones (667)	4 355	5 429	5 185	5 838	6 162	41.5	14.9
Special transactions not classified by kind (931)	872	833	891	917	897	2.9	2.2
Oil (not crude) (334)	340	622	827	484	829	143.8	2.0
Medicaments (including veterinary medicaments) (542)	208	272	503	535	703	238.0	1.7
Telecommunications equipment (764)	793	1 114	926	605	616	-22.3	1.5
Women's or girls' coats, jackets, etc. not knit (842)	349	460	532	499	557	59.6	1.3
Articles of apparel of textile fabrics (845)	283	345	388	434	455	60.8	1.1
Organic chemicals (516)	388	688	571	488	448	15.5	1.1
Aircraft and associated equipment (792)	280	333	373	386	390	39.3	0.9
Jewelry, goldsmiths' and silversmiths' wares (897)	323	325	321	335	325	0.6	0.8
Thermionic, cold cathode, and photocathode valves (776)	69	502	247	295	314	355.1	0.8
Women's or girls' coats, jackets, etc. knit (844)	190	239	226	274	314	65.3	0.8
Electrical machinery and apparatus (778)	153	553	260	309	294	92.2	0.7
Electro-diagnostic apparatus (774)	101	140	169	212	268	165.3	0.6
Fertilizers (except crude) (562)	61	138	197	109	265	334.4	0.6
Men's or boys' coats, jackets, etc. not knit (841)	236	286	254	228	238	0.8	0.6
Measuring/checking/analyzing instruments (874)	231	379	329	257	230	-0.4	0.6
Nonelectric engines and motors (714)	145	146	167	169	172	18.6	0.4
Alcohols, phenols, and halogenated derivatives (512)	102	133	152	123	148	45.1	0.4

Table C-15. U.S. Trade by Commodity with Other Asia, 1999–2003

(Millions of dollars; total exports, f.a.s.; general imports, Customs; top 20 commodities based on 2003 dollar value.)

Commodity and SITC code	1999	2000	2001	2002	2003	Percent change, 1999–2003	Percent share of total, 2003
EXPORTS							
Total	130 012	153 123	136 204	132 602	141 986	9.2	100.0
Food and live animals (0)	13 351	13 878	13 380	12 757	13 562	1.6	9.6
Beverages and tobacco (1)	2 515	2 853	2 008	1 590	1 601	-36.3	1.1
Crude materials, inedible, except fuels (2)	8 091	10 470	10 469	10 192	14 277	76.5	10.1
Mineral fuels, lubricants and related materials (3)	1 618	1 512	988	1 031	1 353	-16.4	1.0
Animal and vegetable oils, fats and waxes (4)	385	232	181	333	317	-17.7	0.2
Chemicals and related products (5)	14 533	16 454	15 477	16 813	19 065	31.2	13.4
Manufactured goods classified chiefly by material (6)	7 361	8 925	7 856	7 577	8 841	20.1	6.2
Machinery and transport equipment (7)	64 689	77 429	65 339	63 403	63 654	-1.6	44.8
Miscellaneous manufactured articles (8)	14 580	18 326	17 588	16 042	16 447	12.8	11.6
Commodities and transactions not classified elsewhere (9)	2 888	3 044	2 918	2 864	2 869	-0.7	2.0
Top 20 Commodities	70 172	84 552	71 772	69 196	74 307	5.9	52.3
Thermionic, cold cathode, and photocathode valves (776)	16 615	19 791	14 487	15 378	16 795	1.1	11.8
Aircraft and associated equipment (792)	11 323	9 071	9 890	11 078	10 737	-5.2	7.6
Measuring/checking/analyzing instruments (874)	4 661	6 525	5 499	5 164	5 311	13.9	3.7
Oil seeds and oleaginous fruits (222)	1 782	2 461	2 411	2 418	4 523	153.8	3.2
Telecommunications equipment (764)	5 177	6 453	5 743	4 898	4 434	-14.4	3.1
Automatic data processing machines (752)	5 114	7 409	6 382	4 729	4 224	-17.4	3.0
Machinery and equipment specialized for particular industries (728)	3 831	6 996	4 117	3 470	3 442	-10.2	2.4
Parts for office machines and a.d.p. machines (759)	3 800	5 273	4 255	2 980	2 843	-25.2	2.0
Miscellaneous chemical products (598)	1 362	1 720	1 763	1 864	2 261	66.0	1.6
Electrical machinery and apparatus (778)	1 734	2 278	1 852	2 182	2 212	27.6	1.6
Maize (not including sweet corn) unmilled (044)	2 497	2 106	2 096	2 129	2 173	-13.0	1.5
Meat of bovine animals (011)	1 784	2 165	1 698	1 562	2 046	14.7	1.4
Nonelectric engines and motors (714)	1 808	1 980	2 143	2 178	1 989	10.0	1.4
Medical instruments and appliances (872)	1 385	1 516	1 669	1 596	1 776	28.2	1.3
Parts and accessories of motor vehicles (784)	1 640	1 915	1 722	1 732	1 767	7.7	1.2
Cotton textile fibers (263)	321	589	859	793	1 616	403.4	1.1
Other meat and edible offal (012)	1 751	1 903	1 853	1 536	1 581	-9.7	1.1
Hydrocarbons and specified derivatives (511)	872	1 186	609	784	1 547	77.4	1.1
Pulp and waste paper (251)	1 256	1 496	1 162	1 286	1 528	21.7	1.1
Estimated low value shipments (994)	1 459	1 719	1 562	1 439	1 502	2.9	1.1
IMPORTS							
Total	306 093	357 889	325 106	343 497	369 149	20.6	100.0
Food and live animals (0)	2 773	2 973	2 914	3 331	3 891	40.3	1.1
Beverages and tobacco (1)	133	147	172	206	188	41.4	0.1
Crude materials, inedible, except fuels (2)	1 265	1 533	1 400	1 389	1 579	24.8	0.4
Mineral fuels, lubricants and related materials (3)	885	1 821	1 717	1 390	1 478	67.0	0.4
Animal and vegetable oils, fats and waxes (4)	79	85	69	61	70	-11.4	0.0
Chemicals and related products (5)	9 961	11 173	11 004	11 825	13 862	39.2	3.8
Manufactured goods classified chiefly by material (6)	30 129	34 143	31 320	35 064	37 986	26.1	10.3
Machinery and transport equipment (7)	172 433	205 948	177 364	186 615	198 675	15.2	53.8
Miscellaneous manufactured articles (8)	81 180	92 184	91 264	96 062	103 570	27.6	28.1
Commodities and transactions not classified elsewhere (9)	7 256	7 882	7 881	7 555	7 851	8.2	2.1
Top 20 Commodities	186 163	218 365	197 327	211 902	225 903	21.3	61.2
All motor vehicles (781)	32 185	37 082	37 607	42 020	40 284	25.2	10.9
Automatic data processing machines (752)	22 389	27 315	20 904	23 008	25 630	14.5	6.9
Telecommunications equipment (764)	12 221	16 186	15 136	15 994	18 989	55.4	5.1
Toys and sporting goods (894)	15 616	16 757	17 451	18 342	18 506	18.5	5.0
Parts for office machines and a.d.p. machines (759)	14 723	16 600	13 367	14 084	15 211	3.3	4.1
Footwear (851)	8 893	9 624	10 138	10 549	10 883	22.4	2.9
Sound and television recorders (763)	6 991	8 729	7 650	9 557	10 499	50.2	2.8
Thermionic, cold cathode, and photocathode valves (776)	19 340	23 570	13 309	11 129	10 418	-46.1	2.8
Furniture and bedding accessories (821)	4 644	5 920	6 226	8 188	10 018	115.7	2.7
Parts and accessories of motor vehicles (784)	7 398	8 752	8 260	8 874	9 629	30.2	2.6
Articles of apparel of textile fabrics (845)	7 101	7 955	8 016	8 030	8 445	18.9	2.3
Electrical machinery and apparatus (778)	7 026	8 651	7 341	7 336	7 735	10.1	2.1
Women's or girls' coats, jackets, etc. not knit (842)	6 065	6 758	6 542	6 660	7 272	19.9	2.0
Internal combustion piston engines (713)	5 351	5 840	5 296	5 176	5 107	-4.6	1.4
Articles of plastics (893)	3 247	3 730	3 816	4 378	4 939	52.1	1.3
Household type electrical and nonelectrical equipment (775)	2 670	3 275	3 629	4 288	4 820	80.5	1.3
Television receivers (761)	678	1 138	1 856	2 953	4 681	590.4	1.3
Special transactions not classified by kind (931)	4 501	4 612	4 927	4 550	4 565	1.4	1.2
Made-up articles of textile materials (658)	2 211	2 542	2 764	3 316	4 214	90.6	1.1
Musical instruments and accessories (898)	2 913	3 329	3 092	3 470	4 058	39.3	1.1

Table C-16. U.S. Trade by Commodity with Australia and Oceania, 1999–2003

(Millions of dollars; total exports, f.a.s.; general imports, Customs; top 20 commodities based on 2003 dollar value.)

Commodity and SITC code	1999	2000	2001	2002	2003	Percent change, 1999–2003	Percent share of total, 2003
EXPORTS							
Total	14 165	14 812	13 418	15 184	15 251	7.7	100.0
Food and live animals (0)	410	424	405	431	712	73.7	4.7
Beverages and tobacco (1)	97	112	100	105	112	15.5	0.7
Crude materials, inedible, except fuels (2)	176	165	149	149	147	-16.5	1.0
Mineral fuels, lubricants and related materials (3)	168	158	174	202	156	-7.1	1.0
Animal and vegetable oils, fats and waxes (4)	5	4	3	8	5	0.0	0.0
Chemicals and related products (5)	1 908	2 026	2 007	1 876	2 079	9.0	13.6
Manufactured goods classified chiefly by material (6)	936	855	770	817	860	-8.1	5.6
Machinery and transport equipment (7)	7 707	8 292	7 389	9 181	8 542	10.8	56.0
Miscellaneous manufactured articles (8)	1 736	1 852	1 699	1 666	1 795	3.4	11.8
Commodities and transactions not classified elsewhere (9)	1 023	923	721	749	844	-17.5	5.5
Top 20 Commodities	7 657	8 137	7 478	9 091	8 504	11.1	55.8
Aircraft and associated equipment (792)	1 740	1 586	1 747	3 483	2 396	37.7	15.7
Estimated low value shipments (994)	656	677	609	615	661	0.8	4.3
Automatic data processing machines (752)	755	727	660	494	506	-33.0	3.3
Parts and accessories of motor vehicles (784)	388	525	442	422	486	25.3	3.2
Telecommunications equipment (764)	471	803	472	487	483	2.5	3.2
Nonelectric engines and motors (714)	421	374	370	381	409	-2.9	2.7
Internal combustion piston engines (713)	272	312	302	335	349	28.3	2.3
Medicaments (including veterinary medicaments) (542)	156	235	229	298	338	116.7	2.2
Civil engineering and contractors' plant and equipment (723)	378	345	409	354	338	-10.6	2.2
Measuring/checking/analyzing instruments (874)	316	298	339	299	334	5.7	2.2
All motor vehicles (781)	211	238	264	343	319	51.2	2.1
Medical instruments and appliances (872)	209	238	239	255	294	40.7	1.9
Live animals other than animals of division 03 (001)	17	9	8	8	233	1 270.6	1.5
Parts for office machines and a.d.p. machines (759)	487	641	370	257	229	-53.0	1.5
Fertilizers (except crude) (562)	251	205	229	208	214	-14.7	1.4
Printed matter (892)	242	219	189	191	199	-17.8	1.3
Agricultural machinery (excluding tractors) and parts (721)	184	230	163	208	195	6.0	1.3
Electrical machinery and apparatus (778)	188	206	165	158	174	-7.4	1.1
Mechanical handling equipment (744)	157	124	132	134	174	10.8	1.1
Electro-diagnostic apparatus (774)	158	145	140	161	173	9.5	1.1
IMPORTS							
Total	7 393	8 831	9 037	9 127	9 196	24.4	100.0
Food and live animals (0)	1 926	2 256	2 477	2 581	2 694	39.9	29.3
Beverages and tobacco (1)	227	312	388	512	704	210.1	7.7
Crude materials, inedible, except fuels (2)	934	1 137	974	908	736	-21.2	8.0
Mineral fuels, lubricants and related materials (3)	418	688	493	651	432	3.3	4.7
Animal and vegetable oils, fats and waxes (4)	4	4	5	6	8	100.0	0.1
Chemicals and related products (5)	541	603	742	551	729	34.8	7.9
Manufactured goods classified chiefly by material (6)	882	1 013	1 006	923	854	-3.2	9.3
Machinery and transport equipment (7)	1 142	1 372	1 361	1 382	1 332	16.6	14.5
Miscellaneous manufactured articles (8)	634	821	920	922	904	42.6	9.8
Commodities and transactions not classified elsewhere (9)	685	624	672	690	802	17.1	8.7
Top 20 Commodities	4 282	5 331	5 479	6 034	5 975	39.5	65.0
Meat of bovine animals (011)	838	1 113	1 332	1 344	1 363	62.6	14.8
Special transactions not classified by kind (931)	517	523	579	595	695	34.4	7.6
Alcoholic beverages (112)	224	306	375	498	679	203.1	7.4
Crude oil (333)	280	523	347	619	420	50.0	4.6
Other meat and edible offal (012)	213	255	284	321	401	88.3	4.4
Starches, inulin and wheat gluten; albuminoidal substances (592)	235	274	297	227	271	15.3	2.9
Articles of apparel of textile fabrics (845)	169	236	268	292	260	53.8	2.8
Parts and accessories of motor vehicles (784)	177	217	170	210	238	34.5	2.6
Ores and concentrates of base metals (287)	129	192	167	212	202	56.6	2.2
Wood, simply worked (248)	139	135	176	211	192	38.1	2.1
Aluminum ores and concentrates (285)	428	493	327	272	167	-61.0	1.8
Medical instruments and appliances (872)	63	86	96	128	150	138.1	1.6
All motor vehicles (781)	139	237	279	312	142	2.2	1.5
Medicaments (including veterinary medicaments) (542)	41	49	147	122	126	207.3	1.4
Fish, fresh, chilled or frozen (034)	158	124	114	141	119	-24.7	1.3
Aircraft and associated equipment (792)	139	108	133	112	112	-19.4	1.2
Milk, cream, milk products except butter or cheese (022)	79	102	97	97	112	41.8	1.2
Pearls, precious and semiprecious stones (667)	97	110	107	120	109	12.4	1.2
Crustaceans (036)	84	110	88	102	109	29.8	1.2
Fruit and nuts (not including oil nuts), fresh or dried (057)	133	138	96	99	108	-18.8	1.2

Table C-17. U.S. Trade by Commodity with Africa, 1999–2003

(Millions of dollars; total exports, f.a.s.; general imports, Customs; top 20 commodities based on 2003 dollar value.)

Commodity and SITC code	1999	2000	2001	2002	2003	Percent change, 1999–2003	Percent share of total, 2003
EXPORTS							
Total	9 909	10 960	12 369	10 658	10 685	7.8	100.0
Food and live animals (0)	1 820	2 068	1 850	1 964	2 153	18.3	20.1
Beverages and tobacco (1)	225	89	35	25	28	-87.6	0.3
Crude materials, inedible, except fuels (2)	282	297	320	279	308	9.2	2.9
Mineral fuels, lubricants and related materials (3)	181	221	213	224	250	38.1	2.3
Animal and vegetable oils, fats and waxes (4)	174	117	125	190	230	32.2	2.2
Chemicals and related products (5)	756	898	1 151	896	897	18.7	8.4
Manufactured goods classified chiefly by material (6)	699	709	598	651	634	-9.3	5.9
Machinery and transport equipment (7)	4 550	5 284	6 749	5 206	5 009	10.1	46.9
Miscellaneous manufactured articles (8)	909	936	905	856	836	-8.0	7.8
Commodities and transactions not classified elsewhere (9)	314	341	424	368	342	8.9	3.2
Top 20 Commodities	5 651	6 605	7 880	6 737	6 532	15.6	61.1
Aircraft and associated equipment (792)	1 287	1 973	2 588	1 820	1 273	-1.1	11.9
Wheat and meslin, unmilled (041)	844	974	750	698	1 038	23.0	9.7
Civil engineering and contractors' plant and equipment (723)	586	626	882	945	983	67.7	9.2
Maize (not including sweet corn) unmilled (044)	521	596	617	720	559	7.3	5.2
Telecommunications equipment (764)	347	364	553	324	338	-2.6	3.2
All motor vehicles (781)	119	91	188	196	257	116.0	2.4
Arms and ammunition (891)	338	357	284	326	246	-27.2	2.3
Estimated low value shipments (994)	196	208	255	210	216	10.2	2.0
Special purpose motor vehicles (782)	115	97	156	129	191	66.1	1.8
Measuring/checking/analyzing instruments (874)	148	136	165	140	171	15.5	1.6
Fixed vegetable fats and oils (421)	126	67	93	120	149	18.3	1.4
Machinery and equipment specialized for particular industries (728)	110	126	125	106	141	28.2	1.3
Automatic data processing machines (752)	175	203	172	122	129	-26.3	1.2
Feeding stuff for animals (081)	97	161	176	165	128	32.0	1.2
Mechanical handling equipment (744)	107	105	143	135	123	15.0	1.2
Residual petroleum products (335)	79	97	118	122	122	54.4	1.1
Parts and accessories of motor vehicles (784)	95	152	258	83	122	28.4	1.1
Special transactions not classified by kind (931)	79	104	158	150	119	50.6	1.1
Parts for office machines and a.d.p. machines (759)	119	119	92	87	114	-4.2	1.1
Iron and steel tubes, pipes and fittings (679)	163	49	107	139	113	-30.7	1.1
IMPORTS							
Total	16 956	27 638	25 425	22 144	32 035	88.9	100.0
Food and live animals (0)	729	793	744	842	1 076	47.6	3.4
Beverages and tobacco (1)	92	61	79	88	78	-15.2	0.2
Crude materials, inedible, except fuels (2)	772	728	655	621	647	-16.2	2.0
Mineral fuels, lubricants and related materials (3)	10 702	20 279	17 678	14 258	23 077	115.6	72.0
Animal and vegetable oils, fats and waxes (4)	14	12	17	6	10	-28.6	0.0
Chemicals and related products (5)	248	335	464	409	570	129.8	1.8
Manufactured goods classified chiefly by material (6)	2 318	3 029	2 966	2 720	3 016	30.1	9.4
Machinery and transport equipment (7)	466	550	803	792	926	98.7	2.9
Miscellaneous manufactured articles (8)	1 237	1 491	1 682	1 771	2 243	81.3	7.0
Commodities and transactions not classified elsewhere (9)	377	360	337	637	392	4.0	1.2
Top 20 Commodities	14 284	24 744	22 675	19 452	29 119	103.9	90.9
Crude oil (333)	8 228	16 290	14 283	12 222	19 926	142.2	62.2
Oil (not crude) (334)	2 210	3 553	2 700	1 731	2 237	1.2	7.0
Silver, platinum, and other platinum group metals (681)	1 023	1 529	1 534	1 173	1 272	24.3	4.0
Pearls, precious and semiprecious stones (667)	386	454	527	587	718	86.0	2.2
Articles of apparel of textile fabrics (845)	264	368	435	463	584	121.2	1.8
Women's or girls' coats, jackets, etc. not knit (842)	250	322	395	407	553	121.2	1.7
Men's or boys' coats, jackets, etc. not knit (841)	368	435	427	431	502	36.4	1.6
Natural gas, whether or not liquefied (343)	134	155	362	110	483	260.4	1.5
Cocoa (072)	333	311	276	323	469	40.8	1.5
Liquefied propane and butane (342)	105	210	296	153	398	279.0	1.2
All motor vehicles (781)	0	23	256	267	374	X	1.2
Special transactions not classified by kind (931)	249	320	288	588	326	30.9	1.0
Pig iron and iron and steel powders (671)	265	276	183	183	223	-15.8	0.7
Spices (075)	28	42	100	136	211	653.6	0.7
Women's or girls' coats, jackets, etc. knit (844)	73	81	108	146	199	172.6	0.6
Men's or boys' coats, jackets, etc. knit (843)	68	65	90	106	159	133.8	0.5
Nonferrous base metal waste and scrap (288)	187	169	148	160	142	-24.1	0.4
Alcohols, phenols, and halogenated derivatives (512)	5	8	45	68	127	2 440.0	0.4
Fruit and nuts (not including oil nuts), fresh or dried (057)	64	57	48	64	109	70.3	0.3
Pumps, air or gas compressors and fans (743)	44	76	174	134	107	143.2	0.3

X = Not applicable.

Table C-18. U.S. Trade by Commodity with Developed Countries, 1999–2003

(Millions of dollars; total exports, f.a.s.; general imports, Customs; top 20 commodities based on 2003 dollar value.)

Commodity and SITC code	1999	2000	2001	2002	2003	Percent change, 1999–2003	Percent share of total, 2003
EXPORTS							
Total	403 477	440 473	412 541	386 743	404 218	0.2	100.0
Food and live animals (0)	20 579	21 175	21 128	21 012	22 617	9.9	5.6
Beverages and tobacco (1)	4 859	4 958	4 011	3 349	3 549	-27.0	0.9
Crude materials, inedible, except fuels (2)	13 779	15 469	14 053	13 735	14 417	4.6	3.6
Mineral fuels, lubricants and related materials (3)	4 900	5 720	6 486	4 985	6 218	26.9	1.5
Animal and vegetable oils, fats and waxes (4)	562	488	512	557	627	11.6	0.2
Chemicals and related products (5)	43 908	49 530	50 003	51 052	57 621	31.2	14.3
Manufactured goods classified chiefly by material (6)	35 876	40 549	37 402	36 030	37 067	3.3	9.2
Machinery and transport equipment (7)	213 861	229 951	206 730	191 594	193 020	-9.7	47.8
Miscellaneous manufactured articles (8)	49 289	55 240	54 025	49 071	51 800	5.1	12.8
Commodities and transactions not classified elsewhere (9)	15 863	17 394	18 192	15 358	17 282	8.9	4.3
Top 20 Commodities	204 643	221 122	204 457	191 107	197 859	-3.3	48.9
Aircraft and associated equipment (792)	29 869	26 111	24 037	24 494	22 848	-23.5	5.7
Parts and accessories of motor vehicles (784)	22 016	22 260	20 145	21 122	20 431	-7.2	5.1
All motor vehicles (781)	13 363	12 789	13 074	15 558	17 816	33.3	4.4
Automatic data processing machines (752)	17 155	18 369	15 831	12 582	12 894	-24.8	3.2
Measuring/checking/analyzing instruments (874)	11 384	13 121	12 537	11 009	11 573	1.7	2.9
Nonelectric engines and motors (714)	11 067	12 046	13 140	11 951	11 275	1.9	2.8
Telecommunications equipment (764)	12 545	15 457	13 434	10 990	10 477	-16.5	2.6
Thermionic, cold cathode, and photocathode valves (776)	15 314	19 463	14 195	10 474	9 905	-35.3	2.5
Medicaments (including veterinary medicaments) (542)	4 869	5 994	7 658	7 749	9 591	97.0	2.4
Internal combustion piston engines (713)	9 893	10 125	9 345	9 732	9 499	-4.0	2.3
Parts for office machines and a.d.p. machines (759)	13 162	15 788	12 641	9 005	8 950	-32.0	2.2
Estimated low value shipments (994)	6 910	7 637	9 288	8 264	8 761	26.8	2.2
Medicinal products, except medicaments (541)	4 450	4 955	5 199	5 894	6 950	56.2	1.7
Medical instruments and appliances (872)	5 143	5 351	6 072	5 919	6 594	28.2	1.6
Special purpose motor vehicles (782)	4 729	5 172	4 404	5 056	6 183	30.7	1.5
Miscellaneous chemical products (598)	4 351	5 010	4 881	4 863	5 390	23.9	1.3
Electrical machinery and apparatus (778)	5 747	6 736	5 590	5 181	5 171	-10.0	1.3
Electrical apparatus for switching or protecting elec. circuits (772)	5 581	6 635	5 623	5 004	4 891	-12.4	1.2
Gold, nonmonetary (971)	4 681	5 394	4 318	2 966	4 517	-3.5	1.1
Miscellaneous manufactured articles (899)	2 414	2 709	3 045	3 294	4 143	71.6	1.0
IMPORTS							
Total	553 133	629 540	595 994	591 170	621 874	12.4	100.0
Food and live animals (0)	14 943	16 113	17 209	18 223	18 830	26.0	3.0
Beverages and tobacco (1)	6 480	6 821	7 008	7 673	8 718	34.5	1.4
Crude materials, inedible, except fuels (2)	15 472	15 726	14 179	13 607	13 077	-15.5	2.1
Mineral fuels, lubricants and related materials (3)	24 387	45 036	46 133	43 334	56 411	131.3	9.1
Animal and vegetable oils, fats and waxes (4)	792	806	758	864	1 038	31.1	0.2
Chemicals and related products (5)	51 724	59 948	63 616	70 410	81 693	57.9	13.1
Manufactured goods classified chiefly by material (6)	66 354	73 991	68 814	66 749	69 597	4.9	11.2
Machinery and transport equipment (7)	283 015	310 742	280 941	274 866	277 154	-2.1	44.6
Miscellaneous manufactured articles (8)	57 381	65 172	62 493	60 639	62 387	8.7	10.0
Commodities and transactions not classified elsewhere (9)	32 586	35 184	34 845	34 806	32 968	1.2	5.3
Top 20 Commodities	276 352	324 883	317 872	324 534	342 340	23.9	55.0
All motor vehicles (781)	83 849	88 547	85 311	93 123	93 378	11.4	15.0
Parts and accessories of motor vehicles (784)	19 676	21 330	19 762	21 366	23 554	19.7	3.8
Medicaments (including veterinary medicaments) (542)	8 887	9 484	12 498	17 530	22 358	151.6	3.6
Special transactions not classified by kind (931)	22 157	23 444	24 348	24 423	22 081	-0.3	3.6
Crude oil (333)	10 425	19 704	15 645	19 371	21 788	109.0	3.5
Natural gas, whether or not liquefied (343)	6 022	10 369	15 357	11 428	18 249	203.0	2.9
Organo-inorganic and heterocyclic compounds (515)	11 185	15 740	16 441	17 205	17 982	60.8	2.9
Aircraft and associated equipment (792)	13 110	15 885	18 200	15 208	14 231	8.6	2.3
Internal combustion piston engines (713)	11 728	12 509	10 975	11 290	11 966	2.0	1.9
Oil (not crude) (334)	5 058	9 739	9 866	9 016	11 697	131.3	1.9
Paper and paperboard (641)	10 010	11 077	10 588	10 111	10 258	2.5	1.6
Special purpose motor vehicles (782)	10 432	10 469	9 773	10 096	10 037	-3.8	1.6
Telecommunications equipment (764)	12 148	18 946	11 874	10 680	9 610	-20.9	1.5
Estimate of low value import transactions (984)	8 075	9 223	8 923	8 580	9 170	13.6	1.5
Measuring/checking/analyzing instruments (874)	7 412	9 125	8 674	7 944	8 330	12.4	1.3
Nonelectric engines and motors (714)	9 509	10 075	12 486	9 828	7 874	-17.2	1.3
Alcoholic beverages (112)	5 556	5 916	6 079	6 746	7 695	38.5	1.2
Parts for office machines and a.d.p. machines (759)	10 532	11 420	9 213	7 902	7 620	-27.6	1.2
Furniture and bedding accessories (821)	6 840	7 644	7 034	7 041	7 366	7.7	1.2
Medicinal products, except medicaments (541)	3 741	4 237	4 825	5 646	7 096	89.7	1.1

Table C-19. U.S. Trade by Commodity with Developing Countries, 1999–2003

(Millions of dollars; total exports, f.a.s.; general imports, Customs; top 20 commodities based on 2003 dollar value.)

Commodity and SITC code	1999	2000	2001	2002	2003	Percent change, 1999–2003	Percent share of total, 2003
EXPORTS							
Total	288 973	339 639	318 222	306 251	319 339	10.5	100.0
Food and live animals (0)	17 525	19 015	19 950	19 226	20 584	17.5	6.4
Beverages and tobacco (1)	1 906	1 863	1 633	1 322	1 239	-35.0	0.4
Crude materials, inedible, except fuels (2)	10 160	13 330	13 859	14 263	19 016	87.2	6.0
Mineral fuels, lubricants and related materials (3)	5 026	7 620	6 380	6 705	7 829	55.8	2.5
Animal and vegetable oils, fats and waxes (4)	1 372	951	867	1 358	1 385	0.9	0.4
Chemicals and related products (5)	28 081	33 012	32 320	32 541	36 532	30.1	11.4
Manufactured goods classified chiefly by material (6)	26 281	31 441	29 256	29 029	30 629	16.5	9.6
Machinery and transport equipment (7)	155 437	182 247	168 338	158 065	158 737	2.1	49.7
Miscellaneous manufactured articles (8)	32 341	37 943	34 498	33 066	33 064	2.2	10.4
Commodities and transactions not classified elsewhere (9)	10 844	12 215	11 120	10 674	10 323	-4.8	3.2
Top 20 Commodities	151 157	181 493	166 129	159 323	163 096	7.9	51.1
Thermionic, cold cathode, and photocathode valves (776)	34 037	43 361	33 427	34 045	37 865	11.2	11.9
Aircraft and associated equipment (792)	19 742	14 843	20 652	19 305	16 789	-15.0	5.3
Telecommunications equipment (764)	11 836	13 706	12 699	10 597	9 886	-16.5	3.1
Parts for office machines and a.d.p. machines (759)	7 648	9 679	8 228	8 170	9 792	28.0	3.1
Automatic data processing machines (752)	9 559	12 561	11 555	9 231	8 701	-9.0	2.7
Parts and accessories of motor vehicles (784)	7 382	9 381	9 021	8 127	7 896	7.0	2.5
Measuring/checking/analyzing instruments (874)	6 772	9 031	7 850	7 632	7 833	15.7	2.5
Estimated low value shipments (994)	6 847	8 070	7 554	7 016	7 066	3.2	2.2
Electrical apparatus for switching or protecting elec. circuits (772)	6 832	8 493	6 875	6 644	6 950	1.7	2.2
Oil (not crude) (334)	3 328	5 362	4 624	4 702	5 806	74.5	1.8
Electrical machinery and apparatus (778)	5 559	7 434	5 760	5 941	5 717	2.8	1.8
Oil seeds and oleaginous fruits (222)	2 428	3 141	3 263	3 384	5 592	130.3	1.8
Civil engineering and contractors' plant and equipment (723)	4 133	4 696	5 176	5 576	5 212	26.1	1.6
All motor vehicles (781)	3 697	4 445	5 290	5 548	4 961	34.2	1.6
Machinery and equipment specialized for particular industries (728)	5 982	9 016	5 905	5 204	4 733	-20.9	1.5
Nonelectric engines and motors (714)	3 896	3 583	4 405	4 464	4 333	11.2	1.4
Articles of plastics (893)	3 587	4 719	4 224	4 023	3 867	7.8	1.2
Pumps, air or gas compressors and fans (743)	2 969	3 495	3 839	3 476	3 527	18.8	1.1
Pearls, precious and semiprecious stones (667)	1 948	2 543	2 451	2 919	3 290	68.9	1.0
Manufactures of base metal (699)	2 975	3 934	3 331	3 319	3 280	10.3	1.0
IMPORTS							
Total	471 632	587 347	545 965	572 379	637 522	35.2	100.0
Food and live animals (0)	20 150	20 679	20 018	20 965	24 070	19.5	3.8
Beverages and tobacco (1)	2 135	2 439	2 727	3 097	3 260	52.7	0.5
Crude materials, inedible, except fuels (2)	6 246	6 640	6 075	6 164	6 937	11.1	1.1
Mineral fuels, lubricants and related materials (3)	50 815	88 554	76 741	73 760	99 150	95.1	15.6
Animal and vegetable oils, fats and waxes (4)	616	594	432	480	546	-11.4	0.1
Chemicals and related products (5)	10 483	13 685	15 254	15 647	19 357	84.7	3.0
Manufactured goods classified chiefly by material (6)	50 642	59 977	54 247	60 188	63 328	25.1	9.9
Machinery and transport equipment (7)	196 856	242 445	218 932	230 778	246 463	25.2	38.7
Miscellaneous manufactured articles (8)	119 293	135 730	135 593	144 595	156 550	31.2	24.6
Commodities and transactions not classified elsewhere (9)	14 397	16 605	15 944	16 704	17 860	24.1	2.8
Top 20 Commodities	285 890	373 064	337 882	350 246	390 766	36.7	61.3
Crude oil (333)	40 236	70 081	59 618	59 997	79 935	98.7	12.5
Automatic data processing machines (752)	35 456	42 239	38 607	42 665	45 486	28.3	7.1
Telecommunications equipment (764)	16 934	25 402	26 063	27 010	30 921	82.6	4.9
All motor vehicles (781)	13 040	21 067	21 695	21 301	21 343	63.7	3.3
Articles of apparel of textile fabrics (845)	16 403	18 944	19 219	19 260	20 214	23.2	3.2
Toys and sporting goods (894)	14 488	16 008	15 856	18 246	19 118	32.0	3.0
Thermionic, cold cathode, and photocathode valves (776)	26 756	34 483	21 440	19 725	18 515	-30.8	2.9
Parts for office machines and a.d.p. machines (759)	21 373	21 932	16 803	16 855	17 342	-18.9	2.7
Furniture and bedding accessories (821)	9 338	11 283	11 577	14 531	16 990	81.9	2.7
Oil (not crude) (334)	9 467	16 626	14 674	11 685	15 038	58.8	2.4
Women's or girls' coats, jackets, etc. not knit (842)	11 513	13 383	13 229	13 075	14 433	25.4	2.3
Footwear (851)	11 889	12 683	13 167	13 447	13 733	15.5	2.2
Special transactions not classified by kind (931)	9 625	11 128	11 019	11 470	11 541	19.9	1.8
Men's or boys' coats, jackets, etc. not knit (841)	10 743	12 120	11 281	10 684	11 396	6.1	1.8
Pearls, precious and semiprecious stones (667)	7 829	9 234	8 223	9 587	9 904	26.5	1.6
Television receivers (761)	5 808	6 446	6 704	8 285	9 819	69.1	1.5
Electrical machinery and apparatus (778)	7 020	8 839	7 929	8 572	9 539	35.9	1.5
Parts and accessories of motor vehicles (784)	6 368	7 110	7 146	8 398	9 334	46.6	1.5
Sound and television recorders (763)	4 738	6 444	6 565	7 976	8 580	81.1	1.3
Equipment for distributing electricity (773)	6 866	7 612	7 067	7 477	7 585	10.5	1.2

Table C-20. U.S. Trade by Commodity with Asian Pacific Economic Cooperation (APEC-20), 1999–2003

(Millions of dollars; total exports, f.a.s.; general imports, Customs; top 20 commodities based on 2003 dollar value.)

Commodity and SITC code	1999	2000	2001	2002	2003	Percent change, 1999–2003	Percent share of total, 2003
EXPORTS							
Total	436 518	505 771	460 848	448 819	469 619	7.6	100.0
Food and live animals (0)	26 815	28 982	29 851	29 043	31 286	16.7	6.7
Beverages and tobacco (1)	3 337	3 771	2 959	2 491	2 488	-25.4	0.5
Crude materials, inedible, except fuels (2)	16 219	19 731	18 981	19 092	23 858	47.1	5.1
Mineral fuels, lubricants and related materials (3)	6 666	9 185	8 837	7 904	9 056	35.9	1.9
Animal and vegetable oils, fats and waxes (4)	989	765	633	954	963	-2.6	0.2
Chemicals and related products (5)	41 151	47 452	45 584	47 424	52 452	27.5	11.2
Manufactured goods classified chiefly by material (6)	44 037	51 992	46 055	45 342	46 855	6.4	10.0
Machinery and transport equipment (7)	236 115	273 668	240 935	233 339	237 645	0.6	50.6
Miscellaneous manufactured articles (8)	47 862	55 392	51 720	49 314	50 969	6.5	10.9
Commodities and transactions not classified elsewhere (9)	13 327	14 833	15 291	13 914	14 046	5.4	3.0
Top 20 Commodities	223 699	264 618	233 366	226 803	232 107	3.8	49.4
Thermionic, cold cathode, and photocathode valves (776)	42 115	52 522	39 045	37 210	40 613	-3.6	8.6
Parts and accessories of motor vehicles (784)	25 003	26 947	24 372	25 329	24 647	-1.4	5.2
Aircraft and associated equipment (792)	18 459	15 023	19 579	21 149	19 788	7.2	4.2
All motor vehicles (781)	12 942	13 694	13 382	14 808	14 820	14.5	3.2
Automatic data processing machines (752)	15 269	18 906	16 647	13 997	13 776	-9.8	2.9
Telecommunications equipment (764)	13 644	17 603	15 589	13 021	12 355	-9.4	2.6
Measuring/checking/analyzing instruments (874)	10 808	14 032	12 261	11 555	11 862	9.8	2.5
Parts for office machines and a.d.p. machines (759)	10 117	13 223	11 054	9 794	11 107	9.8	2.4
Internal combustion piston engines (713)	10 131	11 155	9 897	10 100	9 941	-1.9	2.1
Estimated low value shipments (994)	7 533	8 970	10 067	9 250	9 569	27.0	2.0
Electrical apparatus for switching or protecting elec. circuits (772)	9 440	11 520	9 155	8 737	8 957	-5.1	1.9
Electrical machinery and apparatus (778)	8 188	10 264	8 025	8 173	7 946	-3.0	1.7
Special purpose motor vehicles (782)	4 777	5 964	5 016	5 812	6 939	45.3	1.5
Oil seeds and oleaginous fruits (222)	3 161	3 865	3 910	4 091	6 487	105.2	1.4
Machinery and equipment specialized for particular industries (728)	7 684	11 791	7 739	6 617	6 349	-17.4	1.4
Manufactures of base metal (699)	5 451	7 452	5 936	6 022	5 894	8.1	1.3
Articles of plastics (893)	5 185	6 423	5 881	5 794	5 768	11.2	1.2
Nonelectric engines and motors (714)	5 046	5 182	5 962	5 967	5 573	10.4	1.2
Pumps, air or gas compressors and fans (743)	4 439	5 073	5 261	4 977	5 086	14.6	1.1
Paper and paperboard (641)	4 307	5 009	4 588	4 400	4 630	7.5	1.0
IMPORTS							
Total	692 896	812 271	750 814	767 389	813 988	17.5	100.0
Food and live animals (0)	21 972	23 877	25 225	26 473	28 704	30.6	3.5
Beverages and tobacco (1)	2 540	2 963	3 225	3 521	3 836	51.0	0.5
Crude materials, inedible, except fuels (2)	16 418	16 896	15 118	14 573	14 403	-12.3	1.8
Mineral fuels, lubricants and related materials (3)	27 824	49 644	49 292	47 110	63 660	128.8	7.8
Animal and vegetable oils, fats and waxes (4)	917	825	662	738	847	-7.6	0.1
Chemicals and related products (5)	23 773	27 458	28 079	29 277	33 997	43.0	4.2
Manufactured goods classified chiefly by material (6)	73 221	81 924	76 115	78 593	82 231	12.3	10.1
Machinery and transport equipment (7)	376 171	438 834	386 695	393 467	404 355	7.5	49.7
Miscellaneous manufactured articles (8)	119 904	136 051	133 760	140 401	149 502	24.7	18.4
Commodities and transactions not classified elsewhere (9)	30 156	33 797	32 644	33 236	32 453	7.6	4.0
Top 20 Commodities	389 788	469 769	423 708	435 007	458 416	17.6	56.3
All motor vehicles (781)	76 670	87 267	83 023	87 126	83 055	8.3	10.2
Automatic data processing machines (752)	44 628	51 390	44 349	47 188	48 982	9.8	6.0
Telecommunications equipment (764)	25 701	38 967	32 100	31 414	34 713	35.1	4.3
Crude oil (333)	14 861	26 794	21 079	25 039	31 780	113.8	3.9
Parts and accessories of motor vehicles (784)	21 132	23 468	22 147	24 431	26 539	25.6	3.3
Parts for office machines and a.d.p. machines (759)	27 109	29 078	23 257	22 117	22 230	-18.0	2.7
Thermionic, cold cathode, and photocathode valves (776)	35 396	44 434	27 414	23 070	21 285	-39.9	2.6
Special transactions not classified by kind (931)	19 909	21 839	22 339	22 645	21 145	6.2	2.6
Furniture and bedding accessories (821)	13 293	15 555	15 288	18 114	20 614	55.1	2.5
Toys and sporting goods (894)	17 568	18 752	19 487	20 806	20 345	15.8	2.5
Natural gas, whether or not liquefied (343)	6 034	10 383	15 357	11 450	18 261	202.6	2.2
Special purpose motor vehicles (782)	14 179	14 796	16 093	16 337	16 781	18.4	2.1
Articles of apparel of textile fabrics (845)	11 018	12 298	12 385	12 401	13 068	18.6	1.6
Electrical machinery and apparatus (778)	11 532	13 634	11 787	11 951	12 758	10.6	1.6
Sound and television recorders (763)	9 180	11 412	10 134	11 799	12 554	36.8	1.5
Footwear (851)	10 461	11 141	11 610	12 039	12 305	17.6	1.5
Television receivers (761)	6 142	7 108	7 919	9 853	11 710	90.7	1.4
Internal combustion piston engines (713)	11 679	12 481	10 814	11 022	11 600	-0.7	1.4
Electrical apparatus for switching or protecting elec. circuits (772)	9 261	11 752	9 422	9 068	9 365	1.1	1.2
Oil (not crude) (334)	4 035	7 220	7 704	7 137	9 326	131.1	1.1

Table C-21. U.S. Trade by Commodity with Algeria, 1999–2003

(Millions of dollars; total exports, f.a.s.; general imports, Customs; top 20 commodities based on 2003 dollar value.)

Commodity and SITC code	1999	2000	2001	2002	2003	Percent change, 1999–2003	Percent share of total, 2003
EXPORTS							
Total	456	867	1 047	984	487	6.8	100.0
Food and live animals (0)	192	254	181	232	192	0.0	39.4
Beverages and tobacco (1)	0	0	0	0	0	X	0.0
Crude materials, inedible, except fuels (2)	3	7	15	16	5	66.7	1.0
Mineral fuels, lubricants and related materials (3)	14	14	16	17	20	42.9	4.1
Animal and vegetable oils, fats and waxes (4)	27	0	38	25	7	-74.1	1.4
Chemicals and related products (5)	10	11	11	22	24	140.0	4.9
Manufactured goods classified chiefly by material (6)	43	22	35	68	31	-27.9	6.4
Machinery and transport equipment (7)	157	538	727	576	187	19.1	38.4
Miscellaneous manufactured articles (8)	8	17	16	26	18	125.0	3.7
Commodities and transactions not classified elsewhere (9)	1	4	8	3	3	200.0	0.6
Top 20 Commodities	408	753	903	857	411	0.7	84.4
Maize (not including sweet corn) unmilled (044)	79	101	110	131	101	27.8	20.7
Civil engineering and contractors' plant and equipment (723)	73	67	105	81	68	-6.8	14.0
Wheat and meslin, unmilled (041)	67	87	20	44	41	-38.8	8.4
Feeding stuff for animals (081)	36	40	35	42	39	8.3	8.0
Aircraft and associated equipment (792)	14	268	265	363	27	92.9	5.5
Coal, pulverized or not (321)	14	13	12	16	20	42.9	4.1
Telecommunications equipment (764)	15	85	233	49	16	6.7	3.3
Nonelectric engines and motors (714)	12	21	12	4	14	16.7	2.9
Iron and steel tubes, pipes and fittings (679)	36	8	13	51	14	-61.1	2.9
Mechanical handling equipment (744)	6	13	6	9	13	116.7	2.7
Machinery and equipment specialized for particular industries (728)	10	4	6	6	13	30.0	2.7
Measuring/checking/analyzing instruments (874)	4	5	10	10	8	100.0	1.6
Plastics (575)	0	0	1	1	7	X	1.4
Fixed vegetable fats and oils (421)	27	0	38	25	7	-74.1	1.4
Fruit and nuts (not including oil nuts), fresh or dried (057)	0	0	0	1	5	X	1.0
Mineral manufactures (663)	1	5	4	4	4	300.0	0.8
Parts and accessories of motor vehicles (784)	3	3	6	3	4	33.3	0.8
Vegetables, roots, tubers and other edible vegetable products (054)	6	11	12	5	4	-33.3	0.8
Pumps, air or gas compressors and fans (743)	4	18	7	6	3	-25.0	0.6
Special purpose motor vehicles (782)	1	4	8	6	3	200.0	0.6
IMPORTS							
Total	1 831	2 724	2 694	2 365	4 753	159.6	100.0
Food and live animals (0)	1	0	0	0	0	X	0.0
Beverages and tobacco (1)	0	0	0	0	0	X	0.0
Crude materials, inedible, except fuels (2)	0	0	0	0	0	X	0.0
Mineral fuels, lubricants and related materials (3)	1 768	2 716	2 655	2 354	4 692	165.4	98.7
Animal and vegetable oils, fats and waxes (4)	0	0	0	0	0	X	0.0
Chemicals and related products (5)	16	6	19	4	27	68.8	0.6
Manufactured goods classified chiefly by material (6)	0	0	3	3	0	X	0.0
Machinery and transport equipment (7)	0	0	16	0	0	X	0.0
Miscellaneous manufactured articles (8)	0	0	0	0	0	X	0.0
Commodities and transactions not classified elsewhere (9)	45	2	2	4	33	-26.7	0.7
Top 20 Commodities	1 787	2 684	2 677	2 351	4 752	165.9	100.0
Crude oil (333)	104	0	517	1 250	2 858	2 648.1	60.1
Oil (not crude) (334)	1 459	2 403	1 717	863	1 233	-15.5	25.9
Liquefied propane and butane (342)	71	160	232	141	343	383.1	7.2
Natural gas, whether or not liquefied (343)	134	114	186	89	255	90.3	5.4
Special transactions not classified by kind (931)	3	1	2	4	33	1 000.0	0.7
Fertilizers (except crude) (562)	0	0	10	4	14	X	0.3
Hydrocarbons and specified derivatives (511)	16	6	10	0	13	-18.8	0.3
Petroleum gases and other gaseous hydrocarbons (344)	0	0	0	0	3	X	0.1
Fruit and nuts (not including oil nuts), fresh or dried (057)	0	0	0	0	0	X	0.0
Trailers and semi-trailers (786)	0	0	0	0	0	X	0.0
Works of art, collectors' pieces, and antiques (896)	0	0	0	0	0	X	0.0
Estimate of low value import transactions (984)	0	0	0	0	0	X	0.0
Automatic data processing machines (752)	0	0	0	0	0	X	0.0
Alcoholic beverages (112)	0	0	0	0	0	X	0.0
Rotating electric plant and parts (716)	0	0	0	0	0	X	0.0
Electrical machinery and apparatus (778)	0	0	0	0	0	X	0.0
Nonelectric engines and motors (714)	0	0	0	0	0	X	0.0
Telecommunications equipment (764)	0	0	0	0	0	X	0.0
Iron and steel tubes, pipes and fittings (679)	0	0	3	0	0	X	0.0
Miscellaneous manufactured articles (899)	0	0	0	0	0	X	0.0

X = Not applicable.

Table C-22. U.S. Trade by Commodity with Angola, 1999–2003

(Millions of dollars; total exports, f.a.s.; general imports, Customs; top 20 commodities based on 2003 dollar value.)

Commodity and SITC code	1999	2000	2001	2002	2003	Percent change, 1999–2003	Percent share of total, 2003
EXPORTS							
Total	252	226	276	372	492	95.2	100.0
Food and live animals (0)	22	44	27	42	58	163.6	11.8
Beverages and tobacco (1)	0	0	0	0	0	X	0.0
Crude materials, inedible, except fuels (2)	2	4	4	6	7	250.0	1.4
Mineral fuels, lubricants and related materials (3)	1	1	1	2	3	200.0	0.6
Animal and vegetable oils, fats and waxes (4)	1	10	0	4	7	600.0	1.4
Chemicals and related products (5)	9	5	14	11	22	144.4	4.5
Manufactured goods classified chiefly by material (6)	18	13	20	16	38	111.1	7.7
Machinery and transport equipment (7)	182	130	194	276	333	83.0	67.7
Miscellaneous manufactured articles (8)	12	12	9	7	12	0.0	2.4
Commodities and transactions not classified elsewhere (9)	5	6	5	8	12	140.0	2.4
Top 20 Commodities	165	164	219	333	437	164.8	88.8
Civil engineering and contractors' plant and equipment (723)	90	55	125	198	209	132.2	42.5
Aircraft and associated equipment (792)	14	15	13	32	55	292.9	11.2
Other meat and edible offal (012)	5	14	19	24	33	560.0	6.7
Iron and steel tubes, pipes and fittings (679)	10	2	10	9	21	110.0	4.3
Machinery and equipment specialized for particular industries (728)	10	19	15	11	18	80.0	3.7
Telecommunications equipment (764)	8	13	4	5	14	75.0	2.8
Hydrocarbons and specified derivatives (511)	1	0	7	5	13	1 200.0	2.6
Maize (not including sweet corn) unmilled (044)	1	6	1	9	10	900.0	2.0
Wheat and meslin, unmilled (041)	0	2	0	1	7	X	1.4
Metal structures and parts of iron, steel,or aluminum (691)	0	1	0	1	7	X	1.4
Estimated low value shipments (994)	4	3	4	5	7	75.0	1.4
All motor vehicles (781)	3	2	2	4	6	100.0	1.2
Vegetables, roots, tubers and other edible vegetable products (054)	4	8	5	6	6	50.0	1.2
Worn clothing and other worn textile articles (269)	2	3	3	5	6	200.0	1.2
Special transactions not classified by kind (931)	0	2	1	3	6	X	1.2
Measuring/checking/analyzing instruments (874)	4	8	4	3	5	25.0	1.0
Fixed vegetable fats and oils; crude (422)	1	6	0	4	4	300.0	0.8
Automatic data processing machines (752)	3	2	2	4	4	33.3	0.8
Internal combustion piston engines (713)	3	2	3	3	3	0.0	0.6
Special purpose motor vehicles (782)	2	1	1	1	3	50.0	0.6
IMPORTS							
Total	2 425	3 557	3 100	3 115	4 264	75.8	100.0
Food and live animals (0)	0	0	0	0	0	X	0.0
Beverages and tobacco (1)	0	0	0	0	0	X	X
Crude materials, inedible, except fuels (2)	0	0	0	0	0	X	0.0
Mineral fuels, lubricants and related materials (3)	2 414	3 544	3 093	3 107	4 238	75.6	99.4
Animal and vegetable oils, fats and waxes (4)	0	0	0	0	0	X	X
Chemicals and related products (5)	0	0	0	0	0	X	0.0
Manufactured goods classified chiefly by material (6)	9	7	0	0	21	133.3	0.5
Machinery and transport equipment (7)	0	0	0	3	0	X	0.0
Miscellaneous manufactured articles (8)	0	0	0	0	0	X	0.0
Commodities and transactions not classified elsewhere (9)	1	5	6	5	5	400.0	0.1
Top 20 Commodities	2 424	3 555	3 099	3 112	4 264	75.9	100.0
Crude oil (333)	2 346	3 391	2 990	2 991	4 105	75.0	96.3
Oil (not crude) (334)	68	152	103	116	133	95.6	3.1
Pearls, precious and semiprecious stones (667)	9	7	0	0	21	133.3	0.5
Special transactions not classified by kind (931)	1	5	6	5	5	400.0	0.1
Automatic data processing machines (752)	0	0	0	0	0	X	0.0
Works of art, collectors' pieces, and antiques (896)	0	0	0	0	0	X	0.0
Mechanical handling equipment (744)	0	0	0	0	0	X	0.0
Machine tools working by removing metal or other (731)	0	0	0	0	0	X	0.0
Jewelry, goldsmiths' and silversmiths' wares (897)	0	0	0	0	0	X	0.0
Telecommunications equipment (764)	0	0	0	0	0	X	0.0
Measuring/checking/analyzing instruments (874)	0	0	0	0	0	X	0.0
Musical instruments and accessories (898)	0	0	0	0	0	X	0.0
Photographic and cinematographic supplies (882)	0	0	0	0	0	X	0.0
Manufactures of base metal (699)	0	0	0	0	0	X	0.0
Aircraft and associated equipment (792)	0	0	0	0	0	X	0.0
Electrical machinery and apparatus (778)	0	0	0	0	0	X	0.0
Watches and clocks (885)	0	0	0	0	0	X	0.0
Pumps for liquids and liquid elevators (742)	0	0	0	0	0	X	0.0
Spices (075)	0	0	0	0	0	X	0.0
Television receivers (761)	0	0	0	0	0	X	0.0

X = Not applicable.

Table C-23. U.S. Trade by Commodity with Argentina, 1999–2003

(Millions of dollars; total exports, f.a.s.; general imports, Customs; top 20 commodities based on 2003 dollar value.)

Commodity and SITC code	1999	2000	2001	2002	2003	Percent change, 1999–2003	Percent share of total, 2003
EXPORTS							
Total	4 939	4 700	3 928	1 591	2 435	-50.7	100.0
Food and live animals (0)	88	76	67	29	23	-73.9	0.9
Beverages and tobacco (1)	6	5	4	2	3	-50.0	0.1
Crude materials, inedible, except fuels (2)	100	117	96	55	70	-30.0	2.9
Mineral fuels, lubricants and related materials (3)	23	49	24	19	26	13.0	1.1
Animal and vegetable oils, fats and waxes (4)	3	8	5	1	7	133.3	0.3
Chemicals and related products (5)	952	1 101	1 127	613	840	-11.8	34.5
Manufactured goods classified chiefly by material (6)	301	257	213	76	119	-60.5	4.9
Machinery and transport equipment (7)	2 849	2 484	1 871	603	1 057	-62.9	43.4
Miscellaneous manufactured articles (8)	447	432	379	131	210	-53.0	8.6
Commodities and transactions not classified elsewhere (9)	171	171	142	61	79	-53.8	3.2
Top 20 Commodities	2 822	2 657	2 240	868	1 370	-51.5	56.3
Parts for office machines and a.d.p. machines (759)	344	354	244	60	120	-65.1	4.9
Automatic data processing machines (752)	328	337	247	47	115	-64.9	4.7
Carboxylic acids, halides, and derivities (513)	62	43	73	102	113	82.3	4.6
Civil engineering and contractors' plant and equipment (723)	162	91	102	43	103	-36.4	4.2
Fertilizers (except crude) (562)	39	65	62	40	91	133.3	3.7
Telecommunications equipment (764)	551	529	313	47	89	-83.8	3.7
Pumps, air or gas compressors and fans (743)	108	60	98	94	71	-34.3	2.9
Estimated low value shipments (994)	143	140	120	49	69	-51.7	2.8
Measuring/checking/analyzing instruments (874)	115	119	119	32	68	-40.9	2.8
Organo-inorganic and heterocyclic compounds (515)	108	170	217	45	56	-48.1	2.3
Medicaments (including veterinary medicaments) (542)	72	83	75	44	56	-22.2	2.3
Parts and accessories of motor vehicles (784)	89	147	81	28	56	-37.1	2.3
Plastics (575)	63	62	53	39	55	-12.7	2.3
Aircraft and associated equipment (792)	364	117	110	36	53	-85.4	2.2
Nitrogen-function compounds (514)	55	99	79	40	49	-10.9	2.0
Alcohols, phenols, and halogenated derivatives (512)	24	28	33	37	46	91.7	1.9
Mechanical handling equipment (744)	64	77	62	26	42	-34.4	1.7
Pigments, paints, varnishes and related materials (533)	35	37	31	24	40	14.3	1.6
Agricultural machinery (excluding tractors) and parts (721)	39	37	38	5	40	2.6	1.6
Miscellaneous chemical products (598)	57	62	83	30	38	-33.3	1.6
IMPORTS							
Total	2 599	3 102	3 016	3 185	3 169	21.9	100.0
Food and live animals (0)	611	591	547	502	479	-21.6	15.1
Beverages and tobacco (1)	76	63	74	80	75	-1.3	2.4
Crude materials, inedible, except fuels (2)	93	96	69	75	67	-28.0	2.1
Mineral fuels, lubricants and related materials (3)	748	1 037	1 106	1 299	1 367	82.8	43.1
Animal and vegetable oils, fats and waxes (4)	17	21	14	25	25	47.1	0.8
Chemicals and related products (5)	141	156	154	161	216	53.2	6.8
Manufactured goods classified chiefly by material (6)	538	642	534	549	518	-3.7	16.3
Machinery and transport equipment (7)	110	120	112	143	146	32.7	4.6
Miscellaneous manufactured articles (8)	157	237	286	247	205	30.6	6.5
Commodities and transactions not classified elsewhere (9)	107	139	119	103	72	-32.7	2.3
Top 20 Commodities	1 747	2 285	2 304	2 472	2 411	38.0	76.1
Oil (not crude) (334)	270	460	590	588	682	152.6	21.5
Crude oil (333)	457	557	499	682	609	33.3	19.2
Furniture and bedding accessories (821)	105	183	224	189	141	34.3	4.4
Leather (611)	258	259	209	172	120	-53.5	3.8
Aluminum (684)	40	119	93	123	114	185.0	3.6
Fruit/vegetable juices, unfermented (59)	134	122	113	95	100	-25.4	3.2
Parts and accessories of motor vehicles (784)	38	35	43	54	65	71.1	2.1
Special transactions not classified by kind (931)	79	127	108	91	61	-22.8	1.9
Meat and edible offal, prepared or preserved (17)	74	66	70	56	55	-25.7	1.7
Fish, fresh, chilled or frozen (034)	72	69	58	51	54	-25.0	1.7
Fruit and nuts (not including oil nuts), fresh or dried (057)	46	57	71	50	48	4.3	1.5
Alcohols, phenols, and halogenated derivatives (512)	12	12	10	14	46	283.3	1.5
Iron and steel bars, rods, angles, shapes and section (676)	8	25	18	48	43	437.5	1.4
Iron and steel tubes, pipes and fittings (679)	10	40	45	36	43	330.0	1.4
Residual petroleum products (335)	20	21	17	30	43	115.0	1.4
Wood, simply worked (248)	18	15	16	39	41	127.8	1.3
Alcoholic beverages (112)	23	34	37	35	39	69.6	1.2
Sugar confectionery (62)	14	23	20	42	38	171.4	1.2
Tobacco, unmanufactured; tobacco refuse (121)	53	27	37	44	35	-34.0	1.1
Essential oils, perfume and flavor materials (551)	16	34	26	33	34	112.5	1.1

Table C-24. U.S. Trade by Commodity with Aruba, 1999–2003

(Millions of dollars; total exports, f.a.s.; general imports, Customs; top 20 commodities based on 2003 dollar value.)

Commodity and SITC code	1999	2000	2001	2002	2003	Percent change, 1999–2003	Percent share of total, 2003
EXPORTS							
Total	307	289	279	465	355	15.6	100.0
Food and live animals (0)	25	25	25	24	23	-8.0	6.5
Beverages and tobacco (1)	8	5	6	8	10	25.0	2.8
Crude materials, inedible, except fuels (2)	4	4	4	3	4	0.0	1.1
Mineral fuels, lubricants and related materials (3)	28	35	32	55	37	32.1	10.4
Animal and vegetable oils, fats and waxes (4)	1	1	1	1	1	0.0	0.3
Chemicals and related products (5)	26	26	16	15	18	-30.8	5.1
Manufactured goods classified chiefly by material (6)	28	24	20	27	31	10.7	8.7
Machinery and transport equipment (7)	113	82	107	226	117	3.5	33.0
Miscellaneous manufactured articles (8)	54	66	49	79	92	70.4	25.9
Commodities and transactions not classified elsewhere (9)	21	21	18	27	21	0.0	5.9
Top 20 Commodities	138	153	129	320	258	87.0	72.7
Jewelry, goldsmiths' and silversmiths' wares (897)	25	35	26	54	65	160.0	18.3
Oil (not crude) (334)	28	33	32	55	37	32.1	10.4
Civil engineering and contractors' plant and equipment (723)	3	3	0	124	35	1 066.7	9.9
Mechanical handling equipment (744)	5	3	2	3	28	460.0	7.9
Estimated low value shipments (994)	19	18	16	26	20	5.3	5.6
Telecommunications equipment (764)	3	14	11	8	10	233.3	2.8
Pearls, precious and semiprecious stones (667)	1	1	2	3	7	600.0	2.0
Alcoholic beverages (112)	3	3	4	5	7	133.3	2.0
All motor vehicles (781)	8	6	5	6	7	-12.5	2.0
Edible products and preparations, n.e.s. (098)	4	5	6	6	6	50.0	1.7
Perfumery, cosmetics or toilet preparations, excluding soaps (553)	5	6	6	5	5	0.0	1.4
Watches and clocks (885)	3	4	4	5	5	66.7	1.4
Automatic data processing machines (752)	5	3	3	4	5	0.0	1.4
Special purpose motor vehicles (782)	3	2	2	1	3	0.0	0.8
Furniture and bedding accessories (821)	5	3	2	2	3	-40.0	0.8
Metal structures and parts of iron, steel or aluminum (691)	2	2	1	3	3	50.0	0.8
Ships, boats, and floating structures (793)	1	1	1	2	3	200.0	0.8
Toys and sporting goods (894)	2	4	2	3	3	50.0	0.8
Miscellaneous chemical products (598)	10	3	1	2	3	-70.0	0.8
Medicaments (including veterinary medicaments) (542)	3	4	3	3	3	0.0	0.8
IMPORTS							
Total	675	1 511	1 052	771	964	42.8	100.0
Food and live animals (0)	0	0	1	0	0	X	0.0
Beverages and tobacco (1)	0	1	0	0	0	X	0.0
Crude materials, inedible, except fuels (2)	0	1	0	0	1	X	0.1
Mineral fuels, lubricants and related materials (3)	638	1 434	1 031	746	943	47.8	97.8
Animal and vegetable oils, fats and waxes (4)	0	0	0	0	0	X	0.0
Chemicals and related products (5)	0	0	0	7	0	X	0.0
Manufactured goods classified chiefly by material (6)	0	0	0	0	0	X	0.0
Machinery and transport equipment (7)	0	0	0	0	0	X	0.0
Miscellaneous manufactured articles (8)	0	1	0	0	0	X	0.0
Commodities and transactions not classified elsewhere (9)	37	73	20	18	20	-45.9	2.1
Top 20 Commodities	674	1 508	1 049	764	963	42.9	99.9
Oil (not crude) (334)	625	1 403	1 021	739	930	48.8	96.5
Gold, nonmonetary (971)	5	6	6	12	14	180.0	1.5
Residual petroleum products (335)	12	31	7	7	12	0.0	1.2
Special transactions not classified by kind (931)	30	62	10	3	3	-90.0	0.3
Estimate of low value import transactions (984)	2	5	4	3	3	50.0	0.3
Ferrous waste and scrap (282)	0	0	0	0	1	X	0.1
Thermionic, cold cathode, and photocathode valves (776)	0	0	0	0	0	X	0.0
Automatic data processing machines (752)	0	0	0	0	0	X	0.0
Crustaceans (036)	0	0	1	0	0	X	0.0
Jewelry, goldsmiths' and silversmiths' wares (897)	0	1	0	0	0	X	0.0
Miscellaneous chemical products (598)	0	0	0	0	0	X	0.0
Pumps for liquids and liquid elevators (742)	0	0	0	0	0	X	0.0
Sound and television recorders (763)	0	0	0	0	0	X	0.0
Nonelectric engines and motors (714)	0	0	0	0	0	X	0.0
Measuring/checking/analyzing instruments (874)	0	0	0	0	0	X	0.0
Paper and paperboard, cut to size or shape, and articles (642)	0	0	0	0	0	X	0.0
Works of art, collectors' pieces, and antiques (896)	0	0	0	0	0	X	0.0
Perfumery, cosmetics or toilet preparations, excluding soaps (553)	0	0	0	0	0	X	0.0
Motorcycles and cycles, motorized and not motorized (785)	0	0	0	0	0	X	0.0
Electrical machinery and apparatus (778)	0	0	0	0	0	X	0.0

X = Not applicable.

Table C-25. U.S. Trade by Commodity with Australia, 1999–2003

(Millions of dollars; total exports, f.a.s.; general imports, Customs; top 20 commodities based on 2003 dollar value.)

Commodity and SITC code	1999	2000	2001	2002	2003	Percent change, 1999–2003	Percent share of total, 2003
EXPORTS							
Total	11 811	12 460	10 945	13 084	13 104	10.9	100.0
Food and live animals (0)	264	270	238	275	519	96.6	4.0
Beverages and tobacco (1)	77	89	85	85	90	16.9	0.7
Crude materials, inedible, except fuels (2)	130	130	109	112	115	-11.5	0.9
Mineral fuels, lubricants and related materials (3)	132	127	140	161	134	1.5	1.0
Animal and vegetable oils, fats and waxes (4)	4	3	2	6	5	25.0	0.0
Chemicals and related products (5)	1 686	1 773	1 750	1 637	1 809	7.3	13.8
Manufactured goods classified chiefly by material (6)	772	724	660	706	749	-3.0	5.7
Machinery and transport equipment (7)	6 403	7 001	5 943	8 087	7 472	16.7	57.0
Miscellaneous manufactured articles (8)	1 528	1 638	1 484	1 462	1 567	2.6	12.0
Commodities and transactions not classified elsewhere (9)	813	705	534	553	645	-20.7	4.9
Top 20 Commodities	6 239	6 788	5 934	7 954	7 429	19.1	56.7
Aircraft and associated equipment (792)	1 204	1 182	989	3 149	2 228	85.0	17.0
Estimated low value shipments (994)	490	497	451	447	484	-1.2	3.7
Parts and accessories of motor vehicles (784)	380	516	435	412	475	25.0	3.6
Automatic data processing machines (752)	677	661	590	429	453	-33.1	3.5
Telecommunications equipment (764)	388	610	372	411	403	3.9	3.1
Medicaments (including veterinary medicaments) (542)	151	229	220	288	328	117.2	2.5
Civil engineering and contractors' plant and equipment (723)	334	326	393	332	318	-4.8	2.4
Internal combustion piston engines (713)	245	276	271	307	296	20.8	2.3
Measuring/checking/analyzing instruments (874)	280	256	294	259	291	3.9	2.2
All motor vehicles (781)	191	216	229	291	275	44.0	2.1
Medical instruments and appliances (872)	185	214	214	232	264	42.7	2.0
Live animals other than animals of division 03 (001)	15	8	7	7	203	1 253.3	1.5
Parts for office machines and a.d.p. machines (759)	447	581	340	227	201	-55.0	1.5
Nonelectric engines and motors (714)	262	204	248	223	195	-25.6	1.5
Fertilizers (except crude) (562)	240	193	207	186	192	-20.0	1.5
Printed matter (892)	211	188	166	170	174	-17.5	1.3
Agricultural machinery (excluding tractors) and parts (721)	166	211	149	190	174	4.8	1.3
Tractors (722)	112	119	108	130	159	42.0	1.2
Electrical machinery and apparatus (778)	168	185	145	142	158	-6.0	1.2
Special purpose motor vehicles (782)	93	116	106	122	158	69.9	1.2
IMPORTS							
Total	5 290	6 439	6 479	6 478	6 414	21.2	100.0
Food and live animals (0)	970	1 186	1 301	1 335	1 386	42.9	21.6
Beverages and tobacco (1)	206	283	349	462	628	204.9	9.8
Crude materials, inedible, except fuels (2)	717	909	724	636	475	-33.8	7.4
Mineral fuels, lubricants and related materials (3)	332	678	477	615	411	23.8	6.4
Animal and vegetable oils, fats and waxes (4)	2	4	4	6	7	250.0	0.1
Chemicals and related products (5)	358	358	442	367	526	46.9	8.2
Manufactured goods classified chiefly by material (6)	682	799	826	719	627	-8.1	9.8
Machinery and transport equipment (7)	969	1 115	1 122	1 118	1 020	5.3	15.9
Miscellaneous manufactured articles (8)	474	617	698	700	677	42.8	10.6
Commodities and transactions not classified elsewhere (9)	582	492	534	519	656	12.7	10.2
Top 20 Commodities	3 159	4 102	4 334	4 675	4 610	45.9	71.9
Meat of bovine animals (011)	504	667	870	878	882	75.0	13.8
Alcoholic beverages (112)	205	283	349	462	628	206.3	9.8
Special transactions not classified by kind (931)	438	426	473	459	591	34.9	9.2
Crude oil (333)	201	523	347	583	400	99.0	6.2
Other meat and edible offal (012)	118	155	177	192	252	113.6	3.9
Ores and concentrates of base metals (287)	129	192	167	212	202	56.6	3.1
Articles of apparel of textile fabrics (845)	120	159	195	222	193	60.8	3.0
Parts and accessories of motor vehicles (784)	150	161	124	151	175	16.7	2.7
Aluminum ores and concentrates (285)	428	493	327	272	167	-61.0	2.6
All motor vehicles (781)	138	236	279	311	141	2.2	2.2
Medicaments (including veterinary medicaments) (542)	40	49	147	121	121	202.5	1.9
Aircraft and associated equipment (792)	137	105	132	111	111	-19.0	1.7
Medical instruments and appliances (872)	45	63	68	91	109	142.2	1.7
Radioactive and associated materials (525)	68	59	26	38	107	57.4	1.7
Nickel (683)	77	136	121	77	101	31.2	1.6
Starches, inulin and wheat gluten; albuminoidal substances (592)	69	73	62	67	95	37.7	1.5
Measuring/checking/analyzing instruments (874)	70	114	127	121	95	35.7	1.5
Iron and nonalloy steel flat-roll products (673)	61	89	71	74	88	44.3	1.4
Pearls, precious and semiprecious stones (667)	66	72	80	91	79	19.7	1.2
Aluminum (684)	95	47	192	142	73	-23.2	1.1

Table C-26. U.S. Trade by Commodity with Austria, 1999–2003

(Millions of dollars; total exports, f.a.s.; general imports, Customs; top 20 commodities based on 2003 dollar value.)

Commodity and SITC code	1999	2000	2001	2002	2003	Percent change, 1999–2003	Percent share of total, 2003
EXPORTS							
Total	456	867	1 047	984	487	6.8	100.0
Food and live animals (0)	192	254	181	232	192	0.0	39.4
Beverages and tobacco (1)	0	0	0	0	0	X	0.0
Crude materials, inedible, except fuels (2)	3	7	15	16	5	66.7	1.0
Mineral fuels, lubricants and related materials (3)	14	14	16	17	20	42.9	4.1
Animal and vegetable oils, fats and waxes (4)	27	0	38	25	7	-74.1	1.4
Chemicals and related products (5)	10	11	11	22	24	140.0	4.9
Manufactured goods classified chiefly by material (6)	43	22	35	68	31	-27.9	6.4
Machinery and transport equipment (7)	157	538	727	576	187	19.1	38.4
Miscellaneous manufactured articles (8)	8	17	16	26	18	125.0	3.7
Commodities and transactions not classified elsewhere (9)	1	4	8	3	3	200.0	0.6
Top 20 Commodities	408	753	903	857	411	0.7	84.4
Maize (not including sweet corn) unmilled (044)	79	101	110	131	101	27.8	20.7
Civil engineering and contractors' plant and equipment (723)	73	67	105	81	68	-6.8	14.0
Wheat and meslin, unmilled (041)	67	87	20	44	41	-38.8	8.4
Feeding stuff for animals (081)	36	40	35	42	39	8.3	8.0
Aircraft and associated equipment (792)	14	268	265	363	27	92.9	5.5
Coal, pulverized or not (321)	14	13	12	16	20	42.9	4.1
Telecommunications equipment (764)	15	85	233	49	16	6.7	3.3
Nonelectric engines and motors (714)	12	21	12	4	14	16.7	2.9
Iron and steel tubes, pipes and fittings (679)	36	8	13	51	14	-61.1	2.9
Mechanical handling equipment (744)	6	13	6	9	13	116.7	2.7
Machinery and equipment specialized for particular industries (728)	10	4	6	6	13	30.0	2.7
Measuring/checking/analyzing instruments (874)	4	5	10	10	8	100.0	1.6
Plastics (575)	0	0	1	1	7	X	1.4
Fixed vegetable fats and oils (421)	27	0	38	25	7	-74.1	1.4
Fruit and nuts (not including oil nuts), fresh or dried (057)	0	0	0	1	5	X	1.0
Mineral manufactures (663)	1	5	4	4	4	300.0	0.8
Parts and accessories of motor vehicles (784)	3	3	6	3	4	33.3	0.8
Vegetables, roots, tubers and other edible vegetable products (054)	6	11	12	5	4	-33.3	0.8
Pumps, air or gas compressors and fans (743)	4	18	7	6	3	-25.0	0.6
Special purpose motor vehicles (782)	1	4	8	6	3	200.0	0.6
IMPORTS							
Total	1 831	2 724	2 694	2 365	4 753	159.6	100.0
Food and live animals (0)	1	0	0	0	0	X	0.0
Beverages and tobacco (1)	0	0	0	0	0	X	0.0
Crude materials, inedible, except fuels (2)	0	0	0	0	0	X	0.0
Mineral fuels, lubricants and related materials (3)	1 768	2 716	2 655	2 354	4 692	165.4	98.7
Animal and vegetable oils, fats and waxes (4)	0	0	0	0	0	X	0.0
Chemicals and related products (5)	16	6	19	4	27	68.8	0.6
Manufactured goods classified chiefly by material (6)	0	0	3	3	0	X	0.0
Machinery and transport equipment (7)	0	0	16	0	0	X	0.0
Miscellaneous manufactured articles (8)	0	0	0	0	0	X	0.0
Commodities and transactions not classified elsewhere (9)	45	2	2	4	33	-26.7	0.7
Top 20 Commodities	1 787	2 684	2 677	2 351	4 752	165.9	100.0
Crude oil (333)	104	0	517	1 250	2 858	2 648.1	60.1
Oil (not crude) (334)	1 459	2 403	1 717	863	1 233	-15.5	25.9
Liquefied propane and butane (342)	71	160	232	141	343	383.1	7.2
Natural gas, whether or not liquefied (343)	134	114	186	89	255	90.3	5.4
Special transactions not classified by kind (931)	3	1	2	4	33	1 000.0	0.7
Fertilizers (except crude) (562)	0	0	10	4	14	X	0.3
Hydrocarbons and specified derivatives (511)	16	6	10	0	13	-18.8	0.3
Petroleum gases and other gaseous hydrocarbons (344)	0	0	0	0	3	X	0.1
Fruit and nuts (not including oil nuts), fresh or dried (057)	0	0	0	0	0	X	0.0
Trailers and semi-trailers (786)	0	0	0	0	0	X	0.0
Works of art, collectors' pieces, and antiques (896)	0	0	0	0	0	X	0.0
Estimate of low value import transactions (984)	0	0	0	0	0	X	0.0
Automatic data processing machines (752)	0	0	0	0	0	X	0.0
Alcoholic beverages (112)	0	0	0	0	0	X	0.0
Rotating electric plant and parts (716)	0	0	0	0	0	X	0.0
Electrical machinery and apparatus (778)	0	0	0	0	0	X	0.0
Nonelectric engines and motors (714)	0	0	0	0	0	X	0.0
Telecommunications equipment (764)	0	0	0	0	0	X	0.0
Iron and steel tubes, pipes and fittings (679)	0	0	3	0	0	X	0.0
Miscellaneous manufactured articles (899)	0	0	0	0	0	X	0.0

X = Not applicable.

Table C-27. U.S. Trade by Commodity with Bahamas, 1999–2003

(Millions of dollars; total exports, f.a.s.; general imports, Customs; top 20 commodities based on 2003 dollar value.)

Commodity and SITC code	1999	2000	2001	2002	2003	Percent change, 1999–2003	Percent share of total, 2003
EXPORTS							
Total	844	1 065	1 022	975	1 084	28.4	100.0
Food and live animals (0)	98	108	120	119	117	19.4	10.8
Beverages and tobacco (1)	17	15	14	13	18	5.9	1.7
Crude materials, inedible, except fuels (2)	35	41	28	31	29	-17.1	2.7
Mineral fuels, lubricants and related materials (3)	40	73	98	169	253	532.5	23.3
Animal and vegetable oils, fats and waxes (4)	2	2	2	2	3	50.0	0.3
Chemicals and related products (5)	60	75	73	77	65	8.3	6.0
Manufactured goods classified chiefly by material (6)	122	147	131	125	110	-9.8	10.1
Machinery and transport equipment (7)	271	349	328	217	238	-12.2	22.0
Miscellaneous manufactured articles (8)	99	118	110	102	118	19.2	10.9
Commodities and transactions not classified elsewhere (9)	99	137	119	120	132	33.3	12.2
Top 20 Commodities	406	552	561	545	653	60.8	60.2
Oil (not crude) (334)	36	68	95	166	249	591.7	23.0
Estimated low value shipments (994)	81	105	97	99	110	35.8	10.1
All motor vehicles (781)	49	58	43	42	42	-14.3	3.9
Civil engineering and contractors' plant and equipment (723)	11	22	30	24	27	145.5	2.5
Telecommunications equipment (764)	21	21	22	24	23	9.5	2.1
Furniture and bedding accessories (821)	20	25	18	16	21	5.0	1.9
Edible products and preparations, n.e.s. (098)	24	30	29	25	18	-25.0	1.7
Hydrocarbons and specified derivatives (511)	14	19	22	19	16	14.3	1.5
Jewelry, goldsmiths' and silversmiths' wares (897)	19	19	17	14	15	-21.1	1.4
Vegetables, roots and tubers, prepared or preserved (56)	5	10	9	13	14	180.0	1.3
Exports not over $20,000 not identified by kind (992)	17	31	21	18	13	-23.5	1.2
Manufactures of base metal (699)	5	11	10	14	13	160.0	1.2
Paper and paperboard, cut to size or shape, and articles (642)	11	14	13	12	13	18.2	1.2
Other meat and edible offal (012)	17	8	10	10	12	-29.4	1.1
Articles of plastics (893)	7	10	9	12	12	71.4	1.1
Wood, simply worked (248)	18	17	12	12	12	-33.3	1.1
Ships, boats, and floating structures (793)	34	35	41	7	11	-67.6	1.0
Toys and sporting goods (894)	4	6	8	5	11	175.0	1.0
Meat of bovine animals (011)	4	4	10	10	11	175.0	1.0
Aircraft and associated equipment (792)	9	39	45	3	10	11.1	0.9
IMPORTS							
Total	195	275	313	458	479	145.6	100.0
Food and live animals (0)	49	63	49	57	67	36.7	14.0
Beverages and tobacco (1)	4	5	4	5	5	25.0	1.0
Crude materials, inedible, except fuels (2)	31	24	27	30	37	19.4	7.7
Mineral fuels, lubricants and related materials (3)	24	58	121	232	210	775.0	43.8
Animal and vegetable oils, fats and waxes (4)	0	0	0	0	1	X	0.2
Chemicals and related products (5)	64	86	84	69	88	37.5	18.4
Manufactured goods classified chiefly by material (6)	0	8	2	8	1	X	0.2
Machinery and transport equipment (7)	0	1	2	2	1	X	0.2
Miscellaneous manufactured articles (8)	1	3	2	2	2	100.0	0.4
Commodities and transactions not classified elsewhere (9)	21	27	23	54	69	228.6	14.4
Top 20 Commodities	162	239	289	443	479	195.7	100.0
Oil (not crude) (334)	24	58	111	232	210	775.0	43.8
Polymers of styrene (572)	36	53	67	64	84	133.3	17.5
Special transactions not classified by kind (931)	20	26	22	52	67	235.0	14.0
Crustaceans (036)	47	62	46	54	63	34.0	13.2
Stone, sand and gravel (273)	11	12	13	20	22	100.0	4.6
Crude minerals (278)	11	10	12	8	13	18.2	2.7
Alcoholic beverages (112)	4	4	3	3	5	25.0	1.0
Fruit and nuts (not including oil nuts), fresh or dried (057)	1	1	3	2	2	100.0	0.4
Medicinal products, except medicaments (541)	3	5	6	2	2	-33.3	0.4
Estimate of low value import transactions (984)	1	1	1	1	2	100.0	0.4
Medicaments (including veterinary medicaments) (542)	0	0	0	0	1	X	0.2
Toys and sporting goods (894)	1	2	2	1	1	0.0	0.2
Tobacco, manufactured (122)	0	1	0	1	1	X	0.2
Nonferrous base metal waste and scrap (288)	1	1	1	1	1	0.0	0.2
Metallic salts and peroxysalts of inorganic acids (523)	1	2	1	1	1	0.0	0.2
Fish, crustaceans and molluscs (37)	0	0	0	0	1	X	0.2
Crude animal materials (291)	1	1	1	1	1	0.0	0.2
Animal oils and fats (411)	0	0	0	0	1	X	0.2
Metal containers for storage or transport (692)	0	0	0	0	1	X	0.2
Fish, fresh, chilled or frozen (034)	0	0	0	0	0	X	0.0

X = Not applicable.

Table C-28. U.S. Trade by Commodity with Bahrain, 1999–2003

(Millions of dollars; total exports, f.a.s.; general imports, Customs; top 20 commodities based on 2003 dollar value.)

Commodity and SITC code	1999	2000	2001	2002	2003	Percent change, 1999–2003	Percent share of total, 2003
EXPORTS							
Total	348	449	433	419	509	46.3	100.0
Food and live animals (0)	14	10	22	18	12	-14.3	2.4
Beverages and tobacco (1)	10	9	8	6	6	-40.0	1.2
Crude materials, inedible, except fuels (2)	1	1	8	11	5	400.0	1.0
Mineral fuels, lubricants and related materials (3)	3	13	19	5	2	-33.3	0.4
Animal and vegetable oils, fats and waxes (4)	11	0	0	0	0	X	0.0
Chemicals and related products (5)	13	10	10	10	9	-30.8	1.8
Manufactured goods classified chiefly by material (6)	11	8	12	11	11	0.0	2.2
Machinery and transport equipment (7)	157	305	228	181	343	118.5	67.4
Miscellaneous manufactured articles (8)	63	41	62	84	47	-25.4	9.2
Commodities and transactions not classified elsewhere (9)	65	50	65	93	72	10.8	14.1
Top 20 Commodities	248	368	329	335	433	74.6	85.1
Aircraft and associated equipment (792)	38	223	104	75	243	539.5	47.7
Estimated low value shipments (994)	57	42	61	72	55	-3.5	10.8
All motor vehicles (781)	15	12	20	27	26	73.3	5.1
Special transactions not classified by kind (931)	7	8	3	20	17	142.9	3.3
Arms and ammunition (891)	38	19	29	58	12	-68.4	2.4
Measuring/checking/analyzing instruments (874)	5	7	13	7	11	120.0	2.2
Nonelectric engines and motors (714)	28	7	4	9	9	-67.9	1.8
Civil engineering and contractors' plant and equipment (723)	13	2	4	9	7	-46.2	1.4
Furniture and bedding accessories (821)	6	4	5	4	6	0.0	1.2
Telecommunications equipment (764)	6	6	3	3	6	0.0	1.2
Automatic data processing machines (752)	6	5	7	4	6	0.0	1.2
Heating and cooling equipment (741)	6	5	6	9	6	0.0	1.2
Tobacco, manufactured (122)	8	7	6	4	5	-37.5	1.0
Pumps, air or gas compressors and fans (743)	7	12	12	7	4	-42.9	0.8
Edible products and preparations, n.e.s. (098)	3	3	5	3	4	33.3	0.8
Cotton textile fibers (263)	0	0	6	10	4	X	0.8
Ships, boats, and floating structures (793)	0	2	33	8	4	X	0.8
Special purpose motor vehicles (782)	3	2	4	3	3	0.0	0.6
Musical instruments and accessories (898)	1	1	1	1	3	200.0	0.6
Iron and steel tubes, pipes and fittings (679)	1	1	3	2	2	100.0	0.4
IMPORTS							
Total	225	338	424	395	378	68.0	100.0
Food and live animals (0)	1	0	0	0	0	X	0.0
Beverages and tobacco (1)	0	0	0	0	0	X	0.0
Crude materials, inedible, except fuels (2)	0	0	0	0	4	X	1.1
Mineral fuels, lubricants and related materials (3)	6	11	20	0	5	-16.7	1.3
Animal and vegetable oils, fats and waxes (4)	0	0	0	0	0	X	0.0
Chemicals and related products (5)	20	49	67	41	56	180.0	14.8
Manufactured goods classified chiefly by material (6)	83	100	64	88	61	-26.5	16.1
Machinery and transport equipment (7)	2	2	0	0	0	X	0.0
Miscellaneous manufactured articles (8)	97	155	193	179	165	70.1	43.7
Commodities and transactions not classified elsewhere (9)	16	20	80	86	85	431.3	22.5
Top 20 Commodities	225	336	423	394	376	67.1	99.5
Women's or girls' coats, jackets, etc. not knit (842)	56	91	128	116	108	92.9	28.6
Special transactions not classified by kind (931)	16	19	79	85	85	431.3	22.5
Men's or boys' coats, jackets, etc. not knit (841)	24	43	35	49	52	116.7	13.8
Aluminum (684)	81	83	46	64	37	-54.3	9.8
Alcohols, phenols, and halogenated derivatives (512)	8	18	21	17	32	300.0	8.5
Fertilizers (except crude) (562)	12	30	46	25	24	100.0	6.3
Cotton fabrics, woven (652)	2	10	13	16	10	400.0	2.6
Made-up articles of textile materials (658)	0	0	1	1	9	X	2.4
Oil (not crude) (334)	6	11	20	0	5	-16.7	1.3
Fertilizer, crude (272)	0	0	0	0	4	X	1.1
Textile yarn (651)	1	8	4	5	4	300.0	1.1
Articles of apparel of textile fabrics (845)	14	19	18	7	3	-78.6	0.8
Estimate of low value import transactions (984)	0	1	1	1	1	X	0.3
Articles of plastics (893)	0	0	0	0	1	X	0.3
Women's or girls' coats, jackets, etc. knit (844)	2	1	2	1	1	-50.0	0.3
Men's or boys' coats, jackets, etc. knit (843)	2	2	6	5	0	X	0.0
Woven fabrics of manmade textile materials (653)	0	0	0	2	0	X	0.0
Jewelry, goldsmiths' and silversmiths' wares (897)	0	0	3	0	0	X	0.0
Crustaceans (036)	1	0	0	0	0	X	0.0
Lime, cement, and fabricated construction materials (661)	0	0	0	0	0	X	0.0

X = Not applicable.

Table C-29. U.S. Trade by Commodity with Bangladesh, 1999–2003

(Millions of dollars; total exports, f.a.s.; general imports, Customs; top 20 commodities based on 2003 dollar value.)

Commodity and SITC code	1999	2000	2001	2002	2003	Percent change, 1999–2003	Percent share of total, 2003
EXPORTS							
Total	275	239	308	269	227	-17.5	100.0
Food and live animals (0)	85	27	41	34	26	-69.4	11.5
Beverages and tobacco (1)	2	3	2	1	2	0.0	0.9
Crude materials, inedible, except fuels (2)	46	65	94	85	81	76.1	35.7
Mineral fuels, lubricants and related materials (3)	0	0	0	0	0	X	0.0
Animal and vegetable oils, fats and waxes (4)	2	2	16	25	0	X	0.0
Chemicals and related products (5)	45	21	39	27	29	-35.6	12.8
Manufactured goods classified chiefly by material (6)	23	26	26	16	15	-34.8	6.6
Machinery and transport equipment (7)	57	80	72	60	61	7.0	26.9
Miscellaneous manufactured articles (8)	11	11	13	18	11	0.0	4.8
Commodities and transactions not classified elsewhere (9)	4	3	4	3	3	-25.0	1.3
Top 20 Commodities	193	164	220	183	164	-15.0	72.2
Cotton textile fibers (263)	29	50	76	67	59	103.4	26.0
Pulp and waste paper (251)	7	6	8	8	14	100.0	6.2
Wheat and meslin, unmilled (041)	63	16	25	17	10	-84.1	4.4
Rotating electric plant and parts (716)	12	16	14	11	10	-16.7	4.4
Feeding stuff for animals (081)	1	1	10	9	8	700.0	3.5
Fertilizers (except crude) (562)	32	7	20	9	7	-78.1	3.1
Medicinal products, except medicaments (541)	2	5	7	7	7	250.0	3.1
Textile and leather machinery & pts (724)	2	5	6	7	7	250.0	3.1
Civil engineering and contractors' plant and equipment (723)	1	3	2	2	6	500.0	2.6
Aircraft and associated equipment (792)	11	22	3	6	5	-54.5	2.2
Mineral manufactures (663)	0	4	6	5	5	X	2.2
Telecommunications equipment (764)	8	9	19	7	5	-37.5	2.2
Crude animal materials (291)	6	5	7	6	5	-16.7	2.2
Measuring/checking/analyzing instruments (874)	3	5	5	11	4	33.3	1.8
Special yarns, special textile fabrics, etc. (657)	7	3	3	2	2	-71.4	0.9
Manmade fibers for spinning (267)	2	2	2	3	2	0.0	0.9
Electrical apparatus for switching or protecting elec. circuits (772)	1	1	1	1	2	100.0	0.9
Estimated low value shipments (994)	3	2	3	3	2	-33.3	0.9
Internal combustion piston engines (713)	1	1	1	1	2	100.0	0.9
Nonelectric engines and motors (714)	2	1	2	1	2	0.0	0.9
IMPORTS							
Total	1 918	2 418	2 359	2 134	2 074	8.1	100.0
Food and live animals (0)	115	149	95	90	86	-25.2	4.1
Beverages and tobacco (1)	0	0	0	0	1	X	0.0
Crude materials, inedible, except fuels (2)	1	1	0	1	0	X	0.0
Mineral fuels, lubricants and related materials (3)	0	0	7	0	0	X	0.0
Animal and vegetable oils, fats and waxes (4)	0	0	0	0	0	X	0.0
Chemicals and related products (5)	0	13	0	0	3	X	0.1
Manufactured goods classified chiefly by material (6)	88	98	116	121	115	30.7	5.5
Machinery and transport equipment (7)	0	1	0	2	0	X	0.0
Miscellaneous manufactured articles (8)	1 711	2 154	2 140	1 919	1 867	9.1	90.0
Commodities and transactions not classified elsewhere (9)	1	3	1	1	1	0.0	0.0
Top 20 Commodities	1 906	2 407	2 344	2 127	2 067	8.4	99.7
Men's or boys' coats, jackets, etc. not knit (841)	520	668	651	559	570	9.6	27.5
Women's or girls' coats, jackets, etc. not knit (842)	490	615	604	540	527	7.6	25.4
Articles of apparel of textile fabrics (845)	345	486	507	460	442	28.1	21.3
Women's or girls' coats, jackets, etc. knit (844)	95	94	103	115	129	35.8	6.2
Made-up articles of textile materials (658)	66	75	95	101	99	50.0	4.8
Apparel and accessories except textile; headgear (848)	153	176	173	130	91	-40.5	4.4
Men's or boys' coats, jackets, etc. knit (843)	69	72	59	80	88	27.5	4.2
Crustaceans (036)	112	146	92	88	82	-26.8	4.0
Toys and sporting goods (894)	14	14	13	12	8	-42.9	0.4
Textile yarn (651)	4	6	6	7	7	75.0	0.3
Articles of plastics (893)	0	1	1	5	6	X	0.3
Fertilizers (except crude) (562)	0	13	0	0	3	X	0.1
Pottery (666)	2	3	3	2	3	50.0	0.1
Clothing accessories (846)	6	7	5	3	3	-50.0	0.1
Trunks, suitcases, vanity cases, and briefcases (831)	17	18	20	14	2	-88.2	0.1
Fish, fresh, chilled or frozen (034)	2	2	2	2	2	0.0	0.1
Cotton fabrics, woven (652)	2	4	3	2	2	0.0	0.1
Fish, crustaceans and molluscs (37)	0	0	0	0	1	X	0.0
Woven fabrics of textile material, not cotton or manmade fibers (654)	8	6	6	6	1	-87.5	0.0
Furniture and bedding accessories (821)	1	1	1	1	1	0.0	0.0

X = Not applicable.

Table C-30. U.S. Trade by Commodity with Belgium, 1999–2003

(Millions of dollars; total exports, f.a.s.; general imports, Customs; top 20 commodities based on 2003 dollar value.)

Commodity and SITC code	1999	2000	2001	2002	2003	Percent change, 1999–2003	Percent share of total, 2003
EXPORTS							
Total	12 385	13 960	13 524	13 343	15 218	22.9	100.0
Food and live animals (0)	309	262	250	242	252	-18.4	1.7
Beverages and tobacco (1)	480	278	284	223	264	-45.0	1.7
Crude materials, inedible, except fuels (2)	786	926	824	745	760	-3.3	5.0
Mineral fuels, lubricants and related materials (3) ...	147	168	161	160	155	5.4	1.0
Animal and vegetable oils, fats and waxes (4)	9	7	4	3	4	-55.6	0.0
Chemicals and related products (5)	3 485	4 305	4 215	5 014	6 636	90.4	43.6
Manufactured goods classified chiefly by material (6) ...	1 600	2 053	2 095	2 016	2 235	39.7	14.7
Machinery and transport equipment (7)	4 235	4 559	4 205	3 625	3 457	-18.4	22.7
Miscellaneous manufactured articles (8)	1 092	1 149	1 196	1 020	1 151	5.4	7.6
Commodities and transactions not classified elsewhere (9) ...	243	251	290	295	303	24.7	2.0
Top 20 Commodities	5 575	6 956	7 054	7 479	9 082	62.9	59.7
Pearls, precious and semiprecious stones (667) ...	775	1 009	1 099	1 175	1 361	75.6	8.9
Organo-inorganic and heterocyclic compounds (515)	417	344	442	346	1 253	200.5	8.2
Medicaments (including veterinary medicaments) (542)	138	383	415	758	953	590.6	6.3
Medicinal products, except medicaments (541) ...	487	548	535	798	908	86.4	6.0
Plastics (575)	382	511	523	559	600	57.1	3.9
Medical instruments and appliances (872)	322	346	491	386	446	38.5	2.9
Miscellaneous chemical products (598)	235	327	323	363	406	72.8	2.7
Carboxylic acids, halides, and derivities (513) ...	123	141	142	235	360	192.7	2.4
Internal combustion piston engines (713)	237	312	259	314	311	31.2	2.0
Pigments, paints, varnishes and related materials (533)	195	231	166	251	302	54.9	2.0
Civil engineering and contractors' plant and equipment (723)	630	715	705	393	292	-53.7	1.9
Polymers of ethylene (571)	172	225	179	237	253	47.1	1.7
Parts and accessories of motor vehicles (784) ...	220	248	209	256	224	1.8	1.5
Nitrogen-function compounds (514)	209	212	172	190	220	5.3	1.4
Estimated low value shipments (994)	180	199	200	192	209	16.1	1.4
Aircraft and associated equipment (792)	206	495	439	249	205	-0.5	1.3
Synthetic rubber and reclaim rubber (232)	190	215	236	228	203	6.8	1.3
Nonelectric engines and motors (714)	183	201	190	264	197	7.7	1.3
Measuring/checking/analyzing instruments (874) ...	215	224	182	180	194	-9.8	1.3
Tobacco, unmanufactured; tobacco refuse (121) ...	59	70	147	105	185	213.6	1.2
IMPORTS							
Total	9 208	9 931	10 129	9 835	10 141	10.1	100.0
Food and live animals (0)	131	120	130	131	145	10.7	1.4
Beverages and tobacco (1)	19	41	27	29	35	84.2	0.3
Crude materials, inedible, except fuels (2)	73	86	65	64	61	-16.4	0.6
Mineral fuels, lubricants and related materials (3) ...	354	675	824	836	1 060	199.4	10.5
Animal and vegetable oils, fats and waxes (4)	2	3	3	3	8	300.0	0.1
Chemicals and related products (5)	1 812	1 544	1 995	1 972	1 828	0.9	18.0
Manufactured goods classified chiefly by material (6) ...	2 875	3 807	3 253	3 289	3 448	19.9	34.0
Machinery and transport equipment (7)	2 869	2 561	2 581	2 322	2 354	-18.0	23.2
Miscellaneous manufactured articles (8)	518	635	574	566	515	-0.6	5.1
Commodities and transactions not classified elsewhere (9) ...	556	459	677	624	687	23.6	6.8
Top 20 Commodities	6 707	7 206	7 647	7 475	7 856	17.1	77.5
Pearls, precious and semiprecious stones (667) ...	1 969	2 586	2 143	2 300	2 600	32.0	25.6
Oil (not crude) (334)	343	656	799	810	1 032	200.9	10.2
All motor vehicles (781)	1 294	910	1 077	983	946	-26.9	9.3
Special transactions not classified by kind (931) ...	487	393	606	556	619	27.1	6.1
Medicinal products, except medicaments (541) ...	378	356	435	343	422	11.6	4.2
Organo-inorganic and heterocyclic compounds (515)	718	385	670	724	413	-42.5	4.1
Medicaments (including veterinary medicaments) (542)	107	151	223	315	374	249.5	3.7
Photographic and cinematographic supplies (882) ...	206	260	206	197	207	0.5	2.0
Electrical machinery and apparatus (778)	114	111	116	143	166	45.6	1.6
Veneers, plywood and particle board (634)	4	6	44	81	138	3 350.0	1.4
Floor coverings (659)	93	96	99	108	119	28.0	1.2
Civil engineering and contractors' plant and equipment (723)	147	163	205	142	107	-27.2	1.1
Silver, platinum, and other platinum group metals (681)	165	396	373	229	99	-40.0	1.0
Trasmission shafts and cranks (748)	112	94	88	87	97	-13.4	1.0
Works of art, collectors' pieces, and antiques (896)	58	82	89	131	93	60.3	0.9
Perfumery, cosmetics or toilet preparations, excluding soaps (553)	80	79	77	77	90	12.5	0.9
Road motor vehicles (783)	175	166	142	38	87	-50.3	0.9
Automatic data processing machines (752)	92	112	79	73	85	-7.6	0.8
Pumps, air or gas compressors and fans (743) ...	93	117	95	77	83	-10.8	0.8
Nonelectric engines and motors (714)	72	87	81	61	79	9.7	0.8

Table C-31. U.S. Trade by Commodity with Brazil, 1999–2003

(Millions of dollars; total exports, f.a.s.; general imports, Customs; top 20 commodities based on 2003 dollar value.)

Commodity and SITC code	1999	2000	2001	2002	2003	Percent change, 1999–2003	Percent share of total, 2003
EXPORTS							
Total	13 249	15 360	15 929	12 409	11 218	-15.3	100.0
Food and live animals (0)	144	147	151	234	253	75.7	2.3
Beverages and tobacco (1)	6	9	6	7	4	-33.3	0.0
Crude materials, inedible, except fuels (2)	239	333	255	275	328	37.2	2.9
Mineral fuels, lubricants and related materials (3)	304	342	339	297	272	-10.5	2.4
Animal and vegetable oils, fats and waxes (4)	5	2	8	6	4	-20.0	0.0
Chemicals and related products (5)	2 538	2 853	2 957	2 647	2 799	10.3	25.0
Manufactured goods classified chiefly by material (6)	770	782	674	511	505	-34.4	4.5
Machinery and transport equipment (7)	7 851	9 201	9 995	7 154	6 050	-22.9	53.9
Miscellaneous manufactured articles (8)	1 085	1 361	1 194	1 017	762	-29.8	6.8
Commodities and transactions not classified elsewhere (9)	307	331	351	262	242	-21.2	2.2
Top 20 Commodities	8 184	9 397	9 652	7 379	6 532	-20.2	58.2
Aircraft and associated equipment (792)	955	760	1 569	1 235	736	-22.9	6.6
Nonelectric engines and motors (714)	750	955	1 327	1 032	734	-2.1	6.5
Thermionic, cold cathode, and photocathode valves (776)	697	1 181	895	656	658	-5.6	5.9
Parts for office machines and a.d.p. machines (759)	741	931	861	623	591	-20.2	5.3
Civil engineering and contractors' plant and equipment (723)	243	371	432	338	398	63.8	3.5
Telecommunications equipment (764)	1 299	1 396	915	518	389	-70.1	3.5
Automatic data processing machines (752)	746	906	765	423	371	-50.3	3.3
Parts and accessories of motor vehicles (784)	325	339	284	247	298	-8.3	2.7
Fertilizers (except crude) (562)	115	155	190	174	290	152.2	2.6
Organo-inorganic and heterocyclic compounds (515)	338	329	340	187	250	-26.0	2.2
Measuring/checking/analyzing instruments (874)	342	346	346	316	231	-32.5	2.1
Plastics (575)	175	180	169	208	213	21.7	1.9
Medicaments (including veterinary medicaments) (542)	204	213	159	199	204	0.0	1.8
Internal combustion piston engines (713)	82	114	158	182	187	128.0	1.7
Miscellaneous chemical products (598)	160	169	208	165	174	8.8	1.6
Electrical machinery and apparatus (778)	244	288	236	182	172	-29.5	1.5
Insecticides, disinfectants (591)	208	201	195	193	168	-19.2	1.5
Estimated low value shipments (994)	210	234	244	188	168	-20.0	1.5
Coal, pulverized or not (321)	175	159	180	166	157	-10.3	1.4
Electro-diagnostic apparatus (774)	175	170	179	147	143	-18.3	1.3
IMPORTS							
Total	11 314	13 855	14 462	15 812	17 884	58.1	100.0
Food and live animals (0)	1 319	1 082	904	1 054	1 377	4.4	7.7
Beverages and tobacco (1)	143	145	175	231	238	66.4	1.3
Crude materials, inedible, except fuels (2)	973	1 136	1 033	1 033	1 187	22.0	6.6
Mineral fuels, lubricants and related materials (3)	290	794	1 109	1 209	1 935	567.2	10.8
Animal and vegetable oils, fats and waxes (4)	16	16	17	16	12	-25.0	0.1
Chemicals and related products (5)	488	675	552	556	664	36.1	3.7
Manufactured goods classified chiefly by material (6)	2 463	2 920	2 638	3 218	3 508	42.4	19.6
Machinery and transport equipment (7)	3 569	4 299	5 524	5 986	6 178	73.1	34.5
Miscellaneous manufactured articles (8)	1 351	1 657	1 694	1 738	1 762	30.4	9.9
Commodities and transactions not classified elsewhere (9)	701	1 130	817	771	1 022	45.8	5.7
Top 20 Commodities	6 459	8 405	9 606	10 576	11 764	82.1	65.8
Aircraft and associated equipment (792)	1 204	1 474	1 950	1 847	1 845	53.2	10.3
Oil (not crude) (334)	268	687	973	645	1 144	326.9	6.4
Footwear (851)	961	1 151	1 155	1 084	1 047	8.9	5.9
Telecommunications equipment (764)	59	383	946	1 071	991	1 579.7	5.5
Special transactions not classified by kind (931)	377	729	528	563	827	119.4	4.6
Crude oil (333)	4	67	112	514	744	18 500.0	4.2
Internal combustion piston engines (713)	370	345	248	474	575	55.4	3.2
All motor vehicles (781)	2	166	625	622	546	27 200.0	3.1
Pig iron and iron and steel powders (671)	345	445	435	455	489	41.7	2.7
Parts and accessories of motor vehicles (784)	478	420	343	412	456	-4.6	2.5
Pulp and waste paper (251)	334	476	387	348	438	31.1	2.4
Wood, simply worked (248)	320	310	335	369	401	25.3	2.2
Iron or steel & semifinish products (672)	472	607	394	581	369	-21.8	2.1
Veneers, plywood and particle board (634)	146	153	151	208	320	119.2	1.8
Coffee and coffee substitutes (071)	512	293	194	230	308	-39.8	1.7
Pumps, air or gas compressors and fans (743)	234	240	230	304	307	31.2	1.7
Furniture and bedding accessories (821)	90	115	161	252	292	224.4	1.6
Lime, cement, and fabricated construction materials (661)	70	105	115	167	229	227.1	1.3
Tobacco, unmanufactured; tobacco refuse (121)	142	141	172	220	219	54.2	1.2
Wood manufactures (635)	71	98	152	210	217	205.6	1.2

Table C-32. U.S. Trade by Commodity with Cambodia, 1999–2003

(Millions of dollars; total exports, f.a.s.; general imports, Customs; top 20 commodities based on 2003 dollar value.)

Commodity and SITC code	1999	2000	2001	2002	2003	Percent change, 1999–2003	Percent share of total, 2003
EXPORTS							
Total	20	32	30	29	58	190.0	100.0
Food and live animals (0)	1	11	7	2	3	200.0	5.2
Beverages and tobacco (1)	1	1	0	0	1	0.0	1.7
Crude materials, inedible, except fuels (2)	4	6	4	5	4	0.0	6.9
Mineral fuels, lubricants and related materials (3)	0	0	0	0	0	X	0.0
Animal and vegetable oils, fats and waxes (4)	0	0	2	1	0	X	0.0
Chemicals and related products (5)	1	0	0	0	0	X	0.0
Manufactured goods classified chiefly by material (6)	0	3	1	2	3	X	5.2
Machinery and transport equipment (7)	6	8	11	14	42	600.0	72.4
Miscellaneous manufactured articles (8)	1	1	3	1	2	100.0	3.4
Commodities and transactions not classified elsewhere (9)	5	2	1	4	3	-40.0	5.2
Top 20 Commodities	13	18	16	22	49	276.9	84.5
Aircraft and associated equipment (792)	0	0	1	0	25	X	43.1
All motor vehicles (781)	3	3	5	8	9	200.0	15.5
Parts and accessories of motor vehicles (784)	0	1	3	3	4	X	6.9
Special transactions not classified by kind (931)	4	1	1	4	3	-25.0	5.2
Worn clothing and other worn textile articles (269)	4	5	3	4	2	-50.0	3.4
Cotton textile fibers (263)	0	0	0	1	2	X	3.4
Edible products and preparations, n.e.s. (098)	1	7	1	1	1	0.0	1.7
Cotton fabrics, woven (652)	0	0	0	0	1	X	1.7
Telecommunications equipment (764)	1	1	1	0	1	0.0	1.7
Fruit and nuts (not including oil nuts), fresh or dried (057)	0	0	0	1	1	X	1.7
Heating and cooling equipment (741)	0	0	0	0	0	X	0.0
Television receivers (761)	0	0	0	0	0	X	0.0
Toys and sporting goods (894)	0	0	0	0	0	X	0.0
Furniture and bedding accessories (821)	0	0	0	0	0	X	0.0
Medical instruments and appliances (872)	0	0	1	0	0	X	0.0
Leather (611)	0	0	0	0	0	X	0.0
Automatic data processing machines (752)	0	0	0	0	0	X	0.0
Alcoholic beverages (112)	0	0	0	0	0	X	0.0
Polyacetals and epoxide resins (574)	0	0	0	0	0	X	0.0
Vegetables, roots and tubers, prepared or preserved (56)	0	0	0	0	0	X	0.0
IMPORTS							
Total	592	826	963	1 071	1 263	113.3	100.0
Food and live animals (0)	1	1	0	1	1	0.0	0.1
Beverages and tobacco (1)	0	0	0	0	0	X	0.0
Crude materials, inedible, except fuels (2)	1	1	1	1	1	0.0	0.1
Mineral fuels, lubricants and related materials (3)	0	0	0	0	0	X	0.0
Animal and vegetable oils, fats and waxes (4)	0	0	0	0	0	X	0.0
Chemicals and related products (5)	0	0	0	0	0	X	0.0
Manufactured goods classified chiefly by material (6)	2	6	17	18	12	500.0	1.0
Machinery and transport equipment (7)	0	0	0	0	0	X	0.0
Miscellaneous manufactured articles (8)	588	816	943	1 050	1 247	112.1	98.7
Commodities and transactions not classified elsewhere (9)	1	2	1	1	2	100.0	0.2
Top 20 Commodities	592	823	961	1 070	1 262	113.2	99.9
Women's or girls' coats, jackets, etc. not knit (842)	109	225	275	334	445	308.3	35.2
Articles of apparel of textile fabrics (845)	189	244	290	260	248	31.2	19.6
Men's or boys' coats, jackets, etc. not knit (841)	210	235	198	222	246	17.1	19.5
Women's or girls' coats, jackets, etc. knit (844)	40	60	109	129	183	357.5	14.5
Men's or boys' coats, jackets, etc. knit (843)	32	35	46	80	107	234.4	8.5
Apparel and accessories except textile; headgear (848)	2	7	15	16	11	450.0	0.9
Made-up articles of textile materials (658)	1	3	12	12	9	800.0	0.7
Jewelry, goldsmiths' and silversmiths' wares (897)	1	2	4	3	3	200.0	0.2
Woven fabrics of manmade textile materials (653)	0	2	4	6	3	X	0.2
Articles of plastics (893)	0	0	0	1	3	X	0.2
Estimate of low value import transactions (984)	1	1	1	1	1	0.0	0.1
Works of art, collectors' pieces, and antiques (896)	1	2	1	1	1	0.0	0.1
Natural rubber in primary forms (231)	1	1	1	1	1	0.0	0.1
Fish, fresh, chilled or frozen (034)	1	1	0	1	1	0.0	0.1
Toys and sporting goods (894)	0	0	0	0	0	X	0.0
Special transactions not classified by kind (931)	0	1	0	0	0	X	0.0
Miscellaneous manufactured articles (899)	0	0	0	0	0	X	0.0
Clothing accessories (846)	4	2	3	1	0	X	0.0
Trunks, suitcases, vanity cases, and briefcases (831)	0	2	2	2	0	X	0.0
Fruit and nuts (not including oil nuts), fresh or dried (057)	0	0	0	0	0	X	0.0

X = Not applicable.

Table C-33. U.S. Trade by Commodity with Canada, 1999–2003

(Millions of dollars; total exports, f.a.s.; general imports, Customs; top 20 commodities based on 2003 dollar value.)

Commodity and SITC code	1999	2000	2001	2002	2003	Percent change, 1999–2003	Percent share of total, 2003
EXPORTS							
Total	163 913	176 430	163 724	160 799	169 481	3.4	100.0
Food and live animals (0)	7 271	7 683	8 077	8 585	9 244	27.1	5.5
Beverages and tobacco (1)	392	395	409	401	470	19.9	0.3
Crude materials, inedible, except fuels (2)	4 240	4 726	4 382	4 320	4 593	8.3	2.7
Mineral fuels, lubricants and related materials (3)	2 237	2 763	3 768	2 652	4 074	82.1	2.4
Animal and vegetable oils, fats and waxes (4)	187	201	183	214	273	46.0	0.2
Chemicals and related products (5)	14 825	16 151	15 857	16 344	17 891	20.7	10.6
Manufactured goods classified chiefly by material (6)	21 716	24 487	21 951	22 152	22 519	3.7	13.3
Machinery and transport equipment (7)	91 760	97 330	85 559	83 935	86 751	-5.5	51.2
Miscellaneous manufactured articles (8)	17 179	18 193	17 423	16 879	18 172	5.8	10.7
Commodities and transactions not classified elsewhere (9)	4 106	4 501	6 115	5 318	5 495	33.8	3.2
Top 20 Commodities	82 540	89 460	79 430	78 754	81 568	-1.2	48.1
Parts and accessories of motor vehicles (784)	17 354	16 986	15 169	16 507	16 222	-6.5	9.6
All motor vehicles (781)	9 509	9 508	8 900	10 463	11 078	16.5	6.5
Internal combustion piston engines (713)	7 471	7 449	6 595	6 399	6 469	-13.4	3.8
Special purpose motor vehicles (782)	4 033	4 445	3 946	4 651	5 684	40.9	3.4
Automatic data processing machines (752)	5 592	6 130	5 052	4 759	5 132	-8.2	3.0
Estimated low value shipments (994)	1 750	1 989	3 753	3 332	3 654	108.8	2.2
Telecommunications equipment (764)	3 915	5 092	4 256	3 530	3 609	-7.8	2.1
Measuring/checking/analyzing instruments (874)	3 253	3 575	3 404	3 157	3 301	1.5	1.9
Manufactures of base metal (699)	2 683	3 718	2 786	2 839	2 699	0.6	1.6
Electrical machinery and apparatus (778)	2 972	3 158	2 561	2 506	2 500	-15.9	1.5
Thermionic, cold cathode, and photocathode valves (776)	5 732	6 690	3 769	2 433	2 423	-57.7	1.4
Electrical apparatus for switching or protecting elec. circuits (772)	2 896	3 429	2 738	2 437	2 400	-17.1	1.4
Printed matter (892)	2 009	2 046	2 008	2 004	2 250	12.0	1.3
Furniture and bedding accessories (821)	2 383	2 592	2 280	2 136	2 174	-8.8	1.3
Paper and paperboard (641)	1 764	1 975	1 972	1 908	2 057	16.6	1.2
Articles of plastics (893)	1 761	1 870	1 901	1 959	2 053	16.6	1.2
Medicaments (including veterinary medicaments) (542)	1 317	1 655	1 633	1 755	2 035	54.5	1.2
Pumps, air or gas compressors and fans (743)	1 955	2 135	2 045	1 958	2 002	2.4	1.2
Parts for office machines and a.d.p. machines (759)	2 230	3 058	2 838	2 087	1 954	-12.4	1.2
Heating and cooling equipment (741)	1 961	1 960	1 824	1 934	1 872	-4.5	1.1
IMPORTS							
Total	198 324	229 209	216 969	210 590	224 166	13.0	100.0
Food and live animals (0)	8 387	9 247	10 419	11 016	10 971	30.8	4.9
Beverages and tobacco (1)	920	924	951	881	920	0.0	0.4
Crude materials, inedible, except fuels (2)	11 987	12 014	10 786	10 111	9 717	-18.9	4.3
Mineral fuels, lubricants and related materials (3)	17 214	31 483	34 258	29 592	41 378	140.4	18.5
Animal and vegetable oils, fats and waxes (4)	375	301	293	310	361	-3.7	0.2
Chemicals and related products (5)	10 012	11 579	12 001	12 108	13 492	34.8	6.0
Manufactured goods classified chiefly by material (6)	31 013	33 578	32 136	32 095	33 241	7.2	14.8
Machinery and transport equipment (7)	90 334	97 457	85 810	83 412	84 181	-6.8	37.6
Miscellaneous manufactured articles (8)	13 196	15 562	14 237	14 300	14 583	10.5	6.5
Commodities and transactions not classified elsewhere (9)	14 886	17 065	16 078	16 763	15 322	2.9	6.8
Top 20 Commodities	125 471	147 265	138 973	135 225	147 837	17.8	65.9
All motor vehicles (781)	34 282	34 178	30 827	31 264	30 799	-10.2	13.7
Natural gas, whether or not liquefied (343)	6 006	10 361	15 355	11 428	18 249	203.8	8.1
Crude oil (333)	6 570	12 715	10 146	11 225	14 196	116.1	6.3
Parts and accessories of motor vehicles (784)	9 339	9 758	8 975	10 001	10 902	16.7	4.9
Special transactions not classified by kind (931)	9 701	10 845	10 981	11 523	10 008	3.2	4.5
Special purpose motor vehicles (782)	9 217	9 365	8 846	9 162	9 075	-1.5	4.0
Paper and paperboard (641)	7 622	8 370	8 190	7 509	7 401	-2.9	3.3
Aircraft and associated equipment (792)	3 799	4 744	6 092	5 265	6 343	67.0	2.8
Oil (not crude) (334)	2 158	3 673	4 064	3 971	5 149	138.6	2.3
Wood, simply worked (248)	7 267	6 491	6 107	5 644	5 018	-30.9	2.2
Furniture and bedding accessories (821)	4 337	4 859	4 411	4 424	4 552	5.0	2.0
Aluminum (684)	3 434	3 757	3 816	3 693	4 136	20.4	1.8
Estimate of low value import transactions (984)	3 365	3 910	3 788	3 576	3 810	13.2	1.7
Internal combustion piston engines (713)	3 841	3 963	3 171	3 260	3 564	-7.2	1.6
Veneers, plywood and particle board (634)	2 453	2 312	2 107	2 225	3 157	28.7	1.4
Telecommunications equipment (764)	5 120	9 790	4 510	3 495	3 000	-41.4	1.3
Articles of plastics (893)	1 875	2 230	2 268	2 434	2 656	41.7	1.2
Pulp and waste paper (251)	2 154	2 754	2 116	1 884	1 983	-7.9	0.9
Polymers of ethylene (571)	1 197	1 499	1 581	1 501	1 957	63.5	0.9
Wood manufactures (635)	1 734	1 691	1 622	1 741	1 882	8.5	0.8

Table C-34. U.S. Trade by Commodity with Chile, 1999–2003

(Millions of dollars; total exports, f.a.s.; general imports, Customs; top 20 commodities based on 2003 dollar value.)

Commodity and SITC code	1999	2000	2001	2002	2003	Percent change, 1999–2003	Percent share of total, 2003
EXPORTS							
Total	12 385	13 960	13 524	13 343	15 218	22.9	100.0
Food and live animals (0)	309	262	250	242	252	-18.4	1.7
Beverages and tobacco (1)	480	278	284	223	264	-45.0	1.7
Crude materials, inedible, except fuels (2)	786	926	824	745	760	-3.3	5.0
Mineral fuels, lubricants and related materials (3)	147	168	161	160	155	5.4	1.0
Animal and vegetable oils, fats and waxes (4)	9	7	4	3	4	-55.6	0.0
Chemicals and related products (5)	3 485	4 305	4 215	5 014	6 636	90.4	43.6
Manufactured goods classified chiefly by material (6)	1 600	2 053	2 095	2 016	2 235	39.7	14.7
Machinery and transport equipment (7)	4 235	4 559	4 205	3 625	3 457	-18.4	22.7
Miscellaneous manufactured articles (8)	1 092	1 149	1 196	1 020	1 151	5.4	7.6
Commodities and transactions not classified elsewhere (9)	243	251	290	295	303	24.7	2.0
Top 20 Commodities	5 575	6 956	7 054	7 479	9 082	62.9	59.7
Pearls, precious and semiprecious stones (667)	775	1 009	1 099	1 175	1 361	75.6	8.9
Organo-inorganic and heterocyclic compounds (515)	417	344	442	346	1 253	200.5	8.2
Medicaments (including veterinary medicaments) (542)	138	383	415	758	953	590.6	6.3
Medicinal products, except medicaments (541)	487	548	535	798	908	86.4	6.0
Plastics (575)	382	511	523	559	600	57.1	3.9
Medical instruments and appliances (872)	322	346	491	386	446	38.5	2.9
Miscellaneous chemical products (598)	235	327	323	363	406	72.8	2.7
Carboxylic acids, halides, and derivities (513)	123	141	142	235	360	192.7	2.4
Internal combustion piston engines (713)	237	312	259	314	311	31.2	2.0
Pigments, paints, varnishes and related materials (533)	195	231	166	251	302	54.9	2.0
Civil engineering and contractors' plant and equipment (723)	630	715	705	393	292	-53.7	1.9
Polymers of ethylene (571)	172	225	179	237	253	47.1	1.7
Parts and accessories of motor vehicles (784)	220	248	209	256	224	1.8	1.5
Nitrogen-function compounds (514)	209	212	172	190	220	5.3	1.4
Estimated low value shipments (994)	180	199	200	192	209	16.1	1.4
Aircraft and associated equipment (792)	206	495	439	249	205	-0.5	1.3
Synthetic rubber and reclaim rubber (232)	190	215	236	228	203	6.8	1.3
Nonelectric engines and motors (714)	183	201	190	264	197	7.7	1.3
Measuring/checking/analyzing instruments (874)	215	224	182	180	194	-9.8	1.3
Tobacco, unmanufactured; tobacco refuse (121)	59	70	147	105	185	213.6	1.2
IMPORTS							
Total	9 208	9 931	10 129	9 835	10 141	10.1	100.0
Food and live animals (0)	131	120	130	131	145	10.7	1.4
Beverages and tobacco (1)	19	41	27	29	35	84.2	0.3
Crude materials, inedible, except fuels (2)	73	86	65	64	61	-16.4	0.6
Mineral fuels, lubricants and related materials (3)	354	675	824	836	1 060	199.4	10.5
Animal and vegetable oils, fats and waxes (4)	2	3	3	3	8	300.0	0.1
Chemicals and related products (5)	1 812	1 544	1 995	1 972	1 828	0.9	18.0
Manufactured goods classified chiefly by material (6)	2 875	3 807	3 253	3 289	3 448	19.9	34.0
Machinery and transport equipment (7)	2 869	2 561	2 581	2 322	2 354	-18.0	23.2
Miscellaneous manufactured articles (8)	518	635	574	566	515	-0.6	5.1
Commodities and transactions not classified elsewhere (9)	556	459	677	624	687	23.6	6.8
Top 20 Commodities	6 707	7 206	7 647	7 475	7 856	17.1	77.5
Pearls, precious and semiprecious stones (667)	1 969	2 586	2 143	2 300	2 600	32.0	25.6
Oil (not crude) (334)	343	656	799	810	1 032	200.9	10.2
All motor vehicles (781)	1 294	910	1 077	983	946	-26.9	9.3
Special transactions not classified by kind (931)	487	393	606	556	619	27.1	6.1
Medicinal products, except medicaments (541)	378	356	435	343	422	11.6	4.2
Organo-inorganic and heterocyclic compounds (515)	718	385	670	724	413	-42.5	4.1
Medicaments (including veterinary medicaments) (542)	107	151	223	315	374	249.5	3.7
Photographic and cinematographic supplies (882)	206	260	206	197	207	0.5	2.0
Electrical machinery and apparatus (778)	114	111	116	143	166	45.6	1.6
Veneers, plywood and particle board (634)	4	6	44	81	138	3 350.0	1.4
Floor coverings (659)	93	96	99	108	119	28.0	1.2
Civil engineering and contractors' plant and equipment (723)	147	163	205	142	107	-27.2	1.1
Silver, platinum, and other platinum group metals (681)	165	396	373	229	99	-40.0	1.0
Trasmission shafts and cranks (748)	112	94	88	87	97	-13.4	1.0
Works of art, collectors' pieces, and antiques (896)	58	82	89	131	93	60.3	0.9
Perfumery, cosmetics or toilet preparations, excluding soaps (553)	80	79	77	77	90	12.5	0.9
Road motor vehicles (783)	175	166	142	38	87	-50.3	0.9
Automatic data processing machines (752)	92	112	79	73	85	-7.6	0.8
Pumps, air or gas compressors and fans (743)	93	117	95	77	83	-10.8	0.8
Nonelectric engines and motors (714)	72	87	81	61	79	9.7	0.8

Table C-35. U.S. Trade by Commodity with China, 1999–2003

(Millions of dollars; total exports, f.a.s.; general imports, Customs; top 20 commodities based on 2003 dollar value.)

Commodity and SITC code	1999	2000	2001	2002	2003	Percent change, 1999–2003	Percent share of total, 2003
EXPORTS							
Total	13 118	16 253	19 235	22 053	28 418	116.6	100.0
Food and live animals (0)	326	473	511	554	811	148.8	2.9
Beverages and tobacco (1)	11	5	6	6	12	9.1	0.0
Crude materials, inedible, except fuels (2)	1 178	2 567	3 146	3 336	6 860	482.3	24.1
Mineral fuels, lubricants and related materials (3)	123	60	93	94	133	8.1	0.5
Animal and vegetable oils, fats and waxes (4)	74	21	14	28	103	39.2	0.4
Chemicals and related products (5)	2 089	2 325	2 211	2 960	3 622	73.4	12.7
Manufactured goods classified chiefly by material (6)	901	1 272	1 107	1 310	2 005	122.5	7.1
Machinery and transport equipment (7)	7 149	8 068	10 285	11 778	12 546	75.5	44.1
Miscellaneous manufactured articles (8)	1 058	1 240	1 653	1 756	2 057	94.4	7.2
Commodities and transactions not classified elsewhere (9)	209	223	209	229	268	28.2	0.9
Top 20 Commodities	8 165	9 996	12 310	14 011	17 524	114.6	61.7
Oil seeds and oleaginous fruits (222)	354	1 020	1 014	890	2 832	700.0	10.0
Thermionic, cold cathode, and photocathode valves (776)	812	901	1 133	1 622	2 475	204.8	8.7
Aircraft and associated equipment (792)	2 317	1 691	2 448	3 428	2 451	5.8	8.6
Measuring/checking/analyzing instruments (874)	467	483	751	772	985	110.9	3.5
Telecommunications equipment (764)	548	781	1 159	1 026	844	54.0	3.0
Cotton textile fibers (263)	24	61	48	150	769	3 104.2	2.7
Nonferrous base metal waste and scrap (288)	144	331	439	459	740	413.9	2.6
Automatic data processing machines (752)	578	942	957	739	736	27.3	2.6
Ferrous waste and scrap (282)	97	218	424	455	685	606.2	2.4
Machinery and equipment specialized for particular industries (728)	231	365	456	620	646	179.7	2.3
Pulp and waste paper (251)	194	276	330	414	601	209.8	2.1
Parts for office machines and a.d.p. machines (759)	258	541	638	443	527	104.3	1.9
Fertilizers (except crude) (562)	932	666	420	667	459	-50.8	1.6
Heating and cooling equipment (741)	207	306	399	414	451	117.9	1.6
Hides and skins, raw (211)	96	233	398	390	444	362.5	1.6
Pumps, air or gas compressors and fans (743)	186	208	298	313	410	120.4	1.4
Plastics (575)	143	157	212	254	403	181.8	1.4
Electrical apparatus for switching or protecting elec. circuits (772)	145	264	252	307	360	148.3	1.3
Paper and paperboard (641)	290	321	264	326	359	23.8	1.3
Electrical machinery and apparatus (778)	142	231	270	322	347	144.4	1.2
IMPORTS							
Total	81 786	100 063	102 280	125 168	152 379	86.3	100.0
Food and live animals (0)	863	1 021	1 144	1 505	2 001	131.9	1.3
Beverages and tobacco (1)	19	33	40	48	35	84.2	0.0
Crude materials, inedible, except fuels (2)	511	614	595	634	773	51.3	0.5
Mineral fuels, lubricants and related materials (3)	248	730	387	416	451	81.9	0.3
Animal and vegetable oils, fats and waxes (4)	6	7	6	6	9	50.0	0.0
Chemicals and related products (5)	1 674	1 809	2 065	2 423	3 026	80.8	2.0
Manufactured goods classified chiefly by material (6)	8 315	10 287	10 804	13 374	16 217	95.0	10.6
Machinery and transport equipment (7)	26 397	34 947	34 944	46 217	60 848	130.5	39.9
Miscellaneous manufactured articles (8)	42 819	49 475	51 068	59 136	67 210	57.0	44.1
Commodities and transactions not classified elsewhere (9)	933	1 139	1 228	1 408	1 808	93.8	1.2
Top 20 Commodities	58 221	70 555	72 892	89 854	108 205	85.9	71.0
Toys and sporting goods (894)	11 639	12 925	12 672	14 869	16 448	41.3	10.8
Automatic data processing machines (752)	4 116	6 310	5 961	9 145	15 268	270.9	10.0
Footwear (851)	8 434	9 195	9 758	10 227	10 565	25.3	6.9
Furniture and bedding accessories (821)	3 262	4 476	5 018	6 957	8 750	168.2	5.7
Telecommunications equipment (764)	3 434	4 579	4 690	6 401	7 922	130.7	5.2
Parts for office machines and a.d.p. machines (759)	3 208	3 843	4 052	5 216	6 560	104.5	4.3
Sound and television recorders (763)	1 754	2 585	3 065	4 488	5 327	203.7	3.5
Household type electrical and nonelectrical equipment (775)	1 836	2 380	2 802	3 232	3 774	105.6	2.5
Articles of plastics (893)	2 111	2 481	2 653	3 175	3 611	71.1	2.4
Articles of apparel of textile fabrics (845)	2 126	2 263	2 362	2 767	3 360	58.0	2.2
Trunks, suitcases, vanity cases, and briefcases (831)	1 972	2 210	2 172	2 773	3 320	68.4	2.2
Electrical machinery and apparatus (778)	1 560	2 040	2 295	2 703	3 135	101.0	2.1
Lighting fixtures and fittings (813)	2 052	2 524	2 340	2 887	3 081	50.1	2.0
Women's or girls' coats, jackets, etc. not knit (842)	2 158	2 335	2 403	2 469	3 003	39.2	2.0
Apparel and accessories except textile; headgear (848)	1 580	2 281	2 437	2 467	2 693	70.4	1.8
Miscellaneous manufactured articles (899)	1 986	2 070	2 177	2 377	2 552	28.5	1.7
Made-up articles of textile materials (658)	957	1 095	1 201	1 650	2 359	146.5	1.5
Household equipment of base metal (697)	876	1 199	1 398	1 868	2 259	157.9	1.5
Radio-broadcast receivers (762)	2 189	2 591	2 105	2 525	2 242	2.4	1.5
Manufactures of base metal (699)	971	1 173	1 331	1 658	1 976	103.5	1.3

Table C-36. U.S. Trade by Commodity with Colombia, 1999–2003

(Millions of dollars; total exports, f.a.s.; and general imports, Customs; top 20 commodities based on 2003 dollar value.)

Commodity and SITC code	1999	2000	2001	2002	2003	Percent change, 1999–2003	Percent share of total, 2003
EXPORTS							
Total	3 532	3 689	3 606	3 589	3 755	6.3	100.0
Food and live animals (0)	354	333	347	399	387	9.3	10.3
Beverages and tobacco (1)	7	2	2	2	1	-85.7	0.0
Crude materials, inedible, except fuels (2)	101	135	134	156	164	62.4	4.4
Mineral fuels, lubricants and related materials (3)	23	33	21	29	54	134.8	1.4
Animal and vegetable oils, fats and waxes (4)	32	14	19	19	15	-53.1	0.4
Chemicals and related products (5)	747	873	814	883	966	29.3	25.7
Manufactured goods classified chiefly by material (6)	305	325	303	279	324	6.2	8.6
Machinery and transport equipment (7)	1 496	1 505	1 545	1 406	1 420	-5.1	37.8
Miscellaneous manufactured articles (8)	354	350	303	305	316	-10.7	8.4
Commodities and transactions not classified elsewhere (9)	112	120	117	111	108	-3.6	2.9
Top 20 Commodities	1 685	1 870	1 750	1 842	1 971	17.0	52.5
Hydrocarbons and specified derivatives (511)	142	218	136	192	254	78.9	6.8
Automatic data processing machines (752)	179	192	229	217	201	12.3	5.4
Telecommunications equipment (764)	177	215	219	169	187	5.6	5.0
Maize (not including sweet corn) unmilled (044)	150	161	152	183	173	15.3	4.6
Parts for office machines and a.d.p. machines (759)	104	106	87	109	132	26.9	3.5
Civil engineering and contractors' plant and equipment (723)	156	148	137	90	124	-20.5	3.3
Wheat and meslin, unmilled (041)	91	69	69	98	108	18.7	2.9
Aircraft and associated equipment (792)	133	140	100	188	94	-29.3	2.5
Estimated low value shipments (994)	78	80	79	74	80	2.6	2.1
Paper and paperboard (641)	66	68	68	62	71	7.6	1.9
Machinery and equipment specialized for particular industries (728)	88	78	95	64	68	-22.7	1.8
Plastics (575)	51	61	59	61	63	23.5	1.7
Mechanical handling equipment (744)	36	62	45	35	63	75.0	1.7
Polymers of ethylene (571)	53	60	41	48	60	13.2	1.6
Fertilizers (except crude) (562)	52	54	50	57	57	9.6	1.5
Oil (not crude) (334)	17	26	17	25	50	194.1	1.3
Pumps, air or gas compressors and fans (743)	24	25	31	35	49	104.2	1.3
Cotton textile fibers (263)	19	27	31	36	47	147.4	1.3
Organo-inorganic and heterocyclic compounds (515)	31	36	55	44	46	48.4	1.2
Measuring/checking/analyzing instruments (874)	38	44	50	55	44	15.8	1.2
IMPORTS							
Total	6 276	6 969	5 696	5 606	6 385	1.7	100.0
Food and live animals (0)	873	810	644	656	692	-20.7	10.8
Beverages and tobacco (1)	4	6	25	40	72	1 700.0	1.1
Crude materials, inedible, except fuels (2)	379	377	332	314	370	-2.4	5.8
Mineral fuels, lubricants and related materials (3)	3 493	4 100	3 248	3 173	3 209	-8.1	50.3
Animal and vegetable oils, fats and waxes (4)	0	0	1	2	3	X	0.0
Chemicals and related products (5)	330	334	272	112	101	-69.4	1.6
Manufactured goods classified chiefly by material (6)	285	309	296	334	381	33.7	6.0
Machinery and transport equipment (7)	13	26	40	33	36	176.9	0.6
Miscellaneous manufactured articles (8)	478	526	464	466	661	38.3	10.4
Commodities and transactions not classified elsewhere (9)	420	480	374	475	861	105.0	13.5
Top 20 Commodities	5 533	6 212	4 998	5 038	5 738	3.7	89.9
Crude oil (333)	2 950	3 402	2 416	2 401	2 239	-24.1	35.1
Oil (not crude) (334)	396	490	502	488	523	32.1	8.2
Gold, nonmonetary (971)	82	71	36	148	478	482.9	7.5
Coal, pulverized or not (321)	133	201	330	284	440	230.8	6.9
Coffee and coffee substitutes (071)	519	451	318	328	374	-27.9	5.9
Crude vegetable materials (292)	345	350	307	294	348	0.9	5.5
Estimate of low value import transactions (984)	272	322	266	246	285	4.8	4.5
Men's or boys' coats, jackets, etc. not knit (841)	139	157	134	131	195	40.3	3.1
Fruit and nuts (not including oil nuts), fresh or dried (057)	224	220	185	187	166	-25.9	2.6
Women's or girls' coats, jackets, etc. not knit (842)	68	85	83	90	108	58.8	1.7
Articles of apparel of textile fabrics (845)	82	98	79	61	108	31.7	1.7
Special transactions not classified by kind (931)	66	87	72	81	99	50.0	1.6
Lime, cement, and fabricated construction materials (661)	53	61	67	60	68	28.3	1.1
Tobacco, manufactured (122)	0	2	19	34	63	X	1.0
Pearls, precious and semiprecious stones (667)	65	70	60	71	55	-15.4	0.9
Plates, sheets, film, foil and strip of plastics (582)	37	35	32	39	46	24.3	0.7
Sugars, molasses, and honey (061)	30	40	31	36	46	53.3	0.7
Women's or girls' coats, jackets, etc. knit (844)	42	35	25	23	37	-11.9	0.6
Iron and steel tubes, pipes and fittings (679)	9	22	24	19	30	233.3	0.5
Men's or boys' coats, jackets, etc. knit (843)	21	13	12	17	30	42.9	0.5

X = Not applicable.

Table C-37. U.S. Trade by Commodity with Costa Rica, 1999–2003

(Millions of dollars; total exports, f.a.s.; general imports, Customs; top 20 commodities based on 2003 dollar value.)

Commodity and SITC code	1999	2000	2001	2002	2003	Percent change, 1999–2003	Percent share of total, 2003
EXPORTS							
Total	2 380	2 445	2 496	3 132	3 414	43.4	100.0
Food and live animals (0)	133	136	147	163	175	31.6	5.1
Beverages and tobacco (1)	3	2	2	2	1	-66.7	0.0
Crude materials, inedible, except fuels (2)	64	67	71	81	91	42.2	2.7
Mineral fuels, lubricants and related materials (3)	45	45	59	66	98	117.8	2.9
Animal and vegetable oils, fats and waxes (4)	5	4	5	6	7	40.0	0.2
Chemicals and related products (5)	221	264	295	321	383	73.3	11.2
Manufactured goods classified chiefly by material (6)	358	327	297	316	336	-6.1	9.8
Machinery and transport equipment (7)	818	814	879	1 449	1 631	99.4	47.8
Miscellaneous manufactured articles (8)	604	667	636	593	544	-9.9	15.9
Commodities and transactions not classified elsewhere (9)	129	119	106	135	147	14.0	4.3
Top 20 Commodities	1 129	1 282	1 388	1 978	2 292	103.0	67.1
Thermionic, cold cathode, and photocathode valves (776)	182	230	247	846	1 012	456.0	29.6
Estimated low value shipments (994)	96	100	101	122	131	36.5	3.8
Paper and paperboard (641)	130	115	108	97	113	-13.1	3.3
Measuring/checking/analyzing instruments (874)	47	63	80	91	102	117.0	3.0
Monofilaments of plastics (583)	2	39	52	72	93	4 550.0	2.7
Oil (not crude) (334)	43	42	55	63	89	107.0	2.6
Men's or boys' coats, jackets, etc. not knit (841)	120	130	90	92	85	-29.2	2.5
Telecommunications equipment (764)	59	40	76	46	82	39.0	2.4
Parts for office machines and a.d.p. machines (759)	45	49	63	71	77	71.1	2.3
Clothing accessories (846)	54	90	111	89	57	5.6	1.7
Maize (not including sweet corn) unmilled (044)	39	47	48	51	57	46.2	1.7
Oil seeds and oleaginous fruits (222)	33	37	38	49	52	57.6	1.5
Polymers of ethylene (571)	34	38	42	35	51	50.0	1.5
Automatic data processing machines (752)	48	59	64	52	48	0.0	1.4
Electrical apparatus for switching or protecting elec. circuits (772)	46	39	30	42	48	4.3	1.4
Electrical machinery and apparatus (778)	43	43	40	36	42	-2.3	1.2
Articles of plastics (893)	23	29	40	32	41	78.3	1.2
Medical instruments and appliances (872)	19	22	26	28	38	100.0	1.1
Miscellaneous manufactured articles (899)	12	12	15	21	38	216.7	1.1
Women's or girls' coats, jackets, etc. knit (844)	54	58	62	43	36	-33.3	1.1
IMPORTS							
Total	3 958	3 547	2 887	3 142	3 362	-15.1	100.0
Food and live animals (0)	851	849	844	839	879	3.3	26.1
Beverages and tobacco (1)	4	3	1	0	0	X	0.0
Crude materials, inedible, except fuels (2)	44	48	44	49	63	43.2	1.9
Mineral fuels, lubricants and related materials (3)	0	0	0	12	4	X	0.1
Animal and vegetable oils, fats and waxes (4)	0	0	0	0	0	X	0.0
Chemicals and related products (5)	37	44	27	28	31	-16.2	0.9
Manufactured goods classified chiefly by material (6)	111	105	88	100	102	-8.1	3.0
Machinery and transport equipment (7)	1 742	1 263	618	750	937	-46.2	27.9
Miscellaneous manufactured articles (8)	1 063	1 117	1 158	1 207	1 182	11.2	35.2
Commodities and transactions not classified elsewhere (9)	106	118	105	156	164	54.7	4.9
Top 20 Commodities	3 483	3 123	2 527	2 717	2 904	-16.6	86.4
Thermionic, cold cathode, and photocathode valves (776)	72	203	327	449	627	770.8	18.6
Fruit and nuts (not including oil nuts), fresh or dried (057)	505	481	506	475	508	0.6	15.1
Medical instruments and appliances (872)	85	186	280	336	434	410.6	12.9
Men's or boys' coats, jackets, etc. not knit (841)	280	290	235	193	164	-41.4	4.9
Coffee and coffee substitutes (071)	133	123	102	121	125	-6.0	3.7
Articles of apparel of textile fabrics (845)	158	163	166	162	116	-26.6	3.5
Special transactions not classified by kind (931)	53	72	69	114	116	118.9	3.5
Women's or girls' coats, jackets, etc. knit (844)	205	176	151	142	105	-48.8	3.1
Parts for office machines and a.d.p. machines (759)	1 468	832	104	108	100	-93.2	3.0
Electrical apparatus for switching or protecting elec. circuits (772)	57	81	57	68	78	36.8	2.3
Clothing accessories (846)	44	64	90	90	75	70.5	2.2
Men's or boys' coats, jackets, etc. knit (843)	64	69	72	70	69	7.8	2.1
Fish, fresh, chilled or frozen (034)	42	62	67	72	64	52.4	1.9
Women's or girls' coats, jackets, etc. not knit (842)	72	64	58	70	61	-15.3	1.8
Crude vegetable materials (292)	39	41	37	42	51	30.8	1.5
Vegetables, roots, tubers and other edible vegetable products (054)	45	46	52	49	46	2.2	1.4
Household type electrical and nonelectrical equipment (775)	60	52	53	46	45	-25.0	1.3
Estimate of low value import transactions (984)	47	42	32	36	42	-10.6	1.2
Articles of rubber (629)	34	34	34	35	40	17.6	1.2
Fruit/vegetable juices, unfermented (59)	20	42	35	39	38	90.0	1.1

X = Not applicable.

Table C-38. U.S. Trade by Commodity with Czech Republic, 1999–2003

(Millions of dollars; total exports, f.a.s.; general imports, Customs; top 20 commodities based on 2003 dollar value.)

Commodity and SITC code	1999	2000	2001	2002	2003	Percent change, 1999–2003	Percent share of total, 2003
EXPORTS							
Total	610	733	707	654	672	10.2	100.0
Food and live animals (0)	6	7	8	10	13	116.7	1.9
Beverages and tobacco (1)	37	40	32	13	14	-62.2	2.1
Crude materials, inedible, except fuels (2)	9	9	11	11	18	100.0	2.7
Mineral fuels, lubricants and related materials (3)	0	0	0	0	1	X	0.1
Animal and vegetable oils, fats and waxes (4)	0	0	0	0	0	X	0.0
Chemicals and related products (5)	39	37	35	35	37	-5.1	5.5
Manufactured goods classified chiefly by material (6)	39	39	35	29	47	20.5	7.0
Machinery and transport equipment (7)	362	474	451	411	385	6.4	57.3
Miscellaneous manufactured articles (8)	81	85	90	93	107	32.1	15.9
Commodities and transactions not classified elsewhere (9)	36	42	47	52	51	41.7	7.6
Top 20 Commodities	415	548	526	483	456	9.9	67.9
Parts for office machines and a.d.p. machines (759)	22	41	70	76	60	172.7	8.9
Aircraft and associated equipment (792)	124	178	140	106	49	-60.5	7.3
Thermionic, cold cathode, and photocathode valves (776)	16	28	29	57	43	168.8	6.4
Measuring/checking/analyzing instruments (874)	41	40	42	41	40	-2.4	6.0
Estimated low value shipments (994)	30	32	35	31	38	26.7	5.7
Telecommunications equipment (764)	25	25	27	28	33	32.0	4.9
Electrical machinery and apparatus (778)	12	13	10	18	27	125.0	4.0
Automatic data processing machines (752)	39	46	35	25	24	-38.5	3.6
Power generating machinery and parts (718)	0	1	29	1	20	X	3.0
Medical instruments and appliances (872)	7	10	14	16	20	185.7	3.0
Pumps, air or gas compressors and fans (743)	4	6	3	5	16	300.0	2.4
Electrical apparatus for switching or protecting elec. circuits (772)	10	28	11	7	13	30.0	1.9
Special transactions not classified by kind (931)	3	8	11	20	12	300.0	1.8
Pulp and waste paper (251)	7	7	8	8	11	57.1	1.6
Medicinal products, except medicaments (541)	8	7	10	7	11	37.5	1.6
Tobacco, manufactured (122)	35	38	29	9	10	-71.4	1.5
Electro-diagnostic apparatus (774)	5	5	5	7	8	60.0	1.2
Machinery and equipment specialized for particular industries (728)	17	23	6	7	7	-58.8	1.0
Heating and cooling equipment (741)	9	12	8	7	7	-22.2	1.0
Special yarns, special textile fabrics, etc. (657)	1	0	4	7	7	600.0	1.0
IMPORTS							
Total	754	1 071	1 120	1 232	1 394	84.9	100.0
Food and live animals (0)	5	6	10	11	16	220.0	1.1
Beverages and tobacco (1)	7	8	12	14	12	71.4	0.9
Crude materials, inedible, except fuels (2)	1	5	20	17	18	1 700.0	1.3
Mineral fuels, lubricants and related materials (3)	0	0	0	0	0	X	0.0
Animal and vegetable oils, fats and waxes (4)	0	0	0	0	0	X	0.0
Chemicals and related products (5)	68	79	82	101	100	47.1	7.2
Manufactured goods classified chiefly by material (6)	161	186	204	247	254	57.8	18.2
Machinery and transport equipment (7)	335	584	590	640	767	129.0	55.0
Miscellaneous manufactured articles (8)	154	166	159	166	180	16.9	12.9
Commodities and transactions not classified elsewhere (9)	23	35	44	36	47	104.3	3.4
Top 20 Commodities	387	587	576	658	817	111.1	58.6
Parts for office machines and a.d.p. machines (759)	3	9	44	101	123	4 000.0	8.8
Electrical machinery and apparatus (778)	105	212	89	74	93	-11.4	6.7
Pumps for liquids and liquid elevators (742)	6	13	38	61	73	1 116.7	5.2
Glassware (665)	61	69	70	65	67	9.8	4.8
Aircraft and associated equipment (792)	8	7	23	36	60	650.0	4.3
Parts and accessories of motor vehicles (784)	25	27	33	39	43	72.0	3.1
Internal combustion piston engines (713)	13	17	14	18	35	169.2	2.5
Iron and steel tubes, pipes and fittings (679)	6	11	14	11	31	416.7	2.2
Estimate of low value import transactions (984)	15	22	24	26	30	100.0	2.2
Iron and steel bars, rods, angles, shapes and section (676)	4	5	31	35	30	650.0	2.2
Textile and leather machinery and pts (724)	18	25	20	21	29	61.1	2.1
Made-up articles of textile materials (658)	17	20	16	21	25	47.1	1.8
Furniture and bedding accessories (821)	17	23	21	22	25	47.1	1.8
Toys and sporting goods (894)	21	20	21	18	23	9.5	1.6
Medical instruments and appliances (872)	6	4	8	16	23	283.3	1.6
Organo-inorganic and heterocyclic compounds (515)	4	6	8	23	22	450.0	1.6
Automatic data processing machines (752)	13	22	12	11	22	69.2	1.6
Electrical apparatus for switching or protecting elec. circuits (772)	13	36	40	23	22	69.2	1.6
Nonelectric engines and motors (714)	5	11	17	21	21	320.0	1.5
Machine tools working by removing metal or other (731)	27	28	33	16	20	-25.9	1.4

X = Not applicable.

Table C-39. U.S. Trade by Commodity with Denmark, 1999–2003

(Millions of dollars; total exports, f.a.s.; general imports, Customs; top 20 commodities based on 2003 dollar value.)

Commodity and SITC code	1999	2000	2001	2002	2003	Percent change, 1999–2003	Percent share of total, 2003
EXPORTS							
Total	1 719	1 513	1 611	1 496	1 548	-9.9	100.0
Food and live animals (0)	91	81	84	65	82	-9.9	5.3
Beverages and tobacco (1)	54	59	43	46	52	-3.7	3.4
Crude materials, inedible, except fuels (2)	38	37	39	50	54	42.1	3.5
Mineral fuels, lubricants and related materials (3)	3	5	5	5	13	333.3	0.8
Animal and vegetable oils, fats and waxes (4)	1	0	3	0	2	100.0	0.1
Chemicals and related products (5)	131	128	158	139	180	37.4	11.6
Manufactured goods classified chiefly by material (6)	71	77	65	65	80	12.7	5.2
Machinery and transport equipment (7)	1 035	807	858	758	757	-26.9	48.9
Miscellaneous manufactured articles (8)	220	248	245	283	241	9.5	15.6
Commodities and transactions not classified elsewhere (9)	75	70	112	85	88	17.3	5.7
Top 20 Commodities	1 130	940	1 059	951	931	-17.6	60.1
Aircraft and associated equipment (792)	426	191	259	228	172	-59.6	11.1
Automatic data processing machines (752)	88	76	62	76	80	-9.1	5.2
Measuring/checking/analyzing instruments (874)	49	75	72	62	61	24.5	3.9
Heating and cooling equipment (741)	33	33	38	29	54	63.6	3.5
Estimated low value shipments (994)	57	55	55	50	53	-7.0	3.4
Parts for office machines and a.d.p. machines (759)	53	42	43	49	50	-5.7	3.2
Medical instruments and appliances (872)	31	39	43	60	48	54.8	3.1
Telecommunications equipment (764)	57	69	92	64	45	-21.1	2.9
Medicaments (including veterinary medicaments) (542)	8	8	24	22	42	425.0	2.7
Tobacco, unmanufactured; tobacco refuse (121)	41	45	35	39	40	-2.4	2.6
Thermionic, cold cathode, and photocathode valves (776)	61	80	52	34	38	-37.7	2.5
Miscellaneous manufactured articles (899)	32	34	31	29	37	15.6	2.4
Machinery and equipment specialized for particular industries (728)	23	39	38	35	36	56.5	2.3
Special transactions not classified by kind (931)	11	9	55	34	35	218.2	2.3
Fruit and nuts (not including oil nuts), fresh or dried (057)	20	20	20	21	28	40.0	1.8
Electro-diagnostic apparatus (774)	17	22	26	23	25	47.1	1.6
Agricultural machinery (excluding tractors) and parts (721)	20	20	16	19	24	20.0	1.6
Electrical apparatus for switching or protecting elec. circuits (772)	40	33	33	28	21	-47.5	1.4
Organic chemicals (516)	23	18	34	25	21	-8.7	1.4
Feeding stuff for animals (081)	40	32	31	24	21	-47.5	1.4
IMPORTS							
Total	2 825	2 974	3 400	3 236	3 718	31.6	100.0
Food and live animals (0)	312	357	351	362	409	31.1	11.0
Beverages and tobacco (1)	10	14	15	18	26	160.0	0.7
Crude materials, inedible, except fuels (2)	73	67	79	69	53	-27.4	1.4
Mineral fuels, lubricants and related materials (3)	27	130	43	38	166	514.8	4.5
Animal and vegetable oils, fats and waxes (4)	0	0	0	0	1	X	0.0
Chemicals and related products (5)	453	532	652	785	969	113.9	26.1
Manufactured goods classified chiefly by material (6)	167	149	166	150	164	-1.8	4.4
Machinery and transport equipment (7)	921	855	1 191	908	1 087	18.0	29.2
Miscellaneous manufactured articles (8)	691	718	727	670	686	-0.7	18.5
Commodities and transactions not classified elsewhere (9)	171	152	175	236	158	-7.6	4.2
Top 20 Commodities	1 551	1 590	2 064	2 055	2 488	60.4	66.9
Medicinal products, except medicaments (541)	157	191	342	453	577	267.5	15.5
Rotating electric plant and parts (716)	184	57	406	158	289	57.1	7.8
Furniture and bedding accessories (821)	180	196	159	146	189	5.0	5.1
Other meat and edible offal (012)	104	142	144	134	157	51.0	4.2
Medicaments (including veterinary medicaments) (542)	14	43	39	76	127	807.1	3.4
Miscellaneous manufactured articles (899)	93	105	97	105	121	30.1	3.3
Crude oil (333)	0	77	0	28	114	X	3.1
Organic chemicals (516)	66	76	86	90	96	45.5	2.6
Toys and sporting goods (894)	150	84	127	141	94	-37.3	2.5
Estimate of low value import transactions (984)	66	71	83	76	89	34.8	2.4
Telecommunications equipment (764)	64	79	64	88	77	20.3	2.1
Measuring/checking/analyzing instruments (874)	61	68	68	70	75	23.0	2.0
Electro-diagnostic apparatus (774)	29	34	43	63	73	151.7	2.0
Medical instruments and appliances (872)	43	41	68	64	70	62.8	1.9
Special transactions not classified by kind (931)	105	81	92	159	69	-34.3	1.9
Cheese and curd (24)	54	52	51	57	67	24.1	1.8
Heating and cooling equipment (741)	66	55	52	51	54	-18.2	1.5
Cereal preparations (48)	54	55	63	56	52	-3.7	1.4
Oil (not crude) (334)	27	53	43	8	50	85.2	1.3
Pumps, air or gas compressors and fans (743)	34	30	37	32	48	41.2	1.3

X = Not applicable.

Table C-40. U.S. Trade by Commodity with Dominican Republic, 1999–2003

(Millions of dollars; total exports, f.a.s.; general imports, Customs; top 20 commodities based on 2003 dollar value.)

Commodity and SITC code	1999	2000	2001	2002	2003	Percent change, 1999–2003	Percent share of total, 2003
EXPORTS							
Total	4 086	4 443	4 436	4 262	4 214	3.1	100.0
Food and live animals (0)	378	361	398	377	333	-11.9	7.9
Beverages and tobacco (1)	148	122	114	121	108	-27.0	2.6
Crude materials, inedible, except fuels (2)	85	81	87	113	123	44.7	2.9
Mineral fuels, lubricants and related materials (3)	58	141	113	107	365	529.3	8.7
Animal and vegetable oils, fats and waxes (4)	30	23	25	38	27	-10.0	0.6
Chemicals and related products (5)	209	248	317	348	319	52.6	7.6
Manufactured goods classified chiefly by material (6)	573	620	849	939	977	70.5	23.2
Machinery and transport equipment (7)	1 048	1 189	1 121	1 006	754	-28.1	17.9
Miscellaneous manufactured articles (8)	1 422	1 520	1 246	1 079	1 051	-26.1	24.9
Commodities and transactions not classified elsewhere (9)	135	138	167	135	157	16.3	3.7
Top 20 Commodities	2 086	2 276	2 194	2 238	2 462	18.0	58.4
Oil (not crude) (334)	52	127	106	98	343	559.6	8.1
Cotton fabrics, woven (652)	35	55	204	281	231	560.0	5.5
Articles of apparel of textile fabrics (845)	260	302	224	219	227	-12.7	5.4
Electrical apparatus for switching or protecting elec. circuits (772)	159	139	122	137	144	-9.4	3.4
Jewelry, goldsmiths' and silversmiths' wares (897)	56	51	98	124	142	153.6	3.4
Knitted or crocheted fabrics (655)	32	31	45	71	124	287.5	2.9
Men's or boys' coats, jackets, etc. not knit (841)	300	377	213	165	116	-61.3	2.8
Men's or boys' coats, jackets, etc. knit (843)	98	107	118	114	112	14.3	2.7
Telecommunications equipment (764)	139	184	188	125	111	-20.1	2.6
Maize (not including sweet corn) unmilled (044)	91	91	93	104	101	11.0	2.4
Woven fabrics of manmade textile materials (653)	7	15	66	81	97	1 285.7	2.3
Clothing accessories (846)	193	130	77	55	93	-51.8	2.2
Tulles, lace, embroidery, ribbons, trimmings, etc. (656)	57	79	84	97	89	56.1	2.1
Medical instruments and appliances (872)	100	97	92	90	88	-12.0	2.1
Estimated low value shipments (994)	85	93	92	88	87	2.4	2.1
Feeding stuff for animals (081)	64	77	84	81	83	29.7	2.0
Electrical machinery and apparatus (778)	104	98	85	94	79	-24.0	1.9
Articles of plastics (893)	50	56	60	60	73	46.0	1.7
Tobacco, unmanufactured; tobacco refuse (121)	138	106	94	94	64	-53.6	1.5
Paper and paperboard (641)	66	61	49	60	58	-12.1	1.4
IMPORTS							
Total	4 282	4 384	4 183	4 169	4 455	4.0	100.0
Food and live animals (0)	190	196	203	216	241	26.8	5.4
Beverages and tobacco (1)	227	233	233	231	233	2.6	5.2
Crude materials, inedible, except fuels (2)	17	24	28	26	30	76.5	0.7
Mineral fuels, lubricants and related materials (3)	0	0	2	0	1	X	0.0
Animal and vegetable oils, fats and waxes (4)	0	0	0	0	0	X	0.0
Chemicals and related products (5)	15	19	30	44	63	320.0	1.4
Manufactured goods classified chiefly by material (6)	114	153	128	186	234	105.3	5.3
Machinery and transport equipment (7)	359	380	309	330	395	10.0	8.9
Miscellaneous manufactured articles (8)	3 227	3 239	3 114	2 977	3 043	-5.7	68.3
Commodities and transactions not classified elsewhere (9)	132	140	136	159	216	63.6	4.8
Top 20 Commodities	3 869	3 950	3 744	3 717	3 965	2.5	89.0
Men's or boys' coats, jackets, etc. not knit (841)	834	912	881	870	849	1.8	19.1
Articles of apparel of textile fabrics (845)	665	625	549	539	537	-19.2	12.1
Medical instruments and appliances (872)	350	347	350	354	441	26.0	9.9
Men's or boys' coats, jackets, etc. knit (843)	208	197	210	267	295	41.8	6.6
Women's or girls' coats, jackets, etc. not knit (842)	353	415	371	275	225	-36.3	5.1
Jewelry, goldsmiths' and silversmiths' wares (897)	172	152	173	194	203	18.0	4.6
Electrical apparatus for switching or protecting elec. circuits (772)	250	205	175	188	201	-19.6	4.5
Tobacco, manufactured (122)	182	192	189	192	197	8.2	4.4
Footwear (851)	237	181	193	140	138	-41.8	3.1
Women's or girls' coats, jackets, etc. knit (844)	196	185	175	139	127	-35.2	2.9
Special transactions not classified by kind (931)	79	91	89	99	117	48.1	2.6
Sugars, molasses, and honey (061)	77	88	78	80	88	14.3	2.0
Electrical machinery and apparatus (778)	53	67	66	79	86	62.3	1.9
Articles of plastics (893)	25	30	50	61	78	212.0	1.8
Gold, nonmonetary (971)	30	25	24	36	71	136.7	1.6
Pig iron and iron and steel powders (671)	44	70	29	45	69	56.8	1.5
Clothing accessories (846)	51	56	40	44	66	29.4	1.5
Made-up articles of textile materials (658)	15	12	28	42	64	326.7	1.4
Electric power machinery, and parts (771)	30	85	46	36	58	93.3	1.3
Cocoa (072)	18	15	28	37	55	205.6	1.2

X = Not applicable.

Table C-41. U.S. Trade by Commodity with Ecuador, 1999–2003

(Millions of dollars; total exports, f.a.s.; general imports, Customs; top 20 commodities based on 2003 dollar value.)

Commodity and SITC code	1999	2000	2001	2002	2003	Percent change, 1999–2003	Percent share of total, 2003
EXPORTS							
Total	920	1 037	1 420	1 607	1 448	57.4	100.0
Food and live animals (0)	83	69	80	110	76	-8.4	5.2
Beverages and tobacco (1)	1	0	1	1	1	0.0	0.1
Crude materials, inedible, except fuels (2)	42	59	54	50	49	16.7	3.4
Mineral fuels, lubricants and related materials (3)	46	46	66	82	116	152.2	8.0
Animal and vegetable oils, fats and waxes (4)	2	4	1	2	1	-50.0	0.1
Chemicals and related products (5)	163	176	202	193	198	21.5	13.7
Manufactured goods classified chiefly by material (6)	174	192	204	196	168	-3.4	11.6
Machinery and transport equipment (7)	322	396	673	809	698	116.8	48.2
Miscellaneous manufactured articles (8)	50	55	98	107	91	82.0	6.3
Commodities and transactions not classified elsewhere (9)	36	41	41	56	50	38.9	3.5
Top 20 Commodities	479	560	760	850	854	78.3	59.0
Telecommunications equipment (764)	21	28	61	87	118	461.9	8.1
Civil engineering and contractors' plant and equipment (723)	80	105	130	203	115	43.8	7.9
Oil (not crude) (334)	42	37	66	68	115	173.8	7.9
Paper and paperboard (641)	122	126	111	99	91	-25.4	6.3
Automatic data processing machines (752)	25	40	63	62	65	160.0	4.5
Mechanical handling equipment (744)	18	29	63	46	41	127.8	2.8
Parts for office machines and a.d.p. machines (759)	10	14	21	32	33	230.0	2.3
Polymers of ethylene (571)	32	29	35	37	32	0.0	2.2
Estimated low value shipments (994)	26	24	31	37	32	23.1	2.2
Pumps, air or gas compressors and fans (743)	7	6	14	13	30	328.6	2.1
Cotton textile fibers (263)	9	26	21	18	24	166.7	1.7
Maize (not including sweet corn) unmilled (044)	21	13	14	30	23	9.5	1.6
Pumps for liquids and liquid elevators (742)	8	11	16	14	22	175.0	1.5
Parts and accessories of motor vehicles (784)	8	11	31	17	20	150.0	1.4
Heating and cooling equipment (741)	11	12	20	23	17	54.5	1.2
Electrical apparatus for switching or protecting elec. circuits (772)	5	6	10	12	17	240.0	1.2
Fertilizers (except crude) (562)	15	12	15	10	16	6.7	1.1
Rotating electric plant and parts (716)	6	15	9	12	15	150.0	1.0
Machinery and equipment specialized for particular industries (728)	7	8	18	16	14	100.0	1.0
Electrical machinery and apparatus (778)	6	8	11	14	14	133.3	1.0
IMPORTS							
Total	1 814	2 210	2 042	2 146	2 721	50.0	100.0
Food and live animals (0)	1 014	713	763	840	916	-9.7	33.7
Beverages and tobacco (1)	7	7	11	10	16	128.6	0.6
Crude materials, inedible, except fuels (2)	106	103	111	96	116	9.4	4.3
Mineral fuels, lubricants and related materials (3)	530	1 223	971	1 041	1 469	177.2	54.0
Animal and vegetable oils, fats and waxes (4)	0	0	0	0	0	X	0.0
Chemicals and related products (5)	2	9	3	4	2	0.0	0.1
Manufactured goods classified chiefly by material (6)	40	42	37	38	53	32.5	1.9
Machinery and transport equipment (7)	11	6	8	13	12	9.1	0.4
Miscellaneous manufactured articles (8)	43	50	59	48	47	9.3	1.7
Commodities and transactions not classified elsewhere (9)	61	58	78	55	91	49.2	3.3
Top 20 Commodities	1 736	2 126	1 964	2 072	2 639	52.0	97.0
Crude oil (333)	490	1 055	861	950	1 393	184.3	51.2
Fruit and nuts (not including oil nuts), fresh or dried (057)	331	264	274	309	300	-9.4	11.0
Crustaceans (036)	408	194	221	194	208	-49.0	7.6
Fish, crustaceans and molluscs (37)	89	86	91	148	157	76.4	5.8
Fish, fresh, chilled or frozen (034)	52	82	80	93	121	132.7	4.4
Crude vegetable materials (292)	92	89	100	88	106	15.2	3.9
Oil (not crude) (334)	40	166	110	91	74	85.0	2.7
Cocoa (072)	53	32	31	35	57	7.5	2.1
Estimate of low value import transactions (984)	30	37	35	35	45	50.0	1.7
Special transactions not classified by kind (931)	24	18	42	19	44	83.3	1.6
Veneers, plywood and particle board (634)	15	15	11	13	19	26.7	0.7
Wood manufactures (635)	16	14	14	14	18	12.5	0.7
Vegetables, roots, tubers and other edible vegetable products (054)	3	5	11	14	17	466.7	0.6
Fruit preserved and fruit preparations (58)	14	12	14	14	17	21.4	0.6
Sanitary, plumbing & heating fixtures (812)	4	7	11	12	15	275.0	0.6
Tobacco, unmanufactured; tobacco refuse (121)	7	6	9	9	15	114.3	0.6
Coffee and coffee substitutes (071)	43	15	13	9	10	-76.7	0.4
Vegetables, roots and tubers, prepared or preserved(56)	5	6	11	9	9	80.0	0.3
Jewelry, goldsmiths' and silversmiths' wares (897)	9	11	12	9	7	-22.2	0.3
Articles of apparel of textile fabrics (845)	11	12	13	7	7	-36.4	0.3

X = Not applicable.

Table C-42. U.S. Trade by Commodity with Egypt, 1999–2003

(Millions of dollars; total exports, f.a.s.; general imports, Customs; top 20 commodities based on 2003 dollar value.)

Commodity and SITC code	1999	2000	2001	2002	2003	Percent change, 1999–2003	Percent share of total, 2003
EXPORTS							
Total	3 025	3 329	3 778	2 866	2 660	-12.1	100.0
Food and live animals (0)	893	985	949	775	903	1.1	33.9
Beverages and tobacco (1)	118	20	2	4	3	-97.5	0.1
Crude materials, inedible, except fuels (2)	72	72	111	68	69	-4.2	2.6
Mineral fuels, lubricants and related materials (3)	28	46	47	41	66	135.7	2.5
Animal and vegetable oils, fats and waxes (4)	55	22	27	43	56	1.8	2.1
Chemicals and related products (5)	134	174	375	183	161	20.1	6.1
Manufactured goods classified chiefly by material (6)	97	96	94	137	112	15.5	4.2
Machinery and transport equipment (7)	1 085	1 402	1 667	1 162	919	-15.3	34.5
Miscellaneous manufactured articles (8)	485	452	404	392	323	-33.4	12.1
Commodities and transactions not classified elsewhere (9)	58	59	101	61	49	-15.5	1.8
Top 20 Commodities	2 007	2 464	2 597	2 151	2 029	1.1	76.3
Wheat and meslin, unmilled (041)	479	496	388	252	419	-12.5	15.8
Maize (not including sweet corn) unmilled (044)	283	345	398	385	363	28.3	13.6
Aircraft and associated equipment (792)	257	633	826	561	253	-1.6	9.5
Arms and ammunition (891)	329	350	273	314	236	-28.3	8.9
Civil engineering and contractors' plant and equipment (723)	102	80	80	110	112	9.8	4.2
Telecommunications equipment (764)	123	95	121	93	94	-23.6	3.5
Feeding stuff for animals (081)	31	88	107	90	75	141.9	2.8
Fixed vegetable fats and oils (421)	46	17	26	40	52	13.0	2.0
Heating and cooling equipment (741)	46	31	27	16	50	8.7	1.9
Special purpose motor vehicles (782)	23	15	10	27	49	113.0	1.8
Mechanical handling equipment (744)	35	39	42	37	45	28.6	1.7
Coal, pulverized or not (321)	15	33	23	17	40	166.7	1.5
Pumps, air or gas compressors and fans (743)	53	55	39	41	39	-26.4	1.5
Parts and accessories of motor vehicles (784)	29	18	18	18	38	31.0	1.4
Special transactions not classified by kind (931)	33	36	80	44	32	-3.0	1.2
Paper and paperboard (641)	24	23	22	24	31	29.2	1.2
Oil seeds and oleaginous fruits (222)	18	26	43	34	29	61.1	1.1
Residual petroleum products (335)	8	11	20	20	24	200.0	0.9
Nonelectric engines and motors (714)	28	44	10	8	24	-14.3	0.9
Measuring/checking/analyzing instruments (874)	45	29	44	20	24	-46.7	0.9
IMPORTS							
Total	617	888	879	1 352	1 144	85.4	100.0
Food and live animals (0)	12	15	15	17	14	16.7	1.2
Beverages and tobacco (1)	0	0	1	1	2	X	0.2
Crude materials, inedible, except fuels (2)	15	28	13	27	36	140.0	3.1
Mineral fuels, lubricants and related materials (3)	57	113	159	204	184	222.8	16.1
Animal and vegetable oils, fats and waxes (4)	0	0	0	0	0	X	0.0
Chemicals and related products (5)	11	23	63	37	74	572.7	6.5
Manufactured goods classified chiefly by material (6)	111	138	157	231	251	126.1	21.9
Machinery and transport equipment (7)	2	4	3	3	18	800.0	1.6
Miscellaneous manufactured articles (8)	377	453	431	382	424	12.5	37.1
Commodities and transactions not classified elsewhere (9)	32	113	37	450	141	340.6	12.3
Top 20 Commodities	554	800	804	1 278	1 058	91.0	92.5
Oil (not crude) (334)	36	111	104	189	148	311.1	12.9
Special transactions not classified by kind (931)	30	110	34	444	137	356.7	12.0
Men's or boys' coats, jackets, etc. not knit (841)	108	124	110	102	119	10.2	10.4
Women's or girls' coats, jackets, etc. not knit (842)	78	121	132	108	112	43.6	9.8
Articles of apparel of textile fabrics (845)	73	91	79	78	88	20.5	7.7
Floor coverings (659)	44	46	44	57	71	61.4	6.2
Fertilizers (except crude) (562)	8	20	53	12	49	512.5	4.3
Iron and steel bars, rods, angles, shapes and section (676)	5	8	12	34	45	800.0	3.9
Men's or boys' coats, jackets, etc. knit (843)	39	35	35	33	42	7.7	3.7
Made-up articles of textile materials (658)	18	23	28	31	40	122.2	3.5
Iron and nonalloy steel flat-roll products (673)	0	0	9	58	33	X	2.9
Textile yarn (651)	24	26	37	33	32	33.3	2.8
Cotton textile fibers (263)	7	19	4	19	24	242.9	2.1
Crude oil (333)	21	0	54	0	23	9.5	2.0
Inorganic chemical elements (522)	0	0	7	22	23	X	2.0
Women's or girls' coats, jackets, etc. knit (844)	30	31	28	26	21	-30.0	1.8
Furniture and bedding accessories (821)	20	21	19	16	17	-15.0	1.5
Electrical machinery and apparatus (778)	0	0	0	0	14	X	1.2
Works of art, collectors' pieces, and antiques (896)	13	14	15	8	12	-7.7	1.0
Liquefied propane and butane (342)	0	0	0	8	8	X	0.7

X = Not applicable.

Table C-43. U.S. Trade by Commodity with El Salvador, 1999–2003

(Millions of dollars; total exports, f.a.s.; general imports, Customs; top 20 commodities based on 2003 dollar value.)

Commodity and SITC code	1999	2000	2001	2002	2003	Percent change, 1999–2003	Percent share of total, 2003
EXPORTS							
Total	1 520	1 775	1 771	1 665	1 824	20.0	100.0
Food and live animals (0)	153	166	191	168	181	18.3	9.9
Beverages and tobacco (1)	2	1	1	1	3	50.0	0.2
Crude materials, inedible, except fuels (2)	32	42	43	43	44	37.5	2.4
Mineral fuels, lubricants and related materials (3)	20	30	32	59	83	315.0	4.6
Animal and vegetable oils, fats and waxes (4)	33	22	19	25	25	-24.2	1.4
Chemicals and related products (5)	97	111	109	93	118	21.6	6.5
Manufactured goods classified chiefly by material (6)	156	207	404	448	509	226.3	27.9
Machinery and transport equipment (7)	377	294	300	284	352	-6.6	19.3
Miscellaneous manufactured articles (8)	580	793	553	439	385	-33.6	21.1
Commodities and transactions not classified elsewhere (9)	71	108	119	106	124	74.6	6.8
Top 20 Commodities	825	1 084	1 066	1 000	1 222	48.1	67.0
Knitted or crocheted fabrics (655)	9	18	81	153	266	2 855.6	14.6
Clothing accessories (846)	199	199	131	106	115	-42.2	6.3
Articles of apparel of textile fabrics (845)	139	290	180	127	99	-28.8	5.4
Oil (not crude) (334)	17	26	29	46	75	341.2	4.1
Estimated low value shipments (994)	56	65	65	61	67	19.6	3.7
Nonelectric engines and motors (714)	0	0	1	7	56	X	3.1
Special transactions not classified by kind (931)	7	36	53	41	53	657.1	2.9
Woven fabrics of manmade textile materials (653)	6	15	42	43	51	750.0	2.8
Maize (not including sweet corn) unmilled (044)	34	39	44	34	47	38.2	2.6
Telecommunications equipment (764)	101	69	51	36	45	-55.4	2.5
Electrical machinery and apparatus (778)	41	38	40	47	40	-2.4	2.2
Wheat and meslin, unmilled (041)	24	26	31	24	39	62.5	2.1
Women's or girls' coats, jackets, etc. knit (844)	38	66	58	47	38	0.0	2.1
Feeding stuff for animals (081)	28	33	37	33	38	35.7	2.1
Textile yarn (651)	6	20	44	40	36	500.0	2.0
Automatic data processing machines (752)	31	32	34	24	35	12.9	1.9
Paper and paperboard (641)	48	50	50	40	35	-27.1	1.9
Cotton fabrics, woven (652)	8	18	43	56	34	325.0	1.9
Cotton textile fibers (263)	14	22	24	18	27	92.9	1.5
Polymers of ethylene (571)	19	22	28	17	26	36.8	1.4
IMPORTS							
Total	1 605	1 933	1 882	1 982	2 019	25.8	100.0
Food and live animals (0)	124	181	100	78	108	-12.9	5.3
Beverages and tobacco (1)	1	3	4	4	6	500.0	0.3
Crude materials, inedible, except fuels (2)	5	7	4	5	6	20.0	0.3
Mineral fuels, lubricants and related materials (3)	0	6	0	0	0	X	0.0
Animal and vegetable oils, fats and waxes (4)	0	0	0	0	0	X	0.0
Chemicals and related products (5)	7	9	5	7	9	28.6	0.4
Manufactured goods classified chiefly by material (6)	47	50	54	87	66	40.4	3.3
Machinery and transport equipment (7)	31	34	39	28	24	-22.6	1.2
Miscellaneous manufactured articles (8)	1 346	1 623	1 656	1 697	1 750	30.0	86.7
Commodities and transactions not classified elsewhere (9)	43	19	19	76	52	20.9	2.6
Top 20 Commodities	1 562	1 877	1 835	1 934	1 978	26.6	98.0
Articles of apparel of textile fabrics (845)	528	667	677	729	804	52.3	39.8
Women's or girls' coats, jackets, etc. knit (844)	198	227	235	251	256	29.3	12.7
Men's or boys' coats, jackets, etc. not knit (841)	178	180	181	195	199	11.8	9.9
Men's or boys' coats, jackets, etc. knit (843)	161	231	238	226	199	23.6	9.9
Women's or girls' coats, jackets, etc. not knit (842)	162	204	213	154	145	-10.5	7.2
Clothing accessories (846)	101	94	90	120	118	16.8	5.8
Special transactions not classified by kind (931)	39	15	15	71	47	20.5	2.3
Coffee and coffee substitutes (071)	67	136	37	32	45	-32.8	2.2
Sugars, molasses, and honey (061)	24	18	33	24	37	54.2	1.8
Made-up articles of textile materials (658)	23	23	23	25	28	21.7	1.4
Electrical machinery and apparatus (778)	26	29	32	27	22	-15.4	1.1
Paper and paperboard, cut to size or shape, and articles (642)	5	7	12	28	20	300.0	1.0
Miscellaneous manufactured articles (899)	5	7	8	7	12	140.0	0.6
Alcohols, phenols, and halogenated derivatives (512)	6	8	4	6	8	33.3	0.4
Footwear (851)	4	5	7	6	8	100.0	0.4
Vegetables, roots, tubers and other edible vegetable products (054)	3	3	5	6	7	133.3	0.3
Crustaceans (036)	25	16	17	7	7	-72.0	0.3
Trunks, suitcases, vanity cases, and briefcases (831)	6	4	4	6	6	0.0	0.3
Alcoholic beverages (112)	1	3	4	4	5	400.0	0.2
Iron and nonalloy steel flat-roll products (673)	0	0	0	10	5	X	0.2

X = Not applicable.

Table C-44. U.S. Trade by Commodity with Equatorial Guinea, 1999–2003

(Millions of dollars; total exports, f.a.s.; general imports, Customs; top 20 commodities based on 2003 dollar value.)

Commodity and SITC code	1999	2000	2001	2002	2003	Percent change, 1999–2003	Percent share of total, 2003
EXPORTS							
Total	221	95	80	109	336	52.0	100.0
Food and live animals (0)	0	0	1	1	1	X	0.3
Beverages and tobacco (1)	0	0	0	0	0	X	0.0
Crude materials, inedible, except fuels (2)	0	0	0	0	0	X	0.0
Mineral fuels, lubricants and related materials (3)	0	0	1	0	1	X	0.3
Animal and vegetable oils, fats and waxes (4)	0	0	0	0	0	X	0.0
Chemicals and related products (5)	1	8	1	1	3	200.0	0.9
Manufactured goods classified chiefly by material (6)	39	11	11	15	42	7.7	12.5
Machinery and transport equipment (7)	174	72	63	86	271	55.7	80.7
Miscellaneous manufactured articles (8)	1	1	1	3	14	1 300.0	4.2
Commodities and transactions not classified elsewhere (9)	5	2	1	2	5	0.0	1.5
Top 20 Commodities	101	78	70	101	315	211.9	93.8
Civil engineering and contractors' plant and equipment (723)	60	57	53	70	141	135.0	42.0
Machinery and equipment specialized for particular industries (728)	0	1	2	3	46	X	13.7
Aircraft and associated equipment (792)	0	0	0	0	40	X	11.9
Iron and steel tubes, pipes and fittings (679)	5	3	8	10	22	340.0	6.5
Pumps, air or gas compressors and fans (743)	0	1	0	0	11	X	3.3
Prefabricated buildings (811)	0	0	0	0	8	X	2.4
Mechanical handling equipment (744)	0	1	2	5	7	X	2.1
Iron or steel and semifinish products (672)	0	0	0	0	5	X	1.5
Estimated low value shipments (994)	1	2	1	2	4	300.0	1.2
Taps, cocks, valves & similar appliances (747)	1	0	0	3	4	300.0	1.2
Manufactures of base metal (699)	2	1	0	0	4	100.0	1.2
Mineral manufactures (663)	0	2	2	3	4	X	1.2
Heating and cooling equipment (741)	0	1	2	2	3	X	0.9
Rotating electric plant and parts (716)	1	5	0	0	3	200.0	0.9
Metal structures and parts of iron, steel, or aluminum (691)	30	4	0	0	3	-90.0	0.9
Furniture and bedding accessories (821)	0	0	0	2	3	X	0.9
Pumps for liquids and liquid elevators (742)	1	0	0	1	2	100.0	0.6
Measuring/checking/analyzing instruments (874)	0	0	0	0	2	X	0.6
Electrical apparatus for switching or protecting elec. circuits (772)	0	0	0	0	2	X	0.6
Equipment for distributing electricity (773)	0	0	0	0	1	X	0.3
IMPORTS							
Total	43	155	445	520	904	2 002.3	100.0
Food and live animals (0)	0	0	0	0	0	X	0.0
Beverages and tobacco (1)	0	0	0	0	0	X	0.0
Crude materials, inedible, except fuels (2)	0	0	0	0	0	X	0.0
Mineral fuels, lubricants and related materials (3)	42	153	417	463	802	1 809.5	88.7
Animal and vegetable oils, fats and waxes (4)	0	0	0	0	0	X	0.0
Chemicals and related products (5)	0	0	25	52	94	X	10.4
Manufactured goods classified chiefly by material (6)	1	1	0	0	1	0.0	0.1
Machinery and transport equipment (7)	0	0	0	0	1	X	0.1
Miscellaneous manufactured articles (8)	0	0	0	1	0	X	0.0
Commodities and transactions not classified elsewhere (9)	1	1	3	5	7	600.0	0.8
Top 20 Commodities	43	156	445	520	904	2 002.3	100.0
Crude oil (333)	15	107	378	463	793	5 186.7	87.7
Alcohols, phenols, and halogenated derivatives (512)	0	0	25	52	94	X	10.4
Oil (not crude) (334)	27	46	39	0	8	-70.4	0.9
Estimate of low value import transactions (984)	0	1	1	2	3	X	0.3
Special transactions not classified by kind (931)	0	1	2	3	3	X	0.3
Liquefied propane and butane (342)	0	0	0	0	1	X	0.1
Mechanical handling equipment (744)	0	0	0	0	1	X	0.1
Veneers, plywood and particle board (634)	1	1	0	0	1	0.0	0.1
Wood, simply worked (248)	0	0	0	0	0	X	0.0
Coffee and coffee substitutes (071)	0	0	0	0	0	X	0.0
Live animals other than animals of division 03 (001)	0	0	0	0	0	X	0.0
Measuring/checking/analyzing instruments (874)	0	0	0	0	0	X	0.0
Gold, nonmonetary (971)	0	0	0	0	0	X	0.0
Taps, cocks, valves & similar appliances (747)	0	0	0	0	0	X	0.0
Electrical apparatus for switching or protecting elec. circuits (772)	0	0	0	0	0	X	0.0
Telecommunications equipment (764)	0	0	0	0	0	X	0.0
Automatic data processing machines (752)	0	0	0	0	0	X	0.0
Metal containers for storage or transport (692)	0	0	0	0	0	X	0.0
Musical instruments and accessories (898)	0	0	0	0	0	X	0.0
Hydrocarbons and specified derivatives (511)	0	0	0	0	0	X	0.0

X = Not applicable.

Table C-45. U.S. Trade by Commodity with Finland, 1999–2003

(Millions of dollars; total exports, f.a.s.; general imports, Customs; top 20 commodities based on 2003 dollar value.)

Commodity and SITC code	1999	2000	2001	2002	2003	Percent change, 1999–2003	Percent share of total, 2003
EXPORTS							
Total	1 668	1 571	1 554	1 537	1 714	2.8	100.0
Food and live animals (0)	48	33	27	29	29	-39.6	1.7
Beverages and tobacco (1)	21	19	15	9	10	-52.4	0.6
Crude materials, inedible, except fuels (2)	98	107	102	79	168	71.4	9.8
Mineral fuels, lubricants and related materials (3)	10	17	48	44	43	330.0	2.5
Animal and vegetable oils, fats and waxes (4)	0	0	0	0	0	X	0.0
Chemicals and related products (5)	90	80	79	67	88	-2.2	5.1
Manufactured goods classified chiefly by material (6)	62	65	66	64	69	11.3	4.0
Machinery and transport equipment (7)	1 049	921	901	961	989	-5.7	57.7
Miscellaneous manufactured articles (8)	195	246	231	197	212	8.7	12.4
Commodities and transactions not classified elsewhere (9)	94	82	84	87	106	12.8	6.2
Top 20 Commodities	1 089	995	987	1 063	1 192	9.5	69.5
All motor vehicles (781)	37	24	27	62	187	405.4	10.9
Telecommunications equipment (764)	114	174	154	136	105	-7.9	6.1
Aircraft and associated equipment (792)	311	124	102	188	93	-70.1	5.4
Estimated low value shipments (994)	80	74	78	66	78	-2.5	4.6
Ferrous waste and scrap (282)	0	0	0	4	74	X	4.3
Measuring/checking/analyzing instruments (874)	64	82	98	62	73	14.1	4.3
Automatic data processing machines (752)	95	109	98	62	72	-24.2	4.2
Thermionic, cold cathode, and photocathode valves (776)	96	138	115	122	68	-29.2	4.0
Parts for office machines and a.d.p. machines (759)	54	56	73	57	62	14.8	3.6
Crude minerals (278)	65	69	52	55	60	-7.7	3.5
Electrical apparatus for switching or protecting elec. circuits (772)	18	22	23	41	53	194.4	3.1
Special purpose motor vehicles (782)	4	1	1	14	46	1 050.0	2.7
Electrical machinery and apparatus (778)	32	45	31	49	39	21.9	2.3
Oil (not crude) (334)	1	2	41	36	30	2 900.0	1.8
Toys and sporting goods (894)	20	15	18	22	28	40.0	1.6
Nonelectrical machinery and tools (745)	15	13	21	18	27	80.0	1.6
Parts and accessories of motor vehicles (784)	12	8	9	12	27	125.0	1.6
Medical instruments and appliances (872)	20	19	21	21	24	20.0	1.4
Special transactions not classified by kind (931)	8	3	4	18	24	200.0	1.4
Electro-diagnostic apparatus (774)	43	17	21	18	22	-48.8	1.3
IMPORTS							
Total	2 910	3 250	3 394	3 444	3 598	23.6	100.0
Food and live animals (0)	47	39	67	71	68	44.7	1.9
Beverages and tobacco (1)	26	24	26	26	24	-7.7	0.7
Crude materials, inedible, except fuels (2)	33	36	66	76	88	166.7	2.4
Mineral fuels, lubricants and related materials (3)	137	288	163	276	261	90.5	7.3
Animal and vegetable oils, fats and waxes (4)	3	0	0	0	0	X	0.0
Chemicals and related products (5)	185	219	277	297	373	101.6	10.4
Manufactured goods classified chiefly by material (6)	923	985	901	927	1 124	21.8	31.2
Machinery and transport equipment (7)	1 263	1 396	1 621	1 538	1 374	8.8	38.2
Miscellaneous manufactured articles (8)	214	187	180	179	212	-0.9	5.9
Commodities and transactions not classified elsewhere (9)	80	74	92	54	73	-8.8	2.0
Top 20 Commodities	1 954	2 362	2 539	2 591	2 718	39.1	75.5
Paper and paperboard (641)	609	668	613	654	810	33.0	22.5
Telecommunications equipment (764)	129	157	305	487	475	268.2	13.2
Oil (not crude) (334)	136	288	163	275	259	90.4	7.2
Electro-diagnostic apparatus (774)	49	64	95	103	121	146.9	3.4
All motor vehicles (781)	406	468	447	301	114	-71.9	3.2
Medicaments (including veterinary medicaments) (542)	17	26	62	68	105	517.6	2.9
Measuring/checking/analyzing instruments (874)	98	108	108	105	102	4.1	2.8
Ships, boats, and floating structures (793)	11	15	12	92	89	709.1	2.5
Mechanical handling equipment (744)	66	75	60	62	87	31.8	2.4
Pulp and waste paper (251)	7	9	39	54	72	928.6	2.0
Civil engineering and contractors' plant and equipment (723)	60	65	51	61	66	10.0	1.8
Miscellaneous chemical products (598)	41	54	56	60	59	43.9	1.6
Electric power machinery, and parts (771)	81	58	54	53	57	-29.6	1.6
Nickel (683)	24	37	49	25	52	116.7	1.4
Paper mill and pulp mill machines (725)	50	83	192	41	51	2.0	1.4
Machinery and equipment specialized for particular industries (728)	73	92	97	53	45	-38.4	1.3
Special transactions not classified by kind (931)	55	46	63	24	42	-23.6	1.2
Organo-inorganic and heterocyclic compounds (515)	17	24	26	35	39	129.4	1.1
Rotating electric plant and parts (716)	14	21	31	15	37	164.3	1.0
Medicinal products, except medicaments (541)	11	4	16	23	36	227.3	1.0

X = Not applicable.

Table C-46. U.S. Trade by Commodity with France, 1999–2003

(Millions of dollars; total exports, f.a.s.; general imports, Customs; top 20 commodities based on 2003 dollar value.)

Commodity and SITC code	1999	2000	2001	2002	2003	Percent change, 1999–2003	Percent share of total, 2003
EXPORTS							
Total	18 838	20 253	19 896	19 019	17 068	-9.4	100.0
Food and live animals (0)	310	285	285	316	340	9.7	2.0
Beverages and tobacco (1)	46	41	56	73	58	26.1	0.3
Crude materials, inedible, except fuels (2)	335	371	371	333	330	-1.5	1.9
Mineral fuels, lubricants and related materials (3)	178	202	181	135	115	-35.4	0.7
Animal and vegetable oils, fats and waxes (4)	5	4	5	4	28	460.0	0.2
Chemicals and related products (5)	2 422	2 706	2 963	3 238	3 411	40.8	20.0
Manufactured goods classified chiefly by material (6)	953	1 040	1 179	841	847	-11.1	5.0
Machinery and transport equipment (7)	11 388	11 811	11 287	10 897	8 810	-22.6	51.6
Miscellaneous manufactured articles (8)	2 618	3 135	2 965	2 606	2 544	-2.8	14.9
Commodities and transactions not classified elsewhere (9)	584	657	605	575	586	0.3	3.4
Top 20 Commodities	12 864	13 458	13 521	13 573	11 594	-9.9	67.9
Nonelectric engines and motors (714)	2 662	2 861	3 100	2 914	2 371	-10.9	13.9
Aircraft and associated equipment (792)	2 774	1 822	2 166	2 849	1 541	-44.4	9.0
Medicaments (including veterinary medicaments) (542)	400	389	545	480	947	136.8	5.5
Measuring/checking/analyzing instruments (874)	811	1 017	880	759	864	6.5	5.1
Medicinal products, except medicaments (541)	562	724	887	1 123	853	51.8	5.0
Telecommunications equipment (764)	544	577	514	533	480	-11.8	2.8
Automatic data processing machines (752)	679	594	509	415	457	-32.7	2.7
Parts for office machines and a.d.p. machines (759)	676	789	680	555	455	-32.7	2.7
Estimated low value shipments (994)	466	519	516	461	436	-6.4	2.6
Thermionic, cold cathode, and photocathode valves (776)	733	1 077	621	464	430	-41.3	2.5
Electro-diagnostic apparatus (774)	307	295	378	405	417	35.8	2.4
Medical instruments and appliances (872)	486	397	478	425	380	-21.8	2.2
Miscellaneous chemical products (598)	249	284	248	251	297	19.3	1.7
Photographic and cinematographic supplies (882)	152	300	237	324	285	87.5	1.7
Pumps, air or gas compressors and fans (743)	250	321	318	275	284	13.6	1.7
Organo-inorganic and heterocyclic compounds (515)	287	315	271	370	282	-1.7	1.7
Parts and accessories of motor vehicles (784)	154	226	302	227	239	55.2	1.4
Works of art, collectors' pieces, and antiques (896)	206	310	313	267	205	-0.5	1.2
Electrical machinery and apparatus (778)	284	387	305	249	191	-32.7	1.1
Electrical apparatus for switching or protecting elec. circuits (772)	182	254	253	227	180	-1.1	1.1
IMPORTS							
Total	25 910	29 782	30 296	28 408	29 221	12.8	100.0
Food and live animals (0)	360	299	302	348	405	12.5	1.4
Beverages and tobacco (1)	1 740	1 697	1 591	1 807	2 101	20.7	7.2
Crude materials, inedible, except fuels (2)	199	198	197	191	198	-0.5	0.7
Mineral fuels, lubricants and related materials (3)	203	594	524	355	488	140.4	1.7
Animal and vegetable oils, fats and waxes (4)	4	5	10	23	19	375.0	0.1
Chemicals and related products (5)	3 642	4 040	4 783	5 062	6 635	82.2	22.7
Manufactured goods classified chiefly by material (6)	2 460	2 578	2 303	2 156	2 142	-12.9	7.3
Machinery and transport equipment (7)	12 045	14 227	14 507	13 101	12 033	-0.1	41.2
Miscellaneous manufactured articles (8)	3 831	4 435	4 386	3 975	3 745	-2.2	12.8
Commodities and transactions not classified elsewhere (9)	1 426	1 711	1 694	1 389	1 455	2.0	5.0
Top 20 Commodities	16 674	20 184	21 403	19 994	20 467	22.7	70.0
Aircraft and associated equipment (792)	3 636	5 240	5 728	5 131	4 206	15.7	14.4
Medicaments (including veterinary medicaments) (542)	358	589	1 252	1 579	2 171	506.4	7.4
Nonelectric engines and motors (714)	2 675	2 912	3 147	2 575	2 092	-21.8	7.2
Alcoholic beverages (112)	1 621	1 578	1 476	1 704	2 015	24.3	6.9
Works of art, collectors' pieces, and antiques (896)	1 826	2 312	2 205	1 841	1 392	-23.8	4.8
Special transactions not classified by kind (931)	1 049	1 299	1 265	994	1 057	0.8	3.6
Parts and accessories of motor vehicles (784)	993	836	921	940	997	0.4	3.4
Perfumery, cosmetics or toilet preparations, excluding soaps (553)	688	762	797	832	982	42.7	3.4
Organo-inorganic and heterocyclic compounds (515)	421	424	519	464	725	72.2	2.5
Medicinal products, except medicaments (541)	321	422	442	564	677	110.9	2.3
Telecommunications equipment (764)	318	538	493	506	579	82.1	2.0
Thermionic, cold cathode, and photocathode valves (776)	606	653	610	516	577	-4.8	2.0
Radioactive and associated materials (525)	293	238	174	272	576	96.6	2.0
Oil (not crude) (334)	194	571	504	340	470	142.3	1.6
Measuring/checking/analyzing instruments (874)	348	393	454	400	466	33.9	1.6
Estimate of low value import transactions (984)	349	402	420	388	394	12.9	1.3
Electro-diagnostic apparatus (774)	167	166	221	258	278	66.5	1.0
Machinery and equipment specialized for particular industries (728)	366	289	246	211	273	-25.4	0.9
Electrical apparatus for switching or protecting elec. circuits (772)	285	358	305	253	272	-4.6	0.9
Miscellaneous chemical products (598)	160	202	224	226	268	67.5	0.9

Table C-47. U.S. Trade by Commodity with Gabon, 1999–2003

(Millions of dollars; total exports, f.a.s.; general imports, Customs; top 20 commodities based on 2003 dollar value.)

Commodity and SITC code	1999	2000	2001	2002	2003	Percent change, 1999–2003	Percent share of total, 2003
EXPORTS							
Total	45	63	74	66	63	40.0	100.0
Food and live animals (0)	2	3	4	4	2	0.0	3.2
Beverages and tobacco (1)	3	2	0	0	0	X	0.0
Crude materials, inedible, except fuels (2)	1	1	1	2	2	100.0	3.2
Mineral fuels, lubricants and related materials (3)	0	1	1	0	3	X	4.8
Animal and vegetable oils, fats and waxes (4)	0	0	0	0	0	X	0.0
Chemicals and related products (5)	2	1	1	2	2	0.0	3.2
Manufactured goods classified chiefly by material (6)	6	3	5	3	8	33.3	12.7
Machinery and transport equipment (7)	30	47	57	51	41	36.7	65.1
Miscellaneous manufactured articles (8)	1	3	3	2	4	300.0	6.3
Commodities and transactions not classified elsewhere (9)	1	2	2	1	1	0.0	1.6
Top 20 Commodities	32	47	60	52	56	75.0	88.9
Civil engineering and contractors' plant and equipment (723)	16	34	41	37	28	75.0	44.4
Iron and steel tubes, pipes and fittings (679)	5	2	3	1	6	20.0	9.5
Mechanical handling equipment (744)	2	1	2	4	3	50.0	4.8
Coke and semicoke of coal (325)	0	1	1	0	3	X	4.8
Footwear (851)	0	0	1	0	2	X	3.2
Other meat and edible offal (012)	1	2	2	3	2	100.0	3.2
Telecommunications equipment (764)	3	1	1	1	1	-66.7	1.6
Machinery and equipment specialized for particular industries (728)	1	2	2	2	1	0.0	1.6
Essential oils, perfume and flavor materials (551)	0	0	0	0	1	X	1.6
Estimated low value shipments (994)	1	1	1	1	1	0.0	1.6
Worn clothing and other worn textile articles (269)	1	0	1	1	1	0.0	1.6
Measuring/checking/analyzing instruments (874)	0	1	1	0	1	X	1.6
Aircraft and associated equipment (792)	1	1	1	1	1	0.0	1.6
Agricultural machinery (excluding tractors) and parts (721)	0	0	0	0	1	X	1.6
Articles of plastics (893)	0	0	1	0	1	X	1.6
Heating and cooling equipment (741)	0	0	0	0	1	X	1.6
Pumps for liquids and liquid elevators (742)	0	1	1	1	1	X	1.6
All motor vehicles (781)	1	0	0	0	1	0.0	1.6
Tools for use in the hand or in machines (695)	0	0	0	0	0	X	0.0
Rubber tires and accessories (625)	0	0	1	0	0	X	0.0
IMPORTS							
Total	1 520	2 209	1 655	1 592	1 970	29.6	100.0
Food and live animals (0)	1	0	1	0	0	X	0.0
Beverages and tobacco (1)	0	0	0	0	0	X	0.0
Crude materials, inedible, except fuels (2)	26	27	22	20	21	-19.2	1.1
Mineral fuels, lubricants and related materials (3)	1 431	2 172	1 622	1 558	1 937	35.4	98.3
Animal and vegetable oils, fats and waxes (4)	0	0	0	0	0	X	0.0
Chemicals and related products (5)	0	0	0	0	0	X	0.0
Manufactured goods classified chiefly by material (6)	5	6	5	5	5	0.0	0.3
Machinery and transport equipment (7)	53	0	0	0	0	X	0.0
Miscellaneous manufactured articles (8)	2	1	3	2	2	0.0	0.1
Commodities and transactions not classified elsewhere (9)	2	2	2	6	3	50.0	0.2
Top 20 Commodities	1 454	2 180	1 656	1 591	1 969	35.4	99.9
Crude oil (333)	1 419	2 144	1 622	1 558	1 937	36.5	98.3
Ores and concentrates of base metals (287)	26	27	22	19	19	-26.9	1.0
Veneers, plywood and particle board (634)	5	6	5	5	5	0.0	0.3
Special transactions not classified by kind (931)	1	1	2	6	3	200.0	0.2
Works of art, collectors' pieces, and antiques (896)	2	1	3	2	2	0.0	0.1
Wood, simply worked (248)	0	0	0	1	2	X	0.1
Estimate of low value import transactions (984)	0	1	1	0	1	X	0.1
Wood in the rough (247)	0	0	0	0	0	X	0.0
Crude vegetable materials (292)	0	0	0	0	0	X	0.0
Feeding stuff for animals (081)	1	0	1	0	0	X	0.0
Pumps, air or gas compressors and fans (743)	0	0	0	0	0	X	0.0
Printed matter (892)	0	0	0	0	0	X	0.0
Wood manufactures (635)	0	0	0	0	0	X	0.0
Mineral manufactures (663)	0	0	0	0	0	X	0.0
Measuring/checking/analyzing instruments (874)	0	0	0	0	0	X	0.0
Rotating electric plant and parts (716)	0	0	0	0	0	X	0.0
Telecommunications equipment (764)	0	0	0	0	0	X	0.0
Automatic data processing machines (752)	0	0	0	0	0	X	0.0
Trailers and semi-trailers (786)	0	0	0	0	0	X	0.0
Parts and accessories of motor vehicles (784)	0	0	0	0	0	X	0.0

X = Not applicable.

Table C-48. U.S. Trade by Commodity with Germany, 1999–2003

(Millions of dollars; total exports, f.a.s.; general imports, Customs; top 20 commodities based on 2003 dollar value.)

Commodity and SITC code	1999	2000	2001	2002	2003	Percent change, 1999–2003	Percent share of total, 2003
EXPORTS							
Total	26 789	29 244	30 114	26 628	28 848	7.7	100.0
Food and live animals (0)	415	426	545	494	492	18.6	1.7
Beverages and tobacco (1)	348	408	389	288	274	-21.3	0.9
Crude materials, inedible, except fuels (2)	872	956	814	940	966	10.8	3.3
Mineral fuels, lubricants and related materials (3)	63	80	64	50	38	-39.7	0.1
Animal and vegetable oils, fats and waxes (4)	10	9	15	12	11	10.0	0.0
Chemicals and related products (5)	2 748	2 722	2 770	2 671	3 598	30.9	12.5
Manufactured goods classified chiefly by material (6)	1 734	1 845	1 985	1 672	1 859	7.2	6.4
Machinery and transport equipment (7)	16 017	17 580	18 146	15 902	17 044	6.4	59.1
Miscellaneous manufactured articles (8)	3 613	4 102	4 279	3 548	3 507	-2.9	12.2
Commodities and transactions not classified elsewhere (9)	969	1 115	1 107	1 053	1 058	9.2	3.7
Top 20 Commodities	17 348	18 782	19 605	17 347	19 261	11.0	66.8
All motor vehicles (781)	1 178	1 184	1 776	2 791	3 941	234.6	13.7
Thermionic, cold cathode and photocathode valves (776)	984	1 370	1 489	1 589	1 548	57.3	5.4
Nonelectric engines and motors (714)	1 175	1 537	1 785	1 485	1 512	28.7	5.2
Aircraft & associated equipment (792)	3 274	3 137	2 787	1 558	1 398	-57.3	4.8
Measuring/checking/analysing instuments (874)	1 233	1 494	1 523	1 230	1 289	4.5	4.5
Parts for office machines & adp machines (759)	1 708	1 820	1 682	1 072	1 089	-36.2	3.8
Automatic data process machines (752)	1 530	1 282	1 124	966	1 017	-33.5	3.5
Electro-diagnostic apparatus (774)	701	708	790	866	1 002	42.9	3.5
Medicinal products, except medicaments (541)	466	452	477	451	821	76.2	2.8
Miscellaneous chemical products (598)	764	663	573	560	781	2.2	2.7
Telecommunications equipment (764)	843	985	1 021	808	767	-9.0	2.7
Estimated low value shipments (994)	594	649	690	623	678	14.1	2.4
Parts and accessories of motor vehicles (784)	577	648	720	638	617	6.9	2.1
Medical instruments & appliances (872)	504	495	629	567	616	22.2	2.1
Electrical apparatus for switching or protecting (772)	353	372	475	417	454	28.6	1.6
Machinery specialized for particular industries (728)	433	816	772	495	402	-7.2	1.4
Electrical machinery and apparatus (778)	301	452	458	350	380	26.2	1.3
Special transactions not classified by kind (931)	288	383	368	389	338	17.4	1.2
Medicaments (including veterinary medicaments) (542)	260	198	363	220	314	20.8	1.1
Oil seeds and oleaginous fruit (222)	182	137	103	272	297	63.2	1.0
IMPORTS							
Total	55 094	58 737	59 151	62 480	68 047	23.5	100.0
Food and live animals (0)	419	437	401	395	446	6.4	0.7
Beverages and tobacco (1)	238	242	260	288	348	46.2	0.5
Crude materials, inedible, except fuels (2)	254	328	350	420	446	75.6	0.7
Mineral fuels, lubricants and related materials (3)	280	506	437	506	597	113.2	0.9
Animal and vegetable oils, fats and waxes (4)	7	9	7	12	15	114.3	0.0
Chemicals and related products (5)	7 699	6 876	7 176	8 466	9 239	20.0	13.6
Manufactured goods classified chiefly by material (6)	4 737	5 431	5 123	4 942	5 245	10.7	7.7
Machinery and transport equipment (7)	34 098	36 928	37 671	39 308	43 153	26.6	63.4
Miscellaneous manufactured articles (8)	4 674	5 270	4 920	4 961	5 611	20.0	8.2
Commodities and transactions not classified elsewhere (9)	2 686	2 709	2 806	3 181	2 947	9.7	4.3
Top 20 Commodities	33 932	36 280	37 434	40 898	44 527	31.2	65.4
All motor vehicles (781)	13 480	14 650	15 007	17 807	19 726	46.3	29.0
Medicaments (including veterinary medicaments) (542)	2 754	1 700	1 810	2 134	2 658	-3.5	3.9
Parts and accessories of motor vehicles (784)	1 319	1 496	1 531	1 730	2 294	73.9	3.4
Internal combustion piston engines (713)	1 633	1 727	1 594	1 861	2 242	37.3	3.3
Measuring/checking/analysing instuments (874)	1 494	1 868	1 724	1 557	1 715	14.8	2.5
Special transactions not classified by kind (931)	1 616	1 565	1 645	1 998	1 626	0.6	2.4
Machinery specialized for particular industries (728)	1 564	1 590	1 349	1 134	1 378	-11.9	2.0
Medicinal products, except medicaments (541)	492	584	710	1 054	1 367	177.8	2.0
Electro-diagnostic apparatus (774)	831	865	939	1 161	1 356	63.2	2.0
Estimate of low valued import transactions (984)	1 062	1 139	1 155	1 172	1 313	23.6	1.9
Electrical apparatus for switching or protecting (772)	859	984	835	974	1 174	36.7	1.7
Aircraft & associated equipment (792)	1 706	2 333	2 614	1 663	1 091	-36.0	1.6
Organo-inorganic & heterocyclic compounds (515)	845	866	962	1 370	958	13.4	1.4
Thermionic, cold cathode and photocathode valves (776)	683	848	958	971	854	25.0	1.3
Medical instruments & appliances (872)	469	522	595	676	849	81.0	1.2
Nonelectrical machinery and tools (745)	589	603	698	721	843	43.1	1.2
Nonelectric engines and motors (714)	1 004	1 149	1 476	1 026	807	-19.6	1.2
Electrical machinery and apparatus (778)	614	672	663	663	800	30.3	1.2
Telecommunications equipment (764)	345	423	524	613	743	115.4	1.1
Pumps, air or other gas compressors and fans (743)	573	696	645	613	733	27.9	1.1

Table C-49. U.S. Trade by Commodity with Greece, 1999–2003

(Millions of dollars; total exports, f.a.s.; general imports, Customs; top 20 commodities based on 2003 dollar value.)

Commodity and SITC code	1999	2000	2001	2002	2003	Percent change, 1999–2003	Percent share of total, 2003
EXPORTS							
Total	994	1 218	1 296	1 153	1 191	19.8	100.0
Food and live animals (0)	45	47	50	57	73	62.2	6.1
Beverages and tobacco (1)	10	10	10	10	10	0.0	0.8
Crude materials, inedible, except fuels (2)	63	57	74	64	57	-9.5	4.8
Mineral fuels, lubricants and related materials (3)	10	15	16	17	12	20.0	1.0
Animal and vegetable oils, fats and waxes (4)	5	1	1	4	0	X	0.0
Chemicals and related products (5)	77	88	74	65	81	5.2	6.8
Manufactured goods classified chiefly by material (6)	36	53	38	47	52	44.4	4.4
Machinery and transport equipment (7)	509	522	724	547	595	16.9	50.0
Miscellaneous manufactured articles (8)	201	385	231	282	264	31.3	22.2
Commodities and transactions not classified elsewhere (9)	38	40	77	60	46	21.1	3.9
Top 20 Commodities	602	797	900	808	816	35.5	68.5
Aircraft and associated equipment (792)	165	193	297	144	213	29.1	17.9
Arms and ammunition (891)	84	262	81	149	111	32.1	9.3
All motor vehicles (781)	12	22	18	44	82	583.3	6.9
Telecommunications equipment (764)	107	62	200	182	70	-34.6	5.9
Nonelectric engines and motors (714)	11	16	6	15	37	236.4	3.1
Medical instruments and appliances (872)	26	29	30	32	33	26.9	2.8
Fruit and nuts (not including oil nuts), fresh or dried (057)	10	7	9	16	32	220.0	2.7
Estimated low value shipments (994)	26	30	28	34	29	11.5	2.4
Measuring/checking/analyzing instruments (874)	21	28	44	38	28	33.3	2.4
Oil seeds and oleaginous fruits (222)	38	26	42	33	28	-26.3	2.4
Miscellaneous manufactured articles (899)	18	19	18	19	20	11.1	1.7
Other meat and edible offal (012)	9	11	19	15	17	88.9	1.4
Special transactions not classified by kind (931)	6	5	48	24	16	166.7	1.3
Rotating electric plant and parts (716)	3	2	3	1	16	433.3	1.3
Automatic data processing machines (752)	24	37	16	14	16	-33.3	1.3
Medicaments (including veterinary medicaments) (542)	8	10	12	12	15	87.5	1.3
Electro-diagnostic apparatus (774)	15	19	13	15	14	-6.7	1.2
Photographic apparatus and equipment (881)	3	1	1	1	13	333.3	1.1
Miscellaneous chemical products (598)	10	12	10	10	13	30.0	1.1
Nonelectrical machinery and tools (745)	6	6	5	10	13	116.7	1.1
IMPORTS							
Total	571	592	506	546	616	7.9	100.0
Food and live animals (0)	75	92	91	118	110	46.7	17.9
Beverages and tobacco (1)	58	36	42	50	62	6.9	10.1
Crude materials, inedible, except fuels (2)	80	14	13	16	20	-75.0	3.2
Mineral fuels, lubricants and related materials (3)	18	62	35	28	58	222.2	9.4
Animal and vegetable oils, fats and waxes (4)	9	11	10	11	13	44.4	2.1
Chemicals and related products (5)	16	21	16	27	40	150.0	6.5
Manufactured goods classified chiefly by material (6)	185	184	182	182	180	-2.7	29.2
Machinery and transport equipment (7)	21	27	18	24	33	57.1	5.4
Miscellaneous manufactured articles (8)	82	84	78	70	75	-8.5	12.2
Commodities and transactions not classified elsewhere (9)	28	60	22	20	27	-3.6	4.4
Top 20 Commodities	367	422	365	401	458	24.8	74.4
Vegetables, roots and tubers, prepared or preserved (56)	39	36	39	54	59	51.3	9.6
Lime, cement, and fabricated construction materials (661)	96	70	70	77	54	-43.8	8.8
Oil (not crude) (334)	18	62	35	28	52	188.9	8.4
Tobacco, unmanufactured; tobacco refuse (121)	49	22	26	32	46	-6.1	7.5
Aluminum (684)	34	35	32	32	43	26.5	7.0
Cutlery (696)	10	17	15	12	25	150.0	4.1
Special transactions not classified by kind (931)	23	55	19	17	23	0.0	3.7
Works of art, collectors' pieces, and antiques (896)	39	33	24	18	19	-51.3	3.1
Polymers of styrene (572)	0	1	2	7	17	X	2.8
Crude minerals (278)	8	7	6	9	13	62.5	2.1
Cheese and curd (24)	10	10	11	12	13	30.0	2.1
Fixed vegetable fats and oils (421)	9	11	10	11	13	44.4	2.1
Aircraft and associated equipment (792)	4	3	4	12	12	200.0	1.9
Fruit preserved and fruit preparations (58)	6	24	20	30	12	100.0	1.9
Apparel and accessories except textile; headgear (848)	7	12	16	14	11	57.1	1.8
Alcoholic beverages (112)	8	8	8	9	10	25.0	1.6
Iron and steel tubes, pipes and fittings (679)	1	8	18	13	10	900.0	1.6
Plates, sheets, film, foil and strip of plastics (582)	5	7	7	9	10	100.0	1.6
Furniture and bedding accessories (821)	1	1	3	3	8	700.0	1.3
Equipment for distributing electricity (773)	0	0	0	2	8	X	1.3

X = Not applicable.

Table C-50. U.S. Trade by Commodity with Guatemala, 1999–2003

(Millions of dollars; total exports, f.a.s.; general imports, Customs; top 20 commodities based on 2003 dollar value.)

Commodity and SITC code	1999	2000	2001	2002	2003	Percent change, 1999–2003	Percent share of total, 2003
EXPORTS							
Total	1 812	1 895	1 877	2 042	2 274	25.5	100.0
Food and live animals (0)	212	197	235	266	268	26.4	11.8
Beverages and tobacco (1)	4	1	1	2	1	-75.0	0.0
Crude materials, inedible, except fuels (2)	37	57	53	62	101	173.0	4.4
Mineral fuels, lubricants and related materials (3)	71	150	115	127	268	277.5	11.8
Animal and vegetable oils, fats and waxes (4)	41	21	26	35	38	-7.3	1.7
Chemicals and related products (5)	216	233	250	270	267	23.6	11.7
Manufactured goods classified chiefly by material (6)	225	287	403	468	438	94.7	19.3
Machinery and transport equipment (7)	602	514	436	494	518	-14.0	22.8
Miscellaneous manufactured articles (8)	297	313	239	193	217	-26.9	9.5
Commodities and transactions not classified elsewhere (9)	107	123	121	124	157	46.7	6.9
Top 20 Commodities	683	791	822	1 021	1 224	79.2	53.8
Oil (not crude) (334)	61	133	100	103	236	286.9	10.4
Cotton fabrics, woven (652)	17	27	82	121	105	517.6	4.6
Telecommunications equipment (764)	114	107	58	94	92	-19.3	4.0
Paper and paperboard (641)	67	76	77	77	81	20.9	3.6
Estimated low value shipments (994)	65	67	69	73	80	23.1	3.5
Special transactions not classified by kind (931)	21	8	32	31	60	185.7	2.6
Textile yarn (651)	9	17	30	48	55	511.1	2.4
Maize (not including sweet corn) unmilled (044)	42	46	48	59	54	28.6	2.4
Parts for office machines and a.d.p. machines (759)	44	43	49	57	52	18.2	2.3
Polymers of ethylene (571)	46	49	48	75	50	8.7	2.2
Wheat and meslin, unmilled (041)	11	10	17	48	44	300.0	1.9
Feeding stuff for animals (081)	37	41	38	37	44	18.9	1.9
Other meat and edible offal (012)	16	22	30	33	42	162.5	1.8
Synthetic fibers suitable for spinning (266)	2	2	2	9	37	1 750.0	1.6
All motor vehicles (781)	29	27	20	28	37	27.6	1.6
Electrical machinery and apparatus (778)	16	11	11	12	33	106.3	1.5
Automatic data processing machines (752)	48	49	31	29	33	-31.3	1.5
Woven fabrics of manmade textile materials (653)	14	20	44	37	32	128.6	1.4
Liquefied propane and butane (342)	8	14	11	22	29	262.5	1.3
Articles of plastics (893)	16	22	25	28	28	75.0	1.2
IMPORTS							
Total	2 266	2 605	2 589	2 800	2 945	30.0	100.0
Food and live animals (0)	661	668	585	652	730	10.4	24.8
Beverages and tobacco (1)	14	13	9	19	11	-21.4	0.4
Crude materials, inedible, except fuels (2)	51	52	50	51	49	-3.9	1.7
Mineral fuels, lubricants and related materials (3)	94	154	101	169	177	88.3	6.0
Animal and vegetable oils, fats and waxes (4)	0	0	0	0	0	X	0.0
Chemicals and related products (5)	46	39	33	37	27	-41.3	0.9
Manufactured goods classified chiefly by material (6)	30	33	37	42	41	36.7	1.4
Machinery and transport equipment (7)	1	4	4	4	5	400.0	0.2
Miscellaneous manufactured articles (8)	1 341	1 601	1 724	1 783	1 868	39.3	63.4
Commodities and transactions not classified elsewhere (9)	28	41	47	44	37	32.1	1.3
Top 20 Commodities	2 125	2 463	2 444	2 636	2 794	31.5	94.9
Articles of apparel of textile fabrics (845)	341	508	570	664	737	116.1	25.0
Women's or girls' coats, jackets, etc. not knit (842)	405	469	448	391	416	2.7	14.1
Fruit and nuts (not including oil nuts), fresh or dried (057)	193	249	291	335	334	73.1	11.3
Women's or girls' coats, jackets, etc. knit (844)	115	157	201	221	256	122.6	8.7
Men's or boys' coats, jackets, etc. not knit (841)	287	266	279	270	251	-12.5	8.5
Coffee and coffee substitutes (071)	302	302	175	168	213	-29.5	7.2
Crude oil (333)	94	154	101	168	177	88.3	6.0
Men's or boys' coats, jackets, etc. knit (843)	79	83	107	108	95	20.3	3.2
Sugars, molasses, and honey (061)	87	38	38	60	85	-2.3	2.9
Vegetables, roots, tubers and other edible vegetable products (054)	42	39	34	40	49	16.7	1.7
Crude vegetable materials (292)	24	25	25	26	24	0.0	0.8
Jewelry, goldsmiths' and silversmiths' wares (897)	4	11	19	44	22	450.0	0.7
Miscellaneous manufactured articles (899)	56	51	38	25	22	-60.7	0.7
Special transactions not classified by kind (931)	15	25	33	29	21	40.0	0.7
Apparel and accessories except textile; headgear (848)	9	14	19	17	20	122.2	0.7
Crustaceans (036)	16	16	19	16	19	18.8	0.6
Estimate of low value import transactions (984)	13	15	14	15	16	23.1	0.5
Wood manufactures (635)	7	8	9	13	14	100.0	0.5
Oil seeds and oleaginous fruits (222)	16	16	12	12	12	-25.0	0.4
Soap, cleansing and polishing preparations (554)	20	17	12	14	11	-45.0	0.4

X = Not applicable.

Table C-51. U.S. Trade by Commodity with Haiti, 1999–2003

(Millions of dollars; total exports, f.a.s.; general imports, Customs; top 20 commodities based on 2003 dollar value.)

Commodity and SITC code	1999	2000	2001	2002	2003	Percent change, 1999–2003	Percent share of total, 2003
EXPORTS							
Total	615	576	550	583	640	4.1	100.0
Food and live animals (0)	173	149	149	147	173	0.0	27.0
Beverages and tobacco (1)	6	5	5	6	3	-50.0	0.5
Crude materials, inedible, except fuels (2)	18	15	16	14	13	-27.8	2.0
Mineral fuels, lubricants and related materials (3)	11	10	8	14	39	254.5	6.1
Animal and vegetable oils, fats and waxes (4)	37	25	21	14	13	-64.9	2.0
Chemicals and related products (5)	22	18	21	21	19	-13.6	3.0
Manufactured goods classified chiefly by material (6)	39	38	53	54	51	30.8	8.0
Machinery and transport equipment (7)	101	84	79	87	82	-18.8	12.8
Miscellaneous manufactured articles (8)	146	178	140	144	172	17.8	26.9
Commodities and transactions not classified elsewhere (9)	63	54	59	80	75	19.0	11.7
Top 20 Commodities	329	355	335	402	482	46.5	75.3
Articles of apparel of textile fabrics (845)	77	114	80	87	118	53.2	18.4
Rice (42)	70	64	50	65	89	27.1	13.9
Special transactions not classified by kind (931)	23	17	26	46	39	69.6	6.1
Oil (not crude) (334)	10	9	8	14	39	290.0	6.1
Estimated low value shipments (994)	31	29	28	28	32	3.2	5.0
Wheat and meslin, unmilled (041)	11	18	18	18	23	109.1	3.6
All motor vehicles (781)	11	16	12	17	17	54.5	2.7
Vegetables, roots, tubers and other edible vegetable products (054)	12	10	13	11	17	41.7	2.7
Other meat and edible offal (012)	27	14	15	15	15	-44.4	2.3
Men's or boys' coats, jackets, etc. knit (843)	7	4	4	5	14	100.0	2.2
Knitted or crocheted fabrics (655)	1	3	8	4	11	1 000.0	1.7
Women's or girls' coats, jackets, etc. knit (844)	2	4	10	19	11	450.0	1.7
Rotating electric plant and parts (716)	5	6	17	17	10	100.0	1.6
Special purpose motor vehicles (782)	10	8	6	7	9	-10.0	1.4
Edible products and preparations, n.e.s. (098)	7	9	8	10	8	14.3	1.3
Worn clothing and other worn textile articles (269)	9	7	8	9	7	-22.2	1.1
Animal or vegetable fats and oils, processed (431)	5	11	6	5	7	40.0	1.1
Perfumery, cosmetics or toilet preparations, excluding soaps (553)	5	4	4	5	6	20.0	0.9
Cotton fabrics, woven (652)	1	2	9	13	5	400.0	0.8
Articles of plastics (893)	5	6	5	7	5	0.0	0.8
IMPORTS							
Total	301	297	263	255	332	10.3	100.0
Food and live animals (0)	12	12	8	12	11	-8.3	3.3
Beverages and tobacco (1)	0	0	0	0	1	X	0.3
Crude materials, inedible, except fuels (2)	2	1	1	1	2	0.0	0.6
Mineral fuels, lubricants and related materials (3)	0	0	0	0	0	X	0.0
Animal and vegetable oils, fats and waxes (4)	0	0	0	0	0	X	0.0
Chemicals and related products (5)	1	1	1	1	1	0.0	0.3
Manufactured goods classified chiefly by material (6)	13	13	10	9	8	-38.5	2.4
Machinery and transport equipment (7)	3	2	2	2	6	100.0	1.8
Miscellaneous manufactured articles (8)	264	265	238	224	299	13.3	90.1
Commodities and transactions not classified elsewhere (9)	6	3	4	5	6	0.0	1.8
Top 20 Commodities	287	286	253	248	324	12.9	97.6
Articles of apparel of textile fabrics (845)	159	157	135	140	201	26.4	60.5
Women's or girls' coats, jackets, etc. knit (844)	32	36	40	31	32	0.0	9.6
Men's or boys' coats, jackets, etc. not knit (841)	25	25	23	22	26	4.0	7.8
Men's or boys' coats, jackets, etc. knit (843)	24	20	16	13	21	-12.5	6.3
Clothing accessories (846)	10	13	8	8	9	-10.0	2.7
Women's or girls' coats, jackets, etc. not knit (842)	7	7	9	7	5	-28.6	1.5
Fruit and nuts (not including oil nuts), fresh or dried (057)	7	7	3	6	4	-42.9	1.2
Cocoa (072)	1	1	1	4	4	300.0	1.2
Special transactions not classified by kind (931)	4	1	2	3	4	0.0	1.2
Equipment for distributing electricity (773)	0	0	0	0	3	X	0.9
Made-up articles of textile materials (658)	2	3	2	2	2	0.0	0.6
Estimate of low value import transactions (984)	2	2	2	2	2	0.0	0.6
Toys and sporting goods (894)	2	3	2	2	2	0.0	0.6
Leather (611)	4	4	4	2	2	-50.0	0.6
Electric power machinery, and parts (771)	1	1	1	1	2	100.0	0.6
Essential oils, perfume and flavor materials (551)	1	1	1	1	1	0.0	0.3
Household equipment of base metal (697)	1	1	1	1	1	0.0	0.3
Crustaceans (036)	3	3	2	2	1	-66.7	0.3
Special yarns, special textile fabrics, etc. (657)	1	1	1	1	1	0.0	0.3
Crude vegetable materials (292)	1	0	0	0	1	0.0	0.3

X = Not applicable.

Table C-52. U.S. Trade by Commodity with Honduras, 1999–2003

(Millions of dollars; total exports, f.a.s. and general imports, customs; top 20 commodities based on 2003 dollar value.)

Commodity and SITC code	1999	2000	2001	2002	2003	Percent change, 1999–2003	Percent share of total, 2003
EXPORTS							
Total	2 369	2 575	2 437	2 565	2 845	20.1	100.0
Food and live animals (0)	171	171	177	143	170	-0.6	6.0
Beverages and tobacco (1)	11	17	13	18	12	9.1	0.4
Crude materials, inedible, except fuels (2)	16	24	22	33	43	168.8	1.5
Mineral fuels, lubricants and related materials (3)	59	63	27	65	233	294.9	8.2
Animal and vegetable oils, fats and waxes (4)	14	10	8	16	19	35.7	0.7
Chemicals and related products (5)	111	113	123	113	116	4.5	4.1
Manufactured goods classified chiefly by material (6)	300	381	549	828	937	212.3	32.9
Machinery and transport equipment (7)	350	329	305	307	366	4.6	12.9
Miscellaneous manufactured articles (8)	1 132	1 310	1 063	885	784	-30.7	27.6
Commodities and transactions not classified elsewhere (9)	205	158	151	156	166	-19.0	5.8
Top 20 Commodities	1 519	1 804	1 718	1 905	2 113	39.1	74.3
Knitted or crocheted fabrics (655)	25	27	87	244	340	1 260.0	12.0
Articles of apparel of textile fabrics (845)	482	641	501	398	327	-32.2	11.5
Textile yarn (651)	40	67	95	156	288	620.0	10.1
Oil (not crude) (334)	57	61	17	55	215	277.2	7.6
Estimated low value shipments (994)	127	135	131	136	150	18.1	5.3
Clothing accessories (846)	250	254	233	157	124	-50.4	4.4
Men's or boys' coats, jackets, etc. not knit (841)	171	151	95	89	118	-31.0	4.1
Cotton fabrics, woven (652)	34	48	99	141	59	73.5	2.1
Men's or boys' coats, jackets, etc. knit (843)	78	91	80	72	56	-28.2	2.0
Tulles, lace, embroidery, ribbons, trimmings, etc (656)	38	56	107	123	54	42.1	1.9
Parts & access for metal work machine tools (735)	5	8	11	44	52	940.0	1.8
Paper and paperboard (641)	26	38	39	40	49	88.5	1.7
Textile and leather machinery and pts (724)	31	28	39	30	49	58.1	1.7
Woven fabrics of manmade textile materials (653)	15	15	9	23	44	193.3	1.5
Women's or girls' coats, jackets, etc. knit (844)	36	42	37	49	42	16.7	1.5
Articles of plastics (893)	33	42	42	42	34	3.0	1.2
Feeding stuff for animals (081)	16	17	20	19	32	100.0	1.1
Maize (not including sweet corn) unmilled (044)	9	17	23	24	29	222.2	1.0
Wheat and meslin, unmilled (041)	23	31	22	32	27	17.4	0.9
Special yarns, special textile fabrics, etc. (657)	23	35	31	31	24	4.3	0.8
IMPORTS							
Total	2 713	3 090	3 126	3 264	3 312	22.1	100.0
Food and live animals (0)	234	366	342	349	335	43.2	10.1
Beverages and tobacco (1)	56	60	64	73	71	26.8	2.1
Crude materials, inedible, except fuels (2)	13	14	14	14	14	7.7	0.4
Mineral fuels, lubricants and related materials (3)	0	0	0	0	0	X	0.0
Animal and vegetable oils, fats and waxes (4)	0	0	0	0	0	X	0.0
Chemicals and related products (5)	1	2	2	2	4	300.0	0.1
Manufactured goods classified chiefly by material (6)	29	27	23	22	28	-3.4	0.8
Machinery and transport equipment (7)	51	83	60	82	109	113.7	3.3
Miscellaneous manufactured articles (8)	2 271	2 486	2 507	2 567	2 626	15.6	79.3
Commodities and transactions not classified elsewhere (9)	58	51	115	155	126	117.2	3.8
Top 20 Commodities	2 630	3 000	3 047	3 181	3 227	22.7	97.4
Articles of apparel of textile fabrics (845)	1 167	1 401	1 470	1 555	1 577	35.1	47.6
Men's or boys' coats, jackets, etc. not knit (841)	379	373	335	295	306	-19.3	9.2
Men's or boys' coats, jackets, etc. knit (843)	331	309	293	280	286	-13.6	8.6
Women's or girls' coats, jackets, etc. knit (844)	183	194	192	227	243	32.8	7.3
Fruit and nuts (not including oil nuts), fresh or dried (057)	50	108	146	153	149	198.0	4.5
Crustaceans (036)	103	120	110	113	106	2.9	3.2
Women's or girls' coats, jackets, etc. not knit (842)	126	122	125	101	104	-17.5	3.1
Equipment for distributing electricity (773)	37	58	46	67	91	145.9	2.7
Gold, nonmonetary (971)	6	9	53	74	68	1 033.3	2.1
Tobacco, manufactured (122)	48	50	52	56	60	25.0	1.8
Special transactions not classified by kind (931)	47	36	56	75	52	10.6	1.6
Clothing accessories (846)	10	16	24	46	50	400.0	1.5
Furniture and bedding accessories (821)	42	40	42	35	31	-26.2	0.9
Coffee and coffee substitutes (071)	49	97	36	27	24	-51.0	0.7
Fish, fresh, chilled or frozen (034)	5	9	11	19	19	280.0	0.6
Wood manufactures (635)	19	16	15	13	16	-15.8	0.5
Miscellaneous manufactured articles (899)	10	12	11	14	15	50.0	0.5
Sugars, molasses, and honey (061)	6	8	14	8	13	116.7	0.4
Tobacco, unmanufactured; tobacco refuse (121)	7	10	11	15	9	28.6	0.3
Parts and accessories of motor vehicles (784)	5	12	5	8	8	60.0	0.2

X = Not applicable.

Table C-53. U.S. Trade by Commodity with Hong Kong, 1999–2003

(Millions of dollars; total exports, f.a.s.; general imports, Customs; top 20 commodities based on 2003 dollar value.)

Commodity and SITC code	1999	2000	2001	2002	2003	Percent change, 1999–2003	Percent share of total, 2003
EXPORTS							
Total	12 647	14 625	14 072	12 612	13 542	7.1	100.0
Food and live animals (0)	1 028	1 044	953	838	789	-23.2	5.8
Beverages and tobacco (1)	93	91	68	52	48	-48.4	0.4
Crude materials, inedible, except fuels (2)	386	482	501	521	574	48.7	4.2
Mineral fuels, lubricants and related materials (3)	19	22	29	29	65	242.1	0.5
Animal and vegetable oils, fats and waxes (4)	29	20	10	14	9	-69.0	0.1
Chemicals and related products (5)	1 147	1 390	1 339	1 305	1 426	24.3	10.5
Manufactured goods classified chiefly by material (6)	1 395	1 689	1 525	1 494	1 647	18.1	12.2
Machinery and transport equipment (7)	6 612	7 720	7 142	6 290	6 769	2.4	50.0
Miscellaneous manufactured articles (8)	1 512	1 719	2 099	1 738	1 867	23.5	13.8
Commodities and transactions not classified elsewhere (9)	427	448	406	331	347	-18.7	2.6
Top 20 Commodities	7 982	9 523	9 089	7 969	8 596	7.7	63.5
Thermionic, cold cathode, and photocathode valves (776)	2 392	2 897	2 250	2 403	2 838	18.6	21.0
Automatic data processing machines (752)	880	1 227	1 250	801	687	-21.9	5.1
Pearls, precious and semiprecious stones (667)	413	625	534	528	588	42.4	4.3
Parts for office machines and a.d.p. machines (759)	671	757	695	554	583	-13.1	4.3
Telecommunications equipment (764)	552	559	628	564	553	0.2	4.1
Measuring/checking/analyzing instruments (874)	306	383	394	378	417	36.3	3.1
Jewelry, goldsmiths' and silversmiths' wares (897)	208	212	273	290	305	46.6	2.3
Electrical apparatus for switching or protecting elec. circuits (772)	231	309	261	288	303	31.2	2.2
Electrical machinery and apparatus (778)	379	363	263	255	295	-22.2	2.2
Estimated low value shipments (994)	269	301	294	254	260	-3.3	1.9
Other meat and edible offal (012)	439	437	383	280	238	-45.8	1.8
Plastics (575)	170	239	201	198	234	37.6	1.7
Fruit and nuts (not including oil nuts), fresh or dried (057)	160	229	229	232	227	41.9	1.7
Toys and sporting goods (894)	136	111	110	134	168	23.5	1.2
Hides and skins, raw (211)	25	53	107	102	167	568.0	1.2
Polyacetals and epoxide resins (574)	123	171	113	168	164	33.3	1.2
Leather (611)	154	145	153	156	164	6.5	1.2
Plates, sheets, film, foil and strip of plastics (582)	107	117	105	114	138	29.0	1.0
Optical goods (884)	79	130	446	96	134	69.6	1.0
Aircraft and associated equipment (792)	288	258	400	174	133	-53.8	1.0
IMPORTS							
Total	10 531	11 452	9 650	9 328	8 850	-16.0	100.0
Food and live animals (0)	76	82	72	91	70	-7.9	0.8
Beverages and tobacco (1)	5	5	5	5	5	0.0	0.1
Crude materials, inedible, except fuels (2)	18	29	15	14	13	-27.8	0.1
Mineral fuels, lubricants and related materials (3)	5	0	1	0	0	X	0.0
Animal and vegetable oils, fats and waxes (4)	1	1	1	1	1	0.0	0.0
Chemicals and related products (5)	42	41	40	53	54	28.6	0.6
Manufactured goods classified chiefly by material (6)	762	936	858	724	649	-14.8	7.3
Machinery and transport equipment (7)	2 350	2 544	1 696	1 794	1 646	-30.0	18.6
Miscellaneous manufactured articles (8)	6 637	7 057	6 337	6 023	5 805	-12.5	65.6
Commodities and transactions not classified elsewhere (9)	634	756	625	623	607	-4.3	6.9
Top 20 Commodities	8 345	9 203	7 766	7 570	7 171	-14.1	81.0
Articles of apparel of textile fabrics (845)	1 801	1 971	1 862	1 582	1 469	-18.4	16.6
Women's or girls' coats, jackets, etc. not knit (842)	1 179	1 218	1 151	1 225	1 209	2.5	13.7
Men's or boys' coats, jackets, etc. not knit (841)	780	841	716	652	649	-16.8	7.3
Special transactions not classified by kind (931)	530	637	529	529	514	-3.0	5.8
Jewelry, goldsmiths' and silversmiths' wares (897)	527	619	489	548	480	-8.9	5.4
Telecommunications equipment (764)	127	150	160	264	366	188.2	4.1
Women's or girls' coats, jackets, etc. knit (844)	358	333	371	341	318	-11.2	3.6
Printed matter (892)	310	315	320	323	283	-8.7	3.2
Pearls, precious and semiprecious stones (667)	290	408	343	305	270	-6.9	3.1
Toys and sporting goods (894)	273	271	230	230	245	-10.3	2.8
Thermionic, cold cathode, and photocathode valves (776)	1 172	1 180	638	461	234	-80.0	2.6
Automatic data processing machines (752)	95	160	114	226	209	120.0	2.4
Articles of plastics (893)	104	132	128	145	168	61.5	1.9
Musical instruments and accessories (898)	81	144	105	127	143	76.5	1.6
Sound and television recorders (763)	21	76	28	58	122	481.0	1.4
Furniture and bedding accessories (821)	75	84	99	90	109	45.3	1.2
Electrical machinery and apparatus (778)	201	216	133	123	108	-46.3	1.2
Electrical apparatus for switching or protecting elec. circuits (772)	180	188	124	112	96	-46.7	1.1
Parts for office machines and a.d.p. machines (759)	138	142	131	138	91	-34.1	1.0
Estimate of low value import transactions (984)	103	118	95	91	88	-14.6	1.0

X = Not applicable.

Table C-54. U.S. Trade by Commodity with Hungary, 1999–2003

(Millions of dollars; total exports, f.a.s.; general imports, Customs; top 20 commodities based on 2003 dollar value.)

Commodity and SITC code	1999	2000	2001	2002	2003	Percent change, 1999–2003	Percent share of total, 2003
EXPORTS							
Total	503	569	687	688	934	85.7	100.0
Food and live animals (0)	10	13	17	19	22	120.0	2.4
Beverages and tobacco (1)	2	3	2	2	1	-50.0	0.1
Crude materials, inedible, except fuels (2)	12	4	6	9	7	-41.7	0.7
Mineral fuels, lubricants and related materials (3)	0	3	2	1	0	X	0.0
Animal and vegetable oils, fats and waxes (4)	0	0	0	0	0	X	0.0
Chemicals and related products (5)	37	34	54	63	68	83.8	7.3
Manufactured goods classified chiefly by material (6)	63	109	121	77	38	-39.7	4.1
Machinery and transport equipment (7)	288	313	406	433	722	150.7	77.3
Miscellaneous manufactured articles (8)	68	64	51	58	49	-27.9	5.2
Commodities and transactions not classified elsewhere (9)	23	26	27	27	26	13.0	2.8
Top 20 Commodities	258	286	397	434	730	182.9	78.2
Aircraft and associated equipment (792)	4	10	3	7	304	7 500.0	32.5
Parts and accessories of motor vehicles (784)	49	27	24	51	67	36.7	7.2
Thermionic, cold cathode, and photocathode valves (776)	9	21	49	94	46	411.1	4.9
Parts for office machines and a.d.p. machines (759)	26	31	23	31	42	61.5	4.5
Nonelectric engines and motors (714)	2	2	57	31	34	1 600.0	3.6
Electrical machinery and apparatus (778)	14	18	9	14	24	71.4	2.6
Estimated low value shipments (994)	20	22	25	24	23	15.0	2.5
Automatic data processing machines (752)	40	53	80	43	23	-42.5	2.5
Electrical apparatus for switching or protecting elec. circuits (772)	8	14	15	24	22	175.0	2.4
Medicaments (including veterinary medicaments) (542)	4	5	10	10	20	400.0	2.1
Telecommunications equipment (764)	27	33	34	13	18	-33.3	1.9
Measuring/checking/analyzing instruments (874)	12	12	14	21	16	33.3	1.7
Tractors (722)	4	5	5	10	16	300.0	1.7
Perfumery, cosmetics or toilet preparations, excluding soaps (553)	6	5	8	12	14	133.3	1.5
Machinery and equipment specialized for particular industries (728)	20	12	21	19	12	-40.0	1.3
Electro-diagnostic apparatus (774)	5	6	6	9	11	120.0	1.2
Trasmission shafts and cranks (748)	3	4	5	6	11	266.7	1.2
Taps, cocks, valves and similar appliances (747)	1	2	3	5	10	900.0	1.1
Civil engineering and contractors' plant and equipment (723)	1	1	1	2	9	800.0	1.0
Edible products and preparations, n.e.s. (098)	3	3	5	8	8	166.7	0.9
IMPORTS							
Total	1 892	2 716	2 965	2 639	2 699	42.7	100.0
Food and live animals (0)	19	28	29	31	21	10.5	0.8
Beverages and tobacco (1)	1	2	3	3	3	200.0	0.1
Crude materials, inedible, except fuels (2)	12	9	5	8	8	-33.3	0.3
Mineral fuels, lubricants and related materials (3)	1	1	1	1	1	0.0	0.0
Animal and vegetable oils, fats and waxes (4)	0	0	0	0	0	X	0.0
Chemicals and related products (5)	55	443	756	770	693	1 160.0	25.7
Manufactured goods classified chiefly by material (6)	105	116	118	131	94	-10.5	3.5
Machinery and transport equipment (7)	1 532	1 950	1 702	1 465	1 631	6.5	60.4
Miscellaneous manufactured articles (8)	129	134	315	142	162	25.6	6.0
Commodities and transactions not classified elsewhere (9)	36	33	37	88	87	141.7	3.2
Top 20 Commodities	1 603	2 344	2 364	2 217	2 315	44.4	85.8
Carboxylic acids, halides, and derivities (513)	3	381	676	651	541	17 933.3	20.0
Automatic data processing machines (752)	1 040	1 206	767	509	519	-50.1	19.2
Parts and accessories of motor vehicles (784)	78	94	78	159	263	237.2	9.7
All motor vehicles (781)	48	201	335	237	194	304.2	7.2
Electrical machinery and apparatus (778)	109	122	119	93	103	-5.5	3.8
Sound and television recorders (763)	47	65	35	74	101	114.9	3.7
Organo-inorganic and heterocyclic compounds (515)	10	19	38	69	89	790.0	3.3
Road motor vehicles (783)	27	39	55	50	70	159.3	2.6
Special transactions not classified by kind (931)	23	15	16	69	67	191.3	2.5
Nonelectric engines and motors (714)	1	1	19	35	59	5 800.0	2.2
Telecommunications equipment (764)	3	5	3	14	48	1 500.0	1.8
Rotating electric plant and parts (716)	13	11	43	50	44	238.5	1.6
Medicinal products, except medicaments (541)	16	16	19	25	34	112.5	1.3
Pumps, air or gas compressors and fans (743)	6	8	6	14	31	416.7	1.1
Parts for office machines and a.d.p. machines (759)	78	52	56	65	30	-61.5	1.1
Women's or girls' coats, jackets, etc. not knit (842)	21	17	20	21	28	33.3	1.0
Thermionic, cold cathode, and photocathode valves (776)	23	32	21	22	26	13.0	1.0
Pumps for liquids and liquid elevators (742)	17	24	17	18	24	41.2	0.9
Electrical apparatus for switching or protecting elec. circuits (772)	9	10	11	15	23	155.6	0.9
Footwear (851)	31	26	30	27	21	-32.3	0.8

X = Not applicable.

Table C-55. U.S. Trade by Commodity with India, 1999–2003

(Millions of dollars; total exports, f.a.s.; general imports, Customs; top 20 commodities based on 2003 dollar value.)

Commodity and SITC code	1999	2000	2001	2002	2003	Percent change, 1999–2003	Percent share of total, 2003
EXPORTS							
Total	3 707	3 663	3 764	4 098	4 986	34.5	100.0
Food and live animals (0)	107	144	129	127	125	16.8	2.5
Beverages and tobacco (1)	0	1	1	2	1	X	0.0
Crude materials, inedible, except fuels (2)	162	203	405	298	403	148.8	8.1
Mineral fuels, lubricants and related materials (3)	52	82	85	54	134	157.7	2.7
Animal and vegetable oils, fats and waxes (4)	33	29	14	46	26	-21.2	0.5
Chemicals and related products (5)	903	588	566	755	1 112	23.1	22.3
Manufactured goods classified chiefly by material (6)	370	342	316	362	469	26.8	9.4
Machinery and transport equipment (7)	1 653	1 782	1 700	1 804	2 013	21.8	40.4
Miscellaneous manufactured articles (8)	329	395	447	557	596	81.2	12.0
Commodities and transactions not classified elsewhere (9)	98	97	102	93	107	9.2	2.1
Top 20 Commodities	2 215	2 181	2 316	2 521	3 256	47.0	65.3
Miscellaneous chemical products (598)	41	58	74	223	471	1 048.8	9.4
Aircraft and associated equipment (792)	376	308	387	303	318	-15.4	6.4
Telecommunications equipment (764)	108	163	153	259	298	175.9	6.0
Pearls, precious and semiprecious stones (667)	186	149	143	202	275	47.8	5.5
Automatic data processing machines (752)	153	260	246	256	274	79.1	5.5
Measuring/checking/analyzing instruments (874)	117	111	146	151	170	45.3	3.4
Cotton textile fibers (263)	7	30	196	89	152	2 071.4	3.0
Nonelectric engines and motors (714)	125	210	115	80	138	10.4	2.8
Jewelry, goldsmiths' and silversmiths' wares (897)	36	42	53	69	124	244.4	2.5
Musical instruments and accessories (898)	54	89	67	157	118	118.5	2.4
Pulp and waste paper (251)	74	80	89	87	117	58.1	2.3
Fertilizers (except crude) (562)	470	87	87	34	105	-77.7	2.1
Civil engineering and contractors' plant and equipment (723)	87	82	54	85	98	12.6	2.0
Electro-diagnostic apparatus (774)	48	57	85	96	98	104.2	2.0
Fruit and nuts (not including oil nuts), fresh or dried (057)	42	73	69	79	93	121.4	1.9
Thermionic, cold cathode, and photocathode valves (776)	53	69	79	78	91	71.7	1.8
Hydrocarbons and specified derivatives (511)	98	104	66	74	86	-12.2	1.7
Estimated low value shipments (994)	63	63	64	68	82	30.2	1.6
Residual petroleum products (335)	19	47	54	38	75	294.7	1.5
Parts for office machines and a.d.p. machines (759)	58	99	89	93	73	25.9	1.5
IMPORTS							
Total	9 083	10 686	9 738	11 818	13 053	43.7	100.0
Food and live animals (0)	805	824	732	828	873	8.4	6.7
Beverages and tobacco (1)	13	8	16	24	21	61.5	0.2
Crude materials, inedible, except fuels (2)	200	229	193	165	191	-4.5	1.5
Mineral fuels, lubricants and related materials (3)	1	82	197	224	239	23 800.0	1.8
Animal and vegetable oils, fats and waxes (4)	45	45	33	24	30	-33.3	0.2
Chemicals and related products (5)	448	553	721	832	1 133	152.9	8.7
Manufactured goods classified chiefly by material (6)	4 193	4 876	3 954	5 205	5 315	26.8	40.7
Machinery and transport equipment (7)	499	611	671	816	1 009	102.2	7.7
Miscellaneous manufactured articles (8)	2 743	3 267	3 098	3 579	4 086	49.0	31.3
Commodities and transactions not classified elsewhere (9)	138	192	124	122	156	13.0	1.2
Top 20 Commodities	6 404	7 386	6 819	8 536	9 412	47.0	72.1
Pearls, precious and semiprecious stones (667)	2 396	2 631	2 034	2 746	2 730	13.9	20.9
Jewelry, goldsmiths' and silversmiths' wares (897)	588	713	605	912	1 224	108.2	9.4
Women's or girls' coats, jackets, etc. not knit (842)	699	834	729	867	927	32.6	7.1
Made-up articles of textile materials (658)	386	469	496	612	706	82.9	5.4
Floor coverings (659)	343	354	324	384	425	23.9	3.3
Crustaceans (036)	171	251	266	370	416	143.3	3.2
Men's or boys' coats, jackets, etc. not knit (841)	293	339	364	359	404	37.9	3.1
Articles of apparel of textile fabrics (845)	335	402	422	456	403	20.3	3.1
Medicaments (including veterinary medicaments) (542)	7	5	94	223	359	5 028.6	2.8
Oil (not crude) (334)	0	76	191	216	237	X	1.8
Men's or boys' coats, jackets, etc. knit (843)	163	173	187	183	213	30.7	1.6
Fruit and nuts (not including oil nuts), fresh or dried (057)	287	242	217	214	186	-35.2	1.4
Lime, cement, and fabricated construction materials (661)	77	106	115	140	183	137.7	1.4
Household equipment of base metal (697)	162	167	149	156	166	2.5	1.3
Manufactures of base metal (699)	140	154	141	158	162	15.7	1.2
Furniture and bedding accessories (821)	58	82	95	117	149	156.9	1.1
Crude vegetable materials (292)	136	152	139	118	135	-0.7	1.0
Parts and accessories of motor vehicles (784)	86	113	100	132	130	51.2	1.0
Electric power machinery, and parts (771)	14	45	53	74	130	828.6	1.0
Organo-inorganic and heterocyclic compounds (515)	63	78	98	99	127	101.6	1.0

X = Not applicable.

Table C-56. U.S. Trade by Commodity with Indonesia, 1999–2003

(Millions of dollars; total exports, f.a.s.; general imports, Customs; top 20 commodities based on 2003 dollar value.)

Commodity and SITC code	1999	2000	2001	2002	2003	Percent change, 1999–2003	Percent share of total, 2003
EXPORTS							
Total	1 939	2 547	2 499	2 581	2 520	30.0	100.0
Food and live animals (0)	233	326	439	320	379	62.7	15.0
Beverages and tobacco (1)	9	12	15	15	17	88.9	0.7
Crude materials, inedible, except fuels (2)	478	570	604	656	756	58.2	30.0
Mineral fuels, lubricants and related materials (3)	18	25	25	18	39	116.7	1.5
Animal and vegetable oils, fats and waxes (4)	1	2	1	2	2	100.0	0.1
Chemicals and related products (5)	391	474	385	373	375	-4.1	14.9
Manufactured goods classified chiefly by material (6)	166	168	141	148	140	-15.7	5.6
Machinery and transport equipment (7)	538	857	760	939	663	23.2	26.3
Miscellaneous manufactured articles (8)	72	76	94	80	110	52.8	4.4
Commodities and transactions not classified elsewhere (9)	31	36	35	30	40	29.0	1.6
Top 20 Commodities	995	1 497	1 542	1 671	1 569	57.7	62.3
Oil seeds and oleaginous fruits (222)	202	164	245	255	324	60.4	12.9
Cotton textile fibers (263)	81	166	194	197	247	204.9	9.8
Feeding stuff for animals (081)	32	112	219	156	198	518.8	7.9
Aircraft and associated equipment (792)	40	44	105	247	135	237.5	5.4
Civil engineering and contractors' plant and equipment (723)	84	289	152	203	91	8.3	3.6
Additives for mineral oils (597)	32	49	49	69	81	153.1	3.2
Pulp and waste paper (251)	89	120	59	76	73	-18.0	2.9
Telecommunications equipment (764)	25	54	63	48	48	92.0	1.9
Miscellaneous chemical products (598)	51	90	51	57	43	-15.7	1.7
Nonelectric engines and motors (714)	19	29	26	31	34	78.9	1.3
Fruit and nuts (not including oil nuts), fresh or dried (057)	19	26	31	35	33	73.7	1.3
Automatic data processing machines (752)	24	25	35	30	33	37.5	1.3
Metallic salts and peroxysalts of inorganic acids (523)	43	32	61	34	32	-25.6	1.3
Pumps, air or gas compressors and fans (743)	20	33	22	50	32	60.0	1.3
Rotating electric plant and parts (716)	14	7	21	18	31	121.4	1.2
Thermionic, cold cathode, and photocathode valves (776)	79	109	58	36	29	-63.3	1.2
Wheat and meslin, unmilled (041)	54	61	72	47	27	-50.0	1.1
Measuring/checking/analyzing instruments (874)	22	22	29	24	26	18.2	1.0
Paper and paperboard (641)	30	38	26	35	26	-13.3	1.0
Manmade fibers for spinning (267)	35	27	24	23	26	-25.7	1.0
IMPORTS							
Total	9 514	10 385	10 105	9 644	9 520	0.1	100.0
Food and live animals (0)	855	815	830	860	1 012	18.4	10.6
Beverages and tobacco (1)	19	27	23	26	20	5.3	0.2
Crude materials, inedible, except fuels (2)	512	500	406	466	654	27.7	6.9
Mineral fuels, lubricants and related materials (3)	537	586	573	474	468	-12.8	4.9
Animal and vegetable oils, fats and waxes (4)	90	94	24	37	26	-71.1	0.3
Chemicals and related products (5)	142	197	233	205	212	49.3	2.2
Manufactured goods classified chiefly by material (6)	1 275	1 271	1 067	1 009	957	-24.9	10.1
Machinery and transport equipment (7)	2 274	2 524	2 485	2 261	2 009	-11.7	21.1
Miscellaneous manufactured articles (8)	3 729	4 293	4 411	4 246	4 096	9.8	43.0
Commodities and transactions not classified elsewhere (9)	82	78	53	61	65	-20.7	0.7
Top 20 Commodities	6 229	6 856	6 802	6 764	6 562	5.3	68.9
Women's or girls' coats, jackets, etc. not knit (842)	594	716	788	734	836	40.7	8.8
Articles of apparel of textile fabrics (845)	454	623	664	629	619	36.3	6.5
Natural rubber in primary forms (231)	376	417	331	405	596	58.5	6.3
Footwear (851)	747	731	726	729	576	-22.9	6.1
Sound and television recorders (763)	434	435	626	659	553	27.4	5.8
Furniture and bedding accessories (821)	436	493	496	540	524	20.2	5.5
Men's or boys' coats, jackets, etc. not knit (841)	483	540	560	483	476	-1.4	5.0
Automatic data processing machines (752)	444	504	442	374	339	-23.6	3.6
Crude oil (333)	414	412	376	396	301	-27.3	3.2
Cocoa (072)	231	142	174	198	254	10.0	2.7
Veneers, plywood and particle board (634)	298	242	199	216	192	-35.6	2.0
Radio-broadcast receivers (762)	334	342	322	289	171	-48.8	1.8
Crustaceans (036)	161	186	155	143	169	5.0	1.8
Toys and sporting goods (894)	159	208	184	172	163	2.5	1.7
Fish, crustaceans and molluscs (37)	97	96	142	158	155	59.8	1.6
Thermionic, cold cathode, and photocathode valves (776)	183	281	201	157	141	-23.0	1.5
Wood manufactures (635)	121	147	127	125	127	5.0	1.3
Electrical machinery and apparatus (778)	120	159	107	105	126	5.0	1.3
Optical goods (884)	80	102	86	141	123	53.8	1.3
Musical instruments and accessories (898)	63	80	96	111	121	92.1	1.3

Table C-57. U.S. Trade by Commodity with Iraq, 1999–2003

(Millions of dollars; total exports, f.a.s.; general imports, Customs; top 20 commodities based on 2003 dollar value.)

Commodity and SITC code	1999	2000	2001	2002	2003	Percent change, 1999–2003	Percent share of total, 2003
EXPORTS							
Total	10	10	46	32	316	3 060.0	100.0
Food and live animals (0)	9	8	8	0	61	577.8	19.3
Beverages and tobacco (1)	0	0	0	0	0	X	0.0
Crude materials, inedible, except fuels (2)	1	0	0	0	0	X	0.0
Mineral fuels, lubricants and related materials (3)	0	0	0	0	0	X	0.0
Animal and vegetable oils, fats and waxes (4)	0	0	0	0	20	X	6.3
Chemicals and related products (5)	0	0	0	0	1	X	0.3
Manufactured goods classified chiefly by material (6)	0	0	2	1	2	X	0.6
Machinery and transport equipment (7)	0	2	37	30	208	X	65.8
Miscellaneous manufactured articles (8)	0	0	0	1	13	X	4.1
Commodities and transactions not classified elsewhere (9)	0	0	0	0	10	X	3.2
Top 20 Commodities	8	8	8	3	294	3 575.0	93.0
Rotating electric plant and parts (716)	0	0	1	0	96	X	30.4
Nonelectric engines and motors (714)	0	0	0	0	82	X	25.9
Vegetables, roots, tubers and other edible vegetable products (054)	0	0	0	0	24	X	7.6
Fixed vegetable fats and oils (421)	0	0	0	0	14	X	4.4
Milk, cream, milk products except butter or cheese (022)	0	0	0	0	12	X	3.8
Special transactions not classified by kind (931)	0	0	0	0	10	X	3.2
Rice (42)	0	8	0	0	10	X	3.2
Wheat and meslin, unmilled (041)	8	0	0	0	9	12.5	2.8
Telecommunications equipment (764)	0	0	0	0	7	X	2.2
Fixed vegetable fats and oils; crude (422)	0	0	0	0	6	X	1.9
Aircraft and associated equipment (792)	0	0	0	0	5	X	1.6
Meal and flour of wheat and meslin (46)	0	0	0	0	3	X	0.9
Special purpose motor vehicles (782)	0	0	7	2	3	X	0.9
Prefabricated buildings (811)	0	0	0	0	3	X	0.9
Measuring/checking/analyzing instruments (874)	0	0	0	1	3	X	0.9
Automatic data processing machines (752)	0	0	0	0	2	X	0.6
All motor vehicles (781)	0	0	0	0	2	X	0.6
Edible products and preparations, n.e.s. (098)	0	0	0	0	1	X	0.3
Printed matter (892)	0	0	0	0	1	X	0.3
Pumps for liquids and liquid elevators (742)	0	0	0	0	1	X	0.3
IMPORTS							
Total	4 193	6 111	5 801	3 593	4 574	9.1	100.0
Food and live animals (0)	0	0	0	0	0	X	0.0
Beverages and tobacco (1)	0	0	0	0	0	X	0.0
Crude materials, inedible, except fuels (2)	0	1	0	0	0	X	0.0
Mineral fuels, lubricants and related materials (3)	4 193	6 110	5 801	3 593	4 573	9.1	100.0
Animal and vegetable oils, fats and waxes (4)	0	0	0	0	0	X	0.0
Chemicals and related products (5)	0	0	0	0	0	X	0.0
Manufactured goods classified chiefly by material (6)	0	0	0	0	0	X	0.0
Machinery and transport equipment (7)	0	0	0	0	0	X	0.0
Miscellaneous manufactured articles (8)	0	0	0	0	0	X	0.0
Commodities and transactions not classified elsewhere (9)	0	0	0	0	1	X	0.0
Top 20 Commodities	4 194	6 111	5 801	3 592	4 574	9.1	100.0
Crude oil (333)	4 190	6 097	5 796	3 590	4 562	8.9	99.7
Oil (not crude) (334)	3	12	5	2	11	266.7	0.2
Special transactions not classified by kind (931)	0	0	0	0	1	X	0.0
Crude vegetable materials (292)	0	0	0	0	0	X	0.0
Floor coverings (659)	0	0	0	0	0	X	0.0
Copper (682)	0	0	0	0	0	X	0.0
Inorganic chemical elements (522)	0	0	0	0	0	X	0.0
Petroleum gases and other gaseous hydrocarbons (344)	0	1	0	0	0	X	0.0
Sulfur and unroasted iron pyrites (274)	0	1	0	0	0	X	0.0
Crude minerals (278)	0	0	0	0	0	X	0.0
Residual petroleum products (335)	0	0	0	0	0	X	0.0
Liquefied propane and butane (342)	1	0	0	0	0	X	0.0
Natural gas, whether or not liquefied (343)	0	0	0	0	0	X	0.0
Coal gas, water gas and producer gas (345)	0	0	0	0	0	X	0.0
Hydrocarbons and specified derivatives (511)	0	0	0	0	0	X	0.0
Works of art, collectors' pieces, and antiques (896)	0	0	0	0	0	X	0.0
Rotating electric plant and parts (716)	0	0	0	0	0	X	0.0
Nonelectric engines and motors (714)	0	0	0	0	0	X	0.0
Vegetables, roots, tubers and other edible vegetable products (054)	0	0	0	0	0	X	0.0
Fixed vegetable fats and oils (421)	0	0	0	0	0	X	0.0

X = Not applicable.

Table C-58. U.S. Trade by Commodity with Ireland, 1999–2003

(Millions of dollars; total exports, f.a.s.; general imports, Customs; top 20 commodities based on 2003 dollar value.)

Commodity and SITC code	1999	2000	2001	2002	2003	Percent change, 1999–2003	Percent share of total, 2003
EXPORTS							
Total	6 375	7 727	7 150	6 749	7 699	20.8	100.0
Food and live animals (0)	160	248	205	169	166	3.8	2.2
Beverages and tobacco (1)	17	18	17	14	17	0.0	0.2
Crude materials, inedible, except fuels (2)	70	86	75	88	65	-7.1	0.8
Mineral fuels, lubricants and related materials (3)	36	18	16	30	14	-61.1	0.2
Animal and vegetable oils, fats and waxes (4)	2	2	1	1	7	250.0	0.1
Chemicals and related products (5)	714	1 183	1 052	1 204	1 328	86.0	17.2
Manufactured goods classified chiefly by material (6)	232	277	237	269	272	17.2	3.5
Machinery and transport equipment (7)	4 233	4 857	4 249	3 586	3 937	-7.0	51.1
Miscellaneous manufactured articles (8)	679	836	1 117	1 219	1 716	152.7	22.3
Commodities and transactions not classified elsewhere (9)	231	202	181	168	176	-23.8	2.3
Top 20 Commodities	4 659	5 963	5 643	5 285	6 313	35.5	82.0
Miscellaneous manufactured articles (899)	89	160	466	626	1 098	1 133.7	14.3
Aircraft and associated equipment (792)	515	566	639	705	911	76.9	11.8
Parts for office machines and a.d.p. machines (759)	762	898	673	658	698	-8.4	9.1
Thermionic, cold cathode, and photocathode valves (776)	383	506	413	277	519	35.5	6.7
Medicaments (including veterinary medicaments) (542)	83	299	426	431	491	491.6	6.4
Automatic data processing machines (752)	864	810	648	411	445	-48.5	5.8
Carboxylic acids, halides, and derivities (513)	145	285	143	245	252	73.8	3.3
Measuring/checking/analyzing instruments (874)	139	188	143	158	221	59.0	2.9
Medical instruments and appliances (872)	145	185	225	225	215	48.3	2.8
Electrical machinery and apparatus (778)	87	152	143	143	209	140.2	2.7
Electrical apparatus for switching or protecting elec. circuits (772)	242	377	297	272	204	-15.7	2.6
Telecommunications equipment (764)	390	505	603	393	193	-50.5	2.5
Machinery and equipment specialized for particular industries (728)	144	212	84	85	186	29.2	2.4
Estimated low value shipments (994)	144	175	165	151	165	14.6	2.1
Nonelectric engines and motors (714)	191	250	220	193	117	-38.7	1.5
Feeding stuff for animals (081)	108	94	112	102	109	0.9	1.4
Miscellaneous chemical products (598)	38	75	76	57	77	102.6	1.0
Nitrogen-function compounds (514)	31	21	32	35	74	138.7	1.0
Medicinal products, except medicaments (541)	37	86	47	59	68	83.8	0.9
Heating and cooling equipment (741)	122	119	88	59	61	-50.0	0.8
IMPORTS							
Total	11 002	16 410	18 539	22 388	25 841	134.9	100.0
Food and live animals (0)	97	109	120	110	121	24.7	0.5
Beverages and tobacco (1)	243	264	252	273	342	40.7	1.3
Crude materials, inedible, except fuels (2)	68	87	51	51	54	-20.6	0.2
Mineral fuels, lubricants and related materials (3)	22	67	27	36	58	163.6	0.2
Animal and vegetable oils, fats and waxes (4)	0	0	0	0	0	X	0.0
Chemicals and related products (5)	6 392	11 555	13 354	16 366	19 257	201.3	74.5
Manufactured goods classified chiefly by material (6)	262	240	215	199	200	-23.7	0.8
Machinery and transport equipment (7)	2 703	2 463	2 238	2 645	1 956	-27.6	7.6
Miscellaneous manufactured articles (8)	688	1 014	1 644	2 053	3 234	370.1	12.5
Commodities and transactions not classified elsewhere (9)	528	611	640	655	618	17.0	2.4
Top 20 Commodities	9 976	15 219	17 504	21 324	24 772	148.3	95.9
Organo-inorganic and heterocyclic compounds (515)	5 390	10 459	10 786	10 531	11 649	116.1	45.1
Medicaments (including veterinary medicaments) (542)	381	463	1 875	5 024	5 126	1 245.4	19.8
Miscellaneous manufactured articles (899)	111	316	857	1 225	1 726	1 455.0	6.7
Medical instruments and appliances (872)	330	405	489	499	1 064	222.4	4.1
Essential oils, perfume and flavor materials (551)	44	8	9	10	908	1 963.6	3.5
Nitrogen-function compounds (514)	84	160	138	175	769	815.5	3.0
Parts for office machines and a.d.p. machines (759)	924	839	686	767	633	-31.5	2.4
Automatic data processing machines (752)	991	595	509	723	569	-42.6	2.2
Medicinal products, except medicaments (541)	258	234	296	338	488	89.1	1.9
Special transactions not classified by kind (931)	442	487	492	484	419	-5.2	1.6
Alcoholic beverages (112)	242	261	249	271	341	40.9	1.3
Estimate of low value import transactions (984)	85	124	147	171	198	132.9	0.8
Measuring/checking/analyzing instruments (874)	48	52	92	113	172	258.3	0.7
Thermionic, cold cathode, and photocathode valves (776)	209	269	172	99	122	-41.6	0.5
Telecommunications equipment (764)	97	200	336	503	120	23.7	0.5
Optical goods (884)	28	46	58	74	115	310.7	0.4
Starches, inulin and wheat gluten; albuminoidal substances (592)	96	109	103	98	103	7.3	0.4
Perfumery, cosmetics or toilet preparations, excluding soaps (553)	44	33	65	74	92	109.1	0.4
Pumps, air or gas compressors and fans (743)	79	78	72	69	86	8.9	0.3
Glassware (665)	93	81	73	76	72	-22.6	0.3

X = Not applicable.

Table C-59. U.S. Trade by Commodity with Israel, 1999–2003

(Millions of dollars; total exports, f.a.s.; general imports, Customs; top 20 commodities based on 2003 dollar value.)

Commodity and SITC code	1999	2000	2001	2002	2003	Percent change, 1999–2003	Percent share of total, 2003
EXPORTS							
Total	7 694	7 750	7 482	7 039	6 878	-10.6	100.0
Food and live animals (0)	302	371	317	332	346	14.6	5.0
Beverages and tobacco (1)	105	107	81	57	61	-41.9	0.9
Crude materials, inedible, except fuels (2)	160	177	164	174	124	-22.5	1.8
Mineral fuels, lubricants and related materials (3)	99	80	100	123	131	32.3	1.9
Animal and vegetable oils, fats and waxes (4)	17	12	13	11	15	-11.8	0.2
Chemicals and related products (5)	352	425	468	411	453	28.7	6.6
Manufactured goods classified chiefly by material (6)	1 492	1 808	1 824	2 112	2 331	56.2	33.9
Machinery and transport equipment (7)	4 080	3 664	3 378	2 861	2 458	-39.8	35.7
Miscellaneous manufactured articles (8)	847	856	909	764	756	-10.7	11.0
Commodities and transactions not classified elsewhere (9)	240	252	229	193	205	-14.6	3.0
Top 20 Commodities	5 574	5 334	5 288	4 909	5 016	-10.0	72.9
Pearls, precious and semiprecious stones (667)	1 127	1 444	1 492	1 823	2 046	81.5	29.7
Aircraft and associated equipment (792)	1 542	616	959	774	726	-52.9	10.6
Thermionic, cold cathode, and photocathode valves (776)	234	559	365	267	245	4.7	3.6
Automatic data processing machines (752)	313	335	304	187	211	-32.6	3.1
Telecommunications equipment (764)	590	549	365	249	209	-64.6	3.0
Measuring/checking/analyzing instruments (874)	268	253	261	208	207	-22.8	3.0
Arms and ammunition (891)	168	151	251	206	207	23.2	3.0
Estimated low value shipments (994)	158	178	171	150	130	-17.7	1.9
Oil (not crude) (334)	77	71	89	114	124	61.0	1.8
Nonelectric engines and motors (714)	208	202	193	157	119	-42.8	1.7
Electrical machinery and apparatus (778)	117	160	155	161	105	-10.3	1.5
Parts for office machines and a.d.p. machines (759)	147	179	125	97	93	-36.7	1.4
Electrical apparatus for switching or protecting elec. circuits (772)	78	119	123	96	83	6.4	1.2
Maize (not including sweet corn) unmilled (044)	53	71	49	68	78	47.2	1.1
Internal combustion piston engines (713)	19	11	11	11	78	310.5	1.1
Machinery and equipment specialized for particular industries (728)	238	194	116	64	76	-68.1	1.1
Special transactions not classified by kind (931)	51	47	45	39	72	41.2	1.0
Miscellaneous nonferrous base metals (689)	36	53	57	55	72	100.0	1.0
Medical instruments and appliances (872)	47	46	61	64	69	46.8	1.0
Oil seeds and oleaginous fruits (222)	103	96	96	119	66	-35.9	1.0
IMPORTS							
Total	9 870	12 975	11 971	12 442	12 770	29.4	100.0
Food and live animals (0)	86	82	95	100	124	44.2	1.0
Beverages and tobacco (1)	4	5	4	5	9	125.0	0.1
Crude materials, inedible, except fuels (2)	44	46	50	46	44	0.0	0.3
Mineral fuels, lubricants and related materials (3)	3	46	15	65	17	466.7	0.1
Animal and vegetable oils, fats and waxes (4)	0	1	1	0	1	X	0.0
Chemicals and related products (5)	623	757	988	1 013	1 248	100.3	9.8
Manufactured goods classified chiefly by material (6)	4 801	5 927	5 687	6 363	6 673	39.0	52.3
Machinery and transport equipment (7)	2 241	3 797	2 933	2 716	2 752	22.8	21.6
Miscellaneous manufactured articles (8)	1 518	1 715	1 629	1 576	1 433	-5.6	11.2
Commodities and transactions not classified elsewhere (9)	550	599	571	557	469	-14.7	3.7
Top 20 Commodities	8 264	10 999	10 054	10 418	10 768	30.3	84.3
Pearls, precious and semiprecious stones (667)	4 325	5 397	5 144	5 807	6 113	41.3	47.9
Medicaments (including veterinary medicaments) (542)	208	271	503	534	703	238.0	5.5
Telecommunications equipment (764)	792	1 112	925	604	614	-22.5	4.8
Special transactions not classified by kind (931)	501	532	509	494	404	-19.4	3.2
Aircraft and associated equipment (792)	279	330	371	384	389	39.4	3.0
Thermionic, cold cathode, and photocathode valves (776)	69	502	247	294	314	355.1	2.5
Electrical machinery and apparatus (778)	150	549	256	306	289	92.7	2.3
Electro-diagnostic apparatus (774)	101	140	169	212	268	165.3	2.1
Measuring/checking/analyzing instruments (874)	230	378	328	256	229	-0.4	1.8
Jewelry, goldsmiths' and silversmiths' wares (897)	243	241	239	275	216	-11.1	1.7
Nonelectric engines and motors (714)	144	144	161	169	170	18.1	1.3
Articles of apparel of textile fabrics (845)	186	194	175	152	150	-19.4	1.2
Women's or girls' coats, jackets, etc. knit (844)	156	193	157	168	149	-4.5	1.2
Medical instruments and appliances (872)	275	177	152	140	131	-52.4	1.0
Organo-inorganic and heterocyclic compounds (515)	98	116	121	120	129	31.6	1.0
Articles of plastics (893)	92	109	126	126	124	34.8	1.0
Automatic data processing machines (752)	109	245	183	112	115	5.5	0.9
Printing and bookbinding machinery (726)	93	114	96	98	92	-1.1	0.7
Tools for use in the hand or in machines (695)	87	102	96	89	87	0.0	0.7
Electrical apparatus for switching or protecting elec. circuits (772)	126	153	96	78	82	-34.9	0.6

X = Not applicable.

Table C-60. U.S. Trade by Commodity with Italy, 1999–2003

(Millions of dollars; total exports, f.a.s.; general imports, Customs; top 20 commodities based on 2003 dollar value.)

Commodity and SITC code	1999	2000	2001	2002	2003	Percent change, 1999–2003	Percent share of total, 2003
EXPORTS							
Total	10 094	11 000	9 916	10 089	10 570	4.7	100.0
Food and live animals (0)	328	325	337	298	344	4.9	3.3
Beverages and tobacco (1)	62	60	40	46	46	-25.8	0.4
Crude materials, inedible, except fuels (2)	681	882	819	863	839	23.2	7.9
Mineral fuels, lubricants and related materials (3)	295	287	359	244	257	-12.9	2.4
Animal and vegetable oils, fats and waxes (4)	37	47	24	26	11	-70.3	0.1
Chemicals and related products (5)	1 630	2 122	1 453	1 510	1 677	2.9	15.9
Manufactured goods classified chiefly by material (6)	760	851	911	744	963	26.7	9.1
Machinery and transport equipment (7)	4 557	4 746	4 185	4 611	4 789	5.1	45.3
Miscellaneous manufactured articles (8)	1 409	1 362	1 472	1 412	1 312	-6.9	12.4
Commodities and transactions not classified elsewhere (9)	335	318	314	336	333	-0.6	3.2
Top 20 Commodities	5 811	6 152	5 609	5 920	6 320	8.8	59.8
Aircraft and associated equipment (792)	1 068	659	600	1 499	1 465	37.2	13.9
Nonelectric engines and motors (714)	384	322	418	550	600	56.3	5.7
Medicaments (including veterinary medicaments) (542)	575	552	428	455	574	-0.2	5.4
Measuring/checking/analyzing instruments (874)	436	463	437	386	456	4.6	4.3
Medicinal products, except medicaments (541)	232	382	328	336	410	76.7	3.9
Pulp and waste paper (251)	271	372	314	330	372	37.3	3.5
Thermionic, cold cathode, and photocathode valves (776)	487	738	453	281	244	-49.9	2.3
Medical instruments and appliances (872)	203	231	250	250	230	13.3	2.2
Estimated low value shipments (994)	212	230	221	207	219	3.3	2.1
Telecommunications equipment (764)	311	415	334	177	196	-37.0	1.9
Automatic data processing machines (752)	254	238	199	174	192	-24.4	1.8
Silver, platinum, and other platinum group metals (681)	160	231	280	199	168	5.0	1.6
Internal combustion piston engines (713)	141	174	159	180	168	19.1	1.6
Machinery and equipment specialized for particular industries (728)	242	274	202	122	162	-33.1	1.5
Parts for office machines and a.d.p. machines (759)	226	266	249	144	156	-31.0	1.5
Miscellaneous chemical products (598)	173	161	129	108	152	-12.1	1.4
All motor vehicles (781)	76	74	117	141	151	98.7	1.4
Electro-diagnostic apparatus (774)	129	135	136	161	145	12.4	1.4
Coal, pulverized or not (321)	186	165	258	151	139	-25.3	1.3
Leather (611)	45	70	97	69	121	168.9	1.1
IMPORTS							
Total	22 438	25 050	23 824	24 290	25 437	13.4	100.0
Food and live animals (0)	563	566	574	614	708	25.8	2.8
Beverages and tobacco (1)	666	719	758	915	1 098	64.9	4.3
Crude materials, inedible, except fuels (2)	112	137	117	113	102	-8.9	0.4
Mineral fuels, lubricants and related materials (3)	127	547	559	496	562	342.5	2.2
Animal and vegetable oils, fats and waxes (4)	240	324	283	326	375	56.3	1.5
Chemicals and related products (5)	2 281	2 685	2 216	2 199	2 386	4.6	9.4
Manufactured goods classified chiefly by material (6)	3 325	3 887	3 749	3 713	3 922	18.0	15.4
Machinery and transport equipment (7)	6 781	7 257	6 891	7 113	7 494	10.5	29.5
Miscellaneous manufactured articles (8)	7 556	8 162	7 943	7 976	8 051	6.6	31.7
Commodities and transactions not classified elsewhere (9)	787	767	734	824	739	-6.1	2.9
Top 20 Commodities	10 561	12 077	11 428	11 960	12 691	20.2	49.9
Furniture and bedding accessories (821)	1 070	1 300	1 265	1 310	1 363	27.4	5.4
Footwear (851)	1 189	1 264	1 261	1 184	1 245	4.7	4.9
Jewelry, goldsmiths' and silversmiths' wares (897)	1 495	1 506	1 408	1 536	1 242	-16.9	4.9
Alcoholic beverages (112)	622	668	713	863	1 029	65.4	4.0
Clay and refractory construction materials (662)	489	559	554	627	720	47.2	2.8
Medicaments (including veterinary medicaments) (542)	632	1 078	603	552	629	-0.5	2.5
Machinery and equipment specialized for particular industries (728)	585	588	523	444	553	-5.5	2.2
Lime, cement, and fabricated construction materials (661)	448	510	518	510	545	21.7	2.1
Parts and accessories of motor vehicles (784)	402	421	395	453	540	34.3	2.1
Oil (not crude) (334)	122	522	546	478	533	336.9	2.1
Nonelectrical machinery and tools (745)	304	312	355	416	524	72.4	2.1
Men's or boys' coats, jackets, etc. not knit (841)	490	476	447	436	486	-0.8	1.9
Women's or girls' coats, jackets, etc. not knit (842)	366	381	421	444	474	29.5	1.9
Optical goods (884)	363	418	454	425	467	28.7	1.8
Organo-inorganic and heterocyclic compounds (515)	444	405	403	466	467	5.2	1.8
Special transactions not classified by kind (931)	481	425	407	497	391	-18.7	1.5
Works of art, collectors' pieces, and antiques (896)	378	403	346	402	376	-0.5	1.5
Fixed vegetable fats and oils (421)	238	321	280	322	371	55.9	1.5
Trunks, suitcases, vanity cases, and briefcases (831)	263	299	305	293	368	39.9	1.4
All motor vehicles (781)	180	221	224	302	368	104.4	1.4

Table C-61. U.S. Trade by Commodity with Jamaica, 1999–2003

(Millions of dollars; total exports, f.a.s.; general imports, Customs; top 20 commodities based on 2003 dollar value.)

Commodity and SITC code	1999	2000	2001	2002	2003	Percent change, 1999–2003	Percent share of total, 2003
EXPORTS							
Total	1 295	1 378	1 407	1 420	1 470	13.5	100.0
Food and live animals (0)	170	156	164	164	165	-2.9	11.2
Beverages and tobacco (1)	5	6	7	8	9	80.0	0.6
Crude materials, inedible, except fuels (2)	36	32	29	22	22	-38.9	1.5
Mineral fuels, lubricants and related materials (3)	133	188	160	183	275	106.8	18.7
Animal and vegetable oils, fats and waxes (4)	13	11	8	12	15	15.4	1.0
Chemicals and related products (5)	140	167	175	185	163	16.4	11.1
Manufactured goods classified chiefly by material (6)	122	133	135	131	115	-5.7	7.8
Machinery and transport equipment (7)	278	304	398	392	391	40.6	26.6
Miscellaneous manufactured articles (8)	306	275	216	192	183	-40.2	12.4
Commodities and transactions not classified elsewhere (9)	92	104	114	130	133	44.6	9.0
Top 20 Commodities	564	663	752	792	877	55.5	59.7
Oil (not crude) (334)	131	186	158	181	268	104.6	18.2
Telecommunications equipment (764)	28	42	86	115	92	228.6	6.3
Special transactions not classified by kind (931)	20	31	47	66	65	225.0	4.4
Estimated low value shipments (994)	57	58	61	59	62	8.8	4.2
Inorganic chemical elements (522)	35	50	57	65	49	40.0	3.3
Nonelectric engines and motors (714)	1	1	39	2	40	3 900.0	2.7
Articles of apparel of textile fabrics (845)	67	55	50	38	36	-46.3	2.4
Automatic data processing machines (752)	25	34	35	43	30	20.0	2.0
Wheat and meslin, unmilled (041)	22	22	23	21	27	22.7	1.8
Jewelry, goldsmiths' and silversmiths' wares (897)	14	17	17	28	26	85.7	1.8
Articles of plastics (893)	14	22	23	21	24	71.4	1.6
Maize (not including sweet corn) unmilled (044)	23	21	21	27	23	0.0	1.6
Feeding stuff for animals (081)	20	17	19	22	23	15.0	1.6
Mechanical handling equipment (744)	11	10	12	12	19	72.7	1.3
Furniture and bedding accessories (821)	17	23	18	20	18	5.9	1.2
Aircraft and associated equipment (792)	9	6	20	13	17	88.9	1.2
Edible products and preparations, n.e.s. (098)	20	20	20	17	15	-25.0	1.0
Wood, simply worked (248)	28	27	20	15	15	-46.4	1.0
Printed matter (892)	10	9	11	12	14	40.0	1.0
Medicaments (including veterinary medicaments) (542)	12	12	15	15	14	16.7	1.0
IMPORTS							
Total	679	648	461	392	495	-27.1	100.0
Food and live animals (0)	52	43	48	49	47	-9.6	9.5
Beverages and tobacco (1)	37	33	21	29	33	-10.8	6.7
Crude materials, inedible, except fuels (2)	114	92	123	125	210	84.2	42.4
Mineral fuels, lubricants and related materials (3)	0	0	1	4	0	X	0.0
Animal and vegetable oils, fats and waxes (4)	0	0	0	0	0	X	0.0
Chemicals and related products (5)	26	33	40	35	50	92.3	10.1
Manufactured goods classified chiefly by material (6)	62	150	16	2	10	-83.9	2.0
Machinery and transport equipment (7)	1	1	1	2	2	100.0	0.4
Miscellaneous manufactured articles (8)	347	271	189	126	107	-69.2	21.6
Commodities and transactions not classified elsewhere (9)	40	25	21	20	35	-12.5	7.1
Top 20 Commodities	544	531	398	367	478	-12.1	96.6
Aluminum ores and concentrates (285)	109	87	119	121	206	89.0	41.6
Articles of apparel of textile fabrics (845)	144	101	75	62	61	-57.6	12.3
Alcohols, phenols, and halogenated derivatives (512)	23	29	36	32	48	108.7	9.7
Special transactions not classified by kind (931)	36	20	18	17	30	-16.7	6.1
Alcoholic beverages (112)	25	23	19	25	27	8.0	5.5
Women's or girls' coats, jackets, etc. knit (844)	42	41	38	38	23	-45.2	4.6
Men's or boys' coats, jackets, etc. knit (843)	8	11	9	12	13	62.5	2.6
Vegetables, roots, tubers and other edible vegetable products (054)	11	8	11	11	11	0.0	2.2
Edible products and preparations, n.e.s. (098)	6	8	10	10	9	50.0	1.8
Clay and refractory construction materials (662)	61	148	15	0	9	-85.2	1.8
Crustaceans (036)	11	7	7	6	6	-45.5	1.2
Men's or boys' coats, jackets, etc. not knit (841)	37	24	18	7	5	-86.5	1.0
Nonalcoholic beverages (111)	1	1	2	4	5	400.0	1.0
Estimate of low value import transactions (984)	4	5	3	3	5	25.0	1.0
Fruit and nuts (not including oil nuts), fresh or dried (057)	4	5	4	5	4	0.0	0.8
Cereal preparations (48)	3	3	4	4	4	33.3	0.8
Fruit preserved and fruit preparations (58)	0	1	2	3	4	X	0.8
Women's or girls' coats, jackets, etc. not knit (842)	15	4	2	2	3	-80.0	0.6
Coffee and coffee substitutes (071)	2	3	4	3	3	50.0	0.6
Spices (075)	2	2	2	2	2	0.0	0.4

X = Not applicable.

Table C-62. U.S. Trade by Commodity with Japan, 1999–2003

(Millions of dollars; total exports, f.a.s.; general imports, Customs; top 20 commodities based on 2003 dollar value.)

Commodity and SITC code	1999	2000	2001	2002	2003	Percent change, 1999–2003	Percent share of total, 2003
EXPORTS							
Total	57 484	65 254	57 639	51 440	52 064	-9.4	100.0
Food and live animals (0)	8 625	9 042	8 584	7 916	8 222	-4.7	15.8
Beverages and tobacco (1)	2 203	2 492	1 673	1 351	1 363	-38.1	2.6
Crude materials, inedible, except fuels (2)	3 615	3 848	3 185	2 891	2 971	-17.8	5.7
Mineral fuels, lubricants and related materials (3)	760	845	519	564	592	-22.1	1.1
Animal and vegetable oils, fats and waxes (4)	76	55	57	69	70	-7.9	0.1
Chemicals and related products (5)	5 794	6 547	6 510	6 501	6 804	17.4	13.1
Manufactured goods classified chiefly by material (6)	2 937	3 549	2 940	2 544	2 585	-12.0	5.0
Machinery and transport equipment (7)	24 117	27 866	23 467	20 430	20 233	-16.1	38.9
Miscellaneous manufactured articles (8)	8 037	9 680	9 309	7 788	7 846	-2.4	15.1
Commodities and transactions not classified elsewhere (9)	1 320	1 331	1 396	1 386	1 378	4.4	2.6
Top 20 Commodities	31 036	35 315	30 534	27 109	27 740	-10.6	53.3
Aircraft and associated equipment (792)	4 620	3 394	2 737	3 813	4 844	4.8	9.3
Thermionic, cold cathode, and photocathode valves (776)	3 673	4 679	3 619	2 819	2 499	-32.0	4.8
Measuring/checking/analyzing instruments (874)	2 047	2 682	2 474	2 083	2 068	1.0	4.0
Automatic data processing machines (752)	2 211	2 878	2 542	1 779	1 650	-25.4	3.2
Maize (not including sweet corn) unmilled (044)	1 428	1 427	1 331	1 557	1 602	12.2	3.1
Telecommunications equipment (764)	2 418	2 857	2 401	1 723	1 569	-35.1	3.0
Medical instruments and appliances (872)	1 002	1 081	1 188	1 103	1 201	19.9	2.3
Meat of bovine animals (011)	1 367	1 517	1 243	833	1 157	-15.4	2.2
Parts and accessories of motor vehicles (784)	1 054	1 393	1 185	1 219	1 071	1.6	2.1
Nonelectric engines and motors (714)	988	1 256	1 408	1 252	1 063	7.6	2.0
Tobacco, manufactured (122)	1 812	2 096	1 299	979	1 013	-44.1	1.9
Parts for office machines and a.d.p. machines (759)	2 011	2 452	1 909	1 108	1 012	-49.7	1.9
Oil seeds and oleaginous fruits (222)	808	795	747	842	973	20.4	1.9
Other meat and edible offal (012)	1 106	1 228	1 255	1 006	973	-12.0	1.9
Miscellaneous chemical products (598)	628	832	856	834	935	48.9	1.8
Machinery and equipment specialized for particular industries (728)	1 122	1 992	1 295	753	902	-19.6	1.7
Fish, fresh, chilled or frozen (034)	903	917	934	910	832	-7.9	1.6
Radioactive and associated materials (525)	540	594	584	909	817	51.3	1.6
Special transactions not classified by kind (931)	533	453	659	770	785	47.3	1.5
Electro-diagnostic apparatus (774)	765	792	868	817	774	1.2	1.5
IMPORTS							
Total	131 404	146 577	126 602	121 494	118 029	-10.2	100.0
Food and live animals (0)	347	351	312	328	364	4.9	0.3
Beverages and tobacco (1)	71	72	71	74	61	-14.1	0.1
Crude materials, inedible, except fuels (2)	236	277	242	243	232	-1.7	0.2
Mineral fuels, lubricants and related materials (3)	318	370	324	237	233	-26.7	0.2
Animal and vegetable oils, fats and waxes (4)	22	25	23	23	24	9.1	0.0
Chemicals and related products (5)	6 536	7 220	6 679	7 008	8 013	22.6	6.8
Manufactured goods classified chiefly by material (6)	7 834	8 098	6 928	6 593	6 707	-14.4	5.7
Machinery and transport equipment (7)	99 367	111 949	94 258	92 005	88 498	-10.9	75.0
Miscellaneous manufactured articles (8)	12 750	14 209	13 783	11 371	10 371	-18.7	8.8
Commodities and transactions not classified elsewhere (9)	3 921	4 005	3 982	3 613	3 527	-10.0	3.0
Top 20 Commodities	92 240	104 950	87 779	86 720	83 773	-9.2	71.0
All motor vehicles (781)	29 261	32 154	31 183	35 110	32 227	10.1	27.3
Parts and accessories of motor vehicles (784)	6 155	7 320	6 650	6 854	7 286	18.4	6.2
Internal combustion piston engines (713)	5 198	5 678	5 099	4 916	4 771	-8.2	4.0
Parts for office machines and a.d.p. machines (759)	5 157	5 921	4 813	4 629	4 663	-9.6	4.0
Sound and television recorders (763)	4 486	5 011	3 588	3 879	4 051	-9.7	3.4
Automatic data processing machines (752)	9 456	9 332	5 924	4 565	3 403	-64.0	2.9
Electrical machinery and apparatus (778)	3 976	4 797	3 553	3 079	2 943	-26.0	2.5
Thermionic, cold cathode, and photocathode valves (776)	7 010	8 797	4 948	3 219	2 804	-60.0	2.4
Telecommunications equipment (764)	4 540	5 290	3 442	2 656	2 538	-44.1	2.2
Special transactions not classified by kind (931)	2 496	2 382	2 568	2 296	2 208	-11.5	1.9
Measuring/checking/analyzing instruments (874)	2 135	2 966	2 501	2 119	2 206	3.3	1.9
Motorcycles and cycles, motorized and not motorized (785)	1 444	2 083	2 271	2 212	2 149	48.8	1.8
Medicaments (including veterinary medicaments) (542)	1 031	1 237	1 319	1 528	2 040	97.9	1.7
Television receivers (761)	337	664	1 232	1 573	1 924	470.9	1.6
Electrical apparatus for switching or protecting elec. circuits (772)	2 230	2 652	1 860	1 570	1 530	-31.4	1.3
Musical instruments and accessories (898)	1 462	1 532	1 318	1 364	1 517	3.8	1.3
Machinery and equipment specialized for particular industries (728)	2 061	3 135	2 111	1 701	1 503	-27.1	1.3
Civil engineering and contractors' plant and equipment (723)	1 520	1 355	1 094	1 154	1 464	-3.7	1.2
Estimate of low value import transactions (984)	1 424	1 622	1 412	1 314	1 317	-7.5	1.1
Pumps, air or gas compressors and fans (743)	861	1 022	893	982	1 229	42.7	1.0

Table C-63. U.S. Trade by Commodity with Jordan, 1999–2003

(Millions of dollars; total exports, f.a.s.; general imports, Customs; top 20 commodities based on 2003 dollar value.)

Commodity and SITC code	1999	2000	2001	2002	2003	Percent change, 1999–2003	Percent share of total, 2003
EXPORTS							
Total	276	313	343	404	492	78.3	100.0
Food and live animals (0)	62	81	110	66	66	6.5	13.4
Beverages and tobacco (1)	11	17	18	11	9	-18.2	1.8
Crude materials, inedible, except fuels (2)	15	27	18	23	18	20.0	3.7
Mineral fuels, lubricants and related materials (3)	1	1	0	1	0	X	0.0
Animal and vegetable oils, fats and waxes (4)	24	8	11	18	17	-29.2	3.5
Chemicals and related products (5)	13	16	22	19	24	84.6	4.9
Manufactured goods classified chiefly by material (6)	12	11	13	26	18	50.0	3.7
Machinery and transport equipment (7)	91	106	105	159	263	189.0	53.5
Miscellaneous manufactured articles (8)	31	35	32	66	52	67.7	10.6
Commodities and transactions not classified elsewhere (9)	15	10	13	17	26	73.3	5.3
Top 20 Commodities	160	175	206	245	361	125.6	73.4
Aircraft and associated equipment (792)	28	19	27	43	119	325.0	24.2
Telecommunications equipment (764)	5	14	13	21	35	600.0	7.1
Wheat and meslin, unmilled (041)	27	59	87	42	30	11.1	6.1
All motor vehicles (781)	6	5	5	12	27	350.0	5.5
Arms and ammunition (891)	8	12	6	32	24	200.0	4.9
Special transactions not classified by kind (931)	8	2	6	9	18	125.0	3.7
Fixed vegetable fats and oils (421)	20	6	10	16	15	-25.0	3.0
Automatic data processing machines (752)	4	6	6	8	10	150.0	2.0
Electro-diagnostic apparatus (774)	3	3	4	12	9	200.0	1.8
Maize (not including sweet corn) unmilled (044)	11	3	1	5	9	-18.2	1.8
Civil engineering and contractors' plant and equipment (723)	5	2	2	3	8	60.0	1.6
Special purpose motor vehicles (782)	1	0	1	4	8	700.0	1.6
Estimated low value shipments (994)	5	6	6	7	7	40.0	1.4
Tobacco, unmanufactured; tobacco refuse (121)	0	0	0	0	7	X	1.4
Pulp and waste paper (251)	7	15	8	6	7	0.0	1.4
Edible products and preparations, n.e.s. (098)	3	5	5	4	6	100.0	1.2
Iron and steel tubes, pipes and fittings (679)	2	0	1	8	6	200.0	1.2
Pumps, air or gas compressors and fans (743)	7	10	8	5	6	-14.3	1.2
Furniture and bedding accessories (821)	3	3	5	4	5	66.7	1.0
Measuring/checking/analyzing instruments (874)	7	5	5	4	5	-28.6	1.0
IMPORTS							
Total	31	73	229	412	673	2 071.0	100.0
Food and live animals (0)	0	1	1	1	2	X	0.3
Beverages and tobacco (1)	0	0	0	0	0	X	0.0
Crude materials, inedible, except fuels (2)	1	1	3	2	1	0.0	0.1
Mineral fuels, lubricants and related materials (3)	0	0	0	0	0	X	0.0
Animal and vegetable oils, fats and waxes (4)	0	0	0	0	0	X	0.0
Chemicals and related products (5)	1	1	2	3	3	200.0	0.4
Manufactured goods classified chiefly by material (6)	1	1	1	2	1	0.0	0.1
Machinery and transport equipment (7)	1	1	5	2	4	300.0	0.6
Miscellaneous manufactured articles (8)	8	64	210	399	635	7 837.5	94.4
Commodities and transactions not classified elsewhere (9)	19	4	7	3	27	42.1	4.0
Top 20 Commodities	24	57	205	405	672	2 700.0	99.9
Articles of apparel of textile fabrics (845)	0	12	83	176	205	X	30.5
Women's or girls' coats, jackets, etc. not knit (842)	0	14	40	77	142	X	21.1
Women's or girls' coats, jackets, etc. knit (844)	0	4	23	60	123	X	18.3
Men's or boys' coats, jackets, etc. knit (843)	0	2	18	45	70	X	10.4
Jewelry, goldsmiths' and silversmiths' wares (897)	4	9	8	11	50	1 150.0	7.4
Men's or boys' coats, jackets, etc. not knit (841)	1	11	19	26	42	4 100.0	6.2
Special transactions not classified by kind (931)	19	4	7	3	26	36.8	3.9
Estimate of low value import transactions (984)	0	0	1	1	2	X	0.3
Heating and cooling equipment (741)	0	0	0	1	2	X	0.3
Printed matter (892)	0	1	0	1	1	X	0.1
Articles of plastics (893)	0	0	0	1	1	X	0.1
Perfumery, cosmetics or toilet preparations, excluding soaps (553)	0	0	1	0	1	X	0.1
Parts and accessories of motor vehicles (784)	0	0	1	0	1	X	0.1
Soap, cleansing and polishing preparations (554)	0	0	1	0	1	X	0.1
Machinery and equipment specialized for particular industries (728)	0	0	0	0	1	X	0.1
Medicinal products, except medicaments (541)	0	0	0	1	1	X	0.1
Ores and concencentrate of precious metal (289)	0	0	1	0	1	X	0.1
Crude minerals (278)	0	0	2	2	1	X	0.1
Edible products and preparations, n.e.s. (098)	0	0	0	0	1	X	0.1
Carboxylic acids, halides, and derivities (513)	0	0	0	0	0	X	0.0

X = Not applicable.

Table C-64. U.S. Trade by Commodity with South Korea, 1999–2003

(Millions of dollars; total exports, f.a.s.; general imports, Customs; top 20 commodities based on 2003 dollar value.)

Commodity and SITC code	1999	2000	2001	2002	2003	Percent change, 1999–2003	Percent share of total, 2003
EXPORTS							
Total	22 954	27 902	22 197	22 596	24 099	5.0	100.0
Food and live animals (0)	1 767	1 761	1 824	1 988	2 251	27.4	9.3
Beverages and tobacco (1)	120	170	164	101	92	-23.3	0.4
Crude materials, inedible, except fuels (2)	1 627	2 096	1 891	1 788	2 022	24.3	8.4
Mineral fuels, lubricants and related materials (3)	487	354	191	228	324	-33.5	1.3
Animal and vegetable oils, fats and waxes (4)	128	77	30	79	46	-64.1	0.2
Chemicals and related products (5)	2 146	2 744	2 538	2 821	3 397	58.3	14.1
Manufactured goods classified chiefly by material (6)	922	1 122	1 172	1 015	1 123	21.8	4.7
Machinery and transport equipment (7)	13 556	16 865	12 003	12 052	12 299	-9.3	51.0
Miscellaneous manufactured articles (8)	1 776	2 258	1 993	2 098	2 123	19.5	8.8
Commodities and transactions not classified elsewhere (9)	425	456	390	426	419	-1.4	1.7
Top 20 Commodities	14 551	18 644	13 560	13 810	14 919	2.5	61.9
Thermionic, cold cathode, and photocathode valves (776)	6 074	6 104	3 496	3 899	4 697	-22.7	19.5
Aircraft and associated equipment (792)	1 564	1 910	2 634	2 330	1 822	16.5	7.6
Machinery and equipment specialized for particular industries (728)	895	1 721	1 030	867	1 010	12.8	4.2
Meat of bovine animals (011)	330	532	361	608	742	124.8	3.1
Telecommunications equipment (764)	955	1 353	806	788	736	-22.9	3.1
Measuring/checking/analyzing instruments (874)	756	1 007	740	651	717	-5.2	3.0
Electrical machinery and apparatus (778)	305	439	311	419	589	93.1	2.4
Hydrocarbons and specified derivatives (511)	142	249	149	236	580	308.5	2.4
Automatic data processing machines (752)	825	1 478	813	694	519	-37.1	2.2
Hides and skins, raw (211)	324	527	562	432	407	25.6	1.7
Nitrogen-function compounds (514)	145	292	250	288	373	157.2	1.5
Fish, fresh, chilled or frozen (034)	169	194	296	289	357	111.2	1.5
Ferrous waste and scrap (282)	215	242	192	236	352	63.7	1.5
Pulp and waste paper (251)	383	461	239	306	318	-17.0	1.3
Nonelectric engines and motors (714)	301	271	222	366	318	5.6	1.3
Oil seeds and oleaginous fruits (222)	226	260	230	258	296	31.0	1.2
Miscellaneous chemical products (598)	222	260	276	273	288	29.7	1.2
Pumps, air or gas compressors and fans (743)	181	304	358	358	282	55.8	1.2
Alcohols, phenols, and halogenated derivatives (512)	166	172	129	178	259	56.0	1.1
Parts for office machines and a.d.p. machines (759)	373	868	466	334	257	-31.1	1.1
IMPORTS							
Total	31 262	40 300	35 185	35 575	36 963	18.2	100.0
Food and live animals (0)	150	166	176	187	189	26.0	0.5
Beverages and tobacco (1)	17	22	32	46	54	217.6	0.1
Crude materials, inedible, except fuels (2)	145	209	198	173	218	50.3	0.6
Mineral fuels, lubricants and related materials (3)	300	629	701	451	408	36.0	1.1
Animal and vegetable oils, fats and waxes (4)	0	2	2	1	1	X	0.0
Chemicals and related products (5)	757	869	872	870	907	19.8	2.5
Manufactured goods classified chiefly by material (6)	3 428	3 769	3 282	3 471	3 313	-3.4	9.0
Machinery and transport equipment (7)	21 631	29 475	24 962	25 778	27 682	28.0	74.9
Miscellaneous manufactured articles (8)	4 234	4 488	4 216	3 831	3 474	-17.9	9.4
Commodities and transactions not classified elsewhere (9)	600	670	743	765	717	19.5	1.9
Top 20 Commodities	22 854	30 607	26 136	26 987	28 578	25.0	77.3
All motor vehicles (781)	2 879	4 839	6 344	6 803	7 938	175.7	21.5
Telecommunications equipment (764)	2 195	3 618	4 830	4 947	6 289	186.5	17.0
Thermionic, cold cathode, and photocathode valves (776)	6 681	7 608	3 562	3 499	3 405	-49.0	9.2
Automatic data processing machines (752)	3 686	4 885	3 150	2 769	2 140	-41.9	5.8
Parts for office machines and a.d.p. machines (759)	1 737	2 841	1 433	1 791	1 540	-11.3	4.2
Television receivers (761)	161	155	221	312	780	384.5	2.1
Household type electrical and nonelectrical equipment (775)	600	624	573	777	778	29.7	2.1
Sound and television recorders (763)	486	774	767	918	702	44.4	1.9
Articles of apparel of textile fabrics (845)	696	708	727	724	588	-15.5	1.6
Electrical machinery and apparatus (778)	388	510	398	446	553	42.5	1.5
Special transactions not classified by kind (931)	459	480	573	598	541	17.9	1.5
Parts and accessories of motor vehicles (784)	291	327	359	471	516	77.3	1.4
Rubber tires and accessories (625)	314	312	336	436	470	49.7	1.3
Oil (not crude) (334)	267	600	691	426	391	46.4	1.1
Heating and cooling equipment (741)	246	347	350	382	380	54.5	1.0
Men's or boys' coats, jackets, etc. not knit (841)	479	563	506	423	376	-21.5	1.0
Paper and paperboard (641)	195	283	230	275	335	71.8	0.9
Women's or girls' coats, jackets, etc. not knit (842)	480	508	459	366	295	-38.5	0.8
Musical instruments and accessories (898)	403	386	352	313	282	-30.0	0.8
Knitted or crocheted fabrics (655)	211	239	275	311	279	32.2	0.8

X = Not applicable.

Table C-65. U.S. Trade by Commodity with Kuwait, 1999–2003

(Millions of dollars; total exports, f.a.s.; general imports, Customs; top 20 commodities based on 2003 dollar value.)

Commodity and SITC code	1999	2000	2001	2002	2003	Percent change, 1999–2003	Percent share of total, 2003
EXPORTS							
Total	909	791	906	1 015	1 509	66.0	100.0
Food and live animals (0)	43	38	49	47	117	172.1	7.8
Beverages and tobacco (1)	45	45	35	20	25	-44.4	1.7
Crude materials, inedible, except fuels (2)	12	8	8	5	6	-50.0	0.4
Mineral fuels, lubricants and related materials (3)	2	2	2	1	2	0.0	0.1
Animal and vegetable oils, fats and waxes (4)	11	8	6	7	13	18.2	0.9
Chemicals and related products (5)	49	47	49	52	59	20.4	3.9
Manufactured goods classified chiefly by material (6)	46	40	37	68	75	63.0	5.0
Machinery and transport equipment (7)	479	460	576	666	972	102.9	64.4
Miscellaneous manufactured articles (8)	174	115	119	120	178	2.3	11.8
Commodities and transactions not classified elsewhere (9)	46	29	24	29	63	37.0	4.2
Top 20 Commodities	655	561	644	738	1 097	67.5	72.7
All motor vehicles (781)	143	159	223	297	384	168.5	25.4
Special purpose motor vehicles (782)	26	60	58	24	84	223.1	5.6
Aircraft and associated equipment (792)	22	16	32	58	67	204.5	4.4
Telecommunications equipment (764)	13	18	11	10	61	369.2	4.0
Pumps, air or gas compressors and fans (743)	25	41	32	32	47	88.0	3.1
Arms and ammunition (891)	95	43	38	41	43	-54.7	2.8
Heating and cooling equipment (741)	70	22	30	38	42	-40.0	2.8
Measuring/checking/analyzing instruments (874)	16	6	14	19	38	137.5	2.5
Civil engineering and contractors' plant and equipment (723)	49	26	40	34	37	-24.5	2.5
Parts and accessories of motor vehicles (784)	21	20	19	19	31	47.6	2.1
Special transactions not classified by kind (931)	26	11	6	8	30	15.4	2.0
Automatic data processing machines (752)	12	9	17	13	30	150.0	2.0
Miscellaneous chemical products (598)	26	23	20	20	28	7.7	1.9
Estimated low value shipments (994)	17	15	15	18	27	58.8	1.8
Edible products and preparations, n.e.s. (098)	14	15	18	19	27	92.9	1.8
Furniture and bedding accessories (821)	27	25	26	25	26	-3.7	1.7
Meat of bovine animals (011)	2	2	3	2	26	1 200.0	1.7
Iron and steel tubes, pipes and fittings (679)	3	3	3	38	23	666.7	1.5
Electrical apparatus for switching or protecting elec. circuits (772)	3	2	5	4	23	666.7	1.5
Tobacco, manufactured (122)	45	45	34	19	23	-48.9	1.5
IMPORTS							
Total	1 446	2 762	1 993	1 940	2 277	57.5	100.0
Food and live animals (0)	0	0	0	0	0	X	0.0
Beverages and tobacco (1)	0	0	0	0	0	X	0.0
Crude materials, inedible, except fuels (2)	0	0	8	0	4	X	0.2
Mineral fuels, lubricants and related materials (3)	1 410	2 693	1 871	1 879	2 107	49.4	92.5
Animal and vegetable oils, fats and waxes (4)	0	0	0	0	0	X	0.0
Chemicals and related products (5)	6	4	16	5	73	1 116.7	3.2
Manufactured goods classified chiefly by material (6)	0	0	0	0	0	X	0.0
Machinery and transport equipment (7)	0	1	0	0	2	X	0.1
Miscellaneous manufactured articles (8)	10	17	19	29	36	260.0	1.6
Commodities and transactions not classified elsewhere (9)	19	46	78	27	56	194.7	2.5
Top 20 Commodities	1 444	2 760	1 973	1 939	2 276	57.6	100.0
Crude oil (333)	1 353	2 537	1 692	1 762	1 977	46.1	86.8
Oil (not crude) (334)	23	126	130	96	106	360.9	4.7
Fertilizers (except crude) (562)	6	4	12	3	71	1 083.3	3.1
Special transactions not classified by kind (931)	19	46	78	27	55	189.5	2.4
Residual petroleum products (335)	34	31	33	21	24	-29.4	1.1
Men's or boys' coats, jackets, etc. not knit (841)	9	14	13	14	18	100.0	0.8
Women's or girls' coats, jackets, etc. not knit (842)	0	1	4	14	14	X	0.6
Ores and concencentrate of precious metal (289)	0	0	8	0	4	X	0.2
Perfumery, cosmetics or toilet preparations, excluding soaps (553)	0	0	1	1	2	X	0.1
Articles of apparel of textile fabrics (845)	0	1	1	1	1	X	0.0
Telecommunications equipment (764)	0	0	0	0	1	X	0.0
Men's or boys' coats, jackets, etc. knit (843)	0	0	1	0	1	X	0.0
Automatic data processing machines (752)	0	0	0	0	1	X	0.0
Women's or girls' coats, jackets, etc. knit (844)	0	0	0	0	1	X	0.0
Glass (664)	0	0	0	0	0	X	0.0
Estimate of low value import transactions (984)	0	0	0	0	0	X	0.0
Toys and sporting goods (894)	0	0	0	0	0	X	0.0
Nonelectric engines and motors (714)	0	0	0	0	0	X	0.0
Cereal preparations (48)	0	0	0	0	0	X	0.0
Inorganic chemicals; precious metal compounds (524)	0	0	0	0	0	X	0.0

X = Not applicable.

Table C-66. U.S. Trade by Commodity with Macao, 1999–2003

(Millions of dollars; total exports, f.a.s.; general imports, Customs; top 20 commodities based on 2003 dollar value.)

Commodity and SITC code	1999	2000	2001	2002	2003	Percent change, 1999–2003	Percent share of total, 2003
EXPORTS							
Total	42	70	71	79	55	31.0	100.0
Food and live animals (0)	2	2	3	1	1	-50.0	1.8
Beverages and tobacco (1)	1	0	1	1	0	X	0.0
Crude materials, inedible, except fuels (2)	0	0	0	1	2	X	3.6
Mineral fuels, lubricants and related materials (3)	0	0	0	0	0	X	0.0
Animal and vegetable oils, fats and waxes (4)	0	0	0	0	0	X	0.0
Chemicals and related products (5)	1	2	1	1	1	0.0	1.8
Manufactured goods classified chiefly by material (6)	3	6	4	6	6	100.0	10.9
Machinery and transport equipment (7)	21	42	45	49	27	28.6	49.1
Miscellaneous manufactured articles (8)	5	4	4	6	6	20.0	10.9
Commodities and transactions not classified elsewhere (9)	9	13	14	13	10	11.1	18.2
Top 20 Commodities	28	52	53	66	45	60.7	81.8
Estimated low value shipments (994)	8	11	13	13	10	25.0	18.2
Telecommunications equipment (764)	1	5	25	11	7	600.0	12.7
Aircraft and associated equipment (792)	2	3	4	14	6	200.0	10.9
Nonelectric engines and motors (714)	0	0	0	14	3	X	5.5
Textile yarn (651)	0	1	1	2	2	X	3.6
Electrical machinery and apparatus (778)	2	17	2	2	2	0.0	3.6
Thermionic, cold cathode, and photocathode valves (776)	7	3	1	1	2	-71.4	3.6
Wood, simply worked (248)	0	0	0	1	1	X	1.8
Toys and sporting goods (894)	1	0	0	2	1	0.0	1.8
Cotton fabrics, woven (652)	0	0	0	0	1	X	1.8
Paper and paperboard (641)	1	2	1	1	1	0.0	1.8
Measuring/checking/analyzing instruments (874)	1	1	1	2	1	0.0	1.8
Mechanical handling equipment (744)	0	1	0	0	1	X	1.8
Optical instruments and apparatus (871)	0	1	0	0	1	X	1.8
Steam turbines and other vapor turbines (712)	0	0	0	0	1	X	1.8
Automatic data processing machines (752)	1	2	3	1	1	0.0	1.8
Electric power machinery, and parts (771)	4	5	2	2	1	-75.0	1.8
Medical instruments and appliances (872)	0	0	0	0	1	X	1.8
Optical goods (884)	0	0	0	0	1	X	1.8
Furskins, raw (212)	0	0	0	0	1	X	1.8
IMPORTS							
Total	1 124	1 266	1 224	1 232	1 356	20.6	100.0
Food and live animals (0)	2	2	1	2	2	0.0	0.1
Beverages and tobacco (1)	0	0	0	0	0	X	0.0
Crude materials, inedible, except fuels (2)	0	0	0	0	0	X	0.0
Mineral fuels, lubricants and related materials (3)	0	0	0	0	0	X	0.0
Animal and vegetable oils, fats and waxes (4)	0	0	0	0	0	X	0.0
Chemicals and related products (5)	7	15	7	7	5	-28.6	0.4
Manufactured goods classified chiefly by material (6)	26	19	9	3	2	-92.3	0.1
Machinery and transport equipment (7)	27	33	14	9	16	-40.7	1.2
Miscellaneous manufactured articles (8)	1 059	1 195	1 166	1 202	1 315	24.2	97.0
Commodities and transactions not classified elsewhere (9)	3	3	26	9	16	433.3	1.2
Top 20 Commodities	1 083	1 223	1 207	1 222	1 347	24.4	99.3
Articles of apparel of textile fabrics (845)	428	455	443	438	437	2.1	32.2
Women's or girls' coats, jackets, etc. not knit (842)	157	201	219	247	310	97.5	22.9
Women's or girls' coats, jackets, etc. knit (844)	195	198	208	233	268	37.4	19.8
Men's or boys' coats, jackets, etc. not knit (841)	157	189	158	134	181	15.3	13.3
Men's or boys' coats, jackets, etc. knit (843)	57	64	55	74	70	22.8	5.2
Apparel and accessories except textile; headgear (848)	29	42	42	20	16	-44.8	1.2
Special transactions not classified by kind (931)	2	1	24	7	14	600.0	1.0
Lighting fixtures and fittings (813)	20	30	24	19	13	-35.0	1.0
Household type electrical and nonelectrical equipment (775)	0	0	0	4	8	X	0.6
Footwear (851)	3	3	3	5	6	100.0	0.4
Medicinal products, except medicaments (541)	5	4	7	6	5	0.0	0.4
Miscellaneous manufactured articles (899)	5	6	6	25	5	0.0	0.4
Electric power machinery, and parts (771)	17	21	10	4	4	-76.5	0.3
Parts for office machines and a.d.p. machines (759)	5	4	1	0	3	-40.0	0.2
Articles of plastics (893)	0	1	1	2	2	X	0.1
Crustaceans (036)	1	1	1	1	1	0.0	0.1
Estimate of low value import transactions (984)	1	2	2	1	1	0.0	0.1
Musical instruments and accessories (898)	0	0	2	1	1	X	0.1
Works of art, collectors' pieces, and antiques (896)	0	0	0	0	1	X	0.1
Furniture and bedding accessories (821)	1	1	1	1	1	0.0	0.1

X = Not applicable.

Table C-67. U.S. Trade by Commodity with Malaysia, 1999–2003

(Millions of dollars; total exports, f.a.s.; general imports, Customs; top 20 commodities based on 2003 dollar value.)

Commodity and SITC code	1999	2000	2001	2002	2003	Percent change, 1999–2003	Percent share of total, 2003
EXPORTS							
Total	9 079	10 996	9 380	10 348	10 921	20.3	100.0
Food and live animals (0)	184	194	264	246	287	56.0	2.6
Beverages and tobacco (1)	52	67	81	66	32	-38.5	0.3
Crude materials, inedible, except fuels (2)	126	131	167	177	204	61.9	1.9
Mineral fuels, lubricants and related materials (3)	15	19	30	27	24	60.0	0.2
Animal and vegetable oils, fats and waxes (4)	21	4	2	7	2	-90.5	0.0
Chemicals and related products (5)	496	564	524	496	553	11.5	5.1
Manufactured goods classified chiefly by material (6)	387	407	370	327	299	-22.7	2.7
Machinery and transport equipment (7)	6 941	8 461	7 071	8 139	8 704	25.4	79.7
Miscellaneous manufactured articles (8)	684	939	694	672	602	-12.0	5.5
Commodities and transactions not classified elsewhere (9)	174	210	175	192	213	22.4	2.0
Top 20 Commodities	7 298	9 000	7 415	8 625	9 321	27.7	85.3
Thermionic, cold cathode, and photocathode valves (776)	4 693	5 500	3 974	4 947	6 450	37.4	59.1
Measuring/checking/analyzing instruments (874)	326	550	408	457	414	27.0	3.8
Parts for office machines and a.d.p. machines (759)	341	423	400	429	350	2.6	3.2
Automatic data processing machines (752)	357	413	407	371	289	-19.0	2.6
Aircraft and associated equipment (792)	421	263	604	822	233	-44.7	2.1
Telecommunications equipment (764)	147	209	238	297	227	54.4	2.1
Electrical apparatus for switching or protecting elec. circuits (772)	192	266	160	147	193	0.5	1.8
Nonelectric engines and motors (714)	115	68	123	209	159	38.3	1.5
Estimated low value shipments (994)	126	155	128	137	151	19.8	1.4
Machinery and equipment specialized for particular industries (728)	145	392	282	154	131	-9.7	1.2
Electrical machinery and apparatus (778)	68	299	214	168	130	91.2	1.2
Fruit and nuts (not including oil nuts), fresh or dried (057)	25	42	75	77	88	252.0	0.8
Pumps, air or gas compressors and fans (743)	50	87	77	67	76	52.0	0.7
Edible products and preparations, n.e.s. (098)	46	47	42	48	76	65.2	0.7
Ferrous waste and scrap (282)	4	9	36	33	73	1 725.0	0.7
Manufactures of base metal (699)	20	28	29	39	60	200.0	0.5
Paper and paperboard (641)	74	78	56	58	57	-23.0	0.5
Organo-inorganic and heterocyclic compounds (515)	33	33	40	48	56	69.7	0.5
Electric power machinery, and parts (771)	31	76	49	56	56	80.6	0.5
Miscellaneous chemical products (598)	84	62	73	61	52	-38.1	0.5
IMPORTS							
Total	21 429	25 568	22 336	24 010	25 438	18.7	100.0
Food and live animals (0)	110	111	101	91	145	31.8	0.6
Beverages and tobacco (1)	4	6	6	7	5	25.0	0.0
Crude materials, inedible, except fuels (2)	147	171	109	122	159	8.2	0.6
Mineral fuels, lubricants and related materials (3)	267	588	402	246	327	22.5	1.3
Animal and vegetable oils, fats and waxes (4)	188	160	124	161	213	13.3	0.8
Chemicals and related products (5)	236	374	357	287	285	20.8	1.1
Manufactured goods classified chiefly by material (6)	567	584	518	481	491	-13.4	1.9
Machinery and transport equipment (7)	17 108	20 668	17 841	19 659	20 900	22.2	82.2
Miscellaneous manufactured articles (8)	2 427	2 507	2 419	2 382	2 391	-1.5	9.4
Commodities and transactions not classified elsewhere (9)	375	399	458	573	522	39.2	2.1
Top 20 Commodities	19 004	22 760	19 812	21 836	23 166	21.9	91.1
Automatic data processing machines (752)	3 695	4 658	4 824	6 882	7 782	110.6	30.6
Telecommunications equipment (764)	1 190	2 248	2 294	2 624	3 837	222.4	15.1
Thermionic, cold cathode, and photocathode valves (776)	5 061	6 336	4 557	4 275	3 585	-29.2	14.1
Parts for office machines and a.d.p. machines (759)	3 753	3 472	2 510	2 192	2 168	-42.2	8.5
Television receivers (761)	648	754	768	1 246	993	53.2	3.9
Sound and television recorders (763)	931	1 232	1 180	832	849	-8.8	3.3
Radio-broadcast receivers (762)	914	941	832	769	791	-13.5	3.1
Furniture and bedding accessories (821)	469	492	431	497	533	13.6	2.1
Apparel and accessories except textile; headgear (848)	527	498	472	453	482	-8.5	1.9
Special transactions not classified by kind (931)	215	204	287	394	331	54.0	1.3
Measuring/checking/analyzing instruments (874)	48	97	187	201	274	470.8	1.1
Articles of apparel of textile fabrics (845)	211	219	238	256	215	1.9	0.8
Crude oil (333)	137	355	123	99	192	40.1	0.8
Estimate of low value import transactions (984)	154	186	167	176	185	20.1	0.7
Fixed vegetable fats and oils; crude (422)	178	120	101	139	181	1.7	0.7
Electrical apparatus for switching or protecting elec. circuits (772)	214	276	167	168	168	-21.5	0.7
Electrical machinery and apparatus (778)	174	172	171	183	161	-7.5	0.6
Men's or boys' coats, jackets, etc. not knit (841)	241	246	235	168	156	-35.3	0.6
Household type electrical and nonelectrical equipment (775)	70	93	97	106	151	115.7	0.6
Toys and sporting goods (894)	174	161	171	176	132	-24.1	0.5

Table C-68. U.S. Trade by Commodity with Mexico, 1999–2003

(Millions of dollars; total exports, f.a.s.; general imports, Customs; top 20 commodities based on 2003 dollar value.)

Commodity and SITC code	1999	2000	2001	2002	2003	Percent change, 1999–2003	Percent share of total, 2003
EXPORTS							
Total	87 044	111 721	101 509	97 531	97 457	12.0	100.0
Food and live animals (0)	3 885	4 621	5 335	5 047	5 483	41.1	5.6
Beverages and tobacco (1)	111	127	139	145	156	40.5	0.2
Crude materials, inedible, except fuels (2)	2 603	3 138	3 013	3 248	3 478	33.6	3.6
Mineral fuels, lubricants and related materials (3)	2 268	4 303	3 288	3 270	2 879	26.9	3.0
Animal and vegetable oils, fats and waxes (4)	360	303	273	457	380	5.6	0.4
Chemicals and related products (5)	7 187	8 944	8 527	8 768	9 911	37.9	10.2
Manufactured goods classified chiefly by material (6)	12 409	15 790	13 756	13 175	13 040	5.1	13.4
Machinery and transport equipment (7)	43 770	57 144	51 437	47 941	47 215	7.9	48.4
Miscellaneous manufactured articles (8)	10 336	12 332	11 466	11 576	11 222	8.6	11.5
Commodities and transactions not classified elsewhere (9)	4 115	5 020	4 277	3 902	3 694	-10.2	3.8
Top 20 Commodities	46 059	61 960	55 737	52 756	51 527	11.9	52.9
Thermionic, cold cathode, and photocathode valves (776)	6 393	9 379	7 894	6 669	6 063	-5.2	6.2
Parts and accessories of motor vehicles (784)	5 460	7 325	6 819	6 482	5 937	8.7	6.1
Electrical apparatus for switching or protecting elec. circuits (772)	4 315	5 423	4 274	4 078	4 253	-1.4	4.4
Parts for office machines and a.d.p. machines (759)	1 805	1 942	1 626	2 665	3 954	119.1	4.1
Telecommunications equipment (764)	3 007	4 151	3 991	3 287	3 107	3.3	3.2
Estimated low value shipments (994)	2 901	3 670	3 353	3 146	3 003	3.5	3.1
Articles of plastics (893)	2 574	3 338	2 998	2 931	2 815	9.4	2.9
Automatic data processing machines (752)	1 840	2 629	2 877	2 722	2 688	46.1	2.8
All motor vehicles (781)	2 175	2 778	3 260	3 149	2 510	15.4	2.6
Electrical machinery and apparatus (778)	2 775	3 694	2 768	2 710	2 480	-10.6	2.5
Manufactures of base metal (699)	2 072	2 998	2 435	2 318	2 171	4.8	2.2
Oil (not crude) (334)	1 743	3 208	2 430	2 219	2 164	24.2	2.2
Internal combustion piston engines (713)	1 425	2 427	2 178	2 111	2 000	40.4	2.1
Equipment for distributing electricity (773)	1 870	2 306	2 046	1 875	1 748	-6.5	1.8
Measuring/checking/analyzing instruments (874)	1 185	1 533	1 536	1 386	1 276	7.7	1.3
Plastics (575)	783	978	964	1 016	1 106	41.3	1.1
Paper and paperboard, cut to size or shape, and articles (642)	1 081	1 182	1 173	1 085	1 073	-0.7	1.1
Rotating electric plant and parts (716)	978	1 102	1 005	977	1 067	9.1	1.1
Oil seeds and oleaginous fruits (222)	716	804	840	936	1 061	48.2	1.1
Pumps, air or gas compressors and fans (743)	961	1 093	1 270	994	1 051	9.4	1.1
IMPORTS							
Total	109 706	135 911	131 433	134 732	138 073	25.9	100.0
Food and live animals (0)	4 429	4 521	4 527	4 526	5 257	18.7	3.8
Beverages and tobacco (1)	1 010	1 299	1 410	1 633	1 759	74.2	1.3
Crude materials, inedible, except fuels (2)	812	817	752	724	742	-8.6	0.5
Mineral fuels, lubricants and related materials (3)	7 217	12 763	10 210	12 209	15 497	114.7	11.2
Animal and vegetable oils, fats and waxes (4)	41	29	26	23	43	4.9	0.0
Chemicals and related products (5)	1 612	1 783	1 810	1 917	2 158	33.9	1.6
Manufactured goods classified chiefly by material (6)	7 993	9 128	8 730	9 438	9 476	18.6	6.9
Machinery and transport equipment (7)	63 805	79 479	78 265	77 193	75 883	18.9	55.0
Miscellaneous manufactured articles (8)	17 924	20 220	19 924	21 289	21 308	18.9	15.4
Commodities and transactions not classified elsewhere (9)	4 864	5 873	5 779	5 781	5 951	22.3	4.3
Top 20 Commodities	71 579	93 047	90 956	93 339	96 632	35.0	70.0
Crude oil (333)	6 781	11 953	9 511	11 500	14 428	112.8	10.4
All motor vehicles (781)	10 065	15 770	14 310	13 530	11 826	17.5	8.6
Telecommunications equipment (764)	5 666	9 128	8 803	7 801	7 258	28.1	5.3
Special purpose motor vehicles (782)	4 251	4 853	6 816	6 705	7 226	70.0	5.2
Automatic data processing machines (752)	4 998	6 413	7 914	7 188	6 138	22.8	4.4
Parts and accessories of motor vehicles (784)	4 097	4 639	4 643	5 259	5 661	38.2	4.1
Equipment for distributing electricity (773)	5 189	5 602	5 114	5 612	5 511	6.2	4.0
Television receivers (761)	4 267	4 573	4 732	4 846	5 249	23.0	3.8
Furniture and bedding accessories (821)	2 885	3 202	3 212	3 825	4 275	48.2	3.1
Special transactions not classified by kind (931)	3 558	4 285	4 245	4 196	4 250	19.4	3.1
Electrical apparatus for switching or protecting elec. circuits (772)	2 953	3 713	3 344	3 494	3 794	28.5	2.7
Electrical machinery and apparatus (778)	2 778	3 144	2 833	2 948	3 406	22.6	2.5
Internal combustion piston engines (713)	2 470	2 676	2 344	2 565	2 867	16.1	2.1
Articles of apparel of textile fabrics (845)	2 733	2 875	2 867	2 626	2 486	-9.0	1.8
Measuring/checking/analyzing instruments (874)	1 578	1 845	1 865	2 141	2 331	47.7	1.7
Men's or boys' coats, jackets, etc. not knit (841)	2 042	2 349	2 105	2 149	2 154	5.5	1.6
Vegetables, roots, tubers and other edible vegetable products (054)	1 489	1 573	1 781	1 793	2 115	42.0	1.5
Rotating electric plant and parts (716)	1 732	1 901	1 780	1 935	2 050	18.4	1.5
Medical instruments and appliances (872)	756	998	1 177	1 482	1 816	140.2	1.3
Manufactures of base metal (699)	1 291	1 555	1 560	1 744	1 791	38.7	1.3

Table C-69. U.S. Trade by Commodity with Morocco, 1999–2003

(Millions of dollars; total exports, f.a.s.; general imports, Customs; top 20 commodities based on 2003 dollar value.)

Commodity and SITC code	1999	2000	2001	2002	2003	Percent change, 1999–2003	Percent share of total, 2003
EXPORTS							
Total	574	525	286	566	465	-19.0	100.0
Food and live animals (0)	106	145	71	65	77	-27.4	16.6
Beverages and tobacco (1)	33	6	0	0	3	-90.9	0.6
Crude materials, inedible, except fuels (2)	31	39	30	50	74	138.7	15.9
Mineral fuels, lubricants and related materials (3)	4	36	25	11	27	575.0	5.8
Animal and vegetable oils, fats and waxes (4)	26	2	1	20	14	-46.2	3.0
Chemicals and related products (5)	19	17	22	17	18	-5.3	3.9
Manufactured goods classified chiefly by material (6)	94	15	22	17	21	-77.7	4.5
Machinery and transport equipment (7)	239	238	84	358	197	-17.6	42.4
Miscellaneous manufactured articles (8)	16	23	23	19	21	31.3	4.5
Commodities and transactions not classified elsewhere (9)	6	5	8	8	14	133.3	3.0
Top 20 Commodities	368	397	167	461	379	3.0	81.5
Aircraft and associated equipment (792)	143	148	17	295	131	-8.4	28.2
Oil seeds and oleaginous fruits (222)	19	16	14	35	55	189.5	11.8
Wheat and meslin, unmilled (041)	40	59	18	11	40	0.0	8.6
Maize (not including sweet corn) unmilled (044)	48	64	42	39	35	-27.1	7.5
Coal, pulverized or not (321)	0	24	9	4	18	X	3.9
Special transactions not classified by kind (931)	1	2	6	6	11	1 000.0	2.4
Fixed vegetable fats and oils (421)	22	0	0	16	10	-54.5	2.2
Telecommunications equipment (764)	12	18	12	7	10	-16.7	2.2
Sulfur and unroasted iron pyrites (274)	1	6	3	6	9	800.0	1.9
Internal combustion piston engines (713)	16	15	10	12	9	-43.8	1.9
Residual petroleum products (335)	3	11	14	6	8	166.7	1.7
Civil engineering and contractors' plant and equipment (723)	8	4	4	6	8	0.0	1.7
Paper and paperboard (641)	2	4	4	4	7	250.0	1.5
Iron and nonalloy steel flat-roll products (673)	0	0	0	0	6	X	1.3
Measuring/checking/analyzing instruments (874)	3	3	5	3	6	100.0	1.3
Polyacetals and epoxide resins (574)	4	5	3	4	4	0.0	0.9
Special purpose motor vehicles (782)	6	3	1	0	3	-50.0	0.6
Animal oils and fats (411)	4	2	1	3	3	-25.0	0.6
Automatic data processing machines (752)	4	7	4	4	3	-25.0	0.6
Tobacco, manufactured (122)	32	6	0	0	3	-90.6	0.6
IMPORTS							
Total	390	444	435	392	385	-1.3	100.0
Food and live animals (0)	54	52	49	63	82	51.9	21.3
Beverages and tobacco (1)	0	0	0	0	0	X	0.0
Crude materials, inedible, except fuels (2)	86	69	73	91	78	-9.3	20.3
Mineral fuels, lubricants and related materials (3)	7	39	64	9	22	214.3	5.7
Animal and vegetable oils, fats and waxes (4)	7	0	0	2	1	-85.7	0.3
Chemicals and related products (5)	13	20	34	13	8	-38.5	2.1
Manufactured goods classified chiefly by material (6)	12	8	9	14	6	-50.0	1.6
Machinery and transport equipment (7)	103	143	86	103	94	-8.7	24.4
Miscellaneous manufactured articles (8)	99	105	108	84	85	-14.1	22.1
Commodities and transactions not classified elsewhere (9)	9	8	11	13	8	-11.1	2.1
Top 20 Commodities	349	419	403	367	362	3.7	94.0
Thermionic, cold cathode, and photocathode valves (776)	101	141	82	96	88	-12.9	22.9
Fertilizer, crude (272)	38	31	36	50	42	10.5	10.9
Women's or girls' coats, jackets, etc. not knit (842)	28	41	30	27	32	14.3	8.3
Fruit and nuts (not including oil nuts), fresh or dried (057)	6	1	0	13	30	400.0	7.8
Crude minerals (278)	34	29	30	35	28	-17.6	7.3
Vegetables, roots and tubers, prepared or preserved (56)	27	26	26	30	27	0.0	7.0
Women's or girls' coats, jackets, etc. knit (844)	15	11	18	19	23	53.3	6.0
Oil (not crude) (334)	7	39	57	9	22	214.3	5.7
Fish, crustaceans and molluscs (37)	18	23	21	18	22	22.2	5.7
Men's or boys' coats, jackets, etc. not knit (841)	8	11	21	17	12	50.0	3.1
Crude vegetable materials (292)	8	9	8	6	9	12.5	2.3
Articles of apparel of textile fabrics (845)	38	31	26	12	7	-81.6	1.8
Special transactions not classified by kind (931)	7	5	8	11	5	-28.6	1.3
Inorganic chemical elements (522)	10	13	19	7	3	-70.0	0.8
Footwear (851)	2	2	4	2	2	0.0	0.5
Estimate of low value import transactions (984)	2	2	2	2	2	0.0	0.5
Rotating electric plant and parts (716)	0	0	2	1	2	X	0.5
Fertilizers (except crude) (562)	0	4	12	4	2	X	0.5
Equipment for distributing electricity (773)	0	0	1	0	2	X	0.5
Iron and nonalloy steel flat-roll products (673)	0	0	0	8	2	X	0.5

X = Not applicable.

Table C-70. U.S. Trade by Commodity with Netherlands, 1999–2003

(Millions of dollars; total exports, f.a.s.; general imports, Customs; top 20 commodities based on 2003 dollar value.)

Commodity and SITC code	1999	2000	2001	2002	2003	Percent change, 1999–2003	Percent share of total, 2003
EXPORTS							
Total	19 412	21 974	19 525	18 334	20 703	6.7	100.0
Food and live animals (0)	664	595	576	676	715	7.7	3.5
Beverages and tobacco (1)	366	223	212	134	165	-54.9	0.8
Crude materials, inedible, except fuels (2)	859	1 065	995	788	751	-12.6	3.6
Mineral fuels, lubricants and related materials (3)	386	500	482	254	216	-44.0	1.0
Animal and vegetable oils, fats and waxes (4)	39	27	50	41	34	-12.8	0.2
Chemicals and related products (5)	3 570	3 812	3 682	4 057	5 162	44.6	24.9
Manufactured goods classified chiefly by material (6)	718	741	710	650	670	-6.7	3.2
Machinery and transport equipment (7)	9 704	11 684	9 699	8 654	9 498	-2.1	45.9
Miscellaneous manufactured articles (8)	2 746	2 920	2 737	2 765	3 155	14.9	15.2
Commodities and transactions not classified elsewhere (9)	360	407	382	316	337	-6.4	1.6
Top 20 Commodities	11 645	13 367	11 364	11 414	13 552	16.4	65.5
Aircraft and associated equipment (792)	1 377	1 676	1 191	1 248	2 405	74.7	11.6
Automatic data processing machines (752)	2 018	2 270	2 118	1 463	1 380	-31.6	6.7
Parts for office machines and a.d.p. machines (759)	2 060	2 619	1 687	1 220	1 188	-42.3	5.7
Medicinal products, except medicaments (541)	371	237	340	636	1 130	204.6	5.5
Medical instruments and appliances (872)	635	701	622	777	1 080	70.1	5.2
Telecommunications equipment (764)	847	1 127	931	1 228	1 074	26.8	5.2
Medicaments (including veterinary medicaments) (542)	339	364	528	717	821	142.2	4.0
Organo-inorganic and heterocyclic compounds (515)	374	517	360	267	567	51.6	2.7
Measuring/checking/analyzing instruments (874)	620	661	600	531	545	-12.1	2.6
Thermionic, cold cathode, and photocathode valves (776)	555	577	576	567	444	-20.0	2.1
Miscellaneous chemical products (598)	404	400	371	386	358	-11.4	1.7
Electro-diagnostic apparatus (774)	195	242	312	388	354	81.5	1.7
Miscellaneous manufactured articles (899)	177	178	199	241	320	80.8	1.5
Nitrogen-function compounds (514)	196	230	244	220	308	57.1	1.5
Electrical machinery and apparatus (778)	211	265	207	272	294	39.3	1.4
Nonelectric engines and motors (714)	208	175	251	243	285	37.0	1.4
Musical instruments and accessories (898)	292	261	202	234	270	-7.5	1.3
Estimated low value shipments (994)	268	298	274	256	268	0.0	1.3
Plastics (575)	250	237	183	220	247	-1.2	1.2
Hydrocarbons and specified derivatives (511)	248	332	168	300	214	-13.7	1.0
IMPORTS							
Total	8 473	9 704	9 500	9 864	10 972	29.5	100.0
Food and live animals (0)	439	473	461	502	574	30.8	5.2
Beverages and tobacco (1)	688	841	917	1 029	1 072	55.8	9.8
Crude materials, inedible, except fuels (2)	332	334	310	311	339	2.1	3.1
Mineral fuels, lubricants and related materials (3)	270	514	604	706	1 099	307.0	10.0
Animal and vegetable oils, fats and waxes (4)	12	15	15	12	32	166.7	0.3
Chemicals and related products (5)	1 270	1 467	1 492	1 556	1 793	41.2	16.3
Manufactured goods classified chiefly by material (6)	699	772	663	685	645	-7.7	5.9
Machinery and transport equipment (7)	2 470	2 892	2 631	2 439	2 579	4.4	23.5
Miscellaneous manufactured articles (8)	1 165	1 390	1 297	1 575	1 508	29.4	13.7
Commodities and transactions not classified elsewhere (9)	1 127	1 006	1 109	1 048	1 330	18.0	12.1
Top 20 Commodities	4 719	5 576	5 656	6 165	7 191	52.4	65.5
Special transactions not classified by kind (931)	975	827	937	870	1 128	15.7	10.3
Alcoholic beverages (112)	678	827	906	1 016	1 057	55.9	9.6
Oil (not crude) (334)	241	445	529	664	1 004	316.6	9.2
Photographic apparatus and equipment (881)	374	596	399	613	614	64.2	5.6
Electro-diagnostic apparatus (774)	229	255	318	340	364	59.0	3.3
Organo-inorganic and heterocyclic compounds (515)	90	172	183	212	364	304.4	3.3
Crude vegetable materials (292)	257	257	257	264	280	8.9	2.6
All motor vehicles (781)	343	657	456	332	274	-20.1	2.5
Automatic data processing machines (752)	157	157	108	166	267	70.1	2.4
Medicinal products, except medicaments (541)	180	182	240	247	261	45.0	2.4
Estimate of low value import transactions (984)	149	178	172	177	201	34.9	1.8
Radioactive and associated materials (525)	53	87	69	106	192	262.3	1.7
Photographic and cinematographic supplies (882)	110	137	95	179	186	69.1	1.7
Works of art, collectors' pieces, and antiques (896)	216	156	202	184	167	-22.7	1.5
Cocoa (072)	71	70	91	113	164	131.0	1.5
Measuring/checking/analyzing instruments (874)	103	89	142	130	163	58.3	1.5
Mechanical handling equipment (744)	106	120	125	123	140	32.1	1.3
Household type electrical and nonelectrical equipment (775)	132	141	137	147	139	5.3	1.3
Medicaments (including veterinary medicaments) (542)	147	123	181	173	119	-19.0	1.1
Vegetables, roots, tubers and other edible vegetable products (054)	108	100	109	109	107	-0.9	1.0

Table C-71. U.S. Trade by Commodity with Netherlands Antilles, 1999–2003

(Millions of dollars; total exports, f.a.s.; general imports, Customs; top 20 commodities based on 2003 dollar value.)

Commodity and SITC code	1999	2000	2001	2002	2003	Percent change, 1999–2003	Percent share of total, 2003
EXPORTS							
Total	603	674	818	742	747	23.9	100.0
Food and live animals (0)	69	67	58	52	50	-27.5	6.7
Beverages and tobacco (1)	14	13	12	10	12	-14.3	1.6
Crude materials, inedible, except fuels (2)	9	9	13	6	9	0.0	1.2
Mineral fuels, lubricants and related materials (3)	70	143	154	132	122	74.3	16.3
Animal and vegetable oils, fats and waxes (4)	2	1	1	1	1	-50.0	0.1
Chemicals and related products (5)	36	35	33	31	32	-11.1	4.3
Manufactured goods classified chiefly by material (6)	43	49	47	53	58	34.9	7.8
Machinery and transport equipment (7)	140	124	240	146	123	-12.1	16.5
Miscellaneous manufactured articles (8)	181	186	205	267	293	61.9	39.2
Commodities and transactions not classified elsewhere (9)	40	46	53	44	46	15.0	6.2
Top 20 Commodities	369	454	538	530	581	57.5	77.8
Jewelry, goldsmiths' and silversmiths' wares (897)	126	130	155	214	225	78.6	30.1
Oil (not crude) (334)	66	141	153	125	112	69.7	15.0
Estimated low value shipments (994)	34	38	47	38	44	29.4	5.9
Pearls, precious and semiprecious stones (667)	8	17	20	31	37	362.5	5.0
All motor vehicles (781)	14	17	11	13	20	42.9	2.7
Telecommunications equipment (764)	24	12	47	7	15	-37.5	2.0
Watches and clocks (885)	8	11	10	11	13	62.5	1.7
Edible products and preparations, n.e.s. (098)	14	13	11	12	13	-7.1	1.7
Photographic apparatus and equipment (881)	4	5	5	6	12	200.0	1.6
Automatic data processing machines (752)	13	12	15	10	11	-15.4	1.5
Measuring/checking/analyzing instruments (874)	5	2	3	3	11	120.0	1.5
Residual petroleum products (335)	3	0	1	7	10	233.3	1.3
Civil engineering and contractors' plant and equipment (723)	8	11	24	15	9	12.5	1.2
Sound and television recorders (763)	7	9	4	4	8	14.3	1.1
Ships, boats, and floating structures (793)	3	5	4	6	8	166.7	1.1
Alcoholic beverages (112)	6	6	7	6	7	16.7	0.9
Parts for office machines and a.d.p. machines (759)	8	6	5	6	7	-12.5	0.9
Perfumery, cosmetics or toilet preparations, excluding soaps (553)	10	10	9	8	7	-30.0	0.9
Medicaments (including veterinary medicaments) (542)	7	8	6	7	6	-14.3	0.8
Radio-broadcast receivers (762)	1	1	1	1	6	500.0	0.8
IMPORTS							
Total	383	718	488	362	620	61.9	100.0
Food and live animals (0)	15	16	1	3	8	-46.7	1.3
Beverages and tobacco (1)	2	2	1	1	0	X	0.0
Crude materials, inedible, except fuels (2)	5	17	13	10	14	180.0	2.3
Mineral fuels, lubricants and related materials (3)	245	559	345	239	433	76.7	69.8
Animal and vegetable oils, fats and waxes (4)	0	0	0	0	0	X	0.0
Chemicals and related products (5)	2	4	5	1	1	-50.0	0.2
Manufactured goods classified chiefly by material (6)	0	0	0	1	1	X	0.2
Machinery and transport equipment (7)	2	6	7	5	3	50.0	0.5
Miscellaneous manufactured articles (8)	8	1	5	11	19	137.5	3.1
Commodities and transactions not classified elsewhere (9)	104	113	110	90	141	35.6	22.7
Top 20 Commodities	379	702	478	358	617	62.8	99.5
Oil (not crude) (334)	227	529	344	235	428	88.5	69.0
Special transactions not classified by kind (931)	101	112	109	89	140	38.6	22.6
Photographic apparatus and equipment (881)	0	0	3	8	16	X	2.6
Crude minerals (278)	4	16	12	10	14	250.0	2.3
Fish, fresh, chilled or frozen (034)	15	16	1	3	8	-46.7	1.3
Residual petroleum products (335)	18	22	1	4	5	-72.2	0.8
Equipment for distributing electricity (773)	0	3	3	2	2	X	0.3
Jewelry, goldsmiths' and silversmiths' wares (897)	7	0	1	3	1	-85.7	0.2
Estimate of low value import transactions (984)	1	1	1	1	1	0.0	0.2
Miscellaneous chemical products (598)	1	0	0	0	1	0.0	0.2
Electric power machinery, and parts (771)	2	2	2	1	1	-50.0	0.2
Watches and clocks (885)	0	0	0	0	0	X	0.0
Alcoholic beverages (112)	1	1	1	1	0	X	0.0
Nonferrous base metal waste and scrap (288)	0	0	0	0	0	X	0.0
Gold, nonmonetary (971)	2	0	0	1	0	X	0.0
Lime, cement, and fabricated construction materials (661)	0	0	0	0	0	X	0.0
Trailers and semi-trailers (786)	0	0	0	0	0	X	0.0
Works of art, collectors' pieces, and antiques (896)	0	0	0	0	0	X	0.0
Floor coverings (659)	0	0	0	0	0	X	0.0
Crude vegetable materials (292)	0	0	0	0	0	X	0.0

X = Not applicable.

Table C-72. U.S. Trade by Commodity with New Zealand, 1999–2003

(Millions of dollars; total exports, f.a.s.; general imports, Customs; top 20 commodities based on 2003 dollar value.)

Commodity and SITC code	1999	2000	2001	2002	2003	Percent change, 1999–2003	Percent share of total, 2003
EXPORTS							
Total	1 934	1 974	2 134	1 814	1 849	-4.4	100.0
Food and live animals (0)	86	87	102	96	131	52.3	7.1
Beverages and tobacco (1)	12	14	6	13	14	16.7	0.8
Crude materials, inedible, except fuels (2)	27	16	23	17	17	-37.0	0.9
Mineral fuels, lubricants and related materials (3)	27	29	32	33	22	-18.5	1.2
Animal and vegetable oils, fats and waxes (4)	0	1	1	1	1	X	0.1
Chemicals and related products (5)	212	241	241	225	253	19.3	13.7
Manufactured goods classified chiefly by material (6)	136	107	92	95	93	-31.6	5.0
Machinery and transport equipment (7)	1 087	1 126	1 305	998	958	-11.9	51.8
Miscellaneous manufactured articles (8)	177	177	180	175	198	11.9	10.7
Commodities and transactions not classified elsewhere (9)	168	176	151	161	163	-3.0	8.8
Top 20 Commodities	1 155	1 225	1 428	1 065	1 091	-5.5	59.0
Nonelectric engines and motors (714)	153	164	115	154	202	32.0	10.9
Aircraft and associated equipment (792)	419	315	687	312	153	-63.5	8.3
Estimated low value shipments (994)	134	145	127	136	145	8.2	7.8
Telecommunications equipment (764)	73	187	95	63	70	-4.1	3.8
Rotating electric plant and parts (716)	8	4	6	5	65	712.5	3.5
Automatic data processing machines (752)	73	62	66	61	51	-30.1	2.8
Internal combustion piston engines (713)	24	33	27	25	50	108.3	2.7
Measuring/checking/analyzing instruments (874)	29	35	37	32	38	31.0	2.1
All motor vehicles (781)	17	18	32	49	36	111.8	1.9
Feeding stuff for animals (081)	20	22	29	40	32	60.0	1.7
Live animals other than animals of division 03 (001)	2	1	1	1	30	1 400.0	1.6
Medical instruments and appliances (872)	21	22	23	21	28	33.3	1.5
Motorcycles and cycles, motorized and not motorized (785)	19	19	15	23	25	31.6	1.4
Fruit and nuts (not including oil nuts), fresh or dried (057)	17	17	16	15	25	47.1	1.4
Toys and sporting goods (894)	15	24	33	24	24	60.0	1.3
Miscellaneous chemical products (598)	19	17	23	21	24	26.3	1.3
Parts for office machines and a.d.p. machines (759)	36	57	28	27	24	-33.3	1.3
Organo-inorganic and heterocyclic compounds (515)	32	42	34	19	24	-25.0	1.3
Printed matter (892)	28	24	19	18	23	-17.9	1.2
Nonelectrical machinery and tools (745)	16	17	15	19	22	37.5	1.2
IMPORTS							
Total	1 749	2 080	2 200	2 283	2 403	37.4	100.0
Food and live animals (0)	861	999	1 049	1 108	1 180	37.0	49.1
Beverages and tobacco (1)	18	23	26	38	52	188.9	2.2
Crude materials, inedible, except fuels (2)	211	223	243	268	256	21.3	10.7
Mineral fuels, lubricants and related materials (3)	7	10	16	0	1	-85.7	0.0
Animal and vegetable oils, fats and waxes (4)	0	1	1	0	1	X	0.0
Chemicals and related products (5)	183	244	298	183	201	9.8	8.4
Manufactured goods classified chiefly by material (6)	159	143	138	167	184	15.7	7.7
Machinery and transport equipment (7)	171	256	235	263	308	80.1	12.8
Miscellaneous manufactured articles (8)	60	78	91	109	123	105.0	5.1
Commodities and transactions not classified elsewhere (9)	79	104	103	147	98	24.1	4.1
Top 20 Commodities	1 366	1 546	1 704	1 823	1 859	36.1	77.4
Meat of bovine animals (011)	334	446	462	466	481	44.0	20.0
Wood, simply worked (248)	135	133	173	208	187	38.5	7.8
Starches, inulin and wheat gluten; albuminoidal substances (592)	166	201	235	159	176	6.0	7.3
Other meat and edible offal (012)	95	100	108	129	149	56.8	6.2
Milk, cream, milk products except butter or cheese (022)	61	75	88	86	111	82.0	4.6
Fish, fresh, chilled or frozen (034)	115	86	73	97	82	-28.7	3.4
Cheese and curd (24)	85	68	94	91	80	-5.9	3.3
Special transactions not classified by kind (931)	64	87	85	129	79	23.4	3.3
Edible products and preparations, n.e.s. (098)	10	30	59	74	74	640.0	3.1
Fruit and nuts (not including oil nuts), fresh or dried (057)	83	80	57	61	66	-20.5	2.7
Parts and accessories of motor vehicles (784)	26	56	46	59	63	142.3	2.6
Alcoholic beverages (112)	18	23	26	36	51	183.3	2.1
Medical instruments and appliances (872)	18	23	28	37	41	127.8	1.7
Crustaceans (036)	33	41	35	44	37	12.1	1.5
Household type electrical and nonelectrical equipment (775)	14	15	25	30	35	150.0	1.5
Aluminum (684)	40	3	12	23	33	-17.5	1.4
Electrical apparatus for switching or protecting elec. circuits (772)	19	23	23	26	33	73.7	1.4
Butter and other fats and oils (23)	22	16	38	25	30	36.4	1.2
Tools for use in the hand or in machines (695)	18	22	21	26	26	44.4	1.1
Telecommunications equipment (764)	10	18	16	17	25	150.0	1.0

X = Not applicable.

Table C-73. U.S. Trade by Commodity with Nicaragua, 1999–2003

(Millions of dollars; total exports, f.a.s.; general imports, Customs; top 20 commodities based on 2003 dollar value.)

Commodity and SITC code	1999	2000	2001	2002	2003	Percent change, 1999–2003	Percent share of total, 2003
EXPORTS							
Total	374	379	443	438	503	34.5	100.0
Food and live animals (0)	67	60	77	63	73	9.0	14.5
Beverages and tobacco (1)	1	2	2	2	1	0.0	0.2
Crude materials, inedible, except fuels (2)	10	6	9	8	10	0.0	2.0
Mineral fuels, lubricants and related materials (3)	4	2	5	4	15	275.0	3.0
Animal and vegetable oils, fats and waxes (4)	12	11	18	13	20	66.7	4.0
Chemicals and related products (5)	27	27	24	29	29	7.4	5.8
Manufactured goods classified chiefly by material (6)	31	33	46	55	63	103.2	12.5
Machinery and transport equipment (7)	121	113	112	101	111	-8.3	22.1
Miscellaneous manufactured articles (8)	68	84	73	74	71	4.4	14.1
Commodities and transactions not classified elsewhere (9)	33	41	77	89	109	230.3	21.7
Top 20 Commodities	162	175	244	272	339	109.3	67.4
Special transactions not classified by kind (931)	13	21	57	70	87	569.2	17.3
Telecommunications equipment (764)	13	14	13	17	30	130.8	6.0
Articles of apparel of textile fabrics (845)	24	31	22	28	24	0.0	4.8
Rice (42)	20	13	27	19	23	15.0	4.6
Estimated low value shipments (994)	16	16	18	18	21	31.3	4.2
Wheat and meslin, unmilled (041)	12	6	13	12	18	50.0	3.6
Oil (not crude) (334)	4	2	5	4	15	275.0	3.0
Fixed vegetable fats and oils (421)	8	8	11	8	13	62.5	2.6
Woven fabrics of manmade textile materials (653)	0	1	2	9	13	X	2.6
Parts for office machines and a.d.p. machines (759)	6	6	12	13	12	100.0	2.4
Paper and paperboard (641)	4	8	9	11	11	175.0	2.2
Cotton fabrics, woven (652)	1	0	4	5	11	1 000.0	2.2
Men's or boys' coats, jackets, etc. not knit (841)	11	12	12	9	10	-9.1	2.0
Automatic data processing machines (752)	11	13	10	19	9	-18.2	1.8
Maize (not including sweet corn) unmilled (044)	7	7	7	7	8	14.3	1.6
Knitted or crocheted fabrics (655)	0	0	3	3	8	X	1.6
Perfumery, cosmetics or toilet preparations, excluding soaps (553)	3	5	7	7	7	133.3	1.4
Animal oils and fats (411)	3	3	3	4	7	133.3	1.4
Electrical apparatus for switching or protecting elec. circuits (772)	3	3	3	2	6	100.0	1.2
Feeding stuff for animals (081)	3	6	6	7	6	100.0	1.2
IMPORTS							
Total	493	590	605	679	769	56.0	100.0
Food and live animals (0)	150	212	166	174	180	20.0	23.4
Beverages and tobacco (1)	11	11	14	22	22	100.0	2.9
Crude materials, inedible, except fuels (2)	6	9	13	11	6	0.0	0.8
Mineral fuels, lubricants and related materials (3)	0	0	0	0	0	X	0.0
Animal and vegetable oils, fats and waxes (4)	1	0	5	3	3	200.0	0.4
Chemicals and related products (5)	0	0	0	1	1	X	0.1
Manufactured goods classified chiefly by material (6)	2	2	1	1	1	-50.0	0.1
Machinery and transport equipment (7)	0	0	0	4	39	X	5.1
Miscellaneous manufactured articles (8)	281	341	387	442	493	75.4	64.1
Commodities and transactions not classified elsewhere (9)	42	15	18	23	23	-45.2	3.0
Top 20 Commodities	477	569	587	662	755	58.3	98.2
Men's or boys' coats, jackets, etc. not knit (841)	135	166	182	186	215	59.3	28.0
Articles of apparel of textile fabrics (845)	61	90	96	132	117	91.8	15.2
Women's or girls' coats, jackets, etc. not knit (842)	66	67	72	79	94	42.4	12.2
Crustaceans (036)	75	99	72	74	61	-18.7	7.9
Women's or girls' coats, jackets, etc. knit (844)	5	10	20	28	48	860.0	6.2
Coffee and coffee substitutes (071)	25	59	36	31	40	60.0	5.2
Equipment for distributing electricity (773)	0	0	0	3	39	X	5.1
Meat of bovine animals (011)	14	21	29	33	36	157.1	4.7
Tobacco, manufactured (122)	9	9	13	21	20	122.2	2.6
Gold, nonmonetary (971)	36	9	13	17	18	-50.0	2.3
Fruit and nuts (not including oil nuts), fresh or dried (057)	10	4	11	10	15	50.0	2.0
Sugars, molasses, and honey (061)	15	14	2	9	11	-26.7	1.4
Fish, fresh, chilled or frozen (034)	7	8	10	10	9	28.6	1.2
Men's or boys' coats, jackets, etc. knit (843)	10	5	9	9	9	-10.0	1.2
Sanitary, plumbing & heating fixtures (812)	2	1	5	6	7	250.0	0.9
Vegetables, roots, tubers and other edible vegetable products (054)	2	3	4	3	4	100.0	0.5
Estimate of low value import transactions (984)	3	3	3	3	4	33.3	0.5
Wood, simply worked (248)	1	1	4	3	3	200.0	0.4
Fixed vegetable fats and oils (421)	1	0	5	3	3	200.0	0.4
Cheese and curd (24)	0	0	1	2	2	X	0.3

X = Not applicable.

Table C-74. U.S. Trade by Commodity with Nigeria, 1999–2003

(Millions of dollars; total exports, f.a.s.; general imports, Customs; top 20 commodities based on 2003 dollar value.)

Commodity and SITC code	1999	2000	2001	2002	2003	Percent change, 1999–2003	Percent share of total, 2003
EXPORTS							
Total	628	718	957	1 057	1 029	63.9	100.0
Food and live animals (0)	156	157	227	276	295	89.1	28.7
Beverages and tobacco (1)	7	12	8	8	9	28.6	0.9
Crude materials, inedible, except fuels (2)	7	7	7	11	12	71.4	1.2
Mineral fuels, lubricants and related materials (3)	25	11	16	27	16	-36.0	1.6
Animal and vegetable oils, fats and waxes (4)	9	8	7	16	16	77.8	1.6
Chemicals and related products (5)	40	59	65	65	59	47.5	5.7
Manufactured goods classified chiefly by material (6)	34	38	57	54	42	23.5	4.1
Machinery and transport equipment (7)	315	391	514	540	521	65.4	50.6
Miscellaneous manufactured articles (8)	26	21	45	47	46	76.9	4.5
Commodities and transactions not classified elsewhere (9)	10	15	11	13	12	20.0	1.2
Top 20 Commodities	443	463	686	773	766	72.9	74.4
Wheat and meslin, unmilled (41)	149	152	217	255	271	81.9	26.3
Civil engineering and contractors' plant and equipmen (723)	67	99	163	165	134	100.0	13.0
Telecommunications equipment (764)	20	20	42	55	72	260.0	7.0
Aircraft and associated equipment (792)	3	16	21	50	40	1 233.3	3.9
All motor vehicles (781)	16	14	23	20	34	112.5	3.3
Mechanical handling equipment (744)	23	12	32	44	22	-4.3	2.1
Automatic data process machines (752)	10	7	16	15	16	60.0	1.6
Animal oils and fats (411)	9	8	7	16	16	77.8	1.6
Ships, boats and floatng structures (793)	65	65	20	19	16	-75.4	1.6
Special purpose motor vehicles (782)	3	6	13	7	16	433.3	1.6
Measuring/checking/analysing instuments (874)	7	5	14	11	15	114.3	1.5
Parts for office machines and adp machines (759)	5	5	5	4	15	200.0	1.5
Road motor vehicles (783)	1	3	8	4	15	1 400.0	1.5
Electrical machinery and apparatus (778)	5	2	3	5	15	200.0	1.5
Oil (not crude) (334)	25	11	14	27	14	-44.0	1.4
Pumps for liquids and liquid elevators (742)	6	8	19	16	13	116.7	1.3
Plastics (575)	6	8	11	6	11	83.3	1.1
Iron and steel tubes, pipes and fittings (679)	11	13	24	17	11	0.0	1.1
Machinery specialized for particular industries (728)	9	7	17	18	10	11.1	1.0
Rotating electric plant and parts (716)	3	2	17	19	10	233.3	1.0
IMPORTS							
Total	4 361	10 549	8 786	5 964	10 394	138.3	100.0
Food and live animals (0)	7	4	8	14	46	557.1	0.4
Beverages and tobacco (1)	0	0	0	0	0	X	0.0
Crude materials, inedible, except fuels (2)	3	18	13	1	2	-33.3	0.0
Mineral fuels, lubricants and related materials (3)	4 337	10 516	8 756	5 930	10 326	138.1	99.3
Animal and vegetable oils, fats and waxes (4)	0	0	0	0	0	X	0.0
Chemicals and related products (5)	0	1	0	0	3	X	0.0
Manufactured goods classified chiefly by material (6)	2	2	2	2	1	-50.0	0.0
Machinery and transport equipment (7)	3	0	0	2	0	X	0.0
Miscellaneous manufactured articles (8)	5	3	2	2	2	-60.0	0.0
Commodities and transactions not classified elsewhere (9)	4	4	4	12	13	225.0	0.1
Top 20 Commodities	4 352	10 523	8 771	5 955	10 389	138.7	100.0
Crude oil (333)	3 858	10 024	8 126	5 579	9 629	149.6	92.6
Oil (not crude) (334)	442	405	399	326	429	-2.9	4.1
Natural gas, whether or not liquefied (343)	0	41	176	21	228	X	2.2
Cocoa (72)	3	0	1	8	40	1 233.3	0.4
Liquefied propane and butane (342)	34	39	54	0	39	14.7	0.4
Special transactions not classified by kind (931)	4	3	4	12	12	200.0	0.1
Feeding stuff for animals (81)	2	2	5	3	4	100.0	0.1
Hydrocarbons and specified derivatives (511)	0	1	0	0	3	X	0.0
Works of art, collectors' pieces and antiques (896)	5	3	1	2	2	-60.0	0.0
Crude vegetable materials (292)	1	1	1	0	1	0.0	0.0
Crustacean (36)	0	0	1	2	1	X	0.0
Estimate of low valued import transactions (984)	0	1	1	1	1	X	0.0
Spices (75)	0	0	0	0	0	X	0.0
Natural rubber in primary form (231)	1	1	0	0	0	X	0.0
Leather (611)	0	1	2	1	0	X	0.0
Wood, simply worked (248)	1	1	0	0	0	X	0.0
Pearls, precious and semiprecious stones (667)	0	0	0	0	0	X	0.0
Cotton fabrics, woven (652)	1	0	0	0	0	X	0.0
Parts and accessories of motor vehicles (784)	0	0	0	0	0	X	0.0
Meal and flour of wheat and meslin (46)	0	0	0	0	0	X	0.0

X = Not applicable.

Table C-75. U.S. Trade by Commodity with Norway, 1999–2003

(Millions of dollars; total exports, f.a.s.; general imports, Customs; top 20 commodities based on 2003 dollar value.)

Commodity and SITC code	1999	2000	2001	2002	2003	Percent change, 1999–2003	Percent share of total, 2003
EXPORTS							
Total	1 440	1 544	1 838	1 407	1 468	1.9	100.0
Food and live animals (0)	75	71	75	70	68	-9.3	4.6
Beverages and tobacco (1)	9	10	13	9	9	0.0	0.6
Crude materials, inedible, except fuels (2)	14	16	17	16	25	78.6	1.7
Mineral fuels, lubricants and related materials (3)	39	28	34	46	33	-15.4	2.2
Animal and vegetable oils, fats and waxes (4)	8	3	8	5	11	37.5	0.7
Chemicals and related products (5)	101	167	110	90	145	43.6	9.9
Manufactured goods classified chiefly by material (6)	68	76	72	60	61	-10.3	4.2
Machinery and transport equipment (7)	785	918	1 269	860	784	-0.1	53.4
Miscellaneous manufactured articles (8)	255	171	158	171	243	-4.7	16.6
Commodities and transactions not classified elsewhere (9)	85	85	83	80	90	5.9	6.1
Top 20 Commodities	845	984	999	957	976	15.5	66.5
Measuring/checking/analyzing instruments (874)	72	50	61	75	140	94.4	9.5
Civil engineering and contractors' plant and equipment (723)	99	84	104	116	114	15.2	7.8
Nonelectric engines and motors (714)	36	81	73	74	94	161.1	6.4
All motor vehicles (781)	32	23	31	27	93	190.6	6.3
Aircraft and associated equipment (792)	167	295	265	242	88	-47.3	6.0
Estimated low value shipments (994)	75	74	70	68	79	5.3	5.4
Telecommunications equipment (764)	64	46	47	38	47	-26.6	3.2
Automatic data processing machines (752)	64	52	42	41	47	-26.6	3.2
Mechanical handling equipment (744)	34	41	47	57	31	-8.8	2.1
Residual petroleum products (335)	33	22	29	43	30	-9.1	2.0
Nitrogen-function compounds (514)	32	38	36	10	29	-9.4	2.0
Medicaments (including veterinary medicaments) (542)	2	5	9	9	26	1 200.0	1.8
Electro-diagnostic apparatus (774)	17	21	24	24	22	29.4	1.5
Thermionic, cold cathode, and photocathode valves (776)	37	53	50	19	22	-40.5	1.5
Electrical machinery and apparatus (778)	19	19	20	15	21	10.5	1.4
Internal combustion piston engines (713)	10	11	16	23	21	110.0	1.4
Inorganic chemical elements (522)	2	2	4	11	19	850.0	1.3
Fruit and nuts (not including oil nuts), fresh or dried (057)	13	16	13	14	18	38.5	1.2
Fish, fresh, chilled or frozen (034)	16	23	28	23	18	12.5	1.2
Machinery and equipment specialized for particular industries (728)	21	28	30	28	17	-19.0	1.2
IMPORTS							
Total	4 051	5 710	5 207	5 830	5 212	28.7	100.0
Food and live animals (0)	194	187	149	158	161	-17.0	3.1
Beverages and tobacco (1)	0	1	1	4	6	X	0.1
Crude materials, inedible, except fuels (2)	9	12	10	12	7	-22.2	0.1
Mineral fuels, lubricants and related materials (3)	2 261	3 949	3 431	4 078	3 366	48.9	64.6
Animal and vegetable oils, fats and waxes (4)	9	13	10	18	20	122.2	0.4
Chemicals and related products (5)	262	293	324	342	327	24.8	6.3
Manufactured goods classified chiefly by material (6)	570	612	501	412	523	-8.2	10.0
Machinery and transport equipment (7)	506	396	441	503	480	-5.1	9.2
Miscellaneous manufactured articles (8)	140	154	258	215	211	50.7	4.0
Commodities and transactions not classified elsewhere (9)	99	92	83	90	110	11.1	2.1
Top 20 Commodities	3 269	5 049	4 453	5 098	4 509	37.9	86.5
Crude oil (333)	1 962	3 353	2 844	3 733	2 690	37.1	51.6
Oil (not crude) (334)	261	576	495	278	432	65.5	8.3
Liquefied propane and butane (342)	37	20	91	46	230	521.6	4.4
Nickel (683)	139	158	112	58	159	14.4	3.1
Paper and paperboard (641)	133	142	128	108	111	-16.5	2.1
Telecommunications equipment (764)	52	52	64	96	103	98.1	2.0
Special transactions not classified by kind (931)	81	68	59	64	91	12.3	1.7
Fish, fresh, chilled or frozen (034)	134	110	84	89	86	-35.8	1.7
Medicinal products, except medicaments (541)	15	17	31	67	80	433.3	1.5
Measuring/checking/analyzing instruments (874)	40	48	89	81	68	70.0	1.3
Nonelectric engines and motors (714)	37	64	80	89	65	75.7	1.2
Silver, platinum, and other platinum group metals (681)	25	48	58	68	63	152.0	1.2
Nitrogen-function compounds (514)	94	105	107	100	57	-39.4	1.1
Pig iron and iron and steel powders (671)	85	82	40	31	47	-44.7	0.9
Arms and ammunition (891)	15	13	21	41	46	206.7	0.9
Furniture and bedding accessories (821)	36	42	39	41	43	19.4	0.8
Fertilizers (except crude) (562)	43	38	28	35	39	-9.3	0.7
Miscellaneous nonferrous base metals (689)	49	51	37	26	37	-24.5	0.7
Cheese and curd (24)	29	36	28	27	31	6.9	0.6
Medicaments (including veterinary medicaments) (542)	2	26	18	20	31	1 450.0	0.6

X = Not applicable.

Table C-76. U.S. Trade by Commodity with Oman, 1999–2003

(Millions of dollars; total exports, f.a.s.; general imports, Customs; top 20 commodities based on 2003 dollar value.)

Commodity and SITC code	1999	2000	2001	2002	2003	Percent change, 1999–2003	Percent share of total, 2003
EXPORTS							
Total	188	200	306	357	323	71.8	100.0
Food and live animals (0)	13	10	13	12	9	-30.8	2.8
Beverages and tobacco (1)	10	9	7	5	5	-50.0	1.5
Crude materials, inedible, except fuels (2)	6	4	5	8	13	116.7	4.0
Mineral fuels, lubricants and related materials (3)	0	2	2	1	0	X	0.0
Animal and vegetable oils, fats and waxes (4)	4	1	2	3	2	-50.0	0.6
Chemicals and related products (5)	14	21	21	19	23	64.3	7.1
Manufactured goods classified chiefly by material (6)	7	7	8	13	14	100.0	4.3
Machinery and transport equipment (7)	111	118	216	265	217	95.5	67.2
Miscellaneous manufactured articles (8)	13	15	20	22	23	76.9	7.1
Commodities and transactions not classified elsewhere (9)	10	12	14	10	17	70.0	5.3
Top 20 Commodities	123	140	229	288	256	108.1	79.3
Aircraft and associated equipment (792)	3	4	67	148	69	2 200.0	21.4
Civil engineering and contractors' plant and equipment (723)	20	19	25	28	34	70.0	10.5
All motor vehicles (781)	15	18	25	18	20	33.3	6.2
Nonelectric engines and motors (714)	16	15	14	8	16	0.0	5.0
Pumps, air or gas compressors and fans (743)	3	4	2	11	14	366.7	4.3
Measuring/checking/analyzing instruments (874)	5	7	11	11	12	140.0	3.7
Heating and cooling equipment (741)	4	2	6	3	11	175.0	3.4
Stone, sand and gravel (273)	3	2	0	5	10	233.3	3.1
Estimated low value shipments (994)	7	8	9	8	9	28.6	2.8
Plastics (575)	3	10	7	3	8	166.7	2.5
Special transactions not classified by kind (931)	3	4	4	1	8	166.7	2.5
Telecommunications equipment (764)	6	7	9	6	8	33.3	2.5
Edible products and preparations, n.e.s. (098)	7	7	7	7	6	-14.3	1.9
Machinery and equipment specialized for particular industries (728)	5	7	11	4	6	20.0	1.9
Mechanical handling equipment (744)	3	2	5	5	6	100.0	1.9
Pumps for liquids and liquid elevators (742)	7	13	16	5	5	-28.6	1.5
Mineral manufactures (663)	0	0	1	5	4	X	1.2
Tobacco, manufactured (122)	9	8	7	4	4	-55.6	1.2
Arms and ammunition (891)	3	1	1	5	3	0.0	0.9
Additives for mineral oils (597)	1	2	2	3	3	200.0	0.9
IMPORTS							
Total	219	257	420	401	695	217.4	100.0
Food and live animals (0)	11	8	12	15	16	45.5	2.3
Beverages and tobacco (1)	0	0	0	0	0	X	0.0
Crude materials, inedible, except fuels (2)	0	0	0	0	0	X	0.0
Mineral fuels, lubricants and related materials (3)	0	38	209	130	427	X	61.4
Animal and vegetable oils, fats and waxes (4)	0	0	0	0	0	X	0.0
Chemicals and related products (5)	0	0	0	0	0	X	0.0
Manufactured goods classified chiefly by material (6)	1	3	6	6	7	600.0	1.0
Machinery and transport equipment (7)	0	1	2	0	0	X	0.0
Miscellaneous manufactured articles (8)	198	203	185	157	175	-11.6	25.2
Commodities and transactions not classified elsewhere (9)	9	4	6	93	69	666.7	9.9
Top 20 Commodities	217	253	415	398	695	220.3	100.0
Crude oil (333)	0	19	155	125	394	X	56.7
Women's or girls' coats, jackets, etc. not knit (842)	74	77	74	69	74	0.0	10.6
Special transactions not classified by kind (931)	9	3	5	92	68	655.6	9.8
Jewelry, goldsmiths' and silversmiths' wares (897)	55	48	36	29	39	-29.1	5.6
Natural gas, whether or not liquefied (343)	0	19	54	5	34	X	4.9
Men's or boys' coats, jackets, etc. not knit (841)	43	47	34	24	32	-25.6	4.6
Articles of apparel of textile fabrics (845)	7	11	14	10	14	100.0	2.0
Crustaceans (036)	10	7	8	12	14	40.0	2.0
Women's or girls' coats, jackets, etc. knit (844)	7	8	10	12	6	-14.3	0.9
Men's or boys' coats, jackets, etc. knit (843)	11	10	13	10	6	-45.5	0.9
Iron and steel tubes, pipes and fittings (679)	0	1	3	4	6	X	0.9
Furniture and bedding accessories (821)	0	0	2	2	3	X	0.4
Estimate of low value import transactions (984)	0	0	1	1	2	X	0.3
Vegetables, roots and tubers, prepared or preserved (56)	0	1	1	1	1	X	0.1
Lime, cement, and fabricated construction materials (661)	1	1	3	1	1	0.0	0.1
Articles of plastics (893)	0	1	2	1	1	X	0.1
Cereal preparations (48)	0	0	0	0	0	X	0.0
Carboxylic acids, halides, and derivities (513)	0	0	0	0	0	X	0.0
Fruit/vegetable juices, unfermented (59)	0	0	0	0	0	X	0.0
Made-up articles of textile materials (658)	0	0	0	0	0	X	0.0

X = Not applicable.

Table C-77. U.S. Trade by Commodity with Pakistan, 1999–2003

(Millions of dollars; total exports, f.a.s.; general imports, Customs; top 20 commodities based on 2003 dollar value.)

Commodity and SITC code	1999	2000	2001	2002	2003	Percent change, 1999–2003	Percent share of total, 2003
EXPORTS							
Total	426	462	542	694	840	97.2	100.0
Food and live animals (0)	64	17	12	40	22	-65.6	2.6
Beverages and tobacco (1)	4	2	3	1	0	X	0.0
Crude materials, inedible, except fuels (2)	28	47	112	132	208	642.9	24.8
Mineral fuels, lubricants and related materials (3)	11	1	1	5	10	-9.1	1.2
Animal and vegetable oils, fats and waxes (4)	6	7	25	48	28	366.7	3.3
Chemicals and related products (5)	131	138	132	100	131	0.0	15.6
Manufactured goods classified chiefly by material (6)	29	27	27	26	43	48.3	5.1
Machinery and transport equipment (7)	126	183	198	303	342	171.4	40.7
Miscellaneous manufactured articles (8)	18	29	22	27	42	133.3	5.0
Commodities and transactions not classified elsewhere (9)	11	11	10	13	14	27.3	1.7
Top 20 Commodities	223	260	325	454	613	174.9	73.0
Cotton textile fibers (263)	12	28	61	95	178	1 383.3	21.2
Aircraft and associated equipment (792)	39	44	30	51	83	112.8	9.9
Fertilizers (except crude) (562)	61	47	50	30	46	-24.6	5.5
Textile and leather machinery and pts (724)	9	14	30	34	41	355.6	4.9
Civil engineering and contractors' plant and equipment (723)	11	18	13	25	39	254.5	4.6
Nonelectric engines and motors (714)	2	3	15	25	29	1 350.0	3.5
Telecommunications equipment (764)	5	13	11	32	24	380.0	2.9
Pumps, air or gas compressors and fans (743)	13	7	6	21	21	61.5	2.5
Rotating electric plant and parts (716)	4	14	11	25	17	325.0	2.0
Iron and natural steel flat-rolled products (674)	9	7	7	6	16	77.8	1.9
Medicinal products, except medicaments (541)	20	14	17	13	15	-25.0	1.8
Nitrogen-function compounds (514)	10	7	11	11	15	50.0	1.8
Measuring/checking/analyzing instruments (874)	4	10	8	11	15	275.0	1.8
Fixed vegetable fats and oils (421)	0	0	21	23	13	X	1.5
Automatic data processing machines (752)	5	7	9	11	12	140.0	1.4
Estimated low value shipments (994)	6	6	7	10	11	83.3	1.3
Heating and cooling equipment (741)	5	4	4	6	10	100.0	1.2
Plastics (575)	3	5	6	6	10	233.3	1.2
Animal oils and fats (411)	2	6	0	6	9	350.0	1.1
Pulp and waste paper (251)	3	6	8	13	9	200.0	1.1
IMPORTS							
Total	1 740	2 167	2 249	2 305	2 531	45.5	100.0
Food and live animals (0)	31	31	37	30	31	0.0	1.2
Beverages and tobacco (1)	0	0	0	0	0	X	0.0
Crude materials, inedible, except fuels (2)	14	11	10	11	16	14.3	0.6
Mineral fuels, lubricants and related materials (3)	0	9	0	0	0	X	0.0
Animal and vegetable oils, fats and waxes (4)	0	0	0	0	0	X	0.0
Chemicals and related products (5)	1	2	1	1	4	300.0	0.2
Manufactured goods classified chiefly by material (6)	775	956	1 026	1 127	1 208	55.9	47.7
Machinery and transport equipment (7)	2	3	3	3	3	50.0	0.1
Miscellaneous manufactured articles (8)	912	1 148	1 166	1 127	1 263	38.5	49.9
Commodities and transactions not classified elsewhere (9)	5	7	6	5	7	40.0	0.3
Top 20 Commodities	1 672	2 084	2 165	2 221	2 440	45.9	96.4
Made-up articles of textile materials (658)	395	476	560	561	652	65.1	25.8
Articles of apparel of textile fabrics (845)	287	384	386	376	448	56.1	17.7
Cotton fabrics, woven (652)	157	205	212	301	309	96.8	12.2
Men's or boys' coats, jackets, etc. knit (843)	197	209	212	191	232	17.8	9.2
Men's or boys' coats, jackets, etc. not knit (841)	130	164	140	121	122	-6.2	4.8
Floor coverings (659)	91	105	96	97	99	8.8	3.9
Women's or girls' coats, jackets, etc. knit (844)	43	45	51	58	83	93.0	3.3
Apparel and accessories except textile; headgear (848)	68	87	87	93	80	17.6	3.2
Women's or girls' coats, jackets, etc. not knit (842)	62	95	106	90	74	19.4	2.9
Clothing accessories (846)	22	32	39	47	64	190.9	2.5
Textile yarn (651)	56	84	72	69	62	10.7	2.4
Furniture and bedding accessories (821)	14	15	28	40	54	285.7	2.1
Woven fabrics of manmade textile materials (653)	35	41	39	53	40	14.3	1.6
Toys and sporting goods (894)	33	38	39	39	34	3.0	1.3
Medical instruments and appliances (872)	26	27	26	29	29	11.5	1.1
Jewelry, goldsmiths' and silversmiths' wares (897)	18	33	32	22	19	5.6	0.8
Cutlery (696)	16	19	17	15	14	-12.5	0.6
Rice (42)	7	9	7	8	10	42.9	0.4
Crude vegetable materials (292)	10	9	8	5	8	-20.0	0.3
Trunks, suitcases, vanity cases, and briefcases (831)	5	7	8	6	7	40.0	0.3

X = Not applicable.

Table C-78. U.S. Trade by Commodity with Panama, 1999–2003

(Millions of dollars; total exports, f.a.s.; general imports, Customs; top 20 commodities based on 2003 dollar value.)

Commodity and SITC code	1999	2000	2001	2002	2003	Percent change, 1999–2003	Percent share of total, 2003
EXPORTS							
Total	1 741	1 609	1 333	1 408	1 848	6.1	100.0
Food and live animals (0)	171	155	161	167	177	3.5	9.6
Beverages and tobacco (1)	17	13	17	13	15	-11.8	0.8
Crude materials, inedible, except fuels (2)	14	15	17	13	10	-28.6	0.5
Mineral fuels, lubricants and related materials (3)	95	179	154	192	432	354.7	23.4
Animal and vegetable oils, fats and waxes (4)	11	7	5	9	7	-36.4	0.4
Chemicals and related products (5)	224	223	250	201	240	7.1	13.0
Manufactured goods classified chiefly by material (6)	164	144	117	103	107	-34.8	5.8
Machinery and transport equipment (7)	766	620	383	502	622	-18.8	33.7
Miscellaneous manufactured articles (8)	197	179	170	154	166	-15.7	9.0
Commodities and transactions not classified elsewhere (9)	82	74	60	54	72	-12.2	3.9
Top 20 Commodities	946	928	736	902	1 296	37.0	70.1
Oil (not crude) (334)	94	175	149	186	426	353.2	23.1
Aircraft and associated equipment (792)	221	180	17	191	261	18.1	14.1
Medicaments (including veterinary medicaments) (542)	78	60	85	64	90	15.4	4.9
Estimated low value shipments (994)	62	58	53	46	63	1.6	3.4
Telecommunications equipment (764)	77	64	60	57	60	-22.1	3.2
Parts for office machines and a.d.p. machines (759)	41	45	29	41	50	22.0	2.7
Feeding stuff for animals (081)	23	22	27	32	36	56.5	1.9
Perfumery, cosmetics or toilet preparations, excluding soaps (553)	44	50	63	42	36	-18.2	1.9
Paper and paperboard (641)	38	42	36	32	35	-7.9	1.9
Maize (not including sweet corn) unmilled (044)	28	28	27	31	34	21.4	1.8
Automatic data processing machines (752)	44	42	35	26	33	-25.0	1.8
Medicinal products, except medicaments (541)	8	6	11	16	26	225.0	1.4
All motor vehicles (781)	21	24	23	22	26	23.8	1.4
Musical instruments and accessories (898)	32	22	17	19	21	-34.4	1.1
Photographic apparatus and equipment (881)	19	17	19	22	19	0.0	1.0
Wheat and meslin, unmilled (041)	13	14	16	14	18	38.5	1.0
Edible products and preparations, n.e.s. (098)	31	22	21	19	17	-45.2	0.9
Toys and sporting goods (894)	14	12	15	13	16	14.3	0.9
Heating and cooling equipment (741)	28	20	17	15	16	-42.9	0.9
Civil engineering and contractors' plant and equipment (723)	30	25	16	14	13	-56.7	0.7
IMPORTS							
Total	365	307	293	302	301	-17.5	100.0
Food and live animals (0)	176	143	144	138	148	-15.9	49.2
Beverages and tobacco (1)	1	2	2	1	3	200.0	1.0
Crude materials, inedible, except fuels (2)	8	11	9	9	8	0.0	2.7
Mineral fuels, lubricants and related materials (3)	23	41	33	30	14	-39.1	4.7
Animal and vegetable oils, fats and waxes (4)	0	0	0	0	0	X	0.0
Chemicals and related products (5)	10	8	6	5	6	-40.0	2.0
Manufactured goods classified chiefly by material (6)	9	11	8	8	13	44.4	4.3
Machinery and transport equipment (7)	27	13	6	8	10	-63.0	3.3
Miscellaneous manufactured articles (8)	22	18	18	15	20	-9.1	6.6
Commodities and transactions not classified elsewhere (9)	89	60	65	88	79	-11.2	26.2
Top 20 Commodities	312	270	262	270	265	-15.1	88.0
Special transactions not classified by kind (931)	83	53	55	77	66	-20.5	21.9
Fish, fresh, chilled or frozen (034)	20	25	30	41	56	180.0	18.6
Crustaceans (036)	67	60	64	52	46	-31.3	15.3
Sugars, molasses, and honey (061)	21	19	18	15	13	-38.1	4.3
Coffee and coffee substitutes (071)	19	15	10	8	12	-36.8	4.0
Oil (not crude) (334)	23	41	33	29	11	-52.2	3.7
Gold, nonmonetary (971)	3	4	7	8	10	233.3	3.3
Fish, crustaceans and molluscs (37)	4	8	10	9	8	100.0	2.7
Fruit and nuts (not including oil nuts), fresh or dried (057)	40	12	8	7	7	-82.5	2.3
Miscellaneous manufactured articles (899)	5	5	4	4	4	-20.0	1.3
Sound and television recorders (763)	4	4	2	1	4	0.0	1.3
Glassware (665)	0	1	0	1	4	X	1.3
Jewelry, goldsmiths' and silversmiths' wares (897)	1	1	1	0	4	300.0	1.3
Vegetables, roots, tubers and other edible vegetable products (054)	2	2	3	4	3	50.0	1.0
Crude oil (333)	0	0	0	0	3	X	1.0
Nonferrous base metal waste and scrap (288)	7	10	7	5	3	-57.1	1.0
Estimate of low value import transactions (984)	4	3	3	3	3	-25.0	1.0
Paper and paperboard, cut to size or shape, and articles (642)	2	2	2	1	3	50.0	1.0
Articles of plastics (893)	1	2	2	2	3	200.0	1.0
Articles of apparel of textile fabrics (845)	6	3	3	3	2	-66.7	0.7

X = Not applicable.

Table C-79. U.S. Trade by Commodity with Peru, 1999–2003

(Millions of dollars; total exports, f.a.s.; general imports, Customs; top 20 commodities based on 2003 dollar value.)

Commodity and SITC code	1999	2000	2001	2002	2003	Percent change, 1999–2003	Percent share of total, 2003
EXPORTS							
Total	1 701	1 662	1 567	1 556	1 707	0.4	100.0
Food and live animals (0)	245	121	151	141	147	-40.0	8.6
Beverages and tobacco (1)	9	3	2	2	2	-77.8	0.1
Crude materials, inedible, except fuels (2)	41	49	53	56	79	92.7	4.6
Mineral fuels, lubricants and related materials (3)	23	24	46	56	92	300.0	5.4
Animal and vegetable oils, fats and waxes (4)	28	22	21	28	33	17.9	1.9
Chemicals and related products (5)	190	257	248	273	297	56.3	17.4
Manufactured goods classified chiefly by material (6)	125	137	96	85	99	-20.8	5.8
Machinery and transport equipment (7)	764	808	727	700	767	0.4	44.9
Miscellaneous manufactured articles (8)	124	114	106	111	113	-8.9	6.6
Commodities and transactions not classified elsewhere (9)	153	128	117	103	79	-48.4	4.6
Top 20 Commodities	747	828	882	901	1 044	39.8	61.2
Civil engineering and contractors' plant and equipment (723)	105	141	144	142	158	50.5	9.3
Telecommunications equipment (764)	86	101	118	114	128	48.8	7.5
Wheat and meslin, unmilled (041)	69	30	76	66	101	46.4	5.9
Automatic data processing machines (752)	87	116	93	76	93	6.9	5.4
Oil (not crude) (334)	19	22	41	51	90	373.7	5.3
Polyacetals and epoxide resins (574)	5	28	31	39	59	1 080.0	3.5
Parts for office machines and a.d.p. machines (759)	61	70	54	54	57	-6.6	3.3
Cotton textile fibers (263)	13	19	30	36	47	261.5	2.8
Estimated low value shipments (994)	47	43	41	40	43	-8.5	2.5
Heating and cooling equipment (741)	19	15	12	43	37	94.7	2.2
Nitrogen-function compounds (514)	8	28	22	27	33	312.5	1.9
Internal combustion piston engines (713)	19	20	16	16	27	42.1	1.6
Fertilizers (except crude) (562)	21	18	26	22	25	19.0	1.5
Gold, nonmonetary (971)	79	71	68	53	24	-69.6	1.4
Measuring/checking/analyzing instruments (874)	29	22	24	26	22	-24.1	1.3
Polymers of ethylene (571)	16	17	18	28	21	31.3	1.2
Pumps, air or gas compressors and fans (743)	14	16	15	13	20	42.9	1.2
Parts and accessories of motor vehicles (784)	14	10	16	17	20	42.9	1.2
Paper and paperboard (641)	24	28	18	18	20	-16.7	1.2
Toys and sporting goods (894)	12	13	19	20	19	58.3	1.1
IMPORTS							
Total	1 928	1 996	1 840	1 932	2 407	24.8	100.0
Food and live animals (0)	254	219	225	261	306	20.5	12.7
Beverages and tobacco (1)	1	1	2	6	9	800.0	0.4
Crude materials, inedible, except fuels (2)	127	90	88	103	94	-26.0	3.9
Mineral fuels, lubricants and related materials (3)	160	180	198	220	249	55.6	10.3
Animal and vegetable oils, fats and waxes (4)	1	0	0	1	0	X	0.0
Chemicals and related products (5)	12	17	14	14	22	83.3	0.9
Manufactured goods classified chiefly by material (6)	598	825	712	650	734	22.7	30.5
Machinery and transport equipment (7)	8	8	9	11	11	37.5	0.5
Miscellaneous manufactured articles (8)	432	503	490	502	600	38.9	24.9
Commodities and transactions not classified elsewhere (9)	334	153	100	163	383	14.7	15.9
Top 20 Commodities	1 758	1 830	1 666	1 749	2 192	24.7	91.1
Copper (682)	343	595	514	447	445	29.7	18.5
Gold, nonmonetary (971)	244	123	63	131	342	40.2	14.2
Articles of apparel of textile fabrics (845)	178	249	243	247	302	69.7	12.5
Oil (not crude) (334)	43	144	151	172	138	220.9	5.7
Men's or boys' coats, jackets, etc. knit (843)	82	83	77	82	120	46.3	5.0
Crude oil (333)	117	36	48	48	111	-5.1	4.6
Vegetables, roots, tubers and other edible vegetable products (054)	60	57	77	92	110	83.3	4.6
Tin (687)	61	80	70	83	97	59.0	4.0
Silver, platinum, and other platinum group metals (681)	49	22	26	31	89	81.6	3.7
Jewelry, goldsmiths' and silversmiths' wares (897)	113	101	100	94	72	-36.3	3.0
Coffee and coffee substitutes (071)	89	86	48	58	62	-30.3	2.6
Women's or girls' coats, jackets, etc. knit (844)	34	30	29	38	55	61.8	2.3
Wood, simply worked (248)	40	37	41	60	48	20.0	2.0
Zinc (686)	101	80	55	31	37	-63.4	1.5
Special transactions not classified by kind (931)	82	23	31	26	34	-58.5	1.4
Fruit and nuts (not including oil nuts), fresh or dried (057)	19	17	22	34	30	57.9	1.2
Ores and concentrates of base metals (287)	64	41	19	22	27	-57.8	1.1
Lime, cement, and fabricated construction materials (661)	3	6	14	21	27	800.0	1.1
Crustaceans (036)	27	13	11	15	25	-7.4	1.0
Sugars, molasses, and honey (061)	9	7	27	17	21	133.3	0.9

X = Not applicable.

Table C-80. U.S. Trade by Commodity with Philippines, 1999–2003

(Millions of dollars; total exports, f.a.s.; general imports, Customs; top 20 commodities based on 2003 dollar value.)

Commodity and SITC code	1999	2000	2001	2002	2003	Percent change, 1999–2003	Percent share of total, 2003
EXPORTS							
Total	7 226	8 790	7 665	7 270	7 992	10.6	100.0
Food and live animals (0)	625	729	667	650	516	-17.4	6.5
Beverages and tobacco (1)	28	37	25	26	19	-32.1	0.2
Crude materials, inedible, except fuels (2)	216	224	169	160	148	-31.5	1.9
Mineral fuels, lubricants and related materials (3)	9	7	8	8	11	22.2	0.1
Animal and vegetable oils, fats and waxes (4)	5	2	2	2	2	-60.0	0.0
Chemicals and related products (5)	279	355	339	330	320	14.7	4.0
Manufactured goods classified chiefly by material (6)	206	259	226	167	153	-25.7	1.9
Machinery and transport equipment (7)	5 328	6 375	5 587	5 477	6 293	18.1	78.7
Miscellaneous manufactured articles (8)	369	604	459	309	387	4.9	4.8
Commodities and transactions not classified elsewhere (9)	160	198	184	141	144	-10.0	1.8
Top 20 Commodities	5 751	6 965	6 074	6 016	6 832	18.8	85.5
Thermionic, cold cathode, and photocathode valves (776)	4 133	4 863	4 437	4 582	5 446	31.8	68.1
Measuring/checking/analyzing instruments (874)	164	311	207	158	249	51.8	3.1
Wheat and meslin, unmilled (041)	235	246	229	253	223	-5.1	2.8
Estimated low value shipments (994)	106	125	116	104	116	9.4	1.5
Parts for office machines and a.d.p. machines (759)	108	167	121	88	82	-24.1	1.0
Feeding stuff for animals (081)	158	197	162	185	79	-50.0	1.0
Machinery and equipment specialized for particular industries (728)	119	123	64	52	74	-37.8	0.9
Aircraft and associated equipment (792)	73	125	50	65	62	-15.1	0.8
Electrical apparatus for switching or protecting elec. circuits (772)	148	185	125	96	59	-60.1	0.7
Automatic data processing machines (752)	87	85	86	57	56	-35.6	0.7
Paper and paperboard (641)	63	63	44	42	47	-25.4	0.6
Equipment for distributing electricity (773)	49	55	25	48	47	-4.1	0.6
Telecommunications equipment (764)	107	129	111	71	47	-56.1	0.6
Oil seeds and oleaginous fruits (222)	55	69	53	56	42	-23.6	0.5
Parts and accessories of motor vehicles (784)	8	10	9	13	38	375.0	0.5
Rice (42)	0	25	28	9	37	X	0.5
Electric power machinery, and parts (771)	37	54	107	50	34	-8.1	0.4
Heating and cooling equipment (741)	43	63	34	24	32	-25.6	0.4
Pulp and waste paper (251)	40	44	35	32	32	-20.0	0.4
Essential oils, perfume and flavor materials (551)	18	26	31	31	30	66.7	0.4
IMPORTS							
Total	12 380	13 937	11 331	10 985	10 061	-18.7	100.0
Food and live animals (0)	435	393	397	413	508	16.8	5.0
Beverages and tobacco (1)	11	11	21	25	13	18.2	0.1
Crude materials, inedible, except fuels (2)	34	36	43	28	33	-2.9	0.3
Mineral fuels, lubricants and related materials (3)	1	0	0	0	0	X	0.0
Animal and vegetable oils, fats and waxes (4)	181	193	147	158	149	-17.7	1.5
Chemicals and related products (5)	32	29	31	38	38	18.8	0.4
Manufactured goods classified chiefly by material (6)	320	344	290	282	303	-5.3	3.0
Machinery and transport equipment (7)	8 231	9 638	7 136	7 040	6 089	-26.0	60.5
Miscellaneous manufactured articles (8)	2 899	3 057	2 979	2 725	2 646	-8.7	26.3
Commodities and transactions not classified elsewhere (9)	238	235	286	277	282	18.5	2.8
Top 20 Commodities	10 904	12 453	9 913	9 624	8 595	-21.2	85.4
Thermionic, cold cathode, and photocathode valves (776)	4 413	5 531	3 549	3 293	2 889	-34.5	28.7
Automatic data processing machines (752)	1 449	1 920	1 951	2 073	1 618	11.7	16.1
Women's or girls' coats, jackets, etc. not knit (842)	538	632	665	600	668	24.2	6.6
Articles of apparel of textile fabrics (845)	518	566	585	566	531	2.5	5.3
Equipment for distributing electricity (773)	273	351	326	321	349	27.8	3.5
Men's or boys' coats, jackets, etc. not knit (841)	370	368	316	289	305	-17.6	3.0
Electric power machinery, and parts (771)	319	339	239	244	271	-15.0	2.7
Parts for office machines and a.d.p. machines (759)	1 060	739	414	354	254	-76.0	2.5
Telecommunications equipment (764)	356	354	310	376	253	-28.9	2.5
Furniture and bedding accessories (821)	256	287	239	237	222	-13.3	2.2
Special transactions not classified by kind (931)	114	94	170	167	182	59.6	1.8
Women's or girls' coats, jackets, etc. knit (844)	179	159	159	191	178	-0.6	1.8
Fixed vegetable fats and oils; crude (422)	177	190	140	141	129	-27.1	1.3
Men's or boys' coats, jackets, etc. knit (843)	128	110	108	123	122	-4.7	1.2
Electrical apparatus for switching or protecting elec. circuits (772)	67	94	81	98	112	67.2	1.1
Fruit preserved and fruit preparations (58)	111	115	102	105	111	0.0	1.1
Electrical machinery and apparatus (778)	118	113	90	106	104	-11.9	1.0
Trunks, suitcases, vanity cases, and briefcases (831)	252	292	283	152	101	-59.9	1.0
Estimate of low value import transactions (984)	124	141	116	110	100	-19.4	1.0
Fish, crustaceans and molluscs (37)	82	58	70	78	96	17.1	1.0

X = Not applicable.

Table C-81. U.S. Trade by Commodity with Poland, 1999–2003

(Millions of dollars; total exports, f.a.s.; general imports, Customs; top 20 commodities based on 2003 dollar value.)

Commodity and SITC code	1999	2000	2001	2002	2003	Percent change, 1999–2003	Percent share of total, 2003
EXPORTS							
Total	825	757	788	687	759	-8.0	100.0
Food and live animals (0)	55	42	71	50	49	-10.9	6.5
Beverages and tobacco (1)	39	3	1	1	1	-97.4	0.1
Crude materials, inedible, except fuels (2)	26	37	63	58	61	134.6	8.0
Mineral fuels, lubricants and related materials (3) ..	0	0	1	1	2	X	0.3
Animal and vegetable oils, fats and waxes (4)	0	0	0	1	1	X	0.1
Chemicals and related products (5)	87	89	103	90	120	37.9	15.8
Manufactured goods classified chiefly by material (6)	48	37	44	35	42	-12.5	5.5
Machinery and transport equipment (7)	418	395	370	349	359	-14.1	47.3
Miscellaneous manufactured articles (8)	92	107	96	71	84	-8.7	11.1
Commodities and transactions not classified elsewhere (9)	59	47	40	31	40	-32.2	5.3
Top 20 Commodities	482	474	502	428	479	-0.6	63.1
Telecommunications equipment (764)	130	85	78	106	68	-47.7	9.0
Pulp and waste paper (251)	17	25	41	38	39	129.4	5.1
Medicaments (including veterinary medicaments) (542)	13	12	27	30	34	161.5	4.5
Automatic data processing machines (752)	54	77	48	22	32	-40.7	4.2
Other meat and edible offal (012)	35	30	58	35	31	-11.4	4.1
Nitrogen-function compounds (514)	12	16	17	11	31	158.3	4.1
Thermionic, cold cathode, and photocathode valves (776)	8	14	9	15	31	287.5	4.1
Measuring/checking/analyzing instruments (874)	25	33	29	19	28	12.0	3.7
Special transactions not classified by kind (931) ...	35	25	22	15	23	-34.3	3.0
Parts and accessories of motor vehicles (784)	24	17	19	19	22	-8.3	2.9
Aircraft and associated equipment (792)	16	17	28	27	22	37.5	2.9
Machinery and equipment specialized for particular industries (728)	18	23	36	16	20	11.1	2.6
Estimated low value shipments (994)	17	16	16	15	15	-11.8	2.0
Medical instruments and appliances (872)	18	17	16	12	13	-27.8	1.7
Electro-diagnostic apparatus (774)	7	9	8	8	12	71.4	1.6
Synthetic rubber and reclaim rubber (232)	0	1	8	7	12	X	1.6
Parts for office machines and a.d.p. machines (759)	26	24	16	9	12	-53.8	1.6
All motor vehicles (781)	13	13	10	8	12	-7.7	1.6
Electrical apparatus for switching or protecting elec. circuits (772)	7	11	9	9	11	57.1	1.4
Nonelectrical machinery and tools (745)	7	9	7	7	11	57.1	1.4
IMPORTS							
Total	813	1 040	953	1 101	1 326	63.1	100.0
Food and live animals (0)	76	83	99	131	143	88.2	10.8
Beverages and tobacco (1)	32	36	51	57	71	121.9	5.4
Crude materials, inedible, except fuels (2)	8	5	7	7	8	0.0	0.6
Mineral fuels, lubricants and related materials (3) ..	0	0	18	8	13	X	1.0
Animal and vegetable oils, fats and waxes (4)	0	0	0	0	0	X	0.0
Chemicals and related products (5)	33	52	64	56	97	193.9	7.3
Manufactured goods classified chiefly by material (6)	213	322	245	258	247	16.0	18.6
Machinery and transport equipment (7)	276	288	247	317	389	40.9	29.3
Miscellaneous manufactured articles (8)	156	197	195	240	329	110.9	24.8
Commodities and transactions not classified elsewhere (9)	20	57	28	26	30	50.0	2.3
Top 20 Commodities	373	463	456	549	747	100.3	56.3
Furniture and bedding accessories (821)	31	67	61	67	89	187.1	6.7
Measuring/checking/analyzing instruments (874)	1	2	2	28	76	7 500.0	5.7
Alcoholic beverages (112)	31	35	50	55	68	119.4	5.1
Glassware (665)	54	68	62	56	59	9.3	4.4
Fertilizers (except crude) (562)	4	8	14	7	37	825.0	2.8
Starches, inulin and wheat gluten; albuminoidal substances (592)	8	12	20	20	35	337.5	2.6
Rubber tires and accessories (625)	7	26	30	27	34	385.7	2.6
Civil engineering and contractors' plant and equipment (723)	55	32	13	13	33	-40.0	2.5
Toys and sporting goods (894)	35	39	41	42	31	-11.4	2.3
Parts and accessories of motor vehicles (784)	6	6	8	11	29	383.3	2.2
Rotating electric plant and parts (716)	23	21	17	64	29	26.1	2.2
Meat and edible offal, prepared or preserved (17) ...	28	31	30	30	28	0.0	2.1
Internal combustion piston engines (713)	6	21	21	18	27	350.0	2.0
Ball or roller bearings (746)	14	18	12	15	26	85.7	2.0
Electrical machinery and apparatus (778)	14	13	16	19	26	85.7	2.0
Footwear (851)	15	12	8	9	26	73.3	2.0
Telecommunications equipment (764)	19	21	10	21	25	31.6	1.9
Men's or boys' coats, jackets, etc. not knit (841)	15	16	19	21	25	66.7	1.9
Fruit and nuts (not including oil nuts), fresh or dried (057)	0	0	8	14	23	X	1.7
Nonelectric engines and motors (714)	7	15	14	12	21	200.0	1.6

X = Not applicable.

Table C-82. U.S. Trade by Commodity with Portugal, 1999–2003

(Millions of dollars; total exports, f.a.s.; general imports, Customs; top 20 commodities based on 2003 dollar value.)

Commodity and SITC code	1999	2000	2001	2002	2003	Percent change, 1999–2003	Percent share of total, 2003
EXPORTS							
Total	1 091	957	1 258	863	863	-20.9	100.0
Food and live animals (0)	125	96	97	91	104	-16.8	12.1
Beverages and tobacco (1)	7	15	17	21	23	228.6	2.7
Crude materials, inedible, except fuels (2)	88	77	103	162	158	79.5	18.3
Mineral fuels, lubricants and related materials (3)	29	28	29	9	21	-27.6	2.4
Animal and vegetable oils, fats and waxes (4)	0	0	0	0	0	X	0.0
Chemicals and related products (5)	52	43	60	56	52	0.0	6.0
Manufactured goods classified chiefly by material (6)	43	44	46	40	49	14.0	5.7
Machinery and transport equipment (7)	628	529	778	384	362	-42.4	41.9
Miscellaneous manufactured articles (8)	88	89	85	71	68	-22.7	7.9
Commodities and transactions not classified elsewhere (9)	32	35	44	29	26	-18.8	3.0
Top 20 Commodities	766	610	891	566	587	-23.4	68.0
Aircraft and associated equipment (792)	262	72	75	102	130	-50.4	15.1
Oil seeds and oleaginous fruits (222)	43	31	67	123	108	151.2	12.5
Feeding stuff for animals (081)	63	64	55	55	51	-19.0	5.9
Nonelectric engines and motors (714)	45	39	33	42	35	-22.2	4.1
Wood, simply worked (248)	22	22	18	23	26	18.2	3.0
Thermionic, cold cathode, and photocathode valves (776)	103	135	359	22	23	-77.7	2.7
Parts and accessories of motor vehicles (784)	6	20	48	24	22	266.7	2.5
Estimated low value shipments (994)	21	23	31	19	20	-4.8	2.3
Tobacco, unmanufactured; tobacco refuse (121)	4	12	14	17	19	375.0	2.2
Measuring/checking/analyzing instruments (874)	26	25	17	16	18	-30.8	2.1
Wheat and meslin, unmilled (041)	6	4	0	5	18	200.0	2.1
Medical instruments and appliances (872)	14	14	16	15	17	21.4	2.0
Automatic data processing machines (752)	29	22	23	16	16	-44.8	1.9
Fish, fresh, chilled or frozen (034)	31	14	22	18	15	-51.6	1.7
Coal, pulverized or not (321)	25	18	23	4	14	-44.0	1.6
Electrical machinery and apparatus (778)	6	16	11	13	14	133.3	1.6
Telecommunications equipment (764)	37	47	46	23	13	-64.9	1.5
Nitrogen-function compounds (514)	1	3	10	11	10	900.0	1.2
Electrical apparatus for switching or protecting elec. circuits (772)	12	22	17	12	9	-25.0	1.0
Wood in the rough (247)	10	7	6	6	9	-10.0	1.0
IMPORTS							
Total	1 357	1 579	1 556	1 673	1 967	45.0	100.0
Food and live animals (0)	16	16	16	21	21	31.3	1.1
Beverages and tobacco (1)	64	56	54	67	59	-7.8	3.0
Crude materials, inedible, except fuels (2)	7	10	11	12	11	57.1	0.6
Mineral fuels, lubricants and related materials (3)	130	138	139	114	231	77.7	11.7
Animal and vegetable oils, fats and waxes (4)	2	2	2	4	7	250.0	0.4
Chemicals and related products (5)	63	72	48	51	64	1.6	3.3
Manufactured goods classified chiefly by material (6)	511	527	523	556	577	12.9	29.3
Machinery and transport equipment (7)	290	459	471	579	708	144.1	36.0
Miscellaneous manufactured articles (8)	218	230	234	207	235	7.8	11.9
Commodities and transactions not classified elsewhere (9)	56	70	58	60	55	-1.8	2.8
Top 20 Commodities	916	1 137	1 180	1 256	1 538	67.9	78.2
Thermionic, cold cathode, and photocathode valves (776)	13	195	198	215	314	2 315.4	16.0
Oil (not crude) (334)	129	137	138	109	207	60.5	10.5
Made-up articles of textile materials (658)	229	226	215	214	199	-13.1	10.1
Cork manufactures (633)	127	133	145	150	158	24.4	8.0
Footwear (851)	98	99	113	101	96	-2.0	4.9
Parts for office machines and a.d.p. machines (759)	1	1	37	76	83	8 200.0	4.2
Alcoholic beverages (112)	62	53	51	63	55	-11.3	2.8
Nonelectric parts & accessories of machinery (749)	39	42	31	31	46	17.9	2.3
Paper and paperboard (641)	0	0	2	28	46	X	2.3
Articles of apparel of textile fabrics (845)	25	30	29	28	43	72.0	2.2
Medicinal products, except medicaments (541)	20	27	26	31	42	110.0	2.1
Pottery (666)	50	48	45	37	41	-18.0	2.1
Radio-broadcast receivers (762)	13	6	14	30	38	192.3	1.9
Special transactions not classified by kind (931)	43	55	42	44	34	-20.9	1.7
Men's or boys' coats, jackets, etc. not knit (841)	28	32	33	24	30	7.1	1.5
Parts and accessories of motor vehicles (784)	12	16	21	25	24	100.0	1.2
Residual petroleum products (335)	0	0	2	5	22	X	1.1
Household type electrical and nonelectrical equipment (775)	5	10	9	11	21	320.0	1.1
Estimate of low value import transactions (984)	12	15	16	16	20	66.7	1.0
Special yarns, special textile fabrics, etc. (657)	10	12	13	18	19	90.0	1.0

X = Not applicable.

Table C-83. U.S. Trade by Commodity with Republic of South Africa, 1999–2003

(Millions of dollars; total exports, f.a.s.; general imports, Customs; top 20 commodities based on 2003 dollar value.)

Commodity and SITC code	1999	2000	2001	2002	2003	Percent change, 1999–2003	Percent share of total, 2003
EXPORTS							
Total	2 582	3 085	2 962	2 525	2 821	9.3	100.0
Food and live animals (0)	136	97	60	115	114	-16.2	4.0
Beverages and tobacco (1)	16	10	11	7	8	-50.0	0.3
Crude materials, inedible, except fuels (2)	68	73	55	48	52	-23.5	1.8
Mineral fuels, lubricants and related materials (3)	81	83	75	87	87	7.4	3.1
Animal and vegetable oils, fats and waxes (4)	5	2	2	8	8	60.0	0.3
Chemicals and related products (5)	403	488	455	439	433	7.4	15.3
Manufactured goods classified chiefly by material (6)	284	374	202	184	225	-20.8	8.0
Machinery and transport equipment (7)	1 206	1 567	1 713	1 290	1 522	26.2	54.0
Miscellaneous manufactured articles (8)	259	265	272	230	254	-1.9	9.0
Commodities and transactions not classified elsewhere (9)	125	125	117	118	119	-4.8	4.2
Top 20 Commodities	1 119	1 572	1 710	1 312	1 546	38.2	54.8
Aircraft and associated equipment (792)	210	606	665	310	357	70.0	12.7
All motor vehicles (781)	54	40	136	138	162	200.0	5.7
Civil engineering and contractors' plant and equipment (723)	101	118	136	110	117	15.8	4.1
Estimated low value shipments (994)	107	108	105	101	108	0.9	3.8
Special purpose motor vehicles (782)	48	32	57	62	89	85.4	3.2
Residual petroleum products (335)	45	53	65	73	73	62.2	2.6
Telecommunications equipment (764)	64	62	63	59	64	0.0	2.3
Measuring/checking/analyzing instruments (874)	60	57	63	59	64	6.7	2.3
Parts for office machines and a.d.p. machines (759)	68	60	32	33	60	-11.8	2.1
Medical instruments and appliances (872)	40	45	53	57	55	37.5	1.9
Automatic data processing machines (752)	105	100	63	44	46	-56.2	1.6
Wheat and meslin, unmilled (041)	14	16	4	9	46	228.6	1.6
Power generating machinery and parts (718)	2	3	27	39	45	2 150.0	1.6
Tractors (722)	20	24	22	36	43	115.0	1.5
Parts and accessories of motor vehicles (784)	42	57	41	36	40	-4.8	1.4
Medicaments (including veterinary medicaments) (542)	37	34	38	26	40	8.1	1.4
Organo-inorganic and heterocyclic compounds (515)	21	32	27	22	37	76.2	1.3
Nitrogen-function compounds (514)	24	36	32	31	35	45.8	1.2
Miscellaneous chemical products (598)	34	52	51	46	34	0.0	1.2
Toys and sporting goods (894)	23	37	30	21	31	34.8	1.1
IMPORTS							
Total	3 195	4 204	4 428	4 027	4 638	45.2	100.0
Food and live animals (0)	123	150	115	132	143	16.3	3.1
Beverages and tobacco (1)	9	12	13	19	27	200.0	0.6
Crude materials, inedible, except fuels (2)	409	374	335	314	319	-22.0	6.9
Mineral fuels, lubricants and related materials (3)	18	50	42	22	25	38.9	0.5
Animal and vegetable oils, fats and waxes (4)	0	0	1	1	1	X	0.0
Chemicals and related products (5)	192	271	293	262	338	76.0	7.3
Manufactured goods classified chiefly by material (6)	1 763	2 614	2 575	2 257	2 513	42.5	54.2
Machinery and transport equipment (7)	280	372	676	653	780	178.6	16.8
Miscellaneous manufactured articles (8)	163	219	255	272	349	114.1	7.5
Commodities and transactions not classified elsewhere (9)	237	141	123	96	143	-39.7	3.1
Top 20 Commodities	2 301	3 179	3 514	3 117	3 646	58.5	78.6
Silver, platinum, and other platinum group metals (681)	1 023	1 529	1 534	1 173	1 272	24.3	27.4
Pearls, precious and semiprecious stones (667)	145	342	454	486	621	328.3	13.4
All motor vehicles (781)	0	23	256	267	374	X	8.1
Pig iron and iron and steel powders (671)	225	243	168	175	205	-8.9	4.4
Nonferrous base metal waste and scrap (288)	187	169	145	160	142	-24.1	3.1
Pumps, air or gas compressors and fans (743)	41	76	174	134	106	158.5	2.3
Parts and accessories of motor vehicles (784)	78	88	69	75	102	30.8	2.2
Special transactions not classified by kind (931)	167	128	109	76	100	-40.1	2.2
Aluminum (684)	36	92	93	95	98	172.2	2.1
Hydrocarbons and specified derivatives (511)	43	78	83	62	78	81.4	1.7
Men's or boys' coats, jackets, etc. not knit (841)	33	42	44	47	77	133.3	1.7
Ores and concentrates of base metals (287)	88	84	82	75	75	-14.8	1.6
Inorganic chemical elements (522)	51	69	52	47	65	27.5	1.4
Articles of apparel of textile fabrics (845)	37	70	83	74	63	70.3	1.4
Fruit and nuts (not including oil nuts), fresh or dried (057)	45	39	40	43	62	37.8	1.3
Women's or girls' coats, jackets, etc. not knit (842)	13	11	22	33	61	369.2	1.3
Jewelry, goldsmiths' and silversmiths' wares (897)	7	17	22	30	44	528.6	0.9
Special purpose motor vehicles (782)	27	31	27	20	37	37.0	0.8
Alcohols, phenols, and halogenated derivatives (512)	4	7	20	15	33	725.0	0.7
Crude minerals (278)	51	41	37	30	31	-39.2	0.7

X = Not applicable.

Table C-84. U.S. Trade by Commodity with Romania, 1999–2003

(Millions of dollars; total exports, f.a.s.; general imports, Customs; top 20 commodities based on 2003 dollar value.)

Commodity and SITC code	1999	2000	2001	2002	2003	Percent change, 1999–2003	Percent share of total, 2003
EXPORTS							
Total	177	233	375	248	367	107.3	100.0
Food and live animals (0)	9	11	15	25	55	511.1	15.0
Beverages and tobacco (1)	2	1	1	2	12	500.0	3.3
Crude materials, inedible, except fuels (2)	6	6	8	16	4	-33.3	1.1
Mineral fuels, lubricants and related materials (3)	14	23	5	2	3	-78.6	0.8
Animal and vegetable oils, fats and waxes (4)	0	0	0	0	0	X	0.0
Chemicals and related products (5)	8	7	8	8	12	50.0	3.3
Manufactured goods classified chiefly by material (6)	7	10	13	10	12	71.4	3.3
Machinery and transport equipment (7)	98	139	242	146	234	138.8	63.8
Miscellaneous manufactured articles (8)	14	19	67	23	26	85.7	7.1
Commodities and transactions not classified elsewhere (9)	17	17	15	15	8	-52.9	2.2
Top 20 Commodities	61	96	235	143	294	382.0	80.1
Aircraft and associated equipment (792)	2	33	105	8	109	5 350.0	29.7
Telecommunications equipment (764)	11	13	64	41	44	300.0	12.0
Other meat and edible offal (012)	3	5	13	21	26	766.7	7.1
Wheat and meslin, unmilled (041)	0	0	0	0	22	X	6.0
Measuring/checking/analyzing instruments (874)	5	7	8	12	15	200.0	4.1
Automatic data processing machines (752)	5	5	6	10	13	160.0	3.5
Parts and accessories of motor vehicles (784)	1	0	1	3	10	900.0	2.7
Tobacco, manufactured (122)	2	0	0	1	9	350.0	2.5
Electrical apparatus for switching or protecting elec. circuits (772)	2	4	1	2	7	250.0	1.9
Special transactions not classified by kind (931)	14	14	13	13	6	-57.1	1.6
Parts for office machines and a.d.p. machines (759)	5	5	6	8	6	20.0	1.6
Nonelectric engines and motors (714)	1	1	7	2	4	300.0	1.1
Electric power machinery, and parts (771)	0	0	0	2	3	X	0.8
Fish, fresh, chilled or frozen (034)	0	0	0	0	3	X	0.8
Heating and cooling equipment (741)	5	2	1	8	3	-40.0	0.8
Residual petroleum products (335)	0	1	4	1	3	X	0.8
Thermionic, cold cathode, and photocathode valves (776)	1	0	1	1	3	200.0	0.8
Electrical machinery and apparatus (778)	2	5	3	6	3	50.0	0.8
Musical instruments and accessories (898)	1	1	1	2	3	200.0	0.8
Medicaments (including veterinary medicaments) (542)	1	0	1	2	2	100.0	0.5
IMPORTS							
Total	434	470	520	695	730	68.2	100.0
Food and live animals (0)	1	2	2	3	6	500.0	0.8
Beverages and tobacco (1)	1	1	1	1	2	100.0	0.3
Crude materials, inedible, except fuels (2)	1	1	1	0	0	X	0.0
Mineral fuels, lubricants and related materials (3)	42	4	33	168	95	126.2	13.0
Animal and vegetable oils, fats and waxes (4)	0	0	0	0	0	X	0.0
Chemicals and related products (5)	8	10	20	17	45	462.5	6.2
Manufactured goods classified chiefly by material (6)	143	171	125	155	187	30.8	25.6
Machinery and transport equipment (7)	61	74	121	115	125	104.9	17.1
Miscellaneous manufactured articles (8)	174	194	211	224	259	48.9	35.5
Commodities and transactions not classified elsewhere (9)	4	12	8	10	10	150.0	1.4
Top 20 Commodities	315	309	344	513	586	86.0	80.3
Oil (not crude) (334)	42	3	33	165	94	123.8	12.9
Footwear (851)	39	27	42	48	59	51.3	8.1
Furniture and bedding accessories (821)	14	16	20	41	52	271.4	7.1
Women's or girls' coats, jackets, etc. not knit (842)	37	39	44	39	48	29.7	6.6
Fertilizers (except crude) (562)	0	0	11	12	41	X	5.6
Iron and steel tubes, pipes and fittings (679)	21	18	42	35	35	66.7	4.8
Iron and nonalloy steel flat-roll products (673)	72	93	11	35	28	-61.1	3.8
Rubber tires and accessories (625)	9	8	4	10	28	211.1	3.8
Musical instruments and accessories (898)	5	5	5	4	24	380.0	3.3
Television receivers (761)	0	0	0	0	21	X	2.9
Ball or roller bearings (746)	9	11	19	19	20	122.2	2.7
Iron and steel bars, rods, angles, shapes and section (676)	1	3	10	7	19	1 800.0	2.6
Pig iron and iron and steel powders (671)	0	4	6	11	18	X	2.5
Taps, cocks, valves and similar appliances (747)	7	13	21	11	18	157.1	2.5
Glassware (665)	17	17	16	19	17	0.0	2.3
Men's or boys' coats, jackets, etc. not knit (841)	9	18	14	12	16	77.8	2.2
Articles of apparel of textile fabrics (845)	18	22	19	18	15	-16.7	2.1
Rotating electric plant and parts (716)	4	5	13	13	13	225.0	1.8
Aluminum (684)	0	0	3	5	10	X	1.4
Toys and sporting goods (894)	11	7	11	9	10	-9.1	1.4

X = Not applicable.

Table C-85. U.S. Trade by Commodity with Russia, 1999–2003

(Millions of dollars; total exports, f.a.s.; general imports, Customs; top 20 commodities based on 2003 dollar value.)

Commodity and SITC code	1999	2000	2001	2002	2003	Percent change, 1999–2003	Percent share of total, 2003
EXPORTS							
Total	1 845	2 318	2 724	2 399	2 450	32.8	100.0
Food and live animals (0)	461	770	854	526	532	15.4	21.7
Beverages and tobacco (1)	29	68	116	83	44	51.7	1.8
Crude materials, inedible, except fuels (2)	33	20	15	13	31	-6.1	1.3
Mineral fuels, lubricants and related materials (3)	7	7	13	8	7	0.0	0.3
Animal and vegetable oils, fats and waxes (4)	23	18	15	6	6	-73.9	0.2
Chemicals and related products (5)	55	244	354	371	305	454.5	12.4
Manufactured goods classified chiefly by material (6)	52	70	91	93	106	103.8	4.3
Machinery and transport equipment (7)	1 039	917	935	1 073	1 189	14.4	48.5
Miscellaneous manufactured articles (8)	128	171	311	209	215	68.0	8.8
Commodities and transactions not classified elsewhere (9)	18	33	20	16	16	-11.1	0.7
Top 20 Commodities	1 117	1 456	1 835	1 664	1 629	45.8	66.5
Other meat and edible offal (012)	136	462	740	433	431	216.9	17.6
Civil engineering and contractors' plant and equipment (723)	152	196	276	332	305	100.7	12.4
Radioactive and associated materials (525)	0	133	196	209	102	X	4.2
Parts for office machines and a.d.p. machines (759)	31	41	49	57	84	171.0	3.4
Pumps for liquids and liquid elevators (742)	38	41	50	60	81	113.2	3.3
All motor vehicles (781)	6	13	28	24	73	1 116.7	3.0
Automatic data processing machines (752)	40	51	63	60	72	80.0	2.9
Measuring/checking/analyzing instruments (874)	44	53	70	79	66	50.0	2.7
Thermionic, cold cathode, and photocathode valves (776)	7	21	33	30	52	642.9	2.1
Telecommunications equipment (764)	65	67	71	51	52	-20.0	2.1
Special purpose motor vehicles (782)	21	18	20	33	38	81.0	1.6
Electro-diagnostic apparatus (774)	22	14	18	22	35	59.1	1.4
Starches, inulin and wheat gluten; albuminoidal substances (592)	1	2	6	7	34	3 300.0	1.4
Toys and sporting goods (894)	6	10	15	30	34	466.7	1.4
Tobacco, manufactured (122)	15	49	71	69	33	120.0	1.3
Mechanical handling equipment (744)	13	18	42	31	30	130.8	1.2
Heating and cooling equipment (741)	36	46	33	40	28	-22.2	1.1
Tractors (722)	3	7	23	16	27	800.0	1.1
Medical instruments and appliances (872)	13	12	20	15	27	107.7	1.1
Aircraft and associated equipment (792)	468	202	11	66	25	-94.7	1.0
IMPORTS							
Total	5 805	7 796	6 261	6 825	8 598	48.1	100.0
Food and live animals (0)	305	259	219	276	259	-15.1	3.0
Beverages and tobacco (1)	80	73	96	81	66	-17.5	0.8
Crude materials, inedible, except fuels (2)	72	77	48	70	61	-15.3	0.7
Mineral fuels, lubricants and related materials (3)	523	830	883	2 012	3 364	543.2	39.1
Animal and vegetable oils, fats and waxes (4)	0	0	0	0	0	X	0.0
Chemicals and related products (5)	795	1 236	1 297	1 064	1 427	79.5	16.6
Manufactured goods classified chiefly by material (6)	3 524	4 704	3 138	2 685	2 574	-27.0	29.9
Machinery and transport equipment (7)	94	120	100	72	212	125.5	2.5
Miscellaneous manufactured articles (8)	232	449	453	476	595	156.5	6.9
Commodities and transactions not classified elsewhere (9)	180	49	27	90	39	-78.3	0.5
Top 20 Commodities	4 697	6 646	5 334	5 851	7 810	66.3	90.8
Oil (not crude) (334)	414	751	873	1 310	1 846	345.9	21.5
Crude oil (333)	108	77	0	695	1 515	1 302.8	17.6
Aluminum (684)	1 162	1 286	686	1 064	1 067	-8.2	12.4
Radioactive and associated materials (525)	610	955	930	784	937	53.6	10.9
Silver, platinum, and other platinum group metals (681)	1 442	2 256	1 497	509	456	-68.4	5.3
Inorganic chemical elements (522)	47	78	98	89	263	459.6	3.1
Nickel (683)	77	167	57	160	236	206.5	2.7
Crustaceans (036)	152	160	165	222	205	34.9	2.4
Articles of apparel of textile fabrics (845)	49	87	111	134	171	249.0	2.0
Pig iron and iron and steel powders (671)	91	93	68	79	143	57.1	1.7
Men's or boys' coats, jackets, etc. not knit (841)	39	99	128	122	129	230.8	1.5
Pearls, precious and semiprecious stones (667)	54	65	127	86	117	116.7	1.4
Veneers, plywood and particle board (634)	75	89	104	130	116	54.7	1.3
Miscellaneous nonferrous base metals (689)	114	103	112	88	113	-0.9	1.3
Copper (682)	72	115	48	123	105	45.8	1.2
Fertilizers (except crude) (562)	51	92	132	89	102	100.0	1.2
Women's or girls' coats, jackets, etc. not knit (842)	28	44	48	41	86	207.1	1.0
Aircraft and associated equipment (792)	22	37	30	8	70	218.2	0.8
Women's or girls' coats, jackets, etc. knit (844)	10	20	24	37	67	570.0	0.8
Alcoholic beverages (112)	80	72	96	81	66	-17.5	0.8

X = Not applicable.

Table C-86. U.S. Trade by Commodity with Saudi Arabia, 1999–2003

(Millions of dollars; total exports, f.a.s.; general imports, Customs; top 20 commodities based on 2003 dollar value.)

Commodity and SITC code	1999	2000	2001	2002	2003	Percent change, 1999–2003	Percent share of total, 2003
EXPORTS							
Total	7 902	6 230	5 971	4 778	4 596	-41.8	100.0
Food and live animals (0)	377	420	377	267	243	-35.5	5.3
Beverages and tobacco (1)	234	270	190	126	128	-45.3	2.8
Crude materials, inedible, except fuels (2)	73	91	117	125	119	63.0	2.6
Mineral fuels, lubricants and related materials (3)	12	18	12	10	12	0.0	0.3
Animal and vegetable oils, fats and waxes (4)	44	38	31	39	58	31.8	1.3
Chemicals and related products (5)	331	327	362	330	362	9.4	7.9
Manufactured goods classified chiefly by material (6)	307	288	269	266	266	-13.4	5.8
Machinery and transport equipment (7)	5 587	4 019	3 894	2 838	2 637	-52.8	57.4
Miscellaneous manufactured articles (8)	515	394	434	414	438	-15.0	9.5
Commodities and transactions not classified elsewhere (9)	421	367	285	364	333	-20.9	7.2
Top 20 Commodities	6 076	4 380	4 060	3 006	2 936	-51.7	63.9
All motor vehicles (781)	376	307	623	861	648	72.3	14.1
Aircraft and associated equipment (792)	3 071	1 910	1 386	276	326	-89.4	7.1
Special transactions not classified by kind (931)	328	291	230	311	280	-14.6	6.1
Nonelectric engines and motors (714)	289	129	109	94	193	-33.2	4.2
Civil engineering and contractors' plant and equipment (723)	169	121	152	174	161	-4.7	3.5
Pumps, air or gas compressors and fans (743)	170	108	189	165	144	-15.3	3.1
Tobacco, manufactured (122)	232	268	189	125	126	-45.7	2.7
Measuring/checking/analyzing instruments (874)	89	85	113	108	119	33.7	2.6
Heating and cooling equipment (741)	172	115	127	142	113	-34.3	2.5
Telecommunications equipment (764)	308	128	84	137	112	-63.6	2.4
Miscellaneous chemical products (598)	59	68	69	63	97	64.4	2.1
Arms and ammunition (891)	190	42	41	19	82	-56.8	1.8
Rotating electric plant and parts (716)	69	42	68	70	81	17.4	1.8
Parts and accessories of motor vehicles (784)	91	98	83	79	77	-15.4	1.7
Electrical apparatus for switching or protecting elec. circuits (772)	59	52	67	58	70	18.6	1.5
Electrical machinery and apparatus (778)	53	51	58	52	65	22.6	1.4
Edible products and preparations, n.e.s. (098)	65	60	70	62	63	-3.1	1.4
Special purpose motor vehicles (782)	187	376	274	89	60	-67.9	1.3
Medical instruments and appliances (872)	38	52	61	59	60	57.9	1.3
Internal combustion piston engines (713)	61	77	67	62	59	-3.3	1.3
IMPORTS							
Total	8 237	14 219	13 334	13 143	18 069	119.4	100.0
Food and live animals (0)	4	6	8	6	10	150.0	0.1
Beverages and tobacco (1)	0	0	0	0	0	X	0.0
Crude materials, inedible, except fuels (2)	7	8	1	4	12	71.4	0.1
Mineral fuels, lubricants and related materials (3)	7 575	13 373	12 596	12 599	17 334	128.8	95.9
Animal and vegetable oils, fats and waxes (4)	0	0	0	0	0	X	0.0
Chemicals and related products (5)	428	617	532	430	578	35.0	3.2
Manufactured goods classified chiefly by material (6)	24	39	26	35	41	70.8	0.2
Machinery and transport equipment (7)	11	33	31	10	14	27.3	0.1
Miscellaneous manufactured articles (8)	38	53	47	13	3	-92.1	0.0
Commodities and transactions not classified elsewhere (9)	150	89	92	46	77	-48.7	0.4
Top 20 Commodities	8 166	14 103	13 231	13 091	18 033	120.8	99.8
Crude oil (333)	7 364	13 083	12 151	12 376	16 887	129.3	93.5
Oil (not crude) (334)	204	258	330	195	403	97.5	2.2
Organic chemicals (516)	291	431	301	263	320	10.0	1.8
Alcohols, phenols, and halogenated derivatives (512)	87	107	115	102	110	26.4	0.6
Fertilizers (except crude) (562)	20	59	78	42	76	280.0	0.4
Special transactions not classified by kind (931)	149	88	90	45	75	-49.7	0.4
Hydrocarbons and specified derivatives (511)	11	7	10	14	40	263.6	0.2
Inorganic chemical elements (522)	17	8	20	3	22	29.4	0.1
Liquefied propane and butane (342)	0	9	90	0	19	X	0.1
Residual petroleum products (335)	0	15	5	26	18	X	0.1
Metal structures and parts of iron, steel, or aluminum (691)	5	0	0	4	12	140.0	0.1
Crustaceans (036)	3	5	7	5	9	200.0	0.0
Floor coverings (659)	4	6	7	9	8	100.0	0.0
Silver, platinum, and other platinum group metals (681)	1	8	0	0	8	700.0	0.0
Petroleum gases and other gaseous hydrocarbons (344)	6	8	21	2	6	0.0	0.0
Ores and concencentrate of precious metal (289)	0	0	0	0	6	X	0.0
Miscellaneous chemical products (598)	0	2	4	0	5	X	0.0
Synthetic fibers suitable for spinning (266)	0	0	0	0	3	X	0.0
Special yarns, special textile fabrics, etc. (657)	0	1	1	2	3	X	0.0
Nonferrous base metal waste and scrap (288)	4	8	1	3	3	-25.0	0.0

X = Not applicable.

Table C-87. U.S. Trade by Commodity with Singapore, 1999–2003

(Millions of dollars; total exports, f.a.s.; general imports, Customs; top 20 commodities based on 2003 dollar value.)

Commodity and SITC code	1999	2000	2001	2002	2003	Percent change, 1999–2003	Percent share of total, 2003
EXPORTS							
Total	16 246	17 816	17 692	16 221	16 576	2.0	100.0
Food and live animals (0)	176	205	203	218	235	33.5	1.4
Beverages and tobacco (1)	72	80	54	41	32	-55.6	0.2
Crude materials, inedible, except fuels (2)	99	77	64	75	76	-23.2	0.5
Mineral fuels, lubricants and related materials (3)	282	311	475	615	461	63.5	2.8
Animal and vegetable oils, fats and waxes (4)	12	10	4	11	5	-58.3	0.0
Chemicals and related products (5)	1 409	1 633	1 471	1 578	1 738	23.3	10.5
Manufactured goods classified chiefly by material (6)	646	724	558	662	753	16.6	4.5
Machinery and transport equipment (7)	10 771	11 853	12 562	10 773	10 851	0.7	65.5
Miscellaneous manufactured articles (8)	2 246	2 350	1 742	1 734	1 854	-17.5	11.2
Commodities and transactions not classified elsewhere (9)	533	573	557	514	570	6.9	3.4
Top 20 Commodities	12 265	13 159	13 519	12 169	12 464	1.6	75.2
Aircraft and associated equipment (792)	1 546	839	3 544	2 828	2 615	69.1	15.8
Thermionic, cold cathode, and photocathode valves (776)	3 104	3 805	2 724	2 186	2 375	-23.5	14.3
Parts for office machines and a.d.p. machines (759)	921	1 197	923	837	1 082	17.5	6.5
Measuring/checking/analyzing instruments (874)	731	1 053	720	814	859	17.5	5.2
Nonelectric engines and motors (714)	581	583	709	757	814	40.1	4.9
Automatic data processing machines (752)	1 237	1 204	924	660	670	-45.8	4.0
Oil (not crude) (334)	266	289	454	592	428	60.9	2.6
Civil engineering and contractors' plant and equipment (723)	408	307	511	440	426	4.4	2.6
Electrical apparatus for switching or protecting elec. circuits (772)	368	381	288	379	359	-2.4	2.2
Estimated low value shipments (994)	379	435	369	350	355	-6.3	2.1
Musical instruments and accessories (898)	775	522	324	234	351	-54.7	2.1
Electrical machinery and apparatus (778)	325	461	301	350	348	7.1	2.1
Telecommunications equipment (764)	333	345	371	331	326	-2.1	2.0
Machinery and equipment specialized for particular industries (728)	512	906	532	423	303	-40.8	1.8
Manufactures of base metal (699)	164	115	90	189	262	59.8	1.6
Special transactions not classified by kind (931)	95	89	169	142	200	110.5	1.2
Pumps, air or gas compressors and fans (743)	119	152	157	172	186	56.3	1.1
Additives for mineral oils (597)	118	145	149	179	177	50.0	1.1
Miscellaneous chemical products (598)	178	219	134	145	168	-5.6	1.0
Plates, sheets, film, foil and strip of plastics (582)	105	112	126	161	160	52.4	1.0
IMPORTS							
Total	18 188	19 186	14 979	14 793	15 158	-16.7	100.0
Food and live animals (0)	92	102	88	95	114	23.9	0.8
Beverages and tobacco (1)	2	3	2	2	1	-50.0	0.0
Crude materials, inedible, except fuels (2)	62	24	12	12	15	-75.8	0.1
Mineral fuels, lubricants and related materials (3)	187	368	203	172	94	-49.7	0.6
Animal and vegetable oils, fats and waxes (4)	4	4	4	4	5	25.0	0.0
Chemicals and related products (5)	630	706	925	1 667	2 432	286.0	16.0
Manufactured goods classified chiefly by material (6)	99	119	105	70	100	1.0	0.7
Machinery and transport equipment (7)	14 857	15 251	11 256	10 532	10 118	-31.9	66.8
Miscellaneous manufactured articles (8)	1 195	1 324	1 270	1 222	1 235	3.3	8.1
Commodities and transactions not classified elsewhere (9)	1 060	1 286	1 115	1 016	1 044	-1.5	6.9
Top 20 Commodities	16 827	17 780	13 789	13 648	13 972	-17.0	92.2
Automatic data processing machines (752)	8 340	6 915	5 685	5 216	4 952	-40.6	32.7
Parts for office machines and a.d.p. machines (759)	2 876	3 126	2 192	2 352	2 343	-18.5	15.5
Organo-inorganic and heterocyclic compounds (515)	513	557	790	1 508	2 214	331.6	14.6
Thermionic, cold cathode, and photocathode valves (776)	1 992	3 338	1 764	1 278	1 300	-34.7	8.6
Special transactions not classified by kind (931)	936	1 156	1 013	921	950	1.5	6.3
Telecommunications equipment (764)	360	442	399	459	400	11.1	2.6
Medical instruments and appliances (872)	222	264	277	297	270	21.6	1.8
Measuring/checking/analyzing instruments (874)	241	236	242	233	260	7.9	1.7
Electrical apparatus for switching or protecting elec. circuits (772)	278	294	232	204	195	-29.9	1.3
Articles of apparel of textile fabrics (845)	146	157	135	138	146	0.0	1.0
Miscellaneous manufactured articles (899)	97	145	133	136	142	46.4	0.9
Radio-broadcast receivers (762)	161	245	233	180	133	-17.4	0.9
Printed matter (892)	121	122	126	124	130	7.4	0.9
Electrical machinery and apparatus (778)	83	117	84	96	99	19.3	0.7
Oil (not crude) (334)	187	365	201	170	94	-49.7	0.6
Estimate of low value import transactions (984)	110	116	94	88	91	-17.3	0.6
Women's or girls' coats, jackets, etc. knit (844)	81	87	79	72	69	-14.8	0.5
Aircraft and associated equipment (792)	56	59	73	62	64	14.3	0.4
Pumps, air or gas compressors and fans (743)	23	29	24	74	62	169.6	0.4
Polyacetals and epoxide resins (574)	4	10	13	40	58	1 350.0	0.4

Table C-88. U.S. Trade by Commodity with Slovakia, 1999–2003

(Millions of dollars; total exports, f.a.s.; general imports, Customs; top 20 commodities based on 2003 dollar value.)

Commodity and SITC code	1999	2000	2001	2002	2003	Percent change, 1999–2003	Percent share of total, 2003
EXPORTS							
Total	127	110	70	93	115	-9.4	100.0
Food and live animals (0)	1	1	1	1	1	0.0	0.9
Beverages and tobacco (1)	0	0	0	0	0	X	0.0
Crude materials, inedible, except fuels (2)	0	0	0	0	0	X	0.0
Mineral fuels, lubricants and related materials (3)	0	0	0	0	0	X	0.0
Animal and vegetable oils, fats and waxes (4)	0	0	0	0	0	X	0.0
Chemicals and related products (5)	6	9	6	4	7	16.7	6.1
Manufactured goods classified chiefly by material (6)	9	7	14	8	16	77.8	13.9
Machinery and transport equipment (7)	93	75	36	65	66	-29.0	57.4
Miscellaneous manufactured articles (8)	10	10	9	10	18	80.0	15.7
Commodities and transactions not classified elsewhere (9)	8	7	4	4	6	-25.0	5.2
Top 20 Commodities	93	84	44	63	89	-4.3	77.4
Aircraft and associated equipment (792)	0	0	0	20	19	X	16.5
Telecommunications equipment (764)	8	5	11	14	11	37.5	9.6
Measuring/checking/analyzing instruments (874)	4	3	2	2	9	125.0	7.8
Special yarns, special textile fabrics, etc. (657)	2	2	4	5	6	200.0	5.2
Estimated low value shipments (994)	7	6	4	4	5	-28.6	4.3
Automatic data processing machines (752)	8	6	5	3	5	-37.5	4.3
Electrical apparatus for switching or protecting elec. circuits (772)	1	1	1	1	4	300.0	3.5
Clay and refractory construction materials (662)	0	0	3	0	4	X	3.5
Miscellaneous chemical products (598)	3	6	2	1	3	0.0	2.6
Machinery and equipment specialized for particular industries (728)	1	1	0	3	3	200.0	2.6
Pumps for liquids and liquid elevators (742)	0	0	0	0	2	X	1.7
Miscellaneous manufactured articles (899)	1	1	1	1	2	100.0	1.7
Medical instruments and appliances (872)	1	2	2	2	2	100.0	1.7
Parts for office machines and a.d.p. machines (759)	55	32	3	1	2	-96.4	1.7
Electrical machinery and apparatus (778)	1	4	1	1	2	100.0	1.7
Plates, sheets, film, foil and strip of plastics (582)	0	1	1	1	2	X	1.7
Electro-diagnostic apparatus (774)	0	0	1	0	2	X	1.7
Equipment for distributing electricity (773)	1	0	1	2	2	100.0	1.7
Thermionic, cold cathode, and photocathode valves (776)	0	14	1	1	2	X	1.7
Made-up articles of textile materials (658)	0	0	1	1	2	X	1.7
IMPORTS							
Total	169	241	237	255	1 013	499.4	100.0
Food and live animals (0)	2	1	2	3	1	-50.0	0.1
Beverages and tobacco (1)	0	0	0	0	0	X	0.0
Crude materials, inedible, except fuels (2)	0	1	1	2	3	X	0.3
Mineral fuels, lubricants and related materials (3)	0	0	0	1	1	X	0.1
Animal and vegetable oils, fats and waxes (4)	0	0	0	0	0	X	0.0
Chemicals and related products (5)	11	14	13	9	8	-27.3	0.8
Manufactured goods classified chiefly by material (6)	72	86	59	82	71	-1.4	7.0
Machinery and transport equipment (7)	48	84	78	90	827	1 622.9	81.6
Miscellaneous manufactured articles (8)	34	52	82	65	93	173.5	9.2
Commodities and transactions not classified elsewhere (9)	2	3	2	3	9	350.0	0.9
Top 20 Commodities	107	170	176	192	947	785.0	93.5
All motor vehicles (781)	0	0	0	0	714	X	70.5
Footwear (851)	9	15	27	22	32	255.6	3.2
Electric power machinery, and parts (771)	0	1	3	7	22	X	2.2
Ball or roller bearings (746)	11	13	16	23	21	90.9	2.1
Furniture and bedding accessories (821)	5	10	9	12	18	260.0	1.8
Glassware (665)	10	10	11	15	17	70.0	1.7
Pumps, air or gas compressors and fans (743)	2	18	22	19	17	750.0	1.7
Rubber tires and accessories (625)	23	28	25	17	15	-34.8	1.5
Jewelry, goldsmiths' and silversmiths' wares (897)	0	6	17	2	13	X	1.3
Toys and sporting goods (894)	2	3	9	12	10	400.0	1.0
Leather (611)	0	0	6	13	10	X	1.0
Iron and nonalloy steel flat-roll products (673)	31	35	1	18	9	-71.0	0.9
Men's or boys' coats, jackets, etc. not knit (841)	5	8	8	5	8	60.0	0.8
Estimate of low value import transactions (984)	1	2	1	2	7	600.0	0.7
Parts and accessories of motor vehicles (784)	2	3	2	2	7	250.0	0.7
Transmission shafts and cranks (748)	2	5	6	5	7	250.0	0.7
Parts for office machines and a.d.p. machines (759)	1	2	2	5	6	500.0	0.6
Electrical apparatus for switching or protecting elec. circuits (772)	0	4	2	3	5	X	0.5
Iron and steel tubes, pipes and fittings (679)	2	3	6	5	5	150.0	0.5
Electrical machinery and apparatus (778)	1	4	3	5	4	300.0	0.4

X = Not applicable.

Table C-89. U.S. Trade by Commodity with Spain, 1999–2003

(Millions of dollars; total exports, f.a.s.; general imports, Customs; top 20 commodities based on 2003 dollar value.)

Commodity and SITC code	1999	2000	2001	2002	2003	Percent change, 1999–2003	Percent share of total, 2003
EXPORTS							
Total	6 132	6 323	5 811	5 226	5 935	-3.2	100.0
Food and live animals (0)	375	353	375	409	528	40.8	8.9
Beverages and tobacco (1)	130	142	121	86	69	-46.9	1.2
Crude materials, inedible, except fuels (2)	564	601	563	620	690	22.3	11.6
Mineral fuels, lubricants and related materials (3)	157	172	194	215	147	-6.4	2.5
Animal and vegetable oils, fats and waxes (4)	39	24	13	12	8	-79.5	0.1
Chemicals and related products (5)	548	593	825	614	721	31.6	12.1
Manufactured goods classified chiefly by material (6)	328	341	330	326	377	14.9	6.4
Machinery and transport equipment (7)	3 122	3 187	2 318	2 103	2 356	-24.5	39.7
Miscellaneous manufactured articles (8)	660	698	736	590	710	7.6	12.0
Commodities and transactions not classified elsewhere (9)	210	210	335	250	327	55.7	5.5
Top 20 Commodities	3 376	3 543	2 924	2 590	3 301	-2.2	55.6
Parts for office machines and a.d.p. machines (759)	82	73	65	70	412	402.4	6.9
Aircraft and associated equipment (792)	1 196	1 291	575	522	389	-67.5	6.6
Oil seeds and oleaginous fruits (222)	239	236	271	263	341	42.7	5.7
Nonelectric engines and motors (714)	134	82	141	170	218	62.7	3.7
Fruit and nuts (not including oil nuts), fresh or dried (057)	109	105	114	142	198	81.7	3.3
Special transactions not classified by kind (931)	65	67	195	128	178	173.8	3.0
Medicinal products, except medicaments (541)	106	147	203	134	156	47.2	2.6
Measuring/checking/analyzing instruments (874)	169	180	167	143	149	-11.8	2.5
Medical instruments and appliances (872)	118	120	148	124	145	22.9	2.4
Estimated low value shipments (994)	124	127	133	117	139	12.1	2.3
Medicaments (including veterinary medicaments) (542)	78	54	57	67	116	48.7	2.0
Wood, simply worked (248)	153	160	133	120	116	-24.2	2.0
Automatic data processing machines (752)	158	118	108	99	115	-27.2	1.9
Works of art, collectors' pieces, and antiques (896)	61	77	85	35	111	82.0	1.9
Telecommunications equipment (764)	261	288	205	113	99	-62.1	1.7
Parts and accessories of motor vehicles (784)	54	77	59	67	99	83.3	1.7
Electro-diagnostic apparatus (774)	84	95	60	64	98	16.7	1.7
Coal, pulverized or not (321)	95	96	62	74	76	-20.0	1.3
Nitrogen-function compounds (514)	31	55	74	67	73	135.5	1.2
Civil engineering and contractors' plant and equipment (723)	59	95	69	71	73	23.7	1.2
IMPORTS							
Total	5 055	5 731	5 192	5 678	6 708	32.7	100.0
Food and live animals (0)	538	506	480	513	595	10.6	8.9
Beverages and tobacco (1)	165	152	164	174	187	13.3	2.8
Crude materials, inedible, except fuels (2)	79	74	67	78	84	6.3	1.3
Mineral fuels, lubricants and related materials (3)	138	397	443	261	360	160.9	5.4
Animal and vegetable oils, fats and waxes (4)	57	64	57	85	97	70.2	1.4
Chemicals and related products (5)	437	460	510	781	1 164	166.4	17.4
Manufactured goods classified chiefly by material (6)	1 355	1 473	1 300	1 234	1 295	-4.4	19.3
Machinery and transport equipment (7)	1 036	1 241	1 082	1 195	1 622	56.6	24.2
Miscellaneous manufactured articles (8)	1 043	914	888	1 118	950	-8.9	14.2
Commodities and transactions not classified elsewhere (9)	207	451	202	239	354	71.0	5.3
Top 20 Commodities	2 433	2 778	2 561	2 949	3 756	54.4	56.0
Organo-inorganic and heterocyclic compounds (515)	66	64	69	176	351	431.8	5.2
Parts for office machines and a.d.p. machines (759)	14	44	43	41	340	2 328.6	5.1
Oil (not crude) (334)	101	349	425	219	308	205.0	4.6
Special transactions not classified by kind (931)	166	404	158	193	299	80.1	4.5
Vegetables, roots and tubers, prepared or preserved (56)	263	231	229	246	283	7.6	4.2
Parts and accessories of motor vehicles (784)	226	199	184	219	280	23.9	4.2
Medicaments (including veterinary medicaments) (542)	3	3	26	120	258	8 500.0	3.8
Footwear (851)	327	325	273	269	235	-28.1	3.5
Clay and refractory construction materials (662)	198	208	200	227	234	18.2	3.5
Alcoholic beverages (112)	134	115	122	146	173	29.1	2.6
Lime, cement, and fabricated construction materials (661)	168	145	139	124	140	-16.7	2.1
Works of art, collectors' pieces, and antiques (896)	184	99	135	328	136	-26.1	2.0
Fruit and nuts (not including oil nuts), fresh or dried (057)	117	108	82	80	115	-1.7	1.7
Electrical machinery and apparatus (778)	67	64	68	91	112	67.2	1.7
Fixed vegetable fats and oils (421)	56	64	55	84	96	71.4	1.4
Rubber tires and accessories (625)	142	113	98	95	91	-35.9	1.4
Furniture and bedding accessories (821)	60	84	90	78	83	38.3	1.2
Perfumery, cosmetics or toilet preparations, excluding soaps (553)	40	50	49	63	83	107.5	1.2
Manufactures of base metal (699)	56	51	62	73	71	26.8	1.1
Toys and sporting goods (894)	45	58	54	77	68	51.1	1.0

Table C-90. U.S. Trade by Commodity with Sri Lanka, 1999–2003

(Millions of dollars; total exports, f.a.s.; general imports, Customs; top 20 commodities based on 2003 dollar value.)

Commodity and SITC code	1999	2000	2001	2002	2003	Percent change, 1999–2003	Percent share of total, 2003
EXPORTS							
Total	167	204	183	172	155	-7.2	100.0
Food and live animals (0)	53	52	65	26	17	-67.9	11.0
Beverages and tobacco (1)	1	1	5	2	4	300.0	2.6
Crude materials, inedible, except fuels (2)	4	5	5	8	9	125.0	5.8
Mineral fuels, lubricants and related materials (3)	0	0	0	0	0	X	0.0
Animal and vegetable oils, fats and waxes (4)	0	0	0	0	0	X	0.0
Chemicals and related products (5)	10	10	10	8	10	0.0	6.5
Manufactured goods classified chiefly by material (6)	30	34	30	26	31	3.3	20.0
Machinery and transport equipment (7)	53	86	50	87	63	18.9	40.6
Miscellaneous manufactured articles (8)	11	12	13	10	16	45.5	10.3
Commodities and transactions not classified elsewhere (9)	5	4	4	4	3	-40.0	1.9
Top 20 Commodities	105	150	128	113	109	3.8	70.3
Automatic data processing machines (752)	9	7	9	28	16	77.8	10.3
Electrical apparatus for switching or protecting elec. circuits (772)	2	16	1	1	15	650.0	9.7
Wheat and meslin, unmilled (041)	46	48	62	23	14	-69.6	9.0
Telecommunications equipment (764)	10	38	12	16	11	10.0	7.1
Pearls, precious and semiprecious stones (667)	4	3	4	4	7	75.0	4.5
Special yarns, special textile fabrics, etc. (657)	6	9	7	5	6	0.0	3.9
Measuring/checking/analyzing instruments (874)	2	3	2	3	5	150.0	3.2
Tobacco, unmanufactured; tobacco refuse (121)	1	1	5	2	4	300.0	2.6
Paper and paperboard (641)	3	3	2	3	4	33.3	2.6
Tulles, lace, embroidery, ribbons, trimmings, etc (656)	4	1	3	2	3	-25.0	1.9
Synthetic rubber and reclaim rubber (232)	2	3	2	5	3	50.0	1.9
Cotton textile fibers (263)	0	0	1	1	3	X	1.9
Textile yarn (651)	0	1	1	3	3	X	1.9
Machinery and equipment specialized for particular industries (728)	1	1	1	1	3	200.0	1.9
Estimated low value shipments (994)	3	3	3	3	2	-33.3	1.3
Knitted or crocheted fabrics (655)	3	5	4	2	2	-33.3	1.3
Jewelry, goldsmiths' and silversmiths' wares (897)	2	0	1	0	2	0.0	1.3
Medical instruments and appliances (872)	1	2	2	2	2	100.0	1.3
Woven fabrics of manmade textile materials (653)	3	3	4	2	2	-33.3	1.3
Aircraft and associated equipment (792)	3	3	2	7	2	-33.3	1.3
IMPORTS							
Total	1 742	2 002	1 984	1 810	1 807	3.7	100.0
Food and live animals (0)	33	40	31	32	39	18.2	2.2
Beverages and tobacco (1)	0	0	0	0	0	X	0.0
Crude materials, inedible, except fuels (2)	6	6	6	7	10	66.7	0.6
Mineral fuels, lubricants and related materials (3)	0	0	0	0	0	X	0.0
Animal and vegetable oils, fats and waxes (4)	0	0	0	0	0	X	0.0
Chemicals and related products (5)	9	10	8	9	9	0.0	0.5
Manufactured goods classified chiefly by material (6)	196	229	204	184	176	-10.2	9.7
Machinery and transport equipment (7)	14	19	14	20	20	42.9	1.1
Miscellaneous manufactured articles (8)	1 476	1 686	1 714	1 552	1 546	4.7	85.6
Commodities and transactions not classified elsewhere (9)	8	12	8	6	7	-12.5	0.4
Top 20 Commodities	1 646	1 894	1 894	1 724	1 724	4.7	95.4
Women's or girls' coats, jackets, etc. not knit (842)	476	530	505	511	563	18.3	31.2
Articles of apparel of textile fabrics (845)	333	421	425	382	352	5.7	19.5
Men's or boys' coats, jackets, etc. not knit (841)	306	343	373	313	306	0.0	16.9
Women's or girls' coats, jackets, etc. knit (844)	62	56	83	95	118	90.3	6.5
Men's or boys' coats, jackets, etc. knit (843)	57	77	79	80	72	26.3	4.0
Rubber tires and accessories (625)	30	42	41	44	48	60.0	2.7
Pearls, precious and semiprecious stones (667)	24	36	32	35	44	83.3	2.4
Apparel and accessories except textile; headgear (848)	44	51	49	43	44	0.0	2.4
Made-up articles of textile materials (658)	55	63	63	37	31	-43.6	1.7
Clothing accessories (846)	23	30	22	26	20	-13.0	1.1
Articles of plastics (893)	7	10	11	15	17	142.9	0.9
Trunks, suitcases, vanity cases, and briefcases (831)	106	106	109	51	17	-84.0	0.9
Tea and mate (74)	13	13	13	15	15	15.4	0.8
Toys and sporting goods (894)	25	22	18	16	13	-48.0	0.7
Pottery (666)	25	21	18	17	13	-48.0	0.7
Crustaceans (036)	9	15	9	5	12	33.3	0.7
Footwear (851)	15	11	11	8	11	-26.7	0.6
Textile yarn (651)	10	15	12	9	10	0.0	0.6
Woven fabrics of manmade textile materials (653)	18	23	13	14	9	-50.0	0.5
Articles of rubber (629)	8	9	8	8	9	12.5	0.5

X = Not applicable.

Table C-91. U.S. Trade by Commodity with Sweden, 1999–2003

(Millions of dollars; total exports, f.a.s.; general imports, Customs; top 20 commodities based on 2003 dollar value.)

Commodity and SITC code	1999	2000	2001	2002	2003	Percent change, 1999–2003	Percent share of total, 2003
EXPORTS							
Total	4 239	4 557	3 548	3 154	3 225	-23.9	100.0
Food and live animals (0)	77	70	71	70	70	-9.1	2.2
Beverages and tobacco (1)	22	21	22	9	10	-54.5	0.3
Crude materials, inedible, except fuels (2)	102	113	112	135	137	34.3	4.2
Mineral fuels, lubricants and related materials (3)	37	40	58	27	25	-32.4	0.8
Animal and vegetable oils, fats and waxes (4)	5	1	1	2	4	-20.0	0.1
Chemicals and related products (5)	243	301	301	323	346	42.4	10.7
Manufactured goods classified chiefly by material (6)	160	168	179	145	144	-10.0	4.5
Machinery and transport equipment (7)	2 830	3 012	1 942	1 672	1 704	-39.8	52.8
Miscellaneous manufactured articles (8)	529	589	624	581	597	12.9	18.5
Commodities and transactions not classified elsewhere (9)	233	242	236	189	189	-18.9	5.9
Top 20 Commodities	2 953	3 219	2 225	2 071	2 130	-27.9	66.0
Aircraft and associated equipment (792)	979	919	244	235	250	-74.5	7.8
Nonelectric engines and motors (714)	334	435	368	261	206	-38.3	6.4
Miscellaneous manufactured articles (899)	85	94	112	158	184	116.5	5.7
Parts and accessories of motor vehicles (784)	166	98	88	121	173	4.2	5.4
Measuring/checking/analyzing instruments (874)	167	192	199	193	168	0.6	5.2
Estimated low value shipments (994)	173	188	180	157	159	-8.1	4.9
Telecommunications equipment (764)	138	149	128	110	153	10.9	4.7
Thermionic, cold cathode, and photocathode valves (776)	195	286	174	132	103	-47.2	3.2
Medicinal products, except medicaments (541)	38	65	62	95	92	142.1	2.9
Miscellaneous chemical products (598)	48	61	84	77	90	87.5	2.8
Medical instruments and appliances (872)	79	93	108	80	81	2.5	2.5
Parts for office machines and a.d.p. machines (759)	81	93	68	67	75	-7.4	2.3
Internal combustion piston engines (713)	73	57	63	64	66	-9.6	2.0
Automatic data processing machines (752)	117	114	98	63	61	-47.9	1.9
Electrical machinery and apparatus (778)	56	134	59	70	53	-5.4	1.6
Agricultural machinery (excluding tractors) and parts (721)	32	30	31	57	50	56.3	1.6
Electrical apparatus for switching or protecting elec. circuits (772)	64	64	47	61	48	-25.0	1.5
All motor vehicles (781)	72	74	56	28	41	-43.1	1.3
Civil engineering and contractors' plant and equipment (723)	15	30	36	16	39	160.0	1.2
Medicaments (including veterinary medicaments) (542)	41	43	20	26	38	-7.3	1.2
IMPORTS							
Total	8 111	9 603	8 851	9 287	11 125	37.2	100.0
Food and live animals (0)	78	65	72	85	74	-5.1	0.7
Beverages and tobacco (1)	205	224	286	310	337	64.4	3.0
Crude materials, inedible, except fuels (2)	97	113	133	198	185	90.7	1.7
Mineral fuels, lubricants and related materials (3)	73	338	281	200	292	300.0	2.6
Animal and vegetable oils, fats and waxes (4)	3	2	3	2	3	0.0	0.0
Chemicals and related products (5)	831	1 052	962	1 101	1 924	131.5	17.3
Manufactured goods classified chiefly by material (6)	898	975	854	849	1 035	15.3	9.3
Machinery and transport equipment (7)	5 068	5 811	5 241	5 573	6 238	23.1	56.1
Miscellaneous manufactured articles (8)	516	567	538	547	604	17.1	5.4
Commodities and transactions not classified elsewhere (9)	340	456	481	423	434	27.6	3.9
Top 20 Commodities	5 258	6 523	6 167	6 730	8 158	55.2	73.3
All motor vehicles (781)	2 098	2 182	2 187	2 113	2 875	37.0	25.8
Medicaments (including veterinary medicaments) (542)	507	683	585	734	1 380	172.2	12.4
Telecommunications equipment (764)	510	987	806	1 328	902	76.9	8.1
Alcoholic beverages (112)	201	221	279	306	336	67.2	3.0
Oil (not crude) (334)	73	334	268	199	290	297.3	2.6
Estimate of low value import transactions (984)	162	188	178	182	218	34.6	2.0
Special transactions not classified by kind (931)	178	268	303	241	216	21.3	1.9
Medicinal products, except medicaments (541)	22	22	42	62	215	877.3	1.9
Measuring/checking/analyzing instruments (874)	138	167	186	185	185	34.1	1.7
Paper and paperboard (641)	121	120	113	137	168	38.8	1.5
Civil engineering and contractors' plant and equipment (723)	205	164	137	130	160	-22.0	1.4
Nonelectrical machinery and tools (745)	151	147	138	133	154	2.0	1.4
Household type electrical and nonelectrical equipment (775)	136	137	118	142	153	12.5	1.4
Mechanical handling equipment (744)	109	147	138	135	153	40.4	1.4
Internal combustion piston engines (713)	105	111	92	101	149	41.9	1.3
Tools for use in the hand or in machines (695)	133	153	116	118	128	-3.8	1.2
Pumps, air or gas compressors and fans (743)	106	105	91	97	123	16.0	1.1
Machinery and equipment specialized for particular industries (728)	138	200	126	113	122	-11.6	1.1
Nonelectric engines and motors (714)	129	145	182	138	117	-9.3	1.1
Wood, simply worked (248)	36	42	82	136	114	216.7	1.0

Table C-92. U.S. Trade by Commodity with Switzerland, 1999–2003

(Millions of dollars; total exports, f.a.s.; general imports, Customs; top 20 commodities based on 2003 dollar value.)

Commodity and SITC code	1999	2000	2001	2002	2003	Percent change, 1999–2003	Percent share of total, 2003
EXPORTS							
Total	8 365	9 942	9 835	7 782	8 660	3.5	100.0
Food and live animals (0)	80	85	83	73	94	17.5	1.1
Beverages and tobacco (1)	92	70	70	99	157	70.7	1.8
Crude materials, inedible, except fuels (2)	36	64	65	44	105	191.7	1.2
Mineral fuels, lubricants and related materials (3)	2	6	19	30	2	0.0	0.0
Animal and vegetable oils, fats and waxes (4)	1	1	2	1	3	200.0	0.0
Chemicals and related products (5)	1 386	1 446	1 406	1 408	1 545	11.5	17.8
Manufactured goods classified chiefly by material (6)	589	641	694	877	600	1.9	6.9
Machinery and transport equipment (7)	1 788	2 070	1 893	1 538	1 324	-26.0	15.3
Miscellaneous manufactured articles (8)	1 601	1 911	2 246	1 760	1 817	13.5	21.0
Commodities and transactions not classified elsewhere (9)	2 790	3 648	3 359	1 952	3 012	8.0	34.8
Top 20 Commodities	6 142	7 672	7 278	5 485	7 055	14.9	81.5
Gold, nonmonetary (971)	2 555	3 353	3 054	1 704	2 715	6.3	31.4
Medicaments (including veterinary medicaments) (542)	370	346	315	375	728	96.8	8.4
Works of art, collectors' pieces, and antiques (896)	572	957	1 081	581	714	24.8	8.2
Pearls, precious and semiprecious stones (667)	380	357	322	275	362	-4.7	4.2
Medicinal products, except medicaments (541)	165	272	212	200	313	89.7	3.6
Miscellaneous manufactured articles (899)	155	225	232	273	299	92.9	3.5
Aircraft and associated equipment (792)	330	636	340	293	234	-29.1	2.7
Jewelry, goldsmiths' and silversmiths' wares (897)	287	206	325	324	224	-22.0	2.6
Estimated low value shipments (994)	198	252	255	189	220	11.1	2.5
Internal combustion piston engines (713)	10	11	138	211	171	1 610.0	2.0
Measuring/checking/analyzing instruments (874)	190	171	210	201	169	-11.1	2.0
Nonelectric engines and motors (714)	277	218	206	217	158	-43.0	1.8
Medical instruments and appliances (872)	86	92	117	122	138	60.5	1.6
Tobacco, unmanufactured; tobacco refuse (121)	45	31	44	81	122	171.1	1.4
Watches and clocks (885)	79	57	60	72	101	27.8	1.2
Miscellaneous chemical products (598)	34	50	32	102	92	170.6	1.1
Automatic data processing machines (752)	202	152	142	84	88	-56.4	1.0
Special transactions not classified by kind (931)	18	30	44	49	74	311.1	0.9
Perfumery, cosmetics or toilet preparations, excluding soaps (553)	28	44	52	39	69	146.4	0.8
Organo-inorganic and heterocyclic compounds (515)	161	212	97	93	64	-60.2	0.7
IMPORTS							
Total	9 596	10 174	9 574	9 382	10 668	11.2	100.0
Food and live animals (0)	116	116	114	142	169	45.7	1.6
Beverages and tobacco (1)	21	82	10	13	14	-33.3	0.1
Crude materials, inedible, except fuels (2)	27	26	20	19	18	-33.3	0.2
Mineral fuels, lubricants and related materials (3)	26	6	36	27	44	69.2	0.4
Animal and vegetable oils, fats and waxes (4)	1	2	2	4	6	500.0	0.1
Chemicals and related products (5)	2 319	2 259	2 457	2 544	2 820	21.6	26.4
Manufactured goods classified chiefly by material (6)	1 068	1 146	949	692	800	-25.1	7.5
Machinery and transport equipment (7)	2 692	2 948	2 492	2 214	2 268	-15.8	21.3
Miscellaneous manufactured articles (8)	2 378	2 737	2 420	2 841	3 601	51.4	33.8
Commodities and transactions not classified elsewhere (9)	948	852	1 074	885	928	-2.1	8.7
Top 20 Commodities	5 896	6 312	6 218	6 487	7 588	28.7	71.1
Watches and clocks (885)	1 060	1 199	1 111	1 208	1 478	39.4	13.9
Medicaments (including veterinary medicaments) (542)	691	667	911	944	1 081	56.4	10.1
Miscellaneous manufactured articles (899)	94	145	207	479	922	880.9	8.6
Special transactions not classified by kind (931)	703	647	770	701	698	-0.7	6.5
Organo-inorganic and heterocyclic compounds (515)	583	494	394	424	496	-14.9	4.6
Medicinal products, except medicaments (541)	344	378	435	403	466	35.5	4.4
Measuring/checking/analyzing instruments (874)	283	334	314	301	321	13.4	3.0
Works of art, collectors' pieces, and antiques (896)	153	286	200	263	267	74.5	2.5
Medical instruments and appliances (872)	128	126	152	174	217	69.5	2.0
Machinery and equipment specialized for particular industries (728)	251	276	242	221	217	-13.5	2.0
Pearls, precious and semiprecious stones (667)	357	352	173	146	210	-41.2	2.0
Electrical apparatus for switching or protecting elec. circuits (772)	199	264	229	215	207	4.0	1.9
Nitrogen-function compounds (514)	172	169	196	211	174	1.2	1.6
Estimate of low value import transactions (984)	160	172	167	156	174	8.8	1.6
Aircraft and associated equipment (792)	138	154	160	149	137	-0.7	1.3
Nonelectric engines and motors (714)	113	174	138	85	117	3.5	1.1
Tools for use in the hand or in machines (695)	102	86	89	92	107	4.9	1.0
Nonelectrical machinery and tools (745)	107	102	105	108	104	-2.8	1.0
Machine tools working by removing metal or other (731)	187	207	156	132	99	-47.1	0.9
Heating and cooling equipment (741)	71	80	69	75	96	35.2	0.9

Table C-93. U.S. Trade by Commodity with Taiwan, 1999–2003

(Millions of dollars; total exports, f.a.s.; general imports, Customs; top 20 commodities based on 2003 dollar value.)

Commodity and SITC code	1999	2000	2001	2002	2003	Percent change, 1999–2003	Percent share of total, 2003
EXPORTS							
Total	19 121	24 380	18 152	18 394	17 488	-8.5	100.0
Food and live animals (0)	1 282	1 302	1 255	1 211	1 291	0.7	7.4
Beverages and tobacco (1)	80	87	84	72	77	-3.8	0.4
Crude materials, inedible, except fuels (2)	1 045	1 156	1 128	1 130	1 144	9.5	6.5
Mineral fuels, lubricants and related materials (3)	165	146	70	57	95	-42.4	0.5
Animal and vegetable oils, fats and waxes (4)	37	21	13	19	19	-48.6	0.1
Chemicals and related products (5)	2 255	2 687	2 127	2 328	2 531	12.2	14.5
Manufactured goods classified chiefly by material (6)	751	856	707	777	912	21.4	5.2
Machinery and transport equipment (7)	11 319	14 693	10 360	10 410	9 245	-18.3	52.9
Miscellaneous manufactured articles (8)	1 815	2 976	2 029	2 033	1 864	2.7	10.7
Commodities and transactions not classified elsewhere (9)	373	456	378	358	310	-16.9	1.8
Top 20 Commodities	12 291	16 454	11 776	12 137	11 411	-7.2	65.3
Thermionic, cold cathode, and photocathode valves (776)	3 595	5 137	3 901	4 552	4 188	16.5	23.9
Aircraft and associated equipment (792)	2 100	1 411	1 240	889	1 068	-49.1	6.1
Measuring/checking/analyzing instruments (874)	956	1 840	974	1 100	922	-3.6	5.3
Machinery and equipment specialized for particular industries (728)	1 444	2 754	1 165	1 100	760	-47.4	4.3
Maize (not including sweet corn) unmilled (044)	465	457	473	474	514	10.5	2.9
Oil seeds and oleaginous fruits (222)	392	385	386	415	420	7.1	2.4
Electrical machinery and apparatus (778)	309	498	338	562	395	27.8	2.3
Parts for office machines and a.d.p. machines (759)	422	550	451	442	384	-9.0	2.2
Telecommunications equipment (764)	565	670	525	408	375	-33.6	2.1
Hydrocarbons and specified derivatives (511)	307	387	133	208	336	9.4	1.9
Automatic data processing machines (752)	448	606	548	416	325	-27.5	1.9
Nitrogen-function compounds (514)	122	193	169	205	238	95.1	1.4
Miscellaneous chemical products (598)	253	288	217	249	234	-7.5	1.3
Arms and ammunition (891)	119	233	344	165	209	75.6	1.2
Estimated low value shipments (994)	206	279	214	213	198	-3.9	1.1
Glass (664)	15	24	50	123	186	1 140.0	1.1
Polyacetals and epoxide resins (574)	144	199	170	143	171	18.8	1.0
Plastics (575)	157	154	138	173	164	4.5	0.9
Optical goods (884)	50	93	76	98	163	226.0	0.9
Heating and cooling equipment (741)	222	296	264	202	161	-27.5	0.9
IMPORTS							
Total	35 198	40 514	33 391	32 199	31 600	-10.2	100.0
Food and live animals (0)	347	307	313	237	235	-32.3	0.7
Beverages and tobacco (1)	8	8	8	10	10	25.0	0.0
Crude materials, inedible, except fuels (2)	131	155	139	138	124	-5.3	0.4
Mineral fuels, lubricants and related materials (3)	13	2	101	61	103	692.3	0.3
Animal and vegetable oils, fats and waxes (4)	4	4	4	5	4	0.0	0.0
Chemicals and related products (5)	486	639	610	622	707	45.5	2.2
Manufactured goods classified chiefly by material (6)	4 481	4 836	4 103	4 227	4 250	-5.2	13.4
Machinery and transport equipment (7)	22 143	26 364	20 803	19 971	18 952	-14.4	60.0
Miscellaneous manufactured articles (8)	6 578	7 108	6 180	5 932	6 218	-5.5	19.7
Commodities and transactions not classified elsewhere (9)	1 007	1 090	1 132	996	998	-0.9	3.2
Top 20 Commodities	25 192	29 686	24 189	23 502	22 736	-9.7	71.9
Automatic data processing machines (752)	5 017	6 616	5 748	6 295	4 601	-8.3	14.6
Thermionic, cold cathode, and photocathode valves (776)	3 757	5 176	3 453	3 137	3 055	-18.7	9.7
Parts for office machines and a.d.p. machines (759)	4 468	3 833	2 923	2 294	2 333	-47.8	7.4
Telecommunications equipment (764)	1 911	2 531	2 003	1 715	1 852	-3.1	5.9
Musical instruments and accessories (898)	555	810	805	895	1 181	112.8	3.7
Nails, screws, nuts, etc, (694)	825	928	783	836	957	16.0	3.0
Electrical machinery and apparatus (778)	870	1 044	918	948	947	8.9	3.0
Furniture and bedding accessories (821)	1 009	1 032	766	795	749	-25.8	2.4
Manufactures of base metal (699)	776	829	718	754	742	-4.4	2.3
Electrical apparatus for switching or protecting elec. circuits (772)	1 030	1 447	933	720	682	-33.8	2.2
Parts and accessories of motor vehicles (784)	554	545	572	635	671	21.1	2.1
Articles of apparel of textile fabrics (845)	698	763	688	612	647	-7.3	2.0
Toys and sporting goods (894)	688	818	721	680	644	-6.4	2.0
Special transactions not classified by kind (931)	582	587	714	604	612	5.2	1.9
Articles of plastics (893)	584	610	576	574	593	1.5	1.9
Motorcycles and cycles, motorized and not motorized (785)	531	549	435	474	584	10.0	1.8
Tools for use in the hand or in machines (695)	485	491	473	497	525	8.2	1.7
Television receivers (761)	50	130	136	216	519	938.0	1.6
Machinery and equipment specialized for particular industries (728)	436	530	443	442	429	-1.6	1.4
Taps, cocks, valves and similar appliances (747)	366	417	381	379	413	12.8	1.3

Table C-94. U.S. Trade by Commodity with Thailand, 1999–2003

(Millions of dollars; total exports, f.a.s.; general imports, Customs; top 20 commodities based on 2003 dollar value.)

Commodity and SITC code	1999	2000	2001	2002	2003	Percent change, 1999–2003	Percent share of total, 2003
EXPORTS							
Total	4 984	6 643	5 995	4 859	5 842	17.2	100.0
Food and live animals (0)	193	225	259	293	281	45.6	4.8
Beverages and tobacco (1)	27	27	26	25	14	-48.1	0.2
Crude materials, inedible, except fuels (2)	308	412	422	462	631	104.9	10.8
Mineral fuels, lubricants and related materials (3)	41	55	54	39	40	-2.4	0.7
Animal and vegetable oils, fats and waxes (4)	3	2	1	1	2	-33.3	0.0
Chemicals and related products (5)	538	625	649	644	707	31.4	12.1
Manufactured goods classified chiefly by material (6)	257	359	401	365	380	47.9	6.5
Machinery and transport equipment (7)	3 059	4 255	3 674	2 505	3 245	6.1	55.5
Miscellaneous manufactured articles (8)	437	525	349	395	405	-7.3	6.9
Commodities and transactions not classified elsewhere (9)	121	158	161	130	137	13.2	2.3
Top 20 Commodities	3 288	4 558	3 934	2 881	3 836	16.7	65.7
Thermionic, cold cathode, and photocathode valves (776)	1 279	2 216	1 604	889	905	-29.2	15.5
Aircraft and associated equipment (792)	583	532	561	232	782	34.1	13.4
Parts for office machines and a.d.p. machines (759)	233	323	327	285	422	81.1	7.2
Oil seeds and oleaginous fruits (222)	136	145	114	114	181	33.1	3.1
Cotton textile fibers (263)	28	69	104	125	156	457.1	2.7
Measuring/checking/analyzing instruments (874)	152	159	125	112	134	-11.8	2.3
Pumps, air or gas compressors and fans (743)	103	118	116	115	133	29.1	2.3
Automatic data processing machines (752)	97	146	137	137	125	28.9	2.1
Electrical apparatus for switching or protecting elec. circuits (772)	69	135	120	117	124	79.7	2.1
Telecommunications equipment (764)	116	102	104	136	117	0.9	2.0
Pearls, precious and semiprecious stones (667)	39	59	55	78	91	133.3	1.6
Estimated low value shipments (994)	81	110	103	84	90	11.1	1.5
Plastics (575)	47	46	53	64	82	74.5	1.4
Ferrous waste and scrap (282)	7	16	4	22	79	1 028.6	1.4
Jewelry, goldsmiths' and silversmiths' wares (897)	23	46	43	63	79	243.5	1.4
Feeding stuff for animals (081)	73	82	95	100	79	8.2	1.4
Machinery and equipment specialized for particular industries (728)	54	88	98	50	72	33.3	1.2
Pulp and waste paper (251)	65	77	52	64	70	7.7	1.2
Hides and skins, raw (211)	17	38	56	51	58	241.2	1.0
Nonelectric engines and motors (714)	86	51	63	43	57	-33.7	1.0
IMPORTS							
Total	14 324	16 389	14 729	14 799	15 181	6.0	100.0
Food and live animals (0)	2 022	2 240	2 066	1 812	2 003	-0.9	13.2
Beverages and tobacco (1)	31	38	42	39	53	71.0	0.3
Crude materials, inedible, except fuels (2)	218	325	237	271	328	50.5	2.2
Mineral fuels, lubricants and related materials (3)	30	68	85	26	37	23.3	0.2
Animal and vegetable oils, fats and waxes (4)	1	1	2	2	2	100.0	0.0
Chemicals and related products (5)	98	169	169	177	268	173.5	1.8
Manufactured goods classified chiefly by material (6)	1 387	1 689	1 464	1 593	1 550	11.8	10.2
Machinery and transport equipment (7)	6 403	7 013	5 747	6 078	5 847	-8.7	38.5
Miscellaneous manufactured articles (8)	3 930	4 632	4 707	4 580	4 825	22.8	31.8
Commodities and transactions not classified elsewhere (9)	204	216	209	221	267	30.9	1.8
Top 20 Commodities	9 985	11 384	9 973	10 058	10 249	2.6	67.5
Automatic data processing machines (752)	2 394	2 340	1 806	1 801	1 663	-30.5	11.0
Telecommunications equipment (764)	610	618	468	516	832	36.4	5.5
Jewelry, goldsmiths' and silversmiths' wares (897)	521	653	682	714	808	55.1	5.3
Fish, crustaceans and molluscs (37)	728	774	749	763	773	6.2	5.1
Articles of apparel of textile fabrics (845)	649	882	915	810	753	16.0	5.0
Television receivers (761)	413	511	456	682	660	59.8	4.3
Thermionic, cold cathode, and photocathode valves (776)	1 104	1 416	837	629	618	-44.0	4.1
Crustaceans (036)	791	974	824	540	598	-24.4	3.9
Apparel and accessories except textile; headgear (848)	249	295	312	355	414	66.3	2.7
Women's or girls' coats, jackets, etc. not knit (842)	325	369	369	365	413	27.1	2.7
Furniture and bedding accessories (821)	267	302	302	392	413	54.7	2.7
Sound and television recorders (763)	183	254	263	439	349	90.7	2.3
Toys and sporting goods (894)	242	297	299	283	295	21.9	1.9
Footwear (851)	322	328	314	280	285	-11.5	1.9
Parts for office machines and a.d.p. machines (759)	198	218	318	430	262	32.3	1.7
Natural rubber in primary forms (231)	145	256	168	202	258	77.9	1.7
Electric power machinery, and parts (771)	265	291	265	247	222	-16.2	1.5
Men's or boys' coats, jackets, etc. knit (843)	176	183	191	207	218	23.9	1.4
Men's or boys' coats, jackets, etc. not knit (841)	233	250	239	212	209	-10.3	1.4
Household equipment of base metal (697)	170	173	196	191	206	21.2	1.4

Table C-95. U.S. Trade by Commodity with Trinidad and Tobago, 1999–2003

(Millions of dollars; total exports, f.a.s.; general imports, Customs; top 20 commodities based on 2003 dollar value.)

Commodity and SITC code	1999	2000	2001	2002	2003	Percent change, 1999–2003	Percent share of total, 2003
EXPORTS							
Total	785	1 097	1 090	1 018	1 064	35.5	100.0
Food and live animals (0)	84	85	91	91	93	10.7	8.7
Beverages and tobacco (1)	2	2	2	2	3	50.0	0.3
Crude materials, inedible, except fuels (2)	27	35	36	39	30	11.1	2.8
Mineral fuels, lubricants and related materials (3)	6	6	11	5	19	216.7	1.8
Animal and vegetable oils, fats and waxes (4)	6	3	4	3	5	-16.7	0.5
Chemicals and related products (5)	86	100	116	108	110	27.9	10.3
Manufactured goods classified chiefly by material (6)	94	115	162	146	131	39.4	12.3
Machinery and transport equipment (7)	363	637	514	485	537	47.9	50.5
Miscellaneous manufactured articles (8)	52	50	77	73	67	28.8	6.3
Commodities and transactions not classified elsewhere (9)	66	64	77	66	68	3.0	6.4
Top 20 Commodities	401	409	631	525	619	54.4	58.2
Ships, boats, and floating structures (793)	7	14	12	77	125	1 685.7	11.7
Civil engineering and contractors' plant and equipment (723)	80	78	159	79	100	25.0	9.4
Estimated low value shipments (994)	48	48	65	55	56	16.7	5.3
Telecommunications equipment (764)	30	42	41	43	41	36.7	3.9
Mechanical handling equipment (744)	19	26	41	33	32	68.4	3.0
Pumps, air or gas compressors and fans (743)	9	8	13	9	30	233.3	2.8
Metal structures and parts of iron, steel, or aluminum (691)	4	14	24	11	22	450.0	2.1
Automatic data processing machines (752)	17	25	22	24	22	29.4	2.1
Iron and steel tubes, pipes and fittings (679)	9	20	38	51	20	122.2	1.9
Feeding stuff for animals (081)	13	16	16	16	18	38.5	1.7
Measuring/checking/analyzing instruments (874)	18	8	29	19	18	0.0	1.7
Oil (not crude) (334)	5	6	11	4	17	240.0	1.6
Heating and cooling equipment (741)	35	13	65	17	17	-51.4	1.6
Wheat and meslin, unmilled (041)	17	16	17	17	17	0.0	1.6
Oil seeds and oleaginous fruits (222)	11	18	17	22	16	45.5	1.5
Nonelectric engines and motors (714)	47	14	12	9	15	-68.1	1.4
Miscellaneous chemical products (598)	9	13	12	11	15	66.7	1.4
Polymers of ethylene (571)	10	11	12	11	14	40.0	1.3
Taps, cocks, valves and similar appliances (747)	5	5	13	6	12	140.0	1.1
Machinery and equipment specialized for particular industries (728)	8	14	12	11	12	50.0	1.1
IMPORTS							
Total	1 294	2 228	2 381	2 437	4 322	234.0	100.0
Food and live animals (0)	57	43	38	42	50	-12.3	1.2
Beverages and tobacco (1)	5	7	6	6	6	20.0	0.1
Crude materials, inedible, except fuels (2)	9	5	25	1	10	11.1	0.2
Mineral fuels, lubricants and related materials (3)	710	1 435	1 414	1 593	3 012	324.2	69.7
Animal and vegetable oils, fats and waxes (4)	0	0	0	0	0	0.0	0.0
Chemicals and related products (5)	355	590	719	578	1 093	207.9	25.3
Manufactured goods classified chiefly by material (6)	117	107	130	153	102	-12.8	2.4
Machinery and transport equipment (7)	3	3	3	4	4	33.3	0.1
Miscellaneous manufactured articles (8)	8	8	8	8	8	0.0	0.2
Commodities and transactions not classified elsewhere (9)	31	30	36	52	36	16.1	0.8
Top 20 Commodities	1 250	2 189	2 332	2 403	4 296	243.7	99.4
Natural gas, whether or not liquefied (343)	105	327	486	566	1 767	1 582.9	40.9
Crude oil (333)	298	564	481	603	782	162.4	18.1
Inorganic chemical elements (522)	226	332	386	312	689	204.9	15.9
Oil (not crude) (334)	305	543	447	416	455	49.2	10.5
Alcohols, phenols, and halogenated derivatives (512)	100	224	283	221	341	241.0	7.9
Fertilizers (except crude) (562)	24	32	47	40	58	141.7	1.3
Pig iron and iron steel powders (671)	7	7	20	28	41	485.7	0.9
Iron and steel bars, rods, angles, shapes and section (676)	83	70	88	98	39	-53.0	0.9
Special transactions not classified by kind (931)	28	25	31	47	26	-7.1	0.6
Fish, fresh, chilled or frozen (034)	46	31	27	28	25	-45.7	0.6
Rubber tires and accessories (625)	14	17	17	20	16	14.3	0.4
Fish, crustaceans and molluscs (37)	0	0	0	0	14	X	0.3
Estimate of low value import transactions (984)	3	5	6	5	10	233.3	0.2
Liquefied propane and butane (342)	1	0	0	3	9	800.0	0.2
Fertilizer, crude (272)	0	0	0	0	9	X	0.2
Alcoholic beverages (112)	4	5	4	4	4	0.0	0.1
Sugars, molasses, and honey (061)	3	2	3	3	3	0.0	0.1
Miscellaneous manufactured articles (899)	1	2	2	2	3	200.0	0.1
Lighting fixtures and fittings (813)	1	1	2	2	3	200.0	0.1
Nonalcoholic beverages (111)	1	2	2	2	2	100.0	0.0

X = Not applicable.

Table C-96. U.S. Trade by Commodity with Turkey, 1999–2003

(Millions of dollars; total exports, f.a.s.; general imports, Customs; top 20 commodities based on 2003 dollar value.)

Commodity and SITC code	1999	2000	2001	2002	2003	Percent change, 1999–2003	Percent share of total, 2003
EXPORTS							
Total	3 197	3 731	3 107	3 107	2 904	-9.2	100.0
Food and live animals (0)	207	208	145	184	257	24.2	8.8
Beverages and tobacco (1)	152	223	165	97	68	-55.3	2.3
Crude materials, inedible, except fuels (2)	171	368	369	492	696	307.0	24.0
Mineral fuels, lubricants and related materials (3)	54	88	56	44	73	35.2	2.5
Animal and vegetable oils, fats and waxes (4)	100	75	100	110	115	15.0	4.0
Chemicals and related products (5)	280	345	287	245	334	19.3	11.5
Manufactured goods classified chiefly by material (6)	161	163	101	106	141	-12.4	4.9
Machinery and transport equipment (7)	1 669	1 945	1 612	1 540	881	-47.2	30.3
Miscellaneous manufactured articles (8)	343	265	218	221	263	-23.3	9.1
Commodities and transactions not classified elsewhere (9)	60	51	52	68	76	26.7	2.6
Top 20 Commodities	1 806	2 309	2 089	2 146	1 841	1.9	63.4
Cotton textile fibers (263)	46	209	173	241	410	791.3	14.1
Aircraft and associated equipment (792)	893	1 203	774	952	313	-64.9	10.8
Maize (not including sweet corn) unmilled (044)	73	87	44	72	111	52.1	3.8
Oil seeds and oleaginous fruits (222)	56	59	72	96	96	71.4	3.3
Nonelectric engines and motors (714)	60	111	339	140	87	45.0	3.0
Ferrous waste and scrap (282)	0	0	24	37	71	X	2.4
Nitrogen-function compounds (514)	30	50	27	24	67	123.3	2.3
Arms and ammunition (891)	142	20	43	56	67	-52.8	2.3
Fixed vegetable fats and oils (421)	62	40	73	66	66	6.5	2.3
Tobacco, manufactured (122)	93	133	109	93	66	-29.0	2.3
Rotating electric plant and parts (716)	15	5	68	16	60	300.0	2.1
Measuring/checking/analyzing instruments (874)	59	77	60	59	59	0.0	2.0
Carboxylic acids, halides, and derivities (513)	52	72	48	47	52	0.0	1.8
Animal oils and fats (411)	38	34	27	43	49	28.9	1.7
Coal, pulverized or not (321)	31	63	29	27	48	54.8	1.7
Feeding stuff for animals (081)	72	52	65	53	47	-34.7	1.6
Pulp and waste paper (251)	35	46	51	50	45	28.6	1.5
Plastics (575)	21	22	33	18	44	109.5	1.5
Special transactions not classified by kind (931)	21	15	21	39	42	100.0	1.4
Other meat and edible offal (012)	7	11	9	17	41	485.7	1.4
IMPORTS							
Total	2 627	3 042	3 054	3 515	3 788	44.2	100.0
Food and live animals (0)	114	107	114	123	148	29.8	3.9
Beverages and tobacco (1)	178	111	174	127	126	-29.2	3.3
Crude materials, inedible, except fuels (2)	89	77	65	62	66	-25.8	1.7
Mineral fuels, lubricants and related materials (3)	25	75	74	197	146	484.0	3.9
Animal and vegetable oils, fats and waxes (4)	29	13	22	12	35	20.7	0.9
Chemicals and related products (5)	40	43	52	49	66	65.0	1.7
Manufactured goods classified chiefly by material (6)	650	913	842	1 102	1 163	78.9	30.7
Machinery and transport equipment (7)	188	277	279	245	315	67.6	8.3
Miscellaneous manufactured articles (8)	1 086	1 369	1 349	1 532	1 683	55.0	44.4
Commodities and transactions not classified elsewhere (9)	228	56	83	65	40	-82.5	1.1
Top 20 Commodities	1 754	2 188	2 257	2 693	2 862	63.2	75.6
Articles of apparel of textile fabrics (845)	252	307	296	363	373	48.0	9.8
Women's or girls' coats, jackets, etc. not knit (842)	233	321	351	364	367	57.5	9.7
Made-up articles of textile materials (658)	151	205	218	277	291	92.7	7.7
Women's or girls' coats, jackets, etc. knit (844)	192	216	205	239	278	44.8	7.3
Jewelry, goldsmiths' and silversmiths' wares (897)	182	231	200	199	250	37.4	6.6
Lime, cement, and fabricated construction materials (661)	69	111	110	146	218	215.9	5.8
Iron and steel bars, rods, angles, shapes and section (676)	51	116	105	178	151	196.1	4.0
Men's or boys' coats, jackets, etc. not knit (841)	71	124	124	127	145	104.2	3.8
Tobacco, unmanufactured; tobacco refuse (121)	178	111	174	126	125	-29.8	3.3
Oil (not crude) (334)	14	60	59	173	125	792.9	3.3
Men's or boys' coats, jackets, etc. knit (843)	78	68	53	74	65	-16.7	1.7
Nonelectric engines and motors (714)	45	55	71	60	61	35.6	1.6
Iron and steel tubes, pipes and fittings (679)	6	17	27	37	60	900.0	1.6
Fruit and nuts (not including oil nuts), fresh or dried (057)	62	50	41	50	59	-4.8	1.6
Woven fabrics of manmade textile materials (653)	59	65	57	64	58	-1.7	1.5
Tractors (722)	19	35	14	14	50	163.2	1.3
Cotton fabrics, woven (652)	40	45	53	69	49	22.5	1.3
Iron and nonalloy steel flat-roll products (673)	28	26	69	94	48	71.4	1.3
Household type electrical and nonelectrical equipment (775)	6	4	7	8	46	666.7	1.2
Clay and refractory construction materials (662)	18	21	23	31	43	138.9	1.1

X = Not applicable.

Table C-97. U.S. Trade by Commodity with United Arab Emirates, 1999–2003

(Millions of dollars; total exports, f.a.s.; general imports, Customs; top 20 commodities based on 2003 dollar value.)

Commodity and SITC code	1999	2000	2001	2002	2003	Percent change, 1999–2003	Percent share of total, 2003
EXPORTS							
Total	2 713	2 291	2 640	3 598	3 510	29.4	100.0
Food and live animals (0)	154	216	259	257	220	42.9	6.3
Beverages and tobacco (1)	41	39	43	49	27	-34.1	0.8
Crude materials, inedible, except fuels (2)	30	34	26	25	38	26.7	1.1
Mineral fuels, lubricants and related materials (3)	37	31	27	28	35	-5.4	1.0
Animal and vegetable oils, fats and waxes (4)	20	14	19	18	18	-10.0	0.5
Chemicals and related products (5)	175	172	201	220	232	32.6	6.6
Manufactured goods classified chiefly by material (6)	185	181	176	245	241	30.3	6.9
Machinery and transport equipment (7)	1 636	1 172	1 409	2 322	2 245	37.2	64.0
Miscellaneous manufactured articles (8)	347	256	300	307	355	2.3	10.1
Commodities and transactions not classified elsewhere (9)	87	177	180	129	99	13.8	2.8
Top 20 Commodities	1 647	1 258	1 498	2 440	2 294	39.3	65.4
Aircraft and associated equipment (792)	769	241	280	973	732	-4.8	20.9
Civil engineering and contractors' plant and equipment (723)	105	114	195	310	244	132.4	7.0
All motor vehicles (781)	46	54	118	149	237	415.2	6.8
Measuring/checking/analyzing instruments (874)	74	73	88	97	126	70.3	3.6
Telecommunications equipment (764)	81	79	67	75	101	24.7	2.9
Mechanical handling equipment (744)	48	44	62	75	88	83.3	2.5
Nonelectric engines and motors (714)	45	45	69	93	71	57.8	2.0
Estimated low value shipments (994)	47	49	56	62	66	40.4	1.9
Machinery and equipment specialized for particular industries (728)	26	38	43	55	61	134.6	1.7
Pearls, precious and semiprecious stones (667)	16	20	36	82	60	275.0	1.7
Heating and cooling equipment (741)	80	76	78	85	59	-26.3	1.7
Fruit and nuts (not including oil nuts), fresh or dried (057)	28	40	41	52	59	110.7	1.7
Live animals other than animals of division 03 (001)	42	78	95	68	59	40.5	1.7
Automatic data processing machines (752)	48	67	56	64	59	22.9	1.7
Parts for office machines and a.d.p. machines (759)	46	67	56	39	49	6.5	1.4
Pumps, air or gas compressors and fans (743)	54	46	44	43	47	-13.0	1.3
Perfumery, cosmetics or toilet preparations, excluding soaps (553)	42	33	40	46	46	9.5	1.3
Rotating electric plant and parts (716)	10	26	16	13	45	350.0	1.3
Special purpose motor vehicles (782)	22	45	33	15	44	100.0	1.3
Electrical machinery and apparatus (778)	18	23	25	44	41	127.8	1.2
IMPORTS							
Total	711	972	1 194	937	1 129	58.8	100.0
Food and live animals (0)	11	15	16	31	21	90.9	1.9
Beverages and tobacco (1)	1	2	5	3	3	200.0	0.3
Crude materials, inedible, except fuels (2)	4	7	5	1	1	-75.0	0.1
Mineral fuels, lubricants and related materials (3)	23	111	331	116	233	913.0	20.6
Animal and vegetable oils, fats and waxes (4)	0	0	0	0	0	X	0.0
Chemicals and related products (5)	86	118	167	128	124	44.2	11.0
Manufactured goods classified chiefly by material (6)	92	192	195	185	198	115.2	17.5
Machinery and transport equipment (7)	10	11	21	24	117	1 070.0	10.4
Miscellaneous manufactured articles (8)	336	385	342	295	289	-14.0	25.6
Commodities and transactions not classified elsewhere (9)	147	129	112	153	144	-2.0	12.8
Top 20 Commodities	626	876	1 116	846	1 059	69.2	93.8
Special transactions not classified by kind (931)	144	126	109	149	141	-2.1	12.5
Oil (not crude) (334)	15	79	189	52	137	813.3	12.1
Women's or girls' coats, jackets, etc. not knit (842)	128	144	141	113	106	-17.2	9.4
Crude oil (333)	0	28	142	64	95	X	8.4
Aluminum (684)	25	95	105	96	81	224.0	7.2
Organic chemicals (516)	77	98	138	110	81	5.2	7.2
Ships, boats, and floating structures (793)	0	0	5	0	61	X	5.4
Articles of apparel of textile fabrics (845)	54	71	58	61	56	3.7	5.0
Men's or boys' coats, jackets, etc. not knit (841)	71	72	59	46	49	-31.0	4.3
Civil engineering and contractors' plant and equipment (723)	0	0	0	0	44	X	3.9
Pearls, precious and semiprecious stones (667)	28	29	39	28	43	53.6	3.8
Nails, screws, nuts, etc, (694)	18	29	21	30	37	105.6	3.3
Women's or girls' coats, jackets, etc. knit (844)	19	25	23	22	25	31.6	2.2
Fertilizers (except crude) (562)	0	4	10	0	23	X	2.0
Men's or boys' coats, jackets, etc. knit (843)	17	23	23	17	21	23.5	1.9
Perfumery, cosmetics or toilet preparations, excluding soaps (553)	8	15	17	16	16	100.0	1.4
Crustaceans (036)	9	11	11	11	13	44.4	1.2
Cotton fabrics, woven (652)	8	16	12	15	12	50.0	1.1
Sanitary, plumbing and heating fixtures (812)	2	6	8	9	10	400.0	0.9
Printed matter (892)	3	5	6	7	8	166.7	0.7

X = Not applicable.

Table C-98. U.S. Trade by Commodity with United Kingdom, 1999–2003

(Millions of dollars; total exports, f.a.s.; general imports, Customs; top 20 commodities based on 2003 dollar value.)

Commodity and SITC code	1999	2000	2001	2002	2003	Percent change, 1999–2003	Percent share of total, 2003
EXPORTS							
Total	38 338	41 579	40 798	33 253	33 895	-11.6	100.0
Food and live animals (0)	781	704	758	686	698	-10.6	2.1
Beverages and tobacco (1)	230	226	258	298	332	44.3	1.0
Crude materials, inedible, except fuels (2)	880	903	909	868	812	-7.7	2.4
Mineral fuels, lubricants and related materials (3)	192	187	207	149	114	-40.6	0.3
Animal and vegetable oils, fats and waxes (4)	18	15	29	31	31	72.2	0.1
Chemicals and related products (5)	3 256	4 014	5 471	4 877	4 835	48.5	14.3
Manufactured goods classified chiefly by material (6)	2 366	2 705	2 683	2 280	2 318	-2.0	6.8
Machinery and transport equipment (7)	22 425	23 189	21 822	16 575	16 646	-25.8	49.1
Miscellaneous manufactured articles (8)	5 437	6 711	6 252	5 439	5 547	2.0	16.4
Commodities and transactions not classified elsewhere (9)	2 753	2 925	2 408	2 049	2 562	-6.9	7.6
Top 20 Commodities	24 492	25 692	25 600	19 704	20 763	-15.2	61.3
Aircraft and associated equipment (792)	6 111	4 622	4 936	2 859	3 097	-49.3	9.1
Nonelectric engines and motors (714)	2 098	2 193	2 122	1 895	2 147	2.3	6.3
Medicaments (including veterinary medicaments) (542)	718	1 041	2 136	1 580	1 546	115.3	4.6
Automatic data processing machines (752)	1 948	2 208	1 980	1 390	1 340	-31.2	4.0
Gold, nonmonetary (971)	1 358	1 478	944	766	1 298	-4.4	3.8
Parts for office machines and a.d.p. machines (759)	2 123	2 388	1 813	1 300	1 244	-41.4	3.7
Measuring/checking/analyzing instruments (874)	1 329	1 425	1 439	1 218	1 239	-6.8	3.7
Telecommunications equipment (764)	1 366	1 588	1 410	1 106	1 148	-16.0	3.4
Thermionic, cold cathode, and photocathode valves (776)	1 744	2 333	1 785	1 159	1 008	-42.2	3.0
Estimated low value shipments (994)	979	1 090	1 097	928	907	-7.4	2.7
All motor vehicles (781)	549	353	549	660	903	64.5	2.7
Works of art, collectors' pieces, and antiques (896)	662	902	1 080	707	876	32.3	2.6
Internal combustion piston engines (713)	523	712	879	822	707	35.2	2.1
Miscellaneous chemical products (598)	357	533	654	622	592	65.8	1.7
Printed matter (892)	485	553	516	512	518	6.8	1.5
Medical instruments and appliances (872)	317	326	407	438	484	52.7	1.4
Electrical apparatus for switching or protecting elec. circuits (772)	632	751	568	491	462	-26.9	1.4
Organo-inorganic and heterocyclic compounds (515)	168	168	393	467	434	158.3	1.3
Parts and accessories of motor vehicles (784)	671	620	497	410	430	-35.9	1.3
Toys and sporting goods (894)	354	408	395	374	383	8.2	1.1
IMPORTS							
Total	39 191	43 459	41 397	40 870	42 667	8.9	100.0
Food and live animals (0)	448	426	356	369	412	-8.0	1.0
Beverages and tobacco (1)	881	936	905	953	987	12.0	2.3
Crude materials, inedible, except fuels (2)	304	253	221	240	248	-18.4	0.6
Mineral fuels, lubricants and related materials (3)	2 406	4 130	3 371	4 702	5 534	130.0	13.0
Animal and vegetable oils, fats and waxes (4)	12	11	12	11	14	16.7	0.0
Chemicals and related products (5)	6 217	6 591	6 976	7 946	9 085	46.1	21.3
Manufactured goods classified chiefly by material (6)	3 281	3 908	3 651	2 826	2 810	-14.4	6.6
Machinery and transport equipment (7)	17 046	17 657	16 808	15 483	16 015	-6.0	37.5
Miscellaneous manufactured articles (8)	5 242	5 905	5 213	4 693	4 570	-12.8	10.7
Commodities and transactions not classified elsewhere (9)	3 355	3 642	3 885	3 646	2 992	-10.8	7.0
Top 20 Commodities	24 043	27 460	27 015	28 096	29 868	24.2	70.0
All motor vehicles (781)	2 353	2 797	2 701	4 020	5 006	112.7	11.7
Crude oil (333)	1 687	2 986	2 297	3 801	4 368	158.9	10.2
Medicaments (including veterinary medicaments) (542)	1 594	1 899	2 382	2 808	4 031	152.9	9.4
Special transactions not classified by kind (931)	2 524	2 776	3 074	2 907	2 208	-12.5	5.2
Nonelectric engines and motors (714)	3 417	2 682	3 530	2 689	2 022	-40.8	4.7
Organo-inorganic and heterocyclic compounds (515)	1 528	1 277	1 296	1 670	1 417	-7.3	3.3
Measuring/checking/analyzing instruments (874)	1 251	1 498	1 486	1 289	1 360	8.7	3.2
Medicinal products, except medicaments (541)	530	799	729	853	1 096	106.8	2.6
Oil (not crude) (334)	684	1 097	999	839	1 071	56.6	2.5
Alcoholic beverages (112)	858	916	888	934	968	12.8	2.3
Aircraft and associated equipment (792)	1 358	1 363	1 263	932	934	-31.2	2.2
Works of art, collectors' pieces, and antiques (896)	1 101	1 240	1 158	1 053	933	-15.3	2.2
Estimate of low value import transactions (984)	663	746	727	699	732	10.4	1.7
Automatic data processing machines (752)	908	1 015	722	506	647	-28.7	1.5
Telecommunications equipment (764)	580	933	839	537	625	7.8	1.5
Internal combustion piston engines (713)	475	558	574	593	586	23.4	1.4
Electrical machinery and apparatus (778)	636	737	603	558	534	-16.0	1.3
Printed matter (892)	467	502	471	440	460	-1.5	1.1
Parts for office machines and a.d.p. machines (759)	944	1 093	832	538	443	-53.1	1.0
Parts and accessories of motor vehicles (784)	485	546	444	430	427	-12.0	1.0

Table C-99. U.S. Trade by Commodity with Venezuela, 1999–2003

(Millions of dollars; total exports, f.a.s.; general imports, Customs; top 20 commodities based on 2003 dollar value.)

Commodity and SITC code	1999	2000	2001	2002	2003	Percent change, 1999–2003	Percent share of total, 2003
EXPORTS							
Total	5 373	5 552	5 684	4 447	2 840	-47.1	100.0
Food and live animals (0)	350	341	343	269	295	-15.7	10.4
Beverages and tobacco (1)	2	4	4	2	1	-50.0	0.0
Crude materials, inedible, except fuels (2)	118	144	119	100	88	-25.4	3.1
Mineral fuels, lubricants and related materials (3)	52	118	81	90	173	232.7	6.1
Animal and vegetable oils, fats and waxes (4)	37	27	18	39	47	27.0	1.7
Chemicals and related products (5)	598	789	888	637	450	-24.7	15.8
Manufactured goods classified chiefly by material (6)	415	464	452	275	192	-53.7	6.8
Machinery and transport equipment (7)	3 261	3 057	3 155	2 178	1 364	-58.2	48.0
Miscellaneous manufactured articles (8)	390	456	488	351	173	-55.6	6.1
Commodities and transactions not classified elsewhere (9)	150	152	136	505	57	-62.0	2.0
Top 20 Commodities	2 449	2 648	2 688	2 008	1 533	-37.4	54.0
Civil engineering and contractors' plant and equipment (723)	411	436	449	302	172	-58.2	6.1
Telecommunications equipment (764)	378	292	263	254	124	-67.2	4.4
Wheat and meslin, unmilled (041)	60	66	69	89	118	96.7	4.2
Oil (not crude) (334)	12	67	36	36	112	833.3	3.9
Mechanical handling equipment (744)	160	284	193	117	104	-35.0	3.7
Parts and accessories of motor vehicles (784)	201	334	434	202	97	-51.7	3.4
Aircraft and associated equipment (792)	206	48	70	94	96	-53.4	3.4
Rotating electric plant and parts (716)	42	34	38	38	78	85.7	2.7
Parts for office machines and a.d.p. machines (759)	110	124	129	95	74	-32.7	2.6
Maize (not including sweet corn) unmilled (044)	105	106	96	70	67	-36.2	2.4
Automatic data processing machines (752)	169	205	221	111	65	-61.5	2.3
Pumps, air or gas compressors and fans (743)	92	144	119	75	60	-34.8	2.1
Residual petroleum products (335)	39	51	44	52	59	51.3	2.1
Feeding stuff for animals (081)	75	72	62	40	52	-30.7	1.8
Estimated low value shipments (994)	95	104	113	88	51	-46.3	1.8
Measuring/checking/analyzing instruments (874)	73	66	90	83	47	-35.6	1.7
Plastics (575)	52	65	69	46	45	-13.5	1.6
Nonelectric engines and motors (714)	70	33	31	126	38	-45.7	1.3
Pumps for liquids and liquid elevators (742)	63	65	71	37	37	-41.3	1.3
Hydrocarbons and specified derivatives (511)	36	52	91	53	37	2.8	1.3
IMPORTS							
Total	11 269	18 648	15 236	15 108	17 144	52.1	100.0
Food and live animals (0)	208	216	139	121	126	-39.4	0.7
Beverages and tobacco (1)	6	7	5	4	4	-33.3	0.0
Crude materials, inedible, except fuels (2)	164	160	114	130	51	-68.9	0.3
Mineral fuels, lubricants and related materials (3)	9 610	16 695	13 460	13 298	15 403	60.3	89.8
Animal and vegetable oils, fats and waxes (4)	1	0	0	0	0	X	0.0
Chemicals and related products (5)	200	362	450	426	442	121.0	2.6
Manufactured goods classified chiefly by material (6)	712	765	713	813	780	9.6	4.5
Machinery and transport equipment (7)	209	256	188	190	193	-7.7	1.1
Miscellaneous manufactured articles (8)	39	41	45	46	49	25.6	0.3
Commodities and transactions not classified elsewhere (9)	121	146	121	80	97	-19.8	0.6
Top 20 Commodities	10 726	18 128	14 874	14 725	16 810	56.7	98.1
Crude oil (333)	6 678	12 393	10 118	10 916	12 691	90.0	74.0
Oil (not crude) (334)	2 705	4 028	3 010	2 050	2 329	-13.9	13.6
Aluminum (684)	228	239	273	333	302	32.5	1.8
Pig iron and iron and steel powders (671)	114	174	145	203	223	95.6	1.3
Alcohols, phenols, and halogenated derivatives (512)	58	132	161	108	176	203.4	1.0
Parts and accessories of motor vehicles (784)	165	195	145	158	160	-3.0	0.9
Coal, pulverized or not (321)	63	62	125	130	156	147.6	0.9
Residual petroleum products (335)	105	157	148	168	127	21.0	0.7
Organic chemicals (516)	99	180	191	184	116	17.2	0.7
Inorganic chemical elements (522)	5	11	64	95	82	1 540.0	0.5
Special transactions not classified by kind (931)	115	139	115	75	75	-34.8	0.4
Crustaceans (036)	101	154	99	73	75	-25.7	0.4
Liquefied propane and butane (342)	54	53	59	34	74	37.0	0.4
Lime, cement, and fabricated construction materials (661)	89	78	64	54	59	-33.7	0.3
Fertilizers (except crude) (562)	5	7	14	21	50	900.0	0.3
Rubber tires and accessories (625)	39	37	11	11	29	-25.6	0.2
Iron and steel bars, rods, angles, shapes and section (676)	37	23	29	30	26	-29.7	0.2
Iron and steel tubes, pipes and fittings (679)	13	32	64	22	22	69.2	0.1
Iron and nonalloy steel flat-roll products (673)	43	15	24	48	21	-51.2	0.1
Fish, crustaceans and molluscs (37)	10	19	15	12	17	70.0	0.1

X = Not applicable.

Table C-100. U.S. Trade by Commodity with Vietnam, 1999–2003

(Millions of dollars; total exports, f.a.s.; general imports, Customs; top 20 commodities based on 2003 dollar value.)

Commodity and SITC code	1999	2000	2001	2002	2003	Percent change, 1999–2003	Percent share of total, 2003
EXPORTS							
Total	291	368	461	580	1 324	355.0	100.0
Food and live animals (0)	27	37	49	49	48	77.8	3.6
Beverages and tobacco (1)	0	1	0	1	1	X	0.1
Crude materials, inedible, except fuels (2)	12	30	56	69	91	658.3	6.9
Mineral fuels, lubricants and related materials (3)	1	0	1	0	2	100.0	0.2
Animal and vegetable oils, fats and waxes (4)	0	0	0	0	0	X	0.0
Chemicals and related products (5)	77	72	69	83	109	41.6	8.2
Manufactured goods classified chiefly by material (6)	22	23	38	42	57	159.1	4.3
Machinery and transport equipment (7)	95	149	187	271	922	870.5	69.6
Miscellaneous manufactured articles (8)	49	48	51	53	86	75.5	6.5
Commodities and transactions not classified elsewhere (9)	8	7	10	11	9	12.5	0.7
Top 20 Commodities	162	187	237	311	1 028	534.6	77.6
Aircraft and associated equipment (792)	1	3	53	79	716	71 500.0	54.1
Cotton textile fibers (263)	4	15	29	27	35	775.0	2.6
Civil engineering and contractors' plant and equipment (723)	8	15	14	30	31	287.5	2.3
Fertilizers (except crude) (562)	47	29	19	26	24	-48.9	1.8
Measuring/checking/analyzing instruments (874)	6	7	10	11	24	300.0	1.8
Footwear (851)	30	27	19	18	23	-23.3	1.7
Plastics (575)	5	9	12	15	22	340.0	1.7
Automatic data processing machines (752)	6	9	12	15	16	166.7	1.2
Telecommunications equipment (764)	13	14	13	12	15	15.4	1.1
Paper and paperboard, cut to size or shape, and articles (642)	4	3	7	8	14	250.0	1.1
Nonelectric engines and motors (714)	2	1	0	4	13	550.0	1.0
Feeding stuff for animals (081)	5	9	8	13	13	160.0	1.0
Special purpose motor vehicles (782)	1	2	2	3	12	1 100.0	0.9
Wood, simply worked (248)	1	1	4	11	12	1 100.0	0.9
Steam turbines and other vapor turbines (712)	13	22	1	0	11	-15.4	0.8
Oil seeds and oleaginous fruit for vegetable oil (223)	0	0	3	1	10	X	0.8
Edible products and preparations, n.e.s. (098)	5	7	8	7	10	100.0	0.8
Electrical apparatus for switching or protecting elec. circuits (772)	4	5	6	9	9	125.0	0.7
Pulp and waste paper (251)	3	6	9	9	9	200.0	0.7
Heating and cooling equipment (741)	4	3	8	13	9	125.0	0.7
IMPORTS							
Total	609	822	1 053	2 395	4 555	647.9	100.0
Food and live animals (0)	294	497	632	799	969	229.6	21.3
Beverages and tobacco (1)	1	1	1	1	3	200.0	0.1
Crude materials, inedible, except fuels (2)	4	7	4	13	20	400.0	0.4
Mineral fuels, lubricants and related materials (3)	101	88	183	181	284	181.2	6.2
Animal and vegetable oils, fats and waxes (4)	0	0	0	0	0	X	0.0
Chemicals and related products (5)	1	1	1	3	3	200.0	0.1
Manufactured goods classified chiefly by material (6)	11	16	18	56	106	863.6	2.3
Machinery and transport equipment (7)	3	3	3	35	111	3 600.0	2.4
Miscellaneous manufactured articles (8)	189	198	199	1 292	3 037	1 506.9	66.7
Commodities and transactions not classified elsewhere (9)	6	11	11	15	22	266.7	0.5
Top 20 Commodities	566	755	996	2 233	4 297	659.2	94.3
Articles of apparel of textile fabrics (845)	6	11	12	275	722	11 933.3	15.9
Women's or girls' coats, jackets, etc. not knit (842)	5	4	6	201	609	12 080.0	13.4
Men's or boys' coats, jackets, etc. not knit (841)	13	19	13	192	551	4 138.5	12.1
Crustaceans (036)	83	193	315	374	476	473.5	10.5
Footwear (851)	146	125	132	225	327	124.0	7.2
Crude oil (333)	101	88	183	181	278	175.2	6.1
Women's or girls' coats, jackets, etc. knit (844)	2	3	5	113	262	13 000.0	5.8
Men's or boys' coats, jackets, etc. knit (843)	5	5	7	89	189	3 680.0	4.1
Furniture and bedding accessories (821)	4	9	13	80	188	4 600.0	4.1
Fish, crustaceans and molluscs (37)	31	58	94	138	164	429.0	3.6
Fruit and nuts (not including oil nuts), fresh or dried (057)	23	50	48	70	99	330.4	2.2
Fish, fresh, chilled or frozen (034)	25	49	69	103	91	264.0	2.0
Trunks, suitcases, vanity cases, and briefcases (831)	1	2	1	50	86	8 500.0	1.9
Coffee and coffee substitutes (071)	100	113	76	53	76	-24.0	1.7
Automatic data processing machines (752)	0	0	0	10	55	X	1.2
Apparel and accessories except textile; headgear (848)	0	0	0	25	40	X	0.9
Made-up articles of textile materials (658)	0	1	1	7	23	X	0.5
Toys and sporting goods (894)	0	0	1	16	21	X	0.5
Spices (075)	17	19	12	19	21	23.5	0.5
Estimate of low value import transactions (984)	4	6	8	12	19	375.0	0.4

X = Not applicable.

SECTION D. U.S. COMMODITY TRADE HIGHLIGHTS

ABOUT THE DATA

Section D provides another view of foreign trade, by highlighting the United States' top exported and imported commodities with their 3-digit Standard International Trade Classification (SITC) groupings (see "Understanding Foreign Trade Statistics" for definitions). Each commodity table includes details on the chief foreign purchasers (exports) and suppliers (imports), as well as the countries with the largest trade surpluses and deficits. Table D-1 gives the aggregate picture for total commodities, and commodity detail is presented in tables D-2 to D-31.

These tables present the top 20 U.S. commodity exports and the top 20 commodity imports ranked by 2003 values, and listed in order by SITC code. There is some overlap between these exports and imports. For example, "All motor vehicles (SITC 781)" is the fourth largest

export as well as the top import. Section D contains tables for 30 different commodities. The top 20 exports and top 20 imports are ranked below.

These data are taken from the Office of Trade and Economic Analysis (OTEA) in the Commerce Department's International Trade Administration (ITA). In turn, the OTEA presents data that was collected by the Bureau of Economic Analysis (BEA) and the Census Bureau. The data are generally revised annually.

The arrangement of tables in this section generally matches *U.S. Foreign Trade Highlights*, formerly published by the OTEA. These tables are now available online on the OTEA's Web site at <www.ita.doc.gov/td/industry/otea/usfth/>. Data for all 265 3-digit SITC commodities can be found there as well, and also on the ITA's custom tables on TradeStats Express at <tse.export.gov>.

TOP 20 EXPORTS, 2003

1. Thermionic, cold cathode, and photocathode valves (SITC 776)
2. Aircraft and associated equipment (SITC 792)
3. Parts and accessories of motor vehicles (SITC 784)
4. All motor vehicles (SITC 781)
5. Automatic data processing machines (SITC 752)
6. Telecommunications equipment (SITC 764)
7. Measuring/checking/analyzing instruments (SITC 874)
8. Parts for office machines and automatic data processing machines (SITC 759)
9. Estimated low value shipments (SITC 994)
10. Nonelectric engines and motors (SITC 714)
11. Internal combustion piston engines (SITC 713)
12. Electrical apparatus for switching or protecting electrical circuits (SITC 772)
13. Medicaments, including veterinary medicaments (SITC 542)
14. Electrical machinery and apparatus (SITC 778)
15. Medical instruments and appliances (SITC 872)
16. Civil engineering and contractors' plants and equipment (SITC 723)
17. Machinery specialized for particular industries (SITC 728)
18. Miscellaneous chemical products (SITC 598)
19. Oil seeds and oleaginous fruits (SITC 222)
20. Medicinal products, except medicaments (SITC 541)

TOP 20 IMPORTS, 2003

1. All motor vehicles (SITC 781)
2. Crude oil (SITC 333)
3. Automatic data processing machines (SITC 752)
4. Telecommunications equipment (SITC 764)
5. Special transactions not classified by kind (SITC 931)
6. Parts and accessories of motor vehicles (SITC 784)
7. Oil, not crude (SITC 334)
8. Thermionic, cold cathode, and photocathode valves (SITC 776)
9. Parts for office machines and automatic data processing machines (SITC 759)
10. Furniture and bedding accessories (SITC 821)
11. Medicaments, including veterinary medicaments (SITC 542)
12. Articles of apparel of textile fabrics (SITC 845)
13. Baby carriages, toys, games, and sporting goods (SITC 894)
14. Organo-inorganic and heterocyclic compounds (SITC 515)
15. Natural gas, whether or not liquefied (SITC 343)
16. Special purpose motor vehicles (SITC 782)
17. Aircraft and associated equipment (SITC 792)
18. Electrical machinery and apparatus (SITC 778)
19. Internal combustion piston engines (SITC 713)
20. Women's or girls' coats, jackets, etc., not knit (SITC 842)

HIGHLIGHTS

Among the top five U.S. exports and imports, there are two commodities, all motor vehicles and automotive data processing machines, that fall on both lists. For total commodities (Table D-1), Canada is both the top importer and top exporter, while the United States has the highest surplus with Netherlands and the biggest deficit with China. Trading partners vary widely for most of these commodities.

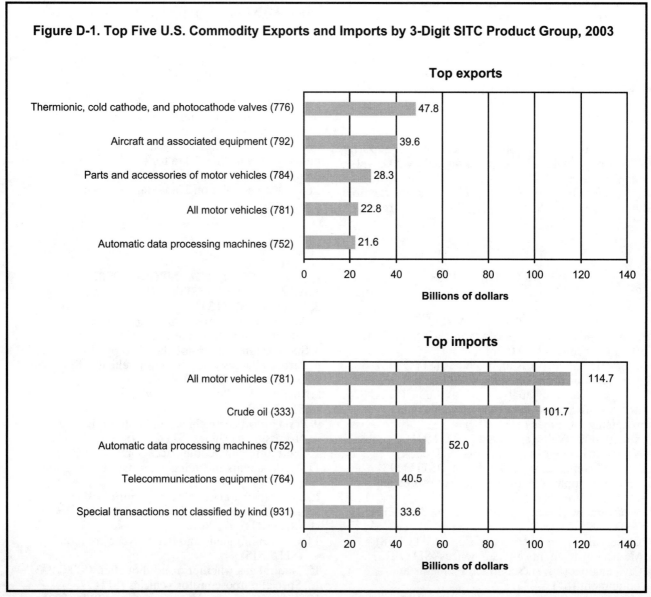

Figure D-1. Top Five U.S. Commodity Exports and Imports by 3-Digit SITC Product Group, 2003

Source: International Trade Administration.

The top commodity export in 2003 was "thermionic, cold cathode, and photocathode valves (SITC 776)," primarily computer components (see Table D-18). This commodity was also the eighth highest import. The largest purchaser was Malaysia, which was also the largest supplier to the United States, though different types of products within this SITC category were being exported and imported. For this commodity, the United States ran its largest trade surplus with Mexico, followed by Malaysia, while it had the largest deficit with Japan.

Motor vehicles (SITC 781) were the top import in 2003, as well as the fourth highest export, though the value of imports dwarfed that of exports (see Table D-20). They were purchased largely by Canada, while U.S. purchases of this commodity from abroad came largely from Japan, Canada, and Germany. The largest trade surplus in this commodity was in U.S. trade with Saudi Arabia, while trade with Japan in this commodity resulted in the biggest deficit.

Table D-1. U.S. Trade Highlights for Total Commodities (SITC 000)

(Millions of dollars; ranked by 2003 value; total exports, f.a.s.; general imports, Customs.)

Country	1999	2000	2001	2002	2003	Percent change, 1999–2003
LARGEST EXPORTS						
World	692 821	780 419	731 026	693 257	723 743	4.5
Canada	163 913	176 430	163 724	160 799	169 481	3.4
Mexico	87 044	111 721	101 509	97 531	97 457	12.0
Japan	57 484	65 254	57 639	51 440	52 064	-9.4
United Kingdom	38 338	41 579	40 798	33 253	33 895	-11.6
Germany	26 789	29 244	30 114	26 628	28 848	7.7
China	13 118	16 253	19 235	22 053	28 418	116.6
South Korea	22 954	27 902	22 197	22 596	24 099	5.0
Netherlands	19 412	21 974	19 525	18 334	20 703	6.7
Taiwan	19 121	24 380	18 152	18 394	17 488	-8.5
France	18 838	20 253	19 896	19 019	17 068	-9.4
LARGEST IMPORTS						
World	1 024 766	1 216 888	1 141 959	1 163 549	1 259 396	22.9
Canada	198 324	229 209	216 969	210 590	224 166	13.0
China	81 786	100 063	102 280	125 168	152 379	86.3
Mexico	109 706	135 911	131 433	134 732	138 073	25.9
Japan	131 404	146 577	126 602	121 494	118 029	-10.2
Germany	55 094	58 737	59 151	62 480	68 047	23.5
United Kingdom	39 191	43 459	41 397	40 870	42 667	8.9
South Korea	31 262	40 300	35 185	35 575	36 963	18.2
Taiwan	35 198	40 514	33 391	32 199	31 600	-10.2
France	25 910	29 782	30 296	28 408	29 221	12.8
Ireland	11 002	16 410	18 539	22 388	25 841	134.9
LARGEST SURPLUSES						
Netherlands	10 939	12 270	10 024	8 471	9 731	-11.0
Australia	6 520	6 021	4 466	6 606	6 690	2.6
Belgium	3 177	4 029	3 395	3 508	5 077	59.8
Hong Kong	2 116	3 173	4 423	3 283	4 692	121.7
United Arab Emirates	2 002	1 319	1 446	2 661	2 381	18.9
Panama	1 376	1 302	1 040	1 105	1 547	12.4
Egypt	2 408	2 441	2 899	1 514	1 516	-37.0
Singapore	-1 941	-1 370	2 712	1 429	1 418	-173.1
Jamaica	616	730	946	1 028	975	58.3
Bahamas	648	790	709	517	605	-6.6
LARGEST DEFICITS						
China	-68 668	-83 810	-83 046	-103 115	-123 961	80.5
Japan	-73 920	-81 322	-68 963	-70 055	-65 965	-10.8
Canada	-34 411	-52 779	-53 244	-49 790	-54 685	58.9
Mexico	-22 662	-24 190	-29 924	-37 202	-40 616	79.2
Germany	-28 305	-29 493	-29 037	-35 852	-39 199	38.5
Ireland	-4 628	-8 683	-11 390	-15 639	-18 142	292.0
Italy	-12 344	-14 050	-13 908	-14 201	-14 867	20.4
Malaysia	-12 350	-14 573	-12 956	-13 662	-14 517	17.5
Venezuela	-5 896	-13 096	-9 552	-10 662	-14 305	142.6
Taiwan	-16 077	-16 134	-15 240	-13 805	-14 112	-12.2

Table D-2. U.S. Trade Highlights for Oil Seeds and Oleaginous Fruits (SITC 222)

(Millions of dollars; ranked by 2003 value; total exports, f.a.s.; general imports, Customs.)   **19th highest export**

Country	1999	2000	2001	2002	2003	Percent change, 1999–2003
LARGEST EXPORTS						
World	4 936	5 722	5 815	6 051	8 303	68.2
China	354	1 020	1 014	890	2 832	700.0
Mexico	716	804	840	936	1 061	48.2
Japan	808	795	747	842	973	20.4
Taiwan	392	385	386	415	420	7.1
Spain	239	236	271	263	341	42.7
Indonesia	202	164	245	255	324	60.4
Germany	182	137	103	272	297	63.2
South Korea	226	260	230	258	296	31.0
Canada	184	190	250	271	293	59.2
Netherlands	435	564	468	306	205	-52.9
LARGEST IMPORTS						
World	250	288	246	205	180	-28.0
Canada	102	108	107	103	120	17.6
Guatemala	16	16	12	12	12	-25.0
India	8	10	10	10	11	37.5
Argentina	41	62	34	17	7	-82.9
Mexico	15	19	15	9	6	-60.0
China	1	1	2	4	5	400.0
Venezuela	6	10	7	4	3	-50.0
Australia	31	39	39	31	3	-90.3
Chile	3	3	1	1	2	-33.3
Ethiopia	3	5	4	3	2	-33.3
LARGEST SURPLUSES						
China	353	1 018	1 012	887	2 827	700.8
Mexico	701	785	825	927	1 054	50.4
Japan	807	795	747	842	973	20.6
Taiwan	391	384	385	414	419	7.2
Spain	239	236	271	263	341	42.7
Indonesia	202	164	245	255	324	60.4
Germany	182	137	103	272	297	63.2
South Korea	226	260	230	258	296	31.0
Netherlands	433	563	468	306	204	-52.9
Thailand	136	145	114	114	181	33.1
LARGEST DEFICITS						
India	-8	-10	-9	-10	-11	37.5
Guatemala	-16	-15	-9	-10	-10	-37.5
Argentina	-39	-60	-33	-16	-6	-84.6
Venezuela	8	9	11	6	-3	-137.5
Chile	-1	-3	-1	-1	-2	100.0
Ethiopia	-3	-5	-4	-3	-2	-33.3
Switzerland	3	2	10	-1	-1	-133.3
Nicaragua	-1	-5	-5	-5	-1	0.0
El Salvador	-1	-1	-1	-1	*	X
Brazil	7	-1	-1	-1	*	X

* = Trade between -$0.5 million and $0.5 million.
X = Not applicable.

Table D-3. U.S. Trade Highlights for Crude Oil (SITC 333)

(Millions of dollars; ranked by 2003 value; total exports, f.a.s.; general imports, Customs.)   **2nd highest import**

Country	1999	2000	2001	2002	2003	Percent change, 1999–2003
LARGEST EXPORTS						
World	786	482	248	92	155	-80.3
Canada	284	193	247	90	154	-45.8
China	57	*	*	*	*	X
Mexico	*	1	*	1	*	X
South Korea	228	103	*	*	*	X
Australia	*	*	*	*	*	X
Ukraine	*	*	*	*	*	X
United Kingdom	*	*	*	*	*	X
Venezuela	*	*	*	*	*	X
Peru	*	*	*	*	*	X
Antigua and Barbuda	*	*	*	*	*	X
LARGEST IMPORTS						
World	50 662	89 786	75 263	79 368	101 722	100.8
Saudi Arabia	7 364	13 083	12 151	12 376	16 887	129.3
Mexico	6 781	11 953	9 511	11 500	14 428	112.8
Canada	6 570	12 715	10 146	11 225	14 196	116.1
Venezuela	6 678	12 393	10 118	10 916	12 691	90.0
Nigeria	3 858	10 024	8 126	5 579	9 629	149.6
Iraq	4 190	6 097	5 796	3 590	4 562	8.9
United Kingdom	1 687	2 986	2 297	3 801	4 368	158.9
Angola	2 346	3 391	2 990	2 991	4 105	75.0
Algeria	104	*	517	1 250	2 858	2 648.1
Norway	1 962	3 353	2 844	3 733	2 690	37.1
LARGEST SURPLUSES						
South Korea	228	103	*	*	*	X
Germany	*	-21	*	*	*	X
Italy	-3	*	*	*	*	X
Netherlands	-2	*	-11	*	*	X
Netherlands Antilles	*	-9	*	*	*	X
Singapore	*	-3	*	*	*	X
Taiwan	22	*	*	*	*	X
Ukraine	*	*	*	*	-20	X
Egypt	-21	*	-54	*	-23	9.5
China	-19	-403	-121	-182	-110	478.9
LARGEST DEFICITS						
Saudi Arabia	-7 364	-13 083	-12 151	-12 376	-16 887	129.3
Mexico	-6 781	-11 953	-9 511	-11 498	-14 428	112.8
Canada	-6 286	-12 523	-9 898	-11 136	-14 042	123.4
Venezuela	-6 678	-12 393	-10 118	-10 916	-12 691	90.0
United Kingdom	-1 687	-2 986	-2 297	-3 801	-4 368	158.9
Trinidad and Tobago	-298	-564	-481	-603	-782	162.4
Brazil	-4	-67	-112	-513	-744	18 500.0
Argentina	-457	-557	-499	-682	-609	33.3
Australia	-201	-523	-347	-583	-400	99.0
Malaysia	-137	-355	-123	-99	-192	40.1

* = Trade between -$0.5 million and $0.5 million.
X = Not applicable.

Table D-4. U.S. Trade Highlights for Oil, Not Crude (SITC 334)

(Millions of dollars; ranked by 2003 value; total exports, f.a.s.; general imports, Customs.)   **7th highest import**

Country	1999	2000	2001	2002	2003	Percent change, 1999–2003
LARGEST EXPORTS						
World	4 576	7 107	6 411	6 157	7 350	60.6
Mexico	1 743	3 208	2 430	2 219	2 164	24.2
Canada	703	963	1 020	844	1 051	49.5
Singapore	266	289	454	592	428	60.9
Panama	94	175	149	186	426	353.2
Dominican Republic	52	127	106	98	343	559.6
Jamaica	131	186	158	181	268	104.6
Japan	173	261	173	197	266	53.8
Bahamas	36	68	95	166	249	591.7
Guatemala	61	133	100	103	236	286.9
Honduras	57	61	17	55	215	277.2
LARGEST IMPORTS						
World	14 525	26 365	24 541	20 702	26 735	84.1
Canada	2 158	3 673	4 064	3 971	5 149	138.6
Venezuela	2 705	4 028	3 010	2 050	2 329	-13.9
Russia	414	751	873	1 310	1 846	345.9
Algeria	1 459	2 403	1 717	863	1 233	-15.5
Brazil	268	687	973	645	1 144	326.9
United Kingdom	684	1 097	999	839	1 071	56.6
Mexico	399	757	652	658	1 036	159.6
Belgium	343	656	799	810	1 032	200.9
Netherlands	241	445	529	664	1 004	316.6
Aruba	625	1 403	1 021	739	930	48.8
LARGEST SURPLUSES						
Mexico	1 344	2 451	1 777	1 561	1 129	-16.0
Panama	70	134	116	157	415	492.9
Dominican Republic	52	127	106	98	343	559.6
Singapore	80	-76	253	423	335	318.8
Jamaica	131	186	158	177	268	104.6
Guatemala	61	133	100	103	236	286.9
Honduras	57	61	17	55	215	277.2
Japan	37	82	14	120	179	383.8
Israel	74	26	74	49	107	44.6
Costa Rica	43	42	55	51	84	95.3
LARGEST DEFICITS						
Canada	-1 455	-2 710	-3 044	-3 127	-4 098	181.6
Venezuela	-2 694	-3 961	-2 974	-2 013	-2 216	-17.7
Russia	-408	-744	-864	-1 305	-1 839	350.7
Algeria	-1 459	-2 402	-1 716	-862	-1 233	-15.5
Brazil	-215	-614	-912	-602	-1 121	421.4
United Kingdom	-646	-1 066	-950	-799	-1 048	62.2
Belgium	-322	-628	-776	-795	-1 010	213.7
Netherlands	-94	-189	-258	-559	-960	921.3
Aruba	-597	-1 370	-989	-685	-894	49.7
Argentina	-250	-418	-575	-577	-667	166.8

Table D-5. U.S. Trade Highlights for Natural Gas, Whether or Not Liquefied (SITC 343)

(Millions of dollars; ranked by 2003 value; total exports, f.a.s.; general imports, Customs.)   **15th highest import**

Country	1999	2000	2001	2002	2003	Percent change, 1999–2003
LARGEST EXPORTS						
World	218	411	538	994	1 300	496.3
Canada	58	153	191	382	1 078	1 758.6
Japan	141	145	145	141	148	5.0
Mexico	18	111	201	471	73	305.6
Guatemala	*	*	*	*	*	X
Costa Rica	*	*	*	*	*	X
Italy	*	*	*	*	*	X
Argentina	*	*	*	*	*	X
India	*	*	*	*	*	X
Taiwan	*	*	*	*	*	X
Hong Kong	*	*	*	*	*	X
LARGEST IMPORTS						
World	6 304	10 966	16 303	12 220	20 621	227.1
Canada	6 006	10 361	15 355	11 428	18 249	203.8
Trinidad and Tobago	105	327	486	566	1 767	1 582.9
Algeria	134	114	186	89	255	90.3
Nigeria	*	41	176	21	228	X
Qatar	23	77	44	89	60	160.9
Oman	*	19	54	5	34	X
Venezuela	*	*	*	*	16	X
Malaysia	3	*	*	2	11	266.7
Mexico	9	10	*	11	1	-88.9
Italy	*	*	*	*	*	X
LARGEST SURPLUSES						
Mexico	9	101	201	460	72	700.0
Italy	*	*	*	*	*	X
Argentina	*	*	*	*	*	X
Australia	-16	-8	-2	*	*	X
United Kingdom	*	*	*	*	*	X
Brunei	*	*	*	-9	*	X
Chile	*	*	*	*	*	X
Colombia	*	*	*	*	*	X
Germany	*	*	*	*	*	X
Netherlands	*	*	*	*	*	X
LARGEST DEFICITS						
Canada	-5 948	-10 208	-15 164	-11 047	-17 170	188.7
Trinidad and Tobago	-105	-327	-486	-566	-1 767	1 582.9
Venezuela	*	*	*	*	-16	X
Malaysia	-3	*	*	-2	-11	266.7
Brunei	*	*	*	-9	*	X
Chile	*	*	*	*	*	X
Colombia	*	*	*	*	*	X
Germany	*	*	*	*	*	X
Netherlands	*	*	*	*	*	X
Peru	*	*	*	*	*	X

* = Trade between -$0.5 million and $0.5 million.
X = Not applicable.

Table D-6. U.S. Trade Highlights for Organo-Inorganic and Heterocyclic Compounds (SITC 515)

(Millions of dollars; ranked by 2003 value; total exports, f.a.s.; general imports, Customs.) **14th highest import**

Country	1999	2000	2001	2002	2003	Percent change, 1999–2003
LARGEST EXPORTS						
World	4 118	4 608	4 349	3 610	4 819	17.0
Belgium	417	344	442	346	1 253	200.5
Netherlands	374	517	360	267	567	51.6
United Kingdom	168	168	393	467	434	158.3
Canada	548	401	408	341	311	-43.2
France	287	315	271	370	282	-1.7
Brazil	338	329	340	187	250	-26.0
Germany	99	138	110	143	182	83.8
Japan	294	193	190	185	179	-39.1
China	42	50	64	106	152	261.9
Mexico	168	171	224	149	151	-10.1
LARGEST IMPORTS						
World	12 242	16 868	17 840	19 378	20 973	71.3
Ireland	5 390	10 459	10 786	10 531	11 649	116.1
Singapore	513	557	790	1 508	2 214	331.6
United Kingdom	1 528	1 277	1 296	1 670	1 417	-7.3
Germany	845	866	962	1 370	958	13.4
Japan	863	937	910	950	877	1.6
France	421	424	519	464	725	72.2
Switzerland	583	494	394	424	496	-14.9
Italy	444	405	403	466	467	5.2
Belgium	718	385	670	724	413	-42.5
Netherlands	90	172	183	212	364	304.4
LARGEST SURPLUSES						
Belgium	-302	-41	-228	-377	840	-378.1
Canada	512	362	363	293	263	-48.6
Brazil	308	303	301	158	229	-25.6
Netherlands	284	345	178	55	203	-28.5
Mexico	109	129	177	103	125	14.7
South Korea	45	47	56	63	75	66.7
Australia	110	72	61	63	70	-36.4
Hong Kong	21	22	35	13	64	204.8
Taiwan	100	117	92	65	56	-44.0
Malaysia	29	28	38	47	55	89.7
LARGEST DEFICITS						
Ireland	-5 191	-10 277	-10 667	-10 406	-11 593	123.3
Singapore	-446	-483	-687	-1 456	-2 122	375.8
United Kingdom	-1 359	-1 109	-903	-1 203	-983	-27.7
Germany	-746	-728	-852	-1 227	-776	4.0
Japan	-570	-744	-720	-765	-698	22.5
France	-134	-108	-248	-95	-443	230.6
Switzerland	-422	-283	-298	-331	-432	2.4
Italy	-346	120	-344	-395	-420	21.4
Spain	-29	-37	108	-119	-322	1 010.3
China	-86	-118	-107	-91	-124	44.2

Table D-7. U.S. Trade Highlights for Medicinal Products, Except Medicaments (SITC 541)

(Millions of dollars; ranked by 2003 value; total exports, f.a.s.; general imports, Customs.)   **20th highest export**

Country	1999	2000	2001	2002	2003	Percent change, 1999–2003
LARGEST EXPORTS						
World	5 424	5 957	6 446	7 075	8 181	50.8
Netherlands	371	237	340	636	1 130	204.6
Belgium	487	548	535	798	908	86.4
France	562	724	887	1 123	853	51.8
Germany	466	452	477	451	821	76.2
Canada	521	527	558	627	716	37.4
Japan	810	745	762	706	701	-13.5
Italy	232	382	328	336	410	76.7
United Kingdom	296	388	433	320	372	25.7
Switzerland	165	272	212	200	313	89.7
Mexico	154	190	201	209	244	58.4
LARGEST IMPORTS						
World	4 371	4 872	5 399	6 234	7 839	79.3
Germany	492	584	710	1 054	1 367	177.8
United Kingdom	530	799	729	853	1 096	106.8
France	321	422	442	564	677	110.9
Denmark	157	191	342	453	577	267.5
Ireland	258	234	296	338	488	89.1
Switzerland	344	378	435	403	466	35.5
China	376	386	314	329	430	14.4
Belgium	378	356	435	343	422	11.6
Japan	270	285	286	334	354	31.1
Netherlands	180	182	240	247	261	45.0
LARGEST SURPLUSES						
Netherlands	191	55	100	388	870	355.5
Belgium	110	192	100	456	486	341.8
Canada	282	302	302	384	464	64.5
Japan	540	460	476	371	347	-35.7
Mexico	106	142	148	155	194	83.0
France	241	303	445	558	177	-26.6
Italy	-15	140	60	154	170	-1 233.3
Australia	64	81	69	91	107	67.2
Spain	54	103	172	90	102	88.9
South Korea	48	51	132	103	85	77.1
LARGEST DEFICITS						
United Kingdom	-234	-411	-296	-534	-725	209.8
Denmark	-142	-180	-332	-440	-558	293.0
Germany	-25	-131	-233	-604	-546	2 084.0
Ireland	-221	-149	-249	-279	-420	90.0
China	-342	-348	-265	-231	-341	-0.3
Slovenia	-2	-2	-4	-43	-155	7 650.0
Switzerland	-178	-106	-222	-203	-153	-14.0
Sweden	17	43	20	33	-123	-823.5
Norway	-4	37	-24	-56	-64	1 500.0
Croatia	-38	-58	-45	-59	-51	34.2

Table D-8. U.S. Trade Highlights for Medicaments, Including Veterinary Medicaments (SITC 542)

(Millions of dollars; ranked by 2003 value; total exports, f.a.s.; general imports, Customs.)   **11th highest import, 13th highest export**

Country	1999	2000	2001	2002	2003	Percent change, 1999–2003
LARGEST EXPORTS						
World	5 823	7 165	8 975	9 075	11 028	89.4
Canada	1 317	1 655	1 633	1 755	2 035	54.5
United Kingdom	718	1 041	2 136	1 580	1 546	115.3
Belgium	138	383	415	758	953	590.6
France	400	389	545	480	947	136.8
Netherlands	339	364	528	717	821	142.2
Switzerland	370	346	315	375	728	96.8
Italy	575	552	428	455	574	-0.2
Japan	284	317	419	465	506	78.2
Ireland	83	299	426	431	491	491.6
Australia	151	229	220	288	328	117.2
LARGEST IMPORTS						
World	9 171	9 823	13 225	18 486	23 677	158.2
Ireland	381	463	1 875	5 024	5 126	1 245.4
United Kingdom	1 594	1 899	2 382	2 808	4 031	152.9
Germany	2 754	1 700	1 810	2 134	2 658	-3.5
France	358	589	1 252	1 579	2 171	506.4
Japan	1 031	1 237	1 319	1 528	2 040	97.9
Canada	462	604	878	990	1 607	247.8
Sweden	507	683	585	734	1 380	172.2
Switzerland	691	667	911	944	1 081	56.4
Israel	208	271	503	534	703	238.0
Italy	632	1 078	603	552	629	-0.5
LARGEST SURPLUSES						
Netherlands	192	241	347	544	703	266.1
Belgium	31	232	192	444	579	1 767.7
Canada	855	1 051	755	764	428	-49.9
Australia	111	181	73	167	206	85.6
Brazil	202	212	158	198	204	1.0
Mexico	105	199	149	109	102	-2.9
Panama	74	55	82	63	88	18.9
Taiwan	48	61	74	77	76	58.3
South Korea	18	48	44	50	64	255.6
Argentina	70	82	73	42	54	-22.9
LARGEST DEFICITS						
Ireland	-299	-164	-1 449	-4 592	-4 635	1 450.2
United Kingdom	-876	-858	-247	-1 229	-2 484	183.6
Germany	-2 494	-1 502	-1 447	-1 913	-2 344	-6.0
Japan	-747	-920	-900	-1 063	-1 533	105.2
Sweden	-466	-640	-566	-708	-1 343	188.2
France	42	-200	-706	-1 100	-1 225	-3 016.7
Israel	-170	-229	-466	-477	-660	288.2
Austria	-140	-130	-176	-336	-440	214.3
Switzerland	-321	-321	-597	-570	-354	10.3
India	-2	3	-64	-212	-351	17 450.0

Table D-9. U.S. Trade Highlights for Miscellaneous Chemical Products (SITC 598)

(Millions of dollars; ranked by 2003 value; total exports, f.a.s.; general imports, Customs.)   **18th highest export**

Country	1999	2000	2001	2002	2003	Percent change, 1999–2003
LARGEST EXPORTS						
World	6 627	7 712	7 626	7 535	8 381	26.5
Canada	1 125	1 263	1 159	1 166	1 248	10.9
Japan	628	832	856	834	935	48.9
Germany	764	663	573	560	781	2.2
United Kingdom	357	533	654	622	592	65.8
Mexico	483	575	510	561	582	20.5
India	41	58	74	223	471	1 048.8
Belgium	235	327	323	363	406	72.8
Netherlands	404	400	371	386	358	-11.4
France	249	284	248	251	297	19.3
South Korea	222	260	276	273	288	29.7
LARGEST IMPORTS						
World	3 110	3 624	3 799	4 071	4 386	41.0
Japan	856	1 035	997	1 050	1 127	31.7
Germany	476	531	546	627	670	40.8
Canada	344	411	518	553	618	79.7
United Kingdom	334	335	335	416	394	18.0
France	160	202	224	226	268	67.5
China	62	91	105	124	193	211.3
Mexico	121	112	155	120	136	12.4
South Korea	59	80	99	108	104	76.3
Italy	77	82	71	85	92	19.5
Netherlands	93	94	90	90	91	-2.2
LARGEST SURPLUSES						
Canada	781	852	640	613	629	-19.5
India	35	48	64	205	459	1 211.4
Mexico	361	463	355	442	446	23.5
Belgium	189	286	265	316	364	92.6
Netherlands	311	305	281	296	268	-13.8
United Kingdom	23	198	319	206	198	760.9
South Korea	163	181	177	164	184	12.9
Taiwan	227	200	143	193	177	-22.0
Brazil	143	145	172	132	151	5.6
Singapore	171	206	116	122	150	-12.3
LARGEST DEFICITS						
Japan	-228	-203	-141	-216	-191	-16.2
Finland	-28	-46	-49	-52	-49	75.0
Denmark	-29	-30	-36	-29	-26	-10.3
Norway	-8	-10	-6	-16	-22	175.0
Sri Lanka (Ceylon)	-6	-7	-6	-7	-7	16.7
Czech Republic	-2	*	-5	-5	-6	200.0
Russia	1	6	13	-1	-4	-500.0
Malaysia	-15	-50	13	-5	-4	-73.3
Luxembourg	-1	-3	*	-1	-1	0.0
Ukraine	*	-1	*	*	-1	X

* = Trade between -$0.5 million and $0.5 million.
X = Not applicable.

Table D-10. U.S. Trade Highlights for Internal Combustion Piston Engines (SITC 713)

(Millions of dollars; ranked by 2003 value; total exports, f.a.s.; general imports, Customs.) **11th highest export, 19th highest import**

Country	1999	2000	2001	2002	2003	Percent change, 1999–2003
LARGEST EXPORTS						
World	12 388	13 700	12 632	12 862	12 619	1.9
Canada	7 471	7 449	6 595	6 399	6 469	-13.4
Mexico	1 425	2 427	2 178	2 111	2 000	40.4
United Kingdom	523	712	879	822	707	35.2
Japan	531	487	377	814	637	20.0
Belgium	237	312	259	314	311	31.2
Australia	245	276	271	307	296	20.8
Brazil	82	114	158	182	187	128.0
Switzerland	10	11	138	211	171	1 610.0
Italy	141	174	159	180	168	19.1
Germany	237	241	239	232	163	-31.2
LARGEST IMPORTS						
World	14 785	15 771	13 850	14 695	15 933	7.8
Japan	5 198	5 678	5 099	4 916	4 771	-8.2
Canada	3 841	3 963	3 171	3 260	3 564	-7.2
Mexico	2 470	2 676	2 344	2 565	2 867	16.1
Germany	1 633	1 727	1 594	1 861	2 242	37.3
United Kingdom	475	558	574	593	586	23.4
Brazil	370	345	248	474	575	55.4
Italy	94	75	90	139	201	113.8
Austria	141	151	121	146	200	41.8
Sweden	105	111	92	101	149	41.9
China	59	55	62	100	147	149.2
LARGEST SURPLUSES						
Canada	3 630	3 486	3 424	3 139	2 905	-20.0
Belgium	200	282	227	282	288	44.0
Australia	223	253	241	279	266	19.3
Switzerland	4	3	131	203	160	3 900.0
United Kingdom	48	154	305	230	121	152.1
Singapore	105	122	137	116	109	3.8
Netherlands	80	68	80	87	105	31.3
Israel	15	9	8	9	76	406.7
Saudi Arabia	61	76	66	62	59	-3.3
New Zealand	23	31	25	21	47	104.3
LARGEST DEFICITS						
Japan	-4 667	-5 191	-4 722	-4 101	-4 134	-11.4
Germany	-1 396	-1 486	-1 355	-1 629	-2 080	49.0
Mexico	-1 045	-249	-166	-454	-867	-17.0
Brazil	-288	-230	-90	-293	-388	34.7
Austria	-98	-123	-86	-97	-131	33.7
Sweden	-32	-54	-29	-37	-83	159.4
Thailand	21	12	-4	2	-39	-285.7
Italy	47	98	69	41	-33	-170.2
Czech Republic	-9	-13	-11	-13	-32	255.6
China	-10	23	24	-17	-32	220.0

Table D-11. U.S. Trade Highlights for Nonelectric Engines and Motors (SITC 714)

(Millions of dollars; ranked by 2003 value; total exports, f.a.s.; general imports, Customs.)   **10th highest export**

Country	1999	2000	2001	2002	2003	Percent change, 1999–2003
LARGEST EXPORTS						
World	14 964	15 629	17 545	16 415	15 609	4.3
France	2 662	2 861	3 100	2 914	2 371	-10.9
United Kingdom	2 098	2 193	2 122	1 895	2 147	2.3
Canada	1 698	1 848	2 042	1 805	1 679	-1.1
Germany	1 175	1 537	1 785	1 485	1 512	28.7
Japan	988	1 256	1 408	1 252	1 063	7.6
Singapore	581	583	709	757	814	40.1
Brazil	750	955	1 327	1 032	734	-2.1
Italy	384	322	418	550	600	56.3
Mexico	343	382	569	594	483	40.8
South Korea	301	271	222	366	318	5.6
LARGEST IMPORTS						
World	10 117	10 707	13 347	10 673	8 714	-13.9
France	2 675	2 912	3 147	2 575	2 092	-21.8
United Kingdom	3 417	2 682	3 530	2 689	2 022	-40.8
Canada	1 452	1 942	2 451	2 267	1 571	8.2
Germany	1 004	1 149	1 476	1 026	807	-19.6
Japan	250	452	836	438	593	137.2
Italy	202	289	383	253	230	13.9
Mexico	96	146	167	176	217	126.0
Israel	144	144	161	169	170	18.1
South Korea	94	124	224	178	132	40.4
Sweden	129	145	182	138	117	-9.3
LARGEST SURPLUSES						
Singapore	556	550	659	693	757	36.2
Brazil	672	940	1 306	1 015	728	8.3
Germany	171	387	309	459	704	311.7
Japan	738	804	572	814	470	-36.3
Italy	182	33	34	297	370	103.3
France	-13	-51	-46	340	279	-2 246.2
Mexico	246	236	403	419	266	8.1
Netherlands	180	146	220	193	235	30.6
China	172	46	108	159	220	27.9
Spain	123	74	132	149	202	64.2
LARGEST DEFICITS						
Israel	63	58	32	-11	-51	-181.0
Hungary	1	*	38	-4	-25	-2 600.0
Russia	-19	-25	-27	-15	-21	10.5
Czech Republic	-2	-9	-16	-20	-20	900.0
Poland	-1	-11	-9	-9	-19	1 800.0
Romania	-1	-4	-3	-12	-2	100.0
Mauritius	*	*	*	*	*	X
Croatia	24	-7	-3	1	*	X
Swaziland	*	*	*	*	*	X
Albania	*	*	*	*	*	X

* = Trade between -$0.5 million and $0.5 million.
X = Not applicable.

Table D-12. U.S. Trade Highlights for Civil Engineering and Contractors' Plants and Equipment (SITC 723)

(Millions of dollars; ranked by 2003 value; total exports, f.a.s.; general imports, Customs.)   **16th highest export**

Country	1999	2000	2001	2002	2003	Percent change, 1999–2003
LARGEST EXPORTS						
World	7 924	8 663	9 166	8 996	8 860	11.8
Canada	1 347	1 513	1 386	1 335	1 635	21.4
Mexico	376	515	429	502	521	38.6
Singapore	408	307	511	440	426	4.4
Brazil	243	371	432	338	398	63.8
United Kingdom	330	346	409	374	346	4.8
Australia	334	326	393	332	318	-4.8
Russia	152	196	276	332	305	100.7
Belgium	630	715	705	393	292	-53.7
China	105	207	163	259	282	168.6
United Arab Emirates	105	114	195	310	244	132.4
LARGEST IMPORTS						
World	5 062	4 740	4 335	4 304	4 983	-1.6
Japan	1 520	1 355	1 094	1 154	1 464	-3.7
Canada	435	457	499	486	552	26.9
Germany	429	459	391	417	523	21.9
Mexico	293	347	392	349	353	20.5
United Kingdom	495	367	337	375	338	-31.7
Italy	411	429	395	284	334	-18.7
France	339	304	270	239	264	-22.1
South Korea	222	221	139	161	189	-14.9
Brazil	152	110	112	150	166	9.2
Sweden	205	164	137	130	160	-22.0
LARGEST SURPLUSES						
Canada	912	1 056	886	849	1 082	18.6
Singapore	397	302	506	419	409	3.0
Russia	152	196	276	332	302	98.7
Australia	303	299	371	315	291	-4.0
Brazil	92	261	320	188	232	152.2
Angola	90	55	125	195	209	132.2
China	75	168	119	203	203	170.7
United Arab Emirates	104	114	195	310	201	93.3
Belgium	483	551	499	251	185	-61.7
Mexico	83	168	36	153	168	102.4
LARGEST DEFICITS						
Japan	-1 371	-1 211	-959	-1 056	-1 379	0.6
Germany	-290	-295	-211	-274	-320	10.3
Italy	-336	-337	-302	-189	-219	-34.8
France	-207	-191	-161	-139	-156	-24.6
Sweden	-189	-135	-101	-114	-120	-36.5
South Korea	-95	-131	-83	-102	-83	-12.6
Austria	-33	-49	-58	-45	-72	118.2
Finland	-42	-54	-29	-52	-55	31.0
Poland	-49	-25	-6	-10	-25	-49.0
Czech Republic	-4	-6	-10	-13	-16	300.0

Table D-13. U.S. Trade Highlights for Machinery Specialized for Particular Industries (SITC 728)

(Millions of dollars; ranked by 2003 value; total exports, f.a.s.; general imports, Customs.)   **17th highest export**

Country	1999	2000	2001	2002	2003	Percent change, 1999–2003
LARGEST EXPORTS						
World	10 792	15 927	11 216	9 058	8 795	-18.5
Canada	1 518	1 682	1 344	1 332	1 392	-8.3
South Korea	895	1 721	1 030	867	1 010	12.8
Japan	1 122	1 992	1 295	753	902	-19.6
Taiwan	1 444	2 754	1 165	1 100	760	-47.4
Mexico	1 251	1 378	1 027	920	745	-40.4
China	231	365	456	620	646	179.7
Germany	433	816	772	495	402	-7.2
Singapore	512	906	532	423	303	-40.8
United Kingdom	356	526	477	292	271	-23.9
Ireland	144	212	84	85	186	29.2
LARGEST IMPORTS						
World	7 915	9 397	7 488	6 639	7 179	-9.3
Japan	2 061	3 135	2 111	1 701	1 503	-27.1
Germany	1 564	1 590	1 349	1 134	1 378	-11.9
Canada	1 088	1 171	972	971	1 077	-1.0
Italy	585	588	523	444	553	-5.5
Taiwan	436	530	443	442	429	-1.6
China	109	118	153	245	381	249.5
United Kingdom	403	418	395	314	342	-15.1
France	366	289	246	211	273	-25.4
Switzerland	251	276	242	221	217	-13.5
Austria	153	162	156	152	142	-7.2
LARGEST SURPLUSES						
South Korea	829	1 628	958	800	920	11.0
Mexico	1 194	1 318	961	871	691	-42.1
Taiwan	1 008	2 224	722	658	331	-67.2
Canada	430	511	372	361	315	-26.7
Singapore	494	868	507	398	270	-45.3
China	122	247	303	375	265	117.2
Ireland	124	184	60	52	162	30.6
Malaysia	133	363	260	132	104	-21.8
Brazil	130	133	106	87	79	-39.2
Hong Kong	86	117	111	73	72	-16.3
LARGEST DEFICITS						
Germany	-1 132	-773	-577	-639	-976	-13.8
Japan	-938	-1 143	-816	-948	-601	-35.9
Italy	-343	-315	-320	-322	-391	14.0
Switzerland	-203	-219	-161	-167	-155	-23.6
Austria	-133	-107	-80	-131	-123	-7.5
Sweden	-61	-123	-65	-84	-98	60.7
France	-133	301	51	-12	-96	-27.8
United Kingdom	-47	108	82	-21	-71	51.1
Luxembourg	4	*	*	1	-32	-900.0
Finland	-52	-74	-79	-39	-31	-40.4

* = Trade between -$0.5 million and $0.5 million.

Table D-14. U.S. Trade Highlights for Automatic Data Processing Machines (SITC 752)

(Millions of dollars; ranked by 2003 value; total exports, f.a.s.; general imports, Customs.)

3rd highest import, 5th highest export

Country	1999	2000	2001	2002	2003	Percent change, 1999–2003
LARGEST EXPORTS						
World	26 715	30 929	27 386	21 812	21 595	-19.2
Canada	5 592	6 130	5 052	4 759	5 132	-8.2
Mexico	1 840	2 629	2 877	2 722	2 688	46.1
Japan	2 211	2 878	2 542	1 779	1 650	-25.4
Netherlands	2 018	2 270	2 118	1 463	1 380	-31.6
United Kingdom	1 948	2 208	1 980	1 390	1 340	-31.2
Germany	1 530	1 282	1 124	966	1 017	-33.5
China	578	942	957	739	736	27.3
Hong Kong	880	1 227	1 250	801	687	-21.9
Singapore	1 237	1 204	924	660	670	-45.8
South Korea	825	1 478	813	694	519	-37.1
LARGEST IMPORTS						
World	49 173	55 909	47 596	50 035	52 012	5.8
China	4 116	6 310	5 961	9 145	15 268	270.9
Malaysia	3 695	4 658	4 824	6 882	7 782	110.6
Mexico	4 998	6 413	7 914	7 188	6 138	22.8
Singapore	8 340	6 915	5 685	5 216	4 952	-40.6
Taiwan	5 017	6 616	5 748	6 295	4 601	-8.3
Japan	9 456	9 332	5 924	4 565	3 403	-64.0
South Korea	3 686	4 885	3 150	2 769	2 140	-41.9
Thailand	2 394	2 340	1 806	1 801	1 663	-30.5
Philippines	1 449	1 920	1 951	2 073	1 618	11.7
Canada	886	1 314	806	613	788	-11.1
LARGEST SURPLUSES						
Canada	4 706	4 816	4 246	4 147	4 344	-7.7
Netherlands	1 861	2 113	2 010	1 297	1 113	-40.2
United Kingdom	1 039	1 193	1 259	884	693	-33.3
Germany	1 141	893	764	606	624	-45.3
Hong Kong	785	1 068	1 136	575	478	-39.1
Australia	625	638	570	401	431	-31.0
Brazil	730	888	740	397	349	-52.2
France	481	391	381	308	345	-28.3
India	135	248	240	247	266	97.0
Colombia	179	191	229	216	201	12.3
LARGEST DEFICITS						
China	-3 538	-5 369	-5 003	-8 406	-14 533	310.8
Malaysia	-3 338	-4 244	-4 417	-6 510	-7 494	124.5
Singapore	-7 104	-5 710	-4 762	-4 556	-4 283	-39.7
Taiwan	-4 569	-6 010	-5 199	-5 878	-4 276	-6.4
Mexico	-3 158	-3 784	-5 038	-4 466	-3 450	9.2
Japan	-7 244	-6 454	-3 382	-2 786	-1 753	-75.8
South Korea	-2 861	-3 407	-2 337	-2 075	-1 622	-43.3
Philippines	-1 362	-1 835	-1 866	-2 015	-1 562	14.7
Thailand	-2 297	-2 194	-1 669	-1 664	-1 538	-33.0
Hungary	-1 000	-1 153	-687	-466	-496	-50.4

Table D-15. U.S. Trade Highlights for Parts for Office Machines and Automatic Data Processing Machines (SITC 759)

(Millions of dollars; ranked by 2003 value; total exports, f.a.s.; general imports, Customs.)

8th highest export, 9th highest import

Country	1999	2000	2001	2002	2003	Percent change, 1999–2003
LARGEST EXPORTS						
World	20 811	25 467	20 869	17 175	18 742	-9.9
Mexico	1 805	1 942	1 626	2 665	3 954	119.1
Canada	2 230	3 058	2 838	2 087	1 954	-12.4
United Kingdom	2 123	2 388	1 813	1 300	1 244	-41.4
Netherlands	2 060	2 619	1 687	1 220	1 188	-42.3
Germany	1 708	1 820	1 682	1 072	1 089	-36.2
Singapore	921	1 197	923	837	1 082	17.5
Japan	2 011	2 452	1 909	1 108	1 012	-49.7
Ireland	762	898	673	658	698	-8.4
Brazil	741	931	861	623	591	-20.2
Hong Kong	671	757	695	554	583	-13.1
LARGEST IMPORTS						
World	31 906	33 352	26 016	24 757	24 962	-21.8
China	3 208	3 843	4 052	5 216	6 560	104.5
Japan	5 157	5 921	4 813	4 629	4 663	-9.6
Singapore	2 876	3 126	2 192	2 352	2 343	-18.5
Taiwan	4 468	3 833	2 923	2 294	2 333	-47.8
Malaysia	3 753	3 472	2 510	2 192	2 168	-42.2
South Korea	1 737	2 841	1 433	1 791	1 540	-11.3
Mexico	2 042	2 386	2 257	1 571	1 320	-35.4
Ireland	924	839	686	767	633	-31.5
Canada	2 304	2 330	1 978	1 042	589	-74.4
United Kingdom	944	1 093	832	538	443	-53.1
LARGEST SURPLUSES						
Mexico	-238	-444	-631	1 094	2 634	-1 206.7
Canada	-74	728	859	1 045	1 365	-1 944.6
Netherlands	1 925	2 488	1 585	1 127	1 103	-42.7
Germany	1 279	1 489	1 451	824	827	-35.3
United Kingdom	1 179	1 296	981	762	801	-32.1
Brazil	666	864	806	581	569	-14.6
Hong Kong	534	615	564	416	492	-7.9
France	520	489	558	441	376	-27.7
Australia	423	561	322	212	189	-55.3
Thailand	35	105	9	-145	160	357.1
LARGEST DEFICITS						
China	-2 949	-3 302	-3 413	-4 772	-6 033	104.6
Japan	-3 146	-3 469	-2 904	-3 521	-3 651	16.1
Taiwan	-4 046	-3 283	-2 471	-1 852	-1 950	-51.8
Malaysia	-3 412	-3 050	-2 111	-1 764	-1 818	-46.7
South Korea	-1 363	-1 973	-967	-1 457	-1 282	-5.9
Singapore	-1 955	-1 929	-1 270	-1 516	-1 261	-35.5
Philippines	-952	-572	-293	-267	-172	-81.9
Italy	-82	11	30	-70	-150	82.9
Portugal	13	12	-23	-68	-77	-692.3
Indonesia	-134	-186	-198	-71	-73	-45.5

Table D-16. U.S. Trade Highlights for Telecommunications Equipment (SITC 764)

(Millions of dollars; ranked by 2003 value; total exports, f.a.s.; general imports, Customs.)   **4th highest import, 6th highest export**

Country	1999	2000	2001	2002	2003	Percent change, 1999–2003
LARGEST EXPORTS						
World	24 381	29 163	26 133	21 587	20 364	-16.5
Canada	3 915	5 092	4 256	3 530	3 609	-7.8
Mexico	3 007	4 151	3 991	3 287	3 107	3.3
Japan	2 418	2 857	2 401	1 723	1 569	-35.1
United Kingdom	1 366	1 588	1 410	1 106	1 148	-16.0
Netherlands	847	1 127	931	1 228	1 074	26.8
China	548	781	1 159	1 026	844	54.0
Germany	843	985	1 021	808	767	-9.0
South Korea	955	1 353	806	788	736	-22.9
Hong Kong	552	559	628	564	553	0.2
France	544	577	514	533	480	-11.8
LARGEST IMPORTS						
World	29 082	44 349	37 937	37 690	40 531	39.4
China	3 434	4 579	4 690	6 401	7 922	130.7
Mexico	5 666	9 128	8 803	7 801	7 258	28.1
South Korea	2 195	3 618	4 830	4 947	6 289	186.5
Malaysia	1 190	2 248	2 294	2 624	3 837	222.4
Canada	5 120	9 790	4 510	3 495	3 000	-41.4
Japan	4 540	5 290	3 442	2 656	2 538	-44.1
Taiwan	1 911	2 531	2 003	1 715	1 852	-3.1
Brazil	59	383	946	1 071	991	1 579.7
Sweden	510	987	806	1 328	902	76.9
Thailand	610	618	468	516	832	36.4
LARGEST SURPLUSES						
Netherlands	823	1 098	905	1 205	1 025	24.5
Canada	-1 205	-4 698	-254	35	609	-150.5
United Kingdom	785	655	572	570	523	-33.4
Australia	352	540	316	369	353	0.3
India	100	149	144	248	276	176.0
Hong Kong	425	409	467	300	187	-56.0
Colombia	176	213	218	168	186	5.7
Peru	86	100	117	114	128	48.8
Chile	311	317	264	157	128	-58.8
Venezuela	378	288	262	253	123	-67.5
LARGEST DEFICITS						
China	-2 886	-3 798	-3 531	-5 375	-7 078	145.3
South Korea	-1 240	-2 265	-4 024	-4 159	-5 553	347.8
Mexico	-2 659	-4 976	-4 811	-4 514	-4 150	56.1
Malaysia	-1 043	-2 039	-2 057	-2 327	-3 610	246.1
Taiwan	-1 346	-1 862	-1 478	-1 306	-1 476	9.7
Japan	-2 122	-2 433	-1 042	-932	-969	-54.3
Sweden	-372	-838	-678	-1 217	-749	101.3
Thailand	-495	-516	-364	-380	-716	44.6
Brazil	1 241	1 013	-31	-552	-602	-148.5
Israel	-202	-563	-560	-354	-405	100.5

Table D-17. U.S. Trade Highlights for Electrical Apparatus for Switching or Protecting Electrical Circuits (SITC 772)

(Millions of dollars; ranked by 2003 value; total exports, f.a.s.; general imports, Customs.)   **12th highest export**

Country	1999	2000	2001	2002	2003	Percent change, 1999–2003
LARGEST EXPORTS						
World	12 413	15 129	12 498	11 648	11 841	-4.6
Mexico	4 315	5 423	4 274	4 078	4 253	-1.4
Canada	2 896	3 429	2 738	2 437	2 400	-17.1
United Kingdom	632	751	568	491	462	-26.9
Germany	353	372	475	417	454	28.6
Japan	453	487	410	313	376	-17.0
China	145	264	252	307	360	148.3
Singapore	368	381	288	379	359	-2.4
Hong Kong	231	309	261	288	303	31.2
South Korea	220	194	154	196	210	-4.5
Ireland	242	377	297	272	204	-15.7
LARGEST IMPORTS						
World	12 161	15 185	12 334	11 959	12 476	2.6
Mexico	2 953	3 713	3 344	3 494	3 794	28.5
Japan	2 230	2 652	1 860	1 570	1 530	-31.4
China	822	1 219	1 030	1 131	1 304	58.6
Germany	859	984	835	974	1 174	36.7
Canada	1 048	1 270	1 150	1 088	1 015	-3.1
Taiwan	1 030	1 447	933	720	682	-33.8
United Kingdom	381	451	383	326	296	-22.3
France	285	358	305	253	272	-4.6
South Korea	255	356	272	253	243	-4.7
Switzerland	199	264	229	215	207	4.0
LARGEST SURPLUSES						
Canada	1 848	2 159	1 588	1 348	1 385	-25.1
Mexico	1 362	1 710	930	583	459	-66.3
Hong Kong	51	120	138	176	207	305.9
United Kingdom	250	299	185	165	166	-33.6
Netherlands	83	149	214	168	165	98.8
Singapore	89	87	56	175	163	83.1
Ireland	152	243	173	188	150	-1.3
Australia	73	69	67	120	87	19.2
Saudi Arabia	58	52	67	58	68	17.2
Brazil	106	151	166	60	53	-50.0
LARGEST DEFICITS						
Japan	-1 777	-2 165	-1 449	-1 258	-1 154	-35.1
China	-677	-955	-778	-825	-944	39.4
Germany	-506	-613	-360	-557	-721	42.5
Taiwan	-776	-1 223	-756	-548	-538	-30.7
Switzerland	-146	-215	-193	-185	-182	24.7
France	-103	-105	-52	-25	-93	-9.7
Indonesia	-43	-68	-91	-102	-77	79.1
Dominican Republic	-91	-66	-52	-52	-57	-37.4
Philippines	81	91	44	-2	-53	-165.4
Sweden	-39	-69	-57	-36	-40	2.6

Table D-18. U.S. Trade Highlights for Thermionic, Cold Cathode, and Photocathode Valves (SITC 776)

(Millions of dollars; ranked by 2003 value; total exports, f.a.s.; general imports, Customs.)   **1st highest export, 8th highest import**

Country	1999	2000	2001	2002	2003	Percent change, 1999–2003
LARGEST EXPORTS						
World	49 351	62 824	47 622	44 518	47 770	-3.2
Malaysia	4 693	5 500	3 974	4 947	6 450	37.4
Mexico	6 393	9 379	7 894	6 669	6 063	-5.2
Philippines	4 133	4 863	4 437	4 582	5 446	31.8
South Korea	6 074	6 104	3 496	3 899	4 697	-22.7
Taiwan	3 595	5 137	3 901	4 552	4 188	16.5
Hong Kong	2 392	2 897	2 250	2 403	2 838	18.6
Japan	3 673	4 679	3 619	2 819	2 499	-32.0
China	812	901	1 133	1 622	2 475	204.8
Canada	5 732	6 690	3 769	2 433	2 423	-57.7
Singapore	3 104	3 805	2 724	2 186	2 375	-23.5
LARGEST IMPORTS						
World	38 564	49 210	31 405	26 955	25 417	-34.1
Malaysia	5 061	6 336	4 557	4 275	3 585	-29.2
South Korea	6 681	7 608	3 562	3 499	3 405	-49.0
Taiwan	3 757	5 176	3 453	3 137	3 055	-18.7
Philippines	4 413	5 531	3 549	3 293	2 889	-34.5
Japan	7 010	8 797	4 948	3 219	2 804	-60.0
Singapore	1 992	3 338	1 764	1 278	1 300	-34.7
Mexico	1 350	1 829	1 429	1 231	1 252	-7.3
Canada	1 962	2 134	1 779	1 080	1 068	-45.6
China	688	778	669	781	898	30.5
Germany	683	848	958	971	854	25.0
LARGEST SURPLUSES						
Mexico	5 043	7 549	6 465	5 439	4 811	-4.6
Malaysia	-367	-836	-583	673	2 865	-880.7
Hong Kong	1 220	1 717	1 612	1 941	2 604	113.4
Philippines	-280	-669	888	1 288	2 557	-1 013.2
China	124	123	464	841	1 576	1 171.0
Canada	3 770	4 557	1 990	1 353	1 354	-64.1
South Korea	-606	-1 504	-65	401	1 292	-313.2
Taiwan	-162	-39	448	1 414	1 133	-799.4
Singapore	1 111	466	959	908	1 075	-3.2
United Kingdom	1 258	1 807	1 449	919	773	-38.6
LARGEST DEFICITS						
Japan	-3 337	-4 119	-1 328	-400	-305	-90.9
Portugal	90	-60	162	-194	-291	-423.3
Malta and Gozo	-126	-178	-86	-77	-150	19.0
France	126	424	11	-51	-147	-216.7
Indonesia	-104	-172	-143	-121	-112	7.7
Morocco	-92	-134	-81	-94	-86	-6.5
Italy	305	316	241	-102	-83	-127.2
Israel	165	57	118	-28	-69	-141.8
Switzerland	-16	-15	-60	-32	-39	143.8
Slovakia	-1	13	-1	-1	-2	100.0

Table D-19. U.S. Trade Highlights for Electrical Machinery and Apparatus (SITC 778)

(Millions of dollars; ranked by 2003 value; total exports, f.a.s.; general imports, Customs.)   **14th highest export, 18th highest import**

Country	1999	2000	2001	2002	2003	Percent change, 1999–2003
LARGEST EXPORTS						
World	11 306	14 170	11 350	11 122	10 888	-3.7
Canada	2 972	3 158	2 561	2 506	2 500	-15.9
Mexico	2 775	3 694	2 768	2 710	2 480	-10.6
South Korea	305	439	311	419	589	93.1
Japan	542	662	608	565	526	-3.0
Taiwan	309	498	338	562	395	27.8
Germany	301	452	458	350	380	26.2
United Kingdom	525	658	549	400	369	-29.7
Singapore	325	461	301	350	348	7.1
China	142	231	270	322	347	144.4
Hong Kong	379	363	263	255	295	-22.2
LARGEST IMPORTS						
World	14 254	17 149	14 719	14 917	15 989	12.2
Mexico	2 778	3 144	2 833	2 948	3 406	22.6
China	1 560	2 040	2 295	2 703	3 135	101.0
Japan	3 976	4 797	3 553	3 079	2 943	-26.0
Canada	1 065	1 085	1 014	1 040	1 029	-3.4
Taiwan	870	1 044	918	948	947	8.9
Germany	614	672	663	663	800	30.3
South Korea	388	510	398	446	553	42.5
United Kingdom	636	737	603	558	534	-16.0
Israel	150	549	256	306	289	92.7
France	191	213	211	196	194	1.6
LARGEST SURPLUSES						
Canada	1 907	2 073	1 547	1 465	1 472	-22.8
Singapore	242	344	217	254	249	2.9
Netherlands	150	202	146	215	230	53.3
Hong Kong	179	147	129	132	186	3.9
Ireland	64	120	111	116	167	160.9
Australia	130	135	111	113	133	2.3
Brazil	192	226	157	81	92	-52.1
Saudi Arabia	53	51	58	51	63	18.9
Chile	42	69	49	52	47	11.9
United Arab Emirates	16	20	21	42	38	137.5
LARGEST DEFICITS						
China	-1 418	-1 810	-2 025	-2 382	-2 788	96.6
Japan	-3 434	-4 135	-2 944	-2 514	-2 416	-29.6
Mexico	-3	551	-65	-238	-926	30 766.7
Taiwan	-561	-546	-580	-386	-552	-1.6
Germany	-313	-220	-204	-313	-420	34.2
Israel	-34	-389	-101	-145	-183	438.2
United Kingdom	-111	-79	-54	-158	-165	48.6
Indonesia	-111	-148	-99	-96	-117	5.4
Spain	-11	-1	-21	-57	-79	618.2
Hungary	-95	-104	-110	-79	-79	-16.8

Table D-20. U.S. Trade Highlights for All Motor Vehicles (SITC 781)

(Millions of dollars; ranked by 2003 value; total exports, f.a.s.; general imports, Customs.)   **1st highest import, 4th highest export**

Country	1999	2000	2001	2002	2003	Percent change, 1999–2003
LARGEST EXPORTS						
World	17 060	17 234	18 364	21 106	22 777	33.5
Canada	9 509	9 508	8 900	10 463	11 078	16.5
Germany	1 178	1 184	1 776	2 791	3 941	234.6
Mexico	2 175	2 778	3 260	3 149	2 510	15.4
United Kingdom	549	353	549	660	903	64.5
Saudi Arabia	376	307	623	861	648	72.3
Japan	766	751	596	469	474	-38.1
Kuwait	143	159	223	297	384	168.5
Australia	191	216	229	291	275	44.0
United Arab Emirates	46	54	118	149	237	415.2
Finland	37	24	27	62	187	405.4
LARGEST IMPORTS						
World	96 888	109 614	107 006	114 424	114 721	18.4
Japan	29 261	32 154	31 183	35 110	32 227	10.1
Canada	34 282	34 178	30 827	31 264	30 799	-10.2
Germany	13 480	14 650	15 007	17 807	19 726	46.3
Mexico	10 065	15 770	14 310	13 530	11 826	17.5
South Korea	2 879	4 839	6 344	6 803	7 938	175.7
United Kingdom	2 353	2 797	2 701	4 020	5 006	112.7
Sweden	2 098	2 182	2 187	2 113	2 875	37.0
Belgium	1 294	910	1 077	983	946	-26.9
Slovakia	*	*	*	*	714	X
Brazil	2	166	625	622	546	27 200.0
LARGEST SURPLUSES						
Saudi Arabia	376	307	623	861	648	72.3
United Arab Emirates	46	54	118	149	237	415.2
Australia	53	-20	-50	-20	134	152.8
Norway	32	21	27	25	93	190.6
Greece	12	22	18	44	82	583.3
Russia	6	13	28	24	73	1 116.7
Finland	-370	-444	-420	-238	73	-119.7
Hong Kong	23	37	36	25	56	143.5
Chile	35	53	50	51	53	51.4
France	77	75	121	34	48	-37.7
LARGEST DEFICITS						
Japan	-28 495	-31 404	-30 587	-34 641	-31 754	11.4
Canada	-24 773	-24 670	-21 926	-20 801	-19 720	-20.4
Germany	-12 302	-13 466	-13 231	-15 016	-15 785	28.3
Mexico	-7 890	-12 992	-11 050	-10 380	-9 316	18.1
South Korea	-2 860	-4 806	-6 307	-6 710	-7 855	174.7
United Kingdom	-1 804	-2 444	-2 152	-3 361	-4 103	127.4
Sweden	-2 026	-2 109	-2 131	-2 085	-2 834	39.9
Belgium	-885	-836	-895	-837	-819	-7.5
Slovakia	2	3	2	*	-713	-35 750.0
Brazil	19	-145	-613	-616	-533	-2 905.3

* = Trade between -$0.5 million and $0.5 million.
X = Not applicable.

Table D-21. U.S. Trade Highlights for Special Purpose Motor Vehicles (SITC 782)

(Millions of dollars; ranked by 2003 value; total exports, f.a.s.; general imports, Customs.)   **16th highest import**

Country	1999	2000	2001	2002	2003	Percent change, 1999–2003
LARGEST EXPORTS						
World	6 028	7 204	6 076	6 489	7 870	30.6
Canada	4 033	4 445	3 946	4 651	5 684	40.9
Mexico	296	834	628	759	806	172.3
Australia	93	116	106	122	158	69.9
Republic of South Africa	48	32	57	62	89	85.4
Kuwait	26	60	58	24	84	223.1
China	22	40	28	36	69	213.6
Chile	52	141	78	78	63	21.2
Saudi Arabia	187	376	274	89	60	-67.9
Brazil	12	4	55	4	49	308.3
Egypt	23	15	10	27	49	113.0
LARGEST IMPORTS						
World	14 745	15 357	16 596	16 804	17 293	17.3
Canada	9 217	9 365	8 846	9 162	9 075	-1.5
Mexico	4 251	4 853	6 816	6 705	7 226	70.0
Japan	652	546	425	467	473	-27.5
United Kingdom	225	236	204	209	272	20.9
Germany	162	182	160	147	87	-46.3
Sweden	35	43	46	21	71	102.9
Republic of South Africa	27	31	27	20	37	37.0
Brazil	13	1	1	*	26	100.0
Italy	1	5	3	12	8	700.0
Australia	14	*	1	1	3	-78.6
LARGEST SURPLUSES						
Australia	80	116	106	122	155	93.8
China	21	40	27	36	68	223.8
Chile	52	141	78	78	63	21.2
Republic of South Africa	21	2	30	42	51	142.9
Finland	-3	*	*	14	45	-1 600.0
Spain	27	53	41	41	37	37.0
Argentina	17	10	13	2	24	41.2
India	98	*	*	16	24	-75.5
Brazil	-1	2	54	4	23	-2 400.0
Guatemala	21	15	16	15	22	4.8
LARGEST DEFICITS						
Mexico	-3 955	-4 019	-6 188	-5 945	-6 421	62.4
Canada	-5 184	-4 920	-4 900	-4 512	-3 391	-34.6
Japan	-560	-303	-359	-440	-447	-20.2
United Kingdom	-192	-215	-165	-177	-250	30.2
Sweden	-29	-37	-35	-17	-65	124.1
Germany	-133	-151	-131	-125	-45	-66.2
Denmark	-1	*	-1	-1	-2	100.0
Italy	*	-3	1	-6	-1	X
Czech Republic	*	*	*	*	*	X
Slovenia	*	*	*	*	*	X

* = Trade between -$0.5 million and $0.5 million.
X = Not applicable.

Table D-22. U.S. Trade Highlights for Parts and Accessories of Motor Vehicles (SITC 784)

(Millions of dollars; ranked by 2003 value; total exports, f.a.s.; general imports, Customs.)   **3rd highest export, 6th highest import**

Country	1999	2000	2001	2002	2003	Percent change, 1999–2003
LARGEST EXPORTS						
World	29 398	31 641	29 165	29 249	28 327	-3.6
Canada	17 354	16 986	15 169	16 507	16 222	-6.5
Mexico	5 460	7 325	6 819	6 482	5 937	8.7
Japan	1 054	1 393	1 185	1 219	1 071	1.6
Germany	577	648	720	638	617	6.9
Australia	380	516	435	412	475	25.0
United Kingdom	671	620	497	410	430	-35.9
Austria	1 079	957	995	825	411	-61.9
China	157	127	164	196	343	118.5
Brazil	325	339	284	247	298	-8.3
France	154	226	302	227	239	55.2
LARGEST IMPORTS						
World	26 044	28 440	26 908	29 764	32 888	26.3
Canada	9 339	9 758	8 975	10 001	10 902	16.7
Japan	6 155	7 320	6 650	6 854	7 286	18.4
Mexico	4 097	4 639	4 643	5 259	5 661	38.2
Germany	1 319	1 496	1 531	1 730	2 294	73.9
China	306	440	572	771	1 015	231.7
France	993	836	921	940	997	0.4
Taiwan	554	545	572	635	671	21.1
Italy	402	421	395	453	540	34.3
South Korea	291	327	359	471	516	77.3
Brazil	478	420	343	412	456	-4.6
LARGEST SURPLUSES						
Canada	8 015	7 228	6 193	6 506	5 320	-33.6
Austria	1 034	916	949	782	358	-65.4
Australia	231	355	311	261	300	29.9
Mexico	1 364	2 686	2 176	1 223	276	-79.8
Belgium	196	223	182	221	183	-6.6
Netherlands	95	230	208	184	154	62.1
Saudi Arabia	91	98	82	79	76	-16.5
Chile	35	41	79	60	72	105.7
Sweden	-23	-45	-19	8	69	-400.0
Egypt	29	18	18	18	37	27.6
LARGEST DEFICITS						
Japan	-5 100	-5 927	-5 465	-5 635	-6 215	21.9
Germany	-742	-849	-811	-1 092	-1 677	126.0
France	-839	-611	-618	-713	-757	-9.8
China	-149	-314	-408	-575	-672	351.0
Taiwan	-529	-521	-534	-595	-588	11.2
Italy	-343	-354	-305	-371	-430	25.4
South Korea	50	-3	-73	-230	-301	-702.0
Hungary	-29	-67	-54	-107	-196	575.9
Spain	-173	-123	-125	-151	-181	4.6
Brazil	-153	-81	-59	-165	-158	3.3

Table D-23. U.S. Trade Highlights for Aircraft and Associated Equipment (SITC 792)

(Millions of dollars; ranked by 2003 value; total exports, f.a.s.; general imports, Customs.) **2nd highest export, 17th highest import**

Country	1999	2000	2001	2002	2003	Percent change, 1999–2003
LARGEST EXPORTS						
World	49 611	40 954	44 689	43 876	39 638	-20.1
Japan	4 620	3 394	2 737	3 813	4 844	4.8
United Kingdom	6 111	4 622	4 936	2 859	3 097	-49.3
Singapore	1 546	839	3 544	2 828	2 615	69.1
China	2 317	1 691	2 448	3 428	2 451	5.8
Netherlands	1 377	1 676	1 191	1 248	2 405	74.7
Australia	1 204	1 182	989	3 149	2 228	85.0
South Korea	1 564	1 910	2 634	2 330	1 822	16.5
Canada	2 242	2 266	2 625	2 176	1 794	-20.0
France	2 774	1 822	2 166	2 849	1 541	-44.4
Italy	1 068	659	600	1 499	1 465	37.2
LARGEST IMPORTS						
World	14 982	18 160	21 091	17 984	16 990	13.4
Canada	3 799	4 744	6 092	5 265	6 343	67.0
France	3 636	5 240	5 728	5 131	4 206	15.7
Brazil	1 204	1 474	1 950	1 847	1 845	53.2
Germany	1 706	2 333	2 614	1 663	1 091	-36.0
United Kingdom	1 358	1 363	1 263	932	934	-31.2
Japan	1 359	1 187	1 446	1 060	854	-37.2
Israel	279	330	371	384	389	39.4
Italy	624	400	393	578	279	-55.3
Switzerland	138	154	160	149	137	-0.7
Australia	137	105	132	111	111	-19.0
LARGEST SURPLUSES						
Japan	3 261	2 206	1 291	2 754	3 989	22.3
Singapore	1 490	780	3 471	2 766	2 551	71.2
China	2 290	1 657	2 389	3 374	2 389	4.3
Netherlands	1 248	1 536	1 047	1 120	2 298	84.1
United Kingdom	4 753	3 259	3 673	1 927	2 163	-54.5
Australia	1 067	1 077	857	3 037	2 117	98.4
South Korea	1 438	1 776	2 446	2 241	1 736	20.7
Italy	444	260	208	921	1 186	167.1
Taiwan	2 083	1 386	1 210	872	1 032	-50.5
Ireland	505	555	628	692	903	78.8
LARGEST DEFICITS						
Canada	-1 556	-2 478	-3 467	-3 089	-4 549	192.4
France	-862	-3 418	-3 561	-2 282	-2 665	209.2
Brazil	-249	-714	-381	-612	-1 109	345.4
Russia	446	165	-19	58	-45	-110.1
Ukraine	13	-72	-47	63	-23	-276.9
Czech Republic	115	172	118	70	-11	-109.6
Iran	*	*	*	*	*	X
Svalbard and Jan Mayen Island	*	*	*	*	*	X
Christmas Island	*	*	*	*	*	X
Chad	*	*	*	*	*	X

* = Trade between -$0.5 million and $0.5 million.
X = Not applicable.

Table D-24. U.S. Trade Highlights for Furniture and Bedding Accessories (SITC 821)

(Millions of dollars; ranked by 2003 value; total exports, f.a.s.; general imports, Customs.)   **10th highest import**

Country	1999	2000	2001	2002	2003	Percent change, 1999–2003
LARGEST EXPORTS						
World	4 701	5 202	4 720	4 355	4 265	-9.3
Canada	2 383	2 592	2 280	2 136	2 174	-8.8
Mexico	797	1 014	969	867	809	1.5
Japan	221	219	294	336	339	53.4
United Kingdom	273	257	164	159	135	-50.5
China	45	56	51	56	59	31.1
Germany	83	90	87	60	58	-30.1
Saudi Arabia	70	76	83	71	49	-30.0
South Korea	16	31	24	35	37	131.3
Australia	29	36	27	25	36	24.1
Italy	22	26	25	33	33	50.0
LARGEST IMPORTS						
World	16 178	18 927	18 612	21 572	24 356	50.6
China	3 262	4 476	5 018	6 957	8 750	168.2
Canada	4 337	4 859	4 411	4 424	4 552	5.0
Mexico	2 885	3 202	3 212	3 825	4 275	48.2
Italy	1 070	1 300	1 265	1 310	1 363	27.4
Taiwan	1 009	1 032	766	795	749	-25.8
Malaysia	469	492	431	497	533	13.6
Indonesia	436	493	496	540	524	20.2
Thailand	267	302	302	392	413	54.7
Brazil	90	115	161	252	292	224.4
Germany	255	256	233	239	290	13.7
LARGEST SURPLUSES						
Japan	76	78	153	228	204	168.4
Saudi Arabia	70	75	83	71	49	-30.0
Kuwait	27	25	26	25	26	-3.7
Bahamas	20	25	18	16	21	5.0
Jamaica	17	23	18	20	18	5.9
Australia	16	21	11	7	17	6.3
Venezuela	34	30	40	26	15	-55.9
Singapore	20	20	14	10	13	-35.0
United Arab Emirates	20	19	18	19	12	-40.0
Bermuda	15	15	17	14	12	-20.0
LARGEST DEFICITS						
China	-3 217	-4 420	-4 968	-6 900	-8 691	170.2
Mexico	-2 088	-2 188	-2 244	-2 958	-3 466	66.0
Canada	-1 953	-2 266	-2 131	-2 288	-2 378	21.8
Italy	-1 048	-1 275	-1 241	-1 277	-1 329	26.8
Taiwan	-989	-1 012	-751	-784	-741	-25.1
Malaysia	-462	-483	-424	-492	-530	14.7
Indonesia	-432	-488	-492	-537	-520	20.4
Thailand	-259	-295	-294	-387	-406	56.8
Brazil	-54	-81	-136	-239	-283	424.1
Germany	-173	-166	-146	-179	-232	34.1

Table D-25. U.S. Trade Highlights for Women's or Girls' Coats, Jackets, Etc., Not Knit (SITC 842)

(Millions of dollars; ranked by 2003 value; total exports, f.a.s.; general imports, Customs.)   **20th highest import**

Country	1999	2000	2001	2002	2003	Percent change, 1999–2003
LARGEST EXPORTS						
World	809	799	577	501	437	-46.0
Mexico	316	298	207	211	181	-42.7
Canada	119	119	120	107	99	-16.8
Costa Rica	35	40	29	30	29	-17.1
Japan	27	19	17	14	20	-25.9
United Kingdom	7	9	14	18	13	85.7
Honduras	16	20	12	14	10	-37.5
Dominican Republic	137	144	81	26	8	-94.2
Hong Kong	4	4	5	5	7	75.0
Guatemala	37	46	21	9	6	-83.8
Nicaragua	1	1	1	4	5	400.0
LARGEST IMPORTS						
World	12 719	14 736	14 646	14 507	15 903	25.0
China	2 158	2 335	2 403	2 469	3 003	39.2
Mexico	1 652	2 028	1 811	1 683	1 429	-13.5
Hong Kong	1 179	1 218	1 151	1 225	1 209	2.5
India	699	834	729	867	927	32.6
Indonesia	594	716	788	734	836	40.7
Philippines	538	632	665	600	668	24.2
Vietnam	5	4	6	201	609	12 080.0
Sri Lanka (Ceylon)	476	530	505	511	563	18.3
Bangladesh	490	615	604	540	527	7.6
Italy	366	381	421	444	474	29.5
LARGEST SURPLUSES						
Panama	1	*	-1	1	3	200.0
Bermuda	1	1	3	4	2	100.0
Saudi Arabia	-10	-20	-21	-4	1	-110.0
Aruba	*	*	1	*	*	X
Bahamas	*	1	1	*	*	X
Tanzania	*	*	*	*	*	X
Netherlands	3	3	4	2	*	X
Lebanon	*	*	*	*	*	X
Barbados	1	*	*	*	*	X
Sweden	*	*	*	*	*	X
LARGEST DEFICITS						
China	-2 157	-2 335	-2 402	-2 468	-3 002	39.2
Mexico	-1 335	-1 730	-1 604	-1 472	-1 248	-6.5
Hong Kong	-1 175	-1 214	-1 146	-1 220	-1 202	2.3
India	-699	-834	-729	-867	-927	32.6
Indonesia	-593	-716	-788	-734	-834	40.6
Philippines	-537	-632	-665	-600	-668	24.4
Vietnam	-5	-4	-5	-201	-609	12 080.0
Sri Lanka (Ceylon)	-476	-530	-505	-511	-562	18.1
Bangladesh	-490	-615	-604	-540	-527	7.6
Italy	-364	-379	-419	-437	-469	28.8

* = Trade between -$0.5 million and $0.5 million.
X = Not applicable.

Table D-26. U.S. Trade Highlights for Articles of Apparel of Textile Fabrics (SITC 845)

(Millions of dollars; ranked by 2003 value; total exports, f.a.s.; general imports, Customs.)   **12th highest import**

Country	1999	2000	2001	2002	2003	Percent change, 1999–2003
LARGEST EXPORTS						
World	3 010	3 283	2 679	2 352	2 203	-26.8
Mexico	1 085	1 002	871	766	740	-31.8
Honduras	482	641	501	398	327	-32.2
Canada	248	242	245	262	274	10.5
Dominican Republic	260	302	224	219	227	-12.7
Haiti	77	114	80	87	118	53.2
Japan	200	208	171	130	109	-45.5
El Salvador	139	290	180	127	99	-28.8
Jamaica	67	55	50	38	36	-46.3
United Kingdom	29	29	30	30	27	-6.9
Guatemala	38	39	23	16	27	-28.9
LARGEST IMPORTS						
World	17 961	20 794	21 134	21 287	22 225	23.7
China	2 126	2 263	2 362	2 767	3 360	58.0
Mexico	2 733	2 875	2 867	2 626	2 486	-9.0
Honduras	1 167	1 401	1 470	1 555	1 577	35.1
Hong Kong	1 801	1 971	1 862	1 582	1 469	-18.4
El Salvador	528	667	677	729	804	52.3
Thailand	649	882	915	810	753	16.0
Guatemala	341	508	570	664	737	116.1
Vietnam	6	11	12	275	722	11 933.3
Taiwan	698	763	688	612	647	-7.3
Indonesia	454	623	664	629	619	36.3
LARGEST SURPLUSES						
Germany	2	1	7	16	12	500.0
Belgium	10	14	*	2	11	10.0
Netherlands	12	11	9	6	8	-33.3
Saudi Arabia	5	6	3	4	7	40.0
Netherlands Antilles	2	2	3	3	4	100.0
Bahamas	2	3	4	3	3	50.0
Kuwait	3	1	1	*	2	-33.3
Chile	5	8	3	-2	2	-60.0
Venezuela	9	9	22	7	1	-88.9
Bermuda	*	*	*	1	1	X
LARGEST DEFICITS						
China	-2 124	-2 261	-2 336	-2 754	-3 356	58.0
Mexico	-1 648	-1 873	-1 996	-1 859	-1 746	5.9
Hong Kong	-1 785	-1 959	-1 852	-1 561	-1 460	-18.2
Honduras	-684	-760	-969	-1 156	-1 251	82.9
Thailand	-648	-881	-914	-809	-752	16.0
Vietnam	-6	-11	-12	-275	-722	11 933.3
Guatemala	-303	-469	-547	-648	-710	134.3
El Salvador	-389	-377	-496	-602	-705	81.2
Taiwan	-692	-758	-683	-609	-644	-6.9
Indonesia	-454	-623	-664	-627	-617	35.9

* = Trade between -$0.5 million and $0.5 million.
X = Not applicable.

Table D-27. U.S. Trade Highlights for Medical Instruments and Appliances (SITC 872)

(Millions of dollars; ranked by 2003 value; total exports, f.a.s.; general imports, Customs.)   **15th highest export**

Country	1999	2000	2001	2002	2003	Percent change, 1999–2003
LARGEST EXPORTS						
World	6 722	7 115	8 088	7 941	8 930	32.8
Japan	1 002	1 081	1 188	1 103	1 201	19.9
Netherlands	635	701	622	777	1 080	70.1
Canada	802	790	912	887	1 002	24.9
Mexico	406	508	562	673	860	111.8
Germany	504	495	629	567	616	22.2
United Kingdom	317	326	407	438	484	52.7
Belgium	322	346	491	386	446	38.5
France	486	397	478	425	380	-21.8
Australia	185	214	214	232	264	42.7
Italy	203	231	250	250	230	13.3
LARGEST IMPORTS						
World	4 357	4 944	5 500	6 240	7 699	76.7
Mexico	756	998	1 177	1 482	1 816	140.2
Ireland	330	405	489	499	1 064	222.4
Germany	469	522	595	676	849	81.0
China	321	336	345	389	445	38.6
Dominican Republic	350	347	350	354	441	26.0
Costa Rica	85	186	280	336	434	410.6
Japan	383	448	376	364	406	6.0
Singapore	222	264	277	297	270	21.6
United Kingdom	162	175	192	240	265	63.6
Canada	113	124	167	219	239	111.5
LARGEST SURPLUSES						
Netherlands	571	610	480	631	976	70.9
Japan	618	633	811	739	795	28.6
Canada	689	666	746	667	762	10.6
Belgium	307	323	475	370	433	41.0
France	375	285	366	320	272	-27.5
United Kingdom	155	151	215	198	219	41.3
Australia	140	151	146	141	155	10.7
Spain	112	111	139	115	138	23.2
South Korea	79	87	97	103	123	55.7
Italy	143	168	176	163	122	-14.7
LARGEST DEFICITS						
Mexico	-350	-490	-615	-809	-956	173.1
Ireland	-185	-220	-263	-274	-849	358.9
Costa Rica	-66	-164	-254	-308	-395	498.5
Dominican Republic	-250	-250	-258	-264	-352	40.8
China	-263	-266	-245	-285	-321	22.1
Germany	35	-26	35	-109	-233	-765.7
Singapore	-148	-195	-202	-232	-196	32.4
Switzerland	-42	-34	-35	-52	-80	90.5
Israel	-228	-132	-90	-76	-62	-72.8
Taiwan	19	-3	-10	-36	-48	-352.6

Table D-28. U.S. Trade Highlights for Measuring/Checking/Analyzing Instruments (SITC 874)

(Millions of dollars; ranked by 2003 value; total exports, f.a.s.; general imports, Customs.)   **7th highest export**

Country	1999	2000	2001	2002	2003	Percent change, 1999–2003
LARGEST EXPORTS						
World	18 156	22 152	20 388	18 640	19 406	6.9
Canada	3 253	3 575	3 404	3 157	3 301	1.5
Japan	2 047	2 682	2 474	2 083	2 068	1.0
Germany	1 233	1 494	1 523	1 230	1 289	4.5
Mexico	1 185	1 533	1 536	1 386	1 276	7.7
United Kingdom	1 329	1 425	1 439	1 218	1 239	-6.8
China	467	483	751	772	985	110.9
Taiwan	956	1 840	974	1 100	922	-3.6
France	811	1 017	880	759	864	6.5
Singapore	731	1 053	720	814	859	17.5
South Korea	756	1 007	740	651	717	-5.2
LARGEST IMPORTS						
World	10 315	12 689	12 429	12 029	12 994	26.0
Mexico	1 578	1 845	1 865	2 141	2 331	47.7
Japan	2 135	2 966	2 501	2 119	2 206	3.3
Germany	1 494	1 868	1 724	1 557	1 715	14.8
United Kingdom	1 251	1 498	1 486	1 289	1 360	8.7
Canada	967	1 126	1 126	1 177	1 061	9.7
China	322	448	573	671	890	176.4
France	348	393	454	400	466	33.9
Switzerland	283	334	314	301	321	13.4
Malaysia	48	97	187	201	274	470.8
Singapore	241	236	242	233	260	7.9
LARGEST SURPLUSES						
Canada	2 286	2 449	2 278	1 980	2 240	-2.0
Taiwan	786	1 629	786	913	708	-9.9
South Korea	687	921	665	568	632	-8.0
Singapore	490	817	478	581	599	22.2
France	463	624	426	359	399	-13.8
Netherlands	516	572	458	401	382	-26.0
Hong Kong	278	349	370	345	380	36.7
Italy	306	304	308	234	283	-7.5
Philippines	125	289	170	135	230	84.0
Brazil	263	269	281	262	204	-22.4
LARGEST DEFICITS						
Mexico	-393	-313	-329	-755	-1 054	168.2
Germany	-261	-374	-201	-326	-426	63.2
Switzerland	-92	-162	-104	-100	-152	65.2
Japan	-88	-284	-27	-36	-138	56.8
United Kingdom	78	-73	-47	-71	-121	-255.1
Poland	24	31	27	-9	-48	-300.0
Finland	-34	-26	-11	-43	-29	-14.7
Israel	37	-126	-67	-48	-21	-156.8
Sweden	29	26	13	8	-17	-158.6
Denmark	-12	7	4	-8	-14	16.7

Table D-29. U.S. Trade Highlights for Baby Carriages, Toys, Games, and Sporting Goods (SITC 894)

(Millions of dollars; ranked by 2003 value; total exports, f.a.s.; general imports, Customs.)   **13th highest import**

Country	1999	2000	2001	2002	2003	Percent change, 1999–2003
LARGEST EXPORTS						
World	3 928	4 167	3 898	3 666	3 989	1.6
Canada	1 229	1 145	1 207	1 268	1 462	19.0
United Kingdom	354	408	395	374	383	8.2
Japan	579	737	572	383	363	-37.3
Mexico	368	383	326	284	230	-37.5
Hong Kong	136	111	110	134	168	23.5
Australia	95	126	110	123	125	31.6
Netherlands	64	108	74	89	115	79.7
Germany	133	115	106	108	103	-22.6
South Korea	52	84	74	73	91	75.0
France	72	73	71	62	70	-2.8
LARGEST IMPORTS						
World	18 991	20 017	20 909	22 059	21 566	13.6
China	11 639	12 925	12 672	14 869	16 448	41.3
Japan	2 705	2 383	3 468	2 270	886	-67.2
Taiwan	688	818	721	680	644	-6.4
Mexico	728	668	780	1 222	599	-17.7
Canada	621	617	559	543	557	-10.3
Thailand	242	297	299	283	295	21.9
Hong Kong	273	271	230	230	245	-10.3
South Korea	203	252	249	182	184	-9.4
Germany	188	170	165	166	172	-8.5
Indonesia	159	208	184	172	163	2.5
LARGEST SURPLUSES						
Canada	608	528	648	725	905	48.8
United Kingdom	210	287	288	274	270	28.6
Netherlands	25	86	40	72	97	288.0
Australia	80	102	80	82	66	-17.5
Singapore	59	56	45	37	44	-25.4
Paraguay	23	26	15	16	37	60.9
Russia	4	8	12	27	31	675.0
Republic of South Africa	23	35	28	19	28	21.7
Belgium	9	3	5	16	27	200.0
United Arab Emirates	15	12	18	20	25	66.7
LARGEST DEFICITS						
China	-11 601	-12 895	-12 642	-14 843	-16 414	41.5
Taiwan	-645	-771	-687	-647	-615	-4.7
Japan	-2 126	-1 646	-2 895	-1 887	-524	-75.4
Mexico	-360	-285	-455	-938	-369	2.5
Thailand	-234	-281	-287	-267	-283	20.9
Indonesia	-157	-206	-180	-170	-159	1.3
Malaysia	-165	-143	-153	-161	-119	-27.9
Italy	-146	-138	-128	-117	-113	-22.6
South Korea	-151	-168	-174	-109	-93	-38.4
Denmark	-141	-75	-119	-132	-82	-41.8

Table D-30. U.S. Trade Highlights for Special Transactions Not Classified by Kind (SITC 931)

(Millions of dollars; ranked by 2003 value; total exports, f.a.s.; general imports, Customs.)   **5th highest import**

Country	1999	2000	2001	2002	2003	Percent change, 1999–2003
LARGEST EXPORTS						
World	5 500	5 666	6 483	6 554	6 215	13.0
Canada	1 920	2 119	2 137	1 585	1 392	-27.5
Japan	533	453	659	770	785	47.3
Germany	288	383	368	389	338	17.4
United Kingdom	293	255	312	321	337	15.0
Saudi Arabia	328	291	230	311	280	-14.6
Singapore	95	89	169	142	200	110.5
Spain	65	67	195	128	178	173.8
South Korea	104	112	138	180	173	66.3
Mexico	222	183	162	178	160	-27.9
Australia	72	62	72	99	146	102.8
LARGEST IMPORTS						
World	31 783	34 572	35 367	35 893	33 622	5.8
Canada	9 701	10 845	10 981	11 523	10 008	3.2
Mexico	3 558	4 285	4 245	4 196	4 250	19.4
Japan	2 496	2 382	2 568	2 296	2 208	-11.5
United Kingdom	2 524	2 776	3 074	2 907	2 208	-12.5
Germany	1 616	1 565	1 645	1 998	1 626	0.6
Netherlands	975	827	937	870	1 128	15.7
France	1 049	1 299	1 265	994	1 057	0.8
Singapore	936	1 156	1 013	921	950	1.5
Brazil	377	729	528	563	827	119.4
Switzerland	703	647	770	701	698	-0.7
LARGEST SURPLUSES						
Saudi Arabia	179	203	140	266	205	14.5
Nicaragua	10	17	55	68	85	750.0
Guatemala	6	-17	-1	3	38	533.3
Haiti	19	16	24	43	36	89.5
Jamaica	-16	11	29	49	35	-318.8
Tajikistan	2	2	8	21	31	1 450.0
Ukraine	36	22	20	24	29	-19.4
Kyrgyzstan	9	8	20	15	29	222.2
Armenia	24	32	23	24	22	-8.3
Uzbekistan	16	10	18	17	21	31.3
LARGEST DEFICITS						
Canada	-7 781	-8 726	-8 845	-9 938	-8 616	10.7
Mexico	-3 336	-4 102	-4 083	-4 019	-4 090	22.6
United Kingdom	-2 230	-2 521	-2 762	-2 585	-1 871	-16.1
Japan	-1 963	-1 929	-1 909	-1 526	-1 423	-27.5
Germany	-1 328	-1 182	-1 276	-1 609	-1 288	-3.0
Netherlands	-922	-745	-841	-818	-1 064	15.4
France	-975	-1 196	-1 195	-890	-914	-6.3
Brazil	-307	-676	-454	-501	-762	148.2
Singapore	-840	-1 067	-843	-779	-750	-10.7
Switzerland	-684	-617	-726	-651	-624	-8.8

Table D-31. U.S. Trade Highlights for Estimated Low Value Shipments (SITC 994)

(Millions of dollars; ranked by 2003 value; total exports, f.a.s.; general imports, Customs.)   **9th highest export**

Country	1999	2000	2001	2002	2003	Percent change, 1999–2003
LARGEST EXPORTS						
World	13 757	15 707	16 842	15 280	15 826	15.0
Canada	1 750	1 989	3 753	3 332	3 654	108.8
Mexico	2 901	3 670	3 353	3 146	3 003	3.5
United Kingdom	979	1 090	1 097	928	907	-7.4
Germany	594	649	690	623	678	14.1
Japan	614	703	651	556	550	-10.4
Australia	490	497	451	447	484	-1.2
France	466	519	516	461	436	-6.4
Singapore	379	435	369	350	355	-6.3
Netherlands	268	298	274	256	268	0.0
Hong Kong	269	301	294	254	260	-3.3
LARGEST IMPORTS						
World	X	X	X	X	X	X
Canada	X	X	X	X	X	X
Mexico	X	X	X	X	X	X
United Kingdom	X	X	X	X	X	X
Germany	X	X	X	X	X	X
Japan	X	X	X	X	X	X
Australia	X	X	X	X	X	X
France	X	X	X	X	X	X
Singapore	X	X	X	X	X	X
Netherlands	X	X	X	X	X	X
Hong Kong	X	X	X	X	X	X
LARGEST SURPLUSES						
Canada	X	X	X	X	X	X
Mexico	X	X	X	X	X	X
United Kingdom	X	X	X	X	X	X
Germany	X	X	X	X	X	X
Japan	X	X	X	X	X	X
Australia	X	X	X	X	X	X
France	X	X	X	X	X	X
Singapore	X	X	X	X	X	X
Netherlands	X	X	X	X	X	X
Hong Kong	X	X	X	X	X	X
LARGEST DEFICITS						
Canada	X	X	X	X	X	X
Mexico	X	X	X	X	X	X
United Kingdom	X	X	X	X	X	X
Germany	X	X	X	X	X	X
Japan	X	X	X	X	X	X
Australia	X	X	X	X	X	X
France	X	X	X	X	X	X
Singapore	X	X	X	X	X	X
Netherlands	X	X	X	X	X	X
Hong Kong	X	X	X	X	X	X

X = Not applicable.

SECTION E. EXPORTS OF GOODS BY STATE

ABOUT THE DATA

This section presents a detailed export picture of each state. Tables E-1 through E-4 give an aggregate picture of all states, followed by individual tables showing each state or territory's top export products and largest markets abroad. Figures and commentary highlight each state. It should be noted that this section does not provide a complete picture of foreign trade activity by state, as state import data are not published.

Industry exports are grouped by the North American Industry Classification System (NAICS), which replaced the old system of Standard Industrial Classification (SIC) in 1997 to make trade data comparisons within the North American Free Trade Agreement (NAFTA) countries (Canada, Mexico, and the United States) more compatible. These data are from the International Trade Administration (ITA), which is part of the Commerce Department. A limited number of preformatted state tables can be found at <www.ita.doc.gov/td/industry/otea/state/index.html>. Custom tables can be created using multiple variables, including state, NAICS code product, and trading partner, on the ITA's TradeStats Express at <tse.export.gov>. Custom U.S. tables are available as well, and include additional product classification codes.

The **commodity** data in Section E are reported using the Harmonized System (HS) of classification. These data are from the Census Bureau, and can be found at <www.census.gov/foreign-trade/statistics/state/index.html>.

State exports by **country** can be found on both TradeStats and the Census site, however the latter includes only the top 25 countries.

More information on classification codes can be found in this volume's "Understanding Foreign Trade Statistics."

State export data is reported by the exporter or agent, and denote the state from which the merchandise actually starts its journey to the port of export. This may not necessarily be the state where the merchandise is actually grown or manufactured or the actual location of the exporter. This method of calculating state exports is called **origin of movement**. Under this method, the origin of movement may not be the transportation origin.

Whenever shipments are consolidated, the state of origin will reflect the consolidation point. This effect is particularly noticeable for nonmanufactured goods, which are generally exported by intermediaries. For example, intermediaries located in inland states ship agricultural products down the Mississippi River for export from the port of New Orleans. In this case, Louisiana would be reported as the state of origin. The most visible result is a tendency to understate exports from some agricultural states and to overstate exports from states, such as Louisiana, that have ports that handle high-value shipments of farm products.

The series does not represent the production origin and may attribute a sizable amount of manufactured exports to states known to have little manufacturing capability. For example, commodities produced by out-of-state suppliers can be shipped from in-state distribution centers, and shipments of manufactured commodities from in-state warehouses and other distribution centers can be arranged by exporters located out-of-state. In both cases, manufactured exports from the nonindustrial state are overstated. A discussion of these issues can be found in the Census Bureau's document *Description of the Foreign Trade Statistical Program* at <www.census.gov/foreign-trade/guide/>.

Data may not add to total or may appear as zero because of rounding.

HIGHLIGHTS

After implementation of the North American Free Trade Agreement (NAFTA) in January 1994, exports to Canada and Mexico have collectively increased by 88 percent. From 1993 to 2003, total U.S. exports increased by $353 billion, and about $158 billion, or 45 percent, were to Canada and Mexico. In 1997, Mexico eclipsed Japan to become the second largest market for U.S. goods after Canada. In 2003, these two nations purchased about 37 percent of all U.S. exports. Canada and Mexico rank among the top markets for nearly every state.

Figure E-1. Top 10 Exporting States, 2004
(Billions of dollars)

Source: International Trade Administration.

Figure E-1 shows the largest exporting states in 2004: Texas, California, New York, Michigan, Washington, Ohio, Illinois, Florida, Massachusetts, and Louisiana. The lowest exporting states are Hawaii, Montana, Wyoming, South Dakota, North Dakota, Rhode Island, New Mexico, Delaware, New Hampshire, and Nebraska. These 10 states each have exports valued at less than $2.5 billion. (See Table E-1.)

In 2003, computer and electronic products were the nation's leading export, accounting for more than 20 percent of total goods export followed by exports of transportation equipment (18 percent), chemicals (about 13 percent), machinery manufactures (10 percent), and agricultural products (4 percent). (See Table E-4.) California was the leading exporter of computer and electronic products, followed by Texas. Washington, Michigan, and Ohio led the nation in the exports of transportation equipment. The chief exporter of chemicals was Texas; of machinery, California; and of agricultural products, Louisiana (although this probably relates to the use of the port of New Orleans for the shipment of many agricultural products grown inland in other states). (See Table E-2.) As previously noted under the origin of movement concept, the state of consolidation of shipments is designated as the state of exportation.

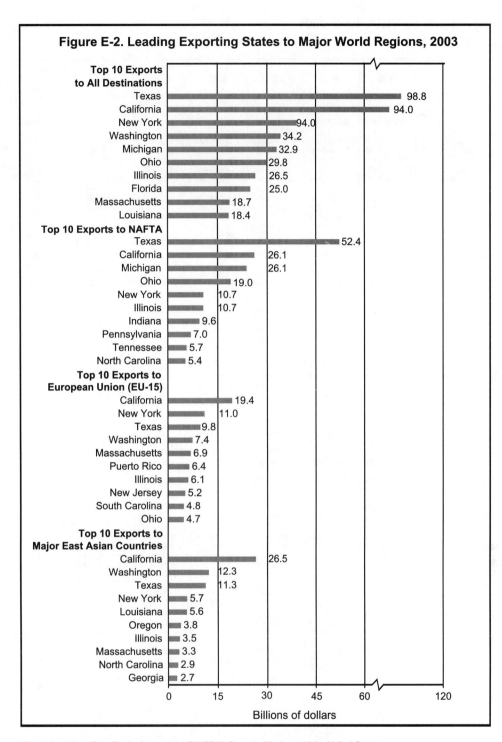

Figure E-2. Leading Exporting States to Major World Regions, 2003

Top 10 Exports to All Destinations

State	Value
Texas	98.8
California	94.0
New York	94.0
Washington	34.2
Michigan	32.9
Ohio	29.8
Illinois	26.5
Florida	25.0
Massachusetts	18.7
Louisiana	18.4

Top 10 Exports to NAFTA

State	Value
Texas	52.4
California	26.1
Michigan	26.1
Ohio	19.0
New York	10.7
Illinois	10.7
Indiana	9.6
Pennsylvania	7.0
Tennessee	5.7
North Carolina	5.4

Top 10 Exports to European Union (EU-15)

State	Value
California	19.4
New York	11.0
Texas	9.8
Washington	7.4
Massachusetts	6.9
Puerto Rico	6.4
Illinois	6.1
New Jersey	5.2
South Carolina	4.8
Ohio	4.7

Top 10 Exports to Major East Asian Countries

State	Value
California	26.5
Washington	12.3
Texas	11.3
New York	5.7
Louisiana	5.6
Oregon	3.8
Illinois	3.5
Massachusetts	3.3
North Carolina	2.9
Georgia	2.7

Billions of dollars

North American Free Trade Agreement (NAFTA): Canada, Mexico, and the United States

European Union (EU-15): Austria, Belgium, Denmark, Finland, France, Germany, Greece, Ireland, Italy, Luxembourg, the Netherlands, Portugal, Spain, Sweden, and United Kingdom.

Major East Asian countries: China, Japan, South Korea, and Taiwan

Source: International Trade Administration.

The top states exporting goods to major foreign markets are shown in Figure E-2. U.S. exports to fellow NAFTA countries dwarf all other regions. In 2003, the top states exporting to Canada and Mexico were Texas, California, and Michigan. Exports to the EU-15 region were led by California, New York, and Texas; and exports to the major East Asian countries of China, Japan, South Korea, and Taiwan were dominated by California, Washington, and Texas.

Table E-1. Total Exports by State, 1999–2004

(Thousands of dollars.)

State/territory	1999	2000	2001	2002	2003	2004	Percent change, 1999–2004	Rank by 2004 value	Percent share of U.S. total, 2004
United States	692 820 620	780 418 628	731 025 906	693 257 300	723 743 177	817 935 849	18.06	X	100.00
Alabama	6 192 431	7 317 040	7 570 360	8 266 884	8 340 387	9 036 641	45.93	25	1.10
Alaska	2 563 798	2 464 139	2 418 284	2 516 220	2 738 558	3 156 911	23.13	38	0.39
Arizona	11 823 753	14 333 689	12 513 510	11 871 004	13 323 392	13 422 913	13.52	17	1.64
Arkansas	2 177 495	2 599 268	2 911 181	2 803 645	2 962 153	3 493 133	60.42	33	0.43
California	97 920 079	119 640 424	106 776 963	92 214 292	93 994 882	109 967 840	12.30	2	13.44
Colorado	5 931 358	6 592 984	6 125 494	5 521 685	6 109 121	6 650 999	12.13	28	0.81
Connecticut	7 231 228	8 046 838	8 610 434	8 313 390	8 136 443	8 559 237	18.36	27	1.05
Delaware	2 286 650	2 197 396	1 984 813	2 003 814	1 886 118	2 053 423	-10.20	44	0.25
District of Columbia	412 165	1 003 177	1 033 602	1 065 873	809 220	1 164 327	182.49	47	0.14
Florida	24 154 695	26 542 976	27 184 581	24 544 204	24 953 414	28 981 515	19.98	8	3.54
Georgia	13 748 662	14 925 063	14 643 686	14 412 700	16 286 235	19 632 738	42.80	11	2.40
Hawaii	273 565	386 813	369 866	513 651	368 227	404 774	47.96	52	0.05
Idaho	2 191 496	3 558 623	2 122 100	1 966 982	2 095 799	2 914 604	33.00	39	0.36
Illinois	29 432 161	31 437 607	30 434 398	25 686 414	26 472 902	30 213 626	2.66	7	3.69
Indiana	12 910 347	15 385 774	14 365 375	14 923 049	16 402 279	19 109 378	48.02	13	2.34
Iowa	4 093 773	4 465 486	4 659 584	4 754 600	5 236 296	6 393 941	56.19	29	0.78
Kansas	4 669 436	5 145 445	5 004 547	4 988 410	4 553 334	4 930 774	5.60	31	0.60
Kentucky	8 877 162	9 612 209	9 047 966	10 606 720	10 733 781	12 991 977	46.35	20	1.59
Louisiana	15 841 781	16 814 289	16 588 957	17 566 658	18 390 130	19 922 346	25.76	10	2.44
Maine	2 014 053	1 778 695	1 812 455	1 973 061	2 188 413	2 432 219	20.76	41	0.30
Maryland	4 009 160	4 592 885	4 974 873	4 473 576	4 940 631	5 746 142	43.33	30	0.70
Massachusetts	16 805 139	20 514 409	17 490 110	16 707 593	18 662 575	21 837 411	29.94	9	2.67
Michigan	31 085 807	33 845 301	32 365 840	33 775 232	32 941 109	35 625 008	14.60	4	4.36
Minnesota	9 372 614	10 302 502	10 524 370	10 402 162	11 265 660	12 677 805	35.26	22	1.55
Mississippi	2 215 735	2 725 551	3 557 419	3 058 008	2 558 259	3 179 374	43.49	36	0.39
Missouri	6 058 992	6 497 147	6 173 043	6 790 778	7 233 937	8 997 288	48.49	26	1.10
Montana	426 902	540 642	488 522	385 735	361 416	564 691	32.28	51	0.07
Nebraska	2 096 385	2 511 183	2 701 795	2 527 632	2 723 670	2 316 114	10.48	42	0.28
Nevada	1 067 171	1 481 897	1 423 225	1 176 999	2 032 599	2 906 689	172.37	40	0.36
New Hampshire	1 929 763	2 373 327	2 401 032	1 863 288	1 931 412	2 285 589	18.44	43	0.28
New Jersey	15 354 453	18 637 554	18 945 751	17 001 514	16 817 673	19 192 131	24.99	12	2.35
New Mexico	3 133 455	2 390 543	1 404 620	1 196 144	2 325 609	2 045 806	-34.71	45	0.25
New York	37 067 481	42 845 957	42 172 062	36 976 801	39 180 708	44 400 729	19.78	3	5.43
North Carolina	15 007 070	17 945 940	16 798 898	14 718 505	16 198 733	18 114 767	20.71	15	2.21
North Dakota	699 225	625 917	806 110	859 383	854 072	1 007 927	44.15	48	0.12
Ohio	24 883 241	26 322 241	27 094 734	27 723 273	29 764 418	31 208 206	25.42	6	3.82
Oklahoma	2 986 579	3 072 177	2 661 344	2 443 578	2 659 603	3 177 874	6.41	37	0.39
Oregon	10 471 154	11 441 272	8 900 414	10 086 397	10 357 199	11 171 751	6.69	24	1.37
Pennsylvania	16 170 424	18 792 448	17 433 129	15 767 794	16 299 212	18 487 253	14.33	14	2.26
Puerto Rico	8 301 033	9 735 372	10 573 285	9 732 153	11 913 947	13 161 778	58.56	19	1.61
Rhode Island	1 116 324	1 185 571	1 268 612	1 121 005	1 177 475	1 286 324	15.23	46	0.16
South Carolina	7 149 890	8 565 126	9 956 333	9 656 247	11 772 894	13 375 890	87.08	18	1.64
South Dakota	494 674	679 366	594 874	596 785	672 268	825 510	66.88	49	0.10
Tennessee	9 867 779	11 591 574	11 320 177	11 621 339	12 611 793	16 122 874	63.39	16	1.97
Texas	83 177 476	103 865 689	94 995 266	95 396 197	98 846 083	117 244 970	40.96	1	14.33
Utah	3 133 520	3 220 823	3 506 386	4 542 725	4 114 540	4 718 350	50.58	32	0.58
Vermont	4 023 270	4 097 073	2 830 360	2 520 955	2 626 922	3 283 135	-18.40	34	0.40
Virgin Islands	154 960	174 320	187 186	257 770	252 719	389 407	151.30	53	0.05
Virginia	11 482 953	11 698 059	11 630 943	10 795 528	10 852 981	11 630 744	1.29	23	1.42
Washington	36 730 711	32 214 701	34 928 533	34 626 549	34 172 826	33 792 504	-8.00	5	4.13
West Virginia	1 892 689	2 219 278	2 241 005	2 237 154	2 379 808	3 261 683	72.33	35	0.40
Wisconsin	9 672 878	10 508 413	10 488 671	10 684 271	11 509 835	12 706 343	31.36	21	1.55
Wyoming	457 954	502 453	503 269	553 361	581 636	680 239	48.54	50	0.08
Unallocated	59 577 666	58 453 978	41 505 557	34 467 615	35 167 868	35 080 226	-41.12	X	4.29

X = Not applicable.

SECTION E. EXPORTS OF GOODS BY STATE   293

Table E-2. Exports by State and Industry (NAICS Code), 2003

(Thousands of dollars.)

State/territory	Total	Manufactures							
		Total	Processed foods (311)	Beverages and tobacco products (312)	Fabric mill products (313)	Non-apparel textile products (314)	Apparel manufactures (315)	Leather and related products (316)	Wood products (321)
United States	723 743 177	644 906 250	27 495 604	3 796 808	7 805 386	2 004 488	5 469 699	2 717 174	4 036 281
Alabama	8 340 387	7 531 494	118 755	1 517	197 445	48 393	489 341	1 864	98 479
Alaska	2 738 558	620 828	54 491	78	156	290	210	196	10 794
Arizona	13 323 392	12 544 140	260 661	6 042	77 279	23 140	25 869	26 320	21 252
Arkansas	2 962 153	2 816 624	575 136	31 537	37 776	5 855	9 496	2 092	12 185
California	93 994 882	84 342 574	4 168 178	742 768	650 306	156 713	1 040 461	264 261	402 698
Colorado	6 109 121	5 923 069	661 298	1 515	12 809	12 332	5 548	17 114	2 993
Connecticut	8 136 443	7 750 544	53 795	11 039	57 076	11 284	3 921	6 155	8 260
Delaware	1 886 118	1 741 957	61 666	61	8 486	7 782	2 347	79	1 437
District of Columbia	809 220	737 201	4 872	23	843	7 000	715	303	225
Florida	24 953 414	23 304 995	996 194	133 858	626 071	76 317	363 739	134 438	120 389
Georgia	16 286 235	14 963 847	623 247	488 323	480 070	367 853	147 142	15 724	129 082
Hawaii	368 227	289 769	24 348	4 875	677	304	1 870	18 304	410
Idaho	2 095 799	1 940 544	268 728	31	572	572	733	2 904	31 147
Illinois	26 472 902	25 336 382	1 297 200	42 643	55 190	38 297	20 905	132 272	42 665
Indiana	16 402 279	16 120 085	247 658	19 413	27 081	28 047	4 230	9 417	134 269
Iowa	5 236 296	4 888 327	1 060 827	8 924	25 801	19 071	4 980	2 635	28 467
Kansas	4 553 334	4 148 788	1 304 111	1 064	9 804	3 375	2 220	89 945	2 542
Kentucky	10 733 781	10 039 362	139 892	142 609	120 593	15 034	73 606	91 691	87 540
Louisiana	18 390 130	8 819 283	2 112 161	77 780	17 329	4 332	12 799	481	34 402
Maine	2 188 413	1 721 583	84 532	5 513	7 458	7 298	2 834	68 147	74 155
Maryland	4 940 631	4 584 840	134 600	18 420	105 922	14 475	12 621	65 939	49 990
Massachusetts	18 662 575	17 735 981	300 498	15 373	226 955	15 381	20 613	65 836	26 389
Michigan	32 941 109	31 535 360	422 286	13 871	62 155	36 025	13 199	121 648	110 227
Minnesota	11 265 660	10 454 885	731 190	15 055	18 834	21 712	3 043	37 384	74 330
Mississippi	2 558 259	2 353 810	119 600	805	99 478	9 251	53 301	3 160	65 377
Missouri	7 233 937	6 980 608	440 463	17 912	21 683	2 908	16 156	148 278	69 270
Montana	361 416	272 722	13 517	19	290	150	1 399	629	21 650
Nebraska	2 723 670	2 248 779	955 428	652	10 957	8 442	246	58 397	2 717
Nevada	2 032 599	1 937 423	8 982	6 771	1 747	2 090	9 515	3 473	2 616
New Hampshire	1 931 412	1 761 787	27 926	197	28 254	1 310	5 557	19 741	48 570
New Jersey	16 817 673	15 311 913	575 521	27 700	108 603	59 313	80 747	56 887	28 719
New Mexico	2 325 609	2 241 454	24 083	30	19 261	290	5 090	353	5 819
New York	39 180 708	34 481 124	620 715	68 033	309 557	89 162	309 590	96 724	211 944
North Carolina	16 198 733	15 319 134	219 818	399 076	1 375 877	129 555	1 118 984	22 655	177 443
North Dakota	854 072	626 128	106 430	1 204	421	152	65	72	1 814
Ohio	29 764 418	28 643 453	470 857	10 791	105 973	48 033	56 625	26 423	179 027
Oklahoma	2 659 603	2 543 072	125 752	2 274	2 641	2 106	27 440	3 488	5 406
Oregon	10 357 199	8 784 760	280 349	3 649	4 825	3 015	11 865	95 219	299 105
Pennsylvania	16 299 212	15 410 397	560 003	22 056	168 660	75 047	137 404	111 506	299 650
Puerto Rico	11 913 947	11 840 043	200 101	34 358	54 775	14 401	204 361	9 107	5 323
Rhode Island	1 177 475	1 020 188	4 892	6	32 108	10 151	2 214	2 115	1 108
South Carolina	11 772 894	11 539 523	175 331	2 714	482 813	81 444	120 968	2 689	59 133
South Dakota	672 268	608 453	178 825	1 488	8 590	4 082	1 076	1 734	204
Tennessee	12 611 793	11 027 359	284 575	243 247	215 629	28 079	101 015	33 721	73 913
Texas	98 846 083	93 676 573	2 755 199	78 657	1 412 689	170 897	504 970	650 640	132 746
Utah	4 114 540	3 960 540	283 210	26 306	3 634	5 176	4 270	6 075	2 671
Vermont	2 626 922	2 541 398	55 576	971	10 073	895	5 653	3 526	27 399
Virgin Islands	252 719	251 451	151	175	202	10	7	16	5
Virginia	10 852 981	9 205 978	241 285	950 934	244 612	75 920	154 931	6 185	166 103
Washington	34 172 826	29 374 419	1 602 185	29 060	16 871	49 390	23 575	12 102	343 458
West Virginia	2 379 808	2 097 318	6 710	10	6 661	321	461	235	95 990
Wisconsin	11 509 835	10 805 422	650 636	45 458	62 020	18 987	75 608	28 700	87 478
Wyoming	581 636	505 692	1 636	458	205	294	214	29	1 776
Unallocated	35 167 868	17 642 868	799 522	39 464	169 589	192 736	173 951	138 146	115 519

Table E-2. Exports by State and Industry (NAICS Code), 2003—*Continued*

(Thousands of dollars.)

State/territory	Paper products (322)	Printing and related products (323)	Petroleum and coal products (324)	Chemical manufactures (325)	Plastics and rubber products (326)	Non-metallic mineral manufactures (327)	Primary metal manufactures (331)	Fabricated metal products (332)	Machinery manufactures (333)
United States	14 504 183	4 983 734	9 659 012	91 017 178	16 509 875	6 405 335	19 125 021	20 364 725	74 925 132
Alabama	658 341	4 724	10 542	1 264 330	215 516	75 438	305 383	123 284	463 039
Alaska	822	255	152 503	202 014	5 090	228	97 426	8 724	21 456
Arizona	179 384	27 300	9 562	233 330	381 826	20 152	109 588	531 489	808 275
Arkansas	194 684	43 915	4 042	431 362	90 579	8 665	117 023	130 432	251 296
California	1 069 151	546 450	892 221	5 963 655	1 575 073	540 007	1 167 545	2 298 694	9 433 880
Colorado	26 646	50 539	19 135	397 569	54 132	47 807	68 269	86 115	456 976
Connecticut	188 637	35 620	84 112	749 024	137 605	41 381	203 147	440 493	784 385
Delaware	32 496	3 128	3 910	803 914	94 198	7 979	16 944	19 469	152 501
District of Columbia	6 912	16 943	45	54 708	2 855	16 411	331	126 792	27 247
Florida	675 167	163 934	57 954	2 920 859	414 552	169 299	369 634	566 528	2 249 041
Georgia	1 361 534	69 314	20 103	2 096 092	315 165	97 192	116 772	286 123	1 555 525
Hawaii	2 250	1 021	74 605	4 261	723	940	163	1 060	21 600
Idaho	112 832	4 417	99	153 179	3 485	3 120	3 267	17 166	76 431
Illinois	489 863	296 154	53 290	3 890 967	796 574	294 716	574 194	1 077 459	6 892 917
Indiana	125 547	142 341	14 061	3 005 403	513 355	177 943	612 346	482 654	2 441 370
Iowa	45 417	21 611	4 248	444 295	165 018	19 065	218 589	168 304	1 297 671
Kansas	34 347	26 077	14 092	250 706	111 294	27 723	18 595	79 577	414 967
Kentucky	126 533	158 237	13 930	2 016 582	220 709	297 224	347 702	341 304	916 961
Louisiana	287 913	3 211	1 206 030	3 708 043	90 695	16 848	124 094	87 762	487 992
Maine	414 834	2 921	2 152	59 300	43 078	7 626	7 784	14 577	88 888
Maryland	68 871	154 044	11 574	838 361	104 557	29 505	175 229	246 313	487 678
Massachusetts	354 686	114 481	17 001	3 216 495	375 026	103 874	425 464	539 263	1 667 509
Michigan	298 676	65 608	65 103	2 785 334	579 474	473 047	912 807	1 200 516	3 372 049
Minnesota	263 408	82 164	7 017	480 716	247 772	109 287	50 390	310 274	1 490 721
Mississippi	307 646	3 929	116 363	614 227	70 496	45 405	20 678	69 008	301 265
Missouri	52 672	141 523	17 848	1 498 826	160 886	32 994	163 639	239 237	741 058
Montana	28 292	148	1 330	64 788	2 201	29 559	6 992	2 974	58 795
Nebraska	7 380	13 983	358	249 362	46 547	4 164	28 415	53 165	293 551
Nevada	4 041	25 076	618	41 824	30 516	5 385	672 231	77 096	107 396
New Hampshire	42 503	16 235	1 224	101 947	62 107	46 712	19 344	76 519	388 637
New Jersey	266 534	584 042	134 532	4 591 251	443 134	169 731	1 008 529	517 902	1 122 679
New Mexico	13 290	1 580	682	31 845	18 955	26 647	12 216	65 380	72 692
New York	571 855	570 970	93 661	4 315 133	742 435	409 252	2 858 120	789 803	4 138 442
North Carolina	553 699	45 861	8 423	3 024 776	793 113	353 911	239 455	402 043	1 557 196
North Dakota	246	860	588	17 033	13 231	1 318	459	3 925	404 714
Ohio	492 394	141 602	70 296	2 834 381	1 138 613	692 292	1 001 277	1 728 345	3 595 682
Oklahoma	21 569	2 927	12 488	164 624	240 309	31 226	59 190	172 485	845 854
Oregon	252 999	34 251	62 623	410 164	79 062	76 300	164 640	160 292	870 516
Pennsylvania	329 742	261 772	159 531	2 612 347	481 013	479 314	1 438 620	669 029	2 131 447
Puerto Rico	29 007	4 266	224 639	8 189 332	54 061	13 998	103 773	45 830	147 618
Rhode Island	20 130	5 073	1 180	123 247	90 561	11 102	61 791	40 391	122 495
South Carolina	564 893	14 850	7 234	1 691 188	842 639	125 903	157 521	269 728	1 270 759
South Dakota	22 743	2 285	215	11 646	5 909	936	1 273	12 698	77 178
Tennessee	332 432	187 452	10 384	1 723 443	473 820	147 519	254 384	353 133	1 264 939
Texas	1 234 343	270 303	4 701 403	17 125 247	2 518 904	540 798	2 097 170	3 073 005	11 407 672
Utah	27 659	21 888	1 800	340 250	74 885	9 956	1 465 736	61 898	141 408
Vermont	38 654	7 654	153	40 570	21 288	8 596	7 461	48 567	126 940
Virgin Islands	33	75	183 535	38 334	308	8	22	136	608
Virginia	469 405	71 255	67 624	1 443 539	365 265	73 978	120 008	260 301	1 131 393
Washington	831 259	38 107	736 788	613 843	137 427	89 389	396 360	200 744	838 962
West Virginia	11 081	12 632	23 911	1 115 503	40 562	43 420	199 531	18 504	204 353
Wisconsin	563 187	183 638	18 505	585 332	347 310	57 191	108 745	352 939	3 217 463
Wyoming	633	21	217	437 882	1 563	1 702	821	9 018	20 229
Unallocated	394 961	285 067	263 527	994 835	674 402	291 150	413 934	1 406 258	2 462 813

Table E-2. Exports by State and Industry (NAICS Code), 2003—*Continued*

(Thousands of dollars.)

State/territory	Manufactures—Continued					Agriculture and livestock products		
	Computer and electronic products (334)	Electrical equipment, appliances, and parts (335)	Transportation equipment (336)	Furniture and related products (337)	Miscellaneous manufactures (339)	Total	Agricultural products (111)	Livestock and livestock products (112)
United States	149 993 323	23 291 636	128 854 240	2 546 044	29 401 371	31 552 607	30 358 839	1 193 767
Alabama	757 216	86 517	2 531 870	23 399	56 101	450 250	405 264	44 987
Alaska	33 623	5 318	23 963	174	3 017	688	476	211
Arizona	6 730 945	525 768	2 135 355	18 467	392 132	452 702	450 614	2 088
Arkansas	127 003	161 449	531 864	14 616	35 619	117 235	73 591	43 644
California	36 714 651	2 936 389	8 643 620	251 918	4 883 936	4 845 564	4 784 249	61 315
Colorado	3 459 736	86 763	286 034	11 176	158 563	20 607	19 399	1 207
Connecticut	789 501	336 127	3 298 121	24 504	486 357	70 754	69 316	1 438
Delaware	266 079	22 181	185 857	3 635	47 807	78 005	76 888	1 117
District of Columbia	108 865	9 719	341 448	3 614	7 329	1 317	1 312	5
Florida	7 286 686	838 896	3 727 991	99 724	1 313 724	626 665	589 731	36 934
Georgia	2 469 331	576 272	3 131 542	31 636	585 803	364 376	309 571	54 805
Hawaii	28 612	1 501	93 434	222	8 587	18 945	14 415	4 530
Idaho	1 206 062	26 794	18 372	1 619	9 012	93 205	91 341	1 865
Illinois	3 664 358	1 710 591	2 950 213	87 674	928 241	273 153	255 162	17 991
Indiana	1 588 809	545 717	5 273 478	47 959	678 986	44 077	38 693	5 384
Iowa	432 074	446 793	267 186	43 011	164 343	275 027	252 925	22 102
Kansas	339 396	90 076	1 270 860	5 758	52 260	258 889	258 500	390
Kentucky	740 343	336 285	3 706 859	22 656	123 070	448 485	20 313	428 172
Louisiana	70 400	101 578	305 441	1 604	68 389	9 388 740	9 378 683	10 057
Maine	605 224	38 446	164 442	7 853	14 522	48 189	19 604	28 585
Maryland	743 738	186 385	1 018 804	9 568	108 246	6 334	5 388	947
Massachusetts	7 687 690	592 145	382 836	17 883	1 570 636	24 917	19 647	5 271
Michigan	1 443 515	739 611	18 086 121	455 909	278 178	288 185	276 895	11 289
Minnesota	3 355 276	289 385	1 141 149	31 467	1 694 310	494 897	488 267	6 630
Mississippi	78 518	76 119	151 477	99 231	48 475	180 479	180 300	179
Missouri	483 625	371 737	2 186 811	44 812	128 269	111 387	106 900	4 487
Montana	13 281	7 077	11 424	142	8 064	26 900	23 188	3 712
Nebraska	132 079	94 630	234 949	15 763	37 595	294 351	293 527	824
Nevada	491 017	22 856	55 967	2 069	366 136	7 236	6 614	622
New Hampshire	613 788	94 675	81 227	4 230	81 086	1 425	1 001	423
New Jersey	2 555 474	479 278	1 396 754	39 183	1 065 400	164 517	161 687	2 830
New Mexico	1 812 957	27 677	86 864	568	15 174	19 713	18 596	1 117
New York	6 305 871	963 493	4 532 868	84 716	6 398 779	232 786	173 754	59 033
North Carolina	2 706 112	447 163	1 164 297	175 622	404 054	546 209	540 873	5 336
North Dakota	13 655	4 570	53 425	1 190	755	178 099	172 464	5 635
Ohio	1 782 790	1 092 247	12 502 378	145 090	528 335	241 412	223 260	18 151
Oklahoma	201 685	113 949	467 236	3 307	37 116	52 764	51 811	952
Oregon	4 601 990	136 353	1 115 550	17 580	104 414	1 289 997	1 288 098	1 899
Pennsylvania	2 057 545	803 281	1 782 665	63 456	766 310	128 069	101 629	26 439
Puerto Rico	1 797 112	281 862	39 184	1 299	385 636	15 080	15 011	69
Rhode Island	258 505	56 904	18 073	4 368	153 774	500	406	94
South Carolina	915 135	296 801	4 332 826	12 329	112 625	86 982	85 349	1 632
South Dakota	218 193	4 934	25 522	288	28 673	27 842	24 790	3 051
Tennessee	1 773 145	460 793	2 390 989	37 879	636 867	1 155 494	1 148 869	6 625
Texas	28 378 198	4 642 580	9 902 792	130 166	1 948 191	2 683 308	2 617 771	65 536
Utah	623 985	85 685	467 223	13 352	293 473	7 211	5 462	1 749
Vermont	1 975 627	44 824	78 607	4 714	33 650	8 571	846	7 725
Virgin Islands	795	14	841	34	26 141	137	137	0
Virginia	1 378 343	277 982	1 464 367	34 275	208 274	597 492	589 454	8 038
Washington	2 353 871	288 442	20 438 422	20 094	314 070	3 421 543	3 333 119	88 424
West Virginia	59 494	4 140	238 856	543	14 400	5 310	243	5 067
Wisconsin	2 042 970	548 561	1 374 288	55 839	380 567	414 950	353 309	61 641
Wyoming	20 860	2 298	5 071	37	729	1 707	1 619	89
Unallocated	3 697 568	870 003	2 736 431	317 821	1 205 172	959 932	938 507	21 426

Table E-2. U.S. Total Exports, by State and Industry (NAICS Code), 2003—*Continued*

(Thousands of dollars.)

State/territory	Total	Other commodities								
		Forestry and logging (113)	Fishing, hunting, and trapping (114)	Oil and gas extraction (211)	Mining (212)	Waste and scrap (910)	Used merchandise (920)	Goods returned to Canada (980)	Special classification provisions (990)	Publishing industries (except Internet) (511)
United States	47 284 320	1 514 647	3 056 153	2 177 138	4 020 330	6 564 409	3 440 634	1 173 075	25 002 037	335 898
Alabama	358 643	10 715	5 522	4	179 938	68 358	8 279	19 053	64 678	2 097
Alaska	2 117 042	141 422	1 401 288	148 371	418 072	1 180	692	3 614	2 404	0
Arizona	326 550	16 124	686	73	26 904	59 216	29 449	7 518	185 980	599
Arkansas	28 294	275	1 210	0	3 685	3 728	1 270	2 932	15 190	3
California	4 806 744	45 703	187 824	315 513	179 900	1 424 290	227 950	70 130	2 245 063	110 370
Colorado	165 446	840	575	4 698	40 407	18 165	10 269	33 661	56 498	333
Connecticut	315 145	4 144	3 389	34	5 842	50 714	9 578	11 150	229 744	551
Delaware	66 157	841	1 005	257	4 797	3 723	43 911	1 576	9 970	77
District of Columbia	70 703	7	152	0	114	324	17 819	2 268	50 019	0
Florida	1 021 754	14 353	104 073	4 363	33 830	222 958	138 800	32 247	430 009	41 122
Georgia	958 013	22 567	8 968	226	582 845	98 766	40 399	19 268	172 344	12 629
Hawaii	59 513	115	7 105	127	175	31 016	5 221	1 791	13 963	0
Idaho	62 050	3 903	1 100	75	39 581	3 659	2 320	3 385	8 005	23
Illinois	863 368	17 920	2 361	183 350	30 311	247 281	47 743	40 559	288 021	5 822
Indiana	238 117	16 788	1 000	399	12 761	44 560	6 523	21 888	118 816	15 381
Iowa	72 942	8 188	1 394	740	29 122	8 988	5 077	4 465	14 653	316
Kansas	145 656	2 977	294	6 144	13 740	13 199	3 249	6 194	99 816	43
Kentucky	245 934	6 965	2 347	44	69 323	28 864	2 604	22 187	107 413	6 188
Louisiana	182 108	3 182	45 120	763	43 324	56 843	4 759	6 428	21 663	26
Maine	418 640	184 867	181 322	0	157	21 705	1 650	18 634	10 293	11
Maryland	349 457	26 664	17 863	12 559	17 941	60 856	24 878	13 129	174 999	569
Massachusetts	901 677	13 311	258 499	728	3 603	190 445	68 028	25 043	335 097	6 923
Michigan	1 117 564	19 370	2 818	526 469	154 010	150 415	30 594	70 699	162 028	1 160
Minnesota	315 878	4 855	7 866	1 140	139 721	42 999	12 791	24 594	77 071	4 842
Mississippi	23 970	1 364	3 395	185	5 289	4 359	2 038	2 268	5 071	0
Missouri	141 942	19 080	1 129	79	22 067	54 156	6 824	11 624	26 866	118
Montana	61 795	107	23	7 391	31 095	6 909	2 709	11 912	1 617	31
Nebraska	180 540	1 218	261	132 749	547	4 972	11 750	4 285	24 735	23
Nevada	87 940	220	388	0	38 221	4 137	4 086	17 333	23 432	123
New Hampshire	168 200	17 788	17 908	124	954	30 987	837	6 612	91 327	1 663
New Jersey	1 341 243	51 195	25 960	35 094	30 123	819 470	118 785	22 265	233 661	4 690
New Mexico	64 442	40	9	18 123	7 050	2 962	4 970	1 818	29 470	0
New York	4 466 798	96 630	35 491	8 247	46 407	908 284	1 661 271	110 164	1 585 529	14 774
North Carolina	333 391	24 660	3 328	39	80 126	48 968	5 467	15 000	149 390	6 413
North Dakota	49 845	19	3 196	19 520	757	4 459	6 676	7 916	7 120	181
Ohio	879 553	47 478	4 654	3 903	362 774	107 555	18 287	93 905	233 890	7 108
Oklahoma	63 768	1 106	0	7 242	3 685	1 935	6 117	5 743	37 131	808
Oregon	282 441	29 690	37 308	43	7 820	123 746	8 730	30 243	44 310	551
Pennsylvania	760 746	70 901	8 047	9 776	138 247	209 005	73 311	29 690	220 439	1 330
Puerto Rico	58 825	292	67	1 241	407	45 006	1 552	677	9 582	0
Rhode Island	156 787	670	18 349	0	1 024	127 122	631	2 017	6 938	36
South Carolina	146 389	4 793	3 269	298	15 892	56 035	4 204	13 934	47 753	211
South Dakota	35 973	114	13	0	5 039	25 773	899	1 018	2 996	120
Tennessee	428 941	9 139	4 571	377	29 196	49 340	8 710	28 202	269 147	30 258
Texas	2 486 202	24 057	25 199	673 356	158 800	486 485	207 200	66 981	814 406	29 718
Utah	146 790	530	1 702	70	43 021	12 646	1 983	6 755	77 860	2 224
Vermont	76 953	24 849	2 588	0	20 316	2 768	640	10 957	14 742	94
Virgin Islands	1 132	7	5	707	62	176	13	105	56	0
Virginia	1 049 511	37 533	44 296	9 791	450 148	86 421	10 684	13 219	396 965	454
Washington	1 376 864	357 821	534 172	22 408	21 327	196 730	46 252	61 591	133 727	2 837
West Virginia	277 180	9 983	211	18	246 101	7 429	2 071	2 465	8 902	0
Wisconsin	289 463	26 517	2 521	18 260	66 468	41 782	15 015	17 424	95 119	6 358
Wyoming	74 236	23	0	308	58 470	3 488	4 337	4 358	2 596	656
Unallocated	16 565 067	90 729	34 315	1 708	98 793	239 051	460 729	110 181	15 513 522	16 038

Table E-3. Total Exports by State to Top 10 Countries, 2003

(Thousands of dollars.)

State and territory	Total	Canada	Mexico	Japan	United Kingdom	Germany	China	South Korea	Netherlands	Taiwan	France
United States	723 743 177	169 480 937	97 457 420	52 063 765	33 895 379	28 847 948	28 418 493	24 098 587	20 702 905	17 487 899	17 068 157
Alabama	8 340 387	1 547 388	751 402	481 403	442 861	1 618 008	355 756	278 896	252 857	130 128	221 344
Alaska	2 738 558	230 523	71 682	1 031 953	12 987	112 603	153 860	566 810	96 800	18 229	19 168
Arizona	13 323 392	1 131 030	3 229 462	466 430	741 864	607 019	741 260	355 319	125 615	338 537	349 843
Arkansas	2 962 153	807 413	244 903	178 063	146 763	58 559	141 452	134 839	132 797	78 039	27 758
California	93 994 882	11 231 567	14 871 836	11 754 708	4 359 964	3 559 740	5 465 042	4 833 318	3 412 235	4 443 027	1 915 067
Colorado	6 109 121	1 431 714	570 428	443 147	237 311	282 016	213 248	424 560	245 595	237 035	267 135
Connecticut	8 136 443	1 352 298	478 003	639 021	512 756	760 141	157 423	282 906	198 610	95 684	1 095 723
Delaware	1 886 118	532 982	254 317	103 709	105 802	149 092	7 215	76 382	38 544	78 381	29 934
District of Columbia	809 220	16 520	7 983	3 177	122 708	7 215	2 113	8 799	2 153	40 706	10 187
Florida	24 953 414	2 368 527	1 814 458	745 765	761 545	499 383	649 474	264 413	407 244	109 960	397 226
Georgia	16 286 235	3 961 627	1 163 241	1 517 338	1 036 087	608 989	644 199	328 482	892 811	248 918	358 360
Hawaii	368 227	19 643	515	147 915	4 512	10 761	12 876	33 613	1 736	2 293	8 741
Idaho	2 095 799	361 855	55 649	269 399	349 616	29 800	106 582	61 948	27 586	131 409	14 390
Illinois	26 472 902	8 558 822	2 152 722	1 964 149	1 543 795	1 209 481	794 203	425 381	785 555	293 934	678 979
Indiana	16 402 279	7 458 458	2 105 233	630 199	1 208 718	552 464	235 552	233 968	288 786	85 878	921 652
Iowa	5 236 296	1 870 676	669 932	576 368	210 733	213 952	92 955	115 606	89 640	55 012	204 105
Kansas	4 553 334	1 020 855	602 032	542 977	249 011	179 909	175 806	320 679	40 400	53 301	121 090
Kentucky	10 733 781	3 424 399	518 087	983 130	850 295	355 342	236 425	217 158	396 242	302 075	740 490
Louisiana	18 390 130	1 246 884	1 776 102	2 482 255	296 794	345 693	2 117 340	625 825	499 852	408 517	190 676
Maine	2 188 413	821 041	24 135	93 005	133 079	17 344	78 307	91 178	44 544	13 174	11 838
Maryland	4 940 631	943 185	300 782	310 653	324 453	183 143	193 955	84 668	189 780	101 121	149 078
Massachusetts	18 662 575	2 641 461	711 767	1 635 760	1 430 033	1 599 264	571 802	558 335	1 759 138	528 255	619 258
Michigan	32 941 109	19 799 054	4 006 426	1 099 943	706 106	973 432	366 702	363 914	278 222	233 087	380 320
Minnesota	11 265 660	2 901 515	393 394	845 593	578 912	436 290	377 559	257 188	575 124	188 368	328 448
Mississippi	2 558 259	584 287	256 252	61 422	90 551	74 564	109 409	48 719	23 695	18 630	30 547
Missouri	7 233 937	3 080 535	748 317	419 690	294 901	236 987	260 181	83 723	119 906	110 771	95 032
Montana	361 416	221 483	11 205	27 266	9 206	7 061	10 249	7 655	11 783	9 006	6 751
Nebraska	2 723 670	700 487	472 448	357 856	44 852	44 960	84 125	166 594	98 683	71 494	33 161
Nevada	2 032 599	467 543	104 465	79 171	78 635	52 037	24 387	32 192	29 023	29 354	37 114
New Hampshire	1 931 412	505 982	84 803	138 462	159 952	108 643	73 267	43 403	127 784	35 969	46 244
New Jersey	16 817 673	3 756 529	830 801	936 084	1 406 993	1 021 799	502 168	562 194	462 997	335 906	602 466
New Mexico	2 325 609	117 921	242 018	33 780	20 355	21 809	206 759	423 702	8 099	201 148	18 333
New York	39 180 708	9 041 414	1 704 740	2 625 127	3 283 052	1 723 245	1 445 174	1 056 106	832 606	621 805	1 261 289
North Carolina	16 198 733	3 896 286	1 463 759	1 590 777	687 303	610 771	649 263	393 353	328 735	287 641	360 475
North Dakota	854 072	475 560	32 216	14 824	13 548	13 348	5 741	4 951	2 665	2 585	8 254
Ohio	29 764 418	16 894 415	2 101 867	1 101 151	1 241 761	727 389	643 691	386 827	512 236	201 475	767 883
Oklahoma	2 659 603	1 054 221	221 105	146 008	79 267	53 966	64 579	25 754	43 521	9 925	49 880
Oregon	10 357 199	1 567 275	393 618	1 275 931	208 504	321 752	574 875	1 363 309	174 995	602 034	194 776
Pennsylvania	16 299 212	5 849 414	1 112 059	819 303	846 416	751 375	564 996	332 616	477 228	246 802	371 578
Puerto Rico	11 913 947	1 212 729	218 744	503 948	942 009	651 323	87 977	58 451	1 139 732	59 711	779 441
Rhode Island	1 177 475	408 102	66 879	35 384	51 261	41 284	35 816	25 242	21 413	17 018	27 666
South Carolina	11 772 894	2 598 006	751 857	476 414	816 671	2 702 653	286 945	161 354	298 907	161 096	275 052
South Dakota	672 268	288 812	123 932	51 245	37 498	25 088	10 425	6 066	5 207	5 354	3 346
Tennessee	12 611 793	4 214 228	1 475 631	528 659	646 179	439 659	636 172	236 854	399 872	178 496	220 593
Texas	98 846 083	10 808 651	41 561 359	2 707 902	2 129 828	1 582 675	3 059 559	2 777 313	1 733 003	2 765 451	905 465
Utah	4 114 540	544 251	111 216	475 556	486 528	118 689	114 031	69 854	124 437	62 773	66 324
Vermont	2 626 922	1 079 076	34 180	147 894	53 353	30 663	31 904	242 585	56 195	416 325	21 347
Virgin Islands	252 719	290	5 392	156	24	10	4 154	35 240	12 253	8 312	7
Virginia	10 852 981	2 106 019	398 995	907 608	723 959	989 887	521 175	246 813	389 232	113 848	200 464
Washington	34 172 826	3 313 881	607 417	5 428 494	1 461 635	785 635	3 211 196	1 673 219	1 739 189	1 958 436	684 058
West Virginia	2 379 808	759 463	80 579	233 491	74 305	55 974	132 576	75 027	79 933	46 305	52 179
Wisconsin	11 509 835	4 349 326	788 033	816 690	493 976	448 464	548 228	258 387	241 869	152 878	371 093
Wyoming	581 636	137 122	62 644	45 205	7 123	5 033	20 688	21 577	12 646	19 427	5 493
Unallocated	35 167 868	13 768 194	4 616 396	1 132 208	1 139 031	831 565	538 512	2 373 159	391 894	522 856	511 035

Table E-4. Total United States Exports, 1999–2003

(Top 25 commodities and top 25 countries based on 2003 dollar value.)

Industry, commodity, and country	Value (millions of dollars)					Percent change, 1999–2003	Percent share of U.S. total				
	1999	2000	2001	2002	2003		1999	2000	2001	2002	2003
TOTAL AND PERCENT SHARE OF U.S. TOTAL	692 820.6	780 418.6	731 025.9	693 257.3	723 743.2	4.46	100.00	100.00	100.00	100.00	100.00
Manufactures (NAICS Code)	627 159.9	707 185.5	656 452.6	622 000.2	644 906.2	2.83	90.52	90.62	89.80	89.72	89.11
Processed foods (311)	24 117.8	25 749.6	27 088.9	25 855.5	27 495.6	14.01	3.48	3.30	3.71	3.73	3.80
Beverages and tobacco products (312)	5 530.6	5 675.4	4 434.9	3 659.2	3 796.8	-31.35	0.80	0.00	0.61	0.53	0.52
Fabric mill products (313)	6 055.0	7 284.2	7 365.2	7 642.4	7 805.4	28.91	0.87	0.93	1.01	1.10	1.08
Non-apparel textile products (314)	2 210.5	2 332.9	2 082.8	1 981.6	2 004.5	-9.32	0.32	0.30	0.28	0.29	0.28
Apparel manufactures (315)	8 193.9	8 557.9	6 956.3	5 994.1	5 469.7	-33.25	1.18	1.10	0.95	0.86	0.76
Leather and related products (316)	2 569.7	2 687.9	2 709.2	2 593.2	2 717.2	5.74	0.37	0.34	0.37	0.37	0.38
Wood products (321)	4 858.7	5 021.9	4 099.4	3 948.2	4 036.3	-16.93	0.70	0.64	0.56	0.57	0.56
Paper products (322)	14 131.2	15 978.5	14 495.9	14 107.3	14 504.2	2.64	2.04	2.05	1.98	2.03	2.00
Printing and related products (323)	4 866.4	5 097.5	5 124.5	4 773.6	4 983.7	2.41	0.70	0.65	0.70	0.69	0.69
Petroleum and coal products (324)	6 006.6	9 028.7	8 416.4	8 048.6	9 659.0	60.81	0.87	1.16	1.15	1.16	1.33
Chemical manufactures (325)	69 870.4	80 259.3	79 034.4	80 504.2	91 017.2	30.27	10.08	10.28	10.81	11.61	12.58
Plastics and rubber products (326)	15 197.0	17 714.7	16 508.4	16 169.0	16 509.9	8.64	2.19	2.27	2.26	2.33	2.28
Non-metallic mineral products (327)	6 526.7	8 173.2	7 744.6	6 325.7	6 405.3	-1.86	0.94	1.05	1.06	0.91	0.89
Primary metal manufactures (331)	18 667.3	21 498.4	19 312.0	16 688.7	19 125.0	2.45	2.69	2.75	2.64	2.41	2.64
Fabricated metal products (332)	20 135.8	22 913.1	20 699.4	20 186.7	20 364.7	1.14	2.91	2.94	2.83	2.91	2.81
Machinery manufactures (333)	76 335.0	89 767.9	81 380.2	74 945.3	74 925.1	-1.85	11.02	11.50	11.13	10.81	10.35
Computer and electronic products (334)	161 542.9	196 234.4	165 345.2	145 847.7	149 993.3	-7.15	23.32	25.14	22.62	21.04	20.72
Electrical equipment, appliances, and parts (335)	23 716.1	27 477.7	24 922.7	22 848.3	23 291.6	-1.79	3.42	3.52	3.41	3.30	3.22
Transportation equipment (336)	132 095.3	128 255.5	130 365.2	130 897.1	128 854.2	-2.45	19.07	16.43	17.83	18.88	17.80
Furniture and related products (337)	2 562.6	3 024.5	2 588.0	2 323.4	2 546.0	-0.65	0.37	0.39	0.35	0.34	0.35
Miscellaneous manufactures (339)	21 970.3	24 452.4	25 779.0	26 660.6	29 401.4	33.82	3.17	3.13	3.53	3.85	4.06
Agricultural and Livestock Products (NAICS Code)	23 771.4	25 715.2	26 186.4	26 828.8	31 552.6	32.73	3.43	3.30	3.58	3.87	4.36
Agricultural products (111)	22 732.5	24 449.1	24 861.3	25 796.9	30 358.8	33.55	3.28	3.13	3.40	3.72	4.19
Livestock and livestock products (112)	1 038.9	1 266.1	1 325.1	1 031.9	1 193.8	14.90	0.15	0.16	0.18	0.15	0.16
Other Commodities (NAICS Code)	41 889.2	47 517.9	48 387.0	44 428.3	47 284.3	12.88	6.05	6.09	6.62	6.41	6.53
Forestry and logging (113)	1 567.8	1 673.3	1 472.4	1 449.7	1 514.6	-3.39	0.23	0.21	0.20	0.21	0.21
Fishing, hunting, and trapping (114)	2 601.3	2 810.4	2 969.4	2 940.8	3 056.2	17.49	0.38	0.36	0.41	0.42	0.42
Oil and gas extraction (211)	1 459.7	1 746.9	1 339.4	1 727.0	2 177.1	49.15	0.21	0.22	0.18	0.25	0.30
Mining (212)	4 450.9	4 537.1	4 239.6	3 910.8	4 020.3	-9.67	0.64	0.58	0.58	0.56	0.56
Waste and scrap (910)	3 623.0	5 128.6	4 823.8	5 165.3	6 564.4	81.19	0.52	0.66	0.66	0.75	0.91
Used merchandise (920)	2 848.5	4 021.2	4 644.5	3 179.3	3 440.6	20.79	0.41	0.52	0.64	0.46	0.48
Goods returned to Canada (980)	1 702.8	1 905.2	1 879.5	1 339.5	1 173.1	-31.11	0.25	0.24	0.26	0.19	0.16
Special classification provisions (990)	23 635.3	25 695.2	27 018.5	24 391.9	25 002.0	5.78	3.41	3.29	3.70	3.52	3.45
Publishing industries (except Internet) (511)	0.0	0.0	0.0	324.0	335.9	X	0.00	0.00	0.00	0.05	0.05
TOTAL AND PERCENT SHARE OF U.S. TOTAL	692 820.6	780 418.6	731 025.9	693 257.3	723 743.2	4.46	100.00	100.00	100.00	100.00	100.00
Top 25 Commodities (HS Code)	588 823.1	666 447.1	621 650.1	589 784.8	615 038.8	4.45	84.99	85.40	85.04	85.07	84.98
1. Nuclear reactors, boilers, machinery; parts (84)	137 321.1	158 919.5	145 087.1	130 206.8	130 803.6	-4.75	19.82	20.36	19.85	18.78	18.07
2. Electric machinery, sound equipment, TV equipment; parts (85)	121 600.8	148 287.2	122 558.7	110 450.7	112 597.9	-7.40	17.55	19.00	16.77	15.93	15.56
3. Vehicles, except railway or tramway, and parts (87)	58 563.1	61 927.6	58 749.5	62 511.2	65 182.4	11.30	8.45	7.94	8.04	9.02	9.01
4. Optic, photo, medic or surgical instruments (90)	38 012.0	45 019.2	44 223.9	41 177.7	44 033.5	15.84	5.49	5.77	6.05	5.94	6.08
5. Aircraft, spacecraft, and parts thereof (88)	49 628.9	40 975.7	44 705.5	43 901.1	39 669.7	-20.07	7.16	5.25	6.12	6.33	5.48
6. Plastics and articles thereof (39)	23 777.6	28 147.7	26 867.6	27 204.1	28 932.3	21.68	3.43	3.61	3.68	3.92	4.00
7. Organic chemicals (29)	17 664.3	21 023.4	19 311.7	19 434.4	23 205.8	31.37	2.55	2.69	2.64	2.80	3.21
8. Special classification provisions (98)	21 440.2	23 502.2	24 407.3	22 634.7	22 733.7	6.03	3.09	3.01	3.34	3.26	3.14
9. Pharmaceutical products (30)	8 920.9	10 531.8	12 507.8	13 073.5	15 939.4	78.67	1.29	1.35	1.71	1.89	2.20
10. Natural/cultured pearls, precious stones, precious metals, coin (71)	12 662.7	15 352.4	14 655.3	13 540.1	15 266.3	20.56	1.83	1.97	2.00	1.95	2.11
11. Mineral fuel, oil; bituminous substances; mineral waxes (27)	9 966.5	13 384.3	12 898.5	11 719.2	14 079.5	41.27	1.44	1.72	1.76	1.69	1.95
12. Miscellaneous chemical products (38)	9 548.6	10 656.7	10 591.6	10 565.4	11 326.5	18.62	1.38	1.37	1.45	1.52	1.56
13. Cereals (10)	10 338.4	9 733.4	9 653.2	10 245.0	10 679.8	3.30	1.49	1.25	1.32	1.48	1.48
14. Paper or paperboard and articles (48)	10 491.2	11 607.5	10 898.6	10 337.4	10 672.5	1.73	1.51	1.49	1.49	1.49	1.47
15. Oil seeds, miscellaneous grain, seed, fruit, plant etc. (12)	5 995.8	6 830.4	6 868.2	7 330.4	9 630.9	60.63	0.87	0.88	0.94	1.06	1.33
16. Articles of iron or steel (73)	8 119.7	9 149.2	8 321.0	8 003.0	8 166.4	0.57	1.17	1.17	1.14	1.15	1.13
17. Meat and edible meat offal (02)	5 932.9	7 063.0	6 806.7	5 910.9	6 780.8	14.29	0.86	0.91	0.93	0.85	0.94
18. Iron and steel (72)	4 239.7	5 226.6	5 007.8	4 978.7	6 639.1	56.59	0.61	0.67	0.69	0.72	0.92
19. Rubber and articles thereof (40)	6 181.2	6 943.3	6 653.9	6 446.8	6 613.5	6.99	0.89	0.89	0.91	0.93	0.91
20. Inorganic chemicals; earth metals; radioactive compounds (28)	5 074.2	5 933.8	6 123.2	5 937.5	6 087.6	19.97	0.73	0.76	0.84	0.86	0.84
21. Furniture; bedding; mattresses; cushions; lamps (94)	5 910.2	6 542.2	6 106.6	5 731.4	5 650.4	-4.40	0.85	0.84	0.84	0.83	0.78
22. Cotton, including yarn and woven fabric thereof (52)	2 473.2	3 784.6	4 032.2	3 982.7	5 229.1	111.43	0.36	0.48	0.55	0.57	0.72
23. Wood and articles of wood; wood charcoal (44)	6 081.7	6 343.3	5 278.0	5 096.6	5 181.3	-14.81	0.88	0.81	0.72	0.74	0.72
24. Aluminum and articles thereof (76)	5 346.5	5 591.0	4 976.7	4 922.5	4 996.4	-6.55	0.77	0.72	0.68	0.71	0.69
25. Essential oils and resinoid; perfumery, cosmetic preparations (33)	3 531.8	3 971.3	4 359.5	4 443.0	4 940.6	39.89	0.51	0.51	0.60	0.64	0.68

X = Not applicable.

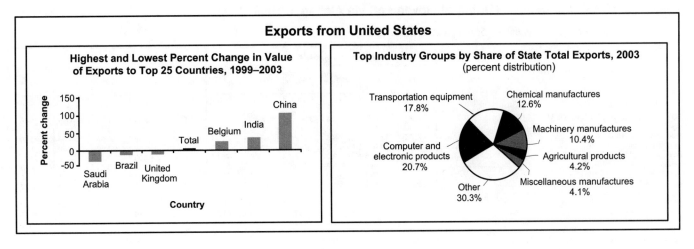

Exports from United States

Highest and Lowest Percent Change in Value of Exports to Top 25 Countries, 1999–2003

Top Industry Groups by Share of State Total Exports, 2003 (percent distribution)

Transportation equipment 17.8% · Chemical manufactures 12.6% · Machinery manufactures 10.4% · Computer and electronic products 20.7% · Agricultural products 4.2% · Miscellaneous manufactures 4.1% · Other 30.3%

- The United States' exports increased 4.4 percent from 2002 to 2003 reaching nearly $724 billion. However, this remains almost $57 billion less than the high of $780 billion in 2000.

- Computer and electronic products are the country's leading export, and amount to $150 billion, or 21 percent of total exports. Transportation equipment, the second largest export, accounts for nearly 18 percent of the United States' total exports.

- Waste and scrap exports grew more than 81 percent, from $3.6 billion in 1999 to about $6.6 billion in 2003. Exports of petroleum and coal products has the second highest growth rate, increasing almost 61 percent from 1999 to 2003.

- The top markets for U.S. exports are Canada (24 percent), Mexico (14 percent), and Japan (8 percent). Exports to China, which ranks sixth with 4 percent, increased by 116 percent from 1999 to 2003.

Table E-4. Total United States Exports, 1999–2003—Continued

(Top 25 commodities and top 25 countries based on 2003 dollar value.)

Industry, commodity, and country	Value (millions of dollars)					Percent change, 1999–2003	Percent share of U.S. total				
	1999	2000	2001	2002	2003		1999	2000	2001	2002	2003
TOTAL AND PERCENT SHARE OF U.S. TOTAL	692 820.6	780 418.6	731 025.9	693 257.3	723 743.2	4.46	100.00	100.00	100.00	100.00	100.00
Top 25 Countries	604 906.0	688 274.4	637 917.3	605 954.3	633 258.4	4.69	87.31	88.19	87.26	87.41	87.50
1. Canada	163 912.8	176 429.6	163 724.5	160 799.2	169 480.9	3.40	23.66	22.61	22.40	23.19	23.42
2. Mexico	87 044.0	111 720.9	101 509.1	97 530.6	97 457.4	11.96	12.56	14.32	13.89	14.07	13.47
3. Japan	57 483.5	65 254.4	57 639.1	51 439.6	52 063.8	-9.43	8.30	8.36	7.88	7.42	7.19
4. United Kingdom	38 337.8	41 579.4	40 797.9	33 253.1	33 895.4	-11.59	5.53	5.33	5.58	4.80	4.68
5. Germany	26 788.9	29 244.0	30 113.9	26 628.4	28 847.9	7.69	3.87	3.75	4.12	3.84	3.99
6. China	13 117.7	16 253.0	19 234.8	22 052.7	28 418.5	116.64	1.89	2.08	2.63	3.18	3.93
7. South Korea	22 954.0	27 901.9	22 196.6	22 595.9	24 098.6	4.99	3.31	3.58	3.04	3.26	3.33
8. Netherlands	19 412.1	21 973.7	19 524.7	18 334.5	20 702.9	6.65	2.80	2.82	2.67	2.64	2.86
9. Taiwan	19 121.1	24 380.3	18 151.6	18 394.3	17 487.9	-8.54	2.76	3.12	2.48	2.65	2.42
10. France	18 838.5	20 252.8	19 895.7	19 018.6	17 068.2	-9.40	2.72	2.60	2.72	2.74	2.36
11. Singapore	16 246.4	17 816.4	17 691.6	16 221.2	16 575.7	2.03	2.34	2.28	2.42	2.34	2.29
12. Belgium	12 384.9	13 960.1	13 523.6	13 342.6	15 217.9	22.87	1.79	1.79	1.85	1.92	2.10
13. Hong Kong	12 647.1	14 625.2	14 072.4	12 611.6	13 542.1	7.08	1.83	1.87	1.93	1.82	1.87
14. Australia	11 810.7	12 459.7	10 944.8	13 083.9	13 103.8	10.95	1.70	1.60	1.50	1.89	1.81
15. Brazil	13 249.0	15 359.6	15 928.6	12 408.8	11 218.3	-15.33	1.91	1.97	2.18	1.79	1.55
16. Malaysia	9 079.0	10 995.7	9 380.2	10 348.1	10 920.6	20.28	1.31	1.41	1.28	1.49	1.51
17. Italy	10 094.0	10 999.8	9 916.1	10 089.0	10 570.1	4.72	1.46	1.41	1.36	1.46	1.46
18. Switzerland	8 364.7	9 942.5	9 835.1	7 781.9	8 660.1	3.53	1.21	1.27	1.35	1.12	1.20
19. Philippines	7 226.2	8 790.2	7 664.5	7 270.2	7 992.2	10.60	1.04	1.13	1.05	1.05	1.10
20. Ireland	6 374.7	7 726.5	7 149.6	6 749.0	7 698.5	20.77	0.92	0.99	0.98	0.97	1.06
21. Israel	7 694.5	7 750.3	7 482.3	7 039.3	6 878.4	-10.61	1.11	0.99	1.02	1.02	0.95
22. Spain	6 131.6	6 322.9	5 810.9	5 225.7	5 935.3	-3.20	0.89	0.81	0.79	0.75	0.82
23. Thailand	4 983.5	6 642.5	5 995.1	4 859.5	5 841.7	17.22	0.72	0.85	0.82	0.70	0.81
24. India	3 707.4	3 662.8	3 764.2	4 097.9	4 986.3	34.50	0.54	0.47	0.51	0.59	0.69
25. Saudi Arabia	7 901.7	6 230.3	5 970.5	4 778.5	4 596.0	-41.84	1.14	0.80	0.82	0.69	0.64

Table E-5. Total U.S. Exports (Origin of Movement) via Alabama, 1999–2003

(Top 25 commodities and top 25 countries based on 2003 dollar value.)

Industry, commodity, and country	Value (millions of dollars)					Percent change, 1999–2003	Percent share of state total				
	1999	2000	2001	2002	2003		1999	2000	2001	2002	2003
TOTAL AND PERCENT SHARE OF U.S. TOTAL	6 192.4	7 317.0	7 570.4	8 266.9	8 340.4	34.69	0.89	0.94	1.04	1.19	1.15
Manufactures (NAICS Code)	5 718.2	6 693.8	6 858.5	7 476.9	7 531.5	31.71	92.34	91.48	90.60	90.44	90.30
Processed foods (311)	89.2	116.0	127.6	124.1	118.8	33.11	1.44	1.58	1.69	1.50	1.42
Beverages and tobacco products (312)	6.1	7.3	8.0	6.0	1.5	-75.27	0.10	0.00	0.11	0.07	0.02
Fabric mill products (313)	128.9	213.9	260.7	204.9	197.4	53.19	2.08	2.92	3.44	2.48	2.37
Non-apparel textile products (314)	63.3	76.4	69.9	50.3	48.4	-23.54	1.02	1.04	0.92	0.61	0.58
Apparel manufactures (315)	255.1	342.2	321.1	306.4	489.3	91.85	4.12	4.68	4.24	3.71	5.87
Leather and related products (316)	2.1	0.9	1.7	1.7	1.9	-9.34	0.03	0.01	0.02	0.02	0.02
Wood products (321)	310.7	234.0	187.7	139.6	98.5	-68.31	5.02	3.20	2.48	1.69	1.18
Paper products (322)	569.5	711.6	613.2	633.6	658.3	15.60	9.20	9.72	8.10	7.66	7.89
Printing and related products (323)	3.8	4.1	5.4	7.7	4.7	24.38	0.06	0.06	0.07	0.09	0.06
Petroleum and coal products (324)	6.3	2.2	6.8	3.4	10.5	66.33	0.10	0.03	0.09	0.04	0.13
Chemical manufactures (325)	825.0	1 118.4	1 200.5	1 317.7	1 264.3	53.26	13.32	15.28	15.86	15.94	15.16
Plastics and rubber products (326)	209.9	223.7	210.4	200.6	215.5	2.67	3.39	3.06	2.78	2.43	2.58
Non-metallic mineral products (327)	63.9	85.8	94.2	68.1	75.4	18.02	1.03	1.17	1.24	0.82	0.90
Primary metal manufactures (331)	228.7	257.1	245.3	309.0	305.4	33.53	3.69	3.51	3.24	3.74	3.66
Fabricated metal products (332)	123.3	179.0	214.6	183.1	123.3	-0.03	1.99	2.45	2.83	2.22	1.48
Machinery manufactures (333)	293.8	322.0	352.3	361.1	463.0	57.61	4.74	4.40	4.65	4.37	5.55
Computer and electronic products (334)	879.6	1 043.9	861.6	918.9	757.2	-13.92	14.20	14.27	11.38	11.12	9.08
Electrical equipment, appliances, and parts (335)	87.8	95.1	84.8	96.0	86.5	-1.42	1.42	1.30	1.12	1.16	1.04
Transportation equipment (336)	1 500.6	1 573.6	1 905.4	2 462.6	2 531.9	68.72	24.23	21.51	25.17	29.79	30.36
Furniture and related products (337)	25.7	39.7	34.7	27.3	23.4	-9.06	0.42	0.54	0.46	0.33	0.28
Miscellaneous manufactures (339)	44.8	46.9	52.8	54.9	56.1	25.10	0.72	0.64	0.70	0.66	0.67
Agricultural and Livestock Products (NAICS Code)	218.8	210.6	377.2	380.4	450.3	105.78	3.53	2.88	4.98	4.60	5.40
Agricultural products (111)	210.4	200.5	356.2	341.1	405.3	92.60	3.40	2.74	4.70	4.13	4.86
Livestock and livestock products (112)	8.4	10.1	21.0	39.3	45.0	437.03	0.14	0.14	0.28	0.48	0.54
Other Commodities (NAICS Code)	255.5	412.7	334.7	409.6	358.6	40.39	4.13	5.64	4.42	4.95	4.30
Forestry and logging (113)	22.9	30.8	12.0	5.7	10.7	-53.23	0.37	0.42	0.16	0.07	0.13
Fishing, hunting, and trapping (114)	9.3	18.6	4.7	6.2	5.5	-40.39	0.15	0.25	0.06	0.08	0.07
Oil and gas extraction (211)	0.0	1.4	0.3	0.6	0.0	X	0.00	0.02	0.00	0.01	0.00
Mining (212)	114.6	224.3	154.2	164.6	179.9	57.02	1.85	3.07	2.04	1.99	2.16
Waste and scrap (910)	27.3	43.9	61.5	103.8	68.4	150.83	0.44	0.60	0.81	1.26	0.82
Used merchandise (920)	6.5	7.1	6.1	6.8	8.3	27.15	0.11	0.10	0.08	0.08	0.10
Goods returned to Canada (980)	11.1	10.0	12.0	34.8	19.1	71.03	0.18	0.14	0.16	0.42	0.23
Special classification provisions (990)	63.8	76.6	83.9	87.0	64.7	1.44	1.03	1.05	1.11	1.05	0.78
Publishing industries (except Internet) (511)	0.0	0.0	0.0	0.0	2.1	X	0.00	0.00	0.00	0.00	0.03
TOTAL AND PERCENT SHARE OF U.S. TOTAL	6 192.4	7 317.0	7 570.4	8 266.9	8 340.4	34.69	0.89	0.94	1.04	1.19	1.15
Top 25 Commodities (HS Code)	2 767.0	3 235.2	3 138.2	4 330.6	4 781.8	72.82	44.68	44.21	41.45	52.38	57.33
1. Passenger vehicles, spark-ignition, > 3,000 cc (870324)	752.9	651.9	509.0	1 327.9	1 699.1	125.67	12.16	8.91	6.72	16.06	20.37
2. Soybeans, whether or not broken (120100)	187.5	161.7	297.5	250.0	310.1	65.39	3.03	2.21	3.93	3.02	3.72
3. Passenger vehicle, spark-ignition, > 1,500 cc < 3,000 cc (870323)	47.1	36.2	140.6	389.6	256.6	444.80	0.76	0.49	1.86	4.71	3.08
4. Kraft paper/paperboard, excluding graphic (481039)	185.7	125.9	137.9	160.9	197.4	6.30	3.00	1.72	1.82	1.95	2.37
5. Lenses, prisms, mirrors, and optical elements (900190)	8.8	22.9	48.2	67.1	174.5	1 882.95	0.14	0.31	0.64	0.81	2.09
6. Parts and accessories for automatic data processing (847330)	84.7	144.6	82.5	208.9	171.6	102.60	1.37	1.98	1.09	2.53	2.06
7. Chemical wood-pulp, semi- or bleached non-coniferous (470329)	144.4	241.6	168.5	170.3	170.2	17.87	2.33	3.30	2.23	2.06	2.04
8. Phenol (hydroxybenzene) and its salts (290711)	0.0	22.8	44.1	58.9	164.2	X	0.00	0.31	0.58	0.71	1.97
9. Polycarbonates in primary forms (390740)	128.2	203.7	160.2	235.9	159.1	24.10	2.07	2.78	2.12	2.85	1.91
10. Parts and accessories of motor vehicles (870899)	305.4	321.3	229.1	180.9	158.6	-48.07	4.93	4.39	3.03	2.19	1.90
11. Parts of airplanes or helicopters (880330)	165.8	150.5	181.7	162.5	155.4	-6.27	2.68	2.06	2.40	1.97	1.86
12. Bituminous coal, not agglomerated (270112)	98.5	183.8	138.4	150.0	149.3	51.57	1.59	2.51	1.83	1.81	1.79
13. Chemical wood-pulp, unbleached non-coniferous (470321)	101.2	174.4	160.9	142.5	137.7	36.07	1.63	2.38	2.13	1.72	1.65
14. Automatic regulating instruments and apparatus (903289)	258.1	273.7	229.1	189.8	135.1	-47.66	4.17	3.74	3.03	2.30	1.62
15. Products and residuals of chemical industry (382490)	63.0	57.1	94.1	74.9	92.9	47.46	1.02	0.78	1.24	0.91	1.11
16. Cotton, not carded or combed (520100)	11.6	24.9	47.7	65.5	81.8	605.17	0.19	0.34	0.63	0.79	0.98
17. Acetone (propanone) (291411)	. . .	13.1	13.7	28.8	78.2	. . .	. . .	0.18	0.18	0.35	0.94
18. Aluminum alloy rectangular plates, > 0.2 mm thick (760612)	70.1	89.4	100.0	92.7	68.2	-2.71	1.13	1.22	1.32	1.12	0.82
19. Magnetic tape unrecorded, width > 6.5 mm (852313)	79.0	59.9	52.5	71.5	67.1	-15.06	1.28	0.82	0.69	0.86	0.80
20. Men's or boys' trousers, not knit, cotton (620342)	. . .	60.1	49.8	42.2	61.0	. . .	. . .	0.82	0.66	0.51	0.73
21. New pneumatic tires of rubber, for buses or trucks (401120)	. . .	48.7	51.4	49.1	60.4	. . .	. . .	0.67	0.68	0.59	0.72
22. Terephthalic acid and its salts (291736)	2.2	0.0	62.1	91.7	59.4	2 600.00	0.04	0.00	0.82	1.11	0.71
23. New pneumatic tires of rubber, for motor cars (401110)	72.8	70.0	68.2	66.1	59.2	-18.68	1.18	0.96	0.90	0.80	0.71
24. Parts of garments and clothing accessories (621790)	. . .	14.7	13.7	10.9	59.0	. . .	. . .	0.20	0.18	0.13	0.71
25. Women's or girls' trousers, not knit, cotton (620462)	. . .	82.3	57.3	42.0	55.7	. . .	. . .	1.12	0.76	0.51	0.67

X = Not applicable.
. . . = Not available.

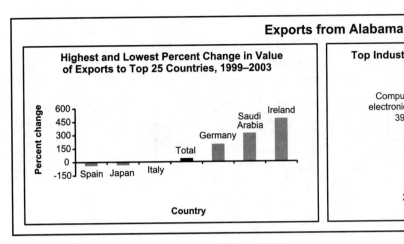

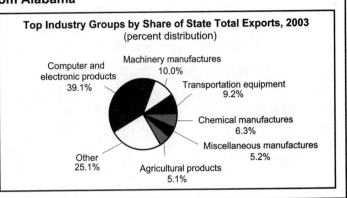

Exports from Alabama

Highest and Lowest Percent Change in Value of Exports to Top 25 Countries, 1999–2003

Top Industry Groups by Share of State Total Exports, 2003
(percent distribution)

- The value of Alabama's total exports grew by more than $2 billion from 1999 to 2003. This is primarily a result of an increase of more than $1.1 billion worth of exports to Germany, the state's top purchaser, over the same period.

- In 2003, Alabama exported more than $1.6 billion worth of goods to Germany, which ranked the state fourth in the nation, behind California, South Carolina, and New York.

- Transportation equipment is Alabama's largest export to Germany, as well as the state's largest export overall. Passenger motor vehicles with spark-ignition internal combustion of various capacities are Alabama's first and third most valuable commodity exports; and soybeans rank second.

- Among the industries experiencing the largest export declines since 1999 are wood exports, which fell by $212 million, or about 68 percent, and computer and electronic products, which decreased by $122 million, or nearly 14 percent.

Table E-5. Total U.S. Exports (Origin of Movement) via Alabama, 1999–2003—*Continued*

(Top 25 commodities and top 25 countries based on 2003 dollar value.)

Industry, commodity, and country	Value (millions of dollars)					Percent change, 1999–2003	Percent share of state total				
	1999	2000	2001	2002	2003		1999	2000	2001	2002	2003
TOTAL AND PERCENT SHARE OF U.S. TOTAL	6 192.4	7 317.0	7 570.4	8 266.9	8 340.4	34.69	0.89	0.94	1.04	1.19	1.15
Top 25 Countries	5 324.7	6 094.5	6 293.0	7 268.0	7 548.4	41.76	85.99	83.29	83.13	87.92	90.50
1. Germany	461.9	455.9	592.8	1 381.0	1 618.0	250.28	7.46	6.23	7.83	16.71	19.40
2. Canada	1 573.2	1 640.1	1 596.3	1 687.7	1 547.4	-1.64	25.41	22.41	21.09	20.42	18.55
3. Mexico	507.8	695.5	656.5	661.9	751.4	47.98	8.20	9.51	8.67	8.01	9.01
4. Japan	636.7	650.6	619.7	513.7	481.4	-24.39	10.28	8.89	8.19	6.21	5.77
5. United Kingdom	352.0	319.7	442.0	504.5	442.9	25.81	5.68	4.37	5.84	6.10	5.31
6. China	102.1	160.5	209.8	234.3	355.8	248.43	1.65	2.19	2.77	2.83	4.27
7. South Korea	130.7	180.1	127.3	194.2	278.9	113.42	2.11	2.46	1.68	2.35	3.34
8. Netherlands	250.1	258.3	214.5	228.4	252.9	1.11	4.04	3.53	2.83	2.76	3.03
9. France	246.1	297.8	317.4	229.7	221.3	-10.07	3.97	4.07	4.19	2.78	2.65
10. Honduras	109.3	125.6	120.3	127.4	170.5	55.98	1.76	1.72	1.59	1.54	2.04
11. Brazil	102.5	139.7	144.9	142.3	137.6	34.28	1.65	1.91	1.91	1.72	1.65
12. Ireland	22.4	31.3	78.4	183.0	134.4	501.50	0.36	0.43	1.04	2.21	1.61
13. Taiwan	97.2	76.0	85.3	97.0	130.1	33.88	1.57	1.04	1.13	1.17	1.56
14. Australia	113.6	134.1	143.8	122.9	125.2	10.21	1.83	1.83	1.90	1.49	1.50
15. Italy	124.5	169.0	224.7	147.1	111.4	-10.51	2.01	2.31	2.97	1.78	1.34
16. Belgium	72.6	112.7	137.2	144.2	105.6	45.44	1.17	1.54	1.81	1.74	1.27
17. Hong Kong	59.7	97.4	103.3	131.9	104.4	74.83	0.96	1.33	1.37	1.60	1.25
18. Saudi Arabia	19.6	42.4	71.3	58.1	91.5	366.91	0.32	0.58	0.94	0.70	1.10
19. Thailand	24.9	22.3	43.0	79.1	81.4	226.75	0.40	0.30	0.57	0.96	0.98
20. Dominican Republic	53.2	62.4	73.4	96.6	75.1	41.01	0.86	0.85	0.97	1.17	0.90
21. Singapore	75.2	192.4	71.5	84.2	74.3	-1.13	1.21	2.63	0.94	1.02	0.89
22. Costa Rica	24.9	75.8	59.9	62.4	70.1	181.71	0.40	1.04	0.79	0.76	0.84
23. El Salvador	33.3	31.6	47.7	53.7	65.8	97.31	0.54	0.43	0.63	0.65	0.79
24. Spain	81.5	88.9	85.2	59.6	60.5	-25.72	1.32	1.22	1.12	0.72	0.73
25. Colombia	49.7	34.5	27.0	43.3	60.5	21.80	0.80	0.47	0.36	0.52	0.73

Table E-6. Total U.S. Exports (Origin of Movement) via Alaska, 1999–2003

(Top 25 commodities and top 25 countries based on 2003 dollar value.)

Industry, commodity, and country	Value (millions of dollars)					Percent change, 1999–2003	Percent share of state total				
	1999	2000	2001	2002	2003		1999	2000	2001	2002	2003
TOTAL AND PERCENT SHARE OF U.S. TOTAL	2 563.8	2 464.1	2 418.3	2 516.2	2 738.6	6.82	0.37	0.32	0.33	0.36	0.38
Manufactures (NAICS Code)	395.5	501.0	586.7	507.7	620.8	56.96	15.43	20.33	24.26	20.18	22.67
Processed foods (311)	71.8	76.5	97.7	65.1	54.5	-24.09	2.80	3.11	4.04	2.59	1.99
Beverages and tobacco products (312)	0.0	0.0	0.8	0.0	0.1	X	0.00	0.00	0.03	0.00	0.00
Fabric mill products (313)	0.6	1.1	0.3	0.2	0.2	-73.20	0.02	0.04	0.01	0.01	0.01
Non-apparel textile products (314)	0.6	0.3	0.2	0.1	0.3	-49.21	0.02	0.01	0.01	0.01	0.01
Apparel manufactures (315)	0.8	0.6	0.7	0.5	0.2	-73.98	0.03	0.02	0.03	0.02	0.01
Leather and related products (316)	0.2	0.1	0.1	0.4	0.2	17.37	0.01	0.01	0.00	0.01	0.01
Wood products (321)	28.5	25.1	13.8	8.6	10.8	-62.15	1.11	1.02	0.57	0.34	0.39
Paper products (322)	11.8	7.5	1.4	0.7	0.8	-93.05	0.46	0.30	0.06	0.03	0.03
Printing and related products (323)	0.2	0.2	0.3	0.2	0.3	50.00	0.01	0.01	0.01	0.01	0.01
Petroleum and coal products (324)	66.0	122.4	134.1	130.3	152.5	130.94	2.58	4.97	5.54	5.18	5.57
Chemical manufactures (325)	131.2	160.2	202.4	166.4	202.0	54.01	5.12	6.50	8.37	6.61	7.38
Plastics and rubber products (326)	1.3	3.1	5.6	2.9	5.1	285.31	0.05	0.12	0.23	0.11	0.19
Non-metallic mineral products (327)	0.4	0.3	0.3	0.2	0.2	-44.53	0.02	0.01	0.01	0.01	0.01
Primary metal manufactures (331)	2.2	2.8	3.9	52.5	97.4	4 302.44	0.09	0.11	0.16	2.09	3.56
Fabricated metal products (332)	16.0	2.1	4.3	2.5	8.7	-45.50	0.62	0.09	0.18	0.10	0.32
Machinery manufactures (333)	15.7	23.9	27.7	17.5	21.5	36.81	0.61	0.97	1.15	0.70	0.78
Computer and electronic products (334)	16.2	20.5	25.0	24.0	33.6	107.83	0.63	0.83	1.03	0.96	1.23
Electrical equipment, appliances, and parts (335)	3.3	2.3	5.6	5.2	5.3	60.71	0.13	0.09	0.23	0.21	0.19
Transportation equipment (336)	26.1	46.3	54.9	28.4	24.0	-8.33	1.02	1.88	2.27	1.13	0.88
Furniture and related products (337)	0.5	0.2	0.6	0.7	0.2	-66.08	0.02	0.01	0.02	0.03	0.01
Miscellaneous manufactures (339)	2.1	5.5	7.0	1.2	3.0	43.26	0.08	0.22	0.29	0.05	0.11
Agricultural and Livestock Products (NAICS Code)	2.1	4.5	4.8	0.5	0.7	-67.75	0.08	0.18	0.20	0.02	0.03
Agricultural products (111)	1.1	4.1	3.0	0.4	0.5	-54.80	0.04	0.16	0.13	0.02	0.02
Livestock and livestock products (112)	1.1	0.5	1.7	0.2	0.2	-80.41	0.04	0.02	0.07	0.01	0.01
Other Commodities (NAICS Code)	2 166.1	1 958.6	1 826.9	2 007.9	2 117.0	-2.27	84.49	79.49	75.54	79.80	77.31
Forestry and logging (113)	194.0	184.4	141.6	120.5	141.4	-27.10	7.57	7.48	5.86	4.79	5.16
Fishing, hunting, and trapping (114)	950.9	1 023.1	1 184.3	1 350.8	1 401.3	47.37	37.09	41.52	48.97	53.68	51.17
Oil and gas extraction (211)	641.1	432.9	145.1	140.9	148.4	-76.86	25.01	17.57	6.00	5.60	5.42
Mining (212)	373.7	309.2	345.7	389.0	418.1	11.87	14.58	12.55	14.29	15.46	15.27
Waste and scrap (910)	0.1	0.5	1.6	1.0	1.2	1 866.67	0.00	0.02	0.07	0.04	0.04
Used merchandise (920)	0.9	0.3	0.8	0.3	0.7	-21.54	0.03	0.01	0.03	0.01	0.03
Goods returned to Canada (980)	3.5	6.2	4.7	3.3	3.6	4.24	0.14	0.25	0.19	0.13	0.13
Special classification provisions (990)	2.0	2.1	3.1	2.1	2.4	17.79	0.08	0.09	0.13	0.08	0.09
Publishing industries (except Internet) (511)	0.0	0.0	0.0	0.0	0.0	X	0.00	0.00	0.00	0.00	0.00
TOTAL AND PERCENT SHARE OF U.S. TOTAL	2 563.8	2 464.1	2 418.3	2 516.2	2 738.6	6.82	0.37	0.32	0.33	0.36	0.38
Top 25 Commodities (HS Code)	1 551.8	1 614.7	1 818.0	2 314.1	2 545.1	64.01	60.53	65.53	75.18	91.97	92.94
1. Zinc ores and concentrates (260800)	309.2	242.6	268.8	314.3	328.8	6.34	12.06	9.85	11.12	12.49	12.01
2. Fish meat, excluding fish steaks, chilled or frozen (030490)	244.4	243.2	252.9	339.8	316.4	29.46	9.53	9.87	10.46	13.50	11.55
3. Fish livers and roes, frozen (030380)	136.3	196.0	261.1	273.4	294.4	115.99	5.32	7.95	10.80	10.87	10.75
4. Fertilizers (310000)	112.8	154.0	189.8	161.6	199.0	76.42	4.40	6.25	7.85	6.42	7.27
5. Natural gas, liquefied (271111)	140.9	145.1	145.1	140.9	148.4	5.32	5.50	5.89	6.00	5.60	5.42
6. Coniferous wood in the rough, not treated (440320)	193.9	184.3	141.6	119.7	141.2	-27.18	7.56	7.48	5.86	4.76	5.16
7. Fish fillets, frozen (030420)	31.6	22.3	118.6	165.9	134.1	324.37	1.23	0.90	4.90	6.59	4.90
8. Fish, with bones, frozen (030379)	78.3	85.8	79.6	92.9	124.8	59.39	3.05	3.48	3.29	3.69	4.56
9. Cod, except fillets, livers, and roes, frozen (030360)	48.8	73.6	91.3	87.1	107.4	120.08	1.90	2.99	3.78	3.46	3.92
10. Light oils and preparations (not crude) from petroleum (271011)	0.0	0.0	0.0	74.5	97.0	X	0.00	0.00	0.00	2.96	3.54
11. Gold, non-monetary, unwrought (710812)	0.0	0.1	0.2	43.1	92.4	X	0.00	0.00	0.01	1.71	3.37
12. Lead ores and concentrates (260700)	25.6	30.0	51.3	65.4	85.0	232.03	1.00	1.22	2.12	2.60	3.10
13. Sockeye salmon, excluding fillets, livers, and roes, frozen (030311)	0.0	0.0	0.0	74.2	82.5	X	0.00	0.00	0.00	2.95	3.01
14. Petroleum oils from bituminous mineral (not crude) (271019)	0.0	0.0	0.0	55.7	55.5	X	0.00	0.00	0.00	2.21	2.03
15. Crabs, including in shell, frozen (030614)	88.1	51.4	25.1	38.4	54.6	-38.02	3.44	2.09	1.04	1.53	1.99
16. Flat fish, except fillets, livers, roes, frozen (030339)	54.3	59.6	48.5	52.7	49.5	-8.84	2.12	2.42	2.01	2.09	1.81
17. Pacific salmon, excluding fillets, liver, roe, frozen (030319)	0.0	0.0	0.0	46.2	48.9	X	0.00	0.00	0.00	1.84	1.79
18. Flour meal and pellet of fish crustaceans, inedible (230120)	8.9	36.2	34.7	37.9	36.8	313.48	0.35	1.47	1.43	1.51	1.34
19. Cod, except fillets, livers, and roes, fresh, chilled (030250)	1.7	2.1	10.8	32.5	32.4	1 805.88	0.07	0.09	0.45	1.29	1.18
20. Halibut and Greenland turbot (030221)	3.3	4.6	17.7	26.4	30.9	836.36	0.13	0.19	0.73	1.05	1.13
21. Pacific, Atlantic, and Danube salmon (030212)	26.9	17.6	11.8	28.5	29.8	10.78	1.05	0.71	0.49	1.13	1.09
22. Flours, meals and pellets of fish, for human consumption (030510)	1.5	16.5	9.0	12.1	15.2	913.33	0.06	0.67	0.37	0.48	0.56
23. Herrings, except fillets, livers, and roes, frozen (030350)	. . .	15.5	20.2	4.4	14.0	. . .	. . .	0.63	0.84	0.17	0.51
24. Fish liver and roe, dried, smoked, salted, or in brine (030520)	36.7	26.4	27.3	13.2	13.2	-64.03	1.43	1.07	1.13	0.52	0.48
25. Parts of airplanes or helicopters (880330)	8.6	7.9	12.8	13.3	12.9	50.00	0.34	0.32	0.53	0.53	0.47

X = Not applicable.

. . . = Not available.

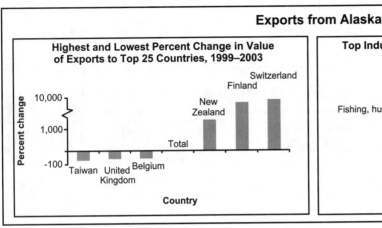

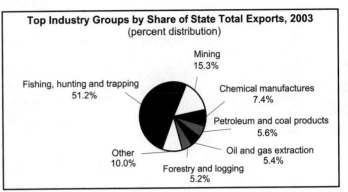

- In 2003, Alaska exported goods worth $2.7 billion, an increase of 6.8 percent from 1999. The fishing, hunting, and trapping industry's exports rose from $951 million in 1999 to $1.4 billion in 2003, solidifying its position as the state's top export. Mining is Alaska's second most valuable industry, with exports worth $418 million.

- Over half of Alaska's top 25 commodities are related to fishing. However, the state's number one commodity is zinc ores and concentrates, which are worth $329 million. Coniferous wood exports, valued at $194 million in 1999, dropped to $142 million in 2003.

- Japan is Alaska's number one market for exports. In 2003, over $1 billion worth of goods were exported from Alaska to Japan. In 1999, Alaska exported less than $1 million worth of goods to Switzerland. By 2003, exports increased to nearly $94 million, placing Switzerland among the top ten countries receiving goods from Alaska. Nearly all (98.7 percent) of the new exports were from the primary metal industry.

Table E-6. Total U.S. Exports (Origin of Movement) via Alaska, 1999–2003—*Continued*

(Top 25 commodities and top 25 countries based on 2003 dollar value.)

Industry, commodity, and country	Value (millions of dollars)					Percent change, 1999–2003	Percent share of state total				
	1999	2000	2001	2002	2003		1999	2000	2001	2002	2003
TOTAL AND PERCENT SHARE OF U.S. TOTAL	2 563.8	2 464.1	2 418.3	2 516.2	2 738.6	6.82	0.37	0.32	0.33	0.36	0.38
Top 25 Countries	2 512.0	2 399.1	2 366.9	2 481.5	2 703.5	7.62	97.98	97.36	97.87	98.62	98.72
1. Japan	1 330.1	1 316.0	1 039.0	1 105.2	1 032.0	-22.42	51.88	53.40	42.96	43.92	37.68
2. South Korea	486.7	448.6	463.1	416.6	566.8	16.46	18.98	18.20	19.15	16.56	20.70
3. Canada	202.8	165.2	188.0	155.0	230.5	13.68	7.91	6.70	7.78	6.16	8.42
4. China	110.9	103.2	102.4	147.8	153.9	38.79	4.32	4.19	4.24	5.88	5.62
5. Germany	21.6	33.8	115.1	117.5	112.6	420.49	0.84	1.37	4.76	4.67	4.11
6. Netherlands	10.1	3.4	30.8	82.8	96.8	857.66	0.39	0.14	1.27	3.29	3.53
7. Switzerland	1.0	3.2	2.1	47.4	93.6	9 693.31	0.04	0.13	0.09	1.89	3.42
8. Mexico	35.3	36.8	82.4	63.3	71.7	103.06	1.38	1.49	3.41	2.51	2.62
9. Belgium	109.5	104.8	81.5	50.4	51.5	-53.01	4.27	4.25	3.37	2.00	1.88
10. Hong Kong	7.2	5.7	9.5	15.4	50.0	593.38	0.28	0.23	0.39	0.61	1.82
11. Spain	4.6	2.3	7.1	67.7	38.0	732.49	0.18	0.09	0.29	2.69	1.39
12. Thailand	20.0	18.9	33.1	31.0	32.6	62.79	0.78	0.77	1.37	1.23	1.19
13. France	12.7	16.5	16.2	24.8	19.2	50.54	0.50	0.67	0.67	0.99	0.70
14. Taiwan	66.9	46.5	30.9	25.0	18.2	-72.76	2.61	1.89	1.28	0.99	0.67
15. Italy	3.3	5.4	23.0	20.1	16.8	404.16	0.13	0.22	0.95	0.80	0.61
16. Australia	17.2	15.2	30.9	21.8	16.6	-3.53	0.67	0.62	1.28	0.87	0.61
17. Finland	0.2	0.1	16.0	0.1	16.5	9 430.06	0.01	0.00	0.66	0.00	0.60
18. Norway	6.2	13.1	20.7	19.8	16.3	164.60	0.24	0.53	0.86	0.79	0.60
19. United Kingdom	34.8	34.1	27.3	24.0	13.0	-62.68	1.36	1.38	1.13	0.96	0.47
20. Portugal	25.5	10.5	23.7	17.9	12.4	-51.44	0.99	0.43	0.98	0.71	0.45
21. Colombia	1.5	4.8	1.7	2.7	11.1	624.31	0.06	0.19	0.07	0.11	0.40
22. United Arab Emirates	1.0	0.8	0.1	0.3	11.0	1 042.49	0.04	0.03	0.01	0.01	0.40
23. Denmark	2.5	3.1	6.8	6.5	9.7	290.48	0.10	0.13	0.28	0.26	0.35
24. Lithuania	0.0	0.8	4.3	8.6	7.3	X	0.00	0.03	0.18	0.34	0.26
25. New Zealand	0.4	6.4	11.1	9.6	5.6	1 324.05	0.02	0.26	0.46	0.38	0.21

X = Not applicable.

Table E-7. Total U.S. Exports (Origin of Movement) via Arizona, 1999–2003

(Top 25 commodities and top 25 countries based on 2003 dollar value.)

Industry, commodity, and country	Value (millions of dollars) 1999	2000	2001	2002	2003	Percent change, 1999–2003	Percent share of state total 1999	2000	2001	2002	2003
TOTAL AND PERCENT SHARE OF U.S. TOTAL	11 823.8	14 333.7	12 513.5	11 871.0	13 323.4	12.68	1.71	1.84	1.71	1.71	1.84
Manufactures (NAICS Code)	11 215.7	13 549.3	11 747.4	11 251.5	12 544.1	11.84	94.86	94.53	93.88	94.78	94.15
Processed foods (311)	108.1	134.1	152.5	174.7	260.7	141.09	0.91	0.94	1.22	1.47	1.96
Beverages and tobacco products (312)	10.2	5.0	3.9	7.2	6.0	-40.61	0.09	0.00	0.03	0.06	0.05
Fabric mill products (313)	33.7	37.7	40.5	51.0	77.3	129.25	0.29	0.26	0.32	0.43	0.58
Non-apparel textile products (314)	55.3	28.3	16.5	20.1	23.1	-58.17	0.47	0.20	0.13	0.17	0.17
Apparel manufactures (315)	80.9	75.5	50.3	32.5	25.9	-68.01	0.68	0.53	0.40	0.27	0.19
Leather and related products (316)	12.8	13.4	11.5	10.3	26.3	105.95	0.11	0.09	0.09	0.09	0.20
Wood products (321)	16.1	14.6	14.5	22.7	21.3	31.90	0.14	0.10	0.12	0.19	0.16
Paper products (322)	240.3	209.0	189.7	171.9	179.4	-25.35	2.03	1.46	1.52	1.45	1.35
Printing and related products (323)	17.6	48.7	27.2	22.8	27.3	55.47	0.15	0.34	0.22	0.19	0.20
Petroleum and coal products (324)	26.0	42.1	43.6	25.0	9.6	-63.29	0.22	0.29	0.35	0.21	0.07
Chemical manufactures (325)	236.5	240.1	213.7	210.0	233.3	-1.32	2.00	1.68	1.71	1.77	1.75
Plastics and rubber products (326)	371.7	557.0	497.9	409.6	381.8	2.72	3.14	3.89	3.98	3.45	2.87
Non-metallic mineral products (327)	48.1	56.5	49.2	27.7	20.2	-58.11	0.41	0.39	0.39	0.23	0.15
Primary metal manufactures (331)	187.0	272.8	165.3	131.7	109.6	-41.39	1.58	1.90	1.32	1.11	0.82
Fabricated metal products (332)	525.7	765.2	594.6	525.7	531.5	1.11	4.45	5.34	4.75	4.43	3.99
Machinery manufactures (333)	667.9	908.6	801.5	684.1	808.3	21.01	5.65	6.34	6.40	5.76	6.07
Computer and electronic products (334)	5 827.0	6 883.6	5 506.6	5 539.8	6 730.9	15.51	49.28	48.02	44.01	46.67	50.52
Electrical equipment, appliances, and parts (335)	582.7	673.5	501.9	547.3	525.8	-9.78	4.93	4.70	4.01	4.61	3.95
Transportation equipment (336)	1 867.5	2 240.8	2 512.9	2 262.1	2 135.4	14.34	15.79	15.63	20.08	19.06	16.03
Furniture and related products (337)	17.7	18.6	15.3	11.7	18.5	4.39	0.15	0.13	0.12	0.10	0.14
Miscellaneous manufactures (339)	282.9	324.2	338.2	363.5	392.1	38.62	2.39	2.26	2.70	3.06	2.94
Agricultural and Livestock Products (NAICS Code)	283.6	337.0	410.1	357.4	452.7	59.60	2.40	2.35	3.28	3.01	3.40
Agricultural products (111)	268.2	316.4	392.1	349.1	450.6	68.02	2.27	2.21	3.13	2.94	3.38
Livestock and livestock products (112)	15.5	20.6	18.0	8.3	2.1	-86.49	0.13	0.14	0.14	0.07	0.02
Other Commodities (NAICS Code)	324.4	447.3	356.0	262.1	326.5	0.66	2.74	3.12	2.85	2.21	2.45
Forestry and logging (113)	2.1	10.7	9.1	5.2	16.1	669.27	0.02	0.07	0.07	0.04	0.12
Fishing, hunting, and trapping (114)	2.0	1.2	0.8	0.6	0.7	-65.73	0.02	0.01	0.01	0.01	0.01
Oil and gas extraction (211)	7.5	4.3	7.7	2.6	0.1	-99.03	0.06	0.03	0.06	0.02	0.00
Mining (212)	77.6	53.9	27.0	18.7	26.9	-65.35	0.66	0.38	0.22	0.16	0.20
Waste and scrap (910)	23.7	90.0	79.1	69.4	59.2	149.92	0.20	0.63	0.63	0.58	0.44
Used merchandise (920)	20.1	29.3	22.8	22.1	29.4	46.67	0.17	0.20	0.18	0.19	0.22
Goods returned to Canada (980)	12.9	14.7	18.7	10.0	7.5	-41.59	0.11	0.10	0.15	0.08	0.06
Special classification provisions (990)	178.5	243.2	190.8	133.3	186.0	4.18	1.51	1.70	1.52	1.12	1.40
Publishing industries (except Internet) (511)	0.0	0.0	0.0	0.0	0.6	X	0.00	0.00	0.00	0.00	0.00
TOTAL AND PERCENT SHARE OF U.S. TOTAL	11 823.8	14 333.7	12 513.5	11 871.0	13 323.4	12.68	1.71	1.84	1.71	1.71	1.84
Top 25 Commodities (HS Code)	3 072.1	4 383.8	4 106.1	7 031.0	8 165.2	165.79	25.98	30.58	32.81	59.23	61.28
1. Digital monolithic integrated circuits (854221)	0.0	0.0	0.0	2 728.3	3 963.3	X	0.00	0.00	0.00	22.98	29.75
2. Airplane and aircraft, unladen weight > 15,000 kg (880240)	72.3	376.5	146.4	265.1	478.1	561.27	0.61	2.63	1.17	2.23	3.59
3. Non-digital monolithic integrated circuits (854229)	0.0	0.0	0.0	667.0	460.5	X	0.00	0.00	0.00	5.62	3.46
4. Parts of airplanes or helicopters (880330)	376.1	446.5	612.0	570.1	423.3	12.55	3.18	3.12	4.89	4.80	3.18
5. Turbojet and turbo-propeller parts (841191)	456.8	461.1	439.0	387.1	370.2	-18.96	3.86	3.22	3.51	3.26	2.78
6. Airplanes and aircraft, unladen wgt > 2,000 kg < 15,000 kg (880230)	129.0	207.5	430.3	488.6	262.6	103.57	1.09	1.45	3.44	4.12	1.97
7. Appliances worn, carried, implanted in body and part (902190)	110.2	148.2	146.1	169.4	183.5	66.52	0.93	1.03	1.17	1.43	1.38
8. Variable or adjustable (pre-set) capacitors (853230)	...	10.4	8.5	3.3	179.8	...	...	0.07	0.07	0.03	1.35
9. Articles of plastics (392690)	211.2	378.7	327.2	216.9	168.4	-20.27	1.79	2.64	2.61	1.83	1.26
10. Wire, rods, tubes, plates, electrodes-base metal (831190)	3.6	24.2	50.0	66.4	153.9	4 175.00	0.03	0.17	0.40	0.56	1.16
11. Bomb mines other ammunitions projections and parts (930690)	119.7	210.3	120.9	125.6	149.0	24.48	1.01	1.47	0.97	1.06	1.12
12. Turbojets of a thrust < 25 kn (84111)	171.0	172.6	319.0	187.1	146.0	-14.62	1.45	1.20	2.55	1.58	1.10
13. Cotton, not carded or combed (520100)	62.0	113.7	146.2	111.6	138.2	122.90	0.52	0.79	1.17	0.94	1.04
14. Electrical apparatus, switches, relays, fuses (853690)	78.8	0.0	0.0	0.0	0.0	-100.00	0.67	0.00	0.00	0.00	0.00
15. Parts and accessories for automatic data processing (847330)	252.5	216.5	200.7	120.2	135.2	-46.46	2.14	1.51	1.60	1.01	1.01
16. Instruments, aeronautical-space nav., no compass (901420)	136.8	153.8	173.1	160.3	112.7	-17.62	1.16	1.07	1.38	1.35	0.85
17. Machine and mechanical appliance, individual function (847989)	147.3	278.9	183.2	126.7	106.9	-27.43	1.25	1.95	1.46	1.07	0.80
18. Diodes, excluding photosensitive or light-emitting (854110)	101.8	206.9	101.5	86.7	105.4	3.54	0.86	1.44	0.81	0.73	0.79
19. Electric plugs and sockets, voltage < 1,000 v (853669)	121.4	236.7	151.9	116.0	98.5	-18.86	1.03	1.65	1.21	0.98	0.74
20. Digital processing units (847150)	112.4	138.3	102.0	69.3	91.8	-18.33	0.95	0.96	0.82	0.58	0.69
21. Parts of apparatus for line telephony or telegraphy (851790)	20.6	82.1	102.5	97.9	91.7	345.15	0.17	0.57	0.82	0.82	0.69
22. Parts, electric apparatus, electric circuit (853890)	262.7	195.8	74.3	97.0	90.9	-65.40	2.22	1.37	0.59	0.82	0.68
23. Printed circuits (853400)	125.9	182.3	105.0	79.2	90.0	-28.51	1.06	1.27	0.84	0.67	0.68
24. Turbojets of a thrust > 25 kn (841112)	...	96.0	129.0	65.3	83.7	...	...	0.67	1.03	0.55	0.63
25. Electrical apparatus for line telephony or telegraphy (851750)	...	46.8	37.3	25.9	81.6	...	...	0.33	0.30	0.22	0.61

X = Not applicable.
. . . = Not available.

Exports from Arizona

Highest and Lowest Percent Change in Value of Exports to Top 25 Countries, 1999–2003

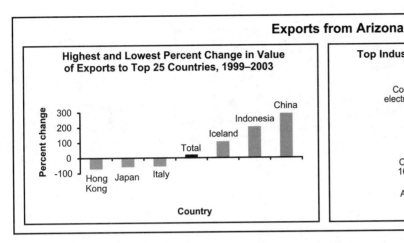

Top Industry Groups by Share of State Total Exports, 2003
(percent distribution)

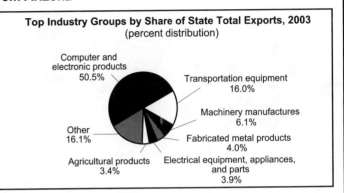

- Computer and electronic products accounted for just over 50 percent, or $6.7 billion, of Arizona's exports in 2003. The transportation industry's exports had the second highest value with $2.1 billion. From 1999 to 2003, both industries' exports grew at rates slightly higher than the state's total growth, which was less than 13 percent.

- Mexico, which shares a border with Arizona, is the top recipient of the state's exports. These exports, valued at $3.2 billion, account for about one-fourth of total exports. In 2003, Arizona exported $1.6 billion worth of goods to Malaysia, ranking the state third, after Texas and California. About 96 percent of those exports were computer and electronic products. Arizona's exports to China increased to $741 million in 2003, up from $193 million in 1999.

- Livestock and livestock products fell to $2 million in 2003, a drop of more than 86 percent from 1999. Oil and gas extraction exports fell from over $7 million in 1999 to just $73,000 in 2003.

Table E-7. Total U.S. Exports (Origin of Movement) via Arizona, 1999–2003—*Continued*

(Top 25 commodities and top 25 countries based on 2003 dollar value.)

Industry, commodity, and country	Value (millions of dollars)					Percent change, 1999–2003	Percent share of state total				
	1999	2000	2001	2002	2003		1999	2000	2001	2002	2003
TOTAL AND PERCENT SHARE OF U.S. TOTAL	11 823.8	14 333.7	12 513.5	11 871.0	13 323.4	12.68	1.71	1.84	1.71	1.71	1.84
Top 25 Countries	11 280.6	13 411.4	11 762.5	11 255.5	12 551.0	11.26	95.41	93.57	94.00	94.82	94.20
1. Mexico	3 251.0	4 651.7	3 581.3	3 044.2	3 229.5	-0.66	27.50	32.45	28.62	25.64	24.24
2. Malaysia	985.1	924.1	915.3	1 211.0	1 628.8	65.33	8.33	6.45	7.31	10.20	12.22
3. Canada	1 193.7	1 490.8	1 335.7	1 167.3	1 131.0	-5.25	10.10	10.40	10.67	9.83	8.49
4. United Kingdom	827.1	925.0	984.0	928.0	741.9	-10.30	6.99	6.45	7.86	7.82	5.57
5. China	193.2	152.1	141.9	380.4	741.3	283.69	1.63	1.06	1.13	3.20	5.56
6. Germany	475.0	445.2	594.5	525.1	607.0	27.79	4.02	3.11	4.75	4.42	4.56
7. Singapore	320.4	436.5	380.9	343.9	509.7	59.06	2.71	3.05	3.04	2.90	3.83
8. Japan	843.0	489.8	478.4	327.8	466.4	-44.67	7.13	3.42	3.82	2.76	3.50
9. Philippines	270.8	269.3	221.9	376.9	444.1	63.98	2.29	1.88	1.77	3.17	3.33
10. South Korea	319.4	397.9	286.8	253.4	355.3	11.23	2.70	2.78	2.29	2.13	2.67
11. France	508.1	556.9	632.0	442.6	349.8	-31.14	4.30	3.88	5.05	3.73	2.63
12. Taiwan	482.1	621.9	332.2	374.4	338.5	-29.78	4.08	4.34	2.65	3.15	2.54
13. Thailand	154.1	385.3	335.2	329.1	322.9	109.52	1.30	2.69	2.68	2.77	2.42
14. Switzerland	162.5	195.9	178.2	245.2	265.5	63.42	1.37	1.37	1.42	2.07	1.99
15. Costa Rica	99.1	127.4	107.9	166.9	233.0	135.18	0.84	0.89	0.86	1.41	1.75
16. Hong Kong	394.2	406.6	304.6	271.8	176.9	-55.12	3.33	2.84	2.43	2.29	1.33
17. Ireland	82.2	58.9	95.1	96.5	160.0	94.65	0.70	0.41	0.76	0.81	1.20
18. Australia	131.8	150.8	124.2	195.4	158.4	20.14	1.12	1.05	0.99	1.65	1.19
19. Israel	74.2	116.8	89.4	153.8	139.4	87.83	0.63	0.82	0.71	1.30	1.05
20. Netherlands	118.8	109.5	122.2	102.3	125.6	5.75	1.00	0.76	0.98	0.86	0.94
21. Brazil	112.0	322.4	230.4	138.9	120.1	7.23	0.95	2.25	1.84	1.17	0.90
22. Indonesia	31.1	16.6	50.2	24.6	95.0	205.50	0.26	0.12	0.40	0.21	0.71
23. Italy	148.3	84.5	155.6	86.9	83.9	-43.38	1.25	0.59	1.24	0.73	0.63
24. Belgium	77.3	74.9	84.6	68.8	64.1	-17.14	0.65	0.52	0.68	0.58	0.48
25. Iceland	26.1	0.6	0.2	0.3	62.7	139.90	0.22	0.00	0.00	0.00	0.47

Table E-8. Total U.S. Exports (Origin of Movement) via Arkansas, 1999–2003

(Top 25 commodities and top 25 countries based on 2003 dollar value.)

Industry, commodity, and country	Value (millions of dollars)					Percent change, 1999–2003	Percent share of state total				
	1999	2000	2001	2002	2003		1999	2000	2001	2002	2003
TOTAL AND PERCENT SHARE OF U.S. TOTAL	2 177.5	2 599.3	2 911.2	2 803.6	2 962.2	36.03	0.31	0.33	0.40	0.40	0.41
Manufactures (NAICS Code)	2 070.7	2 496.0	2 789.9	2 659.5	2 816.6	36.02	95.10	96.03	95.83	94.86	95.09
Processed foods (311)	417.6	510.2	640.6	469.3	575.1	37.72	19.18	19.63	22.01	16.74	19.42
Beverages and tobacco products (312)	15.9	25.9	27.0	31.3	31.5	98.82	0.73	0.00	0.93	1.12	1.06
Fabric mill products (313)	16.6	24.1	32.4	42.6	37.8	127.87	0.76	0.93	1.11	1.52	1.28
Non-apparel textile products (314)	13.1	4.1	3.7	4.0	5.9	-55.21	0.60	0.16	0.13	0.14	0.20
Apparel manufactures (315)	66.1	105.0	23.8	12.9	9.5	-85.64	3.04	4.04	0.82	0.46	0.32
Leather and related products (316)	2.0	2.3	1.9	2.3	2.1	5.82	0.09	0.09	0.07	0.08	0.07
Wood products (321)	21.9	19.0	15.0	12.8	12.2	-44.33	1.01	0.73	0.52	0.46	0.41
Paper products (322)	165.2	190.5	216.2	195.1	194.7	17.84	7.59	7.33	7.43	6.96	6.57
Printing and related products (323)	31.6	68.3	75.7	64.7	43.9	39.02	1.45	2.63	2.60	2.31	1.48
Petroleum and coal products (324)	9.0	23.2	50.7	11.3	4.0	-54.90	0.41	0.89	1.74	0.40	0.14
Chemical manufactures (325)	306.1	396.1	390.2	354.9	431.4	40.94	14.06	15.24	13.41	12.66	14.56
Plastics and rubber products (326)	66.1	68.4	74.6	98.3	90.6	36.94	3.04	2.63	2.56	3.51	3.06
Non-metallic mineral products (327)	13.4	13.3	12.3	9.9	8.7	-35.11	0.61	0.51	0.42	0.35	0.29
Primary metal manufactures (331)	100.2	100.6	111.0	85.8	117.0	16.80	4.60	3.87	3.81	3.06	3.95
Fabricated metal products (332)	141.2	124.8	151.8	98.1	130.4	-7.63	6.48	4.80	5.22	3.50	4.40
Machinery manufactures (333)	187.9	257.8	253.9	246.9	251.3	33.74	8.63	9.92	8.72	8.81	8.48
Computer and electronic products (334)	93.8	117.6	110.0	88.9	127.0	35.46	4.31	4.52	3.78	3.17	4.29
Electrical equipment, appliances, and parts (335)	150.1	171.0	176.6	164.2	161.4	7.54	6.89	6.58	6.07	5.86	5.45
Transportation equipment (336)	207.5	220.8	375.6	613.5	531.9	156.27	9.53	8.49	12.90	21.88	17.96
Furniture and related products (337)	13.3	17.8	15.7	16.2	14.6	9.92	0.61	0.68	0.54	0.58	0.49
Miscellaneous manufactures (339)	32.2	35.3	31.1	36.6	35.6	10.54	1.48	1.36	1.07	1.31	1.20
Agricultural and Livestock Products (NAICS Code)	76.8	70.9	97.4	120.4	117.2	52.70	3.53	2.73	3.35	4.29	3.96
Agricultural products (111)	40.8	38.2	53.7	74.0	73.6	80.37	1.87	1.47	1.85	2.64	2.48
Livestock and livestock products (112)	36.0	32.7	43.7	46.4	43.6	21.31	1.65	1.26	1.50	1.66	1.47
Other Commodities (NAICS Code)	30.0	32.4	23.9	23.8	28.3	-5.78	1.38	1.25	0.82	0.85	0.96
Forestry and logging (113)	0.1	0.3	0.2	0.3	0.3	85.81	0.01	0.01	0.01	0.01	0.01
Fishing, hunting, and trapping (114)	1.4	1.3	0.8	0.1	1.2	-11.36	0.06	0.05	0.03	0.00	0.04
Oil and gas extraction (211)	0.1	0.0	0.0	0.2	0.0	X	0.00	0.00	0.00	0.01	0.00
Mining (212)	5.7	6.8	4.2	10.2	3.7	-35.00	0.26	0.26	0.15	0.36	0.12
Waste and scrap (910)	2.5	3.5	2.3	3.4	3.7	50.32	0.11	0.14	0.08	0.12	0.13
Used merchandise (920)	0.3	0.5	1.9	0.5	1.3	379.25	0.01	0.02	0.07	0.02	0.04
Goods returned to Canada (980)	4.2	5.2	4.7	4.0	2.9	-29.42	0.19	0.20	0.16	0.14	0.10
Special classification provisions (990)	15.9	14.6	9.7	5.1	15.2	-4.20	0.73	0.56	0.33	0.18	0.51
Publishing industries (except Internet) (511)	0.0	0.0	0.0	0.0	0.0	X	0.00	0.00	0.00	0.00	0.00
TOTAL AND PERCENT SHARE OF U.S. TOTAL	2 177.5	2 599.3	2 911.2	2 803.6	2 962.2	36.03	0.31	0.33	0.40	0.40	0.41
Top 25 Commodities (HS Code)	765.2	1 008.8	1 335.4	1 520.5	1 604.1	109.63	35.14	38.81	45.87	54.23	54.15
1. Chicken cuts and edible offal, frozen (020714)	226.8	337.0	454.3	302.2	347.6	53.26	10.42	12.97	15.61	10.78	11.73
2. Airplane and aircraft, unladen weight > 15,000 kg (880240)	0.0	0.0	165.0	423.6	240.9	X	0.00	0.00	5.67	15.11	8.13
3. Airplanes and aircraft, unladen wgt > 2,000 kg < 15,000 kg (880230)	. . .	16.1	59.2	0.8	118.6	. . .	. . .	0.62	2.03	0.03	4.00
4. Paper, paperboard coated with plastic, > 150 g/m2 (481151)	0.0	0.0	0.0	96.7	110.0	X	0.00	0.00	0.00	3.45	3.71
5. Rice, semi-or whole milled, polished or not (100630)	59.1	54.0	58.1	53.9	93.6	58.38	2.71	2.08	2.00	1.92	3.16
6. Phenol or phenol-alcohol derivative, halogen subs. (290810)	45.0	67.3	54.9	61.4	86.3	91.78	2.07	2.59	1.89	2.19	2.91
7. Combined refrigerator-freezers, separate doors (841810)	62.4	64.9	75.6	72.2	60.9	-2.40	2.87	2.50	2.60	2.58	2.06
8. Herbicides, anti-sprouting products, retail (380830)	53.6	41.5	56.4	48.9	52.3	-2.43	2.46	1.60	1.94	1.74	1.77
9. Aromatic ethers and their halo, sulfonated derivatives (290930)	26.4	40.6	32.2	29.5	40.9	54.92	1.21	1.56	1.11	1.05	1.38
10. Road wheels, parts and accessories for motor vehicles (870870)	60.0	61.0	42.7	45.0	40.1	-33.17	2.76	2.35	1.47	1.61	1.35
11. Air conditioning machine with refrigerating unit (841582)	30.8	31.7	34.4	31.3	38.2	24.03	1.41	1.22	1.18	1.12	1.29
12. Printed or illustrated post cards, greeting cards (490900)	25.1	60.9	65.8	58.4	37.1	47.81	1.15	2.34	2.26	2.08	1.25
13. Suspension shock absorbers for motor vehicles (870880)	17.1	24.3	20.3	27.0	34.2	100.00	0.79	0.93	0.70	0.96	1.15
14. Rice husked (brown) (100620)	26.8	26.2	15.4	27.7	33.3	24.25	1.23	1.01	0.53	0.99	1.12
15. Birds' eggs, in shell, fresh, preserved, or cooked (040700)	27.4	22.1	25.4	31.6	30.4	10.95	1.26	0.85	0.87	1.13	1.03
16. Liqueurs and cordials (220870)	6.5	10.4	13.4	27.8	29.1	347.69	0.30	0.40	0.46	0.99	0.98
17. Kraft paper, weighing 225 g/m or more (480452)	29.7	24.7	23.3	17.9	28.8	-3.03	1.36	0.95	0.80	0.64	0.97
18. Rice in the husk (paddy or rough) (100610)	23.5	14.9	7.4	26.7	25.6	8.94	1.08	0.57	0.25	0.95	0.86
19. Chain saws (846781)	11.0	33.2	39.8	34.0	25.0	127.27	0.51	1.28	1.37	1.21	0.84
20. Surface-active, washing, preparations (340290)	0.3	4.2	14.6	17.2	23.7	7 800.00	0.01	0.16	0.50	0.61	0.80
21. Color TVs with or without radios (852812)	. . .	12.6	16.5	12.1	23.1	. . .	. . .	0.48	0.57	0.43	0.78
22. Halogenated derivatives of hydrocarbons (290369)	. . .	11.8	14.8	6.7	22.0	. . .	. . .	0.45	0.51	0.24	0.74
23. Soap, organic surface-active products, toilet use (340111)	25.9	27.0	21.8	18.7	21.6	-16.60	1.19	1.04	0.75	0.67	0.73
24. Casing, oil or gas drilling, iron or steel (730620)	. . .	13.2	7.2	7.7	20.7	. . .	. . .	0.51	0.25	0.27	0.70
25. Tanks and other armored fighting vehicles and parts (871000)	8.1	9.2	16.9	42.3	20.1	148.15	0.37	0.35	0.58	1.51	0.68

X = Not applicable.
. . . = Not available.

Exports from Arkansas

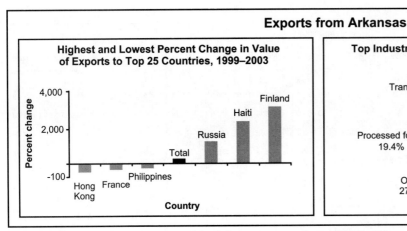

Highest and Lowest Percent Change in Value of Exports to Top 25 Countries, 1999–2003

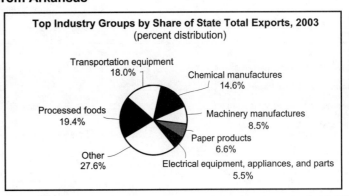

Top Industry Groups by Share of State Total Exports, 2003
(percent distribution)

- Arkansas' exports increased by 36 percent, or about $785 million, from 1999 to 2003, compared with less than 5 percent growth for total U.S. exports. Arkansas ranks third among the 50 states, after Nevada and South Carolina, by rate of growth during this four-year period.

- The transportation industry accounts for about 40 percent of the state's growth, as transportation exports increased from about $208 million in 1999 to $532 million in 2003. Canada is the recipient of 27 percent of Arkansas's exports, with machinery manufactures and transportation equipment each worth about $100 million.

- Processed foods are Arkansas's most valuable export, and Russia is the top market for these exports. From 1999 to 2003, total exports to Russia increased from $10 million to $173 million, 99.8 percent of which were processed foods.

- Chicken cuts and edible offal is the state's number one commodity, and compose nearly 12 percent of Arkansas' total exports. Apparel manufactures exports dropped from $66 million in 1999 to less than $10 million in 2003.

Table E-8. Total U.S. Exports (Origin of Movement) via Arkansas, 1999–2003—*Continued*

(Top 25 commodities and top 25 countries based on 2003 dollar value.)

Industry, commodity, and country	Value (millions of dollars)					Percent change, 1999–2003	Percent share of state total				
	1999	2000	2001	2002	2003		1999	2000	2001	2002	2003
TOTAL AND PERCENT SHARE OF U.S. TOTAL	2 177.5	2 599.3	2 911.2	2 803.6	2 962.2	36.03	0.31	0.33	0.40	0.40	0.41
Top 25 Countries	1 918.9	2 253.9	2 512.8	2 282.9	2 688.4	40.10	88.13	86.71	86.31	81.43	90.76
1. Canada	789.2	848.2	916.6	811.1	807.4	2.30	36.24	32.63	31.48	28.93	27.26
2. Mexico	176.3	201.2	199.6	249.4	244.9	38.90	8.10	7.74	6.86	8.89	8.27
3. Japan	201.3	226.2	224.0	181.3	178.1	-11.56	9.25	8.70	7.69	6.47	6.01
4. Russia	10.3	160.2	297.3	167.8	173.4	1 576.41	0.48	6.16	10.21	5.99	5.86
5. United Kingdom	70.2	99.8	104.8	99.6	146.8	109.02	3.22	3.84	3.60	3.55	4.95
6. China	15.2	29.3	38.5	43.6	141.5	830.97	0.70	1.13	1.32	1.56	4.78
7. South Korea	63.4	91.3	99.7	97.8	134.8	112.70	2.91	3.51	3.43	3.49	4.55
8. Netherlands	65.6	78.3	51.5	58.1	132.8	102.45	3.01	3.01	1.77	2.07	4.48
9. Brazil	41.5	46.5	45.5	74.9	81.6	96.54	1.91	1.79	1.56	2.67	2.75
10. Hong Kong	166.0	103.7	109.1	81.3	81.5	-50.92	7.62	3.99	3.75	2.90	2.75
11. Taiwan	25.6	36.3	42.4	56.7	78.0	204.45	1.18	1.39	1.46	2.02	2.63
12. Italy	20.1	20.5	27.2	15.5	63.3	214.45	0.92	0.79	0.93	0.55	2.14
13. Belgium	56.0	62.6	62.6	47.6	62.4	11.40	2.57	2.41	2.15	1.70	2.11
14. Germany	27.0	36.1	32.3	39.7	58.6	116.97	1.24	1.39	1.11	1.42	1.98
15. Finland	1.4	4.4	9.5	13.9	53.0	3 719.01	0.06	0.17	0.33	0.50	1.79
16. Australia	40.7	45.2	47.2	60.4	52.5	29.04	1.87	1.74	1.62	2.15	1.77
17. Haiti	1.1	0.3	0.1	8.1	29.1	2 610.23	0.05	0.01	0.00	0.29	0.98
18. France	46.0	38.2	35.4	57.7	27.8	-39.63	2.11	1.47	1.22	2.06	0.94
19. Singapore	16.1	24.3	18.1	20.9	26.2	62.79	0.74	0.94	0.62	0.75	0.89
20. Cambodia	0.0	0.0	0.0	0.1	24.9	X	0.00	0.00	0.00	0.01	0.84
21. Saudi Arabia	22.4	25.9	18.6	34.9	23.8	6.55	1.03	1.00	0.64	1.24	0.80
22. Philippines	30.6	32.9	41.2	16.6	20.3	-33.65	1.41	1.26	1.41	0.59	0.69
23. El Salvador	22.8	25.5	16.3	18.7	17.2	-24.60	1.05	0.98	0.56	0.67	0.58
24. Angola	1.2	6.4	8.7	6.9	14.3	1 101.51	0.05	0.25	0.30	0.25	0.48
25. Israel	8.8	10.6	66.8	20.0	14.0	59.56	0.40	0.41	2.30	0.71	0.47

X = Not applicable.

Table E-9. Total U.S. Exports (Origin of Movement) via California, 1999–2003

(Top 25 commodities and top 25 countries based on 2003 dollar value.)

Industry, commodity, and country	Value (millions of dollars)					Percent change, 1999–2003	Percent share of state total				
	1999	2000	2001	2002	2003		1999	2000	2001	2002	2003
TOTAL AND PERCENT SHARE OF U.S. TOTAL	97 920.1	119 640.4	106 777.0	92 214.3	93 994.9	-4.01	14.13	15.33	14.61	13.30	12.99
Manufactures (NAICS Code)	90 809.8	111 529.0	98 431.0	84 052.9	84 342.6	-7.12	92.74	93.22	92.18	91.15	89.73
Processed foods (311)	3 199.2	3 433.7	3 900.6	3 550.9	4 168.2	30.29	3.27	2.87	3.65	3.85	4.43
Beverages and tobacco products (312)	590.1	621.8	660.3	655.5	742.8	25.88	0.60	0.00	0.62	0.71	0.79
Fabric mill products (313)	407.6	464.4	553.7	613.8	650.3	59.56	0.42	0.39	0.52	0.67	0.69
Non-apparel textile products (314)	140.8	149.8	152.9	150.4	156.7	11.28	0.14	0.13	0.14	0.16	0.17
Apparel manufactures (315)	1 018.3	1 128.9	1 119.9	1 115.6	1 040.5	2.17	1.04	0.94	1.05	1.21	1.11
Leather and related products (316)	200.2	247.1	259.9	214.5	264.3	31.99	0.20	0.21	0.24	0.23	0.28
Wood products (321)	412.9	473.1	428.7	392.7	402.7	-2.47	0.42	0.40	0.40	0.43	0.43
Paper products (322)	958.5	1 090.3	1 066.3	1 051.4	1 069.2	11.55	0.98	0.91	1.00	1.14	1.14
Printing and related products (323)	595.8	661.5	667.1	578.8	546.5	-8.28	0.61	0.55	0.62	0.63	0.58
Petroleum and coal products (324)	700.6	921.5	1 007.3	834.1	892.2	27.36	0.72	0.77	0.94	0.90	0.95
Chemical manufactures (325)	4 016.0	4 774.7	5 189.5	5 417.8	5 963.7	48.50	4.10	3.99	4.86	5.88	6.34
Plastics and rubber products (326)	1 324.9	1 672.2	1 639.2	1 537.9	1 575.1	18.88	1.35	1.40	1.54	1.67	1.68
Non-metallic mineral products (327)	485.1	740.9	800.4	733.4	540.0	11.32	0.50	0.62	0.75	0.80	0.57
Primary metal manufactures (331)	957.8	1 270.5	1 114.3	1 013.0	1 167.5	21.89	0.98	1.06	1.04	1.10	1.24
Fabricated metal products (332)	1 915.6	2 095.6	2 450.3	2 157.9	2 298.7	20.00	1.96	1.75	2.29	2.34	2.45
Machinery manufactures (333)	8 720.7	13 774.4	10 695.3	9 517.6	9 433.9	8.18	8.91	11.51	10.02	10.32	10.04
Computer and electronic products (334)	49 457.2	61 442.8	50 311.4	39 671.9	36 714.7	-25.76	50.51	51.36	47.12	43.02	39.06
Electrical equipment, appliances, and parts (335)	2 897.2	3 967.2	3 325.3	2 988.5	2 936.4	1.35	2.96	3.32	3.11	3.24	3.12
Transportation equipment (336)	8 800.8	8 157.7	8 445.3	7 099.7	8 643.6	-1.79	8.99	6.82	7.91	7.70	9.20
Furniture and related products (337)	253.1	332.8	273.3	259.9	251.9	-0.47	0.26	0.28	0.26	0.28	0.27
Miscellaneous manufactures (339)	3 757.4	4 108.2	4 369.8	4 497.7	4 883.9	29.98	3.84	3.43	4.09	4.88	5.20
Agricultural and Livestock Products (NAICS Code)	2 925.8	3 650.1	3 962.9	4 036.6	4 845.6	65.62	2.99	3.05	3.71	4.38	5.16
Agricultural products (111)	2 859.2	3 589.9	3 916.5	3 990.9	4 784.2	67.33	2.92	3.00	3.67	4.33	5.09
Livestock and livestock products (112)	66.6	60.2	46.5	45.7	61.3	-7.98	0.07	0.05	0.04	0.05	0.07
Other Commodities (NAICS Code)	4 184.5	4 461.3	4 383.0	4 124.8	4 806.7	14.87	4.27	3.73	4.10	4.47	5.11
Forestry and logging (113)	43.6	33.0	36.0	41.9	45.7	4.71	0.04	0.03	0.03	0.05	0.05
Fishing, hunting, and trapping (114)	170.2	199.4	190.9	177.0	187.8	10.36	0.17	0.17	0.18	0.19	0.20
Oil and gas extraction (211)	35.0	75.2	53.2	70.2	315.5	800.62	0.04	0.06	0.05	0.08	0.34
Mining (212)	99.5	136.8	138.7	115.5	179.9	80.82	0.10	0.11	0.13	0.13	0.19
Waste and scrap (910)	602.4	899.0	1 040.7	1 059.6	1 424.3	136.44	0.62	0.75	0.97	1.15	1.52
Used merchandise (920)	283.1	308.8	247.6	215.5	228.0	-19.48	0.29	0.26	0.23	0.23	0.24
Goods returned to Canada (980)	129.7	146.1	152.5	89.9	70.1	-45.93	0.13	0.12	0.14	0.10	0.07
Special classification provisions (990)	2 820.9	2 662.8	2 523.4	2 355.2	2 245.1	-20.41	2.88	2.23	2.36	2.55	2.39
Publishing industries (except Internet) (511)	0.0	0.0	0.0	0.0	110.4	X	0.00	0.00	0.00	0.00	0.12
TOTAL AND PERCENT SHARE OF U.S. TOTAL	97 920.1	119 640.4	106 777.0	92 214.3	93 994.9	-4.01	14.13	15.33	14.61	13.30	12.99
Top 25 Commodities (HS Code)	28 360.4	39 021.9	33 614.7	34 336.9	34 207.7	20.62	28.96	32.62	31.48	37.24	36.39
1. Digital monolithic integrated circuits (854221)	0.0	0.0	0.0	6 430.1	5 793.5	X	0.00	0.00	0.00	6.97	6.16
2. Parts, accessories, automatic data processing machines (847330)	6 993.3	9 594.8	7 095.4	4 914.8	4 625.5	-33.86	7.14	8.02	6.65	5.33	4.92
3. Parts of airplanes or helicopters (880330)	3 457.9	3 348.1	3 777.6	3 119.6	3 165.1	-8.47	3.53	2.80	3.54	3.38	3.37
4. Automatic data processing units (847180)	3 648.6	5 153.5	4 282.0	2 084.5	2 018.3	-44.68	3.73	4.31	4.01	2.26	2.15
5. Monolithic integrated circuits, other than digital (854229)	0.0	0.0	0.0	1 406.8	1 761.4	X	0.00	0.00	0.00	1.53	1.87
6. Digital automatic data processing machines, system (847149)	1 835.7	2 397.1	2 712.1	1 975.2	1 510.4	-17.72	1.87	2.00	2.54	2.14	1.61
7. Machine and mechanical appliance, individual function (847989)	1 488.4	3 108.7	1 768.5	1 156.0	1 351.8	-9.18	1.52	2.60	1.66	1.25	1.44
8. Automatic data processing storage units (847170)	2 131.7	2 042.0	1 503.2	1 294.1	1 178.4	-44.72	2.18	1.71	1.41	1.40	1.25
9. Passenger vehicle, spark-ignition, >1500 < 3000 cc (870323)	. . .	253.3	309.3	407.9	966.0	. . .	. . .	0.21	0.29	0.44	1.03
10. Parts, telegraphic apparatus (851790)	1 362.1	1 136.3	878.7	1 422.1	941.1	-30.91	1.39	0.95	0.82	1.54	1.00
11. Airplane and aircraft, unladen weight > 15,000 kg (880240)	. . .	1 191.5	801.8	390.8	892.2	. . .	. . .	1.00	0.75	0.42	0.95
12. Parts, television apparatus (852990)	416.6	557.2	627.8	648.7	873.5	109.67	0.43	0.47	0.59	0.70	0.93
13. Almonds, fresh or dried, shelled (080212)	515.2	508.4	532.5	673.4	829.5	61.01	0.53	0.42	0.50	0.73	0.88
14. Automatic data processing, input or output units (847160)	1 210.7	1 335.9	1 186.5	1 149.1	813.4	-32.82	1.24	1.12	1.11	1.25	0.87
15. Digital processing units (847150)	1 059.7	1 327.7	927.3	756.2	810.8	-23.49	1.08	1.11	0.87	0.82	0.86
16. Electrical apparatus for telephony or line telegraphy (851750)	967.3	1 353.2	1 571.4	1 180.1	802.5	-17.04	0.99	1.13	1.47	1.28	0.85
17. Antisera and other blood fractions (300210)	383.4	552.6	581.5	687.4	794.6	107.25	0.39	0.46	0.54	0.75	0.85
18. Cotton, not carded or combed (520100)	. . .	482.4	657.5	451.9	744.0	. . .	. . .	0.40	0.62	0.49	0.79
19. Composite diagnostic/lab reagents (382200)	416.6	605.8	644.8	644.6	738.5	77.27	0.43	0.51	0.60	0.70	0.79
20. Instruments and appliances for medical science (901890)	567.6	628.8	719.7	674.7	701.7	23.63	0.58	0.53	0.67	0.73	0.75
21. Transmission apparatus for reception apparatus (852520)	643.4	749.9	703.1	589.7	624.4	-2.95	0.66	0.63	0.66	0.64	0.66
22. Parts, liquid crystal device, laser and other optical (901390)	. . .	184.9	271.5	444.9	580.1	. . .	. . .	0.15	0.25	0.48	0.62
23. Cathode-ray TV picture tubes, color monitor (854011)	763.1	1 064.4	1 048.2	866.5	579.6	-24.05	0.78	0.89	0.98	0.94	0.62
24. Optical instrument, inspecting semiconductor wafer (903141)	499.1	1 123.3	729.5	572.1	558.6	11.92	0.51	0.94	0.68	0.62	0.59
25. Diamonds, non-industrial, worked (710239)	. . .	322.1	284.8	395.7	552.8	. . .	. . .	0.27	0.27	0.43	0.59

X = Not applicable.
. . . = Not available.

Exports from California

Highest and Lowest Percent Change in Value of Exports to Top 25 Countries, 1999–2003

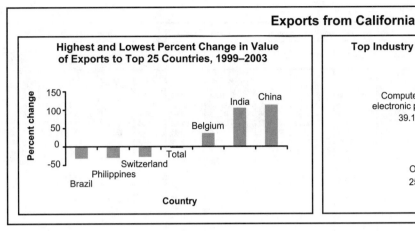

Top Industry Groups by Share of State Total Exports, 2003
(percent distribution)

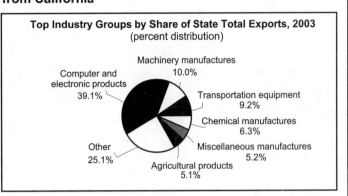

- From 1999 to 2000, the value of California's computer and electronic products exports increased by more than 24 percent, or by close to $12 billion. But since 2000, the value of this industry's exports has dropped substantially, by about $24.7 billion, representing the bulk of the state's loss of $25.6 billion in total exports. The value of computer and electronic products in 2003 was 25 percent, or $12.7 billion, below the 1999 value. This drop accounts for the $11.5 billion drop from 1999 to 2003 in the United States' exports of computer and electronic products.

- California's oil and gas industry has had tremendous growth since 1999, with an increase of 800 percent, or $280 million worth of exports. Agriculture production and chemical manufactures exports each increased in value by nearly $2 billion since 1999.

- Mexico, Japan, and Canada are the top three recipients of California's exports. Since 1999, China's ranking has risen from 11th to fourth by value of exports received from California. China imported over $1 billion more computer and electronic products from California in 2003 than it did in 1999.

Table E-9. Total U.S. Exports (Origin of Movement) via California, 1999–2003—*Continued*

(Top 25 commodities and top 25 countries based on 2003 dollar value.)

Industry, commodity, and country	Value (millions of dollars)					Percent change, 1999–2003	Percent share of state total				
	1999	2000	2001	2002	2003		1999	2000	2001	2002	2003
TOTAL AND PERCENT SHARE OF U.S. TOTAL	97 920.1	119 640.4	106 777.0	92 214.3	93 994.9	-4.01	14.13	15.33	14.61	13.30	12.99
Top 25 Countries	90 986.2	112 826.7	99 943.6	85 754.6	87 481.5	-3.85	92.92	94.30	93.60	92.99	93.07
1. Mexico	13 559.2	17 515.5	16 343.1	16 076.3	14 871.8	9.68	13.85	14.64	15.31	17.43	15.82
2. Japan	12 893.8	16 444.1	14 635.1	11 105.5	11 754.7	-8.83	13.17	13.75	13.71	12.04	12.51
3. Canada	12 381.6	14 075.9	11 816.0	10 075.3	11 231.6	-9.29	12.64	11.77	11.07	10.93	11.95
4. China	2 394.7	3 546.0	4 676.1	4 482.4	5 465.0	128.21	2.45	2.96	4.38	4.86	5.81
5. South Korea	5 343.1	6 917.4	5 034.9	4 711.8	4 833.3	-9.54	5.46	5.78	4.72	5.11	5.14
6. Taiwan	5 398.5	7 362.5	5 664.5	5 391.4	4 443.0	-17.70	5.51	6.15	5.30	5.85	4.73
7. United Kingdom	5 074.4	5 984.5	5 588.8	4 347.3	4 360.0	-14.08	5.18	5.00	5.23	4.71	4.64
8. Hong Kong	3 644.7	4 148.0	3 934.0	3 684.1	4 178.9	14.65	3.72	3.47	3.68	4.00	4.45
9. Germany	4 329.1	5 263.1	4 657.4	3 480.1	3 559.7	-17.77	4.42	4.40	4.36	3.77	3.79
10. Netherlands	3 987.0	4 958.7	4 318.2	3 577.2	3 412.2	-14.42	4.07	4.14	4.04	3.88	3.63
11. Singapore	4 604.5	5 011.1	4 226.8	3 298.4	3 370.8	-26.79	4.70	4.19	3.96	3.58	3.59
12. France	2 254.5	2 942.8	2 242.0	1 885.4	1 915.1	-15.05	2.30	2.46	2.10	2.04	2.04
13. Australia	2 185.2	2 442.0	2 084.5	1 910.1	1 899.4	-13.08	2.23	2.04	1.95	2.07	2.02
14. Malaysia	2 092.0	2 978.4	2 554.2	1 998.6	1 730.8	-17.27	2.14	2.49	2.39	2.17	1.84
15. Belgium	1 032.5	1 087.0	1 131.7	1 244.9	1 425.1	38.03	1.05	0.91	1.06	1.35	1.52
16. Italy	1 276.3	1 534.3	1 393.9	1 095.3	1 355.1	6.17	1.30	1.28	1.31	1.19	1.44
17. Thailand	1 224.8	2 022.4	1 790.1	1 242.2	1 215.6	-0.75	1.25	1.69	1.68	1.35	1.29
18. Ireland	1 131.9	1 231.0	1 030.4	956.6	1 125.1	-0.59	1.16	1.03	0.96	1.04	1.20
19. Philippines	1 492.6	1 930.6	2 011.3	1 100.6	1 008.1	-32.46	1.52	1.61	1.88	1.19	1.07
20. India	416.1	596.3	635.8	674.3	850.4	104.38	0.42	0.50	0.60	0.73	0.90
21. Brazil	1 240.8	1 298.8	1 184.0	782.6	819.9	-33.92	1.27	1.09	1.11	0.85	0.87
22. Israel	867.8	1 073.8	812.2	740.5	752.9	-13.24	0.89	0.90	0.76	0.80	0.80
23. Spain	698.0	814.5	719.8	557.5	686.8	-1.60	0.71	0.68	0.67	0.60	0.73
24. Sweden	595.6	687.8	614.2	627.3	613.7	3.05	0.61	0.57	0.58	0.68	0.65
25. Switzerland	867.7	960.0	844.8	708.9	602.5	-30.57	0.89	0.80	0.79	0.77	0.64

Table E-10. Total U.S. Exports (Origin of Movement) via Colorado, 1999–2003

(Top 25 commodities and top 25 countries based on 2003 dollar value.)

Industry, commodity, and country	Value (millions of dollars)					Percent change, 1999–2003	Percent share of state total				
	1999	2000	2001	2002	2003		1999	2000	2001	2002	2003
TOTAL AND PERCENT SHARE OF U.S. TOTAL	5 931.4	6 593.0	6 125.5	5 521.7	6 109.1	3.00	0.9	0.84	0.84	0.80	0.84
Manufactures (NAICS Code)	5 700.9	6 376.4	5 902.2	5 306.8	5 923.1	3.90	96.1	96.71	96.35	96.11	96.95
Processed foods (311)	436.6	541.9	632.3	592.3	661.3	51.48	7.4	8.22	10.32	10.73	10.82
Beverages and tobacco products (312)	2.3	2.6	2.3	1.9	1.5	-33.41	0.0	0.00	0.04	0.03	0.02
Fabric mill products (313)	10.7	15.7	17.0	14.1	12.8	19.22	0.2	0.24	0.28	0.25	0.21
Non-apparel textile products (314)	15.6	19.3	16.6	16.9	12.3	-20.93	0.3	0.29	0.27	0.31	0.20
Apparel manufactures (315)	10.3	13.0	5.9	5.6	5.5	-46.35	0.2	0.20	0.10	0.10	0.09
Leather and related products (316)	12.2	18.4	15.6	20.5	17.1	40.69	0.2	0.28	0.25	0.37	0.28
Wood products (321)	3.2	2.6	3.2	3.6	3.0	-5.82	0.0	0.04	0.05	0.07	0.05
Paper products (322)	7.6	12.0	21.2	19.6	26.6	251.72	0.1	0.18	0.35	0.36	0.44
Printing and related products (323)	90.6	67.7	47.1	38.7	50.5	-44.23	1.5	1.03	0.77	0.70	0.83
Petroleum and coal products (324)	8.9	1.9	2.1	2.4	19.1	114.23	0.2	0.03	0.03	0.04	0.31
Chemical manufactures (325)	424.8	453.7	363.6	343.4	397.6	-6.42	7.2	6.88	5.94	6.22	6.51
Plastics and rubber products (326)	50.3	69.1	59.2	50.6	54.1	7.57	0.8	1.05	0.97	0.92	0.89
Non-metallic mineral products (327)	59.1	72.8	69.1	52.5	47.8	-19.13	1.0	1.10	1.13	0.95	0.78
Primary metal manufactures (331)	42.2	55.8	75.6	73.0	68.3	61.97	0.7	0.85	1.23	1.32	1.12
Fabricated metal products (332)	90.9	138.4	85.8	79.0	86.1	-5.30	1.5	2.10	1.40	1.43	1.41
Machinery manufactures (333)	458.0	506.7	542.9	459.3	457.0	-0.23	7.7	7.69	8.86	8.32	7.48
Computer and electronic products (334)	3 506.7	3 887.5	3 404.8	3 034.2	3 459.7	-1.34	59.1	58.96	55.58	54.95	56.63
Electrical equipment, appliances, and parts (335)	75.3	108.2	86.9	80.2	86.8	15.18	1.3	1.64	1.42	1.45	1.42
Transportation equipment (336)	261.8	251.6	286.8	264.8	286.0	9.24	4.4	3.82	4.68	4.80	4.68
Furniture and related products (337)	12.0	14.4	12.5	9.2	11.2	-6.63	0.2	0.22	0.20	0.17	0.18
Miscellaneous manufactures (339)	121.8	123.0	151.6	145.0	158.6	30.23	2.0	1.87	2.47	2.63	2.60
Agricultural and Livestock Products (NAICS Code)	20.6	24.1	25.0	25.8	20.6	0.23	0.4	0.37	0.41	0.47	0.34
Agricultural products (111)	18.1	20.6	18.3	20.6	19.4	7.24	0.3	0.31	0.30	0.37	0.32
Livestock and livestock products (112)	2.5	3.5	6.7	5.2	1.2	-51.13	0.0	0.05	0.11	0.09	0.02
Other Commodities (NAICS Code)	209.9	192.5	198.3	189.1	165.4	-21.17	3.5	2.92	3.24	3.43	2.71
Forestry and logging (113)	1.3	2.1	1.0	0.4	0.8	-35.93	0.0	0.03	0.02	0.01	0.01
Fishing, hunting, and trapping (114)	0.3	0.3	1.5	1.0	0.6	119.47	0.0	0.00	0.03	0.02	0.01
Oil and gas extraction (211)	0.2	2.9	3.1	6.6	4.7	2 147.85	0.0	0.04	0.05	0.12	0.08
Mining (212)	74.4	41.8	34.2	41.1	40.4	-45.72	1.3	0.63	0.56	0.74	0.66
Waste and scrap (910)	5.8	11.7	15.2	16.0	18.2	214.60	0.1	0.18	0.25	0.29	0.30
Used merchandise (920)	12.3	13.2	11.5	12.2	10.3	-16.35	0.2	0.20	0.19	0.22	0.17
Goods returned to Canada (980)	11.5	13.9	26.7	16.7	33.7	191.92	0.2	0.21	0.44	0.30	0.55
Special classification provisions (990)	104.1	106.6	105.2	95.0	56.5	-45.72	1.8	1.62	1.72	1.72	0.92
Publishing industries (except Internet) (511)	0.0	0.0	0.0	0.0	0.30	X	0.0	0.00	0.00	0.00	0.01
TOTAL AND PERCENT SHARE OF U.S. TOTAL	5 931.4	6 593.0	6 125.5	5 521.7	6 109.1	3.00	0.9	0.84	0.84	0.80	0.84
Top 25 Commodities (HS Code)	2 408.6	2 663.6	2 741.1	3 218.8	3 655.6	51.77	40.6	40.40	44.75	58.29	59.84
1. Digital monolithic integrated circuits (854221)	0.0	0.0	0.0	559.3	809.2	X	0.0	0.00	0.00	10.13	13.25
2. Parts, accessories, automatic data processing machines (847330)	498.8	561.3	653.1	541.2	520.9	4.43	8.4	8.51	10.66	9.80	8.53
3. Automatic data processing units (847180)	149.6	246.9	342.0	324.7	342.9	129.21	2.5	3.74	5.58	5.88	5.61
4. Meat of bovine animals, boneless, fresh or chilled (020130)	174.4	162.3	173.4	176.9	225.1	29.07	2.9	2.46	2.83	3.20	3.68
5. Automatic data processing, input or output units (847160)	38.8	28.0	76.2	202.2	193.8	399.48	0.6	0.42	1.24	3.66	3.17
6. Monolithic integrated circuits, other than digital (854229)	0.0	0.0	0.0	40.9	167.4	X	0.0	0.00	0.00	0.74	2.74
7. Automatic data processing storage units (847170)	491.3	449.6	427.3	188.3	141.6	-71.18	8.3	6.82	6.98	3.41	2.32
8. Digital processing units (847150)	230.6	85.2	85.6	85.7	136.9	-40.63	3.9	1.29	1.40	1.55	2.24
9. Parts of airplanes or helicopters (880330)	42.7	52.9	106.8	117.3	116.9	173.77	0.7	0.80	1.74	2.12	1.91
10. Color TVs with or without radios (852812)	51.3	68.4	3.1	154.0	108.9	112.28	0.9	1.04	0.05	2.79	1.78
11. Instruments and appliances for medical science (901890)	146.7	168.1	163.0	126.9	92.7	-36.81	2.5	2.55	2.66	2.30	1.52
12. Static converters: automatic data processing power (850440)	61.1	83.3	79.8	61.1	80.9	32.41	1.0	1.26	1.30	1.11	1.32
13. Airplane and aircraft, unladen weight > 15,000 kg (880240)	. . .	0.0	0.0	0.0	68.4	. . .	. . .	0.00	0.00	0.00	1.12
14. Whole hides and skins of bovine/equine <= 8 kg (410120)	0.0	0.0	0.0	69.9	68.4	X	0.0	0.00	0.00	1.19	1.12
15. X-ray plates and flat film (370110)	142.5	134.7	97.2	88.1	68.4	-52.00	2.4	2.04	1.59	1.60	1.12
16. Whole hides and skins of bovine/equine > 16 kg (410150)	0.0	0.0	0.0	69.9	61.6	X	0.0	0.00	0.00	1.27	1.01
17. Parts of instruments for measuring ionizing radiation (903090)	125.2	259.4	182.0	86.4	59.3	-52.64	2.1	3.93	2.97	1.56	0.97
18. Parts for instruments and apparatus measuring liquid (902690)	50.8	60.9	54.9	52.7	55.1	8.46	0.9	0.92	0.90	0.95	0.90
19. Meat of bovine animals, boneless, frozen (020230)	64.7	91.6	58.3	51.9	53.1	-17.93	1.1	1.39	0.95	0.94	0.87
20. Parts, telegraphic apparatus (851790)	84.1	84.4	79.4	65.7	51.6	-38.64	1.4	1.28	1.30	1.19	0.84
21. Animal (not fish) guts, bladders, stomachs and parts (050400)	4.4	7.6	44.8	51.0	51.1	1 061.36	0.1	0.12	0.73	0.92	0.84
22. Portable digital a.d.p. machines < 10 kg (847130)	. . .	5.7	8.4	11.3	51.0	. . .	. . .	0.09	0.14	0.20	0.83
23. Other photographic film rolls for color photograph (370255)	. . .	0.8	3.7	21.6	47.3	. . .	. . .	0.01	0.06	0.39	0.77
24. X-ray film in rolls other than paper (370210)	14.9	15.7	27.4	34.7	42.5	185.23	0.2	0.24	0.45	0.63	0.70
25. Photographic plates and film (370130)	36.7	97.6	74.7	41.3	40.6	10.63	0.6	1.48	1.22	0.75	0.66

X = Not applicable.
. . . = Not available.

Exports from Colorado

Highest and Lowest Percent Change in Value of Exports to Top 25 Countries, 1999–2003

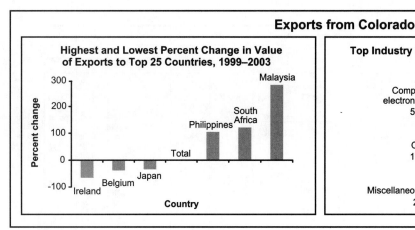

Top Industry Groups by Share of State Total Exports, 2003
(percent distribution)

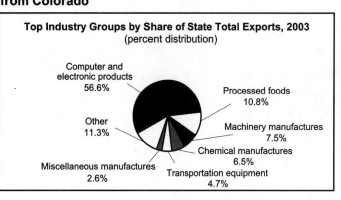

- In 2003, computer and electronic products accounted for nearly 57 percent of Colorado's $6.1 billion worth of exports. Processed foods were the state's second largest export with $661 million in 2003, up from about $437 million in 1999. Paper products increased to nearly $27 million in 2003, a jump from under $8 million in 1999.

- Mining exports dropped to $40.4 million in 2003, down about 46 percent from 1999. Exports of printing and related products decreased 44 percent, about $40 million, from 1999 to 2003.

- Canada receives one-fourth of Colorado's exports, 56 percent of which are computer and electronic products. From 1999 to 2003, exports to Canada increased by $484 million. Exports to Malaysia increased from $95 million in 1999 to $302 million in 2003. Computer and electronic products compose nearly 95 percent of exports to Malaysia. Exports to Ireland fell from $204 million in 1999 to $76 million in 2003, as computer and electronic exports to Ireland dropped by $131 million.

Table E-10. Total U.S. Exports (Origin of Movement) via Colorado, 1999–2003—*Continued*

(Top 25 commodities and top 25 countries based on 2003 dollar value.)

Industry, commodity, and country	Value (millions of dollars)					Percent change, 1999–2003	Percent share of state total				
	1999	2000	2001	2002	2003		1999	2000	2001	2002	2003
TOTAL AND PERCENT SHARE OF U.S. TOTAL	5 931.4	6 593.0	6 125.5	5 521.7	6 109.1	3.00	0.9	0.84	0.84	0.80	0.84
Top 25 Countries	5 610.7	6 283.1	5 818.1	5 265.1	5 848.4	4.24	94.6	95.30	94.98	95.35	95.73
1. Canada	947.8	1 077.1	1 146.1	1 425.5	1 431.7	51.06	16.0	16.34	18.71	25.82	23.44
2. Mexico	296.6	312.6	335.4	370.4	570.4	92.35	5.0	4.74	5.48	6.71	9.34
3. Japan	832.3	891.6	764.7	436.8	443.1	-46.75	14.0	13.52	12.48	7.91	7.25
4. South Korea	284.7	339.5	248.0	320.4	424.6	49.15	4.8	5.15	4.05	5.80	6.95
5. Malaysia	95.2	201.4	228.0	180.9	302.0	217.43	1.6	3.06	3.72	3.28	4.94
6. Germany	457.7	444.8	341.0	290.2	282.0	-38.38	7.7	6.75	5.57	5.26	4.62
7. France	334.8	416.5	339.6	281.5	267.1	-20.20	5.6	6.32	5.54	5.10	4.37
8. Netherlands	302.3	338.8	312.5	209.0	245.6	-18.76	5.1	5.14	5.10	3.79	4.02
9. United Kingdom	387.0	480.8	385.9	288.2	237.3	-38.67	6.5	7.29	6.30	5.22	3.88
10. Taiwan	130.4	196.4	152.5	200.4	237.0	81.72	2.2	2.98	2.49	3.63	3.88
11. Singapore	292.8	318.3	357.0	237.3	236.7	-19.16	4.9	4.83	5.83	4.30	3.87
12. China	127.4	164.6	168.5	153.1	213.2	67.36	2.2	2.50	2.75	2.77	3.49
13. Hong Kong	260.3	233.8	261.6	235.9	202.4	-22.25	4.4	3.55	4.27	4.27	3.31
14. Philippines	66.7	78.3	88.7	77.9	134.4	101.39	1.1	1.19	1.28	1.41	2.20
15. Australia	135.2	133.9	118.6	117.5	112.7	-16.65	2.3	2.03	1.94	2.13	1.85
16. Switzerland	126.9	70.8	71.0	68.2	81.2	-36.02	2.1	1.07	1.16	1.24	1.33
17. Ireland	204.3	227.0	177.4	82.2	76.2	-62.69	3.4	3.44	2.90	1.49	1.25
18. Italy	67.2	76.9	69.5	53.8	62.7	-6.64	1.1	1.17	1.13	0.97	1.03
19. Thailand	55.4	58.3	47.3	60.6	60.3	8.82	0.9	0.88	0.77	1.10	0.99
20. Brazil	61.5	65.3	73.3	57.3	57.2	-6.89	1.0	0.99	1.20	1.04	0.94
21. Israel	23.9	27.4	26.2	21.1	38.1	59.18	0.4	0.42	0.43	0.38	0.62
22. India	19.8	27.0	23.7	26.2	37.9	91.46	0.3	0.41	0.39	0.47	0.62
23. South Africa	15.9	15.4	11.9	10.5	35.6	123.62	0.3	0.23	0.19	0.19	0.58
24. Belgium	68.4	59.3	52.4	32.8	34.6	-49.38	1.2	0.90	0.86	0.59	0.57
25. Turkey	16.5	27.4	27.3	27.5	24.3	46.84	0.3	0.41	0.45	0.50	0.40

Table E-11. Total U.S. Exports (Origin of Movement) via Connecticut, 1999–2003

(Top 25 commodities and top 25 countries based on 2003 dollar value.)

Industry, commodity, and country	Value (millions of dollars)					Percent change, 1999–2003	Percent share of state total				
	1999	2000	2001	2002	2003		1999	2000	2001	2002	2003
TOTAL AND PERCENT SHARE OF U.S. TOTAL	7 231.2	8 046.8	8 610.4	8 313.4	8 136.4	12.52	1.04	1.03	1.18	1.20	1.12
Manufactures (NAICS Code)	6 756.4	7 648.1	8 182.9	7 929.4	7 750.5	14.71	93.43	95.05	95.03	95.38	95.26
Processed foods (311)	38.2	52.0	52.3	67.8	53.8	40.85	0.53	0.65	0.61	0.82	0.66
Beverages and tobacco products (312)	1.9	2.6	6.5	7.2	11.0	492.22	0.03	0.00	0.08	0.09	0.14
Fabric mill products (313)	49.9	48.4	53.3	50.3	57.1	14.31	0.69	0.60	0.62	0.61	0.70
Non-apparel textile products (314)	10.3	11.1	7.8	9.5	11.3	9.77	0.14	0.14	0.09	0.11	0.14
Apparel manufactures (315)	14.5	13.9	12.0	7.1	3.9	-72.97	0.20	0.17	0.14	0.08	0.05
Leather and related products (316)	4.6	4.6	5.8	5.0	6.2	35.10	0.06	0.06	0.07	0.06	0.08
Wood products (321)	8.4	12.3	6.0	6.3	8.3	-1.18	0.12	0.15	0.07	0.08	0.10
Paper products (322)	139.5	150.8	139.5	174.9	188.6	35.18	1.93	1.87	1.62	2.10	2.32
Printing and related products (323)	49.1	46.7	40.8	33.3	35.6	-27.51	0.68	0.58	0.47	0.40	0.44
Petroleum and coal products (324)	99.7	74.8	80.3	33.1	84.1	-15.67	1.38	0.93	0.93	0.40	1.03
Chemical manufactures (325)	547.7	612.8	567.3	499.9	749.0	36.75	7.57	7.62	6.59	6.01	9.21
Plastics and rubber products (326)	153.1	144.5	152.0	141.2	137.6	-10.13	2.12	1.80	1.77	1.70	1.69
Non-metallic mineral products (327)	39.5	60.1	47.3	35.9	41.4	4.84	0.55	0.75	0.55	0.43	0.51
Primary metal manufactures (331)	191.1	247.0	210.1	167.6	203.1	6.28	2.64	3.07	2.44	2.02	2.50
Fabricated metal products (332)	328.5	369.9	391.5	427.4	440.5	34.09	4.54	4.60	4.55	5.14	5.41
Machinery manufactures (333)	755.7	1 005.2	898.0	669.8	784.4	3.79	10.45	12.49	10.43	8.06	9.64
Computer and electronic products (334)	877.6	904.4	804.4	760.0	789.5	-10.03	12.14	11.24	9.34	9.14	9.70
Electrical equipment, appliances, and parts (335)	242.9	292.8	259.8	316.3	336.1	38.37	3.36	3.64	3.02	3.80	4.13
Transportation equipment (336)	2 599.0	3 168.4	3 988.3	4 098.7	3 298.1	26.90	35.94	39.37	46.32	49.30	40.54
Furniture and related products (337)	23.6	30.5	29.5	24.6	24.5	3.85	0.33	0.38	0.34	0.30	0.30
Miscellaneous manufactures (339)	581.5	395.2	430.3	393.6	486.4	-16.36	8.04	4.91	5.00	4.73	5.98
Agricultural and Livestock Products (NAICS Code)	156.0	96.3	102.6	75.8	70.8	-54.63	2.16	1.20	1.19	0.91	0.87
Agricultural products (111)	137.9	84.4	94.2	74.9	69.3	-49.73	1.91	1.05	1.09	0.90	0.85
Livestock and livestock products (112)	18.1	12.0	8.5	0.9	1.4	-92.04	0.25	0.15	0.10	0.01	0.02
Other Commodities (NAICS Code)	318.9	302.4	324.9	308.1	315.1	-1.18	4.41	3.76	3.77	3.71	3.87
Forestry and logging (113)	5.8	5.0	2.4	4.0	4.1	-28.56	0.08	0.06	0.03	0.05	0.05
Fishing, hunting, and trapping (114)	18.8	22.9	23.1	9.9	3.4	-82.02	0.26	0.28	0.27	0.12	0.04
Oil and gas extraction (211)	0.0	0.0	0.0	5.8	0.0	X	0.00	0.00	0.00	0.07	0.00
Mining (212)	59.2	43.3	11.7	11.1	5.8	-90.12	0.82	0.54	0.14	0.13	0.07
Waste and scrap (910)	82.6	81.9	40.5	42.4	50.7	-38.63	1.14	1.02	0.47	0.51	0.62
Used merchandise (920)	4.7	4.8	25.9	13.3	9.6	104.09	0.06	0.06	0.30	0.16	0.12
Goods returned to Canada (980)	18.1	15.5	18.5	16.6	11.2	-38.55	0.25	0.19	0.22	0.20	0.14
Special classification provisions (990)	129.6	129.0	202.6	205.0	229.7	77.25	1.79	1.60	2.35	2.47	2.82
Publishing industries (except Internet) (511)	0.0	0.0	0.0	0.0	0.6	X	0.00	0.00	0.00	0.00	0.01
TOTAL AND PERCENT SHARE OF U.S. TOTAL	7 231.2	8 046.8	8 610.4	8 313.4	8 136.4	12.52	1.04	1.03	1.18	1.20	1.12
Top 25 Commodities (HS Code)	3 200.0	3 631.1	4 565.7	4 719.7	4 339.8	35.62	44.25	45.12	53.03	56.77	53.34
1. Turbojet or turbo-propeller parts (841191)	1 108.8	893.2	1 348.4	1 568.3	1 574.7	42.02	15.33	11.10	15.66	18.86	19.35
2. Turbojets of a thrust exceeding 25 kn (841112)	786.3	1 103.4	1 460.6	1 183.9	1 013.9	28.95	10.87	13.71	16.96	14.24	12.46
3. Parts of airplanes or helicopters (880330)	297.3	410.6	471.4	411.8	366.9	23.41	4.11	5.10	5.47	4.95	4.51
4. Instruments and appliances for medical science (901890)	437.1	244.3	304.4	234.1	309.7	-29.15	6.04	3.04	3.54	2.82	3.81
5. Measured doses of medicaments (300490)	60.9	61.4	60.1	67.1	140.0	129.89	0.84	0.76	0.70	0.81	1.72
6. Automatic circuit breakers (853620)	5.0	3.4	4.1	58.5	81.8	1 536.00	0.07	0.04	0.05	0.70	1.01
7. Medical, surgical, dental, or veterinary furniture (940290)	3.1	0.5	55.7	83.9	78.8	2 441.94	0.04	0.01	0.65	1.01	0.97
8. Helicopters (880212)	167.0	454.6	284.9	449.7	71.5	-57.19	2.31	5.65	3.31	5.41	0.88
9. Petroleum oils from bituminous mineral (not crude) (271019)	. . .	0.0	0.0	23.6	65.7	. . .	. . .	0.00	0.00	0.28	0.81
10. Gas turbine parts (841199)	72.1	98.6	104.1	57.4	56.6	-21.50	1.00	1.23	1.21	0.69	0.70
11. Oils and other products of xylenes (270730)	. . .	0.0	0.1	16.9	49.3	. . .	. . .	0.00	0.00	0.20	0.61
12. Kraft paper, bleached (481032)	. . .	0.3	2.0	17.0	45.6	. . .	. . .	0.00	0.02	0.20	0.56
13. Tobacco, not stemmed/stripped (240110)	97.2	67.8	80.9	67.7	44.4	-54.32	1.34	0.84	0.94	0.81	0.55
14. Taps and cocks for pipe thermostatic control (848180)	41.2	47.2	49.6	47.7	42.6	3.40	0.57	0.59	0.58	0.57	0.52
15. Mail sorting, opening, postage affixing machines (847230)	11.7	8.9	12.3	24.3	42.1	259.83	0.16	0.11	0.14	0.29	0.52
16. Parts of instr. and apparatus for phys/chem. anlys. (902790)	17.5	20.2	27.5	70.4	41.2	135.43	0.24	0.25	0.32	0.85	0.51
17. Other medicaments not in dosage form (300390)	. . .	1.8	1.5	11.7	38.9	. . .	. . .	0.02	0.02	0.14	0.48
18. Parts of measuring and checking instr., appl, and mach. (903190)	12.2	24.6	40.0	33.4	37.6	208.20	0.17	0.31	0.46	0.40	0.46
19. Parts, telegraphic apparatus (851790)	29.3	48.8	44.5	29.9	36.1	23.21	0.41	0.61	0.52	0.36	0.44
20. Electric generating sets (850239)	. . .	1.4	6.7	2.2	36.0	. . .	. . .	0.02	0.08	0.03	0.44
21. Airplane and aircraft, unladen weight > 15,000 kg (880240)	0.0	32.1	110.1	165.4	35.6	X	0.00	0.40	1.28	1.99	0.44
22. Ball bearings (848210)	29.1	28.3	40.1	42.8	34.7	19.24	0.40	0.35	0.47	0.51	0.43
23. Measuring and checking instr., appliances, and machines (903180)	24.2	30.0	32.6	29.5	32.2	33.06	0.33	0.37	0.38	0.35	0.40
24. Parts of spark-ignition internal combustion piston (840999)	. . .	25.5	19.6	18.8	32.1	. . .	. . .	0.32	0.23	0.23	0.39
25. Gas turbines (841182)	. . .	25.0	4.6	3.7	31.8	. . .	. . .	0.31	0.05	0.04	0.39

X = Not applicable.

. . . = Not available.

Exports from Connecticut

Highest and Lowest Percent Change in Value of Exports to Top 25 Countries, 1999–2003

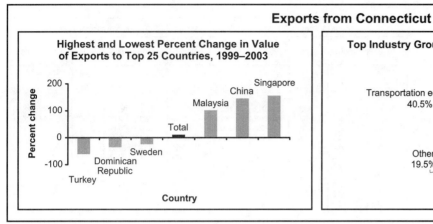

Top Industry Groups by Share of State Total Exports, 2003
(percent distribution)

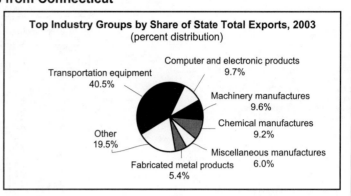

- Transportation equipment is Connecticut's leading export. In 2003, the state exported $3.3 billion worth of transportation exports, composing 40 percent of total exports. Computer and electronic exports fell by 10 percent from 1999 to 2003. However, it remains Connecticut's second largest export. Machinery manufactures are the third leading export with $785 million.

- Mining exports fell substantially from $59 million in 1999 to less than $6 million in 2003. Livestock and livestock products exports declined to less than $2 million in 2003, a drop of 92 percent from 1999.

- Canada is the top market for Connecticut exports. The top three exports to Canada are chemical manufactures (14 percent), transportation equipment (over 12 percent), and machinery manufactures (12 percent). Exports to Canada dropped by more than $425 million from 1999 to 2003. During the same period, exports to Germany increased by $356 million and exports to Singapore by more than $256 million. France imported nearly $1.1 billion worth of Connecticut's products in 2003, making it the second largest importer of Connecticut products.

Table E-11. Total U.S. Exports (Origin of Movement) via Connecticut, 1999–2003—Continued

(Top 25 commodities and top 25 countries based on 2003 dollar value.)

Industry, commodity, and country	Value (millions of dollars)					Percent change, 1999–2003	Percent share of state total				
	1999	2000	2001	2002	2003		1999	2000	2001	2002	2003
TOTAL AND PERCENT SHARE OF U.S. TOTAL	7 231.2	8 046.8	8 610.4	8 313.4	8 136.4	12.52	1.04	1.03	1.18	1.20	1.12
Top 25 Countries	6 749.4	7 555.0	8 033.2	7 634.5	7 462.6	10.57	93.34	93.89	93.30	91.83	91.72
1. Canada	1 780.4	1 831.2	1 728.8	1 492.4	1 352.3	-24.04	24.62	22.76	20.08	17.95	16.62
2. France	959.8	1 112.3	1 416.3	1 178.4	1 095.7	14.16	13.27	13.82	16.45	14.17	13.47
3. Germany	403.8	561.2	675.4	654.1	760.1	88.25	5.58	6.97	7.84	7.87	9.34
4. Japan	516.1	508.3	616.6	606.5	639.0	23.81	7.14	6.32	7.16	7.30	7.85
5. United Kingdom	431.0	471.2	462.4	499.9	512.8	18.98	5.96	5.86	5.37	6.01	6.30
6. Mexico	333.3	404.9	326.6	402.0	478.0	43.44	4.61	5.03	3.79	4.84	5.87
7. Singapore	180.5	198.5	413.5	407.3	437.0	142.14	2.50	2.47	4.80	4.90	5.37
8. South Korea	314.9	158.4	190.9	300.3	282.9	-10.15	4.35	1.97	2.22	3.61	3.48
9. Netherlands	174.5	139.9	143.1	163.6	198.6	13.83	2.41	1.74	1.66	1.97	2.44
10. Belgium	141.4	96.6	159.2	212.8	162.6	15.01	1.96	1.20	1.85	2.56	2.00
11. China	65.4	77.2	119.5	119.2	157.4	140.81	0.90	0.96	1.39	1.43	1.93
12. Switzerland	138.6	191.2	180.6	175.1	149.2	7.70	1.92	2.38	2.10	2.11	1.83
13. Italy	136.4	144.3	165.4	153.6	143.7	5.29	1.89	1.79	1.92	1.85	1.77
14. Australia	81.1	99.2	210.1	207.3	140.2	72.76	1.12	1.23	2.44	2.49	1.72
15. Hong Kong	87.7	100.0	79.6	80.1	126.0	43.71	1.21	1.24	0.92	0.96	1.55
16. Ireland	115.1	154.4	109.1	95.8	110.2	-4.27	1.59	1.92	1.27	1.15	1.35
17. Malaysia	50.1	99.2	94.5	96.3	104.5	108.77	0.69	1.23	1.10	1.16	1.28
18. Spain	107.4	60.8	81.8	73.5	96.4	-10.26	1.49	0.76	0.95	0.88	1.18
19. Taiwan	111.6	374.7	233.6	118.8	95.7	-14.30	1.54	4.66	2.71	1.43	1.18
20. Sweden	138.5	131.0	134.3	105.2	93.9	-32.23	1.92	1.63	1.56	1.27	1.15
21. Dominican Republic	126.9	86.1	93.8	83.6	69.7	-45.07	1.76	1.07	1.09	1.01	0.86
22. Brazil	59.1	96.0	105.3	62.6	68.7	16.32	0.82	1.19	1.22	0.75	0.84
23. Turkey	183.9	292.7	75.2	229.8	67.8	-63.10	2.54	3.64	0.87	2.76	0.83
24. New Zealand	35.5	30.6	146.2	56.7	66.4	87.20	0.49	0.38	1.70	0.68	0.82
25. Israel	76.7	135.2	71.6	59.8	53.9	-29.75	1.06	1.68	0.83	0.72	0.66

Table E-12. Total U.S. Exports (Origin of Movement) via Delaware, 1999–2003

(Top 25 commodities and top 25 countries based on 2003 dollar value.)

Industry, commodity, and country	Value (millions of dollars)					Percent change, 1999–2003	Percent share of state total				
	1999	2000	2001	2002	2003		1999	2000	2001	2002	2003
TOTAL AND PERCENT SHARE OF U.S. TOTAL	2 286.6	2 197.4	1 984.8	2 003.8	1 886.1	-17.52	0.3	0.28	0.27	0.29	0.26
Manufactures (NAICS Code)	2 219.9	2 092.5	1 893.0	1 897.3	1 742.0	-21.53	97.1	95.23	95.37	94.69	92.36
Processed foods (311)	60.0	63.5	53.1	61.5	61.7	2.82	2.6	2.89	2.67	3.07	3.27
Beverages and tobacco products (312)	0.2	0.1	0.2	0.0	0.1	-59.33	0.0	0.00	0.01	0.00	0.00
Fabric mill products (313)	16.4	10.1	12.1	7.3	8.5	-48.41	0.7	0.46	0.61	0.37	0.45
Non-apparel textile products (314)	9.1	8.2	7.5	6.5	7.8	-14.51	0.4	0.37	0.38	0.33	0.41
Apparel manufactures (315)	2.3	3.5	2.4	3.8	2.3	3.21	0.1	0.16	0.12	0.19	0.12
Leather and related products (316)	0.2	0.2	0.4	0.6	0.1	-60.89	0.0	0.01	0.02	0.03	0.00
Wood products (321)	1.0	0.9	1.3	7.5	1.4	47.38	0.0	0.04	0.07	0.38	0.08
Paper products (322)	9.3	19.7	27.5	23.8	32.5	249.42	0.4	0.89	1.39	1.19	1.72
Printing and related products (323)	10.6	12.3	3.1	4.2	3.1	-70.44	0.5	0.56	0.16	0.21	0.17
Petroleum and coal products (324)	9.9	15.4	7.2	4.6	3.9	-60.33	0.4	0.70	0.36	0.23	0.21
Chemical manufactures (325)	1 149.1	1 047.7	916.4	925.8	803.9	-30.04	50.2	47.68	46.17	46.20	42.62
Plastics and rubber products (326)	115.3	116.2	99.0	82.8	94.2	-18.30	5.0	5.29	4.99	4.13	4.99
Non-metallic mineral products (327)	7.5	5.0	4.4	5.2	8.0	6.10	0.3	0.23	0.22	0.26	0.42
Primary metal manufactures (331)	13.7	24.2	18.9	38.9	16.9	23.32	0.6	1.10	0.95	1.94	0.90
Fabricated metal products (332)	63.5	9.6	47.8	15.8	19.5	-69.36	2.8	0.44	2.41	0.79	1.03
Machinery manufactures (333)	115.2	121.0	124.5	134.6	152.5	32.32	5.0	5.51	6.27	6.72	8.09
Computer and electronic products (334)	197.4	197.1	253.1	280.4	266.1	34.77	8.6	8.97	12.75	13.99	14.11
Electrical equipment, appliances, and parts (335)	19.9	20.5	21.4	15.6	22.2	11.25	0.9	0.93	1.08	0.78	1.18
Transportation equipment (336)	346.3	334.9	243.2	227.2	185.9	-46.33	15.2	15.24	12.25	11.34	9.85
Furniture and related products (337)	3.5	8.1	7.6	4.9	3.6	3.65	0.2	0.37	0.38	0.24	0.19
Miscellaneous manufactures (339)	69.3	74.2	41.7	46.2	47.8	-31.03	3.0	3.38	2.10	2.31	2.53
Agricultural and Livestock Products (NAICS Code)	37.1	58.5	65.8	66.9	78.0	110.34	1.6	2.66	3.31	3.34	4.14
Agricultural products (111)	36.9	58.5	65.0	66.5	76.9	108.11	1.6	2.66	3.28	3.32	4.08
Livestock and livestock products (112)	0.1	0.0	0.7	0.4	1.1	697.86	0.0	0.00	0.04	0.02	0.06
Other Commodities (NAICS Code)	29.7	46.4	26.1	39.5	66.2	122.69	1.3	2.11	1.31	1.97	3.51
Forestry and logging (113)	1.3	0.3	0.7	2.2	0.8	-34.60	0.1	0.01	0.04	0.11	0.04
Fishing, hunting, and trapping (114)	0.5	0.3	0.5	1.0	1.0	105.52	0.0	0.01	0.02	0.05	0.05
Oil and gas extraction (211)	0.0	0.0	0.1	0.2	0.3	X	0.0	0.00	0.01	0.01	0.01
Mining (212)	9.4	17.8	8.9	8.8	4.8	-48.77	0.4	0.81	0.45	0.44	0.25
Waste and scrap (910)	1.1	1.1	2.3	1.9	3.7	252.22	0.0	0.05	0.12	0.10	0.20
Used merchandise (920)	3.6	1.5	0.5	8.5	43.9	1 121.45	0.2	0.07	0.03	0.42	2.33
Goods returned to Canada (980)	4.5	2.4	2.8	2.2	1.6	-64.87	0.2	0.11	0.14	0.11	0.08
Special classification provisions (990)	9.4	23.0	10.2	14.8	10.0	5.92	0.4	1.05	0.52	0.74	0.53
Publishing industries (except Internet) (511)	0.0	0.0	0.0	0.0	0.1	X	0.0	0.00	0.00	0.00	0.00
TOTAL AND PERCENT SHARE OF U.S. TOTAL	2 286.6	2 197.4	1 984.8	2 003.8	1 886.1	-17.52	0.3	0.28	0.27	0.29	0.26
Top 25 Commodities (HS Code)	825.4	893.7	814.5	1 026.6	987.8	19.68	36.1	40.67	41.04	51.23	52.37
1. Passenger vehicles, spark-ignition, > 3,000 cc (870324)	198.9	175.8	127.2	126.4	101.0	-49.22	8.7	8.00	6.41	6.31	5.35
2. Retail medicaments in measured dose (300490)	57.7	59.9	36.3	154.9	92.2	59.79	2.5	2.73	1.83	7.73	4.89
3. Parts for machines for working stone and ceramics (846691)	44.5	51.3	47.9	64.9	79.6	78.88	2.0	2.33	2.41	3.24	4.22
4. Polyamide-6,-11,-12,-6,6,-6,9,-6,10 or -6,12 (390810)	64.1	55.9	69.4	72.9	58.3	-9.05	2.8	2.54	3.50	3.64	3.09
5. Dry titanium dioxide (320611)	58.8	71.6	64.4	60.1	57.2	-2.72	2.6	3.26	3.24	3.00	3.03
6. Bananas and plantains, fresh or dried (080300)	19.3	32.6	34.2	44.0	56.0	190.16	0.8	1.48	1.72	2.20	2.97
7. Physical or chemical analysis instruments (902780)	29.6	23.0	42.6	43.6	47.2	59.46	1.3	1.05	2.15	2.18	2.50
8. Chromatographs and electrophoresis instruments (902720)	58.9	50.3	47.3	60.0	45.7	-22.41	2.6	2.29	2.38	2.99	2.42
9. Articles of plastics (392690)	3.4	18.7	25.5	28.8	43.1	1 167.65	0.2	0.85	1.28	1.44	2.29
10. Paintings, drawings, and pastels by hand (970110)	. . .	1.0	0.2	7.5	42.6	. . .	. . .	0.05	0.01	0.37	2.26
11. Parts of instr. and apparatus for phys/chem. anlys. (902790)	37.4	36.2	48.5	41.4	42.0	12.30	1.6	1.65	2.44	2.07	2.23
12. Passenger vehicle, spark-ignition, > 1,500 cc < 3,000 cc (870323)	68.5	72.7	51.7	59.4	32.9	-51.97	3.0	3.31	2.60	2.96	1.74
13. Polytetrafluoroethylene (ptfe) (390461)	. . .	17.0	12.6	17.8	31.6	. . .	. . .	0.77	0.63	0.89	1.68
14. Derivatives of acyclic hydrocarbons (290330)	30.6	21.8	14.2	31.9	29.2	-4.58	1.3	0.99	0.72	1.59	1.55
15. Vaccines for veterinary medicine (300230)	. . .	26.3	20.6	17.5	28.0	. . .	. . .	1.20	1.04	0.87	1.48
16. Instruments using optical radiations (902750)	10.7	16.9	26.5	23.7	25.9	142.06	0.5	0.77	1.34	1.18	1.37
17. Synthetic filament yarn (540232)	40.1	14.1	6.1	19.7	25.5	-36.41	1.8	0.64	0.31	0.98	1.35
18. Photosensitive semiconductor devices (854140)	13.5	21.7	32.8	35.0	24.2	79.26	0.6	0.99	1.65	1.75	1.28
19. Non-ionic organic surface-active agents (340213)	11.6	14.7	16.6	18.5	20.4	75.86	0.5	0.67	0.84	0.92	1.08
20. Propylene copolymers (390230)	41.6	41.0	27.2	31.5	20.3	-51.20	1.8	1.87	1.37	1.57	1.08
21. Plates, sheets, film, foil, non-cellular, of polymers of propylene (392020)	. . .	15.8	11.7	15.4	18.8	. . .	. . .	0.72	0.59	0.77	1.00
22. Cellulose and its chemical derivatives in primary forms (391290)	. . .	8.6	13.6	14.5	17.7	. . .	. . .	0.39	0.69	0.72	0.94
23. Frozen orange juice (200911)	36.2	32.1	20.9	19.0	16.7	-53.87	1.6	1.46	1.05	0.95	0.89
24. Parts and accessories for automatic data processing (847330)	. . .	2.4	3.4	2.3	15.9	. . .	. . .	0.11	0.17	0.11	0.84
25. Chicken cuts and edible offal, frozen (020714)	. . .	13.3	13.3	15.9	15.8	. . .	. . .	0.61	0.67	0.79	0.84

X = Not applicable.
. . . = Not available.

Exports from Delaware

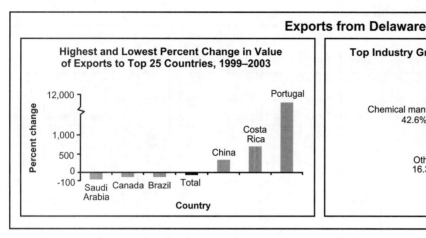

Highest and Lowest Percent Change in Value of Exports to Top 25 Countries, 1999–2003

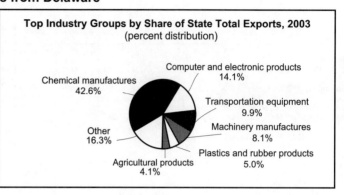

Top Industry Groups by Share of State Total Exports, 2003
(percent distribution)

Chemical manufactures 42.6%
Computer and electronic products 14.1%
Transportation equipment 9.9%
Machinery manufactures 8.1%
Plastics and rubber products 5.0%
Agricultural products 4.1%
Other 16.3%

- The value of exports from Delaware declined from $2.3 billion in 1999 to $1.9 billion in 2003. This drop of over 17 percent is the third highest in the nation, behind only Vermont and New Mexico.

- From 1999 to 2003, chemical manufactures exports dropped by $345 million, transportation equipment fell by $160 million, and fabricated metal products lost $44 million. Together, these three industries added up to a loss of nearly $550 million, which was offset somewhat by the computer and electronic products' gain of nearly $69 million, and the used merchandise increase of $40 million.

- Despite a drop of $576 million in exports to Canada, the country remains Delaware's top market. Exports to Mexico, the second largest market, increased by nearly 28 percent, or $55 million, from 1999 to 2003. Exports to Germany, ranked third, also increased, reaching $149 million in 2003.

Table E-12. Total U.S. Exports (Origin of Movement) via Delaware, 1999–2003—*Continued*

(Top 25 commodities and top 25 countries based on 2003 dollar value.)

Industry, commodity, and country	Value (millions of dollars)					Percent change, 1999–2003	Percent share of state total				
	1999	2000	2001	2002	2003		1999	2000	2001	2002	2003
TOTAL AND PERCENT SHARE OF U.S. TOTAL	2 286.7	2 197.4	1 984.8	2 003.8	1 886.1	-17.52	0.3	0.28	0.27	0.29	0.26
Top 25 Countries	2 102.3	2 076.7	1 802.5	1 876.0	1 769.9	-15.81	91.9	94.51	90.81	93.62	93.84
1. Canada	1 109.1	919.4	642.1	594.6	533.0	-51.94	48.5	41.84	32.35	29.67	28.26
2. Mexico	198.9	267.5	317.5	320.0	254.3	27.85	8.7	12.17	16.00	15.97	13.48
3. Germany	98.8	105.7	137.8	121.5	149.1	50.88	4.3	4.81	6.94	6.06	7.90
4. United Kingdom	81.9	131.2	105.5	213.9	105.8	29.21	3.6	5.97	5.32	10.67	5.61
5. Japan	127.5	110.6	105.1	102.7	103.7	-18.69	5.6	5.03	5.30	5.13	5.50
6. Taiwan	35.0	72.1	58.8	69.8	78.4	124.04	1.5	3.28	2.96	3.48	4.16
7. China	15.9	15.8	31.1	56.8	76.4	381.51	0.7	0.72	1.57	2.84	4.05
8. Netherlands	60.6	78.7	39.8	44.0	59.8	-1.30	2.6	3.58	2.01	2.20	3.17
9. Belgium	83.5	84.3	61.2	52.9	58.0	-30.55	3.6	3.84	3.08	2.64	3.08
10. Switzerland	26.2	26.2	14.9	21.1	47.5	80.96	1.2	1.19	0.75	1.05	2.52
11. Singapore	19.9	28.9	26.2	35.4	43.5	118.79	0.9	1.31	1.32	1.77	2.31
12. South Korea	21.8	22.6	31.7	33.1	38.5	76.48	1.0	1.03	1.59	1.65	2.04
13. Hong Kong	17.1	22.1	23.8	31.4	30.4	77.11	0.8	1.01	1.20	1.57	1.61
14. France	19.5	20.5	21.7	19.1	29.9	53.15	0.8	0.93	1.09	0.95	1.59
15. Colombia	20.1	29.2	21.5	17.4	23.6	17.63	0.9	1.33	1.08	0.87	1.25
16. Spain	31.5	18.2	23.3	13.0	21.2	-32.59	1.4	0.83	1.17	0.65	1.13
17. Brazil	32.2	31.6	33.2	38.7	20.4	-36.82	1.4	1.44	1.67	1.93	1.08
18. Costa Rica	2.1	5.0	20.0	13.2	20.2	844.96	0.1	0.23	1.01	0.66	1.07
19. Italy	13.3	16.2	15.8	16.1	15.9	20.27	0.6	0.74	0.79	0.80	0.85
20. Ireland	10.5	16.2	13.6	12.6	12.0	14.11	0.5	0.74	0.68	0.63	0.64
21. Australia	14.9	11.8	12.6	14.3	11.7	-21.73	0.6	0.54	0.64	0.71	0.62
22. Portugal	0.1	0.4	0.6	0.2	9.9	11 058.40	0.0	0.02	0.03	0.01	0.53
23. Thailand	4.9	4.7	5.9	9.8	9.3	91.20	0.2	0.21	0.30	0.49	0.49
24. Chile	12.3	12.5	14.7	11.0	9.0	-26.65	0.5	0.57	0.74	0.55	0.48
25. Saudi Arabia	44.6	25.3	24.2	13.5	8.4	-81.19	2.0	1.15	1.22	0.67	0.44

Table E-13. Total U.S. Exports (Origin of Movement) via District of Columbia, 1999–2003

(Top 25 commodities and top 25 countries based on 2003 dollar value.)

Industry, commodity, and country	Value (millions of dollars)					Percent change, 1999–2003	Percent share of city total				
	1999	2000	2001	2002	2003		1999	2000	2001	2002	2003
TOTAL AND PERCENT SHARE OF U.S. TOTAL	412.2	1 003.2	1 033.6	1 065.9	809.2	96.33	0.06	0.13	0.14	0.15	0.11
Manufactures (NAICS Code)	343.6	898.8	958.9	997.4	737.2	114.52	83.37	89.59	92.77	93.58	91.10
Processed foods (311)	15.6	21.3	19.1	7.8	4.9	-68.68	3.77	2.13	1.84	0.73	0.60
Beverages and tobacco products (312)	0.1	0.0	0.1	0.0	0.0	-78.90	0.03	0.00	0.01	0.00	0.00
Fabric mill products (313)	0.2	0.4	0.4	0.4	0.8	278.03	0.05	0.04	0.04	0.04	0.10
Non-apparel textile products (314)	0.2	2.9	2.2	3.2	7.0	2 828.87	0.06	0.29	0.21	0.30	0.87
Apparel manufactures (315)	1.0	0.8	0.4	1.0	0.7	-31.64	0.25	0.08	0.04	0.09	0.09
Leather and related products (316)	0.1	1.7	0.3	0.2	0.3	380.95	0.02	0.17	0.02	0.02	0.04
Wood products (321)	0.1	0.1	0.2	0.8	0.2	164.71	0.02	0.01	0.02	0.08	0.03
Paper products (322)	7.9	6.1	13.6	17.2	6.9	-12.21	1.91	0.61	1.32	1.62	0.85
Printing and related products (323)	3.4	14.5	13.0	13.6	16.9	403.06	0.82	1.44	1.26	1.27	2.09
Petroleum and coal products (324)	0.1	0.2	0.1	0.0	0.0	X	0.02	0.02	0.01	0.00	0.01
Chemical manufactures (325)	64.4	42.3	56.0	36.2	54.7	-15.03	15.62	4.22	5.42	3.39	6.76
Plastics and rubber products (326)	0.5	3.7	2.2	3.6	2.9	466.47	0.12	0.37	0.22	0.34	0.35
Non-metallic mineral products (327)	0.9	0.9	1.2	1.2	16.4	1 760.66	0.21	0.09	0.12	0.12	2.03
Primary metal manufactures (331)	0.1	1.1	0.2	0.6	0.3	206.48	0.03	0.11	0.02	0.06	0.04
Fabricated metal products (332)	4.2	172.8	146.9	251.4	126.8	2 923.90	1.02	17.23	14.21	23.59	15.67
Machinery manufactures (333)	9.9	80.4	20.2	12.2	27.2	174.92	2.40	8.02	1.95	1.14	3.37
Computer and electronic products (334)	59.1	85.8	90.4	84.8	108.9	84.25	14.34	8.55	8.75	7.96	13.45
Electrical equipment, appliances, and parts (335)	3.4	6.0	6.7	5.3	9.7	189.95	0.81	0.60	0.65	0.49	1.20
Transportation equipment (336)	166.9	442.5	576.4	545.9	341.4	104.56	40.50	44.11	55.76	51.22	42.19
Furniture and related products (337)	1.4	0.4	1.1	1.4	3.6	155.41	0.34	0.04	0.11	0.13	0.45
Miscellaneous manufactures (339)	4.3	14.8	8.2	10.5	7.3	71.92	1.03	1.48	0.80	0.99	0.91
Agricultural and Livestock Products (NAICS Code)	3.7	1.5	1.2	6.6	1.3	-63.99	0.89	0.15	0.11	0.62	0.16
Agricultural products (111)	3.6	1.5	1.2	6.6	1.3	-64.03	0.88	0.15	0.11	0.62	0.16
Livestock and livestock products (112)	0.0	0.0	0.0	0.0	0.0	X	0.00	0.00	0.00	0.00	0.00
Other Commodities (NAICS Code)	64.9	102.9	73.6	61.8	70.7	9.00	15.74	10.26	7.12	5.80	8.74
Forestry and logging (113)	0.0	0.5	0.4	1.0	0.0	X	0.00	0.05	0.04	0.10	0.00
Fishing, hunting, and trapping (114)	0.0	0.1	0.0	0.0	0.2	X	0.00	0.01	0.00	0.00	0.02
Oil and gas extraction (211)	0.0	0.0	0.0	0.0	0.0	X	0.00	0.00	0.00	0.00	0.00
Mining (212)	7.3	3.6	0.0	0.0	0.1	-98.45	1.78	0.36	0.00	0.00	0.01
Waste and scrap (910)	0.1	0.3	0.1	0.5	0.3	500.00	0.01	0.03	0.01	0.04	0.04
Used merchandise (920)	42.7	62.1	41.6	28.3	17.8	-58.24	10.35	6.19	4.02	2.66	2.20
Goods returned to Canada (980)	1.8	2.1	2.7	3.2	2.3	26.00	0.44	0.21	0.26	0.30	0.28
Special classification provisions (990)	13.0	34.2	28.7	28.8	50.0	285.50	3.15	3.41	2.78	2.70	6.18
Publishing industries (except Internet) (511)	0.0	0.0	0.0	0.0	0.0	X	0.00	0.00	0.00	0.00	0.00
TOTAL AND PERCENT SHARE OF U.S. TOTAL	412.2	1 003.2	1 033.6	1 065.9	809.2	96.33	0.06	0.13	0.14	0.15	0.11
Top 25 Commodities (HS Code)	250.4	677.0	645.3	836.5	640.9	155.95	60.75	67.49	62.43	78.48	79.20
1. Airplanes and aircraft, unladen wgt > 2,000 kg < 15,000 kg (880230)	4.9	324.2	338.5	415.9	237.6	4 748.98	1.19	32.32	32.75	39.02	29.36
2. Bomb mines other ammunitions projections and parts (930690)	1.2	122.8	124.3	235.5	111.5	9 191.67	0.29	12.24	12.03	22.09	13.78
3. Parts of airplanes or helicopters (880330)	98.5	72.6	39.0	34.0	70.1	-28.83	23.90	7.24	3.77	3.19	8.66
4. Uranium enriched in U235 (284420)	60.4	0.0	20.3	5.3	41.6	-31.13	14.65	0.00	1.96	0.50	5.14
5. Articles donated for relief (980240)	1.6	0.4	0.6	8.8	25.9	1 518.75	0.39	0.04	0.06	0.83	3.20
6. Parts and accessories for automatic data processing (847330)	6.6	13.6	18.0	10.7	20.4	209.09	1.60	1.36	1.74	1.00	2.52
7. Radar apparatus (852610)	0.4	14.3	0.9	6.9	14.3	3 475.00	0.10	1.43	0.09	0.65	1.77
8. Non-woven mats of glass fibers (701931)	...	0.0	0.0	0.0	12.8	...	...	0.00	0.00	0.00	1.58
9. Printed books and brochures (490199)	1.6	11.0	9.9	9.5	12.1	656.25	0.39	1.10	0.96	0.89	1.50
10. Parts of aircraft (880390)	15.2	1.7	1.0	10.6	9.4	-38.16	3.69	0.17	0.10	0.99	1.16
11. Parts of transmission or reception apparatus (852990)	4.8	1.7	1.6	4.7	8.1	68.75	1.16	0.17	0.15	0.44	1.00
12. Vessels and rowboats (890690)	0.0	0.0	0.0	3.5	8.1	X	0.00	0.00	0.00	0.33	1.00
13. Paintings, drawings, and pastels by hand (970110)	36.4	52.4	24.2	20.6	7.6	-79.12	8.83	5.22	2.34	1.93	0.94
14. Exports of military equipment (980320)	8.7	22.0	21.7	12.6	7.0	-19.54	2.11	2.19	2.10	1.18	0.87
15. Chemical wood-pulp, semi- or bleached non-coniferous (470329)	7.6	4.3	13.3	17.0	6.2	-18.42	1.84	0.43	1.29	1.59	0.77
16. Instruments specially designed for telecommunications (903040)	...	0.8	2.6	1.5	6.0	...	...	0.08	0.25	0.14	0.74
17. Digital automatic data processing machines (847149)	...	5.1	6.2	2.8	5.8	...	...	0.51	0.60	0.26	0.72
18. Prepared culture media for dvlp. of microorganisms (382100)	0.2	24.6	20.0	23.1	5.8	2 800.00	0.05	2.45	1.93	2.17	0.72
19. Tanks and other armored fighting vehicles and parts (871000)	0.5	6.7	0.1	5.9	5.7	1 040.00	0.12	0.67	0.01	0.55	0.70
20. Reception apparatus for radiotelephony, telegraphy (852790)	...	0.7	1.3	1.6	5.1	...	...	0.07	0.13	0.15	0.63
21. Electrical machines and apparatus with individ. functions (854389)	...	0.2	0.7	0.4	4.2	...	...	0.02	0.07	0.04	0.52
22. Machine parts with no electrical features (848590)	...	0.5	0.1	0.1	4.0	...	...	0.05	0.01	0.01	0.49
23. Parts of apparatus for line telephony or telegraphy (851790)	...	0.4	0.2	2.4	4.0	...	...	0.04	0.02	0.23	0.49
24. Original sculptures and statuary, in any material (970300)	2.9	0.4	4.4	3.6	3.8	31.03	0.70	0.04	0.43	0.34	0.47
25. Parts for pulley tackle, hoists, winches, and capst (843110)	...	0.2	0.0	0.6	3.8	...	...	0.02	0.00	0.06	0.47

X = Not applicable.
. . . = Not available.

Exports from District of Columbia

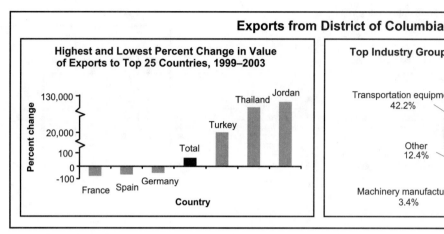

Highest and Lowest Percent Change in Value of Exports to Top 25 Countries, 1999–2003

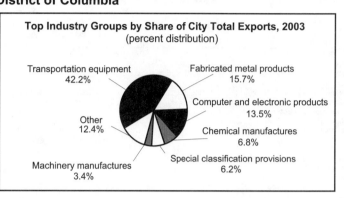

Top Industry Groups by Share of City Total Exports, 2003 (percent distribution)

- The value of total exports from the District of Columbia grew about 96 percent from 1999 to 2003, though the city's exports remain less than $1 billion. As a city, the District of Columbia is not directly comparable to the states, and as the data reflects the origin of movement rather than the production origin, data may be especially imprecise.

- Transportation equipment, fabricated metal products, and computer and electronic products combine to be more than 70 percent of the city's exports. Transportation equipment grew from $167 million to $341 million from 1999 to 2003.

- Thailand is the top recipient for the District of Columbia's goods. Nearly all of the $175 million worth of goods are in the transportation equipment industry. Exports to the United Kingdom and Egypt dropped considerably from 2001 to 2003, primarily because of a decline in transportation exports to those countries. Exports to Jordan increased from $14 million in 2002 to $76 million in 2003, making it the city's the third largest market.

Table E-13. Total U.S. Exports (Origin of Movement) via District of Columbia, 1999–2003—*Continued*

(Top 25 commodities and top 25 countries based on 2003 dollar value.)

Industry, commodity, and country	Value (millions of dollars)					Percent change, 1999–2003	Percent share of city total				
	1999	2000	2001	2002	2003		1999	2000	2001	2002	2003
TOTAL AND PERCENT SHARE OF U.S. TOTAL	412.2	1 003.2	1 033.6	1 065.9	809.2	96.33	0.06	0.13	0.14	0.15	0.11
Top 25 Countries	243.9	606.9	875.6	897.4	695.0	184.89	59.19	60.50	84.71	84.19	85.88
1. Thailand	0.2	9.3	0.5	35.4	175.0	114 998.00	0.04	0.92	0.04	3.32	21.62
2. United Kingdom	34.4	95.2	300.4	180.1	122.7	256.56	8.35	9.49	29.06	16.90	15.16
3. Jordan	0.1	11.7	7.0	14.1	76.3	129 171.00	0.01	1.16	0.68	1.33	9.43
4. Taiwan	0.5	71.9	56.3	41.2	40.7	8 156.80	0.12	7.17	5.45	3.86	5.03
5. Turkey	0.2	1.0	2.5	0.8	38.7	20 270.50	0.05	0.10	0.24	0.07	4.78
6. Italy	3.2	5.7	19.1	50.2	28.9	807.55	0.77	0.57	1.85	4.71	3.57
7. Egypt	0.2	22.0	294.9	411.4	23.8	10 164.20	0.06	2.19	28.53	38.59	2.94
8. Sweden	2.2	1.2	1.5	0.9	21.3	864.66	0.54	0.12	0.14	0.09	2.63
9. Bahrain	0.1	166.2	48.6	38.5	17.0	15 772.90	0.03	16.57	4.71	3.62	2.10
10. Canada	26.5	28.4	27.7	25.0	16.5	-37.73	6.44	2.83	2.68	2.35	2.04
11. Israel	0.6	16.0	18.8	13.3	13.9	2 338.64	0.14	1.59	1.82	1.25	1.72
12. Uzbekistan	0.1	0.0	0.1	1.3	12.8	16 697.30	0.02	0.00	0.01	0.13	1.58
13. New Zealand	0.5	4.2	2.2	2.8	10.9	2 146.91	0.12	0.42	0.21	0.26	1.35
14. Switzerland	6.4	2.3	6.2	7.5	10.5	64.93	1.54	0.23	0.60	0.71	1.30
15. France	121.2	48.3	25.2	9.6	10.2	-91.60	29.41	4.81	2.43	0.90	1.26
16. Austria	0.2	12.4	11.0	3.5	9.9	4 964.10	0.05	1.24	1.07	0.33	1.22
17. South Korea	2.9	39.1	6.3	6.8	8.8	200.31	0.71	3.90	0.61	0.63	1.09
18. Mexico	12.5	16.1	12.7	13.6	8.0	-36.32	3.04	1.61	1.23	1.27	0.99
19. Denmark	0.8	5.9	5.8	6.3	7.9	875.71	0.20	0.59	0.56	0.59	0.98
20. United Arab Emirates	0.5	0.7	0.7	2.2	7.8	1 412.14	0.13	0.07	0.06	0.21	0.97
21. Tunisia	0.6	4.7	5.8	5.9	7.4	1 131.13	0.15	0.47	0.56	0.55	0.92
22. Germany	12.9	38.2	12.5	12.0	7.2	-44.10	3.13	3.81	1.21	1.13	0.89
23. Ireland	0.5	2.1	1.3	0.5	6.4	1 311.09	0.11	0.21	0.13	0.04	0.79
24. Tajikistan	0.1	0.0	0.0	0.9	6.2	4 456.93	0.03	0.00	0.00	0.08	0.77
25. Spain	16.6	4.3	8.7	13.5	6.2	-62.68	4.03	0.43	0.84	1.27	0.77

Table E-14. Total U.S. Exports (Origin of Movement) via Florida, 1999–2003

(Top 25 commodities and top 25 countries based on 2003 dollar value.)

Industry, commodity, and country	Value (millions of dollars)					Percent change, 1999–2003	Percent share of state total				
	1999	2000	2001	2002	2003		1999	2000	2001	2002	2003
TOTAL AND PERCENT SHARE OF U.S. TOTAL	24 154.7	26 543.0	27 184.6	24 544.2	24 953.4	3.31	3.49	3.40	3.72	3.54	3.45
Manufactures (NAICS Code)	22 703.6	24 981.4	25 513.4	23 022.0	23 305.0	2.65	93.99	94.12	93.85	93.80	93.39
Processed foods (311)	995.3	997.2	1 055.0	961.2	996.2	0.09	4.12	3.76	3.88	3.92	3.99
Beverages and tobacco products (312)	64.8	62.1	78.7	91.5	133.9	106.69	0.27	0.00	0.29	0.37	0.54
Fabric mill products (313)	210.5	280.3	534.9	673.5	626.1	197.45	0.87	1.06	1.97	2.74	2.51
Non-apparel textile products (314)	69.3	79.3	78.1	76.3	76.3	10.20	0.29	0.30	0.29	0.31	0.31
Apparel manufactures (315)	1 252.6	1 252.0	703.6	431.4	363.7	-70.96	5.19	4.72	2.59	1.76	1.46
Leather and related products (316)	84.1	87.8	110.0	107.0	134.4	59.85	0.35	0.33	0.40	0.44	0.54
Wood products (321)	170.8	167.2	146.2	129.4	120.4	-29.50	0.71	0.63	0.54	0.53	0.48
Paper products (322)	612.9	779.6	760.1	694.3	675.2	10.17	2.54	2.94	2.80	2.83	2.71
Printing and related products (323)	121.7	123.0	145.8	184.7	163.9	34.72	0.50	0.46	0.54	0.75	0.66
Petroleum and coal products (324)	59.8	53.3	41.8	42.8	58.0	-3.03	0.25	0.20	0.15	0.17	0.23
Chemical manufactures (325)	2 956.6	2 501.8	2 569.9	2 673.2	2 920.9	-1.21	12.24	9.43	9.45	10.89	11.71
Plastics and rubber products (326)	431.1	478.7	481.6	434.8	414.6	-3.85	1.78	1.80	1.77	1.77	1.66
Non-metallic mineral products (327)	136.4	172.5	167.1	152.0	169.3	24.16	0.56	0.65	0.61	0.62	0.68
Primary metal manufactures (331)	352.2	400.8	415.3	353.2	369.6	4.94	1.46	1.51	1.53	1.44	1.48
Fabricated metal products (332)	458.9	524.3	582.4	528.3	566.5	23.44	1.90	1.98	2.14	2.15	2.27
Machinery manufactures (333)	2 473.6	2 727.2	3 129.0	2 354.2	2 249.0	-9.08	10.24	10.27	11.51	9.59	9.01
Computer and electronic products (334)	7 079.7	8 384.4	8 382.6	7 226.1	7 286.7	2.92	29.31	31.59	30.84	29.44	29.20
Electrical equipment, appliances, and parts (335)	968.9	1 136.2	1 141.1	889.0	838.9	-13.42	4.01	4.28	4.20	3.62	3.36
Transportation equipment (336)	2 908.8	3 436.8	3 649.9	3 638.5	3 728.0	28.16	12.04	12.95	13.43	14.82	14.94
Furniture and related products (337)	126.1	128.2	130.6	108.6	99.7	-20.91	0.52	0.48	0.48	0.44	0.40
Miscellaneous manufactures (339)	1 169.6	1 208.9	1 209.6	1 272.2	1 313.7	12.32	4.84	4.55	4.45	5.18	5.26
Agricultural and Livestock Products (NAICS Code)	543.7	569.1	609.3	633.6	626.7	15.25	2.25	2.14	2.24	2.58	2.51
Agricultural products (111)	490.7	534.2	555.1	588.9	589.7	20.17	2.03	2.01	2.04	2.40	2.36
Livestock and livestock products (112)	53.0	34.9	54.2	44.7	36.9	-30.33	0.22	0.13	0.20	0.18	0.15
Other Commodities (NAICS Code)	907.4	992.5	1 061.9	888.6	1 021.8	12.60	3.76	3.74	3.91	3.62	4.09
Forestry and logging (113)	11.5	12.6	12.7	15.9	14.4	25.05	0.05	0.05	0.05	0.06	0.06
Fishing, hunting, and trapping (114)	83.5	92.3	124.6	82.6	104.1	24.58	0.35	0.35	0.46	0.34	0.42
Oil and gas extraction (211)	1.8	3.0	3.4	3.9	4.4	141.85	0.01	0.01	0.01	0.02	0.02
Mining (212)	41.5	46.4	26.6	32.7	33.8	-18.57	0.17	0.17	0.10	0.13	0.14
Waste and scrap (910)	46.8	79.6	95.6	116.8	223.0	376.85	0.19	0.30	0.35	0.48	0.89
Used merchandise (920)	101.8	178.6	225.2	132.9	138.8	36.38	0.42	0.67	0.83	0.54	0.56
Goods returned to Canada (980)	48.0	79.3	70.6	40.1	32.2	-32.87	0.20	0.30	0.26	0.16	0.13
Special classification provisions (990)	572.5	500.7	503.2	463.9	430.0	-24.88	2.37	1.89	1.85	1.89	1.72
Publishing industries (except Internet) (511)	0.0	0.0	0.0	0.0	41.1	X	0.00	0.00	0.00	0.00	0.16
TOTAL AND PERCENT SHARE OF U.S. TOTAL	24 154.7	26 543.0	27 184.6	24 544.2	24 953.4	3.31	3.49	3.40	3.72	3.54	3.45
Top 25 Commodities (HS Code)	6 651.1	8 101.0	8 658.7	8 232.9	8 960.3	34.72	27.54	30.52	31.85	33.54	35.91
1. Fertilizers (310000)	1 786.5	1 236.8	1 161.8	1 227.2	1 417.8	-20.64	7.40	4.66	4.27	5.00	5.68
2. Parts and accessories for automatic data processing (847330)	1 059.3	1 283.7	1 372.8	1 018.6	1 369.8	29.31	4.39	4.84	5.05	4.15	5.49
3. Parts of airplanes or helicopters (880330)	765.7	803.7	732.2	723.9	818.1	6.84	3.17	3.03	2.69	2.95	3.28
4. Transmission and reception apparatus (852520)	879.9	845.5	969.4	807.3	805.8	-8.42	3.64	3.19	3.57	3.29	3.23
5. Digital monolithic integrated circuits (854221)	0.0	0.0	0.0	484.1	604.1	X	0.00	0.00	0.00	1.97	2.42
6. Turbojets of a thrust > 25 kn (841112)	383.7	654.8	706.4	458.9	533.3	38.99	1.59	2.47	2.60	1.87	2.14
7. Automatic data processing input or output units (847160)	122.5	195.6	197.8	198.6	287.1	134.37	0.51	0.74	0.73	0.81	1.15
8. Instruments and appliances for medical sciences (901890)	120.8	159.0	225.1	221.6	240.4	99.01	0.50	0.60	0.83	0.90	0.96
9. Parts of transmission or reception apparatus (852990)	168.6	376.4	379.4	289.8	237.8	41.04	0.70	1.42	1.40	1.18	0.95
10. Jewelry and parts thereof, of precious metal (711319)	141.1	132.4	103.7	154.7	217.9	54.43	0.58	0.50	0.38	0.63	0.87
11. Chemical wood-pulp, unbleached non-coniferous (470321)	84.7	159.4	213.3	205.7	208.3	145.93	0.35	0.60	0.78	0.84	0.83
12. Gas turbine parts (841199)	133.0	237.6	283.2	158.5	191.2	43.76	0.55	0.90	1.04	0.65	0.77
13. Motorboats, other than outboard motorboats (890392)	. . .	97.4	73.8	92.6	186.8	. . .	. . .	0.37	0.27	0.38	0.75
14. Parts of apparatus for line telephony or telegraphy (851790)	349.0	418.5	416.7	440.2	185.1	-46.96	1.44	1.58	1.53	1.79	0.74
15. Automatic data processing storage units (847170)	. . .	105.7	116.4	115.1	174.0	. . .	. . .	0.40	0.43	0.47	0.70
16. Parts of aircraft (880390)	26.3	83.2	185.9	226.5	171.9	553.61	0.11	0.31	0.68	0.92	0.69
17. Passenger vehicle, spark-ignition, > 1,500 cc < 3,000 cc (870323)	. . .	173.1	119.6	137.7	170.1	. . .	. . .	0.65	0.44	0.56	0.68
18. Grapefruit, fresh or dried (080540)	138.9	160.1	154.7	165.1	160.9	15.84	0.58	0.60	0.57	0.67	0.64
19. Portable digital a.d.p. machines < 10 kg (847130)	. . .	92.8	159.1	120.4	160.6	. . .	. . .	0.35	0.59	0.49	0.64
20. Passenger vehicles, spark-ignition, > 3,000 cc (870324)	94.5	48.3	99.5	237.7	151.7	60.53	0.39	0.18	0.37	0.97	0.61
21. Digital automatic data processing machines (847149)	. . .	214.4	193.8	142.4	148.2	. . .	. . .	0.81	0.71	0.58	0.59
22. Turbojet and turbo-propeller parts (841191)	155.0	110.7	238.6	150.0	136.1	-12.19	0.64	0.42	0.88	0.61	0.55
23. A.d.p. machines; mag./opt. rdrs; trnscrb/proc. data (847190)	241.6	264.6	301.1	210.4	128.6	-46.77	1.00	1.00	1.11	0.86	0.52
24. Parts and accessories of motor vehicles (870899)	. . .	112.9	121.0	120.4	128.4	. . .	. . .	0.43	0.45	0.49	0.51
25. Perfumes and toilet waters (330300)	. . .	134.4	133.4	125.5	126.3	. . .	. . .	0.51	0.49	0.51	0.51

X = Not applicable.
. . . = Not available.

Exports from Florida

Highest and Lowest Percent Change in Value of Exports to Top 25 Countries, 1999–2003

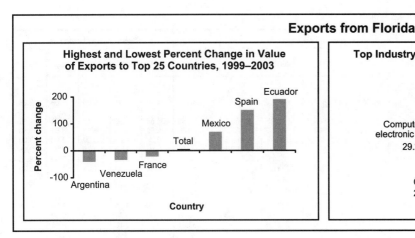

Top Industry Groups by Share of State Total Exports, 2003
(percent distribution)

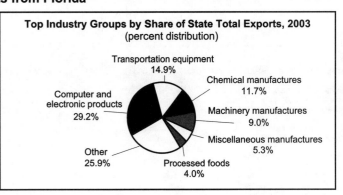

- As one of the nation's top exporters, Florida exported $25 billion worth of goods in 2003, and nearly $7.3 billion in computer and electronic products alone. In 2003, transportation equipment was the second largest export, with $3.7 billion. Waste and scrap exports grew from about $47 million in 1999 to $223 million in 2003. Fabric mill products also had a strong growth rate during this period, nearly tripling from 1999, and reached $626 million in 2003.

- Just over 10 percent of Florida's goods were exported to Brazil, the state's top export country in 2003. Those goods were valued at $2.5 billion. Exports to Mexico increased by nearly 75 percent from 1999 to 2003, making the country the third largest market for Florida's goods. Exports to Ecuador nearly tripled from 1999 to 2003. Computer and electronic products to Ecuador increased from $24 million to $156 million during this period.

- Fertilizers are Florida's top commodity export. However, they declined more than 20 percent from 1999. Parts and accessories for automatic data processing machines rank a close second in commodity exports.

Table E-14. Total U.S. Exports (Origin of Movement) via Florida, 1999–2003—Continued

(Top 25 commodities and top 25 countries based on 2003 dollar value.)

Industry, commodity, and country	Value (millions of dollars)					Percent change, 1999–2003	Percent share of state total				
	1999	2000	2001	2002	2003		1999	2000	2001	2002	2003
TOTAL AND PERCENT SHARE OF U.S. TOTAL	24 154.7	26 543.0	27 184.6	24 544.2	24 953.4	3.31	3.49	3.40	3.72	3.54	3.45
Top 25 Countries	18 361.9	20 338.2	21 158.8	19 131.6	19 129.4	4.18	76.02	76.62	77.83	77.95	76.66
1. Brazil	2 447.7	3 171.9	3 624.9	2 781.5	2 537.0	3.65	10.13	11.95	13.33	11.33	10.17
2. Canada	2 168.1	2 553.0	2 587.8	2 294.3	2 368.5	9.24	8.98	9.62	9.52	9.35	9.49
3. Mexico	1 040.7	1 669.6	1 694.6	1 476.7	1 814.5	74.35	4.31	6.29	6.23	6.02	7.27
4. Dominican Republic	1 216.4	1 365.9	1 398.6	1 278.3	1 059.2	-12.92	5.04	5.15	5.14	5.21	4.24
5. Colombia	919.2	922.1	1 009.6	961.0	1 017.7	10.72	3.81	3.47	3.71	3.92	4.08
6. Venezuela	1 143.0	1 130.5	1 640.7	1 232.9	775.8	-32.13	4.73	4.26	6.04	5.02	3.11
7. United Kingdom	881.2	988.9	929.9	811.3	761.5	-13.58	3.65	3.73	3.42	3.31	3.05
8. Japan	679.2	819.0	845.9	796.5	745.8	9.79	2.81	3.09	3.11	3.25	2.99
9. China	739.7	569.3	514.2	724.5	649.5	-12.19	3.06	2.14	1.89	2.95	2.60
10. Costa Rica	572.0	482.3	465.0	572.8	638.5	11.62	2.37	1.82	1.71	2.33	2.56
11. Chile	522.5	684.4	625.7	601.0	637.0	21.91	2.16	2.58	2.30	2.45	2.55
12. Guatemala	543.4	508.1	532.0	596.3	595.9	9.65	2.25	1.91	1.96	2.43	2.39
13. Spain	210.6	180.8	192.7	304.8	546.3	159.37	0.87	0.68	0.71	1.24	2.19
14. Bahamas	391.0	537.1	518.1	502.3	523.8	33.94	1.62	2.02	1.91	2.05	2.10
15. Germany	511.3	565.7	536.7	479.0	499.4	-2.33	2.12	2.13	1.97	1.95	2.00
16. Argentina	872.9	892.9	756.5	236.1	451.0	-48.33	3.61	3.36	2.78	0.96	1.81
17. Ecuador	149.5	186.5	373.3	488.6	435.6	191.50	0.62	0.70	1.37	1.99	1.75
18. Peru	414.0	402.8	382.2	397.1	428.5	3.48	1.71	1.52	1.41	1.62	1.72
19. Netherlands	489.0	426.3	460.5	411.7	407.2	-16.71	2.02	1.61	1.69	1.68	1.63
20. France	527.7	414.4	398.7	388.4	397.2	-24.73	2.18	1.56	1.47	1.58	1.59
21. Singapore	473.4	422.4	295.0	405.9	384.3	-18.81	1.96	1.59	1.09	1.65	1.54
22. Paraguay	286.6	249.7	260.0	349.7	372.7	30.03	1.19	0.94	0.96	1.42	1.49
23. El Salvador	380.3	382.6	309.7	302.1	362.8	-4.59	1.57	1.44	1.14	1.23	1.45
24. Jamaica	320.4	328.6	407.9	386.8	361.3	12.77	1.33	1.24	1.50	1.58	1.45
25. Honduras	462.1	483.4	398.5	351.9	358.3	-22.46	1.91	1.82	1.47	1.43	1.44

Table E-15. Total U.S. Exports (Origin of Movement) via Georgia, 1999–2003

(Top 25 commodities and top 25 countries based on 2003 dollar value.)

Industry, commodity, and country	Value (millions of dollars)					Percent change, 1999–2003	Percent share of state total				
	1999	2000	2001	2002	2003		1999	2000	2001	2002	2003
TOTAL AND PERCENT SHARE OF U.S. TOTAL	13 748.7	14 925.1	14 643.7	14 412.7	16 286.2	18.46	1.98	1.91	2.00	2.08	2.25
Manufactures (NAICS Code)	12 739.6	13 827.4	13 498.5	13 193.3	14 963.8	17.46	92.66	92.65	92.18	91.54	91.88
Processed foods (311)	388.3	476.8	587.8	549.3	623.2	60.49	2.82	3.19	4.01	3.81	3.83
Beverages and tobacco products (312)	868.8	860.6	439.7	461.3	488.3	-43.79	6.32	0.00	3.00	3.20	3.00
Fabric mill products (313)	262.1	387.6	406.6	467.1	480.1	83.15	1.91	2.60	2.78	3.24	2.95
Non-apparel textile products (314)	455.0	466.2	422.3	364.0	367.9	-19.15	3.31	3.12	2.88	2.53	2.26
Apparel manufactures (315)	322.4	332.6	264.7	187.6	147.1	-54.36	2.35	2.23	1.81	1.30	0.90
Leather and related products (316)	25.3	24.8	22.3	15.3	15.7	-37.84	0.18	0.17	0.15	0.11	0.10
Wood products (321)	92.9	106.6	122.5	123.9	129.1	39.02	0.68	0.71	0.84	0.86	0.79
Paper products (322)	1 167.6	1 455.7	1 401.2	1 341.1	1 361.5	16.61	8.49	9.75	9.57	9.30	8.36
Printing and related products (323)	40.6	51.7	69.9	74.3	69.3	70.89	0.30	0.35	0.48	0.52	0.43
Petroleum and coal products (324)	5.6	19.3	15.6	21.9	20.1	257.01	0.04	0.13	0.11	0.15	0.12
Chemical manufactures (325)	1 265.2	1 510.6	1 740.2	1 872.8	2 096.1	65.68	9.20	10.12	11.88	12.99	12.87
Plastics and rubber products (326)	236.1	302.8	285.5	278.6	315.2	33.51	1.72	2.03	1.95	1.93	1.94
Non-metallic mineral products (327)	102.5	147.6	166.2	100.2	97.2	-5.20	0.75	0.99	1.13	0.70	0.60
Primary metal manufactures (331)	465.0	125.0	116.4	89.7	116.8	-74.89	3.38	0.84	0.79	0.62	0.72
Fabricated metal products (332)	231.3	327.0	259.4	265.8	286.1	23.72	1.68	2.19	1.77	1.84	1.76
Machinery manufactures (333)	1 475.1	1 868.1	1 755.1	1 361.9	1 555.5	5.45	10.73	12.52	11.99	9.45	9.55
Computer and electronic products (334)	1 326.6	1 593.5	1 860.4	1 868.8	2 469.3	86.14	9.65	10.68	12.70	12.97	15.16
Electrical equipment, appliances, and parts (335)	569.9	727.6	797.8	620.2	576.3	1.11	4.15	4.88	5.45	4.30	3.54
Transportation equipment (336)	2 922.5	2 491.9	2 173.8	2 542.2	3 131.5	7.15	21.26	16.70	14.84	17.64	19.23
Furniture and related products (337)	34.2	36.6	33.9	30.6	31.6	-7.52	0.25	0.25	0.23	0.21	0.19
Miscellaneous manufactures (339)	482.7	514.8	557.3	556.8	585.8	21.37	3.51	3.45	3.81	3.86	3.60
Agricultural and Livestock Products (NAICS Code)	123.9	189.9	217.1	318.6	364.4	194.08	0.90	1.27	1.48	2.21	2.24
Agricultural products (111)	101.5	164.1	171.4	256.8	309.6	204.88	0.74	1.10	1.17	1.78	1.90
Livestock and livestock products (112)	22.4	25.8	45.7	61.8	54.8	145.05	0.16	0.17	0.31	0.43	0.34
Other Commodities (NAICS Code)	885.1	907.8	928.0	900.7	958.0	8.24	6.44	6.08	6.34	6.25	5.88
Forestry and logging (113)	6.1	6.9	7.8	16.9	22.6	268.20	0.04	0.05	0.05	0.12	0.14
Fishing, hunting, and trapping (114)	2.0	2.7	8.9	14.2	9.0	354.08	0.01	0.02	0.06	0.10	0.06
Oil and gas extraction (211)	3.2	0.1	0.2	0.2	0.2	-93.01	0.02	0.00	0.00	0.00	0.00
Mining (212)	548.0	616.8	603.5	552.9	582.8	6.36	3.99	4.13	4.12	3.84	3.58
Waste and scrap (910)	56.5	64.8	81.9	81.4	98.8	74.81	0.41	0.43	0.56	0.56	0.61
Used merchandise (920)	18.4	39.3	23.4	21.5	40.4	119.00	0.13	0.26	0.16	0.15	0.25
Goods returned to Canada (980)	37.0	34.9	36.4	25.7	19.3	-47.87	0.27	0.23	0.25	0.18	0.12
Special classification provisions (990)	213.9	142.2	165.9	188.0	172.3	-19.42	1.56	0.95	1.13	1.30	1.06
Publishing industries (except Internet) (511)	0.0	0.0	0.0	0.0	12.6	X	0.00	0.00	0.00	0.00	0.08
TOTAL AND PERCENT SHARE OF U.S. TOTAL	13 748.7	14 925.1	14 643.7	14 412.7	16 286.2	18.46	1.98	1.91	2.00	2.08	2.25
Top 25 Commodities (HS Code)	5 187.4	5 922.7	5 313.8	5 962.5	7 458.6	43.78	37.73	39.68	36.29	41.37	45.80
1. Passenger vehicles, spark-ignition, > 3,000 cc (870324)	710.1	926.6	853.9	944.8	1 188.3	67.34	5.16	6.21	5.83	6.56	7.30
2. Electrical apparatus for line telephony or telegraphy (851750)	3.4	30.5	64.0	177.4	657.6	19 241.18	0.02	0.20	0.44	1.23	4.04
3. Parts of apparatus for line telephony or telegraphy (851790)	38.0	81.8	74.2	344.4	564.8	1 386.32	0.28	0.55	0.51	2.39	3.47
4. Kaolin (250700)	510.2	548.8	527.4	496.7	519.5	1.82	3.71	3.68	3.60	3.45	3.19
5. Gas turbine parts (841199)	278.6	331.5	271.9	310.2	501.6	80.04	2.03	2.22	1.86	2.15	3.08
6. Cigarettes (240220)	831.0	816.6	416.8	430.4	447.2	-46.19	6.04	5.47	2.85	2.99	2.75
7. Parts of airplanes or helicopters (880330)	296.4	267.3	324.5	298.2	374.9	26.48	2.16	1.79	2.22	2.07	2.30
8. Chemical wood-pulp, unbleached non-coniferous (470321)	352.6	432.2	385.8	392.5	341.7	-3.09	2.56	2.90	2.63	2.72	2.10
9. Lactones (293229)	0.1	0.1	218.0	301.0	337.2	337 100.00	0.00	0.00	1.49	2.09	2.07
10. Kraftliner, uncoated and unbleached (480411)	255.2	304.5	241.5	227.4	242.2	-5.09	1.86	2.04	1.65	1.58	1.49
11. Carboxylic acids (291819)	124.0	261.1	134.4	219.9	238.8	92.58	0.90	1.75	0.92	1.53	1.47
12. Airplane and aircraft, unladen weight > 15,000 kg (880240)	868.7	431.3	128.9	234.2	237.6	-72.65	6.32	2.89	0.88	1.62	1.46
13. Contact lenses (900130)	119.9	206.9	225.9	217.7	221.4	84.65	0.87	1.39	1.54	1.51	1.36
14. Chicken cuts and edible offal, frozen (020714)	87.7	126.6	176.7	169.7	201.0	129.19	0.64	0.85	1.21	1.18	1.23
15. Carpets made of nylon (570320)	214.2	257.2	220.3	186.2	191.6	-10.55	1.56	1.72	1.50	1.29	1.18
16. Kraft paper, bleached (481032)	84.8	93.7	135.2	104.5	160.1	88.80	0.62	0.63	0.92	0.73	0.98
17. Chemical wood pulp, dissolving grades (470200)	154.0	152.5	160.6	152.9	153.5	-0.32	1.12	1.02	1.10	1.06	0.94
18. Tractors (870190)	103.5	152.6	130.4	161.1	146.6	41.64	0.75	1.02	0.89	1.12	0.90
19. Parts and accessories of motor vehicles (870899)	71.0	71.2	91.7	98.1	129.9	82.96	0.52	0.48	0.63	0.68	0.80
20. Cotton, not carded or combed (520100)	. . .	22.3	44.2	75.3	109.1	. . .	. . .	0.15	0.30	0.52	0.67
21. Passenger vehicles for snow; golf carts and similar (870310)	84.1	115.5	125.7	105.2	107.6	27.94	0.61	0.77	0.86	0.73	0.66
22. Mixtures of odoriferous substances used in food or drink (330210)	. . .	18.3	29.9	43.5	100.8	. . .	. . .	0.12	0.20	0.30	0.62
23. Automatic data processing units (847180)	. . .	62.6	61.3	70.1	96.2	. . .	. . .	0.42	0.42	0.49	0.59
24. Heterocyclic compounds with nitrogen hetero-atoms (293329)	0.0	23.8	75.0	113.7	96.0	X	0.00	0.16	0.51	0.79	0.59
25. Parts and accessories for automatic data processing (847330)	. . .	187.3	195.6	87.4	93.4	. . .	. . .	1.25	1.34	0.61	0.57

X = Not applicable.
. . . = Not available.

Exports from Georgia

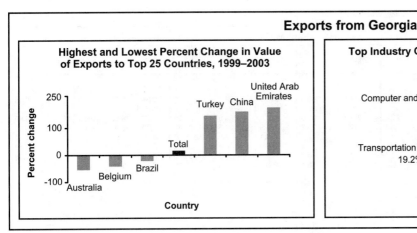

Highest and Lowest Percent Change in Value of Exports to Top 25 Countries, 1999–2003

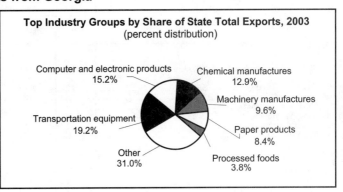

Top Industry Groups by Share of State Total Exports, 2003
(percent distribution)

Computer and electronic products 15.2%
Chemical manufactures 12.9%
Machinery manufactures 9.6%
Paper products 8.4%
Processed foods 3.8%
Other 31.0%
Transportation equipment 19.2%

- Georgia's exports increased 13 percent from 2002 to 2003. Computer and electronic products rose by more than $600 million, or 32 percent, over this one-year period. As a result, this industry increased to 15 percent of the state's total exports. Transportation equipment remains Georgia's largest export, with $3.1 billion in 2003. The largest declines in exports were in primary metals, beverages and tobacco products, and apparel.

- Passenger vehicles are the state's top commodity export. In 2003, they accounted for more than 7 percent of Georgia's exports. Exports of lactones, which are organic compounds used for various purposes, increased from $100,000 in 1999 to over $337 million in 2003.

- Canada is the largest market for Georgia's exports. In 2003, the state exported goods worth close to $4 billion to Canada, up from about $3.1 billion in 1999. More than one-third of these exports were transportation equipment. Exports to China grew from $200 million in 1999 to $644 million in 2003. Paper products and computer and electronic products are Georgia's leading exports to China.

Table E-15. Total U.S. Exports (Origin of Movement) via Georgia, 1999–2003—*Continued*

(Top 25 commodities and top 25 countries based on 2003 dollar value.)

Industry, commodity, and country	Value (millions of dollars)					Percent change, 1999–2003	Percent share of state total				
	1999	2000	2001	2002	2003		1999	2000	2001	2002	2003
TOTAL AND PERCENT SHARE OF U.S. TOTAL	13 748.7	14 925.1	14 643.7	14 412.7	16 286.2	18.46	1.98	1.91	2.00	2.08	2.25
Top 25 Countries	11 562.6	12 540.4	12 002.3	12 075.7	13 883.6	20.07	84.10	84.02	81.96	83.78	85.25
1. Canada	3 149.9	3 571.9	3 750.5	3 637.7	3 961.6	25.77	22.91	23.93	25.61	25.24	24.33
2. Japan	1 670.5	1 685.9	1 366.8	1 248.7	1 517.3	-9.17	12.15	11.30	9.33	8.66	9.32
3. Mexico	946.3	1 106.4	948.2	1 091.4	1 163.2	22.92	6.88	7.41	6.48	7.57	7.14
4. United Kingdom	1 003.9	626.1	782.9	954.3	1 036.1	3.20	7.30	4.19	5.35	6.62	6.36
5. Netherlands	434.4	480.2	425.0	625.8	892.8	105.51	3.16	3.22	2.90	4.34	5.48
6. China	200.4	327.0	390.0	415.6	644.2	221.46	1.46	2.19	2.66	2.88	3.96
7. Germany	536.3	653.4	615.1	561.2	609.0	13.56	3.90	4.38	4.20	3.89	3.74
8. France	278.1	307.4	343.0	338.4	358.4	28.85	2.02	2.06	2.34	2.35	2.20
9. South Korea	188.4	252.1	239.2	221.2	328.5	74.31	1.37	1.69	1.63	1.53	2.02
10. Italy	228.5	450.9	266.4	244.8	316.2	38.38	1.66	3.02	1.82	1.70	1.94
11. Brazil	367.8	334.3	418.8	291.8	310.1	-15.69	2.68	2.24	2.86	2.02	1.90
12. Belgium	471.8	354.8	235.9	234.4	299.8	-36.47	3.43	2.38	1.61	1.63	1.84
13. Australia	544.9	439.9	249.3	252.4	287.6	-47.22	3.96	2.95	1.70	1.75	1.77
14. Hong Kong	228.7	287.5	325.3	276.1	280.4	22.63	1.66	1.93	2.22	1.92	1.72
15. Ireland	189.9	339.0	258.1	315.5	279.9	47.39	1.38	2.27	1.76	2.19	1.72
16. Singapore	208.9	227.1	234.3	236.9	261.1	25.00	1.52	1.52	1.60	1.64	1.60
17. Taiwan	195.8	278.0	241.8	212.6	248.9	27.14	1.42	1.86	1.65	1.47	1.53
18. Saudi Arabia	170.2	149.0	167.3	122.8	179.3	5.37	1.24	1.00	1.14	0.85	1.10
19. Dominican Republic	98.3	137.4	168.9	169.0	164.7	67.53	0.71	0.92	1.15	1.17	1.01
20. Honduras	143.2	142.1	158.6	162.8	150.8	5.31	1.04	0.95	1.08	1.13	0.93
21. Spain	96.8	110.7	134.4	105.3	135.5	39.96	0.70	0.74	0.92	0.73	0.83
22. United Arab Emirates	37.9	53.2	65.2	96.8	126.7	234.73	0.28	0.36	0.45	0.67	0.78
23. Turkey	37.4	66.4	59.1	90.2	116.3	210.83	0.27	0.45	0.40	0.63	0.71
24. India	55.1	83.1	69.6	84.7	107.6	95.37	0.40	0.56	0.48	0.59	0.66
25. Thailand	79.2	76.5	88.7	85.2	107.6	35.81	0.58	0.51	0.61	0.59	0.66

Table E-16. Total U.S. Exports (Origin of Movement) via Hawaii, 1999–2003

(Top 25 commodities and top 25 countries based on 2003 dollar value.)

Industry, commodity, and country	Value (millions of dollars)					Percent change, 1999–2003	Percent share of state total				
	1999	2000	2001	2002	2003		1999	2000	2001	2002	2003
TOTAL AND PERCENT SHARE OF U.S. TOTAL	273.6	386.8	369.9	513.7	368.2	34.60	0.04	0.05	0.05	0.07	0.05
Manufactures (NAICS Code)	221.2	307.8	302.0	420.3	289.8	30.98	80.87	79.59	81.65	81.83	78.69
Processed foods (311)	19.4	28.9	26.2	23.9	24.3	25.47	7.09	7.46	7.08	4.65	6.61
Beverages and tobacco products (312)	0.7	0.8	1.0	1.1	4.9	605.50	0.25	0.00	0.26	0.21	1.32
Fabric mill products (313)	0.5	0.5	0.4	0.3	0.7	30.44	0.19	0.13	0.10	0.05	0.18
Non-apparel textile products (314)	0.7	1.0	0.8	1.5	0.3	-54.90	0.25	0.26	0.21	0.30	0.08
Apparel manufactures (315)	7.9	7.9	6.1	3.5	1.9	-76.35	2.89	2.05	1.65	0.68	0.51
Leather and related products (316)	2.1	2.0	2.8	7.1	18.3	786.82	0.75	0.52	0.75	1.38	4.97
Wood products (321)	0.5	1.0	0.6	0.2	0.4	-23.79	0.20	0.25	0.15	0.03	0.11
Paper products (322)	0.4	2.4	2.4	2.5	2.3	533.80	0.13	0.63	0.66	0.48	0.61
Printing and related products (323)	2.4	1.6	1.7	1.7	1.0	-58.29	0.89	0.41	0.45	0.33	0.28
Petroleum and coal products (324)	74.6	121.5	92.4	77.2	74.6	-0.04	27.28	31.40	24.97	15.02	20.26
Chemical manufactures (325)	3.1	4.7	4.2	3.9	4.3	36.22	1.14	1.22	1.14	0.76	1.16
Plastics and rubber products (326)	0.3	1.0	0.7	0.3	0.7	112.02	0.12	0.26	0.18	0.06	0.20
Non-metallic mineral products (327)	1.4	0.3	0.3	0.1	0.9	-30.37	0.49	0.08	0.08	0.02	0.26
Primary metal manufactures (331)	0.5	1.0	1.1	0.3	0.2	-69.81	0.20	0.27	0.31	0.05	0.04
Fabricated metal products (332)	1.7	0.6	1.6	1.5	1.1	-39.15	0.64	0.15	0.44	0.28	0.29
Machinery manufactures (333)	7.9	11.0	6.5	11.2	21.6	174.60	2.88	2.85	1.75	2.18	5.87
Computer and electronic products (334)	48.7	54.6	59.4	29.1	28.6	-41.25	17.80	14.13	16.06	5.67	7.77
Electrical equipment, appliances, and parts (335)	1.6	7.1	2.0	1.6	1.5	-8.53	0.60	1.83	0.54	0.32	0.41
Transportation equipment (336)	29.9	44.3	79.5	244.3	93.4	212.06	10.94	11.46	21.50	47.57	25.37
Furniture and related products (337)	0.3	0.4	0.7	0.2	0.2	-29.97	0.12	0.12	0.19	0.05	0.06
Miscellaneous manufactures (339)	16.4	15.1	11.8	8.9	8.6	-47.72	6.00	3.90	3.18	1.73	2.33
Agricultural and Livestock Products (NAICS Code)	19.5	21.5	22.9	18.1	18.9	-2.65	7.11	5.55	6.18	3.53	5.14
Agricultural products (111)	15.8	18.0	19.5	13.9	14.4	-8.94	5.79	4.65	5.26	2.71	3.91
Livestock and livestock products (112)	3.6	3.5	3.4	4.2	4.5	24.79	1.33	0.90	0.92	0.81	1.23
Other Commodities (NAICS Code)	32.9	57.5	45.0	75.2	59.5	81.01	12.02	14.87	12.17	14.64	16.16
Forestry and logging (113)	0.1	0.1	0.0	0.1	0.1	59.72	0.03	0.02	0.01	0.01	0.03
Fishing, hunting, and trapping (114)	5.6	6.0	7.0	7.2	7.1	26.81	2.05	1.56	1.90	1.40	1.93
Oil and gas extraction (211)	0.1	0.1	0.1	0.1	0.1	92.42	0.02	0.02	0.02	0.02	0.03
Mining (212)	0.5	0.1	0.2	0.1	0.2	-64.29	0.18	0.04	0.05	0.02	0.05
Waste and scrap (910)	6.7	18.3	17.2	23.2	31.0	364.10	2.44	4.73	4.66	4.52	8.42
Used merchandise (920)	11.4	20.1	9.3	5.4	5.2	-54.03	4.15	5.19	2.51	1.06	1.42
Goods returned to Canada (980)	3.2	2.1	2.2	1.7	1.8	-44.03	1.17	0.55	0.59	0.33	0.49
Special classification provisions (990)	5.4	10.7	9.0	37.4	14.0	158.29	1.98	2.76	2.43	7.29	3.79
Publishing industries (except Internet) (511)	0.0	0.0	0.0	0.0	0.0	X	0.00	0.00	0.00	0.00	0.00
TOTAL AND PERCENT SHARE OF U.S. TOTAL	273.6	386.8	369.9	513.7	368.2	34.60	0.04	0.05	0.05	0.07	0.05
Top 25 Commodities (HS Code)	63.1	96.5	132.4	416.2	271.1	329.64	23.07	24.95	35.80	81.03	73.62
1. Light oils and preparations (not crude) from petroleum (271011)	0.0	0.0	0.0	77.2	71.2	X	0.00	0.00	0.00	15.03	19.34
2. Airplane and aircraft, unladen weight > 15,000 kg (880240)	0.0	0.0	40.0	212.4	56.5	X	0.00	0.00	10.81	41.35	15.34
3. Ferrous waste and scrap (720449)	4.6	11.8	10.0	14.8	18.5	302.17	1.68	3.05	2.70	2.88	5.02
4. Gas turbines (841182)	2.1	0.0	0.1	7.4	14.7	600.00	0.77	0.00	0.03	1.44	3.99
5. Turbojets of a thrust > 25 kn (841112)	9.5	20.8	4.6	12.2	13.9	46.32	3.47	5.38	1.24	2.38	3.77
6. Patent leather handbags (420221)	0.4	0.5	0.5	2.4	11.8	2 850.00	0.15	0.13	0.14	0.47	3.20
7. Papayas, fresh (080720)	11.1	9.9	10.4	8.5	9.1	-18.02	4.06	2.56	2.81	1.65	2.47
8. Parts of airplanes or helicopters (880330)	11.7	10.6	25.2	4.5	7.3	-37.61	4.28	2.74	6.81	0.88	1.98
9. Cocoa preparations (180690)	7.2	8.5	7.8	6.5	6.7	-6.94	2.63	2.20	2.11	1.27	1.82
10. Exports of military equipment (980320)	. . .	2.2	0.1	28.7	6.5	. . .	. . .	0.57	0.03	5.59	1.77
11. Instruments, aeronautical-space nav., no compass (901420)	4.2	3.7	5.9	4.9	5.3	26.19	1.54	0.96	1.60	0.95	1.44
12. Patent leather articles for pocket or handbag (420231)	0.1	0.0	0.1	3.2	4.8	4 700.00	0.04	0.00	0.03	0.62	1.30
13. Pass. vehicles, spark-ignition eng. cylinder cap. < 1,000 cc (870321)	. . .	0.0	0.0	1.2	4.6	. . .	. . .	0.00	0.00	0.23	1.25
14. Seaweed and other algae (121220)	1.5	3.2	3.4	4.0	4.2	180.00	0.55	0.83	0.92	0.78	1.14
15. Paintings, drawings, and pastels by hand (970110)	7.1	12.1	6.2	3.8	3.9	-45.07	2.60	3.13	1.68	0.74	1.06
16. Digital automatic data processing machines (847149)	0.7	3.3	4.6	5.3	3.8	442.86	0.26	0.85	1.24	1.03	1.03
17. Instruments and appliances for medical sciences (901890)	0.1	0.8	0.1	2.2	3.7	3 600.00	0.04	0.21	0.03	0.43	1.00
18. Commingled food exports, donated for relief (980210)	. . .	2.4	3.3	3.1	3.3	. . .	. . .	0.62	0.89	0.60	0.90
19. Waste oils (271099)	. . .	0.0	0.0	0.0	3.3	. . .	. . .	0.00	0.00	0.00	0.90
20. Nuts and seeds, prepared (200819)	1.5	3.3	5.8	4.7	3.2	113.33	0.55	0.85	1.57	0.92	0.87
21. Fermented beverages (220600)	. . .	0.0	0.0	0.0	3.2	. . .	. . .	0.00	0.00	0.00	0.87
22. Motorcycles (871150)	. . .	0.3	0.2	1.8	3.0	. . .	. . .	0.08	0.05	0.35	0.81
23. Stainless steel waste and scrap (720421)	0.0	0.3	0.8	3.0	3.0	X	0.00	0.08	0.22	0.58	0.81
24. Coffee, not roasted, not decaffeinated (090111)	. . .	2.2	3.2	1.8	3.0	. . .	. . .	0.57	0.87	0.35	0.81
25. Live bovine animals (010290)	2.6	2.5	2.0	2.6	2.6	0.00	0.95	0.65	0.54	0.51	0.71

X = Not applicable.
. . . = Not available.

Exports from Hawaii

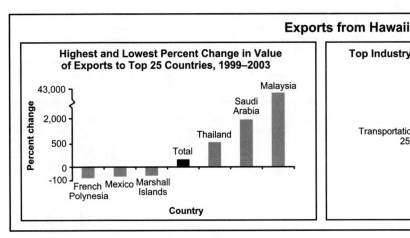

Highest and Lowest Percent Change in Value of Exports to Top 25 Countries, 1999–2003

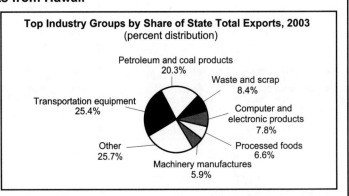

Top Industry Groups by Share of State Total Exports, 2003
(percent distribution)

Petroleum and coal products 20.3%
Waste and scrap 8.4%
Transportation equipment 25.4%
Computer and electronic products 7.8%
Other 25.7%
Processed foods 6.6%
Machinery manufactures 5.9%

- In 2003, Hawaii had the second lowest value of exports among all the states, behind only Montana. From 1999 to 2003, total exports increased 34.6 percent, which was among the highest growth rates in the nation. However, the 2003 total exports were down $145 million from 2002. Exports peaked at $514 million in 2002, which was attributable to a large jump in transportation exports.

- Transportation equipment and petroleum and coal products are Hawaii's leading exports. In 2002, transportation exports were worth $244 million, up $165 million, or 207 percent, from 2001, but by 2003, they were back down to $93.4 million. Leather and related products jumped more than 786 percent from 1999 to 2003, and now account for nearly 5 percent of the state's exports.

- Japan is the top market for Hawaii's exports. Exports to Malaysia grew from $148,000 in 1999 to more than $63 million in 2003. Nearly 90 percent of these exports were transportation equipment. In 2003, Hawaii was the only state or territory without Mexico among its top 20 trading partners.

Table E-16. Total U.S. Exports (Origin of Movement) via Hawaii, 1999–2003—Continued

(Top 25 commodities and top 25 countries based on 2003 dollar value.)

Industry, commodity, and country	Value (millions of dollars)					Percent change, 1999–2003	Percent share of state total				
	1999	2000	2001	2002	2003		1999	2000	2001	2002	2003
TOTAL AND PERCENT SHARE OF U.S. TOTAL	273.6	386.8	369.9	513.7	368.2	34.60	0.04	0.05	0.05	0.07	0.05
Top 25 Countries	267.0	379.7	357.3	503.3	364.2	36.39	97.61	98.17	96.61	97.98	98.91
1. Japan	134.5	211.4	140.3	163.7	147.9	10.00	49.16	54.64	37.93	31.86	40.17
2. Malaysia	0.1	0.5	0.3	6.7	63.5	42 835.80	0.05	0.12	0.08	1.31	17.26
3. South Korea	38.7	45.2	55.6	22.5	33.6	-13.14	14.15	11.69	15.02	4.38	9.13
4. Canada	26.7	30.3	24.2	19.0	19.6	-26.37	9.75	7.83	6.54	3.69	5.33
5. New Zealand	12.7	20.4	63.3	97.9	19.3	51.79	4.64	5.26	17.12	19.06	5.24
6. China	2.0	5.0	13.4	8.0	12.9	530.87	0.75	1.29	3.63	1.56	3.50
7. Germany	2.7	4.3	3.3	3.9	10.8	291.85	1.00	1.10	0.90	0.75	2.92
8. Hong Kong	5.9	9.6	10.5	8.7	10.1	71.41	2.16	2.47	2.85	1.69	2.75
9. France	1.7	2.0	7.7	2.8	8.7	418.45	0.62	0.53	2.09	0.55	2.37
10. Philippines	5.8	4.5	5.3	4.9	6.4	10.61	2.12	1.16	1.44	0.95	1.74
11. Singapore	7.4	9.9	6.6	77.1	5.6	-24.38	2.70	2.57	1.79	15.00	1.52
12. Thailand	0.8	1.7	1.4	3.6	5.3	556.05	0.30	0.43	0.38	0.71	1.44
13. United Kingdom	3.7	3.2	1.9	2.0	4.5	20.77	1.37	0.84	0.51	0.39	1.23
14. Marshall Islands	7.4	9.4	2.8	2.6	3.3	-54.86	2.69	2.43	0.76	0.51	0.90
15. Taiwan	2.9	5.2	7.6	17.0	2.3	-21.01	1.06	1.35	2.07	3.30	0.62
16. Netherlands	1.0	2.0	1.3	2.8	1.7	69.20	0.38	0.51	0.35	0.54	0.47
17. Australia	2.7	6.2	2.1	54.8	1.5	-42.22	0.98	1.59	0.58	10.66	0.42
18. Italy	0.6	0.4	1.7	1.3	1.4	139.90	0.22	0.11	0.45	0.25	0.39
19. Sweden	0.5	0.8	0.3	0.3	1.4	179.38	0.18	0.22	0.08	0.06	0.37
20. Saudi Arabia	0.1	0.0	0.0	0.0	1.2	1 706.25	0.02	0.01	0.00	0.00	0.31
21. Switzerland	0.8	1.4	1.0	0.3	0.8	3.56	0.28	0.36	0.28	0.06	0.21
22. French Polynesia	6.7	0.5	1.4	0.1	0.7	-88.87	2.45	0.13	0.37	0.02	0.20
23. India	0.2	0.3	2.4	0.4	0.5	234.81	0.06	0.07	0.64	0.08	0.14
24. Mexico	1.3	2.4	2.0	2.9	0.5	-59.35	0.46	0.63	0.55	0.56	0.14
25. Chile	0.2	3.3	0.8	0.1	0.4	133.16	0.07	0.85	0.22	0.03	0.12

Table E-17. Total U.S. Exports (Origin of Movement) via Idaho, 1999–2003

(Top 25 commodities and top 25 countries based on 2003 dollar value.)

Industry, commodity, and country	Value (millions of dollars)					Percent change, 1999–2003	Percent share of state total				
	1999	2000	2001	2002	2003		1999	2000	2001	2002	2003
TOTAL AND PERCENT SHARE OF U.S. TOTAL	2 191.5	3 558.6	2 122.1	1 967.0	2 095.8	-4.37	0.32	0.46	0.29	0.28	0.29
Manufactures (NAICS Code)	2 056.7	3 391.5	1 960.9	1 818.4	1 940.5	-5.65	93.85	95.30	92.41	92.45	92.59
Processed foods (311)	202.6	237.7	266.8	258.4	268.7	32.61	9.25	6.68	12.57	13.14	12.82
Beverages and tobacco products (312)	0.1	0.1	0.0	0.1	0.0	-40.38	0.00	0.00	0.00	0.01	0.00
Fabric mill products (313)	0.3	0.2	0.3	0.1	0.6	115.85	0.01	0.01	0.01	0.00	0.03
Non-apparel textile products (314)	0.1	0.1	0.1	0.5	0.6	314.49	0.01	0.00	0.00	0.02	0.03
Apparel manufactures (315)	0.7	1.0	0.7	0.8	0.7	1.52	0.03	0.03	0.03	0.04	0.03
Leather and related products (316)	1.8	1.9	2.2	1.9	2.9	60.53	0.08	0.05	0.10	0.09	0.14
Wood products (321)	21.4	38.5	34.4	31.4	31.1	45.74	0.98	1.08	1.62	1.60	1.49
Paper products (322)	93.9	98.5	98.4	106.3	112.8	20.14	4.29	2.77	4.64	5.40	5.38
Printing and related products (323)	3.1	6.2	3.8	3.5	4.4	43.41	0.14	0.17	0.18	0.18	0.21
Petroleum and coal products (324)	0.4	0.1	0.1	0.0	0.1	-76.81	0.02	0.00	0.00	0.00	0.00
Chemical manufactures (325)	93.5	129.8	112.7	95.7	153.2	63.88	4.27	3.65	5.31	4.87	7.31
Plastics and rubber products (326)	2.6	7.7	8.8	5.5	3.5	32.26	0.12	0.22	0.42	0.28	0.17
Non-metallic mineral products (327)	2.8	3.1	4.6	4.5	3.1	12.35	0.13	0.09	0.22	0.23	0.15
Primary metal manufactures (331)	1.5	1.6	1.5	1.2	3.3	117.08	0.07	0.04	0.07	0.06	0.16
Fabricated metal products (332)	16.2	16.1	13.4	16.6	17.2	6.18	0.74	0.45	0.63	0.84	0.82
Machinery manufactures (333)	88.0	79.1	58.9	79.9	76.4	-13.17	4.02	2.22	2.78	4.06	3.65
Computer and electronic products (334)	1 469.5	2 710.7	1 310.8	1 170.2	1 206.1	-17.93	67.05	76.17	61.77	59.49	57.55
Electrical equipment, appliances, and parts (335)	13.8	16.1	14.8	13.0	26.8	93.95	0.63	0.45	0.70	0.66	1.28
Transportation equipment (336)	33.9	35.0	19.7	19.7	18.4	-45.85	1.55	0.98	0.93	1.00	0.88
Furniture and related products (337)	1.5	1.8	1.3	0.8	1.6	9.76	0.07	0.05	0.06	0.04	0.08
Miscellaneous manufactures (339)	9.0	6.3	7.5	8.4	9.0	-0.13	0.41	0.18	0.36	0.43	0.43
Agricultural and Livestock Products (NAICS Code)	85.7	92.1	91.7	78.9	93.2	8.72	3.91	2.59	4.32	4.01	4.45
Agricultural products (111)	79.7	74.2	79.2	76.0	91.3	14.67	3.63	2.09	3.73	3.86	4.36
Livestock and livestock products (112)	6.1	17.9	12.6	2.9	1.9	-69.31	0.28	0.50	0.59	0.15	0.09
Other Commodities (NAICS Code)	49.1	75.0	69.4	69.7	62.1	26.50	2.24	2.11	3.27	3.54	2.96
Forestry and logging (113)	6.5	10.7	5.1	5.6	3.9	-40.39	0.30	0.30	0.24	0.28	0.19
Fishing, hunting, and trapping (114)	1.5	1.5	1.5	1.3	1.1	-26.72	0.07	0.04	0.07	0.06	0.05
Oil and gas extraction (211)	0.0	0.0	0.0	0.0	0.1	X	0.00	0.00	0.00	0.00	0.00
Mining (212)	20.8	34.0	44.4	46.3	39.6	90.71	0.95	0.95	2.09	2.35	1.89
Waste and scrap (910)	1.4	1.3	1.2	1.1	3.7	155.70	0.07	0.04	0.06	0.06	0.17
Public administration (920)	0.7	0.6	0.8	0.5	2.3	245.75	0.03	0.02	0.04	0.02	0.11
Goods returned to Canada (980)	3.0	2.6	3.6	4.4	3.4	14.05	0.14	0.07	0.17	0.22	0.16
Special classification provisions (990)	15.2	24.3	12.8	10.6	8.0	-47.18	0.69	0.68	0.60	0.54	0.38
Publishing industries (except Internet) (511)	0.0	0.0	0.0	0.0	0.0	X	0.00	0.00	0.00	0.00	0.00
TOTAL AND PERCENT SHARE OF U.S. TOTAL	2 191.5	3 558.6	2 122.1	1 967.0	2 095.8	-4.37	0.32	0.46	0.29	0.28	0.29
Top 25 Commodities (HS Code)	871.2	1 219.5	847.8	1 501.5	1 645.2	88.84	39.75	34.27	39.95	76.34	78.50
1. Digital monolithic integrated circuits (854221)	0.0	0.0	0.0	502.9	558.1	X	0.00	0.00	0.00	25.57	26.63
2. Parts and accessories for automatic data processing (847330)	477.2	721.2	312.7	403.1	469.1	-1.70	21.78	20.27	14.74	20.49	22.38
3. Prepared frozen potatoes (200410)	86.9	91.0	88.4	90.6	94.2	8.40	3.97	2.56	4.17	4.61	4.49
4. Fertilizers (310000)	49.9	82.6	69.6	48.1	89.2	78.76	2.28	2.32	3.28	2.45	4.26
5. Non-digital monolithic integrated circuits (854229)	0.0	0.0	0.0	68.6	83.0	X	0.00	0.00	0.00	3.49	3.96
6. Uncoated Kraft paper and paperboard (480442)	53.3	48.9	63.9	66.4	69.9	31.14	2.43	1.37	3.01	3.38	3.34
7. Automatic data processing storage units (847170)	40.5	32.0	26.5	15.2	26.5	-34.57	1.85	0.90	1.25	0.77	1.26
8. Whole hides and skins of bovine/equine > 16 kg (410150)	0.0	0.0	0.0	20.3	20.6	X	0.00	0.00	0.00	1.03	0.98
9. Beauty and skin care preparations (330499)	7.4	20.0	14.6	16.0	19.9	168.92	0.34	0.56	0.69	0.81	0.95
10. Potato flakes, granules and pellets (110520)	12.1	16.5	13.0	12.0	18.0	48.76	0.55	0.46	0.61	0.61	0.86
11. Lactose (170219)	1.5	1.9	12.0	16.3	17.8	1 086.67	0.07	0.05	0.57	0.83	0.85
12. Sweet corn, not frozen (200580)	9.4	18.8	17.5	14.8	16.2	72.34	0.43	0.53	0.82	0.75	0.77
13. Copper ores and concentrates (260300)	3.8	14.0	21.0	28.5	15.9	318.42	0.17	0.39	0.99	1.45	0.76
14. Lead ores and concentrates (260700)	8.5	13.2	14.2	10.7	13.3	56.47	0.39	0.37	0.67	0.54	0.63
15. Other food preparations (210690)	13.9	12.4	12.3	12.0	13.3	-4.32	0.63	0.35	0.58	0.61	0.63
16. Parts of instruments for measuring radiation (903090)	30.1	22.4	26.8	27.7	13.2	-56.15	1.37	0.63	1.26	1.41	0.63
17. Wood in chips or particles, non-coniferous (440122)	0.0	12.7	14.7	10.9	13.0	X	0.00	0.36	0.69	0.55	0.62
18. Paper, paperboard coated with plastic, > 150 g/m2 (481151)	0.0	0.0	0.0	24.6	12.9	X	0.00	0.00	0.00	1.25	0.62
19. Parts, electric apparatus, electric circuit (853890)	. . .	1.1	0.3	0.1	12.6	. . .	. . .	0.03	0.01	0.01	0.60
20. Dried vegetables (071290)	11.6	11.0	12.0	10.9	12.3	6.03	0.53	0.31	0.57	0.55	0.59
21. Dried shelled peas including seed (071310)	. . .	9.5	9.4	7.6	11.7	. . .	. . .	0.27	0.44	0.39	0.56
22. Cartridges and parts thereof (930630)	9.9	7.4	8.1	10.0	11.5	16.16	0.45	0.21	0.38	0.51	0.55
23. Dried shelled lentils including seed (071340)	. . .	5.4	4.2	6.2	11.0	. . .	. . .	0.15	0.20	0.32	0.52
24. Uncoated paper and paperboard in rolls or sheets (480591)	. . .	0.0	0.0	0.4	11.0	. . .	. . .	0.00	0.00	0.02	0.52
25. Automatic data processing units (847180)	55.2	77.5	106.9	78.1	11.0	-80.07	2.52	2.18	5.04	3.97	0.52

X = Not applicable.
. . . = Not available.

Exports from Idaho

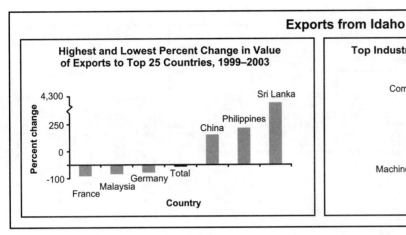

Highest and Lowest Percent Change in Value of Exports to Top 25 Countries, 1999–2003

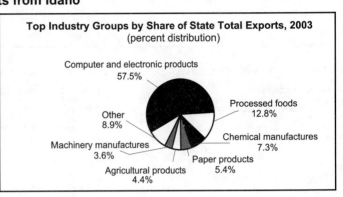

Top Industry Groups by Share of State Total Exports, 2003 (percent distribution)

- Idaho's exports were down about 10 percent, or nearly $224 million, from 1999 to 2002; however, they rebounded in 2003, increasing 6.5 percent from 2002. Computer and electronic products remain the state's leading export, composing nearly 58 percent of Idaho's total exports, though they were down 18 percent from 1999, when computer and electronic products accounted for 67 percent of the state's total exports.

- Processed foods are Idaho's second leading export. They make up nearly 13 percent of the state's total exports, and are up nearly 33 percent from 1999. Chemical manufactures exports increased from less than $94 million in 1999 to $153 million in 2003, to become Idaho's third largest export.

- Canada is the leading market for Idaho's goods, followed by the United Kingdom and Japan. From 1999 to 2003, exports to China and to the Philippines increased $72 million and $54 million, respectively. Both countries are now among Idaho's top 10 markets.

Table E-17. Total U.S. Exports (Origin of Movement) via Idaho, 1999–2003—Continued

(Top 25 commodities and top 25 countries based on 2003 dollar value.)

Industry, commodity, and country	Value (millions of dollars)					Percent change, 1999–2003	Percent share of state total				
	1999	2000	2001	2002	2003		1999	2000	2001	2002	2003
TOTAL AND PERCENT SHARE OF U.S. TOTAL	2 191.5	3 558.6	2 122.1	1 967.0	2 095.8	-4.37	0.32	0.46	0.29	0.28	0.29
Top 25 Countries	2 060.4	3 444.8	2 019.6	1 876.3	2 023.7	-1.78	94.02	96.80	95.17	95.39	96.56
1. Canada	287.7	417.4	353.5	295.4	361.9	25.79	13.13	11.73	16.66	15.02	17.27
2. United Kingdom	363.7	611.8	288.2	322.4	349.6	-3.88	16.60	17.19	13.58	16.39	16.68
3. Japan	255.9	308.2	235.1	259.8	269.4	5.29	11.68	8.66	11.08	13.21	12.85
4. Singapore	260.2	1 026.4	372.9	172.9	204.3	-21.49	11.87	28.84	17.57	8.79	9.75
5. Taiwan	163.2	148.8	123.0	100.2	131.4	-19.50	7.45	4.18	5.80	5.10	6.27
6. Hong Kong	78.4	108.4	47.1	76.2	106.7	36.21	3.58	3.05	2.22	3.87	5.09
7. China	34.1	57.2	68.5	88.3	106.6	212.37	1.56	1.61	3.23	4.49	5.09
8. Philippines	24.1	49.3	88.3	85.8	78.4	225.27	1.10	1.39	4.16	4.36	3.74
9. Malaysia	204.6	145.6	79.5	167.4	77.6	-62.05	9.33	4.09	3.74	8.51	3.70
10. South Korea	36.9	61.3	65.8	58.2	61.9	67.86	1.68	1.72	3.10	2.96	2.96
11. Mexico	63.7	107.4	62.7	60.1	55.6	-12.64	2.91	3.02	2.95	3.05	2.66
12. Germany	77.9	61.6	29.6	27.2	29.8	-61.77	3.56	1.73	1.40	1.38	1.42
13. Netherlands	22.2	37.8	24.2	20.2	27.6	24.17	1.01	1.06	1.14	1.03	1.32
14. Italy	32.8	63.6	45.3	31.6	26.8	-18.28	1.50	1.79	2.14	1.61	1.28
15. Australia	28.9	31.3	19.6	21.3	24.1	-16.55	1.32	0.88	0.92	1.08	1.15
16. United Arab Emirates	16.9	50.5	24.2	14.2	21.0	23.76	0.77	1.42	1.14	0.72	1.00
17. Israel	23.6	42.7	18.8	15.2	20.6	-12.66	1.08	1.20	0.88	0.77	0.99
18. France	43.1	47.7	23.5	13.8	14.4	-66.63	1.97	1.34	1.11	0.70	0.69
19. Thailand	12.4	25.5	9.6	7.0	11.8	-5.17	0.57	0.72	0.45	0.36	0.56
20. India	4.8	2.0	3.1	2.3	11.5	138.48	0.22	0.06	0.14	0.12	0.55
21. Spain	6.8	9.0	6.4	11.3	9.2	34.81	0.31	0.25	0.30	0.57	0.44
22. Indonesia	5.1	4.5	15.2	5.6	6.7	31.53	0.23	0.13	0.72	0.28	0.32
23. Sri Lanka	0.1	0.5	0.4	0.2	6.0	4 245.99	0.01	0.01	0.02	0.01	0.28
24. Ireland	8.8	15.3	6.2	10.2	5.9	-33.28	0.40	0.43	0.29	0.52	0.28
25. Belgium	4.3	11.0	9.0	9.6	4.9	13.82	0.19	0.31	0.43	0.49	0.23

Table E-18. Total U.S. Exports (Origin of Movement) via Illinois, 1999–2003

(Top 25 commodities and top 25 countries based on 2003 dollar value.)

Industry, commodity, and country	Value (millions of dollars)					Percent change, 1999–2003	Percent share of state total				
	1999	2000	2001	2002	2003		1999	2000	2001	2002	2003
TOTAL AND PERCENT SHARE OF U.S. TOTAL	29 432.2	31 437.6	30 434.4	25 686.4	26 472.9	-10.05	4.25	4.03	4.16	3.71	3.66
Manufactures (NAICS Code)	28 608.3	30 452.4	29 434.2	24 696.2	25 336.4	-11.44	97.20	96.87	96.71	96.14	95.71
Processed foods (311)	995.6	1 174.8	1 238.6	1 205.5	1 297.2	30.29	3.38	3.74	4.07	4.69	4.90
Beverages and tobacco products (312)	25.1	27.0	29.7	21.3	42.6	69.92	0.09	0.00	0.10	0.08	0.16
Fabric mill products (313)	53.2	67.5	79.7	58.5	55.2	3.84	0.18	0.21	0.26	0.23	0.21
Non-apparel textile products (314)	34.0	38.0	36.1	32.9	38.3	12.70	0.12	0.12	0.12	0.13	0.14
Apparel manufactures (315)	46.9	54.7	52.7	26.7	20.9	-55.43	0.16	0.17	0.17	0.10	0.08
Leather and related products (316)	35.1	44.0	123.4	157.8	132.3	276.50	0.12	0.14	0.41	0.61	0.50
Wood products (321)	80.0	86.0	77.9	39.4	42.7	-46.65	0.27	0.27	0.26	0.15	0.16
Paper products (322)	545.0	561.4	519.9	510.6	489.9	-10.11	1.85	1.79	1.71	1.99	1.85
Printing and related products (323)	388.1	347.8	345.8	300.7	296.2	-23.69	1.32	1.11	1.14	1.17	1.12
Petroleum and coal products (324)	81.2	114.8	67.4	59.9	53.3	-34.34	0.28	0.37	0.22	0.23	0.20
Chemical manufactures (325)	3 056.2	3 372.7	3 763.0	3 517.5	3 891.0	27.32	10.38	10.73	12.36	13.69	14.70
Plastics and rubber products (326)	756.6	875.6	876.6	822.7	796.6	5.29	2.57	2.79	2.88	3.20	3.01
Non-metallic mineral products (327)	208.6	235.6	248.0	239.2	294.7	41.27	0.71	0.75	0.81	0.93	1.11
Primary metal manufactures (331)	490.5	603.4	588.3	511.9	574.2	17.07	1.67	1.92	1.93	1.99	2.17
Fabricated metal products (332)	896.5	962.2	909.8	957.5	1 077.5	20.19	3.05	3.06	2.99	3.73	4.07
Machinery manufactures (333)	7 334.6	7 471.8	7 108.7	6 528.3	6 892.9	-6.02	24.92	23.77	23.36	25.42	26.04
Computer and electronic products (334)	5 408.4	5 116.2	4 367.4	3 939.9	3 664.4	-32.25	18.38	16.27	14.35	15.34	13.84
Electrical equipment, appliances, and parts (335)	1 592.2	1 800.7	1 884.6	1 625.3	1 710.6	7.44	5.41	5.73	6.19	6.33	6.46
Transportation equipment (336)	5 590.4	6 448.2	6 037.4	3 254.4	2 950.2	-47.23	18.99	20.51	19.84	12.67	11.14
Furniture and related products (337)	97.7	94.1	88.0	72.9	87.7	-10.30	0.33	0.30	0.29	0.28	0.33
Miscellaneous manufactures (339)	892.6	955.9	991.3	813.3	928.2	3.99	3.03	3.04	3.26	3.17	3.51
Agricultural and Livestock Products (NAICS Code)	191.6	220.3	204.5	286.9	273.2	42.60	0.65	0.70	0.67	1.12	1.03
Agricultural products (111)	164.7	199.2	183.8	255.5	255.2	54.90	0.56	0.63	0.60	0.99	0.96
Livestock and livestock products (112)	26.8	21.1	20.7	31.4	18.0	-32.95	0.09	0.07	0.07	0.12	0.07
Other Commodities (NAICS Code)	632.3	764.8	795.7	703.4	863.4	36.54	2.15	2.43	2.61	2.74	3.26
Forestry and logging (113)	9.2	9.6	10.9	15.0	17.9	94.53	0.03	0.03	0.04	0.06	0.07
Fishing, hunting, and trapping (114)	1.6	2.7	1.7	1.6	2.4	45.38	0.01	0.01	0.01	0.01	0.01
Oil and gas extraction (211)	36.3	55.3	75.6	102.7	183.4	405.71	0.12	0.18	0.25	0.40	0.69
Mining (212)	32.6	32.8	47.1	28.8	30.3	-7.12	0.11	0.10	0.15	0.11	0.11
Waste and scrap (910)	98.1	161.1	155.3	192.7	247.3	151.97	0.33	0.51	0.51	0.75	0.93
Used merchandise (920)	91.6	117.1	191.9	56.8	47.7	-47.88	0.31	0.37	0.63	0.22	0.18
Goods returned to Canada (980)	89.5	66.6	63.1	49.8	40.6	-54.70	0.30	0.21	0.21	0.19	0.15
Special classification provisions (990)	273.3	319.6	250.1	256.1	288.0	5.37	0.93	1.02	0.82	1.00	1.09
Publishing industries (except Internet) (511)	0.0	0.0	0.0	0.0	5.8	X	0.00	0.00	0.00	0.00	0.02
TOTAL AND PERCENT SHARE OF U.S. TOTAL	29 432.2	31 437.6	30 434.4	25 686.4	26 472.9	-10.05	4.25	4.03	4.16	3.71	3.66
Top 25 Commodities (HS Code)	8 194.3	8 300.7	7 857.1	6 984.2	7 440.3	-9.20	27.84	26.40	25.82	27.19	28.11
1. Other parts and attachments for derricks (843149)	429.5	487.9	372.6	484.0	730.8	70.15	1.46	1.55	1.22	1.88	2.76
2. Parts and accessories of motor vehicles (870899)	539.7	699.4	649.7	640.4	604.4	11.99	1.83	2.22	2.13	2.49	2.28
3. Dumpers designed for off-highway use (870410)	347.0	451.9	486.4	437.1	536.8	54.70	1.18	1.44	1.60	1.70	2.03
4. Compression-ignition internal combustion engines (840820)	634.6	590.4	481.3	572.1	486.2	-23.38	2.16	1.88	1.58	2.23	1.84
5. Parts and accessories of motor vehicles bodies (870829)	181.0	221.1	215.5	296.5	425.2	134.92	0.61	0.70	0.71	1.15	1.61
6. Passenger vehicle, spark-ignition, > 1,500 cc < 3,000 cc (870323)	1 307.0	1 759.4	1 624.4	638.9	395.9	-69.71	4.44	5.60	5.34	2.49	1.50
7. Composite diagnostic or laboratory reagents (382200)	296.5	310.2	350.0	345.3	376.8	27.08	1.01	0.99	1.15	1.34	1.42
8. Retail medicaments in measured dose (300490)	215.8	189.9	454.6	312.2	375.2	73.86	0.73	0.60	1.49	1.22	1.42
9. Mechanical front-end shovel loaders (842951)	285.5	283.9	247.9	231.3	321.9	12.75	0.97	0.90	0.81	0.90	1.22
10. Parts of spark-ignition internal combustion piston (840999)	179.7	180.2	175.9	285.8	292.6	62.83	0.61	0.57	0.58	1.11	1.11
11. Transmission and reception apparatus (852520)	1 344.1	946.9	589.6	496.9	289.6	-78.45	4.57	3.01	1.94	1.93	1.09
12. Other compression-ignition internal combustion engines (840890)	196.7	180.2	158.6	173.7	257.1	30.71	0.67	0.57	0.52	0.68	0.97
13. Combine harvester-threshers (843351)	203.8	210.0	192.0	203.9	244.6	20.02	0.69	0.67	0.63	0.79	0.92
14. Boards, panels, consoles for electrical control (853710)	189.1	182.3	187.9	191.1	215.5	13.96	0.64	0.58	0.62	0.74	0.81
15. Lysine and its esters; salts thereof (292241)	105.3	114.7	139.4	140.5	211.5	100.85	0.36	0.36	0.46	0.55	0.80
16. Parts of transmission or reception apparatus (852990)	987.5	458.7	347.6	207.5	206.8	-79.06	3.36	1.46	1.14	0.81	0.78
17. Digital monolithic integrated circuits (854221)	0.0	0.0	0.0	259.4	196.5	X	0.00	0.00	0.00	1.01	0.74
18. Track-laying tractors (870130)	186.2	175.9	195.9	201.8	183.8	-1.29	0.63	0.56	0.64	0.79	0.69
19. Parts of airplanes or helicopters (880330)	177.2	171.3	209.9	187.2	173.6	-2.03	0.60	0.54	0.69	0.73	0.66
20. X-ray/high tension generators (902290)	107.4	126.5	142.3	169.2	164.9	53.54	0.36	0.40	0.47	0.66	0.62
21. Graders and levelers, self-propelled (842920)	92.3	112.7	117.9	134.3	159.3	72.59	0.31	0.36	0.39	0.52	0.60
22. Generating sets, compression-ignition engines (850213)	. . .	141.9	119.1	85.9	157.4	. . .	. . .	0.45	0.39	0.33	0.59
23. Electro-diagnostic apparatus and parts (901819)	. . .	24.6	64.8	65.5	146.1	. . .	. . .	0.08	0.21	0.25	0.55
24. Chassis with engines for motor vehicles (870600)	. . .	81.1	152.7	83.1	145.4	. . .	. . .	0.26	0.50	0.32	0.55
25. Articles of plastics (392690)	188.4	199.6	181.1	140.6	142.4	-24.42	0.64	0.63	0.60	0.55	0.54

X = Not applicable.
. . . = Not available.

Exports from Illinois

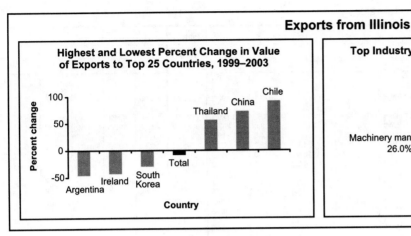

Highest and Lowest Percent Change in Value of Exports to Top 25 Countries, 1999–2003

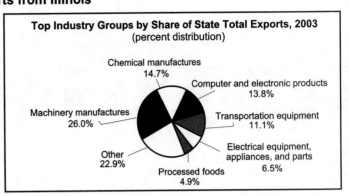

Top Industry Groups by Share of State Total Exports, 2003
(percent distribution)

- Chemical manufactures 14.7%
- Computer and electronic products 13.8%
- Machinery manufactures 26.0%
- Transportation equipment 11.1%
- Electrical equipment, appliances, and parts 6.5%
- Other 22.9%
- Processed foods 4.9%

- Illinois ranks seventh in the United States for total exports, with nearly $26.5 billion. While this is an increase of 3 percent from 2002, total exports are down 10 percent from 1999. Two industries that suffered big losses are computer and electronic products, down $1.7 billion, and transportation equipment, down $2.6 billion.

- From 1999 to 2003, chemical manufactures exports increased about $835 million and processed foods were up $302 million. Oil and gas extraction exports had the largest growth from 1999 to 2003, increasing more than 400 percent, or $147 million.

- Canada is the recipient of more than 32 percent of Illinois' exports, which is down considerably from 1999, when nearly 39 percent of the state's exports went to Canada. Exports to Mexico are up about 16 percent from 1999. Mexico is the second largest market, exceeding Japan, where exports were down more than 8 percent from 1999. Among the top 25 markets, exports to Chile grew the most, nearly doubling from 1999 to 2003.

Table E-18. Total U.S. Exports (Origin of Movement) via Illinois, 1999–2003—Continued

(Top 25 commodities and top 25 countries based on 2003 dollar value.)

Industry, commodity, and country	Value (millions of dollars)					Percent change, 1999–2003	Percent share of state total				
	1999	2000	2001	2002	2003		1999	2000	2001	2002	2003
TOTAL AND PERCENT SHARE OF U.S. TOTAL	29 432.2	31 437.6	30 434.4	25 686.4	26 472.9	-10.05	4.25	4.03	4.16	3.71	3.66
Top 25 Countries	26 753.9	28 981.3	27 726.8	23 454.1	23 931.2	-10.55	90.90	92.19	91.10	91.31	90.40
1. Canada	11 413.4	12 235.3	11 435.6	8 175.3	8 558.8	-25.01	38.78	38.92	37.57	31.83	32.33
2. Mexico	1 862.1	2 393.0	2 260.2	2 102.6	2 152.7	15.61	6.33	7.61	7.43	8.19	8.13
3. Japan	2 146.4	2 313.3	2 089.4	2 090.1	1 964.1	-8.49	7.29	7.36	6.87	8.14	7.42
4. United Kingdom	1 655.4	1 832.5	1 674.1	1 605.1	1 543.8	-6.74	5.62	5.83	5.50	6.25	5.83
5. Germany	1 371.7	1 380.1	1 368.4	1 176.0	1 209.5	-11.82	4.66	4.39	4.50	4.58	4.57
6. Australia	827.2	804.6	933.9	909.7	924.7	11.79	2.81	2.56	3.07	3.54	3.49
7. Belgium	914.6	998.3	956.8	876.0	824.6	-9.85	3.11	3.18	3.14	3.41	3.11
8. China	438.0	533.5	700.7	660.6	794.2	81.34	1.49	1.70	2.30	2.57	3.00
9. Netherlands	570.9	609.6	689.6	728.0	785.6	37.61	1.94	1.94	2.27	2.83	2.97
10. Brazil	788.6	713.6	847.6	745.2	697.4	-11.57	2.68	2.27	2.78	2.90	2.63
11. France	728.9	693.4	709.5	623.1	679.0	-6.85	2.48	2.21	2.33	2.43	2.56
12. Singapore	570.9	677.6	683.7	617.5	629.2	10.21	1.94	2.16	2.25	2.40	2.38
13. South Korea	656.3	734.8	527.2	478.8	425.4	-35.19	2.23	2.34	1.73	1.86	1.61
14. Hong Kong	378.2	436.9	422.0	452.4	412.0	8.93	1.28	1.39	1.39	1.76	1.56
15. Italy	403.7	381.8	299.3	298.2	309.0	-23.46	1.37	1.21	0.98	1.16	1.17
16. Taiwan	335.2	469.1	402.8	289.2	293.9	-12.32	1.14	1.49	1.32	1.13	1.11
17. Spain	267.1	310.1	298.6	220.3	238.1	-10.87	0.91	0.99	0.98	0.86	0.90
18. India	167.8	168.1	138.0	265.9	230.1	37.16	0.57	0.53	0.45	1.04	0.87
19. Malaysia	145.5	193.6	196.4	198.1	226.7	55.82	0.49	0.62	0.65	0.77	0.86
20. South Africa	200.4	198.0	232.1	222.8	225.0	12.26	0.68	0.63	0.76	0.87	0.85
21. Ireland	329.5	270.3	211.6	177.6	170.4	-48.29	1.12	0.86	0.70	0.69	0.64
22. Chile	85.8	172.4	190.2	147.0	170.0	98.11	0.29	0.55	0.62	0.57	0.64
23. Saudi Arabia	105.6	131.8	172.9	189.6	161.2	52.68	0.36	0.42	0.57	0.74	0.61
24. Thailand	95.9	127.0	134.3	152.2	155.4	61.98	0.33	0.40	0.44	0.59	0.59
25. Argentina	295.1	202.6	151.9	52.9	150.8	-48.92	1.00	0.64	0.50	0.21	0.57

Table E-19. Total U.S. Exports (Origin of Movement) via Indiana, 1999–2003

(Top 25 commodities and top 25 countries based on 2003 dollar value.)

Industry, commodity, and country	Value (millions of dollars)					Percent change, 1999–2003	Percent share of state total				
	1999	2000	2001	2002	2003		1999	2000	2001	2002	2003
TOTAL AND PERCENT SHARE OF U.S. TOTAL	12 910.3	15 385.8	14 365.4	14 923.1	16 402.3	27.05	1.86	1.97	1.97	2.15	2.27
Manufactures (NAICS Code)	12 595.5	15 032.8	14 051.2	14 603.2	16 120.1	27.98	97.56	97.71	97.81	97.86	98.28
Processed foods (311)	183.0	242.8	216.0	212.9	247.7	35.37	1.42	1.58	1.50	1.43	1.51
Beverages and tobacco products (312)	19.2	23.5	26.5	24.8	19.4	0.86	0.15	0.00	0.18	0.17	0.12
Fabric mill products (313)	19.9	19.1	24.1	23.7	27.1	36.13	0.15	0.12	0.17	0.16	0.17
Non-apparel textile products (314)	9.1	11.2	12.0	12.3	28.0	206.63	0.07	0.07	0.08	0.08	0.17
Apparel manufactures (315)	13.6	8.8	4.2	4.1	4.2	-68.82	0.11	0.06	0.03	0.03	0.03
Leather and related products (316)	10.6	10.1	10.0	10.8	9.4	-11.20	0.08	0.07	0.07	0.07	0.06
Wood products (321)	135.6	143.7	123.3	126.3	134.3	-0.99	1.05	0.93	0.86	0.85	0.82
Paper products (322)	94.7	115.6	114.1	99.6	125.5	32.62	0.73	0.75	0.79	0.67	0.77
Printing and related products (323)	147.7	117.7	123.4	131.3	142.3	-3.66	1.14	0.76	0.86	0.88	0.87
Petroleum and coal products (324)	19.8	16.5	17.3	16.7	14.1	-29.07	0.15	0.11	0.12	0.11	0.09
Chemical manufactures (325)	1 941.8	2 222.7	2 286.7	2 440.5	3 005.4	54.78	15.04	14.45	15.92	16.35	18.32
Plastics and rubber products (326)	405.4	477.7	488.6	491.4	513.4	26.61	3.14	3.10	3.40	3.29	3.13
Non-metallic mineral products (327)	185.6	188.9	147.6	161.5	177.9	-4.13	1.44	1.23	1.03	1.08	1.08
Primary metal manufactures (331)	520.8	711.9	627.7	526.3	612.3	17.57	4.03	4.63	4.37	3.53	3.73
Fabricated metal products (332)	448.2	574.8	510.6	494.1	482.7	7.69	3.47	3.74	3.55	3.31	2.94
Machinery manufactures (333)	1 712.9	2 338.1	2 223.2	2 350.7	2 441.4	42.53	13.27	15.20	15.48	15.75	14.88
Computer and electronic products (334)	1 174.2	1 384.2	1 448.6	1 529.7	1 588.8	35.31	9.09	9.00	10.08	10.25	9.69
Electrical equipment, appliances, and parts (335)	519.9	723.7	488.7	505.2	545.7	4.96	4.03	4.70	3.40	3.39	3.33
Transportation equipment (336)	4 397.0	5 092.2	4 510.5	4 786.0	5 273.5	19.93	34.06	33.10	31.40	32.07	32.15
Furniture and related products (337)	55.8	61.0	61.8	61.7	48.0	-14.04	0.43	0.40	0.43	0.41	0.29
Miscellaneous manufactures (339)	580.6	548.6	586.5	593.7	679.0	16.95	4.50	3.57	4.08	3.98	4.14
Agricultural and Livestock Products (NAICS Code)	63.3	61.4	65.5	46.6	44.1	-30.39	0.49	0.40	0.46	0.31	0.27
Agricultural products (111)	60.9	58.1	61.5	42.1	38.7	-36.47	0.47	0.38	0.43	0.28	0.24
Livestock and livestock products (112)	2.4	3.3	4.0	4.4	5.4	122.48	0.02	0.02	0.03	0.03	0.03
Other Commodities (NAICS Code)	251.5	291.6	248.6	273.3	238.1	-5.33	1.95	1.90	1.73	1.83	1.45
Forestry and logging (113)	6.9	10.7	17.5	16.4	16.8	141.62	0.05	0.07	0.12	0.11	0.10
Fishing, hunting, and trapping (114)	0.5	1.2	0.9	0.4	1.0	86.57	0.00	0.01	0.01	0.00	0.01
Oil and gas extraction (211)	0.1	0.1	0.1	0.0	0.4	587.93	0.00	0.00	0.00	0.00	0.00
Mining (212)	8.6	8.2	10.2	8.9	12.8	49.25	0.07	0.05	0.07	0.06	0.08
Waste and scrap (910)	30.8	44.3	33.3	45.6	44.6	44.47	0.24	0.29	0.23	0.31	0.27
Used merchandise (920)	6.3	2.0	7.4	24.5	6.5	4.13	0.05	0.01	0.05	0.16	0.04
Goods returned to Canada (980)	32.3	32.3	41.1	30.2	21.9	-32.28	0.25	0.21	0.29	0.20	0.13
Special classification provisions (990)	166.0	192.9	138.2	147.2	118.8	-28.42	1.29	1.25	0.96	0.99	0.72
Publishing industries (except Internet) (511)	0.0	0.0	0.0	0.0	15.4	X	0.00	0.00	0.00	0.00	0.09
TOTAL AND PERCENT SHARE OF U.S. TOTAL	12 910.3	15 385.8	14 365.4	14 923.1	16 402.3	27.05	1.86	1.97	1.97	2.15	2.27
Top 25 Commodities (HS Code)	5 185.3	6 256.7	5 879.7	7 098.4	8 136.2	56.91	40.16	40.67	40.93	47.57	49.60
1. Gear boxes for motor vehicles (870840)	899.2	1 252.4	1 106.6	1 136.7	924.8	2.85	6.96	8.14	7.70	7.62	5.64
2. Compression-ignition internal combustion engines (840820)	226.7	612.0	528.7	761.2	906.1	299.69	1.76	3.98	3.68	5.10	5.52
3. Parts and accessories of motor vehicles (870899)	804.4	767.8	690.0	735.6	903.8	12.36	6.23	4.99	4.80	4.93	5.51
4. Parts and accessories of motor vehicles bodies (870829)	527.6	520.9	477.9	514.7	534.6	1.33	4.09	3.39	3.33	3.45	3.26
5. Composite diagnostic or laboratory reagents (382200)	290.2	353.9	313.4	443.7	523.0	80.22	2.25	2.30	2.18	2.97	3.19
6. Goods vehicles, with spark-ignition piston engines (870431)	380.0	427.6	384.7	473.1	468.0	23.16	2.94	2.78	2.68	3.17	2.85
7. Passenger vehicle, spark-ignition, > 1,500 cc < 3,000 cc (870323)	. . .	23.5	40.0	81.2	412.9	. . .	. . .	0.15	0.28	0.54	2.52
8. Insulin and its salts (293712)	0.0	0.0	0.0	231.7	326.3	X	0.00	0.00	0.00	1.55	1.99
9. Retail medicaments in measured dose (300490)	109.6	137.2	170.6	188.7	275.2	151.09	0.85	0.89	1.19	1.26	1.68
10. Artificial joints and parts and accessories thereof (902131)	0.0	0.0	0.0	220.4	245.1	X	0.00	0.00	0.00	1.48	1.49
11. Other antibiotics (294190)	347.9	316.3	273.6	288.0	245.1	-29.55	2.69	2.06	1.90	1.93	1.49
12. Trailers and semi-trailers for housing or camping (871610)	123.3	133.2	123.0	169.6	234.7	90.35	0.96	0.87	0.86	1.14	1.43
13. Glycosides, natural or synthetic and their derivatives (293890)	85.6	144.2	198.7	196.7	233.7	173.01	0.66	0.94	1.38	1.32	1.42
14. Automatic regulating instruments and apparatus (903289)	110.4	133.5	122.6	160.9	222.8	101.81	0.86	0.87	0.85	1.08	1.36
15. Piperidine and its salts (293332)	. . .	1.1	2.2	44.7	212.2	. . .	. . .	0.01	0.02	0.30	1.29
16. Parts and accessories for automatic data processing (847330)	80.6	141.1	183.1	171.3	203.4	152.36	0.62	0.92	1.27	1.15	1.24
17. Gas turbine parts (841199)	76.7	101.1	117.0	112.1	168.1	119.17	0.59	0.66	0.81	0.75	1.02
18. Other compression-ignition internal combustion engines (840890)	84.0	159.9	174.7	168.0	161.6	92.38	0.65	1.04	1.22	1.13	0.99
19. Parts of spark-ignition internal combustion piston (840999)	165.6	206.6	194.2	154.2	147.6	-10.87	1.28	1.34	1.35	1.03	0.90
20. Turbojet and turbo-propeller parts (841191)	109.3	97.3	87.0	132.5	146.9	34.40	0.85	0.63	0.61	0.89	0.90
21. Passenger vehicles, spark-ignition, > 3,000 cc (870324)	125.1	216.0	125.8	172.9	145.9	16.63	0.97	1.40	0.88	1.16	0.89
22. Instruments and appliances for medical sciences (901890)	171.1	121.6	200.4	161.7	141.4	-17.36	1.33	0.79	1.40	1.08	0.86
23. Steering wheels, columns and boxes for motor vehicles (870894)	179.5	151.7	113.7	127.5	118.9	-33.76	1.39	0.99	0.79	0.85	0.72
24. Spark-ignition engine parts (840991)	166.8	143.4	155.9	145.3	118.1	-29.20	1.29	0.93	1.09	0.97	0.72
25. Printed books and brochures (490199)	121.7	94.4	95.9	106.0	116.0	-4.68	0.94	0.61	0.67	0.71	0.71

X = Not applicable.
. . . = Not available.

Exports from Indiana

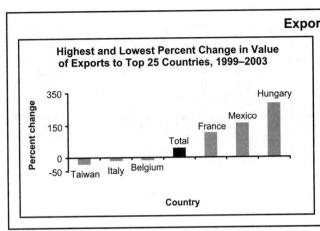

Highest and Lowest Percent Change in Value of Exports to Top 25 Countries, 1999–2003

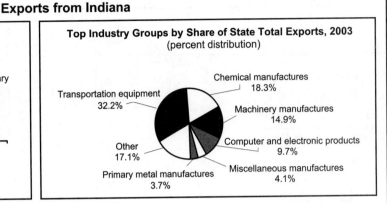

Top Industry Groups by Share of State Total Exports, 2003
(percent distribution)

Transportation equipment 32.2%
Chemical manufactures 18.3%
Machinery manufactures 14.9%
Computer and electronic products 9.7%
Other 17.1%
Miscellaneous manufactures 4.1%
Primary metal manufactures 3.7%

- Indiana's exports increased $3.5 billion, or 27 percent, from 1999 to 2003. Transportation equipment remains the state's largest export, accounting for 32 percent, or nearly $5.3 billion, of Indiana's total exports.

- Chemical manufactures and machinery manufactures are two other leading exports for Indiana. Together, these exports were valued at $5.4 billion in 2003. Both exports had considerable growth from 1999 to 2003. In 1999, the two exports were worth about $3.6 billion combined.

- Indiana's top commodities are related to motor vehicles. Exports of compression-ignition internal combustion piston engines for vehicles, which are Indiana's second largest export commodity, grew from less than $227 million in 1999 to $906 million in 2003.

- Canada and Mexico are the markets for 58 percent of Indiana's exports. Exports to Mexico increased nearly 187 percent from 1999 to 2003. Machinery manufactures compose nearly half of the state's exports to Mexico.

Table E-19. Total U.S. Exports (Origin of Movement) via Indiana, 1999–2003—*Continued*

(Top 25 commodities and top 25 countries based on 2003 dollar value.)

Industry, commodity, and country	Value (millions of dollars)					Percent change, 1999–2003	Percent share of state total				
	1999	2000	2001	2002	2003		1999	2000	2001	2002	2003
TOTAL AND PERCENT SHARE OF U.S. TOTAL	12 910.3	15 385.8	14 365.4	14 923.0	16 402.3	27.05	1.86	1.97	1.97	2.15	2.27
Top 25 Countries	12 220.4	14 491.3	13 454.6	14 211.0	15 635.6	27.95	94.66	94.19	93.66	95.23	95.33
1. Canada	7 002.1	7 105.9	6 201.0	6 819.3	7 458.5	6.52	54.24	46.19	43.17	45.70	45.47
2. Mexico	734.6	2 031.4	1 770.1	1 942.5	2 105.2	186.57	5.69	13.20	12.32	13.02	12.84
3. United Kingdom	817.5	839.9	941.0	1 006.7	1 208.7	47.85	6.33	5.46	6.55	6.75	7.37
4. France	412.7	512.3	669.0	637.6	921.7	123.31	3.20	3.33	4.66	4.27	5.62
5. Japan	702.8	823.7	700.8	714.1	630.2	-10.32	5.44	5.35	4.88	4.79	3.84
6. Germany	382.8	425.3	553.8	525.1	552.5	44.31	2.97	2.76	3.86	3.52	3.37
7. Netherlands	263.1	557.9	307.1	295.3	288.8	9.78	2.04	3.63	2.14	1.98	1.76
8. Brazil	215.9	303.5	290.5	194.4	276.9	28.23	1.67	1.97	2.02	1.30	1.69
9. Australia	203.3	262.8	235.4	227.8	238.9	17.48	1.58	1.71	1.64	1.53	1.46
10. China	135.0	166.5	200.3	187.2	235.6	74.44	1.05	1.08	1.39	1.25	1.44
11. South Korea	147.2	180.7	220.9	244.7	234.0	58.94	1.14	1.17	1.54	1.64	1.43
12. Singapore	162.7	266.4	215.3	252.7	230.0	41.41	1.26	1.73	1.50	1.69	1.40
13. Spain	86.5	68.0	95.5	120.4	188.2	117.68	0.67	0.44	0.66	0.81	1.15
14. Belgium	161.3	129.4	131.3	118.3	142.2	-11.87	1.25	0.84	0.91	0.79	0.87
15. Italy	161.2	163.5	173.3	152.3	140.5	-12.85	1.25	1.06	1.21	1.02	0.86
16. Hong Kong	124.0	134.6	120.4	130.7	132.2	6.59	0.96	0.88	0.84	0.88	0.81
17. Ireland	96.2	98.2	131.8	131.7	125.7	30.74	0.74	0.64	0.92	0.88	0.77
18. Sweden	69.4	63.9	82.3	97.0	104.2	50.15	0.54	0.42	0.57	0.65	0.64
19. Taiwan	108.0	98.0	96.4	80.6	85.9	-20.45	0.84	0.64	0.67	0.54	0.52
20. Austria	81.0	48.7	92.3	98.2	77.3	-4.61	0.63	0.32	0.64	0.66	0.47
21. Saudi Arabia	35.6	78.7	76.5	86.3	55.8	56.70	0.28	0.51	0.53	0.58	0.34
22. Thailand	34.2	43.4	48.8	54.1	54.7	60.01	0.26	0.28	0.34	0.36	0.33
23. India	38.8	35.6	39.9	37.7	53.8	38.59	0.30	0.23	0.28	0.25	0.33
24. Malaysia	34.1	39.8	45.5	39.3	52.4	53.45	0.26	0.26	0.32	0.26	0.32
25. Hungary	10.4	13.2	15.4	16.9	42.0	305.13	0.08	0.09	0.11	0.11	0.26

Table E-20. Total U.S. Exports (Origin of Movement) via Iowa, 1999–2003

(Top 25 commodities and top 25 countries based on 2003 dollar value.)

Industry, commodity, and country	Value (millions of dollars)					Percent change, 1999–2003	Percent share of state total				
	1999	2000	2001	2002	2003		1999	2000	2001	2002	2003
TOTAL AND PERCENT SHARE OF U.S. TOTAL	4 093.8	4 465.5	4 659.6	4 754.6	5 236.3	27.91	0.59	0.57	0.64	0.69	0.72
Manufactures (NAICS Code)	3 852.0	4 229.0	4 378.1	4 493.1	4 888.3	26.91	94.09	94.71	93.96	94.50	93.35
Processed foods (311)	713.8	777.8	951.0	938.8	1 060.8	48.62	17.44	17.42	20.41	19.75	20.26
Beverages and tobacco products (312)	6.3	2.7	8.3	8.4	8.9	40.96	0.15	0.00	0.18	0.18	0.17
Fabric mill products (313)	25.4	35.3	26.3	19.0	25.8	1.65	0.62	0.79	0.56	0.40	0.49
Non-apparel textile products (314)	15.2	14.1	15.1	13.9	19.1	25.12	0.37	0.32	0.32	0.29	0.36
Apparel manufactures (315)	2.5	2.5	5.0	3.3	5.0	98.25	0.06	0.06	0.11	0.07	0.10
Leather and related products (316)	3.4	3.8	2.3	6.1	2.6	-22.00	0.08	0.08	0.05	0.13	0.05
Wood products (321)	20.4	24.0	29.1	28.0	28.5	39.27	0.50	0.54	0.62	0.59	0.54
Paper products (322)	39.2	33.2	35.7	39.3	45.4	15.80	0.96	0.74	0.77	0.83	0.87
Printing and related products (323)	31.6	30.6	39.2	26.0	21.6	-31.64	0.77	0.68	0.84	0.55	0.41
Petroleum and coal products (324)	1.6	2.7	3.4	3.6	4.2	163.52	0.04	0.06	0.07	0.08	0.08
Chemical manufactures (325)	358.6	395.4	426.6	448.4	443.3	23.90	8.76	8.85	9.15	9.43	8.48
Plastics and rubber products (326)	146.4	135.0	125.7	132.2	165.0	12.72	3.58	3.02	2.70	2.78	3.15
Non-metallic mineral products (327)	7.1	11.4	8.9	10.1	19.1	168.75	0.17	0.25	0.19	0.21	0.36
Primary metal manufactures (331)	136.3	264.5	213.7	174.7	218.6	60.34	3.33	5.92	4.59	3.67	4.17
Fabricated metal products (332)	131.0	137.8	144.3	159.7	168.3	28.46	3.20	3.09	3.10	3.36	3.21
Machinery manufactures (333)	965.0	1 092.6	1 034.3	1 216.1	1 297.7	34.48	23.57	24.47	22.20	25.58	24.78
Computer and electronic products (334)	398.9	367.5	409.5	434.9	432.1	8.31	9.74	8.23	8.79	9.15	8.25
Electrical equipment, appliances, and parts (335)	300.5	340.5	389.6	394.0	446.8	48.70	7.34	7.63	8.36	8.29	8.53
Transportation equipment (336)	355.1	358.0	321.6	245.4	267.2	-24.77	8.68	8.02	6.90	5.16	5.10
Furniture and related products (337)	38.2	44.5	37.1	27.7	43.0	12.61	0.93	1.00	0.80	0.58	0.82
Miscellaneous manufactures (339)	155.3	155.3	151.5	163.5	164.3	5.82	3.79	3.48	3.25	3.44	3.14
Agricultural and Livestock Products (NAICS Code)	179.1	186.4	206.8	204.2	275.0	53.55	4.38	4.18	4.44	4.29	5.25
Agricultural products (111)	159.4	165.4	186.6	183.5	252.9	58.70	3.89	3.70	4.00	3.86	4.83
Livestock and livestock products (112)	19.7	21.0	20.2	20.6	22.1	11.97	0.48	0.47	0.43	0.43	0.42
Other Commodities (NAICS Code)	62.7	50.0	74.7	57.3	72.9	16.33	1.53	1.12	1.60	1.21	1.39
Forestry and logging (113)	2.0	1.4	2.2	5.5	8.2	311.87	0.05	0.03	0.05	0.12	0.16
Fishing, hunting, and trapping (114)	2.2	0.9	3.2	1.1	1.4	-35.16	0.05	0.02	0.07	0.02	0.03
Oil and gas extraction (211)	0.0	0.0	0.0	0.3	0.7	X	0.00	0.00	0.00	0.01	0.01
Mining (212)	14.9	8.0	19.7	10.3	29.1	95.12	0.36	0.18	0.42	0.22	0.56
Waste and scrap (910)	4.2	6.2	13.1	4.7	9.0	115.95	0.10	0.14	0.28	0.10	0.17
Public administration (920)	3.5	3.4	4.0	5.1	5.1	45.60	0.09	0.08	0.08	0.11	0.10
Goods returned to Canada (980)	9.2	7.7	7.5	6.0	4.5	-51.44	0.22	0.17	0.16	0.13	0.09
Special classification provisions (990)	26.8	22.3	25.0	24.3	14.7	-45.31	0.65	0.50	0.54	0.51	0.28
Publishing industries (except Internet) (511)	0.0	0.0	0.0	0.0	0.3	X	0.00	0.00	0.00	0.00	0.01
TOTAL AND PERCENT SHARE OF U.S. TOTAL	4 093.8	4 465.5	4 659.6	4 754.6	5 236.3	27.91	0.59	0.57	0.64	0.69	0.72
Top 25 Commodities (HS Code)	1 305.5	1 513.9	1 641.1	1 854.7	2 108.8	61.53	31.89	33.90	35.22	39.01	40.27
1. Tractors (870190)	296.7	304.8	280.8	464.5	416.4	40.34	7.25	6.83	6.03	9.77	7.95
2. Corn, other than seed corn (100590)	64.4	48.7	41.5	61.6	151.5	135.25	1.57	1.09	0.89	1.30	2.89
3. Meat of swine, frozen (020329)	56.2	85.8	187.3	164.9	145.2	158.36	1.37	1.92	4.02	3.47	2.77
4. Meat of swine, fresh or chilled (020319)	64.3	102.4	109.3	134.4	139.9	117.57	1.57	2.29	2.35	2.83	2.67
5. Combined refrigerator-freezers, separate doors (841810)	57.2	77.0	67.9	86.7	106.7	86.54	1.40	1.72	1.46	1.82	2.04
6. Soybean oilcake and other solid residue (230400)	48.6	40.3	63.8	76.8	93.3	91.98	1.19	0.90	1.37	1.62	1.78
7. Grains, worked corn (110423)	. . .	0.0	0.0	7.5	88.8	. . .	. . .	0.00	0.00	0.16	1.70
8. Parts and accessories of motor vehicles (870899)	72.0	59.3	74.3	50.7	82.7	14.86	1.76	1.33	1.59	1.07	1.58
9. Washing machines (845011)	58.0	71.6	78.3	75.4	76.6	32.07	1.42	1.60	1.68	1.59	1.46
10. Aluminum alloy rectangular plates, > 0.2 mm thick (760612)	7.9	114.1	98.6	46.5	73.6	831.65	0.19	2.56	2.12	0.98	1.41
11. Vaccines for veterinary medicine (300230)	53.2	63.4	75.1	78.9	65.5	23.12	1.30	1.42	1.61	1.66	1.25
12. Soybeans, whether or not broken (120100)	63.9	73.6	100.4	74.2	63.6	-0.47	1.56	1.65	2.15	1.56	1.21
13. Mechanical shovels and excavators (842959)	42.4	52.8	61.6	45.5	56.6	33.49	1.04	1.18	1.32	0.96	1.08
14. Transmission and reception apparatus (852520)	53.7	37.6	43.8	60.7	56.4	5.03	1.31	0.84	0.94	1.28	1.08
15. Parts and accessories of motor vehicles bodies (870829)	47.8	43.0	37.6	38.0	54.0	12.97	1.17	0.96	0.81	0.80	1.03
16. Mechanical front-end shovel loaders (842951)	40.0	37.7	28.2	43.9	52.7	31.75	0.98	0.84	0.61	0.92	1.01
17. Radio navigational aid apparatus (852691)	82.8	71.2	53.3	49.6	49.1	-40.70	2.02	1.59	1.14	1.04	0.94
18. Gelatin and derivatives (350300)	19.1	17.6	26.4	39.4	48.1	151.83	0.47	0.39	0.57	0.83	0.92
19. Parts for taps and cocks, for pipes (848190)	. . .	9.2	8.9	19.0	45.4	. . .	. . .	0.21	0.19	0.40	0.87
20. Radar apparatus (852610)	. . .	15.7	21.0	27.6	42.2	. . .	. . .	0.35	0.45	0.58	0.81
21. Meat of bovine animals, boneless, frozen (020230)	103.0	105.4	76.6	79.9	41.1	-60.10	2.52	2.36	1.64	1.68	0.78
22. Animal feed, except dog or cat food (230990)	31.3	37.0	38.3	39.4	40.8	30.35	0.76	0.83	0.82	0.83	0.78
23. Agricultural, horticultural, or forestry machines (843280)	. . .	1.0	2.5	17.8	40.6	. . .	. . .	0.02	0.05	0.37	0.78
24. Adhesive dressings (300510)	43.0	40.8	43.2	47.3	39.4	-8.37	1.05	0.91	0.93	0.99	0.75
25. Sausages, similar products of meat (160100)	. . .	4.9	22.4	24.5	38.6	. . .	. . .	0.11	0.48	0.52	0.74

X = Not applicable.
. . . = Not available.

Exports from Iowa

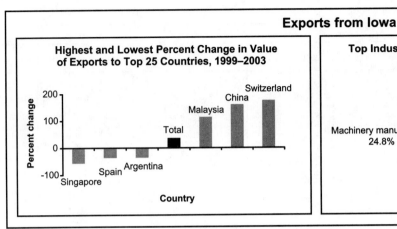

Highest and Lowest Percent Change in Value of Exports to Top 25 Countries, 1999–2003

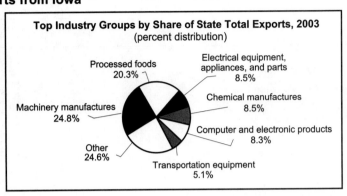

Top Industry Groups by Share of State Total Exports, 2003
(percent distribution)

- Iowa's exports grew from $4.1 billion in 1999 to over $5.2 billion in 2003, an increase of nearly 28 percent. In 2003, machinery manufactures were the leading export, accounting for nearly 25 percent of Iowa's total exports.

- Processed foods, which are Iowa's second largest export, grew from $714 million in 1999 to $1 billion in 2003. Transportation equipment exports fell from $355 million in 1999 to $267 million in 2003, a drop of about 25 percent.

- Canada receives nearly 36 percent of Iowa's exports. These exports are mostly manufactured goods, led by machinery manufactures. Processed food exports to Canada increased from $158 million in 1999 to $256 million in 2003.

- Agricultural products grew about 59 percent since 1999, reaching $253 million in 2003. About 75 percent of these products are exported to Mexico. Exports to China increased 160 percent from 1999 to 2003. Chemical manufactures exports to China grew from $440,000 in 1999 to over $12 million in 2003.

Table E-20. Total U.S. Exports (Origin of Movement) via Iowa, 1999–2003—*Continued*

(Top 25 commodities and top 25 countries based on 2003 dollar value.)

Industry, commodity, and country	Value (millions of dollars)					Percent change, 1999–2003	Percent share of state total				
	1999	2000	2001	2002	2003		1999	2000	2001	2002	2003
TOTAL AND PERCENT SHARE OF U.S. TOTAL	4 093.8	4 465.5	4 659.6	4 754.6	5 236.3	27.91	0.59	0.57	0.64	0.69	0.72
Top 25 Countries	3 801.6	4 120.8	4 231.2	4 336.8	4 828.6	27.01	92.86	92.28	90.81	91.21	92.21
1. Canada	1 528.9	1 582.6	1 581.7	1 675.7	1 870.7	22.35	37.35	35.44	33.95	35.24	35.73
2. Mexico	313.9	345.6	372.3	396.4	669.9	113.46	7.67	7.74	7.99	8.34	12.79
3. Japan	462.3	548.9	647.4	605.1	576.4	24.67	11.29	12.29	13.89	12.73	11.01
4. Germany	284.8	259.8	246.0	239.7	214.0	-24.87	6.96	5.82	5.28	5.04	4.09
5. United Kingdom	190.3	189.3	207.4	192.3	210.7	10.75	4.65	4.24	4.45	4.04	4.02
6. France	154.1	170.8	157.0	196.5	204.1	32.47	3.76	3.83	3.37	4.13	3.90
7. Australia	120.2	115.3	114.9	115.3	144.1	19.85	2.94	2.58	2.47	2.43	2.75
8. South Korea	68.1	71.3	89.2	114.0	115.6	69.76	1.66	1.60	1.91	2.40	2.21
9. Brazil	46.8	63.9	70.3	55.6	99.0	111.29	1.14	1.43	1.51	1.17	1.89
10. China	35.8	45.0	83.3	78.3	93.0	159.69	0.87	1.01	1.79	1.65	1.78
11. Netherlands	91.2	110.7	95.9	76.7	89.6	-1.74	2.23	2.48	2.06	1.61	1.71
12. Belgium	54.9	104.0	117.0	79.8	70.4	28.27	1.34	2.33	2.51	1.68	1.34
13. Taiwan	45.5	65.0	58.4	69.2	55.0	20.94	1.11	1.46	1.25	1.46	1.05
14. Ireland	41.8	61.9	44.0	46.0	49.8	19.30	1.02	1.39	0.94	0.97	0.95
15. Hong Kong	38.7	53.7	45.7	43.0	43.8	13.07	0.95	1.20	0.98	0.90	0.84
16. Singapore	86.7	73.6	51.9	57.3	42.1	-51.40	2.12	1.65	1.11	1.20	0.80
17. Italy	45.9	60.3	58.5	53.5	41.2	-10.17	1.12	1.35	1.25	1.12	0.79
18. Switzerland	14.2	21.9	23.4	25.6	37.8	166.84	0.35	0.49	0.50	0.54	0.72
19. Spain	52.1	48.3	37.6	28.0	37.7	-27.51	1.27	1.08	0.81	0.59	0.72
20. South Africa	17.1	29.8	22.3	36.1	36.3	112.28	0.42	0.67	0.48	0.76	0.69
21. Malaysia	12.9	20.5	27.1	26.2	27.9	116.03	0.32	0.46	0.58	0.55	0.53
22. Saudi Arabia	21.4	18.7	26.2	60.6	26.6	24.15	0.52	0.42	0.56	1.28	0.51
23. Sweden	23.9	19.2	15.9	28.6	26.5	11.01	0.58	0.43	0.34	0.60	0.51
24. Argentina	33.2	26.2	21.7	9.5	24.2	-27.15	0.81	0.59	0.47	0.20	0.46
25. New Zealand	17.0	14.5	16.1	27.7	22.2	30.21	0.42	0.32	0.34	0.58	0.42

Table E-21. Total U.S. Exports (Origin of Movement) via Kansas, 1999–2003

(Top 25 commodities and top 25 countries based on 2003 dollar value.)

Industry, commodity, and country	Value (millions of dollars)					Percent change, 1999–2003	Percent share of state total				
	1999	2000	2001	2002	2003		1999	2000	2001	2002	2003
TOTAL AND PERCENT SHARE OF U.S. TOTAL	4 669.4	5 145.4	5 004.5	4 988.4	4 553.3	-2.49	0.67	0.66	0.68	0.72	0.63
Manufactures (NAICS Code)	4 293.0	4 697.6	4 530.4	4 483.8	4 148.8	-3.36	91.94	91.30	90.52	89.88	91.12
Processed foods (311)	970.1	1 361.6	1 297.5	1 315.8	1 304.1	34.44	20.77	26.46	25.93	26.38	28.64
Beverages and tobacco products (312)	0.7	0.9	0.9	0.8	1.1	48.40	0.02	0.00	0.02	0.02	0.02
Fabric mill products (313)	2.6	3.8	4.0	9.6	9.8	271.22	0.06	0.07	0.08	0.19	0.22
Non-apparel textile products (314)	2.5	2.9	3.5	2.8	3.4	32.56	0.05	0.06	0.07	0.06	0.07
Apparel manufactures (315)	1.5	3.1	3.5	3.2	2.2	48.69	0.03	0.06	0.07	0.06	0.05
Leather and related products (316)	63.4	71.9	103.9	108.8	89.9	41.78	1.36	1.40	2.08	2.18	1.98
Wood products (321)	2.8	3.8	4.9	5.1	2.5	-8.16	0.06	0.07	0.10	0.10	0.06
Paper products (322)	15.0	16.3	23.2	34.3	34.3	129.72	0.32	0.32	0.46	0.69	0.75
Printing and related products (323)	23.3	28.9	31.1	22.3	26.1	12.12	0.50	0.56	0.62	0.45	0.57
Petroleum and coal products (324)	6.2	25.7	12.6	10.2	14.1	127.62	0.13	0.50	0.25	0.20	0.31
Chemical manufactures (325)	170.0	203.4	243.2	242.7	250.7	47.47	3.64	3.95	4.86	4.87	5.51
Plastics and rubber products (326)	99.2	117.2	124.0	106.6	111.3	12.24	2.12	2.28	2.48	2.14	2.44
Non-metallic mineral products (327)	21.4	21.3	23.7	22.4	27.7	29.51	0.46	0.41	0.47	0.45	0.61
Primary metal manufactures (331)	12.2	13.0	13.9	19.0	18.6	52.71	0.26	0.25	0.28	0.38	0.41
Fabricated metal products (332)	51.4	66.2	65.9	65.8	79.6	54.90	1.10	1.29	1.32	1.32	1.75
Machinery manufactures (333)	323.4	431.9	437.0	414.7	415.0	28.32	6.93	8.39	8.73	8.31	9.11
Computer and electronic products (334)	352.8	379.8	340.6	277.0	339.4	-3.80	7.56	7.38	6.80	5.55	7.45
Electrical equipment, appliances, and parts (335)	77.4	78.7	72.9	82.4	90.1	16.42	1.66	1.53	1.46	1.65	1.98
Transportation equipment (336)	2 047.5	1 804.7	1 656.6	1 678.1	1 270.9	-37.93	43.85	35.07	33.10	33.64	27.91
Furniture and related products (337)	4.5	3.6	5.4	6.8	5.8	28.70	0.10	0.07	0.11	0.14	0.13
Miscellaneous manufactures (339)	45.4	58.9	61.9	55.3	52.3	15.23	0.97	1.15	1.24	1.11	1.15
Agricultural and Livestock Products (NAICS Code)	189.1	326.6	284.9	351.1	258.9	36.87	4.05	6.35	5.69	7.04	5.69
Agricultural products (111)	188.9	325.7	284.6	350.0	258.5	36.82	4.05	6.33	5.69	7.02	5.68
Livestock and livestock products (112)	0.2	0.9	0.3	1.1	0.4	77.27	0.00	0.02	0.01	0.02	0.01
Other Commodities (NAICS Code)	187.3	121.2	189.3	153.5	145.7	-22.22	4.01	2.36	3.78	3.08	3.20
Forestry and logging (113)	0.1	3.0	1.2	5.5	3.0	1 939.04	0.00	0.06	0.02	0.11	0.07
Fishing, hunting, and trapping (114)	0.3	0.7	0.0	0.1	0.3	16.67	0.01	0.01	0.00	0.00	0.01
Oil and gas extraction (211)	6.4	14.5	11.2	8.0	6.1	-4.55	0.14	0.28	0.22	0.16	0.13
Mining (212)	2.5	4.5	2.3	0.9	13.7	456.05	0.05	0.09	0.04	0.02	0.30
Waste and scrap (910)	6.0	6.8	12.4	10.9	13.2	119.73	0.13	0.13	0.25	0.22	0.29
Public administration (920)	3.6	1.8	1.4	3.0	3.2	-8.58	0.08	0.03	0.03	0.06	0.07
Goods returned to Canada (980)	14.7	10.6	12.5	7.0	6.2	-57.89	0.32	0.21	0.25	0.14	0.14
Special classification provisions (990)	153.7	79.5	148.5	118.0	99.8	-35.05	3.29	1.54	2.97	2.37	2.19
Publishing industries (except Internet) (511)	0.0	0.0	0.0	0.0	0.0	X	0.00	0.00	0.00	0.00	0.00
TOTAL AND PERCENT SHARE OF U.S. TOTAL	4 669.4	5 145.4	5 004.5	4 988.4	4 553.3	-2.49	0.67	0.66	0.68	0.72	0.63
Top 25 Commodities (HS Code)	2 750.7	3 009.5	2 757.0	3 279.3	2 844.7	3.42	58.91	58.49	55.09	65.74	62.48
1. Airplanes and aircraft, unladen wgt > 2,000 kg < 15,000 kg (880230)	1 151.5	962.9	1 001.5	941.0	742.2	-35.54	24.66	18.71	20.01	18.86	16.30
2. Meat of bovine animals, boneless, fresh or chilled (020130)	274.1	416.6	379.1	437.6	477.2	74.10	5.87	8.10	7.58	8.77	10.48
3. Whole hides and skins of bovine/equine > 16 kg (410150)	0.0	0.0	0.0	256.2	265.9	X	0.00	0.00	0.00	5.14	5.84
4. Wheat and meslin (100190)	97.5	162.8	154.2	237.6	190.4	95.28	2.09	3.16	3.08	4.76	4.18
5. Parts of airplanes or helicopters (880330)	172.2	152.9	161.0	173.3	158.3	-8.07	3.69	2.97	3.22	3.47	3.48
6. Meat of bovine animals, boneless, frozen (020230)	195.9	238.2	165.1	191.0	139.0	-29.05	4.20	4.63	3.30	3.83	3.05
7. Dog and cat food (230910)	136.9	176.7	162.8	126.0	110.2	-19.50	2.93	3.43	3.25	2.53	2.42
8. Turbojet and turbo-propeller parts (841191)	126.6	115.9	45.2	28.1	103.6	-18.17	2.71	2.25	0.90	0.56	2.28
9. Passenger vehicles, spark-ignition, > 3,000 cc (870324)	300.6	349.0	235.9	363.2	76.9	-74.42	6.44	6.78	4.71	7.28	1.69
10. Radio navigational aid apparatus (852691)	68.8	66.0	79.0	77.1	72.9	5.96	1.47	1.28	1.58	1.55	1.60
11. Rare gases (280429)	28.2	34.7	48.7	51.3	57.2	102.84	0.60	0.67	0.97	1.03	1.26
12. Meat of bovine animals, bone in, frozen (020220)	24.7	43.2	35.5	41.0	55.2	123.48	0.53	0.84	0.71	0.82	1.21
13. Grain sorghum (100700)	44.1	75.2	68.9	66.8	48.7	10.43	0.94	1.46	1.38	1.34	1.07
14. Tan hides and skins, of bovine (410411)	0.0	0.0	0.0	45.4	47.1	X	0.00	0.00	0.00	0.91	1.03
15. Instruments, aeronautical-space nav., no compass (901420)	64.6	58.2	52.5	37.9	44.1	-31.73	1.38	1.13	1.05	0.76	0.97
16. Parts and accessories for automatic data processing (847330)	. . .	33.2	17.1	11.4	41.2	. . .	. . .	0.65	0.34	0.23	0.90
17. Mechanical front-end shovel loaders (842951)	1.7	13.6	17.6	35.6	36.6	2 052.94	0.04	0.26	0.35	0.71	0.80
18. Road wheels, parts and accessories for motor vehicles (870870)	37.9	39.8	37.3	37.4	33.3	-12.14	0.81	0.77	0.75	0.75	0.73
19. Footwear (640299)	16.2	16.2	36.3	42.3	24.9	53.70	0.35	0.31	0.73	0.85	0.55
20. Offal of bovine animals, edible, frozen (020629)	. . .	30.1	28.2	16.4	23.7	. . .	. . .	0.58	0.56	0.33	0.52
21. Airplane and aircraft, unladen weight > 15,000 kg (880240)	. . .	1.7	0.0	0.0	19.7	. . .	. . .	0.03	0.00	0.00	0.43
22. Retail medicaments in measured dose (300490)	. . .	1.9	10.3	9.9	19.2	. . .	. . .	0.04	0.21	0.20	0.42
23. Butts/bends/bellies of bovine/equine animals (410190)	0.0	0.0	0.0	18.2	19.2	X	0.00	0.00	0.00	0.36	0.42
24. Whole hides and skins of bovine/equine <= 8 kg (410120)	. . .	0.0	0.0	16.8	19.1	. . .	. . .	0.00	0.00	0.34	0.42
25. Animal (not fish) guts, bladders, stomachs and parts (050400)	9.2	20.7	20.8	17.8	18.9	105.43	0.20	0.40	0.42	0.36	0.42

X = Not applicable.
. . . = Not available.

Exports from Kansas

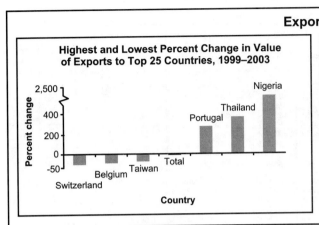

Highest and Lowest Percent Change in Value of Exports to Top 25 Countries, 1999–2003

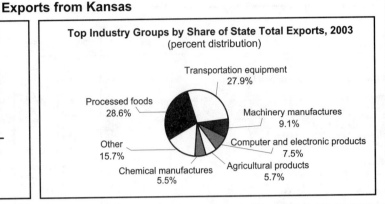

Top Industry Groups by Share of State Total Exports, 2003
(percent distribution)

Transportation equipment 27.9%
Processed foods 28.6%
Machinery manufactures 9.1%
Other 15.7%
Computer and electronic products 7.5%
Chemical manufactures 5.5%
Agricultural products 5.7%

- Exports from Kansas fell from $4.7 billion in 1999 to $4.5 billion in 2003, a decline of 2.5 percent. Transportation equipment exports fell dramatically from over $2 billion in 1999 to $1.3 billion in 2003, which resulted in its share of total exports falling 16 percentage points. However, they remain the state's leading export. Processed foods grew considerably from 1999 to 2003, and composed nearly 29 percent of the state's exports.

- The state's top commodity—airplanes and aircraft—fell more than 35 percent from 1999, and constituted about $742 million of total exports in 2003. Bovine meat became the state's second largest commodity, growing from $274 million in 1999 to $477 million in 2003.

- Canada remains Kansas' top market for exports, and is the recipient of 22 percent of the state's total exports. Exports to Mexico grew considerably from $382 million in 1999 to $602 million in 2003. The lead export to Mexico is processed foods, which doubled from 1999 to 2003.

Table E-21. Total U.S. Exports (Origin of Movement) via Kansas, 1999–2003—*Continued*

(Top 25 commodities and top 25 countries based on 2003 dollar value.)

Industry, commodity, and country	Value (millions of dollars)					Percent change, 1999–2003	Percent share of state total				
	1999	2000	2001	2002	2003		1999	2000	2001	2002	2003
TOTAL AND PERCENT SHARE OF U.S. TOTAL	4 669.4	5 145.4	5 004.5	4 988.4	4 553.3	-2.49	0.67	0.66	0.68	0.72	0.63
Top 25 Countries	4 104.8	4 550.0	4 456.6	4 400.2	4 131.5	0.65	87.91	88.43	89.05	88.21	90.73
1. Canada	1 260.3	1 403.0	1 217.1	1 271.0	1 020.9	-19.00	26.99	27.27	24.32	25.48	22.42
2. Mexico	382.1	523.1	547.3	664.1	602.0	57.56	8.18	10.17	10.94	13.31	13.22
3. Japan	690.2	695.0	709.2	527.9	543.0	-21.33	14.78	13.51	14.17	10.58	11.92
4. South Korea	186.8	261.0	227.5	293.0	320.7	71.66	4.00	5.07	4.55	5.87	7.04
5. United Kingdom	323.7	242.7	303.5	233.3	249.0	-23.08	6.93	4.72	6.06	4.68	5.47
6. Germany	217.9	169.0	192.9	164.9	179.9	-17.44	4.67	3.29	3.85	3.31	3.95
7. China	61.1	125.9	258.9	200.0	175.8	187.96	1.31	2.45	5.17	4.01	3.86
8. Singapore	114.3	113.1	58.1	34.3	129.6	13.35	2.45	2.20	1.16	0.69	2.85
9. France	170.0	124.9	141.6	103.4	121.1	-28.77	3.64	2.43	2.83	2.07	2.66
10. Australia	105.4	69.1	72.0	99.3	108.4	2.89	2.26	1.34	1.44	1.99	2.38
11. South Africa	80.9	40.1	41.1	48.6	86.6	7.04	1.73	0.78	0.82	0.97	1.90
12. Hong Kong	30.2	36.3	47.0	57.1	72.4	139.33	0.65	0.71	0.94	1.14	1.59
13. Brazil	80.8	121.4	105.0	145.4	62.8	-22.26	1.73	2.36	2.10	2.91	1.38
14. Italy	43.9	60.4	68.7	64.5	58.3	32.73	0.94	1.17	1.37	1.29	1.28
15. Nigeria	2.3	24.8	25.2	86.4	57.9	2 440.61	0.05	0.48	0.50	1.73	1.27
16. Taiwan	77.4	73.6	56.4	42.4	53.3	-31.14	1.66	1.43	1.13	0.85	1.17
17. Belgium	71.2	116.8	104.1	79.5	44.4	-37.59	1.52	2.27	2.08	1.59	0.98
18. Netherlands	36.0	64.7	45.2	32.7	40.4	12.29	0.77	1.26	0.90	0.66	0.89
19. Portugal	8.2	19.2	22.0	51.0	31.8	290.42	0.17	0.37	0.44	1.02	0.70
20. Switzerland	52.1	58.5	95.2	53.7	30.8	-40.83	1.12	1.14	1.90	1.08	0.68
21. India	17.0	18.4	12.3	21.0	30.2	77.43	0.36	0.36	0.24	0.42	0.66
22. Thailand	6.2	27.5	18.7	22.4	30.0	386.70	0.13	0.53	0.37	0.45	0.66
23. Egypt	40.6	95.1	39.7	50.0	29.3	-27.99	0.87	1.85	0.79	1.00	0.64
24. Spain	19.2	42.0	30.3	25.2	28.9	50.76	0.41	0.82	0.61	0.50	0.64
25. Colombia	27.0	24.4	17.6	29.0	23.9	-11.67	0.58	0.47	0.35	0.58	0.52

Table E-22. Total U.S. Exports (Origin of Movement) via Kentucky, 1999–2003

(Top 25 commodities and top 25 countries based on 2003 dollar value.)

Industry, commodity, and country	Value (millions of dollars)					Percent change, 1999–2003	Percent share of state total				
	1999	2000	2001	2002	2003		1999	2000	2001	2002	2003
TOTAL AND PERCENT SHARE OF U.S. TOTAL	8 877.2	9 612.2	9 048.0	10 606.7	10 733.8	20.91	1.28	1.23	1.24	1.53	1.48
Manufactures (NAICS Code)	8 441.8	9 058.9	8 432.8	10 146.4	10 039.4	18.92	95.10	94.24	93.20	95.66	93.53
Processed foods (311)	79.4	83.7	105.6	130.7	139.9	76.13	0.89	0.87	1.17	1.23	1.30
Beverages and tobacco products (312)	141.7	171.4	210.7	146.4	142.6	0.61	1.60	0.00	2.33	1.38	1.33
Fabric mill products (313)	42.8	42.8	83.2	130.1	120.6	181.86	0.48	0.45	0.92	1.23	1.12
Non-apparel textile products (314)	5.8	26.4	16.7	19.3	15.0	160.46	0.07	0.27	0.18	0.18	0.14
Apparel manufactures (315)	268.0	92.2	110.3	68.1	73.6	-72.53	3.02	0.96	1.22	0.64	0.69
Leather and related products (316)	19.7	6.7	13.4	14.9	91.7	364.42	0.22	0.07	0.15	0.14	0.85
Wood products (321)	66.5	58.6	73.4	75.8	87.5	31.66	0.75	0.61	0.81	0.71	0.82
Paper products (322)	105.0	104.0	91.5	112.9	126.5	20.50	1.18	1.08	1.01	1.06	1.18
Printing and related products (323)	126.5	134.5	116.5	127.7	158.2	25.10	1.42	1.40	1.29	1.20	1.47
Petroleum and coal products (324)	7.9	10.6	8.9	12.8	13.9	76.93	0.09	0.11	0.10	0.12	0.13
Chemical manufactures (325)	1 103.5	1 174.0	1 341.2	1 765.8	2 016.6	82.75	12.43	12.21	14.82	16.65	18.79
Plastics and rubber products (326)	173.5	243.4	223.4	212.4	220.7	27.22	1.95	2.53	2.47	2.00	2.06
Non-metallic mineral products (327)	186.2	206.4	195.7	238.4	297.2	59.58	2.10	2.15	2.16	2.25	2.77
Primary metal manufactures (331)	293.6	278.8	218.1	253.6	347.7	18.41	3.31	2.90	2.41	2.39	3.24
Fabricated metal products (332)	236.0	288.6	302.1	329.9	341.3	44.64	2.66	3.00	3.34	3.11	3.18
Machinery manufactures (333)	782.4	822.9	747.0	823.9	917.0	17.20	8.81	8.56	8.26	7.77	8.54
Computer and electronic products (334)	801.1	1 346.5	1 131.8	826.9	740.3	-7.59	9.02	14.01	12.51	7.80	6.90
Electrical equipment, appliances, and parts (335)	348.7	312.2	279.4	266.7	336.3	-3.56	3.93	3.25	3.09	2.51	3.13
Transportation equipment (336)	3 524.4	3 511.8	3 036.4	4 465.6	3 706.9	5.18	39.70	36.53	33.56	42.10	34.53
Furniture and related products (337)	35.0	56.1	33.5	28.6	22.7	-35.32	0.39	0.58	0.37	0.27	0.21
Miscellaneous manufactures (339)	94.0	87.4	94.0	96.0	123.1	30.90	1.06	0.91	1.04	0.91	1.15
Agricultural and Livestock Products (NAICS Code)	203.3	320.9	353.5	211.8	448.5	120.62	2.29	3.34	3.91	2.00	4.18
Agricultural products (111)	42.4	21.5	36.4	21.8	20.3	-52.10	0.48	0.22	0.40	0.21	0.19
Livestock and livestock products (112)	160.9	299.4	317.1	190.0	428.2	166.15	1.81	3.12	3.50	1.79	3.99
Other Commodities (NAICS Code)	232.1	232.4	261.7	248.6	245.9	5.95	2.61	2.42	2.89	2.34	2.29
Forestry and logging (113)	3.8	4.1	3.4	6.7	7.0	85.14	0.04	0.04	0.04	0.06	0.06
Fishing, hunting, and trapping (114)	0.1	1.3	0.4	0.3	2.3	1 541.26	0.00	0.01	0.00	0.00	0.02
Oil and gas extraction (211)	0.0	0.1	0.2	0.2	0.0	X	0.00	0.00	0.00	0.00	0.00
Mining (212)	82.2	93.9	91.1	88.2	69.3	-15.68	0.93	0.98	1.01	0.83	0.65
Waste and scrap (910)	26.0	19.4	25.6	19.5	28.9	10.89	0.29	0.20	0.28	0.18	0.27
Used merchandise (920)	4.2	5.0	15.7	3.2	2.6	-37.40	0.05	0.05	0.17	0.03	0.02
Goods returned to Canada (980)	15.2	24.4	21.6	16.4	22.2	46.19	0.17	0.25	0.24	0.15	0.21
Special classification provisions (990)	100.6	84.0	103.6	114.1	107.4	6.75	1.13	0.87	1.14	1.08	1.00
Publishing industries (except Internet) (511)	0.0	0.0	0.0	0.0	6.2	X	0.00	0.00	0.00	0.00	0.06
TOTAL AND PERCENT SHARE OF U.S. TOTAL	8 877.2	9 612.2	9 048.0	10 606.7	10 733.8	20.91	1.28	1.23	1.24	1.53	1.48
Top 25 Commodities (HS Code)	4 192.8	4 997.2	4 343.7	5 936.6	5 582.9	33.15	47.23	51.99	48.01	55.97	52.01
1. Turbojet and turbo-propeller parts (841191)	1 417.2	1 613.6	1 165.7	1 622.4	1 544.9	9.01	15.96	16.79	12.88	15.30	14.39
2. Antisera and other blood fractions (300210)	161.0	74.4	220.1	354.2	347.6	115.90	1.81	0.77	2.43	3.34	3.24
3. Purebred breeding animals (010110)	0.0	0.0	0.0	163.7	347.5	X	0.00	0.00	0.00	1.54	3.24
4. Parts and accessories for automatic data processing (847330)	482.2	936.7	750.2	439.9	288.2	-40.23	5.43	9.74	8.29	4.15	2.68
5. Parts and accessories of motor vehicles (870899)	168.6	218.5	278.1	320.1	280.1	66.13	1.90	2.27	3.07	3.02	2.61
6. Parts of airplanes or helicopters (880330)	390.8	369.7	310.3	195.2	258.0	-33.98	4.40	3.85	3.43	1.84	2.40
7. Goods vehicles, with diesel or semi-diesel engines (870421)	0.7	0.1	0.1	350.2	255.9	36 457.10	0.01	0.00	0.00	3.30	2.38
8. Natural uranium and compounds, alloys, and ceramics (284410)	0.0	106.1	36.2	120.2	199.0	X	0.00	1.10	0.40	1.13	1.85
9. Spark-ignition internal combustion piston engines (840734)	39.5	185.0	156.5	290.0	198.0	401.27	0.44	1.92	1.73	2.73	1.84
10. Cast or rolled glass (700319)	57.3	122.4	104.1	137.1	191.0	233.33	0.65	1.27	1.15	1.29	1.78
11. Passenger vehicle, spark-ignition, > 1,500 cc < 3,000 cc (870323)	371.7	258.3	193.5	234.4	141.0	-62.07	4.19	2.69	2.14	2.21	1.31
12. Silicones, in primary forms (391000)	. . .	14.8	19.6	46.8	134.4	. . .	. . .	0.15	0.22	0.44	1.25
13. Passenger vehicles, spark-ignition, > 3,000 cc (870324)	220.9	97.0	100.1	271.3	132.7	-39.93	2.49	1.01	1.11	2.56	1.24
14. Whiskies (220830)	123.9	96.9	117.7	111.4	123.7	-0.16	1.40	1.01	1.30	1.05	1.15
15. Parts of seats (940190)	118.8	122.3	84.3	91.1	116.7	-1.77	1.34	1.27	0.93	0.86	1.09
16. Goods vehicles, with spark-ignition piston engines (870431)	18.6	86.5	53.4	207.7	114.8	517.20	0.21	0.90	0.59	1.96	1.07
17. Spark-ignition engine parts (840991)	130.9	109.5	93.2	109.3	111.7	-14.67	1.47	1.14	1.03	1.03	1.04
18. Uranium enriched in U235 (284420)	0.0	26.2	100.3	208.3	104.7	X	0.00	0.27	1.11	1.96	0.98
19. Aluminum alloy rectangular plates, > 0.2 mm thick (760612)	124.3	109.3	95.9	91.9	103.6	-16.65	1.40	1.14	1.06	0.87	0.97
20. Automatic data processing input or output units (847160)	97.8	83.2	90.0	104.1	103.0	5.32	1.10	0.87	0.99	0.98	0.96
21. Vinyl chloride (chloroethylene) (290321)	. . .	82.6	65.4	57.4	100.5	. . .	. . .	0.86	0.72	0.54	0.94
22. Insulated wiring sets for vehicles, ships, and aircrafts (854430)	81.1	74.4	67.4	103.3	99.7	22.93	0.91	0.77	0.74	0.97	0.93
23. Brakes, servo-brakes, and parts for motor vehicles (870839)	80.1	78.7	88.5	110.9	98.2	22.60	0.90	0.82	0.98	1.05	0.91
24. Acrylic polymers in primary forms (390690)	60.7	65.7	91.5	112.7	97.1	59.97	0.68	0.68	1.01	1.06	0.90
25. Spark-ignition internal combustion engines (840790)	47.4	65.4	61.7	83.0	90.9	91.77	0.53	0.68	0.68	0.78	0.85

X = Not applicable.
. . . = Not available.

Exports from Kentucky

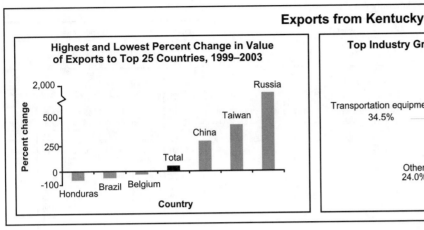

Highest and Lowest Percent Change in Value of Exports to Top 25 Countries, 1999–2003

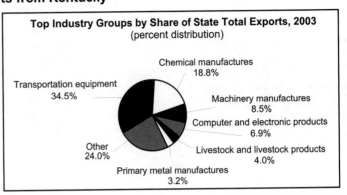

Top Industry Groups by Share of State Total Exports, 2003
(percent distribution)

- Kentucky's exports increased nearly 21 percent from 1999 to 2003. Transportation equipment is the state's largest export, worth $3.7 billion in 2003. Exports of motor vehicles used for the transport of goods ("goods vehicles") increased from about $100,000 in 1999 to $256 million in 2003. These goods vehicles are now among Kentucky's top 10 commodity exports.

- Livestock and livestock products exports increased more than 166 percent from 1999, reaching $428 million in 2003. Purebred breeding animals are Kentucky's third largest commodity export. Before 2002, the state did not export these animals, and in 2003 these animal exports were worth more than $347 million. Chemical manufactures, the second largest export, grew from $1.1 billion in 1999 to just over $2 billion in 2003.

- Canada is by far Kentucky's largest market. Since 1999, more than 30 percent of the state's goods have been exported to Canada. Japan is the second leading recipient of Kentucky exports, having grown from $691 million in 1999 to $983 million in 2003.

Table E-22. Total U.S. Exports (Origin of Movement) via Kentucky, 1999–2003—Continued

(Top 25 commodities and top 25 countries based on 2003 dollar value.)

Industry, commodity, and country	Value (millions of dollars)					Percent change, 1999–2003	Percent share of state total				
	1999	2000	2001	2002	2003		1999	2000	2001	2002	2003
TOTAL AND PERCENT SHARE OF U.S. TOTAL	8 877.2	9 612.2	9 048.0	10 606.7	10 733.8	20.91	1.28	1.23	1.24	1.53	1.48
Top 25 Countries	8 105.6	8 884.1	8 276.5	10 042.1	10 125.3	24.92	91.31	92.43	91.47	94.68	94.33
1. Canada	2 902.0	3 465.2	2 953.9	3 651.8	3 424.4	18.00	32.69	36.05	32.65	34.43	31.90
2. Japan	691.4	919.0	838.2	1 003.0	983.1	42.19	7.79	9.56	9.26	9.46	9.16
3. United Kingdom	765.9	783.8	802.3	824.3	850.3	11.02	8.63	8.15	8.87	7.77	7.92
4. France	779.5	729.5	431.5	795.2	740.5	-5.00	8.78	7.59	4.77	7.50	6.90
5. Mexico	416.9	489.1	433.6	468.9	518.1	24.28	4.70	5.09	4.79	4.42	4.83
6. Netherlands	309.4	298.5	324.9	361.0	396.2	28.08	3.48	3.11	3.59	3.40	3.69
7. Australia	158.6	168.5	218.4	187.7	393.5	148.07	1.79	1.75	2.41	1.77	3.67
8. Germany	379.7	310.8	313.1	346.7	355.3	-6.41	4.28	3.23	3.46	3.27	3.31
9. Taiwan	55.0	51.3	75.5	261.8	302.1	448.94	0.62	0.53	0.83	2.47	2.81
10. Belgium	280.0	216.1	263.9	184.5	236.6	-15.49	3.15	2.25	2.92	1.74	2.20
11. China	63.5	63.9	83.1	129.2	236.4	272.05	0.72	0.66	0.92	1.22	2.20
12. Singapore	124.4	141.8	192.4	232.1	222.4	78.82	1.40	1.48	2.13	2.19	2.07
13. South Korea	105.0	110.8	121.8	188.3	217.2	106.82	1.18	1.15	1.35	1.78	2.02
14. Brazil	245.4	282.7	235.3	173.4	159.4	-35.02	2.76	2.94	2.60	1.63	1.49
15. Spain	93.3	42.4	77.9	116.9	145.1	55.55	1.05	0.44	0.86	1.10	1.35
16. Ireland	79.8	166.5	161.7	159.0	136.2	70.60	0.90	1.73	1.79	1.50	1.27
17. Austria	69.6	18.9	63.4	120.0	133.1	91.34	0.78	0.20	0.70	1.13	1.24
18. Italy	126.9	109.3	133.8	166.5	122.3	-3.60	1.43	1.14	1.48	1.57	1.14
19. Switzerland	100.8	74.1	108.5	136.5	121.3	20.38	1.14	0.77	1.20	1.29	1.13
20. Hong Kong	72.9	89.4	72.7	70.4	107.7	47.73	0.82	0.93	0.80	0.66	1.00
21. Russia	3.5	147.3	125.5	212.1	72.5	1 975.52	0.04	1.53	1.39	2.00	0.68
22. United Arab Emirates	66.7	97.2	114.6	91.1	71.3	6.84	0.75	1.01	1.27	0.86	0.66
23. New Zealand	45.6	33.3	16.6	23.4	65.7	44.04	0.51	0.35	0.18	0.22	0.61
24. Malaysia	52.0	46.2	67.5	89.3	65.1	25.08	0.59	0.48	0.75	0.84	0.61
25. Honduras	117.8	28.4	46.4	49.0	49.4	-58.03	1.33	0.30	0.51	0.46	0.46

Table E-23. Total U.S. Exports (Origin of Movement) via Louisiana, 1999–2003

(Top 25 commodities and top 25 countries based on 2003 dollar value.)

Industry, commodity, and country	Value (millions of dollars)					Percent change, 1999–2003	Percent share of state total				
	1999	2000	2001	2002	2003		1999	2000	2001	2002	2003
TOTAL AND PERCENT SHARE OF U.S. TOTAL	15 841.8	16 814.3	16 589.0	17 566.7	18 390.1	16.09	2.29	2.15	2.27	2.53	2.54
Manufactures (NAICS Code)	8 171.0	9 095.8	8 808.6	8 748.2	8 819.3	7.93	51.58	54.10	53.10	49.80	47.96
Processed foods (311)	2 490.8	2 095.1	2 346.5	2 348.2	2 112.2	-15.20	15.72	12.46	14.15	13.37	11.49
Beverages and tobacco products (312)	73.8	83.8	81.3	87.0	77.8	5.33	0.47	0.00	0.49	0.50	0.42
Fabric mill products (313)	27.8	31.9	33.4	24.9	17.3	-37.60	0.18	0.19	0.20	0.14	0.09
Non-apparel textile products (314)	3.5	2.5	2.8	3.5	4.3	24.81	0.02	0.01	0.02	0.02	0.02
Apparel manufactures (315)	148.5	226.9	83.3	12.0	12.8	-91.38	0.94	1.35	0.50	0.07	0.07
Leather and related products (316)	7.0	5.1	3.6	1.2	0.5	-93.09	0.04	0.03	0.02	0.01	0.00
Wood products (321)	57.6	57.6	42.5	43.0	34.4	-40.32	0.36	0.34	0.26	0.24	0.19
Paper products (322)	221.1	308.0	265.8	268.4	287.9	30.24	1.40	1.83	1.60	1.53	1.57
Printing and related products (323)	2.3	4.5	8.6	6.3	3.2	40.65	0.01	0.03	0.05	0.04	0.02
Petroleum and coal products (324)	684.0	1 281.4	1 188.1	1 090.7	1 206.0	76.31	4.32	7.62	7.16	6.21	6.56
Chemical manufactures (325)	3 017.8	3 737.2	3 442.2	3 038.3	3 708.0	22.87	19.05	22.23	20.75	17.30	20.16
Plastics and rubber products (326)	46.0	77.3	104.2	91.8	90.7	97.28	0.29	0.46	0.63	0.52	0.49
Non-metallic mineral products (327)	18.1	18.5	21.2	17.5	16.8	-7.14	0.11	0.11	0.13	0.10	0.09
Primary metal manufactures (331)	103.3	135.1	95.1	114.9	124.1	20.08	0.65	0.80	0.57	0.65	0.67
Fabricated metal products (332)	76.4	80.6	81.7	98.6	87.8	14.83	0.48	0.48	0.49	0.56	0.48
Machinery manufactures (333)	401.3	358.5	475.1	524.4	488.0	21.59	2.53	2.13	2.86	2.98	2.65
Computer and electronic products (334)	110.2	141.6	116.2	86.7	70.4	-36.13	0.70	0.84	0.70	0.49	0.38
Electrical equipment, appliances, and parts (335)	122.8	137.9	80.0	92.4	101.6	-17.27	0.78	0.82	0.48	0.53	0.55
Transportation equipment (336)	502.2	260.6	281.6	728.9	305.4	-39.18	3.17	1.55	1.70	4.15	1.66
Furniture and related products (337)	6.3	3.9	2.8	1.4	1.6	-74.44	0.04	0.02	0.02	0.01	0.01
Miscellaneous manufactures (339)	50.1	48.0	52.6	68.2	68.4	36.43	0.32	0.29	0.32	0.39	0.37
Agricultural and Livestock Products (NAICS Code)	7 458.9	7 540.0	7 563.8	8 608.9	9 388.7	25.87	47.08	44.84	45.60	49.01	51.05
Agricultural products (111)	7 455.1	7 535.7	7 558.8	8 603.4	9 378.7	25.80	47.06	44.82	45.57	48.98	51.00
Livestock and livestock products (112)	3.8	4.3	5.0	5.5	10.1	165.08	0.02	0.03	0.03	0.03	0.05
Other Commodities (NAICS Code)	211.8	178.4	216.6	209.5	182.1	-14.04	1.34	1.06	1.31	1.19	0.99
Forestry and logging (113)	1.7	4.0	2.8	4.5	3.2	85.65	0.01	0.02	0.02	0.03	0.02
Fishing, hunting, and trapping (114)	55.8	46.1	54.9	63.1	45.1	-19.18	0.35	0.27	0.33	0.36	0.25
Oil and gas extraction (211)	15.9	1.4	2.3	0.6	0.8	-95.21	0.10	0.01	0.01	0.00	0.00
Mining (212)	86.9	42.0	36.8	23.8	43.3	-50.17	0.55	0.25	0.22	0.14	0.24
Waste and scrap (910)	13.3	42.7	75.7	55.9	56.8	326.27	0.08	0.25	0.46	0.32	0.31
Public administration (920)	4.8	6.2	13.3	15.1	4.8	0.04	0.03	0.04	0.08	0.09	0.03
Goods returned to Canada (980)	9.0	10.8	10.8	10.5	6.4	-28.56	0.06	0.06	0.07	0.06	0.03
Special classification provisions (990)	24.4	25.4	20.0	36.1	21.7	-11.06	0.15	0.15	0.12	0.21	0.12
Publishing industries (except Internet) (511)	0.0	0.0	0.0	0.0	0.0	X	0.00	0.00	0.00	0.00	0.00
TOTAL AND PERCENT SHARE OF U.S. TOTAL	15 841.8	16 814.3	16 589.0	17 566.7	18 390.1	16.09	2.29	2.15	2.27	2.53	2.54
Top 25 Commodities (HS Code)	10 497.0	11 002.7	11 053.7	12 326.6	13 549.0	29.07	66.26	65.44	66.63	70.17	73.68
1. Soybeans, whether or not broken (120100)	2 944.0	3 424.9	3 254.5	3 770.0	4 848.0	64.67	18.58	20.37	19.62	21.46	26.36
2. Corn, other than seed corn (100590)	3 422.0	3 054.8	3 193.8	3 600.5	3 119.5	-8.84	21.60	18.17	19.25	20.50	16.96
3. Wheat and meslin (100190)	743.2	672.5	708.7	785.9	877.0	18.00	4.69	4.00	4.27	4.47	4.77
4. Petroleum oils from bituminous mineral (not crude) (271019)	0.0	0.0	0.0	610.6	712.9	X	0.00	0.00	0.00	3.48	3.88
5. Soybean oilcake and other solid residue (230400)	745.6	807.4	988.1	846.5	680.4	-8.74	4.71	4.80	5.96	4.82	3.70
6. Residues of starch manufacture and similar residue (230310)	382.3	400.7	421.8	376.6	382.5	0.05	2.41	2.38	2.54	2.14	2.08
7. Rice in the husk (paddy or rough) (100610)	84.2	118.4	143.9	143.4	258.1	206.53	0.53	0.70	0.87	0.82	1.40
8. Soybean oil and fractions, crude (150710)	285.4	97.3	129.7	255.8	247.0	-13.45	1.80	0.58	0.78	1.46	1.34
9. Miscellaneous organo-inorganic compounds (293100)	423.5	453.5	419.9	140.8	234.4	-44.65	2.67	2.70	2.53	0.80	1.27
10. Petroleum coke, calcined (271312)	225.7	212.5	231.0	268.1	231.9	2.75	1.42	1.26	1.39	1.53	1.26
11. Synthetic rubber (400270)	89.9	130.1	174.8	199.6	204.5	127.47	0.57	0.77	1.05	1.14	1.11
12. Grain sorghum (100700)	177.9	170.1	178.5	195.3	173.7	-2.36	1.12	1.01	1.08	1.11	0.94
13. Isocyanates (292910)	63.5	99.7	93.7	89.8	173.6	173.39	0.40	0.59	0.56	0.51	0.94
14. Amino-resins (390930)	. . .	31.2	34.6	36.0	150.9	. . .	. . .	0.19	0.21	0.20	0.82
15. Parts for boring or sinking machinery (843143)	. . .	46.0	145.2	70.3	141.8	. . .	. . .	0.27	0.88	0.40	0.77
16. Goods vehicles, with spark-ignition piston engines (870431)	133.1	157.7	104.1	125.1	137.4	3.23	0.84	0.94	0.63	0.71	0.75
17. Ethylene dichloride (290315)	. . .	130.4	53.8	46.1	123.3	. . .	. . .	0.78	0.32	0.26	0.67
18. Polymers of ethylene (390190)	126.2	172.1	117.3	122.0	120.7	-4.36	0.80	1.02	0.71	0.69	0.66
19. Rice, semi-or whole milled, polished or not (100630)	212.4	130.6	115.4	118.7	110.5	-47.98	1.34	0.78	0.70	0.68	0.60
20. Oils distilled from coal tar (270799)	66.0	89.6	77.2	94.5	109.8	66.36	0.42	0.53	0.47	0.54	0.60
21. Ethylene glycol (290531)	. . .	48.9	19.1	25.7	106.0	. . .	. . .	0.29	0.12	0.15	0.58
22. Vinyl chloride (chloroethylene) (290321)	76.4	214.5	132.5	92.7	102.2	33.77	0.48	1.28	0.80	0.53	0.56
23. Products and residuals of chemical industry (382490)	57.6	80.0	130.4	121.5	102.1	77.26	0.36	0.48	0.79	0.69	0.56
24. Kraftliner, uncoated and unbleached (480411)	. . .	115.6	101.6	80.5	100.9	. . .	. . .	0.69	0.61	0.46	0.55
25. Fertilizers (310000)	238.1	144.2	84.1	110.6	99.9	-58.04	1.50	0.86	0.51	0.63	0.54

X = Not applicable.
. . . = Not available.

Exports from Louisiana

Highest and Lowest Percent Change in Value of Exports to Top 25 Countries, 1999–2003

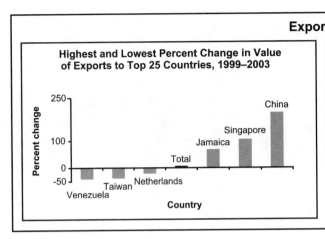

Top Industry Groups by Share of State Total Exports, 2003
(percent distribution)

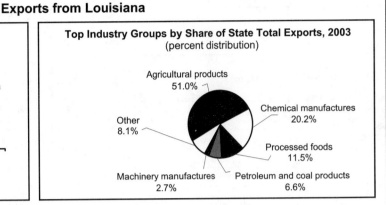

- Exports from Louisiana are worth about $18.4 billion, up 16 percent from 1999. The state has the 10th highest value of exports in the nation. Agricultural products compose more than half of Louisiana's total exports.

- Soybeans, which is Louisiana's top commodity, grew from $2.9 billion in 1999 to $4.8 billion in 2003, an increase of nearly 65 percent. Corn exports account for more than $3 billion, making them the state's second most valuable commodity export.

- Apparel manufactures exports dropped from about $149 million in 1999 to $13 million in 2003. Oil and gas extraction exports also fell significantly during this period, going from $16 million to $763,000.

- Japan is the leading recipient of Louisiana's goods. Of the nearly $2.5 billion worth of exports shipped to Japan in 2003, $2 billion were agricultural products. Exports to China increased from $664 million in 1999 to $2.1 billion in 2003. Agricultural product exports to China accounted for most of this growth.

Table E-23. Total U.S. Exports (Origin of Movement) via Louisiana, 1999–2003—Continued

(Top 25 commodities and top 25 countries based on 2003 dollar value.)

Industry, commodity, and country	Value (millions of dollars)					Percent change, 1999–2003	Percent share of state total				
	1999	2000	2001	2002	2003		1999	2000	2001	2002	2003
TOTAL AND PERCENT SHARE OF U.S. TOTAL	15 841.8	16 814.3	16 589.0	17 566.7	18 390.1	16.09	2.29	2.15	2.27	2.53	2.54
Top 25 Countries	12 026.7	13 026.1	12 723.1	13 439.0	14 726.0	22.44	75.92	77.47	76.70	76.50	80.08
1. Japan	2 040.7	1 963.4	2 136.9	2 521.4	2 482.3	21.63	12.88	11.68	12.88	14.35	13.50
2. China	663.8	1 064.1	682.7	767.9	2 117.3	219.00	4.19	6.33	4.12	4.37	11.51
3. Mexico	1 246.3	1 637.7	1 524.3	1 631.5	1 776.1	42.51	7.87	9.74	9.19	9.29	9.66
4. Canada	1 060.1	1 098.6	1 028.1	1 036.9	1 246.9	17.62	6.69	6.53	6.20	5.90	6.78
5. Egypt	554.6	513.5	656.0	629.5	633.0	14.14	3.50	3.05	3.95	3.58	3.44
6. South Korea	670.4	581.7	549.5	547.8	625.8	-6.64	4.23	3.46	3.31	3.12	3.40
7. Netherlands	660.9	790.0	756.8	569.2	499.9	-24.37	4.17	4.70	4.56	3.24	2.72
8. Spain	359.8	355.5	461.3	429.2	496.6	38.00	2.27	2.11	2.78	2.44	2.70
9. Belgium	498.3	592.8	503.5	467.7	451.5	-9.41	3.15	3.53	3.04	2.66	2.45
10. Taiwan	723.2	735.9	643.4	645.2	408.5	-43.51	4.57	4.38	3.88	3.67	2.22
11. Colombia	267.0	394.9	377.0	416.6	374.4	40.25	1.69	2.35	2.27	2.37	2.04
12. Germany	255.0	247.4	222.2	361.1	345.7	35.57	1.61	1.47	1.34	2.06	1.88
13. Indonesia	276.1	304.3	395.2	335.8	323.4	17.16	1.74	1.81	2.38	1.91	1.76
14. Brazil	316.0	414.8	352.3	316.8	317.6	0.51	1.99	2.47	2.12	1.80	1.73
15. Turkey	211.4	203.8	237.8	259.9	308.5	45.93	1.33	1.21	1.43	1.48	1.68
16. Venezuela	575.0	344.6	326.1	251.0	297.6	-48.24	3.63	2.05	1.97	1.43	1.62
17. United Kingdom	277.8	306.8	336.7	407.7	296.8	6.85	1.75	1.82	2.03	2.32	1.61
18. Dominican Republic	266.5	270.7	249.5	282.6	275.2	3.30	1.68	1.61	1.50	1.61	1.50
19. Jamaica	149.1	163.6	163.5	178.3	241.0	61.67	0.94	0.97	0.99	1.01	1.31
20. Singapore	109.5	149.7	180.9	241.3	221.1	101.85	0.69	0.89	1.09	1.37	1.20
21. Guatemala	161.1	155.2	172.8	224.7	214.0	32.85	1.02	0.92	1.04	1.28	1.16
22. Australia	133.4	150.3	151.6	164.2	199.2	49.28	0.84	0.89	0.91	0.93	1.08
23. Costa Rica	140.3	132.9	168.6	224.8	194.2	38.40	0.89	0.79	1.02	1.28	1.06
24. France	185.8	214.5	237.8	276.6	190.7	2.62	1.17	1.28	1.43	1.57	1.04
25. Israel	224.9	239.3	208.6	251.4	188.8	-16.04	1.42	1.42	1.26	1.43	1.03

Table E-24. Total U.S. Exports (Origin of Movement) via Maine, 1999–2003

(Top 25 commodities and top 25 countries based on 2003 dollar value.)

Industry, commodity, and country	Value (millions of dollars)					Percent change, 1999–2003	Percent share of state total				
	1999	2000	2001	2002	2003		1999	2000	2001	2002	2003
TOTAL AND PERCENT SHARE OF U.S. TOTAL	2 014.1	1 778.7	1 812.5	1 973.1	2 188.4	8.66	0.29	0.23	0.25	0.28	0.30
Manufactures (NAICS Code)	1 582.2	1 281.6	1 294.4	1 538.5	1 721.6	8.81	78.56	72.05	71.42	77.98	78.67
Processed foods (311)	54.2	74.3	68.2	66.2	84.5	56.02	2.69	4.18	3.76	3.36	3.86
Beverages and tobacco products (312)	2.0	6.5	7.7	4.7	5.5	173.06	0.10	0.00	0.42	0.24	0.25
Fabric mill products (313)	6.4	8.0	8.8	7.8	7.5	16.81	0.32	0.45	0.48	0.39	0.34
Non-apparel textile products (314)	9.3	12.6	9.3	7.0	7.3	-21.67	0.46	0.71	0.51	0.36	0.33
Apparel manufactures (315)	6.7	3.0	3.7	3.1	2.8	-57.92	0.33	0.17	0.20	0.16	0.13
Leather and related products (316)	80.2	68.0	69.7	60.5	68.1	-15.05	3.98	3.82	3.85	3.07	3.11
Wood products (321)	60.4	78.0	76.2	65.0	74.2	22.72	3.00	4.38	4.21	3.29	3.39
Paper products (322)	329.1	371.5	354.4	384.9	414.8	26.05	16.34	20.89	19.55	19.51	18.96
Printing and related products (323)	2.3	6.4	5.3	3.1	2.9	26.89	0.11	0.36	0.29	0.16	0.13
Petroleum and coal products (324)	2.3	6.1	1.8	1.5	2.2	-6.72	0.11	0.34	0.10	0.08	0.10
Chemical manufactures (325)	34.9	38.5	53.6	79.0	59.3	69.90	1.73	2.16	2.96	4.01	2.71
Plastics and rubber products (326)	22.1	28.6	27.6	32.2	43.1	95.31	1.10	1.61	1.52	1.63	1.97
Non-metallic mineral products (327)	5.4	3.8	6.0	13.6	7.6	41.54	0.27	0.21	0.33	0.69	0.35
Primary metal manufactures (331)	13.4	14.4	13.5	8.5	7.8	-42.00	0.67	0.81	0.75	0.43	0.36
Fabricated metal products (332)	30.8	18.7	12.5	13.3	14.6	-52.68	1.53	1.05	0.69	0.68	0.67
Machinery manufactures (333)	74.5	93.1	97.9	88.3	88.9	19.26	3.70	5.24	5.40	4.48	4.06
Computer and electronic products (334)	660.4	330.2	347.1	535.4	605.2	-8.35	32.79	18.57	19.15	27.14	27.66
Electrical equipment, appliances, and parts (335)	50.6	46.1	34.4	44.8	38.4	-24.00	2.51	2.59	1.90	2.27	1.76
Transportation equipment (336)	122.2	59.0	79.7	101.2	164.4	34.57	6.07	3.32	4.40	5.13	7.51
Furniture and related products (337)	4.2	3.7	4.0	5.4	7.9	87.96	0.21	0.21	0.22	0.27	0.36
Miscellaneous manufactures (339)	10.8	11.1	13.2	13.0	14.5	34.79	0.53	0.63	0.73	0.66	0.66
Agricultural and Livestock Products (NAICS Code)	52.3	62.8	58.1	40.3	48.2	-7.89	2.60	3.53	3.21	2.04	2.20
Agricultural products (111)	15.5	21.9	19.1	19.6	19.6	26.67	0.77	1.23	1.06	0.99	0.90
Livestock and livestock products (112)	36.8	40.9	39.0	20.7	28.6	-22.41	1.83	2.30	2.15	1.05	1.31
Other Commodities (NAICS Code)	379.5	434.2	459.9	394.2	418.6	10.30	18.84	24.41	25.37	19.98	19.13
Forestry and logging (113)	163.3	177.1	186.9	185.4	184.9	13.19	8.11	9.96	10.31	9.40	8.45
Fishing, hunting, and trapping (114)	143.8	156.5	149.0	166.5	181.3	26.08	7.14	8.80	8.22	8.44	8.29
Oil and gas extraction (211)	0.0	36.3	71.3	0.0	0.0	X	0.00	2.04	3.93	0.00	0.00
Mining (212)	1.7	1.3	0.3	0.3	0.2	-90.66	0.08	0.07	0.02	0.02	0.01
Waste and scrap (910)	14.3	18.5	11.3	13.2	21.7	51.50	0.71	1.04	0.63	0.67	0.99
Public administration (920)	1.5	1.0	2.0	1.4	1.7	7.63	0.08	0.06	0.11	0.07	0.08
Goods returned to Canada (980)	31.3	21.5	22.4	17.8	18.6	-40.50	1.56	1.21	1.23	0.90	0.85
Special classification provisions (990)	23.5	22.0	16.8	9.6	10.3	-56.28	1.17	1.24	0.93	0.49	0.47
Publishing industries (except Internet) (511)	0.0	0.0	0.0	0.0	0.0	X	0.00	0.00	0.00	0.00	0.00
TOTAL AND PERCENT SHARE OF U.S. TOTAL	2 014.1	1 778.7	1 812.5	1 973.1	2 188.4	8.66	0.29	0.23	0.25	0.28	0.30
Top 25 Commodities (HS Code)	475.0	640.4	677.0	1 259.8	1 473.4	210.19	23.58	36.00	37.35	63.85	67.33
1. Non-digital monolithic integrated circuits (854229)	0.0	0.0	0.0	259.9	276.6	X	0.00	0.00	0.00	13.17	12.64
2. Digital monolithic integrated circuits (854221)	0.0	0.0	0.0	148.8	177.0	X	0.00	0.00	0.00	7.54	8.09
3. Chemical wood-pulp, semi- or bleached non-coniferous (470329)	94.2	115.2	79.7	131.9	160.0	69.85	4.68	6.48	4.40	6.69	7.31
4. Lobsters (030622)	106.0	117.7	113.6	141.1	149.4	40.94	5.26	6.62	6.27	7.15	6.83
5. Coniferous wood in the rough, not treated (440320)	122.1	127.6	133.9	130.9	121.4	-0.57	6.06	7.17	7.39	6.63	5.55
6. Airplane and aircraft, unladen weight > 15,000 kg (880240)	0.0	0.0	20.8	44.0	79.2	X	0.00	0.00	1.15	2.23	3.62
7. Paper and paperboard coated in other materials (481190)	33.6	49.6	76.2	56.4	69.8	107.74	1.67	2.79	4.20	2.86	3.19
8. Non-coniferous wood, rough, not treated (440399)	26.1	34.0	35.8	41.6	47.4	81.61	1.30	1.91	1.98	2.11	2.17
9. Coated paper, with mechanically created fibers (481022)	0.0	0.0	0.0	26.9	36.5	X	0.00	0.00	0.00	1.36	1.67
10. Coated paper, without mechanically created fibers (481013)	0.0	0.0	0.0	33.2	35.2	X	0.00	0.00	0.00	1.68	1.61
11. Parts and accessories for automatic data processing (847330)	21.0	7.9	22.5	20.7	33.7	60.48	1.04	0.44	1.24	1.05	1.54
12. Composite diagnostic or laboratory reagents (382200)	13.3	15.0	26.0	38.5	31.6	137.59	0.66	0.84	1.43	1.95	1.44
13. Mucilages and thickeners (130239)	19.9	24.7	23.2	23.3	31.4	57.79	0.99	1.39	1.28	1.18	1.43
14. Leather of bovine or equine animals (410792)	0.0	0.0	0.0	22.8	30.7	X	0.00	0.00	0.00	1.16	1.40
15. Paper and paperboard coated in plastics (481159)	0.0	0.0	0.0	23.9	28.1	X	0.00	0.00	0.00	1.21	1.28
16. Burglar or fire alarms (853110)	. . .	11.3	8.7	11.3	24.6	. . .	. . .	0.64	0.48	0.57	1.12
17. Coniferous wood, sawn, > 6 mm thick (440710)	. . .	29.4	25.1	11.5	20.7	. . .	. . .	1.65	1.38	0.58	0.95
18. Airplanes and aircraft, unladen wgt > 2,000 kg < 15,000 kg (880230)	. . .	4.0	6.1	6.2	16.5	. . .	. . .	0.22	0.34	0.31	0.75
19. Office or school supplies of plastic (392610)	. . .	0.0	0.1	0.0	15.4	. . .	. . .	0.00	0.01	0.00	0.70
20. Pacific, Atlantic, and Danube salmon (030212)	. . .	28.4	26.9	9.7	15.3	. . .	. . .	1.60	1.48	0.49	0.70
21. Parts and accessories of motor vehicles (870899)	12.8	11.1	12.2	15.3	15.2	18.75	0.64	0.62	0.67	0.78	0.69
22. Molluscs (030791)	. . .	20.6	17.4	12.3	15.2	. . .	. . .	1.16	0.96	0.62	0.69
23. Wood in chips or particles, coniferous (440121)	3.0	11.2	16.8	15.0	15.1	403.33	0.15	0.63	0.93	0.76	0.69
24. Parts for discharge lamps (853990)	23.0	20.1	19.3	23.3	13.8	-40.00	1.14	1.13	1.06	1.18	0.63
25. Oak wood, in the rough, not treated (440391)	. . .	12.6	12.8	11.3	13.6	. . .	. . .	0.71	0.71	0.57	0.62

X = Not applicable.
. . . = Not available.

Exports from Maine

Highest and Lowest Percent Change in Value of Exports to Top 25 Countries, 1999–2003

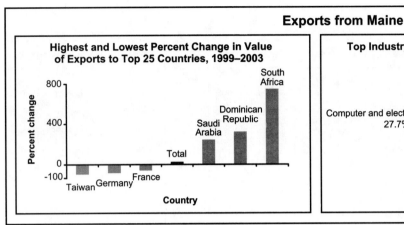

Top Industry Groups by Share of State Total Exports, 2003
(percent distribution)

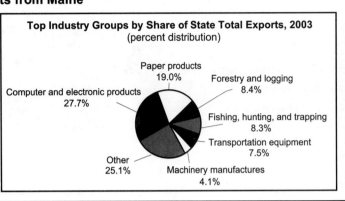

- Computer and electronic products are Maine's largest export. The value of these exports reached $605 million in 2003, after dropping to $330 million in 2000. Plastics and rubber products nearly doubled from $22 million in 1999 to $43 million in 2003.

- Monolithic integrated circuits, both digital and non-digital, are Maine's top commodities. Together, these exports were worth over $453 million in 2003. Lobsters remain among Maine's top five commodity exports, accounting for close to 7 percent of the state's exports.

- In 2003, Canada was the top market for exports. Maine sent 79 percent of its fishing, hunting, and trapping exports to Canada, as well as 99.9 percent of its forestry and logging exports. Nearly one-fourth of the $821 million worth of exports to Canada were forestry and logging products. Malaysia and Singapore each import about 10 percent of Maine's goods. However, exports to Singapore fell from $389 million in 1999 to $224 million in 2003.

Table E-24. Total U.S. Exports (Origin of Movement) via Maine, 1999–2003—Continued

(Top 25 commodities and top 25 countries based on 2003 dollar value.)

Industry, commodity, and country	Value (millions of dollars)					Percent change, 1999–2003	Percent share of state total				
	1999	2000	2001	2002	2003		1999	2000	2001	2002	2003
TOTAL AND PERCENT SHARE OF U.S. TOTAL	2 014.1	1 778.7	1 812.5	1 973.1	2 188.4	8.66	0.29	0.23	0.25	0.28	0.30
Top 25 Countries	1 913.4	1 689.4	1 692.9	1 861.6	2 064.3	7.89	95.00	94.98	93.41	94.35	94.33
1. Canada	717.7	838.9	846.3	791.1	821.0	14.40	35.64	47.16	46.69	40.09	37.52
2. Malaysia	163.7	133.8	132.7	167.6	236.7	44.64	8.13	7.52	7.32	8.50	10.82
3. Singapore	389.2	36.4	105.3	248.3	224.4	-42.34	19.32	2.05	5.81	12.59	10.25
4. United Kingdom	70.1	47.3	36.4	65.9	133.1	89.75	3.48	2.66	2.01	3.34	6.08
5. Japan	79.8	76.6	74.9	85.9	93.0	16.53	3.96	4.31	4.13	4.35	4.25
6. South Korea	51.9	64.4	35.1	80.7	91.2	75.72	2.58	3.62	1.94	4.09	4.17
7. China	35.9	23.2	34.3	48.2	78.3	117.92	1.78	1.30	1.89	2.44	3.58
8. Belgium	50.9	58.2	36.8	49.9	52.9	3.75	2.53	3.27	2.03	2.53	2.42
9. Netherlands	22.9	32.3	21.3	28.5	44.5	94.28	1.14	1.81	1.18	1.44	2.04
10. Italy	15.3	32.2	21.1	30.1	40.3	163.60	0.76	1.81	1.17	1.53	1.84
11. Hong Kong	50.3	50.0	46.8	38.3	34.4	-31.61	2.50	2.81	2.58	1.94	1.57
12. Australia	17.3	40.1	42.0	37.6	28.9	66.74	0.86	2.25	2.32	1.90	1.32
13. Dominican Republic	5.7	9.8	22.8	20.0	25.9	351.99	0.28	0.55	1.26	1.02	1.18
14. Mexico	54.2	36.9	34.2	29.2	24.1	-55.43	2.69	2.08	1.89	1.48	1.10
15. Germany	49.8	35.2	47.4	21.7	17.3	-65.20	2.47	1.98	2.61	1.10	0.79
16. Brazil	18.4	26.6	22.5	14.7	15.9	-13.61	0.91	1.50	1.24	0.75	0.73
17. South Africa	1.7	1.4	2.4	5.4	14.5	749.91	0.08	0.08	0.13	0.28	0.66
18. Taiwan	39.0	42.4	25.3	11.0	13.2	-66.19	1.93	2.38	1.40	0.56	0.60
19. Turkey	4.3	8.8	12.7	11.4	12.3	188.48	0.21	0.49	0.70	0.58	0.56
20. France	28.0	28.3	33.7	36.5	11.8	-57.70	1.39	1.59	1.86	1.85	0.54
21. Israel	12.2	29.3	24.3	9.8	11.3	-6.68	0.60	1.65	1.34	0.50	0.52
22. Spain	6.5	15.3	13.0	9.7	11.0	68.11	0.32	0.86	0.72	0.49	0.50
23. Saudi Arabia	2.8	1.5	1.8	1.9	9.9	248.94	0.14	0.08	0.10	0.10	0.45
24. India	9.4	9.3	9.2	6.2	9.4	-0.39	0.47	0.52	0.51	0.31	0.43
25. Thailand	16.3	11.0	10.6	11.9	9.0	-44.58	0.81	0.62	0.59	0.60	0.41

Table E-25. Total U.S. Exports (Origin of Movement) via Maryland, 1999–2003

(Top 25 commodities and top 25 countries based on 2003 dollar value.)

Industry, commodity, and country	Value (millions of dollars)					Percent change, 1999–2003	Percent share of state total				
	1999	2000	2001	2002	2003		1999	2000	2001	2002	2003
TOTAL AND PERCENT SHARE OF U.S. TOTAL	4 009.2	4 592.9	4 974.9	4 473.6	4 940.6	23.23	0.58	0.59	0.68	0.65	0.68
Manufactures (NAICS Code)	3 751.5	4 291.7	4 620.4	4 172.7	4 584.8	22.21	93.57	93.44	92.88	93.27	92.80
Processed foods (311)	89.7	127.0	111.7	101.3	134.6	50.14	2.24	2.77	2.25	2.26	2.72
Beverages and tobacco products (312)	7.7	13.3	13.8	14.9	18.4	139.47	0.19	0.00	0.28	0.33	0.37
Fabric mill products (313)	101.5	104.3	114.8	109.0	105.9	4.31	2.53	2.27	2.31	2.44	2.14
Non-apparel textile products (314)	13.9	14.4	12.4	12.6	14.5	4.41	0.35	0.31	0.25	0.28	0.29
Apparel manufactures (315)	10.6	4.6	6.2	7.9	12.6	19.44	0.26	0.10	0.12	0.18	0.26
Leather and related products (316)	8.8	8.0	6.7	8.8	65.9	646.00	0.22	0.17	0.13	0.20	1.33
Wood products (321)	46.3	63.5	60.9	49.1	50.0	7.93	1.16	1.38	1.22	1.10	1.01
Paper products (322)	48.2	54.0	71.3	74.7	68.9	42.94	1.20	1.18	1.43	1.67	1.39
Printing and related products (323)	100.1	70.5	76.4	110.8	154.0	53.96	2.50	1.53	1.54	2.48	3.12
Petroleum and coal products (324)	16.3	8.8	9.0	12.0	11.6	-29.02	0.41	0.19	0.18	0.27	0.23
Chemical manufactures (325)	661.1	784.1	628.4	706.7	838.4	26.81	16.49	17.07	12.63	15.80	16.97
Plastics and rubber products (326)	107.6	120.6	104.5	100.6	104.6	-2.83	2.68	2.63	2.10	2.25	2.12
Non-metallic mineral products (327)	31.2	38.8	38.0	35.8	29.5	-5.51	0.78	0.84	0.76	0.80	0.60
Primary metal manufactures (331)	70.9	82.9	117.2	93.7	175.2	147.29	1.77	1.81	2.36	2.09	3.55
Fabricated metal products (332)	139.0	202.0	241.1	279.5	246.3	77.21	3.47	4.40	4.85	6.25	4.99
Machinery manufactures (333)	405.6	473.7	610.9	424.4	487.7	20.24	10.12	10.31	12.28	9.49	9.87
Computer and electronic products (334)	990.0	1 125.5	1 242.3	808.0	743.7	-24.88	24.69	24.50	24.97	18.06	15.05
Electrical equipment, appliances, and parts (335)	136.0	244.5	231.8	182.2	186.4	37.09	3.39	5.32	4.66	4.07	3.77
Transportation equipment (336)	658.1	629.5	802.6	914.3	1 018.8	54.80	16.42	13.71	16.13	20.44	20.62
Furniture and related products (337)	17.4	9.1	9.7	10.2	9.6	-45.14	0.44	0.20	0.19	0.23	0.19
Miscellaneous manufactures (339)	91.5	112.7	110.8	116.2	108.2	18.32	2.28	2.45	2.23	2.60	2.19
Agricultural and Livestock Products (NAICS Code)	44.7	74.3	71.8	9.4	6.3	-85.82	1.11	1.62	1.44	0.21	0.13
Agricultural products (111)	43.5	73.0	70.3	6.6	5.4	-87.61	1.08	1.59	1.41	0.15	0.11
Livestock and livestock products (112)	1.2	1.3	1.5	2.8	0.9	-19.61	0.03	0.03	0.03	0.06	0.02
Other Commodities (NAICS Code)	213.0	226.9	282.7	291.5	349.5	64.06	5.31	4.94	5.68	6.52	7.07
Forestry and logging (113)	21.7	33.3	36.1	30.8	26.7	22.85	0.54	0.72	0.73	0.69	0.54
Fishing, hunting, and trapping (114)	11.6	12.1	13.0	13.7	17.9	53.70	0.29	0.26	0.26	0.31	0.36
Oil and gas extraction (211)	0.0	0.1	0.1	0.0	12.6	X	0.00	0.00	0.00	0.00	0.25
Mining (212)	23.0	27.3	25.1	13.1	17.9	-21.94	0.57	0.59	0.50	0.29	0.36
Waste and scrap (910)	21.0	36.1	37.5	43.5	60.9	189.18	0.52	0.79	0.75	0.97	1.23
Public administration (920)	9.9	14.4	12.5	22.3	24.9	150.43	0.25	0.31	0.25	0.50	0.50
Goods returned to Canada (980)	14.1	18.0	22.0	14.6	13.1	-6.97	0.35	0.39	0.44	0.33	0.27
Special classification provisions (990)	111.6	85.7	136.5	153.5	175.0	56.83	2.78	1.87	2.74	3.43	3.54
Publishing industries (except Internet) (511)	0.0	0.0	0.0	0.0	0.6	X	0.00	0.00	0.00	0.00	0.01
TOTAL AND PERCENT SHARE OF U.S. TOTAL	4 009.2	4 592.9	4 974.9	4 473.6	4 940.6	23.23	0.58	0.59	0.68	0.65	0.68
Top 25 Commodities (HS Code)	1 113.1	1 297.9	1 641.1	1 675.2	1 965.3	76.56	27.76	28.26	32.99	37.45	39.78
1. Parts of airplanes or helicopters (880330)	153.4	132.6	187.4	237.3	286.0	86.44	3.83	2.89	3.77	5.30	5.79
2. Passenger vehicles, spark-ignition, > 3,000 cc (870324)	197.2	162.1	100.4	220.1	282.5	43.26	4.92	3.53	2.02	4.92	5.72
3. Tanks and other armored fighting vehicles and parts (871000)	. . .	27.4	3.8	9.7	123.0	. . .	. . .	0.60	0.08	0.22	2.49
4. Printed books and brochures (490199)	42.0	27.9	30.3	69.5	107.9	156.90	1.05	0.61	0.61	1.55	2.18
5. Parts of transmission or reception apparatus (852990)	51.9	50.1	48.2	49.8	88.5	70.52	1.29	1.09	0.97	1.11	1.79
6. Reaction initiators and accelerators (381590)	26.4	50.0	47.8	60.4	84.1	218.56	0.66	1.09	0.96	1.35	1.70
7. Prepared culture media for dvlp. of microorganisms (382100)	73.7	54.8	51.1	72.9	83.1	12.75	1.84	1.19	1.03	1.63	1.68
8. Helicopters (880212)	0.0	0.0	76.9	192.4	67.8	X	0.00	0.00	1.55	4.30	1.37
9. Transmission and reception apparatus (852520)	76.1	73.7	154.6	56.5	63.1	-17.08	1.90	1.60	3.11	1.26	1.28
10. Goods vehicles, with spark-ignition piston engines (870431)	76.4	73.3	30.5	64.9	62.7	-17.93	1.91	1.60	0.61	1.45	1.27
11. Electrical apparatus for line telephony or telegraphy (851750)	184.5	294.2	259.9	84.3	59.8	-67.59	4.60	6.41	5.22	1.88	1.21
12. Patent leather (411420)	. . .	0.0	0.0	0.4	59.1	. . .	. . .	0.00	0.00	0.01	1.20
13. Double or complex silicates (284210)	6.6	8.4	33.2	43.0	56.4	754.55	0.16	0.18	0.67	0.96	1.14
14. Photosensitive semiconductor devices (854140)	28.0	38.8	50.9	63.4	56.3	101.07	0.70	0.84	1.02	1.42	1.14
15. Textile fabrics impregnated or coated with plastic (590390)	68.2	75.8	82.1	54.5	52.9	-22.43	1.70	1.65	1.65	1.22	1.07
16. Insecticides (380810)	38.8	32.3	35.7	65.3	51.0	31.44	0.97	0.70	0.72	1.46	1.03
17. Exports of military equipment (980320)	. . .	16.4	47.0	51.1	50.6	. . .	. . .	0.36	0.94	1.14	1.02
18. Radar apparatus (852610)	61.7	88.3	164.4	62.9	47.5	-23.01	1.54	1.92	3.30	1.41	0.96
19. Parts of military weapons (930591)	0.0	0.0	0.0	34.6	45.8	X	0.00	0.00	0.00	0.77	0.93
20. Retail medicaments in measured dose (300490)	. . .	8.4	17.3	26.8	43.2	. . .	. . .	0.18	0.35	0.60	0.87
21. Fluoro-polymers (390469)	. . .	0.0	0.0	15.0	43.1	. . .	. . .	0.00	0.00	0.34	0.87
22. Parts of apparatus for line telephony or telegraphy (851790)	19.8	7.7	41.1	34.0	39.5	99.49	0.49	0.17	0.83	0.76	0.80
23. Parts and accessories of motor vehicles (870899)	8.4	25.6	60.5	65.1	38.0	352.38	0.21	0.56	1.22	1.46	0.77
24. Composite diagnostic or laboratory reagents (382200)	. . .	31.3	33.8	27.9	36.8	. . .	. . .	0.68	0.68	0.62	0.74
25. Passenger vehicle, spark-ignition, > 1,500 cc < 3,000 cc (870323)	. . .	18.8	84.2	13.8	36.6	. . .	. . .	0.41	1.69	0.31	0.74

X = Not applicable.
. . . = Not available.

Exports from Maryland

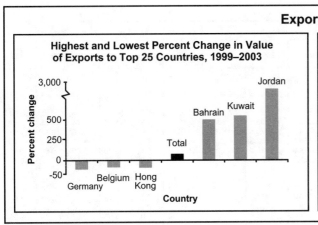

Highest and Lowest Percent Change in Value of Exports to Top 25 Countries, 1999–2003

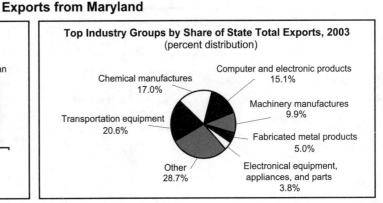

Top Industry Groups by Share of State Total Exports, 2003 (percent distribution)

- Maryland's total exports increased in value from $4 billion in 1999 to $4.9 billion in 2003. Much of this growth was in transportation equipment exports, which increased from $658 million in 1999 to $1 billion in 2003, and now compose 20 percent of the state's total exports. Chemical manufactures are the second leading export, worth $838 million in 2003.

- Exports of airplane and helicopter parts amounted to $286 million in 2003, just edging out passenger vehicles as Maryland's leading commodity export.

- Canada is the top market for Maryland's goods, with 19 percent of the state's total exports. In 1999, Maryland exported goods valued at $93 million to Mexico. By 2003, exports to Mexico had increased to $301 million. Mexico now imports 6 percent of Maryland's goods. Exports to Egypt have also increased, going from $109 million in 1999 to $327 million in 2003. About 70 percent of these exports are transportation equipment.

Table E-25. Total U.S. Exports (Origin of Movement) via Maryland, 1999–2003—*Continued*

(Top 25 commodities and top 25 countries based on 2003 dollar value.)

Industry, commodity, and country	Value (millions of dollars)					Percent change, 1999–2003	Percent share of state total				
	1999	2000	2001	2002	2003		1999	2000	2001	2002	2003
TOTAL AND PERCENT SHARE OF U.S. TOTAL	4 009.2	4 592.9	4 974.9	4 473.6	4 940.6	23.23	0.58	0.59	0.68	0.65	0.68
Top 25 Countries	3 341.4	3 780.8	3 996.1	3 839.4	4 298.9	28.66	83.34	82.32	80.33	85.82	87.01
1. Canada	891.7	858.1	868.5	824.1	943.2	5.77	22.24	18.68	17.46	18.42	19.09
2. Egypt	109.1	83.8	66.2	38.1	327.8	200.49	2.72	1.82	1.33	0.85	6.64
3. United Kingdom	281.6	386.1	313.2	331.4	324.5	15.20	7.03	8.41	6.29	7.41	6.57
4. Japan	227.8	265.5	212.8	261.7	310.7	36.40	5.68	5.78	4.28	5.85	6.29
5. Mexico	93.4	135.9	130.6	241.6	300.8	221.92	2.33	2.96	2.63	5.40	6.09
6. Belgium	294.2	333.0	382.9	196.9	214.1	-27.23	7.34	7.25	7.70	4.40	4.33
7. China	103.5	80.8	125.4	138.1	194.0	87.38	2.58	1.76	2.52	3.09	3.93
8. Netherlands	156.7	202.3	287.3	373.2	189.8	21.11	3.91	4.40	5.77	8.34	3.84
9. Germany	267.3	206.4	223.1	172.8	183.1	-31.47	6.67	4.49	4.49	3.86	3.71
10. France	101.5	184.1	180.4	160.3	149.1	46.92	2.53	4.01	3.63	3.58	3.02
11. Saudi Arabia	59.5	100.1	124.9	123.5	137.0	130.43	1.48	2.18	2.51	2.76	2.77
12. Australia	81.9	113.3	122.1	94.9	110.7	35.14	2.04	2.47	2.45	2.12	2.24
13. Taiwan	65.8	75.8	58.5	54.4	101.1	53.57	1.64	1.65	1.18	1.22	2.05
14. Brazil	91.8	150.4	238.8	126.9	98.1	6.85	2.29	3.27	4.80	2.84	1.99
15. India	42.8	72.6	79.6	68.7	92.2	115.44	1.07	1.58	1.60	1.53	1.87
16. South Korea	103.0	89.8	105.7	186.6	84.7	-17.82	2.57	1.96	2.12	4.17	1.71
17. Italy	75.1	82.6	94.8	77.4	79.4	5.70	1.87	1.80	1.91	1.73	1.61
18. Jordan	2.7	11.0	3.7	3.5	71.6	2 522.14	0.07	0.24	0.08	0.08	1.45
19. Hong Kong	89.6	96.8	106.6	72.1	67.2	-24.99	2.23	2.11	2.14	1.61	1.36
20. Singapore	65.2	64.3	80.9	56.3	64.5	-1.05	1.63	1.40	1.63	1.26	1.31
21. Kuwait	8.9	35.0	15.5	31.1	58.4	553.92	0.22	0.76	0.31	0.69	1.18
22. Sweden	38.9	56.0	49.2	48.6	56.8	45.89	0.97	1.22	0.99	1.09	1.15
23. United Arab Emirates	51.8	43.7	45.0	46.5	55.4	6.97	1.29	0.95	0.91	1.04	1.12
24. Spain	31.6	41.5	48.1	42.9	49.5	56.63	0.79	0.90	0.97	0.96	1.00
25. Bahrain	5.8	11.9	32.3	67.7	35.2	505.22	0.15	0.26	0.65	1.51	0.71

Table E-26. Total U.S. Exports (Origin of Movement) via Massachusetts, 1999–2003

(Top 25 commodities and top 25 countries based on 2003 dollar value.)

Industry, commodity, and country	Value (millions of dollars)					Percent change, 1999–2003	Percent share of state total				
	1999	2000	2001	2002	2003		1999	2000	2001	2002	2003
TOTAL AND PERCENT SHARE OF U.S. TOTAL	16 805.1	20 514.4	17 490.1	16 707.6	18 662.6	11.05	2.43	2.63	2.39	2.41	2.58
Manufactures (NAICS Code)	15 980.8	19 633.0	16 612.3	15 874.1	17 736.0	10.98	95.09	95.70	94.98	95.01	95.04
Processed foods (311)	211.5	232.9	286.1	293.6	300.5	42.10	1.26	1.14	1.64	1.76	1.61
Beverages and tobacco products (312)	7.1	1.6	4.4	20.5	15.4	117.72	0.04	0.00	0.03	0.12	0.08
Fabric mill products (313)	203.7	233.7	218.6	204.3	227.0	11.42	1.21	1.14	1.25	1.22	1.22
Non-apparel textile products (314)	16.5	17.6	14.9	15.7	15.4	-6.60	0.10	0.09	0.09	0.09	0.08
Apparel manufactures (315)	47.7	29.4	30.7	21.6	20.6	-56.81	0.28	0.14	0.18	0.13	0.11
Leather and related products (316)	69.2	74.9	73.1	70.4	65.8	-4.84	0.41	0.37	0.42	0.42	0.35
Wood products (321)	28.9	25.4	22.1	23.1	26.4	-8.72	0.17	0.12	0.13	0.14	0.14
Paper products (322)	363.5	434.6	386.4	372.8	354.6	-2.45	2.16	2.12	2.21	2.23	1.90
Printing and related products (323)	142.6	112.5	126.1	100.2	114.5	-19.71	0.85	0.55	0.72	0.60	0.61
Petroleum and coal products (324)	8.5	4.0	5.6	4.3	17.0	99.50	0.05	0.02	0.03	0.03	0.09
Chemical manufactures (325)	1 356.7	1 600.2	1 533.5	2 267.4	3 216.5	137.08	8.07	7.80	8.77	13.57	17.23
Plastics and rubber products (326)	389.3	373.6	399.9	406.4	375.0	-3.68	2.32	1.82	2.29	2.43	2.01
Non-metallic mineral products (327)	95.7	130.3	120.5	92.5	103.9	8.59	0.57	0.64	0.69	0.55	0.56
Primary metal manufactures (331)	283.4	357.9	271.5	247.5	425.5	50.11	1.69	1.74	1.55	1.48	2.28
Fabricated metal products (332)	601.4	649.8	568.9	691.8	539.3	-10.34	3.58	3.17	3.25	4.14	2.89
Machinery manufactures (333)	1 704.7	2 545.1	2 043.7	1 786.5	1 667.5	-2.18	10.14	12.41	11.68	10.69	8.94
Computer and electronic products (334)	8 055.9	10 213.4	8 121.8	7 023.8	7 687.7	-4.57	47.94	49.79	46.44	42.04	41.19
Electrical equipment, appliances, and parts (335)	720.0	834.0	691.4	649.4	592.1	-17.76	4.28	4.07	3.95	3.89	3.17
Transportation equipment (336)	697.8	658.5	449.0	345.5	382.8	-45.14	4.15	3.21	2.57	2.07	2.05
Furniture and related products (337)	51.3	49.0	31.0	26.2	17.9	-65.16	0.31	0.24	0.18	0.16	0.10
Miscellaneous manufactures (339)	925.4	1 054.7	1 213.0	1 210.5	1 570.6	69.73	5.51	5.14	6.94	7.25	8.42
Agricultural and Livestock Products (NAICS Code)	29.9	22.4	17.0	24.5	24.9	-16.72	0.18	0.11	0.10	0.15	0.13
Agricultural products (111)	23.7	19.1	12.2	16.6	19.6	-17.24	0.14	0.09	0.07	0.10	0.11
Livestock and livestock products (112)	6.2	3.3	4.8	7.9	5.3	-14.71	0.04	0.02	0.03	0.05	0.03
Other Commodities (NAICS Code)	794.4	859.0	860.9	808.9	901.7	13.50	4.73	4.19	4.92	4.84	4.83
Forestry and logging (113)	12.0	11.3	12.1	13.2	13.3	10.64	0.07	0.05	0.07	0.08	0.07
Fishing, hunting, and trapping (114)	224.3	223.2	218.5	239.4	258.5	15.27	1.33	1.09	1.25	1.43	1.39
Oil and gas extraction (211)	3.6	3.9	0.6	0.4	0.7	-79.76	0.02	0.02	0.00	0.00	0.00
Mining (212)	5.0	7.1	5.8	4.4	3.6	-27.68	0.03	0.03	0.03	0.03	0.02
Waste and scrap (910)	74.6	106.0	145.6	183.1	190.4	155.21	0.44	0.52	0.83	1.10	1.02
Public administration (920)	23.0	56.1	52.4	29.3	68.0	195.48	0.14	0.27	0.30	0.18	0.36
Goods returned to Canada (980)	33.7	50.4	37.5	29.6	25.0	-25.70	0.20	0.25	0.21	0.18	0.13
Special classification provisions (990)	418.2	401.1	388.3	309.6	335.1	-19.87	2.49	1.96	2.22	1.85	1.80
Publishing industries (except Internet) (511)	0.0	0.0	0.0	0.0	6.9	X	0.00	0.00	0.00	0.00	0.04
TOTAL AND PERCENT SHARE OF U.S. TOTAL	16 805.1	20 514.4	17 490.1	16 707.6	18 662.6	11.05	2.43	2.63	2.39	2.41	2.58
Top 25 Commodities (HS Code)	4 428.5	6 420.8	5 109.0	6 628.8	8 902.7	101.03	26.35	31.30	29.21	39.68	47.70
1. Digital monolithic integrated circuits (854221)	0.0	0.0	0.0	1 291.0	1 805.8	X	0.00	0.00	0.00	7.73	9.68
2. Antisera and other blood fractions (300210)	89.4	101.2	93.5	343.5	835.7	834.79	0.53	0.49	0.53	2.06	4.48
3. Medical needles, catheters and parts (901839)	364.0	408.0	517.5	509.1	817.9	124.70	2.17	1.99	2.96	3.05	4.38
4. Non-digital monolithic integrated circuits (854229)	0.0	0.0	0.0	427.0	562.2	X	0.00	0.00	0.00	2.56	3.01
5. Hormones (293790)	0.0	0.0	0.0	419.4	529.6	X	0.00	0.00	0.00	2.51	2.84
6. Instruments for checking semiconductor wafers (903082)	160.1	499.6	270.2	334.7	449.5	180.76	0.95	2.44	1.54	2.00	2.41
7. Retail medicaments in measured dose (300490)	214.9	220.7	302.6	396.0	389.7	81.34	1.28	1.08	1.73	2.37	2.09
8. Instruments and appliances for medical sciences (901890)	236.2	246.3	318.9	291.0	372.8	57.83	1.41	1.20	1.82	1.74	2.00
9. Parts and accessories for automatic data processing (847330)	1 153.3	892.9	718.1	429.8	316.9	-72.52	6.86	4.35	4.11	2.57	1.70
10. Polycarbonates in primary forms (390740)	...	46.5	39.5	98.0	269.1	...	...	0.23	0.23	0.59	1.44
11. Gold, non-monetary, unwrought (710812)	...	90.8	13.8	33.5	230.2	...	...	0.44	0.08	0.20	1.23
12. Parts of apparatus for line telephony or telegraphy (851790)	774.4	1 475.0	811.8	160.8	223.3	-71.16	4.61	7.19	4.64	0.96	1.20
13. Electro-diagnostic apparatus and parts (901819)	165.9	169.7	218.9	174.6	220.6	32.97	0.99	0.83	1.25	1.05	1.18
14. Parts of transmission or reception apparatus (852990)	62.7	112.6	166.8	161.9	207.7	231.26	0.37	0.55	0.95	0.97	1.11
15. Automatic data processing units (847180)	442.7	384.6	172.8	154.3	205.5	-53.58	2.63	1.87	0.99	0.92	1.10
16. Parts of instruments for measuring radiation (903090)	148.1	205.1	198.4	184.2	180.5	21.88	0.88	1.00	1.13	1.10	0.97
17. Physical or chemical analysis instruments (902780)	74.7	90.0	105.7	147.0	166.2	122.49	0.44	0.44	0.60	0.88	0.89
18. Composite diagnostic or laboratory reagents (382200)	...	131.7	118.9	120.8	164.0	...	...	0.64	0.68	0.72	0.88
19. Parts of instr. and apparatus for phys/chem. anlys. (902790)	86.6	100.5	122.8	155.4	155.1	79.10	0.52	0.49	0.70	0.93	0.83
20. Turbojet and turbo-propeller parts (841191)	...	92.6	97.9	118.4	142.9	...	...	0.45	0.56	0.71	0.77
21. Ion implanters (854311)	...	483.0	199.3	107.7	137.7	...	...	2.35	1.14	0.64	0.74
22. Lobsters (030622)	...	86.6	86.8	110.3	131.0	...	...	0.42	0.50	0.66	0.70
23. Razors (821210)	205.1	150.0	176.4	161.8	129.8	-36.71	1.22	0.73	1.01	0.97	0.70
24. Parts of electrical machines having individual functions (854390)	78.3	192.8	153.1	139.9	129.7	65.64	0.47	0.94	0.88	0.84	0.69
25. Digital automatic data processing machines (847149)	172.1	240.6	205.3	158.7	129.3	-24.87	1.02	1.17	1.17	0.95	0.69

X = Not applicable.
. . . = Not available.

Exports from Massachusetts

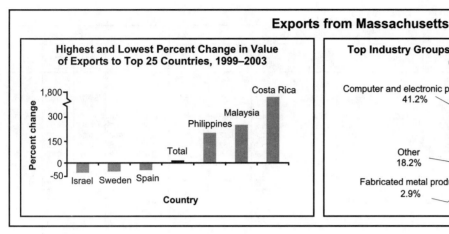

Highest and Lowest Percent Change in Value of Exports to Top 25 Countries, 1999–2003

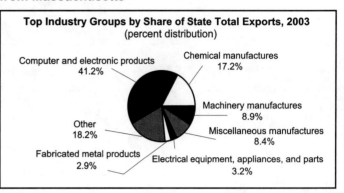

Top Industry Groups by Share of State Total Exports, 2003
(percent distribution)

Computer and electronic products 41.2%
Chemical manufactures 17.2%
Machinery manufactures 8.9%
Miscellaneous manufactures 8.4%
Electrical equipment, appliances, and parts 3.2%
Fabricated metal products 2.9%
Other 18.2%

- In 2003, Massachusetts exported goods worth over $18 billion. This ranked Massachusetts ninth in the nation by value of exports. The state's leading export is computer and electronic products, which were worth $7.7 billion in 2003. Chemical manufactures, the second highest export, increased from $1.4 billion in 1999 to $3.2 billion in 2003.

- Transportation equipment exports, which totaled $698 million in 1999, fell to $383 million in 2003. Apparel manufactures dropped from about $48 million in 1999 to less than $22 million in 2003.

- In 2003, Canada imported $2.6 billion worth of Massachusetts' goods, making it the state's top export market. Exports to the Netherlands increased by more than 50 percent from 1999 to 2003, reaching $1.8 billion. Japan ($1.6 billion), Germany ($1.6 billion), and the United Kingdom ($1.4 billion) all ranked in the top five. Exports to Costa Rica increased from $17 million in 1999 to $313 million in 2003, pushing the country to among Massachusetts' top 20.

Table E-26. Total U.S. Exports (Origin of Movement) via Massachusetts, 1999–2003—Continued

(Top 25 commodities and top 25 countries based on 2003 dollar value.)

Industry, commodity, and country	Value (millions of dollars)					Percent change, 1999–2003	Percent share of state total				
	1999	2000	2001	2002	2003		1999	2000	2001	2002	2003
TOTAL AND PERCENT SHARE OF U.S. TOTAL	16 805.1	20 514.4	17 490.1	16 707.6	18 662.6	11.05	2.43	2.63	2.39	2.41	2.58
Top 25 Countries	15 559.7	19 284.4	16 210.9	15 484.3	17 480.3	12.34	92.59	94.00	92.69	92.68	93.66
1. Canada	3 155.9	3 588.7	2 844.5	2 709.9	2 641.5	-16.30	18.78	17.49	16.26	16.22	14.15
2. Netherlands	1 158.0	1 264.9	820.2	1 054.0	1 759.1	51.92	6.89	6.17	4.69	6.31	9.43
3. Japan	1 771.4	2 183.8	1 964.1	1 598.7	1 635.8	-7.66	10.54	10.65	11.23	9.57	8.76
4. Germany	1 029.0	1 366.2	1 400.7	1 198.5	1 599.3	55.42	6.12	6.66	8.01	7.17	8.57
5. United Kingdom	1 782.4	1 932.9	1 851.0	1 578.9	1 430.0	-19.77	10.61	9.42	10.58	9.45	7.66
6. Malaysia	250.3	402.7	285.4	530.8	928.2	270.87	1.49	1.96	1.63	3.18	4.97
7. Philippines	249.5	433.9	426.2	500.7	820.8	228.96	1.48	2.12	2.44	3.00	4.40
8. Mexico	617.5	701.4	570.9	564.4	711.8	15.27	3.67	3.42	3.26	3.38	3.81
9. France	773.8	1 024.2	864.8	921.5	619.3	-19.97	4.60	4.99	4.94	5.52	3.32
10. Singapore	555.9	702.6	494.8	512.6	576.4	3.69	3.31	3.42	2.83	3.07	3.09
11. China	331.7	502.0	425.4	384.4	571.8	72.37	1.97	2.45	2.43	2.30	3.06
12. South Korea	430.2	746.8	491.0	471.2	558.3	29.77	2.56	3.64	2.81	2.82	2.99
13. Taiwan	646.0	1 053.2	512.6	511.9	528.3	-18.22	3.84	5.13	2.93	3.06	2.83
14. Hong Kong	367.3	483.6	423.7	382.0	496.8	35.27	2.19	2.36	2.42	2.29	2.66
15. Ireland	473.4	664.0	699.5	422.3	381.6	-19.38	2.82	3.24	4.00	2.53	2.04
16. Switzerland	138.9	167.2	123.4	193.8	362.2	160.87	0.83	0.82	0.71	1.16	1.94
17. Italy	356.7	416.5	380.7	344.4	319.7	-10.38	2.12	2.03	2.18	2.06	1.71
18. Costa Rica	17.2	37.6	74.5	349.2	312.8	1 713.71	0.10	0.18	0.43	2.09	1.68
19. Belgium	318.7	302.9	415.5	276.0	265.3	-16.76	1.90	1.48	2.38	1.65	1.42
20. Australia	268.1	256.5	237.6	250.8	253.8	-5.35	1.60	1.25	1.36	1.50	1.36
21. Brazil	214.9	293.3	293.5	257.2	205.5	-4.39	1.28	1.43	1.68	1.54	1.10
22. Spain	180.0	183.2	123.4	115.3	135.3	-24.87	1.07	0.89	0.71	0.69	0.72
23. Israel	207.5	264.5	232.9	156.4	132.5	-36.17	1.23	1.29	1.33	0.94	0.71
24. Sweden	171.0	192.8	170.9	117.4	123.2	-27.94	1.02	0.94	0.98	0.70	0.66
25. Thailand	94.4	118.8	83.8	81.9	111.1	17.68	0.56	0.58	0.48	0.49	0.60

Table E-27. Total U.S. Exports (Origin of Movement) via Michigan, 1999–2003

(Top 25 commodities and top 25 countries based on 2003 dollar value.)

Industry, commodity, and country	Value (millions of dollars)					Percent change, 1999–2003	Percent share of state total				
	1999	2000	2001	2002	2003		1999	2000	2001	2002	2003
TOTAL AND PERCENT SHARE OF U.S. TOTAL	31 085.8	33 845.3	32 365.8	33 775.2	32 941.1	5.97	4.49	4.34	4.43	4.87	4.55
Manufactures (NAICS Code)	30 258.2	32 889.8	31 401.2	32 684.9	31 535.4	4.22	97.34	97.18	97.02	96.77	95.73
Processed foods (311)	182.8	211.4	269.6	315.2	422.3	130.96	0.59	0.62	0.83	0.93	1.28
Beverages and tobacco products (312)	33.8	23.6	11.3	11.1	13.9	-58.91	0.11	0.00	0.04	0.03	0.04
Fabric mill products (313)	36.3	55.3	62.3	65.1	62.2	71.12	0.12	0.16	0.19	0.19	0.19
Non-apparel textile products (314)	23.2	39.9	43.6	45.2	36.0	55.45	0.07	0.12	0.13	0.13	0.11
Apparel manufactures (315)	10.7	9.2	10.0	9.7	13.2	22.94	0.03	0.03	0.03	0.03	0.04
Leather and related products (316)	85.5	89.0	204.8	108.5	121.6	42.27	0.28	0.26	0.63	0.32	0.37
Wood products (321)	82.0	86.9	82.8	89.1	110.2	34.43	0.26	0.26	0.26	0.26	0.33
Paper products (322)	198.8	259.2	223.0	232.5	298.7	50.21	0.64	0.77	0.69	0.69	0.91
Printing and related products (323)	73.1	70.7	65.6	61.1	65.6	-10.24	0.24	0.21	0.20	0.18	0.20
Petroleum and coal products (324)	46.1	52.9	50.5	41.3	65.1	41.24	0.15	0.16	0.16	0.12	0.20
Chemical manufactures (325)	2 123.6	2 467.6	2 524.5	2 822.6	2 785.3	31.16	6.83	7.29	7.80	8.36	8.46
Plastics and rubber products (326)	451.3	632.5	654.1	592.7	579.5	28.39	1.45	1.87	2.02	1.75	1.76
Non-metallic mineral products (327)	480.3	508.7	490.7	474.4	473.0	-1.51	1.55	1.50	1.52	1.40	1.44
Primary metal manufactures (331)	691.4	882.2	775.8	838.2	912.8	32.02	2.22	2.61	2.40	2.48	2.77
Fabricated metal products (332)	1 136.1	1 504.4	1 125.6	1 219.2	1 200.5	5.67	3.65	4.44	3.48	3.61	3.64
Machinery manufactures (333)	3 918.3	3 978.7	3 489.2	3 583.6	3 372.0	-13.94	12.60	11.76	10.78	10.61	10.24
Computer and electronic products (334)	1 057.4	1 374.6	1 464.4	1 404.2	1 443.5	36.52	3.40	4.06	4.52	4.16	4.38
Electrical equipment, appliances, and parts (335)	512.4	585.8	688.4	645.3	739.6	44.33	1.65	1.73	2.13	1.91	2.25
Transportation equipment (336)	18 539.0	19 416.2	18 558.5	19 582.8	18 086.1	-2.44	59.64	57.37	57.34	57.98	54.90
Furniture and related products (337)	323.7	397.8	365.5	287.2	455.9	40.83	1.04	1.18	1.13	0.85	1.38
Miscellaneous manufactures (339)	252.3	243.0	240.9	255.8	278.2	10.28	0.81	0.72	0.74	0.76	0.84
Agricultural and Livestock Products (NAICS Code)	182.2	176.7	234.4	231.9	288.2	58.19	0.59	0.52	0.72	0.69	0.87
Agricultural products (111)	165.7	155.6	215.4	211.9	276.9	67.07	0.53	0.46	0.67	0.63	0.84
Livestock and livestock products (112)	16.4	21.1	19.0	20.0	11.3	-31.35	0.05	0.06	0.06	0.06	0.03
Other Commodities (NAICS Code)	645.4	778.8	730.2	858.4	1 117.6	73.16	2.08	2.30	2.26	2.54	3.39
Forestry and logging (113)	9.3	17.5	23.7	19.9	19.4	108.37	0.03	0.05	0.07	0.06	0.06
Fishing, hunting, and trapping (114)	6.8	8.2	6.3	5.7	2.8	-58.71	0.02	0.02	0.02	0.02	0.01
Oil and gas extraction (211)	92.0	212.6	191.3	319.3	526.5	472.33	0.30	0.63	0.59	0.95	1.60
Mining (212)	148.3	135.9	151.1	144.1	154.0	3.82	0.48	0.40	0.47	0.43	0.47
Waste and scrap (910)	102.0	108.1	97.5	111.5	150.4	47.53	0.33	0.32	0.30	0.33	0.46
Public administration (920)	11.3	13.3	13.5	11.7	30.6	170.17	0.04	0.04	0.04	0.03	0.09
Goods returned to Canada (980)	130.6	134.3	105.5	101.5	70.7	-45.85	0.42	0.40	0.33	0.30	0.21
Special classification provisions (990)	145.1	149.0	141.3	144.7	162.0	11.67	0.47	0.44	0.44	0.43	0.49
Publishing industries (except Internet) (511)	0.0	0.0	0.0	0.0	1.2	X	0.00	0.00	0.00	0.00	0.00
TOTAL AND PERCENT SHARE OF U.S. TOTAL	31 085.8	33 845.3	32 365.8	33 775.2	32 941.1	5.97	4.49	4.34	4.43	4.87	4.55
Top 25 Commodities (HS Code)	18 395.3	19 852.1	18 929.5	20 466.6	19 124.9	3.97	59.18	58.66	58.49	60.60	58.06
1. Parts and accessories of motor vehicles (870899)	4 120.7	4 209.0	3 669.5	3 506.7	3 014.8	-26.84	13.26	12.44	11.34	10.38	9.15
2. Parts and accessories of motor vehicles bodies (870829)	2 385.1	2 749.6	2 504.0	2 589.0	2 589.4	8.57	7.67	8.12	7.74	7.67	7.86
3. Passenger vehicles, spark-ignition, > 3,000 cc (870324)	2 145.3	1 942.7	2 118.2	2 751.7	2 502.2	16.64	6.90	5.74	6.54	8.15	7.60
4. Spark-ignition internal combustion piston engines (840734)	2 545.8	2 687.3	2 322.7	2 024.4	1 660.6	-34.77	8.19	7.94	7.18	5.99	5.04
5. Passenger vehicle, spark-ignition, > 1,500 cc < 3,000 cc (870323)	1 117.2	1 206.0	1 598.8	2 136.8	1 536.2	37.50	3.59	3.56	4.94	6.33	4.66
6. Gear boxes for motor vehicles (870840)	981.7	1 092.6	1 224.4	1 258.1	1 296.3	32.05	3.16	3.23	3.78	3.72	3.94
7. Goods vehicles, with spark-ignition piston engines (870431)	928.8	869.6	680.0	849.2	1 105.7	19.05	2.99	2.57	2.10	2.51	3.36
8. Spark-ignition engine parts (840991)	824.5	839.4	598.4	601.8	507.5	-38.45	2.65	2.48	1.85	1.78	1.54
9. Parts of seats (940190)	670.5	814.4	685.1	519.7	494.0	-26.32	2.16	2.41	2.12	1.54	1.50
10. Drive axles with differential for motor vehicles (870850)	517.0	657.7	599.9	565.2	487.4	-5.73	1.66	1.94	1.85	1.67	1.48
11. Natural gas, gaseous (271121)	56.4	130.4	156.4	287.5	481.1	753.01	0.18	0.39	0.48	0.85	1.46
12. Brakes, servo-brakes, and parts for motor vehicles (870839)	341.4	368.5	329.1	391.0	448.1	31.25	1.10	1.09	1.02	1.16	1.36
13. Goods vehicles, with diesel or semi-diesel engines (870421)	57.8	62.1	269.4	390.5	443.9	667.99	0.19	0.18	0.83	1.16	1.35
14. Insulated wiring sets for vehicles, ships, and aircrafts (854430)	252.4	292.1	221.2	325.2	287.4	13.87	0.81	0.86	0.68	0.96	0.87
15. Purifying machine and apparatus for gases (842139)	215.3	267.4	267.1	329.7	281.7	30.84	0.69	0.79	0.83	0.98	0.86
16. Rear-view mirrors for vehicles (700910)	160.8	180.2	209.9	212.3	266.2	65.55	0.52	0.53	0.65	0.63	0.81
17. Steering wheels, columns and boxes for motor vehicles (870894)	257.5	306.4	242.5	263.2	261.1	1.40	0.83	0.91	0.75	0.78	0.79
18. Automatic regulating instruments and apparatus (903289)	130.6	191.6	221.6	221.9	230.0	76.11	0.42	0.57	0.68	0.66	0.70
19. Machine and mechanical appliance, individual function (847989)	232.2	146.6	133.9	195.9	192.1	-17.27	0.75	0.43	0.41	0.58	0.58
20. Metal mountings and fittings for motor vehicles (830230)	199.0	216.2	208.1	251.1	191.3	-3.87	0.64	0.64	0.64	0.74	0.58
21. Motor vehicles, trans goods, gvw between 5 and 20 ton (870422)	...	14.6	82.8	110.5	184.0	...	...	0.04	0.26	0.33	0.56
22. Retail medicaments in measured dose (300490)	56.7	82.5	116.2	177.5	173.7	206.35	0.18	0.24	0.36	0.53	0.53
23. Parts of air conditioning machines (841590)	198.6	208.3	179.3	189.8	169.8	-14.50	0.64	0.62	0.55	0.56	0.52
24. Compression-ignition internal combustion engines (840820)	...	176.1	161.5	167.4	160.2	...	...	0.52	0.50	0.50	0.49
25. Iron or steel threaded screws and bolts (731815)	...	140.8	129.5	150.5	160.2	...	...	0.42	0.40	0.45	0.49

X = Not applicable.

. . . = Not available.

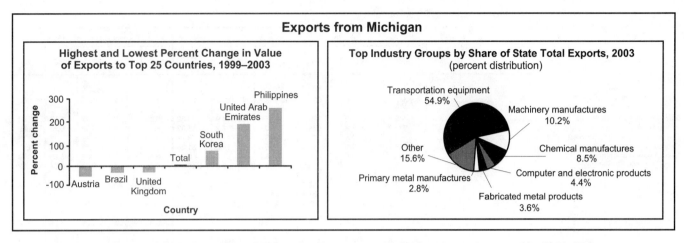

Exports from Michigan

Highest and Lowest Percent Change in Value of Exports to Top 25 Countries, 1999–2003

Top Industry Groups by Share of State Total Exports, 2003
(percent distribution)

Transportation equipment 54.9%
Machinery manufactures 10.2%
Chemical manufactures 8.5%
Computer and electronic products 4.4%
Fabricated metal products 3.6%
Primary metal manufactures 2.8%
Other 15.6%

- Transportation equipment accounted for nearly 55 percent of Michigan's total exports in 2003. However, transportation exports were down about $453 million, or about 2.5 percent, from 1999. A drop also occurred in machine manufacturing, which declined $546 million during the same period. As a share of the state's total exports, machine manufacturing declined from about 12 percent in 1999 to 10 percent in 2003.

- The chemical manufactures and oil and gas extraction industries had the highest dollar increase in exports from 1999 to 2003. During this period, chemical manufactures exports increased $662 million, or 31 percent, and oil and gas extraction exports grew $434 million, or nearly fivefold. The latter's increase can be attributed to the substantial growth in natural gas commodity exports, which rose by nearly $425 million.

- Canada is by far Michigan's largest market, as the recipient of 60 percent of the state's exports. Exports to Mexico, which ranks second, increased more than 67 percent from 1999 to 2003. Since 1999, exports to China and South Korea have grown considerably, each with increases of over $168 million.

Table E-27. Total U.S. Exports (Origin of Movement) via Michigan, 1999–2003—*Continued*

(Top 25 commodities and top 25 countries based on 2003 dollar value.)

Industry, commodity, and country	Value (millions of dollars)					Percent change, 1999–2003	Percent share of state total				
	1999	2000	2001	2002	2003		1999	2000	2001	2002	2003
TOTAL AND PERCENT SHARE OF U.S. TOTAL	31 085.8	33 845.3	32 365.8	33 775.2	32 941.1	5.97	4.49	4.34	4.43	4.87	4.55
Top 25 Countries	29 766.5	32 208.2	30 517.5	32 316.4	31 550.7	5.99	95.76	95.16	94.29	95.68	95.78
1. Canada	19 916.6	20 022.3	17 561.8	19 801.3	19 799.1	-0.59	64.07	59.16	54.26	58.63	60.10
2. Mexico	2 388.0	3 970.8	4 790.9	4 239.0	4 006.4	67.77	7.68	11.73	14.80	12.55	12.16
3. Japan	899.6	1 120.6	1 204.0	1 115.7	1 099.9	22.27	2.89	3.31	3.72	3.30	3.34
4. Germany	765.8	984.6	928.2	989.3	973.4	27.11	2.46	2.91	2.87	2.93	2.96
5. United Kingdom	1 077.4	1 275.9	945.8	778.5	706.1	-34.46	3.47	3.77	2.92	2.30	2.14
6. Australia	453.4	582.6	437.3	552.9	524.5	15.68	1.46	1.72	1.35	1.64	1.59
7. Belgium	574.2	544.0	490.0	461.7	424.4	-26.09	1.85	1.61	1.51	1.37	1.29
8. France	266.8	349.1	370.9	335.2	380.3	42.53	0.86	1.03	1.15	0.99	1.15
9. Austria	704.4	607.1	647.7	665.0	378.2	-46.31	2.27	1.79	2.00	1.97	1.15
10. China	198.2	211.6	251.3	284.8	366.7	84.98	0.64	0.63	0.78	0.84	1.11
11. South Korea	194.2	282.0	398.8	456.6	363.9	87.37	0.62	0.83	1.23	1.35	1.10
12. Saudi Arabia	306.4	215.7	410.4	384.1	324.4	5.89	0.99	0.64	1.27	1.14	0.98
13. Netherlands	231.5	338.4	340.1	300.9	278.2	20.17	0.74	1.00	1.05	0.89	0.84
14. Brazil	395.6	372.9	356.5	281.7	243.9	-38.35	1.27	1.10	1.10	0.83	0.74
15. Taiwan	177.5	173.2	158.4	221.4	233.1	31.35	0.57	0.51	0.49	0.66	0.71
16. Italy	164.1	132.1	166.6	241.6	199.4	21.55	0.53	0.39	0.51	0.72	0.61
17. Kuwait	174.0	132.7	164.5	143.1	189.5	8.90	0.56	0.39	0.51	0.42	0.58
18. Sweden	189.8	146.4	126.0	159.0	185.2	-2.45	0.61	0.43	0.39	0.47	0.56
19. Spain	181.1	206.3	143.1	156.1	154.5	-14.65	0.58	0.61	0.44	0.46	0.47
20. Thailand	91.7	109.2	165.3	158.0	138.7	51.23	0.30	0.32	0.51	0.47	0.42
21. Hong Kong	156.2	142.3	146.8	143.3	125.4	-19.70	0.50	0.42	0.45	0.42	0.38
22. United Arab Emirates	41.2	33.6	38.2	62.1	122.9	198.15	0.13	0.10	0.12	0.18	0.37
23. Philippines	33.9	87.8	96.8	142.2	122.7	262.48	0.11	0.26	0.30	0.42	0.37
24. Malaysia	73.3	58.9	63.0	139.0	112.9	54.11	0.24	0.17	0.19	0.41	0.34
25. Singapore	111.6	108.2	115.0	104.1	96.8	-13.30	0.36	0.32	0.36	0.31	0.29

Table E-28. Total U.S. Exports (Origin of Movement) via Minnesota, 1999–2003

(Top 25 commodities and top 25 countries based on 2003 dollar value.)

Industry, commodity, and country	Value (millions of dollars)					Percent change, 1999–2003	Percent share of state total				
	1999	2000	2001	2002	2003		1999	2000	2001	2002	2003
TOTAL AND PERCENT SHARE OF U.S. TOTAL	9 372.6	10 302.5	10 524.4	10 402.2	11 265.7	20.20	1.35	1.32	1.44	1.50	1.56
Manufactures (NAICS Code)	8 443.8	9 501.2	9 729.8	9 517.6	10 454.9	23.82	90.09	92.22	92.45	91.50	92.80
Processed foods (311)	635.7	675.2	666.3	700.5	731.2	15.03	6.78	6.55	6.33	6.73	6.49
Beverages and tobacco products (312)	8.4	9.8	13.0	13.3	15.1	79.74	0.09	0.00	0.12	0.13	0.13
Fabric mill products (313)	14.4	19.9	12.6	16.0	18.8	31.25	0.15	0.19	0.12	0.15	0.17
Non-apparel textile products (314)	12.0	10.6	9.5	8.9	21.7	80.54	0.13	0.10	0.09	0.09	0.19
Apparel manufactures (315)	5.1	5.5	3.8	3.9	3.0	-40.03	0.05	0.05	0.04	0.04	0.03
Leather and related products (316)	44.1	45.8	52.5	40.1	37.4	-15.23	0.47	0.44	0.50	0.39	0.33
Wood products (321)	81.0	85.7	81.4	83.6	74.3	-8.29	0.86	0.83	0.77	0.80	0.66
Paper products (322)	170.9	210.2	205.4	244.3	263.4	54.14	1.82	2.04	1.95	2.35	2.34
Printing and related products (323)	55.5	54.9	69.5	81.3	82.2	48.00	0.59	0.53	0.66	0.78	0.73
Petroleum and coal products (324)	5.3	5.1	6.0	5.0	7.0	32.92	0.06	0.05	0.06	0.05	0.06
Chemical manufactures (325)	299.8	348.6	447.0	410.4	480.7	60.32	3.20	3.38	4.25	3.95	4.27
Plastics and rubber products (326)	252.2	317.6	254.0	231.8	247.8	-1.74	2.69	3.08	2.41	2.23	2.20
Non-metallic mineral products (327)	251.5	229.6	267.6	166.5	109.3	-56.54	2.68	2.23	2.54	1.60	0.97
Primary metal manufactures (331)	38.5	44.0	32.4	53.7	50.4	30.90	0.41	0.43	0.31	0.52	0.45
Fabricated metal products (332)	407.0	312.7	311.7	288.1	310.3	-23.76	4.34	3.03	2.96	2.77	2.75
Machinery manufactures (333)	1 419.9	1 526.2	1 420.2	1 374.4	1 490.7	4.99	15.15	14.81	13.49	13.21	13.23
Computer and electronic products (334)	3 245.2	3 856.0	3 875.3	3 279.1	3 355.3	3.39	34.62	37.43	36.82	31.52	29.78
Electrical equipment, appliances, and parts (335)	369.2	392.9	361.3	313.2	289.4	-21.61	3.94	3.81	3.43	3.01	2.57
Transportation equipment (336)	619.8	702.1	843.9	1 061.1	1 141.1	84.12	6.61	6.81	8.02	10.20	10.13
Furniture and related products (337)	27.0	29.6	27.3	30.7	31.5	16.36	0.29	0.29	0.26	0.30	0.28
Miscellaneous manufactures (339)	481.4	619.3	769.1	1 111.8	1 694.3	251.94	5.14	6.01	7.31	10.69	15.04
Agricultural and Livestock Products (NAICS Code)	580.3	467.3	489.3	558.8	494.9	-14.71	6.19	4.54	4.65	5.37	4.39
Agricultural products (111)	576.9	463.0	482.6	553.1	488.3	-15.36	6.15	4.49	4.59	5.32	4.33
Livestock and livestock products (112)	3.4	4.3	6.7	5.7	6.6	94.60	0.04	0.04	0.06	0.06	0.06
Other Commodities (NAICS Code)	348.6	334.0	305.2	325.8	315.9	-9.39	3.72	3.24	2.90	3.13	2.80
Forestry and logging (113)	3.0	4.7	6.8	4.6	4.9	59.86	0.03	0.05	0.06	0.04	0.04
Fishing, hunting, and trapping (114)	6.7	5.5	8.5	9.3	7.9	17.16	0.07	0.05	0.08	0.09	0.07
Oil and gas extraction (211)	0.0	0.1	0.0	0.1	1.1	X	0.00	0.00	0.00	0.00	0.01
Mining (212)	125.2	139.7	116.4	158.6	139.7	11.56	1.34	1.36	1.11	1.53	1.24
Waste and scrap (910)	25.8	33.2	24.9	30.4	43.0	66.84	0.27	0.32	0.24	0.29	0.38
Public administration (920)	14.0	8.0	13.3	4.7	12.8	-8.66	0.15	0.08	0.13	0.04	0.11
Goods returned to Canada (980)	38.7	37.2	45.7	28.6	24.6	-36.45	0.41	0.36	0.43	0.27	0.22
Special classification provisions (990)	135.1	105.7	89.6	89.4	77.1	-42.95	1.44	1.03	0.85	0.86	0.68
Publishing industries (except Internet) (511)	0.0	0.0	0.0	0.0	4.8	X	0.00	0.00	0.00	0.00	0.04
TOTAL AND PERCENT SHARE OF U.S. TOTAL	9 372.6	10 302.5	10 524.4	10 402.2	11 265.7	20.20	1.35	1.32	1.44	1.50	1.56
Top 25 Commodities (HS Code)	2 792.2	3 359.9	3 704.7	4 342.9	5 000.2	79.08	29.79	32.61	35.20	41.75	44.38
1. Appliances worn, carried, implanted in body and parts (902190)	116.4	205.3	290.4	583.3	1 084.9	832.04	1.24	1.99	2.76	5.61	9.63
2. Parts and accessories for automatic data processing (847330)	896.5	801.5	704.7	644.5	680.3	-24.12	9.57	7.78	6.70	6.20	6.04
3. Digital processing units (847150)	353.0	653.9	705.4	451.3	397.3	12.55	3.77	6.35	6.70	4.34	3.53
4. Passenger vehicles for snow; golf carts and similar (870310)	140.7	132.5	147.1	145.9	220.1	56.43	1.50	1.29	1.40	1.40	1.95
5. Pass. vehicles, spark-ignition eng. cylinder cap. < 1,000 cc (870321)	84.0	121.1	168.4	174.3	193.2	130.00	0.90	1.18	1.60	1.68	1.71
6. Automatic data processing units (847180)	30.8	52.1	98.9	126.6	184.5	499.03	0.33	0.51	0.94	1.22	1.64
7. Instruments and appliances for medical sciences (901890)	151.8	155.8	159.9	174.7	176.5	16.27	1.62	1.51	1.52	1.68	1.57
8. Corn, other than seed corn (100590)	92.6	51.6	68.2	163.3	156.9	69.44	0.99	0.50	0.65	1.57	1.39
9. Semiconductor device (854150)	4.1	1.2	1.1	179.4	134.4	3 178.05	0.04	0.01	0.01	1.72	1.19
10. Lenses, prisms, mirrors, and optical elements (900190)	60.8	68.3	31.8	87.8	128.1	110.69	0.65	0.66	0.30	0.84	1.14
11. Medical needles, catheters and parts (901839)	76.8	86.6	110.8	119.9	126.0	64.06	0.82	0.84	1.05	1.15	1.12
12. Magnetic tape unrecorded, width > 6.5 mm (852313)	9.4	61.4	62.9	80.5	125.2	1 231.91	0.10	0.60	0.60	0.77	1.11
13. Agglomerated iron ores (260112)	111.7	121.8	98.2	135.6	122.1	9.31	1.19	1.18	0.93	1.30	1.08
14. Soybeans, whether or not broken (120100)	285.5	231.9	217.4	206.1	121.8	-57.34	3.05	2.25	2.07	1.98	1.08
15. Filtering and purifying machinery and parts (842199)	20.6	31.6	52.0	88.7	120.7	485.92	0.22	0.31	0.49	0.85	1.07
16. Spray guns and similar appliances (842420)	40.5	78.8	87.8	93.5	116.6	187.90	0.43	0.76	0.83	0.90	1.04
17. Electro-diagnostic apparatus and parts (901819)	37.7	57.9	147.0	169.0	115.4	206.10	0.40	0.56	1.40	1.62	1.02
18. Automatic data processing input or output units (847160)	32.1	35.0	99.2	103.1	113.0	252.02	0.34	0.34	0.94	0.99	1.00
19. Wheat and meslin (100190)	. . .	77.3	78.3	75.1	111.9	. . .	. . .	0.75	0.74	0.72	0.99
20. Soybean oilcake and other solid residue (230400)	. . .	65.4	72.7	67.5	104.6	. . .	. . .	0.63	0.69	0.65	0.93
21. Printed circuits (853400)	145.0	97.8	94.8	122.0	103.1	-28.90	1.55	0.95	0.90	1.17	0.92
22. Machine and mechanical appliance, individual function (847989)	85.2	105.9	122.8	97.6	96.9	13.73	0.91	1.03	1.17	0.94	0.86
23. Syringes, with or without needles and parts (901831)	. . .	25.8	36.1	56.3	90.5	. . .	. . .	0.25	0.34	0.54	0.80
24. Motor vehicle for the transport of ten persons or more (870210)	17.0	39.4	48.8	83.0	88.7	421.76	0.18	0.38	0.46	0.80	0.79
25. Digital monolithic integrated circuits (854221)	0.0	0.0	0.0	113.9	87.5	X	0.00	0.00	0.00	1.09	0.78

X = Not applicable.
. . . = Not available.

Exports from Minnesota

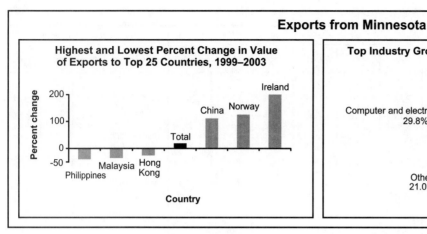

Highest and Lowest Percent Change in Value of Exports to Top 25 Countries, 1999–2003

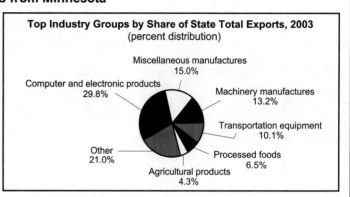

Top Industry Groups by Share of State Total Exports, 2003
(percent distribution)

- Miscellaneous manufactures 15.0%
- Computer and electronic products 29.8%
- Machinery manufactures 13.2%
- Transportation equipment 10.1%
- Processed foods 6.5%
- Agricultural products 4.3%
- Other 21.0%

- Minnesota's top export is computer and electronic products. These exports make up nearly 30 percent of the state's total exports. Miscellaneous manufactures rank second, as a result of growth of more than $1.2 billion from 1999 to 2003. Both machinery manufactures and transportation equipment represent a sizable share of Minnesota's exports.

- About 25 percent, or $2.9 billion, of Minnesota's products are exported to Canada. Ireland ranks second as the recipient of $1.2 billion worth of the state's exports. Exports to Ireland have increased $800 million, or 200 percent, from 1999 to 2003. Exports to Ireland of miscellaneous manufactures alone increased by $917 million, accounting for much of the state's growth in miscellaneous manufactures exports.

- Minnesota's top commodity is 'appliances worn, carried, implanted in the body and parts,' or more specifically parts and accessories of orthopedic appliances, splints, and artificial parts of the body. From 1999 to 2003, this commodity export increased more than ninefold, or by about $969 million. In 2003, it became the state's largest commodity export.

Table E-28. Total U.S. Exports (Origin of Movement) via Minnesota, 1999–2003—*Continued*

(Top 25 commodities and top 25 countries based on 2003 dollar value.)

Industry, commodity, and country	Value (millions of dollars)					Percent change, 1999–2003	Percent share of state total				
	1999	2000	2001	2002	2003		1999	2000	2001	2002	2003
TOTAL AND PERCENT SHARE OF U.S. TOTAL	9 372.6	10 302.5	10 524.4	10 402.2	11 265.7	20.20	1.35	1.32	1.44	1.50	1.56
Top 25 Countries	8 599.4	9 554.5	9 738.1	9 701.1	10 524.3	22.38	91.75	92.74	92.53	93.26	93.42
1. Canada	2 335.9	2 569.7	2 635.4	2 819.3	2 901.5	24.21	24.92	24.94	25.04	27.10	25.76
2. Ireland	402.3	410.4	649.4	767.0	1 203.8	199.20	4.29	3.98	6.17	7.37	10.69
3. Japan	764.7	915.0	1 052.6	840.0	845.6	10.57	8.16	8.88	10.00	8.07	7.51
4. United Kingdom	545.8	551.2	519.3	587.0	578.9	6.07	5.82	5.35	4.93	5.64	5.14
5. Netherlands	325.7	442.2	389.1	406.8	575.1	76.57	3.48	4.29	3.70	3.91	5.11
6. Germany	547.6	492.6	531.6	429.1	436.3	-20.32	5.84	4.78	5.05	4.13	3.87
7. Mexico	373.6	406.8	435.1	426.1	393.4	5.31	3.99	3.95	4.13	4.10	3.49
8. China	168.6	206.7	216.6	304.6	377.6	123.99	1.80	2.01	2.06	2.93	3.35
9. France	350.0	367.8	334.6	353.2	328.4	-6.15	3.73	3.57	3.18	3.40	2.92
10. Hong Kong	377.0	358.2	412.7	322.1	284.5	-24.52	4.02	3.48	3.92	3.10	2.53
11. Thailand	233.4	327.6	265.1	239.8	281.1	20.42	2.49	3.18	2.52	2.31	2.49
12. South Korea	148.2	237.9	302.1	278.4	257.2	73.52	1.58	2.31	2.87	2.68	2.28
13. Belgium	148.2	182.7	187.0	186.8	247.6	67.08	1.58	1.77	1.78	1.80	2.20
14. Singapore	289.3	320.2	274.1	245.3	241.2	-16.63	3.09	3.11	2.60	2.36	2.14
15. Italy	246.7	264.1	214.8	184.3	238.3	-3.38	2.63	2.56	2.04	1.77	2.12
16. Australia	206.4	197.3	191.8	182.5	215.5	4.40	2.20	1.91	1.82	1.75	1.91
17. Malaysia	279.9	283.5	230.0	234.1	195.7	-30.10	2.99	2.75	2.19	2.25	1.74
18. Taiwan	135.1	216.8	171.4	189.1	188.4	39.42	1.44	2.10	1.63	1.82	1.67
19. Philippines	289.8	329.4	246.9	221.6	186.3	-35.72	3.09	3.20	2.35	2.13	1.65
20. Spain	107.9	98.5	102.7	98.2	125.4	16.30	1.15	0.96	0.98	0.94	1.11
21. Norway	41.6	34.7	39.5	35.0	97.9	135.56	0.44	0.34	0.38	0.34	0.87
22. Denmark	55.2	64.6	56.6	57.9	84.6	53.38	0.59	0.63	0.54	0.56	0.75
23. Switzerland	70.8	66.4	69.8	76.9	83.3	17.70	0.75	0.64	0.66	0.74	0.74
24. Sweden	74.2	75.7	75.6	61.4	81.9	10.39	0.79	0.73	0.72	0.59	0.73
25. Brazil	81.8	134.4	134.5	154.6	74.9	-8.53	0.87	1.30	1.28	1.49	0.66

Table E-29. Total U.S. Exports (Origin of Movement) via Mississippi, 1999–2003

(Top 25 commodities and top 25 countries based on 2003 dollar value.)

Industry, commodity, and country	Value (millions of dollars)					Percent change, 1999–2003	Percent share of state total				
	1999	2000	2001	2002	2003		1999	2000	2001	2002	2003
TOTAL AND PERCENT SHARE OF U.S. TOTAL	2 215.7	2 725.6	3 557.4	3 058.0	2 558.3	15.46	0.32	0.35	0.49	0.44	0.35
Manufactures (NAICS Code)	2 105.9	2 582.8	3 419.9	2 512.6	2 353.8	11.77	95.04	94.76	96.14	82.17	92.01
Processed foods (311)	94.0	171.7	114.6	136.2	119.6	27.28	4.24	6.30	3.22	4.46	4.68
Beverages and tobacco products (312)	0.6	0.3	0.3	0.3	0.8	36.21	0.03	0.00	0.01	0.01	0.03
Fabric mill products (313)	77.9	81.5	89.9	162.4	99.5	27.64	3.52	2.99	2.53	5.31	3.89
Non-apparel textile products (314)	11.6	14.8	8.7	10.0	9.3	-19.95	0.52	0.54	0.24	0.33	0.36
Apparel manufactures (315)	123.7	208.5	133.6	197.8	53.3	-56.89	5.58	7.65	3.75	6.47	2.08
Leather and related products (316)	8.4	7.5	4.2	5.0	3.2	-62.27	0.38	0.27	0.12	0.16	0.12
Wood products (321)	35.9	48.9	43.6	64.2	65.4	82.24	1.62	1.80	1.22	2.10	2.56
Paper products (322)	374.0	443.7	390.6	353.9	307.6	-17.75	16.88	16.28	10.98	11.57	12.03
Printing and related products (323)	18.3	17.5	15.0	16.3	3.9	-78.56	0.83	0.64	0.42	0.53	0.15
Petroleum and coal products (324)	37.5	45.4	65.8	64.2	116.4	210.06	1.69	1.67	1.85	2.10	4.55
Chemical manufactures (325)	450.0	560.7	576.1	617.6	614.2	36.49	20.31	20.57	16.19	20.20	24.01
Plastics and rubber products (326)	66.5	65.4	61.1	61.2	70.5	5.95	3.00	2.40	1.72	2.00	2.76
Non-metallic mineral products (327)	41.1	50.9	45.7	47.0	45.4	10.58	1.85	1.87	1.28	1.54	1.77
Primary metal manufactures (331)	25.4	36.9	24.6	13.3	20.7	-18.64	1.15	1.35	0.69	0.44	0.81
Fabricated metal products (332)	53.5	73.8	64.3	51.4	69.0	28.89	2.42	2.71	1.81	1.68	2.70
Machinery manufactures (333)	308.2	262.0	313.5	305.4	301.3	-2.25	13.91	9.61	8.81	9.99	11.78
Computer and electronic products (334)	70.8	89.9	202.0	61.6	78.5	10.87	3.20	3.30	5.68	2.01	3.07
Electrical equipment, appliances, and parts (335)	95.0	108.4	121.3	82.5	76.1	-19.89	4.29	3.98	3.41	2.70	2.98
Transportation equipment (336)	121.7	179.0	1 019.1	122.8	151.5	24.48	5.49	6.57	28.65	4.02	5.92
Furniture and related products (337)	71.6	86.2	95.0	99.2	99.2	38.68	3.23	3.16	2.67	3.24	3.88
Miscellaneous manufactures (339)	20.2	29.7	31.1	40.1	48.5	140.07	0.91	1.09	0.88	1.31	1.89
Agricultural and Livestock Products (NAICS Code)	82.6	113.3	108.6	113.7	180.5	118.48	3.73	4.16	3.05	3.72	7.05
Agricultural products (111)	80.9	112.9	107.9	112.7	180.3	122.92	3.65	4.14	3.03	3.69	7.05
Livestock and livestock products (112)	1.7	0.4	0.7	0.9	0.2	-89.61	0.08	0.02	0.02	0.03	0.01
Other Commodities (NAICS Code)	27.2	29.4	28.9	431.7	24.0	-12.00	1.23	1.08	0.81	14.12	0.94
Forestry and logging (113)	1.3	1.8	2.1	2.5	1.4	8.95	0.06	0.07	0.06	0.08	0.05
Fishing, hunting, and trapping (114)	3.5	3.9	3.0	3.7	3.4	-1.94	0.16	0.14	0.08	0.12	0.13
Oil and gas extraction (211)	0.1	0.1	0.3	0.1	0.2	74.53	0.00	0.00	0.01	0.00	0.01
Mining (212)	4.6	6.7	8.5	7.5	5.3	15.81	0.21	0.24	0.24	0.25	0.21
Waste and scrap (910)	2.1	2.9	2.7	3.6	4.4	105.61	0.10	0.11	0.07	0.12	0.17
Public administration (920)	1.5	1.0	0.3	1.0	2.0	31.82	0.07	0.04	0.01	0.03	0.08
Goods returned to Canada (980)	3.0	4.0	5.1	3.4	2.3	-25.05	0.14	0.15	0.14	0.11	0.09
Special classification provisions (990)	11.2	9.0	7.0	409.9	5.1	-54.55	0.50	0.33	0.20	13.40	0.20
Publishing industries (except Internet) (511)	0.0	0.0	0.0	0.0	0.0	X	0.00	0.00	0.00	0.00	0.00
TOTAL AND PERCENT SHARE OF U.S. TOTAL	2 215.7	2 725.6	3 557.4	3 058.0	2 558.3	15.46	0.32	0.35	0.49	0.44	0.35
Top 25 Commodities (HS Code)	902.3	1 297.2	2 129.0	1 367.9	1 453.5	61.09	40.72	47.59	59.85	44.73	56.82
1. Dry titanium dioxide (320611)	172.8	251.3	207.3	344.5	389.3	125.29	7.80	9.22	5.83	11.27	15.22
2. Chemical wood-pulp, unbleached non-coniferous (470321)	180.1	251.6	219.8	191.0	178.3	-1.00	8.13	9.23	6.18	6.25	6.97
3. Cotton, not carded or combed (520100)	72.2	104.4	99.7	104.1	173.7	140.58	3.26	3.83	2.80	3.40	6.79
4. Petroleum oils from bituminous mineral (not crude) (271019)	...	0.0	0.0	15.0	86.0	...	...	0.00	0.00	0.49	3.36
5. Chicken cuts and edible offal, frozen (020714)	38.2	81.6	66.8	79.1	75.1	96.60	1.72	2.99	1.88	2.59	2.94
6. Kraftliner, uncoated and unbleached (480411)	49.1	62.9	67.9	66.4	52.9	7.74	2.22	2.31	1.91	2.17	2.07
7. Seats with wooden frames, upholstered (940161)	39.4	42.1	48.0	44.7	44.6	13.20	1.78	1.54	1.35	1.46	1.74
8. Floating, submersible drilling, or production platforms (890520)	...	100.0	946.8	0.0	41.2	...	...	3.67	26.61	0.00	1.61
9. Parts of spark-ignition internal combustion piston (840999)	91.3	36.2	35.2	35.2	32.6	-64.29	4.12	1.33	0.99	1.15	1.27
10. Polyvinyl chloride (390410)	0.2	7.9	24.7	24.7	31.6	15 700.00	0.01	0.29	0.69	0.81	1.24
11. Compressors used in refrigerating equipment (841430)	22.4	23.2	42.5	47.9	30.7	37.05	1.01	0.85	1.19	1.57	1.20
12. Parts of airplanes or helicopters (880330)	10.9	16.7	19.5	20.0	28.2	158.72	0.49	0.61	0.55	0.65	1.10
13. Golf equipment, excluding clubs and balls (950639)	5.6	3.1	11.9	21.0	27.8	396.43	0.25	0.11	0.33	0.69	1.09
14. Parts of pumps for liquids (841391)	...	15.4	14.5	12.1	27.5	...	...	0.57	0.41	0.40	1.07
15. Parts of garments and clothing accessories (621790)	51.3	71.2	78.7	120.2	25.8	-49.71	2.32	2.61	2.21	3.93	1.01
16. Parts of furniture (940390)	8.8	8.1	17.4	26.2	25.4	188.64	0.40	0.30	0.49	0.86	0.99
17. Articles of heat or sound-insulating mineral mate (680690)	16.6	24.2	28.2	24.6	24.2	45.78	0.75	0.89	0.79	0.80	0.95
18. Fertilizers (310000)	92.5	61.2	62.5	78.3	22.3	-75.89	4.17	2.25	1.76	2.56	0.87
19. Electrical apparatus, switches, relays, fuses (853690)	34.4	29.1	23.4	27.0	20.7	-39.83	1.55	1.07	0.66	0.88	0.81
20. Office machines (847290)	16.7	21.1	25.4	20.9	20.3	21.56	0.75	0.77	0.71	0.68	0.79
21. Titanium oxides (282300)	...	50.4	47.8	16.8	20.2	...	...	1.85	1.34	0.55	0.79
22. Other parts and attachments for derricks (843149)	...	11.1	10.1	15.0	20.2	...	...	0.41	0.28	0.49	0.79
23. Petroleum coke, not calcined (271311)	...	24.4	30.9	15.2	18.7	...	...	0.90	0.87	0.50	0.73
24. Para-xylene (290243)	...	0.0	0.0	5.6	18.4	...	...	0.00	0.00	0.18	0.72
25. Doors and their frames and thresholds, of wood (441820)	...	0.3	0.7	12.4	17.8	...	...	0.01	0.02	0.41	0.70

X = Not applicable.
. . . = Not available.

Exports from Mississippi

Highest and Lowest Percent Change in Value of Exports to Top 25 Countries, 1999–2003

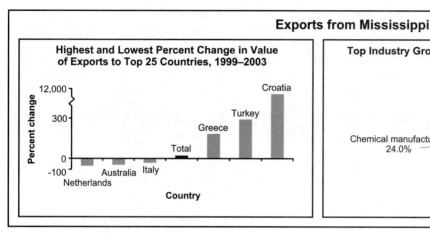

Top Industry Groups by Share of State Total Exports, 2003
(percent distribution)

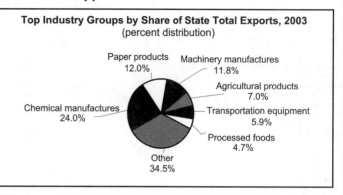

- Mississippi's exports fell by $500 million from 2002 to 2003, but were still up 15 percent from 1999. Chemical manufactures exports increased from $450 million in 1999 to $614 million in 2003. As a result, this industry accounted for 24 percent of Mississippi's total exports and is the state's largest export industry. Despite declines in recent years, the paper products and machinery manufactures industries are Mississippi's two other leading export industries, each accounting for about 12 percent of total exports.

- Dry titanium dioxide is Mississippi's largest commodity export, having increased 125 percent, or $216 million, from 1999 to 2003. Cotton exports grew about 141 percent during the same period, and are the state's third largest commodity export.

- Canada and Mexico are the top recipients of Mississippi's exports. Together, they import about one-third of the state's total exports. Exports to Belgium and China have grown substantially since 1999, and, along with Honduras, round out the state's top five export countries.

Table E-29. Total U.S. Exports (Origin of Movement) via Mississippi, 1999–2003—Continued

(Top 25 commodities and top 25 countries based on 2003 dollar value.)

Industry, commodity, and country	Value (millions of dollars)					Percent change, 1999–2003	Percent share of state total				
	1999	2000	2001	2002	2003		1999	2000	2001	2002	2003
TOTAL AND PERCENT SHARE OF U.S. TOTAL	2 215.7	2 725.6	3 557.4	3 058.0	2 558.3	15.46	0.32	0.35	0.49	0.44	0.35
Top 25 Countries	1 867.7	2 256.5	2 665.9	2 290.0	2 173.0	16.35	84.29	82.79	74.94	74.89	84.94
1. Canada	518.4	521.3	886.8	491.8	584.3	12.72	23.39	19.13	24.93	16.08	22.84
2. Mexico	332.1	410.7	452.8	461.5	256.3	-22.85	14.99	15.07	12.73	15.09	10.02
3. Belgium	121.2	179.0	179.4	193.7	208.4	71.88	5.47	6.57	5.04	6.33	8.15
4. China	67.6	73.9	89.7	138.0	109.4	61.84	3.05	2.71	2.52	4.51	4.28
5. Honduras	94.0	102.8	111.0	86.5	93.9	-0.05	4.24	3.77	3.12	2.83	3.67
6. United Kingdom	100.4	115.4	113.6	87.0	90.6	-9.82	4.53	4.23	3.19	2.85	3.54
7. Germany	83.6	72.8	61.1	117.7	74.6	-10.78	3.77	2.67	1.72	3.85	2.91
8. Hong Kong	44.0	55.7	72.2	94.9	67.5	53.33	1.99	2.05	2.03	3.10	2.64
9. Japan	71.4	80.5	68.2	61.6	61.4	-14.03	3.22	2.95	1.92	2.02	2.40
10. Dominican Republic	26.0	69.8	56.3	53.4	60.2	131.47	1.17	2.56	1.58	1.75	2.35
11. Italy	78.9	95.4	91.7	73.3	59.6	-24.40	3.56	3.50	2.58	2.40	2.33
12. Brazil	39.7	41.3	48.0	54.2	55.7	40.09	1.79	1.52	1.35	1.77	2.18
13. Guatemala	18.3	33.5	51.2	43.8	54.8	198.67	0.83	1.23	1.44	1.43	2.14
14. South Korea	41.7	55.5	57.3	70.2	48.7	16.92	1.88	2.04	1.61	2.29	1.90
15. Panama	15.9	15.5	10.8	24.2	44.1	176.90	0.72	0.57	0.30	0.79	1.72
16. Croatia	0.3	0.0	0.3	0.1	40.0	11 745.50	0.02	0.00	0.01	0.00	1.57
17. Spain	23.5	39.0	41.4	44.8	40.0	70.06	1.06	1.43	1.16	1.46	1.56
18. Turkey	9.3	20.3	29.0	29.5	37.0	298.19	0.42	0.74	0.81	0.96	1.44
19. Singapore	12.5	12.8	73.0	23.6	35.2	182.23	0.56	0.47	2.05	0.77	1.38
20. France	37.5	53.2	51.1	35.0	30.5	-18.43	1.69	1.95	1.44	1.15	1.19
21. Greece	8.3	11.0	8.9	14.2	29.8	257.99	0.38	0.40	0.25	0.46	1.17
22. Netherlands	52.5	45.8	49.6	29.0	23.7	-54.90	2.37	1.68	1.39	0.95	0.93
23. Poland	14.4	9.2	25.4	19.2	22.7	58.50	0.65	0.34	0.71	0.63	0.89
24. Australia	32.9	123.6	17.5	22.2	22.5	-31.68	1.48	4.53	0.49	0.73	0.88
25. Thailand	23.2	18.6	19.7	20.5	22.1	-4.81	1.05	0.68	0.55	0.67	0.86

Table E-30. Total U.S. Exports (Origin of Movement) via Missouri, 1999–2003

(Top 25 commodities and top 25 countries based on 2003 dollar value.)

Industry, commodity, and country	Value (millions of dollars)					Percent change, 1999–2003	Percent share of state total				
	1999	2000	2001	2002	2003		1999	2000	2001	2002	2003
TOTAL AND PERCENT SHARE OF U.S. TOTAL	6 059.0	6 497.1	6 173.0	6 790.8	7 233.9	19.39	0.87	0.83	0.84	0.98	1.00
Manufactures (NAICS Code)	5 799.4	6 228.0	5 962.6	6 583.7	6 980.6	20.37	95.72	95.86	96.59	96.95	96.50
Processed foods (311)	427.6	466.0	432.2	445.0	440.5	3.01	7.06	7.17	7.00	6.55	6.09
Beverages and tobacco products (312)	9.6	8.2	9.9	12.0	17.9	86.56	0.16	0.00	0.16	0.18	0.25
Fabric mill products (313)	19.7	21.7	21.5	22.9	21.7	10.07	0.33	0.33	0.35	0.34	0.30
Non-apparel textile products (314)	9.9	12.0	10.9	4.5	2.9	-70.77	0.16	0.19	0.18	0.07	0.04
Apparel manufactures (315)	68.7	39.5	34.0	26.9	16.2	-76.49	1.13	0.61	0.55	0.40	0.22
Leather and related products (316)	83.5	94.8	105.4	133.5	148.3	77.51	1.38	1.46	1.71	1.97	2.05
Wood products (321)	64.7	67.9	65.7	65.6	69.3	7.07	1.07	1.05	1.06	0.97	0.96
Paper products (322)	54.6	50.7	51.4	48.0	52.7	-3.55	0.90	0.78	0.83	0.71	0.73
Printing and related products (323)	101.7	104.7	119.4	119.9	141.5	39.14	1.68	1.61	1.93	1.77	1.96
Petroleum and coal products (324)	22.6	35.8	28.5	22.7	17.8	-20.92	0.37	0.55	0.46	0.33	0.25
Chemical manufactures (325)	1 042.6	1 039.1	1 010.3	1 206.8	1 498.5	43.76	17.21	15.99	16.37	17.77	20.72
Plastics and rubber products (326)	131.6	156.6	144.9	134.2	160.9	22.26	2.17	2.41	2.35	1.98	2.22
Non-metallic mineral products (327)	39.1	37.7	36.4	37.8	33.0	-15.64	0.65	0.58	0.59	0.56	0.46
Primary metal manufactures (331)	121.4	164.0	172.4	157.7	163.6	34.82	2.00	2.52	2.79	2.32	2.26
Fabricated metal products (332)	229.2	264.3	249.4	226.4	239.2	4.36	3.78	4.07	4.04	3.33	3.31
Machinery manufactures (333)	750.3	781.5	740.1	676.3	741.1	-1.24	12.38	12.03	11.99	9.96	10.24
Computer and electronic products (334)	463.8	607.6	443.5	443.9	483.6	4.28	7.65	9.35	7.19	6.54	6.69
Electrical equipment, appliances, and parts (335)	324.8	446.8	307.4	337.5	371.7	14.45	5.36	6.88	4.98	4.97	5.14
Transportation equipment (336)	1 642.1	1 629.4	1 801.5	2 290.0	2 186.8	33.17	27.10	25.08	29.18	33.72	30.23
Furniture and related products (337)	35.4	41.1	32.5	37.6	44.8	26.51	0.58	0.63	0.53	0.55	0.62
Miscellaneous manufactures (339)	156.3	158.6	145.2	134.5	128.3	-17.95	2.58	2.44	2.35	1.98	1.77
Agricultural and Livestock Products (NAICS Code)	125.8	130.5	91.1	78.7	111.4	-11.48	2.08	2.01	1.48	1.16	1.54
Agricultural products (111)	124.2	128.1	87.4	74.0	106.9	-13.91	2.05	1.97	1.42	1.09	1.48
Livestock and livestock products (112)	1.7	2.4	3.7	4.7	4.5	170.30	0.03	0.04	0.06	0.07	0.06
Other Commodities (NAICS Code)	133.8	138.6	119.4	128.4	141.9	6.10	2.21	2.13	1.93	1.89	1.96
Forestry and logging (113)	7.5	9.0	12.4	15.2	19.1	155.73	0.12	0.14	0.20	0.22	0.26
Fishing, hunting, and trapping (114)	1.1	0.5	0.9	1.3	1.1	4.34	0.02	0.01	0.02	0.02	0.02
Oil and gas extraction (211)	0.1	0.1	0.1	0.1	0.1	6.76	0.00	0.00	0.00	0.00	0.00
Mining (212)	12.0	11.7	10.6	13.6	22.1	83.75	0.20	0.18	0.17	0.20	0.31
Waste and scrap (910)	28.1	33.6	31.6	35.9	54.2	92.49	0.46	0.52	0.51	0.53	0.75
Public administration (920)	8.8	8.6	16.5	8.9	6.8	-22.26	0.14	0.13	0.27	0.13	0.09
Goods returned to Canada (980)	15.2	17.9	14.3	9.5	11.6	-23.39	0.25	0.28	0.23	0.14	0.16
Special classification provisions (990)	61.1	57.4	32.9	43.7	26.9	-56.01	1.01	0.88	0.53	0.64	0.37
Publishing industries (except Internet) (511)	0.0	0.0	0.0	0.0	0.1	X	0.00	0.00	0.00	0.00	0.00
TOTAL AND PERCENT SHARE OF U.S. TOTAL	6 059.0	6 497.1	6 173.0	6 790.8	7 233.9	19.39	0.87	0.83	0.84	0.98	1.00
Top 25 Commodities (HS Code)	2 049.4	2 355.3	2 499.7	3 324.4	3 466.0	69.12	33.82	36.25	40.49	48.95	47.91
1. Passenger vehicle, spark-ignition, > 1,500 cc < 3,000 cc (870323)	25.9	151.7	725.8	810.9	768.5	2 867.18	0.43	2.33	11.76	11.94	10.62
2. Goods vehicles, with spark-ignition piston engines (870431)	489.3	580.6	469.5	694.0	707.4	44.57	8.08	8.94	7.61	10.22	9.78
3. Passenger vehicles, spark-ignition, > 3,000 cc (870324)	582.5	404.1	193.6	360.6	187.3	-67.85	9.61	6.22	3.14	5.31	2.59
4. Retail medicaments in measured dose (300490)	59.2	95.2	100.7	127.7	166.8	181.76	0.98	1.47	1.63	1.88	2.31
5. Peptones, other proteins and derivatives (350400)	127.2	146.6	159.0	146.2	143.8	13.05	2.10	2.26	2.58	2.15	1.99
6. Tan hides and skins, of bovine (410411)	0.0	0.0	0.0	118.6	140.1	X	0.00	0.00	0.00	1.75	1.94
7. Spark-ignition internal combustion engines (840790)	63.8	81.1	94.0	122.8	127.0	99.06	1.05	1.25	1.52	1.81	1.76
8. Printed circuits (853400)	81.8	159.2	78.9	130.5	126.6	54.77	1.35	2.45	1.28	1.92	1.75
9. Herbicides, anti-sprouting products, retail (380830)	190.4	154.4	150.6	142.8	116.7	-38.71	3.14	2.38	2.44	2.10	1.61
10. Other antibiotics (294190)	1.3	1.8	35.4	49.3	75.8	5 730.77	0.02	0.03	0.57	0.73	1.05
11. Printed books and brochures (490199)	66.5	66.6	73.3	71.5	71.9	8.12	1.10	1.03	1.19	1.05	0.99
12. Other antibiotics in dosage form (300420)	. . .	7.7	6.4	24.1	71.1	. . .	. . .	0.12	0.10	0.35	0.98
13. Chemical elements doped for use in electronics (381800)	27.5	49.6	22.0	41.1	69.9	154.18	0.45	0.76	0.36	0.61	0.97
14. Parts of airplanes or helicopters (880330)	161.5	88.8	66.3	52.3	68.9	-57.34	2.67	1.37	1.07	0.77	0.95
15. Mixtures of odoriferous substances used in food or drink (330210)	3.8	7.4	7.3	76.2	66.3	1 644.74	0.06	0.11	0.12	1.12	0.92
16. Other organo-sulfur compounds (293090)	. . .	17.9	12.7	10.5	66.0	. . .	. . .	0.28	0.21	0.15	0.91
17. Miscellaneous organo-inorganic compounds (293100)	. . .	33.8	26.0	2.3	65.9	. . .	. . .	0.52	0.42	0.03	0.91
18. Composite diagnostic or laboratory reagents (382200)	46.9	45.7	64.2	58.7	65.8	40.30	0.77	0.70	1.04	0.86	0.91
19. Primary cells and batteries, manganese dioxide (850610)	34.0	39.6	27.0	39.5	65.8	93.53	0.56	0.61	0.44	0.58	0.91
20. Heterocyclic compound with nitrogen hetero-atom (293399)	0.0	0.0	0.0	46.4	52.2	X	0.00	0.00	0.00	0.68	0.72
21. Brakes, servo-brakes, and parts for motor vehicles (870839)	37.5	32.0	38.9	58.9	51.5	37.33	0.62	0.49	0.63	0.87	0.71
22. Under-carriages and parts for aircraft (880320)	. . .	46.6	25.3	29.5	49.6	. . .	. . .	0.72	0.41	0.43	0.69
23. Soybeans, whether or not broken (120100)	. . .	64.0	39.5	32.3	48.2	. . .	. . .	0.99	0.64	0.48	0.67
24. Parts, electric apparatus, electric circuit (853890)	. . .	41.8	40.7	34.0	47.1	. . .	. . .	0.64	0.66	0.50	0.65
25. Refrigerating or freezing display counters (841850)	50.3	39.1	42.6	43.7	45.8	-8.95	0.83	0.60	0.69	0.64	0.63

X = Not applicable.
. . . = Not available.

Exports from Missouri

Highest and Lowest Percent Change in Value of Exports to Top 25 Countries, 1999–2003

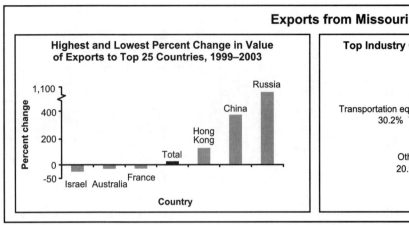

Top Industry Groups by Share of State Total Exports, 2003
(percent distribution)

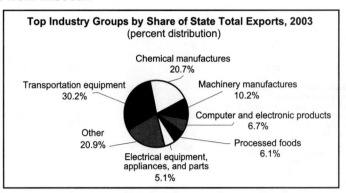

- In 2003, Missouri's total exports were valued at $7.2 billion, up about 19 percent from 1999. The state's top export industry is transportation equipment, which make up 30 percent of Missouri's exports. Chemical manufactures and machinery manufactures are also leading export industries, and together add to 31 percent of total exports. Chemical manufactures exports increased about $456 million from 1999 to 2003, second only to the $545 million increase in transportation exports. Apparel manufactures exports declined $53 million, or about 76 percent, from 1999 to 2003.

- Passenger vehicles with spark-ignition engines of cylinder capacities from 1,500 to 3,000 cc are Missouri's largest commodity export. The value of these exports increased by $742 million from 1999 to 2003, and now compose more than 10 percent of Missouri's total exports.

- Canada and Mexico are Missouri's top export markets. Together, they are recipients of nearly 53 percent of the state's exports. In 2003, China became Missouri's fifth highest export country. Exports to China increased from $52 million in 1999 to $260 million in 2003.

Table E-30. Total U.S. Exports (Origin of Movement) via Missouri, 1999–2003—*Continued*

(Top 25 commodities and top 25 countries based on 2003 dollar value.)

Industry, commodity, and country	Value (millions of dollars)					Percent change, 1999–2003	Percent share of state total				
	1999	2000	2001	2002	2003		1999	2000	2001	2002	2003
TOTAL AND PERCENT SHARE OF U.S. TOTAL	6 059.0	6 497.1	6 173.0	6 790.8	7 233.9	19.39	0.87	0.83	0.84	0.98	1.00
Top 25 Countries	5 336.3	5 957.6	5 577.5	6 334.2	6 766.3	26.80	88.07	91.70	90.35	93.28	93.54
1. Canada	2 586.2	2 703.9	2 517.5	3 116.7	3 080.5	19.12	42.68	41.62	40.78	45.90	42.58
2. Mexico	554.9	685.2	673.0	693.2	748.3	34.85	9.16	10.55	10.90	10.21	10.34
3. Japan	265.8	269.0	310.5	311.3	419.7	57.91	4.39	4.14	5.03	4.58	5.80
4. United Kingdom	305.0	391.6	284.1	335.9	294.9	-3.31	5.03	6.03	4.60	4.95	4.08
5. China	52.1	75.9	108.3	129.7	260.2	399.00	0.86	1.17	1.75	1.91	3.60
6. Germany	214.1	194.0	282.4	241.8	237.0	10.67	3.53	2.99	4.57	3.56	3.28
7. Italy	140.3	97.6	120.9	156.5	186.5	32.91	2.32	1.50	1.96	2.30	2.58
8. Hong Kong	70.9	103.3	89.6	131.8	176.5	148.93	1.17	1.59	1.45	1.94	2.44
9. Belgium	154.1	156.2	124.7	122.3	170.3	10.49	2.54	2.40	2.02	1.80	2.35
10. Australia	161.4	170.7	128.6	126.1	137.2	-15.00	2.66	2.63	2.08	1.86	1.90
11. Singapore	82.6	83.7	61.8	84.8	121.7	47.24	1.36	1.29	1.00	1.25	1.68
12. Netherlands	79.2	97.7	123.7	87.2	119.9	51.42	1.31	1.50	2.00	1.28	1.66
13. Brazil	95.3	116.9	85.4	65.3	111.4	16.87	1.57	1.80	1.38	0.96	1.54
14. Taiwan	76.1	140.3	104.3	111.9	110.8	45.47	1.26	2.16	1.69	1.65	1.53
15. Ireland	117.7	239.2	133.9	138.1	109.0	-7.32	1.94	3.68	2.17	2.03	1.51
16. France	110.9	95.4	99.2	84.1	95.0	-14.32	1.83	1.47	1.61	1.24	1.31
17. South Korea	74.0	78.7	79.7	115.0	83.7	13.16	1.22	1.21	1.29	1.69	1.16
18. Sweden	23.3	52.2	35.9	69.8	57.0	144.48	0.38	0.80	0.58	1.03	0.79
19. Spain	38.8	36.7	41.7	55.6	56.4	45.38	0.64	0.56	0.68	0.82	0.78
20. Russia	3.3	8.2	5.3	5.8	37.9	1 062.57	0.05	0.13	0.09	0.09	0.52
21. Thailand	26.3	34.5	35.0	35.2	36.0	36.94	0.43	0.53	0.57	0.52	0.50
22. Israel	39.4	48.6	38.9	30.3	31.1	-21.00	0.65	0.75	0.63	0.45	0.43
23. South Africa	23.7	21.0	21.5	18.9	30.5	28.43	0.39	0.32	0.35	0.28	0.42
24. Saudi Arabia	27.7	42.9	51.7	49.7	27.4	-1.25	0.46	0.66	0.84	0.73	0.38
25. United Arab Emirates	13.0	14.2	19.8	17.2	27.3	110.84	0.21	0.22	0.32	0.25	0.38

Table E-31. Total U.S. Exports (Origin of Movement) via Montana, 1999–2003

(Top 25 commodities and top 25 countries based on 2003 dollar value.)

Industry, commodity, and country	Value (millions of dollars)					Percent change, 1999–2003	Percent share of state total				
	1999	2000	2001	2002	2003		1999	2000	2001	2002	2003
TOTAL AND PERCENT SHARE OF U.S. TOTAL	426.9	540.6	488.5	385.7	361.4	-15.34	0.06	0.07	0.07	0.06	0.05
Manufactures (NAICS Code)	299.5	373.2	294.5	289.9	272.7	-8.93	70.15	69.03	60.29	75.15	75.46
Processed foods (311)	9.8	8.1	11.0	13.2	13.5	37.51	2.30	1.49	2.25	3.43	3.74
Beverages and tobacco products (312)	1.2	0.0	0.0	0.0	0.0	X	0.28	0.00	0.00	0.00	0.01
Fabric mill products (313)	0.1	0.5	0.2	0.2	0.3	184.31	0.02	0.10	0.05	0.06	0.08
Non-apparel textile products (314)	0.1	0.1	0.1	0.2	0.2	105.48	0.02	0.02	0.01	0.04	0.04
Apparel manufactures (315)	0.5	0.8	1.0	0.6	1.4	162.97	0.12	0.14	0.20	0.16	0.39
Leather and related products (316)	1.2	1.1	0.5	0.4	0.6	-49.27	0.29	0.20	0.11	0.11	0.17
Wood products (321)	16.9	18.8	17.1	20.3	21.7	28.12	3.96	3.48	3.49	5.27	5.99
Paper products (322)	17.7	22.2	18.9	30.0	28.3	59.53	4.15	4.11	3.88	7.78	7.83
Printing and related products (323)	0.5	0.4	0.3	0.2	0.1	-67.69	0.11	0.07	0.06	0.04	0.04
Petroleum and coal products (324)	0.7	0.9	1.5	1.2	1.3	103.68	0.15	0.17	0.31	0.32	0.37
Chemical manufactures (325)	32.9	35.3	50.7	59.5	64.8	96.85	7.71	6.53	10.38	15.43	17.93
Plastics and rubber products (326)	0.6	1.1	1.9	1.7	2.2	242.30	0.15	0.20	0.40	0.44	0.61
Non-metallic mineral products (327)	15.5	16.9	21.6	27.8	29.6	90.30	3.64	3.13	4.43	7.21	8.18
Primary metal manufactures (331)	106.4	122.8	24.6	7.3	7.0	-93.43	24.92	22.72	5.03	1.89	1.93
Fabricated metal products (332)	2.0	3.9	5.2	3.0	3.0	50.13	0.46	0.72	1.07	0.78	0.82
Machinery manufactures (333)	50.8	102.8	101.3	71.8	58.8	15.75	11.90	19.01	20.73	18.61	16.27
Computer and electronic products (334)	17.3	19.4	15.6	17.0	13.3	-23.23	4.05	3.58	3.20	4.42	3.67
Electrical equipment, appliances, and parts (335)	3.4	2.8	4.7	9.4	7.1	109.07	0.79	0.52	0.95	2.44	1.96
Transportation equipment (336)	11.4	8.7	9.4	8.5	11.4	0.11	2.67	1.61	1.93	2.21	3.16
Furniture and related products (337)	0.4	0.4	0.4	0.3	0.1	-64.94	0.09	0.07	0.08	0.09	0.04
Miscellaneous manufactures (339)	10.0	6.2	8.5	17.1	8.1	-19.22	2.34	1.15	1.73	4.43	2.23
Agricultural and Livestock Products (NAICS Code)	72.5	116.0	128.9	34.3	26.9	-62.90	16.99	21.46	26.39	8.90	7.44
Agricultural products (111)	8.5	15.7	35.9	27.3	23.2	172.45	1.99	2.91	7.35	7.07	6.42
Livestock and livestock products (112)	64.0	100.3	93.0	7.0	3.7	-94.20	14.99	18.55	19.04	1.83	1.03
Other Commodities (NAICS Code)	54.9	51.4	65.1	61.5	61.8	12.48	12.87	9.51	13.32	15.95	17.10
Forestry and logging (113)	0.3	0.3	0.3	0.2	0.1	-60.95	0.06	0.05	0.06	0.05	0.03
Fishing, hunting, and trapping (114)	0.0	0.0	0.0	0.0	0.0	X	0.00	0.00	0.00	0.01	0.01
Oil and gas extraction (211)	0.3	0.5	6.8	18.8	7.4	2 856.40	0.06	0.09	1.40	4.88	2.05
Mining (212)	38.1	30.8	35.1	25.2	31.1	-18.31	8.92	5.71	7.18	6.54	8.60
Waste and scrap (910)	2.0	3.4	2.3	1.5	6.9	242.03	0.47	0.62	0.46	0.38	1.91
Public administration (920)	1.9	2.2	3.8	1.5	2.7	46.35	0.43	0.41	0.77	0.39	0.75
Goods returned to Canada (980)	9.3	8.8	15.2	12.6	11.9	27.56	2.19	1.62	3.11	3.27	3.30
Special classification provisions (990)	3.1	5.5	1.6	1.7	1.6	-48.54	0.74	1.02	0.33	0.43	0.45
Publishing industries (except Internet) (511)	0.0	0.0	0.0	0.0	0.0	X	0.00	0.00	0.00	0.00	0.01
TOTAL AND PERCENT SHARE OF U.S. TOTAL	426.9	540.6	488.5	385.7	361.4	-15.34	0.06	0.07	0.07	0.06	0.05
Top 25 Commodities (HS Code)	124.9	189.7	222.9	222.2	236.7	89.51	29.26	35.09	45.63	57.60	65.49
1. Kraftliner, uncoated and unbleached (480411)	16.8	20.1	18.3	29.6	27.5	63.69	3.94	3.72	3.75	7.67	7.61
2. Copper oxides and hydroxides (282550)	15.7	17.6	17.2	20.9	23.1	47.13	3.68	3.26	3.52	5.42	6.39
3. Herbicides, anti-sprouting products, retail (380830)	10.4	9.2	21.4	21.4	19.9	91.35	2.44	1.70	4.38	5.55	5.51
4. Lead ores and concentrates (260700)	0.0	0.0	17.8	10.7	17.2	X	0.00	0.00	3.64	2.77	4.76
5. Natural steatite and talc, crushed or powdered (252620)	6.2	6.5	7.9	12.1	15.1	143.55	1.45	1.20	1.62	3.14	4.18
6. Parts of machines and mechanical appliances (847990)	10.3	25.5	15.9	19.8	14.9	44.66	2.41	4.72	3.25	5.13	4.12
7. Portland cement, except white (252329)	8.3	9.9	12.1	14.3	13.3	60.24	1.94	1.83	2.48	3.71	3.68
8. Barley (100300)	1.1	3.5	9.1	7.0	11.8	972.73	0.26	0.65	1.86	1.81	3.26
9. Machine and mechanical appliance, individual function (847989)	15.0	52.6	56.4	28.7	11.3	-24.67	3.51	9.73	11.55	7.44	3.13
10. Acyclic hydrocarbons, saturated (290110)	0.0	0.0	0.0	3.8	7.9	X	0.00	0.00	0.00	0.99	2.19
11. Crude oil from petroleum and bituminous minerals (270900)	. . .	0.0	0.0	2.3	7.3	. . .	. . .	0.00	0.00	0.60	2.02
12. Fiberboard of wood or other ligneous materials (441121)	2.2	3.3	2.9	4.4	7.0	218.18	0.52	0.61	0.59	1.14	1.94
13. Zinc ores and concentrates (260800)	20.0	14.3	12.3	8.7	6.4	-68.00	4.68	2.64	2.52	2.26	1.77
14. Wheat and meslin (100190)	1.1	4.7	6.7	6.5	6.0	445.45	0.26	0.87	1.37	1.69	1.66
15. Parts for mechanical appliances, project or spray (842490)	. . .	0.0	0.0	2.5	5.8	. . .	. . .	0.00	0.00	0.65	1.60
16. Nickel sulfate (283324)	0.0	2.4	3.0	4.4	5.6	X	0.00	0.44	0.61	1.14	1.55
17. Lasers, other than laser diodes (901320)	. . .	1.3	2.4	2.4	5.5	. . .	. . .	0.24	0.49	0.62	1.52
18. Plywood, at least one outer non-coniferous wood (441214)	. . .	0.9	1.2	0.8	5.4	. . .	. . .	0.17	0.25	0.21	1.49
19. Titanium waste and scrap (810830)	. . .	0.0	0.0	0.0	5.0	. . .	. . .	0.00	0.00	0.00	1.38
20. Pasta, uncooked containing eggs (190211)	0.1	0.8	2.4	4.6	5.0	4 900.00	0.02	0.15	0.49	1.19	1.38
21. Plywood, both outer plies coniferous wood (441219)	8.0	8.2	6.4	7.6	3.7	-53.75	1.87	1.52	1.31	1.97	1.02
22. Platinum metal, semi-manufactured (711019)	0.0	0.0	0.0	3.4	3.3	X	0.00	0.00	0.00	0.88	0.91
23. Combine harvester-threshers (843351)	7.2	4.4	4.3	2.7	3.1	-56.94	1.69	0.81	0.88	0.70	0.86
24. Pasta, uncooked not containing eggs (190219)	2.6	4.9	3.9	3.0	2.9	11.54	0.61	0.91	0.80	0.78	0.80
25. Other compression-ignition internal combustion engines (840890)	. . .	1.3	1.3	1.4	2.7	. . .	. . .	0.24	0.27	0.36	0.75

X = Not applicable.

. . . = Not available.

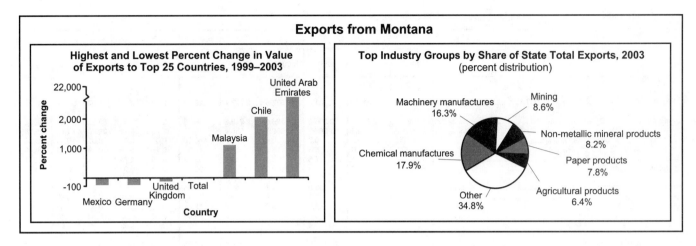

Exports from Montana

Highest and Lowest Percent Change in Value of Exports to Top 25 Countries, 1999–2003

Top Industry Groups by Share of State Total Exports, 2003 (percent distribution)

- Machinery manufactures 16.3%
- Mining 8.6%
- Non-metallic mineral products 8.2%
- Paper products 7.8%
- Agricultural products 6.4%
- Other 34.8%
- Chemical manufactures 17.9%

- Montana ranked among the lowest states by value of exports in 2003. After peaking in 2000 with $541 million, total exports fell to $361 million in 2003. Primary metal manufactures exports have fallen dramatically since 1999, going from 25 percent of the state's exports to just 2 percent in 2003. Livestock and livestock products have also dropped, from $64 million in 1999 to less than $4 million in 2003.

- The state's largest export industry is chemical manufactures. From 1999 to 2003, these exports grew from $33 million to nearly $65 million, which was about 18 percent of Montana's total exports.

- In 2003, more than 60 percent of Montana's goods were exported to Canada. Exports to China increased from about $1 million in 1999 to over $10 million in 2003, moving the country to among the top five purchasers of the state's exports. From 1999 to 2003, exports to Mexico dropped by 84 percent, with much of this attributable to a decline in primary metal manufactures exports, which fell from $66 million to $532,000.

Table E-31. Total U.S. Exports (Origin of Movement) via Montana, 1999–2003—*Continued*

(Top 25 commodities and top 25 countries based on 2003 dollar value.)

Industry, commodity, and country	Value (millions of dollars)					Percent change, 1999–2003	Percent share of state total				
	1999	2000	2001	2002	2003		1999	2000	2001	2002	2003
TOTAL AND PERCENT SHARE OF U.S. TOTAL	426.9	540.6	488.5	385.7	361.4	-15.34	0.06	0.07	0.07	0.06	0.05
Top 25 Countries	402.5	529.9	475.8	374.4	354.4	-11.94	94.28	98.01	97.40	97.05	98.07
1. Canada	229.9	279.5	302.8	235.1	221.5	-3.65	53.85	51.70	61.98	60.94	61.28
2. Japan	35.5	31.5	22.4	27.0	27.3	-23.26	8.32	5.82	4.59	7.01	7.54
3. Netherlands	5.9	13.0	10.7	11.0	11.8	99.24	1.39	2.40	2.20	2.84	3.26
4. Mexico	70.4	73.3	33.9	15.0	11.2	-84.08	16.49	13.56	6.95	3.88	3.10
5. China	1.3	5.0	6.0	5.1	10.2	679.39	0.31	0.92	1.23	1.33	2.84
6. United Kingdom	12.4	13.8	14.7	6.8	9.2	-25.50	2.89	2.55	3.00	1.76	2.55
7. Taiwan	2.7	16.5	23.1	14.0	9.0	233.93	0.63	3.05	4.73	3.62	2.49
8. South Korea	5.1	11.3	7.6	7.0	7.7	51.58	1.18	2.10	1.56	1.81	2.12
9. Germany	20.2	41.7	21.0	22.8	7.1	-65.02	4.73	7.71	4.29	5.91	1.95
10. France	4.0	16.1	10.4	7.9	6.8	68.52	0.94	2.97	2.13	2.06	1.87
11. Singapore	3.6	12.1	4.2	5.2	6.5	79.86	0.84	2.23	0.85	1.36	1.79
12. Chile	0.3	1.2	1.4	2.3	5.5	2 009.20	0.06	0.23	0.28	0.59	1.52
13. Belgium	1.8	0.9	1.0	4.8	3.4	90.69	0.42	0.16	0.20	1.25	0.95
14. Australia	3.4	3.2	3.0	2.0	3.4	0.56	0.79	0.59	0.61	0.53	0.94
15. Italy	1.5	2.4	3.0	1.4	2.4	67.01	0.34	0.44	0.60	0.36	0.68
16. Hong Kong	1.0	0.8	1.6	1.3	1.6	66.28	0.22	0.16	0.33	0.34	0.44
17. Brazil	1.2	0.6	1.0	0.8	1.5	20.26	0.29	0.10	0.21	0.20	0.41
18. United Arab Emirates	0.0	0.1	0.1	0.0	1.4	X	0.00	0.03	0.01	0.01	0.40
19. Denmark	0.8	0.9	0.8	0.6	1.4	64.80	0.20	0.17	0.17	0.17	0.38
20. Malaysia	0.1	3.4	0.4	0.8	1.0	1 221.79	0.02	0.62	0.09	0.20	0.29
21. Israel	0.3	1.3	4.7	0.8	1.0	211.48	0.08	0.24	0.97	0.21	0.29
22. Indonesia	0.3	0.5	0.9	0.4	1.0	288.76	0.06	0.09	0.19	0.10	0.28
23. India	0.1	0.0	0.0	0.1	0.9	1 014.10	0.02	0.00	0.00	0.03	0.24
24. Spain	0.8	0.6	0.5	1.1	0.9	15.25	0.18	0.10	0.10	0.28	0.24
25. New Zealand	0.1	0.4	0.7	1.0	0.8	619.83	0.03	0.07	0.14	0.27	0.23

Table E-32. Total U.S. Exports (Origin of Movement) via Nebraska, 1999–2003

(Top 25 commodities and top 25 countries based on 2003 dollar value.)

Industry, commodity, and country	Value (millions of dollars)					Percent change, 1999–2003	Percent share of state total				
	1999	2000	2001	2002	2003		1999	2000	2001	2002	2003
TOTAL AND PERCENT SHARE OF U.S. TOTAL	2 096.4	2 511.2	2 701.8	2 527.6	2 723.7	29.92	0.30	0.32	0.37	0.36	0.38
Manufactures (NAICS Code)	1 884.6	2 184.7	2 266.5	2 226.0	2 248.8	19.33	89.90	87.00	83.89	88.07	82.56
Processed foods (311)	895.2	982.3	1 069.7	1 052.7	955.4	6.73	42.70	39.12	39.59	41.65	35.08
Beverages and tobacco products (312)	0.2	0.2	0.3	0.4	0.7	188.50	0.01	0.00	0.01	0.01	0.02
Fabric mill products (313)	3.2	4.6	5.1	8.4	11.0	242.62	0.15	0.18	0.19	0.33	0.40
Non-apparel textile products (314)	5.2	6.1	7.6	7.5	8.4	62.82	0.25	0.24	0.28	0.30	0.31
Apparel manufactures (315)	3.5	1.2	0.3	0.5	0.2	-93.04	0.17	0.05	0.01	0.02	0.01
Leather and related products (316)	32.8	40.2	53.9	27.7	58.4	78.26	1.56	1.60	2.00	1.10	2.14
Wood products (321)	4.2	3.9	3.1	3.4	2.7	-35.45	0.20	0.16	0.11	0.13	0.10
Paper products (322)	6.4	12.0	8.6	8.3	7.4	15.84	0.30	0.48	0.32	0.33	0.27
Printing and related products (323)	10.1	8.1	13.6	12.1	14.0	39.08	0.48	0.32	0.50	0.48	0.51
Petroleum and coal products (324)	0.4	0.4	0.4	0.4	0.4	-4.02	0.02	0.02	0.02	0.01	0.01
Chemical manufactures (325)	109.7	157.0	165.6	216.6	249.4	127.34	5.23	6.25	6.13	8.57	9.16
Plastics and rubber products (326)	46.2	57.5	46.2	51.9	46.5	0.65	2.21	2.29	1.71	2.05	1.71
Non-metallic mineral products (327)	2.9	2.6	2.7	4.2	4.2	43.73	0.14	0.10	0.10	0.17	0.15
Primary metal manufactures (331)	19.1	19.5	15.5	17.4	28.4	48.66	0.91	0.78	0.57	0.69	1.04
Fabricated metal products (332)	38.0	52.2	43.3	45.8	53.2	39.85	1.81	2.08	1.60	1.81	1.95
Machinery manufactures (333)	187.4	271.9	268.7	284.2	293.6	56.67	8.94	10.83	9.95	11.24	10.78
Computer and electronic products (334)	185.9	222.1	175.7	131.5	132.1	-28.95	8.87	8.84	6.50	5.20	4.85
Electrical equipment, appliances, and parts (335)	106.2	86.5	75.9	76.4	94.6	-10.92	5.07	3.45	2.81	3.02	3.47
Transportation equipment (336)	180.8	199.4	258.7	211.3	234.9	29.97	8.62	7.94	9.58	8.36	8.63
Furniture and related products (337)	8.1	11.4	12.8	15.4	15.8	94.80	0.39	0.46	0.47	0.61	0.58
Miscellaneous manufactures (339)	39.1	45.6	38.6	50.0	37.6	-3.95	1.87	1.82	1.43	1.98	1.38
Agricultural and Livestock Products (NAICS Code)	185.0	210.5	334.8	257.6	294.4	59.10	8.83	8.38	12.39	10.19	10.81
Agricultural products (111)	184.2	209.6	333.9	256.6	293.5	59.37	8.79	8.35	12.36	10.15	10.78
Livestock and livestock products (112)	0.8	0.9	0.8	1.0	0.8	-0.84	0.04	0.04	0.03	0.04	0.03
Other Commodities (NAICS Code)	26.8	116.0	100.6	44.0	180.5	573.25	1.28	4.62	3.72	1.74	6.63
Forestry and logging (113)	0.1	0.2	1.2	1.0	1.2	890.24	0.01	0.01	0.04	0.04	0.04
Fishing, hunting, and trapping (114)	8.8	79.2	45.1	0.5	0.3	-97.03	0.42	3.16	1.67	0.02	0.01
Oil and gas extraction (211)	0.0	16.9	24.5	11.1	132.7	X	0.00	0.67	0.90	0.44	4.87
Mining (212)	0.2	0.5	0.7	0.9	0.5	154.42	0.01	0.02	0.03	0.04	0.02
Waste and scrap (910)	2.2	3.6	1.6	2.1	5.0	123.36	0.11	0.14	0.06	0.08	0.18
Public administration (920)	4.4	5.9	8.4	8.8	11.8	168.69	0.21	0.24	0.31	0.35	0.43
Goods returned to Canada (980)	4.3	3.8	3.6	3.6	4.3	0.33	0.20	0.15	0.13	0.14	0.16
Special classification provisions (990)	6.8	5.8	15.4	16.0	24.7	265.25	0.32	0.23	0.57	0.63	0.91
Publishing industries (except Internet) (511)	0.0	0.0	0.0	0.0	0.0	X	0.00	0.00	0.00	0.00	0.00
TOTAL AND PERCENT SHARE OF U.S. TOTAL	2 096.4	2 511.2	2 701.8	2 527.6	2 723.7	29.92	0.30	0.32	0.37	0.36	0.38
Top 25 Commodities (HS Code)	943.7	1 063.9	1 251.9	1 426.1	1 603.6	69.93	45.02	42.37	46.34	56.42	58.88
1. Meat of bovine animals, boneless, fresh or chilled (020130)	332.2	358.7	318.0	243.2	179.2	-46.06	15.85	14.28	11.77	9.62	6.58
2. Soybeans, whether or not broken (120100)	77.3	107.1	123.4	110.8	147.9	91.33	3.69	4.26	4.57	4.38	5.43
3. Natural gas, gaseous (271121)	. . .	16.9	24.4	11.1	132.7	X	. . .	0.67	0.90	0.44	4.87
4. Whole hides and skins of bovine/equine > 16 kg (410150)	0.0	0.0	0.0	116.1	118.7	X	0.00	0.00	0.00	4.59	4.36
5. Meat of bovine animals, boneless, frozen (020230)	122.4	146.2	107.6	133.6	102.8	-16.01	5.84	5.82	3.98	5.29	3.77
6. Corn, other than seed corn (100590)	81.7	69.8	128.3	96.5	98.4	20.44	3.90	2.78	4.75	3.82	3.61
7. Lysine and its esters; salts thereof (292241)	0.0	6.6	32.6	47.1	78.6	X	0.00	0.26	1.21	1.86	2.89
8. Agricultural or horticultural mechanical sprayers (842481)	51.8	60.6	65.4	81.9	72.4	39.77	2.47	2.41	2.42	3.24	2.66
9. Pass. vehicles, spark-ignition eng. cylinder cap. < 1,000 cc (870321)	26.3	22.3	44.3	51.3	67.5	156.65	1.25	0.89	1.64	2.03	2.48
10. Grains, worked corn (110423)	0.1	0.0	31.8	64.6	57.4	57 300.00	0.00	0.00	1.18	2.56	2.11
11. Tan hides and skins, of bovine (410411)	0.0	0.0	0.0	25.3	53.4	X	0.00	0.00	0.00	1.00	1.96
12. Offal of bovine animals, edible, frozen (020629)	68.4	25.8	41.0	26.2	52.9	-22.66	3.26	1.03	1.52	1.04	1.94
13. Meat of bovine animals, bone in, frozen (020220)	6.5	16.4	27.7	36.1	52.8	712.31	0.31	0.65	1.03	1.43	1.94
14. Vaccines for veterinary medicine (300230)	39.4	38.3	46.0	52.2	47.9	21.57	1.88	1.53	1.70	2.07	1.76
15. Meat of swine, fresh or chilled (020319)	26.9	26.8	36.8	40.7	44.9	66.91	1.28	1.07	1.36	1.61	1.65
16. Flour meal and pellet meat/meat offal inedible; greave (230110)	23.0	29.5	29.6	33.4	41.2	79.13	1.10	1.17	1.10	1.32	1.51
17. Combine harvester-threshers (843351)	3.0	11.5	10.1	18.9	39.5	1 216.67	0.14	0.46	0.37	0.75	1.45
18. Animal (not fish) guts, bladders, stomachs and parts (050400)	5.0	7.0	29.1	42.4	34.3	586.00	0.24	0.28	1.08	1.68	1.26
19. Parts of seats (940190)	26.2	34.8	39.9	41.3	34.1	30.15	1.25	1.39	1.48	1.63	1.25
20. Meat of swine, frozen (020329)	15.3	9.9	17.0	29.9	29.3	91.50	0.73	0.39	0.63	1.18	1.08
21. Residues of starch manufacture and similar residue (230310)	11.7	23.9	36.1	35.4	25.3	116.24	0.56	0.95	1.34	1.40	0.93
22. Whole hides and skins of bovine/equine <= 8 kg (410120)	0.0	0.0	0.0	33.9	24.3	X	0.00	0.00	0.00	1.34	0.89
23. Insulated optical fiber cables (854470)	. . .	2.9	10.6	11.3	23.2	. . .	. . .	0.12	0.39	0.45	0.85
24. Spark-ignition engine parts (840991)	26.6	34.3	32.1	27.2	23.2	-12.78	1.27	1.37	1.19	1.08	0.85
25. Motorboats, other than outboard motorboats (890392)	. . .	14.6	20.1	15.7	21.7	. . .	. . .	0.58	0.74	0.62	0.80

X = Not applicable.
. . . = Not available.

Exports from Nebraska

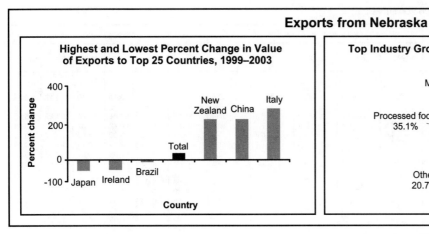

Highest and Lowest Percent Change in Value of Exports to Top 25 Countries, 1999–2003

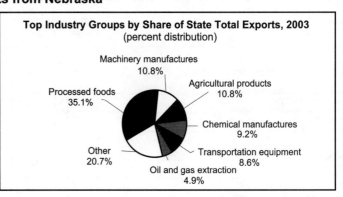

Top Industry Groups by Share of State Total Exports, 2003
(percent distribution)

- Nebraska's exports increased nearly 30 percent from 1999 to 2003. Exports of chemical manufactures increased by nearly $140 million during this period, and exports related to oil and gas extraction grew from $44,000 to nearly $133 million. Processed foods remained Nebraska's largest export, with a value of $955 million in 2003, or 35 percent of the state's total.

- Among Nebraska's leading commodity exports, 'grains, worked corn' had the highest rate of growth, increasing from about $100,000 in 1999 to more than $57 million in 2003. Meat of bovine animals remain the state's top commodity export, although it was down 46 percent from 1999.

- NAFTA members Canada and Mexico are the leading purchasers of Nebraska's exports. In 2003, they accounted for 43 percent of the state's exports. Exports to Mexico grew from $252 million in 1999 to $472 million in 2003. From 1999 to 2003, exports to Italy quadrupled and exports to China (up 269 percent) and South Korea (up 111 percent) also rose substantially.

Table E-32. Total U.S. Exports (Origin of Movement) via Nebraska, 1999–2003—*Continued*

(Top 25 commodities and top 25 countries based on 2003 dollar value.)

Industry, commodity, and country	Value (millions of dollars)					Percent change, 1999–2003	Percent share of state total				
	1999	2000	2001	2002	2003		1999	2000	2001	2002	2003
TOTAL AND PERCENT SHARE OF U.S. TOTAL	2 096.4	2 511.2	2 701.8	2 527.6	2 723.7	29.92	0.30	0.32	0.37	0.36	0.38
Top 25 Countries	1 952.2	2 328.1	2 505.1	2 352.5	2 535.5	29.88	93.12	92.71	92.72	93.07	93.09
1. Canada	545.9	559.1	572.3	561.0	700.5	28.32	26.04	22.27	21.18	22.20	25.72
2. Mexico	251.7	266.1	448.7	465.1	472.4	87.67	12.01	10.60	16.61	18.40	17.35
3. Japan	558.0	683.7	621.0	429.3	357.9	-35.87	26.62	27.23	22.98	16.98	13.14
4. South Korea	79.0	111.3	123.0	178.5	166.6	110.79	3.77	4.43	4.55	7.06	6.12
5. Netherlands	61.5	84.4	101.1	74.3	98.7	60.37	2.94	3.36	3.74	2.94	3.62
6. China	22.8	51.9	68.6	75.6	84.1	268.66	1.09	2.07	2.54	2.99	3.09
7. Taiwan	48.4	71.1	68.7	65.1	71.5	47.76	2.31	2.83	2.54	2.57	2.62
8. Australia	36.9	38.3	41.7	50.8	62.0	68.27	1.76	1.53	1.54	2.01	2.28
9. Italy	15.0	31.9	45.8	28.8	61.0	305.62	0.72	1.27	1.69	1.14	2.24
10. Singapore	37.9	43.3	32.7	31.7	47.2	24.40	1.81	1.72	1.21	1.25	1.73
11. Germany	28.0	31.1	30.1	26.7	45.0	60.32	1.34	1.24	1.11	1.06	1.65
12. United Kingdom	48.2	55.3	61.4	56.6	44.9	-6.86	2.30	2.20	2.27	2.24	1.65
13. Hong Kong	28.5	42.3	34.5	34.7	42.0	47.59	1.36	1.68	1.28	1.37	1.54
14. Thailand	11.1	20.6	42.6	36.2	37.0	234.40	0.53	0.82	1.58	1.43	1.36
15. Belgium	22.3	58.8	22.1	34.6	36.7	64.54	1.06	2.34	0.82	1.37	1.35
16. Indonesia	22.1	19.4	27.8	20.8	33.7	52.38	1.06	0.77	1.03	0.82	1.24
17. France	29.3	31.1	33.0	46.7	33.2	13.17	1.40	1.24	1.22	1.85	1.22
18. Saudi Arabia	20.4	27.4	35.3	23.7	22.0	7.75	0.97	1.09	1.31	0.94	0.81
19. Spain	13.8	12.9	17.6	24.8	21.5	55.55	0.66	0.51	0.65	0.98	0.79
20. Brazil	23.1	27.2	20.3	18.3	21.3	-7.58	1.10	1.08	0.75	0.72	0.78
21. South Africa	7.6	10.7	11.2	23.6	18.2	139.73	0.36	0.43	0.42	0.93	0.67
22. Ireland	24.1	37.7	29.1	24.7	16.7	-31.04	1.15	1.50	1.08	0.98	0.61
23. Dominican Republic	13.1	7.6	6.8	7.2	16.5	25.90	0.63	0.30	0.25	0.29	0.61
24. New Zealand	3.4	5.0	9.7	10.6	12.6	266.06	0.16	0.20	0.36	0.42	0.46
25. Iraq	0.0	0.0	0.0	3.3	12.4	X	0.00	0.00	0.00	0.13	0.46

X = Not applicable.

Table E-33. Total U.S. Exports (Origin of Movement) via Nevada, 1999–2003

(Top 25 commodities and top 25 countries based on 2003 dollar value.)

Industry, commodity, and country	Value (millions of dollars)					Percent change, 1999–2003	Percent share of state total				
	1999	2000	2001	2002	2003		1999	2000	2001	2002	2003
TOTAL AND PERCENT SHARE OF U.S. TOTAL	1 067.2	1 481.9	1 423.2	1 177.0	2 032.6	90.47	0.15	0.19	0.19	0.17	0.28
Manufactures (NAICS Code)	991.8	1 398.7	1 323.6	1 098.1	1 937.4	95.34	92.94	94.38	93.00	93.29	95.32
Processed foods (311)	4.8	6.2	7.4	7.1	9.0	87.95	0.45	0.42	0.52	0.60	0.44
Beverages and tobacco products (312)	14.6	16.7	15.5	6.1	6.8	-53.77	1.37	0.00	1.09	0.52	0.33
Fabric mill products (313)	0.5	2.0	2.0	1.7	1.7	219.96	0.05	0.14	0.14	0.15	0.09
Non-apparel textile products (314)	11.0	5.7	3.0	2.3	2.1	-81.08	1.03	0.39	0.21	0.20	0.10
Apparel manufactures (315)	10.8	10.7	9.6	11.1	9.5	-12.25	1.02	0.72	0.67	0.94	0.47
Leather and related products (316)	2.3	6.0	7.9	7.7	3.5	54.08	0.21	0.40	0.55	0.65	0.17
Wood products (321)	0.6	21.5	1.3	1.3	2.6	336.00	0.06	1.45	0.09	0.11	0.13
Paper products (322)	4.6	5.1	4.2	5.6	4.0	-11.65	0.43	0.34	0.29	0.47	0.20
Printing and related products (323)	11.1	11.8	15.5	22.0	25.1	126.22	1.04	0.80	1.09	1.87	1.23
Petroleum and coal products (324)	0.1	0.7	0.2	0.3	0.6	461.82	0.01	0.05	0.02	0.02	0.03
Chemical manufactures (325)	42.2	54.8	52.4	49.9	41.8	-0.84	3.95	3.69	3.68	4.24	2.06
Plastics and rubber products (326)	27.1	32.6	35.5	43.9	30.5	12.80	2.53	2.20	2.49	3.73	1.50
Non-metallic mineral products (327)	4.3	4.6	6.3	5.0	5.4	24.91	0.40	0.31	0.44	0.43	0.26
Primary metal manufactures (331)	21.8	21.6	31.8	27.2	672.2	2 987.17	2.04	1.46	2.24	2.31	33.07
Fabricated metal products (332)	44.8	49.3	59.4	50.5	77.1	72.27	4.19	3.33	4.17	4.29	3.79
Machinery manufactures (333)	80.8	81.5	82.3	74.2	107.4	32.92	7.57	5.50	5.78	6.30	5.28
Computer and electronic products (334)	331.0	675.1	457.4	412.6	491.0	48.33	31.02	45.55	32.14	35.06	24.16
Electrical equipment, appliances, and parts (335)	27.5	25.8	26.6	24.2	22.9	-17.03	2.58	1.74	1.87	2.05	1.12
Transportation equipment (336)	166.6	129.2	263.5	38.3	56.0	-66.41	15.61	8.72	18.51	3.25	2.75
Furniture and related products (337)	2.6	4.2	2.3	5.9	2.1	-20.70	0.24	0.28	0.16	0.50	0.10
Miscellaneous manufactures (339)	182.7	233.7	239.5	301.2	366.1	100.44	17.12	15.77	16.83	25.59	18.01
Agricultural and Livestock Products (NAICS Code)	5.3	6.7	4.7	5.0	7.2	37.65	0.49	0.45	0.33	0.43	0.36
Agricultural products (111)	4.3	5.5	3.8	4.2	6.6	52.47	0.41	0.37	0.27	0.36	0.33
Livestock and livestock products (112)	0.9	1.2	0.9	0.8	0.6	-32.32	0.09	0.08	0.06	0.07	0.03
Other Commodities (NAICS Code)	70.1	76.6	94.9	73.9	87.9	25.46	6.57	5.17	6.67	6.28	4.33
Forestry and logging (113)	0.0	0.0	0.2	0.1	0.2	X	0.00	0.00	0.01	0.01	0.01
Fishing, hunting, and trapping (114)	0.4	0.0	0.0	0.1	0.4	2.92	0.04	0.00	0.00	0.01	0.02
Oil and gas extraction (211)	0.0	0.0	0.0	0.4	0.0	X	0.00	0.00	0.00	0.03	0.00
Mining (212)	26.2	32.9	39.3	35.8	38.2	45.79	2.46	2.22	2.76	3.04	1.88
Waste and scrap (910)	1.6	1.6	4.2	3.9	4.1	151.03	0.15	0.11	0.29	0.33	0.20
Public administration (920)	3.5	5.1	9.3	4.2	4.1	16.44	0.33	0.35	0.66	0.35	0.20
Goods returned to Canada (980)	18.1	17.8	19.4	13.1	17.3	-4.22	1.70	1.20	1.36	1.12	0.85
Special classification provisions (990)	20.2	19.0	22.5	16.3	23.4	15.89	1.89	1.28	1.58	1.38	1.15
Publishing industries (except Internet) (511)	0.0	0.0	0.0	0.0	0.1	X	0.00	0.00	0.00	0.00	0.01
TOTAL AND PERCENT SHARE OF U.S. TOTAL	1 067.2	1 481.9	1 423.2	1 177.0	2 032.6	90.47	0.15	0.19	0.19	0.17	0.28
Top 25 Commodities (HS Code)	317.2	374.1	399.9	734.8	1 548.8	388.27	29.72	25.24	28.10	62.43	76.20
1. Gold, non-monetary, unwrought (710812)	...	0.0	0.0	0.0	646.7	...	...	0.00	0.00	0.00	31.82
2. Coin/token operated games, not bowling alley equipment (950430)	122.5	130.4	146.6	166.8	245.0	100.00	11.48	8.80	10.30	14.17	12.05
3. Digital monolithic integrated circuits (854221)	0.0	0.0	0.0	184.2	216.6	X	0.00	0.00	0.00	15.65	10.66
4. Measuring and checking instr., appliances, and machines (903180)	50.8	60.3	63.5	73.5	93.4	83.86	4.76	4.07	4.46	6.24	4.60
5. Diamonds, non-industrial, worked (710239)	16.8	50.5	34.3	86.2	70.1	317.26	1.57	3.41	2.41	7.32	3.45
6. Parts and accessories for automatic data processing (847330)	10.1	12.1	10.3	9.6	24.0	137.62	0.95	0.82	0.72	0.82	1.18
7. Non-digital monolithic integrated circuits (854229)	0.0	0.0	0.0	21.1	23.7	X	0.00	0.00	0.00	1.79	1.17
8. Siliceous fossil meals and earths (251200)	13.8	18.8	24.0	20.3	21.8	57.97	1.29	1.27	1.69	1.72	1.07
9. X-ray/high tension generators (902290)	0.0	0.0	3.4	7.0	19.9	X	0.00	0.00	0.24	0.59	0.98
10. Electronic microassemblies (854270)	0.0	0.0	0.0	32.2	19.4	X	0.00	0.00	0.00	2.74	0.95
11. Centrifugal pumps (841370)	13.5	6.6	7.3	8.9	18.7	38.52	1.27	0.45	0.51	0.76	0.92
12. Propeller rotors and parts of gliders and aircraft (880310)	2.9	6.3	12.1	11.3	15.8	444.83	0.27	0.43	0.85	0.96	0.78
13. Socket wrenches with/without handles (820420)	7.0	9.6	13.1	13.2	14.8	111.43	0.66	0.65	0.92	1.12	0.73
14. Game machines, excluding coin-operated (950490)	6.0	15.2	13.0	15.1	13.0	116.67	0.56	1.03	0.91	1.28	0.64
15. Parts of pumps for liquids (841391)	8.2	9.6	10.3	6.5	12.5	52.44	0.77	0.65	0.72	0.55	0.61
16. Printed books and brochures (490199)	5.5	6.5	9.1	10.8	12.1	120.00	0.52	0.44	0.64	0.92	0.60
17. Natural borates and natural boric acid (252890)	10.5	10.9	10.9	11.6	11.0	4.76	0.98	0.74	0.77	0.99	0.54
18. Parts of airplanes or helicopters (880330)	32.5	13.4	14.5	10.1	10.6	-67.38	3.05	0.90	1.02	0.86	0.52
19. Unwrought titanium; powders (810820)	0.0	0.0	0.0	11.2	10.5	X	0.00	0.00	0.00	0.95	0.52
20. Articles of plastics (392690)	3.2	4.5	7.0	19.8	8.8	175.00	0.30	0.30	0.49	1.68	0.43
21. Helicopters (880212)	...	0.0	0.0	0.5	8.7	...	...	0.00	0.00	0.04	0.43
22. Military weapons, other than revolvers and pistols (930190)	...	0.0	0.0	1.5	8.7	...	...	0.00	0.00	0.13	0.43
23. Taps and cocks for pipe thermostatic control (848180)	...	2.7	3.2	2.6	8.6	...	...	0.18	0.22	0.22	0.42
24. Blotting pads, book covers, and articles of stationary (482090)	...	0.0	1.8	5.4	8.0	...	...	0.00	0.13	0.46	0.39
25. Waters, incl. mineral and aerated, sweetened or flavored (220210)	13.9	16.7	15.5	5.9	6.4	-53.96	1.30	1.13	1.09	0.50	0.31

X = Not applicable.
. . . = Not available.

Exports from Nevada

Highest and Lowest Percent Change in Value of Exports to Top 25 Countries, 1999–2003

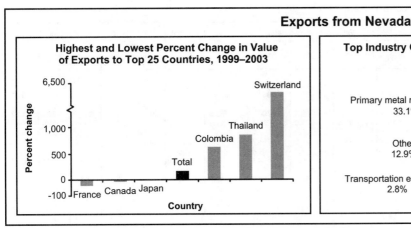

Top Industry Groups by Share of State Total Exports, 2003
(percent distribution)

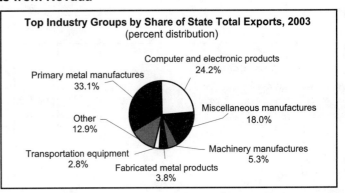

- From 1999 to 2003, Nevada's exports increased by 90 percent, which was the highest rate of growth among the 50 states. Primary metal manufactures exports rose from $22 million to $672 million, a jump of over 30-fold, largely attributable to exports of gold. These exports accounted for one-third of Nevada's total exports. Miscellaneous manufactures exports also grew considerably, increasing from $183 million to $366 million from 1999 to 2003.

- Transportation equipment exports fell from $167 million in 1999 to $56 million in 2003, a drop of about 66 percent. Non-apparel textile products and fabric mill products also declined during this period.

- Gold became Nevada's top commodity export in 2003, with exports valued at $646.7 million. In previous years, Nevada did not export gold. The majority of these exports went to Switzerland, making it Nevada's top export recipient in 2003. Canada and Mexico ranked second and third, respectively.

Table E-33. Total U.S. Exports (Origin of Movement) via Nevada, 1999–2003—*Continued*

(Top 25 commodities and top 25 countries based on 2003 dollar value.)

Industry, commodity, and country	Value (millions of dollars)					Percent change, 1999–2003	Percent share of state total				
	1999	2000	2001	2002	2003		1999	2000	2001	2002	2003
TOTAL AND PERCENT SHARE OF U.S. TOTAL	1 067.2	1 481.9	1 423.2	1 177.0	2 032.6	90.47	0.15	0.19	0.19	0.17	0.28
Top 25 Countries	991.6	1 382.1	1 303.5	1 057.1	1 909.4	92.56	92.92	93.26	91.59	89.81	93.94
1. Switzerland	10.5	9.4	8.5	8.9	658.4	6 173.75	0.98	0.63	0.60	0.75	32.39
2. Canada	486.8	585.8	580.5	379.9	467.5	-3.95	45.62	39.53	40.79	32.28	23.00
3. Mexico	57.4	119.4	125.1	71.0	104.5	82.09	5.38	8.06	8.79	6.03	5.14
4. Japan	78.8	99.7	85.2	75.9	79.2	0.44	7.39	6.73	5.99	6.44	3.90
5. United Kingdom	52.7	67.5	86.0	71.9	78.6	49.26	4.94	4.55	6.04	6.11	3.87
6. Australia	14.3	43.9	38.7	49.5	52.3	266.47	1.34	2.96	2.72	4.21	2.57
7. Germany	49.3	52.4	54.5	45.7	52.0	5.64	4.62	3.54	3.83	3.88	2.56
8. Israel	13.1	38.2	26.3	35.5	49.6	277.91	1.23	2.58	1.85	3.02	2.44
9. France	72.1	34.9	26.2	29.3	37.1	-48.50	6.75	2.36	1.84	2.49	1.83
10. Belgium	9.0	30.8	22.3	61.3	32.3	258.79	0.84	2.08	1.57	5.21	1.59
11. South Korea	24.3	17.2	14.9	20.5	32.2	32.24	2.28	1.16	1.05	1.75	1.58
12. Taiwan	17.5	28.9	27.2	26.2	29.4	67.31	1.64	1.95	1.91	2.23	1.44
13. Netherlands	16.9	26.3	36.4	23.6	29.0	71.38	1.59	1.78	2.56	2.00	1.43
14. Hong Kong	12.0	44.3	48.4	39.5	27.4	128.06	1.13	2.99	3.40	3.36	1.35
15. China	10.9	9.3	13.6	20.1	24.4	124.27	1.02	0.63	0.96	1.71	1.20
16. Singapore	6.0	21.5	19.1	20.9	24.1	303.50	0.56	1.45	1.34	1.78	1.19
17. Thailand	2.2	5.2	7.7	6.5	20.6	836.64	0.21	0.35	0.54	0.55	1.01
18. Italy	13.1	13.2	18.0	18.3	18.0	36.99	1.23	0.89	1.27	1.56	0.88
19. South Africa	9.1	18.7	14.6	9.6	16.8	84.28	0.85	1.26	1.03	0.82	0.83
20. Malaysia	8.3	23.5	17.4	19.6	16.0	91.56	0.78	1.59	1.22	1.67	0.79
21. Colombia	2.0	61.9	2.3	4.9	14.8	653.27	0.18	4.18	0.16	0.42	0.73
22. Chile	3.7	7.2	8.1	4.6	13.1	255.52	0.35	0.48	0.57	0.39	0.65
23. Argentina	9.5	8.9	12.1	3.7	11.1	17.53	0.89	0.60	0.85	0.32	0.55
24. Finland	6.8	4.0	3.7	2.2	11.0	63.53	0.63	0.27	0.26	0.19	0.54
25. Spain	5.4	10.0	6.5	8.0	9.9	84.53	0.50	0.67	0.46	0.68	0.49

Table E-34. Total U.S. Exports (Origin of Movement) via New Hampshire, 1999–2003

(Top 25 commodities and top 25 countries based on 2003 dollar value.)

Industry, commodity, and country	Value (millions of dollars)					Percent change, 1999–2003	Percent share of state total				
	1999	2000	2001	2002	2003		1999	2000	2001	2002	2003
TOTAL AND PERCENT SHARE OF U.S. TOTAL	1 929.8	2 373.3	2 401.0	1 863.3	1 931.4	0.09	0.28	0.30	0.33	0.27	0.27
Manufactures (NAICS Code)	1 821.0	2 234.2	2 269.4	1 700.1	1 761.8	-3.25	94.36	94.14	94.52	91.24	91.22
Processed foods (311)	15.3	18.5	23.0	23.4	27.9	82.33	0.79	0.78	0.96	1.25	1.45
Beverages and tobacco products (312)	1.6	2.2	3.0	3.7	0.2	-87.45	0.08	0.00	0.13	0.20	0.01
Fabric mill products (313)	33.3	24.0	21.5	24.7	28.3	-15.23	1.73	1.01	0.90	1.33	1.46
Non-apparel textile products (314)	6.8	3.2	1.7	1.5	1.3	-80.61	0.35	0.14	0.07	0.08	0.07
Apparel manufactures (315)	6.1	6.4	10.0	9.1	5.6	-9.60	0.32	0.27	0.42	0.49	0.29
Leather and related products (316)	76.4	62.6	68.6	32.2	19.7	-74.17	3.96	2.64	2.86	1.73	1.02
Wood products (321)	34.4	42.7	42.6	42.7	48.6	41.11	1.78	1.80	1.78	2.29	2.51
Paper products (322)	41.6	50.5	29.8	29.4	42.5	2.17	2.16	2.13	1.24	1.58	2.20
Printing and related products (323)	16.0	12.7	13.6	16.8	16.2	1.70	0.83	0.53	0.56	0.90	0.84
Petroleum and coal products (324)	2.2	1.6	0.9	1.1	1.2	-44.89	0.12	0.07	0.04	0.06	0.06
Chemical manufactures (325)	90.1	103.2	143.2	97.0	101.9	13.09	4.67	4.35	5.97	5.20	5.28
Plastics and rubber products (326)	77.1	84.4	60.8	66.7	62.1	-19.42	3.99	3.56	2.53	3.58	3.22
Non-metallic mineral products (327)	27.3	38.0	50.8	48.8	46.7	71.18	1.41	1.60	2.12	2.62	2.42
Primary metal manufactures (331)	19.2	24.3	18.1	17.6	19.3	0.62	1.00	1.03	0.75	0.95	1.00
Fabricated metal products (332)	159.7	109.2	97.0	73.2	76.5	-52.07	8.27	4.60	4.04	3.93	3.96
Machinery manufactures (333)	283.1	409.3	466.5	385.3	388.6	37.27	14.67	17.25	19.43	20.68	20.12
Computer and electronic products (334)	710.7	999.3	884.6	569.5	613.8	-13.64	36.83	42.11	36.84	30.57	31.78
Electrical equipment, appliances, and parts (335)	117.3	119.6	205.1	99.7	94.7	-19.27	6.08	5.04	8.54	5.35	4.90
Transportation equipment (336)	52.0	59.5	59.8	77.9	81.2	56.18	2.70	2.51	2.49	4.18	4.21
Furniture and related products (337)	2.2	2.5	1.8	5.0	4.2	93.95	0.11	0.10	0.07	0.27	0.22
Miscellaneous manufactures (339)	48.5	60.4	67.1	74.6	81.1	67.03	2.52	2.54	2.79	4.00	4.20
Agricultural and Livestock Products (NAICS Code)	2.8	1.8	0.8	1.4	1.4	-49.05	0.14	0.08	0.03	0.07	0.07
Agricultural products (111)	1.7	0.8	0.5	0.5	1.0	-40.42	0.09	0.03	0.02	0.03	0.05
Livestock and livestock products (112)	1.1	1.0	0.3	0.8	0.4	-62.06	0.06	0.04	0.01	0.05	0.02
Other Commodities (NAICS Code)	106.0	137.3	130.8	161.8	168.2	58.72	5.49	5.78	5.45	8.69	8.71
Forestry and logging (113)	20.6	28.5	24.0	24.8	17.8	-13.63	1.07	1.20	1.00	1.33	0.92
Fishing, hunting, and trapping (114)	16.7	20.1	17.4	16.0	17.9	7.38	0.86	0.85	0.73	0.86	0.93
Oil and gas extraction (211)	0.0	0.9	2.3	0.6	0.1	X	0.00	0.04	0.10	0.03	0.01
Mining (212)	1.5	1.1	0.2	0.6	1.0	-36.86	0.08	0.05	0.01	0.03	0.05
Waste and scrap (910)	5.8	8.8	6.0	12.7	31.0	435.92	0.30	0.37	0.25	0.68	1.60
Public administration (920)	0.9	0.8	0.8	1.3	0.8	-6.06	0.05	0.03	0.03	0.07	0.04
Goods returned to Canada (980)	10.0	8.6	11.5	8.8	6.6	-34.08	0.52	0.36	0.48	0.47	0.34
Special classification provisions (990)	50.5	68.5	68.6	97.0	91.3	80.92	2.62	2.88	2.86	5.21	4.73
Publishing industries (except Internet) (511)	0.0	0.0	0.0	0.0	1.7	X	0.00	0.00	0.00	0.00	0.09
TOTAL AND PERCENT SHARE OF U.S. TOTAL	1 929.8	2 373.3	2 401.0	1 863.3	1 931.4	0.09	0.28	0.30	0.33	0.27	0.27
Top 25 Commodities (HS Code)	446.4	752.4	748.0	689.6	799.6	79.12	23.13	31.70	31.15	37.01	41.40
1. Parts and accessories for automatic data processing (847330)	96.8	128.6	117.4	68.9	100.4	3.72	5.02	5.42	4.89	3.70	5.20
2. Parts for printing and ancillary to printing machinery (844390)	31.9	53.4	81.0	55.8	57.7	80.88	1.65	2.25	3.37	2.99	2.99
3. Automatic data processing units (847180)	106.0	83.9	99.4	61.5	56.1	-47.08	5.49	3.54	4.14	3.30	2.90
4. Electrical apparatus for line telephony or telegraphy (851750)	7.8	61.5	46.2	35.5	50.3	544.87	0.40	2.59	1.92	1.91	2.60
5. Laser discs for reproducing other than sound/image (852431)	5.9	20.8	12.1	21.8	49.3	735.59	0.31	0.88	0.50	1.17	2.55
6. Parts of apparatus for line telephony or telegraphy (851790)	21.5	51.2	37.3	25.0	47.1	119.07	1.11	2.16	1.55	1.34	2.44
7. Ink-jet printing machinery, except units of 8471 (844351)	17.8	46.0	53.3	48.6	39.6	122.47	0.92	1.94	2.22	2.61	2.05
8. Digital monolithic integrated circuits (854221)	0.0	0.0	0.0	32.0	30.2	X	0.00	0.00	0.00	1.72	1.56
9. Electronic integrated circuits and microassemblies parts (854290)	2.3	7.8	28.0	23.7	28.8	1 152.17	0.12	0.33	1.17	1.27	1.49
10. Chemical preparations for photo use (370790)	18.6	23.5	10.6	23.2	27.8	49.46	0.96	0.99	0.44	1.25	1.44
11. Parts and accessories for use with machine tools (846693)	22.2	29.8	28.2	21.2	27.7	24.77	1.15	1.26	1.17	1.14	1.43
12. Instruments for measuring voltage current (903039)	2.0	26.6	27.0	24.3	26.7	1 235.00	0.10	1.12	1.12	1.30	1.38
13. Electric plugs and sockets, voltage < 1,000 v (853669)	11.4	45.7	32.3	22.9	25.3	121.93	0.59	1.93	1.35	1.23	1.31
14. Printing ink, other than black (321519)	. . .	10.6	4.7	9.3	22.9	. . .	. . .	0.45	0.20	0.50	1.19
15. Parts and accessories of motor vehicles bodies (870829)	7.8	11.1	11.5	22.3	22.7	191.03	0.40	0.47	0.48	1.20	1.18
16. Non-coniferous wood, sawn, sliced, > 6 mm (440799)	12.6	17.0	20.8	19.8	21.6	71.43	0.65	0.72	0.87	1.06	1.12
17. Mounted piezoelectric crystals (854160)	13.9	28.6	22.6	14.6	21.2	52.52	0.72	1.21	0.94	0.78	1.10
18. Exports of military equipment (980320)	12.1	13.8	30.6	45.0	21.1	74.38	0.63	0.58	1.27	2.42	1.09
19. Non-digital monolithic integrated circuits (854229)	0.0	0.0	0.0	17.0	19.6	X	0.00	0.00	0.00	0.91	1.01
20. Articles of plastics (392690)	19.2	17.9	18.7	20.7	19.1	-0.52	0.99	0.75	0.78	1.11	0.99
21. Tungsten halogen electric filament lamps (853921)	15.0	18.7	14.2	22.3	17.7	18.00	0.78	0.79	0.59	1.20	0.92
22. Parts and accessories of bicycles (871499)	. . .	0.1	0.8	9.3	17.4	. . .	. . .	0.00	0.03	0.50	0.90
23. Oak wood, sawn, sliced, > 6 mm thick (440791)	14.1	16.2	14.8	15.0	17.1	21.28	0.73	0.68	0.62	0.81	0.89
24. Machines for uses ancillary to printing (844360)	7.5	39.7	37.3	25.1	16.2	116.00	0.39	1.67	1.55	1.35	0.84
25. Ferrous waste and scrap (720449)	. . .	0.0	0.3	4.8	16.0	. . .	. . .	0.00	0.01	0.26	0.83

X = Not applicable.
. . . = Not available.

Exports from New Hampshire

Highest and Lowest Percent Change in Value of Exports to Top 25 Countries, 1999–2003

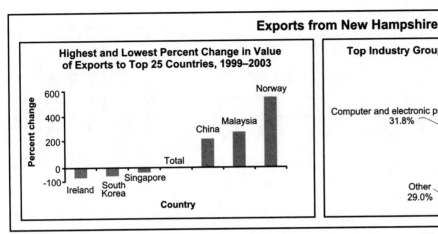

Top Industry Groups by Share of State Total Exports, 2003
(percent distribution)

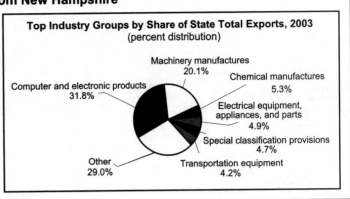

- Computer and electronic products and machinery manufactures are New Hampshire's top exporting industries. Together, they totaled $1 billion, or just over half of the state's total exports in 2003. Machinery manufactures exports increased over $100 million between 1999 and 2003, but computers and electronic products fell by $97 million, declining steeply in 2002.

- From 1999 to 2003, waste and scrap exports increased by $25 million, or more than fivefold. During the same period, furniture and related products (up 94 percent) and processed foods (up 82 percent) also had high rates of growth, but fabricated metal products fell from about $160 million in 1999 to under $77 million in 2003.

- In 2003, more than one-fourth of New Hampshire's exports were to Canada. This share was down 5 percentage points from 1999. Among the top export countries, exports to Japan and the Netherlands had the highest growth rates, as exports to both nations increased about 74 percent from 1999 to 2003. In 2003, exports to China reached $73 million, more than triple that of those in 1999. As a result, China ranked seventh in 2003 among New Hampshire's export markets.

Table E-34. Total U.S. Exports (Origin of Movement) via New Hampshire, 1999–2003—Continued

(Top 25 commodities and top 25 countries based on 2003 dollar value.)

Industry, commodity, and country	Value (millions of dollars)					Percent change, 1999–2003	Percent share of state total				
	1999	2000	2001	2002	2003		1999	2000	2001	2002	2003
TOTAL AND PERCENT SHARE OF U.S. TOTAL	1 929.8	2 373.3	2 401.0	1 863.3	1 931.4	0.09	0.28	0.30	0.33	0.27	0.27
Top 25 Countries	1 781.1	2 241.4	2 190.9	1 705.6	1 769.0	-0.68	92.30	94.44	91.25	91.54	91.59
1. Canada	608.5	742.7	593.9	514.3	506.0	-16.84	31.53	31.30	24.73	27.60	26.20
2. United Kingdom	162.3	213.4	365.6	163.5	160.0	-1.45	8.41	8.99	15.22	8.78	8.28
3. Japan	79.2	145.5	198.2	126.8	138.5	74.89	4.10	6.13	8.25	6.80	7.17
4. Netherlands	73.5	88.1	82.3	90.1	127.8	73.83	3.81	3.71	3.43	4.84	6.62
5. Germany	100.1	198.0	143.4	128.4	108.6	8.56	5.19	8.34	5.97	6.89	5.63
6. Mexico	73.3	82.6	81.8	63.7	84.8	15.64	3.80	3.48	3.41	3.42	4.39
7. China	21.9	29.9	48.6	42.0	73.3	234.13	1.14	1.26	2.02	2.25	3.79
8. Hong Kong	49.5	66.2	82.5	50.1	66.3	33.94	2.57	2.79	3.44	2.69	3.43
9. Italy	23.3	31.3	52.2	65.6	54.2	132.89	1.21	1.32	2.18	3.52	2.81
10. Ireland	168.3	168.3	77.2	50.2	53.0	-68.53	8.72	7.09	3.21	2.70	2.74
11. Singapore	93.4	58.1	41.8	31.8	47.6	-49.05	4.84	2.45	1.74	1.71	2.47
12. France	44.8	75.1	65.9	63.7	46.2	3.15	2.32	3.17	2.74	3.42	2.39
13. South Korea	93.3	23.8	28.6	55.2	43.4	-53.47	4.83	1.00	1.19	2.96	2.25
14. Taiwan	37.4	50.8	35.6	36.2	36.0	-3.85	1.94	2.14	1.48	1.94	1.86
15. Malaysia	9.0	60.6	47.7	26.1	33.3	270.87	0.47	2.55	1.99	1.40	1.73
16. Australia	20.3	29.9	23.7	20.1	32.7	60.65	1.05	1.26	0.99	1.08	1.69
17. Israel	20.8	28.4	22.1	24.3	30.9	48.46	1.08	1.20	0.92	1.30	1.60
18. Belgium	13.0	16.1	38.4	36.5	22.4	72.57	0.67	0.68	1.60	1.96	1.16
19. Thailand	13.2	13.8	12.4	6.6	18.7	41.63	0.68	0.58	0.52	0.36	0.97
20. Switzerland	8.8	11.0	12.2	12.7	17.2	94.73	0.46	0.46	0.51	0.68	0.89
21. Brazil	18.1	44.3	59.9	27.9	16.0	-11.92	0.94	1.87	2.50	1.50	0.83
22. Spain	22.5	16.7	26.2	40.3	14.4	-36.08	1.17	0.70	1.09	2.16	0.74
23. Norway	1.8	7.4	13.3	7.6	12.9	596.38	0.10	0.31	0.56	0.41	0.67
24. Sweden	20.7	31.3	22.8	13.1	12.8	-37.95	1.07	1.32	0.95	0.70	0.66
25. Denmark	4.0	8.0	14.9	8.8	12.2	206.02	0.21	0.34	0.62	0.47	0.63

Table E-35. Total U.S. Exports (Origin of Movement) via New Jersey, 1999–2003

(Top 25 commodities and top 25 countries based on 2003 dollar value.)

Industry, commodity, and country	Value (millions of dollars)					Percent change, 1999–2003	Percent share of state total				
	1999	2000	2001	2002	2003		1999	2000	2001	2002	2003
TOTAL AND PERCENT SHARE OF U.S. TOTAL	15 354.5	18 637.6	18 945.7	17 001.5	16 817.7	9.53	2.22	2.39	2.59	2.45	2.32
Manufactures (NAICS Code)	14 355.2	17 219.9	17 562.4	15 609.6	15 311.9	6.66	93.49	92.39	92.70	91.81	91.05
Processed foods (311)	520.0	480.2	695.5	595.0	575.5	10.67	3.39	2.58	3.67	3.50	3.42
Beverages and tobacco products (312)	9.0	14.9	7.5	17.9	27.7	207.71	0.06	0.08	0.04	0.11	0.16
Fabric mill products (313)	163.3	150.8	130.4	114.1	108.6	-33.50	1.06	0.81	0.69	0.67	0.65
Non-apparel textile products (314)	47.5	63.9	62.4	61.5	59.3	24.92	0.31	0.34	0.33	0.36	0.35
Apparel manufactures (315)	100.8	105.0	107.9	87.6	80.7	-19.86	0.66	0.56	0.57	0.52	0.48
Leather and related products (316)	72.5	76.7	52.5	40.4	56.9	-21.50	0.47	0.41	0.28	0.24	0.34
Wood products (321)	30.2	34.3	30.5	29.8	28.7	-5.05	0.20	0.18	0.16	0.18	0.17
Paper products (322)	268.3	259.2	260.1	286.1	266.5	-0.64	1.75	1.39	1.37	1.68	1.58
Printing and related products (323)	398.5	425.1	454.1	522.4	584.0	46.57	2.60	2.28	2.40	3.07	3.47
Petroleum and coal products (324)	100.6	83.8	113.6	222.2	134.5	33.77	0.65	0.45	0.60	1.31	0.80
Chemical manufactures (325)	4 448.0	5 204.0	4 924.0	4 507.9	4 591.3	3.22	28.97	27.92	25.99	26.51	27.30
Plastics and rubber products (326)	382.7	406.3	425.7	381.5	443.1	15.79	2.49	2.18	2.25	2.24	2.63
Non-metallic mineral products (327)	190.7	237.0	245.2	167.1	169.7	-10.98	1.24	1.27	1.29	0.98	1.01
Primary metal manufactures (331)	786.6	1 340.1	1 491.0	1 112.9	1 008.5	28.21	5.12	7.19	7.87	6.55	6.00
Fabricated metal products (332)	384.7	469.0	468.7	641.6	517.9	34.63	2.51	2.52	2.47	3.77	3.08
Machinery manufactures (333)	1 139.1	1 272.7	1 316.9	1 032.5	1 122.7	-1.44	7.42	6.83	6.95	6.07	6.68
Computer and electronic products (334)	2 477.8	3 325.1	3 586.1	2 589.4	2 555.5	3.14	16.14	17.84	18.93	15.23	15.20
Electrical equipment, appliances, and parts (335)	466.4	566.4	513.6	488.2	479.3	2.77	3.04	3.04	2.71	2.87	2.85
Transportation equipment (336)	1 542.0	1 730.9	1 564.0	1 557.4	1 396.8	-9.42	10.04	9.29	8.26	9.16	8.31
Furniture and related products (337)	40.0	41.5	45.7	46.8	39.2	-1.98	0.26	0.22	0.24	0.28	0.23
Miscellaneous manufactures (339)	786.7	932.9	1 067.1	1 107.3	1 065.4	35.42	5.12	5.01	5.63	6.51	6.34
Agricultural and Livestock Products (NAICS Code)	154.7	147.1	168.1	166.5	164.5	6.34	1.01	0.79	0.89	0.98	0.98
Agricultural products (111)	139.8	132.7	137.2	133.7	161.7	15.63	0.91	0.71	0.72	0.79	0.96
Livestock and livestock products (112)	14.9	14.5	30.9	32.9	2.8	-80.98	0.10	0.08	0.16	0.19	0.02
Other Commodities (NAICS Code)	844.6	1 270.5	1 215.3	1 225.4	1 341.2	58.80	5.50	6.82	6.41	7.21	7.98
Forestry and logging (113)	36.1	34.1	42.6	44.1	51.2	41.79	0.24	0.18	0.23	0.26	0.30
Fishing, hunting, and trapping (114)	35.7	24.9	28.5	23.6	26.0	-27.29	0.23	0.13	0.15	0.14	0.15
Oil and gas extraction (211)	17.1	59.1	31.8	7.3	35.1	104.84	0.11	0.32	0.17	0.04	0.21
Mining (212)	33.9	41.6	40.7	26.8	30.1	-11.17	0.22	0.22	0.21	0.16	0.18
Waste and scrap (910)	433.7	764.0	689.4	728.9	819.5	88.93	2.82	4.10	3.64	4.29	4.87
Used merchandise (920)	45.6	81.3	108.0	97.7	118.8	160.59	0.30	0.44	0.57	0.57	0.71
Goods returned to Canada (980)	38.0	41.0	50.4	30.5	22.3	-41.42	0.25	0.22	0.27	0.18	0.13
Special classification provisions (990)	204.4	224.5	223.8	266.5	233.7	14.31	1.33	1.20	1.18	1.57	1.39
Publishing industries (except Internet) (511)	0.0	0.0	0.0	0.0	4.7	X	0.00	0.00	0.00	0.00	0.03
TOTAL AND PERCENT SHARE OF U.S. TOTAL	15 354.5	18 637.6	18 945.7	17 001.5	16 817.7	9.53	2.22	2.39	2.59	2.45	2.32
Top 25 Commodities (HS Code)	2 517.4	3 639.1	4 327.5	4 641.5	4 969.8	97.42	16.40	19.53	22.84	27.30	29.55
1. Parts of airplanes or helicopters (880330)	629.2	703.4	734.1	572.3	631.5	0.37	4.10	3.77	3.87	3.37	3.75
2. Retail medicaments in measured dose (300490)	379.6	417.7	429.0	513.2	575.6	51.63	2.47	2.24	2.26	3.02	3.42
3. Platinum, unwrought or powder (711011)	76.6	155.7	219.8	249.1	371.3	384.73	0.50	0.84	1.16	1.47	2.21
4. Newspapers, appearing fewer than 4 times per week (490290)	106.6	130.7	167.6	247.3	303.0	184.24	0.69	0.70	0.88	1.45	1.80
5. Jewelry and parts thereof, of precious metal (711319)	86.6	23.4	286.6	238.3	297.2	243.19	0.56	0.13	1.51	1.40	1.77
6. Platinum waste and scrap, without other precious metals (711292)	0.0	0.0	0.0	173.5	258.7	X	0.00	0.00	0.00	1.02	1.54
7. Palladium, unwrought or in powder form (711021)	252.7	506.9	606.2	386.5	195.6	-22.60	1.65	2.72	3.20	2.27	1.16
8. Gold waste and scrap, without other precious metals (711291)	0.0	0.0	0.0	119.0	190.0	X	0.00	0.00	0.00	0.70	1.13
9. Printed books and brochures (490199)	207.2	217.4	204.0	190.1	185.4	-10.52	1.35	1.17	1.08	1.12	1.10
10. Ferrous waste and scrap (720449)	20.5	13.5	58.3	151.2	185.1	802.93	0.13	0.07	0.31	0.89	1.10
11. Additives for lubricating oil containing petroleum (381121)	74.0	70.5	75.0	111.9	148.7	100.95	0.48	0.38	0.40	0.66	0.88
12. Parts of apparatus for line telephony or telegraphy (851790)	174.7	314.6	404.5	254.4	146.1	-16.37	1.14	1.69	2.14	1.50	0.87
13. Instruments and appliances for medical sciences (901890)	96.7	96.9	147.4	123.9	143.2	48.09	0.63	0.52	0.78	0.73	0.85
14. Perfumes and toilet waters (330300)	93.5	102.2	113.1	121.5	140.6	50.37	0.61	0.55	0.60	0.71	0.84
15. Sulfonamides (293500)	103.6	88.1	91.0	131.5	128.5	24.03	0.67	0.47	0.48	0.77	0.76
16. Photographic plates and film (370130)	. . .	80.9	44.8	67.6	122.2	. . .	. . .	0.43	0.24	0.40	0.73
17. Parts and accessories for automatic data processing (847330)	. . .	143.7	119.2	103.2	119.6	. . .	. . .	0.77	0.63	0.61	0.71
18. Mixtures of odoriferous substances (330290)	. . .	107.3	115.2	102.6	116.2	. . .	. . .	0.58	0.61	0.60	0.69
19. Beauty and skin care preparations (330499)	84.5	116.9	153.7	141.7	114.4	35.38	0.55	0.63	0.81	0.83	0.68
20. Instruments, aeronautical-space nav., no compass (901420)	. . .	58.5	95.8	84.4	108.3	. . .	. . .	0.31	0.51	0.50	0.64
21. Medical needles, catheters and parts (901839)	124.7	145.9	121.6	109.3	103.3	-17.16	0.81	0.78	0.64	0.64	0.61
22. Mixtures of odoriferous substances used in food or drink (330210)	. . .	74.9	76.0	87.2	102.3	. . .	. . .	0.40	0.40	0.51	0.61
23. Petroleum oils from bituminous mineral (not crude) (271019)	0.0	0.0	0.0	142.8	97.3	X	0.00	0.00	0.00	0.84	0.58
24. Medical, surgical, or laboratory sterilizers (841920)	6.7	43.4	52.3	120.9	93.8	1 300.00	0.04	0.23	0.28	0.71	0.56
25. Electronic integrated circuits and microassemblies parts (854290)	. . .	26.6	12.3	98.1	91.9	. . .	. . .	0.14	0.06	0.58	0.55

X = Not applicable.

. . . = Not available.

Exports from New Jersey

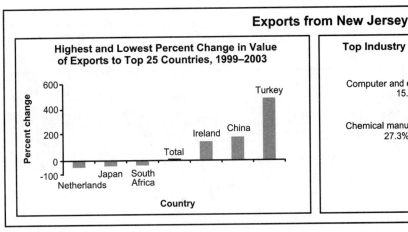

Highest and Lowest Percent Change in Value of Exports to Top 25 Countries, 1999–2003

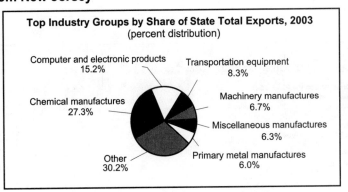

Top Industry Groups by Share of State Total Exports, 2003
(percent distribution)

Computer and electronic products 15.2%

Transportation equipment 8.3%

Chemical manufactures 27.3%

Machinery manufactures 6.7%

Miscellaneous manufactures 6.3%

Other 30.2%

Primary metal manufactures 6.0%

- In 2003, New Jersey ranked 11th among the states in terms of the highest value of exports. Of the $16.8 billion total, chemical manufactures exports compose 27 percent, or $4.6 billion. Computer and electronic products were the state's second largest export. Waste and scrap exports, the fourth largest, reached $819 million in 2003, up $386 million from 1999. That industry was among the fastest growing over the period.

- Beverages and tobacco products exports had the highest growth, tripling from 1999 to 2003. Also showing high percentage increases were exports of used merchandise, up 161 percent, and oil and gas extraction, up 105 percent. Livestock and livestock products had the largest percentage decrease, down 81 percent, and transportation equipment had the largest dollar drop, with a decline of $145 million.

- New Jersey exported more than 22 percent of its products to Canada, followed by the United Kingdom (8 percent), and Germany (6 percent). Exports to Turkey, ranked 19th, increased sixfold from 1999 to 2003. More than half of these products were classified as transportation equipment.

Table E-35. Total U.S. Exports (Origin of Movement) via New Jersey, 1999–2003—Continued

(Top 25 commodities and top 25 countries based on 2003 dollar value.)

Industry, commodity, and country	Value (millions of dollars)					Percent change, 1999–2003	Percent share of state total				
	1999	2000	2001	2002	2003		1999	2000	2001	2002	2003
TOTAL AND PERCENT SHARE OF U.S. TOTAL	15 354.5	18 637.6	18 945.8	17 001.5	16 817.7	9.53	2.22	2.39	2.59	2.45	2.32
Top 25 Countries	13 493.2	16 654.9	16 914.8	15 191.2	15 012.6	11.26	87.88	89.36	89.28	89.35	89.27
1. Canada	3 727.7	4 193.9	3 914.2	3 705.3	3 756.5	0.77	24.28	22.50	20.66	21.79	22.34
2. United Kingdom	1 199.7	1 772.8	1 638.6	1 335.5	1 407.0	17.28	7.81	9.51	8.65	7.86	8.37
3. Germany	693.0	748.7	1 036.5	910.5	1 021.8	47.46	4.51	4.02	5.47	5.36	6.08
4. Israel	799.4	958.6	948.6	887.0	938.5	17.39	5.21	5.14	5.01	5.22	5.58
5. Japan	1 271.6	1 414.0	1 469.5	930.4	936.1	-26.38	8.28	7.59	7.76	5.47	5.57
6. Mexico	820.6	1 076.7	1 106.6	861.7	830.8	1.25	5.34	5.78	5.84	5.07	4.94
7. France	493.9	533.5	657.6	622.0	602.5	21.97	3.22	2.86	3.47	3.66	3.58
8. South Korea	292.5	416.1	725.7	680.2	562.2	92.20	1.91	2.23	3.83	4.00	3.34
9. Belgium	388.3	398.5	600.6	539.9	556.9	43.42	2.53	2.14	3.17	3.18	3.31
10. China	190.1	258.8	397.7	423.4	502.2	164.18	1.24	1.39	2.10	2.49	2.99
11. Italy	309.6	885.4	546.0	456.5	470.4	51.92	2.02	4.75	2.88	2.68	2.80
12. Netherlands	828.7	824.0	611.0	482.5	463.0	-44.13	5.40	4.42	3.22	2.84	2.75
13. Hong Kong	263.9	322.7	417.8	306.2	365.0	38.33	1.72	1.73	2.21	1.80	2.17
14. Taiwan	321.3	446.6	531.0	720.5	335.9	4.54	2.09	2.40	2.80	4.24	2.00
15. Australia	241.6	506.0	272.0	274.3	306.8	26.98	1.57	2.71	1.44	1.61	1.82
16. Switzerland	276.9	300.5	435.4	462.3	275.5	-0.49	1.80	1.61	2.30	2.72	1.64
17. Singapore	262.5	272.6	311.9	258.1	275.4	4.90	1.71	1.46	1.65	1.52	1.64
18. Saudi Arabia	285.8	285.3	238.8	236.8	253.8	-11.16	1.86	1.53	1.26	1.39	1.51
19. Turkey	42.1	48.7	147.4	163.5	253.1	501.51	0.27	0.26	0.78	0.96	1.51
20. Brazil	289.1	337.3	286.0	247.9	232.6	-19.54	1.88	1.81	1.51	1.46	1.38
21. Ireland	99.5	141.3	244.7	248.0	200.6	101.51	0.65	0.76	1.29	1.46	1.19
22. Spain	126.7	125.9	108.5	123.5	129.3	2.10	0.82	0.68	0.57	0.73	0.77
23. India	68.4	72.8	116.1	148.7	129.3	89.05	0.45	0.39	0.61	0.87	0.77
24. South Africa	141.3	224.1	78.3	92.2	105.6	-25.26	0.92	1.20	0.41	0.54	0.63
25. Thailand	59.1	90.0	74.0	74.1	101.9	72.34	0.38	0.48	0.39	0.44	0.61

Table E-36. Total U.S. Exports (Origin of Movement) via New Mexico, 1999–2003

(Top 25 commodities and top 25 countries based on 2003 dollar value.)

Industry, commodity, and country	Value (millions of dollars)					Percent change, 1999–2003	Percent share of state total				
	1999	2000	2001	2002	2003		1999	2000	2001	2002	2003
TOTAL AND PERCENT SHARE OF U.S. TOTAL	3 133.5	2 390.5	1 404.6	1 196.1	2 325.6	-25.78	0.45	0.31	0.19	0.17	0.32
Manufactures (NAICS Code)	3 099.0	2 346.1	1 353.0	1 076.7	2 241.5	-27.67	98.90	98.14	96.32	90.02	96.38
Processed foods (311)	4.5	8.0	10.9	10.1	24.1	430.70	0.14	0.33	0.77	0.84	1.04
Beverages and tobacco products (312)	0.1	0.1	0.0	0.0	0.0	X	0.00	0.00	0.00	0.00	0.00
Fabric mill products (313)	0.7	1.8	2.3	4.7	19.3	2 616.64	0.02	0.07	0.16	0.39	0.83
Non-apparel textile products (314)	0.9	1.0	0.8	0.6	0.3	-67.74	0.03	0.04	0.06	0.05	0.01
Apparel manufactures (315)	1.3	0.7	1.3	1.2	5.1	299.53	0.04	0.03	0.09	0.10	0.22
Leather and related products (316)	0.4	0.2	0.3	0.4	0.4	-12.84	0.01	0.01	0.02	0.03	0.02
Wood products (321)	3.1	3.7	4.6	6.8	5.8	84.79	0.10	0.15	0.33	0.57	0.25
Paper products (322)	2.7	1.4	1.6	8.1	13.3	391.13	0.09	0.06	0.12	0.68	0.57
Printing and related products (323)	1.2	0.8	0.6	1.7	1.6	29.08	0.04	0.03	0.04	0.14	0.07
Petroleum and coal products (324)	0.8	0.2	1.8	1.0	0.7	-13.89	0.03	0.01	0.13	0.08	0.03
Chemical manufactures (325)	87.8	90.5	45.5	26.2	31.8	-63.72	2.80	3.79	3.24	2.19	1.37
Plastics and rubber products (326)	6.4	22.8	12.4	3.8	19.0	196.40	0.20	0.95	0.88	0.31	0.82
Non-metallic mineral products (327)	2.5	2.5	15.5	20.7	26.6	984.53	0.08	0.10	1.10	1.73	1.15
Primary metal manufactures (331)	3.6	9.1	6.6	6.6	12.2	242.57	0.11	0.38	0.47	0.56	0.53
Fabricated metal products (332)	9.7	36.1	18.2	13.0	65.4	572.91	0.31	1.51	1.29	1.09	2.81
Machinery manufactures (333)	38.0	46.4	53.0	79.3	72.7	91.06	1.21	1.94	3.77	6.63	3.13
Computer and electronic products (334)	2 860.7	2 043.7	1 107.0	788.0	1 813.0	-36.63	91.30	85.49	78.81	65.88	77.96
Electrical equipment, appliances, and parts (335)	11.3	19.9	16.9	29.3	27.7	144.45	0.36	0.83	1.20	2.45	1.19
Transportation equipment (336)	51.6	40.4	31.0	57.9	86.9	68.38	1.65	1.69	2.21	4.84	3.74
Furniture and related products (337)	0.4	0.6	1.9	0.5	0.6	32.40	0.01	0.03	0.14	0.04	0.02
Miscellaneous manufactures (339)	11.2	16.0	20.9	16.8	15.2	35.65	0.36	0.67	1.49	1.40	0.65
Agricultural and Livestock Products (NAICS Code)	9.1	17.8	15.5	16.8	19.7	115.99	0.29	0.74	1.11	1.40	0.85
Agricultural products (111)	6.0	11.8	10.4	13.5	18.6	212.17	0.19	0.50	0.74	1.13	0.80
Livestock and livestock products (112)	3.2	5.9	5.2	3.3	1.1	-64.76	0.10	0.25	0.37	0.27	0.05
Other Commodities (NAICS Code)	25.3	26.6	36.1	102.7	64.4	154.29	0.81	1.11	2.57	8.58	2.77
Forestry and logging (113)	0.1	0.1	0.3	0.0	0.0	X	0.00	0.00	0.02	0.00	0.00
Fishing, hunting, and trapping (114)	0.0	0.0	0.0	0.2	0.0	X	0.00	0.00	0.00	0.02	0.00
Oil and gas extraction (211)	3.4	6.1	4.0	11.3	18.1	436.82	0.11	0.25	0.28	0.95	0.78
Mining (212)	7.5	4.1	6.8	9.4	7.1	-5.89	0.24	0.17	0.49	0.79	0.30
Waste and scrap (910)	0.2	0.4	1.3	13.6	3.0	1 652.66	0.01	0.02	0.09	1.14	0.13
Public administration (920)	1.4	3.7	2.5	41.1	5.0	259.36	0.04	0.16	0.18	3.44	0.21
Goods returned to Canada (980)	2.7	2.5	2.3	2.7	1.8	-33.48	0.09	0.10	0.16	0.23	0.08
Special classification provisions (990)	10.1	9.7	18.9	24.2	29.5	191.81	0.32	0.41	1.34	2.02	1.27
Publishing industries (except Internet) (511)	0.0	0.0	0.0	0.0	0.0	0.0	0.00	0.00	0.00	0.00	0.00
TOTAL AND PERCENT SHARE OF U.S. TOTAL	3 133.5	2 390.5	1 404.6	1 196.1	2 325.6	-25.78	0.45	0.31	0.19	0.17	0.32
Top 25 Commodities (HS Code)	154.4	209.2	189.1	820.4	1 952.3	1 164.44	4.93	8.75	13.46	68.59	83.95
1. Digital monolithic integrated circuits (854221)	0.0	0.0	0.0	623.2	1 617.6	X	0.45	0.31	0.19	0.17	69.56
2. Non-digital monolithic integrated circuits (854229)	0.0	0.0	0.0	29.9	55.1	X	0.00	0.00	0.00	2.50	2.37
3. Ceramic receptacles for agriculture (690990)	1.1	0.2	11.3	18.1	23.9	2 072.73	0.04	0.01	0.80	1.51	1.03
4. Taps and cocks for pipe thermostatic control (848180)	...	8.8	5.0	5.0	21.8	...	...	0.37	0.36	0.42	0.94
5. Vacuum pumps (841410)	1.8	6.1	9.4	13.7	20.5	1 038.89	0.06	0.26	0.67	1.15	0.88
6. Electrical apparatus for line telephony or line telegraphy (851780)	7.3	21.3	37.7	13.3	17.6	141.10	0.23	0.89	2.68	1.11	0.76
7. Parts of airplanes or helicopters (880330)	16.0	1.1	2.5	10.6	14.6	-8.75	0.51	0.05	0.18	0.89	0.63
8. Passenger vehicles, spark-ignition, > 3,000 cc (870324)	1.0	0.5	0.1	11.7	13.4	1 240.00	0.03	0.02	0.01	0.98	0.58
9. Parts of apparatus for line telephony or telegraphy (851790)	3.2	30.3	9.9	6.4	13.2	312.50	0.10	1.27	0.70	0.54	0.57
10. Parts for taps and cocks, for pipes (848190)	...	2.1	1.6	0.1	13.0	...	...	0.09	0.11	0.01	0.56
11. Articles of iron or steel (732690)	...	11.5	6.1	0.9	13.0	...	...	0.48	0.43	0.08	0.56
12. Electrical apparatus for line telephony or telegraphy (851750)	...	0.5	0.5	4.6	12.1	...	...	0.02	0.04	0.38	0.52
13. Swelling or roasting cereal and product (190410)	...	0.3	2.6	1.2	10.3	...	...	0.01	0.19	0.10	0.44
14. Fuel, lubricating/cooling pumps for piston engines (841330)	0.0	3.5	2.6	13.7	9.9	X	0.00	0.15	0.19	1.15	0.43
15. Propane, liquefied (271112)	...	3.3	1.1	5.3	9.3	...	...	0.14	0.08	0.44	0.40
16. Articles of plastics (392690)	...	13.8	6.5	0.7	9.2	...	...	0.58	0.46	0.06	0.40
17. Parts and accessories of motor vehicles (870899)	...	2.6	3.9	2.6	9.1	...	...	0.11	0.28	0.22	0.39
18. Exports of military equipment (980320)	2.9	3.2	10.3	7.4	8.9	206.90	0.09	0.13	0.73	0.62	0.38
19. Petroleum gases, liquified (271119)	1.8	2.8	2.9	6.0	8.8	388.89	0.06	0.12	0.21	0.50	0.38
20. Fertilizers (310000)	77.6	77.7	29.6	15.0	8.8	-88.66	2.48	3.25	2.11	1.25	0.38
21. Passenger vehicles for snow; golf carts and similar (870310)	...	0.1	0.1	2.1	8.6	...	...	0.00	0.01	0.18	0.37
22. Parts of aircraft (880390)	22.3	9.8	16.2	13.1	8.6	-61.43	0.71	0.41	1.15	1.10	0.37
23. Nuts, fresh or dried, shelled or not (080290)	1.5	0.5	1.5	5.7	8.6	473.33	0.05	0.02	0.11	0.48	0.37
24. Parts of transmission or reception apparatus (852990)	18.9	11.3	28.4	11.8	8.5	-55.03	0.60	0.47	2.02	0.99	0.37
25. Sewing thread synthetic filaments, retail or not (540110)	...	0.0	0.0	0.0	7.9	...	...	0.00	0.00	0.00	0.34

X = Not applicable.
. . . = Not available.

Exports from New Mexico

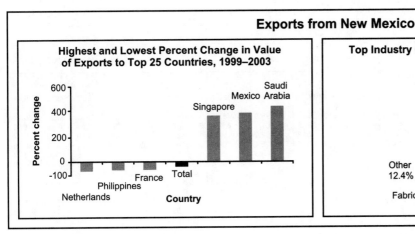

Highest and Lowest Percent Change in Value of Exports to Top 25 Countries, 1999–2003

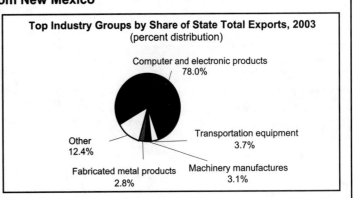

Top Industry Groups by Share of State Total Exports, 2003
(percent distribution)

- The value of New Mexico's exports fell from $3.1 billion in 1999 to $2.3 billion in 2003. As a result, the state's national ranking by value of exports fell from 34th to 40th. A decline in exports of computer and electronic products, down $1 billion, accounted for New Mexico's drop in total exports of $808 million. Despite this, computer and electronic products remained by far the state's leading export, accounting for 91 percent of total exports in 1999, and 78 percent of total exports in 2003.

- In 2002, New Mexico began exporting digital monolithic integrated circuits. By 2003, they became the state's top commodity export. While valued at $623 million in 2002, they jumped to $1.6 billion in 2003.

- The Philippines and South Korea were the top recipients of New Mexico's exports in 2003. Computer and electronic exports represented 99.9 percent of the exports to the Philippines and nearly 85 percent of those to South Korea.

Table E-36. Total U.S. Exports (Origin of Movement) via New Mexico, 1999–2003—*Continued*

(Top 25 commodities and top 25 countries based on 2003 dollar value.)

Industry, commodity, and country	Value (millions of dollars)					Percent change, 1999–2003	Percent share of state total				
	1999	2000	2001	2002	2003		1999	2000	2001	2002	2003
TOTAL AND PERCENT SHARE OF U.S. TOTAL	3 133.5	2 390.5	1 404.6	1 196.1	2 325.6	-25.78	0.45	0.31	0.19	0.17	0.32
Top 25 Countries	3 075.8	2 331.8	1 344.5	1 111.6	2 291.2	-25.51	98.16	97.54	95.72	92.94	98.52
1. Philippines	1 021.0	416.9	258.5	180.4	441.1	-56.80	32.58	17.44	18.40	15.08	18.97
2. South Korea	860.4	461.0	101.0	105.3	423.7	-50.76	27.46	19.28	7.19	8.80	18.22
3. Mexico	49.9	126.6	111.7	116.6	242.0	384.66	1.59	5.30	7.95	9.75	10.41
4. Malaysia	389.1	359.1	167.9	91.7	224.9	-42.22	12.42	15.02	11.95	7.67	9.67
5. China	220.4	118.8	34.7	47.7	206.8	-6.19	7.03	4.97	2.47	3.99	8.89
6. Taiwan	72.4	161.2	89.3	71.9	201.1	177.95	2.31	6.74	6.36	6.01	8.65
7. Canada	77.4	134.0	96.4	98.2	117.9	52.29	2.47	5.60	6.86	8.21	5.07
8. Costa Rica	38.3	57.1	86.9	122.6	103.9	170.86	1.22	2.39	6.19	10.25	4.47
9. Ireland	56.9	58.7	49.7	31.9	74.7	31.14	1.82	2.45	3.54	2.67	3.21
10. Thailand	46.0	55.3	57.9	16.5	38.4	-16.48	1.47	2.32	4.12	1.38	1.65
11. Japan	56.4	167.3	73.2	50.3	33.8	-40.05	1.80	7.00	5.21	4.20	1.45
12. Israel	25.1	83.5	52.3	24.5	31.3	24.47	0.80	3.49	3.72	2.05	1.34
13. Germany	33.5	23.5	35.6	24.5	21.8	-34.91	1.07	0.98	2.53	2.04	0.94
14. Singapore	4.4	5.8	12.4	19.3	21.1	376.45	0.14	0.24	0.88	1.61	0.91
15. United Kingdom	18.0	18.1	19.9	31.5	20.4	13.22	0.57	0.76	1.41	2.63	0.88
16. France	42.0	36.7	44.7	15.0	18.3	-56.34	1.34	1.54	3.18	1.25	0.79
17. Saudi Arabia	2.4	2.0	2.2	3.8	13.8	479.36	0.08	0.08	0.15	0.32	0.59
18. Belgium	2.6	3.5	2.5	7.5	11.7	352.34	0.08	0.14	0.18	0.62	0.50
19. Italy	2.2	1.7	4.8	3.9	8.8	299.32	0.07	0.07	0.34	0.33	0.38
20. Netherlands	19.9	16.5	20.1	29.8	8.1	-59.22	0.63	0.69	1.43	2.49	0.35
21. Hong Kong	12.3	5.0	5.0	5.3	7.5	-39.26	0.39	0.21	0.36	0.44	0.32
22. Australia	14.3	4.4	10.0	5.7	6.5	-54.49	0.46	0.18	0.72	0.47	0.28
23. Brazil	4.6	10.2	2.4	3.5	5.9	28.09	0.15	0.43	0.17	0.29	0.25
24. Austria	5.3	4.0	5.1	4.3	4.3	-18.68	0.17	0.17	0.37	0.36	0.18
25. Egypt	0.9	0.9	0.2	0.0	3.5	281.47	0.03	0.04	0.01	0.00	0.15

Table E-37. Total U.S. Exports (Origin of Movement) via New York, 1999–2003

(Top 25 commodities and top 25 countries based on 2003 dollar value.)

Industry, commodity, and country	Value (millions of dollars)					Percent change, 1999–2003	Percent share of state total				
	1999	2000	2001	2002	2003		1999	2000	2001	2002	2003
TOTAL AND PERCENT SHARE OF U.S. TOTAL	37 067.5	42 846.0	42 172.1	36 976.8	39 180.7	5.70	5.35	5.49	5.77	5.33	5.41
Manufactures (NAICS Code)	32 950.3	37 643.7	36 399.1	32 275.3	34 481.1	4.65	88.89	87.86	86.31	87.29	88.01
Processed foods (311)	482.7	554.5	661.2	701.1	620.7	28.60	1.30	1.29	1.57	1.90	1.58
Beverages and tobacco products (312)	77.9	77.6	76.6	62.7	68.0	-12.67	0.21	0.00	0.18	0.17	0.17
Fabric mill products (313)	402.2	423.6	382.0	328.4	309.6	-23.04	1.09	0.99	0.91	0.89	0.79
Non-apparel textile products (314)	67.7	87.1	106.2	89.3	89.2	31.68	0.18	0.20	0.25	0.24	0.23
Apparel manufactures (315)	350.5	391.8	423.1	347.7	309.6	-11.67	0.95	0.91	1.00	0.94	0.79
Leather and related products (316)	130.1	141.9	135.6	108.2	96.7	-25.68	0.35	0.33	0.32	0.29	0.25
Wood products (321)	210.7	224.3	192.5	207.9	211.9	0.57	0.57	0.52	0.46	0.56	0.54
Paper products (322)	551.9	640.4	670.4	536.5	571.9	3.62	1.49	1.49	1.59	1.45	1.46
Printing and related products (323)	653.2	740.8	839.2	578.2	571.0	-12.59	1.76	1.73	1.99	1.56	1.46
Petroleum and coal products (324)	58.3	89.5	145.6	158.4	93.7	60.69	0.16	0.21	0.35	0.43	0.24
Chemical manufactures (325)	3 901.5	4 680.0	4 406.7	3 939.9	4 315.1	10.60	10.53	10.92	10.45	10.66	11.01
Plastics and rubber products (326)	544.8	768.3	702.7	744.5	742.4	36.27	1.47	1.79	1.67	2.01	1.89
Non-metallic mineral products (327)	351.8	467.3	494.7	393.3	409.3	16.32	0.95	1.09	1.17	1.06	1.04
Primary metal manufactures (331)	4 318.3	4 766.7	3 892.9	1 676.0	2 858.1	-33.81	11.65	11.13	9.23	4.53	7.29
Fabricated metal products (332)	781.0	759.4	705.8	727.5	789.8	1.13	2.11	1.77	1.67	1.97	2.02
Machinery manufactures (333)	4 625.1	4 994.9	4 823.6	4 181.3	4 138.4	-10.52	12.48	11.66	11.44	11.31	10.56
Computer and electronic products (334)	6 001.1	7 438.9	6 537.6	6 297.3	6 305.9	5.08	16.19	17.36	15.50	17.03	16.09
Electrical equipment, appliances, and parts (335)	901.5	1 139.1	1 100.4	987.7	963.5	6.87	2.43	2.66	2.61	2.67	2.46
Transportation equipment (336)	3 865.6	3 959.2	4 467.0	4 509.5	4 532.9	17.26	10.43	9.24	10.59	12.20	11.57
Furniture and related products (337)	78.4	97.8	84.7	88.8	84.7	7.99	0.21	0.23	0.20	0.24	0.22
Miscellaneous manufactures (339)	4 595.7	5 200.8	5 550.7	5 611.2	6 398.8	39.23	12.40	12.14	13.16	15.17	16.33
Agricultural and Livestock Products (NAICS Code)	261.2	242.2	268.8	305.8	232.8	-10.88	0.70	0.57	0.64	0.83	0.59
Agricultural products (111)	174.6	157.6	192.1	251.9	173.8	-0.46	0.47	0.37	0.46	0.68	0.44
Livestock and livestock products (112)	86.6	84.6	76.7	53.9	59.0	-31.87	0.23	0.20	0.18	0.15	0.15
Other Commodities (NAICS Code)	3 856.0	4 960.0	5 504.1	4 395.7	4 466.8	15.84	10.40	11.58	13.05	11.89	11.40
Forestry and logging (113)	67.1	81.7	71.6	76.5	96.6	43.96	0.18	0.19	0.17	0.21	0.25
Fishing, hunting, and trapping (114)	53.9	55.6	41.3	46.9	35.5	-34.11	0.15	0.13	0.10	0.13	0.09
Oil and gas extraction (211)	1.9	2.4	1.7	2.0	8.2	330.20	0.01	0.01	0.00	0.01	0.02
Mining (212)	31.4	35.5	41.3	48.1	46.4	47.65	0.08	0.08	0.10	0.13	0.12
Waste and scrap (910)	398.6	533.9	637.8	677.4	908.3	127.84	1.08	1.25	1.51	1.83	2.32
Used merchandise (920)	1 519.4	2 217.5	2 761.5	1 720.9	1 661.3	9.34	4.10	5.18	6.55	4.65	4.24
Goods returned to Canada (980)	240.7	202.7	184.0	139.2	110.2	-54.22	0.65	0.47	0.44	0.38	0.28
Special classification provisions (990)	1 543.0	1 830.7	1 765.2	1 684.7	1 585.5	2.76	4.16	4.27	4.19	4.56	4.05
Publishing industries (except Internet) (511)	0.0	0.0	0.0	0.0	14.8	X	0.00	0.00	0.00	0.00	0.04
TOTAL AND PERCENT SHARE OF U.S. TOTAL	37 067.5	42 846.0	42 172.1	36 976.8	39 180.7	5.70	5.35	5.49	5.77	5.33	5.41
Top 25 Commodities (HS Code)	13 511.3	16 276.5	16 283.4	14 339.4	16 745.0	23.93	36.45	37.99	38.61	38.78	42.74
1. Diamonds, non-industrial, worked (710239)	2 591.9	3 162.7	3 293.1	3 473.5	4 082.6	57.51	6.99	7.38	7.81	9.39	10.42
2. Gold, non-monetary, unwrought (710812)	3 060.0	3 424.5	2 592.8	318.9	1 623.2	-46.95	8.26	7.99	6.15	0.86	4.14
3. Paintings, drawings, and pastels by hand (970110)	830.7	1 611.1	1 929.2	1 234.8	1 243.0	49.63	2.24	3.76	4.57	3.34	3.17
4. Parts and accessories for automatic data processing (847330)	795.2	956.2	994.5	1 035.1	1 114.8	40.19	2.15	2.23	2.36	2.80	2.85
5. Parts of airplanes or helicopters (880330)	903.3	898.2	974.4	979.2	950.4	5.21	2.44	2.10	2.31	2.65	2.43
6. Jewelry and parts thereof, of precious metal (711319)	677.8	429.5	815.1	778.9	847.7	25.07	1.83	1.00	1.93	2.11	2.16
7. Digital monolithic integrated circuits (854221)	0.0	0.0	0.0	748.5	742.0	X	0.00	0.00	0.00	2.02	1.89
8. Turbojet and turbo-propeller parts (841191)	483.4	648.9	652.2	500.0	556.3	15.08	1.30	1.51	1.55	1.35	1.42
9. Spark-ignition internal combustion piston engines (840734)	456.9	466.7	541.9	590.4	539.7	18.12	1.23	1.09	1.28	1.60	1.38
10. Gas turbines (841182)	236.1	142.1	222.7	474.8	502.8	112.96	0.64	0.33	0.53	1.28	1.28
11. Aluminum alloy rectangular plates, > 0.2 mm thick (760612)	553.6	594.2	473.0	514.4	494.8	-10.62	1.49	1.39	1.12	1.39	1.26
12. Other photographic film rolls for color photograph (370255)	445.5	595.0	466.2	479.3	491.6	10.35	1.20	1.39	1.11	1.30	1.25
13. Gas turbine parts (841199)	640.1	639.0	659.1	527.5	401.4	-37.29	1.73	1.49	1.56	1.43	1.02
14. Printed circuits (853400)	391.9	442.0	446.9	354.2	377.1	-3.78	1.06	1.03	1.06	0.96	0.96
15. Automatic data processing input or output units (847160)	397.3	466.0	423.9	420.2	326.0	-17.95	1.07	1.09	1.01	1.14	0.83
16. Parts and accessories of motor vehicles bodies (870829)	244.4	216.8	193.9	298.0	288.3	17.96	0.66	0.51	0.46	0.81	0.74
17. Under-carriages and parts for aircraft (880320)	324.7	255.3	343.0	353.1	288.1	-11.27	0.88	0.60	0.81	0.95	0.74
18. Printed books and brochures (490199)	295.2	348.2	350.0	310.9	266.6	-9.69	0.80	0.81	0.83	0.84	0.68
19. Retail medicaments in measured dose (300490)	. . .	201.2	239.7	146.0	264.9	. . .	. . .	0.47	0.57	0.39	0.68
20. Gold waste and scrap, without other precious metals (711291)	. . .	0.0	0.0	176.6	262.7	. . .	. . .	0.00	0.00	0.48	0.67
21. Beauty and skin care preparations (330499)	. . .	217.6	217.6	180.5	255.6	. . .	. . .	0.51	0.52	0.49	0.65
22. Radar apparatus (852610)	. . .	21.5	52.2	52.7	232.2	. . .	. . .	0.05	0.12	0.14	0.59
23. Refrigerating/freezing equipment (841869)	. . .	35.8	32.0	33.6	212.9	. . .	. . .	0.08	0.08	0.09	0.54
24. Diamonds excluding industrial unworked (710231)	183.3	209.4	168.2	205.7	190.6	3.98	0.49	0.49	0.40	0.56	0.49
25. Parts of transmission or reception apparatus (852990)	. . .	294.6	201.8	152.6	189.7	. . .	. . .	0.69	0.48	0.41	0.48

X = Not applicable.
. . . = Not available.

Exports from New York

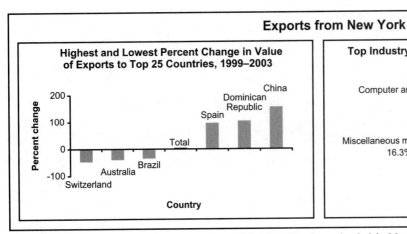

Highest and Lowest Percent Change in Value of Exports to Top 25 Countries, 1999–2003

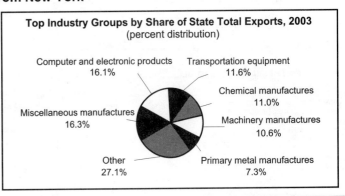

Top Industry Groups by Share of State Total Exports, 2003
(percent distribution)

Computer and electronic products 16.1%
Transportation equipment 11.6%
Chemical manufactures 11.0%
Machinery manufactures 10.6%
Primary metal manufactures 7.3%
Other 27.1%
Miscellaneous manufactures 16.3%

- With exports worth $39 billion in 2003, New York ranked third behind California and Texas as a major exporting state. The two largest export industries are miscellaneous manufactures and computer and electronic products, which together account for more than 32 percent of New York's exports. Miscellaneous manufactures increased by more than $1.8 billion from 1999 to 2003, which represented the bulk of New York's total dollar increase of $2.1 billion during that period. Since 1999, primary metal manufactures have fallen nearly $1.5 billion, or almost 34 percent. These exports accounted for just over 7 percent in 2003 of New York's total, down from close to 12 percent in 1999.

- In 2003, non-industrial diamonds exports were New York's top commodity. With these exports worth $4.1 billion, up more than 57 percent from 1999, they accounted for more than 10 percent of the state's total exports in 2003. Non-monetary gold ranked second with $1.6 billion, or 4 percent of exports.

- While Canada remains the top export country, the value of exports from New York fell more than 14 percent from 1999 to 2003. Exports to China, ranked ninth, were up 147 percent from 1999, making it the fastest growing destination for the state's exports.

Table E-37. Total U.S. Exports (Origin of Movement) via New York, 1999–2003—Continued

(Top 25 commodities and top 25 countries based on 2003 dollar value.)

Industry, commodity, and country	Value (millions of dollars)					Percent change, 1999–2003	Percent share of state total				
	1999	2000	2001	2002	2003		1999	2000	2001	2002	2003
TOTAL AND PERCENT SHARE OF U.S. TOTAL	37 067.5	42 846.0	42 172.1	36 976.8	39 180.7	5.70	5.35	5.49	5.77	5.33	5.41
Top 25 Countries	34 044.6	39 595.7	38 549.8	33 342.1	35 434.7	4.08	91.84	92.41	91.41	90.17	90.44
1. Canada	10 580.7	11 229.9	9 760.1	9 221.3	9 041.4	-14.55	28.54	26.21	23.14	24.94	23.08
2. United Kingdom	2 887.7	3 747.3	3 130.8	2 369.1	3 283.1	13.69	7.79	8.75	7.42	6.41	8.38
3. Japan	2 510.2	3 487.8	3 613.3	2 823.2	2 625.1	4.58	6.77	8.14	8.57	7.64	6.70
4. Israel	1 681.2	1 857.9	2 021.1	2 139.9	2 371.7	41.07	4.54	4.34	4.79	5.79	6.05
5. Switzerland	3 449.4	3 945.1	4 058.1	1 319.4	1 770.3	-48.68	9.31	9.21	9.62	3.57	4.52
6. Germany	1 610.4	1 795.9	1 801.4	1 499.6	1 723.2	7.01	4.34	4.19	4.27	4.06	4.40
7. Mexico	1 406.0	1 773.8	1 851.8	1 897.7	1 704.7	21.25	3.79	4.14	4.39	5.13	4.35
8. Belgium	1 028.9	1 275.8	1 355.3	1 366.9	1 669.4	62.25	2.78	2.98	3.21	3.70	4.26
9. China	584.8	777.8	1 036.2	1 118.1	1 445.2	147.11	1.58	1.82	2.46	3.02	3.69
10. Hong Kong	1 072.9	1 409.3	1 373.2	1 291.1	1 377.6	28.40	2.89	3.29	3.26	3.49	3.52
11. France	1 068.7	1 417.0	1 481.2	1 317.4	1 261.3	18.02	2.88	3.31	3.51	3.56	3.22
12. South Korea	636.1	902.9	880.2	1 038.1	1 056.1	66.02	1.72	2.11	2.09	2.81	2.70
13. Netherlands	718.7	717.9	938.5	867.0	832.6	15.86	1.94	1.68	2.23	2.34	2.13
14. Italy	539.4	658.7	676.9	796.3	735.5	36.35	1.46	1.54	1.61	2.15	1.88
15. India	431.4	518.5	525.8	547.6	660.5	53.13	1.16	1.21	1.25	1.48	1.69
16. Taiwan	528.9	641.2	562.1	551.6	621.8	17.56	1.43	1.50	1.33	1.49	1.59
17. Ireland	266.7	337.1	241.5	253.2	446.0	67.27	0.72	0.79	0.57	0.68	1.14
18. Singapore	440.4	546.4	473.6	458.2	424.1	-3.69	1.19	1.28	1.12	1.24	1.08
19. Spain	227.0	352.5	711.2	460.3	413.0	81.89	0.61	0.82	1.69	1.24	1.05
20. Brazil	643.3	693.3	532.3	530.8	395.9	-38.47	1.74	1.62	1.26	1.44	1.01
21. Australia	706.0	583.4	403.1	365.5	392.4	-44.41	1.90	1.36	0.96	0.99	1.00
22. Saudi Arabia	510.9	302.6	329.6	313.2	347.5	-31.97	1.38	0.71	0.78	0.85	0.89
23. Dominican Republic	161.8	164.9	228.6	250.3	315.9	95.33	0.44	0.38	0.54	0.68	0.81
24. Thailand	188.0	294.9	274.6	261.1	292.5	55.55	0.51	0.69	0.65	0.70	0.75
25. United Arab Emirates	165.2	163.6	289.6	286.0	227.7	37.87	0.45	0.38	0.69	0.77	0.58

Table E-38. Total U.S. Exports (Origin of Movement) via North Carolina, 1999–2003

(Top 25 commodities and top 25 countries based on 2003 dollar value.)

Industry, commodity, and country	Value (millions of dollars)					Percent change, 1999–2003	Percent share of state total				
	1999	2000	2001	2002	2003		1999	2000	2001	2002	2003
TOTAL AND PERCENT SHARE OF U.S. TOTAL	15 007.1	17 945.9	16 798.9	14 718.5	16 198.7	7.94	2.17	2.30	2.30	2.12	2.24
Manufactures (NAICS Code)	13 854.7	16 829.1	15 726.4	13 817.2	15 319.1	10.57	92.32	93.78	93.62	93.88	94.57
Processed foods (311)	155.6	201.8	266.0	215.2	219.8	41.29	1.04	1.12	1.58	1.46	1.36
Beverages and tobacco products (312)	776.1	904.1	657.2	462.6	399.1	-48.58	5.17	0.00	3.91	3.14	2.46
Fabric mill products (313)	929.6	1 279.0	1 204.7	1 297.0	1 375.9	48.01	6.19	7.13	7.17	8.81	8.49
Non-apparel textile products (314)	211.8	171.5	152.3	146.6	129.6	-38.85	1.41	0.96	0.91	1.00	0.80
Apparel manufactures (315)	1 028.1	1 196.3	1 242.0	1 153.8	1 119.0	8.84	6.85	6.67	7.39	7.84	6.91
Leather and related products (316)	93.3	104.2	66.4	35.2	22.7	-75.72	0.62	0.58	0.40	0.24	0.14
Wood products (321)	200.4	202.4	164.6	178.4	177.4	-11.44	1.34	1.13	0.98	1.21	1.10
Paper products (322)	526.6	652.8	561.8	535.8	553.7	5.15	3.51	3.64	3.34	3.64	3.42
Printing and related products (323)	39.0	38.7	55.2	70.9	45.9	17.62	0.26	0.22	0.33	0.48	0.28
Petroleum and coal products (324)	5.9	7.5	13.8	12.9	8.4	43.25	0.04	0.04	0.08	0.09	0.05
Chemical manufactures (325)	1 925.0	2 309.6	2 313.7	2 355.8	3 024.8	57.14	12.83	12.87	13.77	16.01	18.67
Plastics and rubber products (326)	588.4	758.8	702.3	714.1	793.1	34.78	3.92	4.23	4.18	4.85	4.90
Non-metallic mineral products (327)	748.9	1 162.6	1 092.9	349.8	353.9	-52.74	4.99	6.48	6.51	2.38	2.18
Primary metal manufactures (331)	289.1	271.2	282.8	229.2	239.5	-17.17	1.93	1.51	1.68	1.56	1.48
Fabricated metal products (332)	420.0	429.9	430.7	422.9	402.0	-4.28	2.80	2.40	2.56	2.87	2.48
Machinery manufactures (333)	1 288.9	1 674.0	1 658.4	1 450.3	1 557.2	20.82	8.59	9.33	9.87	9.85	9.61
Computer and electronic products (334)	2 694.1	3 309.6	2 813.3	2 400.1	2 706.1	0.44	17.95	18.44	16.75	16.31	16.71
Electrical equipment, appliances, and parts (335)	473.8	536.5	574.4	404.3	447.2	-5.62	3.16	2.99	3.42	2.75	2.76
Transportation equipment (336)	981.9	1 083.2	905.5	855.8	1 164.3	18.58	6.54	6.04	5.39	5.81	7.19
Furniture and related products (337)	145.2	160.6	169.5	153.0	175.6	20.99	0.97	0.90	1.01	1.04	1.08
Miscellaneous manufactures (339)	333.1	374.8	398.8	373.7	404.1	21.32	2.22	2.09	2.37	2.54	2.49
Agricultural and Livestock Products (NAICS Code)	808.7	759.9	730.1	586.4	546.2	-32.46	5.39	4.23	4.35	3.98	3.37
Agricultural products (111)	803.0	754.1	723.3	583.3	540.9	-32.64	5.35	4.20	4.31	3.96	3.34
Livestock and livestock products (112)	5.7	5.8	6.8	3.1	5.3	-6.86	0.04	0.03	0.04	0.02	0.03
Other Commodities (NAICS Code)	343.7	356.9	342.5	314.9	333.4	-3.00	2.29	1.99	2.04	2.14	2.06
Forestry and logging (113)	12.4	15.1	12.7	21.2	24.7	99.47	0.08	0.08	0.08	0.14	0.15
Fishing, hunting, and trapping (114)	6.6	3.7	2.2	2.4	3.3	-49.70	0.04	0.02	0.01	0.02	0.02
Oil and gas extraction (211)	0.2	0.0	0.0	0.2	0.0	X	0.00	0.00	0.00	0.00	0.00
Mining (212)	46.1	55.8	97.0	86.6	80.1	73.66	0.31	0.31	0.58	0.59	0.49
Waste and scrap (910)	27.8	31.8	40.3	34.1	49.0	75.90	0.19	0.18	0.24	0.23	0.30
Used merchandise (920)	5.2	2.3	5.6	8.6	5.5	5.66	0.03	0.01	0.03	0.06	0.03
Goods returned to Canada (980)	24.9	39.7	34.9	19.4	15.0	-39.76	0.17	0.22	0.21	0.13	0.09
Special classification provisions (990)	220.5	208.3	149.8	142.3	149.4	-32.25	1.47	1.16	0.89	0.97	0.92
Publishing industries (except Internet) (511)	0.0	0.0	0.0	0.0	6.4	X	0.00	0.00	0.00	0.00	0.04
TOTAL AND PERCENT SHARE OF U.S. TOTAL	15 007.1	17 945.9	16 798.9	14 718.5	16 198.7	7.94	2.17	2.30	2.30	2.12	2.24
Top 25 Commodities (HS Code)	4 590.3	6 013.3	5 174.7	4 636.0	5 359.8	16.76	30.59	33.51	30.80	31.50	33.09
1. Uranium enriched in U235 (284420)	183.3	222.5	288.2	508.7	520.5	183.96	1.22	1.24	1.72	3.46	3.21
2. Tobacco, partly or wholly stemmed/stripped (240120)	749.5	705.2	660.6	512.5	455.3	-39.25	4.99	3.93	3.93	3.48	2.81
3. Parts and accessories for automatic data processing (847330)	576.1	698.3	530.4	403.3	376.2	-34.70	3.84	3.89	3.16	2.74	2.32
4. Non-digital monolithic integrated circuits (854229)	0.0	0.0	0.0	326.6	366.6	X	0.00	0.00	0.00	2.22	2.26
5. Cigarettes (240220)	732.4	860.6	605.9	424.3	359.0	-50.98	4.88	4.80	3.61	2.88	2.22
6. Chemical wood-pulp, unbleached non-coniferous (470321)	200.3	288.2	242.6	262.3	287.4	43.48	1.33	1.61	1.44	1.78	1.77
7. Automatic data processing units (847180)	192.5	82.8	96.6	128.3	244.4	26.96	1.28	0.46	0.58	0.87	1.51
8. Parts of apparatus for line telephony or telegraphy (851790)	382.5	635.6	310.7	184.6	233.2	-39.03	2.55	3.54	1.85	1.25	1.44
9. Photosensitive semiconductor devices (854140)	39.2	107.6	116.0	124.1	229.5	485.46	0.26	0.60	0.69	0.84	1.42
10. Antisera and other blood fractions (300210)	. . .	81.8	98.2	78.4	211.4	. . .	. . .	0.46	0.58	0.53	1.31
11. Digital processing units (847150)	112.9	204.8	116.1	197.0	204.1	80.78	0.75	1.14	0.69	1.34	1.26
12. Optical fibers, optical fiber bundles, and cables (900110)	631.1	973.6	915.1	207.7	202.4	-67.93	4.21	5.43	5.45	1.41	1.25
13. Retail medicaments in measured dose (300490)	107.5	120.8	117.3	158.9	181.8	69.12	0.72	0.67	0.70	1.08	1.12
14. T-shirts, singlets, tank tops, knit, cotton (610910)	163.7	214.0	233.5	206.9	179.8	9.84	1.09	1.19	1.39	1.41	1.11
15. Socks and other hosiery of cotton, knit (611592)	34.5	64.7	89.3	102.0	165.1	378.55	0.23	0.36	0.53	0.69	1.02
16. Parts and accessories of motor vehicles (870899)	142.7	135.9	103.0	104.7	160.7	12.61	0.95	0.76	0.61	0.71	0.99
17. Turbojet and turbo-propeller parts (841191)	. . .	52.1	28.1	43.8	144.0	. . .	. . .	0.29	0.17	0.30	0.89
18. Airplane and aircraft, unladen weight > 15,000 kg (880240)	. . .	64.2	80.0	18.4	132.6	. . .	. . .	0.36	0.48	0.13	0.82
19. Knitted or crocheted fabrics, cotton, dyed (600622)	. . .	0.0	0.0	75.3	114.1	. . .	. . .	0.00	0.00	0.51	0.70
20. Drive axles with differential for motor vehicles (870850)	136.0	131.5	107.1	120.8	105.8	-22.21	0.91	0.73	0.64	0.82	0.65
21. Woven cotton fabrics, blue denim >= 85 percent cotton (520942)	47.1	110.9	125.3	136.4	103.2	119.11	0.31	0.62	0.75	0.93	0.64
22. Men's or boys' trousers, not knit, cotton (620342)	81.4	126.2	101.8	93.2	100.2	23.10	0.54	0.70	0.61	0.63	0.62
23. Monofilament, cross-section > 1 mm, rods, plastics (391690)	. . .	17.2	38.0	70.9	96.6	. . .	. . .	0.10	0.23	0.48	0.60
24. Medical needles, catheters and parts (901839)	77.6	98.3	105.1	101.0	94.4	21.65	0.52	0.55	0.63	0.69	0.58
25. Medicaments containing insulin, no antibiotics (300431)	. . .	16.5	65.8	45.9	91.5	. . .	. . .	0.09	0.39	0.31	0.56

X = Not applicable.
. . . = Not available.

Exports from North Carolina

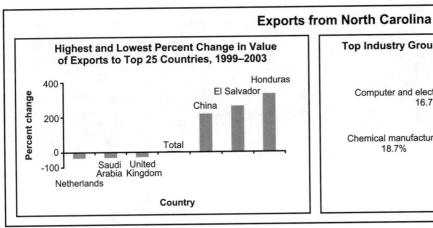

Highest and Lowest Percent Change in Value of Exports to Top 25 Countries, 1999–2003

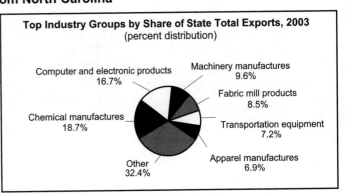

Top Industry Groups by Share of State Total Exports, 2003
(percent distribution)

Computer and electronic products 16.7%
Machinery manufactures 9.6%
Fabric mill products 8.5%
Chemical manufactures 18.7%
Transportation equipment 7.2%
Other 32.4%
Apparel manufactures 6.9%

- North Carolina's exports are valued at $16.2 billion. Exports from manufacturing industries are up nearly 10 percent from 1999, while agricultural and livestock exports are down more than 32 percent. Chemical manufactures represent more than 18 percent of North Carolina's total exports, up from less than 13 percent in 1999, and increased by more than $1 billion during this period. Computer and electronic products account for 16.7 percent, or $2.7 billion, of the state's total exports.

- Tobacco and cigarettes remain two of North Carolina's top five commodity exports. However, in 1999, they totaled nearly 10 percent of the state's exports, and by 2003 were down to about 5 percent. Uranium became North Carolina's top commodity export in 2003, with growth of 184 percent from 1999 to 2003.

- In 2003, North Carolina's top export markets were Canada ($3.9 billion), Japan ($1.6 billion), and Mexico ($1.5 billion). Exports to Honduras grew more than 327 percent from 1999, increasing from $163 million to $696 million. More than half of these exports were fabric mill products.

Table E-38. Total U.S. Exports (Origin of Movement) via North Carolina, 1999–2003—*Continued*

(Top 25 commodities and top 25 countries based on 2003 dollar value.)

Industry, commodity, and country	Value (millions of dollars)					Percent change, 1999–2003	Percent share of state total				
	1999	2000	2001	2002	2003		1999	2000	2001	2002	2003
TOTAL AND PERCENT SHARE OF U.S. TOTAL	15 007.1	17 945.9	16 798.9	14 718.5	16 198.7	7.94	2.17	2.30	2.30	2.12	2.24
Top 25 Countries	13 157.7	15 849.9	14 767.7	12 932.1	14 369.4	9.21	87.68	88.32	87.91	87.86	88.71
1. Canada	4 220.2	4 940.7	4 085.7	3 738.6	3 896.3	-7.68	28.12	27.53	24.32	25.40	24.05
2. Japan	1 310.9	1 540.4	1 372.3	1 417.2	1 590.8	21.35	8.73	8.58	8.17	9.63	9.82
3. Mexico	1 564.2	1 975.1	1 625.6	1 329.6	1 463.8	-6.42	10.42	11.01	9.68	9.03	9.04
4. Honduras	162.7	284.5	427.8	575.3	695.9	327.60	1.08	1.59	2.55	3.91	4.30
5. United Kingdom	959.1	1 199.6	969.6	735.0	687.3	-28.34	6.39	6.68	5.77	4.99	4.24
6. China	222.4	350.0	393.9	365.8	649.3	191.88	1.48	1.95	2.34	2.49	4.01
7. Germany	674.9	767.1	683.4	604.5	610.8	-9.50	4.50	4.27	4.07	4.11	3.77
8. Hong Kong	307.5	384.4	753.4	420.4	424.1	37.92	2.05	2.14	4.48	2.86	2.62
9. South Korea	225.9	416.4	423.1	369.2	393.4	74.13	1.51	2.32	2.52	2.51	2.43
10. France	378.1	435.0	347.8	251.8	360.5	-4.66	2.52	2.42	2.07	1.71	2.23
11. Netherlands	514.9	453.5	415.8	298.9	328.7	-36.16	3.43	2.53	2.48	2.03	2.03
12. Costa Rica	220.5	299.0	319.5	328.0	320.3	45.25	1.47	1.67	1.90	2.23	1.98
13. El Salvador	87.1	187.3	248.0	278.2	315.5	262.43	0.58	1.04	1.48	1.89	1.95
14. Belgium	354.1	374.2	487.9	322.0	299.8	-15.34	2.36	2.09	2.90	2.19	1.85
15. Taiwan	225.9	267.4	305.3	274.9	287.6	27.32	1.51	1.49	1.82	1.87	1.78
16. Dominican Republic	137.1	190.5	205.4	232.2	278.7	103.26	0.91	1.06	1.22	1.58	1.72
17. Australia	234.5	247.0	222.5	215.9	262.4	11.90	1.56	1.38	1.32	1.47	1.62
18. Brazil	223.1	278.7	285.2	167.1	235.1	5.39	1.49	1.55	1.70	1.14	1.45
19. Italy	228.5	260.3	244.3	208.4	229.5	0.46	1.52	1.45	1.45	1.42	1.42
20. Switzerland	79.5	162.8	94.0	114.2	224.9	182.69	0.53	0.91	0.56	0.78	1.39
21. Malaysia	127.1	162.0	193.9	184.7	211.2	66.09	0.85	0.90	1.15	1.25	1.30
22. Saudi Arabia	286.5	233.8	227.3	160.7	193.7	-32.41	1.91	1.30	1.35	1.09	1.20
23. Singapore	180.6	194.2	180.1	131.6	173.6	-3.87	1.20	1.08	1.07	0.89	1.07
24. Spain	146.6	165.3	162.2	127.6	123.0	-16.13	0.98	0.92	0.97	0.87	0.76
25. Denmark	85.6	80.5	93.7	80.3	113.5	32.54	0.57	0.45	0.56	0.55	0.70

Table E-39. Total U.S. Exports (Origin of Movement) via North Dakota, 1999–2003

(Top 25 commodities and top 25 countries based on 2003 dollar value.)

Industry, commodity, and country	Value (millions of dollars)					Percent change, 1999–2003	Percent share of state total				
	1999	2000	2001	2002	2003		1999	2000	2001	2002	2003
TOTAL AND PERCENT SHARE OF U.S. TOTAL	699.2	625.9	806.1	859.4	854.1	22.15	0.10	0.08	0.11	0.12	0.12
Manufactures (NAICS Code)	545.8	495.7	632.3	644.9	626.1	14.71	78.06	79.19	78.44	75.04	73.31
Processed foods (311)	92.9	79.6	86.7	105.6	106.4	14.59	13.28	12.72	10.75	12.29	12.46
Beverages and tobacco products (312)	0.3	0.3	1.2	0.7	1.2	279.81	0.05	0.00	0.15	0.09	0.14
Fabric mill products (313)	0.3	0.4	0.2	0.4	0.4	54.21	0.04	0.06	0.02	0.04	0.05
Non-apparel textile products (314)	0.2	0.1	0.1	0.3	0.2	-9.52	0.02	0.02	0.01	0.04	0.02
Apparel manufactures (315)	0.1	0.2	0.3	0.2	0.1	-44.44	0.02	0.03	0.04	0.03	0.01
Leather and related products (316)	0.1	0.1	0.1	0.1	0.1	-39.50	0.02	0.02	0.01	0.01	0.01
Wood products (321)	0.7	1.6	1.5	2.9	1.8	145.14	0.11	0.25	0.19	0.33	0.21
Paper products (322)	0.5	0.4	0.2	0.2	0.2	-54.78	0.08	0.07	0.02	0.03	0.03
Printing and related products (323)	0.6	0.4	1.2	1.3	0.9	52.21	0.08	0.07	0.14	0.15	0.10
Petroleum and coal products (324)	0.1	0.2	0.3	0.7	0.6	302.74	0.02	0.02	0.03	0.09	0.07
Chemical manufactures (325)	37.3	29.3	25.2	18.1	17.0	-54.35	5.34	4.67	3.13	2.10	1.99
Plastics and rubber products (326)	8.0	8.4	8.9	10.3	13.2	65.82	1.14	1.35	1.10	1.20	1.55
Non-metallic mineral products (327)	0.2	0.6	0.7	0.4	1.3	485.78	0.03	0.10	0.09	0.05	0.15
Primary metal manufactures (331)	0.4	0.3	0.6	0.1	0.5	27.50	0.05	0.05	0.07	0.02	0.05
Fabricated metal products (332)	4.2	5.6	9.4	5.3	3.9	-7.34	0.61	0.89	1.16	0.62	0.46
Machinery manufactures (333)	282.2	242.7	401.3	424.8	404.7	43.40	40.36	38.77	49.78	49.44	47.39
Computer and electronic products (334)	18.7	8.8	11.5	9.9	13.7	-26.93	2.67	1.40	1.43	1.16	1.60
Electrical equipment, appliances, and parts (335)	4.0	2.4	5.2	3.7	4.6	13.29	0.58	0.39	0.65	0.43	0.54
Transportation equipment (336)	93.0	84.2	75.3	56.9	53.4	-42.54	13.30	13.45	9.35	6.62	6.26
Furniture and related products (337)	1.5	1.6	1.5	1.2	1.2	-18.38	0.21	0.26	0.19	0.14	0.14
Miscellaneous manufactures (339)	0.5	28.3	1.0	1.5	0.8	53.77	0.07	4.52	0.13	0.17	0.09
Agricultural and Livestock Products (NAICS Code)	126.9	95.7	135.0	177.6	178.1	40.39	18.14	15.29	16.74	20.67	20.85
Agricultural products (111)	117.9	87.9	128.6	174.5	172.5	46.27	16.86	14.04	15.95	20.31	20.19
Livestock and livestock products (112)	9.0	7.8	6.4	3.1	5.6	-37.07	1.28	1.25	0.79	0.36	0.66
Other Commodities (NAICS Code)	26.5	34.6	38.8	36.9	49.8	88.01	3.79	5.52	4.81	4.30	5.84
Forestry and logging (113)	0.0	0.1	0.2	0.0	0.0	X	0.00	0.01	0.02	0.00	0.00
Fishing, hunting, and trapping (114)	2.9	3.0	3.9	4.5	3.2	9.72	0.42	0.48	0.49	0.53	0.37
Oil and gas extraction (211)	1.1	11.0	10.4	10.0	19.5	1 642.86	0.16	1.75	1.29	1.16	2.29
Mining (212)	0.6	0.7	0.5	0.6	0.8	22.89	0.09	0.10	0.07	0.07	0.09
Waste and scrap (910)	1.6	1.6	2.7	1.7	4.5	186.02	0.22	0.25	0.34	0.20	0.52
Used merchandise (920)	3.3	3.1	4.4	2.7	6.7	102.67	0.47	0.49	0.55	0.31	0.78
Goods returned to Canada (980)	7.4	8.3	8.7	9.1	7.9	7.07	1.06	1.33	1.08	1.06	0.93
Special classification provisions (990)	9.6	6.9	7.9	8.3	7.1	-25.96	1.38	1.11	0.98	0.96	0.83
Publishing industries (except Internet) (511)	0.0	0.0	0.0	0.0	0.2	X	0.00	0.00	0.00	0.00	0.02
TOTAL AND PERCENT SHARE OF U.S. TOTAL	699.2	625.9	806.1	859.4	854.1	22.15	0.10	0.08	0.11	0.12	0.12
Top 25 Commodities (HS Code)	362.0	312.9	496.1	630.2	651.8	80.06	51.77	49.99	61.54	73.33	76.32
1. Mechanical front-end shovel loaders (842951)	93.2	103.9	100.7	97.0	113.0	21.24	13.33	16.60	12.49	11.29	13.23
2. Self-propelled bulldozers with a 360 degree superstructure (842952) ...	103.3	57.0	147.4	143.9	99.9	-3.29	14.77	9.11	18.29	16.74	11.70
3. Tractors (870190)	10.0	14.5	48.9	53.4	60.1	501.00	1.43	2.32	6.07	6.21	7.04
4. Corn, other than seed corn (100590)	4.2	3.7	15.0	37.0	39.9	850.00	0.60	0.59	1.86	4.31	4.67
5. Soybean oilcake and other solid residue (230400)	2.7	0.5	13.4	32.2	38.6	1 329.63	0.39	0.08	1.66	3.75	4.52
6. Seeders, planters, and transplanters (843230)	4.8	4.7	5.3	19.7	35.8	645.83	0.69	0.75	0.66	2.29	4.19
7. Low erucic acid rape/colza seeds, whether or not broken (120510)	0.0	0.0	0.0	33.8	35.7	X	0.00	0.00	0.00	3.93	4.18
8. Sunflower seeds, whether or not broken (120600)	43.8	32.3	38.3	40.4	34.6	-21.00	6.26	5.16	4.75	4.70	4.05
9. Motor vehicle for the transport of ten persons or more (870210)	47.3	33.9	29.3	16.5	32.0	-32.35	6.76	5.42	3.63	1.92	3.75
10. Other parts and attachments for derricks (843149)	29.5	15.0	37.3	42.9	30.4	3.05	4.22	2.40	4.63	4.99	3.56
11. Crude oil from petroleum and bituminous minerals (270900)	0.1	4.5	2.1	9.1	19.5	19 400.00	0.01	0.72	0.26	1.06	2.28
12. Sunflower-seed or safflower oil (151219)	5.8	5.2	5.7	12.4	15.0	158.62	0.83	0.83	0.71	1.44	1.76
13. Rape or colza seeds, whether or not broken (120590)	0.0	0.0	0.0	21.4	15.0	X	0.00	0.00	0.00	2.49	1.76
14. Rape seed/colza oil and fractions, low erucic acid (151411)	0.0	0.0	0.0	5.5	9.2	X	0.00	0.00	0.00	0.64	1.08
15. Beans, dried and shelled, including seed (71339)	6.3	4.1	7.4	8.5	8.1	28.57	0.90	0.66	0.92	0.99	0.95
16. Phenol (hydroxybenzene) and its salts (290711)	4.1	6.6	8.2	8.7	7.9	92.68	0.59	1.05	1.02	1.01	0.92
17. Dried shelled peas including seed (071310)	. . .	0.6	1.0	3.9	7.7	. . .	. . .	0.10	0.12	0.45	0.90
18. Soybeans, whether or not broken (120100)	. . .	3.0	4.7	4.8	7.7	. . .	. . .	0.48	0.58	0.56	0.90
19. Malt, not roasted (110710)	0.2	0.6	2.3	8.1	6.7	3 250.00	0.03	0.10	0.29	0.94	0.78
20. Parts and accessories for automatic data processing (847330)	0.2	3.4	6.2	5.5	6.4	3 100.00	0.03	0.54	0.77	0.64	0.75
21. Combine harvester-threshers (843351)	4.4	8.8	7.7	9.1	6.1	38.64	0.63	1.41	0.96	1.06	0.71
22. Agricultural/forest machinery and lawn/ground roller (843290)	. . .	2.8	5.3	4.8	6.0	. . .	. . .	0.45	0.66	0.56	0.70
23. Laser discs for reproducing other than sound/image (852431)	2.6	3.6	5.8	5.2	5.6	115.38	0.37	0.58	0.72	0.61	0.66
24. Mechanical shovels and excavators (842959)	. . .	0.8	1.7	3.5	5.5	. . .	. . .	0.13	0.21	0.41	0.64
25. Fertilizers (310000)	. . .	5.9	3.4	2.9	5.4	. . .	. . .	0.94	0.42	0.34	0.63

X = Not applicable.
. . . = Not available.

Exports from North Dakota

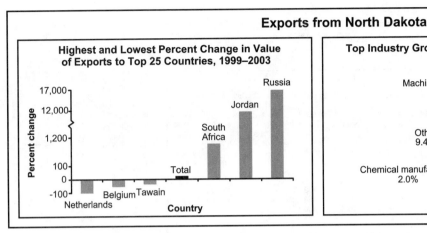

Highest and Lowest Percent Change in Value of Exports to Top 25 Countries, 1999–2003

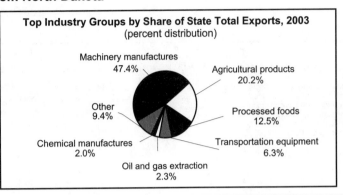

Top Industry Groups by Share of State Total Exports, 2003 (percent distribution)

- North Dakota's exports are worth $854 million, ranking it among the states with the lowest values of exports. However, total overall exports are up 22 percent from 1999. Industries with the greatest dollar increases are machinery manufactures ($122 million), agricultural products ($55 million), and oil and gas extraction ($18 million). Machinery manufactures is by far North Dakota's largest export, representing more than 47 percent of the state's total, and agricultural products rank second with about 20 percent.

- North Dakota's top three commodity exports are front-end shovel loaders, bulldozers, and tractors. Together, they account for 26 percent, or $273 million, of the state's total exports.

- In 2003, nearly 56 percent of North Dakota's exports were to Canada, which is not surprising since they share a border. Belgium ranked second with about 12 percent, followed by Australia with more than 5 percent. Exports to Australia increased more than 152 percent from 1999 to 2003. However, Russia had by far the highest rate of increase, rising from $88,000 to $14.9 million. More than 99 percent of these exports are machinery manufactures.

Table E-39. Total U.S. Exports (Origin of Movement) via North Dakota, 1999–2003—*Continued*

(Top 25 commodities and top 25 countries based on 2003 dollar value.)

Industry, commodity, and country	Value (millions of dollars)					Percent change, 1999–2003	Percent share of state total				
	1999	2000	2001	2002	2003		1999	2000	2001	2002	2003
TOTAL AND PERCENT SHARE OF U.S. TOTAL	699.2	625.9	806.1	859.4	854.1	22.15	0.10	0.08	0.11	0.12	0.12
Top 25 Countries	672.0	593.9	762.0	826.4	812.2	20.86	96.11	94.89	94.52	96.17	95.10
1. Canada	336.4	333.4	393.8	439.6	475.6	41.37	48.11	53.26	48.85	51.16	55.68
2. Belgium	178.0	72.0	155.5	157.8	100.7	-43.43	25.46	11.50	19.29	18.36	11.79
3. Australia	18.6	24.3	25.1	46.5	47.0	152.57	2.66	3.88	3.12	5.41	5.51
4. Mexico	18.2	23.9	38.1	39.1	32.2	77.14	2.60	3.81	4.72	4.54	3.77
5. Italy	21.2	20.3	29.7	26.7	21.5	1.18	3.04	3.24	3.68	3.10	2.52
6. Spain	6.8	12.3	17.2	15.8	17.6	159.65	0.97	1.96	2.13	1.84	2.06
7. Russia	0.1	1.0	2.0	3.1	14.9	16 868.10	0.01	0.17	0.25	0.36	1.75
8. Japan	11.0	15.2	18.7	19.5	14.8	34.60	1.58	2.42	2.32	2.27	1.74
9. United Kingdom	21.7	12.0	21.4	19.9	13.5	-37.45	3.10	1.92	2.66	2.31	1.59
10. Germany	17.8	43.7	20.2	16.9	13.3	-25.20	2.55	6.98	2.51	1.97	1.56
11. South Africa	0.7	1.3	1.7	1.5	8.4	1 142.60	0.10	0.21	0.22	0.17	0.98
12. France	4.9	7.6	16.1	9.9	8.3	68.48	0.70	1.21	2.00	1.15	0.97
13. China	3.6	4.9	1.5	3.7	5.7	57.33	0.52	0.78	0.19	0.43	0.67
14. Turkey	4.3	5.0	4.5	4.6	5.3	25.35	0.61	0.80	0.55	0.53	0.63
15. South Korea	1.5	3.6	2.1	3.3	5.0	241.21	0.21	0.58	0.26	0.38	0.58
16. Denmark	1.6	1.3	1.7	2.1	4.0	158.70	0.22	0.20	0.21	0.24	0.47
17. Saudi Arabia	0.7	0.6	1.3	4.7	3.5	399.57	0.10	0.09	0.16	0.54	0.40
18. Dominican Republic	0.3	0.6	1.5	0.7	2.8	749.55	0.05	0.10	0.19	0.08	0.33
19. Jordan	0.0	0.9	0.5	0.7	2.7	X	0.00	0.14	0.07	0.08	0.31
20. Netherlands	17.3	3.0	3.8	4.1	2.7	-84.62	2.48	0.48	0.47	0.48	0.31
21. Sweden	0.3	0.3	0.8	0.8	2.6	741.85	0.04	0.05	0.10	0.09	0.31
22. Brazil	0.3	2.1	0.8	1.2	2.6	934.25	0.04	0.34	0.10	0.14	0.31
23. Taiwan	4.2	3.6	2.5	2.5	2.6	-37.94	0.60	0.57	0.31	0.29	0.30
24. Iraq	0.0	0.0	0.0	0.0	2.5	X	0.00	0.00	0.00	0.00	0.29
25. New Zealand	2.5	1.2	1.5	1.9	2.2	-13.98	0.36	0.19	0.18	0.23	0.26

X = Not applicable.

Table E-40. Total U.S. Exports (Origin of Movement) via Ohio, 1999–2003

(Top 25 commodities and top 25 countries based on 2003 dollar value.)

Industry, commodity, and country	Value (millions of dollars)					Percent change, 1999–2003	Percent share of state total				
	1999	2000	2001	2002	2003		1999	2000	2001	2002	2003
TOTAL AND PERCENT SHARE OF U.S. TOTAL	24 883.2	26 322.2	27 094.7	27 723.3	29 764.4	19.62	3.59	3.37	3.71	4.00	4.11
Manufactures (NAICS Code)	23 842.0	25 327.5	26 235.5	26 841.4	28 643.5	20.14	95.82	96.22	96.83	96.82	96.23
Processed foods (311)	346.4	382.6	475.6	506.5	470.9	35.93	1.39	1.45	1.76	1.83	1.58
Beverages and tobacco products (312)	13.9	9.2	10.6	13.8	10.8	-22.23	0.06	0.00	0.04	0.05	0.04
Fabric mill products (313)	89.0	111.6	104.4	105.6	106.0	19.04	0.36	0.42	0.39	0.38	0.36
Non-apparel textile products (314)	64.0	69.7	55.2	46.7	48.0	-24.96	0.26	0.26	0.20	0.17	0.16
Apparel manufactures (315)	37.9	58.2	48.9	50.7	56.6	49.33	0.15	0.22	0.18	0.18	0.19
Leather and related products (316)	25.2	30.2	24.6	21.3	26.4	4.84	0.10	0.11	0.09	0.08	0.09
Wood products (321)	150.1	179.3	152.9	162.1	179.0	19.23	0.60	0.68	0.56	0.58	0.60
Paper products (322)	426.6	458.6	464.8	447.2	492.4	15.41	1.71	1.74	1.72	1.61	1.65
Printing and related products (323)	140.8	133.1	130.4	126.4	141.6	0.57	0.57	0.51	0.48	0.46	0.48
Petroleum and coal products (324)	72.0	58.3	81.3	69.7	70.3	-2.35	0.29	0.22	0.30	0.25	0.24
Chemical manufactures (325)	2 432.8	2 495.1	2 588.3	2 532.4	2 834.4	16.51	9.78	9.48	9.55	9.13	9.52
Plastics and rubber products (326)	1 004.7	1 094.2	1 070.9	1 045.7	1 138.6	13.33	4.04	4.16	3.95	3.77	3.83
Non-metallic mineral products (327)	513.1	601.4	609.1	585.5	692.3	34.91	2.06	2.28	2.25	2.11	2.33
Primary metal manufactures (331)	891.0	1 108.4	1 010.8	885.0	1 001.3	12.37	3.58	4.21	3.73	3.19	3.36
Fabricated metal products (332)	1 511.5	1 753.9	1 613.3	1 736.5	1 728.3	14.34	6.07	6.66	5.95	6.26	5.81
Machinery manufactures (333)	3 857.7	4 180.9	4 050.1	3 702.1	3 595.7	-6.79	15.50	15.88	14.95	13.35	12.08
Computer and electronic products (334)	1 882.5	1 941.4	1 676.7	1 836.5	1 782.8	-5.29	7.57	7.38	6.19	6.62	5.99
Electrical equipment, appliances, and parts (335)	966.2	1 026.2	1 038.9	1 044.9	1 092.2	13.05	3.88	3.90	3.83	3.77	3.67
Transportation equipment (336)	8 881.3	9 034.9	10 353.1	11 220.0	12 502.4	40.77	35.69	34.32	38.21	40.47	42.00
Furniture and related products (337)	92.4	112.0	123.7	126.3	145.1	57.03	0.37	0.43	0.46	0.46	0.49
Miscellaneous manufactures (339)	442.7	488.4	552.1	576.5	528.3	19.35	1.78	1.86	2.04	2.08	1.78
Agricultural and Livestock Products (NAICS Code)	225.3	231.2	247.9	112.2	241.4	7.16	0.91	0.88	0.91	0.40	0.81
Agricultural products (111)	201.7	202.9	218.9	88.2	223.3	10.71	0.81	0.77	0.81	0.32	0.75
Livestock and livestock products (112)	23.6	28.3	28.9	23.9	18.2	-23.14	0.09	0.11	0.11	0.09	0.06
Other Commodities (NAICS Code)	816.0	763.5	611.4	769.7	879.6	7.79	3.28	2.90	2.26	2.78	2.96
Forestry and logging (113)	29.1	38.1	44.4	36.3	47.5	63.09	0.12	0.14	0.16	0.13	0.16
Fishing, hunting, and trapping (114)	3.4	3.2	4.0	4.5	4.7	36.48	0.01	0.01	0.01	0.02	0.02
Oil and gas extraction (211)	1.0	0.5	0.5	1.5	3.9	282.65	0.00	0.00	0.00	0.01	0.01
Mining (212)	353.2	272.1	81.4	303.9	362.8	2.71	1.42	1.03	0.30	1.10	1.22
Waste and scrap (910)	60.3	71.6	83.1	83.4	107.6	78.23	0.24	0.27	0.31	0.30	0.36
Used merchandise (920)	10.6	18.8	24.1	21.5	18.3	72.54	0.04	0.07	0.09	0.08	0.06
Goods returned to Canada (980)	76.6	80.6	115.7	77.6	93.9	22.56	0.31	0.31	0.43	0.28	0.32
Special classification provisions (990)	281.6	278.7	258.2	241.0	233.9	-16.95	1.13	1.06	0.95	0.87	0.79
Publishing industries (except Internet) (511)	0.0	0.0	0.0	0.0	7.1	X	0.00	0.00	0.00	0.00	0.02
TOTAL AND PERCENT SHARE OF U.S. TOTAL	24 883.2	26 322.2	27 094.7	27 723.3	29 764.4	19.62	3.59	3.37	3.71	4.00	4.11
Top 25 Commodities (HS Code)	8 754.0	8 995.8	10 290.3	11 682.5	12 586.4	43.78	35.18	34.18	37.98	42.14	42.29
1. Passenger vehicle, spark-ignition, > 1,500 cc < 3,000 cc (870323)	1 388.9	1 111.2	1 408.4	1 621.7	1 805.7	30.01	5.58	4.22	5.20	5.85	6.07
2. Passenger vehicles, spark-ignition, > 3,000 cc (870324)	646.3	580.5	696.7	1 237.1	1 625.5	151.51	2.60	2.21	2.57	4.46	5.46
3. Spark-ignition internal combustion piston engines (840734)	868.7	1 073.3	1 439.8	1 477.6	1 551.4	78.59	3.49	4.08	5.31	5.33	5.21
4. Parts and accessories of motor vehicles bodies (870829)	1 042.3	1 112.1	1 091.8	1 143.3	1 168.5	12.11	4.19	4.22	4.03	4.12	3.93
5. Parts and accessories of motor vehicles (870899)	770.0	824.9	848.2	845.6	786.7	2.17	3.09	3.13	3.13	3.05	2.64
6. Turbojets of a thrust > 25 kn (841112)	121.4	278.1	598.9	762.1	727.9	499.59	0.49	1.06	2.21	2.75	2.45
7. Turbojet and turbo-propeller parts (841191)	1 161.4	982.7	1 330.8	963.0	713.6	-38.56	4.67	3.73	4.91	3.47	2.40
8. Gear boxes for motor vehicles (870840)	438.5	450.7	485.1	486.5	451.5	2.96	1.76	1.71	1.79	1.75	1.52
9. Goods vehicles, with diesel or semi-diesel engines (870421)	. . .	0.7	0.1	76.6	446.7	. . .	. . .	0.00	0.00	0.28	1.50
10. Goods vehicles, with spark-ignition piston engines (870431)	46.9	89.3	10.2	176.9	427.1	810.66	0.19	0.34	0.04	0.64	1.43
11. Bituminous coal, not agglomerated (270112)	318.8	235.6	44.7	268.1	321.2	0.75	1.28	0.90	0.16	0.97	1.08
12. Articles of iron or steel (732690)	241.8	259.9	313.5	394.3	315.5	30.48	0.97	0.99	1.16	1.42	1.06
13. Spark-ignition engine parts (840991)	348.1	333.1	258.8	262.8	253.9	-27.06	1.40	1.27	0.96	0.95	0.85
14. Compressors used in refrigerating equipment (841430)	228.1	225.8	206.0	225.6	219.4	-3.81	0.92	0.86	0.76	0.81	0.74
15. Cathode-ray TV picture tubes, color monitor (854011)	48.7	21.0	51.5	138.6	192.4	295.07	0.20	0.08	0.19	0.50	0.65
16. Motor vehicles, trans goods, gvw between 5 and 20 ton (870422)	. . .	54.4	45.8	114.6	175.9	. . .	. . .	0.21	0.17	0.41	0.59
17. Gas turbines (841182)	163.2	98.4	206.5	307.9	174.5	6.92	0.66	0.37	0.76	1.11	0.59
18. Brakes, servo-brakes, and parts for motor vehicles (870839)	308.0	254.4	189.8	197.0	174.4	-43.38	1.24	0.97	0.70	0.71	0.59
19. Under-carriages and parts for aircraft (880320)	86.2	106.3	138.1	154.7	159.1	84.57	0.35	0.40	0.51	0.56	0.53
20. Surface-active, washing preparations, retail sale (340220)	. . .	95.5	115.1	117.8	158.9	. . .	. . .	0.36	0.42	0.42	0.53
21. Gas turbine parts (841199)	129.7	111.3	129.6	160.9	156.6	20.74	0.52	0.42	0.48	0.58	0.53
22. Air/gas pumps, compressor and fan parts (841490)	. . .	117.9	136.2	100.4	145.7	. . .	. . .	0.45	0.50	0.36	0.49
23. New pneumatic tires of rubber, for motor cars (401110)	193.2	190.4	184.9	157.6	145.5	-24.69	0.78	0.72	0.68	0.57	0.49
24. Parts of airplanes or helicopters (880330)	203.8	197.2	176.3	163.8	144.8	-28.95	0.82	0.75	0.65	0.59	0.49
25. Road wheels, parts and accessories for motor vehicles (870870)	. . .	191.8	183.6	128.0	144.0	. . .	. . .	0.73	0.68	0.46	0.48

X = Not applicable.
. . . = Not available.

Exports from Ohio

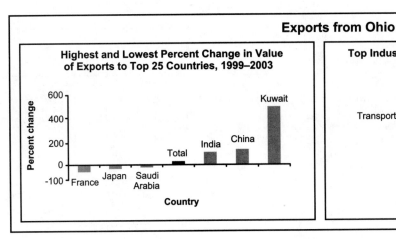

Highest and Lowest Percent Change in Value of Exports to Top 25 Countries, 1999–2003

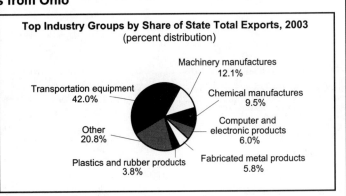

Top Industry Groups by Share of State Total Exports, 2003
(percent distribution)

Transportation equipment 42.0%
Machinery manufactures 12.1%
Chemical manufactures 9.5%
Computer and electronic products 6.0%
Fabricated metal products 5.8%
Plastics and rubber products 3.8%
Other 20.8%

- Ohio's exports increased from nearly $24.9 billion in 1999 to about $29.8 billion in 2003, giving the state the seventh highest value of exports in the nation. In 2003, 42 percent of Ohio's exports were transportation equipment products. While Ohio represents about 4 percent of the United States' total exports, it accounts for close to 10 percent of the transportation equipment exports. The state's transportation equipment exports increased from $8.9 billion in 1999 to $12.5 billion in 2003, a jump of more than 40 percent. In 2003, Ohio's top five commodities were all related to passenger vehicles or engines.

- In 2003, Canada was the recipient of nearly 57 percent of Ohio's exports with $16.9 billion, with transportation equipment representing more than half. Exports to Mexico, which ranked second with $2.1 billion, increased by 53 percent from 1999 to 2003. Transportation equipment accounted for almost one-third of these exports. Exports to Kuwait rose the most from 1999 to 2003, up nearly sixfold, followed by China (163 percent), and India (127 percent).

Table E-40. Total U.S. Exports (Origin of Movement) via Ohio, 1999–2003—*Continued*

(Top 25 commodities and top 25 countries based on 2003 dollar value.)

Industry, commodity, and country	Value (millions of dollars)					Percent change, 1999–2003	Percent share of state total				
	1999	2000	2001	2002	2003		1999	2000	2001	2002	2003
TOTAL AND PERCENT SHARE OF U.S. TOTAL	24 883.2	26 322.2	27 094.7	27 723.3	29 764.4	19.62	3.59	3.37	3.71	4.00	4.11
Top 25 Countries	23 209.3	24 492.5	25 308.2	26 105.6	27 939.9	20.38	93.27	93.05	93.41	94.16	93.87
1. Canada	13 692.0	14 091.7	13 842.9	15 420.4	16 894.4	23.39	55.03	53.54	51.09	55.62	56.76
2. Mexico	1 373.8	1 958.6	2 108.5	2 109.3	2 101.9	53.00	5.52	7.44	7.78	7.61	7.06
3. United Kingdom	1 031.9	1 066.2	1 284.3	1 228.6	1 241.8	20.34	4.15	4.05	4.74	4.43	4.17
4. Japan	1 330.0	1 412.1	1 389.0	1 190.4	1 101.2	-17.20	5.34	5.36	5.13	4.29	3.70
5. France	1 393.3	1 199.0	1 448.5	1 068.1	767.9	-44.89	5.60	4.56	5.35	3.85	2.58
6. Germany	687.5	702.5	758.7	631.1	727.4	5.79	2.76	2.67	2.80	2.28	2.44
7. China	244.8	292.2	449.6	510.7	643.7	162.99	0.98	1.11	1.66	1.84	2.16
8. Netherlands	352.4	450.3	474.9	480.3	512.2	45.34	1.42	1.71	1.75	1.73	1.72
9. Belgium	311.8	339.9	389.7	383.2	449.1	44.03	1.25	1.29	1.44	1.38	1.51
10. Italy	252.3	227.5	286.1	308.8	415.3	64.63	1.01	0.86	1.06	1.11	1.40
11. Australia	323.4	354.9	349.4	339.0	388.9	20.25	1.30	1.35	1.29	1.22	1.31
12. South Korea	391.5	384.5	409.2	347.5	386.8	-1.19	1.57	1.46	1.51	1.25	1.30
13. Brazil	251.8	321.2	370.9	313.1	351.8	39.71	1.01	1.22	1.37	1.13	1.18
14. Singapore	212.8	243.9	257.9	260.2	250.4	17.68	0.86	0.93	0.95	0.94	0.84
15. Hong Kong	189.5	207.5	216.3	217.3	212.4	12.08	0.76	0.79	0.80	0.78	0.71
16. Taiwan	200.5	223.4	198.6	177.7	201.5	0.51	0.81	0.85	0.73	0.64	0.68
17. Thailand	103.1	128.1	153.0	131.0	191.9	86.15	0.41	0.49	0.56	0.47	0.64
18. Saudi Arabia	184.5	107.4	161.2	231.3	169.2	-8.29	0.74	0.41	0.59	0.83	0.57
19. Ireland	170.0	176.3	173.3	155.8	157.0	-7.61	0.68	0.67	0.64	0.56	0.53
20. Kuwait	25.7	33.9	29.3	100.4	152.7	495.20	0.10	0.13	0.11	0.36	0.51
21. India	65.7	82.1	105.6	110.3	149.2	126.91	0.26	0.31	0.39	0.40	0.50
22. Spain	113.8	149.8	146.4	122.4	129.4	13.75	0.46	0.57	0.54	0.44	0.43
23. Switzerland	117.0	149.9	129.4	99.2	125.5	7.24	0.47	0.57	0.48	0.36	0.42
24. South Africa	94.0	93.9	78.2	85.1	115.8	23.25	0.38	0.36	0.29	0.31	0.39
25. Israel	96.3	95.8	97.2	84.5	102.5	6.44	0.39	0.36	0.36	0.30	0.34

Table E-41. Total U.S. Exports (Origin of Movement) via Oklahoma, 1999–2003

(Top 25 commodities and top 25 countries based on 2003 dollar value.)

Industry, commodity, and country	Value (millions of dollars)					Percent change, 1999–2003	Percent share of state total				
	1999	2000	2001	2002	2003		1999	2000	2001	2002	2003
TOTAL AND PERCENT SHARE OF U.S. TOTAL	2 986.6	3 072.2	2 661.3	2 443.6	2 659.6	-10.95	0.43	0.39	0.36	0.35	0.37
Manufactures (NAICS Code)	2 867.2	2 942.8	2 544.3	2 323.5	2 543.1	-11.30	96.00	95.79	95.60	95.09	95.62
Processed foods (311)	85.6	144.2	155.3	138.9	125.8	46.92	2.87	4.69	5.84	5.69	4.73
Beverages and tobacco products (312)	0.0	0.0	0.5	0.3	2.3	X	0.00	0.00	0.02	0.01	0.09
Fabric mill products (313)	1.3	1.6	2.1	1.5	2.6	107.63	0.04	0.05	0.08	0.06	0.10
Non-apparel textile products (314)	1.1	1.7	4.0	1.7	2.1	96.46	0.04	0.06	0.15	0.07	0.08
Apparel manufactures (315)	18.7	25.2	23.9	31.4	27.4	46.50	0.63	0.82	0.90	1.28	1.03
Leather and related products (316)	0.6	0.9	1.1	1.4	3.5	471.80	0.02	0.03	0.04	0.06	0.13
Wood products (321)	6.1	4.8	5.3	5.0	5.4	-11.28	0.20	0.16	0.20	0.20	0.20
Paper products (322)	20.1	19.5	23.3	22.1	21.6	7.39	0.67	0.64	0.88	0.90	0.81
Printing and related products (323)	7.8	6.3	5.1	3.8	2.9	-62.58	0.26	0.21	0.19	0.15	0.11
Petroleum and coal products (324)	25.2	27.7	25.0	14.3	12.5	-50.36	0.84	0.90	0.94	0.58	0.47
Chemical manufactures (325)	152.2	163.9	176.0	154.7	164.6	8.15	5.10	5.34	6.61	6.33	6.19
Plastics and rubber products (326)	163.8	213.7	197.2	224.5	240.3	46.74	5.48	6.96	7.41	9.19	9.04
Non-metallic mineral products (327)	33.3	25.0	28.4	31.1	31.2	-6.35	1.12	0.81	1.07	1.27	1.17
Primary metal manufactures (331)	58.9	61.3	69.2	44.9	59.2	0.49	1.97	2.00	2.60	1.84	2.23
Fabricated metal products (332)	162.6	167.8	186.4	150.0	172.5	6.09	5.44	5.46	7.01	6.14	6.49
Machinery manufactures (333)	713.1	793.5	775.4	656.5	845.9	18.61	23.88	25.83	29.14	26.87	31.80
Computer and electronic products (334)	504.1	271.1	219.3	202.4	201.7	-59.99	16.88	8.82	8.24	8.28	7.58
Electrical equipment, appliances, and parts (335)	100.5	190.0	108.0	98.8	113.9	13.43	3.36	6.18	4.06	4.04	4.28
Transportation equipment (336)	765.6	771.8	494.7	498.9	467.2	-38.97	25.63	25.12	18.59	20.42	17.57
Furniture and related products (337)	3.4	3.2	2.8	2.1	3.3	-2.07	0.11	0.10	0.10	0.09	0.12
Miscellaneous manufactures (339)	43.3	49.6	41.2	39.4	37.1	-14.28	1.45	1.61	1.55	1.61	1.40
Agricultural and Livestock Products (NAICS Code)	40.7	50.6	51.8	42.2	52.8	29.70	1.36	1.65	1.95	1.73	1.98
Agricultural products (111)	39.9	49.8	51.2	41.3	51.8	29.92	1.34	1.62	1.92	1.69	1.95
Livestock and livestock products (112)	0.8	0.8	0.6	0.9	1.0	18.56	0.03	0.03	0.02	0.04	0.04
Other Commodities (NAICS Code)	78.7	78.7	65.2	77.9	63.8	-18.98	2.64	2.56	2.45	3.19	2.40
Forestry and logging (113)	0.3	0.2	1.3	3.5	1.1	280.07	0.01	0.01	0.05	0.14	0.04
Fishing, hunting, and trapping (114)	0.0	0.0	0.0	0.0	0.0	X	0.00	0.00	0.00	0.00	0.00
Oil and gas extraction (211)	2.7	11.2	0.9	2.0	7.2	169.62	0.09	0.36	0.03	0.08	0.27
Mining (212)	20.5	6.2	5.9	4.7	3.7	-82.03	0.69	0.20	0.22	0.19	0.14
Waste and scrap (910)	1.1	3.0	3.5	2.8	1.9	77.85	0.04	0.10	0.13	0.11	0.07
Used merchandise (920)	12.5	4.5	2.3	5.7	6.1	-50.97	0.42	0.15	0.09	0.23	0.23
Goods returned to Canada (980)	15.0	24.8	15.4	4.4	5.7	-61.73	0.50	0.81	0.58	0.18	0.22
Special classification provisions (990)	26.6	28.9	36.0	54.8	37.1	39.50	0.89	0.94	1.35	2.24	1.40
Publishing industries (except Internet) (511)	0.0	0.0	0.0	0.0	0.8	X	0.00	0.00	0.00	0.00	0.03
TOTAL AND PERCENT SHARE OF U.S. TOTAL	2 986.6	3 072.2	2 661.3	2 443.6	2 659.6	-10.95	0.43	0.39	0.36	0.35	0.37
Top 25 Commodities (HS Code)	1 048.3	1 375.5	1 032.6	1 066.5	1 276.4	21.76	35.10	44.77	38.80	43.65	47.99
1. Passenger vehicles, spark-ignition, > 3,000 cc (870324)	204.6	351.3	38.9	127.2	158.6	-22.48	6.85	11.43	1.46	5.21	5.96
2. Parts of pumps for liquids (841391)	72.3	131.8	125.8	98.4	149.9	107.33	2.42	4.29	4.73	4.03	5.64
3. New pneumatic tires of rubber, for motor cars (401110)	92.9	128.8	107.2	128.8	137.3	47.79	3.11	4.19	4.03	5.27	5.16
4. Parts for boring or sinking machinery (843143)	46.1	51.1	79.1	45.3	92.2	100.00	1.54	1.66	2.97	1.85	3.47
5. Parts of airplanes or helicopters (880330)	159.8	162.4	124.4	120.8	91.3	-42.87	5.35	5.29	4.67	4.94	3.43
6. Meat of swine, fresh or chilled (020319)	41.5	89.6	84.1	77.2	72.4	74.46	1.39	2.92	3.16	3.16	2.72
7. Taps and cocks for pipe thermostatic control (848180)	30.1	44.2	48.7	40.9	55.7	85.05	1.01	1.44	1.83	1.67	2.09
8. Centrifugal pumps (841370)	35.6	42.7	42.3	36.3	48.8	37.08	1.19	1.39	1.59	1.49	1.83
9. Air/gas pumps, compressors and fans (841480)	17.2	13.4	42.9	31.8	42.9	149.42	0.58	0.44	1.61	1.30	1.61
10. Heat exchange units, industrial type (841950)	35.8	36.8	34.8	35.1	37.0	3.35	1.20	1.20	1.31	1.44	1.39
11. Inboard engines for marine propulsion (840729)	27.8	34.4	23.7	35.6	36.0	29.50	0.93	1.12	0.89	1.46	1.35
12. Machine and mechanical appliance, individual function (847989)	20.7	38.6	65.7	42.0	34.9	68.60	0.69	1.26	2.47	1.72	1.31
13. Suspension shock absorbers for motor vehicles (870880)	22.8	34.3	29.4	34.6	33.5	46.93	0.76	1.12	1.10	1.42	1.26
14. Turbojet and turbo-propeller parts (841191)	26.9	41.7	25.4	20.4	32.5	20.82	0.90	1.36	0.95	0.83	1.22
15. Navigational instruments and appliances (901480)	. . .	2.8	5.7	14.4	29.2	. . .	. . .	0.09	0.21	0.59	1.10
16. Plates and sheets, non-cellular, polymer (392010)	9.5	12.3	13.2	21.5	27.6	190.53	0.32	0.40	0.50	0.88	1.04
17. New pneumatic tires of rubber, for buses or trucks (401120)	17.6	26.3	24.6	23.7	25.4	44.32	0.59	0.86	0.92	0.97	0.96
18. Rock drilling earth boring tools with working part of cermet (820713)	. . .	18.2	18.0	13.7	25.4	. . .	. . .	0.59	0.68	0.56	0.96
19. Air conditioning machine with refrigerating unit (841582)	27.0	24.1	28.0	25.9	25.3	-6.30	0.90	0.78	1.05	1.06	0.95
20. Dumpers designed for off-highway use (870410)	119.7	32.9	14.5	16.9	22.6	-81.12	4.01	1.07	0.54	0.69	0.85
21. Brassieres, knit or crocheted or not (621210)	13.7	20.2	18.5	24.6	20.7	51.09	0.46	0.66	0.70	1.01	0.78
22. Electric conductors for voltage > 1,000 v (854460)	. . .	4.7	6.6	4.3	19.9	. . .	. . .	0.15	0.25	0.18	0.75
23. Retail medicaments in measured dose (300490)	. . .	4.4	8.9	12.6	19.4	. . .	. . .	0.14	0.33	0.52	0.73
24. Parts and accessories of motor vehicles (870899)	26.7	23.6	17.2	21.2	19.4	-27.34	0.89	0.77	0.65	0.87	0.73
25. Parts for machinery plant or lab equipment (841990)	. . .	4.9	5.0	13.3	18.5	. . .	. . .	0.16	0.19	0.54	0.70

X = Not applicable.
. . . = Not available.

Exports from Oklahoma

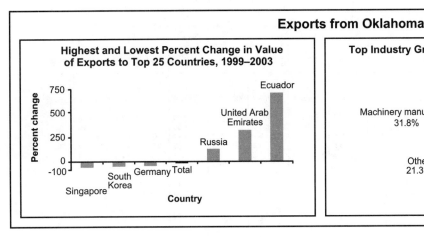

Highest and Lowest Percent Change in Value of Exports to Top 25 Countries, 1999–2003

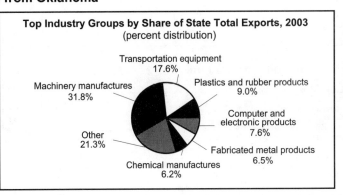

Top Industry Groups by Share of State Total Exports, 2003
(percent distribution)

- Oklahoma's exports were down nearly 11 percent from 1999 to 2003. Computer and electronic products had the greatest dollar loss, with a decline of $302 million. As a result, this industry's share of the state's total fell from about 17 percent in 1999 to less than 8 percent in 2003.

- Exports of transportation equipment, which was the state's largest export industry in 1999 with $766 million, fell to $467 million in 2003. As a result, the industry's share of Oklahoma's total exports dropped from over 25 percent to less than 18 percent. During this period, machinery manufactures exports increased by over 18 percent, and was the leading export in 2003, accounting for 32 percent of the state's total.

- In 2003, Canada imported nearly $1.1 billion, or about 40 percent, of Oklahoma's export products. Mexico ranked second with just over 8 percent, followed by Japan (5 percent) and Russia (3 percent). Exports to Russia increased by 160 percent from 1999 to 2003, with machinery manufactures exports accounting for 89 percent of exports in 2003.

Table E-41. Total U.S. Exports (Origin of Movement) via Oklahoma, 1999–2003—*Continued*

(Top 25 commodities and top 25 countries based on 2003 dollar value.)

Industry, commodity, and country	Value (millions of dollars)					Percent change, 1999–2003	Percent share of state total				
	1999	2000	2001	2002	2003		1999	2000	2001	2002	2003
TOTAL AND PERCENT SHARE OF U.S. TOTAL	2 986.6	3 072.2	2 661.3	2 443.6	2 659.6	-10.95	0.43	0.39	0.36	0.35	0.37
Top 25 Countries	2 463.1	2 698.2	2 269.2	2 083.7	2 343.7	-4.85	82.47	87.83	85.27	85.27	88.12
1. Canada	1 003.6	1 252.3	916.5	925.7	1 054.2	5.04	33.60	40.76	34.44	37.88	39.64
2. Mexico	236.7	226.8	196.4	199.8	221.1	-6.60	7.93	7.38	7.38	8.18	8.31
3. Japan	130.8	188.8	206.2	149.9	146.0	11.59	4.38	6.14	7.75	6.13	5.49
4. Russia	32.5	61.0	71.5	50.5	84.6	160.02	1.09	1.99	2.69	2.07	3.18
5. Singapore	198.6	77.2	76.3	55.6	79.6	-59.90	6.65	2.51	2.87	2.28	2.99
6. United Kingdom	144.4	128.3	142.9	106.8	79.3	-45.11	4.84	4.18	5.37	4.37	2.98
7. China	31.3	41.5	43.7	48.8	64.6	106.12	1.05	1.35	1.64	2.00	2.43
8. United Arab Emirates	13.3	21.5	34.3	41.2	56.3	324.09	0.44	0.70	1.29	1.68	2.12
9. Germany	124.9	127.4	78.6	68.2	54.0	-56.79	4.18	4.15	2.95	2.79	2.03
10. France	84.3	41.9	51.3	37.6	49.9	-40.81	2.82	1.36	1.93	1.54	1.88
11. Brazil	21.9	27.0	69.1	62.7	49.4	125.32	0.73	0.88	2.60	2.57	1.86
12. Australia	48.2	44.4	36.8	41.5	48.8	1.24	1.61	1.45	1.38	1.70	1.83
13. Netherlands	75.3	62.4	54.0	62.0	43.5	-42.19	2.52	2.03	2.03	2.54	1.64
14. Saudi Arabia	62.1	79.6	63.0	20.3	38.1	-38.55	2.08	2.59	2.37	0.83	1.43
15. Belgium	35.4	36.2	32.2	37.6	37.4	5.71	1.19	1.18	1.21	1.54	1.41
16. Venezuela	20.3	65.0	39.1	24.6	29.7	46.22	0.68	2.12	1.47	1.01	1.12
17. Egypt	33.4	13.6	12.6	6.9	28.7	-14.15	1.12	0.44	0.47	0.28	1.08
18. Ecuador	3.6	16.3	6.7	7.2	28.6	705.12	0.12	0.53	0.25	0.30	1.08
19. South Korea	61.3	72.9	45.8	34.1	25.8	-57.96	2.05	2.37	1.72	1.40	0.97
20. Hong Kong	15.7	15.7	11.1	20.0	25.6	62.57	0.53	0.51	0.42	0.82	0.96
21. Argentina	28.4	22.1	19.1	13.4	24.1	-14.91	0.95	0.72	0.72	0.55	0.91
22. Italy	17.0	22.4	23.7	17.4	19.3	13.12	0.57	0.73	0.89	0.71	0.72
23. Kuwait	14.9	13.0	11.5	17.0	18.5	23.92	0.50	0.42	0.43	0.69	0.70
24. Chile	9.7	21.4	10.2	10.8	18.5	91.33	0.32	0.70	0.38	0.44	0.70
25. Nicaragua	15.3	19.3	16.8	24.0	18.0	16.99	0.51	0.63	0.63	0.98	0.68

Table E-42. Total U.S. Exports (Origin of Movement) via Oregon, 1999–2003

(Top 25 commodities and top 25 countries based on 2003 dollar value.)

Industry, commodity, and country	Value (millions of dollars)					Percent change, 1999–2003	Percent share of state total				
	1999	2000	2001	2002	2003		1999	2000	2001	2002	2003
TOTAL AND PERCENT SHARE OF U.S. TOTAL	10 471.2	11 441.3	8 900.4	10 086.4	10 357.2	-1.09	1.51	1.47	1.22	1.45	1.43
Manufactures (NAICS Code)	9 087.5	10 032.4	7 502.1	8 656.1	8 784.8	-3.33	86.79	87.69	84.29	85.82	84.82
Processed foods (311)	284.1	291.1	343.3	301.2	280.3	-1.30	2.71	2.54	3.86	2.99	2.71
Beverages and tobacco products (312)	6.0	3.6	3.2	3.2	3.6	-39.41	0.06	0.00	0.04	0.03	0.04
Fabric mill products (313)	5.0	4.5	13.3	4.2	4.8	-3.63	0.05	0.04	0.15	0.04	0.05
Non-apparel textile products (314)	2.7	4.2	3.3	3.3	3.0	12.21	0.03	0.04	0.04	0.03	0.03
Apparel manufactures (315)	23.2	11.3	10.9	8.2	11.9	-48.86	0.22	0.10	0.12	0.08	0.11
Leather and related products (316)	144.6	135.2	109.7	95.4	95.2	-34.15	1.38	1.18	1.23	0.95	0.92
Wood products (321)	420.2	429.3	332.2	296.3	299.1	-28.83	4.01	3.75	3.73	2.94	2.89
Paper products (322)	165.5	233.1	190.5	222.0	253.0	52.91	1.58	2.04	2.14	2.20	2.44
Printing and related products (323)	23.5	28.7	39.6	31.4	34.3	45.65	0.22	0.25	0.44	0.31	0.33
Petroleum and coal products (324)	25.6	47.4	49.5	55.1	62.6	144.27	0.24	0.41	0.56	0.55	0.60
Chemical manufactures (325)	304.5	336.9	333.7	357.4	410.2	34.71	2.91	2.94	3.75	3.54	3.96
Plastics and rubber products (326)	70.1	56.8	53.4	80.1	79.1	12.74	0.67	0.50	0.60	0.79	0.76
Non-metallic mineral products (327)	82.1	303.3	59.0	65.2	76.3	-7.06	0.78	2.65	0.66	0.65	0.74
Primary metal manufactures (331)	157.9	178.0	179.5	171.3	164.6	4.24	1.51	1.56	2.02	1.70	1.59
Fabricated metal products (332)	149.3	149.5	149.1	139.7	160.3	7.33	1.43	1.31	1.67	1.39	1.55
Machinery manufactures (333)	914.8	1 138.5	932.6	945.8	870.5	-4.84	8.74	9.95	10.48	9.38	8.40
Computer and electronic products (334)	4 952.8	5 594.3	3 842.0	4 682.3	4 602.0	-7.08	47.30	48.90	43.17	46.42	44.43
Electrical equipment, appliances, and parts (335)	120.2	134.2	136.0	112.8	136.4	13.48	1.15	1.17	1.53	1.12	1.32
Transportation equipment (336)	1 136.4	859.1	617.1	965.9	1 115.6	-1.84	10.85	7.51	6.93	9.58	10.77
Furniture and related products (337)	16.1	16.1	18.8	20.0	17.6	9.10	0.15	0.14	0.21	0.20	0.17
Miscellaneous manufactures (339)	82.9	77.4	85.6	95.4	104.4	26.01	0.79	0.68	0.96	0.95	1.01
Agricultural and Livestock Products (NAICS Code)	1 138.3	1 130.6	1 135.2	1 215.4	1 290.0	13.32	10.87	9.88	12.75	12.05	12.46
Agricultural products (111)	1 136.3	1 129.2	1 132.1	1 213.9	1 288.1	13.36	10.85	9.87	12.72	12.04	12.44
Livestock and livestock products (112)	2.0	1.4	3.1	1.4	1.9	-5.43	0.02	0.01	0.03	0.01	0.02
Other Commodities (NAICS Code)	245.3	278.3	263.1	214.9	282.4	15.14	2.34	2.43	2.96	2.13	2.73
Forestry and logging (113)	18.4	30.4	31.3	28.8	29.7	61.75	0.18	0.27	0.35	0.29	0.29
Fishing, hunting, and trapping (114)	25.1	31.4	33.9	34.6	37.3	48.72	0.24	0.27	0.38	0.34	0.36
Oil and gas extraction (211)	0.1	0.1	0.1	0.0	0.0	X	0.00	0.00	0.00	0.00	0.00
Mining (212)	13.1	4.1	8.3	6.2	7.8	-40.32	0.13	0.04	0.09	0.06	0.08
Waste and scrap (910)	65.9	104.1	85.9	80.6	123.7	87.79	0.63	0.91	0.96	0.80	1.19
Used merchandise (920)	8.4	7.9	12.5	6.4	8.7	4.41	0.08	0.07	0.14	0.06	0.08
Goods returned to Canada (980)	16.0	19.1	37.7	13.3	30.2	88.97	0.15	0.17	0.42	0.13	0.29
Special classification provisions (990)	98.3	81.3	53.4	45.0	44.3	-54.94	0.94	0.71	0.60	0.45	0.43
Publishing industries (except Internet) (511)	0.0	0.0	0.0	0.0	0.6	X	0.00	0.00	0.00	0.00	0.01
TOTAL AND PERCENT SHARE OF U.S. TOTAL	10 471.2	11 441.3	8 900.4	10 086.4	10 357.2	-1.09	1.51	1.47	1.22	1.45	1.43
Top 25 Commodities (HS Code)	3 374.0	3 810.1	2 711.6	6 148.6	6 600.1	95.62	32.22	33.30	30.47	60.96	63.72
1. Digital monolithic integrated circuits (854221)	0.0	0.0	0.0	2 877.8	3 028.7	X	0.00	0.00	0.00	28.53	29.24
2. Wheat and meslin (100190)	880.7	837.4	856.8	906.1	940.3	6.77	8.41	7.32	9.63	8.98	9.08
3. Road tractors for semi-trailers (870120)	542.3	359.9	144.0	300.1	384.9	-29.02	5.18	3.15	1.62	2.98	3.72
4. Parts and accessories for automatic data processing (847330)	727.3	647.5	278.0	276.4	225.0	-69.06	6.95	5.66	3.12	2.74	2.17
5. Non-digital monolithic integrated circuits (854229)	0.0	0.0	0.0	212.1	204.5	X	0.00	0.00	0.00	2.10	1.97
6. Fertilizers (310000)	184.7	209.8	176.9	150.0	188.7	2.17	1.76	1.83	1.99	1.49	1.82
7. Motor vehicles, trans goods, gvw between 5 and 20 ton (870422)	34.8	98.6	90.0	136.2	183.7	427.87	0.33	0.86	1.01	1.35	1.77
8. Machine and mechanical appliance, individual function (847989)	26.8	29.0	59.5	109.9	120.2	348.51	0.26	0.25	0.67	1.09	1.16
9. Printed circuits (853400)	56.1	78.7	54.7	112.9	118.6	111.41	0.54	0.69	0.61	1.12	1.15
10. Chemical elements doped for use in electronics (381800)	109.6	171.3	123.5	130.5	114.7	4.65	1.05	1.50	1.39	1.29	1.11
11. Automatic data processing input or output units (847160)	305.5	209.6	130.0	110.5	113.4	-62.88	2.92	1.83	1.46	1.10	1.09
12. Forage products (hay, clover, vetches) (121490)	51.5	75.0	67.9	86.3	92.6	79.81	0.49	0.66	0.76	0.86	0.89
13. Footwear parts; heel cushions, gaiters (640699)	131.7	122.3	100.7	86.4	89.6	-31.97	1.26	1.07	1.13	0.86	0.87
14. Compression-ignition internal combustion engines (840820)	...	75.9	27.0	53.7	84.9	...	...	0.66	0.30	0.53	0.82
15. Airplane and aircraft, unladen weight > 15,000 kg (880240)	...	0.0	0.0	0.0	83.0	...	...	0.00	0.00	0.00	0.80
16. Kraftliner, uncoated and unbleached (480411)	34.0	88.0	62.2	58.7	79.7	134.41	0.32	0.77	0.70	0.58	0.77
17. Instruments and appliances with recording device (903083)	9.3	53.8	92.9	99.8	78.0	738.71	0.09	0.47	1.04	0.99	0.75
18. Coniferous wood, sawn, > 6 mm thick (440710)	175.0	177.8	107.4	73.8	73.1	-58.23	1.67	1.55	1.21	0.73	0.71
19. Parts of instruments for measuring radiation (903090)	57.4	69.6	64.5	69.0	71.7	24.91	0.55	0.61	0.72	0.68	0.69
20. Laser or other light or photon beam machine tools (845610)	47.3	90.9	77.7	61.5	58.3	23.26	0.45	0.79	0.87	0.61	0.56
21. Photographic film, not color, width > 610 mm, length > 200 mm (370242)	0.0	0.0	27.4	77.1	57.0	X	0.00	0.00	0.31	0.76	0.55
22. Wood in chips or particles, coniferous (440121)	...	49.4	44.6	49.8	53.5	...	...	0.43	0.50	0.49	0.52
23. Instruments for checking semiconductor wafers (903082)	...	348.2	97.5	51.5	53.2	...	...	3.04	1.10	0.51	0.51
24. Turbojet and turbo-propeller parts (841191)	...	17.4	22.5	32.5	52.7	...	...	0.15	0.25	0.32	0.51
25. Photographic plates and film (370130)	...	0.0	5.9	26.0	50.1	...	...	0.00	0.07	0.26	0.48

X = Not applicable.
. . . = Not available.

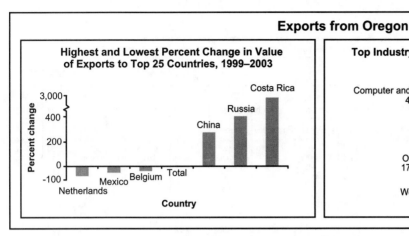

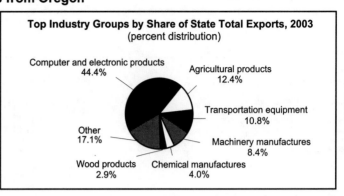

- Oregon's exports exceed $10.3 billion, with about $4.6 billion, or 44 percent, made up of computer and electronic products. Despite a decline of 7 percent from 1999 to 2003, this industry's products remain the state's dominant export. The second largest export industry is agricultural products, which account for about 12 percent of Oregon's total exports. Transportation equipment rank third with just under 11 percent, or $1.1 billion.

- In 2003, digital monolithic integrated circuits were Oregon's leading commodity export, and accounted for more than 29 percent, or over $3 billion, of total exports. Wheat and meslin ranked second with 9 percent and $940 million.

- Fellow NAFTA member Canada was Oregon's top export country, recipient of about 15 percent of the state's exports. South Korea ranked second with 13 percent, followed by Japan with about 12 percent. Exports to all three of these countries have fallen since 1999. Exports to China, ranked sixth, have nearly quadrupled since 1999, an increase of $424 million. In 2003, computer and electronic products accounted for just over 50 percent of Oregon's exports to China.

Table E-42. Total U.S. Exports (Origin of Movement) via Oregon, 1999–2003—Continued

(Top 25 commodities and top 25 countries based on 2003 dollar value.)

Industry, commodity, and country	Value (millions of dollars)					Percent change, 1999–2003	Percent share of state total				
	1999	2000	2001	2002	2003		1999	2000	2001	2002	2003
TOTAL AND PERCENT SHARE OF U.S. TOTAL	10 471.2	11 441.3	8 900.4	10 086.4	10 357.2	-1.09	1.51	1.47	1.22	1.45	1.43
Top 25 Countries	9 903.2	10 558.1	8 233.9	9 461.1	9 719.1	-1.86	94.58	92.28	92.51	93.80	93.84
1. Canada	1 694.6	1 595.6	1 268.8	1 439.9	1 567.3	-7.51	16.18	13.95	14.26	14.28	15.13
2. South Korea	1 641.9	1 183.8	829.3	1 169.6	1 363.3	-16.97	15.68	10.35	9.32	11.60	13.16
3. Japan	1 424.9	1 893.0	1 587.2	1 381.9	1 275.9	-10.46	13.61	16.55	17.83	13.70	12.32
4. Philippines	614.2	760.7	528.1	828.8	767.3	24.92	5.87	6.65	5.93	8.22	7.41
5. Taiwan	471.0	676.2	451.4	603.7	602.0	27.82	4.50	5.91	5.07	5.99	5.81
6. China	150.6	305.0	452.6	681.6	574.9	281.82	1.44	2.67	5.08	6.76	5.55
7. Malaysia	555.6	744.0	339.8	578.7	515.3	-7.25	5.31	6.50	3.82	5.74	4.98
8. Mexico	828.5	481.0	280.1	329.6	393.6	-52.49	7.91	4.20	3.15	3.27	3.80
9. Germany	227.1	360.9	316.1	313.9	321.8	41.66	2.17	3.15	3.55	3.11	3.11
10. Australia	172.2	184.8	160.4	220.2	257.2	49.38	1.64	1.62	1.80	2.18	2.48
11. Singapore	290.1	407.5	425.7	291.0	241.8	-16.65	2.77	3.56	4.78	2.88	2.33
12. Costa Rica	8.1	25.9	11.0	125.1	237.4	2 847.22	0.08	0.23	0.12	1.24	2.29
13. Hong Kong	228.4	309.1	284.6	220.5	208.7	-8.63	2.18	2.70	3.20	2.19	2.01
14. United Kingdom	330.3	279.7	226.2	179.6	208.5	-36.88	3.15	2.44	2.54	1.78	2.01
15. France	160.7	193.9	202.0	281.0	194.8	21.18	1.54	1.69	2.27	2.79	1.88
16. Ireland	83.6	193.5	140.4	140.6	176.3	110.82	0.80	1.69	1.58	1.39	1.70
17. Netherlands	560.9	352.8	167.9	186.0	175.0	-68.80	5.36	3.08	1.89	1.84	1.69
18. Egypt	45.0	97.1	68.5	29.3	130.5	189.85	0.43	0.85	0.77	0.29	1.26
19. Finland	34.6	57.3	50.8	61.8	112.8	226.35	0.33	0.50	0.57	0.61	1.09
20. Italy	87.7	78.4	92.1	93.2	101.5	15.83	0.84	0.68	1.03	0.92	0.98
21. Sweden	50.4	67.5	63.4	46.6	67.7	34.49	0.48	0.59	0.71	0.46	0.65
22. Belgium	113.8	128.3	93.5	82.7	64.8	-43.09	1.09	1.12	1.05	0.82	0.63
23. Russia	11.6	24.3	34.2	37.1	57.8	399.50	0.11	0.21	0.38	0.37	0.56
24. Israel	46.6	84.7	89.1	66.5	52.3	12.35	0.44	0.74	1.00	0.66	0.51
25. Indonesia	71.0	73.2	71.0	72.1	50.7	-28.60	0.68	0.64	0.80	0.71	0.49

Table E-43. Total U.S. Exports (Origin of Movement) via Pennsylvania, 1999–2003

(Top 25 commodities and top 25 countries based on 2003 dollar value.)

Industry, commodity, and country	Value (millions of dollars)					Percent change, 1999–2003	Percent share of state total				
	1999	2000	2001	2002	2003		1999	2000	2001	2002	2003
TOTAL AND PERCENT SHARE OF U.S. TOTAL	16 170.4	18 792.4	17 433.1	15 767.8	16 299.2	0.80	2.33	2.41	2.38	2.27	2.25
Manufactures (NAICS Code)	15 301.1	17 884.9	16 441.9	14 982.6	15 410.4	0.71	94.62	95.17	94.31	95.02	94.55
Processed foods (311)	368.2	405.2	455.1	480.6	560.0	52.08	2.28	2.16	2.61	3.05	3.44
Beverages and tobacco products (312)	14.9	24.0	18.0	10.0	22.1	47.72	0.09	0.00	0.10	0.06	0.14
Fabric mill products (313)	99.4	127.1	143.9	179.0	168.7	69.63	0.61	0.68	0.83	1.14	1.03
Non-apparel textile products (314)	89.5	101.8	90.4	92.7	75.0	-16.16	0.55	0.54	0.52	0.59	0.46
Apparel manufactures (315)	133.3	164.1	198.1	168.0	137.4	3.09	0.82	0.87	1.14	1.07	0.84
Leather and related products (316)	116.7	124.9	129.5	184.3	111.5	-4.49	0.72	0.66	0.74	1.17	0.68
Wood products (321)	287.8	307.1	261.1	289.3	299.7	4.11	1.78	1.63	1.50	1.84	1.84
Paper products (322)	315.4	345.2	315.9	287.2	329.7	4.54	1.95	1.84	1.81	1.82	2.02
Printing and related products (323)	264.1	283.1	273.8	265.3	261.8	-0.88	1.63	1.51	1.57	1.68	1.61
Petroleum and coal products (324)	174.4	182.1	169.1	146.5	159.5	-8.52	1.08	0.97	0.97	0.93	0.98
Chemical manufactures (325)	2 518.6	2 691.1	2 423.7	2 554.7	2 612.3	3.72	15.58	14.32	13.90	16.20	16.03
Plastics and rubber products (326)	439.0	449.5	426.8	450.1	481.0	9.57	2.71	2.39	2.45	2.85	2.95
Non-metallic mineral products (327)	444.3	520.5	514.0	468.6	479.3	7.89	2.75	2.77	2.95	2.97	2.94
Primary metal manufactures (331)	1 267.1	1 437.4	1 418.7	1 306.5	1 438.6	13.53	7.84	7.65	8.14	8.29	8.83
Fabricated metal products (332)	614.8	1 451.9	792.9	683.6	669.0	8.82	3.80	7.73	4.55	4.34	4.10
Machinery manufactures (333)	2 466.9	2 929.1	2 676.8	2 171.7	2 131.4	-13.60	15.26	15.59	15.35	13.77	13.08
Computer and electronic products (334)	2 723.7	3 042.5	2 951.1	2 173.9	2 057.5	-24.46	16.84	16.19	16.93	13.79	12.62
Electrical equipment, appliances, and parts (335)	889.9	1 041.4	863.7	717.5	803.3	-9.74	5.50	5.54	4.95	4.55	4.93
Transportation equipment (336)	1 488.8	1 577.0	1 532.3	1 565.1	1 782.7	19.74	9.21	8.39	8.79	9.93	10.94
Furniture and related products (337)	65.8	91.1	87.2	69.0	63.5	-3.60	0.41	0.48	0.50	0.44	0.39
Miscellaneous manufactures (339)	518.3	588.6	700.1	718.6	766.3	47.84	3.21	3.13	4.02	4.56	4.70
Agricultural and Livestock Products (NAICS Code)	127.3	125.4	117.7	145.9	128.1	0.57	0.79	0.67	0.67	0.93	0.79
Agricultural products (111)	107.2	105.0	91.4	125.4	101.6	-5.19	0.66	0.56	0.52	0.80	0.62
Livestock and livestock products (112)	20.1	20.4	26.2	20.5	26.4	31.25	0.12	0.11	0.15	0.13	0.16
Other Commodities (NAICS Code)	742.0	782.1	873.5	639.2	760.7	2.53	4.59	4.16	5.01	4.05	4.67
Forestry and logging (113)	41.4	49.9	53.4	62.7	70.9	71.16	0.26	0.27	0.31	0.40	0.43
Fishing, hunting, and trapping (114)	1.4	2.7	2.8	4.2	8.0	474.79	0.01	0.01	0.02	0.03	0.05
Oil and gas extraction (211)	5.9	8.3	5.9	8.7	9.8	64.33	0.04	0.04	0.03	0.06	0.06
Mining (212)	258.1	224.4	265.2	187.0	138.2	-46.43	1.60	1.19	1.52	1.19	0.85
Waste and scrap (910)	120.9	194.2	166.6	146.2	209.0	72.89	0.75	1.03	0.96	0.93	1.28
Used merchandise (920)	75.6	85.4	156.4	48.9	73.3	-3.07	0.47	0.45	0.90	0.31	0.45
Goods returned to Canada (980)	55.9	53.6	63.5	36.5	29.7	-46.88	0.35	0.29	0.36	0.23	0.18
Special classification provisions (990)	182.7	163.6	159.7	145.1	220.4	20.63	1.13	0.87	0.92	0.92	1.35
Publishing industries (except Internet) (511)	0.0	0.0	0.0	0.0	1.3	X	0.00	0.00	0.00	0.00	0.01
TOTAL AND PERCENT SHARE OF U.S. TOTAL	16 170.4	18 792.4	17 433.1	15 767.8	16 299.2	0.80	2.33	2.41	2.38	2.27	2.25
Top 25 Commodities (HS Code)	2 657.7	3 064.1	3 059.0	3 002.5	3 155.4	18.73	16.44	16.30	17.55	19.04	19.36
1. Motorcycles (871150)	287.0	356.1	387.9	447.1	464.2	61.74	1.77	1.89	2.23	2.84	2.85
2. Retail medicaments in measured dose (300490)	122.6	156.1	142.0	204.1	185.4	51.22	0.76	0.83	0.81	1.29	1.14
3. Electric plugs and sockets, voltage < 1,000 v (853669)	184.6	242.8	220.8	197.9	175.3	-5.04	1.14	1.29	1.27	1.26	1.08
4. Parts and accessories for automatic data processing (847330)	256.7	239.8	199.7	173.2	170.2	-33.70	1.59	1.28	1.15	1.10	1.04
5. Ozone, oxygen, therapy, respiration apparatus, parts (901920)	64.8	83.9	106.3	121.7	160.2	147.22	0.40	0.45	0.61	0.77	0.98
6. Railway or tramway self-discharging cars not self-propelled (860630)	. . .	11.6	25.5	12.6	156.2	. . .	. . .	0.06	0.15	0.08	0.96
7. Parts of airplanes or helicopters (880330)	156.2	151.9	162.7	153.8	145.4	-6.91	0.97	0.81	0.93	0.98	0.89
8. Diesel electric locomotives (860210)	151.3	119.4	70.6	100.9	124.7	-17.58	0.94	0.64	0.40	0.64	0.77
9. Printed books and brochures (490199)	89.0	91.9	99.0	129.1	119.3	34.04	0.55	0.49	0.57	0.82	0.73
10. Color TVs with or without radios (852812)	105.9	126.6	126.0	130.0	119.1	12.46	0.65	0.67	0.72	0.82	0.73
11. Vaccines for human medicine (300220)	27.9	25.2	48.3	85.6	113.4	306.45	0.17	0.13	0.28	0.54	0.70
12. Parts, electric apparatus, electric circuit (853890)	138.2	107.9	88.1	77.1	108.9	-21.20	0.85	0.57	0.51	0.49	0.67
13. Bituminous coal, not agglomerated (270112)	168.9	150.4	198.0	140.4	100.5	-40.50	1.04	0.80	1.14	0.89	0.62
14. Parts and accessories of motor vehicles (870899)	117.6	157.5	125.6	85.6	99.2	-15.65	0.73	0.84	0.72	0.54	0.61
15. Acrylic polymers in primary forms (390690)	75.4	77.0	59.3	81.7	95.2	26.26	0.47	0.41	0.34	0.52	0.58
16. Other parts and attachments for derricks (843149)	54.1	48.0	59.9	96.8	91.8	69.69	0.33	0.26	0.34	0.61	0.56
17. Non-coniferous wood, sawn, sliced, > 6 mm (440799)	93.2	102.8	85.9	80.7	86.0	-7.73	0.58	0.55	0.49	0.51	0.53
18. Polystyrene, primary forms (390319)	. . .	65.7	76.8	54.3	83.7	. . .	. . .	0.35	0.44	0.34	0.51
19. Transistors, other than photosensitive (854129)	154.2	158.2	104.0	78.6	83.0	-46.17	0.95	0.84	0.60	0.50	0.51
20. Truck, diesel engines, gvw > 20 metric tons (870423)	53.6	52.2	83.6	99.8	82.2	53.36	0.33	0.28	0.48	0.63	0.50
21. Instruments and appliances for medical sciences (901890)	44.4	73.9	96.5	104.3	81.9	84.46	0.27	0.39	0.55	0.66	0.50
22. Self-propelled works trucks and forklifts (842720)	210.3	262.1	312.7	157.0	78.4	-62.72	1.30	1.39	1.79	1.00	0.48
23. Oak wood, sawn, sliced, > 6 mm thick (440791)	101.8	106.5	84.5	76.6	77.6	-23.77	0.63	0.57	0.48	0.49	0.48
24. Veneer sheets, <= 6 mm, non-coniferous (440890)	. . .	59.4	56.5	73.6	77.0	. . .	. . .	0.32	0.32	0.47	0.47
25. Straw or fodder balers, including pick-up balers (843340)	. . .	37.2	38.8	40.0	76.6	. . .	. . .	0.20	0.22	0.25	0.47

X = Not applicable.

. . . = Not available.

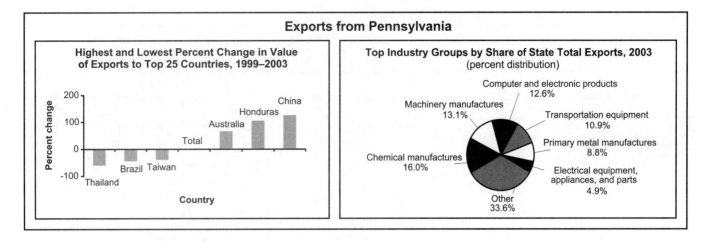

- Pennsylvania's leading export is chemical manufactures. They account for 16 percent of total exports. Transportation equipment exports, the state's fourth largest, had the largest dollar gain from 1999, up $294 million, followed by miscellaneous manufactures, with an increase of $248 million.

- Fishing, hunting, and trapping exports had the largest percentage increase, up nearly sixfold from 1999. From 1999 to 2003, computer and electronic products declined more than 24 percent, or $648 million. As a result, this industry's share of Pennsylvania's total exports declined from nearly 17 percent to less than 13 percent.

- Canada is the largest export market, importing over 35 percent, or $5.8 billion, of the state's exports. Mexico ranks second with just under 7 percent, or $1.1 billion. Exports to China had the largest percentage increase from 1999 to 2003 (115 percent), going from $263 million to $565 million.

Table E-43. Total U.S. Exports (Origin of Movement) via Pennsylvania, 1999–2003—*Continued*

(Top 25 commodities and top 25 countries based on 2003 dollar value.)

Industry, commodity, and country	Value (millions of dollars)					Percent change, 1999–2003	Percent share of state total				
	1999	2000	2001	2002	2003		1999	2000	2001	2002	2003
TOTAL AND PERCENT SHARE OF U.S. TOTAL	16 170.4	18 792.4	17 433.1	15 767.8	16 299.2	0.80	2.33	2.41	2.38	2.27	2.25
Top 25 Countries	14 617.7	16 989.9	15 487.7	14 182.9	14 519.8	-0.67	90.40	90.41	88.84	89.95	89.08
1. Canada	5 831.7	7 133.1	5 667.7	5 557.6	5 849.4	0.30	36.06	37.96	32.51	35.25	35.89
2. Mexico	1 189.9	1 369.5	1 426.9	1 235.9	1 112.1	-6.54	7.36	7.29	8.19	7.84	6.82
3. United Kingdom	942.9	1 338.6	1 204.6	886.8	846.4	-10.23	5.83	7.12	6.91	5.62	5.19
4. Japan	940.5	1 052.0	992.8	861.1	819.3	-12.89	5.82	5.60	5.69	5.46	5.03
5. Germany	705.9	715.8	876.1	714.7	751.4	6.44	4.37	3.81	5.03	4.53	4.61
6. China	263.3	275.9	319.7	424.5	565.0	114.55	1.63	1.47	1.83	2.69	3.47
7. Netherlands	606.9	624.7	703.8	550.1	477.2	-21.37	3.75	3.32	4.04	3.49	2.93
8. Australia	262.7	327.1	254.4	291.2	430.2	63.74	1.62	1.74	1.46	1.85	2.64
9. France	313.4	392.1	440.1	369.0	371.6	18.57	1.94	2.09	2.52	2.34	2.28
10. Belgium	255.0	354.1	339.2	366.1	371.5	45.69	1.58	1.88	1.95	2.32	2.28
11. South Korea	277.0	338.6	363.8	357.4	332.6	20.10	1.71	1.80	2.09	2.27	2.04
12. Singapore	366.3	367.1	290.2	330.4	327.0	-10.74	2.27	1.95	1.66	2.10	2.01
13. Italy	317.7	307.2	351.9	310.8	313.8	-1.25	1.96	1.63	2.02	1.97	1.93
14. Hong Kong	303.2	286.7	307.1	251.1	274.4	-9.50	1.87	1.53	1.76	1.59	1.68
15. Taiwan	381.9	398.6	308.3	223.1	246.8	-35.37	2.36	2.12	1.77	1.42	1.51
16. Malaysia	311.6	322.7	252.1	215.4	209.9	-32.64	1.93	1.72	1.45	1.37	1.29
17. Brazil	324.5	335.5	284.6	186.8	201.2	-38.00	2.01	1.79	1.63	1.18	1.23
18. Spain	203.3	166.4	147.1	169.8	156.3	-23.13	1.26	0.89	0.84	1.08	0.96
19. Israel	101.9	122.2	160.0	142.0	149.5	46.62	0.63	0.65	0.92	0.90	0.92
20. India	83.9	90.5	101.6	100.6	124.0	47.82	0.52	0.48	0.58	0.64	0.76
21. Saudi Arabia	78.3	87.0	121.4	121.8	122.9	56.99	0.48	0.46	0.70	0.77	0.75
22. Thailand	299.1	249.4	181.2	107.4	122.3	-59.11	1.85	1.33	1.04	0.68	0.75
23. Ireland	110.9	130.3	114.9	116.0	117.0	5.45	0.69	0.69	0.66	0.74	0.72
24. Honduras	59.2	99.4	147.7	153.7	114.6	93.45	0.37	0.53	0.85	0.97	0.70
25. Switzerland	86.5	105.6	130.2	139.5	113.5	31.31	0.53	0.56	0.75	0.88	0.70

Table E-44. Total U.S. Exports (Origin of Movement) via Puerto Rico, 1999–2003

(Top 25 commodities and top 25 countries based on 2003 dollar value.)

Industry, commodity, and country	Value (millions of dollars)					Percent change, 1999–2003	Percent share of total				
	1999	2000	2001	2002	2003		1999	2000	2001	2002	2003
TOTAL AND PERCENT SHARE OF U.S. TOTAL	8 301.0	9 735.4	10 573.3	9 732.2	11 913.9	43.52	1.20	1.25	1.45	1.40	1.65
Manufactures (NAICS Code)	8 238.0	9 651.4	10 500.1	9 648.2	11 840.0	43.72	99.24	99.14	99.31	99.14	99.38
Processed foods (311)	549.3	481.2	679.9	531.9	200.1	-63.57	6.62	4.94	6.43	5.47	1.68
Beverages and tobacco products (312)	42.0	58.5	75.8	50.3	34.4	-18.15	0.51	0.00	0.72	0.52	0.29
Fabric mill products (313)	45.6	49.8	42.7	52.9	54.8	20.11	0.55	0.51	0.40	0.54	0.46
Non-apparel textile products (314)	3.9	4.0	2.9	8.2	14.4	273.57	0.05	0.04	0.03	0.08	0.12
Apparel manufactures (315)	143.0	153.4	153.2	199.5	204.4	42.92	1.72	1.58	1.45	2.05	1.72
Leather and related products (316)	60.1	42.0	13.4	9.4	9.1	-84.84	0.72	0.43	0.13	0.10	0.08
Wood products (321)	4.9	4.6	4.0	4.0	5.3	7.99	0.06	0.05	0.04	0.04	0.04
Paper products (322)	14.8	18.2	35.0	30.0	29.0	95.73	0.18	0.19	0.33	0.31	0.24
Printing and related products (323)	4.2	5.0	5.1	4.1	4.3	1.14	0.05	0.05	0.05	0.04	0.04
Petroleum and coal products (324)	55.7	57.6	59.4	116.5	224.6	303.12	0.67	0.59	0.56	1.20	1.89
Chemical manufactures (325)	4 294.2	5 358.7	6 563.8	6 295.2	8 189.3	90.71	51.73	55.04	62.08	64.68	68.74
Plastics and rubber products (326)	36.1	40.3	40.2	35.6	54.1	49.66	0.44	0.41	0.38	0.37	0.45
Non-metallic mineral products (327)	16.0	7.2	12.5	12.9	14.0	-12.75	0.19	0.07	0.12	0.13	0.12
Primary metal manufactures (331)	42.5	25.6	62.2	48.3	103.8	143.96	0.51	0.26	0.59	0.50	0.87
Fabricated metal products (332)	29.6	48.7	80.1	54.9	45.8	54.68	0.36	0.50	0.76	0.56	0.38
Machinery manufactures (333)	161.3	191.5	150.3	158.9	147.6	-8.47	1.94	1.97	1.42	1.63	1.24
Computer and electronic products (334)	2 111.6	2 455.7	1 906.4	1 420.6	1 797.1	-14.89	25.44	25.22	18.03	14.60	15.08
Electrical equipment, appliances, and parts (335)	218.9	224.6	153.4	204.2	281.9	28.79	2.64	2.31	1.45	2.10	2.37
Transportation equipment (336)	57.6	55.7	44.3	45.5	39.2	-31.97	0.69	0.57	0.42	0.47	0.33
Furniture and related products (337)	2.5	3.1	2.6	2.4	1.3	-48.62	0.03	0.03	0.02	0.02	0.01
Miscellaneous manufactures (339)	344.1	366.0	413.1	362.8	385.6	12.06	4.15	3.76	3.91	3.73	3.24
Agricultural and Livestock Products (NAICS Code)	22.4	22.2	12.3	14.8	15.1	-32.78	0.27	0.23	0.12	0.15	0.13
Agricultural products (111)	22.4	22.2	12.2	14.7	15.0	-32.91	0.27	0.23	0.12	0.15	0.13
Livestock and livestock products (112)	0.1	0.0	0.0	0.1	0.1	15.00	0.00	0.00	0.00	0.00	0.00
Other Commodities (NAICS Code)	40.6	61.7	60.9	69.1	58.8	44.90	0.49	0.63	0.58	0.71	0.49
Forestry and logging (113)	0.8	0.8	1.8	2.2	0.3	-64.90	0.01	0.01	0.02	0.02	0.00
Fishing, hunting, and trapping (114)	1.1	0.3	0.9	0.3	0.1	-93.71	0.01	0.00	0.01	0.00	0.00
Oil and gas extraction (211)	0.2	0.4	4.3	2.9	1.2	601.13	0.00	0.00	0.04	0.03	0.01
Mining (212)	0.9	1.5	0.2	0.2	0.4	-55.66	0.01	0.02	0.00	0.00	0.00
Waste and scrap (910)	22.6	40.5	31.3	31.8	45.0	98.91	0.27	0.42	0.30	0.33	0.38
Used merchandise (920)	0.7	1.6	1.2	0.5	1.6	116.46	0.01	0.02	0.01	0.01	0.01
Goods returned to Canada (980)	0.9	1.7	2.8	1.2	0.7	-24.10	0.01	0.02	0.03	0.01	0.01
Special classification provisions (990)	13.4	14.8	18.5	30.0	9.6	-28.33	0.16	0.15	0.18	0.31	0.08
Publishing industries (except Internet) (511)	0.0	0.1	0.0	0.0	0.0	X	0.00	0.00	0.00	0.00	0.00
TOTAL AND PERCENT SHARE OF U.S. TOTAL	8 301.0	9 735.4	10 573.3	9 732.2	11 913.9	43.52	1.20	1.25	1.45	1.40	1.65
Top 25 Commodities (HS Code)	5 310.8	6 724.1	8 053.8	7 551.5	10 224.0	92.51	63.98	69.07	76.17	77.59	85.82
1. Retail medicaments in measured dose (300490)	1 805.6	2 427.9	3 790.4	3 158.4	3 948.7	118.69	21.75	24.94	35.85	32.45	33.14
2. Parts and accessories for automatic data processing (847330)	1 326.9	1 512.6	1 225.4	849.6	1 186.6	-10.57	15.98	15.54	11.59	8.73	9.96
3. Compounds containing an unfused pyridine ring (293339)	12.5	0.7	36.3	110.7	1 044.8	8 258.40	0.15	0.01	0.34	1.14	8.77
4. Composite diagnostic or laboratory reagents (382200)	374.5	358.5	472.1	463.7	633.9	69.27	4.51	3.68	4.47	4.76	5.32
5. Medicaments with hormones, no antibiotics, no doses (300339)	12.3	6.7	1.6	112.3	433.5	3 424.39	0.15	0.07	0.02	1.15	3.64
6. Other antibiotics (294190)	141.1	220.3	266.8	417.2	329.2	133.31	1.70	2.26	2.52	4.29	2.76
7. Erythromycin and its derivatives; salts thereof (294150)	450.8	528.7	595.4	314.9	307.1	-31.88	5.43	5.43	5.63	3.24	2.58
8. Alkaloids (no hormones or antibiotics), dosage form (300440)	103.9	167.9	202.6	237.2	291.0	180.08	1.25	1.72	1.92	2.44	2.44
9. Automatic data processing storage units (847170)	71.3	169.3	187.8	196.0	240.4	237.17	0.86	1.74	1.78	2.01	2.02
10. Other food preparations (210690)	241.4	233.8	251.9	181.4	166.3	-31.11	2.91	2.40	2.38	1.86	1.40
11. Petroleum oils from bituminous mineral (not crude) (271019)	0.0	0.0	0.0	100.6	166.1	X	0.00	0.00	0.00	1.03	1.39
12. Instruments and appliances for medical sciences (901890)	163.6	121.7	115.5	126.5	151.6	-7.33	1.97	1.25	1.09	1.30	1.27
13. Penicillins or streptomycins and derivatives, dosage form (300410)	45.9	35.5	96.1	139.6	149.0	224.62	0.55	0.36	0.91	1.43	1.25
14. Hormones (no antibiotics), dosage form (300439)	22.4	34.8	53.8	88.0	146.4	553.57	0.27	0.36	0.51	0.90	1.23
15. Products and residuals of chemical industry (382490)	111.5	134.5	100.3	96.7	126.2	13.18	1.34	1.38	0.95	0.99	1.06
16. Medicaments containing antibiotics (300320)	13.5	35.4	51.0	134.5	108.5	703.70	0.16	0.36	0.48	1.38	0.91
17. Automatic circuit breakers (853620)	. . .	30.7	37.1	41.3	108.2	. . .	. . .	0.32	0.35	0.42	0.91
18. Pacemakers for stimulating heart muscles (902150)	88.8	96.9	92.1	68.1	107.3	20.83	1.07	1.00	0.87	0.70	0.90
19. Men's or boys' underpants and briefs cotton, knit (610711)	74.3	83.0	91.5	106.6	107.2	44.28	0.90	0.85	0.87	1.10	0.90
20. Automatic data processing units (847180)	119.0	207.7	93.1	67.0	98.8	-16.97	1.43	2.13	0.88	0.69	0.83
21. Parts of electric sound or visual signaling apparatus (853190)	. . .	16.9	19.3	56.7	81.6	. . .	. . .	0.17	0.18	0.58	0.68
22. Herbicides, anti-sprouting products, retail (380830)	44.1	89.4	69.4	132.1	81.4	84.58	0.53	0.92	0.66	1.36	0.68
23. Sulfonamides (293500)	20.8	64.5	28.8	153.4	74.4	257.69	0.25	0.66	0.27	1.58	0.62
24. Organic compounds (294200)	0.1	51.4	88.1	128.0	69.4	69 300.00	0.00	0.53	0.83	1.32	0.58
25. Medical needles, catheters and parts (901839)	66.6	96.0	87.4	71.0	66.4	-0.30	0.80	0.99	0.83	0.73	0.56

X = Not applicable.

. . . = Not available.

Exports from Puerto Rico

Highest and Lowest Percent Change in Value of Exports to Top 25 Countries, 1999–2003

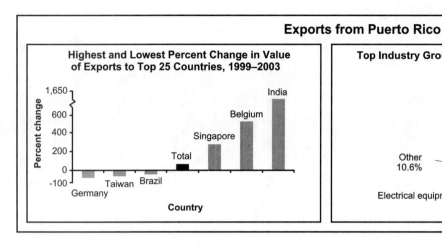

Top Industry Groups by Share of State Total Exports, 2003
(percent distribution)

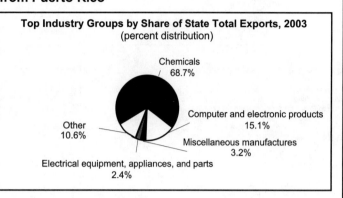

- Puerto Rico's total exports reached $11.9 billion in 2003, a 44 percent increase from 1999. Chemicals is by far the largest export industry, accounting for nearly 69 percent of total exports, or about $8.2 billion. This is an increase of more than 90 percent from 1999. Computer and electronic products rank second, with 15 percent of total exports, or $1.8 billion. Processed foods had the largest dollar decline from 1999 to 2003, down $349 million, or nearly 64 percent.

- About one-third of Puerto Rico's exports are retail medicaments in measured doses, which were worth $3.9 billion 2003, up about 119 percent, or $2.1 billion, from 1999. Both pharmaceutical products (HS code 30) and organic chemicals (HS code 29) are among Puerto Rico's largest and fastest growing commodities.

- Belgium is the top recipient of Puerto Rico's exports. With exports to Belgium worth nearly $2 billion, Puerto Rico is the largest exporter among the states and other areas to Belgium. Exports to Belgium were up 558 percent, or $1.7 billion, from 1999.

Table E-44. Total U.S. Exports (Origin of Movement) via Puerto Rico, 1999–2003—*Continued*

(Top 25 commodities and top 25 countries based on 2003 dollar value.)

Industry, commodity, and country	Value (millions of dollars)					Percent change, 1999–2003	Percent share of total				
	1999	2000	2001	2002	2003		1999	2000	2001	2002	2003
TOTAL AND PERCENT SHARE OF U.S. TOTAL	8 301.0	9 735.4	10 573.3	9 732.2	11 914.0	43.52	1.20	1.25	1.45	1.40	1.65
Top 25 Countries	7 672.3	9 059.5	9 807.8	9 183.8	11 294.9	47.22	92.43	93.06	92.76	94.37	94.80
1. Belgium	300.0	492.7	561.9	980.6	1 974.9	558.30	3.61	5.06	5.31	10.08	16.58
2. Canada	983.0	1 133.1	1 012.5	1 082.3	1 212.7	23.37	11.84	11.64	9.58	11.12	10.18
3. Netherlands	705.3	953.7	835.0	901.7	1 139.7	61.59	8.50	9.80	7.90	9.27	9.57
4. United Kingdom	476.8	838.5	1 868.7	977.0	942.0	97.57	5.74	8.61	17.67	10.04	7.91
5. France	609.1	562.1	614.5	750.8	779.4	27.96	7.34	5.77	5.81	7.71	6.54
6. Dominican Republic	601.9	618.0	626.7	657.3	728.4	21.02	7.25	6.35	5.93	6.75	6.11
7. Germany	1 274.1	1 033.0	1 224.2	603.7	651.3	-48.88	15.35	10.61	11.58	6.20	5.47
8. Italy	650.7	712.0	482.1	522.9	539.0	-17.17	7.84	7.31	4.56	5.37	4.52
9. Singapore	148.6	242.4	147.5	291.3	535.2	260.16	1.79	2.49	1.40	2.99	4.49
10. Switzerland	472.0	432.3	503.9	473.1	527.5	11.76	5.69	4.44	4.77	4.86	4.43
11. Japan	599.5	578.0	642.4	545.1	503.9	-15.95	7.22	5.94	6.08	5.60	4.23
12. India	22.0	26.5	57.0	164.4	377.5	1 615.91	0.27	0.27	0.54	1.69	3.17
13. Ireland	97.4	414.2	252.6	263.2	331.4	240.25	1.17	4.25	2.39	2.70	2.78
14. Mexico	157.6	252.8	180.8	174.1	218.7	38.77	1.90	2.60	1.71	1.79	1.84
15. Hong Kong	34.3	51.8	52.2	51.7	116.0	238.19	0.41	0.53	0.49	0.53	0.97
16. Panama	73.2	58.2	86.5	83.5	115.0	57.10	0.88	0.60	0.82	0.86	0.97
17. Brazil	119.1	108.6	90.2	102.2	94.3	-20.82	1.43	1.12	0.85	1.05	0.79
18. Australia	76.2	140.2	110.5	142.9	92.6	21.52	0.92	1.44	1.05	1.47	0.78
19. China	32.1	47.1	38.1	62.8	88.0	174.14	0.39	0.48	0.36	0.65	0.74
20. Israel	20.4	45.2	118.0	69.3	70.5	245.59	0.25	0.46	1.12	0.71	0.59
21. Taiwan	98.9	86.6	82.3	71.8	59.7	-39.64	1.19	0.89	0.78	0.74	0.50
22. South Korea	36.0	146.9	117.0	96.1	58.5	62.50	0.43	1.51	1.11	0.99	0.49
23. Spain	37.1	30.7	48.3	49.2	46.5	25.34	0.45	0.32	0.46	0.51	0.39
24. Malaysia	33.2	41.1	44.7	36.3	46.4	39.76	0.40	0.42	0.42	0.37	0.39
25. Bahamas	13.8	13.8	10.2	30.5	45.8	231.88	0.17	0.14	0.10	0.31	0.38

Table E-45. Total U.S. Exports (Origin of Movement) via Rhode Island, 1999–2003

(Top 25 commodities and top 25 countries based on 2003 dollar value.)

Industry, commodity, and country	Value (millions of dollars)					Percent change, 1999–2003	Percent share of state total				
	1999	2000	2001	2002	2003		1999	2000	2001	2002	2003
TOTAL AND PERCENT SHARE OF U.S. TOTAL	1 116.3	1 185.6	1 268.6	1 121.0	1 177.5	5.48	0.16	0.15	0.17	0.16	0.16
Manufactures (NAICS Code)	996.1	1 035.8	1 097.5	944.0	1 020.2	2.41	89.23	87.37	86.51	84.21	86.64
Processed foods (311)	4.3	3.8	4.3	8.8	4.9	12.56	0.39	0.32	0.34	0.79	0.42
Beverages and tobacco products (312)	0.0	0.0	0.3	0.0	0.0	X	0.00	0.00	0.02	0.00	0.00
Fabric mill products (313)	28.0	26.1	27.5	31.9	32.1	14.60	2.51	2.20	2.17	2.85	2.73
Non-apparel textile products (314)	7.6	7.5	8.4	7.5	10.2	34.40	0.68	0.63	0.66	0.66	0.86
Apparel manufactures (315)	1.9	2.2	3.1	2.8	2.2	15.19	0.17	0.18	0.24	0.25	0.19
Leather and related products (316)	2.5	2.1	2.4	2.6	2.1	-16.63	0.23	0.17	0.19	0.23	0.18
Wood products (321)	2.0	0.7	1.2	0.7	1.1	-45.07	0.18	0.06	0.09	0.06	0.09
Paper products (322)	25.1	20.4	25.0	23.1	20.1	-19.93	2.25	1.72	1.97	2.06	1.71
Printing and related products (323)	4.8	5.5	5.7	7.0	5.1	6.46	0.43	0.47	0.45	0.62	0.43
Petroleum and coal products (324)	0.4	0.3	0.2	0.5	1.2	197.98	0.04	0.03	0.02	0.04	0.10
Chemical manufactures (325)	86.5	88.4	88.7	126.0	123.2	42.55	7.75	7.46	6.99	11.24	10.47
Plastics and rubber products (326)	54.5	52.6	61.2	75.1	90.6	66.30	4.88	4.43	4.82	6.70	7.69
Non-metallic mineral products (327)	23.3	20.7	21.3	14.0	11.1	-52.42	2.09	1.74	1.68	1.25	0.94
Primary metal manufactures (331)	106.0	93.0	82.4	89.8	61.8	-41.71	9.50	7.85	6.50	8.01	5.25
Fabricated metal products (332)	38.7	40.2	34.1	34.2	40.4	4.49	3.46	3.39	2.68	3.05	3.43
Machinery manufactures (333)	118.2	141.6	236.2	107.7	122.5	3.64	10.59	11.95	18.62	9.60	10.40
Computer and electronic products (334)	261.9	285.2	265.0	206.0	258.5	-1.31	23.46	24.05	20.89	18.37	21.95
Electrical equipment, appliances, and parts (335)	67.3	44.1	38.1	40.7	56.9	-15.48	6.03	3.72	3.00	3.63	4.83
Transportation equipment (336)	28.8	31.9	25.8	20.6	18.1	-37.29	2.58	2.69	2.03	1.84	1.53
Furniture and related products (337)	2.7	3.9	3.1	3.2	4.4	60.82	0.24	0.33	0.25	0.29	0.37
Miscellaneous manufactures (339)	131.5	165.6	163.7	141.8	153.8	16.92	11.78	13.97	12.91	12.65	13.06
Agricultural and Livestock Products (NAICS Code)	1.1	1.1	1.1	0.9	0.5	-55.32	0.10	0.09	0.09	0.08	0.04
Agricultural products (111)	0.9	0.9	0.6	0.8	0.4	-55.14	0.08	0.08	0.04	0.07	0.03
Livestock and livestock products (112)	0.2	0.2	0.6	0.1	0.1	-56.07	0.02	0.02	0.04	0.01	0.01
Other Commodities (NAICS Code)	119.1	148.6	170.0	176.1	156.8	31.67	10.67	12.54	13.40	15.71	13.32
Forestry and logging (113)	1.1	0.7	0.6	1.0	0.7	-38.25	0.10	0.05	0.05	0.09	0.06
Fishing, hunting, and trapping (114)	16.4	13.1	13.2	16.8	18.3	11.97	1.47	1.10	1.04	1.50	1.56
Oil and gas extraction (211)	0.0	0.0	0.0	0.0	0.0	X	0.00	0.00	0.00	0.00	0.00
Mining (212)	0.2	1.0	0.3	0.4	1.0	357.14	0.02	0.08	0.02	0.03	0.09
Waste and scrap (910)	78.5	115.7	141.1	144.8	127.1	62.01	7.03	9.76	11.13	12.92	10.80
Public administration (920)	0.5	0.5	1.3	1.7	0.6	27.47	0.04	0.04	0.10	0.15	0.05
Goods returned to Canada (980)	7.6	4.7	3.7	2.4	2.0	-73.36	0.68	0.40	0.29	0.21	0.17
Special classification provisions (990)	14.8	13.1	9.7	9.1	6.9	-53.26	1.33	1.10	0.77	0.81	0.59
Publishing industries (except Internet) (511)	0.0	0.0	0.0	0.0	0.0	X	0.00	0.00	0.00	0.00	0.00
TOTAL AND PERCENT SHARE OF U.S. TOTAL	1 116.3	1 185.6	1 268.6	1 121.0	1 177.5	5.48	0.16	0.15	0.17	0.16	0.16
Top 25 Commodities (HS Code)	225.3	318.0	464.4	445.7	536.0	137.91	20.18	26.82	36.61	39.76	45.52
1. Waste and scrap of precious metal (711299)	0.0	0.0	0.0	76.8	72.6	X	0.16	0.15	0.17	0.16	6.17
2. Static converters: automatic data processing power (850440)	53.8	77.9	87.8	48.3	54.0	0.37	4.82	6.57	6.92	4.31	4.59
3. Ferrous waste and scrap (720449)	9.8	22.7	42.6	37.9	33.0	236.73	0.88	1.91	3.36	3.38	2.80
4. Chemical preparations for photo use (370790)	9.9	13.3	13.1	20.4	30.0	203.03	0.89	1.12	1.03	1.82	2.55
5. Non-digital monolithic integrated circuits (854229)	. . .	0.0	0.0	2.8	29.4	. . .	. . .	0.00	0.00	0.25	2.50
6. Postage-franking and like machines with calculating device (847090)	22.2	25.2	132.9	12.7	26.8	20.72	1.99	2.13	10.48	1.13	2.28
7. Digital monolithic integrated circuits (854221)	0.0	0.0	0.0	26.4	26.5	X	0.00	0.00	0.00	2.36	2.25
8. Jewelry and parts thereof, of precious metal (711319)	16.9	19.0	17.6	19.1	26.1	54.44	1.51	1.60	1.39	1.70	2.22
9. Cyanides and cyanide oxides (283719)	10.0	7.5	10.0	27.1	25.6	156.00	0.90	0.63	0.79	2.42	2.17
10. Machine and mechanical appliance, individual function (847989)	6.7	7.5	8.6	9.9	18.5	176.12	0.60	0.63	0.68	0.88	1.57
11. Articles of plastics (392690)	8.0	7.9	13.5	18.1	18.3	128.75	0.72	0.67	1.06	1.61	1.55
12. Other imitation jewelry, base metal (711719)	30.6	36.7	29.6	19.6	17.9	-41.50	2.74	3.10	2.33	1.75	1.52
13. Plates, sheets, film, foil, non-cellular, of polymers of propylene (392020) ..	. . .	4.8	3.8	7.4	15.5	. . .	. . .	0.40	0.30	0.66	1.32
14. Plates, non-cellular, polyethylene terephthalate (392062)	5.8	10.3	10.8	9.5	14.9	156.90	0.52	0.87	0.85	0.85	1.27
15. Ball point pens (960810)	13.1	21.7	24.2	16.7	14.9	13.74	1.17	1.83	1.91	1.49	1.27
16. Parts of machines and mechanical appliances (847990)	10.9	12.9	10.4	11.0	14.2	30.28	0.98	1.09	0.82	0.98	1.21
17. Measuring and checking instr., appliances, and machines (903180)	7.0	13.7	18.3	13.7	13.5	92.86	0.63	1.16	1.44	1.22	1.15
18. Electrical switches for voltage < 1,000 v (853650)	. . .	3.4	2.1	5.4	12.6	. . .	. . .	0.29	0.17	0.48	1.07
19. Parts for compasses, navigational instruments (901490)	9.1	5.2	1.3	9.6	11.8	29.67	0.82	0.44	0.10	0.86	1.00
20. Electric plugs and sockets, voltage < 1,000 v (853669)	. . .	5.5	2.2	3.6	11.3	. . .	. . .	0.46	0.17	0.32	0.96
21. Nails, tacks, drawing pins of iron or steel (731700)	3.3	3.9	11.0	12.8	10.8	227.27	0.30	0.33	0.87	1.14	0.92
22. Gold waste and scrap, without other precious metals (711291)	0.0	0.0	0.0	17.5	10.7	X	0.00	0.00	0.00	1.56	0.91
23. Polymers of polyvinyl chloride, plasticized (390422)	8.2	9.5	8.2	8.7	9.2	12.20	0.73	0.80	0.65	0.78	0.78
24. Glass beads imitation pearls precious/semiprecious stones (701810)	. . .	4.8	12.9	7.2	9.0	. . .	. . .	0.40	1.02	0.64	0.76
25. Plates, sheets, and film of plastic (392190)	. . .	4.6	3.5	3.5	8.9	. . .	. . .	0.39	0.28	0.31	0.76

X = Not applicable.
. . . = Not available.

Exports from Rhode Island

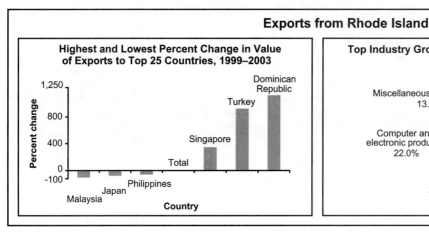

Highest and Lowest Percent Change in Value of Exports to Top 25 Countries, 1999–2003

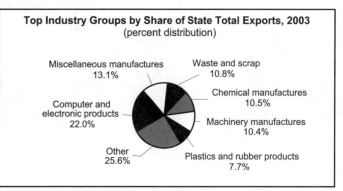

Top Industry Groups by Share of State Total Exports, 2003
(percent distribution)

Miscellaneous manufactures 13.1%
Waste and scrap 10.8%
Chemical manufactures 10.5%
Computer and electronic products 22.0%
Machinery manufactures 10.4%
Other 25.6%
Plastics and rubber products 7.7%

- Rhode Island ranks among the lowest 10 states for value of exports. With exports of $259 million, computer and electronics exports are the state's top export, accounting for 22 percent of the total. Miscellaneous manufactures exports rank second, with $154 million, or 13 percent of Rhode Island's total exports.

- Waste and scrap exports had the largest dollar gain in value from 1999 to 2003, with an increase of $49 million. Primary metal manufactures dropped from $106 million in 1999 to $62 million in 2003. As a result, this industry's exports dropped to just over 5 percent of Rhode Island's total exports, down from more than 9 percent in 1999.

- Exports to Canada account for nearly 35 percent of Rhode Island's total exports. Singapore ranks second, after increasing from less than $23 million in 1999 to $99 million in 2003. Exports of computer and electronic products to Singapore increased 850 percent, or $54 million, from 1999 to 2003. Exports to Mexico fell $42 million from 1999 to 2003.

Table E-45. Total U.S. Exports (Origin of Movement) via Rhode Island, 1999–2003—*Continued*

(Top 25 commodities and top 25 countries based on 2003 dollar value.)

Industry, commodity, and country	Value (millions of dollars)					Percent change, 1999–2003	Percent share of state total				
	1999	2000	2001	2002	2003		1999	2000	2001	2002	2003
TOTAL AND PERCENT SHARE OF U.S. TOTAL	1 116.3	1 185.6	1 268.6	1 121.0	1 177.5	5.48	0.16	0.15	0.17	0.16	0.16
Top 25 Countries	1 006.6	1 085.7	1 137.4	1 026.2	1 088.2	8.11	90.17	91.57	89.66	91.55	92.42
1. Canada	361.1	374.4	352.1	374.9	408.1	13.00	32.35	31.58	27.76	33.44	34.66
2. Singapore	22.5	42.6	60.3	78.9	99.0	339.60	2.02	3.59	4.75	7.04	8.41
3. Mexico	108.9	108.9	69.4	75.0	66.9	-38.58	9.75	9.18	5.47	6.69	5.68
4. United Kingdom	59.2	53.4	125.1	54.5	51.3	-13.43	5.30	4.50	9.86	4.86	4.35
5. Hong Kong	41.1	46.6	34.5	40.4	51.0	24.00	3.68	3.93	2.72	3.60	4.33
6. Belgium	30.0	39.2	35.7	36.9	50.8	69.22	2.69	3.31	2.81	3.29	4.31
7. Germany	31.3	41.2	47.3	43.2	41.3	32.05	2.80	3.48	3.73	3.86	3.51
8. China	10.8	17.5	32.3	31.7	35.8	231.45	0.97	1.48	2.55	2.83	3.04
9. Japan	75.8	67.8	68.0	42.1	35.4	-53.34	6.79	5.72	5.36	3.76	3.01
10. France	20.9	24.3	22.9	23.8	27.7	32.44	1.87	2.05	1.81	2.12	2.35
11. South Korea	21.3	25.4	26.9	36.1	25.2	18.52	1.91	2.14	2.12	3.22	2.14
12. Sweden	18.2	15.4	16.2	23.1	22.3	22.56	1.63	1.30	1.28	2.06	1.89
13. Netherlands	35.7	35.8	40.4	28.7	21.4	-40.03	3.20	3.02	3.18	2.56	1.82
14. Italy	17.2	35.2	26.6	29.6	18.4	7.36	1.54	2.97	2.10	2.64	1.57
15. Taiwan	15.1	20.8	45.1	11.2	17.0	12.48	1.36	1.76	3.55	0.99	1.45
16. Spain	18.8	12.5	17.4	12.3	16.4	-12.59	1.68	1.06	1.37	1.10	1.40
17. Austria	12.1	23.4	20.6	12.0	15.5	28.35	1.08	1.98	1.62	1.07	1.32
18. Philippines	24.2	17.6	22.8	7.7	14.1	-41.71	2.17	1.48	1.79	0.69	1.20
19. Ireland	17.3	26.3	10.8	16.7	13.9	-19.58	1.55	2.22	0.85	1.49	1.18
20. Dominican Republic	0.9	1.4	3.7	3.3	11.7	1 224.15	0.08	0.11	0.29	0.30	0.99
21. Australia	11.2	12.3	19.3	11.3	10.2	-8.84	1.00	1.04	1.52	1.01	0.86
22. Turkey	1.0	4.1	6.4	2.8	10.0	939.52	0.09	0.34	0.50	0.25	0.85
23. Thailand	10.5	8.0	9.2	11.1	9.0	-14.14	0.94	0.67	0.72	0.99	0.76
24. Brazil	8.6	12.6	16.9	10.4	8.7	1.69	0.77	1.07	1.33	0.93	0.74
25. Malaysia	33.0	18.9	7.6	8.8	7.2	-78.24	2.96	1.60	0.60	0.79	0.61

Table E-46. Total U.S. Exports (Origin of Movement) via South Carolina, 1999–2003

(Top 25 commodities and top 25 countries based on 2003 dollar value.)

Industry, commodity, and country	Value (millions of dollars)					Percent change, 1999–2003	Percent share of state total				
	1999	2000	2001	2002	2003		1999	2000	2001	2002	2003
TOTAL AND PERCENT SHARE OF U.S. TOTAL	7 149.9	8 565.1	9 956.3	9 656.2	11 772.9	64.66	1.03	1.10	1.36	1.39	1.63
Manufactures (NAICS Code)	6 952.3	8 353.2	9 761.8	9 444.8	11 539.5	65.98	97.24	97.53	98.05	97.81	98.02
Processed foods (311)	103.2	146.8	155.8	155.4	175.3	69.89	1.44	1.71	1.57	1.61	1.49
Beverages and tobacco products (312)	5.4	4.2	4.9	3.6	2.7	-50.05	0.08	0.00	0.05	0.04	0.02
Fabric mill products (313)	380.8	480.2	507.8	458.9	482.8	26.78	5.33	5.61	5.10	4.75	4.10
Non-apparel textile products (314)	110.1	91.4	98.7	92.0	81.4	-26.04	1.54	1.07	0.99	0.95	0.69
Apparel manufactures (315)	375.5	412.6	272.8	149.5	121.0	-67.78	5.25	4.82	2.74	1.55	1.03
Leather and related products (316)	6.1	2.0	2.3	2.6	2.7	-56.18	0.09	0.02	0.02	0.03	0.02
Wood products (321)	40.0	52.8	57.7	53.9	59.1	47.71	0.56	0.62	0.58	0.56	0.50
Paper products (322)	449.2	572.2	550.5	554.3	564.9	25.76	6.28	6.68	5.53	5.74	4.80
Printing and related products (323)	13.3	11.2	8.5	6.0	14.9	11.79	0.19	0.13	0.09	0.06	0.13
Petroleum and coal products (324)	15.5	12.1	13.4	9.3	7.2	-53.37	0.22	0.14	0.13	0.10	0.06
Chemical manufactures (325)	1 349.9	1 734.2	1 572.7	1 664.8	1 691.2	25.28	18.88	20.25	15.80	17.24	14.37
Plastics and rubber products (326)	715.9	716.8	758.0	804.7	842.6	17.70	10.01	8.37	7.61	8.33	7.16
Non-metallic mineral products (327)	116.1	137.3	151.7	137.6	125.9	8.45	1.62	1.60	1.52	1.42	1.07
Primary metal manufactures (331)	105.5	126.3	96.6	76.4	157.5	49.36	1.48	1.47	0.97	0.79	1.34
Fabricated metal products (332)	267.4	268.4	263.5	291.5	269.7	0.87	3.74	3.13	2.65	3.02	2.29
Machinery manufactures (333)	1 105.4	1 350.6	1 354.8	1 297.7	1 270.8	14.96	15.46	15.77	13.61	13.44	10.79
Computer and electronic products (334)	433.0	415.4	429.4	573.1	915.1	111.36	6.06	4.85	4.31	5.94	7.77
Electrical equipment, appliances, and parts (335)	283.4	238.2	267.6	247.9	296.8	4.72	3.96	2.78	2.69	2.57	2.52
Transportation equipment (336)	995.7	1 476.6	3 099.0	2 760.6	4 332.8	335.16	13.93	17.24	31.13	28.59	36.80
Furniture and related products (337)	15.1	17.9	15.9	12.1	12.3	-18.21	0.21	0.21	0.16	0.13	0.10
Miscellaneous manufactures (339)	65.8	85.9	80.1	92.7	112.6	71.28	0.92	1.00	0.80	0.96	0.96
Agricultural and Livestock Products (NAICS Code)	51.2	67.0	50.0	60.6	87.0	69.80	0.72	0.78	0.50	0.63	0.74
Agricultural products (111)	49.7	66.1	48.9	59.7	85.3	71.64	0.70	0.77	0.49	0.62	0.72
Livestock and livestock products (112)	1.5	0.9	1.1	0.9	1.6	8.73	0.02	0.01	0.01	0.01	0.01
Other Commodities (NAICS Code)	146.3	144.9	144.5	150.8	146.4	0.03	2.05	1.69	1.45	1.56	1.24
Forestry and logging (113)	3.6	2.7	2.7	7.4	4.8	34.71	0.05	0.03	0.03	0.08	0.04
Fishing, hunting, and trapping (114)	4.0	3.7	3.3	2.2	3.3	-19.04	0.06	0.04	0.03	0.02	0.03
Oil and gas extraction (211)	0.0	0.2	0.2	0.1	0.3	X	0.00	0.00	0.00	0.00	0.00
Mining (212)	19.7	31.9	21.3	16.3	15.9	-19.22	0.28	0.37	0.21	0.17	0.13
Waste and scrap (910)	19.8	29.6	36.2	40.6	56.0	183.65	0.28	0.35	0.36	0.42	0.48
Used merchandise (920)	1.7	3.4	4.8	3.7	4.2	150.39	0.02	0.04	0.05	0.04	0.04
Goods returned to Canada (980)	17.5	13.9	15.1	15.0	13.9	-20.34	0.24	0.16	0.15	0.16	0.12
Special classification provisions (990)	80.1	59.6	60.9	65.4	47.8	-40.40	1.12	0.70	0.61	0.68	0.41
Publishing industries (except Internet) (511)	0.0	0.0	0.0	0.0	0.2	X	0.00	0.00	0.00	0.00	0.00
TOTAL AND PERCENT SHARE OF U.S. TOTAL	7 149.9	8 565.1	9 956.3	9 656.2	11 772.9	64.66	1.03	1.10	1.36	1.39	1.63
Top 25 Commodities (HS Code)	1 871.8	2 596.3	3 840.6	4 355.1	6 126.2	227.29	26.18	30.31	38.57	45.10	52.04
1. Passenger vehicle, spark-ignition, > 1,500 cc < 3,000 cc (870323)	463.4	629.9	888.2	635.3	2 000.0	331.59	6.48	7.35	8.92	6.58	16.99
2. Passenger vehicles > 2,500 cc (870333)	0.0	0.5	318.6	896.1	1 081.9	X	0.00	0.01	3.20	9.28	9.19
3. Passenger vehicles, spark-ignition, > 3,000 cc (870324)	10.2	221.5	518.3	496.2	300.4	2 845.10	0.14	2.59	5.21	5.14	2.55
4. New pneumatic tires of rubber, for motor cars (401110)	268.3	252.1	260.7	256.6	258.3	-3.73	3.75	2.94	2.62	2.66	2.19
5. Polyethylene terephthalate, in primary forms (390760)	148.8	194.3	281.3	233.9	256.6	72.45	2.08	2.27	2.83	2.42	2.18
6. Parts and accessories of motor vehicles bodies (870829)	45.2	68.1	111.2	185.8	201.1	344.91	0.63	0.80	1.12	1.92	1.71
7. Chemical wood-pulp, unbleached non-coniferous (470321)	138.0	159.7	151.0	169.3	189.2	37.10	1.93	1.86	1.52	1.75	1.61
8. Cellulose acetates, non-plasticized, primary forms (391211)	98.6	82.0	106.6	115.0	175.8	78.30	1.38	0.96	1.07	1.19	1.49
9. Gas turbine parts (841199)	80.2	129.7	218.8	183.6	151.2	88.53	1.12	1.51	2.20	1.90	1.28
10. Tantalum electrolytic fixed capacitors (853221)	. . .	3.0	3.2	52.5	141.1	. . .	. . .	0.04	0.03	0.54	1.20
11. Fuel elements (cartridges) non-irradiated, and parts (840130)	54.4	59.0	112.8	87.7	134.6	147.43	0.76	0.69	1.13	0.91	1.14
12. New pneumatic tires of rubber, for buses or trucks (401120)	160.3	113.5	139.2	146.3	134.2	-16.28	2.24	1.33	1.40	1.52	1.14
13. Mowers for lawns, parks cutting devices horizontal plane (843311)	104.8	115.5	63.0	102.2	119.5	14.03	1.47	1.35	0.63	1.06	1.02
14. Parts and accessories of motor vehicles (870899)	. . .	30.5	49.5	53.6	117.9	. . .	. . .	0.36	0.50	0.56	1.00
15. Ceramic dielectric, multilayer fixed capacitors (853224)	61.7	55.4	52.8	88.7	116.6	88.98	0.86	0.65	0.53	0.92	0.99
16. Kraftliner, uncoated and unbleached (480411)	26.3	72.2	129.7	99.2	90.8	245.25	0.37	0.84	1.30	1.03	0.77
17. Spark-ignition engine parts (840991)	22.0	56.2	53.1	56.3	88.4	301.82	0.31	0.66	0.53	0.58	0.75
18. Pass. vehicles, spark-ignition eng. cylinder cap. < 1,000 cc (870321)	50.2	59.6	110.3	59.2	81.1	61.55	0.70	0.70	1.11	0.61	0.69
19. Products and residuals of chemical industry (382490)	12.8	40.5	9.5	91.1	79.2	518.75	0.18	0.47	0.10	0.94	0.67
20. Brakes, servo-brakes, and parts for motor vehicles (870839)	67.2	59.1	61.8	80.9	77.7	15.63	0.94	0.69	0.62	0.84	0.66
21. Synthetic staple fibers of polyester (550320)	59.4	75.9	58.0	81.9	77.6	30.64	0.83	0.89	0.58	0.85	0.66
22. Automatic data processing units (847180)	0.3	2.9	7.8	55.0	67.4	22 366.60	0.00	0.03	0.08	0.57	0.57
23. Cotton, not carded or combed (520100)	. . .	39.5	20.1	24.2	64.9	. . .	. . .	0.46	0.20	0.25	0.55
24. Magnetic resonance imaging apparatus (901813)	. . .	5.5	53.0	52.4	61.0	. . .	. . .	0.06	0.53	0.54	0.52
25. Fuel, lubricating/cooling pumps for piston engines (841330)	. . .	70.7	62.1	52.1	59.7	. . .	. . .	0.83	0.62	0.54	0.51

X = Not applicable.
. . . = Not available.

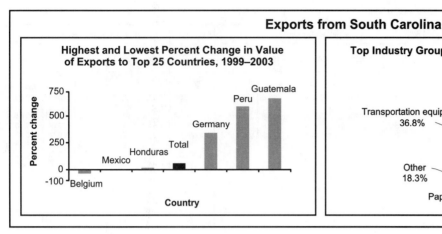

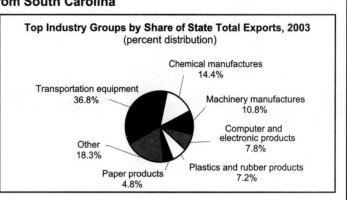

- From 1999 to 2003, the value of South Carolina's exports increased nearly 65 percent, which ranks second after Nevada among the 50 states. Much of this growth can be attributed to an increase in transportation equipment exports, which rose from $996 million in 1999 to $4.3 billion in 2003, a jump of 335 percent. They now account for close to 37 percent of South Carolina's exports, up from 13 percent in 1999.

- Chemical manufactures are the state's second leading export, with about 14 percent of total exports. They increased by $341 million, or 25 percent, from 1999. Apparel manufactures fell from $375 million in 1999 to $121 million in 2003.

- Passenger vehicles represent South Carolina's top three commodities. Exports of vehicles with a spark-ignition engine of cylinder capacity 1,500 to 3,000 cc grew from $463 million in 1999 to $2 billion in 2003. Exports to Germany, the state's leading export market, increased from $651 million to $2.7 billion during this period. About 87 percent of these exports are transportation equipment.

Table E-46. Total U.S. Exports (Origin of Movement) via South Carolina, 1999–2003—*Continued*

(Top 25 commodities and top 25 countries based on 2003 dollar value.)

Industry, commodity, and country	Value (millions of dollars)					Percent change, 1999–2003	Percent share of state total				
	1999	2000	2001	2002	2003		1999	2000	2001	2002	2003
TOTAL AND PERCENT SHARE OF U.S. TOTAL	7 149.9	8 565.1	9 956.3	9 656.2	11 772.9	64.66	1.03	1.10	1.36	1.39	1.63
Top 25 Countries	6 264.3	7 479.6	8 873.0	8 618.5	10 616.6	69.48	87.61	87.33	89.12	89.25	90.18
1. Germany	651.4	895.9	1 454.2	1 685.4	2 702.7	314.93	9.11	10.46	14.61	17.45	22.96
2. Canada	2 098.3	2 442.1	2 352.1	2 411.4	2 598.0	23.82	29.35	28.51	23.62	24.97	22.07
3. United Kingdom	326.0	465.3	1 202.6	555.8	816.7	150.54	4.56	5.43	12.08	5.76	6.94
4. Mexico	735.4	746.3	731.0	781.6	751.9	2.24	10.29	8.71	7.34	8.09	6.39
5. Japan	315.4	455.2	439.5	386.4	476.4	51.04	4.41	5.32	4.41	4.00	4.05
6. Netherlands	202.1	207.4	203.1	213.4	298.9	47.90	2.83	2.42	2.04	2.21	2.54
7. Belgium	350.5	395.2	269.7	258.6	290.7	-17.07	4.90	4.61	2.71	2.68	2.47
8. China	139.0	127.1	172.0	236.5	286.9	106.40	1.94	1.48	1.73	2.45	2.44
9. France	160.1	191.6	260.6	319.9	275.1	71.80	2.24	2.24	2.62	3.31	2.34
10. Australia	97.1	103.6	150.5	171.7	228.3	135.00	1.36	1.21	1.51	1.78	1.94
11. Hong Kong	143.5	130.9	149.5	168.0	219.8	53.11	2.01	1.53	1.50	1.74	1.87
12. Brazil	168.1	233.6	374.5	212.9	207.4	23.36	2.35	2.73	3.76	2.21	1.76
13. South Africa	39.5	37.2	95.9	118.2	162.3	310.47	0.55	0.43	0.96	1.22	1.38
14. South Korea	120.2	147.6	116.7	154.7	161.4	34.19	1.68	1.72	1.17	1.60	1.37
15. Taiwan	143.8	183.5	130.3	117.8	161.1	12.04	2.01	2.14	1.31	1.22	1.37
16. Italy	135.7	149.2	181.0	172.2	160.0	17.93	1.90	1.74	1.82	1.78	1.36
17. Singapore	54.0	51.1	68.3	93.4	158.0	192.54	0.76	0.60	0.69	0.97	1.34
18. Switzerland	103.4	111.6	45.7	129.5	134.0	29.60	1.45	1.30	0.46	1.34	1.14
19. El Salvador	70.6	95.4	123.4	122.1	91.7	29.88	0.99	1.11	1.24	1.26	0.78
20. Spain	73.8	61.7	68.7	73.0	80.9	9.67	1.03	0.72	0.69	0.76	0.69
21. Turkey	28.6	33.5	64.5	42.8	76.9	169.00	0.40	0.39	0.65	0.44	0.65
22. Honduras	68.6	116.1	109.1	67.7	73.4	6.93	0.96	1.36	1.10	0.70	0.62
23. Guatemala	8.5	17.2	24.9	34.2	71.4	735.87	0.12	0.20	0.25	0.35	0.61
24. Peru	10.0	42.7	39.5	48.8	67.6	575.09	0.14	0.50	0.40	0.51	0.57
25. United Arab Emirates	20.6	38.6	45.9	42.1	65.5	217.63	0.29	0.45	0.46	0.44	0.56

Table E-47. Total U.S. Exports (Origin of Movement) via South Dakota, 1999–2003

(Top 25 commodities and top 25 countries based on 2003 dollar value.)

Industry, commodity, and country	Value (millions of dollars)					Percent change, 1999–2003	Percent share of state total				
	1999	2000	2001	2002	2003		1999	2000	2001	2002	2003
TOTAL AND PERCENT SHARE OF U.S. TOTAL	494.7	679.4	594.9	596.8	672.3	35.90	0.07	0.09	0.08	0.09	0.09
Manufactures (NAICS Code)	407.3	619.3	552.8	533.9	608.5	49.38	82.34	91.16	92.93	89.46	90.51
Processed foods (311)	45.6	125.5	153.8	178.8	178.8	292.26	9.22	18.47	25.86	29.96	26.60
Beverages and tobacco products (312)	0.1	0.1	0.1	0.3	1.5	1 466.32	0.02	0.00	0.01	0.05	0.22
Fabric mill products (313)	6.4	6.0	5.0	6.2	8.6	35.25	1.28	0.88	0.84	1.04	1.28
Non-apparel textile products (314)	1.8	2.1	3.5	5.0	4.1	121.61	0.37	0.32	0.58	0.84	0.61
Apparel manufactures (315)	0.9	0.9	0.7	0.3	1.1	24.68	0.17	0.13	0.11	0.05	0.16
Leather and related products (316)	0.2	0.7	1.4	1.5	1.7	868.72	0.04	0.11	0.23	0.25	0.26
Wood products (321)	0.2	0.4	0.2	0.2	0.2	6.81	0.04	0.06	0.04	0.04	0.03
Paper products (322)	17.1	15.3	13.4	15.8	22.7	33.19	3.45	2.25	2.24	2.64	3.38
Printing and related products (323)	3.1	2.3	4.5	4.0	2.3	-26.79	0.63	0.34	0.76	0.67	0.34
Petroleum and coal products (324)	0.5	0.3	0.3	0.1	0.2	-55.30	0.10	0.04	0.05	0.02	0.03
Chemical manufactures (325)	8.8	8.8	13.1	16.1	11.6	31.65	1.78	1.29	2.20	2.69	1.73
Plastics and rubber products (326)	6.3	5.8	7.0	6.9	5.9	-6.77	1.28	0.86	1.18	1.16	0.88
Non-metallic mineral products (327)	1.2	0.5	2.5	0.6	0.9	-21.41	0.24	0.08	0.42	0.10	0.14
Primary metal manufactures (331)	33.0	29.5	23.6	1.0	1.3	-96.14	6.67	4.34	3.96	0.16	0.19
Fabricated metal products (332)	5.6	5.3	7.1	7.0	12.7	127.89	1.13	0.77	1.20	1.18	1.89
Machinery manufactures (333)	53.7	174.5	63.5	64.8	77.2	43.59	10.87	25.69	10.67	10.86	11.48
Computer and electronic products (334)	173.5	179.9	192.1	167.5	218.2	25.77	35.07	26.47	32.28	28.07	32.46
Electrical equipment, appliances, and parts (335)	16.1	22.0	16.7	7.2	4.9	-69.43	3.26	3.25	2.81	1.21	0.73
Transportation equipment (336)	25.3	20.8	22.3	23.2	25.5	0.82	5.12	3.06	3.76	3.90	3.80
Furniture and related products (337)	0.3	1.2	0.3	0.3	0.3	-6.49	0.06	0.17	0.06	0.05	0.04
Miscellaneous manufactures (339)	7.6	17.5	21.8	27.0	28.7	275.55	1.54	2.57	3.66	4.52	4.27
Agricultural and Livestock Products (NAICS Code)	73.4	45.0	23.5	23.3	27.8	-62.05	14.83	6.62	3.94	3.90	4.14
Agricultural products (111)	72.1	43.9	21.3	21.4	24.8	-65.61	14.57	6.46	3.57	3.59	3.69
Livestock and livestock products (112)	1.3	1.1	2.2	1.9	3.1	138.36	0.26	0.17	0.37	0.31	0.45
Other Commodities (NAICS Code)	14.0	15.1	18.6	39.6	36.0	157.07	2.83	2.22	3.12	6.63	5.35
Forestry and logging (113)	0.0	0.0	0.1	0.2	0.1	X	0.00	0.00	0.02	0.03	0.02
Fishing, hunting, and trapping (114)	0.1	0.0	0.0	0.2	0.0	X	0.02	0.00	0.00	0.03	0.00
Oil and gas extraction (211)	0.0	5.1	0.0	0.0	0.0	X	0.00	0.74	0.00	0.00	0.00
Mining (212)	7.8	3.5	4.6	6.4	5.0	-35.26	1.57	0.52	0.78	1.08	0.75
Waste and scrap (910)	0.3	0.4	7.5	26.2	25.8	7 570.54	0.07	0.06	1.26	4.38	3.83
Used merchandise (920)	1.0	0.7	0.6	2.5	0.9	-9.01	0.20	0.11	0.10	0.42	0.13
Goods returned to Canada (980)	1.4	2.5	3.3	1.3	1.0	-27.75	0.28	0.37	0.56	0.22	0.15
Special classification provisions (990)	3.4	2.8	2.4	2.8	3.0	-11.07	0.68	0.41	0.40	0.46	0.45
Publishing industries (except Internet) (511)	0.0	0.0	0.0	0.0	0.1	X	0.00	0.00	0.00	0.00	0.02
TOTAL AND PERCENT SHARE OF U.S. TOTAL	494.7	679.4	594.9	596.8	672.3	35.90	0.07	0.09	0.08	0.09	0.09
Top 25 Commodities (HS Code)	153.6	248.8	272.7	338.3	424.8	176.56	31.05	36.62	45.84	56.69	63.19
1. Parts and accessories for automatic data processing (847330)	94.1	102.1	74.4	59.4	82.7	-12.11	19.02	15.03	12.51	9.95	12.30
2. Meat of bovine animals, boneless, fresh or chilled (020130)	0.6	28.2	36.8	51.7	47.7	7 850.00	0.12	4.15	6.19	8.66	7.10
3. Digital processing units (847150)	0.7	3.3	7.6	11.2	24.9	3 457.14	0.14	0.49	1.28	1.88	3.70
4. Automatic data processing units (847180)	0.5	0.8	24.0	23.0	23.6	4 620.00	0.10	0.12	4.03	3.85	3.51
5. Mechanical front-end shovel loaders (842951)	13.3	11.7	13.2	15.5	19.9	49.62	2.69	1.72	2.22	2.60	2.96
6. Meat of swine, fresh or chilled (020319)	0.0	6.7	19.6	22.8	19.5	X	0.00	0.99	3.29	3.82	2.90
7. Soybean oilcake and other solid residue (230400)	21.6	26.5	23.4	22.2	18.6	-13.89	4.37	3.90	3.93	3.72	2.77
8. Fats, bovine, sheep or goat, raw or rendered (150200)	0.1	3.8	5.0	7.0	18.5	18 400.00	0.02	0.56	0.84	1.17	2.75
9. Corn, other than seed corn (100590)	3.1	9.4	5.8	10.6	15.7	406.45	0.63	1.38	0.97	1.78	2.34
10. Gold waste and scrap, without other precious metals (711291)	0.0	0.0	0.0	14.2	14.4	X	0.00	0.00	0.00	2.38	2.14
11. Parts of apparatus for line telephony or telegraphy (851790)	2.7	8.6	1.3	7.2	14.3	429.63	0.55	1.27	0.22	1.21	2.13
12. Game machines, excluding coin-operated (950490)	1.6	4.4	3.5	10.7	13.9	768.75	0.32	0.65	0.59	1.79	2.07
13. Indicator panels incorporating lcds or leds (853120)	. . .	0.3	2.4	3.2	11.8	. . .	. . .	0.04	0.40	0.54	1.76
14. Digital automatic data processing machines (847149)	6.9	4.9	9.5	17.9	11.3	63.77	1.39	0.72	1.60	3.00	1.68
15. Waste and scrap of precious metal (711299)	0.0	0.0	0.0	11.0	11.2	X	0.00	0.00	0.00	1.84	1.67
16. Sacks and bags (including cones) of polymers of ethylene (392321) ..	5.2	5.9	6.1	7.0	10.8	107.69	1.05	0.87	1.03	1.17	1.61
17. Meat of swine, frozen (020329)	2.0	7.9	10.7	8.8	10.0	400.00	0.40	1.16	1.80	1.47	1.49
18. Offal of bovine animals, edible, frozen (020629)	0.1	2.5	4.3	6.7	9.8	9 700.00	0.02	0.37	0.72	1.12	1.46
19. Offal of swine except livers, edible, frozen (020649)	1.2	5.1	5.4	6.8	9.4	683.33	0.24	0.75	0.91	1.14	1.40
20. Animal (not fish) guts, bladders, stomachs and parts (050400)	1.0	5.1	5.7	4.9	8.0	700.00	0.20	0.75	0.96	0.82	1.19
21. Fans (841459)	. . .	4.8	3.7	4.9	6.8	. . .	. . .	0.71	0.62	0.82	1.01
22. Meat, swine, hams, shoulders, bone in, fresh or chilled (020312)	. . .	1.6	3.6	2.6	6.2	. . .	. . .	0.24	0.61	0.44	0.92
23. Portable digital a.d.p. machines < 10 kg (847130)	. . .	3.0	1.7	3.6	5.7	. . .	. . .	0.44	0.29	0.60	0.85
24. Parts and accessories of motor vehicles bodies (870829)	1.9	2.0	5.0	5.4	5.2	173.68	0.38	0.29	0.84	0.90	0.77
25. Continuous-action elevators and conveyors, for goods (842833)	. . .	1.3	0.6	1.0	4.9	. . .	. . .	0.19	0.10	0.17	0.73

X = Not applicable.

. . . = Not available.

Exports from South Dakota

Highest and Lowest Percent Change in Value of Exports to Top 25 Countries, 1999–2003

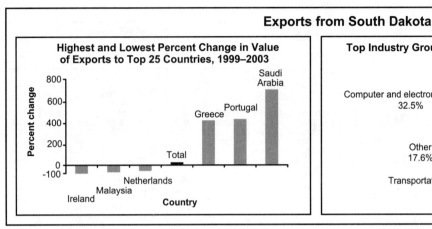

Top Industry Groups by Share of State Total Exports, 2003
(percent distribution)

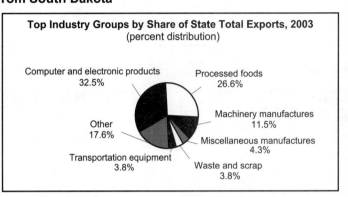

- South Dakota's exports are worth $672 million, ranking it among the lowest in the nation. However, exports from South Dakota increased about 36 percent, or $178 million, since 1999. Computer and electronic products and processed foods are the state's leading export industries, together accounting for 59 percent of total exports. Processed foods exports nearly quadrupled from 1999 to 2003, with an increase of $133 million.

- Many of South Dakota's top commodities had tremendous growth from 1999 to 2003. However, parts and accessories for automatic data processing machines remain the state's number one export commodity, accounting for about 12 percent of total exports in 2003.

- Canada is the top export country, as recipient to 43 percent of South Dakota's exports. Since 1999, exports to Canada increased by $78 million, with about $66 million attributable to an increase in processed food exports. Exports to Japan and Hong Kong have increased substantially since 1999, moving both countries among South Dakota's top trading partners.

Table E-47. Total U.S. Exports (Origin of Movement) via South Dakota, 1999–2003—*Continued*

(Top 25 commodities and top 25 countries based on 2003 dollar value.)

Industry, commodity, and country	Value (millions of dollars)					Percent change, 1999–2003	Percent share of state total				
	1999	2000	2001	2002	2003		1999	2000	2001	2002	2003
TOTAL AND PERCENT SHARE OF U.S. TOTAL	494.7	679.4	594.9	596.8	672.3	35.90	0.07	0.09	0.08	0.09	0.09
Top 25 Countries	477.6	660.1	556.1	574.4	648.5	35.78	96.55	97.16	93.48	96.24	96.47
1. Canada	210.9	272.1	268.8	289.6	288.8	36.97	42.63	40.05	45.18	48.52	42.96
2. Mexico	83.2	69.4	58.0	75.4	123.9	48.97	16.82	10.21	9.76	12.64	18.43
3. Japan	12.6	21.8	41.4	37.4	51.2	306.90	2.55	3.20	6.95	6.26	7.62
4. Hong Kong	13.1	18.3	16.1	35.9	41.5	216.03	2.65	2.69	2.71	6.02	6.17
5. United Kingdom	25.4	46.9	50.1	36.1	37.5	47.83	5.13	6.91	8.42	6.05	5.58
6. Germany	18.4	26.9	30.1	19.5	25.1	36.54	3.71	3.96	5.05	3.27	3.73
7. China	2.2	6.5	5.9	9.7	10.4	373.00	0.45	0.96	0.99	1.63	1.55
8. Thailand	9.7	2.3	15.3	14.1	9.3	-3.92	1.95	0.33	2.57	2.36	1.38
9. Singapore	13.0	11.1	11.7	8.1	9.2	-29.46	2.64	1.63	1.96	1.35	1.37
10. South Korea	4.6	5.5	5.7	6.2	6.1	32.76	0.92	0.81	0.96	1.05	0.90
11. Italy	5.2	14.0	4.7	5.7	5.9	13.71	1.06	2.06	0.79	0.95	0.88
12. Taiwan	8.7	4.6	5.5	5.6	5.4	-38.36	1.76	0.67	0.93	0.94	0.80
13. Netherlands	18.5	12.8	8.4	5.8	5.2	-71.89	3.74	1.89	1.42	0.97	0.77
14. Spain	1.7	2.6	1.1	2.1	3.6	109.40	0.35	0.39	0.19	0.35	0.54
15. Australia	11.1	5.9	8.3	3.7	3.5	-68.67	2.24	0.87	1.39	0.62	0.52
16. France	2.6	3.8	2.7	2.1	3.3	26.89	0.53	0.56	0.45	0.35	0.50
17. Brazil	1.8	2.0	2.8	2.5	3.2	79.73	0.36	0.30	0.48	0.42	0.48
18. Portugal	0.5	0.6	0.9	1.9	3.1	469.46	0.11	0.09	0.15	0.32	0.45
19. Israel	0.9	2.2	1.5	3.7	2.5	162.83	0.19	0.32	0.25	0.62	0.37
20. Belgium	2.2	114.4	3.9	4.2	2.4	8.62	0.45	16.85	0.65	0.70	0.36
21. Ireland	20.9	7.3	6.8	0.2	1.6	-92.22	4.22	1.08	1.14	0.03	0.24
22. Malaysia	9.0	7.6	4.9	2.8	1.6	-81.89	1.81	1.12	0.83	0.46	0.24
23. Greece	0.3	0.4	0.0	0.2	1.4	446.12	0.05	0.05	0.01	0.03	0.21
24. Saudi Arabia	0.2	0.3	1.4	1.7	1.4	773.42	0.03	0.04	0.24	0.29	0.21
25. Austria	1.0	0.9	0.0	0.3	1.4	34.12	0.20	0.13	0.00	0.05	0.20

Table E-48. Total U.S. Exports (Origin of Movement) via Tennessee, 1999–2003

(Top 25 commodities and top 25 countries based on 2003 dollar value.)

Industry, commodity, and country	Value (millions of dollars)					Percent change, 1999–2003	Percent share of state total				
	1999	2000	2001	2002	2003		1999	2000	2001	2002	2003
TOTAL AND PERCENT SHARE OF U.S. TOTAL	9 867.8	11 591.6	11 320.2	11 621.3	12 611.8	27.81	1.42	1.49	1.55	1.68	1.74
Manufactures (NAICS Code)	9 447.4	10 704.5	10 439.5	10 669.9	11 027.4	16.72	95.74	92.35	92.22	91.81	87.44
Processed foods (311)	342.3	327.9	231.5	204.7	284.6	-16.85	3.47	2.83	2.04	1.76	2.26
Beverages and tobacco products (312)	144.9	161.6	206.3	224.4	243.2	67.83	1.47	0.00	1.82	1.93	1.93
Fabric mill products (313)	139.9	150.9	152.6	141.5	215.6	54.13	1.42	1.30	1.35	1.22	1.71
Non-apparel textile products (314)	25.1	31.6	29.9	28.4	28.1	12.09	0.25	0.27	0.26	0.24	0.22
Apparel manufactures (315)	194.5	195.2	102.2	89.3	101.0	-48.06	1.97	1.68	0.90	0.77	0.80
Leather and related products (316)	35.6	38.4	42.1	43.2	33.7	-5.22	0.36	0.33	0.37	0.37	0.27
Wood products (321)	66.4	71.5	71.9	75.9	73.9	11.31	0.67	0.62	0.63	0.65	0.59
Paper products (322)	441.3	463.7	482.5	425.9	332.4	-24.67	4.47	4.00	4.26	3.66	2.64
Printing and related products (323)	154.1	133.8	144.8	169.9	187.5	21.68	1.56	1.15	1.28	1.46	1.49
Petroleum and coal products (324)	5.5	12.1	6.9	2.1	10.4	89.32	0.06	0.10	0.06	0.02	0.08
Chemical manufactures (325)	1 392.7	1 374.6	1 396.6	1 583.6	1 723.4	23.75	14.11	11.86	12.34	13.63	13.67
Plastics and rubber products (326)	432.0	490.1	457.9	493.7	473.8	9.67	4.38	4.23	4.04	4.25	3.76
Non-metallic mineral products (327)	135.1	171.6	149.0	132.3	147.5	9.18	1.37	1.48	1.32	1.14	1.17
Primary metal manufactures (331)	155.2	288.2	266.2	266.1	254.4	63.94	1.57	2.49	2.35	2.29	2.02
Fabricated metal products (332)	351.7	533.0	402.8	357.4	353.1	0.40	3.56	4.60	3.56	3.08	2.80
Machinery manufactures (333)	1 153.1	1 218.7	1 252.4	1 220.5	1 264.9	9.70	11.69	10.51	11.06	10.50	10.03
Computer and electronic products (334)	1 105.4	1 368.6	1 584.4	1 361.1	1 773.1	60.41	11.20	11.81	14.00	11.71	14.06
Electrical equipment, appliances, and parts (335)	483.4	569.6	490.9	462.3	460.8	-4.69	4.90	4.91	4.34	3.98	3.65
Transportation equipment (336)	2 277.6	2 572.6	2 430.7	2 765.9	2 391.0	4.98	23.08	22.19	21.47	23.80	18.96
Furniture and related products (337)	59.0	69.8	39.1	40.2	37.9	-35.80	0.60	0.60	0.35	0.35	0.30
Miscellaneous manufactures (339)	352.8	461.2	499.0	581.4	636.9	80.52	3.58	3.98	4.41	5.00	5.05
Agricultural and Livestock Products (NAICS Code)	202.1	441.1	476.5	676.0	1 155.5	471.80	2.05	3.81	4.21	5.82	9.16
Agricultural products (111)	191.0	433.3	469.5	671.5	1 148.9	501.44	1.94	3.74	4.15	5.78	9.11
Livestock and livestock products (112)	11.1	7.8	7.1	4.5	6.6	-40.09	0.11	0.07	0.06	0.04	0.05
Other Commodities (NAICS Code)	218.3	446.0	404.1	275.5	428.9	96.52	2.21	3.85	3.57	2.37	3.40
Forestry and logging (113)	5.7	8.7	17.4	10.4	9.1	60.08	0.06	0.07	0.15	0.09	0.07
Fishing, hunting, and trapping (114)	3.5	6.2	6.6	4.2	4.6	30.23	0.04	0.05	0.06	0.04	0.04
Oil and gas extraction (211)	0.3	0.2	0.3	0.2	0.4	10.88	0.00	0.00	0.00	0.00	0.00
Mining (212)	22.6	32.6	32.2	26.2	29.2	29.24	0.23	0.28	0.28	0.23	0.23
Waste and scrap (910)	10.1	27.5	27.5	34.9	49.3	388.66	0.10	0.24	0.24	0.30	0.39
Used merchandise (920)	6.2	6.9	19.8	6.1	8.7	40.57	0.06	0.06	0.17	0.05	0.07
Goods returned to Canada (980)	68.1	245.2	152.3	25.5	28.2	-58.58	0.69	2.12	1.35	0.22	0.22
Special classification provisions (990)	101.7	118.8	148.1	168.0	269.1	164.55	1.03	1.02	1.31	1.45	2.13
Publishing industries (except Internet) (511)	0.0	0.0	0.0	0.0	30.3	X	0.00	0.00	0.00	0.00	0.24
TOTAL AND PERCENT SHARE OF U.S. TOTAL	9 867.8	11 591.6	11 320.2	11 621.3	12 611.8	27.81	1.42	1.49	1.55	1.68	1.74
Top 25 Commodities (HS Code)	2 922.5	3 560.0	3 746.9	4 680.0	5 431.4	85.85	29.62	30.71	33.10	40.27	43.07
1. Cotton, not carded or combed (520100)	125.4	396.4	421.0	635.3	1 119.2	792.50	1.27	3.42	3.72	5.47	8.87
2. Parts and accessories of motor vehicles bodies (870829)	375.3	480.3	502.0	604.1	379.6	1.15	3.80	4.14	4.43	5.20	3.01
3. Passenger vehicle, spark-ignition, > 1,500 cc < 3,000 cc (870323)	344.0	394.0	314.3	515.1	362.3	5.32	3.49	3.40	2.78	4.43	2.87
4. Portable digital a.d.p. machines < 10 kg (847130)	15.4	11.0	42.6	104.9	360.2	2 238.96	0.16	0.09	0.38	0.90	2.86
5. Parts and accessories of motor vehicles (870899)	279.5	287.3	303.7	330.0	315.3	12.81	2.83	2.48	2.68	2.84	2.50
6. Parts of airplanes or helicopters (880330)	322.0	252.1	211.6	264.0	315.2	-2.11	3.26	2.17	1.87	2.27	2.50
7. Dry titanium dioxide (320611)	87.2	116.3	105.0	192.6	266.4	205.50	0.88	1.00	0.93	1.66	2.11
8. Whiskies (220830)	132.0	145.5	190.1	207.9	235.6	78.48	1.34	1.26	1.68	1.79	1.87
9. Artificial filament tow (550200)	224.1	202.5	242.8	226.8	215.4	-3.88	2.27	1.75	2.14	1.95	1.71
10. Digital automatic data processing machines (847149)	. . .	28.3	51.3	79.8	178.6	. . .	. . .	0.24	0.45	0.69	1.42
11. Instruments and appliances for medical sciences (901890)	111.3	137.6	161.1	156.2	165.2	48.43	1.13	1.19	1.42	1.34	1.31
12. Discs for laser reading systems (852439)	29.1	45.0	82.9	85.8	153.7	428.18	0.29	0.39	0.73	0.74	1.22
13. Parts of seats (940190)	140.2	143.4	120.9	136.6	149.1	6.35	1.42	1.24	1.07	1.18	1.18
14. Orthopedic or fracture appliances, parts, and accessories (902110)	0.0	0.0	0.0	95.7	129.9	X	0.00	0.00	0.00	0.82	1.03
15. Cellulose and its chemical derivatives in primary forms (391290)	113.0	112.1	102.9	120.2	120.6	6.73	1.15	0.97	0.91	1.03	0.96
16. New pneumatic tires of rubber, for buses or trucks (401120)	168.1	159.2	119.6	127.8	114.2	-32.06	1.70	1.37	1.06	1.10	0.91
17. Parts of spark-ignition internal combustion piston (840999)	88.3	72.1	119.2	83.6	111.7	26.50	0.89	0.62	1.05	0.72	0.89
18. Parts and accessories for automatic data processing (847330)	71.1	103.6	110.6	115.3	102.2	43.74	0.72	0.89	0.98	0.99	0.81
19. Aluminum alloy rectangular plates, > 0.2 mm thick (760612)	20.6	57.2	99.6	129.7	100.9	389.81	0.21	0.49	0.88	1.12	0.80
20. Turbojets of a thrust > 25 kn (841112)	87.4	70.0	92.3	111.3	97.1	11.10	0.89	0.60	0.82	0.96	0.77
21. Parts of instruments for measuring radiation (903090)	. . .	5.4	5.4	8.3	90.5	. . .	. . .	0.05	0.05	0.07	0.72
22. Printed books and brochures (490199)	. . .	52.0	49.8	71.9	89.2	. . .	. . .	0.45	0.44	0.62	0.71
23. Cotton linters pulp (470610)	102.6	112.5	145.7	111.7	87.8	-14.42	1.04	0.97	1.29	0.96	0.70
24. Cylinders for rolling machines, excluding for metals or glass (842091)	85.9	91.8	95.7	104.3	87.1	1.40	0.87	0.79	0.85	0.90	0.69
25. Mowers for lawns, parks cutting devices horizontal plane (843311)	. . .	84.4	56.8	61.1	84.4	. . .	. . .	0.73	0.50	0.53	0.67

X = Not applicable.
. . . = Not available.

Exports from Tennessee

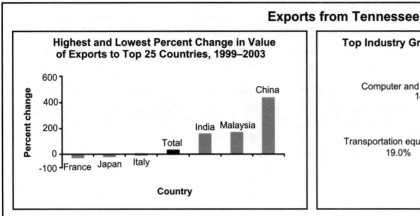

Highest and Lowest Percent Change in Value of Exports to Top 25 Countries, 1999–2003

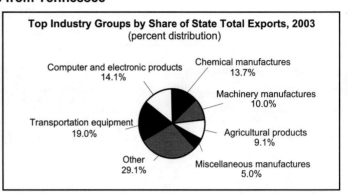

Top Industry Groups by Share of State Total Exports, 2003 (percent distribution)

- Computer and electronic products 14.1%
- Chemical manufactures 13.7%
- Machinery manufactures 10.0%
- Agricultural products 9.1%
- Miscellaneous manufactures 5.0%
- Other 29.1%
- Transportation equipment 19.0%

- Tennessee's exports increased to $12.6 billion in 2003, a nearly 28 percent increase from 1999. In 2003, transportation equipment was the state's largest export, valued at $2.4 billion. The largest increases from 1999 to 2003 were in agricultural products, up $958 million, and computer and electronic products, up $668 million. Agricultural products also had the highest percentage increase, up more than 500 percent during this period.

- Cotton is the state's largest commodity export, representing nearly 9 percent of all exports, up from less than 2 percent in 1999. Cotton exports increased from $125 million in 1999 to $1.1 billion in 2003. Much of these exports are to China. Exports to China increased from $111 million in 1999 to $636 million in 2003, more than 52 percent of which were agricultural products, specifically cotton.

- Canada and Mexico are the leading export markets. Together, they account for 45 percent of Tennessee's exports. Transportation equipment is the leading export to both of these nations.

Table E-48. Total U.S. Exports (Origin of Movement) via Tennessee, 1999–2003—*Continued*

(Top 25 commodities and top 25 countries based on 2003 dollar value.)

Industry, commodity, and country	Value (millions of dollars)					Percent change, 1999–2003	Percent share of state total				
	1999	2000	2001	2002	2003		1999	2000	2001	2002	2003
TOTAL AND PERCENT SHARE OF U.S. TOTAL	9 867.8	11 591.6	11 320.2	11 621.3	12 611.8	27.81	1.42	1.49	1.55	1.68	1.74
Top 25 Countries	8 915.2	10 557.6	10 217.6	10 514.7	11 428.4	28.19	90.35	91.08	90.26	90.48	90.62
1. Canada	3 670.1	4 026.6	4 128.1	3 946.7	4 214.2	14.83	37.19	34.74	36.47	33.96	33.41
2. Mexico	1 062.5	1 759.4	1 369.6	1 419.9	1 475.6	38.89	10.77	15.18	12.10	12.22	11.70
3. United Kingdom	544.3	636.6	655.5	633.0	646.2	18.71	5.52	5.49	5.79	5.45	5.12
4. China	111.4	156.6	184.1	339.2	636.2	471.03	1.13	1.35	1.63	2.92	5.04
5. Japan	580.0	620.4	613.5	599.6	528.7	-8.86	5.88	5.35	5.42	5.16	4.19
6. Germany	400.0	422.8	455.2	444.3	439.7	9.92	4.05	3.65	4.02	3.82	3.49
7. Netherlands	325.6	347.4	339.1	353.8	399.9	22.82	3.30	3.00	3.00	3.04	3.17
8. Belgium	225.6	297.8	238.8	280.0	353.2	56.57	2.29	2.57	2.11	2.41	2.80
9. Brazil	186.7	260.9	191.2	220.3	252.0	35.00	1.89	2.25	1.69	1.90	2.00
10. Hong Kong	184.0	201.6	212.7	225.8	247.9	34.74	1.86	1.74	1.88	1.94	1.97
11. South Korea	135.2	178.8	198.7	235.3	236.9	75.17	1.37	1.54	1.76	2.02	1.88
12. Australia	203.5	174.1	189.0	223.5	224.8	10.49	2.06	1.50	1.67	1.92	1.78
13. France	267.1	346.1	278.9	241.0	220.6	-17.42	2.71	2.99	2.46	2.07	1.75
14. Singapore	189.0	211.6	248.2	224.0	218.9	15.79	1.92	1.83	2.19	1.93	1.74
15. Turkey	100.6	146.7	91.0	127.2	185.9	84.78	1.02	1.27	0.42	1.09	1.47
16. Taiwan	133.7	187.8	156.2	155.5	178.5	33.48	1.36	1.62	1.38	1.34	1.42
17. Italy	157.2	144.9	169.5	162.0	165.3	5.17	1.59	1.25	1.50	1.39	1.31
18. Malaysia	47.8	50.0	93.6	147.4	129.4	170.38	0.48	0.43	0.83	1.27	1.03
19. India	48.6	50.9	88.1	76.4	123.4	153.91	0.49	0.44	0.78	0.66	0.98
20. Indonesia	57.1	67.4	41.9	76.3	99.7	74.71	0.58	0.58	0.37	0.66	0.79
21. Philippines	72.5	64.5	54.2	57.3	97.8	34.98	0.73	0.56	0.48	0.49	0.78
22. Argentina	92.2	64.2	92.4	90.1	97.1	5.28	0.93	0.55	0.82	0.78	0.77
23. Ireland	50.8	43.3	75.5	99.0	94.5	85.92	0.51	0.37	0.67	0.85	0.75
24. Thailand	37.5	48.6	51.7	68.1	85.3	127.40	0.38	0.42	0.46	0.59	0.68
25. Colombia	32.1	48.6	44.4	69.0	76.8	139.37	0.33	0.42	0.39	0.59	0.61

Table E-49. Total U.S. Exports (Origin of Movement) via Texas, 1999–2003

(Top 25 commodities and top 25 countries based on 2003 dollar value.)

Industry, commodity, and country	Value (millions of dollars)					Percent change, 1999–2003	Percent share of state total				
	1999	2000	2001	2002	2003		1999	2000	2001	2002	2003
TOTAL AND PERCENT SHARE OF U.S. TOTAL	83 177.5	103 865.7	94 995.3	95 396.2	98 846.1	18.84	12.01	13.31	12.99	13.76	13.66
Manufactures (NAICS Code)	79 053.6	99 173.4	90 573.5	90 301.8	93 676.6	18.50	95.04	95.48	95.35	94.66	94.77
Processed foods (311)	1 929.2	2 574.8	2 594.3	2 490.0	2 755.2	42.82	2.32	2.48	2.73	2.61	2.79
Beverages and tobacco products (312)	76.1	89.7	89.2	86.3	78.7	3.31	0.09	0.00	0.09	0.09	0.08
Fabric mill products (313)	1 211.4	1 469.5	1 364.1	1 402.2	1 412.7	16.62	1.46	1.41	1.44	1.47	1.43
Non-apparel textile products (314)	232.2	282.5	196.4	179.4	170.9	-26.39	0.28	0.27	0.21	0.19	0.17
Apparel manufactures (315)	1 020.1	973.4	771.4	735.8	505.0	-50.50	1.23	0.94	0.81	0.77	0.51
Leather and related products (316)	539.1	667.8	604.3	717.2	650.6	20.70	0.65	0.64	0.64	0.75	0.66
Wood products (321)	124.2	153.3	123.1	100.7	132.7	6.87	0.15	0.15	0.13	0.11	0.13
Paper products (322)	1 126.3	1 272.6	1 194.1	1 133.5	1 234.3	9.59	1.35	1.23	1.26	1.19	1.25
Printing and related products (323)	220.1	278.3	268.3	208.1	270.3	22.80	0.26	0.27	0.28	0.22	0.27
Petroleum and coal products (324)	2 501.7	4 352.0	3 705.0	3 594.7	4 701.4	87.93	3.01	4.19	3.90	3.77	4.76
Chemical manufactures (325)	12 053.2	15 363.3	14 600.4	15 002.4	17 125.2	42.08	14.49	14.79	15.37	15.73	17.33
Plastics and rubber products (326)	2 582.9	3 229.8	2 763.2	2 714.8	2 518.9	-2.48	3.11	3.11	2.91	2.85	2.55
Non-metallic mineral products (327)	557.3	698.5	650.3	557.6	540.8	-2.96	0.67	0.67	0.68	0.58	0.55
Primary metal manufactures (331)	1 653.8	1 915.9	2 089.3	2 080.9	2 097.2	26.81	1.99	1.84	2.20	2.18	2.12
Fabricated metal products (332)	2 862.1	3 939.5	3 198.8	2 935.7	3 073.0	7.37	3.44	3.79	3.37	3.08	3.11
Machinery manufactures (333)	11 012.7	13 226.9	12 821.2	12 602.2	11 407.7	3.59	13.24	12.73	13.50	13.21	11.54
Computer and electronic products (334)	22 478.8	30 351.5	25 688.5	26 707.0	28 378.2	26.24	27.03	29.22	27.04	28.00	28.71
Electrical equipment, appliances, and parts (335)	4 567.0	4 968.8	4 816.8	4 605.0	4 642.6	1.66	5.49	4.78	5.07	4.83	4.70
Transportation equipment (336)	11 072.7	11 649.9	11 258.1	10 507.7	9 902.8	-10.57	13.31	11.22	11.85	11.01	10.02
Furniture and related products (337)	136.7	181.6	151.3	125.4	130.2	-4.76	0.16	0.17	0.16	0.13	0.13
Miscellaneous manufactures (339)	1 096.0	1 533.6	1 625.3	1 815.2	1 948.2	77.75	1.32	1.48	1.71	1.90	1.97
Agricultural and Livestock Products (NAICS Code)	2 209.7	2 226.2	2 047.4	2 272.5	2 683.3	21.43	2.66	2.14	2.16	2.38	2.71
Agricultural products (111)	2 124.0	2 124.7	1 932.5	2 158.4	2 617.8	23.25	2.55	2.05	2.03	2.26	2.65
Livestock and livestock products (112)	85.8	101.4	114.8	114.1	65.5	-23.60	0.10	0.10	0.12	0.12	0.07
Other Commodities (NAICS Code)	1 914.2	2 466.2	2 374.4	2 821.8	2 486.2	29.88	2.30	2.37	2.50	2.96	2.52
Forestry and logging (113)	21.9	17.2	21.2	20.9	24.1	9.70	0.03	0.02	0.02	0.02	0.02
Fishing, hunting, and trapping (114)	30.9	38.6	25.8	25.2	25.2	-18.38	0.04	0.04	0.03	0.03	0.03
Oil and gas extraction (211)	560.2	737.7	648.8	958.6	673.4	20.21	0.67	0.71	0.68	1.00	0.68
Mining (212)	88.4	143.7	141.2	172.0	158.8	79.72	0.11	0.14	0.15	0.18	0.16
Waste and scrap (910)	191.5	284.4	277.1	346.0	486.5	154.01	0.23	0.27	0.29	0.36	0.49
Used merchandise (920)	134.1	173.1	254.1	223.9	207.2	54.46	0.16	0.17	0.27	0.23	0.21
Goods returned to Canada (980)	98.8	98.0	67.3	65.8	67.0	-32.20	0.12	0.09	0.07	0.07	0.07
Special classification provisions (990)	788.4	973.4	939.0	1 009.4	814.4	3.30	0.95	0.94	0.99	1.06	0.82
Publishing industries (except Internet) (511)	0.0	0.0	0.0	0.0	29.7	X	0.00	0.00	0.00	0.00	0.03
TOTAL AND PERCENT SHARE OF U.S. TOTAL	83 177.5	103 865.7	94 995.3	95 396.2	98 846.1	18.84	12.01	13.31	12.99	13.76	13.66
Top 25 Commodities (HS Code)	17 354.6	23 151.1	20 250.5	33 545.2	37 263.3	114.72	20.86	22.29	21.32	35.16	37.70
1. Digital monolithic integrated circuits (854221)	0.0	0.0	0.0	6 611.8	7 343.7	X	0.00	0.00	0.00	6.93	7.43
2. Parts and accessories for automatic data processing (847330)	1 263.9	1 571.3	1 661.7	2 299.7	3 686.3	191.66	1.52	1.51	1.75	2.41	3.73
3. Parts for boring or sinking machinery (843143)	2 615.6	2 579.4	3 257.8	4 079.3	3 625.0	38.59	3.14	2.48	3.43	4.28	3.67
4. Non-digital monolithic integrated circuits (854229)	0.0	0.0	0.0	2 353.1	2 591.2	X	0.00	0.00	0.00	2.47	2.62
5. Light oils and preparations (not crude) from petroleum (271011)	0.0	0.0	0.0	1 691.3	2 075.4	X	0.00	0.00	0.00	1.77	2.10
6. Petroleum oils from bituminous mineral (not crude) (271019)	0.0	0.0	0.0	1 315.9	1 826.3	X	0.00	0.00	0.00	1.38	1.85
7. Parts of transmission or reception apparatus (852990)	587.2	1 237.5	1 366.0	1 583.3	1 534.1	161.26	0.71	1.19	1.44	1.66	1.55
8. Parts and accessories of motor vehicles bodies (870829)	1 006.5	1 513.4	1 470.3	1 432.3	1 104.6	9.75	1.21	1.46	1.55	1.50	1.12
9. Parts and accessories of motor vehicles (870899)	1 795.2	1 023.7	874.2	833.8	931.5	-48.11	2.16	0.99	0.92	0.87	0.94
10. Automatic data processing input or output units (847160)	...	310.1	292.5	295.8	895.3	...	...	0.30	0.31	0.31	0.91
11. Articles of plastics (392690)	1 132.1	1 454.5	1 145.6	1 014.3	881.1	-22.17	1.36	1.40	1.21	1.06	0.89
12. Passenger vehicles, spark-ignition, > 3,000 cc (870324)	1 358.2	1 402.0	1 285.2	1 186.9	870.4	-35.92	1.63	1.35	1.35	1.24	0.88
13. Parts of airplanes or helicopters (880330)	879.8	899.0	943.2	838.2	869.2	-1.20	1.06	0.87	0.99	0.88	0.88
14. Transmission and reception apparatus (852520)	1 218.6	1 654.9	943.0	743.2	859.4	-29.48	1.47	1.59	0.99	0.78	0.87
15. Cotton, not carded or combed (520100)	...	530.0	609.9	505.5	833.6	...	...	0.51	0.64	0.53	0.84
16. Wheat and meslin (100190)	...	561.6	494.1	583.8	800.3	...	...	0.54	0.52	0.61	0.81
17. Parts, electric apparatus, electric circuit (853890)	639.4	678.7	514.2	640.2	762.1	19.19	0.77	0.65	0.54	0.67	0.77
18. Styrene (290250)	548.0	837.5	352.3	631.3	749.4	36.75	0.66	0.81	0.37	0.66	0.76
19. Machine and mechanical appliance, individual function (847989)	1 561.5	2 711.0	1 292.9	1 050.7	743.5	-52.39	1.88	2.61	1.36	1.10	0.75
20. Instruments and appliances for medical sciences (901890)	269.1	307.2	424.2	640.3	741.5	175.55	0.32	0.30	0.45	0.67	0.75
21. Digital processing units (847150)	909.9	1 115.7	1 014.7	856.2	718.8	-21.00	1.09	1.07	1.07	0.90	0.73
22. Electrical apparatus, switches, relays, fuses (853690)	...	743.0	578.2	589.2	714.5	...	...	0.72	0.61	0.62	0.72
23. Insulated wiring sets for vehicles, ships, and aircrafts (854430)	946.3	887.0	753.3	724.0	713.6	-24.59	1.14	0.85	0.79	0.76	0.72
24. Polyethylene having a specific gravity under 0.94 (390110)	623.3	687.1	642.7	649.6	710.8	14.04	0.75	0.66	0.68	0.68	0.72
25. Para-xylene (290243)	...	446.5	334.5	395.5	681.7	...	...	0.43	0.35	0.41	0.69

X = Not applicable.
. . . = Not available.

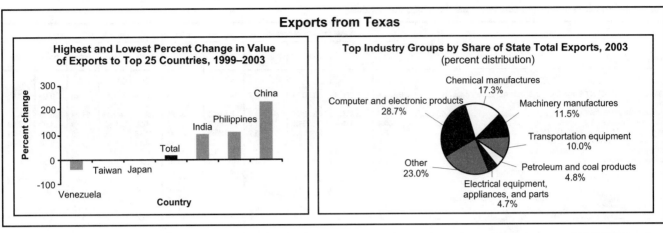

Exports from Texas

Highest and Lowest Percent Change in Value of Exports to Top 25 Countries, 1999–2003

Top Industry Groups by Share of State Total Exports, 2003
(percent distribution)

Chemical manufactures 17.3%
Computer and electronic products 28.7%
Machinery manufactures 11.5%
Transportation equipment 10.0%
Other 23.0%
Petroleum and coal products 4.8%
Electrical equipment, appliances, and parts 4.7%

- Texas is the country's top exporter. Since 1999, Texas' exports increased by about 19 percent, or $15.7 billion. In 2003, the state exported goods worth $98.8 billion, or close to 14 percent of the U.S. total, up from 12 percent in 1999.

- The biggest export industries are computer and electronic products (29 percent of total exports), chemical manufactures (17 percent), machinery manufactures (12 percent), and transportation equipment (10 percent). Among these industries, chemical manufactures had the highest percentage gain from 1999, up 42 percent, or $5 billion, followed by computer and electronic products, up 26 percent, or $5.9 billion.

- Mexico is Texas' largest export market, with 42 percent of the state's total exports. Computer and electronic products represent about 28 percent of these exports, and transportation equipment exports are 13 percent of the total. Canada ranks second, and China third. Exports to China increased 240 percent from 1999 to 2003. Of these $3 billion worth of exports in 2003, chemical manufactures represented 35 percent and computer and electronic products about 31 percent.

Table E-49. Total U.S. Exports (Origin of Movement) via Texas, 1999–2003—*Continued*

(Top 25 commodities and top 25 countries based on 2003 dollar value.)

Industry, commodity, and country	Value (millions of dollars)					Percent change, 1999–2003	Percent share of state total				
	1999	2000	2001	2002	2003		1999	2000	2001	2002	2003
TOTAL AND PERCENT SHARE OF U.S. TOTAL	83 177.5	103 865.7	94 995.3	95 396.2	98 846.1	18.84	12.01	13.31	12.99	13.76	13.66
Top 25 Countries	74 426.4	93 589.5	82 831.9	84 452.6	86 941.9	16.82	89.48	90.11	87.20	88.53	87.96
1. Mexico	37 860.9	47 761.0	41 647.8	41 647.0	41 561.4	9.77	45.52	45.98	43.84	43.66	42.05
2. Canada	10 066.4	11 131.3	10 554.8	9 916.0	10 808.7	7.37	12.10	10.72	11.11	10.39	10.93
3. China	899.7	1 452.3	1 577.8	2 064.3	3 059.6	240.05	1.08	1.40	1.66	2.16	3.10
4. South Korea	1 506.7	2 116.5	1 765.7	2 032.0	2 777.3	84.33	1.81	2.04	1.86	2.13	2.81
5. Taiwan	2 838.1	4 064.6	2 641.5	3 665.2	2 765.5	-2.56	3.41	3.91	2.78	3.84	2.80
6. Japan	2 765.4	4 205.6	2 981.9	2 880.5	2 707.9	-2.08	3.32	4.05	3.14	3.02	2.74
7. Singapore	1 940.6	2 390.0	2 152.7	2 286.2	2 289.0	17.95	2.33	2.30	2.27	2.40	2.32
8. Philippines	1 128.9	1 979.5	1 711.0	2 115.9	2 258.0	100.01	1.36	1.91	1.80	2.22	2.28
9. United Kingdom	2 004.4	2 428.9	2 467.8	2 080.9	2 129.8	6.26	2.41	2.34	2.60	2.18	2.15
10. Malaysia	1 177.1	1 363.1	1 080.1	1 586.2	2 127.0	80.70	1.42	1.31	1.14	1.66	2.15
11. Netherlands	1 399.7	1 956.9	1 989.1	1 718.0	1 733.0	23.81	1.68	1.88	2.09	1.80	1.75
12. Brazil	1 596.4	1 912.9	2 240.2	1 958.8	1 633.8	2.34	1.92	1.84	2.36	2.05	1.65
13. Belgium	1 019.7	1 300.9	1 246.9	1 391.2	1 631.5	60.00	1.23	1.25	1.31	1.46	1.65
14. Germany	1 166.3	1 470.0	1 855.8	1 608.5	1 582.7	35.70	1.40	1.42	1.95	1.69	1.60
15. France	884.7	1 045.6	1 013.8	929.3	905.5	2.34	1.06	1.01	0.05	0.97	0.92
16. Saudi Arabia	836.3	817.9	893.9	931.3	897.1	7.27	1.01	0.79	0.94	0.98	0.91
17. Colombia	741.6	726.9	673.8	690.1	817.9	10.28	0.89	0.70	0.71	0.72	0.83
18. Hong Kong	783.3	1 179.9	885.7	832.8	803.2	2.55	0.94	1.14	0.93	0.87	0.81
19. Venezuela	1 163.7	1 353.6	1 389.2	870.5	783.1	-32.70	1.40	1.30	1.46	0.91	0.79
20. Italy	547.5	646.7	698.2	592.4	754.3	37.78	0.66	0.62	0.73	0.62	0.76
21. Australia	685.2	798.5	739.9	713.0	749.2	9.34	0.82	0.77	0.78	0.75	0.76
22. Turkey	375.2	373.5	312.4	334.3	578.7	54.21	0.45	0.36	0.33	0.35	0.59
23. India	295.5	339.2	364.7	408.2	568.8	92.49	0.36	0.33	0.38	0.43	0.58
24. United Arab Emirates	343.7	314.0	493.9	600.2	521.6	51.78	0.41	0.30	0.52	0.63	0.53
25. Israel	399.3	460.2	419.8	599.8	497.5	24.57	0.48	0.44	0.44	0.63	0.50

Table E-50. Total U.S. Exports (Origin of Movement) via Utah, 1999–2003

(Top 25 commodities and top 25 countries based on 2003 dollar value.)

Industry, commodity, and country	Value (millions of dollars)					Percent change, 1999–2003	Percent share of state total				
	1999	2000	2001	2002	2003		1999	2000	2001	2002	2003
TOTAL AND PERCENT SHARE OF U.S. TOTAL	3 133.5	3 220.8	3 506.4	4 542.7	4 114.5	31.31	0.45	0.41	0.48	0.66	0.57
Manufactures (NAICS Code)	2 897.7	2 926.2	3 306.3	4 376.9	3 960.5	36.68	92.47	90.85	94.29	96.35	96.26
Processed foods (311)	135.4	176.4	231.2	255.3	283.2	109.13	4.32	5.48	6.59	5.62	6.88
Beverages and tobacco products (312)	5.0	3.6	5.3	5.7	26.3	424.44	0.16	0.00	0.15	0.13	0.64
Fabric mill products (313)	3.8	10.0	8.1	7.1	3.6	-3.94	0.12	0.31	0.23	0.16	0.09
Non-apparel textile products (314)	2.4	1.6	1.9	2.1	5.2	119.14	0.08	0.05	0.05	0.05	0.13
Apparel manufactures (315)	6.6	4.4	5.0	3.4	4.3	-34.91	0.21	0.14	0.14	0.08	0.10
Leather and related products (316)	14.5	10.1	7.0	6.6	6.1	-58.06	0.46	0.31	0.20	0.14	0.15
Wood products (321)	1.7	1.1	1.8	2.0	2.7	54.30	0.06	0.03	0.05	0.04	0.06
Paper products (322)	37.4	43.0	45.2	43.5	27.7	-26.08	1.19	1.34	1.29	0.96	0.67
Printing and related products (323)	24.6	21.8	21.6	24.2	21.9	-11.19	0.79	0.68	0.62	0.53	0.53
Petroleum and coal products (324)	2.0	0.2	1.1	2.7	1.8	-11.20	0.06	0.01	0.03	0.06	0.04
Chemical manufactures (325)	153.4	170.5	229.9	264.5	340.3	121.77	4.90	5.29	6.56	5.82	8.27
Plastics and rubber products (326)	30.9	51.6	57.4	65.6	74.9	142.35	0.99	1.60	1.64	1.45	1.82
Non-metallic mineral products (327)	10.0	10.9	12.5	11.2	10.0	-0.25	0.32	0.34	0.36	0.25	0.24
Primary metal manufactures (331)	975.1	661.6	1 008.4	1 913.4	1 465.7	50.31	31.12	20.54	28.76	42.12	35.62
Fabricated metal products (332)	38.9	47.7	57.3	53.9	61.9	59.03	1.24	1.48	1.64	1.19	1.50
Machinery manufactures (333)	188.2	229.5	185.0	140.0	141.4	-24.86	6.01	7.13	5.28	3.08	3.44
Computer and electronic products (334)	499.6	537.7	511.1	758.3	624.0	24.89	15.95	16.69	14.58	16.69	15.17
Electrical equipment, appliances, and parts (335)	100.8	116.8	101.7	102.7	85.7	-15.00	3.22	3.63	2.90	2.26	2.08
Transportation equipment (336)	497.1	619.3	588.8	489.1	467.2	-6.01	15.86	19.23	16.79	10.77	11.36
Furniture and related products (337)	6.4	15.7	11.6	12.3	13.4	107.14	0.21	0.49	0.33	0.27	0.32
Miscellaneous manufactures (339)	163.6	192.7	214.6	213.3	293.5	79.34	5.22	5.98	6.12	4.70	7.13
Agricultural and Livestock Products (NAICS Code)	17.7	22.0	7.5	5.1	7.2	-59.20	0.56	0.68	0.21	0.11	0.18
Agricultural products (111)	17.2	21.5	7.1	4.4	5.5	-68.31	0.55	0.67	0.20	0.10	0.13
Livestock and livestock products (112)	0.4	0.5	0.4	0.7	1.7	300.23	0.01	0.01	0.01	0.02	0.04
Other Commodities (NAICS Code)	218.2	272.6	192.6	160.7	146.8	-32.72	6.96	8.46	5.49	3.54	3.57
Forestry and logging (113)	0.5	0.6	0.5	0.5	0.5	-3.28	0.02	0.02	0.01	0.01	0.01
Fishing, hunting, and trapping (114)	3.0	2.2	5.2	1.3	1.7	-44.14	0.10	0.07	0.15	0.03	0.04
Oil and gas extraction (211)	0.0	0.0	0.0	0.0	0.1	X	0.00	0.00	0.00	0.00	0.00
Mining (212)	130.7	171.5	105.0	62.5	43.0	-67.09	4.17	5.33	2.99	1.38	1.05
Waste and scrap (910)	3.4	5.7	4.9	9.7	12.6	274.81	0.11	0.18	0.14	0.21	0.31
Used merchandise (920)	3.3	3.1	2.6	2.6	2.0	-38.98	0.10	0.10	0.07	0.06	0.05
Goods returned to Canada (980)	6.1	5.7	6.6	16.2	6.8	10.00	0.20	0.18	0.19	0.36	0.16
Special classification provisions (990)	71.1	83.8	67.7	67.9	77.9	9.47	2.27	2.60	1.93	1.50	1.89
Publishing industries (except Internet) (511)	0.0	0.0	0.0	0.0	2.2	X	0.00	0.00	0.00	0.00	0.05
TOTAL AND PERCENT SHARE OF U.S. TOTAL	3 133.5	3 220.8	3 506.4	4 542.7	4 114.5	31.31	0.45	0.41	0.48	0.66	0.57
Top 25 Commodities (HS Code)	1 637.8	1 559.8	1 941.8	3 117.8	2 891.5	76.55	52.27	48.43	55.38	68.63	70.28
1. Gold, non-monetary, unwrought (710812)	891.2	580.0	908.3	1 797.1	1 385.0	55.41	28.44	18.01	25.90	39.56	33.66
2. Parts and accessories of motor vehicles bodies (870829)	172.4	160.8	91.5	121.2	179.0	3.83	5.50	4.99	2.61	2.67	4.35
3. Parts and accessories of motor vehicles (870899)	125.2	187.9	227.0	214.9	176.6	41.05	4.00	5.83	6.47	4.73	4.29
4. Digital monolithic integrated circuits (854221)	0.0	0.0	0.0	201.9	149.9	X	0.00	0.00	0.00	4.44	3.64
5. Other food preparations (210690)	53.3	66.2	82.2	95.0	105.8	98.50	1.70	2.06	2.34	2.09	2.57
6. Transistors excl. photosensitive, dissipation rate < 1 w (854121)	41.3	80.0	62.6	81.4	100.9	144.31	1.32	2.48	1.79	1.79	2.45
7. Beauty and skin care preparations (330499)	21.2	26.8	50.4	63.7	80.2	278.30	0.68	0.83	1.44	1.40	1.95
8. Instruments and appliances for medical sciences (901890)	35.9	41.5	44.5	50.2	75.5	110.31	1.15	1.29	1.27	1.11	1.83
9. X-ray tubes (902230)	60.1	43.0	46.6	59.0	62.7	4.33	1.92	1.34	1.33	1.30	1.52
10. Parts of airplanes or helicopters (880330)	100.7	113.7	108.2	52.2	58.9	-41.51	3.21	3.53	3.09	1.15	1.43
11. Apparatus based on x-ray, medical, surgical, veterinary (902214)	16.6	23.1	44.1	43.7	49.5	198.19	0.53	0.72	1.26	0.96	1.20
12. Medical needles, catheters and parts (901839)	28.4	47.0	45.3	45.1	47.7	67.96	0.91	1.46	1.29	0.99	1.16
13. Electro-diagnostic apparatus and parts (901819)	. . .	2.6	6.7	9.9	46.0	. . .	. . .	0.08	0.19	0.22	1.12
14. Articles donated for relief (980240)	16.1	27.9	34.7	28.7	38.8	140.99	0.51	0.87	0.99	0.63	0.94
15. Articles/equipment for physical exercise; parts (950691)	. . .	17.8	20.4	20.5	35.2	. . .	. . .	0.55	0.58	0.45	0.86
16. Molybdenum ores and concentrates not roasted (261390)	24.6	36.1	24.5	36.7	35.0	42.28	0.79	1.12	0.70	0.81	0.85
17. Safety fuses; detonating fuse; percussion caps (360300)	5.8	6.1	8.9	21.0	34.2	489.66	0.19	0.19	0.25	0.46	0.83
18. Monofilament, cross-section > 1 mm, rods, plastics (391690)	0.1	16.6	17.3	27.5	33.1	33 000.00	0.00	0.52	0.49	0.61	0.80
19. Articles for sports, swimming pools, parts and accessories (950699)	23.9	23.7	42.0	32.8	31.7	32.64	0.76	0.74	1.20	0.72	0.77
20. Ground flying trainers and parts thereof (880529)	0.0	0.0	0.0	36.4	31.3	X	0.00	0.00	0.00	0.80	0.76
21. Mixtures of fruit and/or vegetable juices (200990)	8.0	16.7	22.0	21.7	30.4	280.00	0.26	0.52	0.63	0.48	0.74
22. Interchangeable tools for handtools or machines; and parts (820719)	. . .	17.3	24.8	18.8	30.0	. . .	. . .	0.54	0.71	0.41	0.73
23. Non-electrical articles of graphite or carbon (681510)	13.1	13.0	19.2	23.1	25.6	95.42	0.42	0.40	0.55	0.51	0.62
24. Non-alcoholic beverages (220290)	. . .	2.4	7.1	10.5	25.5	. . .	. . .	0.07	0.20	0.23	0.62
25. Other ophthalmic instruments and appliances and parts (901850)	. . .	9.6	3.5	4.8	23.0	. . .	. . .	0.30	0.10	0.11	0.56

X = Not applicable.
. . . = Not available.

Exports from Utah

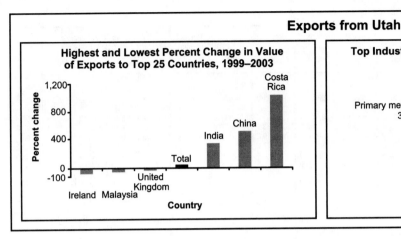

Highest and Lowest Percent Change in Value of Exports to Top 25 Countries, 1999–2003

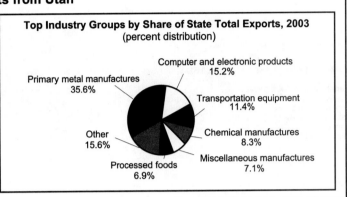

Top Industry Groups by Share of State Total Exports, 2003
(percent distribution)

Computer and electronic products 15.2%
Primary metal manufactures 35.6%
Transportation equipment 11.4%
Chemical manufactures 8.3%
Other 15.6%
Miscellaneous manufactures 7.1%
Processed foods 6.9%

- Utah's exported $4.1 billion worth of goods in 2003. Primary metal manufactures products are by far the state's leading export, representing almost 36 percent of total exports. These exports, primarily gold, increased from $975 million in 1999 to almost $1.5 billion in 2003, a jump of 50 percent. Computer and electronic products rank second with $624 million, or 15 percent of total exports, and transportation equipment third.

- Gold is Utah's top commodity export. In 2003, nearly $1.4 billion worth of gold was exported, representing one-third of Utah's total exports, and 75 percent of primary metal exports.

- Switzerland is Utah's top export country. Exports to Switzerland increased from $400 million in 1999 to $1.1 billion in 2003, an increase of nearly 177 percent. More than 98 percent of these exports are primary metal manufactures, largely gold. Exports to Canada rank second with $544 million, about one-third of which is transportation equipment.

Table E-50. Total U.S. Exports (Origin of Movement) via Utah, 1999–2003—Continued

(Top 25 commodities and top 25 countries based on 2003 dollar value.)

Industry, commodity, and country	Value (millions of dollars)					Percent change, 1999–2003	Percent share of state total				
	1999	2000	2001	2002	2003		1999	2000	2001	2002	2003
TOTAL AND PERCENT SHARE OF U.S. TOTAL	3 133.5	3 220.8	3 506.4	4 542.7	4 114.5	31.31	0.45	0.41	0.48	0.66	0.57
Top 25 Countries	2 934.8	2 998.7	3 259.9	4 333.5	3 862.5	31.61	93.66	93.10	92.97	95.39	93.87
1. Switzerland	399.5	452.9	696.4	1 341.2	1 105.2	176.64	12.75	14.06	19.86	29.52	26.86
2. Canada	568.5	605.8	543.2	513.3	544.3	-4.26	18.14	18.81	15.49	11.30	13.23
3. United Kingdom	628.9	246.0	421.3	710.2	486.5	-22.63	20.07	7.64	12.02	15.63	11.82
4. Japan	378.5	402.1	396.4	427.1	475.6	25.64	12.08	12.48	11.31	9.40	11.56
5. Netherlands	120.8	151.2	154.3	137.8	124.4	3.03	3.85	4.69	4.40	3.03	3.02
6. Germany	75.7	104.5	93.6	68.8	118.7	56.89	2.41	3.25	2.67	1.51	2.88
7. China	17.3	32.6	40.6	64.2	114.0	557.77	0.55	1.01	1.16	1.41	2.77
8. Mexico	78.7	102.1	113.6	134.2	111.2	41.36	2.51	3.17	3.24	2.95	2.70
9. Philippines	79.6	105.2	79.4	84.8	103.6	30.22	2.54	3.27	2.26	1.87	2.52
10. South Korea	67.2	128.9	127.6	88.4	69.9	3.89	2.15	4.00	3.64	1.95	1.70
11. Belgium	53.1	72.8	58.6	62.7	69.4	30.71	1.69	2.26	1.67	1.38	1.69
12. Australia	44.9	59.7	54.1	51.6	67.3	49.93	1.43	1.85	1.54	1.14	1.63
13. France	57.1	46.9	54.1	51.1	66.3	16.25	1.82	1.46	1.54	1.12	1.61
14. Taiwan	43.6	76.3	57.1	59.7	62.8	44.08	1.39	2.37	1.63	1.31	1.53
15. Hong Kong	40.4	58.4	53.2	67.4	58.9	45.85	1.29	1.81	1.52	1.48	1.43
16. Italy	45.9	39.6	37.5	39.1	39.0	-14.98	1.47	1.23	1.07	0.86	0.95
17. Singapore	44.0	54.9	46.3	263.6	38.4	-12.65	1.40	1.70	1.32	5.80	0.93
18. Costa Rica	2.7	18.6	20.8	31.0	32.2	1 113.05	0.08	0.58	0.59	0.68	0.78
19. Thailand	23.4	17.9	23.3	29.0	30.3	29.42	0.75	0.55	0.67	0.64	0.74
20. Spain	15.0	18.2	19.6	23.9	26.8	77.85	0.48	0.57	0.56	0.53	0.65
21. Malaysia	47.3	44.0	50.3	31.2	26.6	-43.69	1.51	1.37	1.43	0.69	0.65
22. Ireland	64.0	98.3	55.3	18.0	24.3	-62.10	2.04	3.05	1.58	0.40	0.59
23. India	5.8	11.8	12.0	12.8	23.5	308.00	0.18	0.37	0.34	0.28	0.57
24. Brazil	24.5	41.1	41.7	12.8	22.9	-6.30	0.78	1.28	1.19	0.28	0.56
25. Israel	8.6	8.9	9.7	9.4	20.4	136.19	0.28	0.28	0.28	0.21	0.50

Table E-51. Total U.S. Exports (Origin of Movement) via Vermont, 1999–2003

(Top 25 commodities and top 25 countries based on 2003 dollar value.)

Industry, commodity, and country	Value (millions of dollars)					Percent change, 1999–2003	Percent share of state total				
	1999	2000	2001	2002	2003		1999	2000	2001	2002	2003
TOTAL AND PERCENT SHARE OF U.S. TOTAL	4 023.3	4 097.1	2 830.4	2 521.0	2 626.9	-34.71	0.58	0.52	0.39	0.36	0.36
Manufactures (NAICS Code)	3 959.2	4 021.8	2 701.1	2 422.3	2 541.4	-35.81	98.41	98.16	95.43	96.08	96.74
Processed foods (311)	101.9	98.4	89.0	63.9	55.6	-45.47	2.53	2.40	3.14	2.54	2.12
Beverages and tobacco products (312)	0.0	0.0	0.0	0.2	1.0	X	0.00	0.00	0.00	0.01	0.04
Fabric mill products (313)	17.5	13.0	8.7	7.8	10.1	-42.56	0.44	0.32	0.31	0.31	0.38
Non-apparel textile products (314)	0.9	0.7	1.0	0.4	0.9	4.43	0.02	0.02	0.04	0.02	0.03
Apparel manufactures (315)	15.0	5.3	5.2	5.2	5.7	-62.26	0.37	0.13	0.18	0.21	0.22
Leather and related products (316)	2.2	2.4	2.4	2.7	3.5	59.62	0.05	0.06	0.08	0.11	0.13
Wood products (321)	38.8	38.6	30.5	30.8	27.4	-29.43	0.97	0.94	1.08	1.22	1.04
Paper products (322)	45.6	45.8	44.1	41.0	38.7	-15.27	1.13	1.12	1.56	1.63	1.47
Printing and related products (323)	7.3	4.5	7.1	6.3	7.7	4.59	0.18	0.11	0.25	0.25	0.29
Petroleum and coal products (324)	0.2	0.1	0.1	0.1	0.2	-25.73	0.01	0.00	0.00	0.00	0.01
Chemical manufactures (325)	32.7	37.9	44.4	37.3	40.6	23.90	0.81	0.93	1.57	1.48	1.54
Plastics and rubber products (326)	18.2	18.4	16.7	20.4	21.3	16.72	0.45	0.45	0.59	0.81	0.81
Non-metallic mineral products (327)	6.9	9.1	12.6	9.8	8.6	24.94	0.17	0.22	0.44	0.39	0.33
Primary metal manufactures (331)	8.2	10.1	11.2	6.6	7.5	-8.59	0.20	0.25	0.40	0.26	0.28
Fabricated metal products (332)	42.9	69.1	80.3	57.6	48.6	13.17	1.07	1.69	2.84	2.28	1.85
Machinery manufactures (333)	81.8	108.7	110.1	103.2	126.9	55.17	2.03	2.65	3.89	4.09	4.83
Computer and electronic products (334)	3 390.0	3 382.0	2 037.1	1 863.8	1 975.6	-41.72	84.26	82.55	71.97	73.93	75.21
Electrical equipment, appliances, and parts (335)	21.1	27.9	34.1	36.2	44.8	112.21	0.52	0.68	1.21	1.44	1.71
Transportation equipment (336)	70.3	103.7	121.9	90.7	78.6	11.76	1.75	2.53	4.31	3.60	2.99
Furniture and related products (337)	2.1	2.1	3.8	3.9	4.7	124.26	0.05	0.05	0.13	0.15	0.18
Miscellaneous manufactures (339)	55.3	43.9	40.7	34.3	33.7	-39.18	1.38	1.07	1.44	1.36	1.28
Agricultural and Livestock Products (NAICS Code)	7.0	9.5	10.3	10.1	8.6	21.89	0.17	0.23	0.37	0.40	0.33
Agricultural products (111)	0.9	0.6	0.5	1.0	0.8	-8.24	0.02	0.01	0.02	0.04	0.03
Livestock and livestock products (112)	6.1	8.9	9.8	9.1	7.7	26.43	0.15	0.22	0.35	0.36	0.29
Other Commodities (NAICS Code)	57.0	65.8	118.9	88.6	77.0	34.89	1.42	1.61	4.20	3.52	2.93
Forestry and logging (113)	14.9	14.5	26.0	23.2	24.8	67.24	0.37	0.35	0.92	0.92	0.95
Fishing, hunting, and trapping (114)	2.0	1.7	2.0	2.1	2.6	29.21	0.05	0.04	0.07	0.08	0.10
Oil and gas extraction (211)	0.0	0.0	0.1	0.0	0.0	X	0.00	0.00	0.00	0.00	0.00
Mining (212)	13.9	11.3	17.7	19.6	20.3	46.54	0.34	0.28	0.63	0.78	0.77
Waste and scrap (910)	2.0	3.5	2.2	2.3	2.8	37.71	0.05	0.09	0.08	0.09	0.11
Used merchandise (920)	0.8	1.0	0.5	1.5	0.6	-20.10	0.02	0.03	0.02	0.06	0.02
Goods returned to Canada (980)	9.9	20.9	52.4	20.3	11.0	10.39	0.25	0.51	1.85	0.81	0.42
Special classification provisions (990)	13.6	12.9	18.0	19.7	14.7	8.51	0.34	0.32	0.64	0.78	0.56
Publishing industries (except Internet) (511)	0.0	0.0	0.0	0.0	0.1	X	0.00	0.00	0.00	0.00	0.00
TOTAL AND PERCENT SHARE OF U.S. TOTAL	4 023.3	4 097.1	2 830.4	2 521.0	2 626.9	-34.71	0.58	0.52	0.39	0.36	0.36
Top 25 Commodities (HS Code)	404.4	386.9	318.6	2 039.1	2 214.5	447.60	10.05	9.44	11.26	80.89	84.30
1. Digital monolithic integrated circuits (854221)	0.0	0.0	0.0	1 492.9	1 689.5	X	0.00	0.00	0.00	59.22	64.31
2. Non-digital monolithic integrated circuits (854229)	0.0	0.0	0.0	226.7	188.6	X	0.00	0.00	0.00	8.99	7.18
3. Injection or compression-type molds for rubber or plastics (848071)	11.7	18.4	20.2	27.9	42.2	260.68	0.29	0.45	0.71	1.11	1.61
4. Parts and accessories for automatic data processing (847330)	137.6	86.3	33.2	28.3	24.0	-82.56	3.42	2.11	1.17	1.12	0.91
5. Turbojet and turbo-propeller parts (841191)	25.1	21.9	14.7	12.8	23.6	-5.98	0.62	0.53	0.52	0.51	0.90
6. Steering wheels, columns and boxes for motor vehicles (870894)	22.1	23.9	26.0	22.9	21.4	X	0.55	0.58	0.92	0.91	0.81
7. Paper/pprboard excl. writing; clay coated > 10 percent mech. (481029)	21.9	23.5	23.4	23.8	20.8	-5.02	0.54	0.57	0.83	0.94	0.79
8. Boards, panels, consoles for electrical control (853710)	2.1	10.6	14.9	16.3	20.3	866.67	0.05	0.26	0.53	0.65	0.77
9. Non-coniferous wood, rough, not treated (440399)	5.2	5.7	11.6	15.7	18.0	246.15	0.13	0.14	0.41	0.62	0.69
10. Iron or steel threaded screws and bolts (731815)	10.8	19.1	22.3	23.4	16.6	53.70	0.27	0.47	0.79	0.93	0.63
11. Parts of airplanes or helicopters (880330)	10.7	16.1	16.4	13.9	15.8	47.66	0.27	0.39	0.58	0.55	0.60
12. Taps and cocks for pipe thermostatic control (848180)	17.2	20.5	14.8	13.2	15.0	-12.79	0.43	0.50	0.52	0.52	0.57
13. Ice cream and other edible ice, with cocoa or not (210500)	4.3	10.8	12.8	12.6	12.7	195.35	0.11	0.26	0.45	0.50	0.48
14. Articles/equipment for physical exercise; parts (950691)	11.5	14.5	14.7	12.1	10.9	X	0.29	0.35	0.52	0.48	0.41
15. Chocolate, prepared, in blocks over 2 kg (180620)	6.8	6.8	9.3	10.0	10.8	58.82	0.17	0.17	0.33	0.40	0.41
16. Granite, crude or roughly trimmed (251611)	4.7	4.3	8.5	9.5	10.1	X	0.12	0.10	0.30	0.38	0.38
17. Printed circuits (853400)	14.0	9.5	5.9	10.7	9.7	-30.71	0.35	0.23	0.21	0.42	0.37
18. Non-coniferous wood, sawn, sliced, > 6 mm (440799)	12.6	11.9	11.3	10.6	9.6	-23.81	0.31	0.29	0.40	0.42	0.37
19. Marble granules, chippings, and powder (251741)	8.4	6.1	8.6	9.5	9.4	11.90	0.21	0.15	0.30	0.38	0.36
20. Instruments for measuring variables of liquids/gases (902680)	. . .	9.1	9.4	9.4	9.3	. . .	. . .	0.22	0.33	0.37	0.35
21. Parts, machines for working rubber/plastics (847790)	. . .	2.4	2.2	6.9	8.0	. . .	. . .	0.06	0.08	0.27	0.30
22. Food preparations for infants, retail sale (190110)	75.2	59.6	26.4	12.5	7.5	-90.03	1.87	1.45	0.93	0.50	0.29
23. Parts of non-electric domestic cooking appliances (732190)	. . .	3.3	4.4	7.2	7.4	. . .	. . .	0.08	0.16	0.29	0.28
24. Lenses, prisms, mirrors, and optical elements (900190)	. . .	0.1	0.4	0.1	7.1	. . .	. . .	0.00	0.01	0.00	0.27
25. Other food preparations (210690)	2.5	2.6	7.6	10.3	6.2	148.00	0.06	0.06	0.27	0.41	0.24

X = Not applicable.
. . . = Not available.

Exports from Vermont

Highest and Lowest Percent Change in Value of Exports to Top 25 Countries, 1999–2003

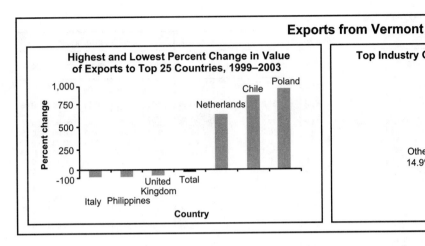

Top Industry Groups by Share of State Total Exports, 2003
(percent distribution)

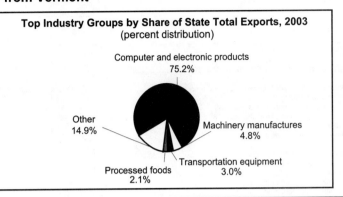

- From 1999 to 2003, Vermont's exports fell almost 35 percent, which was the largest decline of any state in the nation. In 1999, computer and electronics exports accounted for about 84 percent of the state's exports. These exports fell from $3.4 billion in 1999 to under $2 billion in 2003, a drop of almost 42 percent. The decline of this one major industry was the cause of the large drop in Vermont's total exports. Machinery manufactures are the only other export to exceed 3 percent of the state's total.

- Canada remains Vermont's top export market. However, exports to Canada fell by 57 percent from 1999 to 2003. As a result, its portion of Vermont's total exports dropped from 62 percent to 41 percent. During this time, computer and electronic exports to Canada fell from $2.2 billion to $691 million. Exports to Taiwan, which ranks second, grew by 205 percent from 1999 to 2003, as a result of increased exports of computer and electronic products, though this was clearly not enough to offset the reduction of those exports to Canada.

Table E-51. Total U.S. Exports (Origin of Movement) via Vermont, 1999–2003—*Continued*

(Top 25 commodities and top 25 countries based on 2003 dollar value.)

Industry, commodity, and country	Value (millions of dollars)					Percent change, 1999–2003	Percent share of state total				
	1999	2000	2001	2002	2003		1999	2000	2001	2002	2003
TOTAL AND PERCENT SHARE OF U.S. TOTAL	4 023.3	4 097.1	2 830.4	2 521.0	2 626.9	-34.71	0.58	0.52	0.39	0.36	0.36
Top 25 Countries	3 939.8	4 011.0	2 722.9	2 466.6	2 571.2	-34.74	97.92	97.90	96.20	97.85	97.88
1. Canada	2 508.8	2 205.1	1 389.9	1 054.3	1 079.1	-56.99	62.36	53.82	49.11	41.82	41.08
2. Taiwan	136.4	270.7	191.1	325.6	416.3	205.20	3.39	6.61	6.75	12.92	15.85
3. South Korea	147.7	139.3	187.3	331.7	242.6	64.30	3.67	3.40	6.62	13.16	9.23
4. Japan	198.9	207.1	187.3	193.7	147.9	-25.63	4.94	5.05	6.62	7.68	5.63
5. Singapore	56.8	83.0	20.5	41.3	140.9	148.11	1.41	2.03	0.72	1.64	5.37
6. Malaysia	14.2	21.5	26.3	27.3	68.8	383.72	0.35	0.52	0.93	1.08	2.62
7. Ireland	54.0	83.2	91.4	20.3	58.7	8.63	1.34	2.03	3.23	0.80	2.23
8. Netherlands	7.0	29.7	58.4	99.2	56.2	701.18	0.17	0.72	2.06	3.93	2.14
9. United Kingdom	185.9	241.1	177.7	96.5	53.4	-71.29	4.62	5.88	6.28	3.83	2.03
10. Hong Kong	31.2	23.0	50.8	37.1	48.9	56.58	0.78	0.56	1.80	1.47	1.86
11. Thailand	27.9	49.5	30.9	24.4	35.9	28.46	0.69	1.21	1.09	0.97	1.37
12. Mexico	42.0	49.8	18.3	29.7	34.2	-18.69	1.04	1.22	0.65	1.18	1.30
13. China	6.2	13.2	16.2	21.4	31.9	413.09	0.15	0.32	0.57	0.85	1.21
14. Germany	31.0	43.6	48.2	33.5	30.7	-0.98	0.77	1.06	1.70	1.33	1.17
15. Italy	290.9	344.6	103.6	37.7	26.4	-90.91	7.23	8.41	3.66	1.49	1.01
16. France	71.7	122.7	48.5	28.5	21.3	-70.23	1.78	2.99	1.71	1.13	0.81
17. Australia	8.6	10.7	11.4	10.7	12.8	49.04	0.21	0.26	0.40	0.42	0.49
18. Sweden	11.3	30.8	22.3	17.6	12.1	7.92	0.28	0.75	0.79	0.70	0.46
19. Chile	1.1	1.5	1.0	0.3	11.8	937.55	0.03	0.04	0.04	0.01	0.45
20. Philippines	92.3	19.3	18.0	12.5	10.7	-88.40	2.29	0.47	0.64	0.49	0.41
21. Switzerland	7.8	11.0	10.5	10.8	8.7	12.09	0.19	0.27	0.37	0.43	0.33
22. Poland	0.6	0.7	0.9	0.7	6.6	1 000.50	0.01	0.02	0.03	0.03	0.25
23. Belgium	4.1	5.2	8.1	4.7	5.5	33.08	0.10	0.13	0.29	0.19	0.21
24. Spain	2.7	4.5	3.9	5.2	5.5	99.52	0.07	0.11	0.14	0.21	0.21
25. Hungary	0.6	0.2	0.1	2.2	4.4	589.42	0.02	0.01	0.00	0.09	0.17

Table E-52. Total U.S. Exports (Origin of Movement) via Virgin Islands, 1999–2003

(Top 25 commodities and top 25 countries based on 2003 dollar value.)

Industry, commodity, and country	Value (millions of dollars)					Percent change, 1999–2003	Percent share of total				
	1999	2000	2001	2002	2003		1999	2000	2001	2002	2003
TOTAL AND PERCENT SHARE OF U.S. TOTAL	155.0	174.3	187.2	257.8	252.7	63.09	0.02	0.02	0.03	0.04	0.03
Manufactures (NAICS Code)	154.4	173.6	186.9	257.3	251.5	62.90	99.61	99.56	99.84	99.84	99.50
Processed foods (311)	0.1	0.2	0.1	0.2	0.2	31.30	0.07	0.12	0.03	0.09	0.06
Beverages and tobacco products (312)	0.1	0.1	0.1	0.3	0.2	56.25	0.07	0.00	0.03	0.10	0.07
Fabric mill products (313)	0.7	0.4	0.6	0.1	0.2	-70.25	0.44	0.23	0.32	0.04	0.08
Non-apparel textile products (314)	0.1	0.0	1.0	0.0	0.0	X	0.04	0.02	0.52	0.01	0.00
Apparel manufactures (315)	0.0	0.0	0.0	0.0	0.0	X	0.02	0.02	0.00	0.00	0.00
Leather and related products (316)	0.2	0.0	0.0	0.0	0.0	X	0.12	0.00	0.01	0.00	0.01
Wood products (321)	0.1	0.1	0.2	0.2	0.0	X	0.03	0.07	0.12	0.06	0.00
Paper products (322)	0.1	0.2	0.3	0.0	0.0	X	0.03	0.10	0.14	0.02	0.01
Printing and related products (323)	0.0	0.0	0.0	0.0	0.1	X	0.00	0.03	0.02	0.01	0.03
Petroleum and coal products (324)	87.0	131.4	157.5	207.5	183.5	110.85	56.17	75.38	84.15	80.50	72.62
Chemical manufactures (325)	22.9	15.7	6.4	22.4	38.3	X	14.76	9.02	3.41	8.68	15.17
Plastics and rubber products (326)	0.3	1.4	1.5	1.6	0.3	-5.23	0.21	0.79	0.83	0.64	0.12
Non-metallic mineral products (327)	0.1	0.2	0.0	0.0	0.0	X	0.06	0.14	0.02	0.00	0.00
Primary metal manufactures (331)	4.5	7.8	0.1	0.0	0.0	X	2.93	4.50	0.06	0.00	0.01
Fabricated metal products (332)	0.2	0.3	0.1	0.2	0.1	-29.53	0.12	0.15	0.07	0.07	0.05
Machinery manufactures (333)	26.5	2.5	1.4	0.5	0.6	-97.71	17.11	1.44	0.72	0.20	0.24
Computer and electronic products (334)	1.4	3.4	1.0	0.5	0.8	-44.68	0.93	1.93	0.55	0.18	0.31
Electrical equipment, appliances, and parts (335)	2.8	1.4	1.9	0.4	0.0	X	1.84	0.79	1.01	0.17	0.01
Transportation equipment (336)	1.5	0.6	2.3	1.6	0.8	-43.44	0.96	0.35	1.21	0.61	0.33
Furniture and related products (337)	0.1	0.0	0.1	0.0	0.0	X	0.07	0.01	0.05	0.02	0.01
Miscellaneous manufactures (339)	5.6	7.7	12.3	21.8	26.1	365.89	3.62	4.40	6.56	8.44	10.34
Agricultural and Livestock Products (NAICS Code)	0.0	0.0	0.0	0.0	0.1	X	0.00	0.03	0.00	0.00	0.05
Agricultural products (111)	0.0	0.0	0.0	0.0	0.1	X	0.00	0.03	0.00	0.00	0.05
Livestock and livestock products (112)	0.0	0.0	0.0	0.0	0.0	X	0.00	0.00	0.00	0.00	0.00
Other Commodities (NAICS Code)	0.6	0.7	0.3	0.4	1.1	91.05	0.38	0.41	0.16	0.16	0.45
Forestry and logging (113)	0.0	0.0	0.0	0.0	0.0	X	0.00	0.00	0.00	0.01	0.00
Fishing, hunting, and trapping (114)	0.0	0.0	0.0	0.0	0.0	X	0.03	0.00	0.00	0.00	0.00
Oil and gas extraction (211)	0.0	0.0	0.0	0.0	0.7	X	0.00	0.00	0.00	0.00	0.28
Mining (212)	0.1	0.1	0.0	0.1	0.1	-35.42	0.06	0.03	0.02	0.02	0.02
Waste and scrap (910)	0.0	0.0	0.0	0.0	0.2	X	0.00	0.00	0.01	0.00	0.07
Used merchandise (920)	0.0	0.1	0.0	0.0	0.0	X	0.00	0.03	0.01	0.00	0.01
Goods returned to Canada (980)	0.0	0.0	0.0	0.0	0.1	X	0.03	0.02	0.02	0.00	0.04
Special classification provisions (990)	0.4	0.6	0.2	0.3	0.1	-86.17	0.26	0.32	0.11	0.13	0.02
Publishing industries (except Internet) (511)	0.0	0.0	0.0	0.0	0.0	X	0.00	0.00	0.00	0.00	0.00
TOTAL AND PERCENT SHARE OF U.S. TOTAL	155.0	174.3	187.2	257.8	252.7	63.09	0.02	0.02	0.03	0.04	0.03
Top 25 Commodities (HS Code)	12.1	17.3	22.2	247.0	246.4	1 933.74	7.82	9.92	11.86	95.82	97.50
1. Petroleum oils from bituminous mineral (not crude) (271019)	...	0.0	0.0	129.2	97.3	...	...	0.00	0.00	50.12	38.50
2. Light oils and preparations (not crude) from petroleum (271011)	...	0.0	0.0	76.9	28.1	...	...	0.00	0.00	29.83	11.12
3. Toluene (290230)	0.0	0.0	4.7	0.0	25.1	X	0.00	0.00	2.51	0.00	9.93
4. Oils and other products of xylenes (270730)	7.2	2.2	4.6	14.9	21.4	197.54	4.64	1.26	2.46	5.78	8.47
5. Jewelry and parts thereof, of precious metal (711319)	0.8	6.9	9.8	19.6	20.0	2 373.17	0.52	3.96	5.24	7.60	7.91
6. Petroleum coke, not calcined (271311)	...	0.0	0.0	1.1	13.9	...	...	0.00	0.00	0.43	5.50
7. Benzene (290220)	...	0.0	0.0	0.0	10.2	...	...	0.00	0.00	0.00	4.04
8. Benzene (270710)	...	4.7	0.0	1.5	9.7	...	...	2.70	0.00	0.58	3.84
9. Oils distilled from coal tar (270799)	...	0.0	0.0	0.0	8.9	...	...	0.00	0.00	0.00	3.52
10. Sulfur, sublimed or precipitated; colloidal sulfur (280200)	2.0	2.2	1.0	2.4	6.6	228.48	1.30	1.26	0.53	0.93	2.61
11. Articles of precious or semiprecious stones (711620)	2.9	0.1	1.9	1.4	3.6	23.55	1.88	0.06	1.02	0.54	1.42
12. Diamonds, non-industrial, worked (710239)	...	0.0	0.0	0.0	1.6	...	...	0.00	0.00	0.00	0.63
13. Petroleum gases etc., in gaseous state (271129)	...	0.0	0.0	0.0	0.7	...	...	0.00	0.00	0.00	0.28
14. Watch bands of precious metal, parts (911310)	0.0	0.0	0.5	0.0	0.6	X	0.00	0.00	0.27	0.00	0.24
15. Sailboats, with or without auxiliary motors (890391)	1.0	0.0	0.5	0.0	0.6	-37.01	0.61	0.00	0.27	0.00	0.24
16. Plates and sheets, non-cellular, polymer (392010)	0.0	1.3	1.2	1.0	0.3	X	0.00	0.75	0.64	0.39	0.12
17. Herbicides, anti-sprouting products, retail (380830)	...	0.0	0.1	0.9	0.3	...	...	0.00	0.05	0.35	0.12
18. Engines and motors (841280)	...	0.0	0.0	0.0	0.2	...	...	0.00	0.00	0.00	0.08
19. Non-wovens of manmade filaments weighing < 25 g/m2 (560311)	...	0.0	0.0	0.0	0.2	...	...	0.00	0.00	0.00	0.08
20. Sulfuric acid; oleum (280700)	...	0.0	0.0	0.0	0.2	...	...	0.00	0.00	0.00	0.08
21. Game machines, excluding coin-operated (950490)	...	0.0	0.0	0.0	0.2	...	...	0.00	0.00	0.00	0.08
22. Drilling/mortising machines for working wood cork bone (846595)	...	0.0	0.0	0.1	0.2	...	...	0.00	0.00	0.04	0.08
23. Instruments, aeronautical-space nav., no compass (901420)	0.0	0.0	0.3	0.2	0.1	X	0.00	0.00	0.16	0.08	0.04
24. Electrical machines and apparatus with individ. functions (854389)	...	0.0	0.1	0.0	0.1	...	...	0.00	0.05	0.00	0.04
25. Passenger vehicles, spark-ignition, > 3,000 cc (870324)	...	0.0	0.0	0.1	0.1	...	...	0.00	0.00	0.04	0.04

X = Not applicable.
. . . = Not available.

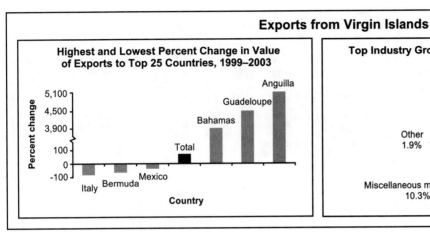

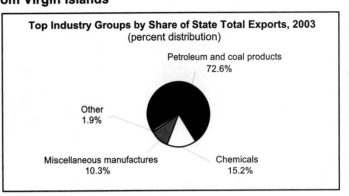

- The Virgin Islands' exports exceeded $252 million in 2003. This was a jump of 63 percent from 1999, and was the fourth highest increase among the 50 states, the District of Columbia, and Puerto Rico. Miscellaneous manufactures had the highest percentage gain, increasing nearly 366 percent from 1999 to 2003.

- The territory's major export industry remains petroleum and coal products. In 2003, these exports accounted for almost 73 percent of the territory's total exports. This industry's exports more than doubled from $87 million in 1999 to close to $184 million in 2003. The chemical manufactures industry had the second highest value of exports in 2003, with $38 million.

- The Virgin Islands' two top commodities are petroleum oils and light oils. Together, they account for half of total exports. The top two export countries, the Netherlands Antilles and the Bahamas, are also located in the Caribbean Sea, as is fourth-ranked St. Lucia. About 14 percent of the Virgin Islands' exports are to South Korea, which ranks third.

Table E-52. Total U.S. Exports (Origin of Movement) via Virgin Islands, 1999–2003—*Continued*

(Top 25 commodities and top 25 countries based on 2003 dollar value.)

Industry, commodity, and country	Value (millions of dollars)					Percent change, 1999–2003	Percent share of total				
	1999	2000	2001	2002	2003		1999	2000	2001	2002	2003
TOTAL AND PERCENT SHARE OF U.S. TOTAL	155.0	174.3	187.2	257.8	252.7	63.03	0.02	0.02	0.03	0.04	0.03
Top 25 Countries	108.3	151.0	4 276.2	241.4	248.2	129.18	69.89	86.62	2284.4	93.64	98.21
1. Netherlands Antilles	16.9	27.9	4 128.1	60.5	49.1	190.53	10.91	16.01	2205.3	23.47	19.43
2. Bahamas	0.9	0.9	25.5	38.4	36.2	3 922.22	0.58	0.52	13.62	14.90	14.32
3. South Korea	5.8	0.1	2.4	11.1	35.2	506.90	3.74	0.06	1.28	4.31	13.93
4. St. Lucia	8.2	16.7	15.6	12.1	15.5	89.02	5.29	9.58	8.33	4.69	6.13
5. Netherlands	8.8	14.3	4.7	1.9	12.3	39.77	5.68	8.20	2.51	0.74	4.87
6. British Virgin Islands	3.7	6.0	8.7	8.2	12.1	227.03	2.39	3.44	4.65	3.18	4.79
7. Venezuela	2.8	33.7	4.4	8.9	9.6	242.86	1.81	19.33	2.35	3.45	3.80
8. Dominican Republic	1.0	0.0	1.8	5.7	9.1	810.00	0.65	0.00	0.96	2.21	3.60
9. Taiwan	0.0	0.0	0.1	3.1	8.3	X	0.00	0.00	0.05	1.20	3.28
10. Brazil	2.3	1.0	0.6	1.7	7.4	221.74	1.48	0.57	0.32	0.66	2.93
11. Bermuda	16.1	11.6	2.9	7.8	6.3	-60.87	10.39	6.65	1.55	3.03	2.49
12. Mexico	8.7	11.0	68.3	62.1	5.4	-37.93	5.61	6.31	36.49	24.09	2.14
13. Spain	0.0	0.0	0.5	0.0	5.3	X	0.00	0.00	0.27	0.00	2.10
14. Anguilla	0.1	0.1	3.0	4.5	5.2	5 100.00	0.06	0.06	1.60	1.75	2.06
15. St. Kitts and Nevis	2.9	0.8	1.2	2.0	4.9	68.97	1.87	0.46	0.64	0.77	1.94
16. Guadeloupe	0.1	0.6	3.6	5.7	4.6	4 500.00	0.06	0.34	1.92	2.21	1.82
17. Italy	28.2	25.5	0.6	3.4	4.2	-85.11	18.20	14.63	0.32	1.32	1.66
18. China	0.0	0.0	0.4	0.0	4.2	X	0.00	0.00	0.21	0.00	1.66
19. Aruba	0.1	0.4	0.0	0.8	3.2	3 100.00	0.06	0.23	0.00	0.31	1.27
20. Turkey	0.0	0.0	0.5	0.0	3.0	X	0.00	0.00	0.27	0.00	1.19
21. Ireland	0.0	0.0	0.0	0.0	2.1	X	0.00	0.00	0.00	0.00	0.83
22. Montserrat	0.0	0.4	1.1	1.2	1.8	X	0.00	0.23	0.59	0.47	0.71
23. Belgium	1.7	0.0	0.0	1.5	1.7	0.00	1.10	0.00	0.00	0.58	0.67
24. Senegal	0.0	0.0	0.0	0.8	0.8	X	0.00	0.00	0.00	0.31	0.32
25. Guatemala	0.0	0.0	2.2	0.0	0.7	X	0.00	0.00	1.18	0.00	0.28

X = Not applicable.

Table E-53. Total U.S. Exports (Origin of Movement) via Virginia, 1999–2003

(Top 25 commodities and top 25 countries based on 2003 dollar value.)

Industry, commodity, and country	Value (millions of dollars)					Percent change, 1999–2003	Percent share of state total				
	1999	2000	2001	2002	2003		1999	2000	2001	2002	2003
TOTAL AND PERCENT SHARE OF U.S. TOTAL	11 483.0	11 698.1	11 630.9	10 795.5	10 853.0	-5.49	1.66	1.50	1.59	1.56	1.50
Manufactures (NAICS Code)	10 198.1	10 328.4	9 875.8	9 252.1	9 206.0	-9.73	88.81	88.29	84.91	85.70	84.82
Processed foods (311)	197.3	212.0	267.9	243.5	241.3	22.32	1.72	1.81	2.30	2.26	2.22
Beverages and tobacco products (312)	2 184.3	2 150.2	1 507.4	978.5	950.9	-56.47	19.02	0.00	12.96	9.06	8.76
Fabric mill products (313)	178.1	208.1	157.6	201.8	244.6	37.38	1.55	1.78	1.35	1.87	2.25
Non-apparel textile products (314)	70.9	81.2	86.9	90.9	75.9	7.09	0.62	0.69	0.75	0.84	0.70
Apparel manufactures (315)	232.1	216.9	227.4	183.0	154.9	-33.26	2.02	1.85	1.96	1.70	1.43
Leather and related products (316)	4.5	3.4	3.9	4.2	6.2	36.99	0.04	0.03	0.03	0.04	0.06
Wood products (321)	147.4	165.4	177.8	173.3	166.1	12.70	1.28	1.41	1.53	1.61	1.53
Paper products (322)	469.0	404.1	401.6	476.3	469.4	0.09	4.08	3.45	3.45	4.41	4.33
Printing and related products (323)	58.9	69.5	61.1	55.5	71.3	21.05	0.51	0.59	0.52	0.51	0.66
Petroleum and coal products (324)	72.1	82.9	50.9	39.9	67.6	-6.23	0.63	0.71	0.44	0.37	0.62
Chemical manufactures (325)	973.2	1 185.6	1 191.0	1 347.9	1 443.5	48.32	8.48	10.14	10.24	12.49	13.30
Plastics and rubber products (326)	316.3	350.1	312.9	322.9	365.3	15.48	2.75	2.99	2.69	2.99	3.37
Non-metallic mineral products (327)	47.5	67.3	68.9	73.2	74.0	55.67	0.41	0.58	0.59	0.68	0.68
Primary metal manufactures (331)	76.3	90.2	95.0	72.1	120.0	57.33	0.66	0.77	0.82	0.67	1.11
Fabricated metal products (332)	370.8	345.7	406.6	275.7	260.3	-29.79	3.23	2.96	3.50	2.55	2.40
Machinery manufactures (333)	936.3	980.1	1 105.4	1 388.9	1 131.4	20.84	8.15	8.38	9.50	12.87	10.42
Computer and electronic products (334)	1 924.6	2 016.7	2 088.0	1 568.7	1 378.3	-28.38	16.76	17.24	17.95	14.53	12.70
Electrical equipment, appliances, and parts (335)	335.9	368.9	377.6	428.2	278.0	-17.25	2.93	3.15	3.25	3.97	2.56
Transportation equipment (336)	1 376.0	1 089.2	1 064.2	1 126.2	1 464.4	6.42	11.98	9.31	9.15	10.43	13.49
Furniture and related products (337)	51.2	61.5	47.2	42.6	34.3	-33.01	0.45	0.53	0.41	0.39	0.32
Miscellaneous manufactures (339)	175.6	179.5	176.6	158.8	208.3	18.63	1.53	1.53	1.52	1.47	1.92
Agricultural and Livestock Products (NAICS Code)	298.4	409.7	557.3	441.3	597.5	100.26	2.60	3.50	4.79	4.09	5.51
Agricultural products (111)	293.2	405.2	553.1	436.9	589.5	101.03	2.55	3.46	4.76	4.05	5.43
Livestock and livestock products (112)	5.1	4.5	4.2	4.4	8.0	56.29	0.04	0.04	0.04	0.04	0.07
Other Commodities (NAICS Code)	986.5	959.9	1 197.9	1 102.1	1 049.5	6.39	8.59	8.21	10.30	10.21	9.67
Forestry and logging (113)	18.5	23.5	30.7	47.3	37.5	102.73	0.16	0.20	0.26	0.44	0.35
Fishing, hunting, and trapping (114)	29.0	24.7	35.9	35.1	44.3	52.96	0.25	0.21	0.31	0.33	0.41
Oil and gas extraction (211)	2.1	0.0	0.0	2.4	9.8	366.02	0.02	0.00	0.00	0.02	0.09
Mining (212)	551.7	481.9	635.4	500.8	450.1	-18.41	4.80	4.12	5.46	4.64	4.15
Waste and scrap (910)	27.7	50.6	65.5	70.5	86.4	211.73	0.24	0.43	0.56	0.65	0.80
Used merchandise (920)	7.4	6.1	5.9	14.9	10.7	44.03	0.06	0.05	0.05	0.14	0.10
Goods returned to Canada (980)	28.3	20.8	24.4	14.8	13.2	-53.21	0.25	0.18	0.21	0.14	0.12
Special classification provisions (990)	321.8	352.2	400.1	416.3	397.0	23.36	2.80	3.01	3.44	3.86	3.66
Publishing industries (except Internet) (511)	0.0	0.0	0.0	0.0	0.5	X	0.00	0.00	0.00	0.00	0.00
TOTAL AND PERCENT SHARE OF U.S. TOTAL	11 483.0	11 698.1	11 630.9	10 795.5	10 853.0	-5.49	1.66	1.50	1.59	1.56	1.50
Top 25 Commodities (HS Code)	4 750.4	4 606.3	4 528.5	4 529.5	4 891.1	2.96	41.37	39.38	38.93	41.96	45.07
1. Cigarettes (240220)	1 615.9	1 526.3	991.0	580.0	586.0	-63.74	14.07	13.05	8.52	5.37	5.40
2. Digital monolithic integrated circuits (854221)	0.0	0.0	0.0	613.9	454.8	X	0.00	0.00	0.00	5.69	4.19
3. Bituminous coal, not agglomerated (270112)	535.7	463.3	618.0	481.3	430.2	-19.69	4.67	3.96	5.31	4.46	3.96
4. Tobacco, partly or wholly stemmed/stripped (240120)	242.6	318.5	407.6	350.6	399.8	64.80	2.11	2.72	3.50	3.25	3.68
5. Parts of airplanes or helicopters (880330)	267.4	283.7	287.0	297.2	340.9	27.49	2.33	2.43	2.47	2.75	3.14
6. Kraft paper, bleached (481032)	331.0	230.9	194.2	238.2	283.3	-14.41	2.88	1.97	1.67	2.21	2.61
7. Road tractors for semi-trailers (870120)	377.8	190.0	120.3	148.9	240.0	-36.47	3.29	1.62	1.03	1.38	2.21
8. Goods vehicles, with spark-ignition piston engines (870431)	. . .	0.3	0.1	38.7	214.1	. . .	. . .	0.00	0.00	0.36	1.97
9. Manufactured tobacco and substitutes; tobacco extracts (240399)	307.1	370.2	283.0	247.2	184.2	-40.02	2.67	3.16	2.43	2.29	1.70
10. Exports of military equipment (980320)	176.0	219.6	194.5	168.9	177.5	0.85	1.53	1.88	1.67	1.56	1.64
11. Compressors used in refrigerating equipment (841430)	131.6	100.9	201.3	185.9	168.2	27.81	1.15	0.86	1.73	1.72	1.55
12. Parts and accessories for automatic data processing (847330)	82.0	112.6	222.3	171.4	165.8	102.20	0.71	0.96	1.91	1.59	1.53
13. Artificial filament tow (550200)	131.9	133.5	154.9	154.7	148.0	12.21	1.15	1.14	1.33	1.43	1.36
14. Parts and accessories of motor vehicles (870899)	103.9	116.7	123.9	132.9	140.4	35.13	0.90	1.00	1.07	1.23	1.29
15. Gas turbine parts (841199)	115.2	69.6	147.3	183.6	138.2	19.97	1.00	0.59	1.27	1.70	1.27
16. Soybeans, whether or not broken (120100)	. . .	7.3	47.8	3.3	123.9	. . .	. . .	0.06	0.41	0.03	1.14
17. Plates, non-cellular, polyethylene terephthalate (392062)	. . .	49.7	42.9	58.4	96.4	. . .	. . .	0.42	0.37	0.54	0.89
18. Smoking tobacco, whether or not containing substitutes (240310)	185.9	152.8	124.1	74.1	96.1	-48.31	1.62	1.31	1.07	0.69	0.89
19. Spacecraft and suborbital and space launch vehicles (880260)	0.5	0.2	2.7	76.8	89.2	17 740.00	0.00	0.00	0.02	0.71	0.82
20. Non-wovens, of manmade filaments > 25 g/m2 < 70 g/m2 (560312)	33.3	51.5	46.0	63.7	86.7	160.36	0.29	0.44	0.40	0.59	0.80
21. Retail medicaments in measured dose (300490)	. . .	18.2	48.7	45.1	70.7	. . .	. . .	0.16	0.42	0.42	0.65
22. Homogenized or reconstituted tobacco (240391)	48.0	71.8	90.6	61.2	67.7	41.04	0.42	0.61	0.78	0.57	0.62
23. Medicinal and pharmaceutical exports, donated (980220)	. . .	32.2	72.4	42.8	65.9	. . .	. . .	0.28	0.62	0.40	0.61
24. Additives for lubricating oil containing petroleum (381121)	. . .	37.4	42.8	49.3	63.2	. . .	. . .	0.32	0.37	0.46	0.58
25. Sweaters, pullovers, knit, cotton (611020)	65.1	49.6	65.2	61.4	59.9	-7.99	0.57	0.42	0.56	0.57	0.55

X = Not applicable.
. . . = Not available.

Exports from Virginia

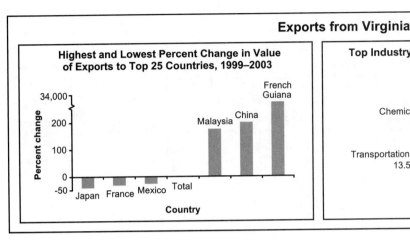

Highest and Lowest Percent Change in Value of Exports to Top 25 Countries, 1999–2003

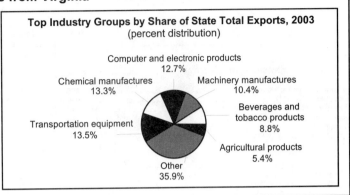

Top Industry Groups by Share of State Total Exports, 2003 (percent distribution)

- Virginia's total exports are about $10.9 billion, which is a decline of more than 5 percent from 1999. Transportation equipment, chemical manufactures, and computer and electronic products are the leading export industries, with each accounting for about 13 percent of the state's total exports. Of the three, chemical manufactures had the greatest percentage gain from 1999 to 2003, increasing 48 percent or about $470 million.

- While cigarettes remain the state's top commodity, these exports fell nearly 64 percent from 1999, which is a drop of over $1 billion. Tobacco exports, the fourth-ranked commodity export, increased by $157 million from 1999 to 2003. Spacecraft and related vehicles are by far the fastest growing commodity export. In 1999, these exports totaled about $500,000, and by 2003 had increased to over $89 million.

- Canada is Virginia's top export country, receiving more than 19 percent of the state's total exports. Germany ranks second, with 9 percent, or $990 million. Exports to French Guiana increased from $281,000 in 1999 to $95 million in 2003, making it the fastest growing market for Virginia's exports.

Table E-53. Total U.S. Exports (Origin of Movement) via Virginia, 1999–2003—*Continued*

(Top 25 commodities and top 25 countries based on 2003 dollar value.)

Industry, commodity, and country	Value (millions of dollars)					Percent change, 1999–2003	Percent share of state total				
	1999	2000	2001	2002	2003		1999	2000	2001	2002	2003
TOTAL AND PERCENT SHARE OF U.S. TOTAL	11 483.0	11 698.1	11 630.9	10 795.5	10 853.0	-5.49	1.66	1.50	1.59	1.56	1.50
Top 25 Countries	9 531.7	9 948.9	9 581.9	9 307.1	9 269.6	-2.75	83.01	85.05	82.38	86.21	85.41
1. Canada	2 157.0	2 104.0	1 780.9	1 838.8	2 106.0	-2.36	18.78	17.99	15.31	17.03	19.40
2. Germany	700.6	783.2	1 079.8	1 157.6	989.9	41.29	6.10	6.69	9.28	10.72	9.12
3. Japan	1 564.5	1 832.2	1 318.1	1 321.9	907.6	-41.99	13.62	15.66	11.33	12.24	8.36
4. United Kingdom	599.2	675.7	732.8	653.7	724.0	20.82	5.22	5.78	6.30	6.06	6.67
5. China	173.6	197.8	262.5	368.6	521.2	200.14	1.51	1.69	2.26	3.41	4.80
6. Belgium	497.1	462.2	422.4	475.9	474.5	-4.56	4.33	3.95	3.63	4.41	4.37
7. Mexico	573.6	646.1	762.1	449.5	399.0	-30.44	5.00	5.52	6.55	4.16	3.68
8. Netherlands	376.6	310.2	299.5	316.6	389.2	3.36	3.28	2.65	2.58	2.93	3.59
9. Malaysia	98.7	138.2	182.8	278.3	280.1	183.75	0.86	1.18	1.57	2.58	2.58
10. Saudi Arabia	336.3	338.2	331.0	255.9	262.0	-22.08	2.93	2.89	2.85	2.37	2.41
11. South Korea	205.5	214.6	212.1	241.4	246.8	20.12	1.79	1.83	1.82	2.24	2.27
12. Brazil	289.7	365.0	360.2	249.3	225.9	-22.02	2.52	3.12	3.10	2.31	2.08
13. Italy	221.8	200.5	308.6	239.6	223.9	0.96	1.93	1.71	2.65	2.22	2.06
14. France	316.6	255.0	248.6	216.9	200.5	-36.68	2.76	2.18	2.14	2.01	1.85
15. Spain	193.8	210.6	191.0	176.5	172.3	-11.10	1.69	1.80	1.64	1.63	1.59
16. Australia	199.0	147.2	122.6	160.9	149.5	-24.85	1.73	1.26	1.05	1.49	1.38
17. Hong Kong	170.9	176.7	192.6	154.8	144.3	-15.55	1.49	1.51	1.66	1.43	1.33
18. Sweden	106.9	106.2	88.5	93.2	138.7	29.75	0.93	0.91	0.76	0.86	1.28
19. Singapore	166.8	164.3	152.4	98.2	117.7	-29.46	1.45	1.40	1.31	0.91	1.08
20. Taiwan	131.1	170.4	90.9	100.6	113.8	-13.13	1.14	1.46	0.78	0.93	1.05
21. Switzerland	115.0	91.6	88.1	91.6	105.6	-8.16	1.00	0.78	0.76	0.85	0.97
22. Turkey	122.6	126.8	150.8	100.6	102.0	-16.75	1.07	1.08	1.30	0.93	0.94
23. Israel	126.6	152.1	136.9	123.0	95.8	-24.33	1.10	1.30	1.18	1.14	0.88
24. French Guiana	0.3	0.0	0.0	78.3	95.2	33 764.00	0.00	0.00	0.00	0.73	0.88
25. Kuwait	88.1	80.0	66.7	65.6	84.1	-4.55	0.77	0.68	0.57	0.61	0.78

Table E-54. Total U.S. Exports (Origin of Movement) via Washington, 1999–2003

(Top 25 commodities and top 25 countries based on 2003 dollar value.)

Industry, commodity, and country	Value (millions of dollars)					Percent change, 1999–2003	Percent share of state total				
	1999	2000	2001	2002	2003		1999	2000	2001	2002	2003
TOTAL AND PERCENT SHARE OF U.S. TOTAL	36 730.7	32 214.7	34 928.5	34 626.5	34 172.8	-6.96	5.30	4.13	4.78	4.99	4.72
Manufactures (NAICS Code)	33 493.8	28 640.1	31 045.8	31 127.0	29 374.4	-12.30	91.19	88.90	88.88	89.89	85.96
Processed foods (311)	1 056.3	1 173.5	1 276.1	1 278.1	1 602.2	51.68	2.88	3.64	3.65	3.69	4.69
Beverages and tobacco products (312)	45.7	30.6	28.0	22.5	29.1	-36.47	0.12	0.00	0.08	0.06	0.09
Fabric mill products (313)	16.3	20.3	18.1	24.3	16.9	3.80	0.04	0.06	0.05	0.07	0.05
Non-apparel textile products (314)	33.2	34.2	34.2	37.7	49.4	48.70	0.09	0.11	0.10	0.11	0.14
Apparel manufactures (315)	22.4	35.1	41.1	33.6	23.6	5.24	0.06	0.11	0.12	0.10	0.07
Leather and related products (316)	22.5	13.4	11.0	11.2	12.1	-46.14	0.06	0.04	0.03	0.03	0.04
Wood products (321)	451.6	428.8	359.6	324.2	343.5	-23.95	1.23	1.33	1.03	0.94	1.01
Paper products (322)	901.4	1 043.7	882.0	817.0	831.3	-7.78	2.45	3.24	2.53	2.36	2.43
Printing and related products (323)	70.8	66.5	41.1	41.9	38.1	-46.17	0.19	0.21	0.12	0.12	0.11
Petroleum and coal products (324)	369.9	324.9	486.2	538.9	736.8	99.20	1.01	1.01	1.39	1.56	2.16
Chemical manufactures (325)	525.3	503.3	548.7	637.3	613.8	16.86	1.43	1.56	1.57	1.84	1.80
Plastics and rubber products (326)	156.1	160.4	140.7	131.8	137.4	-11.96	0.42	0.50	0.40	0.38	0.40
Non-metallic mineral products (327)	52.7	56.7	65.1	64.4	89.4	69.68	0.14	0.18	0.19	0.19	0.26
Primary metal manufactures (331)	543.6	579.1	364.5	287.4	396.4	-27.08	1.48	1.80	1.04	0.83	1.16
Fabricated metal products (332)	177.7	162.0	169.6	164.3	200.7	12.96	0.48	0.50	0.49	0.47	0.59
Machinery manufactures (333)	1 019.1	1 002.0	979.6	800.2	839.0	-17.68	2.77	3.11	2.80	2.31	2.46
Computer and electronic products (334)	1 617.3	2 173.2	2 229.1	1 957.8	2 353.9	45.54	4.40	6.75	6.38	5.65	6.89
Electrical equipment, appliances, and parts (335)	250.6	266.0	260.4	269.6	288.0	15.12	0.68	0.83	0.75	0.78	0.84
Transportation equipment (336)	25 807.0	20 175.3	22 740.2	23 377.4	20 438.4	-20.80	70.26	62.63	65.10	67.51	59.81
Furniture and related products (337)	23.4	34.3	25.4	17.4	20.1	-14.29	0.06	0.11	0.07	0.05	0.06
Miscellaneous manufactures (339)	331.0	356.7	344.9	289.9	314.1	-5.12	0.90	1.11	0.99	0.84	0.92
Agricultural and Livestock Products (NAICS Code)	1 795.2	2 049.7	2 421.7	2 186.7	3 421.5	90.59	4.89	6.36	6.93	6.32	10.01
Agricultural products (111)	1 720.6	1 937.0	2 312.1	2 093.6	3 333.1	93.72	4.68	6.01	6.62	6.05	9.75
Livestock and livestock products (112)	74.6	112.7	109.6	93.1	88.4	18.51	0.20	0.35	0.31	0.27	0.26
Other Commodities (NAICS Code)	1 441.7	1 524.9	1 461.0	1 312.9	1 376.9	-4.50	3.93	4.73	4.18	3.79	4.03
Forestry and logging (113)	563.7	596.0	435.8	386.7	357.8	-36.52	1.53	1.85	1.25	1.12	1.05
Fishing, hunting, and trapping (114)	432.9	511.0	639.5	512.0	534.2	23.40	1.18	1.59	1.83	1.48	1.56
Oil and gas extraction (211)	5.3	10.1	6.6	6.2	22.4	324.88	0.01	0.03	0.02	0.02	0.07
Mining (212)	23.4	34.4	36.8	24.1	21.3	-8.95	0.06	0.11	0.11	0.07	0.06
Waste and scrap (910)	85.3	104.6	109.0	107.9	196.7	130.58	0.23	0.32	0.31	0.31	0.58
Used merchandise (920)	16.2	27.2	14.9	18.8	46.3	186.16	0.04	0.08	0.04	0.05	0.14
Goods returned to Canada (980)	78.5	65.3	70.1	72.4	61.6	-21.52	0.21	0.20	0.20	0.21	0.18
Special classification provisions (990)	236.5	176.5	148.3	184.8	133.7	-43.45	0.64	0.55	0.42	0.53	0.39
Publishing industries (except Internet) (511)	0.0	0.0	0.0	0.0	2.8	X	0.00	0.00	0.00	0.00	0.01
TOTAL AND PERCENT SHARE OF U.S. TOTAL	36 730.7	32 214.7	34 928.5	34 626.5	34 172.8	-6.96	5.30	4.13	4.78	4.99	4.72
Top 25 Commodities (HS Code)	28 573.0	23 555.3	26 462.5	27 656.5	26 628.9	-6.80	77.79	73.12	75.76	79.87	77.92
1. Airplane and aircraft, unladen weight > 15,000 kg (880240)	23 965.4	18 449.8	21 116.5	21 930.2	18 836.6	-21.40	65.25	57.27	60.46	63.33	55.12
2. Soybeans, whether or not broken (120100)	123.8	315.7	607.9	495.4	1 422.9	1 049.35	0.34	0.98	1.74	1.43	4.16
3. Parts of airplanes or helicopters (880330)	1 287.7	1 301.2	1 263.7	1 059.2	1 164.8	-9.54	3.51	4.04	3.62	3.06	3.41
4. Corn, other than seed corn (100590)	654.1	581.4	508.1	354.0	574.1	-12.23	1.78	1.81	1.45	1.02	1.68
5. Digital monolithic integrated circuits (854221)	0.0	0.0	0.0	200.3	566.5	X	0.00	0.00	0.00	0.58	1.66
6. Petroleum oils from bituminous mineral (not crude) (271019)	0.0	0.0	0.0	307.9	524.9	X	0.00	0.00	0.00	0.89	1.54
7. Wheat and meslin (100190)	334.8	339.6	430.5	473.0	483.5	44.41	0.91	1.05	1.23	1.37	1.41
8. Coniferous wood in the rough, not treated (440320)	535.7	574.3	415.5	364.4	339.9	-36.55	1.46	1.78	1.19	1.05	0.99
9. Uranium enriched in U235 (284420)	251.5	253.9	261.3	334.8	305.8	21.59	0.68	0.79	0.75	0.97	0.89
10. Apples, fresh (080810)	206.6	242.8	263.7	257.4	247.6	19.85	0.56	0.75	0.75	0.74	0.72
11. Prepared frozen potatoes (200410)	153.2	167.8	169.0	178.5	196.0	27.94	0.42	0.52	0.48	0.52	0.57
12. Ultrasonic scanning apparatus (901812)	179.8	207.2	197.8	175.5	190.6	6.01	0.49	0.64	0.57	0.51	0.56
13. Newsprint, in rolls or sheets (480100)	235.1	297.2	220.2	187.2	185.9	-20.93	0.64	0.92	0.63	0.54	0.54
14. Paper, paperboard coated with plastic, > 150 g/m2 (481151)	0.0	0.0	0.0	189.8	175.6	X	0.00	0.00	0.00	0.55	0.51
15. Forage products (hay, clover, vetches) (121490)	75.8	109.5	112.5	145.3	160.8	112.14	0.21	0.34	0.32	0.42	0.47
16. Fork-lift and works trucks (842790)	. . .	5.5	13.0	80.8	140.1	. . .	. . .	0.02	0.04	0.23	0.41
17. Meat of bovine animals, boneless, fresh or chilled (020130)	. . .	54.1	43.6	26.9	137.0	. . .	. . .	0.17	0.12	0.08	0.40
18. Petroleum coke, calcined (271312)	87.3	36.3	81.7	136.1	135.1	54.75	0.24	0.11	0.23	0.39	0.40
19. Automatic data processing storage units (847170)	46.7	65.2	106.3	110.4	130.3	179.01	0.13	0.20	0.30	0.32	0.38
20. Salmon, prepared or preserved, whole or pieces (160411)	149.8	109.3	113.2	118.6	128.0	-14.55	0.41	0.34	0.32	0.34	0.37
21. Fish livers and roes, frozen (030380)	28.6	80.2	171.6	138.6	121.7	325.52	0.08	0.25	0.49	0.40	0.36
22. Parts and accessories for automatic data processing (847330)	103.0	144.3	146.8	137.2	121.6	18.06	0.28	0.45	0.42	0.40	0.36
23. Portable digital a.d.p. machines < 10 kg (847130)	39.0	38.7	58.4	95.8	117.7	201.79	0.11	0.12	0.17	0.28	0.34
24. Silicon containing by weight >= 99.99 percent silicon (280461)	115.1	127.5	87.6	84.0	116.4	1.13	0.31	0.40	0.25	0.24	0.34
25. Video games used with TV receiver, parts and accessories (950410)	. . .	53.4	73.6	75.2	105.5	. . .	. . .	0.17	0.21	0.22	0.31

X = Not applicable.
. . . = Not available.

Exports from Washington

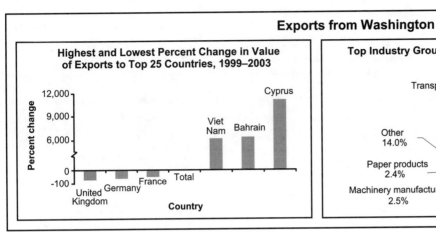

Highest and Lowest Percent Change in Value of Exports to Top 25 Countries, 1999–2003

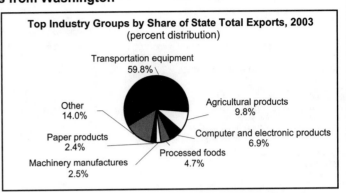

Top Industry Groups by Share of State Total Exports, 2003
(percent distribution)

Transportation equipment 59.8%
Other 14.0%
Paper products 2.4%
Machinery manufactures 2.5%
Processed foods 4.7%
Computer and electronic products 6.9%
Agricultural products 9.8%

- Washington has the fourth highest value of exports in the nation, following only Texas, California, and New York. The state's exports fell 7 percent, or $2.6 billion, from 1999 to 2003. Transportation equipment exports, which exceed $20.4 billion, represent nearly 60 percent of the state's total exports, but this is down almost 21 percent from 1999. While airplane exports are the state's top commodity, they dropped from $24.0 billion to $18.8 billion during this period.

- Exports of agricultural products grew from $1.7 billion in 1999 to $3.3 billion in 2003. Several agricultural commodities are among Washington's top 10 exports. Soybeans rank second, with exports of over $1.4 billion. Also among the top 10 are corn ($574 million), wheat ($484 million), and apples ($248 million).

- The top three export countries are Japan, Canada, and China. Germany, which ranked fourth in 1999, dropped to 12th in 2003, as transportation equipment exports to Germany fell from $1.7 billion to $407 million.

Table E-54. Total U.S. Exports (Origin of Movement) via Washington, 1999–2003—*Continued*

(Top 25 commodities and top 25 countries based on 2003 dollar value.)

Industry, commodity, and country	Value (millions of dollars)					Percent change, 1999–2003	Percent share of state total				
	1999	2000	2001	2002	2003		1999	2000	2001	2002	2003
TOTAL AND PERCENT SHARE OF U.S. TOTAL	36 730.7	32 214.7	34 928.5	34 626.5	34 172.8	-6.96	5.30	4.13	4.78	4.99	4.72
Top 25 Countries	27 605.8	24 240.3	26 586.6	28 604.9	31 026.6	12.39	75.16	75.25	76.12	82.61	90.79
1. Japan	5 502.4	4 594.8	3 383.8	4 349.3	5 428.5	-1.34	14.98	14.26	9.69	12.56	15.89
2. Canada	2 765.9	2 875.9	2 737.3	2 944.2	3 313.9	19.81	7.53	8.93	7.84	8.50	9.70
3. China	2 040.5	1 900.7	2 928.7	3 830.5	3 211.2	57.37	5.56	5.90	8.38	11.06	9.40
4. Singapore	1 279.9	609.8	2 990.9	2 306.4	2 087.0	63.06	3.48	1.89	8.56	6.66	6.11
5. Australia	601.9	511.0	575.7	2 627.0	1 966.9	226.76	1.64	1.59	1.65	7.59	5.76
6. Taiwan	750.8	1 451.8	1 594.2	1 047.3	1 958.4	160.85	2.04	4.51	4.56	3.02	5.73
7. Netherlands	995.2	1 317.4	707.5	765.7	1 739.2	74.76	2.71	4.09	2.03	2.21	5.09
8. South Korea	1 554.9	1 743.4	2 131.3	2 056.2	1 673.2	7.61	4.23	5.41	6.10	5.94	4.90
9. United Kingdom	4 399.6	3 266.7	2 737.3	1 229.8	1 461.6	-66.78	11.98	10.14	7.84	3.55	4.28
10. Italy	764.4	119.6	131.7	1 027.1	1 100.9	44.02	2.08	0.37	0.38	2.97	3.22
11. Ireland	420.0	490.4	613.2	620.9	842.7	100.62	1.14	1.52	1.76	1.79	2.47
12. Germany	2 168.4	2 057.1	1 843.3	1 007.3	785.6	-63.77	5.90	6.39	5.28	2.91	2.30
13. Vietnam	11.5	8.4	16.2	21.1	736.4	6 306.02	0.03	0.03	0.05	0.06	2.16
14. France	1 479.5	1 003.1	1 252.9	1 953.2	684.1	-53.76	4.03	3.11	3.59	5.64	2.00
15. United Arab Emirates	709.7	251.2	271.2	946.6	679.0	-4.33	1.93	0.78	0.78	2.73	1.99
16. Thailand	581.3	467.7	506.7	104.7	648.1	11.49	1.58	1.45	1.45	0.30	1.90
17. Mexico	369.3	467.2	861.5	431.9	607.4	64.47	1.01	1.45	2.47	1.25	1.78
18. Philippines	182.2	185.2	249.3	246.1	366.5	101.17	0.50	0.57	0.71	0.71	1.07
19. Hong Kong	421.7	412.0	506.2	322.2	351.2	-16.72	1.15	1.28	1.45	0.93	1.03
20. Indonesia	84.3	88.9	113.4	189.3	260.5	208.96	0.23	0.28	0.32	0.55	0.76
21. Panama	167.0	176.3	9.2	210.8	256.7	53.76	0.45	0.55	0.03	0.61	0.75
22. Cyprus	2.2	1.4	99.7	101.3	238.7	10 922.30	0.01	0.00	0.29	0.29	0.70
23. India	344.0	230.6	316.0	259.1	228.7	-33.52	0.94	0.72	0.90	0.75	0.67
24. Bahrain	3.0	3.5	5.8	2.5	205.2	6 824.49	0.01	0.01	0.02	0.01	0.60
25. Hungary	6.1	6.3	3.7	4.2	194.8	3 101.78	0.02	0.02	0.01	0.01	0.57

Table E-55. Total U.S. Exports (Origin of Movement) via West Virginia, 1999–2003

(Top 25 commodities and top 25 countries based on 2003 dollar value.)

Industry, commodity, and country	Value (millions of dollars)					Percent change, 1999–2003	Percent share of state total				
	1999	2000	2001	2002	2003		1999	2000	2001	2002	2003
TOTAL AND PERCENT SHARE OF U.S. TOTAL	1 892.7	2 219.3	2 241.0	2 237.2	2 379.8	25.74	0.27	0.28	0.31	0.32	0.33
Manufactures (NAICS Code)	1 572.8	1 778.0	1 804.5	2 006.4	2 097.3	33.35	83.10	80.12	80.52	89.68	88.13
Processed foods (311)	9.5	10.0	6.2	3.0	6.7	-29.24	0.50	0.45	0.28	0.13	0.28
Beverages and tobacco products (312)	0.0	0.0	0.0	0.0	0.0	X	0.00	0.00	0.00	0.00	0.00
Fabric mill products (313)	4.0	2.5	5.3	6.3	6.7	68.42	0.21	0.11	0.24	0.28	0.28
Non-apparel textile products (314)	0.6	0.5	0.5	0.4	0.3	-46.59	0.03	0.02	0.02	0.02	0.01
Apparel manufactures (315)	0.2	1.2	0.7	0.6	0.5	109.55	0.01	0.05	0.03	0.03	0.02
Leather and related products (316)	0.2	0.1	0.1	1.2	0.2	47.80	0.01	0.00	0.01	0.05	0.01
Wood products (321)	75.5	98.6	88.2	94.8	96.0	27.13	3.99	4.44	3.93	4.24	4.03
Paper products (322)	8.2	7.8	12.1	15.9	11.1	34.48	0.44	0.35	0.54	0.71	0.47
Printing and related products (323)	2.2	1.8	1.8	1.6	12.6	479.45	0.12	0.08	0.08	0.07	0.53
Petroleum and coal products (324)	8.5	17.8	33.1	22.4	23.9	181.74	0.45	0.80	1.48	1.00	1.00
Chemical manufactures (325)	1 081.1	1 064.6	934.5	1 050.9	1 115.5	3.18	57.12	47.97	41.70	46.98	46.87
Plastics and rubber products (326)	24.0	26.2	32.8	40.7	40.6	68.97	1.27	1.18	1.46	1.82	1.70
Non-metallic mineral products (327)	38.0	39.3	49.1	44.4	43.4	14.35	2.01	1.77	2.19	1.98	1.82
Primary metal manufactures (331)	151.6	205.6	229.2	217.1	199.5	31.65	8.01	9.26	10.23	9.71	8.38
Fabricated metal products (332)	21.8	21.5	14.0	15.5	18.5	-14.96	1.15	0.97	0.62	0.69	0.78
Machinery manufactures (333)	74.3	169.2	165.7	197.6	204.4	175.18	3.92	7.62	7.39	8.83	8.59
Computer and electronic products (334)	17.0	17.3	33.6	46.4	59.5	249.55	0.90	0.78	1.50	2.07	2.50
Electrical equipment, appliances, and parts (335)	4.6	5.2	8.2	4.6	4.1	-9.43	0.24	0.24	0.37	0.21	0.17
Transportation equipment (336)	47.6	78.3	178.3	229.8	238.9	401.80	2.51	3.53	7.96	10.27	10.04
Furniture and related products (337)	0.7	0.9	1.0	0.5	0.5	-19.56	0.04	0.04	0.04	0.02	0.02
Miscellaneous manufactures (339)	3.5	9.9	10.3	12.7	14.4	315.22	0.18	0.45	0.46	0.57	0.61
Agricultural and Livestock Products (NAICS Code)	6.8	7.3	7.2	6.2	5.3	-21.75	0.36	0.33	0.32	0.28	0.22
Agricultural products (111)	0.2	0.1	0.3	0.0	0.2	25.91	0.01	0.01	0.01	0.00	0.01
Livestock and livestock products (112)	6.6	7.2	6.9	6.2	5.1	-23.15	0.35	0.32	0.31	0.28	0.21
Other Commodities (NAICS Code)	313.1	433.9	429.4	224.6	277.2	-11.47	16.54	19.55	19.16	10.04	11.65
Forestry and logging (113)	7.0	6.8	10.6	12.1	10.0	42.51	0.37	0.31	0.47	0.54	0.42
Fishing, hunting, and trapping (114)	0.0	0.0	0.0	0.2	0.2	X	0.00	0.00	0.00	0.01	0.01
Oil and gas extraction (211)	0.0	0.0	0.3	0.5	0.0	X	0.00	0.00	0.01	0.02	0.00
Mining (212)	287.9	403.9	408.5	199.6	246.1	-14.53	15.21	18.20	18.23	8.92	10.34
Waste and scrap (910)	3.8	10.5	5.5	5.8	7.4	95.45	0.20	0.47	0.25	0.26	0.31
Used merchandise (920)	0.6	0.2	0.1	1.1	2.1	248.65	0.03	0.01	0.00	0.05	0.09
Goods returned to Canada (980)	6.1	3.6	2.5	2.6	2.5	-59.70	0.32	0.16	0.11	0.12	0.10
Special classification provisions (990)	7.6	8.9	1.9	2.6	8.9	16.73	0.40	0.40	0.08	0.12	0.37
Publishing industries (except Internet) (511)	0.0	0.0	0.0	0.0	0.0	X	0.00	0.00	0.00	0.00	0.00
TOTAL AND PERCENT SHARE OF U.S. TOTAL	1 892.7	2 219.3	2 241.0	2 237.2	2 379.8	25.74	0.27	0.28	0.31	0.32	0.33
Top 25 Commodities (HS Code)	917.2	1 209.1	1 226.5	1 189.9	1 460.6	59.25	48.46	54.48	54.73	53.19	61.37
1. Bituminous coal, not agglomerated (270112)	286.6	401.4	406.2	197.9	243.7	-14.97	0.27	0.28	0.31	0.32	10.24
2. Polyamide-6,-11,-12,-6,6,-6,9,-6,10 or -6,12 (390810)	93.8	119.5	104.9	139.3	161.5	72.17	4.96	5.38	4.68	6.23	6.79
3. Polyethers (390720)	28.6	44.1	39.2	75.1	89.1	211.54	1.51	1.99	1.75	3.36	3.74
4. Turbojets of a thrust > 25 kn (841112)	0.0	0.0	39.7	87.6	73.1	X	0.00	0.00	1.77	3.92	3.07
5. Lenses, prisms, mirrors, and optical elements (900190)	0.2	60.7	75.6	92.4	72.7	36 250.00	0.01	2.74	3.37	4.13	3.05
6. Spark-ignition engine parts (840991)	4.4	51.0	39.3	57.2	71.3	1 520.45	0.23	2.30	1.75	2.56	3.00
7. Aluminum alloy rectangular plates, > 0.2 mm thick (760612)	67.4	90.5	75.8	84.6	68.3	1.34	3.56	4.08	3.38	3.78	2.87
8. Phosphoric esters and salts, lactophosphates (291900)	. . .	8.2	8.1	8.9	60.6	. . .	. . .	0.37	0.36	0.40	2.55
9. Polysulfides and polysulfones, primary forms (391190)	24.2	29.7	50.6	58.8	51.3	111.98	1.28	1.34	2.26	2.63	2.16
10. Parts and accessories of motor vehicles bodies (870829)	3.9	12.2	17.6	32.7	47.8	1 125.64	0.21	0.55	0.79	1.46	2.01
11. Polyesters, unsaturated, primary forms (390799)	20.0	28.6	22.0	32.1	43.8	119.00	1.06	1.29	0.98	1.43	1.84
12. Polyacetals, primary forms (390710)	22.7	27.5	21.1	35.8	42.5	87.22	1.20	1.24	0.94	1.60	1.79
13. Polymers of ethylene (390190)	16.3	13.8	22.2	28.5	39.9	144.79	0.86	0.62	0.99	1.27	1.68
14. Parts and accessories of motor vehicles (870899)	. . .	5.4	5.6	7.5	39.8	. . .	. . .	0.24	0.25	0.34	1.67
15. Silicones, in primary forms (391000)	57.3	47.2	36.5	36.7	37.0	-35.43	3.03	2.13	1.63	1.64	1.55
16. Miscellaneous organo-inorganic compounds (293100)	150.8	70.0	48.2	28.3	35.9	-76.19	7.97	3.15	2.15	1.27	1.51
17. Non-ionic organic surface-active agents (340213)	49.5	38.1	52.6	26.4	34.3	-30.71	2.62	1.72	2.35	1.18	1.44
18. Esters of other inorganic acids (292090)	46.7	49.9	35.4	31.7	33.3	-28.69	2.47	2.25	1.58	1.42	1.40
19. Supported catalysts with precious metals and compounds (381512)	. . .	16.5	21.9	19.1	32.2	. . .	. . .	0.74	0.98	0.85	1.35
20. Flat rolled products of iron/non-alloy steel < 0.5 mm thick (721012)	17.4	16.4	20.1	24.9	31.9	83.33	0.92	0.74	0.90	1.11	1.34
21. Bars, rods and profiles of nickel alloys (750512)	. . .	2.8	3.4	2.9	31.8	. . .	. . .	0.13	0.15	0.13	1.34
22. Acyclic aldehydes (291219)	. . .	26.9	22.3	11.9	31.8	. . .	. . .	1.21	1.00	0.53	1.34
23. Plates, non-cellular, polyvinyl (392091)	11.0	14.0	20.1	27.6	31.2	183.64	0.58	0.63	0.90	1.23	1.31
24. Products and residuals of chemical industry (382490)	. . .	17.0	18.2	16.7	28.4	. . .	. . .	0.77	0.81	0.75	1.19
25. Non-coniferous wood, sawn, sliced, > 6 mm thick (440799)	16.6	17.7	19.9	25.3	27.4	65.06	0.88	0.80	0.89	1.13	1.15

X = Not applicable.

. . . = Not available.

Exports from West Virginia

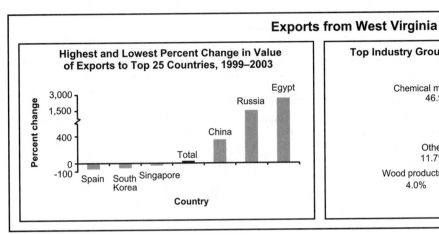

Highest and Lowest Percent Change in Value of Exports to Top 25 Countries, 1999–2003

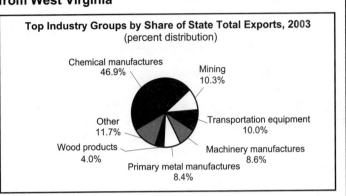

Top Industry Groups by Share of State Total Exports, 2003
(percent distribution)

Chemical manufactures 46.9%
Mining 10.3%
Other 11.7%
Transportation equipment 10.0%
Wood products 4.0%
Machinery manufactures 8.6%
Primary metal manufactures 8.4%

- West Virginia's total exports increased nearly 26 percent from 1999 to 2003. The state's largest export industry is chemical manufactures, which account for about 47 percent, or $1.1 billion, of total exports. Among the state's leading industry exports, transportation equipment had the most growth from 1999 to 2003, increasing fivefold. As a result, its share of West Virginia's total exports climbed from less than 3 percent to 10 percent.

- Mining products remain a leading export. They represent more than 10 percent of all of West Virginia's exports. Coal, which is the state's leading commodity export, represents the bulk of the mining exports.

- Canada is West Virginia's top export market. Exports to Canada rose from $391 million in 1999 to $760 million in 2003. As a result of this growth, Canada received nearly 32 percent of West Virginia's exports in 2003. Chemical manufactures represent almost 28 percent of exports to Canada.

Table E-55. Total U.S. Exports (Origin of Movement) via West Virginia, 1999–2003—*Continued*

(Top 25 commodities and top 25 countries based on 2003 dollar value.)

Industry, commodity, and country	Value (millions of dollars)					Percent change, 1999–2003	Percent share of state total				
	1999	2000	2001	2002	2003		1999	2000	2001	2002	2003
TOTAL AND PERCENT SHARE OF U.S. TOTAL	1 892.7	2 219.3	2 241.0	2 237.2	2 379.8	25.74	0.27	0.28	0.31	0.32	0.33
Top 25 Countries	1 716.9	2 033.2	2 093.2	2 103.0	2 247.5	30.91	90.71	91.61	93.40	94.00	94.44
1. Canada	391.4	648.9	776.1	738.6	759.5	94.02	20.68	29.24	34.63	33.02	31.91
2. Belgium	224.4	246.2	227.4	205.0	235.9	5.13	11.86	11.10	10.15	9.16	9.91
3. Japan	259.6	243.6	213.6	241.6	233.5	-10.06	13.72	10.98	9.53	10.80	9.81
4. China	27.5	35.6	120.4	144.9	132.6	382.67	1.45	1.60	5.37	6.48	5.57
5. Mexico	31.6	28.8	44.4	75.8	80.6	154.66	1.67	1.30	1.98	3.39	3.39
6. Netherlands	86.9	77.6	67.8	69.6	79.9	-8.00	4.59	3.50	3.03	3.11	3.36
7. South Korea	131.9	114.8	68.7	77.7	75.0	-43.12	6.97	5.17	3.07	3.47	3.15
8. United Kingdom	67.1	70.5	66.4	65.4	74.3	10.80	3.54	3.18	2.96	2.93	3.12
9. Hong Kong	54.8	56.2	49.7	68.7	70.8	29.19	2.90	2.53	2.22	3.07	2.98
10. Brazil	62.9	80.1	66.7	63.8	70.3	11.74	3.32	3.61	2.98	2.85	2.95
11. Italy	63.4	72.1	73.6	51.9	65.5	3.29	3.35	3.25	3.28	2.32	2.75
12. Germany	30.2	39.2	53.3	48.7	56.0	85.58	1.59	1.76	2.38	2.18	2.35
13. France	59.0	68.1	80.1	54.1	52.2	-11.60	3.12	3.07	3.58	2.42	2.19
14. Taiwan	56.6	69.0	39.3	46.8	46.3	-18.24	2.99	3.11	1.75	2.09	1.95
15. Australia	31.2	32.8	29.8	30.4	37.5	20.27	1.65	1.48	1.33	1.36	1.58
16. Singapore	47.6	49.0	32.8	33.4	35.5	-25.46	2.51	2.21	1.46	1.49	1.49
17. Turkey	10.9	23.6	13.7	9.4	24.5	124.78	0.58	1.06	0.61	0.42	1.03
18. Egypt	0.9	1.3	1.5	6.3	23.9	2 638.22	0.05	0.06	0.07	0.28	1.01
19. India	12.2	11.9	9.8	18.4	17.4	42.47	0.64	0.54	0.44	0.82	0.73
20. Thailand	16.4	13.0	13.4	14.2	16.5	1.07	0.86	0.59	0.60	0.64	0.70
21. Russia	0.8	0.2	2.8	4.5	15.3	1 926.82	0.04	0.01	0.12	0.20	0.64
22. Colombia	10.8	11.9	12.9	13.5	12.8	18.37	0.57	0.54	0.57	0.61	0.54
23. Spain	25.0	15.5	15.5	15.2	10.7	-57.02	1.32	0.70	0.69	0.68	0.45
24. Bulgaria	13.8	23.0	13.5	4.7	10.5	-24.16	0.73	1.04	0.60	0.21	0.44
25. Morocco	0.0	0.0	0.0	0.0	10.5	X	0.00	0.00	0.00	0.00	0.44

X = Not applicable.

Table E-56. Total U.S. Exports (Origin of Movement) via Wisconsin, 1999–2003

(Top 25 commodities and top 25 countries based on 2003 dollar value.)

Industry, commodity, and country	Value (millions of dollars)					Percent change, 1999–2003	Percent share of state total				
	1999	2000	2001	2002	2003		1999	2000	2001	2002	2003
TOTAL AND PERCENT SHARE OF U.S. TOTAL	9 672.9	10 508.4	10 488.7	10 684.3	11 509.8	18.99	1.40	1.35	1.43	1.54	1.59
Manufactures (NAICS Code)	8 927.5	9 858.4	9 874.8	10 017.6	10 805.4	21.04	92.29	93.81	94.15	93.76	93.88
Processed foods (311)	464.0	552.4	622.8	571.7	650.6	40.22	4.80	5.26	5.94	5.35	5.65
Beverages and tobacco products (312)	11.2	16.6	23.3	29.7	45.5	306.78	0.12	0.00	0.22	0.28	0.39
Fabric mill products (313)	33.8	63.3	88.6	54.4	62.0	83.38	0.35	0.60	0.84	0.51	0.54
Non-apparel textile products (314)	17.0	21.8	19.2	18.1	19.0	11.73	0.18	0.21	0.18	0.17	0.16
Apparel manufactures (315)	47.8	74.3	69.5	55.9	75.6	58.07	0.49	0.71	0.66	0.52	0.66
Leather and related products (316)	57.0	46.1	36.6	29.7	28.7	-49.66	0.59	0.44	0.35	0.28	0.25
Wood products (321)	68.4	79.5	80.6	81.8	87.5	27.93	0.71	0.76	0.77	0.77	0.76
Paper products (322)	518.0	564.0	543.2	528.3	563.2	8.73	5.35	5.37	5.18	4.94	4.89
Printing and related products (323)	134.2	182.1	178.1	168.7	183.6	36.80	1.39	1.73	1.70	1.58	1.60
Petroleum and coal products (324)	18.3	17.9	19.3	18.4	18.5	1.00	0.19	0.17	0.18	0.17	0.16
Chemical manufactures (325)	498.1	505.6	555.5	589.8	585.3	17.50	5.15	4.81	5.30	5.52	5.09
Plastics and rubber products (326)	225.4	294.3	305.8	312.7	347.3	54.11	2.33	2.80	2.92	2.93	3.02
Non-metallic mineral products (327)	53.3	55.2	57.7	56.5	57.2	7.24	0.55	0.53	0.55	0.53	0.50
Primary metal manufactures (331)	81.3	117.4	85.8	95.7	108.7	33.68	0.84	1.12	0.82	0.90	0.94
Fabricated metal products (332)	352.6	383.2	381.8	381.1	352.9	0.09	3.65	3.65	3.64	3.57	3.07
Machinery manufactures (333)	2 658.8	2 883.1	2 860.0	2 978.7	3 217.5	21.01	27.49	27.44	27.27	27.88	27.95
Computer and electronic products (334)	1 668.2	1 811.7	1 929.2	1 999.7	2 043.0	22.46	17.25	17.24	18.39	18.72	17.75
Electrical equipment, appliances, and parts (335)	456.4	527.5	533.1	519.3	548.6	20.18	4.72	5.02	5.08	4.86	4.77
Transportation equipment (336)	1 277.6	1 296.8	1 110.8	1 108.5	1 374.3	7.57	13.21	12.34	10.59	10.38	11.94
Furniture and related products (337)	44.6	56.4	51.6	52.0	55.8	25.16	0.46	0.54	0.49	0.49	0.49
Miscellaneous manufactures (339)	241.3	309.0	322.3	366.8	380.6	57.72	2.49	2.94	3.07	3.43	3.31
Agricultural and Livestock Products (NAICS Code)	457.9	415.2	392.7	456.4	415.0	-9.38	4.73	3.95	3.74	4.27	3.61
Agricultural products (111)	407.1	371.4	348.3	414.3	353.3	-13.20	4.21	3.53	3.32	3.88	3.07
Livestock and livestock products (112)	50.9	43.8	44.4	42.1	61.6	21.17	0.53	0.42	0.42	0.39	0.54
Other Commodities (NAICS Code)	287.5	234.9	221.1	210.3	289.5	0.69	2.97	2.24	2.11	1.97	2.51
Forestry and logging (113)	16.6	17.8	15.8	15.3	26.5	59.33	0.17	0.17	0.15	0.14	0.23
Fishing, hunting, and trapping (114)	0.7	1.6	1.4	1.9	2.5	253.08	0.01	0.02	0.01	0.02	0.02
Oil and gas extraction (211)	1.6	1.1	1.2	1.9	18.3	1 016.14	0.02	0.01	0.01	0.02	0.16
Mining (212)	87.9	32.3	15.7	23.7	66.5	-24.42	0.91	0.31	0.15	0.22	0.58
Waste and scrap (910)	31.4	27.3	22.4	27.0	41.8	33.18	0.32	0.26	0.21	0.25	0.36
Used merchandise (920)	5.4	6.6	8.8	15.4	15.0	179.77	0.06	0.06	0.08	0.14	0.13
Goods returned to Canada (980)	24.4	22.4	21.2	20.0	17.4	-28.67	0.25	0.21	0.20	0.19	0.15
Special classification provisions (990)	119.4	125.8	134.5	105.1	95.1	-20.32	1.23	1.20	1.28	0.98	0.83
Publishing industries (except Internet) (511)	0.0	0.0	0.0	0.0	6.4	X	0.00	0.00	0.00	0.00	0.06
TOTAL AND PERCENT SHARE OF U.S. TOTAL	9 672.9	10 508.4	10 488.7	10 684.3	11 509.8	18.99	1.40	1.35	1.43	1.54	1.59
Top 25 Commodities (HS Code)	2 893.3	3 324.1	3 296.0	3 787.4	3 967.6	37.13	29.91	31.63	31.42	35.45	34.47
1. Spark-ignition internal combustion piston engines (840734)	333.3	402.7	283.3	250.7	402.7	20.82	3.45	3.83	2.70	2.35	3.50
2. Spark-ignition engine parts (840991)	330.7	198.7	201.4	467.0	378.3	14.39	3.42	1.89	1.92	4.37	3.29
3. Electro-diagnostic apparatus and parts (901819)	120.6	146.7	171.2	210.2	249.7	107.05	1.25	1.40	1.63	1.97	2.17
4. Passenger vehicles, spark-ignition, > 3,000 cc (870324)	173.6	176.5	168.5	227.1	238.0	37.10	1.79	1.68	1.61	2.13	2.07
5. Tractors (870190)	67.8	114.8	116.9	148.0	230.7	240.27	0.70	1.09	1.11	1.39	2.00
6. Parts and accessories for automatic data processing (847330)	94.3	263.2	196.7	204.3	209.6	122.27	0.97	2.50	1.88	1.91	1.82
7. Magnetic resonance imaging apparatus (840721)	100.0	147.1	154.4	172.6	187.1	87.10	1.03	1.40	1.47	1.62	1.63
8. Magnetic resonance imaging apparatus (901813)	186.5	219.6	214.3	230.0	176.1	-5.58	1.93	2.09	2.04	2.15	1.53
9. Purifying machine and apparatus for gases (842139)	143.6	150.3	163.8	172.8	159.0	10.72	1.48	1.43	1.56	1.62	1.38
10. Automatic regulating instruments and apparatus (903289)	159.2	162.2	124.0	143.7	158.5	-0.44	1.65	1.54	1.18	1.34	1.38
11. Computed tomography apparatus (902212)	6.3	44.0	96.1	157.6	151.8	2 309.52	0.07	0.42	0.92	1.48	1.32
12. Digital processing units (847150)	105.6	69.4	89.6	152.0	145.6	37.88	1.09	0.66	0.85	1.42	1.27
13. Apparatus based on x-ray, medical, surgical, veterinary (902214)	193.3	211.6	301.1	153.6	144.6	-25.19	2.00	2.01	2.87	1.44	1.26
14. X-ray/high tension generators (902290)	108.5	114.0	131.7	185.6	131.0	20.74	1.12	1.08	1.26	1.74	1.14
15. Wheat and meslin (100190)	93.2	82.0	56.9	137.5	113.8	22.10	0.96	0.78	0.54	1.29	0.99
16. Lenses, prisms, mirrors, and optical elements (900190)	. . .	29.9	44.7	57.8	99.7	. . .	. . .	0.28	0.43	0.54	0.87
17. Other parts and attachments for derricks (843149)	99.7	85.7	92.4	97.1	92.9	-6.82	1.03	0.82	0.88	0.91	0.81
18. Self-propelled bulldozers with a 360 degree superstructure (842952)	. . .	83.8	81.8	65.9	91.2	. . .	. . .	0.80	0.78	0.62	0.79
19. Compression-type heat pump units with heat exchangers (841861)	. . .	10.8	9.0	13.7	90.7	. . .	. . .	0.10	0.09	0.13	0.79
20. Instruments and appliances for medical sciences (901890)	56.5	74.0	81.1	79.5	90.5	60.18	0.58	0.70	0.77	0.74	0.79
21. Soybeans, whether or not broken (120100)	146.2	140.6	101.7	132.7	89.5	-38.78	1.51	1.34	0.97	1.24	0.78
22. Spark-ignition internal combustion engines (840790)	109.6	99.3	111.4	82.3	87.6	-20.07	1.13	0.94	1.06	0.77	0.76
23. Newspapers, appearing fewer than 4 times per week (490290)	68.5	78.5	87.7	68.7	87.3	27.45	0.71	0.75	0.84	0.64	0.76
24. Parts and accessories of motor vehicles (870899)	92.3	109.0	113.0	89.8	84.3	-8.67	0.95	1.04	1.08	0.84	0.73
25. Sanitary napkins, diapers and sanitary articles of paper (481840)	104.0	109.7	103.3	87.2	77.4	-25.58	1.08	1.04	0.98	0.82	0.67

X = Not applicable.
. . . = Not available.

Exports from Wisconsin

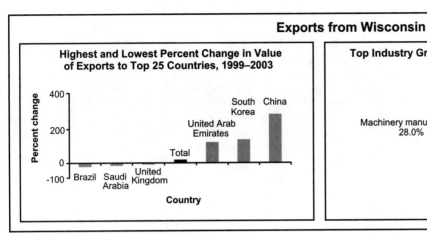

Highest and Lowest Percent Change in Value of Exports to Top 25 Countries, 1999–2003

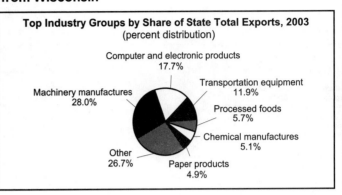

Top Industry Groups by Share of State Total Exports, 2003
(percent distribution)

- Computer and electronic products 17.7%
- Transportation equipment 11.9%
- Processed foods 5.7%
- Chemical manufactures 5.1%
- Paper products 4.9%
- Other 26.7%
- Machinery manufactures 28.0%

- Wisconsin's exports increased 19 percent from 1999 to 2003. The state's largest export industry is machinery manufactures, which represent 28 percent of Wisconsin's total exports. The state's second leading export is computer and electronic products, which are worth over $2 billion. Agricultural product exports had the greatest dollar decrease from 1999 to 2003, falling from $407 million to about $353 million. These exports represent about 3 percent of Wisconsin's total exports.

- The third largest industry export is transportation equipment, to which four of Wisconsin's top five commodities are related. The commodity export of tractors more than tripled from 1999 to 2003, with a jump of about $163 million.

- Canada is the top export country, with exports valued at $4.3 billion. Japan ranks second with $816 million, followed by Mexico ($788 million), and China ($548 million). Exports to China have quadrupled since 1999, up from about $134 million.

Table E-56. Total U.S. Exports (Origin of Movement) via Wisconsin, 1999–2003—*Continued*

(Top 25 commodities and top 25 countries based on 2003 dollar value.)

Industry, commodity, and country	Value (millions of dollars)					Percent change, 1999–2003	Percent share of state total				
	1999	2000	2001	2002	2003		1999	2000	2001	2002	2003
TOTAL AND PERCENT SHARE OF U.S. TOTAL	9 672.9	10 508.4	10 488.7	10 684.3	11 509.8	18.99	1.40	1.35	1.43	1.54	1.59
Top 25 Countries	8 716.1	9 345.5	9 205.6	9 607.3	10 345.4	18.69	90.11	88.93	87.77	89.92	89.88
1. Canada	4 043.7	4 136.4	3 771.3	3 923.2	4 349.3	7.56	41.80	39.36	35.96	36.72	37.79
2. Japan	690.4	748.9	733.0	957.7	816.7	18.29	7.14	7.13	6.99	8.96	7.10
3. Mexico	506.5	673.7	670.1	717.0	788.0	55.58	5.24	6.41	6.39	6.71	6.85
4. China	133.6	177.4	319.6	359.0	548.2	310.44	1.38	1.69	3.05	3.36	4.76
5. United Kingdom	543.4	497.0	448.0	417.2	494.0	-9.09	5.62	4.73	4.27	3.91	4.29
6. Germany	382.5	378.0	376.3	425.1	448.5	17.26	3.95	3.60	3.59	3.98	3.90
7. France	305.0	332.2	366.1	340.1	371.1	21.69	3.15	3.16	3.49	3.18	3.22
8. Australia	254.4	207.5	241.6	255.2	279.9	10.04	2.63	1.97	2.30	2.39	2.43
9. Belgium	169.6	196.3	223.9	256.1	262.7	54.84	1.75	1.87	2.13	2.40	2.28
10. South Korea	106.5	235.3	220.9	214.9	258.4	142.57	1.10	2.24	2.11	2.01	2.24
11. Netherlands	258.5	267.0	312.3	283.2	241.9	-6.45	2.67	2.54	2.98	2.65	2.10
12. Italy	167.9	210.0	254.2	237.4	231.9	38.13	1.74	2.00	2.42	2.22	2.01
13. Hong Kong	148.1	182.2	163.0	155.0	161.8	9.28	1.53	1.73	1.55	1.45	1.41
14. Taiwan	139.8	165.3	153.3	139.8	152.9	9.38	1.44	1.57	1.46	1.31	1.33
15. Singapore	118.1	121.0	112.1	103.0	125.8	6.53	1.22	1.15	1.07	0.96	1.09
16. Brazil	122.6	158.4	169.4	131.5	105.6	-13.86	1.27	1.51	1.61	1.23	0.92
17. Spain	93.2	82.5	72.1	80.3	105.3	13.01	0.96	0.78	0.69	0.75	0.91
18. India	43.3	56.8	82.2	124.6	93.6	115.89	0.45	0.54	0.78	1.17	0.81
19. Saudi Arabia	102.7	57.0	98.2	90.6	90.7	-11.74	1.06	0.54	0.94	0.85	0.79
20. Chile	55.7	120.2	80.9	72.8	84.9	52.37	0.58	1.14	0.77	0.68	0.74
21. Unidentified Countries	156.4	127.4	94.1	121.9	79.2	-49.34	1.62	1.21	0.90	1.14	0.69
22. South Africa	47.5	58.3	54.8	42.1	69.1	45.46	0.49	0.56	0.52	0.39	0.60
23. Ireland	37.0	43.8	50.9	52.0	68.3	84.71	0.38	0.42	0.48	0.49	0.59
24. Sweden	66.2	75.0	92.7	65.6	63.7	-3.65	0.68	0.71	0.88	0.61	0.55
25. United Arab Emirates	23.7	38.0	44.7	42.3	54.1	127.75	0.25	0.36	0.43	0.40	0.47

Table E-57. Total U.S. Exports (Origin of Movement) via Wyoming, 1999–2003

(Top 25 commodities and top 25 countries based on 2003 dollar value.)

Industry, commodity, and country	Value (millions of dollars)					Percent change, 1999–2003	Percent share of state total				
	1999	2000	2001	2002	2003		1999	2000	2001	2002	2003
TOTAL AND PERCENT SHARE OF U.S. TOTAL	458.0	502.5	503.3	553.4	581.6	27.01	0.07	0.06	0.07	0.08	0.08
Manufactures (NAICS Code)	426.1	445.0	432.1	462.7	505.7	18.68	93.04	88.56	85.85	83.61	86.94
Processed foods (311)	1.2	1.4	1.7	1.5	1.6	34.54	0.27	0.27	0.35	0.28	0.28
Beverages and tobacco products (312)	0.0	0.0	0.0	0.0	0.5	X	0.00	0.00	0.00	0.01	0.08
Fabric mill products (313)	0.1	0.1	0.0	0.6	0.2	61.42	0.03	0.02	0.01	0.10	0.04
Non-apparel textile products (314)	0.1	0.0	0.0	0.5	0.3	219.57	0.02	0.01	0.00	0.09	0.05
Apparel manufactures (315)	0.1	0.3	0.1	0.3	0.2	63.36	0.03	0.05	0.02	0.05	0.04
Leather and related products (316)	0.0	0.1	0.0	0.2	0.0	X	0.01	0.01	0.00	0.03	0.00
Wood products (321)	1.0	1.4	1.7	1.5	1.8	80.12	0.22	0.27	0.34	0.27	0.31
Paper products (322)	0.2	0.1	0.1	0.2	0.6	161.57	0.05	0.02	0.02	0.04	0.11
Printing and related products (323)	0.1	0.3	0.1	0.2	0.0	X	0.02	0.05	0.02	0.03	0.00
Petroleum and coal products (324)	0.0	0.2	0.1	0.1	0.2	X	0.00	0.03	0.02	0.02	0.04
Chemical manufactures (325)	389.4	396.9	387.0	418.6	437.9	12.46	85.03	78.99	76.90	75.64	75.28
Plastics and rubber products (326)	1.1	1.0	0.3	0.8	1.6	42.87	0.24	0.21	0.06	0.15	0.27
Non-metallic mineral products (327)	0.3	1.0	1.1	2.5	1.7	528.04	0.06	0.20	0.22	0.44	0.29
Primary metal manufactures (331)	0.9	2.3	1.9	1.5	0.8	-10.57	0.20	0.46	0.39	0.27	0.14
Fabricated metal products (332)	5.5	9.7	8.1	8.3	9.0	65.13	1.19	1.93	1.61	1.50	1.55
Machinery manufactures (333)	5.0	14.5	12.0	14.7	20.2	305.96	1.09	2.89	2.39	2.65	3.48
Computer and electronic products (334)	11.0	9.3	8.2	5.6	20.9	89.83	2.40	1.84	1.64	1.02	3.59
Electrical equipment, appliances, and parts (335)	1.4	4.0	6.4	1.6	2.3	60.92	0.31	0.79	1.27	0.28	0.40
Transportation equipment (336)	7.8	2.3	2.5	3.3	5.1	-34.69	1.70	0.46	0.50	0.60	0.87
Furniture and related products (337)	0.2	0.1	0.0	0.2	0.0	X	0.03	0.01	0.01	0.04	0.01
Miscellaneous manufactures (339)	0.8	0.2	0.4	0.5	0.7	-3.19	0.16	0.04	0.08	0.09	0.13
Agricultural and Livestock Products (NAICS Code)	2.3	2.1	1.6	2.7	1.7	-27.07	0.51	0.41	0.33	0.48	0.29
Agricultural products (111)	0.8	1.1	1.1	2.2	1.6	101.37	0.18	0.22	0.23	0.40	0.28
Livestock and livestock products (112)	1.5	0.9	0.5	0.5	0.1	-94.21	0.34	0.19	0.10	0.08	0.02
Other Commodities (NAICS Code)	29.5	55.4	69.6	88.0	74.2	151.57	6.44	11.03	13.82	15.91	12.76
Forestry and logging (113)	0.0	0.0	0.0	0.0	0.0	X	0.00	0.00	0.00	0.01	0.00
Fishing, hunting, and trapping (114)	0.0	0.0	0.0	0.0	0.0	X	0.00	0.00	0.00	0.00	0.00
Oil and gas extraction (211)	0.0	0.3	2.7	0.5	0.3	X	0.00	0.06	0.54	0.09	0.05
Mining (212)	23.5	47.0	58.2	76.1	58.5	149.02	5.13	9.36	11.56	13.74	10.05
Waste and scrap (910)	0.1	0.1	0.0	0.2	3.5	3 353.47	0.02	0.01	0.00	0.04	0.60
Public administration (920)	0.5	0.6	1.1	2.9	4.3	703.15	0.12	0.11	0.22	0.52	0.75
Goods returned to Canada (980)	3.9	5.0	6.2	5.8	4.4	10.95	0.86	0.99	1.22	1.05	0.75
Special classification provisions (990)	1.5	2.4	1.4	2.5	2.6	78.54	0.32	0.48	0.28	0.46	0.45
Publishing industries (except Internet) (511)	0.0	0.0	0.0	0.0	0.7	X	0.00	0.00	0.00	0.00	0.11
TOTAL AND PERCENT SHARE OF U.S. TOTAL	458.0	502.5	503.3	553.4	581.6	27.01	0.07	0.06	0.07	0.08	0.08
Top 25 Commodities (HS Code)	399.5	428.4	428.2	496.1	528.0	32.17	87.24	85.26	85.08	89.65	90.78
1. Disodium carbonate (283620)	354.5	362.8	356.4	379.8	406.4	14.64	0.07	0.06	0.07	0.08	69.87
2. Bentonite, including calcined (250810)	19.0	21.4	18.5	21.6	26.7	40.53	4.15	4.26	3.68	3.90	4.59
3. Coal, not agglomerated (270119)	0.0	12.5	27.1	45.8	26.1	X	0.00	2.49	5.38	8.28	4.49
4. Parts, television apparatus (852990)	...	0.0	0.0	0.0	9.9	...	...	0.00	0.00	0.00	1.70
5. Rare gases (280429)	2.9	7.0	9.7	9.1	8.6	196.55	0.63	1.39	1.93	1.64	1.48
6. Natural uranium and compounds, alloys, and ceramics (284410)	10.1	9.9	3.3	15.2	5.9	-41.58	2.21	1.97	0.66	2.75	1.01
7. Clays, including ball clays, including calcined (250840)	0.4	0.4	0.3	7.3	5.1	1 175.00	0.09	0.08	0.06	1.32	0.88
8. Fluorosilicates of sodium or of potassium (282620)	0.6	0.3	2.3	1.2	4.0	566.67	0.13	0.06	0.46	0.22	0.69
9. Ash and slag, including seaweed ash (kelp) (262190)	...	0.0	0.0	0.2	3.4	...	...	0.00	0.00	0.04	0.58
10. Fertilizers (310000)	11.2	6.2	6.8	4.5	3.3	-70.54	2.45	1.23	1.35	0.81	0.57
11. Bomb mines other ammunitions projections and parts (930690)	1.8	2.8	2.1	3.7	3.0	66.67	0.39	0.56	0.42	0.67	0.52
12. Parts, accessories, automatic data processing machines (847330)	...	0.2	0.2	0.6	3.0	...	...	0.04	0.04	0.11	0.52
13. Mechanical shovels and excavators, 360 degree superstructure (842952)	...	0.0	0.0	0.0	2.9	...	...	0.00	0.00	0.00	0.50
14. Parts of pumps for liquids (841391)	0.2	0.9	2.0	2.2	2.4	1 100.00	0.04	0.18	0.40	0.40	0.41
15. Products and residuals of chemical industry (382490)	0.5	0.9	0.8	1.6	2.1	320.00	0.11	0.18	0.16	0.29	0.36
16. Other parts and attachments for derricks (843149)	0.3	2.7	0.8	1.6	1.9	533.33	0.07	0.54	0.16	0.29	0.33
17. Bodies for road tractors and motor vehicles (870790)	0.0	0.5	0.3	1.1	1.9	X	0.00	0.10	0.06	0.20	0.33
18. Gears and gearing; ball screws; gear boxes (848340)	...	0.7	0.5	0.4	1.9	...	...	0.14	0.10	0.07	0.33
19. Gear boxes for motor vehicles (870840)	...	0.2	0.0	0.0	1.5	...	...	0.04	0.00	0.00	0.26
20. Tools for pressing, stamping, or punching (820730)	...	0.0	0.0	0.0	1.4	...	...	0.00	0.00	0.00	0.24
21. Parts and accessories of motor vehicles (870899)	...	0.2	0.6	0.3	1.4	...	...	0.04	0.12	0.05	0.24
22. Trailers and semi-trailers for housing or camping (871610)	...	0.2	0.5	0.7	1.4	...	...	0.04	0.10	0.13	0.24
23. Parts and accessories for surveying (901590)	...	3.1	0.5	0.5	1.3	...	...	0.62	0.10	0.09	0.22
24. Plaster boards not ornamental (680911)	0.1	0.3	0.8	1.4	1.3	1 200.00	0.02	0.06	0.16	0.25	0.22
25. Sodium triphosphate (sodium tripolyphosphate) (283531)	...	0.4	0.4	0.7	1.2	...	...	0.08	0.08	0.13	0.21

X = Not applicable.
. . . = Not available.

Exports from Wyoming

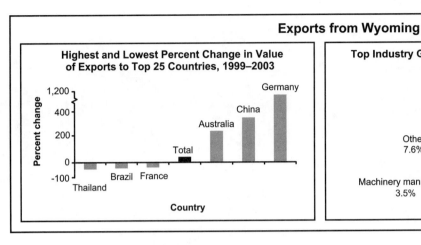

Highest and Lowest Percent Change in Value of Exports to Top 25 Countries, 1999–2003

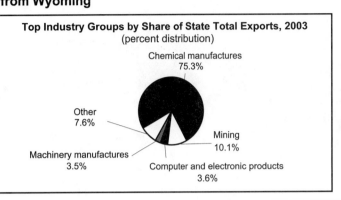

Top Industry Groups by Share of State Total Exports, 2003
(percent distribution)

Chemical manufactures 75.3%
Other 7.6%
Mining 10.1%
Machinery manufactures 3.5%
Computer and electronic products 3.6%

- Wyoming ranks among the states with the lowest value of exports. The state's total exports are valued at about $582 million, up 27 percent from 1999. The chemical manufactures industry represents 75 percent of Wyoming's exports. The value of these exports increased from $389 million in 1999 to about $444 million in 2003. Mining ranks second with exports valued at $149 million, an increase of about 149 percent from 1999.

- Wyoming's top commodity export is disodium carbonate. This commodity, which has many industrial uses, accounts for nearly 70 percent of Wyoming's exports, and almost 93 percent of the state's chemical manufactures industry's exports.

- Canada and Mexico are Wyoming's top export countries. Exports to Canada grew from $75 million in 1999 to $137 million in 2003, an increase of more than 82 percent. Exports to Argentina, ranked seventh, and China, ranked eighth, have grown considerably over the past few years.

Table E-57. Total U.S. Exports (Origin of Movement) via Wyoming, 1999–2003—Continued

(Top 25 commodities and top 25 countries based on 2003 dollar value.)

Industry, commodity, and country	Value (millions of dollars)					Percent change, 1999–2003	Percent share of state total				
	1999	2000	2001	2002	2003		1999	2000	2001	2002	2003
TOTAL AND PERCENT SHARE OF U.S. TOTAL	458.0	502.5	503.3	553.4	581.6	27.01	0.07	0.06	0.07	0.08	0.08
Top 25 Countries	435.8	476.1	473.9	526.2	560.9	28.68	95.17	94.75	94.16	95.09	96.43
1. Canada	75.1	101.3	113.5	140.6	137.1	82.60	16.40	20.17	22.56	25.41	23.58
2. Mexico	55.6	54.4	51.9	57.3	62.6	12.69	12.14	10.83	10.31	10.36	10.77
3. Japan	45.3	53.9	49.4	55.8	45.2	-0.11	9.88	10.73	9.82	10.08	7.77
4. Chile	21.9	23.8	24.6	25.0	29.1	33.01	4.78	4.74	4.90	4.51	5.01
5. Indonesia	31.0	27.0	16.6	27.6	27.1	-12.83	6.78	5.38	3.30	4.99	4.65
6. South Korea	25.9	34.3	33.6	25.1	21.6	-16.61	5.65	6.83	6.68	4.53	3.71
7. Argentina	7.2	13.3	10.1	20.5	20.8	187.55	1.58	2.65	2.00	3.70	3.58
8. China	4.6	10.6	7.2	25.0	20.7	345.57	1.01	2.11	1.42	4.52	3.56
9. Taiwan	21.9	23.2	19.6	22.4	19.4	-11.16	4.77	4.62	3.89	4.06	3.34
10. Brazil	26.6	23.6	18.5	7.0	18.5	-30.32	5.81	4.69	3.67	1.27	3.19
11. Thailand	25.5	19.4	22.6	19.4	17.2	-32.53	5.56	3.85	4.50	3.51	2.95
12. Belgium	7.7	6.0	12.9	14.9	17.2	122.55	1.68	1.19	2.57	2.69	2.95
13. Venezuela	9.2	6.3	5.6	11.9	16.8	83.02	2.01	1.25	1.11	2.15	2.89
14. Australia	4.6	7.7	5.7	5.8	14.8	224.78	1.00	1.53	1.13	1.04	2.55
15. Malaysia	13.8	16.2	13.1	13.5	13.6	-1.71	3.02	3.23	2.60	2.43	2.34
16. Spain	9.5	5.7	8.9	3.7	13.5	42.58	2.06	1.14	1.77	0.66	2.32
17. Netherlands	4.1	3.3	4.3	2.8	12.6	205.68	0.90	0.66	0.86	0.50	2.17
18. Saudi Arabia	9.2	10.3	12.9	11.2	12.0	30.23	2.01	2.06	2.56	2.03	2.06
19. South Africa	10.7	6.8	5.9	4.1	8.2	-23.46	2.33	1.36	1.16	0.73	1.41
20. Philippines	8.8	7.4	9.6	7.9	7.4	-16.38	1.92	1.47	1.91	1.43	1.27
21. United Kingdom	4.7	7.9	9.4	8.2	7.1	50.75	1.03	1.57	1.88	1.48	1.22
22. France	7.4	6.3	7.9	6.7	5.5	-25.69	1.61	1.26	1.56	1.20	0.94
23. Germany	0.4	3.1	3.3	4.6	5.0	1 142.72	0.09	0.61	0.66	0.83	0.87
24. United Arab Emirates	2.0	1.9	4.2	2.8	4.5	122.15	0.44	0.38	0.83	0.51	0.77
25. Peru	3.2	2.4	2.5	2.5	3.3	3.87	0.70	0.47	0.49	0.45	0.57

INDEX